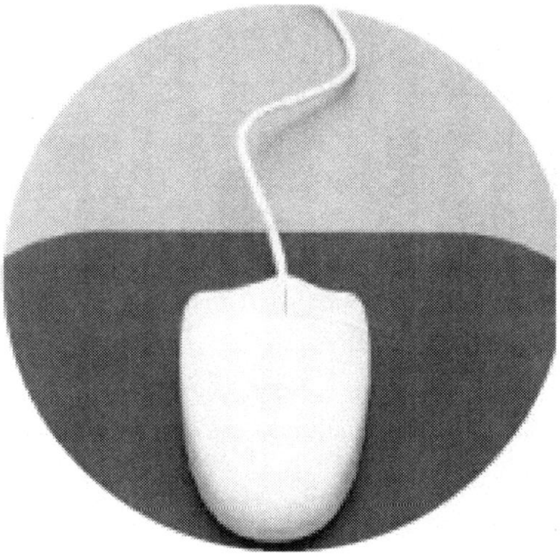

Customer Support Information

Plunkett's Automobile Industry Almanac 2011

Please register your book immediately...

if you did not purchase it directly from Plunkett Research, Ltd. This will enable us to fulfill your requests for assistance. Also, it will enable us to notify you of future editions.

Your purchase includes access to Book Data and Exports online

As a book purchaser, you can register for free, 1-year, 1-seat online access to the latest data for your book's industry trends, statistics and company profiles. This includes tools to export company data. We are migrating from our former CD-ROMs, for supplemental data and export tools, to the web. Simply send us this registration form, and we will send you a user name and password. In this manner, you will have access to our continual updates during the year. Certain restrictions apply.

____ YES, please register me as a purchaser of the book.
I did not buy it directly from Plunkett Research, Ltd.

____ YES, please register me for free online access. I am the actual, original purchaser. (Proof of purchase may be required.)

Customer Name ____

Title ____

Organization ____

Address ____

City ____________________________ State ________ Zip ____________

Country (if other than USA) ___________________________________

Phone ________________________ Fax ___________________________

E-mail ____

Return to: Plunkett Research, Ltd.

Attn: Registration
P.O. Drawer 541737, Houston, TX 77254-1737 USA
713.932.0000 · Fax 713.932.7080 · www.plunkettresearch.com
customersupport@plunkettresearch.com

* Purchasers of used books are not eligible to register. Use of online access is subject to the terms of the end user license agreement.

PLUNKETT'S AUTOMOBILE INDUSTRY ALMANAC 2011

The Only Comprehensive Guide to Automotive Companies and Trends

Jack W. Plunkett

Published by:
Plunkett Research, Ltd., Houston, Texas
www.plunkettresearch.com

PLUNKETT'S AUTOMOBILE INDUSTRY ALMANAC 2011

Editor and Publisher:
Jack W. Plunkett

Executive Editor and Database Manager:
Martha Burgher Plunkett

Senior Editors and Researchers:
Brandon Brison
Michael Esterheld
Addie K. FryeWeaver
Christie Manck

Editors, Researchers and Assistants:
Kalonji Bobb
Elizabeth Braddock
Austin Bunch
Michelle Dotter
Jeremy Faulk
Lucinda Gaines
Leandra Hernandez
Andrew Olsen
Jill Steinberg
Suzanne Zarosky

Enterprise Accounts Manager
Emily Hurley

Information Technology Manager:
Wenping Guo

E-Commerce Managers:
Alejandra Avila
Kelly Burke
Geoffrey Trudeau

Cover Design:
Kim Paxson, Just Graphics
Junction, TX

Special Thanks to:
American Automobile Association (AAA)
Automotive News
National Automobile Dealers Association (NADA)
National Highway Transportation Safety Administration (NHTSA)
R.L. Polk & Co.
Scotiabank Group
U.S. Bureau of Economic Analysis
U.S. Bureau of Transportation Statistics
U.S. Census Bureau
U.S. Department of Commerce
U.S. Department of Transportation
U.S. Energy Information Administration
U.S. Environmental Protection Agency
U.S. Federal Highway Administration

Plunkett Research, Ltd.
P. O. Drawer 541737, Houston, Texas 77254 USA
Phone: 713.932.0000 Fax: 713.932.7080
www.plunkettresearch.com

Published by:
Plunkett Research, Ltd.
P.O. Drawer 541737
Houston, Texas 77254-1737

Phone: 713.932.0000
Fax: 713.932.7080
Internet: www.plunkettresearch.com

ISBN13 # 978-1-59392-181-1
(eBook Edition # 978-1-59392-524-6)

Disclaimer of liability for use and results of use:

PLUNKETT'S AUTOMOBILE INDUSTRY ALMANAC 2011

CONTENTS

Continued on next page

Continued from previous page

A Short Automobile Industry Glossary

10-K: An annual report filed by publicly held companies. It provides a comprehensive overview of the company's business and its finances. By law, it must contain specific information and follow a given form, the "Annual Report on Form 10-K." The U.S. Securities and Exchange Commission requires that it be filed within 90 days after fiscal year end. However, these reports are often filed late due to extenuating circumstances. Variations of a 10-K are often filed to indicate amendments and changes. Most publicly held companies also publish an "annual report" that is not on Form 10-K. These annual reports are more informal and are frequently used by a company to enhance its image with customers, investors and industry peers.

3-D Printing: Refers to systems that use an inkjet-like technology to rapidly apply layers of plastics, ceramics or metal powders to create design prototypes or finished manufactured objects.

802.15.1: See "Bluetooth."

Active Anti-Theft Device: An active device that renders a vehicle inoperative by disabling the fuel, ignition or starting system. The word active refers to a separate manual step, which is needed to engage the device. Also see "Passive Anti-Theft Device."

Active Safety Features: Safety features that are controlled by or interact with the driver (e.g., traction control and anti-lock braking systems).

Actual Cash Value (ACV): An insurance-related term that refers to the amount an insurance company will pay when a vehicle is damaged or declared as a total loss. Actual cash value is recognized as the cost of replacement minus depreciation.

Additive: A resin or chemical from a compounded substance that is designed to improve or enhance certain characteristics such as fuel efficiency.

Aftermarket (Replacement Market): All products and services used to maintain, enhance and repair vehicles after they leave the factory.

AI: See "Artificial Intelligence (AI)."

All-Wheel Drive (AWD): A vehicle drive train in which all wheels are powered by the vehicle's engine at all times. Also see "Four-Wheel Drive (4WD)."

American Automobile Labeling Act (AALA): A regulation requiring manufacturers of vehicles to include content information on vehicle labels for trucks and cars sold in the U.S. after October 1, 1994.

ANPR: See "Automatic Number Plate Recognition (ANPR)."

ANSI: American National Standards Institute. Founded in 1918, ANSI is a private, non-profit organization that administers and coordinates the U.S. voluntary standardization and conformity assessment system. Its mission is to enhance both the global competitiveness of U.S. business and the quality of U.S. life by promoting and facilitating voluntary consensus standards and conformity assessment systems, and safeguarding their integrity. See www.ansi.org.

Antilock Brake System (ABS): A system that senses when wheels lock up or are about to and reduces the braking forces intermittently, lessening the chance of a skid.

APAC: Asia Pacific Advisory Committee. A multi-country committee representing the Asia and Pacific region.

Applied Research: The application of compounds, processes, materials or other items discovered during basic research to practical uses. The goal is to move discoveries along to the final development phase.

Artificial Intelligence (AI): The use of computer technology to perform functions normally associated with human intelligence, such as reasoning, learning and self-improvement.

ASEAN: Association of Southeast Asian Nations. A regional economic development association established in 1967 by five original member countries: Indonesia, Malaysia, Philippines, Singapore, and Thailand. Brunei joined on 8 January 1984, Vietnam on 28 July 1995, Laos and Myanmar on 23 July 1997, and Cambodia on 30 April 1999.

Asia Pacific Economic Cooperation (APEC): An organization established to promote investment and trade in the Pacific basin.

Automated Guided Vehicle System (AGVS): A vehicle equipped with AGVS follows a specific path, stopping at machining or assembly stations for manual loading and unloading of parts.

Automatic Number Plate Recognition (ANPR): A traffic safety and crime prevention technology that uses large numbers of traffic cameras in urban areas. Violators of traffic laws will be automatically photographed, and citations are mailed to them. Britain leads the world in use of this technology, but dozens of U.S. cities have implemented it as well.

Base Model: The least expensive model of a car or truck, often featuring few accessories, a manual transmission and a small engine.

Basic Research: Attempts to discover compounds, materials, processes or other items that may be largely or entirely new and/or unique. Basic research may start with a theoretical concept that has yet to be proven. The goal is to create discoveries that can be moved along to applied research. Basic research is sometimes referred to as "blue sky" research.

Big Three: Ford, Chrysler and General Motors, the three largest car makers in North America.

Biodiesel: A fuel derived when glycerin is separated from vegetable oils or animal fats. The resulting byproducts are methyl esters (the chemical name for biodiesel) and glycerin which can be used in soaps and cleaning products. It has lower emissions than petroleum diesel and is currently used as an additive to that fuel since it helps with lubricity.

Bioethanol: A fuel produced by the fermentation of plant matter such as corn. Fermentation is enhanced through the use of enzymes that are created through biotechnology. Also, see "Ethanol."

Bluetooth: An industry standard for a technology that enables wireless, short-distance infrared connections between devices such as cell phone headsets, Palm Pilots or PDAs, laptops, printers and Internet appliances.

Body Shop: A service outlet that specializes in vehicle body repair work.

BPO: See "Business Process Outsourcing (BPO)."

Branding: A marketing strategy that places a focus on the brand name of a product, service or firm in order to increase the brand's market share, increase sales, establish credibility, improve satisfaction, raise the profile of the firm and increase profits.

BRIC: An acronym representing Brazil, Russia, India and China. The economies of these four countries are seen as some of the fastest growing in the world. A 2003 report by investment bank Goldman Sachs is often credited for popularizing the term; the report suggested that by 2050, BRIC economies will likely outshine those countries which are currently the richest in the world.

B-to-B, or B2B: See "Business-to-Business."

B-to-C, or B2C: See "Business-to-Consumer."

Business Process Outsourcing (BPO): The process of hiring another company to handle business activities. BPO is one of the fastest-growing segments in the offshoring sector. Services include human resources management, billing and purchasing and call centers, as well as many types of customer service or marketing activities, depending on the industry involved. Also, see "Knowledge Process Outsourcing (KPO)."

Business-to-Business: An organization focused on selling products, services or data to commercial customers rather than individual consumers. Also known as B2B.

Business-to-Consumer: An organization focused on selling products, services or data to individual consumers rather than commercial customers. Also known as B2C.

CAFÉ: See "Corporate Average Fuel Economy (CAFÉ)."

CAFTA-DR: See "Central American-Dominican Republic Free Trade Agreement (CAFTA-DR)."

Capital Expenditures: Expenditures to acquire or add to capital assets that will yield benefits over several years.

Captive Finance Company: A finance or leasing company that is affiliated with an automobile distributor or manufacturer.

Captive Import: An imported part or motor vehicle manufactured by another automaker and sold under the brand name of the importer.

Captive Offshoring: Used to describe a company-owned offshore operation. For example, Microsoft owns and operates significant captive offshore research and development centers in China and elsewhere that are offshore from Microsoft's U.S. home base. Also see "Offshoring."

Casting: The process of pouring molten liquid metal into a purpose-built mold.

CEM: Contract electronic manufacturing. See "Contract Manufacturer."

Central American-Dominican Republic Free Trade Agreement (CAFTA-DR): A trade agreement signed into law in 2005 that aimed to open up the Central American and Dominican Republic markets to American goods. Member nations include Guatemala, Nicaragua, Costa Rica, El Salvador, Honduras and the Dominican Republic. Before the law was signed, products from those countries could enter the U.S. almost tariff-free, while American goods heading into those countries faced stiff tariffs. The goal of this agreement was to create U.S. jobs while at the same time offering the non-U.S. member citizens a chance for a better quality of life through access to U.S.-made goods.

Changeover: The refitting of equipment to either neutralize the effects of the just completed model production or to prepare equipment for production of the next scheduled model, or both. This term is frequently used in connection with automotive manufacturing.

Chassis: The structural frame of a vehicle to which wheels, tires, brakes and suspension are attached.

CIS: See "Commonwealth of Independent States (CIS)."

Climate Change (Greenhouse Effect): A theory that assumes an increasing mean global surface temperature of the Earth caused by gases (sometimes referred to as greenhouse gases) in the atmosphere (including carbon dioxide, methane, nitrous oxide, ozone and chlorofluorocarbons). The greenhouse effect allows solar radiation to penetrate the Earth's atmosphere but absorbs the infrared radiation returning to space.

Coachwork: The non-mechanical body and shell work that sit on top of a vehicle's frame.

Coinjection Molding: A hybrid technology, also known as multimaterial injection molding, that creates composite pieces made of plastic and metal parts locked together via injection molding or extrusion. The process combines the strength of steel with the corrosion-resistant properties of plastic. Overall weight is reduced, the need for exterior paint is eliminated and assembly and labor costs are slashed due to more efficient use of machinery.

Collaborative Planning, Forecasting and Replenishment (CPFR): An inventory management practice.

Commerce Chain Management (CCM): Refers to Internet-based tools to facilitate sales, distribution, inventory management and content personalization in the e-commerce industry. Also see "Supply Chain."

Commonwealth of Independent States (CIS): An organization consisting of 11 former members of the Soviet Union: Russia, Ukraine, Armenia, Moldova, Georgia, Belarus, Kazakhstan, Uzbekistan, Azerbaijan, Kyrgyzstan and Tajikistan. It was created in 1991. Turkmenistan recently left the Commonwealth as a permanent member, but remained as an associate member. The Commonwealth seeks to coordinate a variety of economic and social policies, including taxation, pricing, customs and economic regulation, as well as to promote the free movement of capital, goods, services and labor.

Component: In the automobile manufacturing sector, considered to be several distinct parts that have been assembled by a supplier into a subproduct with recognizable features. A component is the next step up from a part such as a bolt. Also see "System" and "Module."

Computer-Aided Design (CAD): A tool used to provide three-dimensional, on-screen design for everything from buildings to automobiles to clothing. It generally runs on workstations.

Computer-Aided Manufacturing (CAM): The use of computers to assist with manufacturing processes, thereby increasing efficiency and productivity.

Concept Vehicle: A vehicle (not currently being produced) that has been modified for new concepts or designs and evaluated for functional feasibility.

Consumer Price Index (CPI): A measure of the average change in consumer prices over time in a fixed market basket of goods and services, such as food, clothing and housing. The CPI is calculated by the U.S. Federal Government and is considered to be one measure of inflation.

Contract Manufacturer: A company that manufactures products that will be sold under the brand names of its client companies. For example, a large number of consumer electronics, such as laptop computers, are manufactured by contract manufacturers for leading brand-name computer companies such as Dell. Many other types of products are made under contract manufacturing, from apparel to pharmaceuticals. Also see "Original Equipment Manufacturer (OEM)" and "Original Design Manufacturer (ODM)."

Contract Manufacturing: See "Contract Manufacturer."

Corporate Average Fuel Economy (CAFÉ): Standards that were first issued by federal regulators in the 1970s as a method of setting average fuel economy standards for carmakers. Each manufacturer must meet a minimum average mpg for passenger cars and a lesser minimum average for SUVs, pickups and minivans.

Coupe: A two-door car.

CPFR: See "Collaborative Planning, Forecasting and Replenishment (CPFR)."

Crossover Utility Vehicle (CUV): A vehicle that has the looks of a sport utility vehicle (SUV), but handling and chassis characteristics more like those of a passenger car than of true SUVs, which tend to handle like light trucks.

Customer Relationship Management (CRM): Refers to the automation, via sophisticated software, of business processes involving existing and prospective customers. CRM may cover aspects such as sales (contact management and contact history), marketing (campaign management and telemarketing) and customer service (call center history and field service history). Well known providers of CRM software include Salesforce, which delivers via a Software as a Service model (see "Software as a Service (Saas)"), Microsoft and Siebel, which as been acquired by Oracle.

CUV: See "Crossover Utility Vehicle (CUV)."

Days' Supply: An estimate of the number of days needed to sell all inventory vehicles, based on the sales rate of the previous month.

DBA: Doing business as.

Dealer Principal: A corporation or individual that owns and controls one or more automobile dealerships.

Demand Chain: A similar concept to a supply chain, but with an emphasis on the end user.

Demographics: The breakdown of the population into statistical categories such as age, income, education and sex.

Design Patent: A patent that may be granted by the U.S. Patent and Trademark Office to anyone who invents a new, original, and ornamental design for an article of manufacture.

Development: The phase of research and development (R&D) in which researchers attempt to create new products from the results of discoveries and applications created during basic and applied research.

Die: A solid or hollow form used to shape materials by pressing, stamping, drawing, threading or extruding.

Displacement Taxes: Taxes levied on vehicles with larger engines.

Distributor: An individual or business involved in marketing, warehousing and/or shipping of products manufactured by others to a specific group of end users. Distributors do not sell to the general public. In order to develop a competitive advantage, distributors often focus on serving one industry or one set of niche clients. For example, within the medical industry, there are major distributors that focus on providing pharmaceuticals, surgical supplies or dental supplies to clinics and hospitals.

Do-it-Yourself (DIY) Market: Market for parts purchased and installed by individual car owners.

Door Rates: Hourly rates charged by a dealer for standard units of service work, which may or may not correspond to an actual hour of work.

E-Commerce: The use of online, Internet-based sales methods. The phrase is used to describe both business-to-consumer and business-to-business sales.

Electronic Data Interchange (EDI): An accepted standard format for the exchange of data between various companies' networks. EDI allows for the transfer of e-mail as well as orders, invoices and other files from one company to another.

Electronic Stability Control (ESC): An advanced safety feature in cars that helps prevent roll over and other control problems.

EMEA: The region comprised of Europe, the Middle East and Africa.

Emission: The release or discharge of a substance into the environment. Generally refers to the release of gases or particulates into the air.

Enterprise Resource Planning (ERP): An integrated information system that helps manage all aspects of a business, including accounting, ordering and human resources, typically across all locations of a major corporation or organization. ERP is considered to be a critical tool for management of large organizations. Suppliers of ERP tools include SAP and Oracle.

ERP: See "Enterprise Resource Planning (ERP)."

ESC: See "Electronic Stability Control (ESC)."

Ethanol: A clear, colorless, flammable, oxygenated hydrocarbon, also called ethyl alcohol. In the U.S., it is used as a gasoline octane enhancer and oxygenate in a 10% blend called E10. Ethanol can be used in higher concentrations (such as an 85% blend called E85) in vehicles designed for its use. It is typically produced chemically from ethylene or biologically from fermentation of various sugars from carbohydrates found in agricultural crops and cellulose residues from crops or wood. Grain ethanol production is typically based on corn or sugarcane. Cellulosic ethanol production is based on agricultural waste, such as wheat stalks, that has been treated with enzymes to break the waste down into component sugars.

EU: See "European Union (EU)."

EU Competence: The jurisdiction in which the EU can take legal action.

European Community (EC): See "European Union (EU)."

European Union (EU): A consolidation of European countries (member states) functioning as one body to facilitate trade. Previously known as the European Community (EC), the EU expanded to include much of Eastern Europe in 2004, raising the total number of member states to 25. In 2002, the EU launched a unified currency, the Euro. See europa.eu.int.

Fab Lab: See "3-D Printing."

Federation International de Automobile (FIA): The sanctioning body of all international car racing.

Fleet Sales: The sale of large quantities of vehicles to business or government agencies.

Forging: A process that transforms solid metal into various thicknesses and shapes, often by heating.

Four-Wheel Drive (4WD): A vehicle drive train in which all four wheels are driven by a transfer case sending power to both axles. Also see "All-Wheel Drive (AWD)."

Franchising: A contractual agreement between a franchiser and a franchisee that allows the franchisee to operate a retail outlet or other type of business using a name and format developed and supported by the franchiser.

Free Trade Agreement of the Americas (FTAA): The effort to unite the economies of the Western Hemisphere into a single free trade agreement.

Front-Wheel Drive: A drive train in which a vehicle is steered by and power is put into the front wheels, pulling the vehicle forward.

Fuel Cell: An environmentally friendly electrochemical engine that generates electricity using hydrogen and oxygen as fuel, emitting only heat and water as byproducts.

GDP: See "Gross Domestic Product (GDP)."

GHG: See "Greenhouse Gas (GHG)."

Global Positioning System (GPS): A satellite system, originally designed by the U.S. Department of Defense for navigation purposes. Today, GPS is in wide use for consumer and business purposes, such as navigation for drivers, boaters and hikers. It utilizes satellites orbiting the earth at 10,900 miles to enable users to pinpoint precise locations using small, electronic wireless receivers.

Global Warming: An increase in the near-surface temperature of the Earth. Global warming has occurred in the distant past as the result of natural influences, but the term is most often used to refer to a theory that warming occurs as a result of increased use of hydrocarbon fuels by man. See "Climate Change (Greenhouse Effect)."

Globalization: The increased mobility of goods, services, labor, technology and capital throughout the world. Although globalization is not a new development, its pace has increased with the advent of new technologies, especially in the areas of telecommunications, finance and shipping.

GPS: See "Global Positioning System (GPS)."

Gray Market: The market for vehicles that have been imported through individual channels outside of authorized dealers.

Greenhouse Gas (GHG): See "Climate Change (Greenhouse Effect)."

Gross Domestic Product (GDP): The total value of a nation's output, income and expenditures produced with a nation's physical borders.

Gross National Product (GNP): A country's total output of goods and services from all forms of economic activity measured at market prices for one calendar year. It differs from Gross Domestic Product (GDP) in that GNP includes income from investments made in foreign nations.

Group of Eight (G8): The eight major industrial countries, including the United States, Japan, Germany, France, the United Kingdom, Italy, Russia and Canada, whose leaders meet at annual economic summits to coordinate economic policies. The group was formerly known as the G7, before Russia was admitted in June 2002.

Heavy-Duty Truck: A vehicle weighing from 26,001 to 33,001 pounds.

Hydraulic Hybrid System: A patented fuel-saving system developed by the Environmental Protection Agency. Used in heavy service vehicles such as garbage trucks and UPS delivery vans, the system utilizes a hydraulic pump and storage tanks that store and use energy that is typically lost when brakes are applied.

Ignition System: An electrical system that includes a battery, induction coil, capacitor, distributor, spark plugs and relevant switches and wiring that produce timed sparks from spark plugs.

Import Nameplate: Vehicles sold by manufacturers primarily located outside North America, whether assembled in North America or overseas.

IMVP: See "International Motor Vehicle Program (IMVP)."

Independent Repair Shop: A service outlet that offers specialized repair services but does not usually sell gasoline and is not associated with a new car dealer.

Initial Public Offering (IPO): A company's first effort to sell its stock to investors (the public). Investors in an up-trending market eagerly seek stocks offered in many IPOs because the stocks of newly public companies that seem to have great promise may appreciate very rapidly in price, reaping great profits for those who were able to get the stock at the first offering. In the United States, IPOs are regulated by the SEC (U.S. Securities Exchange Commission) and by the state-level regulatory agencies of the states in which the IPO shares are offered.

Intelligent Transportation Systems (ITS): Include a broad number of information technologies that can provide an electronic communications link to cars and trucks, enabling drivers to be alerted to road hazards, delays, construction and accidents. At the same time, ITS can transmit driving directions and a wealth of additional driving-related information. ITS enables automated drive-through toll collection and truck pre-clearance along highways and at bridge and tunnel crossings. ITS technologies are likewise in use at border stations, points of entry and customs checkpoints, especially in the NAFTA zone.

International Motor Vehicle Program (IMVP): A research project, launched in 1979, funded by leading global car makers as well as government agencies, focused on research that can enhance automotive design and manufacturing methods. More than 50 senior scientists, management experts, social scientists and engineers have conducted interdisciplinary automotive research at more than 25 universities on six continents. One of IMVP's researchers coined the phrase "lean production."

ISO 9000, 9001, 9002, 9003: Standards set by the International Organization for Standardization. ISO 9000, 9001, 9002 and 9003 are the highest quality certifications awarded to organizations that meet exacting standards in their operating practices and procedures.

IT-Enabled Services (ITES): The portion of the Information Technology industry focused on providing business services, such as call centers, insurance claims processing and medical records transcription, by utilizing the power of IT, especially the Internet. Most ITES functions are considered to be back-office procedures. Also, see "Business Process Outsourcing (BPO)."

Jigs: An accurate machining device that holds goods in place while guiding tools exactly into position.

Just-in-Time (JIT) Delivery: Refers to a supply chain practice whereby manufacturers receive components on or just before the time that they are needed on the assembly line, rather than bearing the cost of maintaining several days' or weeks' supply in a warehouse. This adds greatly to the cost-effectiveness of a manufacturing plant and puts the burden of warehousing and timely delivery on the supplier of the components.

Kaizen: A Japanese manufacturing process concept that is widely studied by the global automotive industry. It is a philosophy based on continuous improvement of the manufacturing and business process. Facets of Kaizen may include just-in-time delivery of components, zero defects, productivity enhancement and a customer-oriented mindset.

Kanban: From the Japanese word for "visual record," a just-in-time methodology, initially attributed to Toyota, whereby sub-assemblies are delivered to a product line at the time required in the appropriate number. Kanban has also come to refer to tag-like cards used to track flow along the product line.

Knowledge Process Outsourcing (KPO): The use of outsourced and/or offshore workers to perform business tasks that require judgment and analysis. Examples include such professional tasks as patent research, legal research, architecture, design, engineering, market research, scientific research, accounting and tax return preparation. Also, see "Business Process Outsourcing (BPO)."

LAC: An acronym for Latin America and the Caribbean.

LDCs: See "Least Developed Countries (LDCs)."

Lean Production: An enhancement of the mass production concept. Lean production, also known as optimum lean production, involves optimizing the factory floor, design team, supply chain and other areas in order to manufacture a higher-quality product in less time at less cost. The phrase was coined by John Krafcik, a member of the research team at IMVP (International Motor Vehicle Program).

Lease (Automotive): A form of contract transferring the use of a vehicle, typically in consideration of a monthly payment. Ownership is retained by the lease company.

Least Developed Countries (LDCs): Nations determined by the U.N. Economic and Social Council to be the poorest and weakest members of the international community. There are currently 50 LDCs, of which 34 are in Africa, 15 are in Asia Pacific and the remaining one (Haiti) is in Latin America. The top 10 on the LDC list, in descending order from top to 10th, are Afghanistan, Angola, Bangladesh, Benin, Bhutan, Burkina Faso, Burundi, Cambodia, Cape Verde and the Central African Republic. Sixteen of the LDCs are also Landlocked Least Developed Countries (LLDCs) which present them with additional difficulties often due to the high cost of transporting trade goods. Eleven of the LDCs are Small Island Developing States (SIDS), which are often at risk of extreme weather phenomenon (hurricanes, typhoons, Tsunami); have fragile ecosystems; are often dependent on foreign energy sources; can have high disease rates for HIV/AIDS and malaria; and can have poor market access and trade terms.

Light Truck: In the U.S., a light truck is a vehicle that weights no more than 13,000 pounds (about 6,300 kg). These are vehicles that are used both by individuals and commercial entities. Vehicles that fall within this classification may include pickups, full-size passenger vans and commercial vans, minivans and SUVs.

LOHAS: Lifestyles of Health and Sustainability. A marketing term that refers to consumers who choose to purchase and/or live with items that are natural, organic, less polluting, etc. Such consumers may also prefer products powered by alternative energy, such as hybrid cars.

Loss Leaders: The use of very low prices to attract customers where merchandise may be sold at or below cost.

Low Emission Vehicle (LEV) Standards: Standards set by federal and state governments for automakers developing vehicles that will output lower emission levels.

Machining: An operation which shapes metal parts by carving away excess material in a sequential process of turning, milling and grinding.

Make-to-Order (MTO): A term applied to products that are manufactured only when an order is confirmed. MTO differs from ETO in that no additional engineering or design is required to make the product.

Manufacturer's Suggested Retail Price (MSRP): The suggested selling price of a vehicle as stated by its manufacturer.

Manufacturing Resource Planning (MRP II): A methodology that supports effective planning with regard to all resources of a manufacturing company, linking MRP with sales and operations planning, production planning and master production scheduling.

Maquila (Maquiladora): A production plant, located in Mexico near the U.S.-Mexican border, that manufactures components but does not perform final assembly of completed products. The U.S. allows duty-free import of these components, which then undergo final assembly at a U.S. plant. Also see "Original Equipment Manufacturer (OEM)."

Market Segmentation: The division of a consumer market into specific groups of buyers based on demographic factors.

Marketing: Includes all planning and management activities and expenses associated with the promotion of a product or service. Marketing can encompass advertising, customer surveys, public relations and many other disciplines. Marketing is distinct from selling, which is the process of sell-through to the end user.

Mass Production: The use of specialized labor, and in some cases moving assembly lines, to manufacture large quantities. This is much faster and much more cost-effective than low-quantity or custom production. Henry Ford is generally credited with making mass production the standard in the automobile industry. He installed the first moving assembly line in 1913 in his Highland Park, Michigan plant.

Material Requirements Planning (MRP): An integrated management technique that uses bill of material data, inventory data and master production schedules to calculate requirements for material. MRP generates recommendations to release or reschedule replenishment orders for materials.

Mechanic Installed Market (MIL): The sale of parts for installation by professional mechanics.

Media Oriented Systems Transport (MOST): A standard adopted in 2004 by the Consumer Electronics Association for the integration of or interface with consumer electronics (such as iPods) into entertainment systems in automobiles.

Medium-Duty Truck: In the U.S., a medium-duty truck is a commercial vehicle weighing between 13,000 pounds and 33,000 pounds.

Merchandising: Any marketing method utilized to foster sales growth.

Model Line: A group of vehicles having the same model name or platform.

Module: In the automobile manufacturing sector, a module is considered to be several distinct systems that have been assembled into a major functional unit of a vehicle, such as an engine. A module is the next step up from a system, which is the next step up from a component, the next step up from a part such as a bolt. Also see "Component" and "System."

Multimaterial Injection Molding: See "Coinjection Molding."

NAFTA: See "North American Free Trade Agreement (NAFTA)."

No Fault Insurance: A system of insurance where both parties in an accident file claims and neither party is held primarily responsible.

North American Free Trade Agreement (NAFTA): A trade agreement signed in December 1992 by U.S. President George H. W. Bush, Canadian Prime Minister Brian Mulroney and Mexican President Carlos Salinas de Gortari. The agreement eliminates tariffs on most goods originating in and traveling between the three member countries. It was approved by the legislatures of the three countries and had entered into force by January 1994. When it was created, NAFTA formed one of the largest free-trade areas of its kind in the world.

ODM: See "Original Design Manufacturer (ODM)."

OECD: See "Organisation for Economic Co-operation and Development (OECD)."

OEM: See "Original Equipment Manufacturer (OEM)."

Off-Highway Vehicle: A vehicle intended to be operated on rough terrain or unpaved surfaces.

Offshoring: The rapidly growing tendency among U.S., Japanese and Western European firms to send knowledge-based and manufacturing work overseas. The intent is to take advantage of lower wages and operating costs in such nations as China, India, Hungary and Russia. The choice of a nation for offshore work may be influenced by such factors as language and education of the local workforce, transportation systems or natural resources. For example, China and India are graduating high numbers of skilled engineers and scientists from their universities. Also, some nations are noted for large numbers of workers skilled in the English language, such as the Philippines and India. Also see "Captive Offshoring" and "Outsourcing."

On Board Diagnostics (OBD): A system that monitors a vehicle for problems and unit failures during normal vehicle operations.

Onshoring: The opposite of "offshoring." Providing or maintaining manufacturing or services within or nearby a company's domestic location. Sometimes referred to as reshoring.

Optimum Lean Production: The practice of fine tuning "lean production" so that it produces the highest profitability and return on investment. In automobile manufacturing, the goal of optimum lean production would be to create a balance between productivity and quality in order to produce the highest profit per vehicle that can be reasonably expected.

Organisation for Economic Co-operation and Development (OECD): A group of more than 30 nations that are strongly committed to the market economy and democracy. Some of the OECD members include Japan, the U.S., Spain, Germany, Australia, Korea, the U.K., Canada and Mexico. Although not members, Estonia, Israel and Russia are invited to member talks; and Brazil, China, India, Indonesia and South Africa have enhanced engagement policies with the OECD. The Organisation provides statistics, as well as social and economic data; and researches social changes, including patterns in evolving fiscal policy, agriculture, technology, trade, the environment and other areas. It publishes over 250 titles annually; publishes a corporate magazine, the OECD Observer; has radio and TV studios; and has centers in Tokyo, Washington, D.C., Berlin and Mexico City that distributed the Organisation's work and organizes events.

Original Design Manufacturer (ODM): A contract manufacturer that offers complete, end-to-end design, engineering and manufacturing services. ODMs design and build products, such as consumer electronics, that client companies can then brand and sell as their own. For example, a large percentage of laptop computers, cell phones and PDAs are made by ODMs. Also see "Original Equipment Manufacturer (OEM)" and "Contract Manufacturer."

Original Equipment Manufacturer (OEM): A company that manufactures a product or component for sale to a customer that will integrate the component into a final product or assembly. The OEM's customer will distribute the end product or resell it to an end user. For example, a personal computer made under a brand name by a given company may contain various components, such as hard drives, graphics cards or speakers, manufactured by several different OEM "vendors," but the firm doing the final assembly/manufacturing process is the final manufacturer. Also see "Original Design Manufacturer (ODM)" and "Contract Manufacturer."

Outbound Logistics: The process related to the movement and storage of products from the end of the production line to the end user.

Outsourcing: The hiring of an outside company to perform a task otherwise performed internally by the company, generally with the goal of lowering costs and/or streamlining work flow. Outsourcing contracts are generally several years in length. Companies that hire outsourced services providers often prefer to focus on their core strengths while sending more routine tasks outside for others to perform. Typical outsourced services include the running of human resources departments, telephone call centers and computer departments. When outsourcing is performed overseas, it may be referred to as offshoring. Also see "Offshoring."

Partnership for a New Generation of Vehicles: A partnership between the U.S. Federal Government and the automotive industry created to establish global technical leadership in the development and production of affordable, fuel-efficient, low-emission vehicles to meet performance standards.

Passenger Vehicle: A four-wheeled motor vehicle, including sport utility vehicles and minivans. The primary purpose of these vehicles is to carry passengers, not cargo.

Passive Anti-Theft Device: A passive device that renders a vehicle inoperative by disabling the fuel, ignition or starting system. The device is passive because a separate manual step is not needed to engage the device. Also see "Active Anti-Theft Device."

Platform: The primary load-bearing structural assembly of a motor vehicle, which determines its basic size and supports its suspension components and driveline.

Plug-in Hybrid Electric Vehicles (PHEV): A PHEV is an automobile that features an extra high-capacity battery bank that gives the vehicle a longer electric-only range than standard hybrids. These cars are designed so that they can be plugged into a standard electric outlet for recharging. The intent is to minimize or eliminate the need to use the car's gasoline engine and rely on the electric engine instead.

Pneumatic Tire: A tire with an outer part made of flexible, hollow rubber which is inflated by air pressure.

Positioning: The design and implementation of a merchandising mix, price structure and style of selling to create an image of the retailer, relative to its competitors, in the customer's mind.

PPP: See "Purchasing Power Parity (PPP) or Point-to-Point Protocol (PPP)."

Product Lifecycle: The prediction of the life of a product or brand. Stages are described as Introduction, Growth, Maturity and finally Sales Decline.

Production Car: A model of vehicle that is in production and for sale to the general public.

Program Cars: Vehicles sold for fleet use, usually in large fleets such as those used by car rental companies.

Purchasing Power Parity (PPP): Currency conversion rates that attempt to reflect the actual purchasing power of a currency in its home market, as opposed to examining price levels and comparing an exchange rate. PPPs are always given in the national currency units per U.S. dollar.

R&D: Research and development. Also see "Applied Research" and "Basic Research."

Rapid Prototyping: See "3-D Printing."

Rear-Wheel Drive: A drive train in which the front wheels of the vehicle steer while the rear wheels push the vehicle forward.

Reefer: A refrigerated trailer.

Refit: In manufacturing, the closure of a plant for the purpose of retooling or conversion.

Registration: Vehicle ownership details that are filed with the state/province and printed out on a certificate of ownership called a title.

Return on Investment (ROI): A measure of a company's profitability, expressed in percentage as net profit (after taxes) divided by total dollar investment.

Saas: See "Software as a Service (Saas)."

Securitization: The process of financing a pool of similar assets (such as mortgages, automobile loans, corporate debt instruments or credit card debts) by issuing to investors interests in the funds generated by that pool. Such pools are generally in the range of $100 million or higher, and may represent the debts of dozens of companies or thousands of consumers. Securitization enables banks and other lenders to have ready markets into which they may sell loans that they generate.

Six Sigma: A quality enhancement strategy designed to reduce the number of products coming from a manufacturing plant that do not conform to specifications. Six Sigma states that no more than 3.4 defects per million parts is the goal of high-quality output. Motorola invented the system in the 1980s in order to enhance its competitive position against Japanese electronics manufacturers.

Software as a Service (SaaS): Refers to the practice of providing users with software applications that are hosted on remote servers and accessed via the Internet. Excellent examples include the CRM (Customer Relationship Management) software provided in SaaS format by Salesforce. An earlier technology that operated in a similar, but less sophisticated, manner was called ASP or Application Service Provider.

Specialty Repair Shop: A retail outlet that focuses on specialized service and repair, such as brake or muffler repair.

Sport Utility Vehicle (SUV): A vehicle designed as a hybrid of a truck and a passenger car. SUVs frequently have four-wheel drive for rough or off-road driving, in addition to extra space for people or cargo and comforts such as additional suspension and luxury options.

Stamping: A process that creates shaped parts from rolled sheet metal by bending or stretching it in a sequence of purpose-built tools fitted to a general-purpose press.

Subsidiary, Wholly-Owned: A company that is wholly controlled by another company through stock ownership.

Supply Chain: The complete set of suppliers of goods and services required for a company to operate its business. For example, a manufacturer's supply chain may include providers of raw materials, components, custom-made parts and packaging materials.

SUV: See "Sport Utility Vehicle (SUV)."

System: In the automobile manufacturing sector, a system is considered to be several distinct components that have been assembled by a supplier into a subproduct that is a functional part of a vehicle, such as an instrument panel. A system is the next step up from a component, which is the next step up from a part such as a bolt. Also see "Component" and "Module."

Telematics: The use of cellular or radio transmission to exchange information between an automobile or truck and a base data center or customer service center. In the trucking industry, telematics is used to provide a headquarters with information about the location and routing of a truck. Telematics can also be used to alert a central service office about the temperature, oil pressure and other vital statistics of a gas or diesel engine. In passenger automobiles, telematics may be used to provide emergency response during accidents or breakdowns. Such emergency response may occur automatically, for example, when an air bag inflates. GM's OnStar service is a well-known example of telematics services for passenger car owners.

Third-Party Logistics (3PL): A specialist firm in logistics, which may provide a variety of transportation, warehousing and logistics-related services to buyers or sellers. These tasks were previously performed in-house by the customer. When 3PL services are provided within the client's own facilities, it can also be referred to as insourcing.

Tier 1 Supplier: A component manufacturer to final vehicle assemblers, responsible for delivery of the finished assembly, product development and continued technology renewal. Tier 1 suppliers work hand-in-hand with automobile manufacturers to design, manufacture and deliver complicated automobile systems and modules, such as significant interior, exterior or drivetrain units. Tier 1 suppliers in turn purchase from tier 2 and tier 3 suppliers, which rank below tier 1.

Tier 2 Supplier: A producer of value-adding parts in the minor sub-assembly phase. Tier 2 suppliers buy from tier 3 and sell to tier 1.

Tier 3 Supplier: A supplier of engineered materials and special services, such as rolls of sheet steel, heat treating and surface treatments. Tier 3 suppliers rank below tier 2 and tier 1 suppliers in terms of the complexity of the products that they provide.

Title: See "Registration."

Total Quality Management (TQM): The management of an operation with the goal of producing a product with zero defects.

Ultrawideband (UWB): A means of low-power, limited-range wireless data transmission that takes advantage of bandwidth set aside by the FCC in 2002. UWB encodes signals in a dramatically different way, sending digital pulses in a relatively secure manner that will not interfere with other wireless systems that may be operating nearby. It has the potential to deliver very large amounts of data to a distance of about 230 feet, even through doors and other obstacles, and requires very little power. Speeds are scalable from approximately 100 Mbps to 2Gbps. UWB works on the 802.15.3 IEEE specification.

Value Added Tax (VAT): A tax that imposes a levy on businesses at every stage of manufacturing based on the value it adds to a product. Each business in the supply chain pays its own VAT and is subsequently repaid by the next link down the chain; hence, a VAT is ultimately paid by the consumer, being the last link in the supply chain, making it comparable to a sales tax. Generally, VAT only applies to goods bought for consumption within a given country; export goods are exempt from VAT, and purchasers from other countries taking goods back home may apply for a VAT refund.

Vehicle Identification Number (VIN): The unique number assigned to a vehicle by its manufacturer for identification and registration purposes.

Vendor: Any firm, such as a manufacturer or distributor, from which a retailer obtains merchandise.

Vertical Integration: A business model in which one company owns many (or all) of the means of production of the many goods that comprise its product line. For example, founder Henry Ford designed Ford Motor Company's early River Rogue plant so that coal, iron ore and other needed raw materials arrived at one end of the plant and were processed into steel, which was then converted on-site into finished components. At the final stage of the plant, completed automobiles were assembled.

World Trade Organization (WTO): One of the only globally active international organizations dealing with the trade rules between nations. Its goal is to assist the free flow of trade goods, ensuring a smooth, predictable supply of goods to help raise the quality of life of member citizens. Members form consensus decisions that are then ratified by their respective parliaments. The WTO's conflict resolution process generally emphasizes interpreting existing commitments and agreements, and discovers how to ensure trade policies to conform to those agreements, with the ultimate aim of avoiding military or political conflict.

WTO: See "World Trade Organization (WTO)."

INTRODUCTION

PLUNKETT'S AUTOMOBILE INDUSTRY ALMANAC, the eighth edition of our guide to the automotive field, is designed to be used as a general source for researchers of all types.

The data and areas of interest covered are intentionally broad, ranging from the trends relating to automotive sales, to emerging technology, to an in-depth look at the major for-profit firms (which we call "THE AUTOMOBILE 400") within the many industry sectors that make up the automotive arena.

This reference book is designed to be a general source for researchers. It is especially intended to assist with market research, strategic planning, employment searches, contact or prospect list creation and financial research, and as a data resource for executives and students of all types.

PLUNKETT'S AUTOMOBILE INDUSTRY ALMANAC takes a rounded approach for the general reader. This book presents a complete overview of the entire automobile and truck industry (see "How To Use This Book"). For example, you will find trends in the passenger car, light truck and heavy truck markets, along with easy-to-use charts and tables on all facets of automobiles in general, from the sales and profits of the automakers, to fuel efficiency, to manufacturing output.

THE AUTOMOBILE 400 is our unique grouping of the biggest, most successful corporations in all segments of the global automotive industry, including cars, trucks, components, specialty vehicles and related services. Tens of thousands of pieces of information, gathered from a wide variety of sources, have been researched and are presented in a unique form that can be easily understood. This section includes thorough indexes to THE AUTOMOBILE 400, by geography, industry, sales, brand names, subsidiary names and many other topics. (See Chapter 4.)

Especially helpful is the way in which PLUNKETT'S AUTOMOBILE INDUSTRY ALMANAC enables readers who have no business background to readily compare the financial records and growth plans of large automotive companies and major industry groups. You'll see the mid-term financial record of each firm, along with the impact of earnings, sales and strategic plans on each company's potential to fuel growth, to serve new markets and to provide investment and employment opportunities.

No other source provides this book's easy-to-understand comparisons of growth, expenditures, technologies, corporations and many other items of great importance to people of all types who may be studying this, one of the largest industries in the world today.

By scanning the data groups and the unique indexes, you can find the best information to fit your personal research needs. The major companies in the automobile field are profiled and then ranked using several different groups of specific criteria. Which firms are the biggest employers? Which companies earn the most profits? These things and much more are easy to find.

In addition to individual company profiles, an overview of automotive markets and trends is provided. This book's job is to help you sort through easy-to-understand summaries of today's trends in a quick and effective manner.

Whatever your purpose for researching the automotive field, you'll find this book to be a valuable guide. Nonetheless, as is true with all resources, this volume has limitations that the reader should be aware of:

- Financial data and other corporate information can change quickly. A book of this type can be no more current than the data that was available as of the time of editing. Consequently, the financial picture, management and ownership of the firm(s) you are studying may have changed since the date of this book. For example, this almanac includes the most up-to-date sales figures and profits available to the editors as of mid-2010. That means that we have typically used corporate financial data as of the end of 2009.

- Corporate mergers, acquisitions and downsizing are occurring at a very rapid rate. Such events may have created significant change, subsequent to the publishing of this book, within a company you are studying.

- Some of the companies in THE AUTOMOBILE 400 are so large in scope and in variety of business endeavors conducted within a parent organization, that we have been unable to completely list all subsidiaries, affiliations, divisions and activities within a firm's corporate structure.

- This volume is intended to be a general guide to a vast industry. That means that researchers should look to this book for an overview and, when conducting in-depth research, should contact the specific corporations or industry associations in question for the very latest changes and data. Where possible, we have listed contact names, toll-free telephone numbers and Internet site addresses for the companies, government agencies and industry associations involved so that the reader may get further details without unnecessary delay.

- Tables of industry data and statistics used in this book include the latest numbers available at the time of printing, generally through the end of 2009. In a few cases, the only complete data available was for earlier years.

- We have used exhaustive efforts to locate and fairly present accurate and complete data. However, when using this book or any other source for business and industry information, the reader should use caution and diligence by conducting further research where it seems appropriate. We wish you success in your endeavors, and we trust that your experience with this book will be both satisfactory and productive.

Jack W. Plunkett
Houston, Texas
September 2010

HOW TO USE THIS BOOK

The two primary sections of this book are devoted first to the automotive industry as a whole and then to the "Individual Data Listings" for THE AUTOMOBILE 400. If time permits, you should begin your research in the front chapters of this book. Also, you will find lengthy indexes in Chapter 4 and in the back of the book.

THE AUTOMOBILE INDUSTRY

Glossary: A short list of automotive industry terms.

Chapter 1: Major Trends Affecting the Automobile Industry. This chapter presents an encapsulated view of the major trends that are creating rapid changes in the automotive industry today.

Chapter 2: Automobile Industry Statistics. This chapter presents in-depth statistics on car sales, manufacturing import/export and more.

Chapter 3: Important Automobile Industry Contacts – Addresses, Telephone Numbers and Internet Sites. This chapter covers contacts for important government agencies, automotive organizations and trade groups. Included are numerous important Internet sites.

THE AUTOMOBILE 400

Chapter 4: THE AUTOMOBILE 400: Who They Are and How They Were Chosen. The companies compared in this book were carefully selected from the automobile industry, largely in the United States. 158 of the firms are based outside the U.S. For a complete description, see THE AUTOMOBILE 400 indexes in this chapter.

Individual Data Listings:

Look at one of the companies in THE AUTOMOBILE 400's Individual Data Listings. You'll find the following information fields:

Company Name:

The company profiles are in alphabetical order by company name. If you don't find the company you are seeking, it may be a subsidiary or division of one of the firms covered in this book. Try looking it up in the Index by Subsidiaries, Brand Names and Selected Affiliations in the back of the book.

Ranks:

Industry Group Code: An NAIC code used to group companies within like segments. (See Chapter 4 for a list of codes.)

Ranks Within This Company's Industry Group: Ranks, within this firm's segment only, for annual sales and annual profits, with 1 being the highest rank.

Business Activities:

A grid arranged into six major industry categories and several sub-categories. A "Y" indicates that the firm operates within the sub-category. A complete Index by Industry is included in the beginning of Chapter 4.

Types of Business:

A listing of the primary types of business specialties conducted by the firm.

Brands/Divisions/Affiliations:

Major brand names, operating divisions or subsidiaries of the firm, as well as major corporate affiliations—such as another firm that owns a significant portion of the company's stock. A complete Index by Subsidiaries, Brand Names and Selected Affiliations is in the back of the book.

Contacts:

The names and titles up to 27 top officers of the company are listed, including human resources contacts.

Address:

The firm's full headquarters address, the headquarters telephone, plus toll-free and fax numbers where available. Also provided is the World Wide Web site address.

Financials:

Annual Sales (2009 or the latest fiscal year available to the editors, plus up to four previous years): These are stated in thousands of dollars (add three zeros if you want the full number). This figure represents consolidated worldwide sales from all operations. 2009 figures may be estimates.

Annual Profits (2009 or the latest fiscal year available to the editors, plus up to four previous years): These are stated in thousands of dollars (add three zeros if you want the full number). This figure represents consolidated, after-tax net profit from all operations. 2009 figures may be estimates.

Stock Ticker, International Exchange, Parent Company: When available, the unique stock market symbol used to identify this firm's common stock for trading and tracking purposes is indicated. Where appropriate, this field may contain "private" or "subsidiary" rather than a ticker symbol. If the firm is a publicly-held company headquartered outside of the U.S., its international ticker and exchange are given. If the firm is a subsidiary, its parent company is listed.

Total Number of Employees: The approximate total number of employees, worldwide, as of the end of 2009 (or the latest data available to the editors).

Apparent Salaries/Benefits:

(The following descriptions generally apply to U.S. employers only.)

A "Y" in appropriate fields indicates "Yes."

Due to wide variations in the manner in which corporations report benefits to the U.S. Government's regulatory bodies, not all plans will have been uncovered or correctly evaluated during our effort to research this data. Also, the availability to employees of such plans will vary according to the qualifications that employees must meet to become eligible. For example, some benefit plans may be available only to salaried workers—others only to employees who work more than 1,000 hours yearly. Benefits that are available to employees of the main or parent company may not be available to employees of the subsidiaries. In addition, employers frequently alter the nature and terms of plans offered.

NOTE: Generally, employees covered by wealth-building benefit plans do not *fully* own ("vest in") funds contributed on their behalf by the employer until as many as five years of service with that employer have passed. All pension plans are voluntary—that is, employers are not obligated to offer pensions.

Pension Plan: The firm offers a pension plan to qualified employees. In this case, in order for a "Y" to appear, the editors believe that the employer offers a defined benefit or cash balance pension plan (see discussions below).The type and generosity of these plans vary widely from firm to firm. Caution: Some employers refer to plans as "pension" or "retirement" plans when they are actually 401(k) savings plans that require a contribution by the employee.

- Defined Benefit Pension Plans: Pension plans that do not require a contribution from the employee are infrequently offered. However, a few companies, particularly larger employers in high-profit-margin industries, offer defined benefit pension plans where the employee is guaranteed to receive a set pension benefit upon retirement. The amount of the benefit is determined by the years of service with the company and the employee's salary during the later years of employment. The longer a person works for the employer, the higher the retirement benefit. These defined benefit plans are funded entirely by the employer. The benefits, up to a reasonable limit, are guaranteed by the Federal Government's Pension Benefit Guaranty Corporation. These plans are not portable—if you leave the company, you cannot transfer your benefits into a different plan. Instead, upon retirement you will receive the benefits that vested during your service with the company. If your employer offers a pension plan, it must give you a summary plan description within 90 days of the date you join the plan. You can also request a summary annual report of the plan, and once every 12 months you may request an individual benefit statement accounting of your interest in the plan.

- Defined Contribution Plans: These are quite different. They do not guarantee a certain amount of pension benefit. Instead, they set out circumstances under which the employer will make a contribution to a plan on your behalf. The most common example is the 401(k) savings plan. Pension benefits are not guaranteed under these plans.
- Cash Balance Pension Plans: These plans were recently invented. These are hybrid plans—part defined benefit and part defined contribution. Many employers have converted their older defined benefit plans into cash balance plans. The employer makes deposits (or credits a given amount of money) on the employee's behalf, usually based on a percentage of pay. Employee accounts grow based on a predetermined interest benchmark, such as the interest rate on Treasury Bonds. There are some advantages to these plans, particularly for younger workers: a) The benefits, up to a reasonable limit, are guaranteed by the Pension Benefit Guaranty Corporation. b) Benefits are portable—they can be moved to another plan when the employee changes companies. c) Younger workers and those who spend a shorter number of years with an employer may receive higher benefits than they would under a traditional defined benefit plan.

ESOP Stock Plan (Employees' Stock Ownership Plan): This type of plan is in wide use. Typically, the plan borrows money from a bank and uses those funds to purchase a large block of the corporation's stock. The corporation makes contributions to the plan over a period of time, and the stock purchase loan is eventually paid off. The value of the plan grows significantly as long as the market price of the stock holds up. Qualified employees are allocated a share of the plan based on their length of service and their level of salary. Under federal regulations, participants in ESOPs are allowed to diversify their account holdings in set percentages that rise as the employee ages and gains years of service with the company. In this manner, not all of the employee's assets are tied up in the employer's stock.

Savings Plan, 401(k): Under this type of plan, employees make a tax-deferred deposit into an account. In the best plans, the company makes annual matching donations to the employees' accounts, typically in some proportion to deposits made by the employees themselves. A good plan will match one-half of employee deposits of up to 6% of wages. For example, an employee earning $30,000 yearly might deposit $1,800 (6%) into the plan. The company will match one-half of the employee's deposit, or $900. The plan grows on a tax-deferred basis, similar to an IRA. A very generous plan will match 100% of employee deposits. However, some plans do not call for the employer to make a matching deposit at all. Other plans call for a matching contribution to be made at the discretion of the firm's board of directors. Actual terms of these plans vary widely from firm to firm. Generally, these savings plans allow employees to deposit as much as 15% of salary into the plan on a tax-deferred basis. However, the portion that the company uses to calculate its matching deposit is generally limited to a maximum of 6%. Employees should take care to diversify the holdings in their 401(k) accounts, and most people should seek professional guidance or investment management for their accounts.

Stock Purchase Plan: Qualified employees may purchase the company's common stock at a price below its market value under a specific plan. Typically, the employee is limited to investing a small percentage of wages in this plan. The discount may range from 5 to 15%. Some of these plans allow for deposits to be made through regular monthly payroll deductions. However, new accounting rules for corporations, along with other factors, are leading many companies to curtail these plans—dropping the discount allowed, cutting the maximum yearly stock purchase or otherwise making the plans less generous or appealing.

Profit Sharing: Qualified employees are awarded an annual amount equal to some portion of a company's profits. In a very generous plan, the pool of money awarded to employees would be 15% of profits. Typically, this money is deposited into a long-term retirement account. Caution: Some employers refer to plans as "profit sharing" when they are actually 401(k) savings plans. True profit sharing plans are rarely offered.

Highest Executive Salary: The highest executive salary paid, typically a 2009 amount (or the latest year available to the editors) and typically paid to the Chief Executive Officer.

Highest Executive Bonus: The apparent bonus, if any, paid to the above person.

Second Highest Executive Salary: The next-highest executive salary paid, typically a 2009 amount (or the latest year available to the editors) and typically paid to the President or Chief Operating Officer.

Second Highest Executive Bonus: The apparent bonus, if any, paid to the above person.

Other Thoughts:

Apparent Women Officers or Directors: It is difficult to obtain this information on an exact basis, and employers generally do not disclose the data in a public way. However, we have indicated what our best efforts reveal to be the apparent number of women who either are in the posts of corporate officers or sit on the board of directors. There is a wide variance from company to company.

Hot Spot for Advancement for Women/Minorities: A "Y" in appropriate fields indicates "Yes." These are firms that appear either to have posted a substantial number of women and/or minorities to high posts or that appear to have a good record of going out of their way to recruit, train, promote and retain women or minorities. (See the Index of Hot Spots For Women and Minorities in the back of the book.) This information may change frequently and can be difficult to obtain and verify. Consequently, the reader should use caution and conduct further investigation where appropriate.

Growth Plans/ Special Features:

Listed here are observations regarding the firm's strategy, hiring plans, plans for growth and product development, along with general information regarding a company's business and prospects.

Locations:

A "Y" in the appropriate field indicates "Yes."

Primary locations outside of the headquarters, categorized by regions of the United States and by international locations. A complete index by locations is also in the front of this chapter.

Chapter 1

MAJOR TRENDS AFFECTING THE AUTOMOBILE INDUSTRY

Major Trends Affecting the Automobile Industry:

1) **Automobile Industry Introduction**
2) **Global Competition Heats Up Among U.S., German, Japanese and Korean Car Makers**
3) **Fuel Efficiency Becomes a Key Selling Element/Stiff Emissions Standards Adopted in the U.S. and Abroad**
4) **Hybrid Cars Gain Market Share**
5) **Electric Cars and Plug-in Hybrids (PHEVs) Will Quickly Gain Popularity**
6) **Major Research in Advanced Lithium Batteries**
7) **Clean Diesel Technology Gains Acceptance**
8) **Natural Gas Powered Vehicles off to a Slow Start**
9) **Ethanol Production Soared, But a Market Glut May Slow Expansion**
10) **Fuel Cell and Hydrogen Power Research Continues**
11) **Outsourcing of Component Design and Manufacturing/Sharing of Parts**
12) **"Optimum Lean Production" Saves Manufacturing Costs**
13) **Car Purchasers Rely on the Internet**
14) **China Becomes the World's Largest Auto Market/Sales Rise in India**
15) **Focus on Safety Improvements by Automakers**
16) **Super-Expensive Cars are Pushed by Manufacturers/Luxury Car Market Is Highly Competitive**
17) **Rethinking SUVs/Small Sedans and Crossovers Gain Market Share**
18) **Big News in Small Cars**
19) **Car and Bike Sharing Programs Proliferate**
20) **Wireless Information Systems Surge Ahead in Vehicles: Telematics, ITS and Real-Time Traffic Information**

1) Automobile Industry Introduction

In the U.S. and around the world, the recession that started in late 2007 had a profound impact on the automobile industry. America's car and light truck market dropped dramatically in 2008, to approximately 13.2 million units sold for the year, down by about 2.9 million from the number of units sold in 2007. In 2009, the market was much worse, with sales for the year totaling 10.4 million units. About 690,000 of those sales were made with the stimulus of a "cash for clunkers" program paid for with federal dollars. This was easily the worst year in decades for the car business, with two giant manufacturers filing for bankruptcy, GM and Chrysler, while a large number of dealerships, suppliers, parts manufacturers and other auto-related businesses also failed.

Estimates of the worldwide automobile market vary substantially from one group to another. Scotiabank Group estimated that 53.96 million new cars and light trucks would be sold globally during 2010. Analysts at R. L. Polk & Co. estimated 2009 global sales of cars and light trucks at 61.9 million, down by 5.1% over 2008.

As widely expected, GM filed for bankruptcy in mid-2009, and was promptly put back in business by a massive federal bailout. Chrysler's significant financial problems led it to file for bankruptcy protection in April 2009. The company secured a large federal bailout and new financing from the U.S., Canadian and Ontario governments. This enabled it to quickly emerge from bankruptcy in a new structure with help from Italian carmaker Fiat, which initially owns about 20% of Chrysler. Fiat will have the right to earn additional shares in the company if certain goals are met, which could lead to Fiat owning a controlling stake. Labor unions received significant stakes in both GM and Chrysler as part of their reorganization. Outside of the U.S., Toyota received some financing from the Japanese government, and car makers throughout Europe and Asia were seeking concessions and/or financial aid.

Analysts at RL Polk expected 2010 car and light truck sales in the U.S. to total approximately 11.5 million units.

The biggest upward trend in auto sales for 2009 and 2010 was in China, where government stimulus helped dealers to sell about 13.6 million units in 2009 and an expected 14 million in 2010. China has become the world's largest car market, and RL Polk expects it to hit 17.5 million units in 2015.

The biggest winner in this tumultuous environment has been Korea, where Kia and Hyundai have enjoyed soaring global sales, as consumers are attracted to their reasonable prices, excellent warranties and world class manufacturing quality. Korean car makers are competing aggressively against leading Japanese firms.

There are approximately 250 million vehicles in operation in the United States. Around the world, there were about 1 billion cars and light trucks on the road in 2010.

The years of 2004 through 2006 will long be remembered as a pivotal period in the automobile industry. It was a period during which high gasoline prices finally created significant demand among U.S. consumers for fuel-efficient vehicles. Gasoline prices of approximately $2.00 per gallon started taking a huge bite out of family budgets in 2004, and many middle-class consumers who owned fuel guzzling SUVs and pickup trucks began to wish they had vehicles that were much less expensive to operate. By 2005-2006, with gasoline prices in the $3.00 range, the party was over for large SUVs and family trucks.

All major car makers will be aggressively pushing their smaller, high efficiency vehicles in 2011-2012. GM is betting heavily on its Chevrolet Cruze, a small sedan capable of 36 mpg on the highway and stuffed with convenience features that consumers will appreciate. Ford's revamped Fusion earned rave reviews in the 2010 model year, and it comes in either a hybrid model or a standard engine version that gets 31 mpg on the highway. Chrysler will be relying heavily on its relationship with Fiat for new, fuel efficient models.

One result of high gasoline costs and frugal consumers has been strong demand for Toyota's Prius gasoline-electric hybrid car over recent years. Also, Toyota made investments in its Georgetown, Kentucky plant to enable it to manufacture hybrid Camrys. There has also been good demand for Toyota's Lexus RX hybrid crossover. Ford launched its hybrids, and other carmakers, including GM, are making their own efforts to bring more hybrids to the market. However, consumers generally aren't as impressed with U.S. hybrid technology as they are with that of Toyota models, and actual mileage results on the road are often disappointing, largely due to driver habits such as quick acceleration which uses more fuel. Hybrids are now available from a wide variety of makers, and technology has steadily improved.

One of the most important trends will be rapid growth in plug-in hybrids (PHEVs) and electric vehicles such as GM's Volt, which will debut as a 2011 model. This car includes a gasoline-powered generator capable of charging its batteries for those occasions when it is not convenient to plug in. Tremendous improvements in battery technology will soon come to market, further enhancing this trend. Nissan offers strong competition in the electric vehicle sector, with the launch of its 2011 all-electric model called Leaf.

Both consumers and emissions regulators are taking a renewed interest in advanced automobile technologies. Clean diesel engines, like those offered in new cars from BMW, Volkswagen and Mercedes-Benz, offer exceptional performance and fuel economy while providing quiet, vibration-free running similar to that found in gasoline-powered cars. Clean diesel offers a particularly attractive alternative to hybrid technology for those who seek fuel efficiency, and it is already widely used in passenger vehicles in Europe. The use of ethanol as a gasoline additive in America has grown rapidly, regardless of whether it makes any environmental or economic sense, thanks to requirements enacted by Congress, backed up by massive government subsidies.

Consumers are keenly interested in quality and serviceability in the cars that they acquire. A stumble in this regard can have devastating consequences for a car maker, as seen in Toyota's recent quality problems that led to slow sales, massive recalls and a humble apology from the firm's leader.

Meanwhile, sales of heavy SUVs have lagged miserably. Ford cancelled production of its larger-than-life Excursion SUV in which some owners reported getting as little as 11 mpg in the city, and GM dumped its Hummer line of SUVs, selling it to a Chinese firm.

The rising affluence of consumers in China is creating both huge opportunities and huge problems. China has become one of the world's largest importers of petroleum products, largely to fuel its burgeoning fleet of cars and trucks. Streets and highways are clogged with cars, to the extent that traffic and smog are nightmarish. Automakers from abroad have raced to establish plants and partnerships in China, with the aim of producing cars both for domestic use and for export. In fact, low labor costs and increasing product quality in China threaten auto plants located in high cost nations such as the U.S. Today, more cars are sold in China than in any other nation, and strong markets have emerged there for everything from inexpensive sedans and vans to Cadillacs and German luxury cars. One of the brightest trends for GM in 2009-2010 has been its great success in selling cars in China.

India has also seen significant growth in its automotive sector. During 2009, local industrial giant Tata launched, with great success, a no-frills car called Nano at a price equal to less than $2,500 U.S dollars.

Not to be overlooked are the vast changes taking place in automobile manufacturing plants. Flexible factories have reduced man-hours and cut costs per car, while offering a much wider range of choices for customization to consumers. Today, more than ever, car manufacturers and their suppliers are cooperating in the design and manufacture of new cars in ways that are revolutionizing the entire process.

Inexpensive cars manufactured in China will soon be on the market in many nations. The question is not whether China will export cars and trucks, but whether consumers in markets such as America will be convinced that they offer safety and reliability. Meanwhile, U.S. automakers have made intense demands on their component suppliers for lower prices—these suppliers are, in turn, looking to low-cost production in China and other emerging nations.

European manufacturers are facing challenges of their own. High costs, tough labor laws, daunting government regulations and a few disappointing model designs have hampered recent results. Meanwhile, European markets suffered from the general economic slowdown, leading to poor automobile sales results.

The Progressive Insurance Automotive X PRIZE offered $10 million in prizes to the competitors able to create viable passenger vehicles capable of operating at the equivalent of 100 miles per gallon. The competition is in conjunction with the X PRIZE Foundation. Of the 111 teams entered, seven remained in final competition. The winners, announced in September 2010, were Edison2, a Virginia-based team of racing engineers who designed and built a four-seat car that gets 102 mpg; Li-ion Motors, a North Carolina firm that produced a two-seat vehicle; and X-Tracer, a Swiss company who produced a motorcycle-type vehicle called the E-Tracer. Edison2 won $5 million, while Li-ion and X-Tracer won $2.5 million each.

2) Global Competition Heats Up Among U.S., German, Japanese and Korean Car Makers

Throughout much of automotive history, the Big Three (GM, Ford and Chrysler) dominated the U.S. market. That dominance was compromised for the first time in July 2006 as unit sales in America for Toyota for that month surpassed those of number two ranked Ford, while Honda briefly surpassed the Chrysler Group (the former U.S. arm of DaimlerChrysler) to rank fourth in unit sales. By the first quarter of 2008, Toyota made worldwide car history by surpassing GM in global automotive sales, selling 2.41 million vehicles compared to GM's 2.25 million. Overall in 2008, Toyota surpassed GM to become the world's biggest auto maker by selling 8.97 million vehicles worldwide compared to GM's 8.35 million (Toyota sales fell 4% in 2008). In 2009, GM slightly pulled ahead of Toyota, selling 7.49 million vehicles worldwide compared to Toyota's 7.24 million. (Meanwhile, Volkswagen is growing rapidly on a global basis, and it may eventually vie for first place.)

Market Share of Cars and Light Trucks sold in America, July 2010	
General Motors	19.0%
Toyota	16.1%
Ford	15.8%
Honda	10.7%
Chrysler	8.9%
Nissan	7.8%

Source: MotorIntelligence.com

By early 2009, the global automobile industry was in a deep slump. Sales were dropping substantially. GM and Chrysler received billions of dollars in federal aid, which was tied to a requirement that the firms develop specific plans for staying afloat. Those plans included concessions from labor unions, fewer workers and fewer plants, along with a reduction in dealerships and models.

Further government aid in the U.S. was announced in 2009 in the form of $25 billion in loans for retooling factories, with a focus on the production of fuel-efficient or electric vehicles. Ford and electric car maker Tesla were among the first to benefit. For others, the road has been more difficult.

GM declared bankruptcy in June 2009, drastically reorganized and emerged from it a month later. Since then, the company reduced its dealerships from a previous total of 6,049 to 5,114 as of August 2010. GM hopes to further reduce its dealer numbers to about 4,500. The U.S. government owns about 60% of the reorganized company, and the Canadian government owns about 12.5%, while former bondholders and the UAW union own the balance. GM shut down its Saturn division, following a failed attempt to sell the company to Penske Automotive Group. In February 2010, the company sold its Saab division to Spyker Cars NV, a Dutch sports car producer. It also sold its Hummer unit and shut down the Pontiac division. GM planned an IPO for late 2010 in order to raise as much as $16 billion. One of the goals of the IPO is to reduce the amount of stock held by governments.

Chrysler's significant financial problems led it to file for bankruptcy protection in April 2009. The company secured a large federal bailout and new financing from the U.S., Canadian and Ontario governments. This enabled it to quickly emerge from bankruptcy in a new structure with help from Italian carmaker Fiat, which initially owns about 20% of Chrysler. Fiat will have the right to earn additional shares in the company if certain goals are met, which could lead to Fiat owning a controlling stake. Fiat's effect on Chrysler vehicles will become apparent to consumers by 2012 when the company returns the popular Alpha Romeo sports car to the U.S. market and introduces the 500, a tiny Fiat that is popular throughout Europe. At the same time, Chrysler will phase out a number of Dodge models including the Grand Caravan minivan and a number of Jeep models.

Meanwhile, Ford has quietly gone about its own reorganization, without government bailouts and without declaring bankruptcy. The company sold its Jaguar, Volvo and Land Rover brands, and in 2010 announced plans to close its Mercury division. Ford also closed a number of its production plants, and shuttered more than 600 dealerships.

The good news is that cost cutting, downsizing and reorganizing, along with a somewhat more stable economy, resulted in growth for the Big Three in sales, profits and hiring in the first part of 2010. Ford earned $4.7 billion in the first 6 months of 2010, its largest profit for that period since 1998. GM was showing a profit and Chrysler announced plans to hire 3,100 new workers. After more than 330,000 jobs at U.S. automakers and suppliers were lost in 2008 according to White House officials, 55,000 jobs have been created since Chrysler and GM emerged from bankruptcy.

In recent years, the appeal of foreign cars and trucks in the U.S., combined with substantial investments made by foreign firms such as Toyota, BMW, Honda and Nissan in American manufacturing plants and dealerships, undermined Detroit's leadership. Beginning in the 1960s, foreign cars slowly infiltrated the U.S. market. By the 1980s American consumers in substantial numbers began to perceive foreign products to be superior in design and quality. Foreign cars began to enjoy higher resale values and higher levels of reliability. American carmakers' share of the U.S. market fell from 73.5% in 1995 to about 57% in 2005. In the critical month of July 2008, those percentages shifted further, with U.S. companies holding just 42.7% of the U.S. auto market, while Asian automakers took 38%. Despite heavy discounting and incentives from U.S. carmakers, consumers were seeking the fuel economy and high quality that they equate with many Asian models, including increasingly popular Korean cars.

The weakened global economy in 2008-09, skyrocketing gasoline prices in 2008 and tightening credit wreaked havoc with U.S. auto manufacturers which posted staggering losses. GM posted a $30.9 billion loss for 2008 on an 11% decline in sales. Ford lost $14.7 billion in the same period, with sales falling 17% to $146.2 billion. At privately-held Chrysler, 2008 losses reached $16.8 billion, although sales fell only 1.2%.

Part of the problem facing the Big Three is the growing shift in American tastes away from gas-guzzling SUVs and light trucks (vehicles that have long been top money-makers for the Big Three as well as for many other manufacturers) to smaller, more fuel efficient cars.

To tackle their problems, the Big Three have been aggressively realigning operations. Tens of thousands of workers have been eliminated. Ford is investing heavily to retool certain existing plants in North America so that they can manufacture at least six small car designs that are good sellers in Europe, and to alter those designs to fit American regulations. For example, in 2010, the firm converted its F-Series truck plant in Mexico to the production of the popular Fiesta, a small four- and five-door vehicle rated at about 40 mpg on the highway. The Fiesta was initially seen as a car to be sold only in Europe and Asia, but it may turn out to be a big hit in the U.S. These initiatives coupled with a massive restructuring put Ford on good financial footing.

Adding to the problems of the U.S. car industry has been the expensive relationship between American carmakers and the United Auto Workers (UAW) labor union. Domestic manufacturers bore the burden of heavy pension and health care costs, both for current and retired workers, as stipulated in contracts with the UAW that have existed for years. This changed dramatically in late 2007 when first GM followed by Ford and Chrysler signed hard-fought deals with the UAW in which a health care trust was established and funded by the union rather than the car manufacturers. This shifted billions in annual health care costs previously paid by the Big Three. In addition, important new agreements with the UAW were reached in 2009 that will dramatically cut labor costs overall.

Cuts in wages and benefits will make U.S. auto labor costs more comparable to those of Japanese firms. Japanese automakers, both in their U.S. and non-U.S. plants, enjoyed significant cost advantages for years because they do not have the pension and labor structures that existed at the Big Three. Their U.S. plants generally are not working under union contracts. However, a number of U.S. plants owned by the Japanese companies are maturing, and workers are earning top wages. According to the Center for Automotive Research, 2009 autoworker costs per hour were $33.00 in the U.S. and $38.63 in Japan. China by far undercuts labor costs with only $3.00 per hour.

Toyota, one of the world's most admired and most successful auto makers, is not immune to the economic slump. Falling sales caused Toyota big problems in excess capacity at its seven North American plants (many of which produce slow-selling trucks and SUVs). For the fiscal year ending March 2009, the company reported a staggering $4.7 billion loss. Global sales were down 21.9% in the 2008-2009 fiscal year. The company recovered significantly in fiscal 2010 despite a number of recalls, ending with approximately $2.48 billion in profit. This is largely due to significant cost cutting, such as revamping its component utilization and instigating its plan to cut the cost of auto parts by 30% by 2013.

A bright spot for manufacturers in late 2009 was the U.S. Government's "Cash for Clunkers" program in the month of August. Officially named the Car Allowance Rebate System (CARS), the program encouraged drivers of vehicles that get 18 miles per gallon fuel efficiency or less to trade in those vehicles for new, more fuel efficient models. Dealers were allowed to give buyers a credit of between $3,500 and $4,500, depending on the price of the new vehicle, paid from a $3 billion federal fund. At the program's end, 690,000 new vehicles were purchased and about $2.9 billion was paid out of government funds.

Many analysts believe that the company to watch in global auto manufacturing is Volkswagen. As of 2010, the firm was already Europe's largest manufacturer. In 2009, Volkswagen sold 6.3 million vehicles worldwide (under the VW, Audi, Bugatti and Scania brands, among others) compared to Toyota's 7.8 million. Volkswagen plans to sell more than 10 million vehicles per year by 2018. In order to boost growth, the company is investing $1 billion in a new midsize sedan production plant in Chattanooga, Tennessee (its first plant in the U.S.) with an initial capacity of 150,000 cars. The firm hopes to triple its sales in America by 2018 to 1 million vehicles yearly, while growing Audi sales to 200,000 units per year. Volkswagen agreed to acquire a 20% stake in Suzuki Motors to increase its presence in India and Southeast Asia. Also, the company plans to invest $11 billion between 2010 and 2013 in order to develop new luxury Audi models to compete with BMW and Mercedes. The Audi brand is enjoying strong sales in the important Chinese market.

All auto manufacturers are gambling on better sales of cars and trucks over the mid- to long-term. Total units sold in the U.S. dropped to 10.4 million in 2009. Based on sales in the first three quarters of 2010, analysts expect sales to total about 11.5 to 12 million units for the year, with the Big Three accounting for about 46%.

3) Fuel Efficiency Becomes a Key Selling Element/Stiff Emissions Standards Adopted in the U.S. and Abroad

By mid-2009, the price per gallon of gasoline in the U.S. averaged around $2.50, which continued more or less into 2010. This followed significantly higher prices in 2008 when consumers were paying more than $4 per gallon. The fluctuating market for gasoline has many consumers reconsidering the vehicles they are willing to drive. Light trucks, usually defined as minivans, pickups and sport utility vehicles (SUVs), have lost market share to smaller, more fuel-efficient vehicles. This was very bad news indeed for the Big Three (General Motors, Ford and Chrysler). U.S. carmakers in the 1990s and early 2000s saw 60% or more of their unit sales in America to be in light trucks, which earned very high profit margins. In contrast, Asian car manufacturers such as Honda, Kia, Hyundai and Nissan offer product lines comprised of more than 50% sedans or smaller vehicles.

This is not to say that light trucks no longer sell in America. In fact, they remain a very large market, although much smaller than in the past. Consumers are now more likely to buy a much smaller vehicle, unless they really need a truck, SUV or minivan in order to carry their typical loads. Light trucks are still needed by certain consumers and by many types of businesses, regardless of the fact that the cost of filling them with fuel has soared. To put this in perspective: In 2004, "truck" sales (primarily pickups, vans and SUVs) hit their peak in the U.S., selling 9.6 million units or about 55.5% of car/truck sales combined. For 2009, the number of trucks sold was down considerably to about 5.0 million, at 47% of the U.S. market. For the manufacturers, gross profits per light truck unit are in the $10,000 to $15,000 range, many times higher than the profits made from small cars.

CAFE (corporate average fuel economy) standards were first issued by U.S. federal regulators in the 1970s as a method of setting average fuel economy standards for carmakers. In December 2007, the U.S. federal government signed a fuel efficiency bill into law that requires automakers to raise their average combined gas mileage fleet-wide to 35 miles per gallon (mpg) by 2020 for all cars and light trucks. The government then established a further requirement of 31.6 mpg for all cars and trucks by 2015. In 2009, the Obama Administration substantially raised those requirements to an average of 35.5 mpg by 2016.

In order to reach such high levels of efficiency, higher costs will impact sticker prices. The Obama Administration estimates that about $1,300 will be added to an average vehicle's price, which might be regained by fuel savings over time. However, some auto industry observers believe that these tough mileage requirements will add much higher manufacturing costs than those estimated by the government.

These new fuel efficiency regulations sparked a furor of protests from automakers, especially U.S. firms. According to Global Insight, GM, Ford and Chrysler would have had to invest nearly $31 billion to meet the 31.6 mpg fleet-wide standards by 2015. Toyota, Honda and Nissan needed to invest about $15 billion since their vehicles are closer to meeting the standards. Hyundai Motor Co. made headlines in late 2008 when it announced that its Hyundai and Kia cars would meet the 35 mpg standard as early as 2015, a full five years before the deadline imposed at the time. The tougher requirements enacted in 2009 place even more pressure on manufacturers already reeling from staggering losses.

According to the U.S. Environmental Protection Agency, the most fuel-efficient 2010 car models included the Toyota Prius hybrid, Ford Fusion hybrid, Honda Civic hybrid, Honda Insight hybrid and Lexus HS250h hybrid.

Not surprisingly, lightweight, advanced diesel models rank highly for mileage, including the Volkswagen Golf TDI, Jetta TDI and Beetle TDI. In Europe, about one-half of all new passenger vehicles sold are diesel-powered.

Meanwhile, in 2008 the EU made a formal proposal for Euro VI emission standards to take effect starting in 2013. The proposal requires an 80% reduction of nitrogen oxide (NOx) and a 66% reduction of the particulate matter (PM) emission limit.

Environmental groups lobbying for lower emissions levels claim that these reductions can be accomplished by updating air conditioning refrigerants, designing more efficient transmissions, and making exterior designs more aerodynamic, while utilizing such things as turbochargers and cylinder deactivators in smaller, more efficient engines. These groups, spearheaded by an organization called the Union of Concerned Scientists, projected that these changes could be made at a cost of $1,960 per vehicle, and that the costs will be recouped by savings at the gas pump. Some observers claim that many of the proposed changes are not feasible, and if they were, they would cost upwards of $4,360 per vehicle.

A study by the National Academy of Sciences projected that improvements of as much as 40% in gasoline-powered automobile fuel economy could be achieved within 10 to 15 years through the use of enhanced technologies. For example, advanced transmissions and fuel-injection systems could minimize fuel usage and curtail unwanted power loss. While the manufacture of lighter vehicles could improve mileage, weight is not the single overriding factor. Technologies are available that could do wonders for fuel efficiency, although they would take considerable time, money and effort to fully deploy.

A study, prepared in part by John DeCicco at Environmental Defense, declared that the adoption of current and emerging technologies could drive the average efficiency of U.S. cars to 46 mpg and SUVs to 40 mpg. The study was co-authored by Feng An of the Argonne National Laboratory and Marc Ross, a physicist and automobile expert at the University of Michigan. They propose that two-thirds of the improvement would come from powertrain technology, while one-third would come from cutting three important factors: vehicle weight, air resistance and rolling resistance. Hyundai is focusing on technologies such as gasoline direct injection, dual continuously variable valve timing and eight-speed automatic transmissions in order to dramatically enhance mileage.

A proven gas-saving measure is an inexpensive shift to a six-speed automatic transmission. The cost for the addition is a mere $400, but the measure can add one to two miles per gallon in efficiency. This kind of transmission was already being used in many new vehicles as of 2008. The 2011 Ford Mustang proves that drivers can enjoy fast acceleration as well as excellent fuel efficiency, since the V-6 model delivers 305 horsepower and 31 mpg on the highway. The car has a six-speed transmission, in addition to lower-rolling resistance tires and an electric (as opposed to a hydraulic) power steering system which reduces engine strain. Ford plans to use this electric steering system on all its models by 2012.

GM claims that an improvement of between 6% and 12% in fuel economy can be achieved through cylinder deactivation technology. In these systems, one-half of an engine's cylinders stop firing once a steady cruising speed is reached.

A bright spot on the fuel efficiency horizon is a new hydraulic-hybrid system that is being tested on large service vehicles such as garbage trucks and UPS delivery vans. The EPA's National Vehicle and Fuel Emissions Laboratory in Ann Arbor, Michigan has designed a hybrid garbage truck that uses a diesel engine, assisted by a hydraulic pump and storage tank system, that replaces the drivetrain and transmission. The pump and tanks makes it possible to store and reuse energy normally lost when brakes are applied, thereby increasing fuel efficiency as much as 60% and reducing carbon monoxide emissions by more than 40%. UPS placed an order with hydraulic manufacturer Eaton Corporation and truck builder Navistar for 200 hybrid electric vehicles which hit the streets in cities across the U.S. in 2010. The EPA projects that the cost per vehicle to add the hybrid components is less than $7,000, while fuel savings over a 20-year lifespan could exceed $50,000.

Internet Research Tip: Hybrid Commercial Trucks:
Hybrid trucks and buses will soon be in high demand by major truck fleet operators such as UPS. For the latest information on pilot projects, technologies and fleet purchases, see Calstart's website at www.calstart.org.

Another new technology of note is an artificial neural network. The network, which is composed of models of neurons embedded on standard silicon chips, detects cylinder misfires and controls idle speeds, thus increasing fuel efficiency. These networks are already in use in large-engine vehicles such as Aston-Martin's 12-cylinder DB9 and Ford's E-Series full-size van. GM and Audi are also working on implementing the technology for use in issues relating to variable valve timing and engine performance improvements. Serious measures such as these will have to be taken across the board by automakers in their vehicle designs in order to meet future emissions and efficiency stipulations.

4) Hybrid Cars Gain Market Share

Toyota and Honda have been selling hybrid gasoline/electric cars in the U.S. since 2001. Since the Prius' Japanese launch in 1997, Toyota had sold more than 2 million of them worldwide as of late 2009. In 2008, 487,000 hybrids of all types were sold around the world, and about the same number sold in 2009 (290.3 thousand in the U.S., or 2.7% of all vehicles sold, according to the Department of

Energy). For the long-term, Toyota hopes to further fuel hybrid sales through the introduction of advanced lithium-ion batteries, as opposed to the nickel-metal-hydride batteries it now uses. However, lithium-ion batteries are faced with safety problems when crushed or overheated. Toyota's third-generation 2010 model offers increased mpg and other enhancements. The firm hoped to sell 400,000 Prius units in the 2010 model year. This may be difficult to achieve, since even hybrid sales have been hit by the global economic recession. Toyota indefinitely delayed construction of a plant in Mississippi that was to begin manufacturing Priuses in May 2010.

For the near term, Toyota plans to introduce six new hybrid vehicles to global markets and two electric cars in the United States by the end of 2012. Ford is expected to unveil an electric version of the Focus in 2012.

A typical hybrid design places two engines in a vehicle, one a traditional internal combustion motor and the other electric. The traditional engine powers the car at startup and when accelerating, and charges the electric engine's battery (separate from the gasoline-powered motor's battery). When slowing down or idling, the standard engine shuts down and the electric motor takes over. The batteries are also charged when a car is rapidly decelerating, bleeding off forward momentum to power the generators. The downside: hybrid cars can cost $2,000 to $10,000 more than their standard powered counterparts, and many drivers have found actual fuel efficiency to be vastly lower than EPA estimates.

The base price for the 2011 Toyota Prius is $21,000. Honda is also competing aggressively in the hybrid market. The Honda Insight hybrid is a sedan similar to the Prius, but with a slightly lower base price. Honda is betting on other hybrid models including a 2011 hybrid Civic sedan, and a 2011 CRZ hybrid sports car.

Other successful hybrids are produced by Lexus, a division of Toyota. The Lexus RX450h, based on the extremely popular RX350 crossover, was the first. The hybrid version was launched in the U.S. in spring 2005, powered by its high-performance Hybrid Synergy Drive system. A pair of electric motors powers both front and rear wheels, in a system that can be configured to boost either total power or fuel economy. For 2010, the new RX450h model had a base price of $41,660; a large increase, as much as $4,000, over the price of the standard-power RX350, but that hasn't stopped it from selling quickly. In 2010, Lexus also launched the HS250h Sport Sedan.

Volkswagen debuted its first hybrid in early 2010, a Touareg that combines a V-6 gasoline engine and a 47-horesepower electric motor with an advanced transmission.

On the commercial side, Daimler Buses North America has sold more than 3,000 Orion VII diesel-electric hybrid buses. The Orion VII utilizes a propulsion system made by BAE Systems which in turn derives power from a Cummins diesel engine and an electric motor powered by a generator and a lithium-ion battery.

India's Eko Vehicles Pvt. Ltd. launched a hybrid moped in late 2009. Priced at about $800, the ET-120 gets about 284 miles per gallon of gasoline (or 120 km per liter) and has a top speed of about 40 mph (65 km).

5) Electric Cars and Plug-in Hybrids (PHEVs) Will Quickly Gain Popularity

For the near term, electric cars will range from 100% electric power vehicles that have relatively short ranges and are plugged-in at home overnight to recharge—to cars like the Chevrolet Volt that will run on an electric motor only, but will include a small gasoline-powered generator engine that will recharge the batteries when needed. The Volt is designed to go up to 40 miles without recharging, and it will have the capability to be recharged by plug-in at home. Many challenges face 100% electric cars. In addition to adequate battery life, engineers are wrestling with the fact that conveniences such as air conditioning, heating and stereos drain a lot of electricity. Technical advances in these accessories may be necessary, since consumers will not buy such cars in volume without them.

A little history is in order: An all-electric car has long sounded logical to many people. GM launched the EV1, an all-electric vehicle, in 1996. Unfortunately, the car was a complete flop, and the $1-billion project was abandoned in 1999. In 2002, Ford announced that it would give up on the Think, an electric car model in which it had invested $123 million. These efforts were an attempt to satisfy government demands, not an attempt to fill early consumer needs. Today's electric cars and hybrids are intended to be major product lines for automakers.

Plug-in hybrids (PHEVs) are similar to standard hybrids, but they enable the owner the option of plugging-in at home overnight to recharge the battery. This will eliminate the need to run the car's gasoline engine, using only battery power as long as the relatively short range isn't exceeded. (Standard hybrids recharge only by running the gasoline-powered side of the car, and by drawing on the drag produced by using the brakes.) Toyota made 500 PHEV versions of its Prius available for testing by selected consumers during 2010 (150 of them in the U.S.).

Meanwhile, GM planned to release its long-awaited Chevy Volt in late 2010. Honda plans a PHEV version for its 2011 Civic.

All-electric cars as well as advanced hybrids are about to make a massive push into the global auto market. This is due to several factors, including:

1) Technical breakthroughs in lithium-ion batteries, making them safer and longer-lasting, are leading to true breakthroughs in electric cars.

2) An electric car research, development and investment focus at major car manufacturers.

3) Toyota quickly proved global consumer acceptance (and technological superiority) by selling more than 2 million Prius hybrid vehicles worldwide from its 1997 debut in Japan. Eventually, Toyota hopes to be selling 1 million hybrid vehicles each year.

4) Electricity is user-friendly, easy to understand, and easy to obtain. Electric utility companies are generally in favor of the electric car trend. Governments are wildly enthusiastic and supportive (including financial support to manufacturers and incentives for consumers).

5) Innovative entrepreneurs are on the electric vehicle bandwagon.

6) Last, but not at all least, in the proper package and at an affordable price, consumers see electric cars as green (low- to no-emissions), highly desirable modes of transportation.

As of late-2010, a few all-electric cars, those that lack gasoline engines and operate entirely on batteries, were already on the market. For example, Irvine, California startup Fisker claimed to have orders for about 1,600 of its $87,900 Karma, and hoped to reach full production of 15,000 cars per month by early 2011.

Another high-end electric vehicle is the Tango T600, made by Commuter Cars Corporation. For $108,000, drivers can take the two-seater (one seat behind the other) from zero to 60 miles per hour in about four seconds, and reach a top speed of more than 130 mph (there is also a $150,000 model which uses more powerful lithium batteries).

Mitsubishi offers a tiny plug-in vehicle, the MiEV, at a price of more than $40,000. The MiEV can travel up to 100 miles on a charge. Mitsubishi hoped to sell 1,400 of the pricey cars in Japan during fiscal 2010, and up to 5,000 in 2011.

However, the big news in electric cars is at Tesla. The $109,000 Tesla Roadster, which can go up to 125 miles per hour and run 244 miles per charge, can also accelerate from zero to 60 mph in about 4 seconds!

Tesla, www.teslamotors.com, is a serious business startup, with substantial amounts of venture capital raised, and another $465 million in federal loans set in 2009. By July 2009, regular production of the Tesla Roadster was underway and 500 vehicles had been delivered. Another Tesla model, the Model S family sedan capable of carrying seven people, was unveiled in 2009, with commercial production hoped to start in 2012. The Model S is to have a base price of less than $60,000. Tesla has taken a simple route to solve the problem of batteries: the Tesla Roadster has 6,831 lithium-ion, laptop computer batteries linked together in the trunk.

In May 2010, the Toyota Motor Corporation purchased a $50 million stake in the firm. As part of the deal, Tesla will take over a large car manufacturing plant in Freemont, California that was formerly operated as a joint venture of Toyota and GM. The new funds and manufacturing facility will give Tesla significant expansion capability.

Toyota and Tesla will jointly develop an electric version of Toyota's compact RAV4 SUV. Toyota also plans to manufacture a compact electric car designed for short urban trips. Both of these new electric vehicles will be on the market in the spring of 2012.

On the lowest end of the electric-powered spectrum are small vehicles that began several years ago as glorified golf carts. Recent technological advances, such as the use of lightweight, long-lasting lithium-ion batteries (the type used in cellular phones and laptop computers) have helped the vehicles evolve into marketable alternatives for short-trip driving. The ZAP Xebra, a three-wheel, four-door vehicle with a sticker price of $11,700, can reach speeds of up to 40 mph and have a range of 40 miles per charge. ZAP stands for "zero air pollution." Chrysler's Global Electric Motorcars LLC subsidiary offers several models, including vehicles with options such as heated seats, steel bumpers and cup holders. Prices start at about $7,395, but buyers may be eligible for a tax credit.

GM is backing a new electric vehicle with release hoped for by November 2010, the Chevy Volt. Although it will have a gasoline-powered generator which runs if the charge in the batteries is depleted, the Volt is designed to run fully on electricity using lithium-ion batteries. GM calls this system "E-Flex." The $40,000 sedan will be able to run at cruising speed for about 40 miles (a range long enough to allow for typical city driving, with plug-ins at home or work between trips). Fuel efficiency for the Volt could reach 230 mpg for city driving. GM hopes that at least 1 million E-Flex vehicles will be produced yearly by 2020. However, the price of the Volt is nearly double that of a Toyota Prius hybrid, and the limited range on batteries will be a huge barrier in the minds of many consumers.

Nissan is taking a different tack with the debut of the Leaf, a fully electric vehicle set for release in December 2010 in Japan and the U.S. With a range of up to 100 miles, the five-seat Leaf sedan is powered by a 480-pound lithium-ion battery that can be recharged overnight on household current. The official retail price had yet to be disclosed, but most analysts expect about $25,000 for the vehicle and another $10,000 for the battery. The first vehicles are being assembled in Japan, but the firm is investing as much as $2 billion to retool its Smyrna, Tennessee plant to begin manufacturing Leafs and lithium-ion batteries by 2012. Nissan got the jump on GM by committing R&D funding to lithium-ion batteries as early as 1990. The company has a next generation battery in the pipeline that promises a range of up to 186 miles per charge. Nissan had developed much of its electric vehicle technology in partnership with Renault.

Ford is using $5.9 billion in U.S. Energy Department loans to develop 13 fuel efficient models, including the manufacture of 5,000 to 10,000 electric vehicles as early as 2011. The funds will be used partly to retool manufacturing plants in Illinois, Kentucky, Michigan, Missouri and Ohio.

GM is collaborating with utility companies in nearly 40 states to work out issues relating to power grids and the added demand that electric vehicles pose. Nissan has similar alliances to promote plug-in stations (it also designated a supplier of home charging stations using a 220-volt plug similar to those used for clothes dryers that promised to recharge batteries in less than eight hours). GM and other manufacturers are working on computer chips and software to imbed in electric vehicles that will communicate with utility systems regarding the best times to recharge for the best prices. Recharging on a summer afternoon, for example, would put a strain on grids already powering air conditioners while off-peak charging would not only be cheaper but more efficient since power plants typically have excess electrical capacity at night.

Many observers believe that two kinds of chargers are necessary, one for home use and another for use in commercial parking spaces. This need opens the door for as much as $12 billion in infrastructure costs. A number of companies are hoping to cash in on PHEV charging needs, including Coulomb Technologies, a California firm which plans to install 4,600 public chargers in nine U.S. cities by the end of 2011 (each station costs between $2,000 and $5,000). ECOtality, a manufacturer based in Arizona, won a $100 million U.S. federal grant to develop its chargers. The company, in collaboration with Nissan, plans to install 11,000 chargers in five U.S. states by 2013.

The U.S. government will likely be an early buyer of PHEVs for its fleets. However, the most successful market for electric cars may be Europe rather than the U.S. European drivers are generally accepting of small vehicles. More importantly, gasoline prices in Europe are extremely expensive, often $5 per gallon or more due to high taxes, providing much greater incentive for plug-in cars. Moreover, European drivers are generally accustomed to taking shorter trips than consumers who drive the wide open spaces of the U.S. and Canada.

FedEx is testing a number of 20-foot electric trucks built by American truck manufacturer Navistar International Corp. and British battery manufacturer Modec. Each truck costs about $150,000 and has a range of between 60 and 100 miles per charge. FedEx believes that since typical delivery routes are fairly short and usually completed by nightfall, electric trucks are ideal. Limited range poses few problems and the trucks can be recharged at night during off-peak hours.

China-based BYD Company Limited entered the car manufacturing business in 2003 by acquiring a small, floundering firm that was owned by the Chinese government. Under BYD, its inexpensive F3 sedan became one of the best-selling cars in China. More importantly, BYD has begun selling a plug-in hybrid in China, the F3DM. This launch was well in advance of the competing plug-in hybrid Toyota Prius expected in 2010. At about $22,000, the F3DM can go about 63 miles in electric-only mode, and can recharge quickly from its backup gasoline engine or from a plug-in feature. Watch for a continuing stream of breakthroughs from this extremely innovative company. It could easily grow to be one of the world's leading makers of inexpensive electric cars, and its new E6 plug-in electric car will be a strong competitor. A subsidiary of America-based Berkshire Hathaway, led by famed investor Warren Buffett, purchased a major stake in BYD in 2008.

Among the biggest problems facing consumer adoption of electric cars is the cost of the batteries, which can run thousands of dollars per vehicle, depending on the type of batteries and the place of manufacture. Factoring this into the initial purchase price of the car makes electric vehicles expensive. Thus, among the big ideas in electric cars is a radical concept spearheaded by Shai Agassi, formerly of enterprise software giant SAP. Agassi's startup, called Better Place (www.betterplace.com), is promoting a business model where drivers would swap depleted batteries for charged batteries, or plug into convenient power stations, paying for their choice of plans: unlimited miles, a monthly maximum or pay as they go. Under one potential business model, electric cars would be purchased by consumers without the battery costs built-in. Instead, the batteries would be owned by Better Place and leased to the car owners. The company would provide swappable, charged batteries as a service at a cost-per-mile driven, or cost-per-battery swapped. The initial price of the car would then be comparable to that of a gasoline-powered vehicle, and the consumer would pay for the battery as used, rather than up-front.

Making consumers comfortable that they can have charged batteries when needed is key to this plan. Better Place would provide convenient, closely-spaced charging stations in places like parking garages and shopping centers. A trial project was underway in Tokyo in 2010, and the firm hopes to develop a long-term relationship with China's Chery Automobile Company. In January 2010, Better Place raised an additional $350 million in venture capital.

Those charging stations will be useful for drivers who have time to wait for a charge between trips to and from work or the grocery store. But what about drivers whose batteries are nearly depleted, or who are on longer non-stop trips? This is where the swappable batteries and swapping stations come in. In early 2009, Better Place demonstrated the first such swapping station, in Tel Aviv, Israel. There, robotic arms can remove a car's battery, clean it of road dirt and install a fully-charged battery. In about the same amount of time it takes to pump a small tank full of gasoline, the driver is back on the road. Such swapping stations are estimated to cost about $500,000 each.

Better Place calls its grid the Electric Recharge Grid Operator (ERGO). Its job is to not only supply the electricity, it would also monitor the electricity needs of the cars on the road and their locations, supply directions to drivers for the nearest power supply (using special software and in-car GPS) and negotiate with the local electricity utility with regard to the power supply and bulk electricity pricing. Hopefully, much of the power will come from solar and wind generation. That may be particularly true in initial markets like Denmark.

Agassi and his staff have made major strides in reaching their goal of independence from oil. Better Place has negotiated with the Israeli government to alter its tax code to make electric vehicles attractive to consumers. The tax proposal calls for a 10% tax on zero-emission vehicles and a 72% tax on traditional vehicles that run on gasoline. Better Place hopes to have recharge points throughout Israel, and has similar plans for Denmark and Portugal. Meanwhile, Agassi signed an agreement with Carlos Ghosn, CEO of Nissan and Renault, to make the cars.

The savings to drivers promise to be substantial. Better Place figures a driver getting 20 mpg in a traditional car and clocking 15,000 miles per year at $4 per gallon would spend about $3,000 for fuel. Better Place's fuel costs for the same 15,000 miles are projected to be approximately $1,050.

Internet Research Tip: Electric Cars

For the latest on electric car manufacturers see:
Better Place, www.betterplace.com
Coda Automotive, www.codaautomotive.com
Commuter Cars Corporation, www.commutercars.com
Electric Drive Transportation Association, www.electricdrive.org
Global Electric Motorcars, www.gemcar.com
Tesla Motors, www.teslamotors.com
Wrightspeed, www.wrightspeed.com
ZAP, www.zapworld.com

6) Major Research in Advanced Lithium Batteries

There are many obstacles to all-electric vehicles. The biggest potential problems are battery capacity and battery cost. Lithium-ion batteries are becoming more powerful, safe and efficient thanks to technological breakthroughs like those of startup manufacturer A123Systems (www.a123systems.com). Lithium-ion batteries pose multiple technical challenges. In the past, the batteries have shown a tendency to overheat, catch fire or explode. However, A123Systems is building batteries made of nanoparticles of lithium iron phosphate modified with trace metals instead of cobalt oxide. The result is a more stable power source with twice as much energy as nickel-metal hydride batteries. A123Systems was selected in August 2009 for a $249 million grant from the U.S. Department of Energy to build advanced battery manufacturing plants in the U.S. This is in addition to $100 million in refundable tax credits awarded from the Michigan Economic Development Corporation earlier in the year. As of mid-2009, A123 manufactured most of its batteries in China and Korea.

Nissan and GM will be powering their PHEVs with lithium-ion batteries that are based on manganese rather than the cobalt oxide technology traditionally used in batteries for laptop computers. The manganese technology provides more stability and is a big leap ahead in battery manufacturing overall.

Despite all of the battery technology investment in the U.S. and Europe, the early leaders in advanced batteries were in Asia, particularly Japan, Korea and China. This is logical when you consider the fact that Asian firms have long been world leaders in advanced batteries for mobile consumer electronics such as cellphones. Without their advances in smaller, longer-lasting batteries, today's tiny mobile phones and iPods would not have been possible.

U.S.-based companies actively trying to become leaders in advanced batteries for electric vehicles also include Quantum Technologies, Altair Nanotechnologies and ActaCell. However, one of A123's top American competitors may be Ener1, www.ener1.com, which owns an advanced lithium-ion electric vehicle battery unit called EnerDel. EnerDel has two cutting-edge manufacturing plants in Indiana and, as of mid-2009, had been promised $118.5 million in federal funding for battery plant construction from the Obama Administration's 2009 economic stimulus package.

A joint venture comprised of U.S.-based Johnson Controls (a leader in automotive systems and a major manufacturer of traditional car batteries) and France-based Saft (a leader in battery technology) plans to convert a former Johnson Controls automobile parts factory in Michigan into an advanced lithium-ion battery plant. The factory will make batteries for Ford's planned plug-in hybrid as early as 2012.

In the U.S. the 2009 American Recovery and Reinvestment Act provided $2.4 billion for investment in lithium-ion batteries. By late 2010, 17 new battery plants in Michigan were in production, under construction or in the planning stages according to the state Department of Energy, Labor and Economic Growth.

Nissan is investing several billion dollars in the construction of manufacturing plants for advanced batteries and retooling existing assembly plants to result in the production of 300,000 to 400,000 vehicles per year on three continents. The lithium manganese battery technology was developed in a joint venture between Nissan and NEC. In Tennessee Nissan is spending $1.6 billion in loans from the U.S. Department of Energy on a lithium-ion battery plant and an electric vehicle assembly line.

Nissan made a significant breakthrough in lithium-ion technology with the development of its laminated battery. Its shape and flexibility allow it to be used in a variety of models and they have two times the capacity and power of traditional batteries of the same weight (but at half the size). Nissan's Leaf runs on a 24-kilowatt-hour laminated battery made of 192 lithium-manganese cells capable of generating enough current to power an AC motor to 107 horsepower.

China is miles ahead in the battery and electric car race. The most exciting developments there are at BYD Company Limited. With $3.9 billion in 2008 revenues, BYD is already a global leader in contract manufacturing of batteries and handsets for mobile phones, even though the firm was founded only a few years ago in 1995. For example, BYD manufactures RAZR cell phone handsets for Motorola, as well as batteries for iPhones and iPods. This background gave it the technical edge that boosted it to a high level in electric automobile technology. The firm is so exciting that Warren' Buffet's Berkshire Hathaway invested $230 million in exchange for 10% of the company's stock in 2009.

Over the long-term, watch for further advances in battery technology that may fuel vehicles for up to 400 miles per charge. That will make a tremendous difference in consumer interest. The expensive Tesla roadster already claims a relatively long range of more than 240 miles.

Companies to Watch in Advanced Battery Technology:

A123 Systems, Inc.
ActaCell
Altair Nanotechnologies
Better Place
BYD
EnerDel division of Ener1
Johnson Controls-Saft joint venture
NEC
Nissan
Panasonic
Quantum Technologies
Sharp
Tesla
Source: Plunkett Research, Ltd.

7) Clean Diesel Technology Gains Acceptance

During the early 1980s, when U.S. drivers were still reeling from Arab oil embargos and fuel rationing, diesel-powered cars were particularly popular in the U.S. Mercedes-Benz made a very high-quality line of diesels at that time, and about 75% of its cars sold in the U.S. were diesel-powered. Diesel cars unfortunately proved to be noisy, polluting and, in some cases, unreliable. American consumers drifted away from diesel for many years, particularly during the 1990s when gasoline was readily available at reasonable prices. However, new, advanced diesel engines appear to be making a comeback in the U.S.

In Europe, extremely fuel-efficient diesels, ranging from Volkswagens to BMWs, achieving from 40 to 71 mpg, account for about 55% of all cars sold. Diesels of this type tend to be small and very inexpensive to operate. This is important in Europe, where parking places are hard to find and fuel is quite expensive. European diesel fuel historically had lower sulfur content that that sold in the U.S., which makes the European engines cleaner. Today, in both the U.S. and Europe, new technologies such as Daimler's BlueTec are in place that reduce nitrogen-oxide emissions.

U.S. environmental regulators, particularly in California, are beginning to make encouraging comments about diesel technology. In late 2006, the U.S. government began requiring oil refineries to produce low-sulfur diesel. That, combined with cleaner emissions provided by new engines and much better mileage than conventional gasoline engines, is making diesel powered cars an attractive commodity in the U.S. The fact is that diesel vehicles can be very efficient, and the diesel option can add less cost per vehicle than a hybrid option. A diesel engine creates more power than a gasoline engine from a similar amount of fuel. Volkswagen, BMW, Mercedes-Benz, Honda and Kia, among others, are selling diesel models in the U.S.

However, two things may put a damper on sales of diesel cars in the U.S. First, diesel prices are sometimes much higher per gallon than gasoline. Adding insult to injury is the additional refining cost of transitioning to low-sulfur diesel fuel and a higher federal excise tax (24.4 cents per gallon or 6 cents higher than on regular gasoline).

The second factor that may slow the sale of diesel cars in America is that nation's focus on boosting hybrid and electric vehicles. Tax rebates and other financial incentives, combined with the promise of using very little liquid fuel, if any, will draw consumers to electric cars who otherwise might have considered diesel.

Volkswagen already offers a diesel engine option to U.S. consumers for its New Beetle, Jetta, Passat and Touareg models. Jeep, a Chrysler vehicle, offers a diesel version of its small Liberty SUV as well as its larger Grand Cherokee. Ford sells a popular F150 Diesel while Dodge has a diesel version of its Ram 1500 pickup.

Internet Research Tip:

Volkswagen does a terrific job of explaining the virtues of its diesel-powered cars and its TDI turbocharged direct injection technology at http://tdi.vw.com . Nearly 70% of VW's cars sold under America's 2009 "cash for clunkers" program were diesels.

Honda is getting into the diesel act as well. Honda's 2.2 CTDi diesel-powered Civic is already sold in the U.K. and the firm will offer an advanced diesel engine in CR-V models in England and in Accords for the European market. The mileage of these diesel models is substantially better than their gasoline-powered siblings. Clearly, since the cars cost only a small amount more than gasoline-powered models, the diesels offer true advantages.

Mercedes, a Daimler subsidiary, sells its E320 CDI BlueTec diesel in the U.S., with fuel economy rated at 23 mpg in the city and 32 on the highway. Priced at about $53,000, it is not a pokey underperformer—this diesel Mercedes goes from zero to 60 miles per hour in a relatively quick 7.1 seconds. "CDI" stands for common-rail direct injection, a technology that also makes diesels allowable in the U.S. regulatory environment. It uses precise, electronic fuel injection that enables the engine to put out more power and less pollution while achieving better fuel economy. In Europe, Mercedes offers the GL350 BlueTec. In addition to the diesel engine, Mercedes uses low resistance tires and a seven-speed automatic transmission to boost fuel economy.

Meanwhile, ultra-low-sulfur diesel fuel was introduced at retail pumps in America in October 2006. New EPA emissions rules took effect across America in 2009 requiring that diesel engines meet exacting standards for low air pollution. The newer clean diesel fuel eliminates 97% of sulfur emissions. While it was previously impossible for automakers to sell diesel-powered cars in several U.S. states, due to tough state-level emissions regulations, new technologies combined with the new clean diesel fuels now make diesels legal in all 50 states. A recent study by the EPA projects that Americans would burn as much as 1.4 million fewer barrels of oil daily if one-third of all light-duty vehicles in America were running on modern diesel engines.

The advent of biodiesel, a fuel derived when glycerin is separated from vegetable oils or animal fats, is altering the landscape in a small way. The resulting byproducts are methyl esters (the chemical name for biodiesel) and glycerin, which can be used in soaps and cleaning products. It has lower emissions than petroleum diesel and is currently used as an additive to that fuel since it helps with lubricity. A small number of public filling stations are offering biodiesel, and it is also available from some petroleum distributors. However, refiners of biodiesel have consistently failed to earn a profit, and many have taken bankruptcy.

8) Natural Gas-Powered Vehicles off to a Slow Start

Cars and trucks that run on either compressed natural gas (CNG) or liquid natural gas (LNG) are already widespread, especially in municipal fleets and school buses. Natural Gas Vehicles for America (www.ngvc.org) estimates that there are 11 million natural gas-powered vehicles worldwide. The International Association of Natural Gas Vehicles projects that there will be more than 50 million natural gas vehicles worldwide by 2020. However, the U.S. count is only about 110,000 as of late 2010. A large percentage of all new public transit buses run on natural gas. This fuel is an attractive technology, not only because it is highly developed, but also because it is economically feasible and environmentally friendly. While initially costing as much as $8,000 more per vehicle than standard fuel equivalents, natural gas engines save 30% or more on fuel costs, making the investment potentially worthwhile over the long term. Emissions are significantly lower overall, and have much lower concentrations of polluting particles and harmful gases. Recognizing the possible economic benefits, UPS has put about 1,500 natural gas trucks in service to haul its packages, including test trucks running on compressed natural gas, liquefied natural gas or propane. Airport buses are often natural gas-powered.

Meanwhile, a natural gas-powered Honda Civic GX is on the U.S. market. Its sticker price is a modest $25,190, and up to $7,000 in state and federal tax credits are available. The downside is that there are only about 1,100 CNG stations in the U.S., making refueling difficult; and the gas tank holds the equivalent of a mere eight gallons of gasoline. However, growing numbers of drivers are looking for economical as well as environmentally friendly alternatives such as the Civic GX. GM plans to offer natural gas powered versions of its Chevrolet Express and GMC Savana full-size vans.

9) Ethanol Production Soared, But a Market Glut May Slow Expansion

High gasoline prices, effective lobbying by agricultural and industrial interests, and a growing interest in cutting reliance on imported oil put a high national focus on bioethanol in America in recent years. Corn and other organic materials, including agricultural waste, can be converted into ethanol through the use of engineered bacteria and superenzymes manufactured by biotechnology firms. This trend has given a boost to the biotech, agriculture and alternative energy sectors. At present, corn is almost the exclusive source for bioethanol in America. This is a shift of a crop from use in the food chain to use in the energy chain that is unprecedented in all of agricultural history—a shift that is having profound effects on prices for consumers, livestock growers (where corn has long been a traditional animal feed) and food processors.

In addition to the use of ethanol in cars and trucks, the chemicals industry, faced with daunting increases in petrochemicals costs, has a new appetite for bioethanol. In fact, bioethanol can be used to create plastics—an area that consumes vast quantities of oil in America and around the globe. Archer Daniels Midland is constructing a plant in Clinton, Iowa that will produce 50,000 tons of plastic per year through the use of biotechnology to convert corn into polymers.

Ethanol is an alcohol produced by a distilling process similar to that used to produce liquors. A small amount of ethanol is added to much of the gasoline sold in America, and most U.S. autos are capable of burning "E10," a gasoline blend that contains 10% ethanol. E85 is an 85% ethanol blend that may grow in popularity due to a shift in automotive manufacturing. Although only about 2,233 of the 170,000 U.S. service stations sold E85 as of the middle of 2010, there may be an increase in demand for ethanol in the U.S. due to mandates by the U.S. government calling for reduced dependence on oil.

Yet, despite the millions of vehicles on the road that can run on E85 and billions of dollars in federal subsidies to participating refiners, many oil companies seem unenthusiastic about the adoption of the higher ethanol mix. E85 requires separate gasoline pumps, trucks and storage tanks, as well as substantial cost to the oil companies (the pumps alone cost about $200,000 per gas station to install). The plants needed to create ethanol cost $500 million or more to build. Many drivers who have tried filling up with E85 once revert to regular unleaded when they find as much as a 25% loss in fuel economy when burning the blend.

Ethanol is a very popular fuel source in Brazil. In fact, Brazil is one of the world's largest producers of ethanol, which provides a significant amount of the fuel used in Brazil's cars. This is due to a concerted effort by the government to reduce dependency on petroleum product imports. After getting an initial boost due to government subsidies and fuel tax strategies beginning in 1975, Brazilian producers developed methods (typically using sugar cane) that enable them to produce ethanol at moderate cost. The fact that Brazil's climate is ideally suited for sugarcane is a great asset. Also, sugar cane can be converted with one less step than corn, which is the primary source for American ethanol. Brazilian automobiles are typically equipped with engines that can burn pure ethanol or a blend of gasoline and ethanol. Brazilian car manufacturing plants operated by Ford, GM and Volkswagen all make such cars.

In America, partly in response to the energy crisis of the 1970s, Congress instituted federal ethanol production subsidies in 1979. Corn-based grain ethanol production picked up quickly, and federal subsidies have amounted to several billion dollars. The size of these subsidies and environmental concerns about the production of grain ethanol produced a steady howl of protest from observers through the years. Nonetheless, the Clean Air Act of 1990 further boosted ethanol production by increasing the use of ethanol as an additive to gasoline. Meanwhile, the largest producers of ethanol, such as Archer Daniels Midland (ADM), have reaped significant subsidies from Washington for their output.

The U.S. Energy Act of 2005 specifically requires that oil refiners mix 7.5 billion gallons of renewable fuels such as ethanol in the nation's gasoline supply by 2012. Ethanol production in the U.S. reached 10.75 billion gallons in 2009, compared to 3.8 billion in 2005, according to the U.S. Energy Information Administration (EIA). Iowa, Illinois, Nebraska, Minnesota and South Dakota are the biggest producers, in that order. Although grain farmers and ethanol producers enjoyed high prices at the onset, a glut of ethanol supply eventually caused market prices to plummet. Next, the Energy Independence and Security Act of 2007 called for even more ethanol production, with a goal of 36 billion gallons per year by 2022 including 21 billion gallons to come from cellulosic and advanced biofuel sources. However, environmental concerns, the sizeable investments needed to construct ethanol refineries and questions about the advisability of using a food grain as a source for fuel may make these goals very unattainable using existing technologies. In addition, the automobile industry expects a significant amount of market share to slowly shift to electric or hybrid-electric vehicles over the long term, which will reduce dependency on liquid fuels, such as gasoline and ethanol.

More recently, some of the largest ethanol production companies have suffered severe financial problems. Notably, VeraSun filed for bankruptcy protection in late 2008, citing high corn prices and difficulty in obtaining trade credit. The Iowa-based company operated 14 ethanol plants in the Midwestern U.S. (Valero, a leading petroleum refiner, purchased some of VeraSun's plants.) The 2008-2009 plummet in the price of crude oil made ethanol look much less attractive from a cost point-of-view. Meanwhile, ethanol factories have generally encountered great difficulty when seeking profitability in the U.S., despite immense federal government support. New plant construction projects have been cancelled or put on hold, and it is looking very unlikely that the industry can meet the production goals set by congressional mandates.

Traditional grain ethanol is typically made from corn or sugarcane. In contrast to grain ethanol, "cellulosic" ethanol is typically made from agricultural waste like corncobs, wheat husks, stems, stalks and leaves, which are treated with specially engineered enzymes to break the waste down into its component sugars. The sugars (or sucrose) are used to make ethanol. Since agricultural waste is plentiful, turning it into energy seems a good strategy. Cellulosic ethanol can also be made from certain types of plants and grasses.

The trick to cellulosic ethanol production is the creation of efficient enzymes to treat the agricultural waste. The U.S. Department of Energy is investing heavily in research, along with major companies such as Dow Chemical, DuPont and Cargill. Another challenge lies in efficient collection and delivery of cellulosic material to the refinery. It may be more costly to make cellulosic ethanol than to make it from corn. In any event, the U.S. remains far behind Brazil in cost-efficiency, as Brazil's use of sugar cane refined in smaller, nearby biorefineries creates ethanol at much lower costs per gallon.

Iogen, a Canadian biotechnology company, makes just such an enzyme and has been operating a test plant to determine how economical the process may be. The company hopes to construct a $300-million, large-scale biorefinery with a potential output of 50 million gallons per year. Its pilot plant in Ottawa utilizes wheat straw and corn stalks. In mid-2009, a Shell gasoline station in Ottawa, Canada became the first retail outlet in that nation to sell a blend of gasoline that features 10% cellulosic ethanol.

In the U.S., the Department of Energy has selected six proposed new cellulosic ethanol refineries to receive a total of $385 million in federal funding. If completed, these six refineries are expected to produce 130 million gallons of ethanol yearly. Iogen's technology will be used in one of the refineries, to be located in Shelley, Idaho. Partners in the refinery include Royal Dutch Shell.

Meanwhile, the Canadian government plans to support the Canadian biofuel industry with up to 500 million Canadian dollars for construction of next-generation plants. Iogen is expected to receive part of those funds for construction of a commercial scale cellulosic ethanol plant.

In the U.S., BP and Verenium announced plans in February 2009 to form a joint venture to build, on a commercial scale, a cellulosic ethanol plant in Highlands County, Florida. In July 2010, BP Biofuels North America acquired Verenium's cellulosic biofuels business and became the sole investor in the new plant. The plant is expected to cost $300 million and have the capacity to produce 36 million gallons of ethanol yearly from agricultural waste.

Other companies, such as Syngenta, DuPont and Ceres, are genetically engineering crops so that they can be more easily converted to ethanol or other energy producing products. Syngenta, for example, is testing a bio-engineered corn that contains the enzyme amylase. Amylase breaks down the corn's starch into sugar, which is then fermented into ethanol. The refining methods currently used with traditional corn crops add amylase to begin the process.

Environmentalists are concerned that genetically engineering crops for use in energy-related yields will endanger the food supply through cross-pollination with traditional plants. Monsanto is focusing on conventional breeding of plants with naturally higher fermentable starch content as an alternative to genetic engineering.

Another concern relating to ethanol use is that its production is not as energy efficient as that of biodiesel made from soybeans. According to a study at the University of Minnesota, the farming and processing of corn grain for ethanol yields only 25% more energy than it consumes compared to 93% for biodiesel. Likewise, greenhouse gas emissions savings are greater for biodiesel. According to one estimate, producing and burning ethanol results in 12% fewer greenhouse gas emissions than burning gasoline, while producing and burning biodiesel results in a 41% reduction compared to making and burning regular diesel fuel. A 2009 vote by Illinois' Air Resources Board requires the use of "lower carbon intensity" fuels starting in 2011, which may have a negative long term effect on the use of ethanol.

Global warming concerns were heightened in 2009 by a report by the International Council for Science (ICSU) that concluded that the production of biofuels, including ethanol, has hurt rather than helped the fight against climate change. The report cites findings by a scientist at the Max Planck Institute for Chemistry in Germany that biofuels expand the harmful effects of a gas called nitrous oxide, which may be 300 times worse for global warming than carbon dioxide. The amounts of nitrous oxide released when farming biofuel crops such as corn may negate any advantage gained by reduced carbon dioxide emissions.

In addition, ethanol production requires enormous amounts of water. To produce one gallon of ethanol, up to four gallons of water are consumed by ethanol refineries. Add in the water needed to grow the corn in the first place, and the number grows to as much as 1,700 gallons of water for each gallon of ethanol.

Other concerns regarding the use of corn to manufacture ethanol include the fact that a great deal of energy is consumed in planting, reaping and transporting the corn in trucks. Also, high demand for corn for use in biorefineries has, from time-to-time, dramatically driven up the cost per bushel, creating burdens on consumers.

As of mid-2009, new technology was being tested that would produce ethanol from corn cobs that have been stripped of edible kernels. Poet, a South Dakota-based producer of ethanol that operates 26 plants in seven U.S. states, is constructing a plant in Emmetsburg, Iowa that will be one of the first in the U.S. to produce ethanol on a large scale using a non-food source. The plant is slated for completion in 2011.

Novozymes, a Danish bioindustrial product manufacturer, has developed an enzyme blend containing an agent called GH-61 that has the potential to speed chemical reactions. Enzymes containing GH-61 may reduce production costs to the extent that producing ethanol can be competitive on a price basis with fossil fuels. Novozymes says that the cost of the enzyme, called Cellic, is about 50 cents per gallon, or less than a third of the projected $1.90 per gallon total cost (naturally, the retail price per gallon would be higher). Poet's Emmetsburg plant will utilize the substance in its ethanol production.

Another potential for ethanol production plants is to retool them to produce other kinds of biochemicals. For example, Houston, Texas startup Glycos Biotechnologies, Inc. is developing an add-on process to use glycerin, a by-product of ethanol, to make chemicals suitable for use in fabrics, insulation and food stuffs. Other firms pursuing similar avenues include Genomatica, Inc., Gevo, Inc. and Myriant Technologies LLC.

SPOTLIGHT: Biofuels

Corn is far from the only source of cellulose for creating biofuels.

Municipal/Agricultural Waste: Cheaply produced, but in limited supply compared to the billions of gallons of fuel needed in the market place.

Wood: Easily harvested and in somewhat healthy supply, however cellulose is more difficult to extract from wood than from other biosources.

Algae: The slimy green stuff does have the potential for high yields per acre, but the process for distilling its cellulose is complex, requiring a source of carbon dioxide to permeate the algae.

Grasses/Wheat: Including switchgrass, miscanthus, sugar cane and wheat straw, the supply would be almost limitless. The challenge here is creating efficient methods for harvesting and infrastructure for delivering it to biorefineries.

Vegetable Oils: Including soybean, canola, sunflower, rapeseed, palm or hemp. It is difficult to keep production costs of these oils low.

SPOTLIGHT: Algae Draws Major Investment

Algae's potential as a source of biofuel got a big boost from an unlikely source in 2009. ExxonMobil announced plans to invest $300 million or more in San Diego, California-based Synthetic Genomics, a company headed by genome pioneer Craig Venter. Dr. Venter is studying ways in which an ideal species of algae can be developed for a unique culturing process. This process induces algae to release their oil (naturally stored as a foodstuff for the organisms), which can then be manipulated so that the oxygen molecules in the oil are disposed of, leaving a pure hydrocarbon suitable for use as biofuel. Another plus to Venter's process is that carbon dioxide claimed from industrial plant exhaust is used in the culturing process and then released in the atmosphere. This does not make algae biofuel production carbon neutral, but it does utilize carbon dioxide twice before it's released. Should the study go well, ExxonMobil has pledged an additional $300 million in funding to further develop the process to an industrial scale.

10) Fuel Cell and Hydrogen Power Research Continues

The fuel cell is nothing new, despite the excitement it is now generating. It has been around since 1839, when Welsh physics professor William Grove created an operating model based on platinum and zinc components. Much later, the U.S. Apollo space program used fuel cells for certain power needs in the Apollo space vehicles that traveled from the Earth to the Moon.

In basic terms, a fuel cell consists of quantities of hydrogen and oxygen separated by a catalyst. Inside the cell, a chemical reaction within the catalyst generates electricity. Byproducts of this reaction include heat and water. Several enhancements to basic fuel cell technology are under research and development at various firms worldwide. These include fuel cell membranes manufactured with advanced nanotechnologies and "solid oxide" technologies that could prove efficient enough to use on aircraft. Another option for fuel cell membranes are those made of hydrocarbon, which cost about one-half a much as membranes using fluorine compounds.

Fuel cells require a steady supply of hydrogen. Therein lies the biggest problem in promoting the widespread use of fuel cells: how to create, transport and store the hydrogen. At present, no one has been able to put a viable plan in place that would create a network of hydrogen fueling stations substantial enough to meet the needs of everyday motorists in the U.S. or anywhere else.

Many currently operating fuel cells burn hydrogen extracted from such sources as gasoline, natural gas or methanol. Each source has its advantages and disadvantages. Unfortunately, burning a hydrocarbon such as oil, natural gas or coal to produce the energy necessary to create hydrogen results in unwanted emissions. Ideally, hydrogen would be created using renewable, non-polluting means, such as solar power or wind power. Also, nuclear or renewable sources could be used to generate electricity that would be used to extract hydrogen molecules from water.

The potential market for fuel cells encompasses diverse uses in fixed applications (such as providing an electric generating plant for a home or a neighborhood), portable systems (such as portable generators for construction sites) or completely mobile uses (powering anything from small hand-held devices to automobiles). The potential advantages of fuel cells as clean, efficient energy sources are enormous. The fuel cell itself is a proven technology—fuel cells are already in use, powering a U.S. Post Office in Alaska, for example. (This project, in Chugach, Alaska, is the result of a joint venture between the local electric association and the U.S. Postal Service to install a one megawatt fuel cell facility.) Tiny fuel cells are also on the market for use in powering cellular phones and laptop computers.

Shipments of fuel cell-equipped mobile devices could grow very rapidly if they can eliminate the need for frequent recharging of current battery-powered models. The "Medis 24/7 Power Pack" is a portable, disposable power source for small electronic devices such as cell phones and MP3 players. Manufactured by Medis Technologies, it is based on Direct Liquid Fuel cell technology, and may be of particular utility in military applications. Elsewhere, MTI MicroFuel Cells manufactures a power pack for portable electronics that is based on direct methanol fuel cell technology that it calls Mobion.

Internet Research Tip: Micro Fuel Cells

For more information on research involving fuel cells for small applications, visit:

MTI MicroFuel Cells	www.mtimicrofuelcells.com
Tekion Solutions, Inc.	www.tekion.com

Electric Vehicles vs. Fuel Cells

Nearly all of the major automobile makers had significant fuel cell research initiatives at one time. While the potential for fuel cell-powered vehicles seemed extremely promising, the automobile industry has made a profound and long-lasting shift toward plug-in electric hybrids and all-electric vehicles as the new technology base of choice. This is due to several reasons, including:

1) The tremendous success and wide consumer acceptance of Toyota's Prius hybrid car. This success gave Toyota early dominance in the electric car field while other makers were still dreaming about fuel cells. An important feature of the Prius is its very affordable price—something that might never be accomplished in a fuel cell vehicle.

2) The technical hurdles of distributing, storing and transporting hydrogen as a fuel have proven extremely difficult to overcome.

3) The costs of building a fuel cell platform for automobiles remains vastly more expensive than building an electric or hybrid vehicle.

4) Consumers, bureaucrats, investors and legislators already understand and trust the safety and ease of use of electricity, whether fixed or portable. This cannot be said for hydrogen.

Now, GM, Nissan and other leading automobile firms have ambitious plans for launching electric-drive vehicles (as opposed to today's hybrid electric cars which run on electricity only part of the time, relying on a gasoline engine the rest of the time). Given the financial constraints that automakers are working under today, these car manufacturers have downgraded or abandoned their focus on fuel cells. In particular, technical breakthroughs in advanced batteries for electric vehicles are occurring quickly. This will spur a huge rush into the electric car market while lessening the near-term interest in fuel cells.

GM has invested $1 billion in fuel cell vehicle research. The company leased 100 fuel cell-equipped Equinox crossover vehicles to customers as a test, starting in early 2008. The Equinox will go about 200 miles on a hydrogen fill up. Initially, the vehicles were provided to government officials, celebrities, journalists and business leaders in New York City, Washington D.C. and Los Angeles. GM has long had aggressive goals for commercializing and producing fuel cell vehicles. However, the financial and technical hurdles would be high, and GM assigned itself a daunting task. It may never happen, unless GM can see its way to real profits from fuel cells. Nonetheless, in January 2008, the firm unveiled a fuel cell concept car, the Cadillac Provoq, at the Consumer Electronics Show, which is held in Las Vegas each year. However, the firm's deep financial problems of 2008-2009 and its intense focus on the Chevy Volt electric car have combined to move GM's fuel cell project to the back burner, perhaps forever.

One of GM's thoughts for eventual commercial development is a wide variety of car and truck bodies that would mount onto a single, radical "skateboard" chassis design, which integrates the engine directly into the chassis. The skateboard stores fuel cell stacks and hydrogen supplies as well as circuitry that manages the flow of electric power through the various systems necessary to stop, start and maneuver the vehicle. The chassis would include a docking port that links the body above to the electronic control systems.

GM is not the only manufacturer with significant investments in fuel cells. Honda leased test models of its "FCX" fuel cell-powered car to small numbers of customers in the U.S. and Japan. Toyota began making a small number of fuel cell-powered cars available on 30-month leases in July 2006. In late 2007, a prototype Highlander hydrogen-hybrid fuel cell vehicle traveled 2,300 miles from Alaska to Vancouver, Canada, getting more than 300 miles per tank of hydrogen. In September 2010, Toyota stated that it hoped to have a fuel-cell vehicle on the market in limited quantities in 2015, but only in a few regions where hydrogen fueling stations would be available.

The former DaimlerChrysler invested about $1 billion in its own fuel cell initiative. In 2008 Chrysler featured its ecoVoyager concept car at the Detroit Auto Show. Nonetheless, Chrysler's bankruptcy of 2009 made risky ventures such as fuel cell research much less feasible. As of 2007, Ford had 30 fuel cell powered Focus compact cars in customer trials, but decided in 2009 to divert hydrogen fuel-cell research funds to focus on electric vehicles.

British startup manufacturer Riversimple developed a fuel cell-powered prototype in 2009 that is about the size of a golf cart. Though small, the vehicle is tough thanks to a body made of carbon composites. There is an electric motor for each of the car's wheels, and ultracapacitors capture and store energy when the brakes are engaged. Riversimple's car has a range of about 199 miles per tank and a top speed of about 50 mph. The company plans to build hydrogen filling stations in British cities.

Mercedes-Benz also has a hydrogen vehicle, the B-Class F-Cell. Twenty of the vehicles were supplied to the city of Hamburg, Germany in a municipal fuel cell project in late 2009. The B-Class F-Cell has a range of 249 miles and a top speed of 109 mph.

Meanwhile, BMW unveiled a hybrid of sorts in 2006 that allows drivers to use either hydrogen or gasoline at the flick of a switch. (The hydrogen is not used in a fuel cell. Instead, it is burned as a fuel in an internal-combustion engine that ordinarily would burn gasoline.) The car uses a V-12 engine that can be powered by either fuel. BMW put 100 of its Hydrogen 7 cars on loan to celebrities in California and Germany in 2007. As of early 2010, BMW was testing a hydrogen-electric drivetrain hybrid that might be used in next-generation Minis and front-wheel-drive BMWs, according to Britain's Autocar web site. Since more hydrogen than gasoline is required to run an engine the same number of miles, the prototype has a hydrogen tank that utilizes space usually reserved for luggage or passengers. The use of hydrogen offers multiple technical challenges.

After the initial enthusiasm over fuel cells, during which many governments planned to introduce large numbers of fuel cell power plants and vehicles, energy agencies have scaled back their goals. The difficulties surrounding the technology are proving much more stubborn than they initially appeared to be. For example, Japan, one of the largest proponents of fuel cell technology, initially wanted 50,000 fuel cell vehicles on the road by 2010, a goal that couldn't be met.

Unfortunately, fuel cells remain grossly expensive due to their limited production and the industry's current low-technology base. Moreover, hydrogen is not readily available to drivers. GM's head of strategic planning projected that 12,000 stations in the largest cities across the U.S. would put

70% of the population within two miles of a hydrogen filling station. The cost would be about $1 million per station. Numerous solutions have been proposed through the years. Honda promoted a Home Energy Station in Southern California that it hoped would convert natural gas into enough hydrogen to power fuel cells that could run a family's vehicle, as well as supply electricity and hot water for the family home.

Another problem is that many people still have concerns about the safety of hydrogen. Naturally gaseous at room temperature, storing hydrogen involves using pressurized tanks that can leak and, if punctured, could cause explosions. It is also difficult to store enough hydrogen in a vehicle to take it the 300+ miles that drivers are used to getting on a tank of gasoline. To do so, hydrogen must be compressed to 10,000 pounds per square inch and stored on board in bulky pressure tanks.

One idea for storage is cooling the hydrogen to a liquid state and storing it in a cooled tank, but this requires constant refrigeration. A mid-term solution to the problem of creation and storage of hydrogen is to use existing fuels, such as methane, gasoline and diesel. These fuels could be broken down in the car, on-demand, to produce hydrogen, which would then power the fuel cell. Although this would relieve the hydrogen storage problems, it would not remove the need for fossil fuels and it would still produce emissions such as carbon dioxide, though in reduced quantities.

The Bush administration launched a "Hydrogen Fuel Initiative" in 2003, and Congress provided over $1 billion for research. In May 2008, the EU's government funded 470 million Euros for fuel cell and hydrogen research, and Germany has promised as much as 500 million Euros. In 2010, U.S. President Obama signed a Nationwide Hydrogen Highway Initiative into law that requires the Federal Transit Administration and the Department of Energy to build up to 200,000 hydrogen fueling stations not more than five miles apart in more regions of the country. Will this be enough to bring fuel cells to the mass market? Maybe not. It remains to be seen whether such stations will be constructed, despite the possibility of up to $2.1 million in subsidies for each new hydrogen filling station, and up to $300,000 for the addition of a hydrogen pump to an existing filling station. In addition, there are still massive challenges to solve in designing and marketing vehicles that can store and burn hydrogen fuel. A U.S. Department of Energy study determined that it would take public funding of $45 billion to get 10 million fuel cell cars on the road by 2025, assuming that mass production would create a dramatic reduction in the cost of manufacturing fuel cells, and that public funding would encourage the development of a network of fueling stations. Meanwhile, electric cars are clearly the next wave.

SPOTLIGHT: Motor Scooters

Don't be surprised to see more and more of your neighbors zipping around on stylish motor scooters. The motor scooter dates back to post-war Europe, where Piaggio made the first Vespa in 1946. While scooters have long been extremely popular in densely-populated cities outside the U.S., such as Rome and Bangkok, Americans have rarely been scooter buyers, turning instead to cars, light trucks and powerful motorcycles.

However, extremely high gasoline prices, the difficulty of parking in some U.S. cities and attractive new scooter models are lighting a fire under U.S. consumers. For example, the Vespa has extremely peppy new models that have room for two people and perhaps a shopping bag, get more than 60 mpg and cost about $4,400. Honda and Yamaha have jumped into the market with scooters that feature storage compartments for groceries or helmets along with engines that are powerful enough for highway cruising. Lighter, new scooters with small engines that get up to 120 mpg are offered by other makers for about $3,000.

Another trend is the restoration of classic, Italian-made Lambretta and Vespa scooters. For example, less than $3,000 will get you a fully restored, classic Vespa from the 1960s. In addition to snappy new scooters, sales of full size motorcycles have grown.

Meanwhile, motorbikes are a massive market in India, where, in a typical year, motorbikes outsell cars and trucks by a factor of seven. Indian manufacturer Hero Honda Motors is India's leading seller, and it saw its net income for 2009 rise by 6% to $273.4 million.

11) Outsourcing of Component Design and Manufacturing/Sharing of Parts

Right along with automakers, parts manufacturers were hit hard by the global recession. Some auto industry experts forecast that as many as 20% of the U.S.'s 1,700 core suppliers could be forced out of business by the end of 2009. However, those that remained in business, many by divesting themselves of unprofitable businesses and focusing on core strengths, managed to turn themselves around in a remarkably short time. For example, Lear

Corporation emerged from bankruptcy in 2009 after selling its automotive interiors business and focused on car seats and electronics. The company reported a second quarter 2010 profit of $159.8 million, compared to a loss of $173.6 million in the same quarter in 2009.

Meanwhile, auto parts suppliers in China are enjoying an upswing to serve the growing market there for light, cost- and fuel-efficient vehicles. In addition, a number of U.S. parts manufacturers, including American Axle & Manufacturing Holdings, Inc. and AvrinMeritor, Inc., opened plants in China and India to diversify their interests and take advantage of the booming markets in those countries.

Automotive manufacturers save vast amounts by outsourcing design and engineering to overseas offices, while sharing component designs across a wide range of models. A growing trend in manufacturing is for American carmakers to utilize engineering and components from foreign plants and manufacture or assemble them domestically. At GM, Chrysler and Ford , a large percentage of models are designed and completed in a cross-platform, globalized way.

Fiat hopes that cross-utilization and globalization of engineering, styling and manufacturing will create tremendous efficiencies and cost-savings in its new partnership with Chrysler (which includes the possibility for Fiat to eventually own a controlling interest in Chrysler). The challenge is to avoid building cars with a cookie-cutter feeling.

At Ford, a sweeping plan to slash the number of global suppliers has been underway. The company hoped to cut its 2,500 current suppliers to less than 1,000 by offering larger long-term contracts to a smaller number of suppliers, thereby streamlining the product process and saving time and money. For example, Ford previously used 28 different seat structures around the world, and now it's been cut down to two. If successful, Ford estimates it could save as much as $7 billion per year through more efficient purchasing. The initial phase of the plan affected vehicles built in 2008 through 2010.

Achieving the "American look," which may include significant changes in bodywork and interiors, is of major importance to car sales in the U.S. Attempts to market the same car, identical in every detail, across global markets are often failures. For example, tastes in Europe often differ from those in the U.S. when it comes to appearance and styling. Likewise, "American look" cars may be difficult to market in other countries.

Nonetheless, the savings from cross-border platform development, when properly marketed, are impressive. The cost to develop a midsize car by an American manufacturer can run $1 billion in the U.S. Using a chassis and engine design from overseas can cut the cost nearly in half.

Automobile makers outside the U.S. are also sharing parts and engineering in a big way. Take, for example, the development of the Nissan March, a compact built on the same chassis created for a Renault. The shared design was projected to save both companies 20% on development costs, and the car is one of the most popular sellers in Japan.

12) "Optimum Lean Production" Saves Manufacturing Costs

The standard in automobile manufacturing today is optimum lean production. This is a business model under which a high (but not necessarily perfect) level of quality is sought while high-efficiency goals are set that save time, money, manpower and floorspace. Optimum lean production applies to the complete manufacturing cycle, from concept design, development and engineering to assembly and shipping. Computer-aided design (CAD), computerized testing and computer-aided manufacturing (CAM) have been a big factor in efficiency gains. As a result, the number of months necessary to fully design and launch a new model has been drastically cut. High manufacturing volume of specific platforms, models or components can be instrumental in achieving optimum efficiency. This is one of the factors that has led to consolidation of manufacturers and to cross-use of components and designs. To a great extent, the more units that are produced, the lower the cost per unit.

While the early mass-production car factories of pioneer Henry Ford's days were vertically integrated, producing nearly all of their own parts and building materials in-house, from glass to steel to batteries to finished cars from basic raw commodities, modern car plants are assemblers more than creators. That is, each manufacturer works very closely with a handful of suppliers to design and price the components necessary to assemble a completed vehicle. Primary suppliers (called tier-one suppliers) deliver complete "systems" or "modules" to the carmakers. Such systems may consist of large interior, exterior or drivetrain units. These tier-one suppliers in turn buy from groups of tier-two and tier-three suppliers that manufacture smaller parts and components.

Meanwhile, manufacturers require that their suppliers bear much of the cost and responsibility of inventory. Under today's just-in-time delivery requirements, suppliers bring their portion of the car to the factory door shortly before it's needed.

The need for suppliers to be able to participate in the design phase, deliver sophisticated systems and provide just-in-time service means that only large, highly evolved companies can compete. As a result, immense consolidation has taken place in the automotive components industry. Carmakers tend to buy from a limited number of suppliers, and to do so in vast quantity.

In the past, that dependence caused many U.S. parts makers to rely too heavily on Detroit manufacturers. Financial problems at the Big Three in recent years hurt the parts companies, bankrupting some, and making others prime targets for takeovers by investors (these investors must have enough capital to restructure and globalize in order to take advantage of booming automotive manufacturing markets in China and other foreign regions).

For some new technologies, it may be better for suppliers to develop their own designs without the control of manufacturers. Manufacturers, in turn, can pick and choose from the best on the market at the most competitive bids. An excellent example is cutting edge lithium-ion batteries for electric and hybrid engines made by A123Systems.

Efficient, fast and cost effective production techniques can make or break a manufacturer. BMW is betting heavily on a new process that creates car bodies from lightweight, extremely strong carbon fibers instead of steel. Its new Megacity plug-in hybrid electric vehicle (PHEV) design utilizes a carbon fiber body which significantly reduces weight and extends the car's range. Carbon fiber is 30% stronger than aluminum and 50% lighter than steel. In order to incorporate carbon fiber, BMW has to redesign its production process in which molds, heat and pressure are used to fuse fibers together with resin into a workable material. The company has reduced the process, which can be performed by robots, to a few minutes from start to finish. BMW plans to launch the Megacity in 2013. Stay tuned to see if its radical new production design is fast and cheap enough to make the project viable.

smart GmbH: The Ultimate Experiment in Outsourcing

The maker of a groundbreaking line of mini-cars, smart GmbH, is a wholly-owned subsidiary of Daimler AG. Based in the Alsace region of France, smart GmbH's "smartville" facility outsources almost every component of its cars from parts and inventory to assembly to delivery. Ten on-site suppliers provide 85% of the cost of goods, and companies other than smart GmbH pay one-half of the workers at the plant.

Suppliers include Eisenmann, which produces powder coating; Magna, which builds bodies; Krupp, which assembles rear modules including engines; Schenker, maker of small parts such as seat belts, levers and wipers; Dynamit Nobel, which provides plastic body panels; and Magna Door Systems. All suppliers have facilities on the smart GmbH site and are connected by conveyor belts to the main assembly building. The entire process is an impressive feat of engineering, which synchronizes all construction and assembly in a line that runs 88 feet per minute.

This vehicle has been designed to achieve 40 plus mpg under normal driving conditions. It is 8.8 feet long, 5.1 feet tall and 5.1 feet wide and comes equipped with many functional and safety features. smart is currently sold in 37 countries. As of January 2008, the smart fortwo model became available in the U.S. smart USA Distributor LLC, headquartered in Bloomfield Hills, Michigan, is the exclusive distributor of the smart fortwo in the United States and Puerto Rico and is a wholly-owned subsidiary of Penske Automotive Group, Inc. In March 2009, joint venture smart-BARBUS GmbH unveiled the smart fortwo BARBUS electric-drive concept car.

13) Car Purchasers Rely on the Internet

In many respects, information about cars and trucks on the Internet has enabled consumers to be better informed than ever before about buying a vehicle. Countless sites document new car models, options and prices, as well as trade-in values of used cars. With a little time spent online, buyers can and do walk into dealerships armed with the knowledge of exactly how much a particular car costs, the options available and approximately how much the dealer paid for that car. (However, consumers frequently are not aware of significant additional commissions and incentives that manufacturers offer to dealers. These programs can greatly reduce a dealer's final cost in a vehicle.)

Various studies find that 80% to 90% of new-car buyers go online for information before making a purchase. However, this trend applies to buyers of both new and used cars. For example, nearly 80 million visitors went to Carfax.com for information on used cars during 2009. Highly popular sites like Kelly Blue Book and Edmunds.com enable prospective car purchasers to research prices and features of cars by model, make and year, and to get detailed information on new and used car prices and trade-in values.

During the Internet boom of the 1990s, some dot-com enthusiasts forecast the end of the traditional auto dealership, once such information was made available to consumers. This is far from the case. To begin with, contracts between auto manufacturers and their dealers, as well as business regulations in most states known as "franchise laws" make it next to impossible to sell new cars strictly via the Internet; physical dealerships are required. In addition, car buyers know that they need to have relationships with physical dealerships for such tasks as warranty work. And, most buyers want a chance to kick some tires or take a test drive. Meanwhile, successful new car dealers today capitalize on the Internet in every way possible. This became all the more critical due to the global economic crisis. Dealers are aware that selling add-ons; facilitating financing, insurance and extended warranties; selling used-car trade-ins; and providing maintenance in the service department make up the majority of dealership profits. Selling new cars serves as the key to establishing customer relations that lead to these additional profits.

The most successful car dealers put the power of the Internet to their advantage. Dealers' web sites are facilitating appointments for sales and service as well as orders for parts. Some dealers make it possible for consumers to search and view their entire car inventories online, including details about each vehicle's color, accessories and price. Savvy car marketers use email campaigns to send out discount offers, new model announcements, coupons and reminders about routine maintenance, such as 10,000-mile checkups. Many dealerships are even placing kiosks on the showroom floor from which shoppers can log onto the web to research consumer reports or pricing and availability at competing dealers. Smart dealers encourage this activity and are willing to concede on matters of price in order to make a sale.

Meanwhile, auto-referral sites such as Autobytel.com, which has relationships with thousands of dealers and generates billions of dollars yearly in sales for dealers, send large quantities of leads to participating dealerships every day. A publicly held company, Autobytel was one of the first e-commerce firms to develop a significant revenue base. On the firm's web site, a prospective car purchaser states his or her needs according to make, model, color, accessories, trade-in and type of financing. Nearby dealerships that subscribe to the Autobytel system respond to the purchaser with a price and availability of inventory. Dealers that are most successful at utilizing online sales methods have specific, well trained salespeople who are dedicated to selling only to purchasers sent by the referral sites. However, Autobytel's revenues have been slipping, and are down considerably from its 2005 peak of $122 million, as competition increases and dealers rely more on their own web sites to generate business. In 2009, in the midst of the global automobile industry slowdown, Autobytel generated revenues of only $53 million.

In addition to referring customers to dealers, these sites screen buyers by collecting information such as name, address and preferred financing method, as well as more specific information relating to likes and dislikes through online questionnaires. The result is that dealerships obtain enough information to distinguish the real buyers from tire-kickers, and to more promptly fulfill the needs of good prospective customers. In early 2010, Autobytel launched iControl, an online application that enables dealers to configure consumer leads according to current inventory, customer location (distance from the dealerships) and lead sourcing.

The online market for used cars is also extremely active. Used-car buyers generally tend to have a willingness to travel farther and try harder to find a car that meets their desires. Used-car sales are an extremely important component of the industry. CarMax, the nationwide chain of used car superstores, uses the Internet extensively to boost sales. Online, car buyers can view the entire used car inventory at CarMax's dozens of locations. For example, if a customer in Dallas sees a car in the Albuquerque inventory that sounds appealing, he can have it shipped to Dallas for a fee of about $250. If he actually purchases the car, one-half of the shipping fees will be refunded.

Popular Auto Referral and Information Sites

AAA.com
www.aaa.com (choose Buy & Maintain Vehicles)
Autobytel
www.autobytel.com
AutoSite
www.autosite.com
AutoTrader.com
www.autotrader.com
Autoweb.com
www.autoweb.com
Cars.com
www.cars.com
CarSmart.com
www.carsmart.com
Edmunds.com
www.edmunds.com
Kelly Blue Book
www.kbb.com
MSN Autos (formerly Carpoint.com)
autos.msn.com
Yahoo! Autos
autos.yahoo.com

Auction Sites

eBay Motors
www.motors.ebay.com

14) China Becomes the World's Largest Auto Market/Sales Rise in India

The emergence of a middle class in China in recent years created a new and lucrative market for automobiles and trucks. China's most successful entrepreneurs have been eager buyers of expensive luxury cars that are imported, while a mass market emerged for inexpensive family cars and vans. In addition, consumers in rural areas are buying their first vehicles, which are typically small, low-cost cars. Beijing's accession to the World Trade Organization brought about a steep reduction in tariffs on vehicle imports. About 13.6 million vehicles were sold in China in 2009, up 46% from 2008. This made China the number one market for vehicle sales behind the U.S. (where about 11.5 million vehicles sold in 2009).

China's growing market sparked efforts by major automotive companies such as GM, Toyota, Honda, Volkswagen and others to export more vehicles into China. These companies also invested directly in manufacturing operations within China. GM operates seven automotive joint ventures in China including Shanghai General Motors (a partnership with Shanghai Automotive Industry Corp.) and Shanghai GM (Shenyang) Norsom Motors Co. GM sold 1.8 million vehicles in China in 2009, up 67% from 2008. Volkswagen maintains two manufacturing facilities in China, one in Shanghai and another in Changchun. The German manufacturer sold 1.4 million vehicles in China in 2009, up 32.4% from 2008. Toyota, a relative latecomer to the Chinese market, plans to invest $215 million to expand its factory in Tianjin in a joint venture with Chinese partner First Auto Works Group. Toyota's 2009 sales in China rose 21% to 709,000 vehicles. The foreign firms aggressively pushed models such as the Buick Sail, Daihatsu Charade and Volkswagen Polo, with average prices of around $13,500.

Recent success stories in the Chinese market include Hyundai's Elantra compact, which, at a price of about $13,600, is selling well to taxi companies and to more affluent private citizens; and the $3,600 QQ mini car made by Chery Automobile Company, a private Chinese firm. Honda's joint venture, Guangzhou Honda Motor Co. is also doing well with its $10,360 Fit compact sedan.

Domestic manufacturers within China are expanding at great rates. Carmakers there were historically owned and operated by the government. The emergence of a private manufacturer, Geely Motor Co. (a subsidiary of Zhejiang Geely Holding Group Co.), opened a new corporate environment in which laborers are not guaranteed their jobs or pensions. A private company is also free to develop and market new models quickly, without waiting for government approval. Geely, which began as a refrigerator builder, first made and sold cars in 1998, with sales of 200 vehicles. The firm sold 325,000 vehicles in 2009, a leap of 59% over 2008. In March 2010, Geely agreed to purchase Ford Motor Company's Volvo Cars unit for $1.8 billion. In July 2010, the company announced plans to construct a local research and development facility and build at least one new factory with an annual production capacity of 300,000 vehicles for Volvo. The firm plans to launch more than 24 new models by the end of 2012.

Another Chinese company, Chery, sold 300,000 vehicles in 50 countries in 2006 and 381,000 in 2007 (119,800 of those were sold in countries other than China). Sales were up to about 500,000 in 2009.

However, Chinese domestic manufacturers have another avenue of support since Chinese-made vehicles are now being exported. In July 2005, the first Chinese cars arrived in Western Europe. China hopes to export to the U.S., but so far is facing challenges meeting safety standards. Chinese manufacturers also face marketing difficulties which have been exacerbated by the recent global recession. For the first three quarters of 2009, Chinese auto exports were down 58% compared to 2008 according to China Central Television (CCTV).

The perception of poor quality dogs Chinese-made products, and, in the U.S. especially, stringent safety and emissions standards will be difficult for Chinese manufacturers to meet. However, these are early days and many analysts predict that China will make short work of the learning curve. BYD, Inc., a maker of both electric and gasoline-powered cars, planned to open a North American headquarters in Los Angeles in 2010. BYD is partly owned by a subsidiary of America's Berkshire Hathaway, and it plans to be a leading contender in the global market for electric cars.

Detroit is far more concerned in the short term with the potential for exports from Chinese companies allied with industry leaders such as GM, Ford, Toyota, Honda and Volkswagen. For years, Chinese automakers have been on the receiving end of Western automotive know-how, which will soon come back to haunt the Westerners. As Chinese cars and trucks hit the global market, China's manufacturers will be in direct competition with their partners. For example, Shanghai Automotive Industry Corp. (SAIC), which has partnered with GM and Volkswagen, plans to sell its products in Europe as well as the U.S. Extremely low-priced, Chinese-built models could eventually have a major impact on sales of U.S. and European cars.

That day is close at hand, since the Chinese automotive market, formerly plagued by high costs for parts, is now enjoying greater exports of automotive parts than imports. Domestic components such as engines and transmissions have improved in quality and remain inexpensive when produced domestically. On the export side, sales to foreign manufacturers are booming. China still offers some of the cheapest labor in the world although wage rates have been growing substantially. In addition, a number of U.S. auto parts companies such as American Axle & Manufacturing Holdings, Inc. and AvrinMeritor, Inc. have opened manufacturing plants in China.

Meanwhile, China has become one of the world's largest importers of oil, thanks to rapidly rising demand for gasoline. Watch for the Chinese Government to become a leading innovator in alternative fuel vehicles. For example, the city of Beijing converted its entire 120,000 vehicle bus fleet to run on compressed natural gas. Automakers in China may become world leaders in the manufacture of electric vehicles.

Car sales slowed in India during the economic crisis of 2008. However, for all of 2009, India saw growth in auto sales to 1.43 million units, up 18.7% from 2008, according to the Society of Indian Automobile Manufacturers. Although India is nowhere near as large a market as China and probably won't be for quite some time, it is attracting the attention of the Big Three and the Japanese manufacturers. India is a market with excellent long-term growth potential. GM opened a second factory in India in September 2008 that doubled its annual production capacity to 300,000 units per year, part of a $500 million expansion program. GM's sales in the first part of 2010 were up, spurring the company to project total sales for the year of more than 100,000 vehicles (compared to 70,000 in 2009). Ford is also jockeying for a piece of the Indian market with the growing success of its Ikon model made specifically for Indian tastes. In addition, Renault-Nissan is having success with its $7,100 Logan, a bare-bones vehicle that the company hopes will reach sales of 50,000 cars per year in India alone.

The port city of Chennai has attracted a number of automobile and parts manufacturers in recent years. Hyundai, Ford, Nissan/Renault and Mercedes/Daimler have invested hundreds of millions (in the case of Hyundai, $2 billion) in new manufacturing facilities. Analysts expect total capacity in the city to reach 1.5 million autos per year over the mid-term.

Tata Group, an Indian industrial conglomerate, is another large presence in the car market. While selling steel to giants such as Honda and Toyota, the company also has its own major automobile venture in India: Tata Motors which makes the Indica economy model. Tata launched a revolutionary new vehicle, the Nano, in 2009. The manufacturing process of this tiny car utilizes every cost-saving measure possible so that it can be sold for an astoundingly low $2,500 or so before taxes. Although Tata Motors received more than 200,000 deposits in its first few days of taking orders, the Nano has not been without its problems. The company had to walk away from a $292 million factory in Singur, West Bengal after farmers protested the government's forced purchase of their land for the 1,000 acre plant site. Tata Motors invested $389 million on a new plant at Sanand in Gujarat, which opened in June 2010. The Sanand plant's capacity is 250,000 units per year, which can be expanded to 500,000 per year. Another low-cost car may eventually enter the market thanks to a joint venture between Nissan, Renault and Indian motorbike manufacturer Bajaj Auto, as early as 2012. The minicar will be priced at around $2,500, putting it into direct competition with the Nano. Nissan and Renault are investing $1 billion to construct a manufacturing plant in Chennai with an initial capacity of 200,000 cars per year.

Another big development in the Indian auto industry is exports. India overtook China in vehicle exports for the first three quarters of 2009. At India's Maruti-Suzuki (a subsidiary of Japan's Suzuki Motor Corporation), vehicle exports doubled during the period to almost 80,000. Europe accounts for 56% of cumulative exports, followed by Algeria, Chile, Sri Lanka and Nepal.

In early 2010, the Indian government increased excise duties on small cars to 10% from 8%. That hike, in addition to rising interest rates, may dampen auto sales growth for the near-term.

15) Focus on Safety Improvements by Automakers

According to U.S. Department of Transportation's NHTSA, the number of fatalities from motor vehicle crashes in the U.S. dropped by a tremendous 9.7% in 2009, to 33,808 from 37,261 the previous year. This is also a vast decrease from the 50,000+ per year in the late 1960s and early 1970s, despite the fact that there are millions more vehicles on the road today. The biggest negative development is a 12-year record of increased motorcycle fatalities. Vehicle safety has progressed a long way beyond seat belts and child restraint seats to deal with these statistics.

Another way to track vehicle safety is by fatality and injury rates per 100 million vehicle miles travelled (VMT). NHTSA reports that these ratios are at historic lows, with fatalities per 100 million VMT down from more than 5.0 in 1965 to 1.13 in 2009. Virtually all new cars have been equipped with air bags for several years, which have reduced driver deaths dramatically.

Today, advanced technologies include adaptive cruise control, electronic stability control, collision sensors and lane-drift warning systems. Adaptive cruise control adjusts a car's speed relative to the speed of the vehicles nearby. Electronic stability control adjusts pressure on individual brakes if a sensor picks up wheel, steering wheel or brake data that suggests a loss of control. The U.S. government will require this technology in all new vehicles by 2012. Collision sensors read tire, steering wheel and brake data and make adjustments such as closing sunroofs or adjusting seats to increase safety factors in the moments before a crash. Lane-drift systems utilize a rear-view mirror camera to detect unusual movement beyond the boundaries of the current lane. A warning sounds or the driver's seat vibrates to alert the driver. All of these options, with the exception of the lane-drift warning system, are currently available on many luxury vehicles, and on a growing number of mid-priced vehicles.

Another safety feature that is rapidly being adopted by manufacturers is active head restraints. In the event of read-end collision, head rests are automatically adjusted forward and upward to cradle drivers' and passengers' heads as they snap backwards after an initial drop forward. The restraints, which help reduce instances of whiplash, are required to earn the Insurance Institute for Highway Safety's "Top Safety Pick" status, which is highly desired by manufacturers. Active head restraints have been in Saabs and Volvos for years, but the systems are now being incorporated in Honda Civics, Acura RDX and MDX models and most Mercedes-Benz models.

In the future, watch for innovations such as those developed by Honda on its ASV-3 (Advanced Safety Vehicle). The car's design includes satellite technology that applies the brakes when a corner is taken too rapidly for safety; radio signals that alert an onboard computer to set off an alarm when a collision is imminent; medical data measuring systems that, in the event of a crash, send driver heart rate and respiratory condition information to emergency personnel.

Since 2007, BMW offers military style night vision systems on its 5-, 6- and 7-series cars. The systems use thermal imaging to see people, animals or other potential obstacles at night. Lexus and Honda offer similar technology.

The only hindrance to the application of these new safety features is cost. Only the most expensive models can absorb the typically $4,300 worth of cutting-edge safety technology. A Bain & Co. consultant estimates that each safety option's cost would have to be limited to $100 to make it standard equipment.

A new business opportunity relating to auto safety is opening up with regard to texting. Text messaging reached 2.5 billion per day in early 2009. However, the combination of driving and texting is deadly. As of mid 2009, 17 U.S. states and the District of Columbia had passed laws prohibiting texting while driving. New applications are emerging that limit a cellphone or personal device's ability to receive or send calls and messages while a vehicle is moving. For example, Safe Driving Systems Corp. is developing an application that overrides a cellphone display when its owner is driving. Aegis Mobility is developing a similar product called DriveAssist that uses a phone's GPS to read when the phone is moving at driving speed. During those times, incoming calls and messages are intercepted and outgoing messages are blocked. The system is available for between $6 and $12 per month.

16) Super-Expensive Cars are Pushed by Manufacturers/Luxury Car Market Is Highly Competitive

The slump suffered by the auto industry overall includes the luxury segment, where sales fell almost 21% in 2008, and even further by 29% in 2009. The popularity of luxury cars rose dramatically between 1990 and 2005, when their share of the overall market peaked at 21%, according to Autodata Corp. A number of manufacturers are concerned that the drop may be a long-term change in tastes rather than a short reaction to the economic recession. Some are designing smaller, less expensive models such as Cadillac's new ATS which is set for a 2011 model year launch. Others are lowering prices, such as Toyota's reduction of its RX SUV model by $900 to start at $36,000. The silver lining on the luxury car market cloud is healthy sales in China through 2009 and into 2010.

Of course, some wealthy buyers remain in the market for cars. Competition is fierce for those privileged few. The market in ultimate spending when it comes to cars is still dominated by Italian makers including Bugatti (a subsidiary of Volkswagen) and Ferrari. The Bugatti 16.4 Veyron goes for a cool $1.6 million and packs a 1,001-hp engine that accelerates from zero to 62.5 mph in 2.5 seconds. Ferrari's Enzo, at about $670,000, is the fastest road car ever produced by the company, accelerating from zero to 60 mph in 3.14 seconds.

German automakers are also claiming a piece of the ultra-high-end market. Mercedes-Benz owns the Maybach brand, offering its models 57 and 62 (priced from $366,200 to $455,500 for 2010 models) while BMW owns the Rolls-Royce brand (with the 2010 Phantom base priced at $380,000). Volkswagen owns the Bentley brand in addition to Bugatti. Bentley's Continental GT is the big success story in upper-end sedans, selling at much higher volume than its competitors. These super-extravagant vehicles, costing $182,800 to $231,400, often offer options such as armor plating, vandal-proof retractable hood ornaments and champagne-flute holders.

For those with shallower pockets but a strong desire for luxury, GM has invested heavily in its Cadillac line. Due to the popularity of high-end cars and SUVs from Lexus, BMW and Infiniti, GM reinvented Cadillacs with the debut of the CTS sedan in 2002 (the 2011 model CTS sedan starts at about $35,165) and the SRX SUV in 2003 (the 2011 model retails for about $33,830 to $48,540).

Porsche launched a four-door coupe called the Panamera. The 2010 model sells for between $89,800 and $132,600, and is the company's attempt to go head-to-head with the Mercedes CLS and the BMW 6-series.

Despite the weaker luxury market, Korean manufacturer Hyundai offers a more expensive sedan that it hopes is competing with Lexus and Mercedes. Hyundai's "Genesis" model is priced from a base of $33,000 for a six-cylinder model to $39,500 for a V-8. The fact that Korean manufacturers are now noted for very high quality vehicles may give a boost to this new car.

Meanwhile, luxury carmakers are pushing all wheel drive (AWD) sedans. Manufacturers such as Lexus, Audi, BMW, Mercedes and Cadillac see AWD sedans as a way to boost features and boost profit margins. While these sedans may not be appropriate for driving off-road, AWD can offer a significant traction and safety boost on snowy roads and in other difficult conditions.

17) Rethinking SUVs/Small Sedans and Crossovers Gain Market Share

Sales of large SUVs dropped precipitously in the U.S. during 2005, slipping from 3 million units sold in 2000 to only 2.4 million. In 2006 through 2007, the trend continued, punctuated by a stunning fall in 2008 when gasoline prices soared above $4 per gallon. These drops proved to be only the first act in a falling sales drama of epic proportions as the global recession hit. Historically, profit margins were very high on large volume production of SUVs compared to typical sedans, so this is a major blow to the Big Three, as well as to Toyota.

Previously, Americans had gravitated in record numbers toward vehicles classified as "light trucks," which include minivans, pickups and sport utility vehicles (SUVs). In 2004, sales of trucks of all types rose to 55.5% (17.3 million units) of the U.S. market, up from about 46% in 1998. Trucks were so important to the Big Three that they made up 78% of DaimlerChrysler's 2003 unit sales, 68% of Ford's and 59% of GM's. By 2008, truck sales were down to 47.7% (13.5 million units) of the market.

With a renewed consumer awareness of harmful emissions, fluctuating gasoline prices and the need for fuel efficiency, customers left trucks and SUVs sitting on dealer lots in 2008 and 2009. However, the beginning of an economic recovery coupled with gasoline prices in the U.S. remaining below $3 per gallon sparked a renewed interest in trucks (including SUVs) in 2010. Manufacturers reported full-size pickup sales rising 29% in July 2010 compared to the same month in 2009. SUV sales rose 17% over the same period. This is partly due to pent-up demand for new trucks for business and commercial use.

An alternative to the SUV is a slightly smaller, more efficient crossover utility vehicle (CUV), such as the Lexus RX 350 and the Ford Edge. Crossovers provide many of the positives afforded by large SUVs (e.g., ample cargo space and room for passengers) but they are built on lighter, and therefore more fuel-efficient, frames, similar to those used for cars. Many offer four-wheel drive. Detractors of these vehicles are quick to point out that crossovers are not designed for off-road driving; however, statistics show that most SUV owners keep to paved roads and highways anyway.

Some of the latest GM trucks including the relatively large Chevy Tahoe, Cadillac Escalade and GMC Yukon offer fuel economy of about 20 mpg because of a system that shuts down four of the engine's eight cylinders while maintaining cruising speeds (this saves as much as 2 to 4 mpg).

Meanwhile, new hybrid versions of crossovers and light SUVs have entered the market. Sales of Lexus' RX450h, the hybrid version of the RX350 crossover, remain strong. Ford's 2011 Escape Hybrid starts at only $24,000 and gets up to 32 mpg in the city.

Meanwhile, sedans are back! Fuel-efficient sedans are gaining new interest, especially as many manufacturers are making them with larger engines and more room for passengers and cargo. In 2008, U.S. sedan unit sales surpassed truck and SUV sales for the first time in years. Top-selling sedans in 2010 in the U.S. include the Toyota Camry, Honda Accord and Chevrolet Malibu. The Accord offers a total passenger and cargo volume of more than 119 cubic feet, making it technically a large sedan rather than a mid-size. A four-cylinder 2010 model gets 23 mpg in the city and 31 mpg on the highway with a five-speed automatic transmission.

Volatile gasoline prices, frugal consumers and concerns about emissions will provide a big boost to the small car market, while sales of large vehicles will be challenged. This presents a significant financial obstacle to automakers, since the largest vehicles, such as full-size pickups and SUVs, traditionally earned significantly higher profits per unit than small cars. The Big Three in particular will continue to be under great pressure to cut overhead and reinvent themselves as lean, low-cost companies. Firms that manufacture and sell small, low-priced cars in growing markets like China and India will face the same challenges. Unit sales may be high, but net profits may be at very low levels per unit.

18) Big News in Small Cars

Fuel prices and tougher emissions standards have catapulted tiny compacts and subcompacts to the forefront of car sales while gas-guzzling trucks and big SUVs languish on car lots. Industry analysts at Ford Motor Co. reported 2009 sales of small cars accounting for 21.6% of the total sold in the U.S., compared to 15% in 2000.

In 2009, the Big Three were struggling to reinvent themselves, and new compact car designs were obvious choices for new models. Ford grabbed headlines with a 2009 U.S. release of its compact Fiesta, which sells for as little as $14,000. The company is also heavily marketing its Focus model, which, for about $30,000, is long on new gadgets such as voice activated entertainment and safety features while remaining short in stature.

Daimler AG's line of "smart" cars (note the trademarked lower-case name) had buyers putting down deposits and waiting sometimes months for delivery when gas prices were high. The smart two passenger coupe is shorter from bumper to bumper by five feet than the Volkswagen Beetle and narrower by a foot, at eight feet, three inches long and five feet wide. These tiny, efficient vehicles deliver more than 40 mpg. The car is a collaborative effort by Mercedes-Benz and the creator of the Swatch line of watches.

Daimler hopes to better smart's performance on the market through a 2010 alliance with Renault-Nissan. The companies will collaborate on small car technology and power trains. Renault-Nissan will provide diesel and gas engines for the smart, which will lower costs significantly. The firms will work together on new generations of their small cars, including Renault's Twingo.

The MINI, currently built by BMW at an English plant in Oxford, is another little car worthy of note. Its first incarnation debuted in 1957 in England in response to an oil crisis in the Suez. Sales were high for the minute car and soared in the U.K. when Queen Elizabeth II was photographed at the wheel of a MINI on the streets of London. The car was sold in the U.S. up until 1968, when it was dropped because it could not meet emissions regulations. The BMW Group acquired the company in 1994 and re-released the brand in the U.S. in 2001.

The base price for the 2010 model MINI is $18,800. Gas mileage for the 2010 MINI with a six-speed manual transmission is 28 mpg in the city and 37 on the highway. Additionally, the MINI is equipped with impressive safety features such as an ultra-hard frame, crumple zones, six airbags and side impact door beams. The 2010 higher-end Cooper "S" model MINI features a boost in horsepower and higher-grade interior materials. Meanwhile, MINI is selling a clean diesel "D" version in Europe that gets approximately 47 mpg in the city and 65 mpg on the highway.

A new contender in the small car market is GM's 2011 Chevrolet Cruze which boasts 40 mpg on the highway. The four-door sedan will sell for between $16,275 and $21,975. GM is banking heavily on this car, which includes an exceptional list of convenience features, to give it a big boost in the small car market.

BMW launched a small, two-door "1 Series" model in 2008. Volvo launched a Volvo C30, a two-door hatchback priced at about $22,700, and Audi's A3 model is a five-door hatchback with 200 horsepower.

Many non-U.S. manufacturers are redesigning subcompact models such as the Toyota Vitz, the Honda Jazz and the Nissan Tiida for the U.S. market. These models have been highly popular in Europe and Asia, and with modifications to meet U.S. emissions and safety standards, are likely to meet the growing demand for fuel-efficient cars.

19) Car and Bike Sharing Programs Proliferate

A car sharing business called Zipcar (www.zipcar.com) is popping up in growing numbers of U.S. cities that offers drivers inexpensive alternatives to owning their own cars. For an annual fee of about $50 (and a $25 application fee), plus hourly rates starting at $8.33 and daily rates starting at $61.20, Zipcar members are issued smart cards that allow them to unlock Zipcar vehicles with a wave of the card over the windshield. The cars are equipped with pre-paid cards for use at gas stations and insurance coverage; and drivers are allowed 180 miles of driving per day. As of early 2010, there were 350,000 members driving 6,500 Zipcars available in 28 North American states and in London in the U.K. Business boomed as gas prices escalated to dizzying heights and then again at the onset of the global economic crisis. Zipcar has spawned a number of similar offerings from competitors including rental car firm Hertz Corp.'s Connect by Hertz (which is available in the U.K., Spain, Germany, France and Canada) and Enterprise Rent-A-Car's WeCar.

Meanwhile, General Motors-sponsored researchers at the Massachusetts Institute of Technology (MIT) are creating a prototype called the CityCar that operates very much like luggage carts found at airports and train stations. CityCars are two-seated, bubble-shaped vehicles with motorized electric wheels that work together to reach speeds of up to 55 miles per hour. When parked, the cars fold to about half their size and stack together, with four stacked cars capable of fitting into a single parking space. Drivers would swipe a credit card in a reader to release a stacked car and restack it at another rack near the driver's destination. The projected cost for using the cars is about $1 per mile.

BMW worked on a similar concept that utilizes collapsible motor scooters that have many safety features typically found on cars such as airbags and seatbelts. The C1 scooter was released in 2001, but sold only 33,700 units before the concept was abandoned.

Advertising firm JCDecaux in Paris launched a bicycle-sharing program in 2007. Sturdy, comfortable gray bikes called Vélibs are currently available at 1,639 rental stations throughout the city. Riders can rent bikes by the day or the week, but there are also annual subscriptions that allow unlimited 30-minute maximum rides for about $46 per year. Members create an account using their credit cards which includes permission for the company to charge about $240 if a bike is not returned. JCDecaux turns rider fees over to the city of Paris, but generates additional income through advertising via more than 1,600 billboards throughout Paris. Initially the program was a success with approximately 42 million rentals in the first 18 months, but by early 2009, about half of the 15,000 Vélibs in the original fleet had been stolen and even more had been vandalized. JCDecaux negotiated with city officials, who agreed to pay $500 per bicycle needing replacement, which will cost up to $2 million per year. Despite the difficulties, bike sharing is catching on and spreading in small ways to cities including London, San Francisco and Singapore.

20) Wireless Information Systems Surge Ahead in Vehicles: Telematics, ITS and Real-Time Traffic Information

Telematics: Many near-term advances in car and truck technology will lie in on-board software, wireless communications and convenience features known broadly as "telematics." Using cellular telephone technology, fee-based telematics networks, which allow drivers to check e-mail and online services for weather, stock quotes or driving directions merely by voicing a command, are already in place. GM's OnStar is a leading telematics system. Such systems offer varying degrees of networked services linking cars to external systems such as global positioning systems (GPS). The external systems monitor the position of each vehicle and can perform tasks such as unlocking doors or switching off lights remotely upon request. They also dispatch service vehicles or medical aid when necessary. More recent innovations include ultrasonic rear sensors that warn drivers when they are about to back into something, and voice-activated phone dialing and navigation plotting.

OnStar services (www.onstar.com) are available in GM cars worldwide, and the firm already had more than 5.5 million subscribers in the U.S. and Canada as of early 2009. OnStar states that it provides the following services for subscribers in an average month: Its operators are notified automatically of 1,000 vehicle accidents that are bad enough to inflate airbags; thanks to GPS technology, it is able to notify police and ambulance services, via 911, of the locations of the accidents immediately; it remotely unlocks the doors of 50,000 cars upon request of locked-out owners; it responds to 27,000 roadside assistance calls; it is able to provide the location of 400 stolen vehicles; and it responds to 353,000 requests for routing directions.

Significant improvements to OnStar's accident-reporting system have been developed. The system is able to notify 911 of further details regarding automobile accidents, including the force and direction of impact and whether the car has rolled over. Through an Advanced Automatic Crash Notification (AACN) system, such data travels in real time to an Internet database that alerts hospitals, police and similar emergency responders. These additional accident details will enable 911 responders to better determine the level of support needed. For example, a high-speed accident with a rollover occurring in a remote area might be more likely to receive an immediate response from a Life Flight helicopter.

In addition to its standard safety features, OnStar offers "Directions & Connections" services at a higher monthly fee. This feature provides recommendations of nearby restaurants and other services. It will make hotel reservations upon request and provides navigation and routing assistance.

By 2007, OnStar was standard equipment on all new GM vehicles. Most other manufacturers are following suit. By 2010, there were about 17 million telematics service subscribers in North America, 1.2 million in Western Europe and 1 million in Asia/Pacific. As the technology grows, it will be able to provide more and more options, whether safety- or entertainment-related.

Another breakthrough in telematics is Ford's Sync, a voice-activated entertainment and communications system developed by Ford in partnership with Microsoft. Sync offers real time traffic information, turn-by-turn directions and personalized sports and weather reports, in addition to hands-free operation of cellphones and sound systems. The cost is a $395 one time activation fee, and the system is available on all 2010 Ford models, as well as a number of Lincoln and Mercury models. Toyota announced plans to offer a similar system in its Lexus and Toyota models by the end of 2010.

ITS (Intelligent Transportation Systems): The FCC set aside the 5.9-gigahertz spectrum for wireless networks providing in-car services known as Intelligent Transportation Systems (ITS). ITS includes a broad number of information technologies that can provide an electronic communications link to cars and trucks, enabling drivers to be alerted to road hazards, delays, construction and accidents. At the same time, ITS can transmit driving directions and a wealth of additional driving-related information. (Services such as this have been available to drivers in Japan for a few years.) ITS enables automated drive-through toll collection and truck pre-clearance along highways and at bridge and tunnel crossings. ITS technologies are likewise in use at border stations, points of entry and customs checkpoints, especially in the NAFTA zone.

More recent developments include communications technology created by Motorola that can sense when a vehicle's braking system is abruptly used (as when a driver reacts to a dog running in front of the car) and transmits that information to other nearby vehicles using GPS. A flashing red light or chime alerts nearby drivers to the situation. Likewise, transponders made by Azulstar, Inc. are being mounted on light poles at intersections with traffic lights. The transponders broadcast the current light status (red, yellow or green) to approaching cars. The onboard computers on those vehicles alert drivers who are perceived to be approaching the light too quickly to react safely.

The U.S. Department of Transportation has a serious effort underway to cooperate with a variety of industries to develop ITS. (See its ITS-specific web site at www.its.dot.gov.)

On-Board Networked Computing in General: A future extension for on-board computing will be cars that run on advanced internal software systems linked to internal and external sensors. These systems could control virtually all of the functions of a vehicle, from acceleration to braking and everything in between. One of the most advanced systems is used in the Lexus LS sedan, which can parallel park itself with the assistance of the driver who must brake when necessary (Lincoln's 2010 MKT has the same feature).

Adaptive cruise control is already in use in many high-end vehicles. For example, Mercedes' Pre-Safe system uses its radar to scan for distances to nearby vehicles and, when a collision seems imminent, primes the braking system, tightens the seat belts and adjusts the car seats to optimum protection positions. Mercedes-Benz claims the system can reduce rear collisions by 75%. Another example of adaptive cruise control is the Acura RL's collision-mitigation braking system. When a driver approaches another vehicle too quickly, a warning light flashes on the dashboard, followed by a tightening of the driver's seat belt and ultimately the braking system is engaged (if the driver has yet to put on the brakes). Similar systems are available in the Volvo XC60, which emits loud beeps and flashes red lights on the dashboard; and the Infiniti EX35, which beeps and pushes back on the accelerator. In a recent study, the Insurance Institute for Highway Safety reports that forward collision warning/avoidance technology may be able to prevent or mitigate up to 2.3 million police-reported crashes in the U.S. each year, or 38% of all vehicle-on-vehicle accidents.

Infiniti's intelligent cruise control matches the speed of a vehicle directly ahead and maintains a preset distance; even when the car in front slows to a stop, the Infiniti stops on its own, and, if the lead car moves forward again in less than two seconds, the Infiniti moves again as well, matching the first car's speed. The 2010 Ford Escape has an electric power-steering system that uses sensors and software to help guide the vehicle in high winds or on roads that are crowned for water drainage. Audi heads a research project called Environmentally Friendly Navigation that is underway at the University of California at Berkeley and the University of California at Riverside. The project focuses on using Wi-Fi to network vehicles with roadway data centers, using information about road surface conditions, temperature and necessary braking and acceleration to optimize engine output and burn the least amount of fuel. Nissan conducted a test over a specific route in the Los Angeles, California area using a similar system to Audi's and found that advanced guidance technology helped reduce travel time by 23% and carbon dioxide emissions by 17%.

Computers bring a new level of efficiency to driving. Optimum acceleration and gear selection by computer, based on the road conditions and terrain, can save as much as 5% in fuel consumption compared to traditional driving. Another possibility is for automobiles to transmit road conditions, such as a slippery surface, wirelessly to nearby cars.

The use of wireless telematics and ITS will be vital to tomorrow's "intelligent" automobiles and trucks. Watch for new developments and ever-increasing ways to link the cars on the road with external and internal networks.

Advanced Onboard Traffic Information: Satellite Radio provider Sirius XM, though best known for satellite-based music, has jumped into advanced onboard traffic information provided by satellite. Previously, GPS navigation systems calculated routes to a destination, with no knowledge of true traffic conditions along the planned route. Sirius XM NavTraffic provides detailed traffic information overlaid on the navigation road map, allowing the navigation system to show the traffic conditions between the driver and his or her destination. The display can show traffic delays, such as accidents or construction, and the average speed of vehicles along the way. The system is already standard on several Acura models and available on the Cadillac CTS. Because the service costs only a few extra dollars monthly for current Sirius XM subscribers, it has the potential to catch on very quickly. (Competitors XM and Sirius finalized a merger in 2008).

Another navigation device called Dash Express hit the market in early 2008. The $299.99 unit (plus a small monthly fee) provides GPS navigation as part of a larger network of other Dash users. Traffic speeds are measured on one unit, beamed to the company's main data center and then broadcast to all Dash Express users. The interactive map in the unit displays color coded speed zones. By 2009, Dash Navigation, Inc. (the company behind Dash Express) offered several Dash Apps, which are applications supported by other companies that complement the unit's traffic and GPS features. For example, Coldwell Banker provides real estate listings and property details about nearby housing via a Coldwell Banker Home Search button. The Trapster Find Traps Now button warns drivers of live speed traps, photo enforcement cameras or other nearby police action.

Chapter 2

AUTOMOBILE INDUSTRY STATISTICS

Tables and Charts:

Automobile Industry Overview

	Quantity	Unit	Date	Source
Sales				
Global Unit Sales, Cars & Light Trucks (estimate)	53.96	Mil.	2010	Scotiabank
General Motors	7.49	Mil.	2009	GM
Toyota	7.24	Mil.	2010*	Toyota
Ford	4.82	Mil.	2009	Ford
Honda	4.47	Mil.	2010*	Honda
Chrysler	0.93	Mil.	2009	Chrysler
Daimler	1.09	Mil.	2009	Daimler
Volkswagen	6.31	Mil.	2009	Volkswagen
Nissan	3.52	Mil.	2009	Nissan
U.S. New Car & Truck Sales				
Cars & Light Trucks Sold, U.S. (estimate)	11.5	Mil.	2010	Scotiabank
Hybrids Sold, U.S.	290.3	Thous.	2009	DOE
Total Number of New-Car Dealerships, U.S., Jan. 1st	18.5	Thous.	2010	NADA
Total Revenue: New-Car & Light Truck Dealers, U.S.	486.9	Bil. US$	2009	NADA
Market Share				
General Motors	19.7	%	2009	Ford
Toyota	16.7	%	2009	Ford
Ford	15.3	%	2009	Ford
Chrysler	8.8	%	2009	Ford
Honda	10.8	%	2009	Ford
Nissan	7.3	%	2009	Ford
All Others	21.4	%	2009	Ford
Car Service & Part Sales	76.21	Bil. US$	2009	NADA
Passenger Cars Sold by Selected Country/Region (estimate)				
Asia	20.39	Mil.	2009	Scotiabank
China	8.77	Mil.	2009	Scotiabank
India	1.72	Mil.	2009	Scotiabank
Western Europe	12.25	Mil.	2009	Scotiabank
South America	4.28	Mil.	2009	Scotiabank
Russia	1.55	Mil.	2009	Scotiabank
Canada	1.53	Mil.	2009	Scotiabank
Mexico	0.85	Mil.	2009	Scotiabank
Operations and Transportation				
Total Vehicles in Operation, Cars & Light Trucks, U.S.	248.4	Mil.	2009	R. L. Polk & Co.
Total Vehicles in Operation, Cars & Light Trucks, Global	1.0	Bil.	2010	R. L. Polk & Co.
Total Highway Miles Traveled, U.S.	260.6	Bil.	May-10	DOT

* Fiscal year ending March 31.

NADA = National Automobile Dealers Association; DOE = Department of Energy; DOT = Department of Transportation.

Scotiabank = Projections by Scotia Economics, "Global Auto Report," July 2010

General Motors Corporation Overview

(Sales in Thousands of Units)

U.S. Car & Truck Sales

Vehicle	2007 Units	2007 As a % of Industry	2008 Units	2008 As a % of Industry	2009 Units	2009 As a % of Industry
Cars	1,489	19.7	1,257	18.6	874	16.3
Trucks	2,377	26.7	1,723	25.6	1,210	23.1
Total U.S.	**3,867**	**23.5**	**2,981**	**22.1**	**2,981**	**19.6**

Worldwide Sales

Sales Division	2007 Units	2007 As a % of Industry	2008 Units	2008 As a % of Industry	2009 Units	2009 As a % of Industry
Canada, Mexico & Other	650	20.6%	585	19.1%	400	16.2%
North America	4,516	23.1%	3,565	21.5%	2,485	19.0%
Europe	2,672	9.5%	2,043	9.3%	1,667	8.9%
GMIO	1,236	9.5%	2,754	9.6%	3,326	10.3%
Total Worldwide	**9,370**	**13.2%**	**8,362**	**12.4%**	**7,478**	**11.6%**

GMIO = General Motors International Operations

Number of Dealerships as of December 31

	2007	2008	2009
North America	7,835	7,360	6,450
Europe	8,902	8,732	8,422
GMIO	5,150	5,510	5,895
Total Worldwide	**21,887**	**21,602**	**20,767**

Note: Most dealerships are independently owned.

Source: General Motors Corporation
Plunkett Research, Ltd.
www.plunkettresearch.com

Ford Motor Company Overview

Vehicles Sold at Wholesale by Automotive Segment (in Thousands of Units)

Segment	2008	2009
Ford North America	2,329	1,959
Ford South America	435	443
Ford Europe	1,820	1,568
Ford Asia Pacific & Africa	464	523
Volvo	359	324
Jaguar, Land Rover and Aston Martin	125	--
Total	**5,532**	**4,817**

Sales & Revenues (in Billions)

Unit	2008	2009
Automotive	129.2	105.9
Financial Services	16.0	12.4

Ford Motor Company Primary Facilities at Dec. 31, 2008

Regional Segment	Plants	Distribution Centers/ Warehouses	Engineering, R&D	Sales Offices
Ford North America	40	31	53	58
Ford South America	7	7	3	9
Ford Europe	20	8	5	19
Volvo	8	11	2	37
Ford Asia Pacific and Africa	12	2	2	13
Total	**87**	**59**	**65**	**136**

* Ford has announced plans to cease operations at a number of North American manufacturing facilities as part of its restructuring actions.

Total Worldwide Number of Ford Dealerships by Vehicle Brands, End of Year

Brand	2007	2008
Ford	11,827	11,682
Mercury	1,871	1,780
Lincoln	1,427	1,376
Volvo	2,341	2,269

Note: Most dealerships are independently owned. Because many of these dealerships distribute more than one of Ford's brands from the same sales location, a single dealership may be counted under more than one brand.

Source: Ford Motor Company
Plunkett Research, Ltd.
www.plunkettresearch.com

Toyota Motor Corporation Overview

(Fiscal Year Ending March 31)

Worldwide Vehicle Unit Sales

Region	2006	2007	2008	2009	2010
Japan	2,364,484	2,273,152	2,188,389	1,944,823	2,162,418
North America	2,556,050	2,942,661	2,958,314	2,212,254	2,097,374
Europe	1,022,781	1,223,628	1,283,793	1,061,954	858,390
Asia	880,661	789,637	956,509	904,892	979,651
Other*	1,150,587	1,295,581	1,526,934	1,443,433	1,139,329
Total	**7,974,563**	**8,524,659**	**8,913,939**	**7,567,356**	**7,237,162**

* "Other" consists of Central and South America, Oceania, Africa and the Middle East, etc.

Toyota Motor Primary Facilities as of March 31, 2010

Region	Cars	Parts	R&D	Other
Japan	11	2	2	1
U.S. & Canada	1	0	0	1
Australia	1	0	0	0
Thailand	1	0	0	0

Note: figures do not include factories under construction in Japan, United States, Canada, China and Russia. Other joint ventures are not listed. Toyota has more than 50 manufacturing plants in 26 countries, but the table lists only the primary plants.

Source: Toyota Motor Corporation
Plunkett Research, Ltd.
www.plunkettresearch.com

Daimler Overview

(Sales in Thousands of Units)

Daimler & Mercedes Benz Worldwide Unit Sales

	2004	2005	2006	2007	2008	2009
Western Europe	820.7	776.6	784.8	779.2	733.2	623.5
Germany	386.9	354.9	353.3	342.9	332.5	297.8
Other	433.8	421.7	431.6	436.3	400.8	325.7
North America	239.9	253.5	271.8	276.1	282.2	235.5
United States	222.5	231.8	248.6	251.8	251.2	203.0
Canada & Mexico	17.4	21.7	23.2	24.7	31.0	32.6
Asia	93.3	107.7	108.5	123.4	144.1	138.9
Japan	41.4	48.3	48.5	46.3	37.0	67.5
Other	51.9	59.4	60.0	77.0	107.2	71.5
Other Markets	72.9	79.0	86.7	114.6	113.5	95.9
Total	**1,226.8**	**1,216.8**	**1,251.8**	**1,293.2**	**1,273.3**	**1,093.9**

Note: Unit sales for 2009, 2008 and 2007 include sales of Mitsubishi pickup trucks (L200) assembled and sold by one of the subsidiaries in South Africa and Mitsubishi Pajero vehicles sold by that subsidiary (5,274; 8,190; and 10,066 units, respectively).

Daimler & Mercedes Benz Unit Sales by Brand

Brand	2007	2008	2009
S-Class (including CL, SL and SLR) and Maybach	107.0	92.9	57.1
E-Class (including CLS)	230.9	172.9	212.1
C-Class (including CLC, CLK and SLK)	386.5	448.4	322.8
A-/B-Class	275.4	250.3	215.5
ML-/R-/G-/GL-/GLK-Class	180.2	161.3	167.2
Smart	103.1	139.0	113.9
Other[1]	10.1	8.2	5.3
Total	1,293.2	1,273.0	1,093.9

[1] This category represents Mitsubishi pickup trucks (L200) assembled and sold by one of the subsidiaries in South Africa and Mitsubishi Pajero vehicles sold by that subsidiary.

Source: Daimler Corporation

Plunkett Research, Ltd.

www.plunkettresearch.com

Honda Motor Corporation Overview

(Fiscal Year Ending March 31)

Worldwide Vehicle and Product Sales in Thousands of Units

	2005	2006	2007	2008	2009	2010
Automobiles	**3,242**	**3,391**	**3,652**	**3,925**	**3,517**	**3,392**
Japan	712	696	672	615	556	646
North America	1,575	1,682	1,788	1,850	1,496	1,297
Europe	267	291	324	391	350	249
Asia	512	521	620	755	793	950
Other Regions[1]	176	201	248	314	322	250
Motorcycles[2]	**10,482**	**10,271**	**10,369**	**9,320**	**10,114**	**9,639**
Japan	378	368	337	311	232	190
North America	643	615	503	453	320	189
Europe	338	353	329	313	276	199
Asia	8192	7,907	7,895	6,633	7,523	7,628
Other Regions[1]	931	1,028	1,305	1,610	1,763	1,433
Power Products[3]	**5,300**	**5,876**	**6,421**	**6,057**	**5,187**	**4,744**

[1] Includes Latin America, the Middle East & Africa and Oceania.

[2] The motorcycle segment includes ATVs and marine watercraft.

[3] Power Products include tillers, portable generators, general-purpose engines, grass cutters, outboard marine engines, water pumps, snow throwers, power carriers, power sprayers, lawn mowers and lawn tractors (riding lawn mowers).

Source: Honda Motor Corporation
Plunkett Research, Ltd.
www.plunkettresearch.com

Motor Vehicle Output, U.S.: 2003-2009

(In Billions of US$)

	2004	2005	2006	2007	2008	2009	Q2 2010
Motor vehicle output	398.9	418.9	412.7	409.9	325.0	248.9	315.9
Auto output	133.1	150.3	155.4	152.4	138.7	94.7	118.8
Truck output	265.8	268.7	257.2	257.5	186.3	154.3	197.2
Final sales of domestic product	394.5	422.6	416.4	417.7	334.1	274.3	298.1
Personal consumption expenditures	359.5	361.6	346.6	349.9	291.0	269.4	285.6
New motor vehicles	252.4	248.9	233.0	233.2	184.9	165.3	174.8
Autos	91.9	97.4	100.0	95.9	85.7	72.1	67.4
Light trucks (including utility vehicles)	160.5	151.4	133.1	137.2	99.2	93.2	107.4
Net purchases of used autos and used light trucks	107.1	112.7	113.5	116.7	106.1	104.1	110.8
Used autos	52.9	55.7	54.2	53.0	48.3	44.4	46.7
Used light trucks (including utility vehicles)	54.2	57.0	59.3	63.7	57.8	59.7	64.1
Private fixed investment	127.6	148.0	163.8	146.6	101.1	42.9	78.8
New motor vehicles	190.7	213.0	230.1	219.4	172.8	116.6	152.2
Autos	72.5	77.8	82.0	83.1	71.3	52.7	69.2
Trucks	118.2	135.2	148.2	136.2	101.6	63.9	82.9
Light trucks (including utility vehicles)	88.8	98.8	107.3	105.4	77.5	47.5	63.9
Other	29.3	36.4	40.8	30.9	24.0	16.5	19.0
Net purchases of used autos and used light trucks	-63.1	-65.0	-66.3	-72.8	-71.7	-73.7	-73.4
Used autos	-31.3	-32.7	-32.3	-34.0	-34.5	-33.5	-34.1
Used light trucks (including utility vehicles)	-31.8	-32.3	-34.0	-38.8	-37.2	-40.1	-39.3
Gross government investment	14.0	15.1	16.9	17.7	18.3	15.1	14.9
Autos	3.2	3.5	3.8	3.9	3.8	3.3	3.2
Trucks	10.9	11.6	13.0	13.7	14.5	11.9	11.7
Net exports	-106.7	-102.1	-110.8	-96.4	-76.3	-53.1	-81.2
Exports	36.5	44.0	49.1	60.8	65.3	40.0	55.0
Autos	16.5	20.4	23.9	31.7	37.2	20.8	27.6
Trucks	20.1	23.6	25.2	29.0	28.1	19.1	27.5
Imports	143.2	146.1	159.9	157.2	141.6	93.1	136.3
Autos	71.7	69.6	77.1	76.6	77.5	54.9	74.2
Trucks	71.5	76.5	82.8	80.6	64.1	38.2	62.1
Change in private inventories	4.4	-3.6	-3.7	-7.8	-9.1	-25.4	17.8
Autos	-0.9	-2.2	0.9	-4.8	4.5	-10.1	12.8
New	-1.4	-1.2	2.6	-3.7	6.2	-12.5	12.0
Used	0.5	-1.0	-1.7	-2.9	4.2	-9.2	7.1
Trucks	5.3	-1.4	-4.7	-0.9	2.0	-3.3	4.9
New	4.8	0.0	-2.7	-1.1	-1.7	2.4	0.8
Used[1]	0.5	-1.5	-2.0	-3.0	-13.6	-15.2	5.0
Addenda:							
Final sales of motor vehicles to domestic purchasers	501.2	524.7	527.2	514.1	410.4	327.4	379.3
Private fixed investment in new autos and new light trucks	161.4	176.5	189.3	188.5	148.8	100.1	133.2
Domestic output of new autos[2]	96.3	107.8	109.2	105.5	101.1	60.6	81.4
Sales of imported new autos[3]	84.4	86.4	96.2	99.6	89	75	81.6

[1] Consists of used light trucks only.

[2] Consists of final sales and change in private inventories of new autos assembled in the United States.

[3] Consists of personal consumption expenditures, private fixed investment, and gross government investment.

Source: U.S. Bureau of Economic Analysis (BEA)
Plunkett Research, Ltd.
www.plunkettesearch.com

Real Motor Vehicle Output, Quantity Indexes, U.S.: 2004-Q2 2010

(2005=100)

	2004	2005	2006	2007	2008	2009	Q2 2010
Motor vehicle output	96.193	100	98.815	98.798	80.384	60.568	75.092
Auto output	89.819	100	102.396	100.899	93.832	62.905	77.757
Truck output	99.748	100	96.791	97.620	72.682	59.266	73.551
Final sales of domestic product	94.305	100	98.875	99.841	81.931	66.201	70.352
Personal consumption expenditures	100.959	100	96.237	98.155	83.389	77.640	78.436
New motor vehicles	101.921	100	94.240	95.338	76.757	67.926	70.551
Autos	95.216	100	101.678	98.093	87.900	73.285	67.882
Light trucks (including utility vehicles)	106.220	100	89.391	93.598	69.341	64.428	72.438
Net purchases of used autos & used light trucks	98.797	100	100.629	104.343	97.989	99.272	95.870
Used autos	98.684	100	97.436	95.884	90.487	85.912	82.291
Used light trucks (including utility vehicles)	98.908	100	103.743	112.596	105.307	112.286	109.088
Private fixed investment	85.717	100	110.634	98.035	68.035	26.089	55.461
New motor vehicles	90.497	100	107.889	103.180	81.892	54.524	70.044
Autos	94.177	100	104.456	106.546	91.636	66.992	87.341
Trucks	88.379	100	109.875	101.221	76.224	47.265	59.968
Light trucks (including utility vehicles)	90.136	100	110.406	110.038	82.802	50.179	66.015
Other	83.531	100	108.469	78.991	59.633	39.659	44.902
Net purchases of used autos & used light trucks	101.655	100	101.651	115.218	114.604	124.472	110.092
Used autos	99.991	100	98.302	106.674	109.481	111.991	101.429
Used light trucks (including utility vehicles)	103.344	100	105.049	123.895	119.802	137.171	118.885
Gross government investment	94.439	100	109.675	112.836	115.340	92.217	90.760
Autos	91.859	100	108.618	110.231	103.983	84.660	87.791
Trucks	95.210	100	109.990	113.609	118.709	94.452	91.644
Net exports							
Exports	84.307	100	110.893	136.119	144.791	88.096	120.365
Autos	81.294	100	116.389	153.513	179.117	99.929	131.476
Trucks	86.934	100	106.131	121.075	115.220	77.803	110.584
Imports	98.978	100	109.010	106.142	93.760	61.443	89.923
Autos	103.695	100	110.684	108.934	108.106	76.635	103.771
Trucks	94.675	100	107.493	103.613	80.788	47.730	77.390
Addenda:							
Final sales of motor vehicles to domestic purchasers	96.442	100	100.694	98.516	79.898	62.898	71.660
Private fixed investment in new autos & new light trucks	91.912	100	107.767	108.500	86.819	57.815	75.707
Domestic output of new autos[1]	90.092	100	100.452	97.206	92.974	54.951	74.182
Sales of imported new autos[2]	98.665	100	110.383	114.931	103.009	86.005	92.687

[1] Consists of final sales and change in private inventories of new autos assembled in the United States.

[2] Consists of personal consumption expenditures, private fixed investment, and gross government investment.

Source: U.S. Bureau of Economic Analysis (BEA)
Plunkett Research, Ltd.
www.plunkettresearch.com

U.S. New Car & Truck Market Shares by Company: 2005-2009

(In Percentages)

New Car Market Share	2005	2006	2007	2008	2009
General Motors	10.2	10.0	9.8	10.0	9.1
Toyota	7.4	8.6	9.2	10.0	10.0
Honda	4.8	4.9	5.3	6.6	6.5
Ford	5.4	5.8	4.6	5.0	5.5
Chrysler	3.3	3.2	3.8	4.4	2.5
Nissan	4.0	4.1	4.2	3.6	4.8
All Other*	10.3	10.6	11.3	12.7	14.1
Total U.S. Car Sales	45.4	47.2	48.2	52.3	52.5

New Truck Market Share	2005	2006	2007	2008	2009
General Motors	15.6	14.1	13.6	12.1	10.6
Ford	11.6	10.2	10.0	9.2	9.8
Chrysler	9.2	8.4	8.4	7.2	6.3
Toyota	5.6	6.3	6.7	6.4	6.7
Honda	3.6	3.9	4.1	4.0	4.3
Nissan	2.9	2.8	2.7	2.7	2.5
All Other*	6.1	7.1	6.3	6.1	7.3
Total U.S. Truck Sales	54.6	52.8	51.8	47.7	47.5

New Car & Truck Market Share	2005	2006	2007	2008	2009
General Motors	25.8	24.1	23.4	22.1	19.7
Toyota	13.0	14.9	15.9	16.4	16.7
Ford	17.0	16.0	14.6	14.2	15.3
Chrysler	13.2	12.5	12.6	10.8	8.8
Honda	8.4	8.8	9.4	10.6	10.8
Nissan	6.2	6.0	6.5	7.1	7.3
All Other*	16.4	17.7	17.6	18.8	21.4
Total U.S. Car & Truck Sales	100	100	100	100	100.0

Note: All U.S. sales data are based on publicly available information from the media and trade publications.

* "All Other" includes primarily companies based in Korea, other Japanese manufacturers and various European manufacturers, and, with respect to the U.S. Truck Market Shares table and U.S. Combined Car and Truck Market Shares table, includes heavy truck manufacturers.

Source: Ford Motor Company
Plunkett Research, Ltd.
www.plunkettresearch.com

New Vehicle Sales by Vehicle Type, U.S.: 2005-2009

(In Millions of Units)

	2005	2006	2007	2008	2009
Cars	7.9	8.1	7.9	7.1	5.6
Trucks	9.6	9.0	8.6	6.4	5.0
Total	**17.5**	**17.1**	**16.5**	**13.5**	**10.6**

(By Percent of Total Sales)

Cars	2005	2006	2007	2008	2009
Small	17.1	19.0	19.8	22.9	23.7
Medium	13.1	13.1	13.6	15.5	16.1
Large	7.4	7.5	7.0	6.1	5.4
Premium	7.8	7.6	7.8	7.8	7.3
Total Car Sales	**45.4**	**47.2**	**48.2**	**52.3**	**52.5**

(By Percent of Total Sales)

Trucks	2005	2006	2007	2008	2009
Compact Pick Up	3.9	3.5	3.2	2.8	2.6
Bus/Van	8.1	7.8	6.6	6.1	5.5
Full Size Pickup	14.6	13.3	13.5	11.9	10.8
SUV/CUV	25.5	25.2	26.5	24.9	27.1
Medium/Heavy	2.5	3.0	2.0	2.0	1.5
Total Truck Sales	**54.6**	**52.8**	**51.8**	**47.7**	**47.5**

	2005	2006	2007	2008	2009
Combined Percentage of Car and Truck Sales	**100**	**100**	**100**	**100**	**100**

Note: Numbers may not add to 100 due to rounding.

Source: Ford Motor Company
Plunkett Research, Ltd.
www.plunkettresearch.com

Highest Fuel Economy by Vehicle Class: 2010 Model Year

Class	Make/Model	MPG City/Highway
Two Seater	Smart fortwo Cabriolet (automatic) Smart fortwo Coupe (automatic) Mazda MX-5 (5 speed manual)	33/41 22/28
Minicompact Car	Mini Cooper (manual) Mini Convertible (automatic) Mini Cooper (automatic)	28/37 25/33
Subcompact Car	Toyota Yaris (manual) Toyota Yaris (automatic)	29/36 29/35
Compact Car	Honda Civic Hybrid (automatic) Volkswagen Jetta (manual, diesel) Volkswagen Golf (manual, diesel)	40/45 30/41
Midsize Car	Toyota Prius (hybrid, automatic) Hyundai Elantra Blue (manual)	51/48 26/35
Large Car	Hyundai Sonata (automatic, 2.4 L) Honda Accord 4 Door Sedan (manual)	22/32 22/31
Small Station Wagon	Audi A3 (automatic, diesel) Volkswagen Jetta SportWagen (automatic, diesel) Volkswagen Jetta SportWagen (manual, diesel)	30/42 30/41
Midsize Station Wagon	Volkswagen Passat Wagon (automatic) BMW 535i Sport Wagon xDrive (manual)	22/31 16/23
Sport Utility Vehicle	Ford Escape Hybrid FWD (automatic) Mazda Tribute Hybrid 2WD (automatic) Mercury Mariner Hybrid FWD (automatic) Jeep Compass 2WD (manual, 2.0 L) Jeep Patriot 2WD (manual, 2.0 L)	34/31 23/29
Minivan	Mazda 5 (manual) Mazda 5 (automatic)	22/28 21/27
Small Pickup Truck	Ford Ranger 2WD (manual, 2.3 L) Toyota Tacoma 2WD (automatic, 2.7 L)	22/27 19/25
Standard Pickup Truck	Chevrolet C15 Silverado 2WD Hybrid (automatic) GMC C15 Sierra 2WD Hybrid (automatic)	21/22
Van (Cargo)	Chevrolet G1500 Van 2WD Cargo GMC G1500 Savana 2WD Cargo	15/20
Van (Passenger)	Chevrolet G1500 Express 2WD (FFV, automatic) Chevrolet H1500 Express AWD (FFV, automatic) GMC G1500 Savana 2WD (FFV, automatic) GMC H1500 Savana AWD (FFV, automatic)	13/17

Source: U.S. Environmental Protection Agency (EPA)
Plunkett Research, Ltd.
www.plunkettresearch.com

Lowest Fuel Economy by Vehicle Class: 2010 Model Year

Class	Make/Model	MPG City/Highway
Two Seater	Lamborghini Murcielago (manual) Lamborghini Murcielago Roadster (manual)	8/13
Minicompact Car	Aston Martin DB9 (manual) Aston Martin DBS (manual)	11/17
Subcompact Car	Bentley Continental GTC	10/17
Compact Car	Bentley Azure Bentley Brooklands	9/15
Midsize Car	Ferrari 612 Scaglietti (automatic)	9/16
Large Car	Maybach 57 Maybach 57 S	10/16
Small Station Wagon	Infiniti EX35 (AWD)	16/23
Midsize Station Wagon	BMW 535i Sport Wagon xDrive (manual)	16/23
Sport Utility Vehicle	Mercedes-Benz ML 63 AMG Mercedes-Benz G550	11/15
Minivan	Toyota Sienna 4WD	16/21
Small Pickup Truck	Ford Ranger 4WD (automatic) Toyota Tacoma 4WD (manual 6 speed)	14/18
Standard Pickup Truck	Nissan Titan 4WD Nissan Titan 4WD FFV	12/17
Van (Passenger)	Chevrolet G1500 Express 2WD (FFV, automatic) Chevrolet H1500 Express AWD (FFV, automatic) GMC G1500 Savana 2WD (FFV, automatic) GMC H1500 Savana AWD (FFV, automatic)	13/17
Van (Cargo)	Chevrolet G1500 Express Cargo Van Conversion 2WD (FFV) Chevrolet H1500 Express Cargo Van Conversion AWD (FFV) Chevrolet H1500 Express AWD Cargo (FFV) GMC G1500 Savana 2WD Cargo Conversion (FFV) GMC H1500 Savana AWD Cargo Conversion (FFV) GMC H1500 Savana AWD Cargo (FFV)	13/17

Source: U.S. Environmental Protection Agency (EPA)

Plunkett Research, Ltd.

www.plunkettresearch.com

Personal Transportation Expenditures, U.S.: 2003-2009

(in Billions of US$)

	2003	2004	2005	2006	2007	2008	2009
Transportation	**857.4**	**909.5**	**979.3**	**1,008.8**	**1,051.6**	**1,033.5**	**890.7**
Motor vehicles	358.2	359.5	361.6	346.6	347.8	291.0	269.4
New motor vehicles	251.6	252.4	248.9	233.0	233.3	184.9	165.3
Net purchases of used motor vehicles	106.6	107.1	112.7	113.5	114.5	106.1	104.1
Motor vehicle operation	430.1	476.0	541.0	581.6	620.5	658.0	544.3
Motor vehicle parts and accessories	43.3	45.2	48.0	50.6	52.5	52.2	50.3
Motor vehicle fuels, lubricants, and fluids	192.8	231.6	283.8	314.7	343.9	383.3	280.8
Motor vehicle maintenance and repair	143.4	148.3	154.9	156.9	162.0	159.7	154.4
Other motor vehicle services	50.6	50.9	54.2	59.5	62.1	62.7	58.7
Public transportation	69.1	73.9	76.8	80.6	83.3	84.5	77.0
Ground transportation[1]	23.3	25.2	26.4	28.4	28.6	29.9	29.3
Air transportation	43.3	46.2	47.7	49.4	51.7	51.6	45.1
Water transportation	2.4	2.6	2.7	2.8	3.0	3.0	2.7

[1] Includes railway transportation, taxicab services, school and employee services, limousine services, and airport bus fares.

Source: U.S. Bureau of Economic Analysis
Plunkett Research, Ltd.
www.plunkettresearch.com

Average Annual Vehicle Distance Traveled

(Billions of Miles)

Year	Miles	Year	Miles	Year	Miles	Year	Miles
1984	1,686	1991	2,149	1998	2,588	2005	2,986
1985	1,745	1992	2,209	1999	2,646	2006	3,003
1986	1,805	1993	2,272	2000	2,734	2007	3,024
1987	1,886	1994	2,321	2001	2,763	2008	3,009
1988	1,977	1995	2,405	2002	2,827	2009	2,966
1989	2,068	1996	2,438	2003	2,862	2010*	2,981
1990	2,136	1997	2,524	2004	2,938		

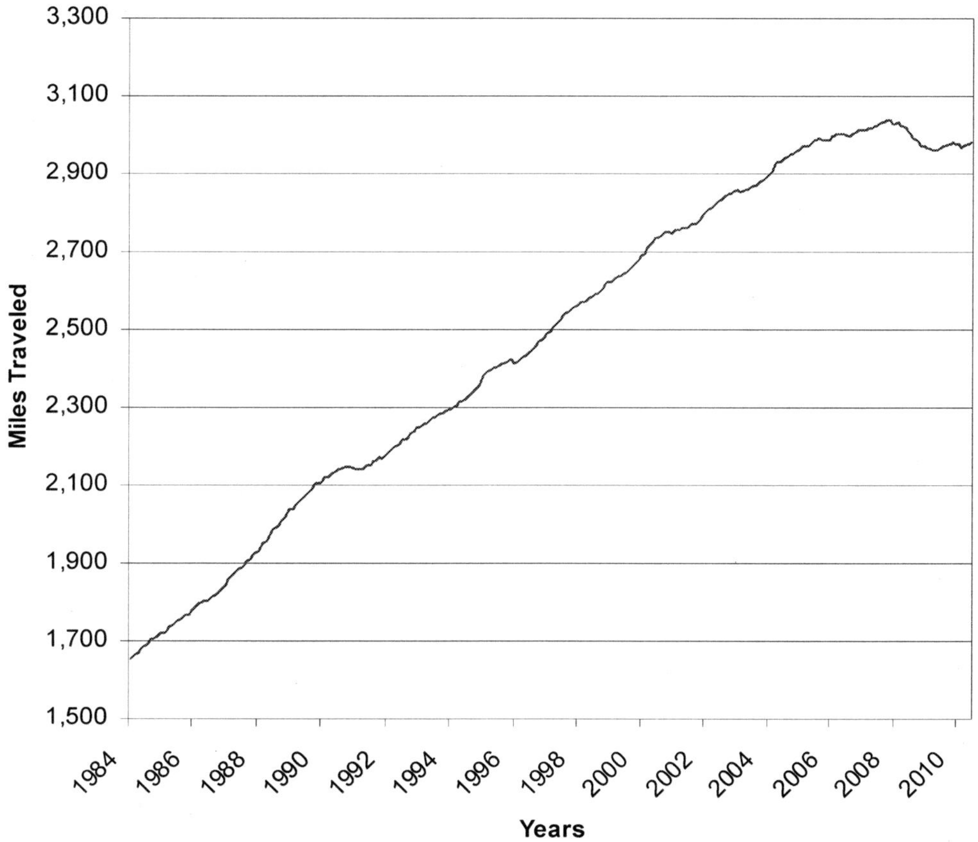

* 2010 is an average of the first six months of the year only.

Source: U.S. Department of Transportation, Federal Highway Administration, Office of Highway Policy Information

Plunkett Research, Ltd.

www.plunkettresearch.com

Average Miles Per Gallon vs. Horsepower, U.S.: 1975-2009

(Lastest Year Available)

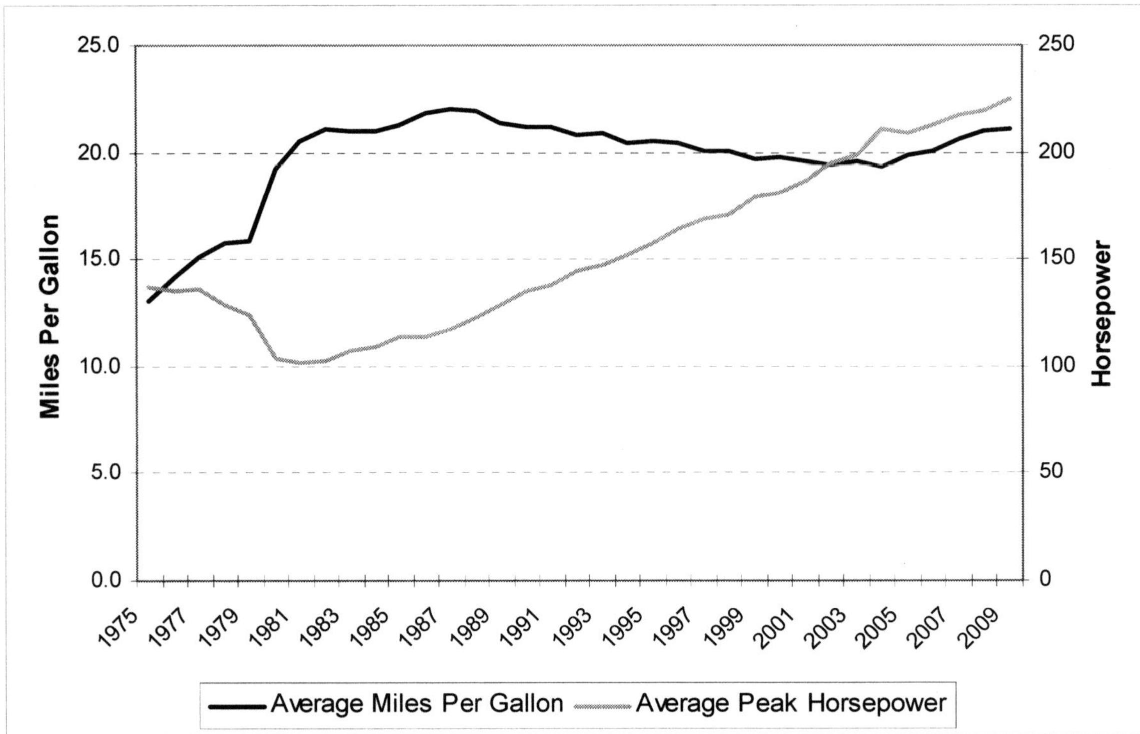

Notes: Motorcycles are not reflected as part of the light-duty fleet. The light truck data used in this series of reports includes vans, SUVs, and trucks with gross vehicle weight ratings (GVWR) up to 8,500 lbs. EPA adjusted the fuel economy figures to reflect real road conditions rather than lab conditions.

Source: U.S. Environmental Protection Agency
Plunkett Research, Ltd.
www.plunkettresearch.com

Automobile Driving Costs, U.S.: 2010

Category	Small Sedan	Midsize Sedan	Large Sedan	Average	4WD Sport Utility Vehicle	Minivan
Examples	Chevrolet Cobalt; Ford Focus; Honda Civic; Nissan Sentra; Toyota Corolla	Chevrolet Impala; Ford Fusion; Honda Accord; Nissan Altima; Toyota Camry	Buick Lucerne; Chrysler 300; Ford Taurus; Nissan Maxima; Toyota Avalon		Chevrolet TrailBlazer; Ford Explorer; Jeep Grand Cherokee; Nissan Pathfinder; Toyota 4Runner	Nissan Quest; Dodge Grand Caravan; Kia Sedona; Honda Odyssey; Toyota Sienna
Operating Costs (Cents/Mile)						
Gas	9.24	11.97	12.88	11.36	16.38	13.70
Maintenance	4.21	4.42	5.00	4.54	4.95	4.86
Tires	0.65	0.91	0.94	0.83	0.98	0.75
Cost per mile	**14.10**	**17.30**	**18.82**	**16.74**	**22.31**	**19.31**
Ownership Costs (US$/Year)						
Full-Coverage Insurance	1,005	1,004	1,084	1,031	964	934
License, Registration & Taxes	427	583	745	585	735	618
Depreciation (15,000 Miles Annually)	2,384	3,451	4,828	3,554	5,003	3,995
Finance Charge (10% down; loan @ 6% for 5 years)	565	803	1,050	806	1,036	857
Cost per year	**4,381**	**5,841**	**7,707**	**5,976**	**7,738**	**6,404**
Cost per day	**12.00**	**16.00**	**21.12**	**16.37**	**21.20**	**17.55**
Total Annual Cost (US$)						
10,000 miles per year						
Cost per year	5,636	7,285	9,259	7,393	9,694	8,060
Cost per mile (in cents)	56.40	72.90	92.60	73.90	96.90	80.60
15,000 miles per year						
Cost per year	6,496	8,436	10,530	8,487	11,085	9,301
Cost per mile (in cents)	43.30	56.20	70.20	56.60	73.90	62.00
20,000 miles per year						
Cost per year	7,321	9,519	11,721	11,721	12,410	10,476
Cost per mile (in cents)	36.60	47.60	58.60	58.60	62.10	62.40

Source: American Automobile Association (AAA)
Plunkett Research, Ltd.
www.plunkettresearch.com

U.S. Highway Vehicle Miles Traveled, Monthly: 1990-2010

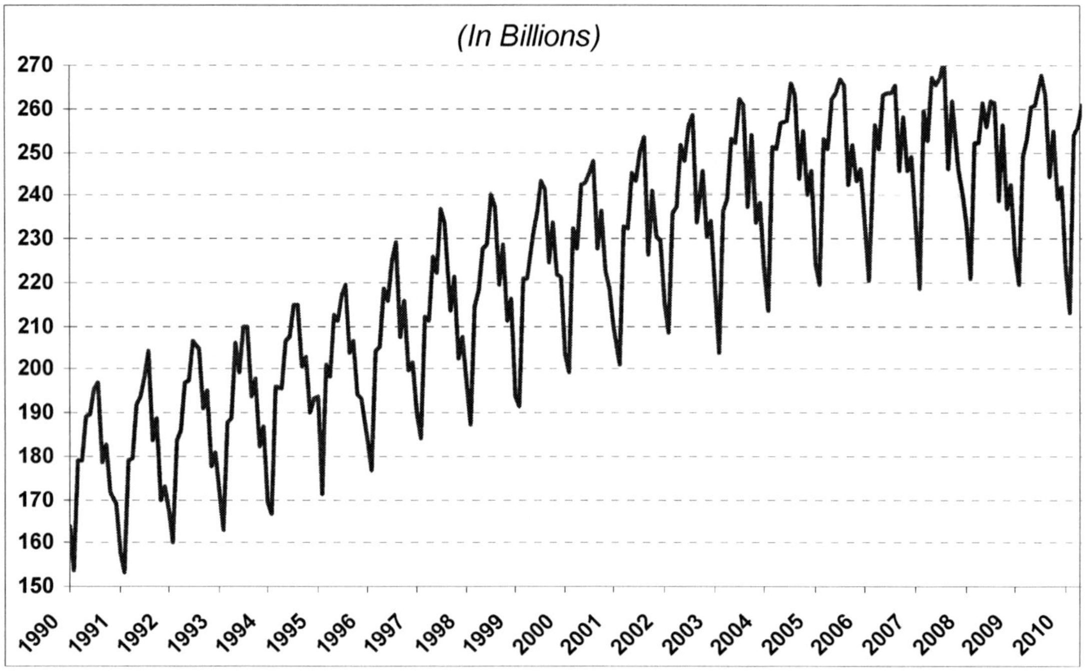

Vehicle Miles Traveled	May-09	May-10
Highway miles (millions)	260,438	260,641
Percent change from same month previous year	-0.35%	0.08%

Vehicle-miles traveled (VMT) are key data for highway planning and management, and a common measure of roadway use. Along with other data, VMT are often used in estimating congestion, air quality, and potential gas-tax revenues, and can provide a general measure of the level of the nation's economic activity.

Source: U.S. Department of Transportation - Federal Highway Administration, Office of Highway Policy Information
Plunkett Research, Ltd.
www.plunkettresearch.com

Motor Vehicle Traffic Accidents in the U.S. by Type of Vehicle & Person: 1999-2008

(Latest Year Available)

	1999	2000	2001	2002	2003	2004	2005	2006	2007	2008
Fatal Vehicle Traffic Accidents	37,140	37,526	37,862	38,491	38,477	38,444	39,252	38,648	37,435	34,017
Vehicle Occupants										
Drivers	22,971	22,914	22,914	23,625	23,352	23,158	23,237	22,831	21,717	19,220
Passengers	10,325	10,451	10,227	10,370	10,171	10,042	9,750	9,187	8,716	7,397
Unknown	96	86	102	110	104	76	83	101	94	72
Total	33,392	33,451	33,243	34,105	33,627	33,276	33,070	32,119	30,527	26,689
Motorcycle Riders	2,483	2,897	3,197	3,270	3,714	4,028	4,576	4,837	5,174	5,290
Nonmotorist										
Pedestrians	4,939	4,763	4,901	4,851	4,774	4,675	4,892	4,795	4,699	4,378
Pedalcyclists	754	693	732	665	629	727	786	772	701	716
Other/Unknown	149	141	123	114	140	130	186	185	158	188
Total	5,842	5,597	5,756	5,630	5,543	5,532	5,864	5,752	5,558	5,282
Total	41,717	41,945	42,196	43,005	42,884	42,836	43,510	42,708	41,259	37,261

Other National Statistics

	1999	2000	2001	2002	2003	2004	2005	2006	2007	2008
Vehicle Miles Traveled (Billions)	2,691	2,747	2,797	2,856	2,890	2,965	2,989	3,014	3,032	2,974
Resident Population (Thousands)	272,691	282,172	285,040	287,727	290,211	292,892	295,561	298,363	301,290	304,060
Registered Vehicles (Thousands)	212,685	217,028	221,230	225,685	230,633	237,949	245,628	251,415	255,748	257,494
Licensed Drivers (Thousands)	187,170	190,625	191,276	194,602	196,166	198,889	200,549	202,810	205,742	208,321

National Rates: Fatalities

	1999	2000	2001	2002	2003	2004	2005	2006	2007	2008
Fatalities per 100 Million Vehicle Miles Traveled	1.55	1.53	1.51	1.51	1.48	1.44	1.46	1.42	1.36	1.25
Fatalities per 100,000 Population	15.30	14.87	14.80	14.95	14.78	14.63	14.72	14.31	13.69	12.25
Fatalities per 100,000 Registered Vehicles	19.61	19.33	19.07	19.06	18.59	18.00	17.71	16.99	16.13	14.47
Fatalities per 100,000 Licensed Drivers	22.29	22.00	22.06	22.10	21.86	21.54	21.7	21.06	20.05	17.89

Source: National Highway Transportation Safety Administration (NHTSA), Fatality Analysis Reporting System (FARS)
Plunkett Research, Ltd.
www.plunkettresearch.com

International Retail Premium Gasoline Prices: August 1996-August 2010

(Includes Taxes; In US$ per Gallon)

Date	Belgium	France	Germany	Italy	Netherlands	U.K.	U.S.
Aug-96	4.04	4.04	4.09	4.21	4.53	3.20	1.39
Aug-97	3.69	3.50	3.43	3.65	3.76	3.83	1.42
Aug-98	3.38	3.39	3.25	3.50	3.51	3.96	1.20
Aug-99	3.64	3.56	3.48	3.64	3.76	4.28	1.41
Aug-00	3.56	3.78	3.49	3.76	4.01	4.53	1.65
Aug-01	3.52	3.55	3.51	3.60	3.94	4.20	1.61
Aug-02	3.63	3.81	3.87	3.89	4.27	4.26	1.59
Aug-03	4.17	4.21	4.55	4.44	4.90	4.53	1.93
Aug-04	5.13	4.99	5.46	5.32	5.88	5.55	2.07
Aug-05	6.16	5.73	6.04	5.91	6.61	6.20	2.80
Aug-06	6.64	6.35	6.54	6.65	7.08	6.86	3.14
Aug-07	6.77	6.54	6.84	6.68	7.47	7.24	2.96
Aug-08	8.20	7.94	8.30	8.10	9.04	7.85	3.92
Aug-09	7.23	6.89	7.21	7.01	7.60	6.52	2.87
Aug-10	6.70	6.34	6.69	6.52	7.09	6.79	2.95

U.S. Retail Premium Gas Prices: 1996-2010

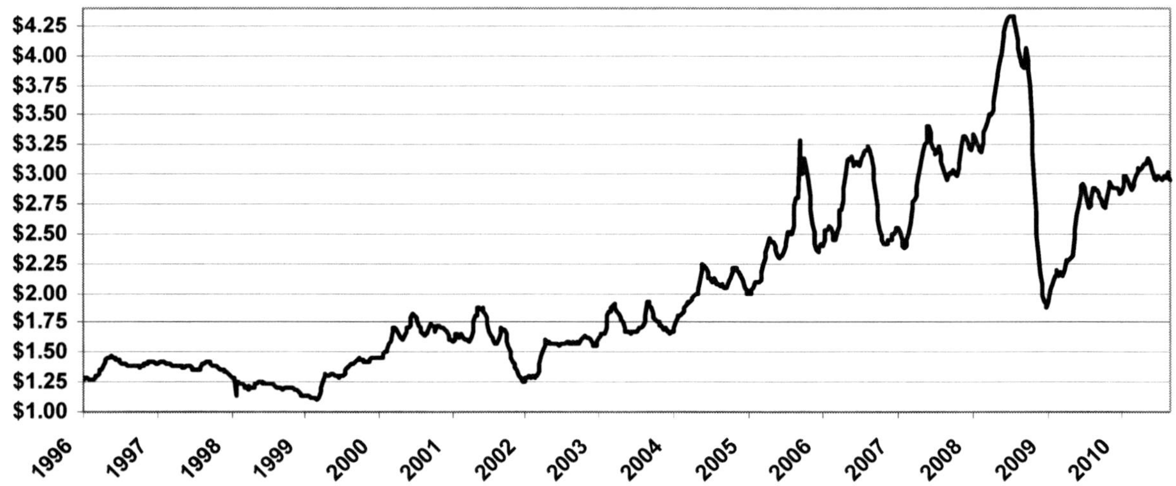

Source: U.S. Energy Information Administration
Plunkett Research, Ltd.
www.plunkettresearch.com

Retail On-Highway Diesel vs. Regular Gasoline Prices, U.S.: 1995-2010

(Weekly Data in US$ per Gallon)

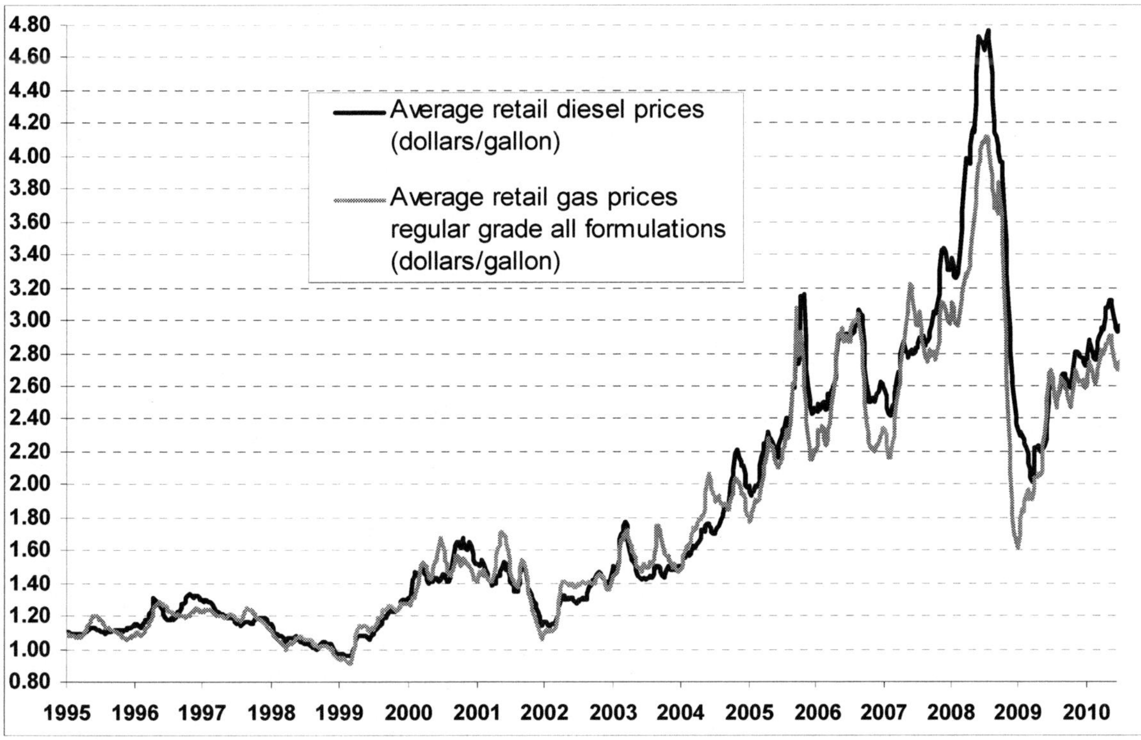

Notes: Motor fuel and gasoline prices are an important cost component of highway transportation. Changes in motor fuel prices impact the behavior of both producers and consumers, and affect the demand for transportation in terms of level and modal mix. Changes in gasoline prices affect the demand for highway transportation, especially as can be seen in vehicle-miles traveled. In the United States, motor gasoline prices follow world crude oil prices more closely than motor diesel prices. Changes in motor fuel prices affect the profit margin of transportation firms, particularly trucking firms.

Source: U.S. Bureau of Transportation Statistics

Plunkett Research, Ltd.

www.plunkettresearch.com

Alternative Fuels in Cars, U.S.: 1992-2008

(Vehicles in Use, Latest Year Available)

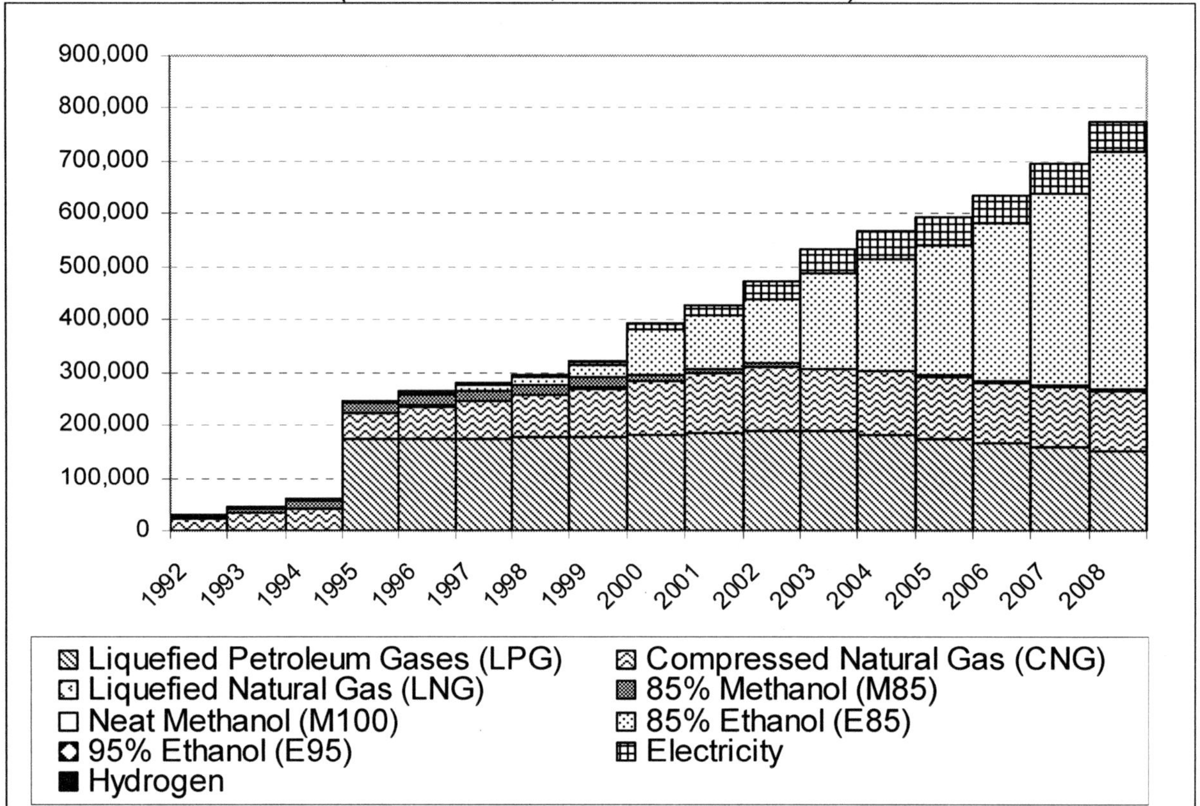

Year	LPG	CNG	LNG	M85	M100	E85	E95	Elec-tricity	Hydro-gen	Total
1992	NA	23,191	90	4,850	404	172	38	1,607	0	NA
1993	NA	32,714	299	10,263	414	441	27	1,690	0	NA
1994	NA	41,227	484	15,484	415	605	33	2,224	0	NA
1995	172,806	50,218	603	18,319	386	1,527	136	2,860	0	246,855
1996	175,585	60,144	663	20,265	172	4,536	361	3,280	0	265,006
1997	175,679	68,571	813	21,040	172	9,130	347	4,453	0	280,205
1998	177,183	78,782	1,172	19,648	200	12,788	14	5,243	0	295,030
1999	178,610	91,267	1,681	18,964	198	24,604	14	6,964	0	322,302
2000	181,994	100,750	2,090	10,426	0	87,570	4	11,830	0	394,664
2001	185,053	111,851	2,576	7,827	0	100,303	0	17,847	0	425,457
2002	187,680	120,839	2,708	5,873	0	120,951	0	33,047	0	471,098
2003	190,369	114,406	2,640	0	0	179,090	0	47,485	9	533,999
2004	182,864	118,532	2,717	0	0	211,800	0	49,536	43	565,492
2005	173,795	117,699	2,748	0	0	246,363	0	51,398	119	592,122
2006	164,846	116,131	2,798	0	0	297,099	0	53,526	159	634,559
2007	158,254	114,391	2,781	0	0	364,384	0	55,730	223	695,763
2008	151,049	113,973	3,101	0	0	450,327	0	56,901	313	775,664

Notes: Vehicles in Use represent accumulated acquisitions, less retirements, as of the end of each calendar year. They do not include concept and demonstration vehicles. E85 designation includes only those E85 vehicles believed to be using E85. Primarily fleet-operated vehicles; excludes other vehicles with E85-fueling capability. For total number of E85 vehicles on the road, see "E85 FFVs in Use." Electric vehicles category does not include hybrid electric vehicles.

Source: U.S. Department of Energy
Plunkett Research, Ltd.
www.plunkettresearch.com

Value of Exports of U.S. Vehicles: 2005-1st Quarter 2010

(In Thousands of US$)

Partner	2005	2006	2007	2008	2009	Q1 2009	Q1 2010
World	**83,686,790**	**92,349,368**	**107,212,567**	**111,697,565**	**73,668,555**	**15,583,287**	**22,802,166**
Canada	43,067,776	46,368,856	50,085,668	45,533,414	31,341,233	6,060,528	10,337,649
Mexico	11,402,106	12,197,072	13,420,252	13,956,213	10,109,930	1,874,884	3,161,375
China	940,624	1,291,004	1,969,912	1,877,383	1,921,802	225,432	1,111,534
Germany	4,878,086	6,480,534	8,459,677	9,919,327	5,682,624	1,258,248	1,042,674
Saudi Arabia	2,359,589	2,342,543	2,555,963	3,778,163	2,383,733	549,868	804,512
Australia	1,675,445	2,060,373	2,300,782	2,567,514	1,607,393	378,695	530,180
United Arab Emirates	1,087,129	996,531	1,651,304	2,785,053	1,232,511	419,154	437,569
United Kingdom	1,667,574	1,781,807	2,216,950	2,059,421	1,308,047	274,138	312,144
Japan	1,612,589	1,731,810	1,872,942	1,973,534	1,063,565	212,462	302,126
Afghanistan	66,322	104,772	145,441	113,814	641,797	183,482	246,503
Kuwait	914,655	735,249	758,045	906,799	608,927	165,267	242,392
Brazil	618,392	684,026	692,935	933,559	642,087	141,192	209,060
Chile	535,806	628,459	765,336	1,029,496	713,532	145,531	194,592
Belgium	604,566	921,815	1,209,559	1,232,337	764,486	229,492	184,959
Nigeria	140,424	252,657	505,614	974,362	774,551	207,364	173,216
South Korea	681,713	756,696	886,669	857,083	462,347	100,257	163,235
Lebanon	138,159	154,633	259,400	607,987	680,405	154,171	153,396
Venezuela	595,428	984,334	1,345,887	907,399	617,353	148,533	147,581
Egypt	345,033	312,622	352,471	258,025	262,002	45,285	139,610
Netherlands	597,006	564,723	757,415	759,682	409,644	93,807	136,034
Jordan	107,597	133,050	127,124	263,846	426,789	92,837	132,216
Hong Kong	189,607	180,199	197,447	288,623	295,366	60,832	123,172
France	483,012	567,701	750,709	697,435	411,720	93,792	114,788
Dominican Republic	241,638	254,156	351,777	379,951	351,420	77,993	110,591
Israel	250,067	286,072	363,543	408,749	280,882	54,318	98,907

Note: "Vehicles" refers to HS (Harmonized System) Code 87, "vehicles, except railway or trainway, and parts etc."

Source: Foreign Trade Division, U.S. Census Bureau
Plunkett Research, Ltd.
www.plunkettresearch.com

Value of Imports of Vehicles to the U.S.: 2005-1st Quarter 2010

(In Thousands of US$)

Partner	2005	2006	2007	2008	2009	Q1 2009	Q1 2010
World Total	**199,661,782**	**215,615,222**	**214,267,258**	**194,989,568**	**131,295,326**	**26,751,012**	**40,481,476**
Canada	61,588,055	61,317,902	60,307,203	47,518,202	31,673,958	6,140,467	10,804,165
Japan	49,593,160	57,773,355	56,501,358	52,661,231	31,490,002	6,092,673	9,673,443
Mexico	26,811,576	33,252,699	33,936,112	32,178,101	26,823,670	4,983,303	9,461,663
Germany	24,405,871	23,531,500	22,299,700	22,979,011	14,710,059	3,114,333	3,698,103
South Korea	10,209,621	10,872,312	10,566,743	9,640,893	7,190,989	1,842,912	1,800,299
China	4,208,608	5,133,984	6,086,925	6,384,198	4,991,817	1,093,243	1,360,090
United Kingdom	7,220,567	6,478,924	5,221,551	5,003,085	2,938,463	556,911	717,412
Taiwan	1,816,651	1,713,177	1,808,941	1,977,681	1,673,379	430,779	405,399
South Africa	294,724	501,490	550,710	1,931,949	1,443,435	344,159	327,629
Italy	1,729,676	1,853,126	2,035,442	2,298,431	1,334,637	394,858	308,678
France	1,530,658	1,317,262	1,284,275	1,474,473	892,155	237,729	218,790
Israel	65,795	75,086	262,797	397,439	471,268	46,216	212,910
Sweden	2,756,044	2,392,614	2,652,954	1,884,375	897,110	133,736	200,807
Belgium	1,425,974	1,237,351	1,029,354	968,442	781,259	245,099	174,760
India	438,917	486,791	622,988	648,209	453,133	126,428	166,031
Turkey	151,440	150,663	132,794	195,094	536,442	40,959	133,417
Slovakia	559,234	913,258	967,239	763,709	256,943	35,249	111,295
Austria	767,694	2,125,189	3,937,471	1,667,380	372,507	111,201	100,251
Brazil	1,328,444	1,220,442	910,771	720,652	339,662	102,199	92,647
Thailand	238,488	321,028	362,061	417,827	324,382	98,201	77,046
Hungary	222,678	217,409	365,102	335,544	142,843	32,797	47,064
Portugal	21,974	167,281	394,522	367,351	93,791	61,144	42,894
Spain	359,196	373,959	317,960	233,776	144,187	35,126	37,658
Switzerland	43,927	51,111	66,297	98,058	193,742	65,836	34,648
Australia	461,251	398,331	187,111	1,028,115	220,285	132,355	32,097

Note: "Vehicles" refers to HS (Harmonized System) Code 87, "vehicles, except railway or trainway, and parts etc."

Source: Foreign Trade Division, U.S. Census Bureau
Plunkett Research, Ltd.
www.plunkettresearch.com

Occupational Employment and Wages for Automotive Service Technicians and Mechanics, May 2009

Employment estimate and mean wage estimates for this occupation:

Employment[1]	Employment RSE[2]	Mean Hourly Wage	Mean Annual Wage[3]	Wage RSE[2]
606,990	0.60%	$18.21	$37,880	0.30%

Percentile wage estimates for this occupation:

Percentile	10%	25%	50% (Median)	75%	90%
Hourly Wage	$9.54	$12.49	$17.03	$22.71	$28.81
Annual Wage[3]	$19,840	$25,970	$35,420	$47,240	$59,920

Industries with the highest levels of employment in this occupation:

Occupation	Employment	Hourly Mean Wage	Annual Mean Wage
Automotive Repair and Maintenance	226,170	$16.74	$34,820
Automobile Dealers	191,090	$20.75	$43,160
Automotive Parts, Accessories, and Tire Stores	57,250	$16.13	$33,550
Gasoline Stations	21,100	$16.27	$33,850
Local Government (OES designation)	20,020	$21.45	$44,620

Note: Category includes those who diagnose, adjust, repair, or overhaul automotive vehicles. Exclude "Automotive Body and Related Repairers" (49-3021), "Bus and Truck Mechanics and Diesel Engine Specialists" (49-3031), and "Electronic Equipment Installers and Repairers, Motor Vehicles" (49-2096).

[1] Estimates for detailed occupations do not sum to the totals because the totals include occupations not shown separately. Estimates do not include self-employed workers.

[2] The relative standard error (RSE) is a measure of the reliability of a survey statistic. The smaller the relative standard error, the more precise the estimate.

[3] Annual wages have been calculated by multiplying the hourly mean wage by a "year-round, full-time" hours figure of 2,080 hours; for those occupations where there is not an hourly mean wage published, the annual wage has been directly calculated from the reported survey data.

Source: U.S. Bureau of Labor Statistics

Plunkett Research, Ltd.

www.plunkettresearch.com

Employment in the Automobile Industry, U.S.: 2003-2009

(Annual Estimates in Thousands of Employed Workers)

NAICS Code[1]	Industry Sector	2003	2004	2005	2006	2007	2008	2009
Manufacturing								
3361,2,3	**Motor vehicles & parts**	**1,125.3**	**1,112.8**	**1,096.7**	**1,070.0**	**994.2**	**875.5**	**666.4**
3361	**Motor vehicles**	**264.6**	**255.9**	**247.6**	**236.5**	**220.0**	**191.6**	**142.5**
33611	Automobiles & light trucks	233.5	221.1	210.0	199.7	185.8	164.2	119.5
336111	Automobiles	156.6	146.3	139.8	134.6	127.8	117.2	89.7
336112	Light trucks & utility vehicles	76.9	74.8	70.2	65.1	58.0	46.9	29.8
33612	Heavy duty trucks	31.1	34.8	37.7	36.8	34.2	27.4	23.0
3362	**Motor vehicle bodies & trailers**	**153.0**	**164.8**	**171.0**	**178.8**	**166.4**	**140.2**	**105.2**
336211	Motor vehicle bodies	61.9	64.5	65.9	67.9	64.8	60.1	51.3
336212	Truck trailers	31.2	33.7	36.7	39.7	37.7	30.8	21.1
336213,4	Motor homes, travel trailers & campers	59.9	66.6	68.4	71.2	63.9	49.4	32.8
3363	**Motor vehicle parts**	**707.8**	**692.1**	**678.1**	**654.7**	**607.9**	**543.7**	**418.7**
33631	Motor vehicle gasoline engine & parts	85.5	80.2	76.3	73.2	68.0	61.7	46.5
33632	Motor vehicle electric equipment	104.0	100.5	95.8	90.8	79.9	70.8	55.7
336321	Vehicular lighting equipment	17.2	16.6	16.8	16.2	13.5	12.7	11.2
336322	Other motor vehicle electric equipment	86.9	83.8	79.0	74.6	66.3	58.1	44.5
33633	Motor vehicle steering & suspension parts	44.6	43.4	43.5	42.4	38.0	33.8	27.7
33634	Motor vehicle brake systems	45.9	45.1	42.9	40.3	36.1	31.3	23.4
33635	Motor vehicle power train components	91.2	85.7	85.0	81.2	76.3	69.9	52.8
33636	Motor vehicle seating & interior trim	62.2	66.1	64.3	62.7	61.4	56.5	44.2
33637	Motor vehicle metal stamping	101.9	99.0	98.6	95.6	89.8	77.9	52.8
33639	Other motor vehicle parts	172.4	172.1	171.7	168.5	158.4	141.8	115.6
Transportation & Warehousing								
484	**Truck transportation**	**1,325.6**	**1,351.7**	**1,397.6**	**1,435.8**	**1,439.2**	**1,389.0**	**1,265.9**
4841	General freight trucking	935.2	949.7	980.5	1,004.6	1,006.8	975.6	884.5
48411	Local	229.8	229.5	231.0	235.5	235.6	228.4	207.5
48412	Long-Distance	705.4	720.2	749.5	769.2	771.3	747.2	677.0
484121	Truckload	496.8	498.2	523.4	538.1	542.5	530.6	484.6
484122	Less-than-Truckload	208.6	222.0	226.1	231.1	228.7	216.6	192.5
4842	Specialized freight trucking	390.4	402.0	417.1	431.2	432.4	413.4	381.3
48421	Used household & office goods moving	98.2	101.6	103.2	103.1	99.6	92.7	83.8
48422	Other specialized trucking, local	189.1	194.6	201.7	209.4	211.3	205.9	188.2
48423	Other specialized trucking, long-distance	103.2	105.8	112.2	118.7	121.6	114.8	109.3
485	**Transit and ground passenger transportation**	**382.2**	**384.9**	**389.2**	**399.3**	**412.1**	**423.3**	**419.3**
4851	Urban transit, interurban and rural bus transportation	59.7	60.3	59.6	59.9	60.5	63.1	61.8
4853	Taxi and limousine service	66.9	66.4	66.3	69.3	72.6	71.2	67.3
48531	Taxi service	31.4	30.6	30.3	30.8	32.2	31.5	31.9
48532	Limousine service	35.5	35.7	36.0	38.5	40.4	39.7	35.4
4855	Charter bus industry	33.2	32.2	31.4	31.2	32.3	33.1	29.8
4859	Other ground passenger transportation	57.7	59.4	63.0	66.6	70.1	73.8	76.0

[1] For a full description of the NAICS codes used in this table, see www.census.gov/epcd/www/naics.html.

Source: U.S. Bureau of Labor Statistics
Plunkett Research, Ltd.
www.plunkettresearch.com

Chapter 3

IMPORTANT AUTOMOBILE INDUSTRY CONTACTS

Addresses, Telephone Numbers and Internet Sites

Contents:

I. Alternative Energy-Clean Transportation

ACEEE's Green Book Online
American Council for an Energy-Efficient Economy (ACEEE)
529 14th St. NW
Washington, DC 20045 US
Phone: 202-507-4000

Fax: 202-429-2248
E-mail Address: *greenercars@aceee.org*
Web Address: www.greenercars.org
Green Book Online is the official web site for the American Council for an Energy-Efficient Economy (ACEEE)'s Green Book publication, which rates cars on how they impact the environment.

Clean Cities Program
U.S. Department of Energy — NETL
3610 Collins Ferry Rd.
Morgantown, WV 26507-0880 US
Phone: 304-285-4535
Toll Free: 877-337-3463
E-mail Address: *Kay.Kelly@netl.doe.gov*
Web Address: www.eere.energy.gov/cleancities
The Clean Cities Program, sponsored by the U.S. Department of Energy, is a federal program to promote the use of alternative transportation fuels in U.S. cities.

II. Alternative Energy-Ethanol

Canadian Renewable Fuels Association (CRFA)
350 Sparks St., Ste. 1005
Ottawa, ON K1R 7S8 Canada
Phone: 613-594-5528
Fax: 613-594-3076
E-mail Address: *R.Speer@greenfuels.org*
Web Address: www.greenfuels.org
The Canadian Renewable Fuels Association (CRFA) is a nonprofit organization whose mission is to promote renewable fuels for automotive transportation through consumer awareness and government liaison activities.

National Ethanol Vehicle Coalition (NEVC)
3216 Emerald Ln., Ste. C
Jefferson City, MO 65109 US
Phone: 573-635-8445
Fax: 573-635-5466
Toll Free: 877-485-8535
E-mail Address: *info@e85fuel.com*
Web Address: www.e85fuel.com
The National Ethanol Vehicle Coalition (NEVC), established in 1996, is a nonprofit organization that is one of the leading advocates in the U.S. for expanding the use of 85% (E85) ethanol motor fuel. It also advocates the production of so-called flexible fuel vehicles, which can run on higher than conventional 10% ethanol fuels.

Renewable Fuels Association (RFA)
1 Massachusetts Ave. NW, Ste. 820
Washington, DC 20001 US
Phone: 202-289-3835
E-mail Address: *info@ethanolrfa.org*
Web Address: www.ethanolrfa.org
The Renewable Fuels Association (RFA) is a trade organization representing the ethanol industry. It publishes a wealth of useful information, including a listing of biorefineries and monthly U.S. fuel ethanol production and demand.

III. Alternative Energy-Fuel Cells

EERE Hydrogen, Fuel Cells & Infrastructure Technologies Program
1000 Independence Ave. SW
Mail Stop EE-1
Washington, DC 20585 US
Phone: 202-586-2480
Toll Free: 877-337-3463
E-mail Address: *JoAnn.Milliken@ee.doe.gov*
Web Address:
www1.eere.energy.gov/hydrogenandfuelcells
The Hydrogen, Fuel Cells & Infrastructure Technologies Program of the Energy Efficiency and Renewable Energy (EERE), a division of the U.S. Department of Energy (DOE), works to develop and successfully introduce fuel cell technologies to the global market.

IV. Automobile Finance and Loans Associations

National Automotive Finance Association (NAF)
7250 Parkway Dr., Ste. 510
Hanover, MD 21076 US
Phone: 410-712-4036
Fax: 410-712-4038
Toll Free: 800-463-8955
Web Address: www.nafassociation.com
The National Automotive Finance Association (NAF) is the only trade association exclusively serving the non-prime auto financing industry. Organized in the fall of 1996, the NAF Association supports its members and the industry with programs and education.

V. Automobile Purchasing-Online

Autobytel, Inc.
18872 MacArthur Blvd.

Irvine, CA 92612 US
Phone: 949-225-4500
E-mail Address: *consumercare@autobytel.com*
Web Address: www.autobytel.com
Autobytel, Inc. is an Internet automotive marketing services company that helps retailers sell cars and manufacturers build brands through marketing and CRM (customer relationship management) tools and programs. Car purchasers can use this popular site to request bids on specific makes and models of new cars and trucks. Participating dealers will respond with detailed prices.

AutoSite
Autobytel, Inc.
18872 MacArthur Blvd.
Irvine, CA 92612 US
Phone: 949-225-4500
E-mail Address: *consumercare@autobytel.com*
Web Address: www.autosite.com
AutoSite customers can find and learn about new and used vehicles through this web site's tools and information. It is owned by industry giant Autobytel, Inc.

Autotrader.com
5775 Peachtree Dunwoody Rd., Ste. A-200
Atlanta, GA 30342 US
Phone: 866-222-0998
Fax: 404-568-3060
Toll Free: 800-353-9350
Web Address: www.autotrader.com
Autotrader.com is designed to give users more control of the buying process and make finding a used vehicle that meets your personal needs easier.

Autoweb
Autobytel, Inc.
18872 MacArthur Blvd.
Irvine, CA 92612 US
Phone: 949-225-4500
Toll Free: 888-422-8999
E-mail Address: *consumercare@autobytel.com*
Web Address: www.autoweb.com
Autoweb helps millions of car shoppers get connected to a local Autoweb-accredited car dealer for up-front pricing and delivery information. It is a subsidiary of Autobytel, Inc.

CARFAX, Inc.
5860 Trinity Pkwy., Ste. 600
Centreville, VA 20120 US
Phone: 703-934-2664
Web Address: www.carfax.com
CARFAX, Inc.'s web site offers Vehicle History Reports that reveal important background information and unearth hidden problems in a vehicle's past that may affect its safety and resale value.

Cars.com
Classified Ventures, LLC
175 W. Jackson Blvd., Ste. 800
Chicago, IL 60604 US
Phone: 312-601-5000
E-mail Address: *kerri@cars.com*
Web Address: www.cars.com
Cars.com, a division of Classified Ventures, LLC, provides users with complete local and national inventories of new and used vehicles, featuring automotive reviews, model reports, advice, a dealer locator, financing information and much more.

CarSmart
Autobytel, Inc.
18872 MacArthur Blvd.
Irvine, CA 92612-1400 US
Phone: 949-225-4500
E-mail Address: *consumercare@autobytel.com*
Web Address: www.carsmart.com
CarSmart is a web site owned by Autobytel, Inc. that provides car model information, free price quotes and online buying assistance.

Classiccar.com
Spider Marketing, LLC
P.O. Box 551164
Dallas, TX 75355 US
Toll Free: 800-480-5080
Web Address: www.classiccar.com
Classiccar.com, powered by Spider Marketing, LLC, is an online forum for buying, selling and discussing classic cars and their restoration.

eBay Motors
eBay, Inc.
2145 Hamilton Ave.
San Jose, CA 95125 US
Phone: 408-376-7400
Fax: 408-376-7401
Web Address: www.ebaymotors.com
eBay Motors, part of eBay, Inc., is a provider of online car and truck vehicle auctions and services. It is an incredibly popular site that makes it possible for buyers and sellers to connect nationwide. It includes listings of used and classic cars and trucks.

Edmunds.com
1620 26th St., Ste. 400 S.
Santa Monica, CA 90404 US
Phone: 310-309-6300
Fax: 310-309-6466
Web Address: www.edmunds.com
Edmunds.com, launched in 1995, was one of the first web sites to offer automotive information to consumers. It provides a database of car values, car reviews, ratings and expert advice to help consumers get a fair deal.

Kelley Blue Book
195 Technology Dr.
Irvine, CA 92618 US
Toll Free: 800-258-3266
Web Address: www.kbb.com
Kelley Blue Book (KBB) is a respected source for pricing information on new and used vehicles. Its web site recently launched a new service, called KBBGreen, which offers information on environmentally friendly vehicles.

Kruse International
P.O. Box 190
5540 County Rd. 11A
Auburn, IN 46706 US
Phone: 260-925-5600
Fax: 260-925-5467
Toll Free: 800-968-4444
E-mail Address: *info@kruse.com*
Web Address: www.kruseinternational.com
Kruse International is one of the world's leading auction firms and the largest collector car auction company. It auctions more than 13,000 cars in more than 30 events and dozens of real estate properties each year.

Motorplace.com
The Cobalt Group, Inc.
2200 1st Ave. S., Ste. 400
Seattle, WA 98134-1408 US
Phone: 206-269-6363
Fax: 206-269-6350
E-mail Address: *comments@MotorPlace.com*
Web Address: www2.motorplace.com
Motorplace.com, a part of The Cobalt Group, Inc., is a leading provider of Internet-based automotive products and services.

MSN Autos
Microsoft Corp.
1 Microsoft Way
Redmond, WA 98052 US
Phone: 425-882-8080
Fax: 425-936-7329
Web Address: www.autos.msn.com
MSN Autos offers extensive information on new cars, used cars, warranties, finance, insurance and automotive news. Consumers will find extensive tools to help them make car-buying decisions.

NADAguides.com
P.O. Box 7800
Costa Mesa, CA 92628 US
Phone: 714-556-8511
Fax: 714-8715
Web Address: www.nadaguides.com
NADAguides.com are appraisal guides that serve as resources for pricing information on used vehicles. The site also has reviews and buying resources for new and used behicles.

Yahoo! Autos
Yahoo! Inc.
701 1st Ave.
Sunnyvale, CA 94089 US
Phone: 408-349-3300
Fax: 408-349-3301
Web Address: www.autos.yahoo.com
Yahoo! Autos is provides a vast amount of information on new and used cars, finance, insurance and car maintenance.

VI. Automotive Industry Associations

Alliance of Automobile Manufacturers
1401 Eye St. NW, Ste. 900
Washington, DC 20005 US
Phone: 202-326-5500
Fax: 202-326-5598
Web Address: www.autoalliance.org
The Alliance of Automobile Manufacturers is a trade association composed of 9 car manufacturing companies including BMW Group, DaimlerChrysler, Ford Motor Company, General Motors, Mazda, Mitsubishi Motors, Porsche, Toyota and Volkswagen. Alliance members account for more than 90% of vehicles sold in the U.S.

American International Automobile Dealers Association (AIADA)
211 N. Union St., Ste. 300
Alexandria, VA 22314 US
Phone: 703-519-7800
Fax: 703-519-7810

Toll Free: 800-462-4232
E-mail Address: *goaiada@aiada.org*
Web Address: www.aiada.org
American International Automobile Dealers Association (AIADA) is the lobbying and communications force in Washington, D.C. for the 10,000 American automobile dealerships that sell and service international nameplate brands.

Association of International Automobile Manufacturers of Canada (AIAMC)
2 Bloor St. W., Ste. 1804, Box 5
Toronto, ON M4W 3E2 Canada
Phone: 416-595-8251
Fax: 416-595-2864
E-mail Address: *auto@aiamc.com*
Web Address: www.aiamc.com
The AIAMC is a trade organization representing 13 of the leading auto manufacturing companies in Canada.

Association of International Automobile Manufacturers, Inc. (AIAM)
2111 Wilson Blvd., Ste. 1150
Arlington, VA 22201 US
Phone: 703-525-7788
Fax: 703-525-8817
E-mail Address: *webmaster2@aiam.org*
Web Address: www.aiam.org
The Association of International Automobile Manufacturers, Inc. (AIAM) is a trade association representing 14 international motor vehicle manufacturers. Members concentrate on improving the safety and efficiency of vehicles, as well as investing in American communities.

Automotive Industry Action Group (AIAG)
26200 Lahser Rd., Ste. 200
Southfield, MI 48033-7100 US
Phone: 248-358-3570
Fax: 248-358-3253
E-mail Address: *order_inquiry@aiag.org*
Web Address: www.aiag.org
The Automotive Industry Action Group (AIAG) is an open forum for members to cooperate in developing and promoting solutions that enhance the prosperity of the automotive industry.

Automotive Service Association (ASA)
1901 Airport Fwy.
Bedford, TX 76095 US
Phone: 817-283-6205
Fax: 817-685-0225
Toll Free: 800-272-7467
E-mail Address: *asainfo@asashop.org*
Web Address: www.asashop.org
The Automotive Service Association (ASA) is a leading organization for owners and managers of automotive service businesses that strive to deliver excellence in service and repairs to consumers.

Canadian Automobile Dealers Association (CADA)
85 Renfrew Dr.
Markham, ON L3R 0N9 Canada
Phone: 905-940-4959
Fax: 905-940-6870
Toll Free: 800-463-5289
E-mail Address: *mail@cada.ca*
Web Address: www.cada.ca
The Canadian Automobile Dealers Association (CADA) represents 3,000 automobile dealers across Canada.

Canadian Transportation Equipment Association (CTEA)
16 Barrie Blvd., Unit 3B
St. Thomas, ON N5P 4B9 Canada
Phone: 519-631-0414
Fax: 519-631-1333
E-mail Address: *transportation@ctea.on.ca*
Web Address: www.ctea.ca
The Canadian Transportation Equipment Association (CTEA) standardizes the commercial vehicle equipment manufacturing industry in Canada.

Canadian Vehicle Manufacturers' Association (CVMA)
170 Attwell Dr., Ste. 400
Toronto, ON M9W 5Z5 Canada
Phone: 416-364-9333
Fax: 416-367-3221
Toll Free: 800-758-7122
E-mail Address: *info@cvma.ca*
Web Address: www.cvma.ca
The Canadian Vehicle Manufacturers' Association (CVMA) is the industry organization representing manufacturers of light and heavy duty motor vehicles in Canada. Association members collaborate to solve industry objectives in the way of consumer protection, the environment and vehicle safety.

China Association of Automobile Manufacturers (CAAM)
46 Fucheng Rd.
Haidian

Beijing, 100036 China
Phone: 86-10-68123210
Fax: 86-10-68127562
E-mail Address: *caa@public.fhnet.cm.net*
Web Address: www.naacam.co.za
China Association of Automobile Manufacturers (CAAM) represents the automobile and vehicle manufacturers in China.

China Automotive Technology & Research Center
No.218 Chenglin Rd.
Dongli District
Tianjin, 300162 China
Phone: 86-22-8477-1317
Fax: 86-22-2437-0843
Web Address: www.catarc.ac.cn
China Automotive Technology & Research Center (CATARC) serves as a technical administrative body with ties to China's State-Owned Assets Supervision and Administration Commission (SASAC) and to the automotive industry throughout China. CATARC works in conjunction with the Chinese government to formulate auto standards and technical regulations, and is also involved in overseeing product certification testing; quality system certification; industry planning and policy research; and automotive technology research. In addition to its headquarters, CATARC maintains various research and testing facilities, as well as offices in Beijing, Shanghai and Wuhan.

European Automobile Manufacturers Association (ACEA)
Avenye des Nerviens 85
Brussels, B-1040 Belgium
Phone: 32-2-732-55-50
Fax: 32-2-738-73-10
E-mail Address: *info@acea.be*
Web Address: www.acea.be
The European Automobile Manufacturers Association, or the Association des Constructeurs Européens d' Automobiles (ACEA), represents the automobile industry in Europe.

Federation of Automobile Dealers Associations (FADA)
805 Surya Kiran
19 K G Marg
New Delhi, 110 001 India
Phone: 011-2332-0095
Fax: 011-2332-0093
E-mail Address: *fada@airtelmail.in*
Web Address: www.fadaweb.com
The Federation of Automobile Dealers Associations (FADA) represents Automobile Dealers of India. It supports and promotes the Indian retail automobile market and members include vehicle manufacturers, tire manufacturers, insurance and finance sectors and other allied industries.

German Association of the Automobile Industry (VDA)
Verband der Automobilindustrie
Markgrafenstr. 43
Berlin, 10117 Germany
Phone: 49 30 89 78 42-15
Fax: 49 30 89 78 42-50
Web Address: www.vda.de
The German Association of the Automobile Industry (VDA) promotes the Germany automotive industry nationally and internationally.

Japan Automobile Manufacturers Association of Canada (JAMA Canada)
151 Bloor St. W., Ste. 460
Toronto, ON M5S 1S4 Canada
Phone: 416-968-0150
Fax: 416-968-7095
E-mail Address: *jama@jama.ca*
Web Address: www.jama.ca
The Japan Automobile Manufacturers Association of Canada (JAMA Canada) represents the interests of members in both the Canadian and Japanese auto industries by promoting closer industrial ties. The association provides up-to-date statistics, newsletters and industry links on its web site.

Japanese Automobile Manufacturers Association, Inc. (JAMA)
Shiba Daimon 1-chome, Minato-ku
Jidosha Kaikan (NBF Twr.), 16th Fl., 1-30
Tokyo, 105-0012 Japan
Phone: 81-3-5405-6126
Web Address: www.jama-english.jp
Japanese Automobile Manufacturers Association, Inc. (JAMA) is a nonprofit industry association that is made up of 14 manufacturers of passenger cars, trucks, buses and motorcycles in Japan. Besides its Tokyo headquarters, JAMA maintains offices in the U.S., Europe and Asia.

Korean Automobile Manufacturing Association (KAMA)
1461-15 Seocho-3 dong, Seocho-gu
Seoul, 137-720 Korea
Phone: 82-2-3660-1853

Fax: 82-2-3660-1900
E-mail Address: *webmaster@kama.or.kr*
Web Address: www.kama.or.kr/eng/K_eng_main.jsp
Korean Automobile Manufacturing Association (KAMA) represents Korean automotive manufacturers in national and international issues affecting the industry.

Motor Traders Association of Singapore
370 Ubi Rd. 3
408651 Singapore
Phone: 65-6472-4934
Fax: 65-6472-4930
Web Address: www.mta.org.sg
Motor Traders Association of Singapore represents the automotive industry in Singapore. It hosts the annual Singapore Motorshow.

National Automobile Dealers Association (NADA)
8400 Westpark Dr.
McLean, VA 22102 US
Phone: 703-821-7000
Toll Free: 800-252-6232
E-mail Address: *nadainfo@nada.org*
Web Address: www.nada.org
The National Automobile Dealers Association (NADA) represents more than 19,700 new car and truck dealers, both import and domestic, operating more than 43,000 separate franchises.

National Institute for Automotive Service Excellence (ASE)
101 Blue Seal Dr. SE, Ste. 101
Leesburg, VA 20175 US
Phone: 703-669-6600
Toll Free: 888-273-8378
E-mail Address: *webmaster@asecert.com*
Web Address: www.ase.com
ASE's mission is to improve the quality of automotive service and repair through the voluntary testing and certification of automotive technicians.

North American Automobile Trade Association (NAATA)
70 E. Beaver Creek Rd., Ste. 30
Richmond Hill, ON L4B 3B2 Canada
Phone: 905-882-7040
E-mail Address: *naata@naata.org*
Web Address: www.naata.org
The North American Automobile Trade Association (NAATA) is a nonprofit organization of automobile dealers that import and export vehicles across international borders.

Society of Indian Automobile Manufacturers (SIAM)
Lodhi Rd.
Core 4-B, 5th Fl., India Habitat Ctr.
New Delhi, 110 003 India
Phone: 91-11-24647810-12
Fax: 91-11-24648222
E-mail Address: *siam@siam.in*
Web Address: www.siamindia.com
The Society of Indian Automobile Manufacturers (SIAM) represents 38 leading vehicle and vehicular engine manufacturers in India. The site contains industry statistics, technical regulations, fuel specifications, industry news and events.

Society of Motor Manufacturers and Traders (SMMT)
Forbes House
Halkin St.
London, SW1X 7DS UK
Phone: 44-(0)20-7235-7000
Fax: 44-(0)20-7235-7112
E-mail Address: *MVRISWeb@smmt.co.uk*
Web Address: www.smmt.co.uk
Society of Motor Manufacturers and Traders (SMMT) represents the automotive and automotive manufacturing industry in the United Kingdom. The site has information regarding the industry's and United Kingdom's automotive statistics.

Special Vehicles and Transportation Equipment Association
1512 Michaud St.
Drummondville, QC J2C 7V3 Canada
Fax: 819-472-6520
Toll Free: 866-499-4494
E-mail Address: *info@ametvs.com*
Web Address: www.ametvs.com
The Special Vehicles and Transportation Equipment Association, or, in French, Association des manufacturiers d'equipements de transport et de vehicules speciaux (AMETVS), is a nonprofit trade organization of specialty vehicle and transportation equipment manufacturers in Canada.

United States Council for Automotive Research Inc. (USCAR)
1000 Town Center Dr., Ste. 300
Southfield, MI 48075 US
Phone: 248-223-9000
Web Address: www.uscar.org
The United States Council for Automotive Research (USCAR) was founded in 1992. Its goal is to further

strengthen the technology base of the U.S. auto industry through cooperative research and development. Its main focus is to create, support and direct U.S. cooperative research and development to advance automotive technologies. USCAR is composed of a number of specialized groups that focus on specific research areas. USCAR is governed by the three-member USCAR Council, whose membership includes the R&D vice presidents from each of the U.S. automakers.

Used Car Dealers Association of Ontario (UCDA)
230 Norseman St.
Toronto, ON M8Z 6A2 Canada
Phone: 416-231-2600
Fax: 416-232-0775
Toll Free: 800-268-2598
E-mail Address: *web@ucda.org*
Web Address: www.ucda.org
The Used Car Dealers Association of Ontario (UCDA) is a nonprofit organization representing the interests of more than 4,400 used car dealers in the Ontario, Canada area.

VII. Automotive Industry Resources

Auto University
55 Brown Ave.
Butler, NJ 07405 US
Fax: 831-789-0256
Toll Free: 800-344-4100
E-mail Address: *shawn.ryder@autouniversity.com*
Web Address: www.autouniversity.com
Part of the Ings Group, Auto University is a leading provider of privately accredited training for employees of automotive manufacturers and dealers.

Automotive Design & Production
705 S. Main St., Ste. 205
Plymouth, MI 48170 US
Phone: 734-416-9705
Fax: 734-416-9707
E-mail Address: *mvohland@autofieldguide.com*
Web Address: www.automfg.com
Automotive Design & Production is dedicated to the automotive design industry offering studies and reports; a magazine with online articles; a calendar of events; supply chain and electronics information and a forum.

Automotive Industries Online
Phone: 313-262-5702
E-mail Address: *enquiries@autoindustry.us*
Web Address: www.ai-online.com
Automotive Industries Online is a monthly publication devoted to providing global coverage of all aspects of the automobile marketplace, with an emphasis on the people, products and processes that shape the industry.

Automotive Learning Center (ALC)
1800 Crooks Rd.
Troy, MI 48084 US
Phone: 248-244-8920
Web Address: www.plastics-car.org
The Automotive Learning Center (ALC), sponsored by the American Chemistry Council's Plastics Division, strives to provide the automobile designer, stylist or engineer with up-to-the-minute research and information on plastics applications in cars.

Autoremarketing.com
301 Cascade Pointe Ln.
Westview at Weston, Ste. 101
Cary, NC 27513 US
Fax: 919-674-6027
Toll Free: 800-608-7500
E-mail Address: *scolby@autoremarketing.com*
Web Address: www.autoremarketing.com
Autoremarketing.com is an online magazine devoted to the auto remarketing industry.

Center for Automotive Research (CAR)
1000 Victors Way, Ste. 200
Ann Arbor, MI 48108 US
Phone: 734-662-1287
Fax: 734-662-5736
E-mail Address: *lhart@cargroup.org*
Web Address: www.cargroup.org
The Center for Automotive Research, a nonprofit organization, is focused on a wide variety of important trends and changes related to the automobile industry and society at the international, federal, state and local levels. CAR conducts industry research, develops new methodologies, forecasts industry trends, advises on public policy, and sponsors multi-stakeholder communication forums.

ConceptCar
P.O. Box 8208
Colchester, CO3 3WU UK
E-mail Address: *admin@conceptcar.co.uk*
Web Address: www.conceptcar.co.uk
ConceptCar is a web site devoted to car design, which provides books, email, message boards and a search directory composed of hundreds of web sites.

Diesel Technology Forum
5291 Corporate Dr., Ste. 102
Frederick, MD 21703 US
Phone: 301-668-7230
Fax: 301-668-7234
E-mail Address: *dtf@dieselforum.org*
Web Address: www.dieselforum.org
The Diesel Technology Forum, which was created by companies in the diesel technology, fuel systems manufacturing and petroleum refining industries, aims to create a new dialogue and encourage the open exchange of information on a range of issues concerning diesel technologies.

DieselNet
Ecopoint Inc.
P.O. Box 47055
Mississauga, ON L5K 2R2 Canada
Phone: 905-990-0775
Fax: 905-990-0776
E-mail Address: *consult2@dieselnet.com*
Web Address: www.dieselnet.com
DieselNet is an online information service on diesel emissions, emission control, diesel engines, fuels and more. Ecopoint Inc. owns and publishes the site.

VIII. Automotive Parts, Repair & Supplies Associations

Automotive Aftermarket Industry Association (AAIA)
7101 Wisconsin Ave., Ste. 1300
Bethesda, MD 20814-3415 US
Phone: 301-654-6664
Fax: 301-654-3299
E-mail Address: *aaia@aftermarket.org*
Web Address: www.aftermarket.org
The Automotive Aftermarket Industry Association (AAIA) provides information about the automotive aftermarket, which maintains, repairs and accessorizes vehicles after they are sold to individuals by a car or truck dealer.

Automotive Component Manufacturers Association of India (ACMA)
Olof Palme Marg, Munirka
6th Fl., The Capital Ct.
New Delhi, 110 067 India
Phone: 91-11-2616-0315
Fax: 91-11-2616-0317
E-mail Address: *acma@vsnl.com*
Web Address: www.acmainfo.com
Automotive Component Manufacturers Association of India (ACMA) is the nodal agency for the Indian auto component industry.

Automotive Industries Association of Canada (AIA)
1272 Wellington St. W.
Ottawa, ON K1Y 3A7 Canada
Fax: 613-728-6021
Toll Free: 800-808-2920
E-mail Address: *info.aia@aiacanada.com*
Web Address: www.aiacanada.com
The Automotive Industries Association of Canada (AIA) is a national trade organization representing the Canadian automotive repair, accessories and tools aftermarket industry.

Automotive Parts Manufacturers' Association (APMA)
10 Four Seasons Pl., Ste. 801
Toronto, ON M9B 6H7 Canada
Phone: 416-620-4220
Fax: 416-620-9730
E-mail Address: *info@apma.ca*
Web Address: www.apma.ca
The Automotive Parts Manufacturers' Association (APMA) is a leading national association representing OEM producers of parts and services for the worldwide automotive industry.

Automotive Recyclers Association
3975 Fair Ridge Dr., Ste. 20-N.
Fairfax, VA 22033 US
Phone: 703-385-1001
Fax: 703-385-1494
Toll Free: 888-385-1005
E-mail Address: *jennifer@a-r-a.org*
Web Address: www.a-r-a.org
The Automotive Recyclers Association is dedicated to the efficient removal and reuse of automotive parts and the safe disposal of inoperable motor vehicles.

Engine Manufacturers Association (EMA)
2 N. LaSalle St., Ste. 2200
Chicago, IL 60602 US
Phone: 312-827-8700
Fax: 312-827-8737
E-mail Address: *ema@enginemanufacturers.org*
Web Address: www.enginemanufacturers.org
The Engine Manufacturers Association (EMA) is the voice of the engine manufacturing industry on domestic and international public policy, as well as regulatory and technical issues that affect

manufacturers of engines used in a broad array of mobile and stationary applications.

Hong Kong Auto Parts Industry Association (HKAPIA)
5/F HKPC Bldg.
78 Tat Chee Ave.
Kowloon, Hong Kong, China
Phone: 852-278-85457
Fax: 852-2788-5543
E-mail Address: *autopart@hkpc.org*
Web Address: www.hkapia.com
The Hong Kong Auto Parts Industry Association (HKAPIA) represents the automotive components industry in Hong Kong. Its members are engaged in the design, manufacturing and business investment in the auto parts industry.

Motor & Equipment Manufacturers Association (MEMA)
10 Laboratory Dr.
P.O. Box 13966
Research Triangle Park, NC 27709-3966 US
Phone: 919-549-4800
Fax: 919-549-4824
E-mail Address: *info@mema.org*
Web Address: www.mema.org
The Motor & Equipment Manufacturers Association (MEMA) exclusively represents and serves manufacturers of motor vehicle components, tools and equipment, automotive chemicals and related products used in the production, repair and maintenance of all classes of motor vehicles.

Specialty Equipment Market Association (SEMA)
P.O. Box 4910
Diamond Bar, CA 91765-0910 US
Phone: 909-396-0289
Fax: 909-860-1709
E-mail Address: *sema@sema.org*
Web Address: www.sema.org
Specialty Equipment Market Association (SEMA) members offer innovative specialty equipment products and services that enhance a vehicle's style, utility and performance.

Transmission Rebuilders Network International (TRNI)
3851 E. Thunderbird Rd., Ste. 111-235
Phoenix, AZ 85032 US
Fax: 602-404-2719
Toll Free: 888-582-8764
E-mail Address: *INFO@trannybuilder.com*
Web Address: www.transbuilder.com
Transmission Rebuilders Network International (TRNI) is a worldwide network of over 1,000 transmission technicians, interacting on topics related to transmission repair.

IX. Automotive Publications

Auto Week Magazine
Crain Communications, Inc.
1155 Gratiot Ave.
Detroit, MI 48207-2997 US
Phone: 313-446-6000
E-mail Address: *kccrain@crain.com*
Web Address: www.autoweek.com
Auto Week Magazine is a publication devoted to the automotive industry and motor sports. It is a service of Crain Communications, Inc.

Automobile Magazine
Source Interlink Companies, Inc.
27500 Riverview Center Blvd., Ste. 400
Bonita Springs, FL 32142-0235 US
Phone: 734-994-3500
Toll Free: 800-289-2886
E-mail Address: *feedback@automobilemag.com*
Web Address: www.automobilemag.com
Automobile Magazine is a monthly magazine featuring the latest automotive news. The magazine is a publication of Source Interlink Media, LLC, which is itself part of Source Interlink Companies, Inc.

Automotive Digest
Automotive Information Network, Inc.
425 32nd St.
Manhattan Beach, CA 90266 US
Phone: 310-265-2225
Fax: 310-796-4591
E-mail Address: *chuck@automotivedigest.com*
Web Address: www.automotivedigest.com
Automotive Digest reviews the massive amount of printed and electronic material published every day for or about the automotive industry and its related market segments and industries in the U.S. and globally. The site is owned and operated by Automotive Information Network, Inc.

Automotive News Group
Crain Communications, Inc.
1155 Gratiot Ave.
Detroit, MI 48207-2997 US
Phone: 313-446-6000

Fax: 313-446-1616
E-mail Address: *info@crain.com*
Web Address: www.autonews.com
The Automotive News Group, a part of the Crain Publishing Company, publishes the weekly magazine, Automotive News. Its web site provides a wealth of up-to-date auto industry news.

Car and Driver Magazine
1585 Eisenhower Pl.
Ann Arbor, MI 48108 US
Phone: 734-971-3600
E-mail Address: *caranddriver@hfnm.com*
Web Address: www.caranddriver.com
Car and Driver Magazine publishes current information on automobiles and the automobile industry. It is published by New York-based Hachette Filipacchi Media, U.S., Inc. (HFMUS), a division of Legardere SCA.

Motor Trend Online
6420 Wilshire Blvd., 7th Fl.
Los Angeles, CA 90048-5515 US
Phone: 323-782-2220
Web Address: www.motortrend.com
Motor Trend Online is an online magazine providing previews on cars, a buyer's guide and current information on the auto industry. It is owned by New York-based Source Interlink Media, LLC.

Road & Track Magazine
1499 Monrovia Ave.
Newport Beach, CA 92663 US
Phone: 949-720-5300
E-mail Address: *RTLettersOnline@HFMUS.com*
Web Address: www.roadandtrack.com
Road & Track Magazine is an automotive magazine providing news and information relating to the auto industry. The company is operated by Hachette Filipacchi Media U.S. (HFMUS), part of Hachette Filipacchi New Media.

Velocity Automotive Journal
P.O. Box 476
Crystal Lake, IL 60039-0476 US
Web Address: www.velocityjournal.com
Velocity Automotive Journal enables viewers to research all of the vehicles currently available in the U.S. domestic market. The group utilizes the Velocity Index tool, which measures 15 performance and drivability criteria and computes them into one easy-to-compare number.

Ward's Auto
3000 Town Ctr., Ste. 2750
Southfield, MI 48075 US
Phone: 248-357-0800
Fax: 248-357-0810
E-mail Address: *wards@wardsauto.com*
Web Address: www.wardsauto.com
Ward's Auto is a highly popular company that provides auto news and in-depth data, in addition to publishing magazines such as Ward's AutoWorld and Ward's Dealer Business.

X. Automotive Safety

American Traffic Safety Services Institute (The) (ATSSA)
15 Riverside Pkwy., Ste. 100
Fredericksburg, VA 22406-1022 US
Phone: 540-368-1701
Fax: 540-368-1717
Toll Free: 800-272-8772
E-mail Address: *jimb@atssa.com*
Web Address: www.atssa.com
The American Traffic Safety Services Institute (ATSSA) is an international trade association whose members provide pavement markings, signage, work zone traffic control devices and other safety features on our nation's roadways.

Insurance Institute for Highway Safety (IIHS)
1005 N. Glebe Rd., Ste. 800
Arlington, VA 22201 US
Phone: 703-247-1500
Fax: 703-247-1588
E-mail Address: *rrader@iihs.org*
Web Address: www.iihs.org
The Insurance Institute for Highway Safety (IIHS) is an independent nonprofit scientific and educational organization dedicated to reducing the numbers of deaths, injuries and property damage in crashes on U.S. highways.

National Safety Council (NSC)
1121 Spring Lake Dr.
Itasca, IL 60143-3201 US
Phone: 630-285-1121
Fax: 630-285-1315
E-mail Address: *info@nsc.org*
Web Address: www.nsc.org
The National Safety Council (NSC) is a nonprofit, international organization that provides safety information and statistics in order to help to prevent accidental injury and death.

SaferCar.gov
NHTSA Headquarters
1200 New Jersey Ave., SE, W. Bldg.
Washington, DC 20590 US
Toll Free: 888-327-4236
E-mail Address: *crash.test@dot.gov*
Web Address: www.safercar.gov
Safercar.gov offers crash test and rollover ratings for all automobiles manufactured since 1990. It also provides tools for checking for automobile recalls, to look into ongoing investigations and to file vehicle complaints. Additionally, safety information regarding child safety seats, electronic stability control, tires, air bags, rollover prevention and hybrid FAQs can all be found on the site. Safecar.gov is operated by the National Highway Traffic Safety Administration (NHTSA), a part of the U.S. Department of Transportation (DOT).

XI. Canadian Government Agencies-Scientific

Industrial Materials Institute (IRI)
75 de Mortagne Blvd.
Boucherville, QC J4B 6Y4 Canada
Phone: 450-641-5000
Fax: 450-641-5102
E-mail Address: *Imi-Info@cnrc-nrc.gc.ca*
Web Address: imi.cnrc-nrc.gc.ca
The Industrial Materials Institute (IRI) is a branch of Canada's National Research Council focusing its research on advanced materials design used in the manufacture of industrial components.

XII. Careers-First Time Jobs/New Grads

Black Collegian Online (The)
140 Carondelet St.
New Orleans, LA 70130 US
Phone: 504-523-0154
Web Address: www.black-collegian.com
The Black Collegian Online features listings for job and internship opportunities, as well as other tools for students of color; it is the web site of The Black Collegian Magazine, published by IMDiversity, Inc. The site includes a list of the top 100 minority corporate employers and an assessment of job opportunities.

Collegegrad.com, Inc.
234 E. College Ave., Ste. 200
State College, PA 16801 US
Phone: 262-375-6700
Toll Free: 1-800-991-4642
Web Address: www.collegegrad.com
Collegegrad.com, Inc. offers in-depth resources for college students and recent grads seeking entry-level jobs.

Job Web
Nat'l Association of Colleges & Employers (NACE)
62 Highland Ave.
Bethlehem, PA 18017-9085 US
Phone: 610-868-1421
Fax: 610-868-0208
Toll Free: 800-544-5272
E-mail Address: *editors@jobweb.com*
Web Address: www.jobweb.com
Job Web, owned and sponsored by National Association of Colleges and Employers (NACE), displays job openings and employer descriptions. The site also offers a database of career fairs, searchable by state or keyword, with contact information.

MBAjobs.net
Fax: 413-556-8849
E-mail Address: *contact@mbajobs.net*
Web Address: www.mbajobs.net
MBAjobs.net is a unique international service for MBA students and graduates, employers, recruiters and business schools. The MBAjobs.net service is provided by WebInfoCo.

MonsterTRAK
11845 W. Olympic Blvd., Ste. 500
Los Angeles, CA 90064 US
Toll Free: 800-999-8725
E-mail Address: *trakstudent@monster.com*
Web Address: www.college.monster.com
MonsterTRAK provides information about internships and entry-level jobs.

National Association of Colleges and Employers (NACE)
62 Highland Ave.
Bethlehem, PA 18017-9085 US
Phone: 610-868-1421
Fax: 610-868-0208
Toll Free: 800-544-5272
E-mail Address: *mcollins@naceweb.org*
Web Address: www.naceweb.org
The National Association of Colleges and Employers (NACE) is a premier U.S. organization representing college placement offices and corporate recruiters who focus on hiring new grads.

XIII. Careers-General Job Listings

Career Exposure, Inc.
805 SW Broadway, Ste. 2250
Portland, OR 97205 US
Phone: 503-221-7779
Fax: 503-221-7780
E-mail Address: *lisam@mackenzie-marketing.com*
Web Address: www.careerexposure.com
Career Exposure, Inc. is an online career center and job placement service, with resources for employers, recruiters and job seekers.

CareerBuilder, Inc.
200 N. LaSalle St., Ste. 1100
Chicago, IL 60601 US
Phone: 773-527-3600
Toll Free: 800-638-4212
Web Address: www.careerbuilder.com
CareerBuilder, Inc. focuses on the needs of companies and also provides a database of job openings. The site has 1.5 million jobs posted by 300,000 employers, and receives an average 23 million unique visitors monthly. The company also operates online career centers for 150 newspapers, 1,000 partners and other online portals such as America Online. Resumes are sent directly to the company, and applicants can set up a special e-mail account for job-seeking purposes. CareerBuilder is primarily a joint venture between three newspaper giants: The McClatchy Company (which recently acquired former partner Knight Ridder), Gannett Co., Inc. and Tribune Company. In 2007, Microsoft acquired a minority interest in CareerBuilder, allowing the site to ally itself with MSN.

CareerOneStop
Toll Free: 877-348-0502
E-mail Address: *info@careeronestop.org*
Web Address: www.careeronestop.org
CareerOneStop is operated by the employment commissions of various state agencies. It contains job listings in both the private sector and in government. CareerOneStop is sponsored by the U.S. Department of Labor. It includes a wide variety of useful career resources and workforce information.

HotJobs
45 W. 18th St., 6th Fl.
New York, NY 10011 US
Phone: 646-351-5300
Web Address: www.hotjobs.yahoo.com
HotJobs, designed for experienced professionals, employers and job seekers, is a Monster-owned site that provides company profiles, a resume posting service and a resume workshop. The site allows posters to block resumes from being viewed by certain companies and provides a notification service of new jobs.

JobCentral
DirectEmployers Association, Inc.
9002 N. Purdue Rd., Quad III, Ste. 100
Indianapolis, IN 46268 US
Phone: 317-874-9000
Fax: 317-874-9100
Toll Free: 866-268-6206
E-mail Address: *info@jobcentral.com*
Web Address: www.jobcentral.com
JobCentral, operated by the nonprofit DirectEmployers Association, Inc., links users directly to hundreds of thousands of job opportunities posted on the sites of participating employers, thus bypassing the usual job search sites. This saves employers money and allows job seekers to access many more job opportunities.

LaborMarketInfo
Employment Dev. Dept., Labor Market Info. Div.
800 Capitol Mall, MIC 83
Sacramento, CA 95814 US
Phone: 916-262-2162
Fax: 916-262-2352
Toll Free: 800-480-3287
Web Address: www.labormarketinfo.edd.ca.gov
LaborMarketInfo, formerly the California Cooperative Occupational Information System, is geared to providing job seekers and employers a wide range of resources, namely the ability to find, access and use labor market information and services. It provides demographical statistics for employment on both a local and regional level, as well as career searching tools for California residents. The web site is sponsored by California's Employment Development Office.

Recruiters Online Network
947 Essex Ln.
Medina, OH 44256 US
Phone: 888-364-4667
Fax: 888-237-8686
E-mail Address: *info@recruitersonline.com*
Web Address: www.recruitersonline.com
The Recruiters Online Network provides job postings from thousands of recruiters, Careers Online

Magazine, a resume database, as well as other career resources.

True Careers, Inc.
Web Address: www.truecareers.com
True Careers, Inc. offers job listings and provides an array of career resources. The company also offers a search of over 2 million scholarships. It is partnered with CareerBuilder.com, which powers its career information and resume posting functions.

USAJOBS
U.S. Office of Personnel Management
1900 E St. NW
Washington, DC 20415 US
Phone: 202-606-1800
Web Address: usajobs.opm.gov
USAJOBS, a program of the U.S. Office of Personnel Management, is the official job site for the U.S. Federal Government. It provides a comprehensive list of U.S. government jobs, allowing users to search for employment by location; agency; type of work, using the Federal Government's numerical identification code, the General Schedule (GS) Series; or by senior executive positions. It also has a special veterans' employment section; an information center, offering resume and interview tips and other useful information such as hiring trends and a glossary of Federal terms; and allows users to create a profile and post a resume.

Wall Street Journal - CareerJournal
Wall Street Journal
200 Liberty St.
New York, NY 10281 US
Phone: 212-416-2000
Toll Free: 800-568-7625
E-mail Address: *onelinejournal@wsj.com*
Web Address: cj.careercast.com/careers/jobsearch
The Wall Street Journal's CareerJournal, an executive career site, features a job database with thousands of available positions; career news and employment related articles; and advice regarding resume writing, interviews, networking, office life and job hunting.

XIV. Careers-Job Reference Tools

NewsVoyager
4401 Wilson Blvd., Ste. 900
Arlington, VA 22203-1867 US
Phone: 571-366-1000
Fax: 571-366-1195
E-mail Address: *sally.clarke@naa.org*
Web Address: www.newsvoyager.com
NewsVoyager, a service of the Newspaper Association of America (NAA), links individuals to local, national and international newspapers. Job seekers can search through thousands of classified sections.

Vault.com, Inc.
75 Varick St., 8th Fl.
New York, NY 10013 US
Phone: 212-366-4212
E-mail Address: *feedback@staff.vault.com*
Web Address: www.vault.com
Vault.com, Inc. is a comprehensive career web site for employers and employees, with job postings and valuable information on a wide variety of industries. Vault gears many of its features toward MBAs. The site has been recognized by Forbes and Fortune Magazines.

XV. Construction Resources-Energy Efficient Buildings

Energy Efficiency Programme Office (E2PO)
140 Hill St., 5th Storey, MICA Bldg.
Singapore, 179369 Singapore
Fax: 65-6235-2611
Toll Free: 800-225-5632
E-mail Address: *contact_NEA@nea.gov.sg*
Web Address: www.e2singapore.gov.sg
To drive energy efficiency improvement in Singapore, the Energy Efficiency Programme Office (E2PO) has been established. The website includes information about energy programs, publications, incentives and development opportunities for power generation, industry, transport, green buildings and the public sector of Singapore.

XVI. Corporate Information Resources

bizjournals.com
120 W. Morehead St., Ste. 400
Charlotte, NC 28202 US
Web Address: www.bizjournals.com
Bizjournals.com is the online media division of American City Business Journals, the publisher of dozens of leading city business journals nationwide. It provides access to research into the latest news regarding companies small and large.

Business Wire
44 Montgomery St., 39th Fl.

San Francisco, CA 94104 US
Phone: 415-986-4422
Fax: 415-788-5335
Toll Free: 800-227-0845
Web Address: www.businesswire.com
Business Wire offers news releases, industry- and company-specific news, top headlines, conference calls, IPOs on the Internet, media services and access to tradeshownews.com and BW Connect On-line through its informative and continuously updated web site.

Edgar Online, Inc.
50 Washington St., 11th Fl.
Norwalk, CT 06854 US
Phone: 203-852-5666
Fax: 203-852-5667
Toll Free: 800-416-6651
Web Address: www.edgar-online.com
Edgar Online, Inc. is a gateway and search tool for viewing corporate documents, such as annual reports on Form 10-K, filed with the U.S. Securities and Exchange Commission.

PR Newswire Association LLC
810 7th Ave., 32nd Fl.
New York, NY 10019 US
Phone: 201-360-6700
Toll Free: 800-832-5522
E-mail Address: *information@prnewswire.com*
Web Address: www.prnewswire.com
PR Newswire Association LLC provides comprehensive communications services for public relations and investor relations professionals ranging from information distribution and market intelligence to the creation of online multimedia content and investor relations web sites. Users can also view recent corporate press releases. The Association is owned by United Business Media plc.

Silicon Investor
100 W. Main
P.O. Box 29
Freeman, MO 64746 US
E-mail Address: *admin_dave@techstocks.com*
Web Address: siliconinvestor.advfn.com
Silicon Investor is focused on providing information about technology companies. The company's web site serves as a financial discussion forum and offers quotes, profiles and charts.

XVII. Economic Data & Research

Eurostat
Phone: 32-2-299-9696
Toll Free: 80-0-6789-1011
Web Address: www.epp.eurostat.ec.europa.eu
Eurostat is the European Union's service that publishes a wide variety of comprehensive statistics on European industries, populations, trade, agriculture, technology, environment and other matters.

India Brand Equity Foundation (IBEF)
249-F Sector 18
Udyog Vihar Phase IV
Gurgaon, Haryana 122015 India
Phone: 91-124-4014060
Fax: 91-124-4013873
E-mail Address: *ceo@ibef.org*
Web Address: www.ibef.org
India Brand Equity Foundation (IBEF) is a public-private partnership between the Ministry of Commerce and Industry, Government of India, and the Confederation of Indian Industry. The Foundation's primary objective is to build positive economic perceptions of India globally. It aims to effectively present the India business perspective and leverage business partnerships in a globalizing market-place.

National Bureau of Statistics (China)
57, Yuetan Nanjie, Sanlihe
Xicheng District
Beijing, 100826 China
Fax: 86-10-68782000
E-mail Address: *info@stats.gov.cn*
Web Address: www.stats.gov.cn/english
The National Bureau of Statistics of China provides statistics and economic data regarding China's economic and social issues.

Statistics Canada
150 Tunney's Pasture Driveway
Ottawa, ON K1A 0T6 Canada
Phone: 613-951-8116
Fax: 613-951-0581
Toll Free: 800-263-1136
Web Address: www.statcan.gc.ca
A complete portal to Canadian economic data and statistics.

STAT-USA/Internet
STAT-USA, HCHB, U.S. Dept. of Commerce

Rm. 4885
Washington, DC 20230 US
Phone: 202-482-1986
Fax: 202-482-2164
Toll Free: 800-782-8872
E-mail Address: *statmail@esa.doc.gov*
Web Address: www.stat-usa.gov
STAT-USA/Internet offers daily economic news, statistical releases and databases relating to export and trade, as well as the domestic economy. It is provided by STAT-USA, which is an agency in the Economics & Statistics Administration of the U.S. Department of Commerce. The site mainly consists of two main databases, the State of the Nation (SOTN), which focuses on the current state of the U.S. economy; and the Global Business Opportunities (GLOBUS) & the National Trade Data Bank (NTDB), which deals with U.S. export opportunities, global political/socio-economic conditions and other world economic issues.

XVIII. Engineering Indices

Engineering Library
Cornell University
Carpenter Hall
Ithaca, NY 14853 US
Phone: 607-255-5933
Fax: 607-255-0278
E-mail Address: *engranswers@cornell.edu*
Web Address:
www.astech.library.cornell.edu/ast/engr
Cornell University's Engineering Library web site has a number of resources concerning engineering research.

XIX. Engineering, Research & Scientific Associations

American National Standards Institute (ANSI)
1819 L St. NW, 6th Fl.
Washington, DC 20036 US
Phone: 202-293-8020
Fax: 202-293-9287
E-mail Address: *info@ansi.org*
Web Address: www.ansi.org
The American National Standards Institute (ANSI) is a private, nonprofit organization that administers and coordinates the U.S. voluntary standardization and conformity assessment system. Its mission is to enhance both the global competitiveness of U.S. business and the quality of life by promoting and facilitating voluntary consensus standards and conformity assessment systems and safeguarding their integrity.

American Society for Testing & Materials (ASTM)
100 Barr Harbor Dr.
P.O. Box C700
West Conshohocken, PA 19428-2959 US
Phone: 610-832-9500
Fax: 610-832-9555
E-mail Address: *service@astm.org*
Web Address: www.astm.org
The American Society for Testing & Materials (ASTM) provides and develops voluntary consensus standards and related technical information, and services that promote public health and safety. It also contributes to the reliability of materials, as well as provides technical standards for industries worldwide.

American Society of Mechanical Engineers (ASME)
3 Park Ave.
New York, NY 10016-5990 US
Phone: 973-882-1170
Fax: 973-882-1717
Toll Free: 800-843-2763
E-mail Address: *infocentral@asme.org*
Web Address: www.asme.org
The American Society of Mechanical Engineers (ASME) offers quality programs and activities in mechanical engineering. It also facilitates the development and application of technology in areas of interest to the mechanical engineering profession.

American Society of Safety Engineers (ASSE)
Customer Service
1800 E. Oakton St.
Des Plaines, IL 60018 US
Phone: 847-699-2929
Fax: 847-768-3434
E-mail Address: *customerservice@asse.org*
Web Address: www.asse.org
The American Society of Safety Engineers (ASSE) is the world's oldest and largest professional safety organization. It manages, supervises and consults on safety, health and environmental issues in industry, insurance, government and education.

ASM International
9639 Kinsman Rd.
Materials Park, OH 44073-0002 US

Phone: 440-338-5151 x0
Fax: 440-338-4634
Toll Free: 800-336-5152
E-mail Address:
customerservice@asminternational.org
Web Address: www.asminternational.org
ASM International is a worldwide network of materials engineers, aimed at advancing industry, technology and applications of metals and materials.

Industrial Research Institute (IRI)
2200 Clarendon Blvd., Ste. 1102
Arlington, VA 22201 US
Phone: 703-647-2580
Fax: 703-647-2581
E-mail Address: *information@iriinc.org*
Web Address: www.iriinc.org
The Industrial Research Institute (IRI) is a nonprofit organization of over 200 leading industrial companies, representing industries such as aerospace, automotive, chemical, computers and electronics, which carry out industrial research efforts in the U.S. manufacturing sector. IRI helps members improve research and development capabilities.

Institute of Electrical and Electronics Engineers (IEEE)
3 Park Ave., 17th Fl.
New York, NY 10016-5997 US
Phone: 212-419-7900
Fax: 212-752-4929
E-mail Address: *ieeeusa@ieee.org*
Web Address: www.ieee.org
The Institute of Electrical and Electronics Engineers (IEEE) is a nonprofit, technical professional association of more than 375,000 individual members in approximately 160 countries. The IEEE sets global technical standards and acts as an authority in technical areas ranging from computer engineering, biomedical technology and telecommunications, to electric power, aerospace and consumer electronics.

International Federation of Automotive Engineering Societies (FISITA)
30 Percy St.
London, W1T 2DB UK
Phone: 44-(0)-20-7299-6630
Fax: 44-(0)-20-7299-6633
E-mail Address: *info@fisita.com*
Web Address: www.fisita.com
The Federation Internationale des Societes d'Ingenieurs des Techniques de l'Automobile (FISITA) was founded in Paris in 1948 with the purpose of bringing engineers from around the world together in a spirit of cooperation to share ideas and advance the technological development of the automobile. FISITA is the umbrella organization for the national automotive societies in 38 countries around the world. Its network of member societies represents more than 147,000 automotive engineers around the globe.

International Standards Organization (ISO)
1 ch. de la Voie-Creuse
Case Postale 56
Geneva 20, CH-1211 Switzerland
Phone: 41-22-749-01-11
Fax: 41-22-733-34-30
E-mail Address: *central@iso.org*
Web Address: www.iso.org
The International Standards Organization (ISO) is a global consortium of national standards institutes from 157 countries. The established International Standards are designed to make products and services more efficient, safe and clean.

Materials Research Society (MRS)
506 Keystone Dr.
Warrendale, PA 15086-7573 US
Phone: 724-779-3003
Fax: 724-779-8313
E-mail Address: *info@mrs.org*
Web Address: www.mrs.org
The Materials Research Society (MRS) is dedicated to basic and applied research on materials of technological importance. MRS emphasizes an interdisciplinary approach to materials science and engineering.

Research in Germany, German Academic Exchange Service (DAAD)
Kennedyallee 50
Bonn, 53175 Germany
Phone: 49(0)228 882 - 0
Fax: 49(0)228 882 - 660
Web Address: www.research-in-germany.de
The Research in Germany portal, German Academic Exchange Service (DAAD),
is an information platform and contact point for those looking to find out more about Germany's research landscape and its latest research achievements. The portal is an initiative of the Federal Ministry of Education and Research.

Royal Society (The)
6-9 Carlton House Ter.

London, SW1Y 5AG UK
Phone: 44-20-7451-2500
Fax: 44-20-7930-2170
E-mail Address: *info@royalsociety.org*
Web Address: www.royalsoc.ac.uk
The Royal Society is the UK's leading scientific organization. It operates as a national academy of science, supporting scientists, engineers, technologists and research. On its website, you will find a wealth of data about the research and development initiatives of its fellows and foreign members.

Society of Automotive Engineers (SAE)
755 W. Big Beaver, Ste. 1600
Troy, MA 48084 US
Phone: 248-273-2455
Fax: 248-273-2494
Toll Free: 877-606-7323
E-mail Address: *automotive_hq@sae.org*
Web Address: www.sae.org
The Society of Automotive Engineers (SAE) is a resource for technical information and expertise used in designing, building, maintaining and operating self-propelled vehicles for use on land, sea, air or space.

Society of Manufacturing Engineers (SME)
1 SME Dr.
Dearborn, MI 48121 US
Phone: 313-425-3000
Fax: 313-425-3412
Toll Free: 800-733-4763
E-mail Address: *communications@sme.org*
Web Address: www.sme.org
The Society of Manufacturing Engineers (SME) a leading professional organization serving engineers in the manufacturing industries.

Society of Plastics Engineers (SPE)
14 Fairfield Dr.
P.O. Box 403
Brookfield, CT 06804-0403 US
Phone: 203-775-0471
Fax: 203-775-8490
E-mail Address: *info@4spe.org*
Web Address: www.4spe.org
The Society of Plastics Engineers (SPE) is a recognized medium of communication among scientists and engineers engaged in the development, conversion and applications of plastics.

XX. Hybrid & Electric Vehicles

EERE FreedomCAR & Vehicle Technologies Program (FCVT)
1000 Independence Ave. SW
Mail Stop EE-2G, Rm. 5G-030
Washington, DC 20585 US
Phone: 202-586-8055
Fax: 202-586-7409
Toll Free: 877-337-3463
E-mail Address: *patrick.davis@ee.doe.gov*
Web Address:
www1.eere.energy.gov/vehiclesandfuels
The FreedomCAR & Vehicle Technologies Program (FCVT) of the Office of Energy Efficiency and Renewable Energy (EERE), a division of the U.S. Department of Energy, works with U.S. industries toward the development of emission- and petroleum-free cars and light trucks. The program focuses on high-risk technological research for fuel cells and advanced hybrid propulsion systems.

Electric Drive Transportation Association (EDTA)
1101 Vermont Ave. NW, Ste. 401
Washington, DC 20005 US
Phone: 202-408-0774
E-mail Address: *info@electricdrive.org*
Web Address: www.electricdrive.org
The Electric Drive Transportation Association (EDTA) is an industry association working to advance electric vehicle transportation technologies and supporting infrastructure through policy, information and market development initiatives.

Hybrid Truck Users Forum (HTUF)
48 S. Chester Ave.
Pasadena, CA 91106 US
Phone: 626-744-5600
Fax: 626-744-5610
E-mail Address: *bvanamburg@calstart.org*
Web Address: www.calstart.org/programs/htuf
The Hybrid Truck Users Forum (HTUF), operated by CALSTART, offers a wealth of information on technologies, pilot projects, test results, fleet purchasing plans and much more.

XXI. Industry Research/Market Research

Forrester Research
400 Technology Sq.
Cambridge, MA 02139 US

Phone: 617-613-6000
Fax: 617-613-5200
Toll Free: 866-367-7378
Web Address: www.forrester.com
Forrester Research identifies and analyzes emerging trends in technology and their impact on business. Among the firm's specialties are the financial services, retail, health care, entertainment, automotive and information technology industries.

Marketresearch.com
11200 Rockville Pike, Ste. 504
Rockville, MD 20852 US
Phone: 240-747-3000
Fax: 240-747-3004
Toll Free: 800-298-5699
E-mail Address:
customerservice@marketresearch.com
Web Address: www.marketresearch.com
Marketresearch.com is a leading broker for professional market research and industry analysis. Users are able to search the company's database of research publications including data on global industries, companies, products and trends.

NPD Group (The)
900 W. Shore Rd.
Port Washington, NY 11050 US
Phone: 516-625-0700
Toll Free: 866-444-1411
E-mail Address: *contactnpd@npd.com*
Web Address: www.npd.com
The NPD Group is one of the world's leading market research firms covering the retailing and related sectors. Its website provides very useful press releases, and it enables users to subscribe to RSS news feeds. NPD covers industries including automotive, beauty, technology, entertainment, fashion, food & beverage, home, software, toys and wireless.

Plunkett Research, Ltd.
P.O. Drawer 541737
Houston, TX 77254-1737 US
Phone: 713-932-0000
Fax: 713-932-7080
E-mail Address:
customersupport@plunkettresearch.com
Web Address: www.plunkettresearch.com
Plunkett Research, Ltd. is a leading provider of market research, industry trends analysis and business statistics. Since 1985, it has served clients worldwide, including corporations, universities, libraries, consultants and government agencies. At the firm's web site, visitors can view product information and pricing and access a great deal of basic market information on industries such as financial services, infotech, e-commerce, health care and biotech.

XXII. Internet Usage Statistics

comScore, Inc.
11950 Democracy Dr.
Reston, VA 20190 US
Phone: 703-438-2000
Fax: 703-438-2051
Toll Free: 866-638-3835
Web Address: www.comscore.com
comScore, Inc. provides data analytics and solutions that help companies build profitable, sustainable businesses. The firm's consumer behavior insights are a guide for marketing and trading strategies.

XXIII. Labor Unions

United Automobile, Aerospace and Agricultural Implement Workers of America (UAW)
8000 E. Jefferson Ave.
Detroit, MI 48214 US
Phone: 313-926-5000
Web Address: www.uaw.org
The United Automobile, Aerospace and Agricultural Implement Workers of America (UAW) is a diverse international union that represents workplaces ranging from multinational corporations, small manufacturers and state and local governments to colleges and universities, hospitals and private nonprofit organizations.

XXIV. Manufacturing Associations-General

Confederation of Indian Industry (CII)
The Mantosh Sondhi Ctr.
23 Institutional Area, Lodi Rd.
New Delhi, 110 003 India
Phone: 91-11-24629994-7
Fax: 91-11-24626149
E-mail Address: *ciico@ciionline.org*
Web Address: www.cii.in
Confederation of Indian Industry (CII) works to develop industry in India. The site provides research reports, a library supporting members and other industry resources and information. CII organizes

trade shows including the Auto Expo held biennially in India.

MAPI/Manufacturers Alliance
1600 Wilson Blvd., 11th Floor
Arlington, VA 22209 US
Phone: 703-841-9000
Fax: 703-841-9514
Web Address: www.mapi.net
Established in 1933, MAPI/Manufacturers Alliance was once known as the Machinery and Allied Products Institute. Today, it represents manufacturers of all types. It publishes extensive research on manufacturing in America.

National Association of Manufacturers (NAM)
1331 Pennsylvania Ave. NW
Washington, DC 20004-1790 US
Phone: 202-637-3000
Fax: 202-637-3182
E-mail Address: *manufacturing@nam.org*
Web Address: www.nam.org
The National Association of Manufacturers (NAM) is one of the largest industrial trade associations in the United States, representing manufacturers and employees in every industrial sector. The association lobbies Congress on behalf of its members and seeks economic growth through the promotion of manufacturing activities and legislation.

XXV. Manufacturing Associations-Machinery & Technology

Association for Manufacturing Technology (AMT)
7901 Westpark Dr.
McLean, VA 22102-4206 US
Phone: 703-893-2900
Fax: 703-893-1151
Toll Free: 800-524-0475
E-mail Address: *amt@amtonline.org*
Web Address: www.amtonline.org
The Association for Manufacturing Technology (AMT) actively supports and promotes American manufacturers of machine tools and manufacturing technology.

Korea Association of Machinery Industry (KOAMI)
Yeouido-dong, Yeongdeungpo-gu
KOAMI Bldg., 13-31
Seoul, 150-729 Korea
Phone: 82-2-369-7851
Fax: 82-2-369-7900
E-mail Address: *trade@koami.or.kr*
Web Address: www.koami.or.kr
The Korea Association of Machinery Industry (KOAMI) is the national trade organization for the Korean machinery industry.

National Center for Manufacturing Sciences (NCMS)
3025 Boardwalk Dr.
Ann Arbor, MI 48108-3230 US
Fax: 734-995-1150
Toll Free: 800-222-6267
Web Address: www.ncms.org
The National Center for Manufacturing Sciences (NCMS) is a nonprofit membership organization dedicated to advancing the global competitiveness of North American industry through collaboration.

National Tooling and Machining Association (NTMA)
9300 Livingston Rd.
Ft. Washington, MD 20744 US
Fax: 301-248-7104
Toll Free: 800-248-6862
E-mail Address: *info@ntma.org*
Web Address: www.ntma.org
The National Tooling and Machining Association (NTMA) helps members of the U.S. precision custom manufacturing industries achieve business success in a global economy through advocacy, advice, networking, information, programs and services.

Precision Metalforming Association (PMA)
6363 Oak Tree Blvd.
Independence, OH 44131 US
Phone: 216-901-8800
Fax: 216-901-9190
Web Address: www.metalforming.com
PMA is a trade association representing the $91-billion metalforming industry of North America. The industry creates precision metal products using stamping, fabricating, spinning, slide forming and roll forming technologies, and other value-added processes. Its nearly 1,100 member companies also include suppliers of equipment, materials and services to the industry.

Singapore Institute of Manufacturing Technology (SIMTech)
71 Nanyang Dr.
638075 Singapore
Phone: 65-6793-8383

E-mail Address: *ido@SIMTech.a-star.edu.sg*
Web Address: www.simtech.a-star.edu.sg
The Singapore Institute of Manufacturing Technology (SIMTech) has completed more than 880 projects with more than 410 companies, big and small, in the electronics, semiconductor, precision engineering, aerospace, automotive, marine, logistics and other sectors.

XXVI. MBA Resources

MBA Depot
Phone: 512-499-8728
Web Address: www.mbadepot.com
MBA Depot is an online community for MBA professionals.

XXVII. Metals & Steel Industry Associations

Aluminum Association (The)
1525 Wilson Blvd., Ste. 600
Arlington, VA 22209 US
Phone: 703-358-2960
Fax: 703-358-2961
E-mail Address: *jsimpson@aluminum.org*
Web Address: www.aluminum.org
The Aluminum Association is the trade association for producers of primary aluminum, recyclers and makers of semi-fabricated aluminum products, as well as suppliers to the industry.

American Iron and Steel Institute
1140 Connecticut Ave. NW, Ste. 705
Washington, DC 20036 US
Phone: 202-452-7100
E-mail Address: *webmaster@steel.org*
Web Address: www.steel.org
AISI provides an in-depth web site with statistics, news, links and various other features geared to members of the steel industry, as well as to students and researchers.

XXVIII. Motorcycle Industry Associations (MIC)

Federation of Asian Motorcycle Industry
c/o Armstrong Auto Parts
Tikam Batu Industrial Estate
Sg. Petani. Kedah, D.A. 08600 Malaysia
Phone: 60-4438-0198
Fax: 60-4438-8626
E-mail Address: *anyenquiry@fami-motorcyle.org*
Web Address: www.fami-motorcycle.org
The Federation of Asian Motorcycle Industries (FAMI) is a nonprofit association currently comprised of seven motorcycle associations in the Asia Pacific: Indonesia, Japan, Malaysia, The Philippines, Singapore, Taiwan, and Thailand.

International Motorcycle Manufacturers Association (IMMA)
E-mail Address: *info@immamotorcycles.org*
Web Address: www.immamotorcycles.org
The International Motorcycle Manufacturers Association (IMMA) is the trade association which represents the motorcycle industry at the global level.

Motorcycle Industry Council (MIC)
2 Jenner St., Ste. 150
Irvine, CA 92618-3806 US
Phone: 949-727-4211
Fax: 949-727-3313
E-mail Address: *ciannello@mic.org*
Web Address: www.mic.org
The Motorcycle Industry Council (MIC) is a not-for-profit, national trade association created to promote and preserve motorcycling and the U.S. motorcycle industry. This is accomplished through its activities in government relations, statistics, communications, technical, and aftermarket programs.

Singapore Motor Cycle Trade Association (SMCTA)
40 Sam Leong Rd.
207930 Singapore
Phone: 65-6297-1991
Fax: 65-6297-1313
E-mail Address: *smcta@singnet.com.sg*
Web Address: www.smcta.org.sg
Singapore Motor Cycle Trade Association (SMCTA) represents the motorcycle trade and related industries in Singapore.

XXIX. Natural Gas Vehicles

Asia Pacific Natural Gas Vehicles Association (ANGVA)
Level 2, Block A, Lot 3288 and 3289
Off Jalan Ayer Hitam, Kawasan Institutusi Bangi
Kajang, Selangor 43000 Malaysia
Phone: 603-8926-1798
Fax: 603-8926-1834
E-mail Address: *leegs@angva.org*
Web Address: www.angva.org

ANGVA serves the needs of fleet operators, vehicle manufacturers, gas suppliers, equipment suppliers, refueling equipment providers, consultants, government representatives, non governmental organizations (NGO) and others involved with the natural gas vehicles industry by promoting the use of natural gas as the fuel for the transportation sector.

Natural Gas Vehicles for America (NGVAmerica)
400 N. Capitol St. NW
Washington, DC 20001 US
Phone: 202-824-7366
Fax: 202-824-7087
E-mail Address: *rkolodziej@ngvamerica.org*
Web Address: www.ngvc.org
Natural Gas Vehicle for America (NGVAmerica) is a national organization dedicated to the development of a growing, sustainable and profitable market for vehicles powered by natural gas or hydrogen. NGVAmerica represents more than 100 companies interested in the promotion and use of natural gas and hydrogen as transportation fuels, including: engine, vehicle and equipment manufacturers fleet operators and service providers natural gas companies and environmental groups and government organizations.

XXX. Patent Organizations

U.S. Patent and Trademark Office (PTO)
U.S. Patent and Trademark Office
Office of Public Affairs, P. O. Box 1450
Alexandria, VA 22313-1450 US
Phone: 571-272-1000
Fax: 571-273-8300
Toll Free: 800-786-9199
E-mail Address: *usptoinfo@uspto.gov*
Web Address: www.uspto.gov
The U.S. Patent and Trademark Office (PTO) administers patent and trademark laws for the U.S. and enables registration of patents and trademarks.

XXXI. Research & Development, Laboratories

Helmholtz Association
AhrstraBe 45
Bonn, 53175 Germany
Phone: 49 228 30818-0
Fax: 49 228 30818-30
E-mail Address: *org@helmholtz.de*
Web Address: www.helmholtz.de/en
The Helmholtz Association is a community of 16 scientific-technical and biological-medical research centers. Helmholtz Centers perform top-class research in strategic programs in six core fields: energy, earth and environment, health, key technologies, structure of matter, aeronautics, space and transport.

International Motor Vehicle Program (IMVP)
MIT Center for Technology, Policy, and Industrial Development
MIT E40-207, 1 Amherst St.
Cambridge, MA 02139-4307 US
Phone: 617-253-8973
Fax: 617-253-7140
E-mail Address: *ctpidcom@mit.edu*
Web Address: imvp.mit.edu
The International Motor Vehicle Program (IMVP) is a research project, funded by leading global car makers as well as government agencies, focused on enhancing automotive design and manufacturing methods. Through the program, more than 50 senior scientists, management experts, social scientists and engineers have conducted interdisciplinary automotive research at more than 25 universities on six continents. The IMVP is based at the Center for Technology, Policy, and Industrial Development (CTPID) at the Massachusetts Institute of Technology (MIT).

National Research Council Canada (NRC)
NRC Communications & Corp. Rel.
1200 Montreal Rd., Bldg. M-58
Ottawa, ON K1A 0R6 Canada
Phone: 613-993-9101
Fax: 613-952-9907
Toll Free: 877-672-2672
E-mail Address: *info@nrc-cnrc.gc.ca*
Web Address: www.nrc-cnrc.gc.ca
National Research Council Canada (NRC) is a government organization of 20 research institutes that carry out multidisciplinary research with partners in industries and sectors key to Canada's economic development.

Sloan Automotive Laboratory
MIT, 77 Massachusetts Ave.
Rm. 31-153
Cambridge, MA 02139-4307 US
Phone: 617-253-4529
Fax: 617-253-9433
E-mail Address: *kstryker@mit.edu*
Web Address: web.mit.edu/sloan-auto-lab

The Sloan Automotive Laboratory at MIT was founded in 1929 by Professor C.F. Taylor, with a grant from Alfred P. Sloan, Jr., CEO of General Motors, as a major laboratory for automotive research in the US and the world. The goals of the Laboratory are to provide the fundamental knowledge base for automotive engineering and to educate students to become technological leaders in the automotive industry.

XXXII. Rubber Industry Associations

Rubber Association of Canada
2000 Argentia Rd.
Plz. 4, Ste. 250
Mississauga, ON L5N 1W1 Canada
Phone: 905-814-1714
Fax: 905-814-1085
E-mail Address: *info@rubberassociation.ca*
Web Address: www.rubberassociation.ca
The Rubber Association of Canada is the national association of rubber manufacturers and distributors in Canada.

Rubber Manufacturers Association (RMA)
1400 K St. NW, Ste. 900
Washington, DC 20005 US
Phone: 202-682-4800
E-mail Address: *info@rma.org*
Web Address: www.rma.org
The Rubber Manufacturers Association (RMA) is the national trade association for the rubber products industry. Its members include more than 100 companies that manufacture various rubber products, such as tires, hoses, belts, seals, molded goods and other finished rubber products.

XXXIII. Sports Leagues

Indy Racing League (IRL)
4565 W. 16th St.
Indianapolis, IN 46222 US
Phone: 317-492-6526
Web Address: www.indycar.com
Indy Racing League, LLC (IRL) is a subsidiary of Hulman and Co., the owner of the Indianapolis Motor Speedway complex. The Indianapolis 500 is the circuit's premier event.

National Association for Stock Car Auto Racing (NASCAR)
P.O. Box 2875
Daytona Beach, FL 32120 US
Phone: 386-253-0611
E-mail Address: *fanfeedback@NASCAR.COM*
Web Address: www.nascar.com
The National Association for Stock Car Auto Racing (NASCAR) is the organizing body for professional stock car racing.

Singapore Motor Sports Association
20 Maxwell Rd.
10-18 Maxwell House
069113 Singapore
Phone: 65-6227-7889
Fax: 65-6227-0911
E-mail Address: *smsa@pacific.net.sg*
Web Address: www.smsa.org.sg
The Singapore Motor Sports Association is a nonproft organization representing and promoting the motor sports and racing in Singapore.

XXXIV. Technology Transfer Associations

Association of University Technology Managers (AUTM)
111 Deer Lake Rd., Ste. 100
Deerfield, IL 60015 US
Phone: 847-559-0846
Fax: 847-480-9282
E-mail Address: *info@autm.net*
Web Address: www.autm.net
The Association of University Technology Managers (AUTM) is a nonprofit professional association whose members belong to over 350 research institutions, universityies, teaching hospitals, government agencies and corporations from 45 countries. The association's mission is to advance the field of technology transfer, and enhance members' ability to bring academic and nonprofit research to people around the world.

Federal Laboratory Consortium for Technology Transfer
950 North Kings Highway, Ste. 208
Cherry Hill, NJ 08304 US
Phone: 856-667-7727
Fax: 856-667-8009
E-mail Address: *flcmso@federallabs.org*
Web Address: www.federallabs.org
In keeping with the aims of the Federal Technology Transfer Act of 1986 and other related legislation, the Federal Laboratory Consortium (FLC) works to facilitate the sharing of research results and technology developments between federal

laboratories and the mainstream U.S. economy. FLC affiliates include federal laboratories, large and small businesses, academic and research institutions, state and local governments, and various federal agencies. The group has regional support offices and local contacts throughout the U.S.

XXXV. Textile & Fabric Associations

Industrial Fabrics Association International (IAFI)
1801 County Rd. B W
Roseville, MN 55113-4061 US
Phone: 651-222-2508
Fax: 651-225-9334
Toll Free: 800-225-4324
E-mail Address: *generalinfo@ifai.com*
Web Address: www.ifai.com
Industrial Fabrics Association International (IAFI) is a not-for-profit trade association that represents the entire range of the specialty fabrics industry. It has over 2,000 member companies.

XXXVI. Trade Associations-General

BUSINESSEUROPE
168 Ave. de Cortenbergh
Brussels, 1000 Belgium
Phone: 32-0-2-237-65-11
Fax: 32-0-2-231-14-45
E-mail Address: *main@businesseurope.eu*
Web Address: www.businesseurope.eu
BUSINESSEUROPE is a major European trade federation that operates in a manner similar to a chamber of commerce. Its members are the central national business federations of the 34 countries throughout Europe from which they come. Companies cannot become direct members of BUSINESSEUROPE, though there is a support group which offers the opportunity for firms to encourage BUSINESSEUROPE objectives in various ways.

The Associated Chambers of Commerce and Industry of India (ASSOCHAM)
1 Community Ctr. Zamrudpur
Kailash Colony
New Delhi, 110 048 India
Phone: 46550555
Fax: 46536481
E-mail Address: *assocham@nic.in*
Web Address: www.assocham.org
The Associated Chambers of Commerce and Industry of India (ASSOCHAM) has a membership of more than 300 chambers and trade associations and serves members from all over India.

XXXVII. Trade Associations-Global

World Trade Organization (WTO)
Centre William Rappard
Rue de Lausanne 154
Geneva 21, CH-1211 Switzerland
Phone: 41-22-739-51-11
Fax: 41-22-731-42-06
E-mail Address: *enquiries@wto.og*
Web Address: www.wto.org
The World Trade Organization (WTO) is a global organization dealing with the rules of trade between nations. To become a member, nations must agree to abide by certain guidelines. Membership increases a nation's ability to import and export efficiently.

XXXVIII. Transportation Industry Associations

American Association of State Highway and Transportation Officials (AASHTO)
444 N. Capitol St. NW, Ste. 249
Washington, DC 20001 US
Phone: 202-624-5800
Fax: 202-624-5806
E-mail Address: *info@aashto.org*
Web Address: www.transportation.org
The American Association of State Highway and Transportation Officials advocates transportation-related policies and provides technical services to support states in their efforts to efficiently and safely move people and goods. The organization's special interests include Intelligent Transportation Systems (ITS), materials, bridges and structures.

American Highway Users Alliance
1101 14th St. NW, Ste. 750
Washington, DC 20005 US
Phone: 202-857-1200
Fax: 202-857-1220
E-mail Address: *info@highways.org*
Web Address: www.highways.org
The American Highway Users Alliance is a nonprofit advocacy organization serving as a united voice of the transportation community and promoting safe, uncongested highways and enhanced freedom of mobility.

ITS America (Intelligent Transportation Society of America)
1100 17th St. NW, Ste. 1200
Washington, DC 20036 US
Phone: 202-484-4847
Fax: 202-484-3483
Toll Free: 800-374-8472
E-mail Address: *info@itsa.org*
Web Address: www.itsa.org
ITS America (Intelligent Transportation Society of America) is a nonprofit organization made up of members interested in furthering intelligent transportation systems.

XXXIX. Travel-Local Transportation, Bus & Car Rental

American Automobile Association (AAA)
1000 AAA Dr.
Heathrow, FL 32746 US
Phone: 407-444-7000
Fax: 407-444-7380
Web Address: www.aaa.com
The American Automobile Association (AAA) offers members roadside assistance, financial services, car rental, a travel agency and a variety of other services.

XL. U.S. Government Agencies

Bureau of Economic Analysis (BEA)
1441 L St. NW
Washington, DC 20230 US
Phone: 202-606-9900
E-mail Address: *customerservice@bea.gov*
Web Address: www.bea.gov
The Bureau of Economic Analysis (BEA), an agency of the U.S. Department of Commerce, is the nation's economic accountant, preparing estimates that illuminate key national, international and regional aspects of the U.S. economy.

Bureau of Labor Statistics (BLS)
2 Massachusetts Ave. NE
Washington, DC 20212-0001 US
Phone: 202-691-5200
Web Address: stats.bls.gov
The Bureau of Labor Statistics (BLS) is the principal fact-finding agency for the Federal Government in the field of labor economics and statistics. It is an independent national statistical agency that collects, processes, analyzes and disseminates statistical data to the American public, U.S. Congress, other federal agencies, state and local governments, business and labor. The BLS also serves as a statistical resource to the Department of Labor.

National Institute of Standards and Technology (NIST)
100 Bureau Dr., Stop 1070
Gaithersburg, MD 20899-1070 US
Phone: 301-975-6478
E-mail Address: *inquiries@nist.gov*
Web Address: www.nist.gov
The National Institute of Standards and Technology (NIST) is an agency of the U.S. Department of Commerce's Technology Administration. It works with various industries to develop and apply technology, measurements and standards.

Occupational Safety and Health Administration (OSHA)
200 Constitution Ave. NW
Washington, DC 20210 US
Phone: 202-693-1999
Fax: 410-865-2068
Toll Free: 800-321-6742
Web Address: www.osha.gov
The Occupational Safety and Health Administration (OSHA), regulates safety within the workplace. Its web site provides an abundance of information on laws and regulations, safety and health, statistics, compliance assistance and news. OSHA is a unit of the U.S. Department of Labor.

Recalls.gov
E-mail Address: *pmargolies@cpsc.gov*
Web Address: www.recalls.gov
Recalls.gov is a one-stop website where six different U.S. government agencies post announcements about product recalls in consumer products, motor vehicles, boats, food, medicine, cosmetics and environmental products.

U.S. Census Bureau
4600 Silver Hill Rd.
Washington, DC 20233-8800 US
Phone: 301-763-4636
Fax: 301-457-3670
Toll Free: 800-923-8282
E-mail Address: *pio@census.gov*
Web Address: www.census.gov
The U.S. Census Bureau is the official collector of data about the people and economy of the U.S. Founded in 1790, it provides official social, demographic and economic information.

U.S. Department of Commerce (DOC)
1401 Constitution Ave. NW
Washington, DC 20230 US
Phone: 202-482-2000
E-mail Address: *cgutierrez@doc.gov*
Web Address: www.commerce.gov
The U.S. Department of Commerce (DOC) regulates trade and provides valuable economic analysis of the economy.

U.S. Department of Labor (DOL)
Frances Perkins Bldg.
200 Constitution Ave. NW
Washington, DC 20210 US
Toll Free: 866-487-2365
Web Address: www.dol.gov
The U.S. Department of Labor (DOL) is the government agency responsible for labor regulations. This site provides tools to help citizens find out whether companies are complying with family and medical-leave requirements.

U.S. Department of Transportation (DOT)
1200 New Jersey Ave. SE
Washington, DC 20590 US
Phone: 202-366-4000
Toll Free: 866-377-8642
E-mail Address: *dot.comments@dot.gov*
Web Address: www.dot.gov
The U.S. Department of Transportation (DOT) is the Government agency in charge of all aspects of the U.S. transportation system. It has agencies dealing with all aspects of transportation, including highways; hazardous materials transportation; pipelines; railroads; marine transportation; aviation; and public transit systems, such as buses and subways. It also has agencies researching transportation statistics, new transportation technologies and even the eventual impact of environmental change on transportation. The DOT web site has links to citizen traveler resources as well as resources for transportation businesses and mainly transportation-related government grants.

U.S. Department of Transportation (US DOT)-Intelligent Transportation Systems (ITS)
U.S. Department of Transportation (US DOT)
1200 New Jersey Ave. SE
Washington, DC 20590 US
Toll Free: 866-367-7487
E-mail Address: *itshelp@fhwa.dot.gov*
Web Address: www.its.dot.gov
The U.S. Department of Transportation's (US DOT) Intelligent Transportation System (ITS) program is based on the creation of an intelligent transportation system through the integration of intelligent vehicles and an intelligent infrastructure. The Federal ITS program supports the overall advancement of ITS through investments in major initiatives, exploratory studies and a crosscutting core program.

U.S. Environmental Protection Agency (EPA) On-road Vehicles and Engines
Office of Transportation and Air Quality (6401A)
1200 Pennsylvania Ave. NW
Washington, DC 20460 US
Phone: 202-564-1682
E-mail Address: *otaqpublicweb@epa.gov*
Web Address: www.epa.gov/otaq/hwy.htm
The U.S. Environmental Protection Agency (EPA) On-road Vehicles and Engines site, part of the EPA's Office of Transportation and Air Quality (OTAQ), provides details about the best and worst cars and trucks in terms of exhaust emissions. Its web site allows people to instantly check the emission rating of any vehicle. The site also contains information about industry emission trends and goals.

U.S. Securities and Exchange Commission (SEC)
100 F St. NE
Washington, DC 20549 US
Phone: 202-551-6000
Toll Free: 888-732-6585
E-mail Address: *publicinfo@sec.gov*
Web Address: www.sec.gov
The U.S. Securities and Exchange Commission (SEC) is a nonpartisan, quasi-judicial regulatory agency responsible for administering federal securities laws. These laws are designed to protect investors in securities markets and ensure that they have access to disclosure of all material information concerning publicly traded securities. Visitors to the web site can access the EDGAR database of corporate financial and business information.

U.S. Trade Representative (USTR)
600 17th St. NW
Washington, DC 20508 US
Phone: 202-395-7360
E-mail Address: *contactustr@ustr.eop.gov*
Web Address: www.ustr.gov
The U.S. Trade Representative (USTR) is the nation's chief trade negotiator and the principal trade policy advisor to the President.

Chapter 4

THE AUTOMOBILE 400: WHO THEY ARE AND HOW THEY WERE CHOSEN

Includes Indexes by Company Name, Industry & Location, And a Complete Table of Sales, Profits and Ranks

The companies chosen to be listed in PLUNKETT'S AUTOMOBILE INDUSTRY ALMANAC comprise a unique list. THE AUTOMOBILE 400 (the actual count is 406 companies) were chosen specifically for their dominance in the many facets of the automotive industry in which they operate. Complete information about each firm can be found in the "Individual Profiles," beginning at the end of this chapter. These profiles are in alphabetical order by company name.

THE AUTOMOBILE 400 includes leading companies from all parts of the United States as well as many other nations, and from all automobile and related industry segments: manufacturers; dealerships; financial services; and many others, including makers of trucks and specialty vehicles.

Simply stated, the list contains 406 of the largest, most successful, fastest growing firms in the automotive and related industries in the world. To be included in our list, the firms had to meet the following criteria:

1) Generally, these are corporations based in the U.S., however, the headquarters of 158 firms are located in other nations.
2) Prominence, or a significant presence, in automotive and supporting fields. (See the following Industry Codes section for a complete list of types of businesses that are covered).
3) The companies in THE AUTOMOBILE 400 do not have to be exclusively in the automotive field.
4) Financial data and vital statistics must have been available to the editors of this book, either directly from the company being written about or from outside sources deemed reliable and accurate by the editors. A small number of companies that we would like to have included are not listed because of a lack of sufficient, objective data.

INDEXES TO THE AUTOMOBILE 400, AS FOUND IN THIS CHAPTER AND IN THE BACK OF THE BOOK:

INDUSTRY LIST, WITH CODES

This book refers to the following list of unique industry codes, based on the 2007 NAIC code system (NAIC is used by many analysts as a replacement for older SIC codes because NAIC is more specific to today's industry sectors, see www.census.gov/NAICS). Companies profiled in this book are given a primary NAIC code, reflecting the main line of business of each firm.

Automotive

Automotive Manufacturing

33611 Automobiles, Manufacturing
336120 Trucks, RVs & Misc. Automotive, Manufacturing
336211 Motor Vehicle Body Manufacturing
3363 Automobile Parts Manufacturing
336350 Automobile Transmission & Power Train Parts Manufacturing

Toys, Sporting Goods & Miscellaneous Manufacturing

336991 Motorcycle, Bicycle, & Parts Manufacturing
336999 Snowmobile Manufacturing

Automotive Distribution

42311 Automobiles, Distribution
423120 Automobile Parts, Wholesale Distribution
441120 Automobile, Used Car Distribution

Automotive Services

5321 Automobile, Rental/Leasing
8111 Automotive Repair & Maintenance
811191 Automotive Oil Change & Lubrication Shops

Entertainment

Broadcasting

515210A Radio Broadcasting via Satellite

Financial Services

Banking, Credit & Finance

522220 Financing--Business

Stocks & Investments

523910 Venture Capital/Private Equity Investments

Insurance

524126 Insurance--Property & Casualty, Specialty, Surety

Health Care

Health Products, Manufacturing

33911 Medical/Dental/Surgical Equipment & Supplies, Manufacturing

InfoTech

Computers & Electronics Manufacturing

334310 Audio & Video Equipment, Consumer Electronics

Software

511210N Computer Software, Product Lifecycle, Engineering, Design & CAD

Internet

519130 Internet Publishing & Web Search Portals

Manufacturing

Chemicals

325 Chemicals, Manufacturing
325510 Paints & Coatings, Manufacturing

Plastics & Rubber

3261 Plastic Products, Manufacturing
3262 Rubber Products & Tires Manufacturing

Ceramics

32712 Ceramic Materials, Fibers and Substrates

Nonmetallic Minerals/Rock/Aggregate

3272 Glass, Manufacturing

Fabricated Metals

332311 Prefabricated Metal Building & Component Manufacturing

Machinery & Manufacturing Equipment

333 Machinery, Manufacturing
3334 Ventilation, Heating & Air-Conditioning Manufacturing

Electrical Equipment, Appliances, Tools

335 Electrical Equipment, Manufacturing
335313 Electrical Switches, Sensors, Microelectronics, Optomechanicals

Manufacturing, Electrical

33591 Battery Manufacturing

Retailing

	Automobiles & Parts Stores
441110	Auto Dealers, Retail
441310	Auto Parts Stores
441320	Tire Stores
	Miscellaneous Retailers
453998	Auctions

Services

	Consulting & Professional Services
541810E	Advertising/Marketing--Online
541910	Market Research
	Management
55111	Management of Companies & Enterprises

Telecommunications

	Telecommunications Equipment
334220	Radio & Wireless Communication, Manufacturing
334290	Security, Detection & Intercom System Manufacturing

Transportation

	Transportation-Manufacturing of Equipment
336214	Travel Trailer & Camper Manufacturing
	Aerospace
33641	Aerospace & Aircraft Related Manufacturing
	Truck
4842	Truck Transportation-Specialized
532120	Trucks, Rental/Leasing

Wholesale Distribution-Other

	Distribution-Durable Goods
4246	Chemicals & Plastics, Distribution

INDEX OF RANKINGS WITHIN INDUSTRY GROUPS

Company	Industry Code	2009 Sales (U.S. $ thousands)	Sales Rank	2009 Profits (U.S. $ thousands)	Profits Rank
Advertising/Marketing--Online					
COBALT GROUP	541810E				
Aerospace & Aircraft Related Manufacturing					
SEQUA CORP	33641				
Auctions					
KAR AUCTION SERVICES INC	453998	1,729,600	1	23,200	1
Audio & Video Equipment, Consumer Electronics					
CLARION CO LTD	334310	1,936,540	1	-213,190	1
Auto Dealers, Retail					
AMERICA'S CAR-MART INC	441110	298,966	10	17,903	7
ANCIRA ENTERPRISES	441110				
ASBURY AUTOMOTIVE GROUP	441110	3,650,600	7	13,400	8
AUTONATION INC	441110	10,757,800	1	198,000	1
BOB ROHRMAN AUTO GROUP	441110				
BRAMAN MANAGEMENT ASSOCIATION	441110				
BROWN AUTOMOTIVE GROUP	441110				
BURT AUTOMOTIVE NETWORK	441110				
CARMAX GROUP	441110	6,974,000	4	59,200	4
CHAPMAN AUTOMOTIVE GROUP	441110				
CONTINENTAL MOTORS GROUP	441110				
DARCARS AUTOMOTIVE GROUP	441110				
DAVID MCDAVID AUTO GROUP	441110				
DAVID WILSON'S AUTOMOTIVE GROUP	441110				
DRIVETIME AUTOMOTIVE GROUP INC	441110				
EARNHARDT'S AUTO CENTERS	441110				
EDARAN OTOMOBIL NASIONAL BERHAD	441110				
ELDER AUTOMOTIVE GROUP	441110				
FAULKNER ORGANIZATION	441110				
FLETCHER JONES MANAGEMENT GROUP INC	441110				
GALPIN MOTORS INC	441110				
GROUP 1 AUTOMOTIVE INC	441110	4,525,707	6	34,845	5
HENDRICK AUTOMOTIVE GROUP	441110				
HERB CHAMBERS COMPANIES	441110				
HOLMAN ENTERPRISES	441110				
HOMETOWN AUTO RETAILERS	441110				
INCHCAPE PLC	441110	8,660,540	3	147,350	2
JIM KOONS AUTOMOTIVE COMPANIES INC	441110				
JORDAN AUTOMOTIVE GROUP	441110				
KELLEY AUTOMOTIVE GROUP	441110				
LARRY H MILLER GROUP	441110				
LITHIA MOTORS INC	441110	1,749,315	8	9,151	9
LUPIENT AUTOMOTIVE GROUP	441110				
MAJOR AUTOMOTIVE COMPANIES INC	441110				
MORSE OPERATIONS INC	441110				
OURISMAN AUTOMOTIVE ENTERPRISES	441110				

Company	Industry Code	2009 Sales (U.S. $ thousands)	Sales Rank	2009 Profits (U.S. $ thousands)	Profits Rank
PENSKE AUTOMOTIVE GROUP	441110	9,523,105	2	76,920	3
PHIL LONG DEALERSHIPS INC	441110				
POTAMKIN AUTOMOTIVE GROUP	441110				
RICART AUTOMOTIVE INC	441110				
RIZZA AUTOMOTIVE GROUP	441110				
ROSENTHAL AUTOMOTIVE ORGANIZATION	441110				
RUSH ENTERPRISES INC	441110	1,239,289	9	5,884	10
RUSS DARROW GROUP INC	441110				
RYBROOK HOLDINGS LIMITED	441110				
RYGOR GROUP LTD	441110				
SAM SWOPE AUTO GROUP INC	441110				
SANSONE AUTO NETWORK	441110				
SANTA MONICA FORD LINCOLN MERCURY	441110				
SHEEHY AUTO STORES	441110				
SONIC AUTOMOTIVE INC	441110	6,131,709	5	31,548	6
SPITZER MANAGEMENT INC	441110				
SYTNER GROUP PLC	441110				
TORESCO ENTERPRISES INC	441110				
TUTTLE-CLICK AUTOMOTIVE GROUP	441110				
VOLVO CARS OF NORTH AMERICA INC	441110				
Auto Parts Stores					
ADVANCE AUTO PARTS INC	441310	5,412,623	3	270,373	4
AUTOZONE INC	441310	6,816,824	2	657,049	1
CARQUEST CORP	441310				
GENUINE PARTS COMPANY	441310	10,057,512	1	399,575	2
O'REILLY AUTOMOTIVE INC	441310	4,847,062	4	307,498	3
PEP BOYS-MANNY MOE & JACK	441310	1,927,788	5	-30,429	5
Automobile Parts Manufacturing					
ABC GROUP	3363				
AGS AUTOMOTIVE SYSTEMS	3363				
AISAN INDUSTRY CO LTD	3363	1,614,405	35	-58,261	41
AISIN SEIKI CO LTD	3363	24,557,400	4	-278,890	52
ALPS AUTOMOTIVE INC	3363				
AMERICAN AXLE & MANUFACTURING HOLDINGS	3363	1,521,600	37	-253,100	51
AMERIGON INC	3363	60,925	60	284	29
APPLIED INDUSTRIAL TECHNOLOGIES INC	3363	1,923,148	31	42,260	15
ARVINMERITOR INC	3363	4,108,000	25	-1,212,000	59
AUTOCAM CORPORATION	3363				
AUTOLIV INC	3363	5,121,000	21	10,000	25
BENTELER GROUP	3363	5,822,710	16		
BORGWARNER BERU SYSTEMS GMBH	3363				
BREMBO SPA	3363	1,067,450	39	13,400	22
CALSONIC KANSEI CORP	3363				
CARLISLE COMPANIES INC	3363	2,379,500	29	144,600	7
CLARCOR INC	3363	907,700	43	71,500	10
COMMERCIAL VEHICLE GROUP INC (CVG)	3363	458,569	50	-81,535	45
COMPAGNIE PLASTIC OMNIUM	3363	3,106,200	27	35,250	17

Company	Industry Code	2009 Sales (U.S. $ thousands)	Sales Rank	2009 Profits (U.S. $ thousands)	Profits Rank
CUMMINS FILTRATION	3363				
CUMMINS INC	3363	10,800,000	11	428,000	4
DANA HOLDINGS CORP	3363	5,228,000	20	-436,000	55
DELPHI CORP	3363	11,755,000	8	9,344,000	1
DENSO CORPORATION	3363	34,011,700	2	-910,020	58
DORMAN PRODUCTS INC	3363	377,378	55	26,495	19
EAGLE OTTAWA LEATHER CO	3363				
EAGLEPICHER CORPORATION	3363				
EAST PENN MANUFACTURING	3363				
EATON CORP	3363	11,873,000	7	383,000	5
EDELBROCK CORPORATION	3363				
FAURECIA SA	3363	11,391,600	10	-511,580	57
FEDERAL MOGUL CORP	3363	5,330,000	19	-45,000	38
FEDERAL SIGNAL CORP	3363	752,500	44	17,700	20
FISHER & COMPANY INC	3363				
FUEL SYSTEMS SOLUTIONS	3363	452,325	51	49,841	13
GENTEX CORPORATION	3363	544,523	47	64,637	11
GEORG FISCHER LTD	3363	2,735,600	28	-230,860	50
GKN PLC	3363	6,491,720	15	-55,340	40
GT TECHNOLOGIES INC	3363				
HAYES LEMMERZ INTERNATIONAL INC	3363	1,848,400	34	-371,700	54
HELLA KGAA HUECK & CO	3363				
HILITE INTERNATIONAL INC	3363				
HYUNDAI MOBIS CO LTD	3363	14,421,900	6	1,311,850	2
INERGY AUTOMOTIVE	3363				
JASON INC	3363				
JOHNSON CONTROLS INC	3363	28,497,000	3	-338,000	53
KEY PLASTICS LLC	3363				
KEY SAFETY SYSTEMS INC	3363				
KOITO MANUFACTURING CO	3363	4,438,340	24	44,820	14
KOLBENSCHMIDT PIERBURG	3363				
LACKS ENTERPRISES INC	3363				
LEAR CORP	3363	9,739,600	13	826,700	3
LINAMAR CORP	3363	1,607,870	36	-45,000	39
LKQ CORP	3363	2,047,942	30	127,521	9
LUND INTERNATIONAL INC	3363				
MAGNA INTERNATIONAL INC	3363	17,367,000	5	-493,000	56
MAGNA MIRRORS	3363				
MAGNETI MARELLI HOLDING	3363	5,706,220	18	31,700	18
MCLAREN PERFORMANCE TECHNOLOGIES	3363				
METALDYNE LLC	3363				
MILLER INDUSTRIES INC	3363	237,567	57	6,016	26
MODINE MANUFACTURING CO	3363	1,408,714	38	-108,612	47
MONTUPET SA	3363	260,330	56	-20,540	33
MOTORCAR PARTS OF AMERICA INC	3363	134,866	58	3,857	27
NEWCOR INC	3363				
NIHON PLAST CO LTD	3363	984,940	41	-37,550	37
NIPPON PISTON RING CO LTD	3363	531,610	48	-58,340	42

Company	Industry Code	2009 Sales (U.S. $ thousands)	Sales Rank	2009 Profits (U.S. $ thousands)	Profits Rank
NYX INC	3363				
ORBITAL CORPORATION LTD	3363	18,871	61	-2,250	30
PETERSON MANUFACTURING	3363				
REMY INTERNATIONAL INC	3363	910,745	42	14,060	21
RHEINMETALL AG	3363	4,661,110	22	-78,910	44
RIETER HOLDING LTD	3363	1,860,310	33	-220,660	49
ROBERT BOSCH GMBH	3363	50,929,800	1	-1,596,980	60
SANLUIS CORPORACION SAB DE CV	3363	415,900	54	-28,790	35
SOGEFI SPA	3363	997,990	40	-9,710	32
SPARTAN MOTORS INC	3363	429,926	52	11,772	24
SPECIAL DEVICES INC	3363				
SPECTRA PREMIUM INDUSTRIES INC	3363				
STANADYNE CORPORATION	3363				
STANDARD MOTOR PRODUCTS	3363	735,424	45	3,483	28
STONERIDGE INC	3363	475,152	49	-32,326	36
STRATTEC SECURITY CORP	3363	126,097	59	-6,122	31
SUPERIOR INDUSTRIES INTERNATIONAL INC	3363	418,846	53	-94,142	46
TELEFLEX INC	3363	1,890,062	32	302,994	6
TENNECO INC	3363	4,649,000	23	-73,000	43
TITAN INTERNATIONAL INC	3363	727,599	46	-24,645	34
TOKAI RIKA CO LTD	3363	3,741,760	26	11,790	23
TOWER AUTOMOTIVE LLC	3363				
TOYODA GOSEI CO LTD	3363	5,798,730	17	41,930	16
TRW AUTOMOTIVE HOLDINGS	3363	11,614,000	9	55,000	12
UNIPART GROUP OF COMPANIES	3363				
VALEO	3363	10,188,400	12	-207,870	48
VISTA PRO AUTOMOTIVE LLC	3363				
VISTEON CORPORATION	3363	6,685,000	14	128,000	8
WANXIANG AMERICA CORP	3363				
WANXIANG GROUP CORP	3363				
WESCAST INDUSTRIES INC	3363				
YAZAKI NORTH AMERICA INC	3363				
Automobile Parts, Wholesale Distribution					
AMERICAN TIRE DISTRIBUTORS	423120				
COAST DISTRIBUTION SYSTEM	423120	103,201	2	99	2
HAHN AUTOMOTIVE WAREHOUSE INC	423120				
KEYSTONE AUTOMOTIVE INDUSTRIES INC	423120				
UNI-SELECT INC	423120	1,339,730	1	36,680	1
Automobile Transmission & Power Train Parts Manufacturing					
ATC TECHNOLOGY CORP	336350	485,017	3	11,707	2
BORGWARNER INC	336350	3,961,800	2	27,000	1
JL FRENCH AUTOMOTIVE CASTINGS	336350				
STACKPOLE LIMITED CO	336350				
TI AUTOMOTIVE	336350				
ZF FRIEDRICHSHAFEN AG	336350	12,006,700	1	-539,410	3
Automobile, Rental/Leasing					
ADA	5321				

Company	Industry Code	2009 Sales (U.S. $ thousands)	Sales Rank	2009 Profits (U.S. $ thousands)	Profits Rank
AVIS EUROPE PLC	5321	1,771,060	4	250	3
DOLLAR THRIFTY AUTOMOTIVE GROUP INC	5321	1,546,249	5	45,022	1
DONLEN CORPORATION	5321				
ENTERPRISE HOLDINGS	5321	13,000,000	1		
HERTZ GLOBAL HOLDINGS INC	5321	7,101,500	2	-111,300	4
RENT-A-WRECK OF AMERICA	5321				
SIXT AKTIENGESELLSCHAFT	5321	2,032,500	3	13,200	2
ZIPCAR INC	5321				
Automobile, Used Car Distribution					
ADESA INC	441120	1,120,000	1		
COPART INC	441120	743,082	2	141,103	1
Automobiles, Distribution					
BEIJING AUTOMOTIVE IMPORT & EXPORT CORP	42311				
GULF STATES TOYOTA INC	42311				
JM FAMILY ENTERPRISES	42311				
SUZUKI AUTOMOBILE (THAILAND) CO LTD	42311				
Automobiles, Manufacturing					
ADAM OPEL AG	33611				
AMERICAN HONDA MOTOR CO	33611				
ASC INCORPORATED	33611				
ASTON MARTIN LAGONDA LTD	33611				
AUDI AG	33611				
AUDI OF AMERICA INC	33611				
AUTOALLIANCE INTERNATIONAL	33611				
AUTOMOBILI LAMBORGHINI HOLDING SPA	33611				
AVTOVAZ OAO	33611				
BENTLEY MOTORS	33611				
BETTER PLACE	33611				
BMW (BAYERISCHE MOTOREN WERKE AG)	33611	69,238,500	9	286,790	12
BMW MANUFACTURING CORP	33611				
BMW OF NORTH AMERICA LLC	33611				
BRILLIANCE CHINA AUTOMOTIVE HOLDINGS LTD	33611	903,200	31	-240,860	21
BYD COMPANY LIMITED	33611	5,774,200	25	554,990	7
CAMI AUTOMOTIVE INC	33611				
CHANGAN AUTOMOBILE GROUP	33611	3,702,070	27	158,420	15
CHRYSLER CANADA INC	33611				
CHRYSLER GROUP LLC	33611				
CODA AUTOMOTIVE INC	33611				
DAIHATSU MOTOR CO LTD	33611	17,867,800	17	241,770	14
DAIMLER AG	33611	107,755,000	3	-3,609,850	30
DONGFENG MOTOR CORP	33611				
FERRARI SPA	33611				
FIAT SPA	33611	67,624,200	10	-1,131,070	27
FIRST AUTOMOTIVE GROUP	33611				
FISKER AUTOMOTIVE	33611				
FORD MOTOR CO	33611	105,893,000	4	2,717,000	2

Company	Industry Code	2009 Sales (U.S. $ thousands)	Sales Rank	2009 Profits (U.S. $ thousands)	Profits Rank
FORD MOTOR COMPANY OF CANADA	33611				
FUJI HEAVY INDUSTRIES LTD (SUBARU)	33611	15,647,200	18	-756,860	26
GAZ GROUP	33611				
GENERAL MOTORS CO (GM)	33611	104,589,000	5	104,690,000	1
GENERAL MOTORS OF CANADA	33611				
GM DAEWOO AUTO AND TECHNOLOGY CO	33611				
GM HOLDEN LTD	33611				
GROUP LOTUS PLC	33611				
HONDA MOTOR CO LTD	33611	101,916,000	6	1,395,000	5
HONDA OF AMERICA MFG INC	33611				
HYUNDAI MOTOR AMERICA	33611				
HYUNDAI MOTOR COMPANY	33611	81,951,000	8	2,664,240	3
ISUZU MOTORS AMERICA INC	33611				
ISUZU MOTORS LTD	33611	15,419,000	19	-290,670	22
JAGUAR CARS LTD	33611				
JARDINE CYCLE AND CARRIAGE	33611	10,640,400	21	502,800	9
KIA MOTORS CORPORATION	33611	26,430,100	15	879,130	6
KOENIGSEGG AUTOMOTIVE AB	33611				
LAND ROVER	33611				
MAHINDRA & MAHINDRA LTD	33611	5,787,960	24	302,170	10
MARUTI SUZUKI INDIA LIMITED	33611	4,392,010	26	260,900	13
MAYBACH	33611				
MAZDA MOTOR CORPORATION	33611	27,445,000	14	-513,950	24
MAZDA NORTH AMERICAN OPERATIONS	33611				
MERCEDES-BENZ USA LLC	33611				
MITSUBISHI MOTORS (THAILAND) CO LTD	33611				
MITSUBISHI MOTORS CORP	33611	21,359,100	16	-593,980	25
MORGAN MOTOR COMPANY	33611				
NISSAN MOTOR CO LTD	33611	89,102,300	7	-2,469,180	29
NISSAN NORTH AMERICA INC	33611				
ORION BUS INDUSTRIES	33611				
PACCAR INC	33611	8,086,500	22	111,900	16
PININFARINA SPA	33611	237,130	33	-38,930	18
PORSCHE AUTOMOBIL HOLDING SE	33611	7,765,930	23	-5,594,549	33
PROTON HOLDINGS BERHAD	33611	1,836,660	28	-85,450	19
PSA PEUGEOT CITROEN SA	33611	64,595,500	11	-1,889,160	28
PT ASTRA INTERNATIONAL TBK	33611				
RENAULT SA	33611	45,865,500	12	-4,251,590	31
ROLLS ROYCE MOTOR CAR LTD	33611				
SAAB AUTOMOBILE AB	33611				
SAAB CARS NORTH AMERICA	33611				
SAIC-GM-WULING AUTOMOBILE	33611				
SALEEN PERFORMANCE VEHICLES	33611				
SEAT SA	33611				
SHANGHAI AUTOMOTIVE INDUSTRY CORP (SAIC)	33611				
SKODA AUTO AS	33611				
SMART GMBH	33611				

Company	Industry Code	2009 Sales (U.S. $ thousands)	Sales Rank	2009 Profits (U.S. $ thousands)	Profits Rank
SSANGYONG MOTOR CO	33611	906,540	30	-292,730	23
SUZUKI MOTOR CORPORATION	33611	32,281,200	13	294,670	11
TATA MOTORS LIMITED	33611	14,455,320	20	510,500	8
TESLA MOTORS INC	33611				
TOYOTA MOTOR CORPORATION	33611	220,547,000	1	-4,693,960	32
TOYOTA MOTOR THAILAND CO	33611				
VAUXHALL MOTORS LTD	33611				
VOLKSWAGEN AG	33611	143,666,000	2	2,533,280	4
VOLKSWAGEN GROUP OF AMERICA INC	33611				
VOLVO CAR CORPORATION	33611				
WABASH NATIONAL CORP	33611	337,840	32	-101,765	20
YULON MOTOR CO LTD	33611	1,525,110	29	35,220	17
ZHEJIANG GEELY HOLDING GROUP	33611				
Automotive Oil Change & Lubrication Shops					
LUCOR INC	811191				
Automotive Repair & Maintenance					
AAMCO TRANSMISSIONS INC	8111				
CALIBER HOLDINGS CORP	8111				
MAACO ENTERPRISES INC	8111				
MIDAS INC	8111	182,800	2	2,600	2
MONRO MUFFLER BRAKE INC	8111	476,106	1	24,088	1
STERLING AUTOBODY CENTERS	8111				
ZIEBART INTERNATIONAL CORP	8111				
Battery Manufacturing					
A123SYSTEMS	33591	91,049	1	-86,589	3
AUTOMOTIVE ENERGY SUPPLY CORPORATION (AESC)	33591				
ENER1 INC	33591	34,800	3	-51,004	2
INTERSTATE BATTERY SYSTEM OF AMERICA	33591				
PRIMEARTH EV ENERGY CO	33591				
YUASA BATTERY (THAILAND)	33591	45,930	2	1,410	1
Ceramics Manufacturing					
CERADYNE	32712	400,575	1	8,515	1
GUARDIAN INDUSTRIES CORP	32712				
Chemicals & Plastics, Distribution					
FINISHMASTER INC	4246	421,391	1	10,946	1
Chemicals, Manufacturing					
E I DU PONT DE NEMOURS & CO (DUPONT)	325	26,109,000	1	1,755,000	1
Computer Software, Product Lifecycle, Engineering, Design & CAD					
NAVTEQ CORPORATION	511210N				
Electrical Equipment, Manufacturing					
SIEMENS AG	335	113,842,000	1	3,404,080	1
Electrical Switches, Sensors, Microelectronics, Optomechanicals					
ALPS ELECTRIC CO LTD	335313	5,790,360	1	-752,690	1
Financing--Business					
ALLY FINANCIAL INC	522220				
CHRYSLER FINANCIAL SERVICES LLC	522220				

Company	Industry Code	2009 Sales (U.S. $ thousands)	Sales Rank	2009 Profits (U.S. $ thousands)	Profits Rank
CONSUMER PORTFOLIO SERVICES INC	522220	223,895	4	-57,207	3
CREDIT ACCEPTANCE CORP	522220	380,664	3	146,255	2
DAIMLER FINANCIAL SERVICES	522220				
DAIMLER FINANCIAL SERVICES AMERICAS LLC	522220				
FIRST INVESTORS FINANCIAL SERVICES GROUP INC	522220				
FORD MOTOR CREDIT CO LLC	522220	12,541,000	1	1,279,000	1
TOYOTA MOTOR CREDIT CORP	522220	8,800,000	2	-623,000	4
Glass, Manufacturing					
ASAHI GLASS COMPANY LTD	3272	13,569,900	1	236,190	1
PILKINGTON PLC	3272				
Insurance--Property & Casualty, Specialty, Surety					
ALLSTATE CORPORATION	524126	32,013,000	2	854,000	2
GEICO CORPORATION	524126				
GMAC INSURANCE HOLDINGS	524126				
PROGRESSIVE CORPORATION	524126	14,563,600	3	1,057,500	1
STATE FARM INSURANCE COMPANIES	524126	32,064,000	1	570,000	3
Internet Publishing & Web Search Portals					
AUTOBYTEL INC	519130	52,918	2	-2,377	2
INTERNET BRANDS INC	519130	99,756	1	12,388	1
Machinery, Manufacturing					
ATS AUTOMATION TOOLING SYSTEMS INC	333	794,820	6	44,620	4
CATERPILLAR INC	333	32,396,000	1	895,000	1
DEERE & CO	333	23,112,400	2	873,500	2
DEUTZ AG	333	1,096,540	5	-157,480	6
KAWASAKI HEAVY INDUSTRIES	333	14,380,400	3	125,980	3
PARK-OHIO HOLDINGS CORP	333	701,047	7	-5,209	5
TEREX CORPORATION	333	4,043,100	4	-398,400	7
Management of Companies & Enterprises					
TATA GROUP	55111	70,900,000	1		
Market Research					
JD POWER & ASSOCIATES	541910				
Medical/Dental/Surgical Equipment & Supplies, Manufacturing					
3M COMPANY	33911	23,123,000	1	3,193,000	1
Motor Vehicle Body Manufacturing					
ACCURIDE CORPORATION	336211	570,193	4	-140,112	5
JB POINDEXTER & CO INC	336211				
KANTO AUTO WORKS LTD	336211	6,615,180	2	3,810	2
NISSAN SHATAI CO LTD	336211	4,915,900	3	108,510	1
SUPREME INDUSTRIES INC	336211	192,036	5	-8,743	3
TOYOTA AUTO BODY CO LTD	336211	19,586,700	1	-12,950	4
Motorcycle, Bicycle, & Parts Manufacturing					
BAJAJ AUTO LTD	336991	1,927,840	4	115,910	2
DUCATI MOTOR HOLDING SPA	336991				
HARLEY-DAVIDSON INC	336991	4,781,909	2	-55,116	6
HERO HONDA MOTORS LTD	336991	2,627,750	3	273,410	1
LDI LTD	336991				

Company	Industry Code	2009 Sales (U.S. $ thousands)	Sales Rank	2009 Profits (U.S. $ thousands)	Profits Rank
PIAGGIO & C SPA	336991	1,885,460	5	58,330	3
S&T MOTORS CO LTD	336991				
SEGWAY LLC	336991				
STELLICAN LTD	336991				
YAMAHA MOTOR CO LTD	336991	17,841,400	1	20,590	4
ZAP	336991	4,068	6	-10,687	5
Paints & Coatings, Manufacturing					
PPG INDUSTRIES INC	325510	12,239,000	1	336,000	1
Plastic Products, Manufacturing					
SRG GLOBAL INC	3261				
TRELLEBORG AB	3261	3,585,020	1	54,190	1
Prefabricated Metal Building & Component Manufacturing					
SKYLINE CORPORATION	332311	166,676	1	-15,434	1
Radio & Wireless Communication, Manufacturing					
ATX GROUP INC	334220				
ONSTAR CORPORATION	334220				
Radio Broadcasting via Satellite					
SIRIUS XM RADIO INC	515210A	2,472,638	1	-342,790	1
Rubber Products & Tires Manufacturing					
BRIDGESTONE BANDAG LLC	3262				
BRIDGESTONE CORPORATION	3262	29,052,100	1	11,670	5
COMPAGNIE GENERALE DES ETABLISSEMENTS MICHELIN	3262	18,288,900	3	130,930	2
CONTINENTAL AG	3262	24,816,600	2	-2,036,630	10
COOPER TIRE & RUBBER CO	3262	2,932,575	8	119,570	3
GOODYEAR TIRE & RUBBER CO	3262	16,301,000	4	-375,000	8
HANKOOK TIRE CO LTD	3262	4,306,490	6	286,410	1
INOUE RUBBER (THAILAND) PCL	3262	144,220	10	8,280	6
KUMHO TIRE CO LTD	3262	1,547,590	9	-633,970	9
MARANGONI SPA	3262				
PIRELLI & C SPA	3262	5,622,600	5	28,480	4
TOYO TIRE & RUBBER CO LTD	3262	3,485,000	7	-113,790	7
Security, Detection & Intercom System Manufacturing					
DEI HOLDINGS INC	334290				
LOJACK CORPORTATION	334290	135,013	1	-35,282	1
Snowmobile Manufacturing					
ARCTIC CAT INC	336999	563,613	2	-9,508	2
POLARIS INDUSTRIES INC	336999	1,565,887	1	101,017	1
Tire Stores					
CANADIAN TIRE CORP LTD	441320	8,262,940	1	318,670	1
DISCOUNT TIRE CO	441320				
LES SCHWAB TIRE CENTERS	441320				
TBC CORPORATION	441320				
TREADWAYS CORP	441320				
Travel Trailer & Camper Manufacturing					
GREAT DANE LIMITED PARTNERSHIP	336214				
THOR INDUSTRIES INC	336214	1,521,896	1	17,143	1

Company	Industry Code	2009 Sales (U.S. $ thousands)	Sales Rank	2009 Profits (U.S. $ thousands)	Profits Rank
Truck Transportation-Specialized					
ALLIED SYSTEMS HOLDINGS	4842				
Trucks, Rental/Leasing					
AMERCO	532120	1,992,266	1	13,410	1
PENSKE CORPORATION	532120				
Trucks, RVs & Misc. Automotive, Manufacturing					
AB VOLVO	336120	28,777,400	1	-1,939,660	6
ALL AMERICAN GROUP	336120	60,623	6	-4,730	2
AM GENERAL LLC	336120				
BLUE BIRD CORPORATION	336120				
COLLINS INDUSTRIES INC	336120				
DAIMLER TRUCKS NORTH AMERICA LLC	336120				
GULF STREAM COACH INC	336120				
HINO MOTOR SALES (THAILAND)	336120				
HINO MOTORS LTD	336120	11,574,600	2	-669,260	4
JAYCO INC	336120				
MACK TRUCKS INC	336120				
MITSUBISHI FUSO TRUCK OF AMERICA INC	336120				
MOTOR COACH INDUSTRIES INTERNATIONAL	336120				
NAVISTAR INC	336120				
NAVISTAR INTERNATIONAL	336120	11,569,000	3	320,000	1
NEWMAR CORP	336120				
NISSAN DIESEL (THAILAND) CO	336120				
OSHKOSH CORPORATION	336120	5,295,200	4	-1,098,800	5
REXHALL INDUSTRIES INC	336120				
SCANIA AB	336120				
TRI PETCH ISUZU SALES CO	336120				
UD TRUCKS CORP	336120				
UTILIMASTER CORP	336120				
UTILITY TRAILER MANUFACTURING CO	336120				
WINNEBAGO INDUSTRIES INC	336120	211,519	5	-78,766	3
Ventilation, Heating & Air-Conditioning Manufacturing					
INGERSOLL-RAND PLC	3334	13,195,300	1	462,900	1
Venture Capital/Private Equity Investments					
CERBERUS CAPITAL MANAGEMENT LP	523910				

ALPHABETICAL INDEX

DAVID MCDAVID AUTO GROUP
DAVID WILSON'S AUTOMOTIVE GROUP
DEERE & CO
DEI HOLDINGS INC
DELPHI CORP
DENSO CORPORATION
DEUTZ AG
DISCOUNT TIRE CO
DOLLAR THRIFTY AUTOMOTIVE GROUP INC
DONGFENG MOTOR CORPORATION
DONLEN CORPORATION
DORMAN PRODUCTS INC
DRIVETIME AUTOMOTIVE GROUP INC
DUCATI MOTOR HOLDING SPA
E I DU PONT DE NEMOURS & CO (DUPONT)
EAGLE OTTAWA LEATHER COMPANY LLC
EAGLEPICHER CORPORATION
EARNHARDT'S AUTO CENTERS
EAST PENN MANUFACTURING CO INC
EATON CORP
EDARAN OTOMOBIL NASIONAL BERHAD
EDELBROCK CORPORATION
ELDER AUTOMOTIVE GROUP
ENER1 INC
ENTERPRISE HOLDINGS
FAULKNER ORGANIZATION (THE)
FAURECIA SA
FEDERAL MOGUL CORP
FEDERAL SIGNAL CORP
FERRARI SPA
FIAT SPA
FINISHMASTER INC
FIRST AUTOMOTIVE GROUP CORPORATION
FIRST INVESTORS FINANCIAL SERVICES GROUP INC
FISHER & COMPANY INC
FISKER AUTOMOTIVE
FLETCHER JONES MANAGEMENT GROUP INC
FORD MOTOR CO
FORD MOTOR COMPANY OF CANADA
FORD MOTOR CREDIT CO LLC
FUEL SYSTEMS SOLUTIONS INC
FUJI HEAVY INDUSTRIES LTD (SUBARU)
GALPIN MOTORS INC
GAZ GROUP
GEICO CORPORATION
GENERAL MOTORS COMPANY (GM)
GENERAL MOTORS OF CANADA LTD
GENTEX CORPORATION
GENUINE PARTS COMPANY
GEORG FISCHER LTD
GKN PLC
GM DAEWOO AUTO AND TECHNOLOGY CO
GM HOLDEN LTD
GMAC INSURANCE HOLDINGS INC
GOODYEAR TIRE & RUBBER COMPANY (THE)
GREAT DANE LIMITED PARTNERSHIP
GROUP 1 AUTOMOTIVE INC
GROUP LOTUS PLC
GT TECHNOLOGIES INC
GUARDIAN INDUSTRIES CORP
GULF STATES TOYOTA INC
GULF STREAM COACH INC
HAHN AUTOMOTIVE WAREHOUSE INC
HANKOOK TIRE CO LTD
HARLEY-DAVIDSON INC
HAYES LEMMERZ INTERNATIONAL INC
HELLA KGAA HUECK & CO
HENDRICK AUTOMOTIVE GROUP
HERB CHAMBERS COMPANIES (THE)
HERO HONDA MOTORS LTD
HERTZ GLOBAL HOLDINGS INC
HILITE INTERNATIONAL INC
HINO MOTOR SALES (THAILAND) LTD
HINO MOTORS LTD
HOLMAN ENTERPRISES
HOMETOWN AUTO RETAILERS INC
HONDA MOTOR CO LTD
HONDA OF AMERICA MFG INC
HYUNDAI MOBIS CO LTD
HYUNDAI MOTOR AMERICA
HYUNDAI MOTOR COMPANY
INCHCAPE PLC
INERGY AUTOMOTIVE
INGERSOLL-RAND PLC
INOUE RUBBER (THAILAND) PCL
INTERNET BRANDS INC
INTERSTATE BATTERY SYSTEM OF AMERICA
ISUZU MOTORS AMERICA INC
ISUZU MOTORS LTD
JAGUAR CARS LTD
JARDINE CYCLE AND CARRIAGE
JASON INC
JAYCO INC
JB POINDEXTER & CO INC
JD POWER & ASSOCIATES
JIM KOONS AUTOMOTIVE COMPANIES INC
JL FRENCH AUTOMOTIVE CASTINGS
JM FAMILY ENTERPRISES
JOHNSON CONTROLS INC
JORDAN AUTOMOTIVE GROUP
KANTO AUTO WORKS LTD
KAR AUCTION SERVICES INC
KAWASAKI HEAVY INDUSTRIES LTD
KELLEY AUTOMOTIVE GROUP
KEY PLASTICS LLC
KEY SAFETY SYSTEMS INC
KEYSTONE AUTOMOTIVE INDUSTRIES INC
KIA MOTORS CORPORATION
KOENIGSEGG AUTOMOTIVE AB
KOITO MANUFACTURING CO LTD
KOLBENSCHMIDT PIERBURG AG
KUMHO TIRE CO LTD
LACKS ENTERPRISES INC
LAND ROVER
LARRY H MILLER GROUP

LDI LTD
LEAR CORP
LES SCHWAB TIRE CENTERS
LINAMAR CORP
LITHIA MOTORS INC
LKQ CORP
LOJACK CORPORTATION
LUCOR INC
LUND INTERNATIONAL INC
LUPIENT AUTOMOTIVE GROUP
MAACO ENTERPRISES INC
MACK TRUCKS INC
MAGNA INTERNATIONAL INC
MAGNA MIRRORS
MAGNETI MARELLI HOLDING SPA
MAHINDRA & MAHINDRA LIMITED
MAJOR AUTOMOTIVE COMPANIES INC
MARANGONI SPA
MARUTI SUZUKI INDIA LIMITED
MAYBACH
MAZDA MOTOR CORPORATION
MAZDA NORTH AMERICAN OPERATIONS
MCLAREN PERFORMANCE TECHNOLOGIES
MERCEDES-BENZ USA LLC
METALDYNE LLC
MIDAS INC
MILLER INDUSTRIES INC
MITSUBISHI FUSO TRUCK OF AMERICA INC
MITSUBISHI MOTORS (THAILAND) CO LTD
MITSUBISHI MOTORS CORP
MODINE MANUFACTURING COMPANY
MONRO MUFFLER BRAKE INC
MONTUPET SA
MORGAN MOTOR COMPANY (THE)
MORSE OPERATIONS INC
MOTOR COACH INDUSTRIES INTERNATIONAL
MOTORCAR PARTS OF AMERICA INC
NAVISTAR INC
NAVISTAR INTERNATIONAL CORP
NAVTEQ CORPORATION
NEWCOR INC
NEWMAR CORP
NIHON PLAST CO LTD
NIPPON PISTON RING CO LTD
NISSAN DIESEL (THAILAND) CO LTD
NISSAN MOTOR CO LTD
NISSAN NORTH AMERICA INC
NISSAN SHATAI CO LTD
NYX INC
ONSTAR CORPORATION
ORBITAL CORPORATION LTD
O'REILLY AUTOMOTIVE INC
ORION BUS INDUSTRIES
OSHKOSH CORPORATION
OURISMAN AUTOMOTIVE ENTERPRISES
PACCAR INC
PARK-OHIO HOLDINGS CORP
PENSKE AUTOMOTIVE GROUP INC
PENSKE CORPORATION
PEP BOYS-MANNY MOE & JACK (THE)
PETERSON MANUFACTURING CO
PHIL LONG DEALERSHIPS INC
PIAGGIO & C SPA
PILKINGTON PLC
PININFARINA SPA
PIRELLI & C SPA
POLARIS INDUSTRIES INC
PORSCHE AUTOMOBIL HOLDING SE
POTAMKIN AUTOMOTIVE GROUP
PPG INDUSTRIES INC
PRIMEARTH EV ENERGY CO LTD
PROGRESSIVE CORPORATION (THE)
PROTON HOLDINGS BERHAD
PSA PEUGEOT CITROEN SA
PT ASTRA INTERNATIONAL TBK
REMY INTERNATIONAL INC
RENAULT SA
RENT-A-WRECK OF AMERICA INC
REXHALL INDUSTRIES INC
RHEINMETALL AG
RICART AUTOMOTIVE INC
RIETER HOLDING LTD
RIZZA AUTOMOTIVE GROUP
ROBERT BOSCH GMBH
ROLLS ROYCE MOTOR CAR LIMITED
ROSENTHAL AUTOMOTIVE ORGANIZATION
RUSH ENTERPRISES INC
RUSS DARROW GROUP INC
RYBROOK HOLDINGS LIMITED
RYGOR GROUP LTD
S&T MOTORS CO LTD
SAAB AUTOMOBILE AB
SAAB CARS NORTH AMERICA INC
SAIC-GM-WULING AUTOMOBILE COMPANY
SALEEN PERFORMANCE VEHICLES
SAM SWOPE AUTO GROUP INC
SANLUIS CORPORACION SAB DE CV
SANSONE AUTO NETWORK
SANTA MONICA FORD LINCOLN MERCURY
SCANIA AB
SEAT SA
SEGWAY LLC
SEQUA CORP
SHANGHAI AUTOMOTIVE INDUSTRY CORP (SAIC)
SHEEHY AUTO STORES
SIEMENS AG
SIRIUS XM RADIO INC
SIXT AKTIENGESELLSCHAFT
SKODA AUTO AS
SKYLINE CORPORATION
SMART GMBH
SOGEFI SPA
SONIC AUTOMOTIVE INC
SPARTAN MOTORS INC
SPECIAL DEVICES INCORPORATED
SPECTRA PREMIUM INDUSTRIES INC

SPITZER MANAGEMENT INC
SRG GLOBAL INC
SSANGYONG MOTOR CO
STACKPOLE LIMITED COMPANY
STANADYNE CORPORATION
STANDARD MOTOR PRODUCTS INC
STATE FARM INSURANCE COMPANIES
STELLICAN LTD
STERLING AUTOBODY CENTERS
STONERIDGE INC
STRATTEC SECURITY CORP
SUPERIOR INDUSTRIES INTERNATIONAL INC
SUPREME INDUSTRIES INC
SUZUKI AUTOMOBILE (THAILAND) CO LTD
SUZUKI MOTOR CORPORATION
SYTNER GROUP PLC
TATA GROUP
TATA MOTORS LIMITED
TBC CORPORATION
TELEFLEX INC
TENNECO INC
TEREX CORPORATION
TESLA MOTORS INC
THOR INDUSTRIES INC
TI AUTOMOTIVE
TITAN INTERNATIONAL INC
TOKAI RIKA CO LTD
TORESCO ENTERPRISES INC
TOWER AUTOMOTIVE LLC
TOYO TIRE & RUBBER CO LTD
TOYODA GOSEI CO LTD
TOYOTA AUTO BODY CO LTD
TOYOTA MOTOR CORPORATION
TOYOTA MOTOR CREDIT CORP
TOYOTA MOTOR THAILAND CO LTD
TREADWAYS CORP
TRELLEBORG AB
TRI PETCH ISUZU SALES CO LTD
TRW AUTOMOTIVE HOLDINGS CORP
TUTTLE-CLICK AUTOMOTIVE GROUP
UD TRUCKS CORP
UNIPART GROUP OF COMPANIES
UNI-SELECT INC
UTILIMASTER CORP
UTILITY TRAILER MANUFACTURING CO
VALEO
VAUXHALL MOTORS LTD
VISTA PRO AUTOMOTIVE LLC
VISTEON CORPORATION
VOLKSWAGEN AG
VOLKSWAGEN GROUP OF AMERICA INC
VOLVO CAR CORPORATION
VOLVO CARS OF NORTH AMERICA INC
WABASH NATIONAL CORP
WANXIANG AMERICA CORPORATION
WANXIANG GROUP CORPORATION
WESCAST INDUSTRIES INC
WINNEBAGO INDUSTRIES INC
YAMAHA MOTOR CO LTD
YAZAKI NORTH AMERICA INC
YUASA BATTERY (THAILAND) PCL
YULON MOTOR CO LTD
ZAP
ZF FRIEDRICHSHAFEN AG
ZHEJIANG GEELY HOLDING GROUP
ZIEBART INTERNATIONAL CORP
ZIPCAR INC

INDEX OF U.S. HEADQUARTERS LOCATION BY STATE

To help you locate the firms geographically, the city and state of the headquarters of each company are in the following index.

JORDAN AUTOMOTIVE GROUP; Mishawaka
KAR AUCTION SERVICES INC; Carmel
KELLEY AUTOMOTIVE GROUP; Fort Wayne
LDI LTD; Indianapolis
NEWMAR CORP; Nappanee
REMY INTERNATIONAL INC; Pendleton
SKYLINE CORPORATION; Elkhart
SUPREME INDUSTRIES INC; Goshen
UTILIMASTER CORP; Wakarusa
WABASH NATIONAL CORP; Lafayette

IOWA
BRIDGESTONE BANDAG LLC; Muscatine
WINNEBAGO INDUSTRIES INC; Forest City

KANSAS
COLLINS INDUSTRIES INC; Hutchinson

KENTUCKY
SAM SWOPE AUTO GROUP INC; Louisville

MARYLAND
DARCARS AUTOMOTIVE GROUP; Silver Spring
GEICO CORPORATION; Chevy Chase
OURISMAN AUTOMOTIVE ENTERPRISES; Marlow Heights
RENT-A-WRECK OF AMERICA INC; Laurel

MASSACHUSETTS
A123SYSTEMS; Watertown
HERB CHAMBERS COMPANIES (THE); Somerville
LOJACK CORPORTATION; Westwood
STERLING AUTOBODY CENTERS; Natick
ZIPCAR INC; Cambridge

MICHIGAN
ALLY FINANCIAL INC; Detroit
ALPS AUTOMOTIVE INC; Auburn Hills
AMERICAN AXLE & MANUFACTURING HOLDINGS INC; Detroit
AMERIGON INC; Northville
ARVINMERITOR INC; Troy
ASC INCORPORATED; Warren
AUDI OF AMERICA INC; Auburn Hills
AUTOALLIANCE INTERNATIONAL INC; Flat Rock
AUTOCAM CORPORATION; Kentwood
BORGWARNER INC; Auburn Hills
CHRYSLER FINANCIAL SERVICES LLC; Farmington Hills
CHRYSLER GROUP LLC; Auburn Hills
CREDIT ACCEPTANCE CORP; Southfield
DAIMLER FINANCIAL SERVICES AMERICAS LLC; Farmington Hills
DELPHI CORP; Troy
EAGLE OTTAWA LEATHER COMPANY LLC; Auburn Hills
EAGLEPICHER CORPORATION; Dearborn
ELDER AUTOMOTIVE GROUP; Troy
FEDERAL MOGUL CORP; Southfield
FISHER & COMPANY INC; St. Clair Shores
FORD MOTOR CO; Dearborn
FORD MOTOR CREDIT CO LLC; Dearborn
GENERAL MOTORS COMPANY (GM); Detroit
GENTEX CORPORATION; Zeeland
GT TECHNOLOGIES INC; Westland
GUARDIAN INDUSTRIES CORP; Auburn Hills
HAYES LEMMERZ INTERNATIONAL INC; Northville
KEY PLASTICS LLC; Northville
KEY SAFETY SYSTEMS INC; Sterling Heights
LACKS ENTERPRISES INC; Grand Rapids
LEAR CORP; Southfield
MAGNA MIRRORS; Holland
MCLAREN PERFORMANCE TECHNOLOGIES; Livonia
METALDYNE LLC; Plymouth
NEWCOR INC; Auburn Hills
NYX INC; Livonia
ONSTAR CORPORATION; Detroit
PENSKE AUTOMOTIVE GROUP INC; Bloomfield Hills
PENSKE CORPORATION; Bloomfield Hills
SAAB CARS NORTH AMERICA INC; Royal Oak
SALEEN PERFORMANCE VEHICLES; Troy
SPARTAN MOTORS INC; Charlotte
SRG GLOBAL INC; Warren
TOWER AUTOMOTIVE LLC; Livonia
TRW AUTOMOTIVE HOLDINGS CORP; Livonia
VISTEON CORPORATION; Van Buren Township
YAZAKI NORTH AMERICA INC; Canton
ZIEBART INTERNATIONAL CORP; Troy

MINNESOTA
3M COMPANY; St. Paul
ARCTIC CAT INC; Thief River Falls
LUPIENT AUTOMOTIVE GROUP; Golden Valley
POLARIS INDUSTRIES INC; Medina

MISSOURI
ENTERPRISE HOLDINGS; St. Louis
GMAC INSURANCE HOLDINGS INC; Winston-Salem
O'REILLY AUTOMOTIVE INC; Springfield
PETERSON MANUFACTURING CO; Grandview

NEVADA
AMERCO; Reno
FLETCHER JONES MANAGEMENT GROUP INC; Las Vegas

NEW HAMPSHIRE
SEGWAY LLC; Bedford

NEW JERSEY
BMW OF NORTH AMERICA LLC; Woodcliff Lake
HERTZ GLOBAL HOLDINGS INC; Park Ridge
HOLMAN ENTERPRISES; Pennsauken
MERCEDES-BENZ USA LLC; Montvale

MITSUBISHI FUSO TRUCK OF AMERICA INC; Logan Township
SANSONE AUTO NETWORK; Neptune
TORESCO ENTERPRISES INC; Springfield
VOLVO CARS OF NORTH AMERICA INC; Rockleigh

NEW YORK
CERBERUS CAPITAL MANAGEMENT LP; New York
ENER1 INC; New York
FUEL SYSTEMS SOLUTIONS INC; New York
HAHN AUTOMOTIVE WAREHOUSE INC; Rochester
MAJOR AUTOMOTIVE COMPANIES INC; Long Island City
MONRO MUFFLER BRAKE INC; Rochester
ORION BUS INDUSTRIES; Oriskany
SIRIUS XM RADIO INC; New York
STANDARD MOTOR PRODUCTS INC; Long Island City

NORTH CAROLINA
AMERICAN TIRE DISTRIBUTORS; Huntersville
CARLISLE COMPANIES INC; Charlotte
CARQUEST CORP; Raleigh
HENDRICK AUTOMOTIVE GROUP; Charlotte
LUCOR INC; Raleigh
MACK TRUCKS INC; Greensboro
SONIC AUTOMOTIVE INC; Charlotte

OHIO
APPLIED INDUSTRIAL TECHNOLOGIES INC; Cleveland
COMMERCIAL VEHICLE GROUP INC (CVG); New Albany
COOPER TIRE & RUBBER COMPANY; Findlay
DANA HOLDINGS CORPORATION; Maumee
EATON CORP; Cleveland
GOODYEAR TIRE & RUBBER COMPANY (THE); Akron
HILITE INTERNATIONAL INC; Cleveland
HONDA OF AMERICA MFG INC; Marysville
PARK-OHIO HOLDINGS CORP; Cleveland
PROGRESSIVE CORPORATION (THE); Mayfield Village
RICART AUTOMOTIVE INC; Columbus
SPITZER MANAGEMENT INC; Elyria
STONERIDGE INC; Warren
THOR INDUSTRIES INC; Jackson Center

OKLAHOMA
DOLLAR THRIFTY AUTOMOTIVE GROUP INC; Tulsa

OREGON
DAIMLER TRUCKS NORTH AMERICA LLC; Portland
LES SCHWAB TIRE CENTERS; Bend
LITHIA MOTORS INC; Medford

PENNSYLVANIA
AAMCO TRANSMISSIONS INC; Horsham
DORMAN PRODUCTS INC; Colmar
EAST PENN MANUFACTURING CO INC; Lyon Station
FAULKNER ORGANIZATION (THE); Trevose
MAACO ENTERPRISES INC; King of Prussia
PEP BOYS-MANNY MOE & JACK (THE); Philadelphia
PPG INDUSTRIES INC; Pittsburgh
TELEFLEX INC; Limerick
TREADWAYS CORP; East Norriton

SOUTH CAROLINA
BMW MANUFACTURING CORP; Greer

TENNESSEE
AUTOZONE INC; Memphis
CLARCOR INC; Franklin
CUMMINS FILTRATION; Nashville
MILLER INDUSTRIES INC; Ooltewah
NISSAN NORTH AMERICA INC; Franklin
VISTA PRO AUTOMOTIVE LLC; Nashville

TEXAS
ANCIRA ENTERPRISES; San Antonio
ATX GROUP INC; Irving
DAVID MCDAVID AUTO GROUP; Irving
FIRST INVESTORS FINANCIAL SERVICES GROUP INC; Houston
GROUP 1 AUTOMOTIVE INC; Houston
GULF STATES TOYOTA INC; Houston
INTERSTATE BATTERY SYSTEM OF AMERICA; Dallas
JB POINDEXTER & CO INC; Houston
RUSH ENTERPRISES INC; New Braunfels

UTAH
LARRY H MILLER GROUP; Sandy

VIRGINIA
ADVANCE AUTO PARTS INC; Roanoke
BROWN AUTOMOTIVE GROUP LTD; Fairfax
CARMAX GROUP; Richmond
JIM KOONS AUTOMOTIVE COMPANIES INC; 112
ROSENTHAL AUTOMOTIVE ORGANIZATION; Arlington
SHEEHY AUTO STORES; Fairfax
VOLKSWAGEN GROUP OF AMERICA INC; Herndon

WASHINGTON
COBALT GROUP (THE); Seattle
PACCAR INC; Bellevue

WISCONSIN
HARLEY-DAVIDSON INC; Milwaukee
JASON INC; Milwaukee
JL FRENCH AUTOMOTIVE CASTINGS; Sheboygan
JOHNSON CONTROLS INC; Milwaukee

INDEX OF NON-U.S. HEADQUARTERS LOCATION BY COUNTRY

VALEO; Paris

GERMANY
ADAM OPEL AG; Russelsheim
AUDI AG; Ingolstadt
BMW (BAYERISCHE MOTOREN WERKE AG); Munich
BORGWARNER BERU SYSTEMS GMBH; Ludwigsburg
CONTINENTAL AG; Hanover
DAIMLER AG; Stuttgart
DAIMLER FINANCIAL SERVICES AG; Berlin
DEUTZ AG; Koln-Porz
HELLA KGAA HUECK & CO; Lippstadt
KOLBENSCHMIDT PIERBURG AG; Neckarsulm
MAYBACH; Stuttgart
PORSCHE AUTOMOBIL HOLDING SE; Stuttgart
RHEINMETALL AG; Dusseldorf
ROBERT BOSCH GMBH; Stuttgart
SIEMENS AG; Munich
SIXT AKTIENGESELLSCHAFT; Pullach im Isartal
SMART GMBH; Boeblingen
VOLKSWAGEN AG; Wolfsburg
ZF FRIEDRICHSHAFEN AG; Friedrichshafen

INDIA
BAJAJ AUTO LTD; Pune
HERO HONDA MOTORS LTD; New Delhi
MAHINDRA & MAHINDRA LIMITED; Mumbai
MARUTI SUZUKI INDIA LIMITED; New Delhi
TATA GROUP; Mumbai
TATA MOTORS LIMITED; Mumbai

INDONESIA
PT ASTRA INTERNATIONAL TBK; Jakarta Utara

ITALY
AUTOMOBILI LAMBORGHINI HOLDING SPA; Sant'Agata Bolognese
BREMBO SPA; Stezzano
DUCATI MOTOR HOLDING SPA; Bologna
FERRARI SPA; Maranello
FIAT SPA; Turin
MAGNETI MARELLI HOLDING SPA; Milano
MARANGONI SPA; Verona
PIAGGIO & C SPA; Pisa
PININFARINA SPA; Turin
PIRELLI & C SPA; Milan
SOGEFI SPA; Milano

JAPAN
AISAN INDUSTRY CO LTD; Obu, Aichi
AISIN SEIKI CO LTD; Kariya
ALPS ELECTRIC CO LTD; Tokyo
ASAHI GLASS COMPANY LIMITED; Tokyo
AUTOMOTIVE ENERGY SUPPLY CORPORATION (AESC); Zama-shi
BRIDGESTONE CORPORATION; Tokyo
CALSONIC KANSEI CORPORATION; Saitama
CLARION CO LTD; Saitama
DAIHATSU MOTOR CO LTD; Ikeda-city, Osaka
DENSO CORPORATION; Kariya
FUJI HEAVY INDUSTRIES LTD (SUBARU); Tokyo
HINO MOTORS LTD; Tokyo
HONDA MOTOR CO LTD; Tokyo
ISUZU MOTORS LTD; Tokyo
KANTO AUTO WORKS LTD; Yokosuka, Kanegawa
KAWASAKI HEAVY INDUSTRIES LTD; Hyogo
KOITO MANUFACTURING CO LTD; Tokyo
MAZDA MOTOR CORPORATION; Hiroshima
MITSUBISHI MOTORS CORP; Tokyo
NIHON PLAST CO LTD; Fuji
NIPPON PISTON RING CO LTD; Saitama City
NISSAN MOTOR CO LTD; Yokohama-shi
NISSAN SHATAI CO LTD; Kanagawa
PRIMEARTH EV ENERGY CO LTD; Shizuoka
SUZUKI MOTOR CORPORATION; Hamamatsu
TOKAI RIKA CO LTD; Aichi
TOYO TIRE & RUBBER CO LTD; Osaka
TOYODA GOSEI CO LTD; Aichi
TOYOTA AUTO BODY CO LTD; Aichi
TOYOTA MOTOR CORPORATION; Aichi
UD TRUCKS CORP; Saitama
YAMAHA MOTOR CO LTD; Shizuoka

KOREA
GM DAEWOO AUTO AND TECHNOLOGY CO; Incheon
HANKOOK TIRE CO LTD; Seoul
HYUNDAI MOBIS CO LTD; Seoul
HYUNDAI MOTOR COMPANY; Seoul
KIA MOTORS CORPORATION; Seoul
KUMHO TIRE CO LTD; Gwangju
S&T MOTORS CO LTD; Changwon, Kyungsangnamdo
SSANGYONG MOTOR CO; Gyeonggi-do

MALAYSIA
EDARAN OTOMOBIL NASIONAL BERHAD; Shah Alam
PROTON HOLDINGS BERHAD; Shah Alam

MEXICO
SANLUIS CORPORACION SAB DE CV; Lomas de Chapultepec

RUSSIA
AVTOVAZ OAO; Togliatti
GAZ GROUP; Nizhny Novgorod

SINGAPORE
JARDINE CYCLE AND CARRIAGE; Singapore

SPAIN
SEAT SA; Martorell

SWEDEN
AB VOLVO; Goteborg
AUTOLIV INC; Stockholm
KOENIGSEGG AUTOMOTIVE AB; Angelholm
SAAB AUTOMOBILE AB; Trollhattan
SCANIA AB; Sodertalje
TRELLEBORG AB; Trelleborg
VOLVO CAR CORPORATION; Goteborg

SWITZERLAND
GEORG FISCHER LTD; Schaffhausen
RIETER HOLDING LTD; Winterthur

TAIWAN
YULON MOTOR CO LTD; Sanyi, Miao li Hsien

THAILAND
HINO MOTOR SALES (THAILAND) LTD; Bangkok
INOUE RUBBER (THAILAND) PCL; Prachatipat
MITSUBISHI MOTORS (THAILAND) CO LTD; Klongluang
NISSAN DIESEL (THAILAND) CO LTD; Ban Klang
SUZUKI AUTOMOBILE (THAILAND) CO LTD; Bangkok
TOYOTA MOTOR THAILAND CO LTD; Samrong Tai
TRI PETCH ISUZU SALES CO LTD; Bangkok
YUASA BATTERY (THAILAND) PCL; Bangkok

UNITED KINGDOM
ASTON MARTIN LAGONDA LTD; Gaydon
AVIS EUROPE PLC; Bracknell
BENTLEY MOTORS; Crewe
GKN PLC; Redditch
GROUP LOTUS PLC; Norwich
INCHCAPE PLC; London
INGERSOLL-RAND PLC; Swords
JAGUAR CARS LTD; Coventry
LAND ROVER; Warwick
MORGAN MOTOR COMPANY (THE); Malvern Link
PILKINGTON PLC; St. Helens
ROLLS ROYCE MOTOR CAR LIMITED; Chichester
RYBROOK HOLDINGS LIMITED; Warwick
RYGOR GROUP LTD; Westbury
STELLICAN LTD; London
SYTNER GROUP PLC; Leicester
TI AUTOMOTIVE; Oxford
UNIPART GROUP OF COMPANIES; Oxford
VAUXHALL MOTORS LTD; Luton

INDEX BY REGIONS OF THE U.S. WHERE THE FIRMS HAVE LOCATIONS

JB POINDEXTER & CO INC
JD POWER & ASSOCIATES
JOHNSON CONTROLS INC
KEYSTONE AUTOMOTIVE INDUSTRIES INC
KIA MOTORS CORPORATION
KOITO MANUFACTURING CO LTD
KUMHO TIRE CO LTD
LAND ROVER
LARRY H MILLER GROUP
LDI LTD
LEAR CORP
LES SCHWAB TIRE CENTERS
LITHIA MOTORS INC
LKQ CORP
LOJACK CORPORTATION
LUND INTERNATIONAL INC
MAACO ENTERPRISES INC
MACK TRUCKS INC
MAZDA MOTOR CORPORATION
MAZDA NORTH AMERICAN OPERATIONS
MERCEDES-BENZ USA LLC
MIDAS INC
MITSUBISHI FUSO TRUCK OF AMERICA INC
MITSUBISHI MOTORS CORP
MOTOR COACH INDUSTRIES INTERNATIONAL
MOTORCAR PARTS OF AMERICA INC
NAVISTAR INC
NAVISTAR INTERNATIONAL CORP
NIPPON PISTON RING CO LTD
NISSAN MOTOR CO LTD
NISSAN NORTH AMERICA INC
O'REILLY AUTOMOTIVE INC
OSHKOSH CORPORATION
PACCAR INC
PENSKE AUTOMOTIVE GROUP INC
PENSKE CORPORATION
PEP BOYS-MANNY MOE & JACK (THE)
PHIL LONG DEALERSHIPS INC
PILKINGTON PLC
POTAMKIN AUTOMOTIVE GROUP
PPG INDUSTRIES INC
PROGRESSIVE CORPORATION (THE)
RENT-A-WRECK OF AMERICA INC
REXHALL INDUSTRIES INC
ROBERT BOSCH GMBH
RUSH ENTERPRISES INC
SAAB CARS NORTH AMERICA INC
SANTA MONICA FORD LINCOLN MERCURY
SEQUA CORP
SIEMENS AG
SKYLINE CORPORATION
SMART GMBH
SONIC AUTOMOTIVE INC
SPECIAL DEVICES INCORPORATED
STANDARD MOTOR PRODUCTS INC
STATE FARM INSURANCE COMPANIES
STERLING AUTOBODY CENTERS
STONERIDGE INC
SUPERIOR INDUSTRIES INTERNATIONAL INC
SUPREME INDUSTRIES INC
SUZUKI MOTOR CORPORATION
TBC CORPORATION
TELEFLEX INC
TENNECO INC
TEREX CORPORATION
TESLA MOTORS INC
THOR INDUSTRIES INC
TITAN INTERNATIONAL INC
TOYO TIRE & RUBBER CO LTD
TOYOTA MOTOR CORPORATION
TOYOTA MOTOR CREDIT CORP
TREADWAYS CORP
TRELLEBORG AB
TUTTLE-CLICK AUTOMOTIVE GROUP
UNI-SELECT INC
UTILITY TRAILER MANUFACTURING CO
VISTA PRO AUTOMOTIVE LLC
VOLKSWAGEN GROUP OF AMERICA INC
VOLVO CAR CORPORATION
VOLVO CARS OF NORTH AMERICA INC
WABASH NATIONAL CORP
YAMAHA MOTOR CO LTD
YAZAKI NORTH AMERICA INC
ZAP
ZF FRIEDRICHSHAFEN AG
ZIEBART INTERNATIONAL CORP
ZIPCAR INC

SOUTHWEST

3M COMPANY
AAMCO TRANSMISSIONS INC
AB VOLVO
ACCURIDE CORPORATION
ADESA INC
ALLIED SYSTEMS HOLDINGS INC
ALLSTATE CORPORATION (THE)
ALLY FINANCIAL INC
ALPS AUTOMOTIVE INC
ALPS ELECTRIC CO LTD
AMERCO
AMERICAN HONDA MOTOR CO INC
AMERICAN TIRE DISTRIBUTORS
AMERICA'S CAR-MART INC
ANCIRA ENTERPRISES
APPLIED INDUSTRIAL TECHNOLOGIES INC
ARVINMERITOR INC
ASBURY AUTOMOTIVE GROUP INC
ASTON MARTIN LAGONDA LTD
ATC TECHNOLOGY CORPORATION
ATX GROUP INC
AUDI AG
AUDI OF AMERICA INC
AUTONATION INC
AUTOZONE INC
BENTELER GROUP (THE)
BENTLEY MOTORS

BMW (BAYERISCHE MOTOREN WERKE AG)
BMW OF NORTH AMERICA LLC
BORGWARNER INC
BRIDGESTONE BANDAG LLC
BRIDGESTONE CORPORATION
BROWN AUTOMOTIVE GROUP LTD
CALIBER HOLDINGS CORP
CARLISLE COMPANIES INC
CARMAX GROUP
CARQUEST CORP
CATERPILLAR INC
CERADYNE
CHAPMAN AUTOMOTIVE GROUP LLC
CHRYSLER FINANCIAL SERVICES LLC
CHRYSLER GROUP LLC
CLARCOR INC
CLARION CO LTD
COAST DISTRIBUTION SYSTEM INC
COBALT GROUP (THE)
COLLINS INDUSTRIES INC
COMMERCIAL VEHICLE GROUP INC (CVG)
COMPAGNIE GENERALE DES ETABLISSEMENTS MICHELIN
COMPAGNIE PLASTIC OMNIUM
CONTINENTAL AG
COOPER TIRE & RUBBER COMPANY
COPART INC
CUMMINS INC
DAIMLER AG
DAIMLER FINANCIAL SERVICES AMERICAS LLC
DAVID MCDAVID AUTO GROUP
DAVID WILSON'S AUTOMOTIVE GROUP
DEERE & CO
DELPHI CORP
DENSO CORPORATION
DISCOUNT TIRE CO
DOLLAR THRIFTY AUTOMOTIVE GROUP INC
DONLEN CORPORATION
DRIVETIME AUTOMOTIVE GROUP INC
E I DU PONT DE NEMOURS & CO (DUPONT)
EAGLEPICHER CORPORATION
EARNHARDT'S AUTO CENTERS
EATON CORP
ENTERPRISE HOLDINGS
FEDERAL MOGUL CORP
FEDERAL SIGNAL CORP
FERRARI SPA
FINISHMASTER INC
FIRST INVESTORS FINANCIAL SERVICES GROUP INC
FISHER & COMPANY INC
FORD MOTOR CO
FORD MOTOR CREDIT CO LLC
GEICO CORPORATION
GENERAL MOTORS COMPANY (GM)
GENUINE PARTS COMPANY
GKN PLC
GMAC INSURANCE HOLDINGS INC
GOODYEAR TIRE & RUBBER COMPANY (THE)
GREAT DANE LIMITED PARTNERSHIP
GROUP 1 AUTOMOTIVE INC
GROUP LOTUS PLC
GUARDIAN INDUSTRIES CORP
GULF STATES TOYOTA INC
HANKOOK TIRE CO LTD
HARLEY-DAVIDSON INC
HENDRICK AUTOMOTIVE GROUP
HERTZ GLOBAL HOLDINGS INC
HILITE INTERNATIONAL INC
HONDA MOTOR CO LTD
HYUNDAI MOTOR AMERICA
INGERSOLL-RAND PLC
INTERSTATE BATTERY SYSTEM OF AMERICA
ISUZU MOTORS AMERICA INC
JAGUAR CARS LTD
JB POINDEXTER & CO INC
JOHNSON CONTROLS INC
KAWASAKI HEAVY INDUSTRIES LTD
KEY SAFETY SYSTEMS INC
KEYSTONE AUTOMOTIVE INDUSTRIES INC
LAND ROVER
LARRY H MILLER GROUP
LDI LTD
LEAR CORP
LITHIA MOTORS INC
LKQ CORP
LOJACK CORPORTATION
MAACO ENTERPRISES INC
MACK TRUCKS INC
MAZDA MOTOR CORPORATION
MAZDA NORTH AMERICAN OPERATIONS
MERCEDES-BENZ USA LLC
MIDAS INC
MITSUBISHI FUSO TRUCK OF AMERICA INC
MODINE MANUFACTURING COMPANY
MOTOR COACH INDUSTRIES INTERNATIONAL
NAVISTAR INC
NAVISTAR INTERNATIONAL CORP
NISSAN MOTOR CO LTD
O'REILLY AUTOMOTIVE INC
OSHKOSH CORPORATION
PACCAR INC
PARK-OHIO HOLDINGS CORP
PENSKE AUTOMOTIVE GROUP INC
PENSKE CORPORATION
PEP BOYS-MANNY MOE & JACK (THE)
PILKINGTON PLC
POTAMKIN AUTOMOTIVE GROUP
PPG INDUSTRIES INC
PROGRESSIVE CORPORATION (THE)
REMY INTERNATIONAL INC
RENT-A-WRECK OF AMERICA INC
ROBERT BOSCH GMBH
RUSH ENTERPRISES INC
SAAB CARS NORTH AMERICA INC
SCANIA AB

SEQUA CORP
SIEMENS AG
SKYLINE CORPORATION
SMART GMBH
SONIC AUTOMOTIVE INC
SPECIAL DEVICES INCORPORATED
SPECTRA PREMIUM INDUSTRIES INC
STANDARD MOTOR PRODUCTS INC
STATE FARM INSURANCE COMPANIES
STELLICAN LTD
STERLING AUTOBODY CENTERS
STONERIDGE INC
STRATTEC SECURITY CORP
SUPREME INDUSTRIES INC
TBC CORPORATION
TELEFLEX INC
TENNECO INC
TEREX CORPORATION
TESLA MOTORS INC
TI AUTOMOTIVE
TITAN INTERNATIONAL INC
TOYODA GOSEI CO LTD
TOYOTA MOTOR CORPORATION
TOYOTA MOTOR CREDIT CORP
TREADWAYS CORP
TRELLEBORG AB
TRW AUTOMOTIVE HOLDINGS CORP
UD TRUCKS CORP
UNI-SELECT INC
UTILITY TRAILER MANUFACTURING CO
VISTA PRO AUTOMOTIVE LLC
VISTEON CORPORATION
VOLKSWAGEN GROUP OF AMERICA INC
VOLVO CAR CORPORATION
VOLVO CARS OF NORTH AMERICA INC
WABASH NATIONAL CORP
YAMAHA MOTOR CO LTD
YAZAKI NORTH AMERICA INC
ZAP
ZF FRIEDRICHSHAFEN AG
ZIEBART INTERNATIONAL CORP
ZIPCAR INC

MIDWEST
3M COMPANY
A123SYSTEMS
AAMCO TRANSMISSIONS INC
AB VOLVO
ABC GROUP
ACCURIDE CORPORATION
ADESA INC
ADVANCE AUTO PARTS INC
AGS AUTOMOTIVE SYSTEMS INC
AISAN INDUSTRY CO LTD
AISIN SEIKI CO LTD
ALL AMERICAN GROUP
ALLIED SYSTEMS HOLDINGS INC
ALLSTATE CORPORATION (THE)
ALLY FINANCIAL INC
ALPS AUTOMOTIVE INC
ALPS ELECTRIC CO LTD
AM GENERAL LLC
AMERCO
AMERICAN AXLE & MANUFACTURING HOLDINGS INC
AMERICAN HONDA MOTOR CO INC
AMERICAN TIRE DISTRIBUTORS
AMERICA'S CAR-MART INC
AMERIGON INC
APPLIED INDUSTRIAL TECHNOLOGIES INC
ARCTIC CAT INC
ARVINMERITOR INC
ASAHI GLASS COMPANY LIMITED
ASBURY AUTOMOTIVE GROUP INC
ASC INCORPORATED
ASTON MARTIN LAGONDA LTD
ATC TECHNOLOGY CORPORATION
ATS AUTOMATION TOOLING SYSTEMS INC
AUDI AG
AUDI OF AMERICA INC
AUTOALLIANCE INTERNATIONAL INC
AUTOBYTEL INC
AUTOCAM CORPORATION
AUTOLIV INC
AUTONATION INC
AUTOZONE INC
BENTELER GROUP (THE)
BENTLEY MOTORS
BMW OF NORTH AMERICA LLC
BOB ROHRMAN AUTO GROUP
BORGWARNER BERU SYSTEMS GMBH
BORGWARNER INC
BREMBO SPA
BRIDGESTONE BANDAG LLC
BRIDGESTONE CORPORATION
BYD COMPANY LIMITED
CALSONIC KANSEI CORPORATION
CARLISLE COMPANIES INC
CARMAX GROUP
CARQUEST CORP
CATERPILLAR INC
CERADYNE
CERBERUS CAPITAL MANAGEMENT LP
CHRYSLER FINANCIAL SERVICES LLC
CHRYSLER GROUP LLC
CLARCOR INC
CLARION CO LTD
COAST DISTRIBUTION SYSTEM INC
COBALT GROUP (THE)
COLLINS INDUSTRIES INC
COMMERCIAL VEHICLE GROUP INC (CVG)
COMPAGNIE GENERALE DES ETABLISSEMENTS MICHELIN
COMPAGNIE PLASTIC OMNIUM
CONSUMER PORTFOLIO SERVICES INC
CONTINENTAL AG

CONTINENTAL MOTORS GROUP
COOPER TIRE & RUBBER COMPANY
COPART INC
CREDIT ACCEPTANCE CORP
CUMMINS INC
DAIMLER AG
DAIMLER FINANCIAL SERVICES AMERICAS LLC
DAIMLER TRUCKS NORTH AMERICA LLC
DANA HOLDINGS CORPORATION
DEERE & CO
DELPHI CORP
DENSO CORPORATION
DISCOUNT TIRE CO
DOLLAR THRIFTY AUTOMOTIVE GROUP INC
DONLEN CORPORATION
DORMAN PRODUCTS INC
E I DU PONT DE NEMOURS & CO (DUPONT)
EAGLE OTTAWA LEATHER COMPANY LLC
EAGLEPICHER CORPORATION
EAST PENN MANUFACTURING CO INC
EATON CORP
ELDER AUTOMOTIVE GROUP
ENER1 INC
ENTERPRISE HOLDINGS
FAURECIA SA
FEDERAL MOGUL CORP
FEDERAL SIGNAL CORP
FERRARI SPA
FINISHMASTER INC
FIRST INVESTORS FINANCIAL SERVICES GROUP INC
FISHER & COMPANY INC
FLETCHER JONES MANAGEMENT GROUP INC
FORD MOTOR CO
FORD MOTOR CREDIT CO LLC
FUEL SYSTEMS SOLUTIONS INC
FUJI HEAVY INDUSTRIES LTD (SUBARU)
GEICO CORPORATION
GENERAL MOTORS COMPANY (GM)
GENTEX CORPORATION
GENUINE PARTS COMPANY
GKN PLC
GMAC INSURANCE HOLDINGS INC
GOODYEAR TIRE & RUBBER COMPANY (THE)
GREAT DANE LIMITED PARTNERSHIP
GROUP 1 AUTOMOTIVE INC
GROUP LOTUS PLC
GT TECHNOLOGIES INC
GUARDIAN INDUSTRIES CORP
GULF STREAM COACH INC
HAHN AUTOMOTIVE WAREHOUSE INC
HANKOOK TIRE CO LTD
HARLEY-DAVIDSON INC
HAYES LEMMERZ INTERNATIONAL INC
HELLA KGAA HUECK & CO
HENDRICK AUTOMOTIVE GROUP
HERTZ GLOBAL HOLDINGS INC
HILITE INTERNATIONAL INC
HINO MOTORS LTD
HONDA MOTOR CO LTD
HONDA OF AMERICA MFG INC
HYUNDAI MOTOR AMERICA
HYUNDAI MOTOR COMPANY
INGERSOLL-RAND PLC
INTERSTATE BATTERY SYSTEM OF AMERICA
ISUZU MOTORS AMERICA INC
ISUZU MOTORS LTD
JAGUAR CARS LTD
JASON INC
JAYCO INC
JB POINDEXTER & CO INC
JD POWER & ASSOCIATES
JL FRENCH AUTOMOTIVE CASTINGS
JM FAMILY ENTERPRISES
JOHNSON CONTROLS INC
JORDAN AUTOMOTIVE GROUP
KAR AUCTION SERVICES INC
KAWASAKI HEAVY INDUSTRIES LTD
KELLEY AUTOMOTIVE GROUP
KEY PLASTICS LLC
KEY SAFETY SYSTEMS INC
KEYSTONE AUTOMOTIVE INDUSTRIES INC
KIA MOTORS CORPORATION
KOITO MANUFACTURING CO LTD
KOLBENSCHMIDT PIERBURG AG
KUMHO TIRE CO LTD
LACKS ENTERPRISES INC
LAND ROVER
LDI LTD
LEAR CORP
LINAMAR CORP
LITHIA MOTORS INC
LKQ CORP
LOJACK CORPORTATION
LUND INTERNATIONAL INC
LUPIENT AUTOMOTIVE GROUP
MAACO ENTERPRISES INC
MACK TRUCKS INC
MAGNA INTERNATIONAL INC
MAGNA MIRRORS
MAGNETI MARELLI HOLDING SPA
MAZDA MOTOR CORPORATION
MAZDA NORTH AMERICAN OPERATIONS
MCLAREN PERFORMANCE TECHNOLOGIES
MERCEDES-BENZ USA LLC
METALDYNE LLC
MIDAS INC
MITSUBISHI FUSO TRUCK OF AMERICA INC
MITSUBISHI MOTORS CORP
MODINE MANUFACTURING COMPANY
MONRO MUFFLER BRAKE INC
MONTUPET SA
MOTOR COACH INDUSTRIES INTERNATIONAL
NAVISTAR INC
NAVISTAR INTERNATIONAL CORP
NAVTEQ CORPORATION

NEWCOR INC
NEWMAR CORP
NIPPON PISTON RING CO LTD
NISSAN MOTOR CO LTD
NYX INC
ONSTAR CORPORATION
ORBITAL CORPORATION LTD
O'REILLY AUTOMOTIVE INC
OSHKOSH CORPORATION
PACCAR INC
PARK-OHIO HOLDINGS CORP
PENSKE AUTOMOTIVE GROUP INC
PENSKE CORPORATION
PEP BOYS-MANNY MOE & JACK (THE)
PETERSON MANUFACTURING CO
PILKINGTON PLC
POLARIS INDUSTRIES INC
PPG INDUSTRIES INC
PROGRESSIVE CORPORATION (THE)
REMY INTERNATIONAL INC
RENT-A-WRECK OF AMERICA INC
RHEINMETALL AG
RICART AUTOMOTIVE INC
RIETER HOLDING LTD
RIZZA AUTOMOTIVE GROUP
ROBERT BOSCH GMBH
RUSH ENTERPRISES INC
RUSS DARROW GROUP INC
SAAB AUTOMOBILE AB
SAAB CARS NORTH AMERICA INC
SALEEN PERFORMANCE VEHICLES
SAM SWOPE AUTO GROUP INC
SANLUIS CORPORACION SAB DE CV
SEQUA CORP
SHANGHAI AUTOMOTIVE INDUSTRY CORP (SAIC)
SIEMENS AG
SKYLINE CORPORATION
SMART GMBH
SOGEFI SPA
SONIC AUTOMOTIVE INC
SPARTAN MOTORS INC
SPECTRA PREMIUM INDUSTRIES INC
SPITZER MANAGEMENT INC
SRG GLOBAL INC
STACKPOLE LIMITED COMPANY
STANDARD MOTOR PRODUCTS INC
STATE FARM INSURANCE COMPANIES
STELLICAN LTD
STERLING AUTOBODY CENTERS
STONERIDGE INC
STRATTEC SECURITY CORP
SUPREME INDUSTRIES INC
TBC CORPORATION
TELEFLEX INC
TENNECO INC
TEREX CORPORATION
THOR INDUSTRIES INC
TI AUTOMOTIVE
TITAN INTERNATIONAL INC
TOKAI RIKA CO LTD
TOWER AUTOMOTIVE LLC
TOYO TIRE & RUBBER CO LTD
TOYODA GOSEI CO LTD
TOYOTA MOTOR CORPORATION
TOYOTA MOTOR CREDIT CORP
TREADWAYS CORP
TRELLEBORG AB
TRW AUTOMOTIVE HOLDINGS CORP
UNI-SELECT INC
UTILIMASTER CORP
UTILITY TRAILER MANUFACTURING CO
VALEO
VISTA PRO AUTOMOTIVE LLC
VISTEON CORPORATION
VOLKSWAGEN GROUP OF AMERICA INC
VOLVO CAR CORPORATION
VOLVO CARS OF NORTH AMERICA INC
WABASH NATIONAL CORP
WANXIANG AMERICA CORPORATION
WANXIANG GROUP CORPORATION
WESCAST INDUSTRIES INC
WINNEBAGO INDUSTRIES INC
YAMAHA MOTOR CO LTD
YAZAKI NORTH AMERICA INC
ZAP
ZF FRIEDRICHSHAFEN AG
ZHEJIANG GEELY HOLDING GROUP
ZIEBART INTERNATIONAL CORP
ZIPCAR INC

SOUTHEAST

3M COMPANY
AAMCO TRANSMISSIONS INC
AB VOLVO
ABC GROUP
ACCURIDE CORPORATION
ADESA INC
ADVANCE AUTO PARTS INC
AGS AUTOMOTIVE SYSTEMS INC
AISIN SEIKI CO LTD
ALLIED SYSTEMS HOLDINGS INC
ALLSTATE CORPORATION (THE)
ALLY FINANCIAL INC
ALPS AUTOMOTIVE INC
ALPS ELECTRIC CO LTD
AMERCO
AMERICAN HONDA MOTOR CO INC
AMERICAN TIRE DISTRIBUTORS
AMERICA'S CAR-MART INC
APPLIED INDUSTRIAL TECHNOLOGIES INC
ARVINMERITOR INC
ASAHI GLASS COMPANY LIMITED
ASBURY AUTOMOTIVE GROUP INC
ASTON MARTIN LAGONDA LTD
AUDI AG
AUDI OF AMERICA INC

AUTOBYTEL INC
AUTONATION INC
AUTOZONE INC
BENTELER GROUP (THE)
BENTLEY MOTORS
BLUE BIRD CORPORATION
BMW OF NORTH AMERICA LLC
BORGWARNER INC
BRAMAN MANAGEMENT ASSOCIATION
BRIDGESTONE BANDAG LLC
BRIDGESTONE CORPORATION
BROWN AUTOMOTIVE GROUP LTD
CALSONIC KANSEI CORPORATION
CARLISLE COMPANIES INC
CARMAX GROUP
CARQUEST CORP
CATERPILLAR INC
CERADYNE
CERBERUS CAPITAL MANAGEMENT LP
CHRYSLER FINANCIAL SERVICES LLC
CHRYSLER GROUP LLC
CLARCOR INC
CLARION CO LTD
COAST DISTRIBUTION SYSTEM INC
COBALT GROUP (THE)
COLLINS INDUSTRIES INC
COMMERCIAL VEHICLE GROUP INC (CVG)
COMPAGNIE GENERALE DES ETABLISSEMENTS MICHELIN
COMPAGNIE PLASTIC OMNIUM
CONSUMER PORTFOLIO SERVICES INC
CONTINENTAL AG
COOPER TIRE & RUBBER COMPANY
COPART INC
CUMMINS FILTRATION
CUMMINS INC
DAIMLER AG
DAIMLER TRUCKS NORTH AMERICA LLC
DANA HOLDINGS CORPORATION
DARCARS AUTOMOTIVE GROUP
DEERE & CO
DELPHI CORP
DENSO CORPORATION
DISCOUNT TIRE CO
DOLLAR THRIFTY AUTOMOTIVE GROUP INC
DONLEN CORPORATION
DORMAN PRODUCTS INC
DRIVETIME AUTOMOTIVE GROUP INC
E I DU PONT DE NEMOURS & CO (DUPONT)
EAGLEPICHER CORPORATION
EATON CORP
ELDER AUTOMOTIVE GROUP
ENER1 INC
ENTERPRISE HOLDINGS
FEDERAL MOGUL CORP
FEDERAL SIGNAL CORP
FERRARI SPA
FINISHMASTER INC
FIRST INVESTORS FINANCIAL SERVICES GROUP INC
FISHER & COMPANY INC
FORD MOTOR CO
FORD MOTOR CREDIT CO LLC
GEICO CORPORATION
GENERAL MOTORS COMPANY (GM)
GENUINE PARTS COMPANY
GEORG FISCHER LTD
GKN PLC
GMAC INSURANCE HOLDINGS INC
GOODYEAR TIRE & RUBBER COMPANY (THE)
GREAT DANE LIMITED PARTNERSHIP
GROUP 1 AUTOMOTIVE INC
GROUP LOTUS PLC
GT TECHNOLOGIES INC
GUARDIAN INDUSTRIES CORP
GULF STATES TOYOTA INC
HANKOOK TIRE CO LTD
HARLEY-DAVIDSON INC
HELLA KGAA HUECK & CO
HENDRICK AUTOMOTIVE GROUP
HERTZ GLOBAL HOLDINGS INC
HOLMAN ENTERPRISES
HONDA MOTOR CO LTD
HONDA OF AMERICA MFG INC
HYUNDAI MOBIS CO LTD
HYUNDAI MOTOR AMERICA
HYUNDAI MOTOR COMPANY
INGERSOLL-RAND PLC
INTERSTATE BATTERY SYSTEM OF AMERICA
ISUZU MOTORS AMERICA INC
JAGUAR CARS LTD
JASON INC
JB POINDEXTER & CO INC
JM FAMILY ENTERPRISES
JOHNSON CONTROLS INC
KAR AUCTION SERVICES INC
KAWASAKI HEAVY INDUSTRIES LTD
KELLEY AUTOMOTIVE GROUP
KEY SAFETY SYSTEMS INC
KEYSTONE AUTOMOTIVE INDUSTRIES INC
KIA MOTORS CORPORATION
KUMHO TIRE CO LTD
LAND ROVER
LDI LTD
LEAR CORP
LKQ CORP
LOJACK CORPORTATION
LUND INTERNATIONAL INC
MAACO ENTERPRISES INC
MACK TRUCKS INC
MAGNA INTERNATIONAL INC
MARANGONI SPA
MAZDA MOTOR CORPORATION
MAZDA NORTH AMERICAN OPERATIONS
MERCEDES-BENZ USA LLC
MIDAS INC

NORTHEAST

COAST DISTRIBUTION SYSTEM INC
COBALT GROUP (THE)
COMMERCIAL VEHICLE GROUP INC (CVG)
COMPAGNIE GENERALE DES ETABLISSEMENTS MICHELIN
COMPAGNIE PLASTIC OMNIUM
CONSUMER PORTFOLIO SERVICES INC
CONTINENTAL AG
COOPER TIRE & RUBBER COMPANY
COPART INC
CUMMINS INC
DAIMLER AG
DAIMLER TRUCKS NORTH AMERICA LLC
DANA HOLDINGS CORPORATION
DARCARS AUTOMOTIVE GROUP
DEERE & CO
DEI HOLDINGS INC
DELPHI CORP
DENSO CORPORATION
DISCOUNT TIRE CO
DOLLAR THRIFTY AUTOMOTIVE GROUP INC
DONLEN CORPORATION
DORMAN PRODUCTS INC
DRIVETIME AUTOMOTIVE GROUP INC
E I DU PONT DE NEMOURS & CO (DUPONT)
EAGLEPICHER CORPORATION
EAST PENN MANUFACTURING CO INC
EATON CORP
ENER1 INC
ENTERPRISE HOLDINGS
FAULKNER ORGANIZATION (THE)
FAURECIA SA
FEDERAL MOGUL CORP
FEDERAL SIGNAL CORP
FERRARI SPA
FINISHMASTER INC
FIRST AUTOMOTIVE GROUP CORPORATION
FIRST INVESTORS FINANCIAL SERVICES GROUP INC
FORD MOTOR CO
FORD MOTOR CREDIT CO LLC
FUEL SYSTEMS SOLUTIONS INC
FUJI HEAVY INDUSTRIES LTD (SUBARU)
GEICO CORPORATION
GENERAL MOTORS COMPANY (GM)
GENUINE PARTS COMPANY
GKN PLC
GMAC INSURANCE HOLDINGS INC
GOODYEAR TIRE & RUBBER COMPANY (THE)
GREAT DANE LIMITED PARTNERSHIP
GROUP 1 AUTOMOTIVE INC
GROUP LOTUS PLC
GUARDIAN INDUSTRIES CORP
HAHN AUTOMOTIVE WAREHOUSE INC
HANKOOK TIRE CO LTD
HARLEY-DAVIDSON INC
HELLA KGAA HUECK & CO
HENDRICK AUTOMOTIVE GROUP
HERB CHAMBERS COMPANIES (THE)
HERTZ GLOBAL HOLDINGS INC
HOLMAN ENTERPRISES
HOMETOWN AUTO RETAILERS INC
HONDA MOTOR CO LTD
HONDA OF AMERICA MFG INC
HYUNDAI MOBIS CO LTD
HYUNDAI MOTOR AMERICA
HYUNDAI MOTOR COMPANY
INERGY AUTOMOTIVE
INGERSOLL-RAND PLC
INTERSTATE BATTERY SYSTEM OF AMERICA
ISUZU MOTORS AMERICA INC
JAGUAR CARS LTD
JASON INC
JB POINDEXTER & CO INC
JD POWER & ASSOCIATES
JIM KOONS AUTOMOTIVE COMPANIES INC
JM FAMILY ENTERPRISES
JOHNSON CONTROLS INC
KAWASAKI HEAVY INDUSTRIES LTD
KEY PLASTICS LLC
KEYSTONE AUTOMOTIVE INDUSTRIES INC
KOITO MANUFACTURING CO LTD
KOLBENSCHMIDT PIERBURG AG
KUMHO TIRE CO LTD
LAND ROVER
LDI LTD
LEAR CORP
LKQ CORP
LOJACK CORPORTATION
LUCOR INC
MAACO ENTERPRISES INC
MACK TRUCKS INC
MAGNA INTERNATIONAL INC
MAGNA MIRRORS
MAJOR AUTOMOTIVE COMPANIES INC
MAYBACH
MAZDA MOTOR CORPORATION
MAZDA NORTH AMERICAN OPERATIONS
MERCEDES-BENZ USA LLC
METALDYNE LLC
MIDAS INC
MILLER INDUSTRIES INC
MITSUBISHI FUSO TRUCK OF AMERICA INC
MODINE MANUFACTURING COMPANY
MONRO MUFFLER BRAKE INC
MOTOR COACH INDUSTRIES INTERNATIONAL
MOTORCAR PARTS OF AMERICA INC
NAVISTAR INC
NAVISTAR INTERNATIONAL CORP
NISSAN MOTOR CO LTD
ORBITAL CORPORATION LTD
O'REILLY AUTOMOTIVE INC
ORION BUS INDUSTRIES
OSHKOSH CORPORATION
OURISMAN AUTOMOTIVE ENTERPRISES
PACCAR INC

PARK-OHIO HOLDINGS CORP
PENSKE AUTOMOTIVE GROUP INC
PENSKE CORPORATION
PEP BOYS-MANNY MOE & JACK (THE)
PILKINGTON PLC
POTAMKIN AUTOMOTIVE GROUP
PPG INDUSTRIES INC
PROGRESSIVE CORPORATION (THE)
PROTON HOLDINGS BERHAD
PSA PEUGEOT CITROEN SA
REMY INTERNATIONAL INC
RENT-A-WRECK OF AMERICA INC
RHEINMETALL AG
ROBERT BOSCH GMBH
ROSENTHAL AUTOMOTIVE ORGANIZATION
SAAB CARS NORTH AMERICA INC
SANSONE AUTO NETWORK
SEGWAY LLC
SEQUA CORP
SHEEHY AUTO STORES
SIEMENS AG
SIRIUS XM RADIO INC
SKYLINE CORPORATION
SMART GMBH
SOGEFI SPA
SONIC AUTOMOTIVE INC
SPARTAN MOTORS INC
SPITZER MANAGEMENT INC
STANADYNE CORPORATION
STANDARD MOTOR PRODUCTS INC
STATE FARM INSURANCE COMPANIES
STELLICAN LTD
STERLING AUTOBODY CENTERS
STONERIDGE INC
SUPREME INDUSTRIES INC
TATA GROUP
TBC CORPORATION
TELEFLEX INC
TENNECO INC
TEREX CORPORATION
TITAN INTERNATIONAL INC
TORESCO ENTERPRISES INC
TOYOTA MOTOR CORPORATION
TOYOTA MOTOR CREDIT CORP
TREADWAYS CORP
TRELLEBORG AB
TRW AUTOMOTIVE HOLDINGS CORP
UNI-SELECT INC
UTILITY TRAILER MANUFACTURING CO
VALEO
VISTA PRO AUTOMOTIVE LLC
VOLKSWAGEN AG
VOLKSWAGEN GROUP OF AMERICA INC
VOLVO CAR CORPORATION
VOLVO CARS OF NORTH AMERICA INC
WABASH NATIONAL CORP
YAMAHA MOTOR CO LTD
YAZAKI NORTH AMERICA INC
ZAP
ZF FRIEDRICHSHAFEN AG
ZHEJIANG GEELY HOLDING GROUP
ZIEBART INTERNATIONAL CORP
ZIPCAR INC

INDEX OF FIRMS WITH INTERNATIONAL OPERATIONS

GAZ GROUP
GENERAL MOTORS COMPANY (GM)
GENERAL MOTORS OF CANADA LTD
GENTEX CORPORATION
GENUINE PARTS COMPANY
GEORG FISCHER LTD
GKN PLC
GM DAEWOO AUTO AND TECHNOLOGY CO
GM HOLDEN LTD
GMAC INSURANCE HOLDINGS INC
GOODYEAR TIRE & RUBBER COMPANY (THE)
GREAT DANE LIMITED PARTNERSHIP
GROUP 1 AUTOMOTIVE INC
GROUP LOTUS PLC
GT TECHNOLOGIES INC
GUARDIAN INDUSTRIES CORP
HANKOOK TIRE CO LTD
HARLEY-DAVIDSON INC
HAYES LEMMERZ INTERNATIONAL INC
HELLA KGAA HUECK & CO
HERO HONDA MOTORS LTD
HERTZ GLOBAL HOLDINGS INC
HILITE INTERNATIONAL INC
HINO MOTOR SALES (THAILAND) LTD
HINO MOTORS LTD
HONDA MOTOR CO LTD
HYUNDAI MOBIS CO LTD
HYUNDAI MOTOR COMPANY
INCHCAPE PLC
INERGY AUTOMOTIVE
INGERSOLL-RAND PLC
INOUE RUBBER (THAILAND) PCL
INTERSTATE BATTERY SYSTEM OF AMERICA
ISUZU MOTORS LTD
JAGUAR CARS LTD
JARDINE CYCLE AND CARRIAGE
JASON INC
JB POINDEXTER & CO INC
JD POWER & ASSOCIATES
JL FRENCH AUTOMOTIVE CASTINGS
JM FAMILY ENTERPRISES
JOHNSON CONTROLS INC
KANTO AUTO WORKS LTD
KAR AUCTION SERVICES INC
KAWASAKI HEAVY INDUSTRIES LTD
KEY PLASTICS LLC
KEY SAFETY SYSTEMS INC
KEYSTONE AUTOMOTIVE INDUSTRIES INC
KIA MOTORS CORPORATION
KOENIGSEGG AUTOMOTIVE AB
KOITO MANUFACTURING CO LTD
KOLBENSCHMIDT PIERBURG AG
KUMHO TIRE CO LTD
LACKS ENTERPRISES INC
LAND ROVER
LEAR CORP
LINAMAR CORP
LOJACK CORPORTATION
MAACO ENTERPRISES INC
MACK TRUCKS INC
MAGNA INTERNATIONAL INC
MAGNA MIRRORS
MAGNETI MARELLI HOLDING SPA
MAHINDRA & MAHINDRA LIMITED
MARANGONI SPA
MARUTI SUZUKI INDIA LIMITED
MAYBACH
MAZDA MOTOR CORPORATION
METALDYNE LLC
MIDAS INC
MILLER INDUSTRIES INC
MITSUBISHI FUSO TRUCK OF AMERICA INC
MITSUBISHI MOTORS (THAILAND) CO LTD
MITSUBISHI MOTORS CORP
MODINE MANUFACTURING COMPANY
MONTUPET SA
MORGAN MOTOR COMPANY (THE)
MOTOR COACH INDUSTRIES INTERNATIONAL
MOTORCAR PARTS OF AMERICA INC
NAVISTAR INC
NAVISTAR INTERNATIONAL CORP
NAVTEQ CORPORATION
NIHON PLAST CO LTD
NIPPON PISTON RING CO LTD
NISSAN DIESEL (THAILAND) CO LTD
NISSAN MOTOR CO LTD
NISSAN NORTH AMERICA INC
NISSAN SHATAI CO LTD
NYX INC
ONSTAR CORPORATION
ORBITAL CORPORATION LTD
ORION BUS INDUSTRIES
OSHKOSH CORPORATION
PACCAR INC
PARK-OHIO HOLDINGS CORP
PENSKE AUTOMOTIVE GROUP INC
PENSKE CORPORATION
PEP BOYS-MANNY MOE & JACK (THE)
PIAGGIO & C SPA
PILKINGTON PLC
PININFARINA SPA
PIRELLI & C SPA
POLARIS INDUSTRIES INC
PORSCHE AUTOMOBIL HOLDING SE
PPG INDUSTRIES INC
PRIMEARTH EV ENERGY CO LTD
PROGRESSIVE CORPORATION (THE)
PROTON HOLDINGS BERHAD
PSA PEUGEOT CITROEN SA
PT ASTRA INTERNATIONAL TBK
REMY INTERNATIONAL INC
RENAULT SA
RENT-A-WRECK OF AMERICA INC
RHEINMETALL AG
RIETER HOLDING LTD
ROBERT BOSCH GMBH

ROLLS ROYCE MOTOR CAR LIMITED
RYBROOK HOLDINGS LIMITED
RYGOR GROUP LTD
S&T MOTORS CO LTD
SAAB AUTOMOBILE AB
SAAB CARS NORTH AMERICA INC
SAIC-GM-WULING AUTOMOBILE COMPANY
SANLUIS CORPORACION SAB DE CV
SCANIA AB
SEAT SA
SEQUA CORP
SHANGHAI AUTOMOTIVE INDUSTRY CORP (SAIC)
SIEMENS AG
SIXT AKTIENGESELLSCHAFT
SKODA AUTO AS
SMART GMBH
SOGEFI SPA
SPECIAL DEVICES INCORPORATED
SPECTRA PREMIUM INDUSTRIES INC
SRG GLOBAL INC
SSANGYONG MOTOR CO
STACKPOLE LIMITED COMPANY
STANADYNE CORPORATION
STANDARD MOTOR PRODUCTS INC
STATE FARM INSURANCE COMPANIES
STELLICAN LTD
STONERIDGE INC
STRATTEC SECURITY CORP
SUPERIOR INDUSTRIES INTERNATIONAL INC
SUZUKI AUTOMOBILE (THAILAND) CO LTD
SUZUKI MOTOR CORPORATION
SYTNER GROUP PLC
TATA GROUP
TATA MOTORS LIMITED
TELEFLEX INC
TENNECO INC
TEREX CORPORATION
TESLA MOTORS INC
THOR INDUSTRIES INC
TI AUTOMOTIVE
TITAN INTERNATIONAL INC
TOKAI RIKA CO LTD
TOWER AUTOMOTIVE LLC
TOYO TIRE & RUBBER CO LTD
TOYODA GOSEI CO LTD
TOYOTA AUTO BODY CO LTD
TOYOTA MOTOR CORPORATION
TOYOTA MOTOR CREDIT CORP
TOYOTA MOTOR THAILAND CO LTD
TRELLEBORG AB
TRI PETCH ISUZU SALES CO LTD
TRW AUTOMOTIVE HOLDINGS CORP
UD TRUCKS CORP
UNIPART GROUP OF COMPANIES
UNI-SELECT INC
UTILITY TRAILER MANUFACTURING CO
VALEO
VAUXHALL MOTORS LTD
VISTA PRO AUTOMOTIVE LLC
VISTEON CORPORATION
VOLKSWAGEN AG
VOLKSWAGEN GROUP OF AMERICA INC
VOLVO CAR CORPORATION
VOLVO CARS OF NORTH AMERICA INC
WABASH NATIONAL CORP
WANXIANG AMERICA CORPORATION
WANXIANG GROUP CORPORATION
WESCAST INDUSTRIES INC
YAMAHA MOTOR CO LTD
YAZAKI NORTH AMERICA INC
YUASA BATTERY (THAILAND) PCL
YULON MOTOR CO LTD
ZF FRIEDRICHSHAFEN AG
ZHEJIANG GEELY HOLDING GROUP
ZIEBART INTERNATIONAL CORP
ZIPCAR INC

Individual Profiles On Each Of THE AUTOMOBILE 400

3M COMPANY

www.3m.com

Industry Group Code: 33911 **Ranks within this company's industry group:** Sales: 1 Profits: 1

Vehicle Manufacturing:		Dealers:		Parts:		Service:		Finance:		Specialty:	
Cars:		Car Dealer New:		Manufacturers:	Y	General Service:		Leasing:		Information Systems:	
Trucks:		Car Dealer Used:		Retail:		Specialty Service:		Auto Loans:		Online Marketing:	
Motorcycles:		Truck Dealer:		Distributors:		Oil Change:		Insurance:		Other:	Y
Specialty:		RV Dealer:		Tires:		Paint and Body:				Publishing:	
Buses:		Motorcycle Dealer:		Batteries:						Rental Cars/Trucks:	
RVs:		Specialty Dealer:									

TYPES OF BUSINESS:

Health Care Products
Specialty Materials & Textiles
Industrial Products
Safety, Security & Protection Products
Display & Graphics Products
Consumer & Office Products
Electronics & Communications Products
Fuel Cell Technology

BRANDS/DIVISIONS/AFFILIATES:

Aearo Technologies Inc
Les Entreprieses Solumed Inc
Quest Technologies Inc
ABRASIVOS SA
Financiere Burgienne
3M Touch Systems
3M Canada
3M Espe

CONTACTS: *Note: Officers with more than one job title may be intentionally listed here more than once.*

George W. Buckley, CEO
George W. Buckley, Pres.
Patrick D. Campbell, CFO/Sr. VP
Robert D. MacDonald, Sr. VP-Mktg. & Sales
Angela S. Lalor, Sr. VP-Human Resources
Frederick J. Palensky, Exec. VP-R&D
Frederick J. Palensky, CTO
Marschall I. Smith, General Counsel/Sr. VP-Legal Affairs
Brad T. Sauer, Exec. VP-Health Care Bus.
H.C. Shin, Exec. VP-Industrial & Transportation Bus.
Joaquin Delgado, Exec. VP-Electro & Comm. Bus.
Joe E. Harlan, Exec. VP-Consumer & Office Bus.
George W. Buckley, Chmn.
Inge Thulin, Exec. VP-Int'l Oper.
John K. Woodworth, Sr. VP-Corp. Supply Chain Oper.

Phone: 651-733-1110	**Fax:** 651-733-9973
Toll-Free: 800-364-3577	
Address: 3M Center, Bldg. 220-11W-02, St. Paul, MN 55144-1000 US	

GROWTH PLANS/SPECIAL FEATURES:

3M Company is involved in the research, manufacturing and marketing of a variety of products. The firm is organized into six segments: health care; consumer and office; display and graphics; electronics and communications; industrial and transportation; and safety, security and protection. The health care segment's products include medical and surgical supplies, skin infection prevention products, drug delivery systems, orthodontic products, health information systems and veterinary products. The consumer and office segment includes office supply, stationery, construction, home improvement, protective material and visual systems products. The display and graphics segment's products include optical film and lenses for electronic displays; touch screens and monitors; screen filters; reflective sheeting; and commercial graphics systems. The electronics and communications segment's products include packaging and interconnection devices (used in circuits); fluids used in computer chips; high-temperature and display tapes; pressure-sensitive tapes and resins; and products for telecommunications systems. The industrial and transportation segment's products include vinyl, polyester, tapes, a variety of non-woven abrasives, adhesives, specialty materials, supply chain execution software, filtration systems, paint finishing products, engineering fluids and components for catalytic converters. The safety, security and protection services segment provides products for personal protection, safety and security, energy control, commercial cleaning and protection, passports and secure cards. In February 2010, the company acquired the Japanese A-One brand of office labels, as well as MTI PolyFab, Inc. In March of 2010, the company signed a research and development agreement with the U.S. Dept. of Energy to assist in developing clear air energy solutions. Also in March 2010, the company announced a partnership with Yushin Precision Equipment Company, Ltd., which will sell and manufacture equipment used in producing 3M's ultrathin wafers for 3-D semi-conductors. In 2010, the firm agreed to acquire Cogent, Inc. for $943 million, Attenti Holdings SA for $230 million and Arizant, Inc. for $810 million.

The company offers a full range of medical and retirement benefits to its employees, including domestic partner benefits; tuition reimbursement; and discounts on company products.

FINANCIALS: **Sales and profits are in thousands of dollars—add 000 to get the full amount. 2009 Note: Financial information for 2009 was not available for all companies at press time.**

2009 Sales: $23,123,000	2009 Profits: $3,193,000	**U.S. Stock Ticker: MMM**
2008 Sales: $25,269,000	2008 Profits: $3,460,000	**Int'l Ticker:** Int'l Exchange:
2007 Sales: $24,462,000	2007 Profits: $4,096,000	Employees: 74,835
2006 Sales: $22,923,000	2006 Profits: $3,851,000	Fiscal Year Ends: 12/31
2005 Sales: $21,167,000	2005 Profits: $3,111,000	Parent Company:

SALARIES/BENEFITS:

Pension Plan:	ESOP Stock Plan: Y	Profit Sharing: Y	Top Exec. Salary: $5,901,401	Bonus: $
Savings Plan: Y	Stock Purch. Plan: Y		Second Exec. Salary: $1,553,068	Bonus: $

OTHER THOUGHTS:

Apparent Women Officers or Directors: 3
Hot Spot for Advancement for Women/Minorities: Y

LOCATIONS: ("Y" = Yes)

West:	Southwest:	Midwest:	Southeast:	Northeast:	International:
Y	Y	Y	Y	Y	Y

Note: Financial information, benefits and other data can change quickly and may vary from those stated here.

A123SYSTEMS

www.a123systems.com

Industry Group Code: 33591 **Ranks within this company's industry group:** Sales: 1 Profits: 3

Vehicle Manufacturing:		Dealers:		Parts:		Service:		Finance:		Specialty:	
Cars:		Car Dealer New:		Manufacturers:	Y	General Service:		Leasing:		Information Systems:	
Trucks:		Car Dealer Used:		Retail:		Specialty Service:		Auto Loans:		Online Marketing:	
Motorcycles:		Truck Dealer:		Distributors:		Oil Change:		Insurance:		Other:	
Specialty:		RV Dealer:		Tires:		Paint and Body:				Publishing:	
Buses:		Motorcycle Dealer:		Batteries:	Y					Rental Cars/Trucks:	
RVs:		Specialty Dealer:									

TYPES OF BUSINESS:

Batteries, Design & Manufacture
Lithium-Ion Batteries
Nanotechnology
Batteries for Electric Automobiles
Nanophosphate

BRANDS/DIVISIONS/AFFILIATES:

A123Systems China
Hymotion, Inc.

CONTACTS:

Note: Officers with more than one job title may be intentionally listed here more than once.

David Vieau, CEO
David Vieau, Pres.
Michael Rubino, CFO
Andy Chu, VP-Mktg. & Comm.
Andrew Cole, VP-Human Resources & Organizational Dev.
Bart Riley, VP-R&D
Bart Riley, CTO
Michael Rubino, VP-Admin.
Eric Pyenson, General Counsel/VP
Louis Golato, VP-Oper.
Kerry Farrell, Public Rel.
Michael Rubino, VP-Finance
Grace Chang, VP-Quality
Robert J. Johnson, VP-Energy Solutions Group
Jason Forcier, VP-Automotive Solutions Group
Chris Tecca, VP-Cell Prod. Group
Desh Deshpande, Chmn.
Tao Zheng, Pres., A123Systems China

Phone: 617-778-5700	**Fax:** 617-778-5749
Toll-Free:	
Address: 321 Arsenal St., Arsenal on the Charles, Watertown, MA 02472 US	

GROWTH PLANS/SPECIAL FEATURES:

A123Systems is the innovator of a powerful, long-lasting, environmentally safe Lithium-Ion battery derived from nanoscale materials, called Nanophosphate lithium battery technology. Founded in 2001 in Watertown, Massachusetts, the company has gone beyond its MIT-research-based design operations to make use of manufacturing space in the U.S., China (through subsidiary A123Systems China) and Korea. The batteries, which currently take the form of cylindrical cells, are presently in mass production after successful testing and customer evaluation. The results indicate that this battery sports numerous features that set it apart from its sister products on the market. For example, it was proven to have discharge rates as high as 100C; deliver power at 3000 watts per kilogram; a fast charge time; high thermal conductivity; very little sensitivity to environmental temperature; virtually no toxicity; and a long cycle life. The battery design is capable of powering a diverse range of high power rechargeable battery applications, including power tools; hybrid electric vehicles, power cells for which are developed through the firm's Hymotion division; heavy duty vehicle fleets; aviation propulsion systems; specialized military equipment, including directed energy weapons and stealth drive applications; and medical devices. The firm has an agreement with General Motors Corp. (GM) to co-develop nanophosphate battery cells for use in GM's electric drive E-Flex system. However, much of the production of batteries for Chevy's upcoming Volt electric car may go to LG Chem. In April 2009, the company announced an agreement with Chrysler to provide batteries for a future Chrysler electric car. In December 2009, the company announced plans to form a joint venture with SAIC Motor Co., Ltd., an automobile manufacturer in China, for the purpose of creating vehicle traction battery systems in hybrid electric and pure electric passenger vehicles, as well as heavy duty trucks and buses in China.

FINANCIALS:

Sales and profits are in thousands of dollars—add 000 to get the full amount. 2009 Note: Financial information for 2009 was not available for all companies at press time.

2009 Sales: $91,049	2009 Profits: $-86,589	**U.S. Stock Ticker: AONE**
2008 Sales: $68,525	2008 Profits: $-80,431	**Int'l Ticker:** Int'l Exchange:
2007 Sales: $41,349	2007 Profits: $-30,993	Employees: 24
2006 Sales: $	2006 Profits: $	Fiscal Year Ends:
2005 Sales: $	2005 Profits: $	Parent Company:

SALARIES/BENEFITS:

Pension Plan:	ESOP Stock Plan:	Profit Sharing:	Top Exec. Salary: $300,000	Bonus: $227,700
Savings Plan:	Stock Purch. Plan:		Second Exec. Salary: $210,000	Bonus: $98,427

OTHER THOUGHTS:

Apparent Women Officers or Directors: 2
Hot Spot for Advancement for Women/Minorities: Y

LOCATIONS: ("Y" = Yes)

West:	Southwest:	Midwest:	Southeast:	Northeast:	International:
		Y		Y	Y

AAMCO TRANSMISSIONS INC

www.aamco.com

Industry Group Code: 8111 **Ranks within this company's industry group:** Sales: Profits:

Vehicle Manufacturing:		Dealers:		Parts:		Service:		Finance:		Specialty:	
Cars:		Car Dealer New:		Manufacturers:		General Service:	Y	Leasing:		Information Systems:	
Trucks:		Car Dealer Used:		Retail:		Specialty Service:	Y	Auto Loans:		Online Marketing:	
Motorcycles:		Truck Dealer:		Distributors:		Oil Change:		Insurance:		Other:	Y
Specialty:		RV Dealer:		Tires:		Paint and Body:				Publishing:	
Buses:		Motorcycle Dealer:		Batteries:						Rental Cars/Trucks:	
RVs:		Specialty Dealer:									

TYPES OF BUSINESS:

Automotive Repair & Maintenance-Transmissions
Automatic Transmission Fluid
Bioethanol Conversion

BRANDS/DIVISIONS/AFFILIATES:

AAMCO Automatic Transmission Fluid
AAMCO Synthetic Blend ATF
AAMCO ATF D/M
AAMCO ATF+3
AAMCO ATF Type F
Cottman Transmissions
Flex-Box Smart Kit
American Capital

CONTACTS: *Note: Officers with more than one job title may be intentionally listed here more than once.*

Marc C. Graham, CEO
Marc C. Graham, Pres.
Mike Sumsky, CFO
Brian O'Donnell, VP-Sales
Bill Larkin, VP-Tech. Svcs.
Jim Goniea, General Counsel/VP-Law
Brian O'Donnell, Sr. VP-Oper.
Mike Sumsky, VP-Finance
Kevin Gordon, VP-Brand Dev.

Phone: 215-643-5885 **Fax:** 215-956-0340
Toll-Free: 800-462-2626
Address: 201 Gibraltar Rd., Horsham, PA 19044-2329 US

GROWTH PLANS/SPECIAL FEATURES:

AAMCO Transmissions, Inc. is a chain of auto transmission shops with more than 850 independently owned and operated franchise locations in the U.S., Canada and Puerto Rico. AAMCO's services include diagnostic, repair and maintenance services for automatic and standard transmissions in cars and trucks; free towing; external inspections; and estimates. The company guarantees its services through a selection of six warranty packages from 90-day limited contracts to lifetime coverage. AAMCO also offers a national fleet program in which more than 500 owners of large fleets of vehicles contract transmission services at discounted prices. Moreover, the firm manufactures a branded automatic transmission fluid, AAMCO Automatic Transmission Fluid (ATF), which is marketed by Exxon Superflo. The ExxonMobil subsidiary blends, packages and markets AAMCO ATF and additional transmission fluid products (AAMCO Mercon V, AAMCO Synthetic Blend ATF, AAMCO ATF D/M, AAMCO ATF+3 and AAMCO ATF Type F) through automotive product retailers across North America. The firm offers its Eco-Green Auto Service at approximately 40 locations in the U.S., which meet eco-friendly standards such as solvent and waste fluid recycling. These locations offer, in addition to standard AAMCO services, a bioethanol fuel conversion kit called the Flex-Box Smart Kit, developed in partnership with Flex Fuel U.S. The investment firm American Capital owns a majority stake in the company, and has stated plans to combine AAMCO with its other portfolio company Cottman Transmissions.

FINANCIALS: **Sales and profits are in thousands of dollars—add 000 to get the full amount. 2009 Note: Financial information for 2009 was not available for all companies at press time.**

2009 Sales: $	2009 Profits: $	**U.S. Stock Ticker: Private**
2008 Sales: $	2008 Profits: $	**Int'l Ticker:** Int'l Exchange:
2007 Sales: $	2007 Profits: $	Employees:
2006 Sales: $	2006 Profits: $	Fiscal Year Ends: 12/31
2005 Sales: $	2005 Profits: $	Parent Company: AMERICAN CAPITAL

SALARIES/BENEFITS:

Pension Plan:	ESOP Stock Plan:	Profit Sharing:	Top Exec. Salary: $	Bonus: $
Savings Plan:	Stock Purch. Plan:		Second Exec. Salary: $	Bonus: $

OTHER THOUGHTS:

Apparent Women Officers or Directors:
Hot Spot for Advancement for Women/Minorities:

LOCATIONS: ("Y" = Yes)

West:	Southwest:	Midwest:	Southeast:	Northeast:	International:
Y	Y	Y	Y	Y	Y

AB VOLVO

www.volvo.com

Industry Group Code: 336120 **Ranks within this company's industry group:** Sales: 1 Profits: 6

Vehicle Manufacturing:		Dealers:		Parts:		Service:		Finance:		Specialty:	
Cars:		Car Dealer New:		Manufacturers:	Y	General Service:		Leasing:		Information Systems:	
Trucks:	Y	Car Dealer Used:		Retail:		Specialty Service:		Auto Loans:	Y	Online Marketing:	
Motorcycles:		Truck Dealer:		Distributors:		Oil Change:		Insurance:	Y	Other:	Y
Specialty:		RV Dealer:		Tires:		Paint and Body:				Publishing:	
Buses:	Y	Motorcycle Dealer:		Batteries:						Rental Cars/Trucks:	
RVs:		Specialty Dealer:									

TYPES OF BUSINESS:

Truck Manufacturer
Engines
Buses
Aerospace Products
Construction Equipment
Financial Services
Intelligent Transport Systems
Overhaul & Repair Services

BRANDS/DIVISIONS/AFFILIATES:

Volvo Trucks
Renault Trucks
Nissan Diesel Motor Co Ltd
Mack Trucks Inc
Volvo Penta
Volvo Aero
Eicher Motors

CONTACTS:

Note: Officers with more than one job title may be intentionally listed here more than once.

Leif Johansson, CEO
Leif Johansson, Pres.
Mikael Bratt, CFO/Sr. VP
Stefan Johnsson, Sr. VP-Human Resources & Bus. Units
Eva Persson, General Counsel/Sr. VP
Per Lojdquist, Sr. VP-Corp. Comm. & Brand Mgmt.
Stefano Chmielewski, Pres., Renault Trucks
Staffan Jufors, Pres., Volvo Truck Corp.
Hakan Karlsson, Pres., Volvo Bus Corp.
Dennis Slagle, Pres./CEO-Mack Trucks, Inc.
Louis Schweitzer, Interim Chmn.
Par Ostberg, Pres., Trucks, Asia

Phone: 46-31-66-10-67 **Fax:** 46-31-53-72-96
Toll-Free:
Address: Volvo Bergegardsvag 1, Torslanda, Goteborg, SE-405 08 Sweden

GROWTH PLANS/SPECIAL FEATURES:

AB Volvo, also called the Volvo Group, is a world leader in the manufacture of trucks and heavy machinery, including buses, construction equipment and marine, industrial and aerospace components. The Volvo Group has nine product-related business areas, Volvo Trucks, Renault Trucks, Mack Trucks, Nissan Diesel, Buses, Construction Equipment, Volvo Penta, Volvo Aero and Financial Services. The firm also has six supporting business units: Volvo 3P, Volvo Powertrain, Volvo Parts, Volvo Technology, Volvo Logistics, Volvo Information Technology and Volvo Technology Transfer. The 3P unit handles purchasing and product planning and development for the three truck businesses, Volvo, Renault and Mack, which mainly manufacture medium-heavy to heavy, long-haul trucks marketed in 130 countries worldwide. Powertrain supplies engine drivelines for Volvo's trucks, busses and Volvo Penta, an engine manufacturer whose engines are used in shipping, leisure boating, power plants and heavy equipment. The Parts unit supports aftermarket (often repair and replacement) activities; the Technology unit is mainly involved in R&D; the Logistics unit offers services from logistics system design to packaging, insurance and distribution; Volvo Information Technology manages complex IT systems for all aspects of the industrial process including product lifecycle management and IT operations; Volvo Technology Transfer a venture capital company. Volvo Aero provides advanced engine components for aircraft and space rockets. It also offers services such as sales of spare parts for aircraft and aircraft engines; sales and leasing of aircraft and aircraft engines; and overhaul and repair. Volvo Financial Services covers customer financing, insurance, treasury, real estate and related services operations.

FINANCIALS:

Sales and profits are in thousands of dollars—add 000 to get the full amount. 2009 Note: Financial information for 2009 was not available for all companies at press time.

2009 Sales: $28,777,400	2009 Profits: $-1,939,660	**U.S. Stock Ticker: VOLV**
2008 Sales: $36,793,200	2008 Profits: $1,213,570	**Int'l Ticker: VOLV B** Int'l Exchange: Stockholm-SSE
2007 Sales: $34,580,500	2007 Profits: $1,820,840	Employees: 90,208
2006 Sales: $44,002,000	2006 Profits: $2,765,600	Fiscal Year Ends: 12/31
2005 Sales: $31,813,343	2005 Profits: $1,804,045	Parent Company:

SALARIES/BENEFITS:

Pension Plan:	ESOP Stock Plan:	Profit Sharing:	Top Exec. Salary: $	Bonus: $
Savings Plan:	Stock Purch. Plan:		Second Exec. Salary: $	Bonus: $

OTHER THOUGHTS:

Apparent Women Officers or Directors: 2
Hot Spot for Advancement for Women/Minorities: Y

LOCATIONS: ("Y" = Yes)

West:	Southwest:	Midwest:	Southeast:	Northeast:	International:
Y	Y	Y	Y	Y	Y

ABC GROUP

www.abcgroupinc.com

Industry Group Code: 3363 **Ranks within this company's industry group:** Sales: Profits:

Vehicle Manufacturing:		Dealers:		Parts:		Service:		Finance:		Specialty:	
Cars:		Car Dealer New:		Manufacturers:	Y	General Service:		Leasing:		Information Systems:	
Trucks:		Car Dealer Used:		Retail:		Specialty Service:		Auto Loans:		Online Marketing:	
Motorcycles:		Truck Dealer:		Distributors:		Oil Change:		Insurance:		Other:	
Specialty:		RV Dealer:		Tires:		Paint and Body:				Publishing:	
Buses:		Motorcycle Dealer:		Batteries:						Rental Cars/Trucks:	
RVs:		Specialty Dealer:									

TYPES OF BUSINESS:

Automotive Plastics
Design & Manufacturing Services
Plastic Packaging & Industrial Parts
Plastic Consumer Products
Decorating & Labeling Services

BRANDS/DIVISIONS/AFFILIATES:

Polybottle Group (The)

CONTACTS:
Note: Officers with more than one job title may be intentionally listed here more than once.

Robert Kunihiro, Co-Managing Dir.
MarkPoynton, Co-Managing Dir.
Helga Schmidt, Chmn.

Phone: 416-246-1782	**Fax:** 416-246-1997
Toll-Free:	
Address: 2 Norelco Dr., Toronto, ON M9L 2X6 Canada	

GROWTH PLANS/SPECIAL FEATURES:

ABC Group is a Canadian-based company that specializes in the design, development and production of plastic automotive systems and components for automotive OEMs (original equipment manufacturers). The company operates over 30 manufacturing facilities within Canada, the U.S, Mexico, Brazil, Germany, Croatia, Spain, the U.K., Japan, China, India, Korea and Poland and 10 sales offices worldwide. Manufacturing techniques of the firm include blow molding, injection molding, thermoforming/sheet extrusion, rotational molding, polyurethane foaming and continuous extrusion. Some of the services of the firm include design and engineering; machine building; research and development; and painting. ABC Group's line of products include interior automotive systems such as instrument panels, seating systems, interior trim and HVAC systems; exterior products such as bumper systems, spoilers and blow-molded running boards and exterior trim; under-hood components such as air induction and fluid management systems; high-performance flexible products that include CVJ boots, prop shaft boots and suspension dust covers. The company is also capable of manufacturing products that meet customer requirements and specifications such as impact, airflow, permeation, temperature and NVH (noise, vibration and harshness) requirements. In addition to its primary automotive line of business, the ABC Group serves industrial manufacturers throughout North America with sports, recreational and consumer goods. Products include computer enclosure doors, stadium seats, tool containers and composters. Through its subsidiary, The Polybottle Group, the company custom-manufactures plastic containers and industrial parts for the food products, household and agriculture, chemicals, automotive and petrochemical industries. The Polybottle Group also offers custom filling of bottles, warehousing services, design and product development services and decorating and labeling services.

FINANCIALS:
Sales and profits are in thousands of dollars—add 000 to get the full amount. 2009 Note: Financial information for 2009 was not available for all companies at press time.

2009 Sales: $	2009 Profits: $	**U.S. Stock Ticker: Private**
2008 Sales: $	2008 Profits: $	**Int'l Ticker:** Int'l Exchange:
2007 Sales: $	2007 Profits: $	Employees:
2006 Sales: $	2006 Profits: $	Fiscal Year Ends:
2005 Sales: $	2005 Profits: $	Parent Company:

SALARIES/BENEFITS:

Pension Plan:	ESOP Stock Plan:	Profit Sharing:	Top Exec. Salary: $	Bonus: $
Savings Plan:	Stock Purch. Plan:		Second Exec. Salary: $	Bonus: $

OTHER THOUGHTS:

Apparent Women Officers or Directors: 1
Hot Spot for Advancement for Women/Minorities:

LOCATIONS: ("Y" = Yes)

West:	Southwest:	Midwest:	Southeast:	Northeast:	International:
		Y	Y		Y

ACCURIDE CORPORATION

www.accuridecorp.com

Industry Group Code: 336211 **Ranks within this company's industry group:** Sales: 4 Profits: 5

Vehicle Manufacturing:		Dealers:		Parts:		Service:		Finance:		Specialty:	
Cars:		Car Dealer New:		Manufacturers:	Y	General Service:		Leasing:		Information Systems:	
Trucks:		Car Dealer Used:		Retail:		Specialty Service:		Auto Loans:		Online Marketing:	
Motorcycles:		Truck Dealer:		Distributors:		Oil Change:		Insurance:		Other:	
Specialty:		RV Dealer:		Tires:		Paint and Body:				Publishing:	
Buses:		Motorcycle Dealer:		Batteries:						Rental Cars/Trucks:	
RVs:		Specialty Dealer:									

TYPES OF BUSINESS:

Commercial Vehicle Components
Wheels & Assemblies
Body & Chassis Parts
Seating Assemblies

BRANDS/DIVISIONS/AFFILIATES:

Accuride Wheels
Gunite Corporation
Brillion Iron Works
Imperial Group
Bostrom Seating
Fabco
Transportation Technologies Industries
Accuride Canada, Inc.

CONTACTS: *Note: Officers with more than one job title may be intentionally listed here more than once.*

William M. Lasky, CEO
William M. Lasky, Interim Pres.
James H. Woodward, Jr., CFO/Sr. VP
Richard F. Schomer, Sr. VP-Sales & Mktg.
James Maniatis, Sr. VP-Human Resources
Kenneth Sparks, VP-Structural Prod.
Stephen A. Martin, General Counsel/VP/Corp. Sec.
Steven J. Holt, Sr. VP-Strategy & Growth
Eva Schmitz, Dir.-Corp. Comm.
Todd Taylor, Contact-Investor Rel.
Gregory A. Risch, Chief Acct. Officer/VP
Leigh A. Wright, Sr. VP-Accuride Wheels
Edward J. Gulda, Sr. VP-Gunite & Brillion
Paul Clark, VP-Mktg.
Jasen Drenth, Dir.-Prod. Mgmt., Gunite
William M. Lasky, Chmn.

Phone: 812-962-5000 **Fax:** 812-962-5400
Toll-Free:
Address: 7140 Office Cir., Evansville, IN 47715 US

GROWTH PLANS/SPECIAL FEATURES:

Accuride Corporation is a North American manufacturer of commercial vehicle components. Accuride produces commercial vehicle wheels, wheel-end parts and assemblies, truck body and chassis parts, seating assemblies and other components. Brands marketed by the company include Accuride, Gunite, Imperial, Bostrom, Fabco and Brillion. The firm operates through six different divisions: Accuride Wheels, Gunite Corporation, Brillion Iron Works, Imperial Group, Bostrom Seating and Fabco. Accuride's customer list is primarily made up of commercial vehicle manufacturers, including Daimler Truck North America, LLC, with its Daimler Truck North America, Sterling and Western Star brands; PACCAR, Inc., with its Peterbilt and Kenworth brand trucks; International Truck and Engine Corporation, with its International brand; and Volvo Truck Corporation, or Volvo/Mack, with its Volvo and Mack brand trucks. Marketed under the Accuride Wheels brand, wheels accounted for approximately 42% of the company's 2009 sales. Wheel-end components and assemblies, marketed under the brand name Gunite, accounted for approximately 27% of sales, and include such products as brake drums, disc wheel hubs, spoke wheels, disc brake rotors and automatic slack adjusters. Truck body and chassis parts, marketed under the brand name Imperial, accounted for approximately 13% of sales; seating assemblies, marketed under the name Bostrom Seating, accounted for approximately 4%; and other components, such as military wheels, steerable drive axles, gear boxes, transmission and engine-related components, industrial components and non-powered farm equipment, accounted for approximately 14%, marketed under the names Brillion and Fabco. The company has a wholly-owned subsidiary, Accuride Canada, Inc., based in Ontario. In February 2010, the firm successfully completed its plan of reorganization and emerged from Chapter 11 bankruptcy.

FINANCIALS: **Sales and profits are in thousands of dollars—add 000 to get the full amount. 2009 Note: Financial information for 2009 was not available for all companies at press time.**

2009 Sales: $570,193 | 2009 Profits: $-140,112
2008 Sales: $931,409 | 2008 Profits: $-328,266
2007 Sales: $1,013,686 | 2007 Profits: $-8,639
2006 Sales: $1,408,155 | 2006 Profits: $65,133
2005 Sales: $1,229,311 | 2005 Profits: $51,229

U.S. Stock Ticker: AURD
Int'l Ticker: Int'l Exchange:
Employees: 2,450
Fiscal Year Ends: 12/31
Parent Company:

SALARIES/BENEFITS:

Pension Plan: | ESOP Stock Plan: | Profit Sharing: Y | Top Exec. Salary: $800,000 | Bonus: $
Savings Plan: Y | Stock Purch. Plan: Y | | Second Exec. Salary: $567,500 | Bonus: $

OTHER THOUGHTS:

Apparent Women Officers or Directors: 2
Hot Spot for Advancement for Women/Minorities: Y

LOCATIONS: ("Y" = Yes)

West:	Southwest:	Midwest:	Southeast:	Northeast:	International:
Y	Y	Y	Y	Y	Y

ADA

www.ada.fr

Industry Group Code: 5321 **Ranks within this company's industry group:** Sales: Profits:

Vehicle Manufacturing:		Dealers:		Parts:		Service:		Finance:		Specialty:	
Cars:		Car Dealer New:		Manufacturers:		General Service:		Leasing:		Information Systems:	
Trucks:		Car Dealer Used:		Retail:		Specialty Service:		Auto Loans:		Online Marketing:	
Motorcycles:		Truck Dealer:		Distributors:		Oil Change:		Insurance:		Other:	
Specialty:		RV Dealer:		Tires:		Paint and Body:				Publishing:	
Buses:		Motorcycle Dealer:		Batteries:						Rental Cars/Trucks:	Y
RVs:		Specialty Dealer:									

TYPES OF BUSINESS:

Automobile Rental

BRANDS/DIVISIONS/AFFILIATES:

G7 Groupe
Holiday Bikes
Via Michelin
A Vendre A Louer
ADA Box
Homebox

CONTACTS:

Note: Officers with more than one job title may be intentionally listed here more than once.

Christopher Plonevez, CEO

Phone: 0-41-27-49-00	**Fax:**
Toll-Free:	
Address: 22-28 rue Henri Barbusse, Clichy, 92585 France	

GROWTH PLANS/SPECIAL FEATURES:

ADA is a franchise car-rental company based in France and the French islands, as well as internationally in Morocco, Luxembourg, Senegal, Dominican Republic, Tunisia and Mauritius. It was established in 1984. As one of the largest private car-rental firms in the world, ADA has nearly 500 locations and offers everything from economy-class cars, electric cars, wagons to minivans. Some agencies also offer commercial vehicles, such as moving vans, dump trucks, all terrain vehicles and weight-bearing porters. Through ADA's partnership with Holiday Bikes, the company also offers two-wheeled vehicles such as bicycles, motorcycles and scooters for rent at most agencies. The company's other partnerships include: ADA Box, a firm that rents storage space to customers; A Vendre A Louer, a provider of real estate classified ads on the internet; Homebox, which rents storage boxes, that are located within the company's secure facility. In addition, most of the firm's agencies offer special equipment, such as baby and child seats; boosters; GPS; and snow chains. The company offers supplemental insurance. The company operates in-terminal locations in nearly all of the major airports in France, including Ajaccio, Bastia, Bordeaux, Brest, Lorient, Lyon, Marseille, Montpellier, Nantes, Nice, Paris Orly, Paris Roissy Charles de Gaulle, Perpignan, Toulouse, Guadeloupe, Guyana and La Reunion. ADA also has agencies at all major railway stations in France. ADA customers can locate the agency of their choice through the company's partnership with Via Michelin, a map, route planner and travel guide service for the U.S. and Europe. ADA is a subsidiary of the G7 Groupe, a global holding company with several subsidiaries. These include Europe's largest taxi company, a software company and numerous real estate holdings.

FINANCIALS:

Sales and profits are in thousands of dollars—add 000 to get the full amount. 2009 Note: Financial information for 2009 was not available for all companies at press time.

2009 Sales: $	2009 Profits: $	**U.S. Stock Ticker: Subsidiary**
2008 Sales: $	2008 Profits: $	**Int'l Ticker:** Int'l Exchange:
2007 Sales: $	2007 Profits: $	Employees:
2006 Sales: $	2006 Profits: $	Fiscal Year Ends: 12/31
2005 Sales: $	2005 Profits: $	Parent Company: G7 GROUPE

SALARIES/BENEFITS:

Pension Plan:	ESOP Stock Plan:	Profit Sharing:	Top Exec. Salary: $	Bonus: $
Savings Plan:	Stock Purch. Plan:		Second Exec. Salary: $	Bonus: $

OTHER THOUGHTS:

Apparent Women Officers or Directors:
Hot Spot for Advancement for Women/Minorities:

LOCATIONS: ("Y" = Yes)

West:	Southwest:	Midwest:	Southeast:	Northeast:	International:
					Y

ADAM OPEL AG

www.opel.com

Industry Group Code: 33611 **Ranks within this company's industry group:** Sales: Profits:

Vehicle Manufacturing:		Dealers:		Parts:		Service:		Finance:		Specialty:	
Cars:	Y	Car Dealer New:		Manufacturers:	Y	General Service:		Leasing:		Information Systems:	
Trucks:		Car Dealer Used:		Retail:		Specialty Service:		Auto Loans:		Online Marketing:	
Motorcycles:		Truck Dealer:		Distributors:		Oil Change:		Insurance:		Other:	
Specialty:	Y	RV Dealer:		Tires:		Paint and Body:				Publishing:	
Buses:		Motorcycle Dealer:		Batteries:						Rental Cars/Trucks:	
RVs:		Specialty Dealer:									

TYPES OF BUSINESS:

Automobile Manufacturing
Alternative Fuel Vehicles

BRANDS/DIVISIONS/AFFILIATES:

Vauxhall
General Motors Corp. (GM)
Ampera
Astra
Zafira
Sports Tourer
Combo
Insignia

CONTACTS:

Note: Officers with more than one job title may be intentionally listed here more than once.

Nick Reilly, CEO
Mark James, CFO
Alain Visser, VP-Mktg. & Sales
Holger Kimmes, VP-Personnel
Rita Forst, VP-Eng.
Reinald Hoben, VP-Mfg.
R. Frank Weber, VP-Corp. & Prod. Planning
Susanne Wegerhoff, VP-Corp. Comm.
Nick Reilly, Pres., GM Europe
Mark Adams, VP-Design
Ulrich Weber, Mgr.-Corp. Comm.
Stefan Weinmann, Dir.-Corp. & Internal Comm.
Walter G. Borst, Chmn.
Thomas A. McMillen, VP-Supply Chain & Purchasing

Phone: 49-061-42-7-70 **Fax:** 49-061-42-7-88-00

Toll-Free:

Address: Friedrich-Lutzmann-Ring, Russelsheim, D-65423 Germany

GROWTH PLANS/SPECIAL FEATURES:

Adam Opel AG, and its sister brand Vauxhall in the U.K., is a European manufacturer of passenger cars, trucks, commercial vehicles, automobile parts and accessories. The company has been a wholly-owned subsidiary of General Motors (GM) since 1929. Beginning with the manufacture of sewing machines and bikes, the company's founder, Adam Opel, began making automobiles in 1899. Organized under the GM Europe business segment, Opel is one of GM's largest non-U.S. subsidiaries. Opel's brand name models include the Agila, Corsa, Meriva, Tigra TwinTop, Astra and Astra TwinTop, Zafira, Insignia, Antara and GTC. The company also builds commercial vehicles, such as the Combo, Corsavan, Astravan, Vivaro and Movano. Opel products are sold in more than 35 countries. In the interest of cutting down on carbon dioxide emissions, the company offers LPG (liquefied petroleum gas) powered models of its Corsa, Meriva, Astra and Zafira vehicles. The firm's 2009 sales totaled 1.2 million vehicles. In January 2009, Opel introduced its first electric car, Ampera at the Geneva Motor Show. In Feb 2009, GM had planned to sell Opel in the spring of 2009, because of its own financial troubles. GM declared chapter 11 bankruptcy protection in June 2009. In November 2009, the firm's parent decided against selling Opel. In July 2009, GM emerges from bankruptcy. GM announced plans for Opel in 2010 that include an investment of $4 billion to cut 8,000 workers, close its Antwerp factory (which will leave 12 plants in operation in eight nations) and redesign products. It plans to restyle car models and invest in technology and fuel efficiency advances.

FINANCIALS:

Sales and profits are in thousands of dollars—add 000 to get the full amount. 2009 Note: Financial information for 2009 was not available for all companies at press time.

2009 Sales: $	2009 Profits: $	**U.S. Stock Ticker: Subsidiary**
2008 Sales: $	2008 Profits: $	**Int'l Ticker:** Int'l Exchange:
2007 Sales: $	2007 Profits: $	Employees: 47,000
2006 Sales: $	2006 Profits: $	Fiscal Year Ends: 12/31
2005 Sales: $	2005 Profits: $	Parent Company: GENERAL MOTORS CORP (GM)

SALARIES/BENEFITS:

Pension Plan:	ESOP Stock Plan:	Profit Sharing:	Top Exec. Salary: $	Bonus: $
Savings Plan:	Stock Purch. Plan:		Second Exec. Salary: $	Bonus: $

OTHER THOUGHTS:

Apparent Women Officers or Directors: 4
Hot Spot for Advancement for Women/Minorities: Y

LOCATIONS: ("Y" = Yes)

West:	Southwest:	Midwest:	Southeast:	Northeast:	International:
					Y

ADESA INC

www.adesainc.com

Industry Group Code: 441120 **Ranks within this company's industry group:** Sales: 1 Profits:

Vehicle Manufacturing:		Dealers:		Parts:		Service:		Finance:		Specialty:	
Cars:		Car Dealer New:		Manufacturers:		General Service:	Y	Leasing:		Information Systems:	Y
Trucks:		Car Dealer Used:		Retail:		Specialty Service:	Y	Auto Loans:		Online Marketing:	
Motorcycles:		Truck Dealer:		Distributors:		Oil Change:		Insurance:		Other:	Y
Specialty:		RV Dealer:		Tires:		Paint and Body:	Y			Publishing:	Y
Buses:		Motorcycle Dealer:		Batteries:						Rental Cars/Trucks:	
RVs:		Specialty Dealer:	Y								

TYPES OF BUSINESS:

Vehicle Auctions-Wholesale
Salvage Vehicle Auctions
Automobile Transportation
Automobile Reconditioning
Automotive Market Analysis

BRANDS/DIVISIONS/AFFILIATES:

ADESA LiveBlock
ADESA DealerBlock
ADESA Run Lists
ADESA Market Guide
ADESA Virtual Inventory
ADESA Notify Me
Kontos Kommentary
KAR Auction Services Inc

CONTACTS: *Note: Officers with more than one job title may be intentionally listed here more than once.*

Tom Caruso, CEO
Tom Caruso, Pres.
Bob Rauschenberg, Exec. VP-Sales & Mktg.
Michelle Mallon, VP-Legal
Paul Lips, Exec. VP-Oper.
Warren Byrd, Exec. VP-Corp. Dev.
Jason Ferreri, VP-e-Bus. Sales & Oper.
Paul Lips, Exec. VP-Finance
Jeff Bescher, Sr. VP-Sales
Mike Caggiano, Regional VP-Eastern Region
Tim DeBerry, Regional VP-Western Region
Tom Kontos, Exec. VP-Customer Strategies & Analytics
Benjamin Skuy, Exec. VP-Int'l Markets

Phone: 317-815-1100	**Fax:** 317-249-4651
Toll-Free: 800-923-3725	
Address: 13085 Hamilton Crossing Blvd., Carmel, IN 46032 US	

GROWTH PLANS/SPECIAL FEATURES:

ADESA, Inc., a wholly-owned subsidiary of KAR Auction Services, Inc., is primarily engaged in automotive auctions, transportation and cosmetic and mechanical reconditioning. The firm operates 62 used-vehicle auction sites across the U.S., with several others in Canada and Mexico. It serves two main client types, institutional buyers and dealers. The firm's institutional customers include vehicle manufacturers; banks, credit unions and other financial institutions; vehicle finance companies; vehicle rental companies; and insurance companies. Dealers buying from ADESA include both licensed franchises and independent wholesale dealers. ADESA's online auction tools include ADESA LiveBlock, an online real-time bidding tool; ADESA Run Lists, a summary of consigned vehicles offered for auction sale; and ADESA DealerBlock, a bulletin board type online auction platform. The firm also offers ADESA Market Guide, a summary of wholesale auction prices, auction sales results, market data and condition reports; ADESA Virtual Inventory, a subscription-based service that allows dealers to embed ADESA Search technology into their web sites; and ADESA Notify Me, an e-mail notification service for dealers looking for particular vehicles. The firm also offers analytical services via monthly, semi-annual and annual market analysis publications including Kontos Kommentary, Pulse and Global Vehicle Remarketing. In September 2009, the company opened a new auction house in Guadalajara, Mexico.

ADESA offers its employees medical, dental and vision coverage; flexible spending accounts; short- and long-term disability; life and AD&D insurance; a 401(k) plan; and an employee assistance program.

FINANCIALS: **Sales and profits are in thousands of dollars—add 000 to get the full amount. 2009 Note: Financial information for 2009 was not available for all companies at press time.**

2009 Sales: $1,120,000	2009 Profits: $	**U.S. Stock Ticker: Subsidiary**
2008 Sales: $1,123,400	2008 Profits: $	**Int'l Ticker:** Int'l Exchange:
2007 Sales: $	2007 Profits: $	Employees: 11,000
2006 Sales: $1,103,900	2006 Profits: $126,300	Fiscal Year Ends: 12/31
2005 Sales: $968,800	2005 Profits: $125,500	Parent Company: KAR AUCTION SERVICES INC

SALARIES/BENEFITS:

Pension Plan:	ESOP Stock Plan:	Profit Sharing:	Top Exec. Salary: $	Bonus: $
Savings Plan: Y	Stock Purch. Plan: Y		Second Exec. Salary: $	Bonus: $

OTHER THOUGHTS:

Apparent Women Officers or Directors: 4
Hot Spot for Advancement for Women/Minorities: Y

LOCATIONS: ("Y" = Yes)

West:	Southwest:	Midwest:	Southeast:	Northeast:	International:
Y	Y	Y	Y	Y	Y

ADVANCE AUTO PARTS INC

www.advanceautoparts.com

Industry Group Code: 441310 **Ranks within this company's industry group:** Sales: 3 Profits: 4

Vehicle Manufacturing:		Dealers:		Parts:		Service:		Finance:		Specialty:	
Cars:		Car Dealer New:		Manufacturers:		General Service:		Leasing:		Information Systems:	
Trucks:		Car Dealer Used:		Retail:	Y	Specialty Service:		Auto Loans:		Online Marketing:	Y
Motorcycles:		Truck Dealer:		Distributors:		Oil Change:		Insurance:		Other:	
Specialty:		RV Dealer:		Tires:	Y	Paint and Body:				Publishing:	
Buses:		Motorcycle Dealer:		Batteries:	Y					Rental Cars/Trucks:	
RVs:		Specialty Dealer:									

TYPES OF BUSINESS:

Auto Parts & Accessories Stores
Online Sales

BRANDS/DIVISIONS/AFFILIATES:

Autopart International (AI)
Advance Discount Auto Parts
Western Auto

CONTACTS: *Note: Officers with more than one job title may be intentionally listed here more than once.*

Darren R. Jackson, CEO
Kevin Freeland, COO
Jim Wade, Pres.
Mike Norona, CFO/Exec. VP
Greg Johnson, Chief Mktg. Officer
Rick Coro, CIO/Sr. VP-IT
Charles Tyson, Sr. VP-Merch.
Sarah Powell, General Counsel/Sr. VP/Corp. Sec.
Derrick Thomas, Sr. VP-Oper., East
Tami Kozikowski, Chief Dev. Officer
Scott Bauhofer, Sr. VP-e-commerce
Judd Nystrom, Sr. VP-Finance
Mike Marolt, Sr. VP-Store Support
Carl Hauch, Sr. VP-Oper., West
Randy Young, Sr. VP-Real Estate
Jack Brouillard, Chmn.
Chas Scheiderer, Sr. VP-Supply Chain

Phone: 540-362-4911	**Fax:** 540-561-1448
Toll-Free: 877-238-2623	
Address: 5008 Airport Rd., Roanoke, VA 24012 US	

GROWTH PLANS/SPECIAL FEATURES:

Advance Auto Parts, Inc. is a leading specialty retailer of automotive aftermarket parts, accessories, batteries and maintenance items. The firm primarily operates in the U.S. and serves both do-it-yourself (DIY) and do-it-for-me (commercial) customers. It operates in two segments: Advance Auto Parts (AAP) and Autopart International (AI). The AAP segment operates 3,264 stores within the U.S., Puerto Rico and the Virgin Islands. It operates 3,238 stores throughout 39 states in the Northeastern, Southeastern and Midwestern regions of the U.S. The stores operate under the Advance Auto Parts brand, while certain stores in Florida operate under the Advance Discount Auto Parts brand. The company also operates 26 stores under the Western Auto and Advance Auto Parts brands in Puerto Rico and the Virgin Islands. The stores' product categories consist of parts, which include alternators, batteries, clutches, engines and engine parts; accessories, including floor mats, mirrors, vent shades and seat and steering wheel covers; chemicals, including antifreeze, freon, fuel additives and car washes and waxes; and oil and other petroleum products. Its stores also provide a variety of services, including battery charging; oil and battery recycling; battery and wiper installation; and electrical system testing. The AI segment operates 156 stores located primarily throughout the Northeast and Mid-Atlantic regions. Its stores serve the commercial market, with an emphasis on parts for imported cars.

The company offers its employees medical, dental and vision benefits; a 401(k) plan; a stock purchase plan; company-paid life insurance; life and AD&D insurance; short- and long-term disability insurance; store discounts; an employee assistance program; business travel accident insurance; a legal benefits plan; dependent scholarships; and bereavement leave.

FINANCIALS: **Sales and profits are in thousands of dollars—add 000 to get the full amount. 2009 Note: Financial information for 2009 was not available for all companies at press time.**

2009 Sales: $5,412,623	2009 Profits: $270,373	**U.S. Stock Ticker: AAP**
2008 Sales: $5,142,255	2008 Profits: $238,038	**Int'l Ticker:** Int'l Exchange:
2007 Sales: $4,844,404	2007 Profits: $238,317	Employees: 49,000
2006 Sales: $4,616,503	2006 Profits: $231,318	Fiscal Year Ends: 12/31
2005 Sales: $4,264,971	2005 Profits: $234,725	Parent Company:

SALARIES/BENEFITS:

Pension Plan:	ESOP Stock Plan:	Profit Sharing:	Top Exec. Salary: $700,000	Bonus: $1,792,000
Savings Plan: Y	Stock Purch. Plan: Y		Second Exec. Salary: $450,008	Bonus: $570,240

OTHER THOUGHTS:

Apparent Women Officers or Directors: 7
Hot Spot for Advancement for Women/Minorities: Y

LOCATIONS: ("Y" = Yes)

West:	Southwest:	Midwest:	Southeast:	Northeast:	International:
Y		Y	Y	Y	

AGS AUTOMOTIVE SYSTEMS INC

www.agsautomotive.com

Industry Group Code: 3363 **Ranks within this company's industry group:** Sales: Profits:

Vehicle Manufacturing:		Dealers:		Parts:		Service:		Finance:		Specialty:	
Cars:		Car Dealer New:		Manufacturers:	Y	General Service:		Leasing:		Information Systems:	
Trucks:		Car Dealer Used:		Retail:		Specialty Service:		Auto Loans:		Online Marketing:	
Motorcycles:		Truck Dealer:		Distributors:		Oil Change:		Insurance:		Other:	
Specialty:		RV Dealer:		Tires:		Paint and Body:				Publishing:	
Buses:		Motorcycle Dealer:		Batteries:						Rental Cars/Trucks:	
RVs:		Specialty Dealer:									

TYPES OF BUSINESS:

Automotive Products, Parts Manufacturing
Chrome Bumpers
Heavy Metal Stamping

BRANDS/DIVISIONS/AFFILIATES:

J2 Management Corporation
Tiercon

CONTACTS:

Note: Officers with more than one job title may be intentionally listed here more than once.

Joseph Leon, Co-Pres.
Michelle Sund, Dir.-Finance
Joe Loparco, Co-Pres.

Phone: 416-438-6650	Fax:
Toll-Free:	
Address: 675 Progress Ave., Toronto, ON M1H 2W9 Canada	

GROWTH PLANS/SPECIAL FEATURES:

AGS Automotive Systems is an automotive parts manufacturer owned by private investor J2 Management Corp. AGS has operations in heavy metal stamping, welding, plating, coating, welding, sequencing and assembly. AGS operations account approximately 38% of the chrome bumper business in North America. The company's impact system assemblies and products include spring hangars, risers, brace rear bumper assemblies, wheelhouses, corner braces, panel rear wheelhouses, front panels, deck panels, assembled rear bumpers, H brackets, rail assemblies, bumper assemblies, crossmembers and floor pans. About 80% of AGS's business consists of supplying impact system assemblies and modules, including bumpers; the other 20% consists of supplying general stampings. The company's stamping capabilities consist of 136 stamping presses, and its stamped products include bumper products, cross members, oil pans, control arms and frame assemblies. The firm operates six plant facilities in Canada and the U.S., with over 2 million square feet of manufacturing space. AGS provides bumper systems and body-in-white structural modules to several original equipment manufacturers (OEM) customers, including General Motors; Chrysler; and International Truck. Its Tier 1 customers include Delphi; Johnson Controls; TI Automotive; and Expert. The company owns and operates Canadian plants in Windsor, Oshawa, Cambridge and Scarborough, Ontario; as well as U.S. facilities in Shreveport, Louisiana, and Sterling Heights, Michigan; plus a sales and engineering office in Sterling Heights. AGS is currently working on a five-year project focused on new developments in bumper systems, flexible manufacturing technologies, alternative energy use and waste reduction and employee training with several million in Canadian government funding. The total $5.6 million investment is split between AGS and Tiercon, a major Canadian provider of plastic molding, painting, coating and assembly services for exterior automotive components. Tiercon is also owned by J2 Management Corp.

FINANCIALS:

Sales and profits are in thousands of dollars—add 000 to get the full amount. 2009 Note: Financial information for 2009 was not available for all companies at press time.

2009 Sales: $	2009 Profits: $	**U.S. Stock Ticker: Private**
2008 Sales: $	2008 Profits: $	**Int'l Ticker:** Int'l Exchange:
2007 Sales: $153,600	2007 Profits: $	Employees:
2006 Sales: $	2006 Profits: $	Fiscal Year Ends: 12/31
2005 Sales: $	2005 Profits: $	Parent Company: J2 MANAGEMENT CORP

SALARIES/BENEFITS:

Pension Plan:	ESOP Stock Plan:	Profit Sharing:	Top Exec. Salary: $	Bonus: $
Savings Plan:	Stock Purch. Plan:		Second Exec. Salary: $	Bonus: $

OTHER THOUGHTS:

Apparent Women Officers or Directors: 1
Hot Spot for Advancement for Women/Minorities:

LOCATIONS: ("Y" = Yes)

West:	Southwest:	Midwest:	Southeast:	Northeast:	International:
		Y	Y		Y

AISAN INDUSTRY CO LTD

www.aisan-ind.co.jp

Industry Group Code: 3363 **Ranks within this company's industry group:** Sales: 35 Profits: 41

Vehicle Manufacturing:		Dealers:		Parts:		Service:		Finance:		Specialty:	
Cars:		Car Dealer New:		Manufacturers:	Y	General Service:		Leasing:		Information Systems:	
Trucks:		Car Dealer Used:		Retail:		Specialty Service:		Auto Loans:		Online Marketing:	
Motorcycles:		Truck Dealer:		Distributors:		Oil Change:		Insurance:		Other:	
Specialty:		RV Dealer:		Tires:		Paint and Body:				Publishing:	
Buses:		Motorcycle Dealer:		Batteries:						Rental Cars/Trucks:	
RVs:		Specialty Dealer:									

TYPES OF BUSINESS:

Automobile Components Manufacturing
Engine Components
Industrial Devices

BRANDS/DIVISIONS/AFFILIATES:

Franklin Precision Industry, Inc.
Aisan Corporation of America
Aisan Corporation Europe S.A.
Hyumdum Industrial Co., Ltd.
Aisan Industry France S.A.
Aisan Industry Czech s.r.o.
Aisan Corporation Gauangzhou Co., Ltd.
Aisan Industry Kumamoto Co., Ltd.

CONTACTS:

Note: Officers with more than one job title may be intentionally listed here more than once.

Nobuo Kobayashi, Pres.
Kenji Naruse, Dir.-Human Resources
Toyohiko Inoue, VP
Shoji Kawakami, Sr. Managing Dir.
Hiroshi Iwahana, Sr. Managing Dir.
Kenji Naruse, Dir.-Gen. Affairs
Hirohide Ichinomiya, Dir.-Logistics

Phone: 81-562-47-1131	**Fax:** 81-562-48-6357
Toll-Free:	
Address: 1-1-1 Kyowa-cho, Obu, Aichi, 474-8588 Japan	

GROWTH PLANS/SPECIAL FEATURES:

Aisan Industry Co., Ltd., founded in 1938, is a Japanese manufacturer of automotive engine components, including electronic fuel injection products, carbon canisters, engine valves and gaseous fuel systems. Aisan operates through three plants in Japan as well as overseas plants in the U.S., Indonesia, China, Korea, France and the Czech Republic. In addition to its overseas plants, the company also has overseas sales and service operations in the U.S., China, Belgium, Thailand and France. Its domestic sales offices are located in Tokyo, Hamamatsu, Osaka, Hiroshima and Honsha. The firm's electronic fuel injection products include throttle bodies, fuel pumps, fuel pump modules, fuel injectors, intake modules and electronic fuel injection (EFI) systems for motorcycles and other vehicles with small engines. It manufactures both mechanical and electronic throttle bodies. Aisan also produces carbon canisters; both traditional steel engine valves and titanium alloy engine valves, which are 40% lighter than the steel version; and gaseous fuel systems, which accommodate either liquefied petroleum gas (LPG) or compressed natural gas (CNG). The company's headquarters are located at its Honsha plant, which manufactures carburetors, intake modules and gaseous fuel products. The firm's operations include the activities of seven domestic and twenty overseas affiliates. Its U.S. production unit, Franklin Precision Industry, Inc., manufactures throttle bodies, carbon canisters and fuel pump modules. Additional subsidiaries of Aisan include Aisan Corporation of America; P.T. Aisan Nasmoco Industri; Aisan Auto Parts Co., Ltd.; Hyumdum Industrial Co., Ltd.; Aisan Industry France S.A.; Aisan Industry Czech s.r.o.; Aisan Industry Louny s.r.o.; Aisan Corporation Gauangzhou Co., Ltd.; and Aisan Corporation Europe S.A. During 2009, the company began construction of a factory in Kyushu, operating as Aisan Industry Kumamoto Co., Ltd.

FINANCIALS:

Sales and profits are in thousands of dollars—add 000 to get the full amount. 2009 Note: Financial information for 2009 was not available for all companies at press time.

2009 Sales: $1,614,405	2009 Profits: $-58,261	**U.S. Stock Ticker:**
2008 Sales: $1,873,594	2008 Profits: $52,476	**Int'l Ticker: 7283** Int'l Exchange: Tokyo-TSE
2007 Sales: $1,469,996	2007 Profits: $27,593	Employees: 7,016
2006 Sales: $1,332,500	2006 Profits: $34,300	Fiscal Year Ends: 3/31
2005 Sales: $1,206,980	2005 Profits: $37,060	Parent Company:

SALARIES/BENEFITS:

Pension Plan:	ESOP Stock Plan:	Profit Sharing:	Top Exec. Salary: $	Bonus: $
Savings Plan:	Stock Purch. Plan:		Second Exec. Salary: $	Bonus: $

OTHER THOUGHTS:

Apparent Women Officers or Directors:
Hot Spot for Advancement for Women/Minorities:

LOCATIONS: ("Y" = Yes)

West:	Southwest:	Midwest:	Southeast:	Northeast:	International:
		Y			Y

AISIN SEIKI CO LTD

www.aisin.co.jp

Industry Group Code: 3363 **Ranks within this company's industry group:** Sales: 4 Profits: 52

Vehicle Manufacturing:		Dealers:		Parts:		Service:		Finance:		Specialty:	
Cars:		Car Dealer New:		Manufacturers:	Y	General Service:		Leasing:		Information Systems:	Y
Trucks:		Car Dealer Used:		Retail:		Specialty Service:		Auto Loans:		Online Marketing:	
Motorcycles:		Truck Dealer:		Distributors:		Oil Change:		Insurance:		Other:	Y
Specialty:		RV Dealer:		Tires:		Paint and Body:				Publishing:	
Buses:		Motorcycle Dealer:		Batteries:						Rental Cars/Trucks:	
RVs:		Specialty Dealer:									

TYPES OF BUSINESS:

Automobile Parts Manufacturing
Sewing & Embroidery Machines
Air Conditioners
Hospital & Biotechnology Equipment
Lasers & Laser Imaging Technology

BRANDS/DIVISIONS/AFFILIATES:

Toyota Motor Corporation
ADVICS

CONTACTS: *Note: Officers with more than one job title may be intentionally listed here more than once.*

Fumio Fujimori, Pres.
Yasuhito Yamauchi, Vice Chmn.
Norio Oku, Exec. VP
Shunichi Nakamura, Exec. VP
Masuji Arai, Exec. VP
Kanshiro Toyoda, Chmn.

Phone: 81-566-24-8441	**Fax:** 81-566-24-8988
Toll-Free:	
Address: 2-1, Asahi-machi, Kariya, 448-8650 Japan	

GROWTH PLANS/SPECIAL FEATURES:

Aisin Seiki Co., Ltd. primarily develops and manufactures automotive parts. It operates three business units: automotive parts and systems; life and energy products; and new business. The automotive parts and systems unit, which generated over 95% of the firm's 2009 sales, manufactures drivetrain, brake, chassis, body and engine products. Drivetrain products generated 16.2% of sales in 2009; brake and chassis products, 22.3%; body products, 35.1%; engine products, 15.3%; and other, 6.2%. Specific products include transmissions, clutches, suspension systems, power seats, oil pumps and exhaust manifolds. This unit also produces information products, such as parking assist systems, lane departure warning systems, front and side monitors, power sliding doors, GPS antenna and daytime running light computers; and casting products, such as cast iron, resin moldings and aluminum die cast products. The company also sells its automotive parts as aftermarket products. The Life and Energy products unit manufactures lifestyle and amenity-related products, including home sewing and embroidery machines; energy system products, such as generators, air conditioners and vacuum devices, often derived from automobile-related technologies; and welfare products including reclining beds. Life and Energy products generated 4.9% of 2009 sales. Lastly, the New Business unit is developing various new technologies for the other two units, including fiber optic lasers, biotechnology, residential fuel cells and laser imaging systems. Aisin maintains 11 manufacturing plants, all located in Japan. In total, the firm has 151 subsidiaries and affiliates, of which 69 are in Japan, with the remainder in the Americas, Asia, Europe and Australia. In September 2009, the firm agreed to sell part of its automobile brake production business, including its Kariya Plant and subsidiary AS Brake Systems to ADVICS, a joint-venture between Aisin Seiki, Toyota and two other companies.

FINANCIALS: **Sales and profits are in thousands of dollars—add 000 to get the full amount. 2009 Note: Financial information for 2009 was not available for all companies at press time.**

2009 Sales: $24,557,400	2009 Profits: $-278,890	**U.S. Stock Ticker:**
2008 Sales: $27,327,200	2008 Profits: $927,510	**Int'l Ticker: 7259** Int'l Exchange: Tokyo-TSE
2007 Sales: $23,786,100	2007 Profits: $668,900	Employees: 61,300
2006 Sales: $21,205,900	2006 Profits: $611,000	Fiscal Year Ends: 3/31
2005 Sales: $18,290,700	2005 Profits: $467,200	Parent Company:

SALARIES/BENEFITS:

Pension Plan:	ESOP Stock Plan:	Profit Sharing:	Top Exec. Salary: $	Bonus: $
Savings Plan:	Stock Purch. Plan:		Second Exec. Salary: $	Bonus: $

OTHER THOUGHTS:

Apparent Women Officers or Directors:
Hot Spot for Advancement for Women/Minorities:

LOCATIONS: ("Y" = Yes)

West:	Southwest:	Midwest:	Southeast:	Northeast:	International:
Y		Y	Y	Y	Y

ALL AMERICAN GROUP

www.allamericangroupinc.com

Industry Group Code: 336120 **Ranks within this company's industry group:** Sales: 6 Profits: 2

Vehicle Manufacturing:		Dealers:		Parts:		Service:		Finance:		Specialty:	
Cars:		Car Dealer New:		Manufacturers:		General Service:		Leasing:		Information Systems:	
Trucks:		Car Dealer Used:		Retail:		Specialty Service:		Auto Loans:		Online Marketing:	
Motorcycles:		Truck Dealer:		Distributors:		Oil Change:		Insurance:		Other:	Y
Specialty:	Y	RV Dealer:		Tires:		Paint and Body:				Publishing:	
Buses:		Motorcycle Dealer:		Batteries:						Rental Cars/Trucks:	
RVs:		Specialty Dealer:									

TYPES OF BUSINESS:

Housing
Specialty Vehicles

BRANDS/DIVISIONS/AFFILIATES:

Coachmen
All American homes
Mod-U-Kraf
All American Building Systems
All American Group
Ameri-Log Homes
Solar Village
All American Specialty Vehicles

CONTACTS:

Note: Officers with more than one job title may be intentionally listed here more than once.

Richard M. Lavers, CEO
Colleen A. Zuhl, CFO
Les G. Thimlar, VP-Human Resources
Todd Woelfer, General Counsel
Rick J. Bedell, Pres., Housing Group
William P. Johnson, Chmn.

Phone: 574-266-2500	**Fax:** 574-266-2559
Toll-Free:	
Address: 2831 Dexter Dr., P.O. Box 3300, Elkhart, IN 46514 US	

GROWTH PLANS/SPECIAL FEATURES:

All American Group, formerly Coachmen Industries, Inc., primarily offers housing and related products, as well as a line of specialty vehicles. The firm's housing segment consists of the manufacturing and distribution of system-built modules for residential buildings. The housing products are branded as All American Homes, Mod-U-Kraf Homes and All American Building Systems. All American Homes and Mod-U-Kraf Homes design, manufacture and market system-built housing structures. All American Homes has operations in Colorado, Indiana, Iowa and North Carolina. Mod-U-Kraf operates from a plant in Virginia. Combined, these plants serve approximately 385 independent builders in 27 states. All American Building Systems designs and markets single-family home subdivisions, apartments, condominiums, townhouses, senior housing facilities and military housing facilities. Housing products include system-built modules for single-family residences, multi-family duplexes, apartments, condominiums, hotels and specialized structures for military use. It has recently added the Ameri-Log Homes and Solar Village brands to its portfolio. In addition, through its All American Specialty Vehicles division, the firm manufactures ADA accessible buses under the Spirit of Mobility brand name. The company operates manufacturing facilities for its buses in Indiana. In May 2009, the firm agreed to sell its former recreational vehicle manufacturing, service and administrative facility in Georgia to Ben Hill County Schools. In November 2009, the firm acquired exclusive rights to market Wick Building Systems' modular home designs, including the brands Artcraft Homes, Marshfield Homes and Rollohome.

The company offers its employees medical, dental, vision and life insurance; short- and long-term disability insurance; a 401(k) plan; an employee stock purchase program; and tuition reimbursement.

FINANCIALS:

Sales and profits are in thousands of dollars—add 000 to get the full amount. 2009 Note: Financial information for 2009 was not available for all companies at press time.

2009 Sales: $60,623	2009 Profits: $-4,730	**U.S. Stock Ticker: COHM**
2008 Sales: $119,596	2008 Profits: $-69,002	**Int'l Ticker:** Int'l Exchange:
2007 Sales: $119,186	2007 Profits: $-38,752	Employees: 612
2006 Sales: $159,672	2006 Profits: $-31,805	Fiscal Year Ends: 12/31
2005 Sales: $702,425	2005 Profits: $-26,350	Parent Company:

SALARIES/BENEFITS:

Pension Plan:	ESOP Stock Plan:	Profit Sharing:	Top Exec. Salary: $275,285	Bonus: $
Savings Plan: Y	Stock Purch. Plan: Y		Second Exec. Salary: $204,253	Bonus: $

OTHER THOUGHTS:

Apparent Women Officers or Directors: 1
Hot Spot for Advancement for Women/Minorities:

LOCATIONS: ("Y" = Yes)

West:	Southwest:	Midwest:	Southeast:	Northeast:	International:
Y		Y		Y	

ALLIED SYSTEMS HOLDINGS INC

www.alliedholdings.com

Industry Group Code: 4842 **Ranks within this company's industry group:** Sales: Profits:

Vehicle Manufacturing:		Dealers:		Parts:		Service:		Finance:		Specialty:	
Cars:		Car Dealer New:		Manufacturers:		General Service:		Leasing:		Information Systems:	
Trucks:		Car Dealer Used:		Retail:		Specialty Service:		Auto Loans:		Online Marketing:	
Motorcycles:		Truck Dealer:		Distributors:		Oil Change:		Insurance:		Other:	Y
Specialty:		RV Dealer:		Tires:		Paint and Body:				Publishing:	
Buses:		Motorcycle Dealer:		Batteries:						Rental Cars/Trucks:	
RVs:		Specialty Dealer:									

TYPES OF BUSINESS:

Automobile Distribution
Railroad Terminal & Loading Services
Logistics Services

BRANDS/DIVISIONS/AFFILIATES:

Allied Automotive Group
Axis Group

CONTACTS: *Note: Officers with more than one job title may be intentionally listed here more than once.*

Mark J. Gendregske, CEO
Mark J. Gendregske, Pres.
Thomas H. King, CFO
Thomas Duffy, General Counsel/Exec. VP/Corp. Sec.
Thomas H. King, Exec. VP-Finance
Joseph Marinelli, Sr. VP-Field Oper., Allied Automotive Group, Inc.
John L. Harrington, Pres., Axis Group
Robert J. Rutland, Chmn.

Phone: 404-370-4206	**Fax:** 404-373-4285
Toll-Free:	
Address: 2302 Parklake Dr., Bldg. 15, Ste. 600, Atlanta, GA 30345 US	

GROWTH PLANS/SPECIAL FEATURES:

Allied Systems Holdings, Inc. is a holding company that operates through its subsidiaries, primarily Allied Automotive Group (AAG) and the Axis Group. AAG is one of the largest automotive distributors and transporters in North America. The company transports automobiles, light trucks and SUVs from manufacturing plants, ports, auctions and railway distribution points to automobile dealerships and provides railroad terminal and loading services. The subsidiary also provides various support services, including yard and inventory management, pick up and delivery of lease return vehicles and support services for safety operations. AAG is primarily involved with the short-haul segment of automotive transportation, meaning it typically hauls cargo less than 200 miles from the point of origin. The subsidiary operates approximately 4,000 modern tractor-trailers from its 90 terminal locations in the U.S. and Canada. It partners with manufacturers, both domestic and international, to deliver over 9 million vehicles per year. General Motors, Ford and DaimlerChrysler are the company's largest customers. AAG also provides services to foreign and import manufacturers, localized automobile dealerships and rental car companies. Through the Axis Group, the company provides logistics solutions to both the new vehicle industry and the pre-owned market, specifically in segments that are complimentary to AAG's operations. These services include vehicle distribution services, automobile inspections, auction and yard management services, vehicle tracking, vehicle accessory and dealer preparatory services.

Allied Systems Holdings offers its employees health services and chaplaincy counseling services.

FINANCIALS: **Sales and profits are in thousands of dollars—add 000 to get the full amount. 2009 Note: Financial information for 2009 was not available for all companies at press time.**

2009 Sales: $	2009 Profits: $	**U.S. Stock Ticker: Private**
2008 Sales: $	2008 Profits: $	**Int'l Ticker:** Int'l Exchange:
2007 Sales: $	2007 Profits: $	Employees:
2006 Sales: $893,837	2006 Profits: $-12,325	Fiscal Year Ends: 12/31
2005 Sales: $892,934	2005 Profits: $-125,724	Parent Company:

SALARIES/BENEFITS:

Pension Plan: Y	ESOP Stock Plan:	Profit Sharing:	Top Exec. Salary: $	Bonus: $
Savings Plan: Y	Stock Purch. Plan:		Second Exec. Salary: $	Bonus: $

OTHER THOUGHTS:

Apparent Women Officers or Directors:
Hot Spot for Advancement for Women/Minorities:

LOCATIONS: ("Y" = Yes)

West:	Southwest:	Midwest:	Southeast:	Northeast:	International:
Y	Y	Y	Y	Y	Y

ALLSTATE CORPORATION (THE)

www.allstate.com

Industry Group Code: 524126 **Ranks within this company's industry group:** Sales: 2 Profits: 2

Vehicle Manufacturing:		**Dealers:**		**Parts:**		**Service:**		**Finance:**		**Specialty:**	
Cars:		Car Dealer New:		Manufacturers:		General Service:		Leasing:		Information Systems:	
Trucks:		Car Dealer Used:		Retail:		Specialty Service:		Auto Loans:		Online Marketing:	
Motorcycles:		Truck Dealer:		Distributors:		Oil Change:		Insurance:	Y	Other:	
Specialty:		RV Dealer:		Tires:		Paint and Body:				Publishing:	
Buses:		Motorcycle Dealer:		Batteries:						Rental Cars/Trucks:	
RVs:		Specialty Dealer:									

TYPES OF BUSINESS:

Insurance, Direct Property & Casualty
Auto Insurance
Homeowners Insurance
Life Insurance
Business Insurance

BRANDS/DIVISIONS/AFFILIATES:

Allstate Insurance Co
Allstate Life Insurance Co
Allstate
Encompass

CONTACTS:

Note: Officers with more than one job title may be intentionally listed here more than once.

Thomas J. Wilson, CEO
Thomas J. Wilson, Pres.
Don Civgin, CFO/Sr. VP
Mark LaNeve, Chief Mktg. Officer-Allstate Insurance Co.
Jim D. DeVries, Sr. VP-Human Resources
Catherine S. Brune, CIO/Sr. VP
Michele Coleman Mayes, General Counsel/VP
Steven P. Sorenson, Sr. VP-Prod. Oper., Allstate Insurance Co.
Joan H. Walker, Sr. VP-Corp. Rel., Allstate Insurance Co.
Joseph Lacher, Jr., Pres., Allstate Protection & Allstate Insurance Co
Judy Greffin, Chief Investment Officer/Sr. VP
Matthew Winter, CEO/Pres., Allstate Financial
Thomas J. Wilson, Chmn.

Phone: 847-402-5000	**Fax:** 847-402-2351
Toll-Free: 800-255-7828	
Address: 2775 Sanders Rd., Northbrook, IL 60062 US	

GROWTH PLANS/SPECIAL FEATURES:

The Allstate Corporation is a holding company for Allstate Insurance Co., through which it principally conducts its business. The firm is primarily engaged in the personal property and casualty insurance business; and the life insurance, retirement and investment products market. Allstate provides insurance products to over 17 million households through a distribution network that utilizes a total of over 14,000 exclusive agencies and exclusive financial specialists in the U.S. and Canada. The company conducts its business through four business segments: Allstate Protection; Allstate Financial; discontinued lines and coverages; and corporate/other. Allstate Protection, which accounts for approximately 93% of the firm's consolidated insurance premiums and contract charges, sells primarily private passenger auto and homeowners insurance (principally through agencies), under the Allstate and Encompass brand names. The segment also sells a wide range of personal property and casualty insurance products; these products are for renters, condominiums, residential fire, manufactured housing, boat owners, loan protection and selected commercial property. Allstate Financial provides life, voluntary accident and health insurance; and retirement and investment products to individual and institutional customers. The discontinued lines and coverages segment includes results from insurance coverage that the company no longer writes and results for certain commercial and other business in run-off. The corporate/other division is comprised of holding company activities and certain non-insurance operations.

The company offers its employees medical, dental, vision, life, AD&D and disability insurance; flexible spending accounts; a retirement plan; a profit sharing fund with 401(k) options; tuition reimbursement; and childcare discounts.

FINANCIALS:

Sales and profits are in thousands of dollars—add 000 to get the full amount. 2009 Note: Financial information for 2009 was not available for all companies at press time.

2009 Sales: $32,013,000	2009 Profits: $854,000	**U.S. Stock Ticker: ALL**
2008 Sales: $29,394,000	2008 Profits: $-1,679,000	**Int'l Ticker:** Int'l Exchange:
2007 Sales: $36,769,000	2007 Profits: $4,636,000	Employees: 36,800
2006 Sales: $35,796,000	2006 Profits: $4,993,000	Fiscal Year Ends: 12/31
2005 Sales: $35,383,000	2005 Profits: $1,765,000	Parent Company:

SALARIES/BENEFITS:

Pension Plan: Y	ESOP Stock Plan:	Profit Sharing: Y	Top Exec. Salary: $1,100,769	Bonus: $1,713,361
Savings Plan: Y	Stock Purch. Plan:		Second Exec. Salary: $657,172	Bonus: $499,980

OTHER THOUGHTS:

Apparent Women Officers or Directors: 7
Hot Spot for Advancement for Women/Minorities: Y

LOCATIONS: ("Y" = Yes)

West:	Southwest:	Midwest:	Southeast:	Northeast:	International:
Y	Y	Y	Y	Y	Y

ALLY FINANCIAL INC

www.ally.com

Industry Group Code: 522220 **Ranks within this company's industry group:** Sales: Profits:

Vehicle Manufacturing:		Dealers:		Parts:		Service:		Finance:		Specialty:	
Cars:		Car Dealer New:		Manufacturers:		General Service:		Leasing:	Y	Information Systems:	
Trucks:		Car Dealer Used:		Retail:		Specialty Service:		Auto Loans:	Y	Online Marketing:	
Motorcycles:		Truck Dealer:		Distributors:		Oil Change:		Insurance:	Y	Other:	Y
Specialty:		RV Dealer:		Tires:		Paint and Body:				Publishing:	
Buses:		Motorcycle Dealer:		Batteries:						Rental Cars/Trucks:	
RVs:		Specialty Dealer:									

TYPES OF BUSINESS:

Automobile Financing
Leasing Services
Insurance
Mortgage Banking
Bank Holding Company
Commercial Credit
Commercial Mortgages
Residential Mortgages

BRANDS/DIVISIONS/AFFILIATES:

GMAC Mortgage
Cerberus Capital Management LP
Residential Capital LLC (ResCap)
Ally Bank
GMAC-CIS
General Motors Acceptance Corporation
Chrysler Financial Services LLC

CONTACTS: *Note: Officers with more than one job title may be intentionally listed here more than once.*

Michael A. Carpenter, CEO
Cliff Skelton, COO
William F. Muir, Pres.
James G. Mackey, Interim CFO
Sanjay Gupta, Chief Mktg. Officer
Anthony S. (Tony) Marino, Chief Human Resources Officer
Cliff Skelton, CTO
William B. Solomon, Jr., General Counsel
Gina Proia, Chief Comm. Officer
Jeffrey Brown, Treas.
Samuel Ramsey, Chief Risk Officer
William (Bill) Hall, Jr., Pres./CEO-GMAC Commercial Finance
Thomas Marano, CEO-GMAC Mortgage
Mark H. Weintraub, Gen. Auditor
Lenard B. Tessler, Chmn.

Phone: 313-556-5000 **Fax:**
Toll-Free:
Address: 200 Renaissance Ctr., Detroit, MI 48265-2000 US

GROWTH PLANS/SPECIAL FEATURES:

Ally Financial, Inc., formerly GMAC, Inc., is a global financial services company providing automotive finance, real estate finance, insurance and commercial finance in roughly 40 countries. GMAC operates in four primary business lines: global automotive finance; mortgage, through wholly-owned subsidiary Residential Capital LLC (ResCap); insurance; and other. The automotive finance segment offers wholesale and retail automotive financing services primarily to GM dealers and their customers. Through ResCap, the company originates, purchases, sells and securitizes residential mortgage loans, primarily in the U.S.; provides collateralized lines of credit; and provides specialty financing and equity capital to residential land developers and homebuilders. GMAC's insurance offerings include automobile service contracts, personal automobile insurance coverages, selected commercial insurance coverages and other consumer products. The company's other solutions include commercial finance services, such as asset-based lending, structured finance, factoring, health capital and resort finance; equity investments; and other corporate offerings. Ally Bank is an online bank offering money market savings accounts and fixed-rate certificates. The U.S. Treasury department owns roughly 56.3% of GMAC; Cerberus Capital Management, L.P., a private equity firm, owns 14.9%; General Motors Trust owns 9.9%; and GM owns 6.7%. The remainder is owned by third party investors. In early 2009, the U.S. federal government injected $7 billion into GMAC in efforts to keep the firm afloat. Another $7.5 billion was allocated to GMAC in May 2009. In April 2009, GMAC Financial Services replaced Chrysler Financial Services LLC as the primary retail and commercial lender for Chrysler dealers. In May 2009, the company re-branded its GMAC Bank division as Ally Bank. Following GM's bankruptcy filing in June 2009, the company announced that it would not be seeking bankruptcy protection. In March 2010, the firm sold its U.S. consumer property and casualty insurance business to American Capital Acquisition Corporation. In April 2010, ResCap agreed to sell its European mortgage assets and businesses. The firm changed its name to Ally Financial, Inc. in 2010.

FINANCIALS: **Sales and profits are in thousands of dollars—add 000 to get the full amount. 2009 Note: Financial information for 2009 was not available for all companies at press time.**

2009 Sales: $	2009 Profits: $	**U.S. Stock Ticker: Private**
2008 Sales: $18,395,000	2008 Profits: $1,868,000	**Int'l Ticker:** Int'l Exchange:
2007 Sales: $21,187,000	2007 Profits: $-2,332,000	Employees: 22,700
2006 Sales: $23,103,000	2006 Profits: $2,125,000	Fiscal Year Ends: 12/31
2005 Sales: $21,312,000	2005 Profits: $2,282,000	Parent Company:

SALARIES/BENEFITS:

Pension Plan:	ESOP Stock Plan:	Profit Sharing:	Top Exec. Salary: $	Bonus: $
Savings Plan:	Stock Purch. Plan:		Second Exec. Salary: $	Bonus: $

OTHER THOUGHTS:

Apparent Women Officers or Directors: 3
Hot Spot for Advancement for Women/Minorities: Y

LOCATIONS: ("Y" = Yes)

West:	Southwest:	Midwest:	Southeast:	Northeast:	International:
Y	Y	Y	Y	Y	Y

ALPS AUTOMOTIVE INC

www.alps.com

Industry Group Code: 3363 **Ranks within this company's industry group:** Sales: Profits:

Vehicle Manufacturing:		Dealers:		Parts:		Service:		Finance:		Specialty:	
Cars:		Car Dealer New:		Manufacturers:	Y	General Service:		Leasing:		Information Systems:	
Trucks:		Car Dealer Used:		Retail:		Specialty Service:		Auto Loans:		Online Marketing:	
Motorcycles:		Truck Dealer:		Distributors:		Oil Change:		Insurance:		Other:	
Specialty:		RV Dealer:		Tires:		Paint and Body:				Publishing:	
Buses:		Motorcycle Dealer:		Batteries:						Rental Cars/Trucks:	
RVs:		Specialty Dealer:									

TYPES OF BUSINESS:

Automotive Components-Electronic
Keyless Entry Systems
Sensors

BRANDS/DIVISIONS/AFFILIATES:

Alps Group
Alps Electric Co Ltd

CONTACTS:

Note: Officers with more than one job title may be intentionally listed here more than once.

Akinori Ito, CEO
Akinori Ito, Pres.
Kogi Seguchi, VP-Mktg. & Sales
Brian Bauer, Mgr.-IT Oper.

Phone: 248-391-9950	**Fax:** 248-391-2500
Toll-Free:	
Address: 1500 Atlantic Blvd., Auburn Hills, MI 48326 US	

GROWTH PLANS/SPECIAL FEATURES:

Alps Automotive, Inc., part of the global Alps Group, is a supplier of electronic and electro-mechanical components to major automobile manufacturers. The company designs, develops and manufactures products in four categories: HMI (human machine interface), internal interface, external interface and car body control power train. HMI products include; power window and mirror switches; climate control panels; passive entry systems; rotary and slide type potentiometers; multi-function control devices; the TACT switch; and the Haptic Commander. Internal interface products comprise a variety of offerings, including steering modules, power seat switch modules, EGR valve position sensors, seat weight sensors and MOST connectors. The external interface products include remote keyless entry units, AM/FM tuners and Bluetooth modules. Alps also manufactures various high precision sensors for car body power trains. Alps Automotive has facilities in Auburn Hills, Michigan; McAllen, Texas; Dublin, Ohio; and Tyrone, Georgia. The company also has a licensing agreement with IQ-mobil GmbH under which it mass-produces and markets a batteryless tire-pressure monitoring system. The company's parent, Alps Electric Company, is based in Tokyo, and makes a variety of electrical components such as sensors, switches and magnetic heads. In recent years, Alps Automotive achieved SPICE (Software Process Improvement and Capability Determination) Capability Level 3 certification in regard to its production of door and seat modules for both domestic and overseas markets.

FINANCIALS:

Sales and profits are in thousands of dollars—add 000 to get the full amount. 2009 Note: Financial information for 2009 was not available for all companies at press time.

2009 Sales: $	2009 Profits: $	**U.S. Stock Ticker: Subsidiary**
2008 Sales: $	2008 Profits: $	**Int'l Ticker:** Int'l Exchange:
2007 Sales: $	2007 Profits: $	Employees:
2006 Sales: $	2006 Profits: $	Fiscal Year Ends: 3/31
2005 Sales: $	2005 Profits: $	Parent Company: ALPS ELECTRIC CO LTD

SALARIES/BENEFITS:

Pension Plan:	ESOP Stock Plan:	Profit Sharing:	Top Exec. Salary: $	Bonus: $
Savings Plan:	Stock Purch. Plan:		Second Exec. Salary: $	Bonus: $

OTHER THOUGHTS:

Apparent Women Officers or Directors:
Hot Spot for Advancement for Women/Minorities:

LOCATIONS: ("Y" = Yes)

West:	Southwest:	Midwest:	Southeast:	Northeast:	International:
	Y	Y	Y		

ALPS ELECTRIC CO LTD

www.alps.com

Industry Group Code: 335313 **Ranks within this company's industry group:** Sales: 1 Profits: 1

Vehicle Manufacturing:		Dealers:		Parts:		Service:		Finance:		Specialty:	
Cars:		Car Dealer New:		Manufacturers:	Y	General Service:		Leasing:		Information Systems:	
Trucks:		Car Dealer Used:		Retail:		Specialty Service:		Auto Loans:		Online Marketing:	
Motorcycles:		Truck Dealer:		Distributors:		Oil Change:		Insurance:		Other:	
Specialty:		RV Dealer:		Tires:		Paint and Body:				Publishing:	
Buses:		Motorcycle Dealer:		Batteries:						Rental Cars/Trucks:	
RVs:		Specialty Dealer:									

TYPES OF BUSINESS:

Electronic Components Manufacturing
Automotive Parts Manufacturing

BRANDS/DIVISIONS/AFFILIATES:

Haptic Commander
GlidePoint
Avnet Electronics Marketing
Alps Green Device

CONTACTS:

Note: Officers with more than one job title may be intentionally listed here more than once.

Masataka Kataoka, Pres.
Toshihiro Kuriyama, Chief Dir.-Tech
Junichi Umehara, Chief Dir.-Admin.
Yozo Yasuoka, Sr. Managing Dir.
Nobuhiko Komeya, Managing Dir.
Seishi Kai, Managing Dir.
Junichi Umehara, Dir.

Phone: 81-3-3726-1211 **Fax:** 81-2-3278-1741
Toll-Free:
Address: 1-7 Yukigaya Otsuka-cho, Ota-Ku, Tokyo, 145-8501 Japan

GROWTH PLANS/SPECIAL FEATURES:

Alps Electric Co., Ltd. is primarily engaged in the manufacture and sale of electronic components, specializing in electronics development and miniaturization. Alps operates via its three divisions: Automotive Division; the Home, Mobile and Industry Division; and the Mechatronics, Materials and Process Division. The Automotive Products Division develops on-board electronics and safety and comfort systems for automotive applications. One of its propriety systems, the Haptic Commander unit, incorporates modules to control various switches, air-conditioning units and passive keyless entry systems. The Home, Mobile and Industry Division consists of the electronic components used in the development of human-to-machine input and output devices, such as keyboards, remote controls, touch sensors, printers and power-saving LCDs. The firm's GlidePoint device is used primarily in the touch pads of laptop PCs and uses electrostatic detection technology to detect the movement of a fingertip. GlidePoint is additionally used in the touch pads of TV remote control units and mobile phone sensor keys. The Mechatronics, Materials and Process Division manufactures human-to-machine interface components, such as switches, variable resistors, sensors and connectors, which are used in automotive components; information and communication devices; and home appliances. The company is composed of over 82 subsidiary and affiliate companies that fall under three primary company headings; Alps Logistics, Company, Ltd., which consists of over 25 companies; Alpine Electronics, Inc., which consists of over 28 companies; and Alps Electronic, Company, Ltd., which consists of over 23 companies. In March 2010, the company announced a joint venture with the Innovation Network Corp. of Japan. The new company, Alps Green Device, will focus on providing power supply devices.

FINANCIALS:

Sales and profits are in thousands of dollars—add 000 to get the full amount. 2009 Note: Financial information for 2009 was not available for all companies at press time.

2009 Sales: $5,790,360	2009 Profits: $-752,690	**U.S. Stock Ticker: APELY.PK**
2008 Sales: $6,926,600	2008 Profits: $44,200	**Int'l Ticker: 6770** Int'l Exchange: Tokyo-TSE
2007 Sales: $7,081,300	2007 Profits: $49,200	Employees:
2006 Sales: $7,096,100	2006 Profits: $188,700	Fiscal Year Ends: 3/31
2005 Sales: $6,436,300	2005 Profits: $163,200	Parent Company:

SALARIES/BENEFITS:

Pension Plan:	ESOP Stock Plan:	Profit Sharing:	Top Exec. Salary: $	Bonus: $
Savings Plan:	Stock Purch. Plan:		Second Exec. Salary: $	Bonus: $

OTHER THOUGHTS:

Apparent Women Officers or Directors:
Hot Spot for Advancement for Women/Minorities:

LOCATIONS: ("Y" = Yes)

West:	Southwest:	Midwest:	Southeast:	Northeast:	International:
Y	Y	Y	Y	Y	Y

AM GENERAL LLC

www.amgeneral.com

Industry Group Code: 336120 **Ranks within this company's industry group:** Sales: Profits:

Vehicle Manufacturing:		Dealers:		Parts:		Service:		Finance:		Specialty:	
Cars:		Car Dealer New:		Manufacturers:	Y	General Service:		Leasing:		Information Systems:	
Trucks:		Car Dealer Used:		Retail:		Specialty Service:		Auto Loans:		Online Marketing:	
Motorcycles:		Truck Dealer:		Distributors:		Oil Change:		Insurance:		Other:	
Specialty:	Y	RV Dealer:		Tires:		Paint and Body:				Publishing:	
Buses:		Motorcycle Dealer:		Batteries:						Rental Cars/Trucks:	
RVs:		Specialty Dealer:									

TYPES OF BUSINESS:

Military Vehicle Manufacturing
Diesel Engines

BRANDS/DIVISIONS/AFFILIATES:

MacAndrews & Forbes Holdings
Renco Group (The)
Humvee
Hummer H1
Hummer H2
Optimizer 6500
General Dynamics Land Systems
General Tactical Vehicles

CONTACTS: *Note: Officers with more than one job title may be intentionally listed here more than once.*

Paul J. Kern, COO
Paul J. Kern, Pres.
James A. Armour, Chmn.

Phone: 574-237-6222	**Fax:** 574-284-2819
Toll-Free:	
Address: 105 N. Niles Ave., P.O. Box 7025, South Bend, IN 46634 US	

GROWTH PLANS/SPECIAL FEATURES:

AM General, LLC, owned by MacAndrews & Forbes Holdings and the Renco Group, designs, engineers, produces and offers technical and parts support for military and special-purpose vehicles. The company's most recognized product is the military High Mobility Multipurpose Wheeled Vehicle (HMMWV), called the Humvee, and its civilian counterparts, the Hummer H1, H2 and H3. The Humvee is sold to the armed forces of over 50 countries and to domestic agencies like the National Guard and Border Patrol. It comes in 15 configurations, has a ground clearance of 16 inches, can ford water 60 inches deep and can carry up to 5,100 pounds. AM General and General Motors Corp. (GM) were partners in the marketing and distribution of the original civilian Hummer, with GM now holding the rights to the Hummer brand name. In addition, through AM General's General Engine Products, Inc. subsidiary, the company produces 6.5-liter diesel engines for its and other companies' vehicles. The subsidiary builds the Optimizer 6500 diesel engines for military and civilian sales, which serve as replacements for the original GM engines in Hummers. The company owns a military training facility in northern Indiana, which has a 320-acre off-road dirt track that AM General uses to train recruits with its own staff. The company's SPLO (Service Parts Logistics Operations) center houses 30,000 part numbers, with 15,000 parts readily available. The ILS (Integrated Logistics Support) segment provides engineering, logistics and manpower to various different projects. AM General also operates a Humvee Spare Parts Distribution Center in the Middle East. The firm recently launched General Tactical Vehicles, a joint venture with General Dynamics Land Systems, to develop the Joint Light Tactical Vehicle (JLTV), a potential replacement for the Humvee. Despite the proposed sale of GM's civilian Hummer business, the company will continue to produce military-use Humvees for the U.S. army.

FINANCIALS: **Sales and profits are in thousands of dollars—add 000 to get the full amount. 2009 Note: Financial information for 2009 was not available for all companies at press time.**

2009 Sales: $	2009 Profits: $	**U.S. Stock Ticker: Joint Venture**
2008 Sales: $	2008 Profits: $	**Int'l Ticker:** Int'l Exchange:
2007 Sales: $	2007 Profits: $	Employees:
2006 Sales: $	2006 Profits: $	Fiscal Year Ends:
2005 Sales: $	2005 Profits: $	Parent Company:

SALARIES/BENEFITS:

Pension Plan:	ESOP Stock Plan:	Profit Sharing:	Top Exec. Salary: $	Bonus: $
Savings Plan:	Stock Purch. Plan:		Second Exec. Salary: $	Bonus: $

OTHER THOUGHTS:

Apparent Women Officers or Directors:
Hot Spot for Advancement for Women/Minorities:

LOCATIONS: ("Y" = Yes)

West:	Southwest:	Midwest:	Southeast:	Northeast:	International:
		Y			

AMERCO

www.amerco.com

Industry Group Code: 532120 **Ranks within this company's industry group:** Sales: 1 Profits: 1

Vehicle Manufacturing:		Dealers:		Parts:		Service:		Finance:		Specialty:	
Cars:		Car Dealer New:		Manufacturers:		General Service:		Leasing:	Y	Information Systems:	
Trucks:		Car Dealer Used:		Retail:		Specialty Service:		Auto Loans:		Online Marketing:	
Motorcycles:		Truck Dealer:		Distributors:		Oil Change:		Insurance:	Y	Other:	Y
Specialty:		RV Dealer:		Tires:		Paint and Body:				Publishing:	
Buses:		Motorcycle Dealer:		Batteries:						Rental Cars/Trucks:	Y
RVs:		Specialty Dealer:									

TYPES OF BUSINESS:

Truck Rental & Leasing Services
Moving & Storage Services & Supplies
Property & Casualty Insurance
Life Insurance
Annuities
Self-Storage Properties

BRANDS/DIVISIONS/AFFILIATES:

U-Haul International, Inc.
Republic Western Insurance Company
Oxford Life Insurance Company
AMERCO Real Estate Company
Safemove
Safetow
Safestor

CONTACTS: *Note: Officers with more than one job title may be intentionally listed here more than once.*

Edward J. Shoen, Pres.
Laurence J. De Respino, General Counsel
Jennifer Flachman, Dir.-Investor Rel.
Jason A. Berg, Principal Acct. Officer
Mark A. Haydukovich, Treas.
Edward J. Shoen, CEO-U-Haul
Carlos Vizcarra, Pres., AMERCO Real Estate Co.
Richard M. Amoroso, Pres., Republic Western Insurance Co.
Edward J. Shoen, Chmn.

Phone: 775-688-6300	**Fax:** 775-688-6338
Toll-Free:	
Address: 1325 Airmotive Way, Ste. 100, Reno, NV 89502 US	

GROWTH PLANS/SPECIAL FEATURES:

AMERCO is a holding company that operates U-Haul International, Inc.'s moving and storage operations; AMERCO Real Estate Company; Republic Western Insurance Company; and Oxford Life Insurance Company. Accordingly, the firm has three reportable business segments: moving and storage; property and casualty insurance; and life insurance. The moving and storage segment consists of U-Haul, with its rental equipment fleet of trucks, trailers and tow dollies being offered by approximately 14,500 independent dealers. It also provides furniture pads, utility dollies and hand trucks; sells a wide selection of other moving supplies; and offers protection packages for moving and storage. U-Haul owns more than 100,000 trucks, 78,500 trailers and 31,100 towing devices. The firm's Emove.com and Uhaul.com online reservation portals are significant drivers of U-Haul's rental transaction volume. The company also offers moving and storage protection packages such as Safemove and Safetow, providing moving and towing customers a damage waiver; cargo protection; and medical and life coverage. Additionally, Safestor protects storage customers from loss on their goods in storage. AMERCO Real Estate Company markets commercial properties available for sale or lease. The property and casualty insurance business consists of Republic Western Insurance Company's business activities, which includes coverage for U-Haul customers, independent dealers, fleet owners and employees of AMERCO. The life insurance operating segment consists of Oxford Life Insurance Company, which offers annuities, credit life and disability, critical illness insurance, single premium whole life, group life and disability coverage as well as Medicare supplement insurance. Oxford also administers self-insured group health and dental plans for AMERCO.

Employees are offered medical, dental and vision insurance; life and AD&D insurance; disability coverage; a 401(k) plan; and an employee stock ownership plan.

FINANCIALS: **Sales and profits are in thousands of dollars—add 000 to get the full amount. 2009 Note: Financial information for 2009 was not available for all companies at press time.**

2009 Sales: $1,992,266	2009 Profits: $13,410	**U.S. Stock Ticker: UHAL**
2008 Sales: $2,049,174	2008 Profits: $67,784	**Int'l Ticker:** Int'l Exchange:
2007 Sales: $2,069,298	2007 Profits: $90,553	Employees: 17,700
2006 Sales: $2,087,525	2006 Profits: $121,154	Fiscal Year Ends: 3/31
2005 Sales: $2,008,100	2005 Profits: $89,400	Parent Company:

SALARIES/BENEFITS:

Pension Plan:	ESOP Stock Plan: Y	Profit Sharing:	Top Exec. Salary: $675,004	Bonus: $
Savings Plan: Y	Stock Purch. Plan:		Second Exec. Salary: $623,077	Bonus: $

OTHER THOUGHTS:

Apparent Women Officers or Directors:
Hot Spot for Advancement for Women/Minorities:

LOCATIONS: ("Y" = Yes)

West:	Southwest:	Midwest:	Southeast:	Northeast:	International:
Y	Y	Y	Y	Y	Y

AMERICAN AXLE & MANUFACTURING HOLDINGS INC

www.aam.com

Industry Group Code: 3363 **Ranks within this company's industry group:** Sales: 37 Profits: 51

Vehicle Manufacturing:		Dealers:		Parts:		Service:		Finance:		Specialty:	
Cars:		Car Dealer New:		Manufacturers:	Y	General Service:		Leasing:		Information Systems:	
Trucks:		Car Dealer Used:		Retail:		Specialty Service:		Auto Loans:		Online Marketing:	
Motorcycles:		Truck Dealer:		Distributors:		Oil Change:		Insurance:		Other:	
Specialty:		RV Dealer:		Tires:		Paint and Body:				Publishing:	
Buses:		Motorcycle Dealer:		Batteries:						Rental Cars/Trucks:	
RVs:		Specialty Dealer:									

TYPES OF BUSINESS:

Automotive Components Manufacturing
Driveline Systems
Chassis Systems
Forged Products

BRANDS/DIVISIONS/AFFILIATES:

SmartBar
TracRite
I-Ride

CONTACTS:
Note: Officers with more than one job title may be intentionally listed here more than once.

Richard E. Dauch, CEO
David C. Dauch, COO
David C. Dauch, Pres.
Michael K. Simonte, CFO
Yogen N. Rahangdale, CTO
Mike S. Barrett, VP-Prod. Dev.
Mike S. Barrett, VP-Eng.
Patrick S. Lancaster, Chief Admin. Officer/Exec. VP
Patrick S. Lancaster, Corp. Sec.
John J. Bellanti, Exec. VP-World Oper.
Alberto L. Satine, VP-Strategic & Bus. Dev.
Christopher M. Son, Dir.-Corp. Comm.
Christopher M. Son, Dir.-Investor Rel.
Michael K. Simonte, Exec. VP-Finance
Curt S. Howell, VP-AAM Americas
Norman Willemse, VP-Global Metal Formed Prod. Bus. Unit
John E. Jerge, VP-Materials, Logistics, Quality, Labor Rel.
John S. Sofia, VP-Commercial Vehicle Bus. Unit
Richard E. Dauch, Chmn.
Steven J. Proctor, Pres., AAM Asia
Michael C. Flynn, Exec. VP-Procurement & Supply Chain Mgmt.

Phone: 313-758-2000	**Fax:** 313-758-4257
Toll-Free: 800-299-2953	
Address: 1 Dauch Dr., Detroit, MI 48211-1198 US	

GROWTH PLANS/SPECIAL FEATURES:

American Axle & Manufacturing Holdings, Inc. (AAM) is a Tier I supplier to the automotive industry and a worldwide leader in the manufacture, engineering, design and validation of driveline and drivetrain systems and related components and chassis modules for light trucks, sport utility vehicles (SUVs), passenger cars and crossover vehicles. AAM brands include TracRite axles, transaxles and transfer case differentials, SmartBar electronic stabilizer systems and I-Ride suspension modules. AAM is the principal supplier of driveline components to General Motors Corporation (GM) for its rear-wheel drive light trucks and SUVs manufactured in North America, supplying substantially all of GM's rear axle and front four-wheel drive/all-wheel drive axle requirements for these vehicle platforms. Sales to GM comprised approximately 78% of the company's sales in 2009. In addition, AAM is the sole-source supplier to GM for certain axles and other driveline products for the life of each GM vehicle program covered by a Lifetime Program Contract. The company is also the principal supplier of driveline system products for the Chrysler Group's heavy-duty Dodge Ram full-size pickup trucks and its derivatives. Sales to Chrysler accounted for approximately 8% of the company's total net sales in 2009. AAM also supplies driveline systems and components to PACCAR, Inc.; Ford Motor Company; Harley-Davidson and other original equipment manufacturers and Tier I supplier companies such as Hino Motors Ltd.; Jatco Ltd.; and the Timken Company. In March 2010, the firm opened a new manufacturing facility in Lancaster, Pennsylvania for welding and bare spindle axle assembly. Also in March, the firm began manufacturing rear axles for Volkswagen's 2010 Amarok, a truck initially launched in South America.

Employees are offered health care; profit sharing; retirement plans; life insurance; disability coverage; and tuition assistance.

FINANCIALS:
Sales and profits are in thousands of dollars—add 000 to get the full amount. 2009 Note: Financial information for 2009 was not available for all companies at press time.

2009 Sales: $1,521,600	2009 Profits: $-253,100	**U.S. Stock Ticker: AXL**
2008 Sales: $2,109,200	2008 Profits: $-1,224,300	**Int'l Ticker:** Int'l Exchange:
2007 Sales: $3,248,200	2007 Profits: $37,000	Employees:
2006 Sales: $3,191,700	2006 Profits: $-222,500	Fiscal Year Ends: 12/31
2005 Sales: $3,387,300	2005 Profits: $56,000	Parent Company:

SALARIES/BENEFITS:

Pension Plan:	ESOP Stock Plan:	Profit Sharing: Y	Top Exec. Salary: $2,156,269	Bonus: $
Savings Plan: Y	Stock Purch. Plan:		Second Exec. Salary: $411,125	Bonus: $

OTHER THOUGHTS:

Apparent Women Officers or Directors: 1
Hot Spot for Advancement for Women/Minorities:

LOCATIONS: ("Y" = Yes)

West:	Southwest:	Midwest:	Southeast:	Northeast:	International:
		Y		Y	Y

AMERICAN HONDA MOTOR CO INC www.corporate.honda.com/america

Industry Group Code: 33611 **Ranks within this company's industry group:** Sales: Profits:

Vehicle Manufacturing:		Dealers:		Parts:		Service:		Finance:		Specialty:	
Cars:	Y	Car Dealer New:		Manufacturers:	Y	General Service:		Leasing:		Information Systems:	
Trucks:		Car Dealer Used:		Retail:	Y	Specialty Service:		Auto Loans:		Online Marketing:	
Motorcycles:	Y	Truck Dealer:		Distributors:		Oil Change:		Insurance:		Other:	
Specialty:	Y	RV Dealer:		Tires:		Paint and Body:				Publishing:	
Buses:		Motorcycle Dealer:		Batteries:						Rental Cars/Trucks:	
RVs:		Specialty Dealer:									

TYPES OF BUSINESS:

Automotive Manufacturing
Motorcycles & ATVs
Power Equipment
Marine Engines
Parts Manufacturing & Retail
Research & Development

BRANDS/DIVISIONS/AFFILIATES:

Honda Motor Co Ltd
Honda of America Manufacturing Inc
Honda R&D Americas Inc
Honda Parts Centers
Civic
Accord
Gold Wing
Acura

CONTACTS:

Note: Officers with more than one job title may be intentionally listed here more than once.

Tetsuo Iwamura, CEO
Tetsuo Iwamura, Pres.
John Mendel, Exec. VP-Sales
Jeffrey Smith, VP-Corp. Comm. & Affairs
Erik Berkman, Pres., Honda Performance Dev.
Takashi Sekiguchi, Exec. VP

Phone: 310-783-2000 **Fax:** 310-783-3023
Toll-Free: 800-999-1009
Address: 1919 Torrance Blvd., Torrance, CA 90501-2746 US

GROWTH PLANS/SPECIAL FEATURES:

American Honda Motor Co., Inc. (AHM) is the U.S. subsidiary of Honda Motor Co., Ltd. The firm manufactures and sells automobiles, motorcycles, ATVs, personal watercraft, marine engines, lawn care equipment, snow equipment, generators and water pumps. The company's car models include the Accord, Civic, Element, Odyssey, CR-V, Pilot and S2000. AHM also produces the Insight, a gas-electric hybrid car; and the Ridgeline pickup truck. In addition, Honda owns the Acura brand of vehicles. AHM's motorcycle models include Gold Wing, ST1300, Shadow Phantom, Nighthawk, Rebel, VTX, Interceptor, NSF, RC51, CBR, 919, CRF450R, CR85R, XR650R and CRF250X. Through Honda of America Manufacturing, the firm operates engine, transmission, automobile, motorcycle, ATV and power equipment plants in Ohio, Indiana, Georgia, Alabama, North Carolina and South Carolina. Through Honda R&D Americas, Inc., AHM also operates office, testing and research/development facilities in North Carolina, Colorado, Ohio, California, Michigan and Toronto, Canada. The company retails auto parts through Honda Parts Centers located in approximately nine states. In October 2009, AHM opened a new port facility in Richmond, California. In March 2010, roughly 68,000 Elements and 344,000 Odysseys made by AHM were recalled by Honda for a potential brake pedal issue.

FINANCIALS:

Sales and profits are in thousands of dollars—add 000 to get the full amount. 2009 Note: Financial information for 2009 was not available for all companies at press time.

2009 Sales: $	2009 Profits: $	**U.S. Stock Ticker: Subsidiary**
2008 Sales: $	2008 Profits: $	**Int'l Ticker:** Int'l Exchange:
2007 Sales: $	2007 Profits: $	Employees:
2006 Sales: $	2006 Profits: $	Fiscal Year Ends: 3/31
2005 Sales: $42,539,100	2005 Profits: $	Parent Company: HONDA MOTOR CO LTD

SALARIES/BENEFITS:

Pension Plan: Y	ESOP Stock Plan:	Profit Sharing:	Top Exec. Salary: $	Bonus: $
Savings Plan:	Stock Purch. Plan:		Second Exec. Salary: $	Bonus: $

OTHER THOUGHTS:

Apparent Women Officers or Directors:
Hot Spot for Advancement for Women/Minorities:

LOCATIONS: ("Y" = Yes)

West:	Southwest:	Midwest:	Southeast:	Northeast:	International:
Y	Y	Y	Y	Y	

AMERICAN TIRE DISTRIBUTORS

www.americantiredistributors.com

Industry Group Code: 423120 **Ranks within this company's industry group:** Sales: Profits:

Vehicle Manufacturing:		Dealers:		Parts:		Service:		Finance:		Specialty:	
Cars:		Car Dealer New:		Manufacturers:		General Service:		Leasing:		Information Systems:	
Trucks:		Car Dealer Used:		Retail:		Specialty Service:		Auto Loans:		Online Marketing:	
Motorcycles:		Truck Dealer:		Distributors:	Y	Oil Change:		Insurance:		Other:	
Specialty:		RV Dealer:		Tires:	Y	Paint and Body:				Publishing:	
Buses:		Motorcycle Dealer:		Batteries:						Rental Cars/Trucks:	
RVs:		Specialty Dealer:									

TYPES OF BUSINESS:

Tires & Related Products, Distribution

BRANDS/DIVISIONS/AFFILIATES:

TPG Inc
Monarch
Silver State Tire Company
ATD Service Bay
Samaritan Wholesale Tire Company
Texas Market Tire

CONTACTS:

Note: Officers with more than one job title may be intentionally listed here more than once.

William E. Berry, CEO
William E. Berry, Pres.
Dave Dyckman, CFO/Exec. VP
Daniel Brown, Sr. VP-Sales
Michael Gaither, General Counsel/Exec. VP
Ron Sinclair, Sr. VP-Mktg.
Phillip Marrett, Sr. VP-Procurement

Phone: 704-992-2000	**Fax:** 704-992-1384
Toll-Free: 800-222-1167	
Address: 12200 Herbert Wayne Ct., Ste. 150, Huntersville, NC 28070 US	

GROWTH PLANS/SPECIAL FEATURES:

American Tire Distributors (ATD) is one of the nation's largest suppliers of tires and wheels, as well as tools and other automotive service equipment. The company serves the replacement tire market through approximately 84 warehouse distribution centers, delivering products to 37 states, with an extensive independent dealer network. ATD offers its tire retailers and service shop clients various tires for passenger vehicles and light trucks, tractor-trailers, buses, farm machinery and specialty and recreational vehicles. The company carries brands including Michelin, Goodyear, Bridgestone/Firestone, Dunlop and BFGoodrich, as well as its Monarch house brand, which is manufactured by Goodyear. Its wheel selection ranges from 13- to 26-inch rims for passenger vehicles and light trucks. The firm runs ATD Service Bay, which provides programs, services, tools and technologies to dealers. ATD owns Texas Market Tire, which expanded the company's presence through Texas, Oklahoma and New Mexico; Silver State Tire Company, in Nevada; Golden State Tire Distributors, which expanded its presence in northern California; and Samaritan Wholesale Tire Company, which expanded service across Minnesota and in western Wisconsin. In April 2010, the company was acquired by TPG Capital for $1.3 billion. In June 2010, the firm opened a new distribution center in Cincinnati, Ohio.

FINANCIALS:

Sales and profits are in thousands of dollars—add 000 to get the full amount. 2009 Note: Financial information for 2009 was not available for all companies at press time.

2009 Sales: $	2009 Profits: $	**U.S. Stock Ticker: Private**
2008 Sales: $	2008 Profits: $	**Int'l Ticker:** Int'l Exchange:
2007 Sales: $1,877,500	2007 Profits: $	Employees:
2006 Sales: $1,578,000	2006 Profits: $-4,600	Fiscal Year Ends: 12/31
2005 Sales: $1,150,900	2005 Profits: $-1,600	Parent Company: TPG INC

SALARIES/BENEFITS:

Pension Plan:	ESOP Stock Plan:	Profit Sharing:	Top Exec. Salary: $	Bonus: $
Savings Plan:	Stock Purch. Plan:		Second Exec. Salary: $	Bonus: $

OTHER THOUGHTS:

Apparent Women Officers or Directors:
Hot Spot for Advancement for Women/Minorities:

LOCATIONS: ("Y" = Yes)

West:	Southwest:	Midwest:	Southeast:	Northeast:	International:
Y	Y	Y	Y	Y	

AMERICA'S CAR-MART INC

www.car-mart.com

Industry Group Code: 441110 **Ranks within this company's industry group:** Sales: 10 Profits: 7

Vehicle Manufacturing:		**Dealers:**		**Parts:**		**Service:**		**Finance:**		**Specialty:**	
Cars:		Car Dealer New:		Manufacturers:		General Service:		Leasing:		Information Systems:	
Trucks:		Car Dealer Used:	Y	Retail:		Specialty Service:		Auto Loans:	Y	Online Marketing:	
Motorcycles:		Truck Dealer:		Distributors:		Oil Change:		Insurance:		Other:	
Specialty:		RV Dealer:		Tires:		Paint and Body:				Publishing:	
Buses:		Motorcycle Dealer:		Batteries:						Rental Cars/Trucks:	
RVs:		Specialty Dealer:									

TYPES OF BUSINESS:

Used Auto Dealers, Retail
Used Car Financing & Servicing

BRANDS/DIVISIONS/AFFILIATES:

America's Car-Mart, Inc.
Car-Mart of Arkansas
Colonial Auto Finance, Inc.

CONTACTS: *Note: Officers with more than one job title may be intentionally listed here more than once.*

William H. Henderson, CEO
Eddie L. Hight, COO
William H. Henderson, Pres.
Jeffrey A. Williams, CFO
Tilman J. Falgout, III, General Counsel
William H. Henderson, Vice Chmn.
Tilman J. Falgout, III, Chmn.

Phone: 479-464-9944	**Fax:** 479-273-7556
Toll-Free:	
Address: 802 Southeast Plz. Ave., Ste. 200, Bentonville, AR 72712 US	

GROWTH PLANS/SPECIAL FEATURES:

America's Car-Mart, Inc. is one of the largest publicly-held automotive retailers focused exclusively on the buy-here/pay-here segment of the used car market in the U.S. America's Car-Mart operates 98 dealerships located primarily in small cities throughout Alabama, Arkansas, Indiana, Kentucky, Missouri, Oklahoma, Tennessee and Texas, with populations from 20,000 to 50,000. However, the company does have a number of dealerships in larger cities such as Tulsa, Oklahoma and Little Rock, Arkansas. The firm operates primarily through its two subsidiaries, America's Car-Mart, Inc., an Arkansas-based company also known as Car-Mart of Arkansas, and Colonial Auto Finance, Inc.
The company targets credit-impaired borrowers living in small to midsize cities and towns who would typically not qualify for conventional financing. Stores are run on a decentralized basis, with each dealership responsible for purchasing (with the help of a corporate buyer), making credit decisions, servicing vehicles and collecting the installment loans it originates. The company operates both regular and satellite stores. Satellite stores tend to be smaller, sell fewer vehicles and have their financing reported with the corresponding regular stores that sponsor them. The majority of the company's vehicles are purchased through wholesalers, new car dealers, individuals and from auctions. Generally, the firm's buyers purchase vehicles between 5-10 years old with 90,000-130,000 miles, paying between $3,000-$6,000 per vehicle. In 2010, the company opened new dealerships in Greenville, Texas; Broken Arrow, Oklahoma; and Clarksville, Tennessee.

Employees are offered medical, dental and life insurance; disability benefits; a 401(k) plan; and educational assistance.

FINANCIALS: **Sales and profits are in thousands of dollars—add 000 to get the full amount. 2009 Note: Financial information for 2009 was not available for all companies at press time.**

2009 Sales: $298,966	2009 Profits: $17,903	**U.S. Stock Ticker: CRMT**
2008 Sales: $274,631	2008 Profits: $15,033	**Int'l Ticker:** Int'l Exchange:
2007 Sales: $240,334	2007 Profits: $4,232	Employees: 915
2006 Sales: $234,207	2006 Profits: $16,705	Fiscal Year Ends: 4/30
2005 Sales: $204,788	2005 Profits: $17,976	Parent Company:

SALARIES/BENEFITS:

Pension Plan:	ESOP Stock Plan:	Profit Sharing:	Top Exec. Salary: $330,000	Bonus: $89,529
Savings Plan: Y	Stock Purch. Plan:		Second Exec. Salary: $300,000	Bonus: $129,204

OTHER THOUGHTS:

Apparent Women Officers or Directors:
Hot Spot for Advancement for Women/Minorities:

LOCATIONS: ("Y" = Yes)

West:	Southwest:	Midwest:	Southeast:	Northeast:	International:
	Y	Y	Y		

AMERIGON INC

www.amerigon.com

Industry Group Code: 3363 **Ranks within this company's industry group:** Sales: 60 Profits: 29

Vehicle Manufacturing:		Dealers:		Parts:		Service:		Finance:		Specialty:	
Cars:		Car Dealer New:		Manufacturers:	Y	General Service:		Leasing:		Information Systems:	
Trucks:		Car Dealer Used:		Retail:		Specialty Service:		Auto Loans:		Online Marketing:	
Motorcycles:		Truck Dealer:		Distributors:		Oil Change:		Insurance:		Other:	
Specialty:		RV Dealer:		Tires:		Paint and Body:				Publishing:	
Buses:		Motorcycle Dealer:		Batteries:						Rental Cars/Trucks:	
RVs:		Specialty Dealer:									

TYPES OF BUSINESS:

Automobile Parts Manufacturing
Thermoelectric Devices
Climate Control Seats

BRANDS/DIVISIONS/AFFILIATES:

BSST LLC
Climate Control Seat (CCS)
Amerigon Asia Pacific, Inc.

CONTACTS: *Note: Officers with more than one job title may be intentionally listed here more than once.*

Dan Coker, CEO
Dan Coker, Pres.
Barry Steele, CFO
Dan Pace, VP-Mktg. & Sales
Barry Steele, Corp. Sec.
Jim Mertes, VP-Oper.
Lon E. Bell, CEO/Pres., BSST LLC
Sandra Grouf, CIO/CFO-BSST LLC
Oscar B. Marx, III, Chmn.

Phone: 248-504-0500 **Fax:** 248-348-9735
Toll-Free:
Address: 21680 Haggerty Rd., Ste. 101, Northville, MI 48167 US

GROWTH PLANS/SPECIAL FEATURES:

Amerigon, Inc. designs, develops and markets products based on its advanced, proprietary thermoelectric device (TED) technologies for a wide range of global markets and heating and cooling applications. The firm's current principal product is its Climate Control Seat (CCS), which it sells to automobile and light truck original equipment manufacturers (OEMs) or Tier 1 suppliers. The CCS actively heats and cools the passenger by using TED technologies. The CCS product is currently offered as an optional feature on 44 automobile models produced by Ford Motor Company, General Motors, Toyota Motor Corporation, Nissan, Hyundai and Tata Motors, Ltd. Tata Motors, Ltd. features CCS on its Jaguar and Land Rover luxury brands. The firm also offers a heated-only variant of the CCS, which has a lower price and is targeted to certain lower cost vehicle models and certain geographical markets. In 2009, the firm's three largest customers were Lear Corporation, accounting for 34% of revenues; Bridgewater Interiors, LLC, accounting for 22%; and NHK Spring Company, Ltd., 10%. The company's subsidiaries include BSST LLC and Amerigon Asia Pacific, Inc. BSST LLC is involved in research and development to improve the efficiency of thermoelectric devices and to develop, market and distribute products based on this technology. Amerigon Asia Pacific, Inc. provides administrative support and engineering activities related to its Japan-based customers. In March 2010, the company, through BSST LLC, reached an agreement with 5N Plus, Inc. to purchase 5N Plus' interest in ZT Plus, a company engaged in the discovery and testing of new materials that show increased thermoelectric efficiency.

FINANCIALS: **Sales and profits are in thousands of dollars—add 000 to get the full amount. 2009 Note: Financial information for 2009 was not available for all companies at press time.**

2009 Sales: $60,925 — 2009 Profits: $ 284
2008 Sales: $63,613 — 2008 Profits: $3,564
2007 Sales: $63,630 — 2007 Profits: $7,375
2006 Sales: $50,609 — 2006 Profits: $3,514
2005 Sales: $35,737 — 2005 Profits: $16,549

U.S. Stock Ticker: ARGN
Int'l Ticker: Int'l Exchange:
Employees: 68
Fiscal Year Ends: 12/31
Parent Company:

SALARIES/BENEFITS:

Pension Plan: ESOP Stock Plan: Profit Sharing: Top Exec. Salary: $291,200 Bonus: $195,000
Savings Plan: Stock Purch. Plan: Second Exec. Salary: $222,000 Bonus: $78,000

OTHER THOUGHTS:

Apparent Women Officers or Directors: 1
Hot Spot for Advancement for Women/Minorities:

LOCATIONS: ("Y" = Yes)

West:	Southwest:	Midwest:	Southeast:	Northeast:	International:
Y		Y			Y

ANCIRA ENTERPRISES

www.ancira.com

Industry Group Code: 441110 **Ranks within this company's industry group:** Sales: Profits:

Vehicle Manufacturing:		Dealers:		Parts:		Service:		Finance:		Specialty:	
Cars:		Car Dealer New:	Y	Manufacturers:		General Service:	Y	Leasing:		Information Systems:	
Trucks:		Car Dealer Used:	Y	Retail:	Y	Specialty Service:		Auto Loans:		Online Marketing:	
Motorcycles:		Truck Dealer:	Y	Distributors:		Oil Change:		Insurance:		Other:	
Specialty:		RV Dealer:	Y	Tires:		Paint and Body:	Y			Publishing:	
Buses:		Motorcycle Dealer:		Batteries:						Rental Cars/Trucks:	
RVs:		Specialty Dealer:									

TYPES OF BUSINESS:

Auto Dealers, Retail
Used Vehicle Sales
Truck & RV Sales
Body Shops

BRANDS/DIVISIONS/AFFILIATES:

Ancira RV

CONTACTS:

Note: Officers with more than one job title may be intentionally listed here more than once.

Ernesto Ancira, Jr., CEO
Ernesto Ancira, Jr., Pres.
Betty Ferguson, CFO
Joey Blackmon, VP-Oper.

Phone: 210-681-4900 **Fax:** 210-681-9413
Toll-Free:
Address: 6111 Bandera Rd., San Antonio, TX 78238 US

GROWTH PLANS/SPECIAL FEATURES:

Ancira Enterprises is a private car, truck and recreational vehicle dealer in Texas. The company has nine car dealerships and two recreational vehicle dealerships predominately located in the greater San Antonio area. Ancira dealerships offer Mercury, Kia, Nissan, Chevrolet, Chrysler, Dodge, Jeep, Volkswagen, Smart, Pontiac, Buick, GMC and Ford brands. The firm also has a used car and trucks division and a body shop, one of the largest in South Texas. Ancira RV, located in Boerne and Alvarado, Texas, sells new and used campers, motorhomes and recreational vehicles. These include diesel motorhomes, class A and C motorhomes, fifth wheels and travel trailers from Winnebago, Fleetwood, Itasca, Allegro and others. Ancira RV also sells parts and accessories for RVs, including bathroom parts, beds, kitchen items, lights, electronics, wheels and brakes, as well as accessories such as camping and hiking gear, flags and flag holders, games, grills and accessories, outdoor furniture cleaners, patio accessories, picnic supplies, books, CDs, coffee makers and health and beauty products. Ancira accepts trade-in vehicles with financing and offers free 23-point vehicle inspections. The company's repair technicians are industry certified in the use of the Genesis System, a computerized and laser-based structure and frame measuring tool, and are also equipped with the Speis Hecker Paint Color Match System.

FINANCIALS:

Sales and profits are in thousands of dollars—add 000 to get the full amount. 2009 Note: Financial information for 2009 was not available for all companies at press time.

2009 Sales: $	2009 Profits: $	**U.S. Stock Ticker: Private**
2008 Sales: $	2008 Profits: $	**Int'l Ticker:** Int'l Exchange:
2007 Sales: $232,500	2007 Profits: $	Employees:
2006 Sales: $	2006 Profits: $	Fiscal Year Ends:
2005 Sales: $	2005 Profits: $	Parent Company:

SALARIES/BENEFITS:

Pension Plan:	ESOP Stock Plan:	Profit Sharing:	Top Exec. Salary: $	Bonus: $
Savings Plan:	Stock Purch. Plan:		Second Exec. Salary: $	Bonus: $

OTHER THOUGHTS:

Apparent Women Officers or Directors: 1
Hot Spot for Advancement for Women/Minorities:

LOCATIONS: ("Y" = Yes)

West:	Southwest:	Midwest:	Southeast:	Northeast:	International:
	Y				

APPLIED INDUSTRIAL TECHNOLOGIES INC

www.applied.com

Industry Group Code: 3363 **Ranks within this company's industry group:** Sales: 31 Profits: 15

Vehicle Manufacturing:		**Dealers:**		**Parts:**		**Service:**		**Finance:**		**Specialty:**	
Cars:		Car Dealer New:		Manufacturers:		General Service:		Leasing:		Information Systems:	
Trucks:		Car Dealer Used:		Retail:		Specialty Service:		Auto Loans:		Online Marketing:	
Motorcycles:		Truck Dealer:		Distributors:	Y	Oil Change:		Insurance:		Other:	
Specialty:		RV Dealer:		Tires:		Paint and Body:				Publishing:	
Buses:		Motorcycle Dealer:		Batteries:						Rental Cars/Trucks:	
RVs:		Specialty Dealer:									

TYPES OF BUSINESS:

Industrial Component Distribution
Automotive Parts & Products, Distribution
Engineering & Maintenance Services

BRANDS/DIVISIONS/AFFILIATES:

Bearing & Transmission
A&H Fluid Technologies
Carolina Fluid Components
Groupe GLM
Applied Mexico
Rafael Benitez Carrillo
Hypower Systems
Vycmex

CONTACTS:

Note: Officers with more than one job title may be intentionally listed here more than once.

David L. Pugh, CEO
Benjamin J. Mondics, COO
Benjamin J. Mondics, Pres.
Mark O. Eisele, CFO
Thomas E. Armold, VP-Mktg. & Strategic Accounts
Michael L. Coticchia, Chief Admin. Officer
Fred D. Bauer, General Counsel/VP/Corp. Sec.
Todd A. Barlett, VP-Global Bus. Dev. & Acquisitions
Richard C. Shaw, VP-Comm.
Daniel T. Brezovec, Corp. Controller
Mark O. Eisele, Treas./VP
Michael L. Coticchia, VP-Gov't Bus.
David L. Pugh, Chmn.
Jeffrey A. Ramras, VP-Supply Chain Mgmt.

Phone: 216-426-4000 **Fax:** 216-426-4845
Toll-Free: 877-279-2799
Address: 1 Applied Plaza, Cleveland, OH 44115 US

GROWTH PLANS/SPECIAL FEATURES:

Applied Industrial Technologies (AIT) is a North American industrial distributor with approximately 460 service centers, seven distribution centers and over 40 specialty repair shops. The company is divided into two segments: the service center-based distribution business and the fluid power business. The service center-based distribution segment provides customers industrial products in 48 U.S. states, Puerto Rico, six Canadian provinces and 13 Mexican states. It also operates regional fabricated rubber shops to modify and repair conveyor belts and hose apparatuses and field crews to install and repair belts and rubber lines at customers' premises. This division operates as Applied Industrial Technologies in the U.S.; Bearing & Transmission and Groupe GLM in Canada; Applied Mexico in Mexico; and Rafael Benitez Carrillo in Puerto Rico. The fluid power businesses segment consists of specialized regional companies that distribute fluid power components and operate shops to assemble fluid power systems and perform equipment repair. Subsidiaries within this segment include A&H Fluid Technologies and Carolina Fluid Components in the U.S.; Hypower Systems in Canada; and Vycmex in Mexico. This segment primarily sells directly to customers. AIT purchases from more than 2,000 product manufacturers and resells the products to customers in a wide variety of industries, including agriculture and food processing; automotive; chemical processing; forest products; industrial machinery and equipment; mining; primary metals; transportation; utilities; and government agencies. Products are also available for purchase through the firm's web site, applied.com, as well as through the company's catalog, which features 42,000 widely used products, including 20,000 bearing and power transmission parts and 9,000 fluid power products.

Employees are offered medical, dental and vision insurance; disability coverage; life insurance; a 401(k) plan; educational assistance; and product discounts.

FINANCIALS:

Sales and profits are in thousands of dollars—add 000 to get the full amount. 2009 Note: Financial information for 2009 was not available for all companies at press time.

2009 Sales: $1,923,148	2009 Profits: $42,260	**U.S. Stock Ticker: AIT**
2008 Sales: $2,089,456	2008 Profits: $95,456	**Int'l Ticker:** Int'l Exchange:
2007 Sales: $2,014,109	2007 Profits: $86,022	Employees: 4,673
2006 Sales: $1,900,780	2006 Profits: $72,299	Fiscal Year Ends: 6/30
2005 Sales: $1,717,055	2005 Profits: $55,339	Parent Company:

SALARIES/BENEFITS:

Pension Plan:	ESOP Stock Plan:	Profit Sharing:	Top Exec. Salary: $945,000	Bonus: $
Savings Plan: Y	Stock Purch. Plan:		Second Exec. Salary: $450,000	Bonus: $

OTHER THOUGHTS:

Apparent Women Officers or Directors: 2
Hot Spot for Advancement for Women/Minorities:

LOCATIONS: ("Y" = Yes)

West:	Southwest:	Midwest:	Southeast:	Northeast:	International:
Y	Y	Y	Y	Y	Y

Note: Financial information, benefits and other data can change quickly and may vary from those stated here.

ARCTIC CAT INC

www.arctic-cat.com

Industry Group Code: 336999 **Ranks within this company's industry group:** Sales: 2 Profits: 2

Vehicle Manufacturing:		Dealers:		Parts:		Service:		Finance:		Specialty:	
Cars:		Car Dealer New:		Manufacturers:	Y	General Service:		Leasing:		Information Systems:	
Trucks:		Car Dealer Used:		Retail:		Specialty Service:		Auto Loans:		Online Marketing:	
Motorcycles:		Truck Dealer:		Distributors:		Oil Change:		Insurance:		Other:	Y
Specialty:	Y	RV Dealer:		Tires:		Paint and Body:				Publishing:	
Buses:		Motorcycle Dealer:		Batteries:						Rental Cars/Trucks:	
RVs:		Specialty Dealer:									

TYPES OF BUSINESS:

All-Terrain Vehicle Manufacturer
Snowmobiles
Parts & Accessories
Cold-Weather Garments

BRANDS/DIVISIONS/AFFILIATES:

Arcticwear
Beracat
Jaguar
Crossfire
Panther
Prowler
Sno Pro

CONTACTS:

Note: Officers with more than one job title may be intentionally listed here more than once.

Christopher A. Twomey, CEO
Claude J. Jordan, COO
Claude J. Jordan, Pres.
Timothy C. Delmore, CFO
Mary Ellen Walker, Gen. Mgr.-Sales, Parts, Garments & Accessories
Terry J. Blount, VP-Human Resources
Roger H. Skime, VP-R&D
Ole E. Tweet, VP-New Prod. Dev.
Timothy C. Delmore, Sec.
Paul Fisher, VP-Oper.
Christopher A. Twomey, Chmn.

Phone: 218-681-8558	**Fax:** 218-681-3162
Toll-Free:	
Address: 601 Brooks Ave. S., Thief River Falls, MN 56701 US	

GROWTH PLANS/SPECIAL FEATURES:

Arctic Cat, Inc. designs, engineers, manufactures and markets snowmobiles and all-terrain vehicles (ATVs) under the Arctic Cat brand name, as well as related parts, winter garments and accessories. The company markets these products through a network of independent dealers in the U.S., Canada and Europe, as well as distributors representing dealers in Europe, the Middle East, Asia and other international markets. The firm manufacturers snowmobiles (51 models); ATVs (19 models); accessories such as electric start kits, reverse gear kits, mirrors, windshields, luggage racks, backrests, saddlebags, bumpers, gauges, tail-light protectors and snowmobile covers; supplies such as oil and fuel additives, track studs and carbide runners; and the Arcticwear line of cold-weather clothing. Artic Cat's snowmobile categories and models include performance snowmobiles (F series, CFR, Z1, Z1 Turbo and Sno Pro); mountain (M series); crossover (Crossfire); touring (T series); and utility (Bearcat). Arctic Cat's ATV line-up includes youth, utility, sport and multi-rider models, including the Prowler Utility Terrain Vehicle. The company owns a distribution center in Bucyrus, Ohio, and contracts with a Taiwanese company for the manufacture of ATV engines. In 2009, the firm received 36% of its revenues from snowmobiles; 42% from ATVs; and 22% from parts, garments and accessories.

FINANCIALS:

Sales and profits are in thousands of dollars—add 000 to get the full amount. 2009 Note: Financial information for 2009 was not available for all companies at press time.

2009 Sales: $563,613	2009 Profits: $-9,508	**U.S. Stock Ticker: ACAT**
2008 Sales: $621,568	2008 Profits: $-3,259	**Int'l Ticker:** Int'l Exchange:
2007 Sales: $782,431	2007 Profits: $22,070	Employees: 1,475
2006 Sales: $732,794	2006 Profits: $23,746	Fiscal Year Ends: 3/31
2005 Sales: $689,100	2005 Profits: $28,300	Parent Company:

SALARIES/BENEFITS:

Pension Plan:	ESOP Stock Plan:	Profit Sharing:	Top Exec. Salary: $521,389	Bonus: $
Savings Plan: Y	Stock Purch. Plan:		Second Exec. Salary: $404,321	Bonus: $

OTHER THOUGHTS:

Apparent Women Officers or Directors: 2
Hot Spot for Advancement for Women/Minorities:

LOCATIONS: ("Y" = Yes)

West:	Southwest:	Midwest:	Southeast:	Northeast:	International:
Y		Y			Y

ARVINMERITOR INC

www.arvinmeritor.com

Industry Group Code: 3363 **Ranks within this company's industry group:** Sales: 25 Profits: 59

Vehicle Manufacturing:		Dealers:		Parts:		Service:		Finance:		Specialty:	
Cars:		Car Dealer New:		Manufacturers:	Y	General Service:		Leasing:		Information Systems:	
Trucks:		Car Dealer Used:		Retail:		Specialty Service:		Auto Loans:		Online Marketing:	
Motorcycles:		Truck Dealer:		Distributors:		Oil Change:		Insurance:		Other:	
Specialty:		RV Dealer:		Tires:		Paint and Body:				Publishing:	
Buses:		Motorcycle Dealer:		Batteries:						Rental Cars/Trucks:	
RVs:		Specialty Dealer:									

TYPES OF BUSINESS:

Auto Parts Manufacturer
Drivetrain Systems & Components
Exhaust Systems
Braking Systems
Driveline Systems & Axles
Undercarriage Systems
Roof & Door Systems

BRANDS/DIVISIONS/AFFILIATES:

Commercial Vehicle Systems
Light Vehicle Systems
OnGuard

CONTACTS:

Note: Officers with more than one job title may be intentionally listed here more than once.

Charles McClure, CEO
Carsten Reinhardt, COO
Charles McClure, Pres.
Jeffrey Craig, CFO/Sr. VP
Vernon Baker, General Counsel/Sr. VP
Mary Lehmann, Sr. VP-Strategic Initiatives
Lin Cummins, Sr. VP-Comm.
Mary Lehmann, Treas.
Barbara Novak, VP/Corp. Sec.
James Donion, Exec. VP
Tim Bowes, VP/Pres., Industrial
Joe Mejaly, VP/Pres., Aftermarket & Trailer
Charles McClure, Chmn.

Phone: 248-435-1000	Fax: 248-435-1393
Toll-Free:	
Address: 2135 W. Maple Rd., Troy, MI 48084 US	

GROWTH PLANS/SPECIAL FEATURES:

ArvinMeritor, Inc., headquartered in Troy, Michigan, is a global supplier of a broad range of integrated systems, modules and components serving light vehicle, commercial truck, trailer and specialty original equipment manufacturers and certain aftermarkets. The company operates approximately 92 manufacturing facilities in 25 countries, participates in 21 joint ventures in 12 of these countries and serves its customers through two businesses: light vehicle systems (LVS) and commercial vehicle systems (CVS). The LVS segment supplies body systems and chassis systems for passenger cars, all-terrain vehicles (ATVs), light trucks and sport utility vehicles (SUVs). CVS supplies drivetrain systems and components, including axles and drivelines, braking systems, suspension systems and ride control products for medium- and heavy-duty trucks, trailers and specialty vehicles. CVS also operates a joint venture with Volvo for the manufacturing of truck axles. North America represents 48% of the company's sales; Europe, 33%, South America, 10%; and Asia Pacific, %. One of the firm's most recent products, OnGuard, is a radar-based adaptive cruise control system with active braking for commercial vehicles in North America. In September 2009, the company completed the sale of its wheel business to Iochpe-Maxion S.A. for approximately $180 million. In October 2009, the firm sold its 57 % stake in the Meritor Suspension Systems Company to Mitsubishi Steel Mfg., Ltd. for approximately $13 million

Employees are offered medical, dental, vision and life insurance; a disability income plan; adoption assistance; and educational assistance.

FINANCIALS:

Sales and profits are in thousands of dollars—add 000 to get the full amount. 2009 Note: Financial information for 2009 was not available for all companies at press time.

2009 Sales: $4,108,000	2009 Profits: $-1,212,000	**U.S. Stock Ticker: ARM**
2008 Sales: $6,390,000	2008 Profits: $-101,000	**Int'l Ticker:** Int'l Exchange:
2007 Sales: $5,720,000	2007 Profits: $-219,000	Employees: 13,200
2006 Sales: $6,415,000	2006 Profits: $-175,000	Fiscal Year Ends: 9/30
2005 Sales: $6,371,000	2005 Profits: $12,000	Parent Company:

SALARIES/BENEFITS:

Pension Plan: Y	ESOP Stock Plan:	Profit Sharing:	Top Exec. Salary: $1,068,542	Bonus: $
Savings Plan: Y	Stock Purch. Plan:		Second Exec. Salary: $653,948	Bonus: $

OTHER THOUGHTS:

Apparent Women Officers or Directors: 4
Hot Spot for Advancement for Women/Minorities: Y

LOCATIONS: ("Y" = Yes)

West:	Southwest:	Midwest:	Southeast:	Northeast:	International:
Y	Y	Y	Y	Y	Y

ASAHI GLASS COMPANY LIMITED

www.agc.co.jp/english

Industry Group Code: 3272 **Ranks within this company's industry group:** Sales: 1 Profits: 1

Vehicle Manufacturing:		Dealers:		Parts:		Service:		Finance:		Specialty:	
Cars:		Car Dealer New:		Manufacturers:	Y	General Service:		Leasing:		Information Systems:	
Trucks:		Car Dealer Used:		Retail:		Specialty Service:		Auto Loans:		Online Marketing:	
Motorcycles:		Truck Dealer:		Distributors:		Oil Change:		Insurance:		Other:	Y
Specialty:		RV Dealer:		Tires:		Paint and Body:				Publishing:	
Buses:		Motorcycle Dealer:		Batteries:						Rental Cars/Trucks:	
RVs:		Specialty Dealer:									

TYPES OF BUSINESS:

Glass Manufacturing
Home & Office Window Glass Manufacturing
Automotive Glass Manufacturing
Specialty Glass Manufacturing
Chemicals Manufacturing
Electronics Components Manufacturing

BRANDS/DIVISIONS/AFFILIATES:

AGC Flat Glass North America, Inc.

CONTACTS:

Note: Officers with more than one job title may be intentionally listed here more than once.

Kazuhiko Ishimura, CEO
Kazuhiko Ishimura, Pres.
Takashi Fujino, CFO/Sr. Exec. VP
Nozomu Taguchi, Gen. Mgr.-Mktg. & Sales, Display Co.
Yasutoshi Hirata, Gen. Mgr.-Human Resources Center
Tomoya Takigawa, Gen. Mgr.-Research Center
Katsuhisa Kato, CTO/Exec. VP
Yasutoshi Hirata, Gen. Mgr.-Admin. Center
Eisuke Yanagisawa, Gen. Mgr.-Legal
Shinji Miyaji, Group Dir.-Corp. Planning
Shukichi Umemoto, Gen. Mgr.-Finance & Control Office
Marehisa Ishiko, Regional Pres., North America, Glass Company
Yuji Nishimi, Sr. Exec. VP/Pres., Electronics Company
Akio Endo, Sr. Exec. VP/Pres., Glass Company
Takuya Shimamura, Pres., Chemicals Company
Masahiro Kadomatsu, Chmn.
Jean-Francois Heris, Regional Pres., Europe, Glass Company
Takashi Shimbo, Gen. Mgr.-Purchase & Logistics Center

Phone: 81-3-3218-5741 **Fax:** 81-3-3218-7815
Toll-Free:
Address: 1-12-1, Yurakucho, Chiyoda-ku, Tokyo, 100-8405 Japan

GROWTH PLANS/SPECIAL FEATURES:

Asahi Glass Co., Ltd. (AGC), founded in 1907, is a global supplier of products, materials and components for glass and related fields. It comprises five main segments: flat glass, automotive glass, display, electronics and energy and chemicals. The flat glass company's products, primarily used in home and office windows, are divided into two categories: glass for construction, which includes float glass, laminated glass, insulating glass units, mirrors, wired glass and heat-resistant glass; and industrial-use processed glass, including double-glazed glass, heater and refrigerating showcase glass, photovoltaic modules and high-transmissivity glass. The automotive glass company strengthens and shapes mostly tempered and laminated flat glass, making it suitable for use in vehicles, primarily in windshields. Other products include privacy glass, acoustic glass and UV-cut glass. Asahi's display company makes glass for traditional cathode ray tube (CRT) monitors, as well as glass for flat-panel displays including liquid crystal displays (LCDs) and plasma display panels. The electronics and energy segment offers electronic components such as lithography process materials, optical filters, LCD backlight tubes, glass powders and pastes, projector materials and aspherical glass lenses. Lastly, the chemicals company supplies chlor-alkalis such as caustic soda, potassium hydroxide, potassium carbonate, chlorine and soda ash, all raw materials for manufacturing glass; fluorochemicals for use in coatings, optical filters and solvents; and urethane products. The firm operates through 178 subsidiaries and affiliated companies, including more than 37 in Japan and 141 in 20 other countries, including U.S.-based AGC Flat Glass North America, Inc., a manufacturer of construction, specialty, solar and automotive glass products. Japan generates the largest share, 47%, of sales, followed by the rest of Asia with 30%, Europe with 17% and the Americas, 6%. In March 2010, the company announced plans to open a new production base for thin-film transistor LCD glass substrates in Jiangsu, China.

FINANCIALS:

Sales and profits are in thousands of dollars—add 000 to get the full amount. 2009 Note: Financial information for 2009 was not available for all companies at press time.

2009 Sales: $13,569,900 | 2009 Profits: $236,190
2008 Sales: $15,336,700 | 2008 Profits: $416,020
2007 Sales: $15,030,000 | 2007 Profits: $620,000
2006 Sales: $13,938,900 | 2006 Profits: $387,040
2005 Sales: $13,160,500 | 2005 Profits: $517,350

U.S. Stock Ticker: ASGLY
Int'l Ticker: 5201 Int'l Exchange: Tokyo-TSE
Employees:
Fiscal Year Ends: 12/31
Parent Company:

SALARIES/BENEFITS:

Pension Plan: ESOP Stock Plan: Profit Sharing: Top Exec. Salary: $ Bonus: $
Savings Plan: Stock Purch. Plan: Second Exec. Salary: $ Bonus: $

OTHER THOUGHTS:

Apparent Women Officers or Directors:
Hot Spot for Advancement for Women/Minorities:

LOCATIONS: ("Y" = Yes)

West:	Southwest:	Midwest:	Southeast:	Northeast:	International:
Y		Y	Y	Y	Y

ASBURY AUTOMOTIVE GROUP INC

www.asburyauto.com

Industry Group Code: 441110 **Ranks within this company's industry group:** Sales: 7 Profits: 8

Vehicle Manufacturing:		Dealers:		Parts:		Service:		Finance:		Specialty:	
Cars:		Car Dealer New:	Y	Manufacturers:		General Service:	Y	Leasing:	Y	Information Systems:	
Trucks:		Car Dealer Used:	Y	Retail:		Specialty Service:		Auto Loans:	Y	Online Marketing:	
Motorcycles:		Truck Dealer:		Distributors:		Oil Change:	Y	Insurance:		Other:	
Specialty:		RV Dealer:		Tires:		Paint and Body:	Y			Publishing:	
Buses:		Motorcycle Dealer:		Batteries:						Rental Cars/Trucks:	
RVs:		Specialty Dealer:									

TYPES OF BUSINESS:

Automotive Dealers, Retail
Finance & Insurance
Vehicle Maintenance & Repair Services
Replacement Parts

BRANDS/DIVISIONS/AFFILIATES:

Smart Car

CONTACTS:

Note: Officers with more than one job title may be intentionally listed here more than once.

Charles R. Oglesby, CEO
Michael S. Kearney, COO/Sr. VP
Charles R. Oglesby, Pres.
Craig Monaghan, CFO/Sr. VP
Joseph G. Parham, Jr., VP-Human Resources
Stephen D. McGee, CIO
Elizabeth B. Chandler, General Counsel/VP
George C. Karolis, VP-Corp. Dev. & Real Estate
Keith Style, VP-Finance
Ronald J. Avallone, VP-Internal Audit & SOX Compliance
Joe Shine, CFO-Dealership Oper.
Kenneth E. Jackson, VP-Field Human Resources
Matthew J. Mees, VP-Manufacturer Rel.
Michael J. Durham, Chmn.

Phone: 770-418-8200 **Fax:**
Toll-Free:
Address: 2905 Premiere Pkwy., Ste. 300, Duluth, GA 30097 US

GROWTH PLANS/SPECIAL FEATURES:

Asbury Automotive Group, Inc. is an U.S. automotive retailer, with 106 franchises at 81 dealership locations. The company offers automotive products and services including new and used vehicles and related financing; vehicle maintenance and repair services; replacement parts; and warranty, insurance and extended service contracts. The firm's franchises include a portfolio of 37 American, European and Asian brands of new vehicles that are sold to individual retail customers and commercial customers. In 2009, Asbury retailed 64,618 new vehicles through its dealerships. The company sells used vehicles at all of its dealerships to individual retail customers and other dealers at auction. The firm sells parts and provides maintenance and repair service at all of its dealerships, primarily for the vehicle brands sold at those dealerships. Asbury maintains 25 freestanding collision repair centers in close proximity to its dealerships. In addition, the company arranges for the financing of the sale or lease of new and used vehicles to customers through third-party vendors. Ashbury's new vehicle sales accounted for 51% of 2009 revenue; new heavy truck sales, 4%; used vehicles sales, 20%; wholesale sales, 5%; parts and service, 17%; and finance and insurance, 3%. The group operates through nine local dealership groups in Florida, New Jersey, Georgia, North Carolina, Virginia, South Carolina, Texas, California, Arkansas, Mississippi and Missouri. The firm also operates several smart-brand car franchises. In January 2010, the company was awarded two Sprinter franchises, which were added to its Mercedes-Benz locations in St. Louis, Missouri and Tampa, Florida.

The company offers its employees medical, dental, vision and life insurance; short- and long-term disability plans; healthcare, dependent-care and adoption assistance flexible spending accounts; a 401(k) plan; and an employee assistance program.

FINANCIALS:

Sales and profits are in thousands of dollars—add 000 to get the full amount. 2009 Note: Financial information for 2009 was not available for all companies at press time.

2009 Sales: $3,650,600	2009 Profits: $13,400	**U.S. Stock Ticker: ABG**
2008 Sales: $4,402,800	2008 Profits: $-343,700	**Int'l Ticker:** Int'l Exchange:
2007 Sales: $5,154,900	2007 Profits: $49,500	Employees: 7,300
2006 Sales: $5,431,100	2006 Profits: $60,749	Fiscal Year Ends: 12/31
2005 Sales: $5,413,193	2005 Profits: $61,081	Parent Company:

SALARIES/BENEFITS:

Pension Plan:	ESOP Stock Plan:	Profit Sharing:	Top Exec. Salary: $779,668	Bonus: $1,250,633
Savings Plan: Y	Stock Purch. Plan:		Second Exec. Salary: $600,000	Bonus: $540,000

OTHER THOUGHTS:

Apparent Women Officers or Directors: 3
Hot Spot for Advancement for Women/Minorities: Y

LOCATIONS: ("Y" = Yes)

West:	Southwest:	Midwest:	Southeast:	Northeast:	International:
Y	Y	Y	Y	Y	

ASC INCORPORATED

www.ascglobal.com

Industry Group Code: 33611 **Ranks within this company's industry group:** Sales: Profits:

Vehicle Manufacturing:		Dealers:		Parts:		Service:		Finance:		Specialty:	
Cars:		Car Dealer New:		Manufacturers:	Y	General Service:		Leasing:		Information Systems:	
Trucks:		Car Dealer Used:		Retail:		Specialty Service:		Auto Loans:		Online Marketing:	
Motorcycles:		Truck Dealer:		Distributors:	Y	Oil Change:		Insurance:		Other:	Y
Specialty:	Y	RV Dealer:		Tires:		Paint and Body:				Publishing:	
Buses:		Motorcycle Dealer:		Batteries:						Rental Cars/Trucks:	
RVs:		Specialty Dealer:									

TYPES OF BUSINESS:

Specialty Car Manufacturing
Automobile Design Services
Manufacturing
Modeling

BRANDS/DIVISIONS/AFFILIATES:

Questor Funds
Saleen Incorporated

CONTACTS:
Note: Officers with more than one job title may be intentionally listed here more than once.

Steven Laurain, CEO
Jeevak Badve, Dir.-Strategic Bus. Dev., Creative Svcs. Div.
Steve Nowicki, Gen. Mgr./Dir.-Design, Creative Svcs. Div.
Chris Mayfield, Dir.-Bus. Dev., Open Air Div.

Phone: 586-446-4701	**Fax:** 586-446-3401
Toll-Free:	
Address: 6115 13 Mile Rd., Warren, MI 48092 US	

GROWTH PLANS/SPECIAL FEATURES:

ASC, Inc., an acronym standing for American Specialty Cars, is a firm based in Warren, Michigan that helps carmakers design, engineer and manufacture high-image low-volume specialty vehicles. The company capitalizes on the recent trend away from standard vehicles towards more personalized, higher-end vehicles. The firm's focus is on automotive; defense, specialty, marine, agricultural and fleet vehicles; commercial trucks; recreational; ATV; aviation; mass transit and material handling. The company operates in two segments, Open-Air Systems and Creative Services. In the Open-Air Systems segment, the company provides Soft tops (topstacks); Retractable Hard Tops (RHT); SkyVu Retractable Glass Panel and fabric panels. The Creative Services segment is divided into seven segments, strategy; research; branding; industrial design; human factors design, which includes ergonomics, user interface and interaction design; graphic design; and concept vehicles. ASC offers manufacturing capabilities that range from body framing to its modeling and prototyping services. The company was involved in developing models such as the Dodge Ram SportSide Concept, Chevrolet SSR, the Buick GNX and the Pontiac Vibe GTR. Clients of the firm include General Motors, Toyota, Chrysler, Nissan, International, Ford, Suzuki, Hyundai, Saleen, CCS, Sea Ray, Freightliner and Honda. ASC has manufacturing facilities in Michigan and Kentucky. The firm is privately held by Questor Funds. The firm has a partnership with Saleen, Inc. as sister companies operating out of common facilities.

FINANCIALS:
Sales and profits are in thousands of dollars—add 000 to get the full amount. 2009 Note: Financial information for 2009 was not available for all companies at press time.

2009 Sales: $	2009 Profits: $	**U.S. Stock Ticker: Private**
2008 Sales: $	2008 Profits: $	**Int'l Ticker:** Int'l Exchange:
2007 Sales: $	2007 Profits: $	Employees:
2006 Sales: $	2006 Profits: $	Fiscal Year Ends:
2005 Sales: $	2005 Profits: $	Parent Company:

SALARIES/BENEFITS:

Pension Plan:	ESOP Stock Plan:	Profit Sharing:	Top Exec. Salary: $	Bonus: $
Savings Plan:	Stock Purch. Plan:		Second Exec. Salary: $	Bonus: $

OTHER THOUGHTS:

Apparent Women Officers or Directors:
Hot Spot for Advancement for Women/Minorities:

LOCATIONS: ("Y" = Yes)

West:	Southwest:	Midwest:	Southeast:	Northeast:	International:
		Y			

ASTON MARTIN LAGONDA LTD

www.astonmartin.com

Industry Group Code: 33611 **Ranks within this company's industry group:** Sales: Profits:

Vehicle Manufacturing:		Dealers:		Parts:		Service:		Finance:		Specialty:	
Cars:	Y	Car Dealer New:	Y	Manufacturers:		General Service:	Y	Leasing:		Information Systems:	
Trucks:		Car Dealer Used:	Y	Retail:		Specialty Service:	Y	Auto Loans:		Online Marketing:	
Motorcycles:		Truck Dealer:		Distributors:		Oil Change:		Insurance:		Other:	Y
Specialty:		RV Dealer:		Tires:		Paint and Body:				Publishing:	
Buses:		Motorcycle Dealer:		Batteries:						Rental Cars/Trucks:	
RVs:		Specialty Dealer:									

TYPES OF BUSINESS:

Automobile Manufacturing
Sports Cars
Antique Vehicle Maintenance & Restoration
Clothing & Fashion Accessories
Automobile Racing

BRANDS/DIVISIONS/AFFILIATES:

DBS
DBS Volante
DB9
V8 Vantage
V12 Vantage
Rapide
Aston Martin Racing
Collection (The)

CONTACTS:

Note: Officers with more than one job title may be intentionally listed here more than once.

Ulrich Bez, CEO
Michael van der Sande, Chief Commercial Officer
Marek Reichman, Dir.-Design
Mark Kenworthy, Gen. Mgr.-Aston Martin, Middle East & North Africa
Ulrich Bez, Chmn.
Adham Charanoglu, CEO-Aston Martin, Middle East & North Africa

Phone: 44-1926-644644	**Fax:** 44-1926-644733
Toll-Free:	
Address: Banbury Rd., Gaydon, Warwickshire CV35 0DB UK	

GROWTH PLANS/SPECIAL FEATURES:

Aston Martin Lagonda, Ltd. is a small British manufacturer of high-performance sports cars. Its current models include the DBS; DBS Volante; DB9; V8 Vantage; V12 Vantage; and the Rapide. Currently, it has two limited edition models, Carbon Black and DBS UB-2010. The company is currently developing Cygnet, a luxury commuter car and will be introducing the One 77 super car. Only 77 cars will be produced of the One 77 super car. The cars are all built by hand and retail for between $130,000 and $280,000. In addition, subsidiary Aston Martin Racing manufactures a line of DBR9 racing cars in partnership with Prodrive Ltd., a British motorsport and vehicle technology company. The Aston Martin Racing division sponsors competitive drivers and a dedicated team. Aston Martin operates a headquarters production facility in Gaydon, Warwickshire in the U.K. with a production capacity of 5,000 vehicles per year. The firm offers a wide variety of customization options and a performance-driving course. It can collect and deliver cars for servicing at its Newport Pagnell, Buckinghamshire facility from anywhere in Europe, and will send service teams to any location in the world if necessary. The company operates a Heritage team dedicated to providing obsolete parts for repair of its older model and antique Aston Martin and Lagonda cars. The firm also markets The Collection, a line of clothing, luggage and fashion accessories. The firm has partnerships with Bang & Olufsen for sound sytems; and Jaeger-LeCoultre, for a special micro-transmitter gentleman's watch designed to lock/unlock the doors. In March 2009, Aston Martin opened its first dealership in Croatia. In May 2009, the firm opened a new dealership in Lyon, France, bringing its total number of dealerships in France to four. In June 2010, Aston Martin opened a new dealership in St. Gallen, Switzerland.

FINANCIALS:

Sales and profits are in thousands of dollars—add 000 to get the full amount. 2009 Note: Financial information for 2009 was not available for all companies at press time.

2009 Sales: $	2009 Profits: $	**U.S. Stock Ticker: Private**
2008 Sales: $	2008 Profits: $	**Int'l Ticker:** Int'l Exchange:
2007 Sales: $515,400	2007 Profits: $	Employees:
2006 Sales: $	2006 Profits: $	Fiscal Year Ends: 12/31
2005 Sales: $	2005 Profits: $	Parent Company:

SALARIES/BENEFITS:

Pension Plan:	ESOP Stock Plan:	Profit Sharing:	Top Exec. Salary: $	Bonus: $
Savings Plan:	Stock Purch. Plan:		Second Exec. Salary: $	Bonus: $

OTHER THOUGHTS:

Apparent Women Officers or Directors:
Hot Spot for Advancement for Women/Minorities:

LOCATIONS: ("Y" = Yes)

West:	Southwest:	Midwest:	Southeast:	Northeast:	International:
Y	Y	Y	Y	Y	Y

Note: Financial information, benefits and other data can change quickly and may vary from those stated here.

ATC TECHNOLOGY CORPORATION

www.goatc.com

Industry Group Code: 336350 **Ranks within this company's industry group:** Sales: 3 Profits: 2

Vehicle Manufacturing:		Dealers:		Parts:		Service:		Finance:		Specialty:	
Cars:		Car Dealer New:		Manufacturers:	Y	General Service:		Leasing:		Information Systems:	
Trucks:		Car Dealer Used:		Retail:		Specialty Service:		Auto Loans:		Online Marketing:	
Motorcycles:		Truck Dealer:		Distributors:	Y	Oil Change:		Insurance:		Other:	Y
Specialty:		RV Dealer:		Tires:		Paint and Body:				Publishing:	
Buses:		Motorcycle Dealer:		Batteries:						Rental Cars/Trucks:	
RVs:		Specialty Dealer:									

TYPES OF BUSINESS:

Engineering & Remanufacturing Services
Logistics Services
Warehousing
Electronics Testing
Turnkey Order Fulfillment

BRANDS/DIVISIONS/AFFILIATES:

ATC Custom Services, Inc.
ATC Drivetrain, Inc
ATC Logistics & Electronics, Inc.
GENCO Distribution System, Inc.

CONTACTS:

Note: Officers with more than one job title may be intentionally listed here more than once.

Todd R. Peters, CEO
Todd R. Peters, Pres.
John Pinkerton, CFO/VP
John J. Machota, VP-Human Resources
Joseph Salamunovich, General Counsel/VP/Sec.
Mary Ryan, VP-Comm.
Mary Ryan, VP-Investor Rel.
Antony Francis, Pres., ATC Logistics & Electronics

Phone: 630-271-8100 **Fax:** 630-271-9999
Toll-Free:
Address: 1400 Opus Place, Ste. 600, Downers Grove, IL 60515 US

GROWTH PLANS/SPECIAL FEATURES:

ATC Technology Corp., formerly Aftermarket Technology Corp., provides outsourced engineering solutions and supply chain logistics services to the light and medium/heavy-duty vehicle aftermarket and consumer electronics industries. The company, who operates through its subsidiaries, functions primarily in two segments: logistics and drivetrain. The logistics business segment, which generates 71% of net sales, offers warehousing, reverse logistics, turnkey order fulfillment, electronics testing, transportation management services and packaging and distribution. Logistics customers are generally wireless carriers, wireless equipment manufacturers (OEMs), or in the consumer electronics and automotive industries. Through the drivetrain business segment, the firm provides customized remanufacturing services focused on complex light and medium/heavy-duty vehicle drivetrain products, such as automatic transmissions and engines, which are primarily sold through the service, repair and parts organizations of its customers. Drivetrain customers include Ford, Chrysler, Allison and GM. This segment generates the remaining 29% of net sales. The firm's subsidiaries include: ATC Custom Services, Inc.; ATC Drivetrain, Inc.; and ATC Logistics & Electronics, Inc. In 2009, the company continued restructuring its drivetrain operations by closing its Springfield, Missouri facility and consolidating the operations into its Oklahoma City, Oklahoma drivetrain facility. In May 2010, ATC sold its U.K. based drivetrain operations.

The company offers its employees medical, dental, vision and life insurance; short- and long-term disability insurance; flexible spending accounts; a 401(k) plan; and education assistance.

FINANCIALS:

Sales and profits are in thousands of dollars—add 000 to get the full amount. 2009 Note: Financial information for 2009 was not available for all companies at press time.

2009 Sales: $485,017	2009 Profits: $11,707	**U.S. Stock Ticker: ATAC**
2008 Sales: $530,560	2008 Profits: $-22,689	**Int'l Ticker:** Int'l Exchange:
2007 Sales: $529,171	2007 Profits: $47,122	Employees: 3,300
2006 Sales: $497,891	2006 Profits: $8,023	Fiscal Year Ends: 12/31
2005 Sales: $419,618	2005 Profits: $31,008	Parent Company:

SALARIES/BENEFITS:

Pension Plan:	ESOP Stock Plan:	Profit Sharing:	Top Exec. Salary: $450,000	Bonus: $202,500
Savings Plan: Y	Stock Purch. Plan:		Second Exec. Salary: $315,000	Bonus: $

OTHER THOUGHTS:

Apparent Women Officers or Directors: 1
Hot Spot for Advancement for Women/Minorities:

LOCATIONS: ("Y" = Yes)

West:	Southwest:	Midwest:	Southeast:	Northeast:	International:
	Y	Y			Y

ATS AUTOMATION TOOLING SYSTEMS INC www.atsautomation.com

Industry Group Code: 333 **Ranks within this company's industry group:** Sales: 6 Profits: 4

Vehicle Manufacturing:		**Dealers:**		**Parts:**		**Service:**		**Finance:**		**Specialty:**	
Cars:		Car Dealer New:		Manufacturers:		General Service:		Leasing:		Information Systems:	
Trucks:		Car Dealer Used:		Retail:		Specialty Service:		Auto Loans:		Online Marketing:	
Motorcycles:		Truck Dealer:		Distributors:		Oil Change:		Insurance:		Other:	Y
Specialty:		RV Dealer:		Tires:		Paint and Body:				Publishing:	
Buses:		Motorcycle Dealer:		Batteries:						Rental Cars/Trucks:	
RVs:		Specialty Dealer:									

TYPES OF BUSINESS:

Automated Systems Manufacturing
Testing Equipment
Manufacturing Consulting
Photovoltaic Cells Manufacturing
Photovoltaic Cells Installation & Design
Photovoltaic Cells Research & Development

BRANDS/DIVISIONS/AFFILIATES:

Automation Systems Group (ATG)
Automated Products Group (APG)
Photowatt Technologies, Inc.
Photowatt France (PWF)
PV Alliance (PVA)
EDF Energies Nouvelles Reparties
Sotimat Group
Photowatt International SA

CONTACTS: *Note: Officers with more than one job title may be intentionally listed here more than once.*

Anthony Caputo, CEO
Maria Perrella, CFO
Doug MacDonald, Dir.-Mktg. & Sales
Ron Keyser, CIO
Stewart McCuaig, General Counsel/VP
Chuck Gyles, VP-Organizational Effectiveness
Hans Reidl, VP-Finance
Mike Fisher, VP-Bus. Dev.
Carl Galloway, Treas./VP
Eric Kiisel, Sr. VP-ASG North America
John Sun, VP/Gen. Mgr.-ASG Asia
Neil D. Arnold, Chmn.
Josef Wildgruber, VP/Gen. Mgr.-ASG Europe

Phone: 519-653-6500	**Fax:** 519-653-6533
Toll-Free:	
Address: 250 Royal Oak Rd., Cambridge, ON N3H 4R6 Canada	

GROWTH PLANS/SPECIAL FEATURES:

ATS Automation Tooling Systems, Inc. manufactures various automated manufacturing and electronics systems. It has two reportable segments: Automation Systems Group (ASG) and Photowatt Technologies. ASG designs and manufactures turn-key automated manufacturing and test systems. It comprises 13 main subsidiaries primarily located in the U.S., Europe, the U.K. and Asia, and is ATS's primary business, generating 69% of 2009 revenues. Primarily multinational corporations operating in the automotive, computer/electronics, healthcare, telecommunications and consumer product industries use this segment's products. In general, when it receives an order, ASG helps the customer design a system, analyze its cost of ownership, prototype it, build it, install it and train the customer's employees to use it, as well as providing after-installation support. It can also offer customers systems designed as part of other projects, instead of custom-designed products. This segment also includes the Automated Products Group (APG), which offers engineering, supply chain management, integration and manufacturing services to customers seeking complex equipment replication. Often, the customer resells APG's products. Wholly-owned subsidiary Photowatt Technologies, Inc., based in Cambridge, Ontario, designs, manufactures and markets solar energy-related products, primarily through Photowatt France (PWF), which makes silicon ingots and wafers, as well as solar cells and solar modules. PWF also sells solar cell installation kits, offers solar power systems design services and offers other valued-added services, mostly in Western Europe. Additionally, PWF owns 40% of the PV Alliance (PVA), a joint venture with EDF Energies Nouvelles Reparties and CEA Valorisation. PVA conducts solar energy research. In total, ATS has 17 manufacturing facilities, including a recently built 60,000-square-foot ASG facility in Penang, Malaysia. In January 2009, as part of a restructuring and consolidation of its business, ATS sold its former segment, the Precision Components Group (PCG). In March 2010, the firm announced plans to acquired Sortimat Group, which specializes in assembly systems for medical and pharmaceutical industries, for $62 million.

FINANCIALS: **Sales and profits are in thousands of dollars—add 000 to get the full amount. 2009 Note: Financial information for 2009 was not available for all companies at press time.**

2009 Sales: $794,820	2009 Profits: $44,620	**U.S. Stock Ticker: ATA**
2008 Sales: $616,540	2008 Profits: $-21,750	**Int'l Ticker: ATA** Int'l Exchange: Toronto-TSX
2007 Sales: $571,180	2007 Profits: $-79,000	Employees: 2,623
2006 Sales: $627,460	2006 Profits: $-69,293	Fiscal Year Ends: 3/31
2005 Sales: $681,857	2005 Profits: $8,223	Parent Company:

SALARIES/BENEFITS:

Pension Plan:	ESOP Stock Plan:	Profit Sharing:	Top Exec. Salary: $	Bonus: $
Savings Plan:	Stock Purch. Plan: Y		Second Exec. Salary: $	Bonus: $

OTHER THOUGHTS:

Apparent Women Officers or Directors: 1
Hot Spot for Advancement for Women/Minorities:

LOCATIONS: ("Y" = Yes)

West:	Southwest:	Midwest:	Southeast:	Northeast:	International:
Y		Y			Y

ATX GROUP INC

www.atxg.com

Industry Group Code: 334220 **Ranks within this company's industry group:** Sales: Profits:

Vehicle Manufacturing:		**Dealers:**		**Parts:**		**Service:**		**Finance:**		**Specialty:**	
Cars:		Car Dealer New:		Manufacturers:		General Service:		Leasing:		Information Systems:	
Trucks:		Car Dealer Used:		Retail:		Specialty Service:	Y	Auto Loans:		Online Marketing:	
Motorcycles:		Truck Dealer:		Distributors:		Oil Change:		Insurance:		Other:	
Specialty:		RV Dealer:		Tires:		Paint and Body:				Publishing:	
Buses:		Motorcycle Dealer:		Batteries:						Rental Cars/Trucks:	
RVs:		Specialty Dealer:									

TYPES OF BUSINESS:

Automotive Telematics
Emergency Response Systems
Stolen Vehicle Tracking
Automobile Operational Analysis
Navigation Tools

GROWTH PLANS/SPECIAL FEATURES:

ATX Group, Inc., a subsidiary of Cross Country Automotive Services, is one of the world's largest providers of telematics (location-based voice and data communication services). It equips more than 600,000 automobiles with its products annually, primarily in North America and Western Europe. The firm's telematics connect the automobile of a subscriber to a support center run by ATX. Its services include location specific emergency response; vehicle breakdown assistance; automatic collision notification; and navigation aids and traffic alerts run in real-time. Satellite driven global positioning systems (GPS) are incorporated into its service package to pinpoint the location of a vehicle, which assists, for example, with stolen vehicle recovery. The firm connects the vehicle owner to a dealer of their preference to address all service needs and vehicle related questions. The company's services for original equipment manufacturers (OEM) include remote access by the OEM to information regarding the vehicle's performance and diagnostics. For instance, the remote access can open doors in the event of a lock out, or provide a repair service with information about the vehicle's engine before it arrives. ATX Group's OEM customers include BMW, Maybach, Rolls-Royce and Mercedes-Benz. Many of the company's services are available in bundled packages. In August 2009, the firm launched a new telematics platform for use in Toyota vehicles through Lexus Enform proprietary telematics programs and Safety Connect. In 2009, the company provided BMW with Automatic Collision Notification (ACN) to provide vehicle-generated data to aid emergency responders with collision information. Also in 2009, ATX introduces hands-free text messaging via voice application in vehicles.

BRANDS/DIVISIONS/AFFILIATES:

ATX
Cross Country Automotive Services
Automatic Collision Notification (ACN)
Safety Connect
Lexus Enform

CONTACTS: *Note: Officers with more than one job title may be intentionally listed here more than once.*

Michael A. Saxton, CEO
Peggy Ward, CFO
Tom Metzger, Sr. VP-Sales & Account Mgmt.
Mark Carbrey, CIO
Tod Farrell, CTO
Peggy Ward, Chief Admin. Officer
Renee T. Kingsley, General Counsel
Niall Berkery, VP-Bus. Dev. & Innovation
Gary Wallace, Chief Privacy Officer/VP-Corp. Rel.
Jimmy Stovall, Sr. VP-Customer Care
Tod Farrell, VP-Customer Solutions
Greg Corley, VP-Sales
Gwen Daniels, VP-Admin & Support Svcs.
Arnaud de Meulemeester, Sr. Dir.-ATX Europe

Phone: 972-753-6200 **Fax:**
Toll-Free:
Address: 8550 Freeport Pkwy., Irving, TX 75063-2547 US

FINANCIALS: **Sales and profits are in thousands of dollars—add 000 to get the full amount. 2009 Note: Financial information for 2009 was not available for all companies at press time.**

2009 Sales: $	2009 Profits: $	**U.S. Stock Ticker: Subsidiary**
2008 Sales: $	2008 Profits: $	**Int'l Ticker:** Int'l Exchange:
2007 Sales: $	2007 Profits: $	Employees:
2006 Sales: $	2006 Profits: $	Fiscal Year Ends: 12/31
2005 Sales: $	2005 Profits: $	Parent Company: CROSS COUNTRY AUTOMOTIVE SERVICES

SALARIES/BENEFITS:

Pension Plan:	ESOP Stock Plan:	Profit Sharing:	Top Exec. Salary: $	Bonus: $
Savings Plan:	Stock Purch. Plan:		Second Exec. Salary: $	Bonus: $

OTHER THOUGHTS:

Apparent Women Officers or Directors: 4
Hot Spot for Advancement for Women/Minorities: Y

LOCATIONS: ("Y" = Yes)

West:	Southwest:	Midwest:	Southeast:	Northeast:	International:
	Y				Y

AUDI AG

www.audi.com

Industry Group Code: 33611 **Ranks within this company's industry group:** Sales: Profits:

Vehicle Manufacturing:		Dealers:		Parts:		Service:		Finance:		Specialty:	
Cars:	Y	Car Dealer New:		Manufacturers:	Y	General Service:		Leasing:		Information Systems:	
Trucks:	Y	Car Dealer Used:		Retail:		Specialty Service:	Y	Auto Loans:		Online Marketing:	
Motorcycles:		Truck Dealer:		Distributors:		Oil Change:		Insurance:		Other:	
Specialty:	Y	RV Dealer:		Tires:		Paint and Body:				Publishing:	
Buses:		Motorcycle Dealer:		Batteries:						Rental Cars/Trucks:	
RVs:		Specialty Dealer:									

TYPES OF BUSINESS:

Automobile Manufacturing
Luxury & Sports Cars
Automobile Customization & Accessories
Engine Manufacturing
Automotive Electronics

BRANDS/DIVISIONS/AFFILIATES:

Audi A8
Audi Hungaria Motor Kft
Quattro Gmbh
Automobili Lamborghini Holding, SpA
Lamborghini
AUTOGERMA SpA
Q7
Volkswagen AG

CONTACTS: *Note: Officers with more than one job title may be intentionally listed here more than once.*

Rupert Stadler, Chmn.-Mgmt. Board
Axel Strotbek, Dir.-Finance & Organization
Peter Schwarzenbauer, Dir.-Mktg. & Sales
Werner Widuckel, Dir.-Human Resources
Michael Dick, Dir.-Tech. Dev.
Frank Dreves, Dir.-Prod.
Martin Winterkorn, Chmn.
Ulf Berkenhagen, Dir.-Purchasing

Phone: 49-841-89-40300	**Fax:** 49-841-89-30900
Toll-Free:	
Address: Postfach 100457, Ingolstadt, D-85045 Germany	

GROWTH PLANS/SPECIAL FEATURES:

Audi AG, a publically listed subsidiary of Volkswagen AG, is a German firm that designs and manufactures high-end luxury cars. Its most popular vehicle series include Audi A8, Audi Q7, Audi TT and Audi RS. The company operates through three main subsidiaries: Audi Hungaria Motor Kft.; Automobili Lamborghini Holding, S.p.A.; and Quattro GmbH. Audi Hungaria Motor Kft., based in Gyor, Hungary, develops and builds engines for Audi, other Volkswagen Group companies and third parties. In addition, this subsidiary produces the Audi TT Coupe and TT Roadster lines of vehicles. Automobili Lamborghini Holding, S.p.A. builds the Lamborghini brand of high-end sports cars, which includes the Gallardo Coupe, Gallardo Spyder, Murcielago LP640 Coupe and Murcielago LP640 Roadster. Additionally, this subsidiary oversees AUTOGERMA S.p.A., which sells Audi and Volkswagen vehicles in Italy. Quattro GmbH, based in Neckarsulm, Germany, designs and manufactures the RS range of vehicles as well as the Avant model. This subsidiary also runs customization operations. Formed in Germany in 1932 from the combination of four separate auto manufacturers, Audi now has production facilities in Germany, Italy, Hungary, Brazil and China, manufacturing over 1 million cars per year. The company also owns and operates various consolidated sales subsidiaries such as Audi Australia Pty Ltd.; Audi Japan K.K.; Audi Volkswagen Korea Ltd.; and Audi Volkswagen Middle East Fze. In November 2009, Audi AG agreed to acquire 9.09% interest in FC Bayern Munchen AG.

FINANCIALS: **Sales and profits are in thousands of dollars—add 000 to get the full amount. 2009 Note: Financial information for 2009 was not available for all companies at press time.**

2009 Sales: $	2009 Profits: $	**U.S. Stock Ticker: Subsidiary**
2008 Sales: $45,246,100	2008 Profits: $4,203,620	**Int'l Ticker:** Int'l Exchange:
2007 Sales: $49,417,000	2007 Profits: $2,431,400	Employees:
2006 Sales: $45,778,700	2006 Profits: $1,974,200	Fiscal Year Ends: 12/31
2005 Sales: $39,088,800	2005 Profits: $1,211,300	Parent Company: VOLKSWAGEN AG

SALARIES/BENEFITS:

Pension Plan:	ESOP Stock Plan:	Profit Sharing:	Top Exec. Salary: $	Bonus: $
Savings Plan:	Stock Purch. Plan:		Second Exec. Salary: $	Bonus: $

OTHER THOUGHTS:

Apparent Women Officers or Directors:
Hot Spot for Advancement for Women/Minorities:

LOCATIONS: ("Y" = Yes)

West:	Southwest:	Midwest:	Southeast:	Northeast:	International:
Y	Y	Y	Y	Y	Y

AUDI OF AMERICA INC

www.audiusa.com

Industry Group Code: 33611 **Ranks within this company's industry group:** Sales: Profits:

Vehicle Manufacturing:		Dealers:		Parts:		Service:		Finance:		Specialty:	
Cars:		Car Dealer New:	Y	Manufacturers:		General Service:		Leasing:	Y	Information Systems:	
Trucks:		Car Dealer Used:	Y	Retail:		Specialty Service:		Auto Loans:	Y	Online Marketing:	
Motorcycles:		Truck Dealer:		Distributors:		Oil Change:		Insurance:		Other:	
Specialty:		RV Dealer:		Tires:		Paint and Body:				Publishing:	
Buses:		Motorcycle Dealer:		Batteries:						Rental Cars/Trucks:	
RVs:		Specialty Dealer:									

TYPES OF BUSINESS:

New & Used Car Dealer
Automotive Accessories
Personal Accessories

BRANDS/DIVISIONS/AFFILIATES:

Volkswagen of America Inc
Audi AG
A6
A8 L
TT Coupe
Quattro
Avant
Q7

CONTACTS:

Note: Officers with more than one job title may be intentionally listed here more than once.

Mark Del Rosso, COO
Johan de Nysschen, Pres.
Scott Keogh, Chief Mktg. Officer

Phone: 248-754-5000	**Fax:** 248-754-5540
Toll-Free: 800-367-2834	
Address: 3800 W. Hamlin Rd., Auburn Hills, MI 48326 US	

GROWTH PLANS/SPECIAL FEATURES:

Audi of America, Inc., a subsidiary of Volkswagen of America, Inc., is the U.S. sales and marketing branch of the Audi car brand. The 19 Audi models available in the U.S. include the A3, A4, A5, A6, A8, R8, TT, the Q5 and the Q7. The models come with various body style options, including sedan, avant, compact, coupe, cabriolet, roadster, sport, crossover and SUV. The vehicles are identifiable through the four ring logo that appears prominently on the grills of all cars. The TT, A4, A6 and A8 are also available in S models, which have additional specially stylized features. Audi equips its luxury cars with options such as GPS navigation and BlueTooth communication. Models range in price from about $27,270 (the A3) to roughly $114,200 (the R8). The subsidiary's parent manufactures a line of car and personal accessories that Audi of America then sells. This line of car accessories allows customers to customize a car at a local dealership, as well as from the manufacturer through the company web site's Build Your Audi function. In addition to new cars, the company offers certified pre-owned models that are subject to a 300+ point inspection process. Service and support programs for these vehicles include roadside assistance, no-charge scheduled maintenance and extended warranties. Audi offers financing services for purchases and leases. Audi of America imports its cars from five main manufacturing facilities in Brazil, Germany, Italy, Hungary and China. In June 2009, Audi launched an ad campaign to raise public awareness of the benefits of TDI (turbocharged direct injection) clean diesel engines. The company launched its 2009 Audi Q7 TDI SUV in 2009. In October 2009, the firm discontinued its Audi Academy Technician Recruitment Program.

FINANCIALS:

Sales and profits are in thousands of dollars—add 000 to get the full amount. 2009 Note: Financial information for 2009 was not available for all companies at press time.

2009 Sales: $	2009 Profits: $	**U.S. Stock Ticker: Subsidiary**
2008 Sales: $	2008 Profits: $	**Int'l Ticker:** Int'l Exchange:
2007 Sales: $	2007 Profits: $	Employees:
2006 Sales: $	2006 Profits: $	Fiscal Year Ends: 12/31
2005 Sales: $	2005 Profits: $	Parent Company: VOLKSWAGEN OF AMERICA INC

SALARIES/BENEFITS:

Pension Plan:	ESOP Stock Plan:	Profit Sharing:	Top Exec. Salary: $	Bonus: $
Savings Plan:	Stock Purch. Plan:		Second Exec. Salary: $	Bonus: $

OTHER THOUGHTS:

Apparent Women Officers or Directors:
Hot Spot for Advancement for Women/Minorities:

LOCATIONS: ("Y" = Yes)

West:	Southwest:	Midwest:	Southeast:	Northeast:	International:
Y	Y	Y	Y	Y	

AUTOALLIANCE INTERNATIONAL INC

media.ford.com/plant_display.cfm?plant_id=62

Industry Group Code: 33611 **Ranks within this company's industry group:** Sales: Profits:

Vehicle Manufacturing:		Dealers:		Parts:		Service:		Finance:		Specialty:	
Cars:	Y	Car Dealer New:		Manufacturers:		General Service:		Leasing:		Information Systems:	
Trucks:		Car Dealer Used:		Retail:		Specialty Service:		Auto Loans:		Online Marketing:	
Motorcycles:		Truck Dealer:		Distributors:		Oil Change:		Insurance:		Other:	
Specialty:		RV Dealer:		Tires:		Paint and Body:				Publishing:	
Buses:		Motorcycle Dealer:		Batteries:						Rental Cars/Trucks:	
RVs:		Specialty Dealer:									

TYPES OF BUSINESS:

Automobile Manufacturing

BRANDS/DIVISIONS/AFFILIATES:

Ford Motor Co
Mazda Motor Corporation
Mercury Cougar
Mazda 626
Ford Probe
Mazda MX-6
Ford Mustang

GROWTH PLANS/SPECIAL FEATURES:

AutoAlliance International, Inc. (AAI) is a joint venture between Ford Motor Company and Mazda Motor Corporation. The company is engaged in the contract manufacturing of mid-priced sedans and sports cars, primarily for sale in North America. Specifically, the firm manufactures the Mazda6 and the Ford Mustang. Past models manufactured at the operations plant have included Mercury Cougar, Mazda 626, Ford Probe and Mazda MX-6. AAI's operations are centered at its 2.9 million square foot manufacturing plant in Flat Rock, Michigan. Employment levels at AAI totaled over 2,500 in 2010, with Ford supplying all of the hourly and substantially all of the salaried labor. Ford Motor Company holds a 13.4% stake in Mazda.

CONTACTS: *Note: Officers with more than one job title may be intentionally listed here more than once.*

Gary A. Roe, CEO
Gary A. Roe, Pres.
Don Gellinas, CFO
Rex Johnson, VP-Human Resources
Don Gellinas, VP-Corp. Planning
Peter Sahlstrom, VP-Purchasing

Phone: 734-782-7800 **Fax:**
Toll-Free:
Address: 1 International Dr., Flat Rock, MI 48134 US

FINANCIALS: **Sales and profits are in thousands of dollars—add 000 to get the full amount. 2009 Note: Financial information for 2009 was not available for all companies at press time.**

2009 Sales: $	2009 Profits: $	**U.S. Stock Ticker: Joint Venture**
2008 Sales: $418,900	2008 Profits: $	**Int'l Ticker:** Int'l Exchange:
2007 Sales: $446,700	2007 Profits: $	Employees: 3,200
2006 Sales: $	2006 Profits: $	Fiscal Year Ends: 12/31
2005 Sales: $	2005 Profits: $	Parent Company:

SALARIES/BENEFITS:

Pension Plan:	ESOP Stock Plan:	Profit Sharing:	Top Exec. Salary: $	Bonus: $
Savings Plan:	Stock Purch. Plan:		Second Exec. Salary: $	Bonus: $

OTHER THOUGHTS:

Apparent Women Officers or Directors:
Hot Spot for Advancement for Women/Minorities:

LOCATIONS: ("Y" = Yes)

West:	Southwest:	Midwest:	Southeast:	Northeast:	International:
		Y			

AUTOBYTEL INC

www.autobytel.com

Industry Group Code: 519130 **Ranks within this company's industry group:** Sales: 2 Profits: 2

Vehicle Manufacturing:		Dealers:		Parts:		Service:		Finance:		Specialty:	
Cars:		Car Dealer New:		Manufacturers:		General Service:		Leasing:		Information Systems:	
Trucks:		Car Dealer Used:		Retail:		Specialty Service:		Auto Loans:		Online Marketing:	Y
Motorcycles:		Truck Dealer:		Distributors:		Oil Change:		Insurance:		Other:	Y
Specialty:		RV Dealer:		Tires:		Paint and Body:				Publishing:	
Buses:		Motorcycle Dealer:		Batteries:						Rental Cars/Trucks:	
RVs:		Specialty Dealer:									

TYPES OF BUSINESS:

Automotive Media & Marketing Services
Online Car Sales Support

BRANDS/DIVISIONS/AFFILIATES:

MyRide.com
Autobytel.com
AutoWeb.com
Car.com
CarSmart.com
AutoSite.com
CarTV.com
iControl by Autobytel

CONTACTS: *Note: Officers with more than one job title may be intentionally listed here more than once.*

Jeffrey Coats, CEO
Jeffrey Coats, Pres.
Curtis E. DeWalt, CFO/Sr. VP
Jim Helberg, Exec. VP-Mktg.
Jim Helberg, Exec. VP-Prod.
Glenn Fuller, Chief Admin. Officer
Glenn Fuller, Chief Legal Officer/Exec. VP/Corp. Sec.
Stephen D. Lind, Exec. VP-Corp. Dev.
Crystal Hartwell, Mgr.-Corp. Comm.
Crystal Hartwell, Mgr.-Investor. Rel.
Lenny McGinley, VP-Dealer Sales
Jim Helberg, Exec. VP-Analytics
Michael Fuchs, Chmn.

Phone: 949-225-4500	**Fax:** 949-225-4541
Toll-Free:	
Address: 18872 MacArthur Blvd., Ste. 200, Irvine, CA 92612 US	

GROWTH PLANS/SPECIAL FEATURES:

Autobytel, Inc. is an automotive media and marketing services company that helps automotive retail dealers and manufacturers market and sell new and used vehicles through its Internet lead referral and online advertising programs. The company owns and operates automotive web sites, including autobytel.com, autoweb.com, car.com, carsmart.com, autosite.com, myride.com and cartv.com. Autobytel.com provides information about new and pre-owned vehicles, including light trucks. Customers can choose from a variety of colors, accessories and methods of payment and then have the site search all retail dealerships within a given radius from the user's home for a car that matches the selected specifications. The firm's other web sites offer various levels of information and access to Autobytel's dealers. Autobytel also provides customer relationship management products and programs, consisting of management products, customer loyalty and retention marketing programs. In December 2009, Autobytel announced that its vehicle price quote and dealer selector platform will power LendingTreeAutos.com, LendingTree LLC's recently-launched car-buying portal. In February 2010, the firm launched iControl by Autobytel, an online application that enables dealers to configure consumer leads according to current inventory, customer location (distance from the dealerships) and lead sourcing. In June 2010, the company partnered with Autoland, Inc. to launch AutoPilot, a new car-buying service for consumers who receive financing from their local credit union or bank.

FINANCIALS: **Sales and profits are in thousands of dollars—add 000 to get the full amount. 2009 Note: Financial information for 2009 was not available for all companies at press time.**

2009 Sales: $52,918	2009 Profits: $-2,377	**U.S. Stock Ticker: ABTL**
2008 Sales: $71,159	2008 Profits: $-79,916	**Int'l Ticker:** Int'l Exchange:
2007 Sales: $84,385	2007 Profits: $-5,355	Employees: 120
2006 Sales: $85,102	2006 Profits: $-31,468	Fiscal Year Ends: 12/31
2005 Sales: $122,054	2005 Profits: $-6,258	Parent Company:

SALARIES/BENEFITS:

Pension Plan:	ESOP Stock Plan:	Profit Sharing:	Top Exec. Salary: $400,588	Bonus: $366,000
Savings Plan: Y	Stock Purch. Plan: Y		Second Exec. Salary: $265,000	Bonus: $151,200

OTHER THOUGHTS:

Apparent Women Officers or Directors: 2
Hot Spot for Advancement for Women/Minorities:

LOCATIONS: ("Y" = Yes)

West:	Southwest:	Midwest:	Southeast:	Northeast:	International:
Y		Y	Y		

AUTOCAM CORPORATION

www.autocam.com

Industry Group Code: 3363 **Ranks within this company's industry group:** Sales: Profits:

Vehicle Manufacturing:		Dealers:		Parts:		Service:		Finance:		Specialty:	
Cars:		Car Dealer New:		Manufacturers:	Y	General Service:		Leasing:		Information Systems:	
Trucks:		Car Dealer Used:		Retail:		Specialty Service:		Auto Loans:		Online Marketing:	
Motorcycles:		Truck Dealer:		Distributors:		Oil Change:		Insurance:		Other:	Y
Specialty:		RV Dealer:		Tires:		Paint and Body:				Publishing:	
Buses:		Motorcycle Dealer:		Batteries:						Rental Cars/Trucks:	
RVs:		Specialty Dealer:									

TYPES OF BUSINESS:

Automobile Parts, Manufacturing
Metal Components
Medical Devices

BRANDS/DIVISIONS/AFFILIATES:

Goldman Sachs Group Inc
Transportation Resource Partners

CONTACTS:

Note: Officers with more than one job title may be intentionally listed here more than once.

John C. Kennedy, CEO

Phone: 616-698-0707	**Fax:** 616-698-6876
Toll-Free: 800-747-6978	
Address: 4436 Broadmoor SE, Kentwood, MI 49512 US	

GROWTH PLANS/SPECIAL FEATURES:

Autocam Corporation, manufactures highly engineered, precision-machined, metal alloy components for many of the world's Tier I automotive parts suppliers. The firm is owned by an investment group comprised of Goldman Sachs Group, Inc., Transportation Resource Partners, Autocam senior management, with the later maintaining a significant stake. With 13 facilities located worldwide, in the U.S., South America, China and Europe, the company's primary focus is on precision-machined automotive components, sub-assemblies and complete assemblies. Autocam has the technological and manufacturing capacity to produce complex parts requiring extremely close tolerances in the single-digit micron range. Autocam manufactures its precision automotive components in five primary product categories: steering, which includes valve assemblies, sleeves, torsion bars, input shafts, pinions and worms; fuel delivery, which includes disk checks, pole pieces, valves, seat guides, diesel pump bodies, diesel cases, sleeves and inlet tubes; braking products, which includes sleeves, push rods, seats and valve rods; electric motors products, which includes gears, gear sub-assemblies and worm shafts; and airbag products, which includes collars, adaptors, projectiles, chargeholders and diffusers. The company also manufactures components and assemblies for other automotive applications and for medical devices, such as hand pieces for ophthalmic surgery; spinal, hip, knee and shoulder implant systems; blood cleaning and separation equipment, ultrasonic imaging equipment and DNA testing equipment; and laser cut coronary and aortic stents. The firm makes its products through a variety of high-tech processes, including precision turning, grinding and milling; forging; plastic injection molding; rotary transfer, precision secondary and laser machining; finishing; heat treating; and precision cleaning. In September 2009, the firm completed a financial restructuring by combining debt of its companies together. With the completion of the restructuring, the company plans to move into the transportation market and capitalize on manufacturing more fuel efficient and environmentally friendly vehicles.

FINANCIALS:

Sales and profits are in thousands of dollars—add 000 to get the full amount. 2009 Note: Financial information for 2009 was not available for all companies at press time.

2009 Sales: $	2009 Profits: $	**U.S. Stock Ticker: Private**
2008 Sales: $	2008 Profits: $	**Int'l Ticker:** Int'l Exchange:
2007 Sales: $	2007 Profits: $	Employees:
2006 Sales: $	2006 Profits: $	Fiscal Year Ends: 6/30
2005 Sales: $	2005 Profits: $	Parent Company:

SALARIES/BENEFITS:

Pension Plan:	ESOP Stock Plan:	Profit Sharing:	Top Exec. Salary: $	Bonus: $
Savings Plan:	Stock Purch. Plan:		Second Exec. Salary: $	Bonus: $

OTHER THOUGHTS:

Apparent Women Officers or Directors:
Hot Spot for Advancement for Women/Minorities:

LOCATIONS: ("Y" = Yes)

West:	Southwest:	Midwest:	Southeast:	Northeast:	International:
Y		Y		Y	Y

AUTOLIV INC

www.autoliv.com

Industry Group Code: 3363 **Ranks within this company's industry group:** Sales: 21 Profits: 25

Vehicle Manufacturing:		Dealers:		Parts:		Service:		Finance:		Specialty:	
Cars:		Car Dealer New:		Manufacturers:	Y	General Service:		Leasing:		Information Systems:	
Trucks:		Car Dealer Used:		Retail:		Specialty Service:		Auto Loans:		Online Marketing:	
Motorcycles:		Truck Dealer:		Distributors:		Oil Change:		Insurance:		Other:	Y
Specialty:		RV Dealer:		Tires:		Paint and Body:				Publishing:	
Buses:		Motorcycle Dealer:		Batteries:						Rental Cars/Trucks:	
RVs:		Specialty Dealer:									

TYPES OF BUSINESS:

Automotive Safety Products Manufacturing
Seat Belts
Airbags
Seat Components
Steering Wheels
Child Seats
Safety Electronics
Anti-Whiplash Systems

BRANDS/DIVISIONS/AFFILIATES:

Inflatable Curtain
Autoliv ASP, Inc.
Active Hood
Pedestrian Protection Airbag
Autoliv AB

CONTACTS:

Note: Officers with more than one job title may be intentionally listed here more than once.

Jan Carlson, CEO
Jan Carlson, Pres.
Mats Wallin, CFO
Mats Adamson, VP-Human Resources
Jan Olsson, VP-Research
Steve Fredin, VP-Eng.
Svante Mogefors, VP-Mfg.
Lars Sjobring, General Counsel/VP-Legal Affairs/Sec.
Ray Pekar, Dir.-Bus. Dev.
Mats Odman, VP-Corp. Comm.
Ray Pekar, Dir.-Investor Rel.
Mats Wallin, VP-Finance
Svante Mogefors, VP-Quality
Lars Westerberg, Chmn.
Gunnar Dahlen, Pres., Autoliv Asia
Halvar Jonzon, VP-Purchasing

Phone: 46-8-587-20-600 **Fax:** 46-8-411-7025
Toll-Free:
Address: Klarabergsviadukten 70, Section E, Stockholm, SE-107 24 Sweden

GROWTH PLANS/SPECIAL FEATURES:

Autoliv, Inc., develops, manufactures and produces automotive safety equipment and systems. Autoliv is the result of a merger of two companies, which continue operations as the firm's primary subsidiaries: Autoliv AB and Autoliv ASP, Inc. Swedish-based Autoliv AB produces restraint systems; steering wheels, seatbelts and seatbelt pretensioners; frontal and side-impact airbags; and seat subsystems. Indiana-based Autoliv ASP, Inc., provides air bag inflators; modules and airbag cushions; seatbelts; and steering wheels. Autoliv's customers include all the leading automobile manufacturers in the world, with nearly half of sales in Europe (49%); North America, (23%); Japan (10%); and the rest of the world, 18%. The firm has nearly 80 plants in 29 countries; and 21 crash tracks and 10 technical centers in 9 countries. Approximately 64% of the firm's sales are derived from airbags and associated products, while 36% are derived from seatbelts and associated products. Autoliv invented one of the world's first side-impact airbags, the Inflatable Curtain. Other products include airbags designed to protect the lower body; a night vision system which uses an infrared camera to project on a display in front of the driver; and the pedestrian protection system. Utilizing the Active Hood, which raises instantly when a sensor system placed in the front bumper is triggered, and the Pedestrian Protection Airbag (a pair of airbags installed near the front windshield), the pedestrian protection system greatly reduces the chances of pedestrian fatality in a car-to-pedestrian impact at 25 mph. In December 2009, the firm announced the closure of four plants in France, Germany, Mexico and Tunisia. In March 2010, Autoliv acquired Visteon's radar systems business. In April 2010 Autoliv completed its acquisition of Delphi's Chinese and Korean Occupant Protection Systems operations.

FINANCIALS:

Sales and profits are in thousands of dollars—add 000 to get the full amount. 2009 Note: Financial information for 2009 was not available for all companies at press time.

2009 Sales: $5,121,000	2009 Profits: $10,000	**U.S. Stock Ticker: ALV**
2008 Sales: $6,473,200	2008 Profits: $164,700	**Int'l Ticker: ALIV** Int'l Exchange: Stockholm-SSE
2007 Sales: $6,769,000	2007 Profits: $287,900	Employees: 37,900
2006 Sales: $6,118,000	2006 Profits: $402,300	Fiscal Year Ends: 12/31
2005 Sales: $6,204,900	2005 Profits: $292,600	Parent Company:

SALARIES/BENEFITS:

Pension Plan:	ESOP Stock Plan:	Profit Sharing:	Top Exec. Salary: $882,353	Bonus: $
Savings Plan:	Stock Purch. Plan:		Second Exec. Salary: $585,714	Bonus: $

OTHER THOUGHTS:

Apparent Women Officers or Directors:
Hot Spot for Advancement for Women/Minorities:

LOCATIONS: ("Y" = Yes)

West:	Southwest:	Midwest:	Southeast:	Northeast:	International:
Y		Y			Y

AUTOMOBILI LAMBORGHINI HOLDING SPA www.lamborghini.com

Industry Group Code: 33611 **Ranks within this company's industry group:** Sales: Profits:

Vehicle Manufacturing:		Dealers:		Parts:		Service:		Finance:		Specialty:	
Cars:	Y	Car Dealer New:		Manufacturers:	Y	General Service:		Leasing:		Information Systems:	
Trucks:		Car Dealer Used:		Retail:		Specialty Service:		Auto Loans:		Online Marketing:	
Motorcycles:		Truck Dealer:		Distributors:		Oil Change:		Insurance:		Other:	Y
Specialty:	Y	RV Dealer:		Tires:		Paint and Body:				Publishing:	
Buses:		Motorcycle Dealer:		Batteries:						Rental Cars/Trucks:	
RVs:		Specialty Dealer:									

TYPES OF BUSINESS:

Automobile Manufacturing
Sports Cars
Powerboat Engines
Vehicle Accessories

BRANDS/DIVISIONS/AFFILIATES:

Volkswagen AG
Audi AG
Automobili Lamborghini S.p.A.
Motori Marini Lamborghini S.p.A.
Lamborghini Artimarca S.p.A.
Gallardo
Murcielago
Lamborghini Gallardo Blancpain Super Trofeo

CONTACTS: *Note: Officers with more than one job title may be intentionally listed here more than once.*

Stephan Winkelmann, CEO
Stephan Winkelmann, Pres.

Phone: 39-051-68-17-611	**Fax:**
Toll-Free:	
Address: Via Modena 12, Sant'Agata Bolognese, 40019 Italy	

GROWTH PLANS/SPECIAL FEATURES:

Automobili Lamborghini Holding S.p.A. (Lamborghini) is a subsidiary of Volkswagen's AUDI business unit, AUDI AG. The company operates through three subsidiaries. Automobili Lamborghini S.p.A. is known worldwide for developing and building high-performance sports cars. It produces and sells approximately 400 cars per year. Motori Marini Lamborghini S.p.A. (MML) produces engines for powerboats. Lamborghini Artimarca S.p.A. is responsible for merchandising, marketing and licensing operations related to Lamborghini-branded products. Lamborghini has two current models: Lamborghini Murcielago and Lamborghini Gallardo. Lamborghini likes to name its models after legendary fighting bulls. The Lamborghini Murcielago is available in the LP 670-4 SV, LP 640 and LP 640 Roadster models. The LP 670-4 SV has a top speed of 212 miles per hour and can accelerate to 62 miles per hour in 3.2 seconds. The Gallardo is available in LP 560-4, LP 560-4 Spyder and LP 550-2 Valentino Balboni models. The LP 560-4 reaches 62 mph in 3.7 seconds and has a top speed of 200 miles per hour. In addition, the firm participates in the sport of racing with its Lamborghini Gallardo Blancpain Super Trofeo racecar. Lamborghini accessories include: outdoor and indoor car covers; seat covers; steering wheel covers; battery charging and maintenance equipment; digital pressure gauges; GPS tracking systems and navigation kits; engine bonnet kits; external rearview mirrors; tire rims; valve caps; lights kits; video recording and telemetry systems; floor mats; headrests; bag sets; selector plates; and media connection devices for USB, iPod and Bluetooth-enabled electronics. The company's largest market is the U.S.; other large markets include China and Italy. In June 2009, the firm announced plans to cut carbon emissions by 35% by 2015. In July 2009, Lamborghini announced its intention to launch an Asia-Pacific regional headquarters in China. In August 2009, the company announced plans to develop a hybrid Gallardo by 2015.

FINANCIALS: **Sales and profits are in thousands of dollars—add 000 to get the full amount. 2009 Note: Financial information for 2009 was not available for all companies at press time.**

2009 Sales: $	2009 Profits: $	**U.S. Stock Ticker: Subsidiary**
2008 Sales: $	2008 Profits: $	**Int'l Ticker:** Int'l Exchange:
2007 Sales: $	2007 Profits: $	Employees:
2006 Sales: $	2006 Profits: $	Fiscal Year Ends: 12/31
2005 Sales: $	2005 Profits: $	Parent Company: AUDI AG

SALARIES/BENEFITS:

Pension Plan:	ESOP Stock Plan:	Profit Sharing:	Top Exec. Salary: $	Bonus: $
Savings Plan:	Stock Purch. Plan:		Second Exec. Salary: $	Bonus: $

OTHER THOUGHTS:

Apparent Women Officers or Directors:
Hot Spot for Advancement for Women/Minorities:

LOCATIONS: ("Y" = Yes)

West:	Southwest:	Midwest:	Southeast:	Northeast:	International:
					Y

AUTOMOTIVE ENERGY SUPPLY CORPORATION (AESC)

www.eco-aesc.com

Industry Group Code: 33591 **Ranks within this company's industry group:** Sales: Profits:

Vehicle Manufacturing:		Dealers:		Parts:		Service:		Finance:		Specialty:	
Cars:		Car Dealer New:		Manufacturers:		General Service:		Leasing:		Information Systems:	
Trucks:		Car Dealer Used:		Retail:		Specialty Service:		Auto Loans:		Online Marketing:	
Motorcycles:		Truck Dealer:		Distributors:		Oil Change:		Insurance:		Other:	
Specialty:		RV Dealer:		Tires:		Paint and Body:				Publishing:	
Buses:		Motorcycle Dealer:		Batteries:	Y					Rental Cars/Trucks:	
RVs:		Specialty Dealer:									

TYPES OF BUSINESS:

Batteries for Electric Automobiles

BRANDS/DIVISIONS/AFFILIATES:

NEC Corporation
Nissan Motor Co Ltd

CONTACTS:

Note: Officers with more than one job title may be intentionally listed here more than once.

Masahiko Otsuka, Pres.

Phone: 046-252-3211	**Fax:**
Toll-Free:	
Address: 10-1 Hironodai 2-chome, Zama-shi, Kanagawa 228-8052 Japan	

GROWTH PLANS/SPECIAL FEATURES:

Automotive Energy Supply Corp. (AESC), a joint venture between Nissan Motor Co. and NEC Corporation, is a manufacturer of advanced lithium-ion battery technology. AESC's primary operating divisions, development and manufacturing, conduct research and development and produce rechargeable lithium-ion batteries in laminate cells, modules and packs that are distributed to original equipment manufacturers (OEMs) and automotive parts suppliers around the world. Some recent applications for the firm's products include a battery-powered forklift manufactured by Nissan, as well as several Nissan-branded electric vehicles (EVs), which operate solely on battery power, and hybrid vehicles, which use an electric motor and battery pack to augment a gasoline engine. Nissan has recently announced plans to introduce an all-electric vehicle by 2010, and aspires to bring EVs to mass-market production by 2012. These vehicles will rely on batteries designed and manufactured by AESC. Nissan owns 51% of the company and NEC Corporation owns 49%. In July 2009, the company began tests on lithium-ion batteries designed for vehicles and plans on marketing the batteries to other companies as well.

FINANCIALS:

Sales and profits are in thousands of dollars—add 000 to get the full amount. 2009 Note: Financial information for 2009 was not available for all companies at press time.

2009 Sales: $	2009 Profits: $	**U.S. Stock Ticker: Joint Venture**
2008 Sales: $	2008 Profits: $	**Int'l Ticker:** Int'l Exchange:
2007 Sales: $	2007 Profits: $	Employees: 80
2006 Sales: $	2006 Profits: $	Fiscal Year Ends:
2005 Sales: $	2005 Profits: $	Parent Company: NISSAN MOTOR CO LTD

SALARIES/BENEFITS:

Pension Plan:	ESOP Stock Plan:	Profit Sharing:	Top Exec. Salary: $	Bonus: $
Savings Plan:	Stock Purch. Plan:		Second Exec. Salary: $	Bonus: $

OTHER THOUGHTS:

Apparent Women Officers or Directors:
Hot Spot for Advancement for Women/Minorities:

LOCATIONS: ("Y" = Yes)

West:	Southwest:	Midwest:	Southeast:	Northeast:	International:
					Y

AUTONATION INC

www.autonation.com

Industry Group Code: 441110 **Ranks within this company's industry group:** Sales: 1 Profits: 1

Vehicle Manufacturing:		Dealers:		Parts:		Service:		Finance:		Specialty:	
Cars:		Car Dealer New:	Y	Manufacturers:		General Service:	Y	Leasing:		Information Systems:	
Trucks:		Car Dealer Used:	Y	Retail:	Y	Specialty Service:		Auto Loans:	Y	Online Marketing:	Y
Motorcycles:		Truck Dealer:		Distributors:		Oil Change:		Insurance:		Other:	
Specialty:		RV Dealer:		Tires:		Paint and Body:				Publishing:	
Buses:		Motorcycle Dealer:		Batteries:						Rental Cars/Trucks:	
RVs:		Specialty Dealer:									

TYPES OF BUSINESS:

Auto Dealer
Online Auto Sales
Vehicle Maintenance & Repair Services
Vehicle Parts
Extended Service Contracts
Vehicle Protection Products

BRANDS/DIVISIONS/AFFILIATES:

CONTACTS:

Note: Officers with more than one job title may be intentionally listed here more than once.

Michael Jackson, CEO
Michael Maroone, COO
Michael Maroone, Pres.
Michael Short, CFO/Exec. VP
Kevin Westfall, Sr. VP-Sales
Jonathan Ferrando, General Counsel/Exec. VP/Corp. Sec.
Donna Parlapiano, Sr. VP-Regional Oper.
Gary Marcotte, Sr. VP-eCommerce
Marc Cannon, Sr. VP-Corp. Comm.
Cheryl Scully, VP-Investor Rel.
Cheryl Scully, Treas.
Donna Parlapiano, Sr. VP-Industry Rel.
Michael Jackson, Chmn.

Phone: 954-769-7000 **Fax:** 954-769-6537
Toll-Free:
Address: 200 SW 1st Ave., Ste.1600, Fort Lauderdale, FL 33301 US

GROWTH PLANS/SPECIAL FEATURES:

AutoNation, Inc. is one of the largest automotive retailers in the U.S. The company offers a diversified range of automotive products and services, including new vehicles; used vehicles; parts and automotive services; and automotive finance and insurance products. The firm also arranges financing for vehicle purchases through third-party finance sources. AutoNation owns and operates 246 new vehicle franchises from 203 stores located in major metropolitan markets, predominantly in the Sunbelt region of the U.S. It retailed approximately 320,000 new and used vehicles through its stores in 2009. The company's stores sell 33 different brands of new vehicles. The core brands of vehicles, representing approximately 96% of the new vehicles the firm sold in 2009, are manufactured by Toyota; Ford; Honda; Nissan; General Motors; Mercedes; BMW; and Chrysler. AutoNation divides its operations into three segments: Domestic, Import and Premium Luxury. The Domestic segment is comprised of retail automotive franchises that sell new vehicles manufactured by General Motors; Ford; and Chrysler. The Import segment consists of franchises that sell Toyota; Honda; and Nissan. The Premium Luxury segment sells Mercedes; BMW; and Lexus. The Domestic segment accounted for 32% of the company's revenue in 2009; Import, 38%; and Premium Luxury, 29%. The company's web site allows prospective buyers to evaluate the trade-in value of a current vehicle, explore nearby car lots, read automotive reviews and even arrange for the purchase of an automobile online. In October 2009, the company signed agreements to acquire Valley Honda and Valley Acura in Spokane, Washington.

Employees are offered health, dental, life and disability insurance; longevity bonuses; a 401(k) plan; and an employee vehicle purchase program.

FINANCIALS:

Sales and profits are in thousands of dollars—add 000 to get the full amount. 2009 Note: Financial information for 2009 was not available for all companies at press time.

2009 Sales: $10,757,800	2009 Profits: $198,000	**U.S. Stock Ticker: AN**
2008 Sales: $13,376,400	2008 Profits: $-1,243,100	**Int'l Ticker:** Int'l Exchange:
2007 Sales: $16,385,200	2007 Profits: $278,700	Employees: 18,000
2006 Sales: $18,626,500	2006 Profits: $316,900	Fiscal Year Ends: 12/31
2005 Sales: $18,729,500	2005 Profits: $496,500	Parent Company:

SALARIES/BENEFITS:

Pension Plan:	ESOP Stock Plan:	Profit Sharing:	Top Exec. Salary: $1,150,000	Bonus: $1,705,833
Savings Plan: Y	Stock Purch. Plan:		Second Exec. Salary: $1,000,000	Bonus: $1,112,500

OTHER THOUGHTS:

Apparent Women Officers or Directors: 2
Hot Spot for Advancement for Women/Minorities:

LOCATIONS: ("Y" = Yes)

West:	Southwest:	Midwest:	Southeast:	Northeast:	International:
Y	Y	Y	Y	Y	

AUTOZONE INC

www.autozone.com

Industry Group Code: 441310 **Ranks within this company's industry group:** Sales: 2 Profits: 1

Vehicle Manufacturing:		Dealers:		Parts:		Service:		Finance:		Specialty:	
Cars:		Car Dealer New:		Manufacturers:		General Service:	Y	Leasing:		Information Systems:	Y
Trucks:		Car Dealer Used:		Retail:	Y	Specialty Service:		Auto Loans:		Online Marketing:	Y
Motorcycles:		Truck Dealer:		Distributors:		Oil Change:		Insurance:		Other:	
Specialty:		RV Dealer:		Tires:		Paint and Body:				Publishing:	
Buses:		Motorcycle Dealer:		Batteries:						Rental Cars/Trucks:	
RVs:		Specialty Dealer:									

TYPES OF BUSINESS:

Auto Parts, Retail
Automotive Software
Online Sales
General Automotive Service

BRANDS/DIVISIONS/AFFILIATES:

Autozone.com
ALLDATA
Loan-a-Tool

CONTACTS: *Note: Officers with more than one job title may be intentionally listed here more than once.*

William C. Rhodes, III, CEO
William C. Rhodes, III, Pres.
William T. Giles, CFO
James A. Shea, Exec. VP-Mktg.
Timothy W. Briggs, Sr. VP-Human Resources
Jon A. Bascom, CIO/Sr. VP
James A. Shea, Exec. VP-Merch.
Harry L. Goldsmith, General Counsel/Exec. VP/Corp. Sec.
Thomas B. Newbern, Sr. VP-Store Oper.
Robert D. Olsen, Corp. Dev. Officer
William T. Giles, Exec. VP-Finance
William T. Giles, Exec. VP-Store Dev. & IT
Larry Roesel, Sr. VP-Commercial
Lisa R. Kranc, Sr. VP-Mktg.
William C. Rhodes, III, Chmn.
James A. Shea, Exec. VP-Supply Chain

Phone: 901-495-6500 **Fax:** 901-495-8300
Toll-Free: 800-288-6966
Address: 123 S. Front St., Memphis, TN 38103 US

GROWTH PLANS/SPECIAL FEATURES:

AutoZone, Inc. is a leading specialty retailer of automotive parts and accessories, targeting do-it-yourself (DIY) customers. With 4,289 stores in the U.S. and Puerto Rico and 202 in Mexico, each AutoZone store carries an extensive product line for cars, sport utility vehicles, vans and light trucks, including new and remanufactured automotive parts, maintenance items, accessories and non-automotive products. Many AutoZone stores have a commercial sales program that provides commercial credit and prompt delivery of parts and other products to local, regional and national repair garages, dealers and service stations. The company has over 800,000 stock keeping units (SKU). Although each of the company's stores carry the same basic product lines, the company does tailor each store's parts inventory to the makes and models of the vehicles in their trade areas. Parts not kept in stock can be ordered and delivered to the store within a few days, or they can be ordered online. AutoZone allows parts ordered online to be returned at any store location. The company also has a Loan-a-Tool program, through which customers can borrow a specialty tool, such as a steering wheel puller, for which they would have little or no use other than for a single job. AutoZone also provides other free services, including check engine light readings; battery charging and installation assistance; and the testing of starters, alternators, batteries, sensors and actuators. The company also offers automotive diagnostic and repair software through its ALLDATA subsidiary.

Employees are offered medical, dental and vision insurance; wellness programs; disability and life insurance; a 401(k) plan; store discounts; tuition reimbursement; ASE certification reimbursement; adoption assistance; a stock purchase plan; a matching gift program; a home mortgage program; and referral bonuses.

FINANCIALS: **Sales and profits are in thousands of dollars—add 000 to get the full amount. 2009 Note: Financial information for 2009 was not available for all companies at press time.**

2009 Sales: $6,816,824	2009 Profits: $657,049	**U.S. Stock Ticker: AZO**
2008 Sales: $6,522,706	2008 Profits: $641,606	**Int'l Ticker:** Int'l Exchange:
2007 Sales: $6,169,804	2007 Profits: $595,672	Employees: 60,000
2006 Sales: $5,948,355	2006 Profits: $569,275	Fiscal Year Ends: 8/31
2005 Sales: $5,710,900	2005 Profits: $571,000	Parent Company:

SALARIES/BENEFITS:

Pension Plan:	ESOP Stock Plan:	Profit Sharing:	Top Exec. Salary: $752,385	Bonus: $1,017,977
Savings Plan: Y	Stock Purch. Plan: Y		Second Exec. Salary: $458,308	Bonus: $372,055

OTHER THOUGHTS:

Apparent Women Officers or Directors: 2
Hot Spot for Advancement for Women/Minorities: Y

LOCATIONS: ("Y" = Yes)

West:	Southwest:	Midwest:	Southeast:	Northeast:	International:
Y	Y	Y	Y	Y	Y

AVIS EUROPE PLC

www.avis-europe.com

Industry Group Code: 5321 **Ranks within this company's industry group:** Sales: 4 Profits: 3

Vehicle Manufacturing:		**Dealers:**		**Parts:**		**Service:**		**Finance:**		**Specialty:**	
Cars:		Car Dealer New:		Manufacturers:		General Service:		Leasing:		Information Systems:	
Trucks:		Car Dealer Used:		Retail:		Specialty Service:		Auto Loans:		Online Marketing:	
Motorcycles:		Truck Dealer:		Distributors:		Oil Change:		Insurance:		Other:	
Specialty:		RV Dealer:		Tires:		Paint and Body:				Publishing:	
Buses:		Motorcycle Dealer:		Batteries:						Rental Cars/Trucks:	Y
RVs:		Specialty Dealer:									

TYPES OF BUSINESS:

Automobile Rental

BRANDS/DIVISIONS/AFFILIATES:

Avis Budget Group, Inc
Budget

CONTACTS:

Note: Officers with more than one job title may be intentionally listed here more than once.

Pascal Bazin, CEO
Martyn Smith, Dir.-Group Finance
Judith Nicholson, Sec.
Stuart Fillingham, Group Treas./VP
Jean-Pierre Bizet, Exec. Deputy Chmn.
Kevin Bradshaw, Managing Dir.-U.K.
John McNicholas, VP-Group Licensees & Budget
Wolfgang Neumann, Dir.-Group Commercial/Managing Dir.-Germany
Alun Cathcart, Chmn.
Roberto Lucchini, Managing Dir.-Italy

Phone: 44-1344-426-644	**Fax:** 44-1344-485-616
Toll-Free:	
Address: Avis House, Park Rd., Bracknell, Berkshire RG12 2EW UK	

GROWTH PLANS/SPECIAL FEATURES:

Avis Europe plc is a leading car rental company with operations in Europe, Africa, the Middle East and Asia. It markets both the Avis and Budget brands in partnership with Avis Budget Group, Inc. Together, these companies market the Avis brand across four continents via a network of over 3,800 locations in 109 countries and through wholly-owned subsidiaries in 13 countries complemented by franchisees in 96 additional countries. The Budget branded business in Europe, Asia and the Middle East serves customers across three continents through over 1,000 rental locations in 65 countries. The firm also has joint ventures in China and France, as well as associate operations in India and Malaysia. Both brands offer basic car rental services. The firm's customer range includes individuals booking directly or through travel companies, tour operators, partnership arrangements and brokers; corporate customers who book through negotiated arrangements with their employers and through vehicle replacement companies; and customers from insurance and leasing companies, dealerships and repair shops with which Avis and Budget have direct contractual relationships. The company's corporate rental revenue by customer was individual, 55%; corporate, 34%; and insurance/replacement, 11%. Avis generated its largest percentage of 2009 annual revenue in France, which accounted for 24%; Italy, 17%; Germany, 16%; the U.K., 16%; Spain, 13%; and other countries, 14%. The company recently entered an exclusive five-year partnership with British Airways as the airline's sole global car rental provider.

FINANCIALS:

Sales and profits are in thousands of dollars—add 000 to get the full amount. 2009 Note: Financial information for 2009 was not available for all companies at press time.

2009 Sales: $1,771,060	2009 Profits: $ 250	**U.S. Stock Ticker: AVE.L**
2008 Sales: $1,890,280	2008 Profits: $1,630	**Int'l Ticker: AVE** Int'l Exchange: London-LSE
2007 Sales: $1,950,400	2007 Profits: $4,400	Employees: 5,671
2006 Sales: $1,846,000	2006 Profits: $2,200	Fiscal Year Ends: 12/31
2005 Sales: $1,876,500	2005 Profits: $17,300	Parent Company:

SALARIES/BENEFITS:

Pension Plan:	ESOP Stock Plan:	Profit Sharing:	Top Exec. Salary: $	Bonus: $
Savings Plan:	Stock Purch. Plan:		Second Exec. Salary: $	Bonus: $

OTHER THOUGHTS:

Apparent Women Officers or Directors: 2
Hot Spot for Advancement for Women/Minorities:

LOCATIONS: ("Y" = Yes)

West:	Southwest:	Midwest:	Southeast:	Northeast:	International:
					Y

AVTOVAZ OAO

www.lada-auto.ru

Industry Group Code: 33611 **Ranks within this company's industry group:** Sales: Profits:

Vehicle Manufacturing:		Dealers:		Parts:		Service:		Finance:		Specialty:	
Cars:	Y	Car Dealer New:		Manufacturers:	Y	General Service:		Leasing:		Information Systems:	
Trucks:		Car Dealer Used:		Retail:		Specialty Service:		Auto Loans:		Online Marketing:	
Motorcycles:		Truck Dealer:		Distributors:		Oil Change:		Insurance:	Y	Other:	Y
Specialty:		RV Dealer:		Tires:		Paint and Body:				Publishing:	
Buses:		Motorcycle Dealer:		Batteries:						Rental Cars/Trucks:	
RVs:		Specialty Dealer:									

TYPES OF BUSINESS:

Auto Manufacturer
Insurance
Vehicle Transportation
Power Supply

BRANDS/DIVISIONS/AFFILIATES:

LADA 4x4
LADA Samara
LADA 110
Chevrolet Niva
LADA KALINA
Opel Astra T-3000
GM-AvtoVAZ
LADA Priori

CONTACTS: *Note: Officers with more than one job title may be intentionally listed here more than once.*

Igor Anatolevich Komarov, Pres.
Maksim Valerevich Nagaytsev, VP-Mktg. & Sales
Dmitry Gennadevich Mikhalenko, VP-Personnel
Hugo Demarchelier, VP-Prod. & Programs
Eduard Karlovich Vayno, VP-External & Shareholder Rel.
Boris Nikolaevich Danilov, VP-Security & Regulation
Sergei Viktorovich Chermezov, Chmn.

Phone: 7-848-273-8097	**Fax:** 7-848-273-8161
Toll-Free:	
Address: 36 Yuzhnoye Shosse, Togliatti, 445633 Russia	

GROWTH PLANS/SPECIAL FEATURES:

AvtoVAZ OAO is the leading manufacturer of passenger cars for the Russian market, as well as for export to Kazakhstan, Ukraine, Azerbaijan, Moldova and Germany. The company's models include the 3- and 5-door LADA 4x4 sport utility vehicle; the LADA Samara; the LADA 110 family sedan; the LADA KALINA; and the LADA Priori. The KALINA, the Samara and the Priori are available in sedan and hatchback versions. The firm also has subsidiaries that specialize in manufacturing components for the vehicles, distribution, vehicle transport and maintenance, power supply, construction and insurance operations. The company's joint venture with General Motors, GM-AvtoVAZ, produces the Chevrolet Niva and the Chevrolet Viva, under the label Opel Astra T-3000. AvtoVaz is 25% owned by Renault-Nissan, 25% owned by Troika Dialog 25% owned by the Russian state government and 25% owned by Russian Technologies. In December 2009, the firm announced plans to sell six of its subsidiaries in the steel making, press-work, mechanical assembly and instrument production sectors. In July 2010, AvtoVAZ sold its 100 % stake in finance and banking firm KB Lada-Kredit ZAO to AKB Novikombank ZAO.

FINANCIALS: **Sales and profits are in thousands of dollars—add 000 to get the full amount. 2009 Note: Financial information for 2009 was not available for all companies at press time.**

2009 Sales: $	2009 Profits: $	**U.S. Stock Ticker:**
2008 Sales: $	2008 Profits: $	**Int'l Ticker: AVAZ** Int'l Exchange: Moscow-RTS
2007 Sales: $	2007 Profits: $	Employees:
2006 Sales: $	2006 Profits: $	Fiscal Year Ends: 12/31
2005 Sales: $	2005 Profits: $	Parent Company:

SALARIES/BENEFITS:

Pension Plan:	ESOP Stock Plan:	Profit Sharing:	Top Exec. Salary: $	Bonus: $
Savings Plan:	Stock Purch. Plan:		Second Exec. Salary: $	Bonus: $

OTHER THOUGHTS:

Apparent Women Officers or Directors:
Hot Spot for Advancement for Women/Minorities:

LOCATIONS: ("Y" = Yes)

West:	Southwest:	Midwest:	Southeast:	Northeast:	International:
					Y

BAJAJ AUTO LTD

www.bajajauto.com

Industry Group Code: 336991 **Ranks within this company's industry group:** Sales: 4 Profits: 2

Vehicle Manufacturing:		Dealers:		Parts:		Service:		Finance:		Specialty:	
Cars:		Car Dealer New:		Manufacturers:		General Service:		Leasing:		Information Systems:	
Trucks:		Car Dealer Used:		Retail:		Specialty Service:		Auto Loans:		Online Marketing:	
Motorcycles:	Y	Truck Dealer:		Distributors:		Oil Change:		Insurance:		Other:	
Specialty:	Y	RV Dealer:		Tires:		Paint and Body:				Publishing:	
Buses:		Motorcycle Dealer:		Batteries:						Rental Cars/Trucks:	
RVs:		Specialty Dealer:									

TYPES OF BUSINESS:

Scooter Manufacturer
Motorcycle Manufacturer
Delivery Van Manufacturer

BRANDS/DIVISIONS/AFFILIATES:

Bajaj Pulsar
Bajaj Avenger
Bajaj Platina
Bajaj Kristal
Auto International Holdings BV
PT Bajaj Indonesia
Bajaj Finserv Limited
KTM Power Sports AG

CONTACTS: *Note: Officers with more than one job title may be intentionally listed here more than once.*

Rajiv Bajaj, Managing Dir.
Amrut Rath, VP-Human Resources
Abraham Joseph, VP-R&D
Pradeep Shrivastava, Pres., Eng.
J. Sridhar, Corp. Sec.
S. Ravikumar, VP-Bus. Dev.
Kevin P. D'sa, VP-Finance
N.H. Hingorani, VP-Commercial
Sanjiv Bajaj, Exec. Dir.
S. Sridhar, CEO-Two Wheelers
R.C. Maheshwari, CEO-Commercial Vehicles
Rahul Bajaj, Chmn.
Rakesh Sharma, CEO-Int'l Bus.

Phone: 91-20-2747-2851 **Fax:** 91-20-2747-3398
Toll-Free:
Address: Bajaj Auto Complex, Mumbai-Pune Rd., Akurdi, Pune, 411 035 India

GROWTH PLANS/SPECIAL FEATURES:

Bajaj Auto Ltd. is a leading India-based manufacturer of motorcycles, scooters and three-wheeled vehicles. The company operates in two segments, automotive and investment, which are operated by two subsidiaries, Bajaj Holdings & Investment Limited (BHIL) and Bajaj FinServ Limited (BFS) respectively. BHIL manages the firm's auto business and all related assets and liabilities including investments in foreign subsidiaries and vendor companies. The operations of BFS include investments in wind power, insurance companies, and consumer finance companies. The company's automotive business accounts for roughly 98% of its total operating revenue and includes two- and three-wheeled vehicles. Motorcycles, which dominate the two-wheeler business, are sold in three categories: the entry segment, 100 cc motorcycles; the executive segment, comprised of 100 cc-135 cc motorcycles such as the XCD and Discover vehicles; and the performance segment, including high performance motorcycles such as the firm's flagship brands, Pulsar and Avenger. Bajaj's three-wheelers include pick-ups, delivery vans and passenger rickshaws, some of which run on compressed natural gas (CNG) and liquefied petroleum gas (LPG). Bajaj is one of the largest Indian exporters of two- and three-wheeled vehicles. The company maintains a distribution network covering approximately 50 countries, with particular emphasis on Sri Lanka, Columbia, Bangladesh, Mexico, Central America, Peru and Egypt. Other subsidiaries include Bajaj Auto International Holdings BV, based in the Netherlands and focused on international ventures; PT Bajaj Indonesia, focused on the assembly and marketing of Pulsars in such Indonesian markets as Jakarta, Java, Sumatra, Bali and Sulawesi. In October 2009, the company launched the Kawasaki Ninja, a 250 cc motorcycle. In December 2009, the company announced plans to exit its scooter business.

FINANCIALS: **Sales and profits are in thousands of dollars—add 000 to get the full amount. 2009 Note: Financial information for 2009 was not available for all companies at press time.**

2009 Sales: $1,927,840	2009 Profits: $115,910	**U.S. Stock Ticker:**
2008 Sales: $1,817,530	2008 Profits: $109,280	**Int'l Ticker: 532977** Int'l Exchange: Bombay-BSE
2007 Sales: $1,855,310	2007 Profits: $152,880	Employees:
2006 Sales: $46,573,960	2006 Profits: $224,910	Fiscal Year Ends: 3/31
2005 Sales: $	2005 Profits: $	Parent Company:

SALARIES/BENEFITS:

Pension Plan:	ESOP Stock Plan:	Profit Sharing:	Top Exec. Salary: $	Bonus: $
Savings Plan:	Stock Purch. Plan:		Second Exec. Salary: $	Bonus: $

OTHER THOUGHTS:

Apparent Women Officers or Directors: 1
Hot Spot for Advancement for Women/Minorities:

LOCATIONS: ("Y" = Yes)

West:	Southwest:	Midwest:	Southeast:	Northeast:	International:
					Y

BEIJING AUTOMOTIVE IMPORT & EXPORT CORP www.baiec.com

Industry Group Code: 42311 **Ranks within this company's industry group:** Sales: Profits:

Vehicle Manufacturing:		Dealers:		Parts:		Service:		Finance:		Specialty:	
Cars:	Y	Car Dealer New:		Manufacturers:		General Service:		Leasing:		Information Systems:	
Trucks:	Y	Car Dealer Used:		Retail:		Specialty Service:		Auto Loans:		Online Marketing:	
Motorcycles:		Truck Dealer:		Distributors:	Y	Oil Change:		Insurance:		Other:	
Specialty:	Y	RV Dealer:		Tires:		Paint and Body:				Publishing:	
Buses:	Y	Motorcycle Dealer:		Batteries:						Rental Cars/Trucks:	
RVs:		Specialty Dealer:									

TYPES OF BUSINESS:

Automobiles Import & Exports
Automotive Parts & Accessories

BRANDS/DIVISIONS/AFFILIATES:

BAIEC

CONTACTS:

Note: Officers with more than one job title may be intentionally listed here more than once.

Phone: 0086-10-66177658	**Fax:** 0086-10-66177325
Toll-Free:	
Address: 2 Xisi Dahongluochang St., Beijing, 100034 China	

GROWTH PLANS/SPECIAL FEATURES:

Beijing Automotive Import and Export Corporation (BAIEC), a subsidiary of Beijing Automotive Industry Holding Co. Ltd., is one of the leading motor suppliers in China, importing and exporting vehicles as well as parts and accessories. BAIEC is globally active and has production based in 26 cites across China and a national sales network. The firm produces 700,000 vehicles per year. The company's passenger vehicle offerings include; the light Off-Road Vehicles (ORV) BJ2023 and QISH120-22MT; the Midi Multi-Purpose Passenger Vehicle; the BJ1021 Pick-up Truck; the Amphibious Vehicle BJ5021-5022; the Towdoor Jeep; the Military Vehicle; the Hyundai Sonata and Elantra; the Mercedes-Benz E300; the Foton MP-X; the Foton SAGA, and the Foton SUP. On the commercial side of trade, the company offers a number of trucks and buses, including the Foton line of pallet, low cab and cargo trucks as well as the new BJ1311VNPJC-3 Pump Truck and the BK6120EV Electric city bus. Its special purpose vehicles include the Isuzu BTL505OTL Cleaning Trucks; the BDK815D Audio Van, which is built on the Mercedes-Benz Vario 815D chassis; the HLT5060ZYS Garbage Truck with Refuse Compactor; the BQJ5051TSL Cleaning Truck; the BDK5200ADSC 2 Mobile Command Unit; and the BQJ5110GSS Cleaning Truck. The company also offers agricultural vehicles such as the Gushen Enricher Combine and the FT series of tractors. Its engineering products include the GTBZ series self-propelled boom lift; the GTJZ self-propelled scissor lifts; GTBY articulating boom and spider boom lifts; GTS6 Single-mast aerial working platform; GTS7 double mast aerial work platform; GTJY manually-propelled scissor lift; GTWY sleeve aerial working platform; the QLY25B and QLY55A Wheel cranes; and a line of truck cranes.

FINANCIALS:

Sales and profits are in thousands of dollars—add 000 to get the full amount. 2009 Note: Financial information for 2009 was not available for all companies at press time.

2009 Sales: $	2009 Profits: $	**U.S. Stock Ticker: Subsidiary**
2008 Sales: $	2008 Profits: $	**Int'l Ticker:** Int'l Exchange:
2007 Sales: $	2007 Profits: $	Employees:
2006 Sales: $	2006 Profits: $	Fiscal Year Ends:
2005 Sales: $	2005 Profits: $	Parent Company: BEIJING AUTOMOTIVE INDUSTRY HOLDING CO LTD

SALARIES/BENEFITS:

Pension Plan:	ESOP Stock Plan:	Profit Sharing:	Top Exec. Salary: $	Bonus: $
Savings Plan:	Stock Purch. Plan:		Second Exec. Salary: $	Bonus: $

OTHER THOUGHTS:

Apparent Women Officers or Directors:
Hot Spot for Advancement for Women/Minorities:

LOCATIONS: ("Y" = Yes)

West:	Southwest:	Midwest:	Southeast:	Northeast:	International:
					Y

BENTELER GROUP (THE)

www.benteler.com

Industry Group Code: 3363 **Ranks within this company's industry group:** Sales: 16 Profits:

Vehicle Manufacturing:		**Dealers:**		**Parts:**		**Service:**		**Finance:**		**Specialty:**	
Cars:		Car Dealer New:		Manufacturers:	Y	General Service:		Leasing:		Information Systems:	
Trucks:		Car Dealer Used:		Retail:		Specialty Service:		Auto Loans:		Online Marketing:	
Motorcycles:		Truck Dealer:		Distributors:		Oil Change:		Insurance:		Other:	Y
Specialty:		RV Dealer:		Tires:		Paint and Body:				Publishing:	
Buses:		Motorcycle Dealer:		Batteries:						Rental Cars/Trucks:	
RVs:		Specialty Dealer:									

TYPES OF BUSINESS:

Automotive Parts Manufacturing
Chassis & Structure Parts Manufacturing
Engine Parts Manufacturing
Exhaust Systems Manufacturing
Engineering Solutions
Design & Testing Services

BRANDS/DIVISIONS/AFFILIATES:

Beneteler AG
Benteler Automotive
Benteler Steel/Tube
Benteler Distribution
Benteler Distribution Deutschland
Benteler-SGL
Benteler Rothrist GmbH
Benteler Tube Management GmbH

CONTACTS: *Note: Officers with more than one job title may be intentionally listed here more than once.*

Hubertus Benteler, Managing Dir.
Hubertus Benteler, Chmn.

Phone: 43-662-2283-0 **Fax:** 43-662-2283-0
Toll-Free:
Address: Schillerstranbe 25-27, Salzberg, 5020 Austria

GROWTH PLANS/SPECIAL FEATURES:

The Benteler Group is one of the 100 largest industrial companies in Germany. It operates through three independent business divisions: Automotive, Steel/Tube and Distribution. The Benteler AG, a management holding company, controls these three divisions. Benteler Automotive's product groups include structures, exhaust systems, engine applications and engineering. It develops and manufactures ready-to-install modules, tool making, components and parts for the body, chassis and engine for nearly all global car manufacturers. The company's product and design solutions address ride comfort and vehicle handling, passenger protection and safety and emission reduction requirements. The firm is the largest supplier of tubular components and modules for the engine in Europe and one of the largest in the world. It is also a leading global manufacturer of fabricated exhaust manifolds and a leading supplier of structural safety products. Most cars worldwide include at least one of its products. In addition, the firm's automotive division manufactures glass processing equipment and fabrication, which includes types of solar; architectural; and automotive glass. The Steel/Tube division's product groups include automotive, energy and industry. Apart from standardized products made of welded and seamless steel tubes above all, it offers solutions matching the specific needs of its customers, supplemented by an extensive range of service. Some of the subsidiaries that are included in the Steel/Tube division include: Benteler Stahl/Rohr GmbH, Benteler Steel/Tube GmbH, Benteler Rothrist GmbH and Benteler Tube Management GmbH. Benteler Distribution's market segments include mechanical engineering, automotive, steel and metal, constructions process engineering, furniture and leisure equipment. The division handles an annual total tonnage of about 525,000 tons. Benteler operates at 150 locations in 38 countries. In February 2009, the firm's subsidiary, Benteler-SGL acquired the Fischer Composite Technology GmbH in Ried, Austria, to create composite components.

FINANCIALS: **Sales and profits are in thousands of dollars—add 000 to get the full amount. 2009 Note: Financial information for 2009 was not available for all companies at press time.**

2009 Sales: $5,822,710	2009 Profits: $	**U.S. Stock Ticker: Private**
2008 Sales: $9,005,300	2008 Profits: $161,730	**Int'l Ticker:** Int'l Exchange:
2007 Sales: $8,993,950	2007 Profits: $199,470	Employees: 23,146
2006 Sales: $8,396,910	2006 Profits: $134,010	Fiscal Year Ends: 12/31
2005 Sales: $7,249,482	2005 Profits: $84,940	Parent Company:

SALARIES/BENEFITS:

Pension Plan:	ESOP Stock Plan:	Profit Sharing:	Top Exec. Salary: $	Bonus: $
Savings Plan:	Stock Purch. Plan:		Second Exec. Salary: $	Bonus: $

OTHER THOUGHTS:

Apparent Women Officers or Directors:
Hot Spot for Advancement for Women/Minorities:

LOCATIONS: ("Y" = Yes)

West:	Southwest:	Midwest:	Southeast:	Northeast:	International:
	Y	Y	Y		Y

BENTLEY MOTORS

www.bentleymotors.com

Industry Group Code: 33611 **Ranks within this company's industry group:** Sales: Profits:

Vehicle Manufacturing:		Dealers:		Parts:		Service:		Finance:		Specialty:	
Cars:	Y	Car Dealer New:	Y	Manufacturers:	Y	General Service:		Leasing:		Information Systems:	
Trucks:		Car Dealer Used:	Y	Retail:		Specialty Service:		Auto Loans:		Online Marketing:	
Motorcycles:		Truck Dealer:		Distributors:		Oil Change:		Insurance:		Other:	Y
Specialty:		RV Dealer:		Tires:		Paint and Body:				Publishing:	
Buses:		Motorcycle Dealer:		Batteries:						Rental Cars/Trucks:	
RVs:		Specialty Dealer:									

TYPES OF BUSINESS:

Automobile Manufacturing
Luxury Automobiles
Luxury Automobile Customization
Automobile Racing
Sports Competition Sponsorship

BRANDS/DIVISIONS/AFFILIATES:

Bentley Mulliner
Continental Supersports
Brooklands
Continental GT
Azure
Continental Flying Spur
Contineta GTC
Muslanne

CONTACTS: *Note: Officers with more than one job title may be intentionally listed here more than once.*

Franz-Josef Paefgen, CEO
Stuart McCullough, Head-Sales & Mktg.
Christine Gaskell, Head-Personnel
Jurgen Hoffman, Head-Info. Systems
Ulrich Eichhorn, Head-Eng.
Doug Dickson, Head-Mfg.
Jurgen Hoffman, Head-Legal
Jurgen Hoffman, Head-Finance
Richard Charlesworth, Dir.-Royal & VIP Rel.
Franz-Josef Paefgen, Chmn.
Michael Mayer, Dir.-Europe & U.K. Region

Phone: 44-1270-255-155 **Fax:**
Toll-Free: 877-300-8803
Address: Pyms Lane, Crewe, Crewe, CW1 3PL UK

GROWTH PLANS/SPECIAL FEATURES:

Bentley Motors Ltd., founded in 1919, designs and manufactures luxury automobiles. The company is a subsidiary of Volkswagen AG. Its current models include the Muslanne; the Continental GT, Supersport, Series 51, Flying Spur and GTC; the Azure and Azure T; and the Brooklands. The company also offers the option of custom designed Bentleys. The firm is represented worldwide through a network of 212 dealer facilities: 24 in the U.K.; 38 in the U.S.; 52 in Europe; 15 in the Middle East and Africa; and 15 in Asia and Australasia, among others. The firm also maintains a used car program. The company's specialist commissioning department, Bentley Mulliner, allows clients to specify the degree of customization, including such options as a front wing vent, longer wheelbase or a specially tailored interior. Jaguar also offers a range of luxury consumer goods, including luggage and small leather accessories, apparel, books and prints, office accessories, gifts, model cars, camp chairs and umbrellas. In April 2009, the company opened a new dealership in Austin, Texas. Also in April 2009, the company opened a showroom in Athens, Greece. In January 2009, the firm's Muslanne and Series 51 made its debut at the North American International Auto Show. In March 2009, the company's Continental Supersports made its debut at the International Geneva Auto Salon. It is capable of running on biofuel and attaining a speed of 60 mph (miles per hour) in just 3.9 seconds with maximum speed of 202 mph. In February 2010, the company expanded into the Kazakhstan market with a new dealership. In March 2010, the firm expanded in the South American market and opened a showroom in Sao Paulo, Brazil.

FINANCIALS: **Sales and profits are in thousands of dollars—add 000 to get the full amount. 2009 Note: Financial information for 2009 was not available for all companies at press time.**

2009 Sales: $	2009 Profits: $	**U.S. Stock Ticker: Subsidiary**
2008 Sales: $	2008 Profits: $	**Int'l Ticker:** Int'l Exchange:
2007 Sales: $	2007 Profits: $	Employees:
2006 Sales: $	2006 Profits: $	Fiscal Year Ends: 12/31
2005 Sales: $	2005 Profits: $	Parent Company: VOLKSWAGEN AG

SALARIES/BENEFITS:

Pension Plan:	ESOP Stock Plan:	Profit Sharing:	Top Exec. Salary: $	Bonus: $
Savings Plan:	Stock Purch. Plan:		Second Exec. Salary: $	Bonus: $

OTHER THOUGHTS:

Apparent Women Officers or Directors: 1
Hot Spot for Advancement for Women/Minorities:

LOCATIONS: ("Y" = Yes)

West:	Southwest:	Midwest:	Southeast:	Northeast:	International:
Y	Y	Y	Y	Y	Y

BETTER PLACE

www.betterplace.com

Industry Group Code: 33611 **Ranks within this company's industry group:** Sales: Profits:

Vehicle Manufacturing:		**Dealers:**		**Parts:**		**Service:**		**Finance:**		**Specialty:**	
Cars:	Y	Car Dealer New:		Manufacturers:		General Service:		Leasing:		Information Systems:	
Trucks:		Car Dealer Used:		Retail:		Specialty Service:		Auto Loans:		Online Marketing:	
Motorcycles:		Truck Dealer:		Distributors:		Oil Change:		Insurance:		Other:	
Specialty:		RV Dealer:		Tires:		Paint and Body:				Publishing:	
Buses:		Motorcycle Dealer:		Batteries:	Y					Rental Cars/Trucks:	
RVs:		Specialty Dealer:									

TYPES OF BUSINESS:

Electric Automobile Battery Services
Electric Automobile Charging Stations

BRANDS/DIVISIONS/AFFILIATES:

Israel Corp.
Ofer Group
VantagePoint Venture Partners
Maniv Energy Capital
Morgan Stanley
Continental
Nissan Motor Company Ltd
Renault SA

CONTACTS: *Note: Officers with more than one job title may be intentionally listed here more than once.*

Shai Agassi, CEO
Charles Stonehill, CFO
Karen Alter, VP-Mktg.
Lior Storfer, VP-R&D
Barak Hershkovitz, CTO
Barak Hershkovitz, VP-Prod. Mgmt.
David Kennedy, General Counsel
Aliza Peleg, VP-Oper. & Planning
Dan Cohen, VP-Strategic Initiatives
Joe Paluska, VP-Comm.
Moshe Kaplinsky, CEO-Better Place Israel
Evan Thornley, CEO-Better Place Australia
Sidney Goodman, VP-Automotive Alliances
Kiyotaka Fujii, Pres., Better Place Japan/Head-Bus. Dev., APAC
Idan Ofer, Chmn.
Jens Moberg, Head-Bus. Dev., EMEA/CEO-Better Place Denmark

Phone: 650-845-2800 **Fax:** 650-845-2850
Toll-Free:
Address: 1070 Arastradero Rd., Ste. 200, Palo Alto, CA 94304 US

GROWTH PLANS/SPECIAL FEATURES:

Better Place is engaged in the design of electric vehicle support networks (EVs) and the operation of charging stations for EVs. The infrastructure envisioned by the firm includes a widespread network of charging spots for battery top-offs, in combination with switching stations enabling cars to swap depleted batteries for fully-charged ones in a few minutes time, thus enabling longer trips. The charging stations would be approximately the size of a parking meter. The battery switching stations would be somewhat similar to gas stations. The customer would pull his or her car into the appropriate bay and an automated process would remove the depleted battery and replace it with a fresh one. Prototypes of Better Places' vehicles use rechargeable lithium ion batteries, but the company is researching other technologies. Better Place envisions that a customer might lease the battery from the company, reducing overall cost of ownership by mitigating initial vehicle costs as well as maintenance costs. The initial battery concept for Better Place was developed by Automotive Energy Supply Corp., a joint partnership of the Renault/Nissan alliance and Japanese manufacturer NEC. A Better Place EV car concept has been developed by Renault/Nissan and is based on the Renault Megane. Discussions or partnerships for the development and installation of Better Place charging systems and EV fleets have been established in Japan, Israel, Denmark, California and Australia. The firm has raised over $500 million in venture capital. Investors include, among others, Morgan Stanley; Israel Corp.; Ofer Group; VantagePoint Venture Partners; and Maniv Energy Capital. In 2009 and 2010, the firm demonstrated its battery switch technology in Japan. In September 2009, the firm partnered with automotive supplier Continental to develop, a network system software for the electric vehicle (EV) to allow car and driver to communicate with the Better Place network, and help EV drivers know where and when to charge.

FINANCIALS: **Sales and profits are in thousands of dollars—add 000 to get the full amount. 2009 Note: Financial information for 2009 was not available for all companies at press time.**

2009 Sales: $	2009 Profits: $	**U.S. Stock Ticker: Private**
2008 Sales: $	2008 Profits: $	**Int'l Ticker:** Int'l Exchange:
2007 Sales: $	2007 Profits: $	Employees:
2006 Sales: $	2006 Profits: $	Fiscal Year Ends:
2005 Sales: $	2005 Profits: $	Parent Company:

SALARIES/BENEFITS:

Pension Plan:	ESOP Stock Plan:	Profit Sharing:	Top Exec. Salary: $	Bonus: $
Savings Plan:	Stock Purch. Plan:		Second Exec. Salary: $	Bonus: $

OTHER THOUGHTS:

Apparent Women Officers or Directors: 2
Hot Spot for Advancement for Women/Minorities: Y

LOCATIONS: ("Y" = Yes)

West:	Southwest:	Midwest:	Southeast:	Northeast:	International:
Y					Y

BLUE BIRD CORPORATION

www.blue-bird.com

Industry Group Code: 336120 **Ranks within this company's industry group:** Sales: Profits:

Vehicle Manufacturing:		**Dealers:**		**Parts:**		**Service:**		**Finance:**		**Specialty:**	
Cars:		Car Dealer New:		Manufacturers:		General Service:		Leasing:		Information Systems:	
Trucks:		Car Dealer Used:		Retail:		Specialty Service:		Auto Loans:	Y	Online Marketing:	
Motorcycles:		Truck Dealer:		Distributors:	Y	Oil Change:		Insurance:		Other:	
Specialty:	Y	RV Dealer:		Tires:		Paint and Body:				Publishing:	
Buses:	Y	Motorcycle Dealer:		Batteries:						Rental Cars/Trucks:	
RVs:		Specialty Dealer:									

TYPES OF BUSINESS:

Bus Manufacturer
Financial Services
School Buses
Bus Parts

BRANDS/DIVISIONS/AFFILIATES:

Cerberus Capital Management LP
Blue Bird VISION
All-American
Micro-Bird
Blue Bird Financial Services
Propane-Powered Micro Bird

CONTACTS: *Note: Officers with more than one job title may be intentionally listed here more than once.*

Greg Bennett, CEO
Mike Horne, COO/Exec. VP
Greg Bennett, Pres.
Roger Howsmon, Chief Mktg. Officer/Sr. VP-Sales
Michael McCurdy, VP-Human Resources
Paul Marcela, General Counsel/VP/Sec.
Travis Kelly, VP-Finance
Bill Danner, VP-School Bus Sales
Ron Smith, Dir.-Mktg.
Ron Sheldon, VP-Int'l Sales
Fred Botero, VP-Purchasing

Phone: 478-825-2021 **Fax:** 478-822-2457
Toll-Free: 800-486-7122
Address: 402 Blue Bird Blvd., Fort Valley, GA 31030 US

GROWTH PLANS/SPECIAL FEATURES:

Blue Bird Corporation, established in 1927, is one of the leading manufacturers of Type A, C and D school and activity buses in the world. The company is owned by Cerberus Capital Management LP. Its products are used in more than 60 countries throughout Africa, Asia, Latin America, the Caribbean, the Middle East and Europe. The firm's school bus lines include the 48-77 seat Blue Bird VISION, the 54-90 seat All-American line and 12 models of Micro Bird 10-30 seat buses. The All American models are available in both front and rear engine configurations. The Blue Bird VISION claims to have the best safety available in a conventional school bus, with 20 more inches of visibility in the loading and unloading zone. Each of these lines can be customized for special needs and transportation requirements, with low-emission, natural gas engines available in many of its models. Other customization options include student safety seats on all of its Micro Bird Type A school buses. Blue Bird buses are contracted through the United States General Services Administration (GSA), the federal government's resource management office. A network of independent distributors sells the company's buses to school districts, public transportation authorities, churches, businesses and nonprofit organizations. Blue Bird also supplies parts for its buses through its distributors in the U.S. and Canada. All of its parts are manufactured in Georgia. Blue Bird Financial Services provides financing programs to cities, countries, states, school districts and nonprofit organizations. In June 2010, the company centralized assembly operations to its Fort Valley, Georgia facility, closing its other Georgia facility. Also in June 2010, the company launched its new line of propane fueled Micro Bird buses. The Propane-Powered Micro Bird is the product of a joint venture between Blue Bird and Girardin begun in 2009.

FINANCIALS: **Sales and profits are in thousands of dollars—add 000 to get the full amount. 2009 Note: Financial information for 2009 was not available for all companies at press time.**

2009 Sales: $
2008 Sales: $
2007 Sales: $201,500
2006 Sales: $
2005 Sales: $

2009 Profits: $
2008 Profits: $
2007 Profits: $
2006 Profits: $
2005 Profits: $

U.S. Stock Ticker: Private
Int'l Ticker: Int'l Exchange:
Employees:
Fiscal Year Ends: 12/31
Parent Company: CERBERUS CAPITAL MANAGEMENT LP

SALARIES/BENEFITS:

Pension Plan:	ESOP Stock Plan:	Profit Sharing:	Top Exec. Salary: $	Bonus: $
Savings Plan:	Stock Purch. Plan:		Second Exec. Salary: $	Bonus: $

OTHER THOUGHTS:

Apparent Women Officers or Directors:
Hot Spot for Advancement for Women/Minorities:

LOCATIONS: ("Y" = Yes)

West:	Southwest:	Midwest:	Southeast:	Northeast:	International:
			Y		Y

Note: Financial information, benefits and other data can change quickly and may vary from those stated here.

BMW (BAYERISCHE MOTOREN WERKE AG)

www.bmw.com

Industry Group Code: 33611 **Ranks within this company's industry group:** Sales: 9 Profits: 12

Vehicle Manufacturing:		Dealers:		Parts:		Service:		Finance:		Specialty:	
Cars:	Y	Car Dealer New:		Manufacturers:	Y	General Service:		Leasing:	Y	Information Systems:	
Trucks:		Car Dealer Used:		Retail:		Specialty Service:		Auto Loans:	Y	Online Marketing:	
Motorcycles:	Y	Truck Dealer:		Distributors:		Oil Change:		Insurance:	Y	Other:	Y
Specialty:		RV Dealer:		Tires:		Paint and Body:				Publishing:	
Buses:		Motorcycle Dealer:		Batteries:						Rental Cars/Trucks:	
RVs:		Specialty Dealer:									

TYPES OF BUSINESS:

Automobile Manufacturing
Financial Services
Motorcycles
Software
Consulting Services
Fleet Management
IT Solutions
Engines

BRANDS/DIVISIONS/AFFILIATES:

MINI
Rolls-Royce Motor Cars
Softlab GmbH
Bavaria Wirtschaftsagentur GmbH
BMW M
BMW Car IT
BMW Motoren
Alphabet Fuhrparkmanagement

CONTACTS: *Note: Officers with more than one job title may be intentionally listed here more than once.*

Norbert Reithoffer, CEO
Ian Robertson, Dir.-Sales & Mktg.
Harald Kruger, Dir.-Human Resources & Industrial Rel.
Frank-Peter Arndt, Head-Prod.
Klaus Draeger, Dir.-Dev.
Friedrich Eichner, Dir.-Finance
Stefan Schmid, Deputy Chmn.
Manfred Schoch, Deputy Chmn.
Stefan Quandt, Deputy Chmn.
Jurgen Strube, Deputy Chmn.
Joachim Milberg, Chmn.
Herbert Diess, Chief Purchasing & Supplier Network Officer

Phone: 49-893-822-3362 **Fax:** 49-893-821-0881
Toll-Free:
Address: Petuelring 130, Munich, D-80788 Germany

GROWTH PLANS/SPECIAL FEATURES:

BMW (Bayerische Motoren Werke AG), based in Munich, Germany, is one of the leading vehicle manufacturers in Europe, with brands including BMW, MINI and Rolls-Royce Motor Cars. The company operates in three primary business segments: automobiles, motorcycles, and financial services. The company's automobile models include the 1 Series coupe and convertible; the 3 Series coupe, sedan, convertible and compact; the 5 Series sedan and touring; the 6 Series coupe and convertible; the 7 Series sedan; the M series coupe, sedan, touring and convertible; the X1, X3, X5 and X6 sport utilities; and the Z4 roadster. The company also manufactures specialty vehicles such as the BMW 5, X5 and 7 Series Security vehicles, armored cars marketed to government officials and diplomats; Vehicles designed for use by law enforcement authorities and emergency service personnel in the 3 Series, 5 Series and X Series models; and vehicles customized for use by U.S. service personnel overseas including DoD personnel and DoD contractors. In addition, BMW produces the MINI brand of cars (One, Cooper, Cooper D, Cooper S and Cabrio) and Rolls-Royce Motor Cars. The BMW brand motorcycles include the K 1300 GT, K 1300 R, R 1200 S, R 1200 GS, F 800 S, F 800 ST, G 650 Xcountry Scramble, G 650 Xchallenge Hard-Enduro and G 650 Xmoto. It also produces related motorcycle apparel, such as leather suits, gloves and boots. The financial services segment manages a range of vehicle related financial services including financing and leasing, asset management, dealer financing and company car pools. Other group activities include the following. Softlab GmbH offers IT consulting, systems integration and software. Bavaria Wirtschaftsagentur GmbH provides insurance and other services to the firm. BMW Car IT is a think tank for automobile IT development and software. BMW Technik works to develop innovative automobile technologies. BKK BMW provides health care to group employees. BMW Motoren manufactures engines. Lastly, subsidiary Alphabet Fuhrparkmanagement manages car fleets. In September 2009, the company established a joint-venture with SGL Group to focus on the development of lightweight carbon fibers for use in the auto industry.

FINANCIALS: **Sales and profits are in thousands of dollars—add 000 to get the full amount. 2009 Note: Financial information for 2009 was not available for all companies at press time.**

2009 Sales: $69,238,500	2009 Profits: $286,790	**U.S. Stock Ticker:**
2008 Sales: $59,737,500	2008 Profits: $517,660	**Int'l Ticker: BMW** Int'l Exchange: Frankfurt-Euronext
2007 Sales: $65,125,700	2007 Profits: $1,596,130	Employees:
2006 Sales: $64,644,400	2006 Profits: $3,791,700	Fiscal Year Ends: 12/31
2005 Sales: $55,254,700	2005 Profits: $2,651,600	Parent Company:

SALARIES/BENEFITS:

Pension Plan:	ESOP Stock Plan:	Profit Sharing:	Top Exec. Salary: $	Bonus: $
Savings Plan:	Stock Purch. Plan:		Second Exec. Salary: $	Bonus: $

OTHER THOUGHTS:

Apparent Women Officers or Directors: 2
Hot Spot for Advancement for Women/Minorities:

LOCATIONS: ("Y" = Yes)

West:	Southwest:	Midwest:	Southeast:	Northeast:	International:
Y	Y			Y	Y

BMW MANUFACTURING CORP

www.bmwusfactory.com

Industry Group Code: 33611 **Ranks within this company's industry group:** Sales: Profits:

Vehicle Manufacturing:		Dealers:		Parts:		Service:		Finance:		Specialty:	
Cars:	Y	Car Dealer New:		Manufacturers:	Y	General Service:		Leasing:		Information Systems:	
Trucks:		Car Dealer Used:		Retail:		Specialty Service:		Auto Loans:		Online Marketing:	
Motorcycles:		Truck Dealer:		Distributors:		Oil Change:		Insurance:		Other:	
Specialty:		RV Dealer:		Tires:		Paint and Body:				Publishing:	
Buses:		Motorcycle Dealer:		Batteries:						Rental Cars/Trucks:	
RVs:		Specialty Dealer:									

TYPES OF BUSINESS:

Automotive Manufacturing

BRANDS/DIVISIONS/AFFILIATES:

BMW (Bayerische Motoren Werke AG)
X6 M
X5 M
X5 Sports Activity Vehicle
Zentrum Museum
X5 xDrive35d
X6 Sports Activity Coupe

CONTACTS:

Note: Officers with more than one job title may be intentionally listed here more than once.

Josef Kerscher, Pres.
Annmarie Higgins, VP-Human Resources
Doug Bartow, VP-Paint
Barbara Bergmeier, VP-Assembly

Phone: 864-968-6000 **Fax:** 864-968-6050
Toll-Free:
Address: 1400 Hwy. 101 S., Greer, SC 29651-6731 US

GROWTH PLANS/SPECIAL FEATURES:

BMW Manufacturing Corp. operates BMW's only manufacturing plant in the U.S. The company has existed as a subsidiary of BMW AG, headquartered in Munich, Germany, since 1992. Located in Greer, South Carolina, the plant is BMW's first full manufacturing facility outside of Germany. The 4-million-square-foot plant exclusively manufactures the X5 M; the X5 xDrive35d; the X5 Sports Activity Vehicle; the X6 M; and the X6 Sports Activity Coupe for the U.S. market. The plant has a daily output average of about 600 vehicles. The firm's Vehicle Assembly Process goes through multiple stages. The first stop before the model gets to the assembly line is sunroof seal station. The firm has a robot stationed above the roof armed with spools of an extruded rubber seals, when the model moves into position, the robot heats the seal and applies it to a flange on the car's roof. Regardless of the vehicle or degree of customization involved, each BMW model begins the same way. The second step is to attach the motor compartment and rear compartment to the floor pan. The motor and rear departments are built at the same time. Then the rear and motor departments are joined with the floor pan to form the underbody. This is the vehicle's structural foundation. While robots accomplish all of the welding, associates assist in the placement of parts on the vehicle. For patrons interested in BMW history, promotions and manufacturing technique, the Zentrum Museum is located next door to the plant. In the first half of 2009, the company produced over 46,000 vehicles. In 2009, the company sold approximately 1.29 million cars and more than 87,000 motorcycles worldwide. In July 2010, the firm announced it would hire over 500 new contingency associates for production of the next generation BMW X3.

FINANCIALS:

Sales and profits are in thousands of dollars—add 000 to get the full amount. 2009 Note: Financial information for 2009 was not available for all companies at press time.

2009 Sales: $ 2009 Profits: $
2008 Sales: $ 2008 Profits: $
2007 Sales: $ 2007 Profits: $
2006 Sales: $ 2006 Profits: $
2005 Sales: $ 2005 Profits: $

U.S. Stock Ticker: Subsidiary
Int'l Ticker: Int'l Exchange:
Employees:
Fiscal Year Ends: 12/31
Parent Company: BMW (BAYERISCHE MOTOREN WERKE AG)

SALARIES/BENEFITS:

Pension Plan: ESOP Stock Plan: Profit Sharing: Top Exec. Salary: $ Bonus: $
Savings Plan: Y Stock Purch. Plan: Second Exec. Salary: $ Bonus: $

OTHER THOUGHTS:

Apparent Women Officers or Directors: 2
Hot Spot for Advancement for Women/Minorities:

LOCATIONS: ("Y" = Yes)

West:	Southwest:	Midwest:	Southeast:	Northeast:	International:
				Y	Y

BMW OF NORTH AMERICA LLC

www.bmwusa.com

Industry Group Code: 33611 **Ranks within this company's industry group:** Sales: Profits:

Vehicle Manufacturing:		Dealers:		Parts:		Service:		Finance:		Specialty:	
Cars:	Y	Car Dealer New:	Y	Manufacturers:		General Service:		Leasing:	Y	Information Systems:	
Trucks:		Car Dealer Used:	Y	Retail:		Specialty Service:	Y	Auto Loans:		Online Marketing:	
Motorcycles:		Truck Dealer:		Distributors:	Y	Oil Change:		Insurance:	Y	Other:	
Specialty:		RV Dealer:		Tires:		Paint and Body:				Publishing:	
Buses:		Motorcycle Dealer:	Y	Batteries:						Rental Cars/Trucks:	
RVs:		Specialty Dealer:									

TYPES OF BUSINESS:

Automobiles, Distribution
Financial Services
Automobile Manufacturing
Automobile Design Services

BRANDS/DIVISIONS/AFFILIATES:

BMW (Bayerische Motoren Werke AG)
DesignworksUSA
MINI
Rolls-Royce Motor Cars
BMW Manufacturing Corporation
Ghost
BMW Financial Services
Z4 Roadster

CONTACTS: *Note: Officers with more than one job title may be intentionally listed here more than once.*

Jim O'Donnell, CEO
Stefan Sengewald, CFO/Exec. VP
Peter Miles, Exec. VP-Oper.

Phone: 201-307-4000 **Fax:** 201-307-0880
Toll-Free: 800-831-1117
Address: 300 Chestnut Ridge Rd., Woodcliff Lake, NJ 07677-7731 US

GROWTH PLANS/SPECIAL FEATURES:

BMW of North America LLC (BMWNA), a subsidiary of BMW, imports BMW, MINI and Rolls-Royce Motor Cars and motorcycles. It markets, sells and provides financial services for 338 BMW car dealerships, 335 BMW sports activity vehicle dealerships, 142 BMW Motorcycle retailers, 90 MINI dealers and 31 Rolls-Royce dealers. The BMW product line includes the 1 series (coupe and convertible); 3 series (sedan, coupe, convertible and sports wagon); 5 series (sedan); 6 series (coupe and convertible); 7 series (sedan); the X3 and X5 Sports Activity Vehicles and the X6 coupe; the Z4 Roadster; and the M3, M5 and M6 series of sedans, convertibles and coupes. The BMW Motorcycle product line includes the BMW G 450 X, the BMW HP2 Sport; the BMW S 1000 RR; BMW k 1300 S; the BMW R 1200 RT; the BMW K 1200 LT; and the BMW K 1300 GT. The MINI line includes the Mini Cooper and the Mini Cooper S (both available in convertible, hardtop and clubman models), and the Rolls-Royce line includes Phantom and Ghost. BMWNA's sister companies include BMW Manufacturing Co., LLC, which operates the exclusive manufacturing plant for all X5 Sports Activity Vehicles and X6 Sports Activity Coupes out of South Carolina; BMW Financial Services NA, LLC., which provides financial tools for buying or leasing a new or used vehicle; and DesignworksUSA, a design consultancy firm.

FINANCIALS: **Sales and profits are in thousands of dollars—add 000 to get the full amount. 2009 Note: Financial information for 2009 was not available for all companies at press time.**

2009 Sales: $
2008 Sales: $
2007 Sales: $
2006 Sales: $16,274,900
2005 Sales: $13,690,500

2009 Profits: $
2008 Profits: $
2007 Profits: $
2006 Profits: $
2005 Profits: $

U.S. Stock Ticker: Subsidiary
Int'l Ticker: Int'l Exchange:
Employees:
Fiscal Year Ends: 12/31
Parent Company: BMW (BAYERISCHE MOTOREN WERKE AG)

SALARIES/BENEFITS:

Pension Plan: ESOP Stock Plan: Profit Sharing: Top Exec. Salary: $ Bonus: $
Savings Plan: Stock Purch. Plan: Second Exec. Salary: $ Bonus: $

OTHER THOUGHTS:

Apparent Women Officers or Directors:
Hot Spot for Advancement for Women/Minorities:

LOCATIONS: ("Y" = Yes)

West:	Southwest:	Midwest:	Southeast:	Northeast:	International:
Y	Y	Y	Y	Y	

BOB ROHRMAN AUTO GROUP

www.rohrman.com

Industry Group Code: 441110 **Ranks within this company's industry group:** Sales: Profits:

Vehicle Manufacturing:		Dealers:		Parts:		Service:		Finance:		Specialty:	
Cars:		Car Dealer New:	Y	Manufacturers:		General Service:	Y	Leasing:	Y	Information Systems:	
Trucks:		Car Dealer Used:	Y	Retail:	Y	Specialty Service:		Auto Loans:	Y	Online Marketing:	
Motorcycles:		Truck Dealer:		Distributors:		Oil Change:		Insurance:		Other:	
Specialty:		RV Dealer:		Tires:		Paint and Body:	Y			Publishing:	
Buses:		Motorcycle Dealer:		Batteries:						Rental Cars/Trucks:	
RVs:		Specialty Dealer:									

TYPES OF BUSINESS:

Auto Dealers, Retail
Auto Service
Financing

BRANDS/DIVISIONS/AFFILIATES:

GROWTH PLANS/SPECIAL FEATURES:

Bob Rohrman Auto Group is a new and used automobile sales company with approximately 40 dealerships in Indiana and Illinois and one collision center in Indiana. The dealerships sell and service a wide variety of cars from most major automotive manufacturers, including DaimlerChrysler, Ford, Honda, Hyundai, Isuzu, Kia, Mitsubishi, Nissan and Toyota. Annually, the company sells more than 36,000 new and used automobiles. In addition to sales, the firm offers car and truck service as well as parts. Bob Rohrman Auto Group's web site provides users with a complete search feature for new and used vehicles. Moreover, customers may book service appointments, order parts online and compare Blue Book values directly on the group's site. The company also offers leasing and financing.

CONTACTS: *Note: Officers with more than one job title may be intentionally listed here more than once.*

Bob Rohrman, CEO
Bob Rohrman, Pres.
Tom Hanlan, CFO
Kim Sharp, Dir.-Human Resources
Craig Gibson, Dir.-Oper.
Tom Hanlan, Comptroller

Phone: 765-448-1000	**Fax:** 765-449-2266
Toll-Free:	
Address: 701 Sagamore Pkwy. S., Lafayette, IN 47905 US	

FINANCIALS: **Sales and profits are in thousands of dollars—add 000 to get the full amount. 2009 Note: Financial information for 2009 was not available for all companies at press time.**

2009 Sales: $	2009 Profits: $	**U.S. Stock Ticker: Private**
2008 Sales: $	2008 Profits: $	**Int'l Ticker:** Int'l Exchange:
2007 Sales: $	2007 Profits: $	Employees:
2006 Sales: $	2006 Profits: $	Fiscal Year Ends: 12/31
2005 Sales: $	2005 Profits: $	Parent Company:

SALARIES/BENEFITS:

Pension Plan:	ESOP Stock Plan:	Profit Sharing:	Top Exec. Salary: $	Bonus: $
Savings Plan:	Stock Purch. Plan:		Second Exec. Salary: $	Bonus: $

OTHER THOUGHTS:

Apparent Women Officers or Directors: 1
Hot Spot for Advancement for Women/Minorities:

LOCATIONS: ("Y" = Yes)

West:	Southwest:	Midwest:	Southeast:	Northeast:	International:
		Y			

BORGWARNER BERU SYSTEMS GMBH

www.beru.com

Industry Group Code: 3363 **Ranks within this company's industry group:** Sales: Profits:

Vehicle Manufacturing:		Dealers:		Parts:		Service:		Finance:		Specialty:	
Cars:		Car Dealer New:		Manufacturers:	Y	General Service:		Leasing:		Information Systems:	
Trucks:		Car Dealer Used:		Retail:		Specialty Service:		Auto Loans:		Online Marketing:	
Motorcycles:		Truck Dealer:		Distributors:		Oil Change:		Insurance:		Other:	
Specialty:		RV Dealer:		Tires:		Paint and Body:				Publishing:	
Buses:		Motorcycle Dealer:		Batteries:						Rental Cars/Trucks:	
RVs:		Specialty Dealer:									

TYPES OF BUSINESS:

Automobile Parts, Manufacturing
Diesel Cold-Start Systems
Ignition Technology
Electronics & Sensors

BRANDS/DIVISIONS/AFFILIATES:

BERU-Eichenauer GmbH
BorgWarner Inc

CONTACTS:

Note: Officers with more than one job title may be intentionally listed here more than once.

Thomas Waldhier, CEO
Ulrich Woehr, Pres.
Marcus Knoedler, CFO
Hans-Peter Vater, Dir.-Mktg. Comm.
Stephanie Schaefer, VP-Investor Rel.
Ulrich Woehr, Gen. Mgr.

Phone: 49-7141-132-0 **Fax:** 49-7141-132-350
Toll-Free:
Address: Moerikestrasse 155, Ludwigsburg, D-71636 Germany

GROWTH PLANS/SPECIAL FEATURES:

BorgWarner BERU Systems GmbH primarily manufactures automotive ignition components. The company is a wholly-owned subsidiary of BorgWarner, Inc. It operates three divisions: diesel cold-start technology; ignition technology; and electronics and sensors. Diesel cold-start products primarily consist of glow plugs, which preheat the air in a diesel engine's cylinder to facilitate starting. Other cold-start products include instant starting systems for use in temperatures as low as -25 degrees Fahrenheit; flame start systems for commercial vehicles; pressure sensor glow plug for diesel engines; and replacement diesel injectors. Ignition technology products include spark plugs; condensers; distributor caps; and ignition coils, modules, contact sets and cables, used mainly in gasoline engines. The firm also produces spark plugs for oil and gas burning heaters. BERU is one of the top major manufacturers of ignition technology for gasoline engines in Europe. Electronics & sensors products comprise automotive heaters, lambda-sensors (an oxygen sensor for catalytic converters), tire pressure control systems, electronic interference suppressors and miscellaneous other sensors, including speed sensors and distance sensors. BERU also manufactures antennas; automotive lighting; cooling air-streams systems, such as fans for the engine; and wiper blades. The company's customers include almost all original equipment manufacturers (OEMs) of automobiles, commercial vehicles and engines. BERU has production companies located in Germany, France, the U.K., Ireland, Italy, Spain, Hungary and Korea; distribution centers in Germany, France, Italy, Japan, Mexico, Singapore and the U.S.; and joint ventures in Germany, India and Korea. In September 2009, BorgWarner, Inc. acquired the company, by purchasing the remaining 4% stock of BERU. In December 2009, the firm changed its name from BERU Aktiengesellschaft to BorgWarner BERU Systems GmbH. Also, the company discontinued its stock exchange listing and officially changed its corporate form to a limited liability company (GmbH). In May 2010, the company acquired BERU-Eichenauer GmbH, which manufactures electric cabin heaters.

FINANCIALS:

Sales and profits are in thousands of dollars—add 000 to get the full amount. 2009 Note: Financial information for 2009 was not available for all companies at press time.

2009 Sales: $	2009 Profits: $
2008 Sales: $582,690	2008 Profits: $-40,480
2007 Sales: $626,020	2007 Profits: $43,910
2006 Sales: $645,400	2006 Profits: $63,200
2005 Sales: $599,400	2005 Profits: $38,300

U.S. Stock Ticker: Subsidiary
Int'l Ticker: Int'l Exchange:
Employees:
Fiscal Year Ends: 3/31
Parent Company: BORGWARNER INC

SALARIES/BENEFITS:

Pension Plan:	ESOP Stock Plan:	Profit Sharing:	Top Exec. Salary: $	Bonus: $
Savings Plan:	Stock Purch. Plan:		Second Exec. Salary: $	Bonus: $

OTHER THOUGHTS:

Apparent Women Officers or Directors: 1
Hot Spot for Advancement for Women/Minorities:

LOCATIONS: ("Y" = Yes)

West:	Southwest:	Midwest:	Southeast:	Northeast:	International:
		Y			Y

BORGWARNER INC

www.bwauto.com

Industry Group Code: 336350 **Ranks within this company's industry group:** Sales: 2 Profits: 1

Vehicle Manufacturing:		**Dealers:**		**Parts:**		**Service:**		**Finance:**		**Specialty:**	
Cars:		Car Dealer New:		Manufacturers:	Y	General Service:		Leasing:		Information Systems:	
Trucks:		Car Dealer Used:		Retail:		Specialty Service:		Auto Loans:		Online Marketing:	
Motorcycles:		Truck Dealer:		Distributors:		Oil Change:		Insurance:		Other:	
Specialty:		RV Dealer:		Tires:		Paint and Body:				Publishing:	
Buses:		Motorcycle Dealer:		Batteries:						Rental Cars/Trucks:	
RVs:		Specialty Dealer:									

TYPES OF BUSINESS:

Automotive Components Manufacturing
Motor Vehicle Transmissions
Power Train Parts
Turbochargers
Cooling Systems
Chain Systems
Industrial Equipment

BRANDS/DIVISIONS/AFFILIATES:

HY-VO
Morse Gemini
Beru
DualTronic
4WD TORQUE-ON-DEMAND
T-Trac
Dytech ENSA
BERU-Eichenauer GmbH

CONTACTS: *Note: Officers with more than one job title may be intentionally listed here more than once.*

Timothy M. Manganello, CEO
Robin J. Adams, CFO
Scott D. Gallett, VP-Mktg., Public Rel. & Internal Comm.
Jan McAdams, VP-Human Resources
Jamal M. Farhat, CIO/VP
Robin J. Adams, Chief Admin. Officer/Exec. VP
John J. Gasparovic, General Counsel/VP/Corp. Sec.
Christopher H. Vance, VP-Bus. Dev.
Mary E. Brevard, VP-Comm.
Mary E. Brevard, VP-Investor Rel.
Jan Bertsch, Treas./VP
John G. Sanderson, Exec. VP/Pres., Drivetrain
Daniel CasaSanta, VP/Pres./Gen. Mgr.-BorgWarner Thermal Sys.
Ron T. Hundzinski, Controller/VP
Roger J. Wood, Exec. VP/Pres, Engine
Timothy M. Manganello, Chmn.

Phone: 248-754-9200	**Fax:** 248-754-9397
Toll-Free:	
Address: 3850 Hamlin Rd., Auburn Hills, MI 48326 US	

GROWTH PLANS/SPECIAL FEATURES:

BorgWarner, Inc. manufactures and sells engineered systems and components, designed to improve fuel efficiency, air quality and vehicle stability, to original equipment manufacturers of passenger cars, sport utility vehicles, trucks, commercial transportation products and industrial equipment worldwide. BorgWarner operates manufacturing and technical facilities at 59 locations in 18 countries, serving customers in North America, South America, Europe and Asia. Products fall into two operating segments: Engine and Drivetrain. The Engine Group produces turbochargers, chain products, emissions systems, thermal systems, diesel cold start and gasoline ignition technology, tire pressure monitoring systems and diesel cabin heaters. Brand names developed by the Engine Group include the HY-VO Front-Wheel Drive transmission and Four-Wheel Drive (4WD) chain and the MORSE GEMINI chain system for light vehicles. Additionally, the Engine Group's products include the results of BorgWarner's German-based subsidiary, Beru Aktiengesellschaft, a global provider of diesel car parts. The Drivetrain Group produces transmission components and systems, as well as all-wheel drive (AWD) torque management systems. Products include friction plates, one-way clutches, transmission bands and torque converter lock-up clutches. Torque-management product brands include the 4WD TORQUE-ON-DEMAND transfer system, that uses electronic sensory input to automatically shift vehicles from 2WD to 4WD; and the T-Trac torque transfer system, which uses electronically controlled clutches to give power to the individual rear wheels when traction is needed. The Drivetrain Group's DualTronic transmission technology, used by the entire VW Group vehicle family, provides smooth-shifting convenience through a two-clutch wet-friction system. In January 2009, the company formed a joint venture with China Automobile Development United Investment Co., Ltd., expanding its DualTronic technology into China. In March 2010, the firm opened two new facilities, one in Shanghai and the other in India. The firm also acquired two companies in 2010, Dytech ENSA and BERU-Eichenauer GmbH, which was formerly a joint venture.

FINANCIALS: **Sales and profits are in thousands of dollars—add 000 to get the full amount. 2009 Note: Financial information for 2009 was not available for all companies at press time.**

2009 Sales: $3,961,800	2009 Profits: $27,000	**U.S. Stock Ticker: BWA**
2008 Sales: $5,263,900	2008 Profits: $-35,600	**Int'l Ticker:** Int'l Exchange:
2007 Sales: $5,328,600	2007 Profits: $288,500	Employees: 12,500
2006 Sales: $4,585,400	2006 Profits: $211,600	Fiscal Year Ends: 12/31
2005 Sales: $4,293,800	2005 Profits: $239,600	Parent Company:

SALARIES/BENEFITS:

Pension Plan: Y	ESOP Stock Plan:	Profit Sharing:	Top Exec. Salary: $946,458	Bonus: $2,997,412
Savings Plan: Y	Stock Purch. Plan:		Second Exec. Salary: $486,135	Bonus: $1,243,419

OTHER THOUGHTS:

Apparent Women Officers or Directors: 4
Hot Spot for Advancement for Women/Minorities: Y

LOCATIONS: ("Y" = Yes)

West:	Southwest:	Midwest:	Southeast:	Northeast:	International:
	Y	Y	Y	Y	Y

BRAMAN MANAGEMENT ASSOCIATION

www.braman.com

Industry Group Code: 441110 **Ranks within this company's industry group:** Sales: Profits:

Vehicle Manufacturing:		Dealers:		Parts:		Service:		Finance:		Specialty:	
Cars:		Car Dealer New:	Y	Manufacturers:		General Service:	Y	Leasing:		Information Systems:	
Trucks:		Car Dealer Used:	Y	Retail:	Y	Specialty Service:		Auto Loans:		Online Marketing:	
Motorcycles:		Truck Dealer:		Distributors:		Oil Change:		Insurance:		Other:	
Specialty:		RV Dealer:		Tires:		Paint and Body:				Publishing:	
Buses:		Motorcycle Dealer:		Batteries:						Rental Cars/Trucks:	
RVs:		Specialty Dealer:									

TYPES OF BUSINESS:

Auto Dealers, Retail
Parts & Service

BRANDS/DIVISIONS/AFFILIATES:

Braman Honda
Braman Honda of Palm Beach
Braman Motors
Braman Motorcars
Mile High Auto Imports
European Motor Cars of Littleton
Prestige Imports
Mercedes Benz of Littleton

CONTACTS: *Note: Officers with more than one job title may be intentionally listed here more than once.*

Norman Braman, CEO
Norman Braman, Pres.

Phone: 305-576-1889	**Fax:** 305-576-9898
Toll-Free:	
Address: 2060 Biscayne Blvd., 2nd Fl., Miami, FL 33137-5024 US	

GROWTH PLANS/SPECIAL FEATURES:

Braman Management Association is a chain of dealerships that primarily sells upscale vehicles, conducting business through seven dealerships in two states. Four of the company's dealerships are in Florida, including Braman Honda in Miami; Braman Honda of Palm Beach in Greenacres; Braman Motors in Miami; and Braman Motorcars in West Palm Beach. The Colorado locations are Mile High Auto Imports in Denver; European Motor Cars of Littleton; Mile High Mitsubishi/Honda/Acura in Denver; Mercedes Benz of Littleton; and Prestige Imports in Lakewood. Each location has a web site where customers can search inventory, apply for financing or schedule a service appointment. Makes of high-end vehicles sold by Braman's dealerships include Acura, Audi, Bentley, BMW, Cadillac, Mercedes, Porsche and Rolls-Royce. The company also sells used cars, as well as new Honda, Mitsubishi and MINI vehicles, and provides part departments and repair services to its customers. The company is also involved in competition racing and participates in charity fundraising events.

FINANCIALS: **Sales and profits are in thousands of dollars—add 000 to get the full amount. 2009 Note: Financial information for 2009 was not available for all companies at press time.**

2009 Sales: $	2009 Profits: $	**U.S. Stock Ticker: Private**
2008 Sales: $	2008 Profits: $	**Int'l Ticker:** Int'l Exchange:
2007 Sales: $	2007 Profits: $	Employees:
2006 Sales: $	2006 Profits: $	Fiscal Year Ends: 12/31
2005 Sales: $	2005 Profits: $	Parent Company:

SALARIES/BENEFITS:

Pension Plan:	ESOP Stock Plan:	Profit Sharing:	Top Exec. Salary: $	Bonus: $
Savings Plan:	Stock Purch. Plan:		Second Exec. Salary: $	Bonus: $

OTHER THOUGHTS:

Apparent Women Officers or Directors:
Hot Spot for Advancement for Women/Minorities:

LOCATIONS: ("Y" = Yes)

West:	Southwest:	Midwest:	Southeast:	Northeast:	International:
Y			Y		

BREMBO SPA

www.brembo.com

Industry Group Code: 3363 **Ranks within this company's industry group:** Sales: 39 Profits: 22

Vehicle Manufacturing:		**Dealers:**		**Parts:**		**Service:**		**Finance:**		**Specialty:**	
Cars:		Car Dealer New:		Manufacturers:	Y	General Service:		Leasing:		Information Systems:	
Trucks:		Car Dealer Used:		Retail:	Y	Specialty Service:		Auto Loans:		Online Marketing:	
Motorcycles:		Truck Dealer:		Distributors:	Y	Oil Change:		Insurance:		Other:	
Specialty:		RV Dealer:		Tires:		Paint and Body:				Publishing:	
Buses:		Motorcycle Dealer:		Batteries:						Rental Cars/Trucks:	
RVs:		Specialty Dealer:									

TYPES OF BUSINESS:

Automobile Parts Manufacturing
Brake Components & Systems
Racing Brake Systems
Seatbelts

BRANDS/DIVISIONS/AFFILIATES:

Brembo Racing
AP Racing
Marchesini
Brembo Foundry Nanjing Co. Ltd.

CONTACTS:

Note: Officers with more than one job title may be intentionally listed here more than once.

Alberto Bombassei, Managing Dir.
Alberto Bombassei, Pres.
Gianfranco de Marchi, Dir.-Comm.
Matteo Tiraboschi, Head-Investor Rel.
Alberto Bombassei, Chmn.

Phone: 39-035-605-2111	**Fax:** 39-035-605290
Toll-Free:	
Address: Viale Europa, 2, Stezzano, 24041 Italy	

GROWTH PLANS/SPECIAL FEATURES:

Brembo S.p.A., based in Italy, designs, develops, produces and manufactures brake discs, components and systems for cars, motorcycles and commercial vehicles, as well as manufacturing clutches, seats and seat belts for the automotive racing market. Brembo divides its products into six segments: passenger cars, which accounted for 64.2% of sales in 2009; commercial vehicles, 13.7%; motorbikes, 12.2%; racing, 6.9%; passive safety, 2.6%; and miscellaneous, less than 1%. The company's car products include brake discs, brake calipers, side-wheel modules and complete braking systems, including integrated engineering services. In the commercial vehicle segment, the company produces various types of braking systems. Motorbike products include brake discs, brake calipers, brake master cylinders, light-alloy wheels and complete braking systems. The firm's racing operations are divided into three brands: Brembo Racing, which offers braking systems for racecars and motorcycles; AP Racing, offering braking systems and clutches for racecars; and Marchesini, offering magnesium and aluminum wheels for racing motorcycles. The passive safety segment manufactures operates in three divisions: the racing division, in which it manufactures and sells safety belts, seats and car racing accessories; the original equipment segment, in which it manufactures and sells special seats for sport road cars; and the child safety segment, in which it produces car seat restraint systems. The company operates in 14 countries on three continents and has 35 production and business sites. Its operations are conducted from nine industrial-commercial facilities in Italy and 26 other countries. In December 2009, the firm agreed to purchase foundry plants and equipment from Donghua Automotive Industrial Co. for $11 million to establish a new manufacturing hub in Nanjing, including a foundry and a machining facility for brake calipers and discs used in cars and commercial vehicles. For the project, the company formed Brembo Foundry Nanjing Co. Ltd. to oversee operations.

FINANCIALS:

Sales and profits are in thousands of dollars—add 000 to get the full amount. 2009 Note: Financial information for 2009 was not available for all companies at press time.

2009 Sales: $1,067,450	2009 Profits: $13,400	**U.S. Stock Ticker:**
2008 Sales: $1,548,360	2008 Profits: $53,650	**Int'l Ticker: BRE** Int'l Exchange: Milan-BI
2007 Sales: $1,448,500	2007 Profits: $94,300	Employees:
2006 Sales: $1,278,500	2006 Profits: $66,600	Fiscal Year Ends: 12/31
2005 Sales: $959,610	2005 Profits: $98,980	Parent Company:

SALARIES/BENEFITS:

Pension Plan:	ESOP Stock Plan:	Profit Sharing:	Top Exec. Salary: $	Bonus: $
Savings Plan:	Stock Purch. Plan:		Second Exec. Salary: $	Bonus: $

OTHER THOUGHTS:

Apparent Women Officers or Directors: 2
Hot Spot for Advancement for Women/Minorities: Y

LOCATIONS: ("Y" = Yes)

West:	Southwest:	Midwest:	Southeast:	Northeast:	International:
		Y			Y

BRIDGESTONE BANDAG LLC

www.bandag.com

Industry Group Code: 3262 **Ranks within this company's industry group:** Sales: Profits:

Vehicle Manufacturing:		Dealers:		Parts:		Service:		Finance:		Specialty:	
Cars:		Car Dealer New:		Manufacturers:		General Service:		Leasing:		Information Systems:	
Trucks:		Car Dealer Used:		Retail:		Specialty Service:		Auto Loans:		Online Marketing:	
Motorcycles:		Truck Dealer:		Distributors:		Oil Change:		Insurance:		Other:	Y
Specialty:		RV Dealer:		Tires:	Y	Paint and Body:				Publishing:	
Buses:		Motorcycle Dealer:		Batteries:						Rental Cars/Trucks:	
RVs:		Specialty Dealer:									

TYPES OF BUSINESS:

Auto Parts, Tire Treads
Retreading Equipment
Management & Outsourcing Services

BRANDS/DIVISIONS/AFFILIATES:

Bridgestone Bandag Tire Solutions
Bridgestone Firestone North American Tire, LLC
Tire Distribution Systems, Inc.
Bridgestone Corporation
Speedco, Inc.

CONTACTS: *Note: Officers with more than one job title may be intentionally listed here more than once.*

Saul Solomon, Pres.
Timothy Chen, VP-Mktg.
John C. McErlane, VP-North America

Phone: 563-262-1400	**Fax:** 563-262-1069
Toll-Free:	
Address: 2905 N. Hwy. 61, Muscatine, IA 52761 US	

GROWTH PLANS/SPECIAL FEATURES:

Bridgestone Bandag, LLC, a subsidiary of Bridgestone Corporation, manufactures and markets tire retreading materials, equipment and tire management services primarily to commercial truck fleets as well as buses, cars and off-road vehicles. The company sells its products through over 2,500 dealers and truck stops. The firm has a sales presence throughout the U.S. as well as in Canada, Europe, the Middle East, South America, Mexico, Australia, New Zealand and South Africa. The company owns two manufacturing facilities in Brazil, one in Belgium, one in Mexico and six in the U.S. Bandag offers roughly 275 types of retreads for a variety of fleet types including over-the-road, pick up and delivery, on/off-road, light truck and severe service. These retreads come with four year workmanship and material warranties and two year casting defect warranties. Other services provided by the firm through local Bandag dealers include trailer and tire inspections; wheel and rim refinishes; and emergency tire assistance. The company also sells fleet management services that reduce unscheduled downtime, improve operational readiness and reduce cost. Tire Distribution Systems, Inc. (TDS), a Bandag subsidiary sells new and retread tires and provides fleet customers with tire management services, such as tire disposal, wheel refurbishing, scarp tire analysis, tire foam fill and wheel alignment and balancing. Another Bandag subsidiary, Speedco, Inc., provides on-highway truck lubrication and routine tire service. Speedco is 87.5% owned by Bandag. Parts of Bandag operate under Bridgestone Bandag Tire Solutions (BBTS), a division of Bridgestone Firestone North American Tire, LLC (BFNAT). BBTS is a combination of Bandag's North American retreading operations, TDS, BFNAT's truck and tire business, GCR Tire Centers and White Tire stores. It sells medium and heavy duty truck tires and offers Bandag retreading services. Bandag's international operations are organized under other Bridgestone Corporation international subsidiaries.

FINANCIALS: **Sales and profits are in thousands of dollars—add 000 to get the full amount. 2009 Note: Financial information for 2009 was not available for all companies at press time.**

2009 Sales: $	2009 Profits: $	**U.S. Stock Ticker: Subsidiary**
2008 Sales: $	2008 Profits: $	**Int'l Ticker:** Int'l Exchange:
2007 Sales: $	2007 Profits: $	Employees:
2006 Sales: $984,100	2006 Profits: $20,000	Fiscal Year Ends: 12/31
2005 Sales: $914,640	2005 Profits: $49,479	Parent Company: BRIDGESTONE CORPORATION

SALARIES/BENEFITS:

Pension Plan:	ESOP Stock Plan:	Profit Sharing:	Top Exec. Salary: $	Bonus: $
Savings Plan:	Stock Purch. Plan:		Second Exec. Salary: $	Bonus: $

OTHER THOUGHTS:

Apparent Women Officers or Directors:
Hot Spot for Advancement for Women/Minorities:

LOCATIONS: ("Y" = Yes)

West:	Southwest:	Midwest:	Southeast:	Northeast:	International:
Y	Y	Y	Y	Y	Y

BRIDGESTONE CORPORATION

www.bridgestone.com

Industry Group Code: 3262 **Ranks within this company's industry group:** Sales: 1 Profits: 5

Vehicle Manufacturing:		Dealers:		Parts:		Service:		Finance:		Specialty:	
Cars:		Car Dealer New:		Manufacturers:	Y	General Service:		Leasing:		Information Systems:	
Trucks:		Car Dealer Used:		Retail:	Y	Specialty Service:		Auto Loans:		Online Marketing:	
Motorcycles:		Truck Dealer:		Distributors:	Y	Oil Change:		Insurance:		Other:	
Specialty:		RV Dealer:		Tires:	Y	Paint and Body:				Publishing:	
Buses:		Motorcycle Dealer:		Batteries:						Rental Cars/Trucks:	
RVs:		Specialty Dealer:									

TYPES OF BUSINESS:

Plastics & Rubber, Manufacturing
Tires
Building Materials
Adhesive Films
Industrial Products
Marine Products
Sporting Goods
Bicycles

BRANDS/DIVISIONS/AFFILIATES:

Bridgestone Americas Holding, Inc.
Firestone
Bridgestone Bandag LLC
Bridgestone Europe NV/SA
Bridgestone India Private Ltd.
Bridgestone Holdings (Thailand) Company, Ltd.
Bridgestone Logistics Company, Ltd.
Bridgestone Retail Operations, LLC.

CONTACTS: *Note: Officers with more than one job title may be intentionally listed here more than once.*

Shoshi Arakawa, CEO
Shoshi Arakawa, Pres.
Akihiro Eto, CFO/VP
Kazuhisa Nishigai, Sr. VP-Japan Tire Sales & Replacement Tire Sales
Hideki Yokoyama, Dir.-Human Resources Div.
Hideki Yokoyama, VP-Central Research
Akihiro Eto, CIO/VP-IT & Network
Mikio Masunaga, VP-Prod. Dev.
Mikio Masunaga, Sr. VP-Prod. Tech.
Koki Takahashi, Sr. VP-Corp. Admin.
Takashi Urano, VP-Int'l. Tire Bus. Oper.
Shuichi Ishibashi, VP-Bus. Dev.
Naomi Eto, VP-Corp. Comm.
Masaaki Tsuya, Chief Revenue Officer/Sr. VP-Internal Auditing
Kazuo Kakehi, VP-Diversified Prod.
Koji Kajiwara, VP-Comm. Tires Solutions
Yasumi Kawasaki, VP-Global Logistics Center
Shoshi Arakawa, Chmn.
Toru Tsuda, CEO/Pres., Bridgestone Europe NV/SA
Masahito Tsuji, VP-Procurement

Phone: 81-3-3567-0111 **Fax:** 81-3-3535-2553
Toll-Free:
Address: 10-1 Kyobashi 1-chome, Chuo-ku, Tokyo, 104-8340 Japan

GROWTH PLANS/SPECIAL FEATURES:

Bridgestone Corporation is a major producer of tires and rubber products. Bridgestone and its 53 subsidiaries and affiliates manufacture a variety of tires and tire materials at 179 plants in 25 countries. The firm operates in eight business units; six of these units focus on the tire business in various locations, while the remaining two units focus on specialty tire and diversified product operations. The tire units, responsible for 83% of 2009 sales, manufacture and market tires for passenger vehicles, aircraft, agricultural machinery, motorcycles and scooters, as well as offering retreading products and services; automotive maintenance and repair work; raw materials for tires; and automotive parts. The diversified products unit supplies chemical and industrial products, including polyurethane foam seat pads, anti-vibration rubber, conveyor belts, multi-rubber bearings, films used in plasma display panels. The firm is focusing on increasing production of ethylene vinyl acetate films, used in the production of solar modules. Some of the firm's larger subsidiaries include Bridgestone Americas, Inc., which oversees the company's operations in the Americas; Bridgestone Tire Hokkaido Hanbai K.K., engaged in the sale of tires; Bridgestone Logistics Co., Ltd, which oversees cargo transportation and warehousing for the group; and Bridgestone Retail Operations, LLC. In February 2010, the company sold its Italian and Chinese steel cord manufacturing subsidiaries to Belgian company Bekaert. That same month, Bridgestone opened the Bridgestone Bandag Retread Center, a plant in Thailand that produces pre-vulcanized tread rubber for its retread tires. In March 2010, Bridgestone India Private announced plans to establish a new plant in Pune, India that will produce passenger radial tires (PSR) as well as truck and bus radial tires (TBR). In May 2010, the company announced the expansion of production capacity of both passenger car radial tires and light truck radial tires at its Karawang Plant in Indonesia.

FINANCIALS: **Sales and profits are in thousands of dollars—add 000 to get the full amount. 2009 Note: Financial information for 2009 was not available for all companies at press time.**

2009 Sales: $29,052,100	2009 Profits: $11,670	**U.S. Stock Ticker: BRDCY**
2008 Sales: $32,344,100	2008 Profits: $104,100	**Int'l Ticker: 5108** Int'l Exchange: Tokyo-TSE
2007 Sales: $30,310,000	2007 Profits: $1,180,000	Employees:
2006 Sales: $25,323,700	2006 Profits: $720,460	Fiscal Year Ends: 12/31
2005 Sales: $23,028,500	2005 Profits: $1,546,200	Parent Company:

SALARIES/BENEFITS:

Pension Plan:	ESOP Stock Plan:	Profit Sharing:	Top Exec. Salary: $	Bonus: $
Savings Plan:	Stock Purch. Plan:		Second Exec. Salary: $	Bonus: $

OTHER THOUGHTS:

Apparent Women Officers or Directors:
Hot Spot for Advancement for Women/Minorities:

LOCATIONS: ("Y" = Yes)

West:	Southwest:	Midwest:	Southeast:	Northeast:	International:
Y	Y	Y	Y	Y	Y

BRILLIANCE CHINA AUTOMOTIVE HOLDINGS LIMITED

www.brillianceauto.com

Industry Group Code: 33611 **Ranks within this company's industry group:** Sales: 31 Profits: 21

Vehicle Manufacturing:		Dealers:		Parts:		Service:		Finance:		Specialty:	
Cars:	Y	Car Dealer New:		Manufacturers:	Y	General Service:		Leasing:		Information Systems:	
Trucks:		Car Dealer Used:		Retail:		Specialty Service:		Auto Loans:		Online Marketing:	
Motorcycles:		Truck Dealer:		Distributors:		Oil Change:		Insurance:		Other:	
Specialty:		RV Dealer:		Tires:		Paint and Body:				Publishing:	
Buses:		Motorcycle Dealer:		Batteries:						Rental Cars/Trucks:	
RVs:		Specialty Dealer:									

TYPES OF BUSINESS:

Automobile Manufacturing
Minibus Manufacturing
Engine & Components Manufacturing

BRANDS/DIVISIONS/AFFILIATES:

Huachen Automotive Group Holdings Co., Ltd.
Shenyang Brilliance JinBei Automobile Co., Ltd.
Zhonghua
Junjie
Kubao
JinBei
Granse
Ningbo Yuming Machinery Industrial Co., Ltd.

CONTACTS: *Note: Officers with more than one job title may be intentionally listed here more than once.*

Qi Yumin, CEO
Qi Yumin, Pres.
Qian Zuming, CFO
Lam Yee Wah Eva, Sec.
He Guohua, Vice Chmn.-Shenyang Brilliance JinBei Automobile
Wu Xiao An, Chmn.

Phone: 852-2523-7227 **Fax:** 852-2526-8472
Toll-Free:
Address: 8 Connaught Rd Central, Charter House, Ste 1602-05, Hong Kong, K3 00000 China

GROWTH PLANS/SPECIAL FEATURES:

Brilliance China Automotive Holdings Limited (Brilliance) is a leading manufacturer of autos and passenger vehicles in the Chinese market. It is 53.38%-owned by Huachen Automotive Group Holdings Co., Ltd. It principally manufactures and sells minibuses and sedans through 51%-owned subsidiary Shenyang Brilliance JinBei Automobile Co., Ltd. (Shenyang Automotive). Brilliance's 33%-owned subsidiary Shenyang JinBei Automotive Co., Ltd. owns 39.1% of Shenyang Automotive. The firm's sedans, based on Mitsubishi engine technology, are sold in China under the Zhonghua, Zunchi, Junjie and Kubao brands. Zhonghua was the firm's first sedan. The Zunchi is a later revision of the Zhonghua, and is a mid-range sedan designed for government institutions, as well as private use. It can be modified for use as a taxi or police car. Brilliance recently expanded its Junjie line up by adding the Junjie FRV (family recreational vehicle). The Kubao is a coupe model jointly designed by Porsche and Shenyang Automotive. BMW Brilliance Automotive Ltd., a 49.5%-owned joint venture with BMW Holding, uses facilities in Shenyang to produce and sell BMW 3-series and 5-series sedans in China. Brilliance's minibus designs, based off Toyota's HIACE and GRANVIA minibuses, are sold in China under the JinBei and Granse brand names. Minibus configurations range from 8-15-passenger models, with additional specialty designs for police and ambulance use. The firm recently sold over 73,860 minibuses, almost 91,360 Zhonghua sedans and 35,070 BMW sedans. Besides manufacturing vehicles, Brilliance's subsidiaries manufacture automotive components, including window moldings, axles and stamped parts, as well as gasoline engines for minibuses, sedans, SUVs and light trucks. These subsidiaries include 50%-owned Shenyang Xinguang Brilliance Automobile Engine Co., Ltd.; 50%-owned Mianyang Xinchen Engine Co., Ltd.; and 51%-owned Ningbo Yuming Machinery Industrial Co, Ltd. Brilliance's distribution network includes 197 minibus distributors, 217 sedan distributors and 90 BMW distributors, as well as service centers.

FINANCIALS: **Sales and profits are in thousands of dollars—add 000 to get the full amount. 2009 Note: Financial information for 2009 was not available for all companies at press time.**

2009 Sales: $903,200 — 2009 Profits: $-240,860
2008 Sales: $803,860 — 2008 Profits: $11,880
2007 Sales: $4,078,300 — 2007 Profits: $14,260
2006 Sales: $1,531,770 — 2006 Profits: $-58,200
2005 Sales: $677,600 — 2005 Profits: $-154,300

U.S. Stock Ticker:
Int'l Ticker: 1114 Int'l Exchange: Hong Kong-HKEX
Employees: 6,360
Fiscal Year Ends: 12/31
Parent Company:

SALARIES/BENEFITS:

Pension Plan: Y — ESOP Stock Plan: — Profit Sharing: — Top Exec. Salary: $ — Bonus: $
Savings Plan: — Stock Purch. Plan: — Second Exec. Salary: $ — Bonus: $

OTHER THOUGHTS:

Apparent Women Officers or Directors: 2
Hot Spot for Advancement for Women/Minorities: Y

LOCATIONS: ("Y" = Yes)

West:	Southwest:	Midwest:	Southeast:	Northeast:	International:
					Y

BROWN AUTOMOTIVE GROUP LTD

www.brownscar.com

Industry Group Code: 441110 **Ranks within this company's industry group:** Sales: Profits:

Vehicle Manufacturing:		Dealers:		Parts:		Service:		Finance:		Specialty:	
Cars:		Car Dealer New:	Y	Manufacturers:		General Service:	Y	Leasing:		Information Systems:	
Trucks:		Car Dealer Used:	Y	Retail:		Specialty Service:		Auto Loans:		Online Marketing:	
Motorcycles:		Truck Dealer:		Distributors:		Oil Change:		Insurance:		Other:	
Specialty:		RV Dealer:		Tires:		Paint and Body:				Publishing:	
Buses:		Motorcycle Dealer:		Batteries:						Rental Cars/Trucks:	
RVs:		Specialty Dealer:									

TYPES OF BUSINESS:

Auto Dealers, Retail
Maintenance & Repair Services

BRANDS/DIVISIONS/AFFILIATES:

GROWTH PLANS/SPECIAL FEATURES:

Brown Automotive Group, Ltd. is one of the leading car dealership for new and pre-owned vehicles. The company sells cars from 14 brands including Mazda, Chrysler, Hyundai, Saab, Dodge, Jaguar, Nissan, Buick, Honda, Subaru, Jeep, Mercedes-Benz, Volkswagen and Toyota through its network of approximately 23 dealerships. These dealerships are located mostly in the eastern U.S., mainly focused in the Washington, D.C., Baltimore, Charlottesville and Richmond areas; however, Brown also owns several dealerships in Texas. Brown Automotive also offers its customers maintenance, collision and repair services. The company's web site contains information regarding its dealerships and the makes and models for sale. Customers are also able to view vehicle inventories and current specials offered by the dealerships. Founded by William Schuiling in 1983, the name of the company originated from the purchase of one of Brown Automotive's Pontiac dealerships in the 1970s.

CONTACTS: *Note: Officers with more than one job title may be intentionally listed here more than once.*

Charles S. Stringfellow, Jr., CEO
Daniel Legge, Pres.
William E. Schuiling, Chmn.

Phone: 703-352-5555	**Fax:** 703-352-5591
Toll-Free:	
Address: 10287 Lee Highway, Fairfax, VA 22030 US	

FINANCIALS: **Sales and profits are in thousands of dollars—add 000 to get the full amount. 2009 Note: Financial information for 2009 was not available for all companies at press time.**

2009 Sales: $	2009 Profits: $	**U.S. Stock Ticker: Private**
2008 Sales: $	2008 Profits: $	**Int'l Ticker:** Int'l Exchange:
2007 Sales: $	2007 Profits: $	Employees:
2006 Sales: $	2006 Profits: $	Fiscal Year Ends: 12/31
2005 Sales: $	2005 Profits: $	Parent Company:

SALARIES/BENEFITS:

Pension Plan:	ESOP Stock Plan:	Profit Sharing:	Top Exec. Salary: $	Bonus: $
Savings Plan:	Stock Purch. Plan:		Second Exec. Salary: $	Bonus: $

OTHER THOUGHTS:

Apparent Women Officers or Directors:
Hot Spot for Advancement for Women/Minorities:

LOCATIONS: ("Y" = Yes)

West:	Southwest:	Midwest:	Southeast:	Northeast:	International:
	Y		Y	Y	

BURT AUTOMOTIVE NETWORK

www.burt.com

Industry Group Code: 441110 **Ranks within this company's industry group:** Sales: Profits:

Vehicle Manufacturing:		**Dealers:**		**Parts:**		**Service:**		**Finance:**		**Specialty:**	
Cars:		Car Dealer New:	Y	Manufacturers:		General Service:	Y	Leasing:	Y	Information Systems:	
Trucks:		Car Dealer Used:	Y	Retail:	Y	Specialty Service:	Y	Auto Loans:	Y	Online Marketing:	Y
Motorcycles:		Truck Dealer:	Y	Distributors:		Oil Change:		Insurance:		Other:	
Specialty:		RV Dealer:		Tires:		Paint and Body:				Publishing:	
Buses:		Motorcycle Dealer:		Batteries:						Rental Cars/Trucks:	
RVs:		Specialty Dealer:									

TYPES OF BUSINESS:

Auto Dealers, Retail
Fleet Sales
Commercial Truck Sales

BRANDS/DIVISIONS/AFFILIATES:

Burt Chevrolet Commercial Trucks
Burt Ford Commercial Trucks

GROWTH PLANS/SPECIAL FEATURES:

Burt Automotive Network is a privately owned auto dealership chain in Colorado. From its five dealerships, the company sells new vehicles from Chevrolet, Ford, GMC, Mazda and Pontiac, as well as pre-owned vehicles from Audi, BMW, Buick, Chevrolet, Honda, Hyundai, Cadillac, Jeep and KIA. The company also offers sales and leasing of new commercial and light- and medium-duty trucks through Burt Chevrolet Commercial Trucks and Burt Ford Commercial Trucks. The firm provides complete fleet sales and services. Burt Automotive offers parts and repair services for its regular customers. In addition, Burt does offer financing and insurance options for all of its automobiles. The company's web site allows customers to view new and used vehicles, learn about the latest specials and promotions, research vehicle recall and apply for credit and purchase programs. Burt is MBE (Minority Business Enterprise) certified, which allows it to manage government or large public sector national car accounts.

CONTACTS: *Note: Officers with more than one job title may be intentionally listed here more than once.*

Lloyd G. Chavez, Jr., CEO
Lloyd G. Chavez, Jr., Pres.

Phone: 303-761-0333 **Fax:** 303-789-6706
Toll-Free: 800-535-2878
Address: 10301 E. Arapahoe Rd., Centennial, CO 80112 US

FINANCIALS: **Sales and profits are in thousands of dollars—add 000 to get the full amount. 2009 Note: Financial information for 2009 was not available for all companies at press time.**

2009 Sales: $	2009 Profits: $	**U.S. Stock Ticker: Private**
2008 Sales: $	2008 Profits: $	**Int'l Ticker:** Int'l Exchange:
2007 Sales: $2,100,000	2007 Profits: $	Employees:
2006 Sales: $	2006 Profits: $	Fiscal Year Ends: 12/31
2005 Sales: $	2005 Profits: $	Parent Company:

SALARIES/BENEFITS:

Pension Plan:	ESOP Stock Plan:	Profit Sharing:	Top Exec. Salary: $	Bonus: $
Savings Plan:	Stock Purch. Plan:		Second Exec. Salary: $	Bonus: $

OTHER THOUGHTS:

Apparent Women Officers or Directors:
Hot Spot for Advancement for Women/Minorities:

LOCATIONS: ("Y" = Yes)

West:	Southwest:	Midwest:	Southeast:	Northeast:	International:
Y					

BYD COMPANY LIMITED

www.byd.com

Industry Group Code: 33611 **Ranks within this company's industry group:** Sales: 25 Profits: 7

Vehicle Manufacturing:		**Dealers:**		**Parts:**		**Service:**		**Finance:**		**Specialty:**	
Cars:	Y	Car Dealer New:		Manufacturers:		General Service:		Leasing:		Information Systems:	
Trucks:		Car Dealer Used:		Retail:		Specialty Service:		Auto Loans:		Online Marketing:	
Motorcycles:		Truck Dealer:		Distributors:		Oil Change:		Insurance:		Other:	
Specialty:	Y	RV Dealer:		Tires:		Paint and Body:				Publishing:	
Buses:		Motorcycle Dealer:		Batteries:	Y					Rental Cars/Trucks:	
RVs:		Specialty Dealer:									

TYPES OF BUSINESS:

Automobile Manufacturing
Cellular Telephone Equipment Manufacturing
Battery Manufacturing
Advanced Battery Technologies
Hybrid and Electric Cars
Contract Electronics Manufacturing

BRANDS/DIVISIONS/AFFILIATES:

BYD Auto Company Limited
F0
F3DM
S8
e6
Hunan Midea Coach
MIDAMERICAN ENERGY HOLDINGS CO
Berkshire Hathaway Inc

CONTACTS:

Note: Officers with more than one job title may be intentionally listed here more than once.

Wang Chuan-fu, CEO
Wang Chuan-fu Wang, Pres.
Jing-Sheng Wu, CFO/VP
Jing-Sheng Wu, Corp. Sec.
Nian-qiang Wang, VP
De-he Mao, VP
Long He, VP
Long-zhong Yang, VP
Wang Chuan-fu, Chmn.

Phone: 86-755-8988-8888	**Fax:** 86-755-8988-8888-64775
Toll-Free:	
Address: No. 3001, Hengping Rd. Pingshan, Longang, Shenzhen, 518118 China	

GROWTH PLANS/SPECIAL FEATURES:

BYD Company Limited is a Chinese company engaged in the design and production of automobiles and in contract electronics manufacturing. The company operates in two divisions: IT industry and automobiles. The firm's IT division produces rechargeable batteries, battery chargers, electro acoustic components, connectors, keypads, microelectronics, cell phone accessories and opto-electronics. The automobile division manufactures low to high-end vehicles, auto molding, auto parts, DM electric cars and all-electric cars. BYD offers a plug-in hybrid, the F3DM. At about $24,800, the F3DM can go about 62 miles in electric-only mode, and can recharge from its backup gasoline engine, its rooftop solar panel charging system or from a plug-in feature. Other models produced include the F0, a four-door compact; F6, a midsized sedan; S8, a hardtop convertible; and e6, a pure electric, zero-emission crossover utility vehicle capable of a 50% charge in 10 minutes. The company is a major manufacturer of cell phone handsets as well as batteries for iPods and iPhones. The firm has nine manufacturing facilities located across China and branch offices in the U.S. (Illinois and California), Europe, Japan, South Korea, India, Taiwan and Hong Kong. MidAmerican Energy Holdings Co., a unit of Berkshire Hathaway Inc., headed by Warren Buffet, owns 10% stake in the company. The company employs about 10,000 engineers. In August 2009 Shenzhen BYD Auto Company Limited, a wholly-owned subsidiary of BYD Company Limited, acquired Hunan Midea Coach, a manufacturer of buses and coaches. In December 2009, the company announced plans to release five new models in 2010. In March 2010, the company began selling a lower carbon version of its F3DM plug-in hybrid to the public in Shenzhen, Guandong Province, China. In April 2010, the company announced plans to open a U.S. headquarters location in Los Angeles. BYD sold 450,000 automobiles in 2009, and had a goal of 600,000 for 2010.

The firm employs about 10,000 engineers.

FINANCIALS:

Sales and profits are in thousands of dollars—add 000 to get the full amount. 2009 Note: Financial information for 2009 was not available for all companies at press time.

2009 Sales: $5,774,200	2009 Profits: $554,990	**U.S. Stock Ticker:**
2008 Sales: $3,900,000	2008 Profits: $180,000	**Int'l Ticker: 1211** Int'l Exchange: Hong Kong-HKEX
2007 Sales: $2,800,000	2007 Profits: $230,000	Employees: 130,000
2006 Sales: $1,700,000	2006 Profits: $144,000	Fiscal Year Ends: 12/31
2005 Sales: $825,000	2005 Profits: $65,000	Parent Company:

SALARIES/BENEFITS:

Pension Plan:	ESOP Stock Plan:	Profit Sharing:	Top Exec. Salary: $	Bonus: $
Savings Plan:	Stock Purch. Plan:		Second Exec. Salary: $	Bonus: $

OTHER THOUGHTS:

Apparent Women Officers or Directors:
Hot Spot for Advancement for Women/Minorities:

LOCATIONS: ("Y" = Yes)

West:	Southwest:	Midwest:	Southeast:	Northeast:	International:
Y		Y			Y

CALIBER HOLDINGS CORP

www.calibernet.com

Industry Group Code: 8111 **Ranks within this company's industry group:** Sales: Profits:

Vehicle Manufacturing:		Dealers:		Parts:		Service:		Finance:		Specialty:	
Cars:		Car Dealer New:		Manufacturers:		General Service:	Y	Leasing:		Information Systems:	
Trucks:		Car Dealer Used:		Retail:		Specialty Service:	Y	Auto Loans:		Online Marketing:	
Motorcycles:		Truck Dealer:		Distributors:		Oil Change:		Insurance:		Other:	
Specialty:		RV Dealer:		Tires:		Paint and Body:	Y			Publishing:	
Buses:		Motorcycle Dealer:		Batteries:						Rental Cars/Trucks:	
RVs:		Specialty Dealer:									

TYPES OF BUSINESS:

Automotive Repair & Maintenance
Body Shops

BRANDS/DIVISIONS/AFFILIATES:

Caliber Collision Centers
CaliberCare Limited Lifetime Warranty

CONTACTS: *Note: Officers with more than one job title may be intentionally listed here more than once.*

Steve Grimshaw, CEO
Mark Sanders, COO
Steve Grimshaw, Pres.
Robert Kliewe, CFO
Ken Mason, Dir.-Mktg.
Anie Chinarian, Sr. VP-Human Resources & Training
Anie Chinarian, Sr. VP-Admin.
Rusty Barsanti, VP-Oper. Texas
Shannon Lynard, Dir.-Corp. Comm.
Robert Tavarez, VP-Client Support
Dan Mossman, VP-Procurement
David Goldstein, VP-Oper. California
Matthew Ohrnstein, Chmn.

Phone: 949-224-0300 **Fax:** 949-224-0313
Toll-Free: 888-225-4237
Address: 17771 Cowan Ave., Ste. 100, Irvine, CA 92614 US

GROWTH PLANS/SPECIAL FEATURES:

Caliber Holdings Corp., one of the largest independent body shop companies in the U.S., operates a chain of 75 automotive repair shops located throughout southern California and Texas, including a large-scale, 90,000-square-foot collision repair center in Santa Monica, California. The company offers comprehensive collision repair, which includes the equipment necessary to repair composites, high-strength steel, aluminum, safety systems, on-board computers and complex finishes. Caliber Collision Centers cooperate with 24-hour-a-day towing services and rental car networks through the Customer Services Division. In addition, the firm has partnered with most insurance companies in order to expedite and simplify repair. Caliber warrantees repair work against defects in materials and workmanship with its CaliberCare Limited Lifetime Warranty for as long as the customer owns the vehicle. The company also keeps its service centers open year-round, 24-hours-a-day.

Caliber offers its employees a benefits package including flexible spending accounts, an employee credit union, technical training and paid educational opportunities for continued advancement.

FINANCIALS: **Sales and profits are in thousands of dollars—add 000 to get the full amount. 2009 Note: Financial information for 2009 was not available for all companies at press time.**

2009 Sales: $	2009 Profits: $	**U.S. Stock Ticker: Private**
2008 Sales: $	2008 Profits: $	**Int'l Ticker:** Int'l Exchange:
2007 Sales: $	2007 Profits: $	Employees:
2006 Sales: $	2006 Profits: $	Fiscal Year Ends: 12/31
2005 Sales: $	2005 Profits: $	Parent Company:

SALARIES/BENEFITS:

Pension Plan:	ESOP Stock Plan:	Profit Sharing:	Top Exec. Salary: $	Bonus: $
Savings Plan: Y	Stock Purch. Plan:		Second Exec. Salary: $	Bonus: $

OTHER THOUGHTS:

Apparent Women Officers or Directors: 2
Hot Spot for Advancement for Women/Minorities:

LOCATIONS: ("Y" = Yes)

West:	Southwest:	Midwest:	Southeast:	Northeast:	International:
Y	Y				

CALSONIC KANSEI CORPORATION

www.calsonickansei.co.jp

Industry Group Code: 3363 **Ranks within this company's industry group:** Sales: Profits:

Vehicle Manufacturing:		Dealers:		Parts:		Service:		Finance:		Specialty:	
Cars:		Car Dealer New:		Manufacturers:	Y	General Service:		Leasing:		Information Systems:	
Trucks:		Car Dealer Used:		Retail:	Y	Specialty Service:		Auto Loans:		Online Marketing:	
Motorcycles:		Truck Dealer:		Distributors:		Oil Change:		Insurance:		Other:	
Specialty:		RV Dealer:		Tires:		Paint and Body:				Publishing:	
Buses:		Motorcycle Dealer:		Batteries:						Rental Cars/Trucks:	
RVs:		Specialty Dealer:									

TYPES OF BUSINESS:

Automobile Parts Manufacturing
Modular Assemblies
Retail Parts & Accessories
Industrial & Construction Equipment

BRANDS/DIVISIONS/AFFILIATES:

Nihon Radiator Manufacturing Co Ltd
CK Sales
Calsonic Kansei North America Inc
Nissan Motor Co Ltd
Daimler AG
Suzuki Motor Corporation
Mitsubishi Motors Corporation
Honda Motor Co

CONTACTS: *Note: Officers with more than one job title may be intentionally listed here more than once.*

Wu Aya Kiyoshi, CEO
Wu Aya Kiyoshi, COO
Wu Aya Kiyoshi, Pres.
Shingo Yamamoto, CFO/Sr. Managing Dir.
Yoshimoto Hiroyuki, CIO/Sr. Managing Dir.
Shigeo Shingyoji, Pres.
Yokoyama Tetsu, Sr. Managing Exec. Officer
Moriya Hiroshi, Sr. Managing Exec. Officer
Huzisaki Akira, Managing Dir.
Itaru Koeda, Chmn.

Phone: 048-660-2111	**Fax:**
Toll-Free:	
Address: 1917 Nichome Nisshin, Kita-ku, Saitama, Japan	

GROWTH PLANS/SPECIAL FEATURES:

Calsonic Kansei Corporation, founded in 1938 as Nihon Radiator Manufacturing Co., Ltd., manufactures automotive parts and accessories, with a particular focus on integrated modular assemblies such as cockpits, front-ends and exhaust systems. With over 50 manufacturing centers across North America, Europe, China and Asia, Calsonic Kansei has 30 consolidated subsidiaries in its global network and 17 affiliated companies. The company's production base in Japan provides manufacturing for nearly 20 affiliates. Modules offer automakers reduced costs and lighter composite weights and provide drivers with engineered efficiencies that increase ease of use and comfort. Calsonic Kansei's cockpit modules integrate instrument panels, air conditioning systems, airbags, electric controls, audio systems, steering columns and other related components in one consolidated unit. Other modules in production and development include front-end modules that combine in one unit a radiator, condenser, internal air cooler, oil cooler, radiator core support, engine fan shroud, as well as headlamps and a bumper reinforcement assembly. Other Calsonic Kansei automotive components and products include air conditioners, exhaust systems and keyless entry devices. The company's CK Sales division sells retail automotive parts and accessories, as well as electronic toll collection devices. Calsonic Kansei additionally markets industrial and construction equipment including control units, instrument clusters, radiators and mufflers. In addition, the company has more than 50 rice production facilities in the world. Calsonic Kansei is a consolidated subsidiary of Nissan Motor. Calsonic Kansei North America, Inc., is the firm's U.S. holding company in Farmington Hills, Michigan. Some of the customers of the company include Audi, Daimler, Isuzu Motors Ltd., BMW, Ford, Volkswagen, Saab, Renault, Mazda Motor Corporation, Honda Motor Co., Mitsubishi Motors Corporation, and Suzuki Motor Corporation.

FINANCIALS: **Sales and profits are in thousands of dollars—add 000 to get the full amount. 2009 Note: Financial information for 2009 was not available for all companies at press time.**

2009 Sales: $	2009 Profits: $	**U.S. Stock Ticker: Subsidiary**
2008 Sales: $7,104,760	2008 Profits: $-586,940	**Int'l Ticker:** Int'l Exchange:
2007 Sales: $6,727,400	2007 Profits: $1,500	Employees:
2006 Sales: $6,868,700	2006 Profits: $184,600	Fiscal Year Ends: 3/31
2005 Sales: $6,247,980	2005 Profits: $167,940	Parent Company: NISSAN MOTOR CO LTD

SALARIES/BENEFITS:

Pension Plan:	ESOP Stock Plan:	Profit Sharing:	Top Exec. Salary: $	Bonus: $
Savings Plan:	Stock Purch. Plan:		Second Exec. Salary: $	Bonus: $

OTHER THOUGHTS:

Apparent Women Officers or Directors:
Hot Spot for Advancement for Women/Minorities:

LOCATIONS: ("Y" = Yes)

West:	Southwest:	Midwest:	Southeast:	Northeast:	International:
		Y	Y		Y

CAMI AUTOMOTIVE INC

www.gm.ca/inm/gmcanada/english/about/Overview/operations_Ingersoll.htm

Industry Group Code: 33611 **Ranks within this company's industry group:** Sales: Profits:

Vehicle Manufacturing:		**Dealers:**		**Parts:**		**Service:**		**Finance:**		**Specialty:**	
Cars:	Y	Car Dealer New:		Manufacturers:		General Service:		Leasing:		Information Systems:	
Trucks:		Car Dealer Used:		Retail:		Specialty Service:		Auto Loans:		Online Marketing:	
Motorcycles:		Truck Dealer:		Distributors:		Oil Change:		Insurance:		Other:	
Specialty:		RV Dealer:		Tires:		Paint and Body:				Publishing:	
Buses:		Motorcycle Dealer:		Batteries:						Rental Cars/Trucks:	
RVs:		Specialty Dealer:									

TYPES OF BUSINESS:

Automobile Manufacturing

BRANDS/DIVISIONS/AFFILIATES:

Suzuki Motor Corporation
General Motors of Canada Ltd
Chevy Equinox
GMC Terrain

CONTACTS:

Note: Officers with more than one job title may be intentionally listed here more than once.

Rafael Urdaneta, VP-Finance
Kevin Williams, Pres., GM Canada

Phone: 519-485-6400	**Fax:**
Toll-Free:	
Address: 300 Ingersoll St., Ingersoll, ON N5C 4A6 Canada	

GROWTH PLANS/SPECIAL FEATURES:

Cami Automotive, Inc., formerly a joint venture between General Motors of Canada, Ltd. and Suzuki Motor Corp, is now a wholly-owned subsidiary of GM Canada and no longer produces any Suzuki models. Based in Canada, the firm manufactures entry-level vehicles and small SUVs. The company is composed of four production units: stamping, welding, paint and assembly. The firm has a manufacturing area of about 1.7 million square feet, and a production capacity of nearly 300,000 vehicles per year. Over the years, the plant manufactured entry-level cars such as Chevy Metro, Pontiac Firefly, Suzuki Swift, Chevy Tracker, Suzuki Sidekick and Suzuki Vitara. The Suzuki XL7, which the firm began making in 2006, is the largest vehicle ever produced by Suzuki: it offers seven passengers seating, and luxury features such as a DVD player, navigation system and leather seating. The company has produced over 2.3 million vehicles, all from its production facility in Ontario. In May 2009, Cami began production of the Chevrolet Equinox, a compact SUV and the first vehicle made at Cami that was largely engineered and developed in Canada for the North American market. The firm also began production of the GMC Terrain at its facility in 2009. In December 2009, GM Canada purchased Suzuki's share in the company.

FINANCIALS:

Sales and profits are in thousands of dollars—add 000 to get the full amount. 2009 Note: Financial information for 2009 was not available for all companies at press time.

2009 Sales: $	2009 Profits: $	**U.S. Stock Ticker: Subsidiary**
2008 Sales: $	2008 Profits: $	**Int'l Ticker:** Int'l Exchange:
2007 Sales: $	2007 Profits: $	Employees:
2006 Sales: $	2006 Profits: $	Fiscal Year Ends:
2005 Sales: $	2005 Profits: $	Parent Company: GENERAL MOTORS OF CANADA LTD

SALARIES/BENEFITS:

Pension Plan:	ESOP Stock Plan:	Profit Sharing:	Top Exec. Salary: $	Bonus: $
Savings Plan:	Stock Purch. Plan:		Second Exec. Salary: $	Bonus: $

OTHER THOUGHTS:

Apparent Women Officers or Directors:
Hot Spot for Advancement for Women/Minorities:

LOCATIONS: ("Y" = Yes)

West:	Southwest:	Midwest:	Southeast:	Northeast:	International:
					Y

CANADIAN TIRE CORP LTD

corp.canadiantire.ca

Industry Group Code: 441320 **Ranks within this company's industry group:** Sales: 1 Profits: 1

Vehicle Manufacturing:		Dealers:		Parts:		Service:		Finance:		Specialty:	
Cars:		Car Dealer New:		Manufacturers:		General Service:	Y	Leasing:		Information Systems:	
Trucks:		Car Dealer Used:		Retail:	Y	Specialty Service:		Auto Loans:		Online Marketing:	
Motorcycles:		Truck Dealer:		Distributors:		Oil Change:	Y	Insurance:	Y	Other:	Y
Specialty:		RV Dealer:		Tires:	Y	Paint and Body:				Publishing:	
Buses:		Motorcycle Dealer:		Batteries:						Rental Cars/Trucks:	
RVs:		Specialty Dealer:									

TYPES OF BUSINESS:

Retail-Auto Parts & Tires
Retail-Auto Accessories
Banking Services
Financial Services-Insurance & Loans
Roadside Assistance
Gas Stations
Convenience Stores
Retail-Sports & Work Apparel

BRANDS/DIVISIONS/AFFILIATES:

Canadian Tire Financial Services
PartSource
Canadian Tire Petroleum
Mark's Work Wearhouse
Canadian Tire Retail
L'Equipeur
Host Kilmer Service Centres

CONTACTS: *Note: Officers with more than one job title may be intentionally listed here more than once.*

Stephen G. Wetmore, CEO
Stephen G. Wetmore, Pres.
Marco Marrone, CFO/Exec. VP-Finance
Sharon J. Patterson, Sr. VP-Human Resources
Kristine Freudenthaler, CIO/Sr. VP-IT
Patrick R. Sinnott, Sr. VP-Tech.
Robyn A. Collver, General Counsel/Sec./Sr. VP
Kenneth Silver, Sr. VP-Strategy & Real Estate
Liz Hamilton, Associate VP-Corp. Comm.
Karen Meagher, Associate VP-Investor Rel.
Stanley W. Pasternak, Treas./Sr. VP
G. Michael Arnett, Pres., Canadian Tire Retail
Dean McCann, Pres., Canadian Tire Financial Svcs. Ltd.
Paul D. Wilson, Pres., Mark's Work Wearhouse Ltd.
Michael B. Medline, Pres., Automotive & Dealer Rel.
Maureen J. Sabia, Chmn.
Patrick R. Sinnott, Sr. VP-Supply Chain

Phone: 416-480-3000 **Fax:** 416-544-7715
Toll-Free: 800-387-8803
Address: 2180 Yonge St., P.O. Box 770, Station K, Toronto, ON M4P 2V8 Canada

GROWTH PLANS/SPECIAL FEATURES:

Canadian Tire Corp., Ltd. is a group of interrelated businesses engaged in tire retail, financial services and petroleum. It operates through five businesses. Canadian Tire Retail (CTR), through its independent associate dealers, operates 479 stores nationwide. CTR offers branded products in the areas of automotive parts, accessories and service; sports and leisure products; and home products. PartSource is an automotive parts specialty retail chain consisting of 87 stores targeting do-it-yourselfers and commercial installers. Canadian Tire Financial Services, Ltd. (CTFS) operates Canadian Tire Bank (CTB), which provides various financial products, including over 5 million branded credit cards in circulation, mostly backed by MasterCard. CTB also offers personal loans, lines of credit, insurance and warranty products. Additionally, CTFS operates a roadside assistance service, Canadian Tire Roadside Assistance. Canadian Tire Petroleum (CTP) is one of Canada's largest independent retailers of gasoline. It operates approximately 272 gas stations, including 267 convenience stores and kiosks, 73 car wash centers, 11 Pit Stop lubrication service centers and 88 stations that supply propane directly to customers. Many of CTP's facilities are co-located. Mark's Work Wearhouse, Ltd. (Mark's), called L'Equipeur in Quebec, offers men's and women's casual clothing and footwear for business-casual, recreational and industrial work environments. The company operates roughly 378 Mark's stores across Canada. CTR generates the largest share of Canadian Tire's earnings, about 55% (PartSource's earnings are included in the CTR segment); followed by CTFS, 27%; Mark's, 13%; and CTP, 5%. In June 2009, the company opened a 1.5 million square foot distribution center in Quebec. In April 2010, the firm announced plans to build and operate 23 fuel and convenience store service centers, in partnership with Host Kilmer Service Centres.

Canadian Tire offers its employees medical, dental and disability coverage; life insurance; a profit sharing plan; a stock purchase plan; and employee discounts.

FINANCIALS: **Sales and profits are in thousands of dollars—add 000 to get the full amount. 2009 Note: Financial information for 2009 was not available for all companies at press time.**

2009 Sales: $8,262,940 | 2009 Profits: $318,670
2008 Sales: $8,358,810 | 2008 Profits: $342,920
2007 Sales: $7,886,680 | 2007 Profits: $377,280
2006 Sales: $7,788,764 | 2006 Profits: $334,095
2005 Sales: $6,729,556 | 2005 Profits: $285,786

U.S. Stock Ticker:
Int'l Ticker: CTC Int'l Exchange: Toronto-TSX
Employees: 7,287
Fiscal Year Ends: 12/31
Parent Company:

SALARIES/BENEFITS:

Pension Plan: | ESOP Stock Plan: | Profit Sharing: Y | Top Exec. Salary: $1,211,207 | Bonus: $1,220,987
Savings Plan: | Stock Purch. Plan: | | Second Exec. Salary: $532,943 | Bonus: $359,163

OTHER THOUGHTS:

Apparent Women Officers or Directors: 7
Hot Spot for Advancement for Women/Minorities: Y

LOCATIONS: ("Y" = Yes)

West:	Southwest:	Midwest:	Southeast:	Northeast:	International:
					Y

CARLISLE COMPANIES INC

www.carlisle.com

Industry Group Code: 3363 **Ranks within this company's industry group:** Sales: 29 Profits: 7

Vehicle Manufacturing:		Dealers:		Parts:		Service:		Finance:		Specialty:	
Cars:		Car Dealer New:		Manufacturers:	Y	General Service:		Leasing:		Information Systems:	
Trucks:	Y	Car Dealer Used:		Retail:		Specialty Service:		Auto Loans:		Online Marketing:	
Motorcycles:		Truck Dealer:		Distributors:	Y	Oil Change:		Insurance:		Other:	
Specialty:		RV Dealer:		Tires:		Paint and Body:				Publishing:	
Buses:		Motorcycle Dealer:		Batteries:						Rental Cars/Trucks:	
RVs:		Specialty Dealer:									

TYPES OF BUSINESS:

Automotive Products, Motors & Parts Manufacturing
Construction Materials
Industrial Components
Transportation Products
Tires & Braking Systems
Rubber & Plastic Components
Foodservice Equipment
Wire & Cables

BRANDS/DIVISIONS/AFFILIATES:

Carlisle Coatings & Waterproofing Incorporated
Carlisle Flight Services, Inc.
Carlisle FoodService Products Incorporated
Insulfoam, LLC
Carlisle International LLC
Carlisle Power Transmission Products, Inc.
Carlisle Roofing Systems, Inc.
Carlyle Incorporated

CONTACTS: *Note: Officers with more than one job title may be intentionally listed here more than once.*

David A. Roberts, CEO
David A. Roberts, Pres.
Steven J. Ford, CFO/VP
Steven J. Ford, General Counsel/VP/Sec.
Scott C. Selbach, VP-Corp. Dev.
Charles D. Siczek, Chief Acct. Officer/Controller
John W. Altmeyer, Group Pres., Construction Materials
Fred A. Sutter, Pres., Engineered Transportation Solutions
D. Christian Koch, Pres., Carlisle Industrial Brake & Friction
Carol P. Lowe, Pres., Trail King Industries, Inc.
David A. Roberts, Chmn.
Kevin Forster, Pres., Asia-Pacific

Phone: 704-501-1100 **Fax:** 704-501-1190
Toll-Free: 866-869-0474
Address: 13925 Ballantyne Corporate Pl., Ste. 400, Charlotte, NC 28277 US

GROWTH PLANS/SPECIAL FEATURES:

Carlisle Companies, Inc. manufactures and distributes a range of products for the roofing, construction, trucking, automotive, foodservice, industrial equipment and aerospace industries. The firm operates through five segments: Construction Materials; Engineered Transportation Solutions; Interconnect Technologies; FoodService Products; and Specialty Products. The Construction Materials segment manufactures and sells rubber (EPDM) and thermoplastic polyolefin (TPO) roofing systems. In addition, the segment markets and sells polyvinyl chloride (PVC) membrane and accessories purchased from third party suppliers. The company also manufactures and distributes energy-efficient rigid foam insulation panels for roofing applications. Through its coatings and waterproofing operation, this segment also manufactures and sells liquid and spray-applied waterproofing membranes, vapor and air barriers, and HVAC duct sealants and hardware for the commercial and residential construction markets. The Engineered Transportation Solutions segment is comprised of three product lines: tire and wheel, including bias-ply, steel-belted radial tires, non-automotive rubber tires and tire and wheel assembly; industrial brake and friction, which includes off-highway braking systems, on-highway brake actuation systems and specialty friction products; and power transmission belt, which includes industrial belts and related components. The Interconnect Technologies segment designs and manufactures high performance wire, cable, fiber optic, RF/microwave connectors, specialty cable assemblies, integrated wired racks and fully integrated airframe subsystem solutions for the aerospace, defense, electronics and test and measurement industries. The FoodService Products business manufactures and distributes commercial and institutional foodservice permanentware, table coverings, display pieces, cookware and supplies to restaurants, hotels, hospitals, nursing homes, schools and correctional facilities; and industrial brooms, brushes, mops and rotary brushes for industrial, commercial and institutional facilities. Lastly, the specialty products segment includes the specialty trailer business and the refrigerated truck bodies business. In September 2009, the firm acquired Jerrik, Inc., a manufacturer of aerospace and military filter connectors. In October 2009, Carlisle acquired Japan Power Brake, Inc. and Electronic Cable Specialists, Inc.

FINANCIALS: **Sales and profits are in thousands of dollars—add 000 to get the full amount. 2009 Note: Financial information for 2009 was not available for all companies at press time.**

2009 Sales: $2,379,500	2009 Profits: $144,600	**U.S. Stock Ticker: CSL**
2008 Sales: $3,110,100	2008 Profits: $55,800	**Int'l Ticker:** Int'l Exchange:
2007 Sales: $2,812,100	2007 Profits: $215,637	Employees: 10,000
2006 Sales: $2,353,500	2006 Profits: $217,075	Fiscal Year Ends: 12/31
2005 Sales: $2,206,965	2005 Profits: $106,365	Parent Company:

SALARIES/BENEFITS:

Pension Plan: Y	ESOP Stock Plan:	Profit Sharing:	Top Exec. Salary: $950,000	Bonus: $963,300
Savings Plan: Y	Stock Purch. Plan:		Second Exec. Salary: $580,000	Bonus: $611,300

OTHER THOUGHTS:

Apparent Women Officers or Directors: 2
Hot Spot for Advancement for Women/Minorities:

LOCATIONS: ("Y" = Yes)

West:	Southwest:	Midwest:	Southeast:	Northeast:	International:
Y	Y	Y	Y	Y	Y

Note: Financial information, benefits and other data can change quickly and may vary from those stated here.

CARMAX GROUP

www.carmax.com

Industry Group Code: 441110 **Ranks within this company's industry group:** Sales: 4 Profits: 4

Vehicle Manufacturing:		Dealers:		Parts:		Service:		Finance:		Specialty:	
Cars:		Car Dealer New:	Y	Manufacturers:		General Service:	Y	Leasing:		Information Systems:	
Trucks:		Car Dealer Used:	Y	Retail:		Specialty Service:		Auto Loans:	Y	Online Marketing:	Y
Motorcycles:		Truck Dealer:		Distributors:		Oil Change:		Insurance:		Other:	
Specialty:		RV Dealer:		Tires:		Paint and Body:				Publishing:	
Buses:		Motorcycle Dealer:		Batteries:						Rental Cars/Trucks:	
RVs:		Specialty Dealer:									

TYPES OF BUSINESS:

Used Auto Dealers, Retail
New Auto Dealers
Online Sales
Vehicle Repair Services
Financial Services

BRANDS/DIVISIONS/AFFILIATES:

CarMax Foundation (The)

CONTACTS:

Note: Officers with more than one job title may be intentionally listed here more than once.

Thomas J. Folliard, CEO
Thomas J. Folliard, Pres.
Keith D. Browning, CFO/Exec. VP
Joseph S. Kunkel, Sr. VP-Mktg. & Strategy
Roberta Douma, VP-Human Resource Dev.
Richard M. Smith, CIO/Sr. VP
Bill Nash, VP-Merch.
Michael K. Dolan, Chief Admin. Officer/Exec. VP
Eric Margolin, General Counsel/Sr. VP/Corp. Sec.
Lynn Mussatt, VP-Bus. Oper.
Anu Agarwal, VP-Bus. Strategy
Trina lee, Dir.-Public Affairs & Comm.
Katharine Kenny, VP-Investor Rel.
Thomas W. Reedy, Jr., Sr. VP-Finance
Laura Donahue, VP-Advertising
Angela S. Chattin, Sr. VP-CarMax Auto Finance
Barbara Harvill, VP-IT
Kim Orcutt, VP/Controller
William R. Tiefel, Chmn.
Mark Adams, Asst. VP-Logistics

Phone: 804-747-0422 **Fax:** 804-967-2918
Toll-Free: 800-519-1511
Address: 12800 Tuckahoe Creek Pkwy., Richmond, VA 23238 US

GROWTH PLANS/SPECIAL FEATURES:

CarMax Group is one of the nation's largest retailers of used cars. The firm purchases, reconditions and sells used vehicles through its 103 used car superstores in 49 metropolitan markets across the U.S. 90% of the cars in the company's used vehicle inventory are between one and six years old and have less than 60,000 miles. Vehicles that do not meet retail standards are sold in closed wholesale auctions. CarMax also sells new vehicles at five of its locations under franchise agreements with four new car manufacturers. The company offers a wide selection of makes and models of both domestic and imported vehicles to appeal to diverse consumer preferences and budgets, including popular brands from manufacturers such as Daimler, Chrysler, Ford, General Motors, Honda, Mitsubishi, Subaru, Toyota and Volkswagen. Vehicles purchased through the company's in-store appraisal process that fall short of retail standards are sold at on-site wholesale auctions restricted to licensed automobile dealers. All store locations provide vehicle repair service and used-car warranty service. In addition, through the company's web site, customers can search new and used cars as well as find information on Kelley Blue Book figures, car buying tips, rebates and incentives. CarMax has finance operations through CarMax Auto Finance that offer revolving credit and automobile installment loans. The company also works through The CarMax Foundation, which supports community service and philanthropic endeavors. The firm sold approximately 357,000 used vehicles retailed in 2009. CarMax opened three new stores in 2010, two in Ohio and one in Georgia.

CarMax offers its employees a benefits package including educational assistance, a daycare savings account, life insurance, adoption assistance, an associate discount program and an employee assistance program. CarMax has been named by Fortune magazine as one of its 2009 100 Best Companies to Work For.

FINANCIALS:

Sales and profits are in thousands of dollars—add 000 to get the full amount. 2009 Note: Financial information for 2009 was not available for all companies at press time.

2009 Sales: $6,974,000	2009 Profits: $59,200	**U.S. Stock Ticker: KMX**
2008 Sales: $8,199,571	2008 Profits: $182,025	**Int'l Ticker:** Int'l Exchange:
2007 Sales: $7,465,656	2007 Profits: $198,597	Employees: 13,035
2006 Sales: $6,259,967	2006 Profits: $134,220	Fiscal Year Ends: 2/28
2005 Sales: $5,260,300	2005 Profits: $112,900	Parent Company:

SALARIES/BENEFITS:

Pension Plan: Y	ESOP Stock Plan:	Profit Sharing:	Top Exec. Salary: $850,000	Bonus: $1,700,000
Savings Plan: Y	Stock Purch. Plan: Y		Second Exec. Salary: $615,835	Bonus: $739,002

OTHER THOUGHTS:

Apparent Women Officers or Directors: 16
Hot Spot for Advancement for Women/Minorities: Y

LOCATIONS: ("Y" = Yes)

West:	Southwest:	Midwest:	Southeast:	Northeast:	International:
Y	Y	Y	Y	Y	

CARQUEST CORP

www.carquest.com

Industry Group Code: 441310 **Ranks within this company's industry group:** Sales: Profits:

Vehicle Manufacturing:		**Dealers:**		**Parts:**		**Service:**		**Finance:**		**Specialty:**	
Cars:		Car Dealer New:		Manufacturers:		General Service:	Y	Leasing:		Information Systems:	
Trucks:		Car Dealer Used:		Retail:	Y	Specialty Service:		Auto Loans:		Online Marketing:	
Motorcycles:		Truck Dealer:		Distributors:	Y	Oil Change:		Insurance:		Other:	
Specialty:		RV Dealer:		Tires:		Paint and Body:				Publishing:	
Buses:		Motorcycle Dealer:		Batteries:						Rental Cars/Trucks:	
RVs:		Specialty Dealer:									

TYPES OF BUSINESS:

Auto Parts Stores
Repair Services

BRANDS/DIVISIONS/AFFILIATES:

TECH-NET Professional Auto Service
CARQUEST eServices
CARQUEST Technical Institute
General Parts, Inc.
Automotive Warehouse, Inc.
CAP Warehouse
BWP Distributors, Inc.
Muffler Warehouse

CONTACTS: *Note: Officers with more than one job title may be intentionally listed here more than once.*

Todd Hack, Pres.
Craig Barnes, Sr. VP-Merch.
John Gardner, Sr. VP-Finance
Temple Sloan III, COO/Pres., General Parts
John Gardner, Sr. VP-Carquest, General Parts
Todd Hack, Sr. VP-Prod. Mgmt., General Parts

Phone: 919-573-3000 **Fax:** 919-573-2501
Toll-Free: 877-735-2233
Address: 2635 E. Millbrook Rd., Raleigh, NC 27604 US

GROWTH PLANS/SPECIAL FEATURES:

CARQUEST Corp. operates a chain of more than 3,000 automotive parts stores, independently and distributor-owned, located throughout the U.S. and parts of Canada. The group also has a network of more than 40 distribution centers. Items available in stores include temperature control and cooling products; steering and suspension products; engine and mechanical systems; brake systems; drivetrain systems; engine performance and emissions control systems; temperature control and cooling systems; and electrical and vision systems. In addition, it provides parts, accessories, supplies and equipment for most models of light and heavy-weight trucks, recreational vehicles, agricultural equipment, buses and off-roading equipment. Within the stores, critical products are marked with a good-better-best system using the colors red, blue and gold. Gold products are the best quality, whereas red products are the least expensive. The firm also sells and distributes tools, equipment, chemicals, paint and accessories. CARQUEST's own branded line of products is sold to the distributor stores, as well as to wholesalers for eventual resale to professional repair shops, service stations, dealerships and do-it-yourself customers. CARQUEST includes five member companies: Automotive Warehouse, Inc.; CAP Warehouse; BWP Distributors, Inc.; General Parts, Inc.; and Muffler Warehouse. In addition, CARQUEST owns TECH-NET Professional Auto Service, a network of independent automotive service facilities, and CARQUEST eServices, which provides professional customers with access to CARQUEST's inventory and catalog through the Internet at any time. The company also maintains the CARQUEST Technical Institute, an online and instructor-led training program for professional technicians and automotive repair facility owners. CARQUEST also offers Direct-Hit, an online diagnostic tool that offers a database of vehicle symptoms with tests and fixes. The company is also the official supplier and sponsor of NASCAR group Hendrick Motorsports.

The company offers its employees a medical, dental and vision insurance; life, AD&D and long-term disability insurance; flexible spending accounts; an employee assistance program; and education reimbursement.

FINANCIALS: **Sales and profits are in thousands of dollars—add 000 to get the full amount. 2009 Note: Financial information for 2009 was not available for all companies at press time.**

2009 Sales: $	2009 Profits: $	**U.S. Stock Ticker: Private**
2008 Sales: $	2008 Profits: $	**Int'l Ticker:** Int'l Exchange:
2007 Sales: $	2007 Profits: $	Employees:
2006 Sales: $	2006 Profits: $	Fiscal Year Ends: 12/31
2005 Sales: $	2005 Profits: $	Parent Company:

SALARIES/BENEFITS:

Pension Plan:	ESOP Stock Plan: Y	Profit Sharing:	Top Exec. Salary: $	Bonus: $
Savings Plan: Y	Stock Purch. Plan:		Second Exec. Salary: $	Bonus: $

OTHER THOUGHTS:

Apparent Women Officers or Directors:
Hot Spot for Advancement for Women/Minorities:

LOCATIONS: ("Y" = Yes)

West:	Southwest:	Midwest:	Southeast:	Northeast:	International:
Y	Y	Y	Y	Y	Y

CATERPILLAR INC

www.cat.com

Industry Group Code: 333 **Ranks within this company's industry group:** Sales: 1 Profits: 1

Vehicle Manufacturing:		Dealers:		Parts:		Service:		Finance:		Specialty:	
Cars:		Car Dealer New:		Manufacturers:	Y	General Service:		Leasing:		Information Systems:	
Trucks:	Y	Car Dealer Used:		Retail:		Specialty Service:	Y	Auto Loans:		Online Marketing:	
Motorcycles:		Truck Dealer:		Distributors:		Oil Change:		Insurance:		Other:	Y
Specialty:	Y	RV Dealer:		Tires:		Paint and Body:				Publishing:	
Buses:		Motorcycle Dealer:		Batteries:						Rental Cars/Trucks:	
RVs:		Specialty Dealer:									

TYPES OF BUSINESS:

Machinery-Earth Moving & Agricultural
Diesel and Turbine Engines
Financing
Fuel Cell Manufacturing
Rail Car Maintenance
Engine & Equipment Remanufacturing
Supply Chain Services
Locomotive Manufacturing and Maintenance

BRANDS/DIVISIONS/AFFILIATES:

Progress Rail Services, Inc.
Navistar International Corp.
Caterpillar Logistics

CONTACTS: *Note: Officers with more than one job title may be intentionally listed here more than once.*

James W. Owens, CEO
David B. Burritt, CFO/VP
Greg Folley, Chief Human Resources Officer
John S. Heller, CIO/VP
Tana L. Utley, CTO/VP
James B. Buda, General Counsel/VP/Corp. Sec.
Robert T. Williams, VP-Americas Oper.
Jananne A. Copeland, Chief Acct. Officer
Jiming Zhu, VP-China Div.
Mary H. Bell, VP-Building Construction Prod. Div.
Steven L. Fisher, VP-Remanufacturing Div.
Bradley M. Halverson, Controller
James W. Owens, Chmn.
Cristiano V. Schena, VP-EMEA
Daniel M. Murphy, VP-Global Purchasing

Phone: 309-675-1000	**Fax:** 309-675-4332
Toll-Free:	
Address: 100 NE Adams St., Peoria, IL 61629 US	

GROWTH PLANS/SPECIAL FEATURES:

Caterpillar, Inc. manufactures construction equipment. The company's three principal lines of business are machinery, engines and financial products. The machinery segment designs, manufactures and markets construction, mining, agricultural and forestry machinery, including track and wheel tractors and loaders, pipe layers, motor graders, wheel tractor-scrapers, track and wheel excavators, backhoe loaders, mining shovels, log skidders and loaders, off-highway trucks, articulated trucks, paving products, telescopic handlers, skid steer loaders and parts. The engines segment designs, manufactures and markets engines for Caterpillar machinery; electric power generation systems; on-highway vehicles and locomotives; marine, petroleum, construction, industrial, agricultural and other applications; and related parts. Caterpillar also manufactures fuel cells, designed to incorporate ethanol, methanol, natural gas, propane, methane, hydrogen and biomass fuels. The firm's Solar Turbines subsidiary is a world leader in industrial gas turbine power system engines. The financial products segment provides financing to customers and dealers for the purchase and lease of Caterpillar and other equipment, financing approximately 60% of equipment sold. Caterpillar has a network of 51 U.S. dealers and 127 outside of the U.S. Worldwide, these dealers serve 182 countries and operate 3,518 places of business, including rental outlets. More than half of the company's sales are to overseas customers. Caterpillar's logistics business provides supply chain services to Caterpillar and 50 other companies worldwide. Caterpillar also holds Progress Rail Services, a remanufacturer of locomotives and railcars. In 2009, the company opened a multi-functional research and development center in China. In 2010, the company announced its intent to join the FutureGen Alliance, a partnership that plans to build a near-zero emissions power plant in Illinois. In June 2010, the company agreed to purchase locomotive maker Electro-Motive Diesel for $ 820 million.

Caterpillar's employees are offered a 401(k) plan; medical insurance; flexible spending accounts; a Healthy Balance program, in which employees receive personalized health information, health club discounts, and health improvement programs; and Work.Life.Solutions, a program that offers counseling and legal advice.

FINANCIALS: **Sales and profits are in thousands of dollars—add 000 to get the full amount. 2009 Note: Financial information for 2009 was not available for all companies at press time.**

2009 Sales: $32,396,000	2009 Profits: $895,000	**U.S. Stock Ticker: CAT**
2008 Sales: $51,324,000	2008 Profits: $3,557,000	**Int'l Ticker:** Int'l Exchange:
2007 Sales: $44,958,000	2007 Profits: $3,541,000	Employees: 93,813
2006 Sales: $41,517,000	2006 Profits: $3,537,000	Fiscal Year Ends: 12/31
2005 Sales: $36,339,000	2005 Profits: $2,854,000	Parent Company:

SALARIES/BENEFITS:

Pension Plan: Y	ESOP Stock Plan:	Profit Sharing:	Top Exec. Salary: $1,550,004	Bonus: $4,353,227
Savings Plan: Y	Stock Purch. Plan:		Second Exec. Salary: $880,993	Bonus: $1,755,385

OTHER THOUGHTS:

Apparent Women Officers or Directors: 6
Hot Spot for Advancement for Women/Minorities: Y

LOCATIONS: ("Y" = Yes)

West:	Southwest:	Midwest:	Southeast:	Northeast:	International:
Y	Y	Y	Y	Y	Y

CERADYNE

www.ceradyne.com

Industry Group Code: 32712 **Ranks within this company's industry group:** Sales: 1 Profits: 1

Vehicle Manufacturing:		Dealers:		Parts:		Service:		Finance:		Specialty:	
Cars:		Car Dealer New:		Manufacturers:	Y	General Service:		Leasing:		Information Systems:	
Trucks:		Car Dealer Used:		Retail:		Specialty Service:		Auto Loans:		Online Marketing:	
Motorcycles:		Truck Dealer:		Distributors:		Oil Change:		Insurance:		Other:	Y
Specialty:		RV Dealer:		Tires:		Paint and Body:				Publishing:	
Buses:		Motorcycle Dealer:		Batteries:						Rental Cars/Trucks:	
RVs:		Specialty Dealer:									

TYPES OF BUSINESS:

Ceramic Materials
Defense & Armoring Products
Industrial Components
Orthodontic Materials
Medical Device Components
Diesel Engine Components

BRANDS/DIVISIONS/AFFILIATES:

Advanced Ceramics Operations
ESK Ceramics
Semicon Associates
Thermo Materials
Ceradyne Canada
Minco Inc
Boron
Diaphorm Technologies LLC

CONTACTS: *Note: Officers with more than one job title may be intentionally listed here more than once.*

Joel P. Moskowitz, CEO
Joel P. Moskowitz, Pres.
Jerrold J. Pellizzon, CFO
Jerrold J. Pellizzon, Corp. Sec.
Kenneth R. Morris, VP-Oper.
Thomas A. Cole, VP-Bus. Dev.
David P. Reed, VP/Pres., North American Oper.
Marc King, VP/Pres., Ceradyne Armor Systems, Inc.
Thomas Juengling, VP/Pres., ESK Ceramics
Bruce Lockhart, VP/Pres., Ceradyne Thermo Materials
Joel P. Moskowitz, Chmn.

Phone: 714-549-0421 **Fax:** 714-549-5787
Toll-Free: 800-839-2189
Address: 3169 Red Hill Ave., Costa Mesa, CA 92626 US

GROWTH PLANS/SPECIAL FEATURES:

Ceradyne, Inc., develops, manufactures and markets advanced technical ceramic products, ceramic powders and components. The firm offers these services for defense, industrial, automotive/diesel and commercial applications. Advanced technical ceramics withstand extremely high temperatures; combine hardness with lightweight; resist corrosion and wear; and have excellent electrical insulation capabilities, special electronic properties and low friction characteristics. Ceradyne conducts its business through 14 divisions and subsidiaries, including its Advanced Ceramics Operations, Semicon Associates, Thermo Materials and Boron Products divisions and ESK Ceramics, SemEquip, Inc. and Ceradyne Canada subsidiaries. Ceradyne's Advanced Ceramics Operations division produces lightweight armor for military applications; ceramic diesel engine components; and translucent ceramic orthodontic brackets. The Semicon Associates division provides ceramic-impregnated dispenser cathodes for microwave tubes, lasers and cathode ray tubes and Samarium cobalt magnets. The Thermo Materials division produces ceramic missile radomes (nose cones) and ceramic crucibles for melting silicon in the photovoltaic solar cell manufacturing process. Boron Products supplies neutron absorbing and reflecting components in materials with specific Boron isotopes, primarily used in the nuclear and semiconductor industries. ESK Ceramics produces water-resistant frictional automotive coatings; evaporation boats for the metallization of materials for packaging and other products; ceramic industrial components for erosion and corrosion resistant applications; ceramic powders used in manufacturing armor; and pump seals. SemEquip, Inc. develops cluster ion implantation sub-systems and advanced ion source materials for the production of memory and logic chips. Ceradyne Canada produces structural neutron absorbing materials in combination with aluminum metal matrix composites that serve as part of a barrier system for spent fuel storage and dry storage in the nuclear industry. The company's proprietary product is a ceramic powder used in ceramic body armor. In June 2009, Ceradyne acquired substantially all of the business, assets, technology and intellectual property of Diaphorm Technologies, LLC.

FINANCIALS: **Sales and profits are in thousands of dollars—add 000 to get the full amount. 2009 Note: Financial information for 2009 was not available for all companies at press time.**

2009 Sales: $400,575	2009 Profits: $8,515	**U.S. Stock Ticker: CRDN**
2008 Sales: $680,197	2008 Profits: $104,480	**Int'l Ticker:** Int'l Exchange:
2007 Sales: $756,835	2007 Profits: $142,183	Employees: 2,039
2006 Sales: $662,888	2006 Profits: $128,404	Fiscal Year Ends: 12/31
2005 Sales: $368,253	2005 Profits: $46,778	Parent Company:

SALARIES/BENEFITS:

Pension Plan: Y	ESOP Stock Plan:	Profit Sharing:	Top Exec. Salary: $710,008	Bonus: $167,747
Savings Plan: Y	Stock Purch. Plan:		Second Exec. Salary: $355,014	Bonus: $244,535

OTHER THOUGHTS:

Apparent Women Officers or Directors:
Hot Spot for Advancement for Women/Minorities:

LOCATIONS: ("Y" = Yes)

West:	Southwest:	Midwest:	Southeast:	Northeast:	International:
Y	Y	Y	Y	Y	Y

CERBERUS CAPITAL MANAGEMENT LP

www.cerberuscapital.com

Industry Group Code: 523910 **Ranks within this company's industry group:** Sales: Profits:

Vehicle Manufacturing:		Dealers:		Parts:		Service:		Finance:		Specialty:	
Cars:		Car Dealer New:	Y	Manufacturers:		General Service:		Leasing:	Y	Information Systems:	
Trucks:		Car Dealer Used:		Retail:		Specialty Service:		Auto Loans:	Y	Online Marketing:	
Motorcycles:		Truck Dealer:		Distributors:		Oil Change:		Insurance:		Other:	Y
Specialty:		RV Dealer:		Tires:		Paint and Body:				Publishing:	
Buses:	Y	Motorcycle Dealer:		Batteries:						Rental Cars/Trucks:	
RVs:	Y	Specialty Dealer:									

TYPES OF BUSINESS:

Private Equity Investments
Retailing Investments
Banking Investments
Bus Industry Investments
Entertainment Investments
Manufacturing Investments

BRANDS/DIVISIONS/AFFILIATES:

Tower Automotive LLC
Dyncorp International, Inc.
Aozora Bank, Ltd.
Albertson's LLC
Blue Bird Corporation
Spyglass Entertainment
NewPage Corp.
North American Bus Industries

CONTACTS: *Note: Officers with more than one job title may be intentionally listed here more than once.*

Stephen Feinberg, CEO
Mark Neporent, COO
Mark Neporent, General Counsel
John W. Snow, Chmn.

Phone: 212-891-2100	**Fax:**
Toll-Free:	
Address: 299 Park Ave., New York, NY 10171 US	

GROWTH PLANS/SPECIAL FEATURES:

Cerberus Capital Management, L.P. is a private equity firm with offices throughout the U.S., Europe and Asia. The firm's portfolio includes companies in the aerospace and defense; apparel; automotive and industrial; building products; commercial services; consumer and retail; financial services; healthcare; manufacturing and distribution; paper, packaging and printing; real estate; technology and telecommunications; transportation; and travel and leisure industries. Cerberus' equity investments include some of the largest companies in their respective sectors, including Albertson's LLC, a food retailer with over 300 stores across the U.S.; Blue Bird, a manufacturer of buses whose products are sold in more than 60 countries; NewPage Corporation, one of the largest printing paper manufacturers in North America; Spyglass Entertainment, a producer, distributor and financer of motion pictures; Tower Automotive, one of the largest global suppliers of automotive metal structural parts, with operations in 13 countries; and Aozora Bank, Ltd., which operates a network of 18 banks in Japan. Cerberus was also the majority owner of automobile manufacturer Chrysler prior to Chrysler's 2009 bankruptcy. By industry, the firm has 14% of its portfolio investments in financial services; 14% in business services; 12% in manufacturing; 9% each in technology and telecommunications; 8% each in automotive and consumer products; 4% each in software and logistics; 3% each in mortgage and healthcare; and 9% in other industries. Cerberus provides general and risk management, operations, human resources, sales and marketing, information technology, legal and procurement services to its investment companies. During 2009, Cerberus announced that major investors were seeking to withdraw about $4.77 billion from two of its funds. In July 2010, the firm acquired DynCorp International, Inc., a Virginia-based defense contractor and government services provider, for $1.5 billion.

FINANCIALS: **Sales and profits are in thousands of dollars—add 000 to get the full amount. 2009 Note: Financial information for 2009 was not available for all companies at press time.**

2009 Sales: $	2009 Profits: $	**U.S. Stock Ticker: Private**
2008 Sales: $	2008 Profits: $	**Int'l Ticker:** Int'l Exchange:
2007 Sales: $	2007 Profits: $	Employees:
2006 Sales: $	2006 Profits: $	Fiscal Year Ends: 12/31
2005 Sales: $	2005 Profits: $	Parent Company:

SALARIES/BENEFITS:

Pension Plan:	ESOP Stock Plan:	Profit Sharing:	Top Exec. Salary: $	Bonus: $
Savings Plan:	Stock Purch. Plan:		Second Exec. Salary: $	Bonus: $

OTHER THOUGHTS:

Apparent Women Officers or Directors:
Hot Spot for Advancement for Women/Minorities:

LOCATIONS: ("Y" = Yes)

West:	Southwest:	Midwest:	Southeast:	Northeast:	International:
Y		Y	Y	Y	Y

CHANGAN AUTOMOBILE GROUP

www.globalchana.com

Industry Group Code: 33611 **Ranks within this company's industry group:** Sales: 27 Profits: 15

Vehicle Manufacturing:		Dealers:		Parts:		Service:		Finance:		Specialty:	
Cars:	Y	Car Dealer New:		Manufacturers:		General Service:		Leasing:		Information Systems:	
Trucks:	Y	Car Dealer Used:		Retail:		Specialty Service:		Auto Loans:		Online Marketing:	
Motorcycles:		Truck Dealer:		Distributors:		Oil Change:		Insurance:		Other:	
Specialty:	Y	RV Dealer:		Tires:		Paint and Body:				Publishing:	
Buses:		Motorcycle Dealer:		Batteries:						Rental Cars/Trucks:	
RVs:		Specialty Dealer:									

TYPES OF BUSINESS:

Automobile Manufacturing

BRANDS/DIVISIONS/AFFILIATES:

CHANA
Chongqig Changang Automobile Company, Ltd.
Chongqing Chana Suzuki Automobile Co.
Chang'an Ford Nanjing Co., Ltd.
Chang'an Ford Maza Engine
Jiangxi Jiangling Co., Ltd.

CONTACTS:

Note: Officers with more than one job title may be intentionally listed here more than once.

Wu Xueson, VP-Chana Automobile Group
Yang Qing, Gen. Mgr.-Chana Int'l Corp.

Phone: 0086-23-67599888	**Fax:** 0086-23-67852882
Toll-Free:	
Address: 199 Wuhong Road, Chongqing, China	

GROWTH PLANS/SPECIAL FEATURES:

Changan Automobile Group is a government-owned Chinese automotive manufacturer that produces both consumer passenger cars and commercial vans and trucks, under the CHANA brand name. The company has four primary production bases in the provinces of Chongqing, Hebei, Jiangsu and Jiangxi. In total, these separate production bases include 11 complete vehicle plants and two engine plants, which feature an annual production capacity of 1.5 million vehicles and an equal number of engines. Changan also has six production bases in other Asian countries, as well as in North and South America, Africa, and Europe. The company's research and development operations include 3,000 technological and researching personnel who are based in five locations: the CHANA Auto European Design Center in Italy; the National Research Institute of Automotive Engineering in Chongqing, China; the Branch Automobile Research Institutes in Beijing and Shanghai; and the CHANA Auto Japan Design Center in Japan. Changan has three other research and development operations in Germany, Belgium and Austria. Its consumer passenger vehicles include the ALSVIN, a four-door compact sedan; the ALSVIN Hatchback; the Z-Shine four-door full-size sedan; the Benni Love, Benni Sport, and Benni Mini, all variations on a four-door compact hatchback. Changan's line of commercial vans includes the CHANA Star 2, Starlight 4500, SC6363, SC 6335, and the SC6395. Its two commercial trucks, the SC1022 and SC 1026, use the same chassis as its vans and include a full size cab with a low-rise or pallet bed. The company also has joint-ventures with Suzuki, Ford Motor Company, Mazda, and Volvo. The company sells its vehicles through independent retailer dealerships in 37 countries around the world. In June 2010, the company expanded its offering of the ALSVIN into Egypt through the Cairo International Auto Show.

FINANCIALS:

Sales and profits are in thousands of dollars—add 000 to get the full amount. 2009 Note: Financial information for 2009 was not available for all companies at press time.

2009 Sales: $3,702,070	2009 Profits: $158,420	**U.S. Stock Ticker: Government-Owned**
2008 Sales: $1,964,670	2008 Profits: $3,580	**Int'l Ticker: 200625** Int'l Exchange: Shanghai-SHE
2007 Sales: $2,015,610	2007 Profits: $97,960	Employees: 9,321
2006 Sales: $	2006 Profits: $	Fiscal Year Ends:
2005 Sales: $	2005 Profits: $	Parent Company:

SALARIES/BENEFITS:

Pension Plan:	ESOP Stock Plan:	Profit Sharing:	Top Exec. Salary: $	Bonus: $
Savings Plan:	Stock Purch. Plan:		Second Exec. Salary: $	Bonus: $

OTHER THOUGHTS:

Apparent Women Officers or Directors:
Hot Spot for Advancement for Women/Minorities:

LOCATIONS: ("Y" = Yes)

West:	Southwest:	Midwest:	Southeast:	Northeast:	International:
					Y

CHAPMAN AUTOMOTIVE GROUP LLC

www.chapmanchoice.com

Industry Group Code: 441110 **Ranks within this company's industry group:** Sales: Profits:

Vehicle Manufacturing:		Dealers:		Parts:		Service:		Finance:		Specialty:	
Cars:		Car Dealer New:	Y	Manufacturers:		General Service:	Y	Leasing:		Information Systems:	
Trucks:		Car Dealer Used:	Y	Retail:	Y	Specialty Service:		Auto Loans:		Online Marketing:	
Motorcycles:		Truck Dealer:		Distributors:		Oil Change:		Insurance:		Other:	Y
Specialty:		RV Dealer:		Tires:		Paint and Body:				Publishing:	
Buses:		Motorcycle Dealer:		Batteries:						Rental Cars/Trucks:	
RVs:		Specialty Dealer:									

TYPES OF BUSINESS:

Auto Dealers, Retail
Parts & Service
Fleet Sales

BRANDS/DIVISIONS/AFFILIATES:

GROWTH PLANS/SPECIAL FEATURES:

Chapman Automotive Group sells new and pre-owned vehicles throughout the states of Nevada and Arizona. With over 17,000 automobiles on its lots at any given time, the company sells Acura, Audi, BMW, Daimler, Chrysler, General Motors, Isuzu, Lincoln-Mercury, Porsche, Chevrolet, Honda, Mercedes and Volkswagen automobiles through approximately 24 dealerships. Chapman Automotive also provides part ordering services and maintenance and repair departments. Additionally, the company supplies the government with parts, trucks and cars and operates a fleet sales division. Jerry Chapman founded the business in 1978. In June 2009, the company opened a four-level, 30,000 square-foot BMW dealership in Phoenix, Arizona.

CONTACTS: *Note: Officers with more than one job title may be intentionally listed here more than once.*

Edward Davault, CEO
Ted Chapman, Pres.
David Bower, CFO
Nick Banker, Gen. Mgr.-Chapman Chrysler Jeep

Phone: 480-970-0740	**Fax:** 480-994-4096
Toll-Free:	
Address: 7455 W. Orchid Ln., Chandler, AZ 85226 US	

FINANCIALS: **Sales and profits are in thousands of dollars—add 000 to get the full amount. 2009 Note: Financial information for 2009 was not available for all companies at press time.**

2009 Sales: $	2009 Profits: $	**U.S. Stock Ticker: Private**
2008 Sales: $	2008 Profits: $	**Int'l Ticker:** Int'l Exchange:
2007 Sales: $	2007 Profits: $	Employees:
2006 Sales: $	2006 Profits: $	Fiscal Year Ends: 12/31
2005 Sales: $	2005 Profits: $	Parent Company:

SALARIES/BENEFITS:

Pension Plan:	ESOP Stock Plan:	Profit Sharing:	Top Exec. Salary: $	Bonus: $
Savings Plan:	Stock Purch. Plan:		Second Exec. Salary: $	Bonus: $

OTHER THOUGHTS:

Apparent Women Officers or Directors:
Hot Spot for Advancement for Women/Minorities:

LOCATIONS: ("Y" = Yes)

West:	Southwest:	Midwest:	Southeast:	Northeast:	International:
Y	Y				

CHRYSLER CANADA INC

www.chryslercanada.ca

Industry Group Code: 33611 **Ranks within this company's industry group:** Sales: Profits:

Vehicle Manufacturing:		Dealers:		Parts:		Service:		Finance:		Specialty:	
Cars:	Y	Car Dealer New:		Manufacturers:	Y	General Service:	Y	Leasing:		Information Systems:	
Trucks:	Y	Car Dealer Used:		Retail:		Specialty Service:		Auto Loans:		Online Marketing:	
Motorcycles:		Truck Dealer:		Distributors:		Oil Change:		Insurance:		Other:	Y
Specialty:		RV Dealer:		Tires:		Paint and Body:				Publishing:	
Buses:		Motorcycle Dealer:		Batteries:						Rental Cars/Trucks:	
RVs:		Specialty Dealer:									

TYPES OF BUSINESS:

Automobile Manufacturing
Automobile Distribution
Parts Manufacturing

BRANDS/DIVISIONS/AFFILIATES:

Chrysler Group LLC
Automotive Research & Development Centre
Mopar
Jeep
Dodge

CONTACTS:

Note: Officers with more than one job title may be intentionally listed here more than once.

Reid Bigland, CEO
Reid Bigland, Pres.
Edward G. Broadbear, VP-Mktg.
Lorraine (Lori) Shalhoub, General Counsel/Sec.
Lorraine (Lori) Shalhoub, VP-External Affairs & Public Policy
David G. Buckingham, VP-Sales

Phone: 519-973-2000	**Fax:** 519-973-2226
Toll-Free:	
Address: 1 Riverside Dr. W., Windsor, ON N9A 5K3 Canada	

GROWTH PLANS/SPECIAL FEATURES:

Chrysler Canada, Inc., a subsidiary of Chrysler Group LLC, manufactures and wholesales passenger cars, trucks and automotive components in Canada, including Chrysler passenger cars; Dodge cars, minivans and trucks; and Jeep SUVs. The company sells its vehicles through a network of approximately 450 dealers. The firm also markets Mopar parts and accessories. Chrysler Canada's vehicle production facilities include the Windsor assembly plant, which builds the Chrysler Town & Country, Dodge Grand Caravan and Volkswagen Routan; the Etobicoke Casting Plant in Toronto, which produces aluminum cast parts; and the Brampton assembly plant, which produces the Chrysler 300, Dodge Charger and Dodge Challenger. The company also operates regional parts distribution centers and sales offices across Canada, and operates the Automotive Research and Development Center in conjunction with the University of Windsor. In April 2009, Chrysler LLC filed for bankruptcy protection and temporarily halted vehicle production. In May 2009, Chrysler announced plans to close 789 dealerships, reducing its dealer network by 25%. In June 2009, Chrysler Group LLC emerged from bankruptcy. A subsidiary of Italian carmaker Fiat owns 20% equity in the new company, with arrangements to increase that ownership equity up to 35% if Chrysler's performance meets certain criteria. The United Auto Workers labor union owns about 55% of the company. The U.S. government owns about 8% and Canadian governments own about 2% of the company. Chrysler has received significant funding from the U.S. and Canadian governments. As part of the finalization of its partnership with Fiat, Chrysler Group LLC resumed production at seven North American plants, including all three of its Canadian facilities. In June 2009, production resumed at the Windsor plant. In August 2009, Chrysler Canada invested $600 million in a new paint shop for its Brampton plant.

FINANCIALS:

Sales and profits are in thousands of dollars—add 000 to get the full amount. 2009 Note: Financial information for 2009 was not available for all companies at press time.

2009 Sales: $	2009 Profits: $	**U.S. Stock Ticker: Subsidiary**
2008 Sales: $	2008 Profits: $	**Int'l Ticker:** Int'l Exchange:
2007 Sales: $	2007 Profits: $	Employees:
2006 Sales: $	2006 Profits: $	Fiscal Year Ends: 12/31
2005 Sales: $	2005 Profits: $	Parent Company: CHRYSLER GROUP LLC

SALARIES/BENEFITS:

Pension Plan:	ESOP Stock Plan:	Profit Sharing:	Top Exec. Salary: $	Bonus: $
Savings Plan:	Stock Purch. Plan:		Second Exec. Salary: $	Bonus: $

OTHER THOUGHTS:

Apparent Women Officers or Directors:
Hot Spot for Advancement for Women/Minorities:

LOCATIONS: ("Y" = Yes)

West:	Southwest:	Midwest:	Southeast:	Northeast:	International:
					Y

CHRYSLER FINANCIAL SERVICES LLC

www.chryslerfinancial.com

Industry Group Code: 522220 **Ranks within this company's industry group:** Sales: Profits:

Vehicle Manufacturing:		**Dealers:**		**Parts:**		**Service:**		**Finance:**		**Specialty:**	
Cars:		Car Dealer New:		Manufacturers:		General Service:		Leasing:	Y	Information Systems:	
Trucks:		Car Dealer Used:		Retail:		Specialty Service:		Auto Loans:	Y	Online Marketing:	
Motorcycles:		Truck Dealer:		Distributors:		Oil Change:		Insurance:	Y	Other:	Y
Specialty:		RV Dealer:		Tires:		Paint and Body:				Publishing:	
Buses:		Motorcycle Dealer:		Batteries:						Rental Cars/Trucks:	
RVs:		Specialty Dealer:									

TYPES OF BUSINESS:

Automobile Financing
Retail & Lease Financing
Property & Casualty Insurance
Dealership Retail Financing

BRANDS/DIVISIONS/AFFILIATES:

Chrysler Financial Services Canada
Cerberus Capital Management LP

CONTACTS:

Note: Officers with more than one job title may be intentionally listed here more than once.

Thomas F. Gilman, CEO
Darryl R. Jackson, COO
Lee Wilson, CFO
Machelle A. McAdory, VP-Human Resources
Machelle A. McAdory, VP-Admin. Svcs.
Tracy Hackman, General Counsel/VP/Sec.
Matt Thibaudeau, VP-Bus. Dev.
Machelle A. McAdory, VP-Comm.
Darcy Walker, Chief Risk Officer
Janet Toronski, VP-Dealer Credit & National Accounts
Thomas F. Gilman, Chmn.

Phone: 248-427-6800 **Fax:** 248-427-6600
Toll-Free:
Address: 27777 Inkster Rd., Farmington Hills, MI 48334 US

GROWTH PLANS/SPECIAL FEATURES:

Chrysler Financial Services LLC, formerly a part Chrysler LLC and a major lender to dealers and customers of Chrysler, provides retail vehicle loans and personal auto insurance. Following Chrysler LLC's filing for Chapter 11 bankruptcy protection in April 2009, GMAC Financial Services replaced Chrysler Financial Services as the primary retail and commercial lender for Chrysler dealers. Chrysler Financial Services has continued to offer a reduced amount of retail loans, while also managing its portfolio of $26 billion in active loans. In partnership with 21st Century Insurance, the firm offers auto insurance to owners of Chrysler, Jeep and Dodge vehicles. Specialty services include 24 hour roadside assistance, safe driver discounts and a guarantee that all repairs are made using genuine Mopar parts. Chrysler Financial Services is owned by private equity firm Cerberus Capital Management L.P. In June 2009, Chrysler Financial Services announced the restructuring of its business operations, including workforce reductions at each of the company's eight business centers, as well as its headquarters; the consolidation of all U.S. retail credit acquisition activities into its Great Lakes Business Center; and the closure of its Kansas City Customer Contact Center. In July 2009, the firm repaid in full its $1.5 billion Troubled Asset Relief Program (TARP) government loans.

Chrysler Financial Services offers its employees medical, dental and vision plans, incentive compensation plans and a 401(k) plan.

FINANCIALS:

Sales and profits are in thousands of dollars—add 000 to get the full amount. 2009 Note: Financial information for 2009 was not available for all companies at press time.

2009 Sales: $ 2009 Profits: $
2008 Sales: $ 2008 Profits: $
2007 Sales: $ 2007 Profits: $
2006 Sales: $ 2006 Profits: $
2005 Sales: $ 2005 Profits: $

U.S. Stock Ticker: Private
Int'l Ticker: Int'l Exchange:
Employees:
Fiscal Year Ends: 12/31
Parent Company: CERBERUS CAPITAL MANAGEMENT LP

SALARIES/BENEFITS:

Pension Plan: ESOP Stock Plan: Profit Sharing: Top Exec. Salary: $ Bonus: $
Savings Plan: Y Stock Purch. Plan: Second Exec. Salary: $ Bonus: $

OTHER THOUGHTS:

Apparent Women Officers or Directors: 4
Hot Spot for Advancement for Women/Minorities: Y

LOCATIONS: ("Y" = Yes)

West:	Southwest:	Midwest:	Southeast:	Northeast:	International:
	Y	Y	Y		

CHRYSLER GROUP LLC

www.chryslergroupllc.com

Industry Group Code: 33611 **Ranks within this company's industry group:** Sales: Profits:

Vehicle Manufacturing:		Dealers:		Parts:		Service:		Finance:		Specialty:	
Cars:	Y	Car Dealer New:		Manufacturers:	Y	General Service:		Leasing:	Y	Information Systems:	
Trucks:	Y	Car Dealer Used:		Retail:		Specialty Service:		Auto Loans:		Online Marketing:	
Motorcycles:		Truck Dealer:		Distributors:		Oil Change:		Insurance:		Other:	Y
Specialty:		RV Dealer:		Tires:		Paint and Body:				Publishing:	
Buses:		Motorcycle Dealer:		Batteries:						Rental Cars/Trucks:	
RVs:		Specialty Dealer:									

TYPES OF BUSINESS:

Auto Manufacturing
Research & Development
Nanotechnology-Coatings
Light Truck Manufacturing
Financial Services

BRANDS/DIVISIONS/AFFILIATES:

Jeep
Fiat SPA
Dodge
Jeep Wrangler Islander
Mopar
Jeep Wrangler Mountain
Liberty Renegade

CONTACTS: *Note: Officers with more than one job title may be intentionally listed here more than once.*

Sergio Marchionne, CEO
Nancy A. Rae, Exec. VP-Human Resources
Scott A. Sandschafer, CIO/VP
Steve Williams, Head-Advance Eng., Planning & Regulatory Affairs
Scott Garberding, Head-Mfg.
Stephen J. Bartoli, Head-Bus. Dev. & Integration
Walter P. Bodden, Jr., Treas./VP
Reid Bigland, Pres./CEO-Chrysler Canada
Doug D. Betts, Sr. VP-Quality
Joe Chama Srour, Pres./CEO-Chrysler Mexico
Michael Manley, Pres./CEO-Jeep Brand
C. Robert Kidder, Chmn.
Stephen J. Bartoli, Head-Int'l Prod. Planning

Phone: 248-576-5741	**Fax:**
Toll-Free: 800-992-1997	
Address: 1000 Chrysler Dr., Auburn Hills, MI 48326-2766 US	

GROWTH PLANS/SPECIAL FEATURES:

Chrysler Group LLC, formerly Chrysler LLC, manufactures, assembles and sells automobiles under the brands Chrysler, Jeep, Ram and Dodge. The firm has facilities in the U.S., Canada and Mexico. It also provides parts and accessories marketed under the Mopar brand. The firm is engaged in automotive-related research and is developing nanotechnologies to reduce air pollution while improving overall fuel-use efficiency. Chrysler Group's Global Electric Motorcars has developed six battery-electric vehicle models that have a maximum speed of 35 miles per hour and are ideal for use around sports stadiums, gated communities, city centers, resorts, job sites and neighborhoods. In April 2009, Chrysler LLC filed for bankruptcy protection. During Chrysler LLC's bankruptcy, GMAC Financial Services replaced Chrysler Financial Services as the primary retail and commercial lender for Chrysler dealers. In 2009, Chrysler closed 789 dealerships, reducing its dealer network by 25%. In June 2009, Chrysler Group LLC emerged from bankruptcy. A subsidiary of Italian carmaker Fiat owns 20% equity in the new company, with arrangements to increase that ownership equity up to 35% if Chrysler's performance meets certain criteria. The deal provides Chrysler access to Fiat's small car engineering and technology. Labor, in the form of the United Auto Workers union, owns about 55% of Chrysler Group. The U.S. government owns about 8% and Canadian governments own about 2% of the company. Upon finalization of the partnership with Fiat (also in June 2009), the new company began production at seven North American plants. In February 2010, Chrysler Group introduced three new Jeep models: Liberty Renegade, Jeep Wrangler Islander and Jeep Wrangler Mountain. Also in February 2010, the firm's Mopar brand launched live mobile television capabilities as an option for new Dodge, Chrylser, Ram and Jeep vehicles.

FINANCIALS: **Sales and profits are in thousands of dollars—add 000 to get the full amount. 2009 Note: Financial information for 2009 was not available for all companies at press time.**

2009 Sales: $	2009 Profits: $	**U.S. Stock Ticker: Private**
2008 Sales: $48,400,000	2008 Profits: $-16,800,000	**Int'l Ticker:** Int'l Exchange:
2007 Sales: $49,000,000	2007 Profits: $1,623,443	Employees: 49,500
2006 Sales: $63,294,342	2006 Profits: $	Fiscal Year Ends: 12/31
2005 Sales: $67,336,201	2005 Profits: $	Parent Company:

SALARIES/BENEFITS:

Pension Plan:	ESOP Stock Plan:	Profit Sharing:	Top Exec. Salary: $	Bonus: $
Savings Plan: Y	Stock Purch. Plan:		Second Exec. Salary: $	Bonus: $

OTHER THOUGHTS:

Apparent Women Officers or Directors: 1
Hot Spot for Advancement for Women/Minorities:

LOCATIONS: ("Y" = Yes)

West:	Southwest:	Midwest:	Southeast:	Northeast:	International:
Y	Y	Y	Y	Y	Y

CLARCOR INC

www.clarcor.com

Industry Group Code: 3363 **Ranks within this company's industry group:** Sales: 43 Profits: 10

Vehicle Manufacturing:		Dealers:		Parts:		Service:		Finance:		Specialty:	
Cars:		Car Dealer New:		Manufacturers:	Y	General Service:		Leasing:		Information Systems:	
Trucks:		Car Dealer Used:		Retail:		Specialty Service:		Auto Loans:		Online Marketing:	
Motorcycles:		Truck Dealer:		Distributors:		Oil Change:		Insurance:		Other:	Y
Specialty:		RV Dealer:		Tires:		Paint and Body:				Publishing:	
Buses:		Motorcycle Dealer:		Batteries:						Rental Cars/Trucks:	
RVs:		Specialty Dealer:									

TYPES OF BUSINESS:

Filtration Products & Services
Consumer Packaging

BRANDS/DIVISIONS/AFFILIATES:

Baldwin
CLC Air
J. L. Clark, Inc.
Airguard
Purolator
Pujiang Novaeastern International Mesh Co., Ltd.
Weifang Yuhua Filters, Ltd.
Quzhou Chinagrace Filter Co., Ltd.

CONTACTS: *Note: Officers with more than one job title may be intentionally listed here more than once.*

Norman E. Johnson, CEO
Christopher L. Conway, COO
Christopher L. Conway, Pres.
David J. Fallon, CFO
David J. Lindsay, VP-Admin./Chief Admin. Officer
Richard M. Wolfson, General Counsel/VP/Corp. Sec.
Richard C. Larson, Pres., Clarcor Air, Clark Filter, USA
Sam Ferrise, Pres., Baldwin Filters
Norman E. Johnson, Chmn.

Phone: 615-771-3100 **Fax:** 615-771-5603
Toll-Free:
Address: 840 Crescent Centre Dr., Ste. 600, Franklin, TN 37067 US

GROWTH PLANS/SPECIAL FEATURES:

Clarcor, Inc. provides filtration products and services organized into three segments: engine/mobile filtration, industrial/environmental filtration and consumer packaging. The engine/mobile filtration segment sells filtration products used on engines and in mobile equipment applications including trucks, automobiles, buses and locomotives; and marine, construction, industrial, mining and agricultural equipment. Products, marketed under the Baldwin, Hastings and Clark brands, include oil, air, fuel, coolant, transmission and hydraulic fluid filters. The segment's filters are sold in the global replacement market. The industrial/environmental filtration segment manufactures and markets filtration products used in industrial and commercial processes and in buildings and infrastructures, including in commercial buildings, hospitals, factories, residential buildings, vehicle cabins and compressors. Products, marketed under brands such as Airguard, ATI, Purolator, Facet, MKI and United Air Specialists, include industrial process liquid filters; pharmaceutical process and beverage filters; filtration systems, filters and coalescers for the oil and natural gas industry; filtration systems for aircraft refueling, anti-pollution, sewage treatment and water recycling; bilge water separators; sand control filters for oil and gas drilling; and woven wire and metallic products for plastics and polymer fiber filtration. Through its subsidiary CLC Air, the firm recently began marketing residential HVAC filters under the Purolator brand. The consumer packaging segment, through subsidiary J. L. Clark, Inc., manufactures different types and sizes of containers and packaging specialties. Manufactured metal, plastic and combination metal/plastic containers are used in packaging a variety of dry and paste form products, such as food specialties, tobacco products, toiletries, playing cards, cosmetics and pharmaceuticals. In 2009, 41% of sales came from the engine/mobile segment, 51% from industrial/environmental and 8% from consumer packaging. In 2009, the firm acquired several Chinese companies: Weifang Yuhua Filters, Ltd.; an 85% interest in Pujiang Novaeastern International Mesh Co., Ltd.; and Quzhou Chinagrace Filter Co., Ltd.

FINANCIALS: **Sales and profits are in thousands of dollars—add 000 to get the full amount. 2009 Note: Financial information for 2009 was not available for all companies at press time.**

2009 Sales: $907,700	2009 Profits: $71,500	**U.S. Stock Ticker: CLC**
2008 Sales: $1,059,601	2008 Profits: $95,654	**Int'l Ticker:** Int'l Exchange:
2007 Sales: $921,191	2007 Profits: $90,659	Employees: 4,958
2006 Sales: $904,347	2006 Profits: $82,710	Fiscal Year Ends: 11/30
2005 Sales: $873,974	2005 Profits: $76,393	Parent Company:

SALARIES/BENEFITS:

Pension Plan:	ESOP Stock Plan:	Profit Sharing:	Top Exec. Salary: $725,962	Bonus: $
Savings Plan:	Stock Purch. Plan:		Second Exec. Salary: $346,511	Bonus: $

OTHER THOUGHTS:

Apparent Women Officers or Directors:
Hot Spot for Advancement for Women/Minorities:

LOCATIONS: ("Y" = Yes)

West:	Southwest:	Midwest:	Southeast:	Northeast:	International:
Y	Y	Y	Y	Y	Y

CLARION CO LTD

www.clarion.com

Industry Group Code: 334310 **Ranks within this company's industry group:** Sales: 1 Profits: 1

Vehicle Manufacturing:		Dealers:		Parts:		Service:		Finance:		Specialty:	
Cars:		Car Dealer New:		Manufacturers:	Y	General Service:		Leasing:		Information Systems:	
Trucks:		Car Dealer Used:		Retail:		Specialty Service:		Auto Loans:		Online Marketing:	
Motorcycles:		Truck Dealer:		Distributors:		Oil Change:		Insurance:		Other:	Y
Specialty:		RV Dealer:		Tires:		Paint and Body:				Publishing:	
Buses:		Motorcycle Dealer:		Batteries:						Rental Cars/Trucks:	
RVs:		Specialty Dealer:									

TYPES OF BUSINESS:

Audio & Video Equipment, Manufacturing
Navigation Systems
Security Systems

BRANDS/DIVISIONS/AFFILIATES:

Clarion Corp. of America
Hitachi Ltd
Xanavi Informatics Corporation

CONTACTS:

Note: Officers with more than one job title may be intentionally listed here more than once.

Tom Hayashi, Pres.
Matt Matsuda, Pres., Clarion Corp. of America

Phone: 81-48-601-3700 **Fax:**
Toll-Free:
Address: 7-2 Shintoshin, Chuo-ku, Saitama-Shi, Saitama, 330-0081 Japan

GROWTH PLANS/SPECIAL FEATURES:

Clarion Co., Ltd., headquartered in Japan, develops audio technology for automobiles and recreational vehicles. Clarion's car audio-visual equipment segment, the firm's core segment, manufactures and sells car audio, navigation and multimedia equipment. These products are sold to individual customers, as well as to original equipment manufacturers in the automotive industry, such as Isuzu, Audi, Honda, Subaru, Mazda, Ford, Nissan, Porsche and Mitsubishi. The car audio-visual division also sells peripheral devices, such as cassettes, compact discs and audio speakers. Many of the company's navigation products also provide integration of software supporting terrestrial digital TV broadcasts, wireless communication using Bluetooths and information sharing with web content. The firm also makes products that connect to other digital media devices, such as iPods, digital cameras, USB drives, cell phones, digital audio players and personal computers, to the navigation, car audio and rear camera systems. Additional products include IT-based location systems and cameras and television checking systems for buses and public transportation, as well as auto-drive systems like the Intelligent Multimode Transit System (ITMS); rear cameras for improved behind-vehicle visibility; and the Drive Recorder system, which captures and records collisions. Clarion also markets its products in the U.S. through its subsidiary Clarion Corporation of America. The firm is a subsidiary of Hitachi, Ltd., a company with interests in IT, biotechnology and nanotechnology. In June 2010, Clarion announced a partnership with Nokia Corporation to develop Terminal Mode, a proposed industry standard for interaction between mobile devices and car information and media systems.

FINANCIALS:

Sales and profits are in thousands of dollars—add 000 to get the full amount. 2009 Note: Financial information for 2009 was not available for all companies at press time.

2009 Sales: $1,936,540 | 2009 Profits: $-213,190
2008 Sales: $2,632,550 | 2008 Profits: $14,700
2007 Sales: $1,683,700 | 2007 Profits: $-7,300
2006 Sales: $1,712,800 | 2006 Profits: $54,500
2005 Sales: $1,660,537 | 2005 Profits: $47,597

U.S. Stock Ticker: Subsidiary
Int'l Ticker: Int'l Exchange:
Employees:
Fiscal Year Ends: 3/31
Parent Company: HITACHI LTD

SALARIES/BENEFITS:

Pension Plan:	ESOP Stock Plan:	Profit Sharing:	Top Exec. Salary: $	Bonus: $
Savings Plan:	Stock Purch. Plan:		Second Exec. Salary: $	Bonus: $

OTHER THOUGHTS:

Apparent Women Officers or Directors:
Hot Spot for Advancement for Women/Minorities:

LOCATIONS: ("Y" = Yes)

West:	Southwest:	Midwest:	Southeast:	Northeast:	International:
Y	Y	Y	Y		Y

COAST DISTRIBUTION SYSTEM INC

www.coastdistribution.com

Industry Group Code: 423120 **Ranks within this company's industry group:** Sales: 2 Profits: 2

Vehicle Manufacturing:		**Dealers:**		**Parts:**		**Service:**		**Finance:**		**Specialty:**	
Cars:		Car Dealer New:		Manufacturers:		General Service:		Leasing:		Information Systems:	
Trucks:		Car Dealer Used:		Retail:		Specialty Service:		Auto Loans:		Online Marketing:	
Motorcycles:		Truck Dealer:		Distributors:	Y	Oil Change:		Insurance:		Other:	Y
Specialty:		RV Dealer:		Tires:		Paint and Body:				Publishing:	
Buses:		Motorcycle Dealer:		Batteries:						Rental Cars/Trucks:	
RVs:		Specialty Dealer:									

TYPES OF BUSINESS:

Automotive Products, Motors & Parts Distribution
Boat & RV Replacement Parts & Accessories

BRANDS/DIVISIONS/AFFILIATES:

Coast

CONTACTS:

Note: Officers with more than one job title may be intentionally listed here more than once.

James I. Musbach, CEO
James I. Musbach, Pres.
Sandra A. Knell, CFO
Dennis A. Castagnola, Exec. VP-Mfg. & New Prod. Dev.
David A. Berger, Exec. VP-Oper.
Sandra A. Knell, Exec. VP-Finance
Thomas R. McGuire, Chmn.
Stephan C. Lussier, Pres., Coast Distribution System (Canada), Inc.

Phone: 408-782-6686	**Fax:** 408-782-7790
Toll-Free:	
Address: 350 Woodview Ave., Morgan Hill, CA 95037 US	

GROWTH PLANS/SPECIAL FEATURES:

Coast Distribution System, Inc. is one of the largest wholesale suppliers of replacement parts, supplies and accessories for recreational vehicles (RVs) and boats in North America. The company supplies roughly 12,000 products and serves more than 18,000 RV dealers, independent RV accessories retailers and boating retailers throughout the U.S. and Canada from 13 regional distribution centers in the U.S., located in California, Texas, Oregon, Arizona, Colorado, Utah, Indiana, Pennsylvania, New York, Georgia, Florida and Wisconsin, and four regional distribution centers in Canada, located in Montreal, Toronto, Calgary and Vancouver. Coast utilizes a computer-based order entry and warehousing system, which enables customers to transmit orders either via telephone or electronically to the company, and enables Coast to prepare and invoice most orders within 24 hours of receipt. The firm's products include optional equipment and accessories, such as awnings, antennae, vents, electrical items, towing equipment and hitches; appliances such as air conditioners, refrigerators, ranges, generators, propane gas equipment, portable toilets and plumbing parts; hardware and tools; specialized recreational vehicle housewares; chemicals and supplies; and various other accessories, such as ladders, jacks, fans, load stabilizers, mirrors and compressors. Coast's boating and marine products include boat covers, stainless steel hardware, depth sounders, anchors, life jackets and other marine safety equipment and fishing equipment. In recent years, the firm has integrated its own brand of products into the market. These proprietary products are specially designed for the company by independent product design firms and manufactured, usually on an exclusive basis, by independent manufacturers primarily located in Asia.

Coast offers medical, dental, life and accident insurance; a 401(k) plan; and an employee stock purchase program, among other benefits.

FINANCIALS:

Sales and profits are in thousands of dollars—add 000 to get the full amount. 2009 Note: Financial information for 2009 was not available for all companies at press time.

2009 Sales: $103,201	2009 Profits: $ 99	**U.S. Stock Ticker: CRV**
2008 Sales: $132,237	2008 Profits: $-1,839	**Int'l Ticker:** Int'l Exchange:
2007 Sales: $164,293	2007 Profits: $ 215	Employees: 265
2006 Sales: $179,103	2006 Profits: $2,973	Fiscal Year Ends: 12/31
2005 Sales: $176,341	2005 Profits: $3,757	Parent Company:

SALARIES/BENEFITS:

Pension Plan:	ESOP Stock Plan:	Profit Sharing:	Top Exec. Salary: $330,770	Bonus: $
Savings Plan: Y	Stock Purch. Plan:		Second Exec. Salary: $250,000	Bonus: $

OTHER THOUGHTS:

Apparent Women Officers or Directors: 1
Hot Spot for Advancement for Women/Minorities:

LOCATIONS: ("Y" = Yes)

West:	Southwest:	Midwest:	Southeast:	Northeast:	International:
Y	Y	Y	Y	Y	Y

COBALT GROUP (THE)

www.cobaltgroup.com

Industry Group Code: 541810E **Ranks within this company's industry group:** Sales: Profits:

Vehicle Manufacturing:		Dealers:		Parts:		Service:		Finance:		Specialty:	
Cars:		Car Dealer New:		Manufacturers:		General Service:		Leasing:		Information Systems:	Y
Trucks:		Car Dealer Used:		Retail:		Specialty Service:		Auto Loans:		Online Marketing:	
Motorcycles:		Truck Dealer:		Distributors:		Oil Change:		Insurance:		Other:	Y
Specialty:		RV Dealer:		Tires:		Paint and Body:				Publishing:	
Buses:		Motorcycle Dealer:		Batteries:						Rental Cars/Trucks:	
RVs:		Specialty Dealer:									

TYPES OF BUSINESS:

Advertising-Automotive Dealerships & Manufacturers
Web-Based Software & CRM Tools
Training & Consulting Services
Media Services
Automotive Data Collection & Reporting
e-Commerce Services

BRANDS/DIVISIONS/AFFILIATES:

Cobalt Prospector
OnStation
Lead Manager Customer Central
Media Tracker
Nitra
PowerSearch Complete
IntegraLink
MotorPlace.com

CONTACTS: *Note: Officers with more than one job title may be intentionally listed here more than once.*

John Holt, CEO
Scott Mathews, COO/Exec. VP
Jim Beach, CFO/Exec. VP
Chris Reed, Chief Mktg. Officer/VP
Greg Meyer, Sr. VP-Tech.
Greg Meyer, Sr. VP-Prod.
Kevin Distelhorst, VP/Gen. Mgr.-IntegraLink
Anna Zornosa, Exec. VP/Gen. Mgr.-Dealix
John Holt, Chmn.

Phone: 206-269-6363 **Fax:** 206-269-6350
Toll-Free: 866-289-2786
Address: 2200 1st Ave. S., Ste. 400, Seattle, WA 98134 US

GROWTH PLANS/SPECIAL FEATURES:

The Cobalt Group provides Internet marketing solutions for auto dealerships and manufacturers. The company partners with two-thirds of major automotive manufacturers worldwide. Cobalt's customer relationship management (CRM) offerings are Cobalt Prospector, automating sales force and showroom floor operations; OnStation, providing e-mail and direct mail marketing campaigns; Lead Manager Customer Central, a lead management and CRM solution; and Media Tracker, an advertising performance measurement system. The company's online retailing products are based on the Nitra brand web site system, which is designed solely for automobile dealers and includes software add-ons for lead management, image marketing, advanced vehicle research, Spanish-language marketing and inventory marketing. Cobalt's PowerSearch Complete provides organic and paid Internet search engine traffic strategies through relationships with Google, Yahoo! and MSN. The company provides third-party leads through its Dealix division. In addition to its software products, the company provides a variety of services. Its automotive marketing services include web site design and management tools; Internet advertising; third-party leads; lead management; owner marketing; and reporting and analytics. Cobalt's program management services include program design consultation; custom solutions and performance reports; and Thought Leadership, providing research-based industry insight. Consulting and training services offered by Cobalt include eDealer Consultants in-person field training and eCare and ProCare customer support. Additional services include dealership management system (DMS) data management, a service offered through the company's Integralink division. Cobalt also operates motorplace.com, a dealer-to-dealer e-commerce marketplace. The firm is owned by investment firms Warburg Pincus; ABS Capital Partners; and Oak Investment Partners.

FINANCIALS: **Sales and profits are in thousands of dollars—add 000 to get the full amount. 2009 Note: Financial information for 2009 was not available for all companies at press time.**

2009 Sales: $	2009 Profits: $	**U.S. Stock Ticker: Private**
2008 Sales: $	2008 Profits: $	**Int'l Ticker:** Int'l Exchange:
2007 Sales: $	2007 Profits: $	Employees:
2006 Sales: $	2006 Profits: $	Fiscal Year Ends: 12/31
2005 Sales: $	2005 Profits: $	Parent Company:

SALARIES/BENEFITS:

Pension Plan:	ESOP Stock Plan:	Profit Sharing:	Top Exec. Salary: $	Bonus: $
Savings Plan:	Stock Purch. Plan:		Second Exec. Salary: $	Bonus: $

OTHER THOUGHTS:

Apparent Women Officers or Directors: 1
Hot Spot for Advancement for Women/Minorities:

LOCATIONS: ("Y" = Yes)

West:	Southwest:	Midwest:	Southeast:	Northeast:	International:
Y	Y	Y	Y	Y	

CODA AUTOMOTIVE INC

www.codaautomotive.com

Industry Group Code: 33611 **Ranks within this company's industry group:** Sales: Profits:

Vehicle Manufacturing:		Dealers:		Parts:		Service:		Finance:		Specialty:	
Cars:	Y	Car Dealer New:		Manufacturers:		General Service:		Leasing:		Information Systems:	
Trucks:		Car Dealer Used:		Retail:		Specialty Service:		Auto Loans:		Online Marketing:	
Motorcycles:		Truck Dealer:		Distributors:		Oil Change:		Insurance:		Other:	
Specialty:		RV Dealer:		Tires:		Paint and Body:				Publishing:	
Buses:		Motorcycle Dealer:		Batteries:	Y					Rental Cars/Trucks:	
RVs:		Specialty Dealer:									

TYPES OF BUSINESS:

Electric Automobile Manufacturing

BRANDS/DIVISIONS/AFFILIATES:

CODA Sedan

CONTACTS:

Note: Officers with more than one job title may be intentionally listed here more than once.

Kevin Czinger, CEO
Kevin Czinger, Pres.
Dan Mosher, CFO
Michael A. Jackson, Sr. VP-Global Sales
Broc TenHouten, Sr. VP-Eng. & Project Mgmt.
Lino Lauro, General Counsel
Sean Blankenship, VP-Mktg., Digital & Media
K. Forrest Beanum, VP-Public Affairs & Comm.
Bruce Shibuya, Sr. VP-Quality Eng., Parts & Service
Phillippe Gow, VP-Battery Systems
Mark Atkeson, Sr. VP-China Oper.
Michael A. Jackson, Sr. VP-Dist.

Phone: 310-390-4890	**Fax:** 310-397-8985
Toll-Free:	
Address: 1601 Wilshire Blvd., Santa Monica, CA 90403 US	

GROWTH PLANS/SPECIAL FEATURES:

CODA Automotive, Inc. designs, develops and, with its joint-venture partners, builds electric vehicles under the CODA Automotive brand name. CODA was launched in 2009 by Miles Rubin, who also founded Miles Electric Vehicles, a manufacturer of low speed electric fleet vehicles. CODA's first car, the CODA Sedan, is assembled in China by Hafei Automobile Group and is based on a Hafei chassis re-engineered by Porsche Engineering. After the chassis is finished in China, it is shipped to the U.S. for installation of electric power-train components. The components for the car are manufactured by American suppliers, including UQM Technologies, which provides the motor; Delphi; BorgWarner; and Nexteer Automotive. The CODA Sedan is powered by a 333V Lithium-Ion battery that can provide 134 horsepower. CODA produces its batteries through a joint venture with Chinese battery cell supplier Tianjin Lishen Power Battery, known as Lio Energy Systems. The Tianjin battery production facility has a capacity of 20,000 battery packs per year. The CODA Sedan has a range of 90-120 miles on a six-hour charge, can accelerate from 0-60 in under 11 seconds and has a maximum speed of 80 miles per hour. The battery pack can be charged at any standard outlet, but charges most efficiently from a 220 volt outlet, such as those used for laundry machines. The CODA Sedan also has a regenerative braking system that stores and reuses the kinetic energy produced when the cars brakes are utilized. The sedan is currently available for pre-sales on the company's website, where potential customers can also sign up for the priority waiting list. Sales will initially be restricted to California.

FINANCIALS:

Sales and profits are in thousands of dollars—add 000 to get the full amount. 2009 Note: Financial information for 2009 was not available for all companies at press time.

2009 Sales: $	2009 Profits: $	**U.S. Stock Ticker: Subsidiary**
2008 Sales: $	2008 Profits: $	**Int'l Ticker:** Int'l Exchange:
2007 Sales: $	2007 Profits: $	Employees:
2006 Sales: $	2006 Profits: $	Fiscal Year Ends:
2005 Sales: $	2005 Profits: $	Parent Company: MILES ELECTRIC VEHICLES

SALARIES/BENEFITS:

Pension Plan:	ESOP Stock Plan:	Profit Sharing:	Top Exec. Salary: $	Bonus: $
Savings Plan:	Stock Purch. Plan:		Second Exec. Salary: $	Bonus: $

OTHER THOUGHTS:

Apparent Women Officers or Directors:
Hot Spot for Advancement for Women/Minorities:

LOCATIONS: ("Y" = Yes)

West:	Southwest:	Midwest:	Southeast:	Northeast:	International:
Y					Y

COLLINS INDUSTRIES INC

www.collinsind.com

Industry Group Code: 336120 **Ranks within this company's industry group:** Sales: Profits:

Vehicle Manufacturing:		Dealers:		Parts:		Service:		Finance:		Specialty:	
Cars:		Car Dealer New:		Manufacturers:		General Service:		Leasing:		Information Systems:	
Trucks:	Y	Car Dealer Used:		Retail:		Specialty Service:		Auto Loans:		Online Marketing:	
Motorcycles:		Truck Dealer:		Distributors:		Oil Change:		Insurance:		Other:	
Specialty:	Y	RV Dealer:		Tires:		Paint and Body:				Publishing:	
Buses:	Y	Motorcycle Dealer:		Batteries:						Rental Cars/Trucks:	
RVs:		Specialty Dealer:									

TYPES OF BUSINESS:

Trucks, RVs & Misc. Automotive, Manufacturing
Buses
Ambulances
Terminal Trucks
Road Construction Equipment
Sweeper Equipment

BRANDS/DIVISIONS/AFFILIATES:

Collins Bus Corporation
Mid Bus Corporation
Corbeil Bus Corporation
Wheeled Coach Industries
Capacity of Texas
World Trans, Inc.
Lay-Mor
Vehicle Acquisition, Inc.

CONTACTS: *Note: Officers with more than one job title may be intentionally listed here more than once.*

Randall Swift, CEO
Randall Swift, Pres.
Hans H. Heinsen, CFO/VP
John L. Dreasher, VP-Human Resources
Ron Sorensen, VP-Risk Mgmt.
Kent Tyler, Pres., Collins Bus Corp.

Phone: 620-663-5551	**Fax:** 620-663-1630
Toll-Free:	
Address: 15 Compound Dr., Hutchinson, KS 67502 US	

GROWTH PLANS/SPECIAL FEATURES:

Collins Industries, Inc., owned by Vehicle Acquisition, Inc., is a mid-sized manufacturer of specialty vehicles and accessories for various basic service niches in the transportation industry. The company's products include ambulances; small school buses; shuttle and mid-sized commercial buses; terminal trucks; commercial bus chassis; road construction equipment; and industrial rental sweepers. The company's innovations include the Moduvan ambulance, the first ambulance of its size with advanced life-support system capability; the Dura-Ride suspension system, the first frame-isolating suspension system for terminal trucks; and the Type A Super Bantam, a relatively small school bus with space for 35 passengers, one of the largest capacities available for that size. Collins is one of the largest U.S. manufacturers of ambulances and terminal trucks, and a leading manufacturer of small school buses and sweepers used in the road construction industry. Subsidiaries include school bus manufacturers Collins Bus Corporation, Mid Bus Corporation and Corbeil Bus Corporation; Wheeled Coach Industries, a leading manufacturer of ambulances and emergency service vehicles; Capacity of Texas, a manufacturer of specialty vehicles used to move semi trailer equipment; World Trans, Inc., a manufacturer of small to mid-sized buses for transit, charter, airport and shuttle applications; and Lay-Mor, a manufacturer of rental equipment, street sweepers and loader backhoes. In April 2009, Collins Bus Corporation entered into an agreement with Azure Dynamics to develop a line of Type A buses based on hybrid electric technology. In September 2009, the company entered an agreement with CleanFUEL USA to develop a Type A bus utilizing autogas with a Liquid Propane Injection (LPI) system. In February 2010, control of the company was purchased from Steel Partners II by Vehicle Acquisition, Inc.

Collins offers its employees tuition reimbursement; an employee assistance program; bonus opportunities; and medical, dental, prescription, life and disability insurance.

FINANCIALS: **Sales and profits are in thousands of dollars—add 000 to get the full amount. 2009 Note: Financial information for 2009 was not available for all companies at press time.**

2009 Sales: $	2009 Profits: $	**U.S. Stock Ticker: Private**
2008 Sales: $	2008 Profits: $	**Int'l Ticker:** Int'l Exchange:
2007 Sales: $127,400	2007 Profits: $	Employees:
2006 Sales: $	2006 Profits: $	Fiscal Year Ends: 10/31
2005 Sales: $269,448	2005 Profits: $2,240	Parent Company: VEHICLE ACQUISITION INC

SALARIES/BENEFITS:

Pension Plan:	ESOP Stock Plan:	Profit Sharing:	Top Exec. Salary: $	Bonus: $
Savings Plan: Y	Stock Purch. Plan:		Second Exec. Salary: $	Bonus: $

OTHER THOUGHTS:

Apparent Women Officers or Directors:
Hot Spot for Advancement for Women/Minorities:

LOCATIONS: ("Y" = Yes)

West:	Southwest:	Midwest:	Southeast:	Northeast:	International:
	Y	Y	Y		

COMMERCIAL VEHICLE GROUP INC (CVG)

www.cvgrp.com

Industry Group Code: 3363 **Ranks within this company's industry group:** Sales: 50 Profits: 45

Vehicle Manufacturing:		Dealers:		Parts:		Service:		Finance:		Specialty:	
Cars:		Car Dealer New:		Manufacturers:	Y	General Service:		Leasing:		Information Systems:	
Trucks:		Car Dealer Used:		Retail:		Specialty Service:		Auto Loans:		Online Marketing:	
Motorcycles:		Truck Dealer:		Distributors:		Oil Change:		Insurance:		Other:	
Specialty:		RV Dealer:		Tires:		Paint and Body:				Publishing:	
Buses:		Motorcycle Dealer:		Batteries:						Rental Cars/Trucks:	
RVs:		Specialty Dealer:									

TYPES OF BUSINESS:

Commercial Cab Structures & Components
Suspension Seat Systems
Interior Trim Systems
Mirrors & Wiper Systems
Electronic Wire Harness Assemblies & Controls
Switches

BRANDS/DIVISIONS/AFFILIATES:

ComforTEK

CONTACTS:

Note: Officers with more than one job title may be intentionally listed here more than once.

Mervin Dunn, CEO
Mervin Dunn, Pres.
Chad M. Utrup, CFO
W. Gordon Boyd, Pres., Seating Systems
Gerald L. Armstrong, Gen. Mgr./Pres., Cab Systems
Kevin R. L. Frailey, Exec. VP/Gen. Mgr.-Electrical Systems
Milton D. Kniss, Exec. VP/Gen. Mgr.-Seating Systems
Richard A. Snell, Chmn.

Phone: 614-289-5360	**Fax:** 614-289-5361
Toll-Free:	
Address: 6530 W. Campus Way, New Albany, OH 43054 US	

GROWTH PLANS/SPECIAL FEATURES:

Commercial Vehicle Group, Inc. (CVG) is a supplier of fully integrated system solutions for the global commercial vehicle market, including the heavy-duty truck market; the construction and agriculture markets; and the specialty and military transportation markets. The company's products include static and suspension seat systems; electronic wire harness assemblies; controls and switches; cab structures and components; interior trim systems, including instrument panels, door panels, headliners, cabinetry and floor systems; and mirrors and wiper systems specifically designed for applications in commercial vehicles. In 2009, the truck market accounted for 48% of the company's 2009 revenues; construction market, 15%; military market, 10%; and aftermarket and service organizations, 14%. The remaining 13% was derived primarily from other global commercial vehicle and specialty markets. The company has U.S. operations in Arizona, Indiana, Illinois, Iowa, Michigan, North Carolina, Ohio, Oregon, Tennessee, Texas, Virginia and Washington; and foreign operations in Australia, Belgium, Czech Republic, China, Mexico, Ukraine and the U.K. In September 2009, the firm launched its ComforTEK high performance flooring system, which uses a layer of bonded, flexible polyurethane foam substructure that maximizes thermal properties. In December 2009, CVG announced plans to close its Norwalk, Ohio truck cab assembly facility. In July 2010, the company was selected by XCMG to be a seat supplier for its family of products. CVG will provide a range of construction seating products for multiple XCMG vehicle lines including mobile cranes, wheel loaders, rollers, graders, excavators, truck cranes and concrete pumps.

Employees are offered medical, dental, vision and life insurance; and a 401(k) plan.

FINANCIALS:

Sales and profits are in thousands of dollars—add 000 to get the full amount. 2009 Note: Financial information for 2009 was not available for all companies at press time.

2009 Sales: $458,569	2009 Profits: $-81,535	**U.S. Stock Ticker: CVGI**
2008 Sales: $763,489	2008 Profits: $-206,759	**Int'l Ticker:** Int'l Exchange:
2007 Sales: $696,786	2007 Profits: $-3,251	Employees: 4,551
2006 Sales: $918,751	2006 Profits: $58,050	Fiscal Year Ends: 12/31
2005 Sales: $754,481	2005 Profits: $49,411	Parent Company:

SALARIES/BENEFITS:

Pension Plan:	ESOP Stock Plan:	Profit Sharing:	Top Exec. Salary: $582,854	Bonus: $
Savings Plan: Y	Stock Purch. Plan:		Second Exec. Salary: $411,268	Bonus: $

OTHER THOUGHTS:

Apparent Women Officers or Directors:
Hot Spot for Advancement for Women/Minorities:

LOCATIONS: ("Y" = Yes)

West:	Southwest:	Midwest:	Southeast:	Northeast:	International:
Y	Y	Y	Y	Y	Y

COMPAGNIE GENERALE DES ETABLISSEMENTS MICHELIN

www.michelin.com

Industry Group Code: 3262 **Ranks within this company's industry group:** Sales: 3 Profits: 2

Vehicle Manufacturing:		**Dealers:**		**Parts:**		**Service:**		**Finance:**		**Specialty:**	
Cars:		Car Dealer New:		Manufacturers:		General Service:		Leasing:		Information Systems:	
Trucks:		Car Dealer Used:		Retail:		Specialty Service:		Auto Loans:		Online Marketing:	
Motorcycles:		Truck Dealer:		Distributors:		Oil Change:		Insurance:		Other:	Y
Specialty:		RV Dealer:		Tires:	Y	Paint and Body:				Publishing:	Y
Buses:		Motorcycle Dealer:		Batteries:						Rental Cars/Trucks:	
RVs:		Specialty Dealer:									

TYPES OF BUSINESS:

Plastics & Rubber, Manufacturing
Tire Production
Tourism Services
Maps, Guidebooks & Atlases

BRANDS/DIVISIONS/AFFILIATES:

Uniroyal
Kleber
BFGoodrich
ViaMichelin
Warrior
Michelin Lifestyle
Manufacture Francaise des Pneumatiques Michelin
Compagnie Financiere Michelin

CONTACTS: *Note: Officers with more than one job title may be intentionally listed here more than once.*

Michel Rollier, Managing Partner
Didier Miraton, Managing Partner
Eric de Cromieres, Dir.-Mktg. & Sales
Jean-Michel Guillon, Dir.-Human Resources & Organization
Jean-Christope Guerin, Dir.-Mfg. Performance
Claire Dorland-Clauzel, Dir.-Comm.
Valerie Magloire, Contact-Investor Rel.
Jean-Dominique Senard, Managing Partner
Florent Menegaux, Dir.-Passenger Car & Light Truck Prod. Line
Pete Selleck, Dir.-Truck Prod. Line
Bernard Vasdeboncoeur, Dir.-Specialty Prod. Lines
Eric Bourdais de Charbonniere, Chmn.
Jean-Christophe Guerin, Supervisor-Supply Chain & Quality

Phone: 33-4-73-32-20-00 **Fax:**

Toll-Free:

Address: 23, place des Carmes-Dechaux, Clermont-Ferrand, 63040 France

GROWTH PLANS/SPECIAL FEATURES:

Compagnie Generale des Etablissements Michelin (CGEM), based in France, is a worldwide corporation best known for its production of Michelin tires for cars, trucks, aircraft, earthmovers and motorcycles. The company is one of the world's largest tire producers, with 72 production facilities in 19 countries and marketing operations in 170 countries. The company operates through two primary subsidiaries: Compagnie Financiere Michelin (CFM), which is responsible for overseeing industrial, commercial and research subsidiaries outside of France; and Manufacture Francaise des Pneumatiques Michelin, which is 40% controlled by CGEM and 60% controlled by CFM and which is responsible for industrial and commercial subsidiaries in France. These subsidiaries offer three lines of products and services consisting of tires, travel assistance services and lifestyle products. The travel assistance services incorporate a number of maps and guides including national maps, local maps, area maps, atlases, city maps, European tourist guidebooks and cultural guidebooks for regions around the world. Michelin's travel assistance services include a number of digital offerings such as navigation software for handheld computers; ViaMichelin, which delivers full color maps to cellular phones and offers a full-service navigational website for drivers, pedestrians, and cyclists; and Michelin Guide, a restaurant and hotel information resource available for mobile phones as well as in print. The company's lifestyle products include automotive and cycle related products such as pumps, pressure gauges, safety accessories, and wheel and tire changing products and transportation accessories. In January 2010, the company announced the end of tire production in Ota, Japan. The site maintains its research and development operations. In February 2010, CGEM sold its 30% share in Shanghai Michelin Warrior Tire Company, Ltd. The Chinese company will continue to allow Michelin usage of the Warrior trademark.

The firm offers North American employees medical, dental and life insurance and employee assistance programs.

FINANCIALS: **Sales and profits are in thousands of dollars—add 000 to get the full amount. 2009 Note: Financial information for 2009 was not available for all companies at press time.**

2009 Sales: $18,288,900	2009 Profits: $130,930	**U.S. Stock Ticker:**
2008 Sales: $22,807,100	2008 Profits: $500,400	**Int'l Ticker: ML** Int'l Exchange: Paris-Euronext
2007 Sales: $23,445,100	2007 Profits: $1,075,900	Employees:
2006 Sales: $22,773,800	2006 Profits: $795,100	Fiscal Year Ends: 12/31
2005 Sales: $19,371,600	2005 Profits: $1,104,600	Parent Company:

SALARIES/BENEFITS:

Pension Plan: Y	ESOP Stock Plan: Y	Profit Sharing:	Top Exec. Salary: $	Bonus: $
Savings Plan: Y	Stock Purch. Plan:		Second Exec. Salary: $	Bonus: $

OTHER THOUGHTS:

Apparent Women Officers or Directors: 3
Hot Spot for Advancement for Women/Minorities: Y

LOCATIONS: ("Y" = Yes)

West:	Southwest:	Midwest:	Southeast:	Northeast:	International:
	Y	Y	Y	Y	Y

COMPAGNIE PLASTIC OMNIUM

www.plasticomnium.com

Industry Group Code: 3363 **Ranks within this company's industry group:** Sales: 27 Profits: 17

Vehicle Manufacturing:		Dealers:		Parts:		Service:		Finance:		Specialty:	
Cars:		Car Dealer New:		Manufacturers:	Y	General Service:		Leasing:		Information Systems:	
Trucks:		Car Dealer Used:		Retail:		Specialty Service:		Auto Loans:		Online Marketing:	
Motorcycles:		Truck Dealer:		Distributors:		Oil Change:		Insurance:		Other:	Y
Specialty:		RV Dealer:		Tires:		Paint and Body:				Publishing:	
Buses:		Motorcycle Dealer:		Batteries:						Rental Cars/Trucks:	
RVs:		Specialty Dealer:									

TYPES OF BUSINESS:

Plastics & Rubber, Manufacturing
Automotive Fuel Systems
Exterior Panels & Trim
Waste Container Manufacturing & Related Services
Playgrounds

BRANDS/DIVISIONS/AFFILIATES:

Inergy Automotive Systems
Plastic Omnium Auto Exterior
Hella-Behr-Plastic Omnium (HBPO)
Inoplast
InoPlastic Omnium (iPO)
Compagnie Signature
Plastic Omnium Environment
Ludoparc SA

CONTACTS:

Note: Officers with more than one job title may be intentionally listed here more than once.

Laurent Burelle, CEO
Paul Henry Lemarie, Co-COO
Jean-Michel Szczerba, Co-COO
Didier Fontaine, CFO/Exec. VP
Phillippe Hugon, Exec. VP-Human Resources
Jean-Luc Petit, Corp. Sec./VP-Legal Affairs
Adeline Mickeler, Exec. VP-Corp. Planning & M&A
Marc Szulewicz, Pres., Plastic Omnium Auto Exterior
Pierre Lecocq, CEO-Inergy Automotive Systems
Michel Kempinski, Pres., Plastic Omnium Environment
Laurent Burelle, Chmn.

Phone: 33-1-40-87-64-00	Fax: 33-1-47-39-78-98
Toll-Free:	
Address: 1 rue du Parc, Levallois, 92593 France	

GROWTH PLANS/SPECIAL FEATURES:

Compagnie Plastic Omnium (PO) is a leading plastics and automotive equipment manufacturer. The company operates in two primary segments: Automotive Equipment, which generated roughly 82% of 2009 revenues, and Environment, which generated approximately 18%. The Automotive Equipment segment consists of two companies. Joint venture Inergy Automotive Systems, with Belgian chemical company Solvay S.A., is a world leader in the supply of automotive fuel systems, including hybrid vehicle fuel systems and fuel tanks adapted to accommodate biodiesel. Plastic Omnium Auto Exterior (PO Auto Exterior) designs and produces bumpers, fenders, front- and rear-end modules and energy absorption systems. PO Auto Exterior also controls 33.3% of Hella-Behr-Plastic Omnium (HBPO), jointly owned with Hella and Behr, which produces front-ends; 100% of Inoplast, one of Europe's leading exterior auto parts producers; and 100% of InoPlastic Omnium (iPO), which makes rear hatchbacks. The Environment segment consists primarily of the following two major companies. Compagnie Signature mainly manufactures road signage for western European countries. Plastic Omnium Environment, meanwhile, serves communities, companies and municipalities worldwide, offering wheeled containers and public waste drop-off structures, with related services including installation, maintenance and repair. It also designs and installs plastic playground equipment through Ludoparc SA. During 2009, France accounted for approximately 30% of sales; the remainder of Europe accounted for 40%; North America accounted for 17%; while Asia, Africa and South America together generated 13% of sales. In June 2009, the company announced that its Inergy Automotive Systems joint venture would build two new fuel systems plants, one located near Beijing, in China, and the other in the vicinity of Chennai, in eastern India. In June 2010, the firm announced plans to acquire Solvay's 50% share of Inergy Automotive Systems, making it a wholly-owned subsidiary of Compagnie Plastic Omnium.

FINANCIALS:

Sales and profits are in thousands of dollars—add 000 to get the full amount. 2009 Note: Financial information for 2009 was not available for all companies at press time.

2009 Sales: $3,106,200	2009 Profits: $35,250	**U.S. Stock Ticker:**
2008 Sales: $3,748,100	2008 Profits: $-90,900	**Int'l Ticker: POM** Int'l Exchange: Paris-Euronext
2007 Sales: $3,732,300	2007 Profits: $68,600	Employees:
2006 Sales: $3,232,600	2006 Profits: $65,300	Fiscal Year Ends: 12/31
2005 Sales: $2,582,950	2005 Profits: $55,450	Parent Company:

SALARIES/BENEFITS:

Pension Plan:	ESOP Stock Plan:	Profit Sharing:	Top Exec. Salary: $	Bonus: $
Savings Plan:	Stock Purch. Plan:		Second Exec. Salary: $	Bonus: $

OTHER THOUGHTS:

Apparent Women Officers or Directors: 3
Hot Spot for Advancement for Women/Minorities: Y

LOCATIONS: ("Y" = Yes)

West:	Southwest:	Midwest:	Southeast:	Northeast:	International:
	Y	Y	Y	Y	Y

CONSUMER PORTFOLIO SERVICES INC www.consumerportfolio.com

Industry Group Code: 522220 **Ranks within this company's industry group:** Sales: 4 Profits: 3

Vehicle Manufacturing:		Dealers:		Parts:		Service:		Finance:		Specialty:	
Cars:		Car Dealer New:		Manufacturers:		General Service:		Leasing:		Information Systems:	
Trucks:		Car Dealer Used:		Retail:		Specialty Service:		Auto Loans:	Y	Online Marketing:	
Motorcycles:		Truck Dealer:		Distributors:		Oil Change:		Insurance:		Other:	
Specialty:		RV Dealer:		Tires:		Paint and Body:				Publishing:	
Buses:		Motorcycle Dealer:		Batteries:						Rental Cars/Trucks:	
RVs:		Specialty Dealer:									

TYPES OF BUSINESS:

Automobile Financing

BRANDS/DIVISIONS/AFFILIATES:

CONTACTS:

Note: Officers with more than one job title may be intentionally listed here more than once.

Charles E. Bradley, Jr., CEO
Charles E. Bradley, Jr., Pres.
Jeffrey P. Fritz, CFO/Sr. VP
Curtis K. Powell, Sr. VP-Mktg.
Mark Creatura, General Counsel/Sr. VP
Jayne E. Jordan, Sr. VP-Oper.
Robery E. Riedl, Chief Investment Officer/Sr. VP
Chris Terry, Sr. VP-Servicing
Teri L. Clements, Sr. VP-Originations
Charles E. Bradley, Jr., Chmn.

Phone: 949-753-6800	**Fax:**
Toll-Free:	
Address: 19500 Jamboree Rd., Irvine, CA 92612 US	

GROWTH PLANS/SPECIAL FEATURES:

Consumer Portfolio Services, Inc. (CPS) is a specialty finance company engaged in purchasing and servicing retail automobile contracts originated primarily by franchised automobile dealers and, to a lesser extent, by select independent dealers in the U.S. in the sale of new and used automobiles, light trucks and passenger vans. Through its automobile contract purchases, the company provides indirect financing to the customers of dealers, who have limited credit histories, low incomes or past credit problems. The firm serves as an alternative source of financing for dealers, facilitating sales to customers who otherwise might not be able to obtain financing from traditional sources, such as commercial banks, credit unions and the captive finance companies affiliated with major automobile manufacturers. Instead of lending money directly to customers, CPS purchases automobile contracts from dealers under several different financing programs. It purchases these contracts with the intention of financing them on a long-term basis through securitizations. Securitizations are transactions in which the firm sells a specified pool of contracts to a special purpose entity, who in turn issues asset-backed securities to fund the purchase of the pool of contracts from the company. CPS offers seven financing programs to its dealership customers, organized according to credit risk from greatest to least risk: First Time Buyer, Mercury/Delta, Standard, Alpha, Alpha Plus, Super Alpha and Preferred. The firm currently has a managed portfolio of $1.1 billion. CPS has 15 marketing representatives and is a party to dealer agreements with over 364 dealers in 45 states.

Employees are offered medical, dental and vision insurance; disability insurance; a 401(k) plan; tuition reimbursement; an employee assistance plan.

FINANCIALS:

Sales and profits are in thousands of dollars—add 000 to get the full amount. 2009 Note: Financial information for 2009 was not available for all companies at press time.

2009 Sales: $223,895	2009 Profits: $-57,207	**U.S. Stock Ticker: CPSS**
2008 Sales: $368,411	2008 Profits: $-26,091	**Int'l Ticker:** Int'l Exchange:
2007 Sales: $394,550	2007 Profits: $13,858	Employees: 525
2006 Sales: $278,863	2006 Profits: $39,555	Fiscal Year Ends: 12/31
2005 Sales: $193,697	2005 Profits: $3,372	Parent Company:

SALARIES/BENEFITS:

Pension Plan:	ESOP Stock Plan:	Profit Sharing:	Top Exec. Salary: $880,000	Bonus: $1,056,000
Savings Plan: Y	Stock Purch. Plan:		Second Exec. Salary: $319,000	Bonus: $182,000

OTHER THOUGHTS:

Apparent Women Officers or Directors: 2
Hot Spot for Advancement for Women/Minorities:

LOCATIONS: ("Y" = Yes)

West:	Southwest:	Midwest:	Southeast:	Northeast:	International:
Y		Y	Y	Y	

CONTINENTAL AG

www.conti-online.com

Industry Group Code: 3262 **Ranks within this company's industry group:** Sales: 2 Profits: 10

Vehicle Manufacturing:		**Dealers:**		**Parts:**		**Service:**		**Finance:**		**Specialty:**	
Cars:		Car Dealer New:		Manufacturers:	Y	General Service:		Leasing:		Information Systems:	
Trucks:		Car Dealer Used:		Retail:		Specialty Service:		Auto Loans:		Online Marketing:	
Motorcycles:		Truck Dealer:		Distributors:		Oil Change:		Insurance:		Other:	
Specialty:		RV Dealer:		Tires:	Y	Paint and Body:				Publishing:	
Buses:		Motorcycle Dealer:		Batteries:						Rental Cars/Trucks:	
RVs:		Specialty Dealer:									

TYPES OF BUSINESS:

Automotive Components
Tires, Plastics & Rubber
Brake Products
Transmissions & Suspensions
Vehicle Interiors
Sealing Systems
Aviation Products
Protective Clothing

BRANDS/DIVISIONS/AFFILIATES:

ContiTech
Viking
Semperit
Benecke-Kaliko Group
Mabor
Barum
Uniroyal
Euzkadi

CONTACTS: *Note: Officers with more than one job title may be intentionally listed here more than once.*

Elmar Degenhart, Chmn.-Exec. Board
Wolfgang Schafer, CFO
Bill Caldwell, VP-Mktg. & Sales, U.S.
Heinz-Gerhard Wente, Dir.-Personnel & Human Resources
Christian von Albrichsfeld, Head-R&D, Continental Auto Romania
Wolfgang Schafer, Dir.-IT
Wolfgang Schafer, Dir.-Law
Felix Gress, Sr. VP-Corp. Comm.
Rolf Woller, Head-Investor Rel.
Elmar Degenhart, Dir.-Finance & Controlling
Hans-Joachim Nikolin, Dir.-Corp. Quality, Environment & Comm., Tires
Elmar Degenhart, Dir.-Powertrain Div.
Helmut Matschi, Dir.-Interiors Div.
Andreas Gerstenberger, Exec. VP-ContiTrade
Rolf Wolfgang Reitzle, Chmn.-Supervisory Board
Samir Salman, CEO-NAFTA Region
Hans-Joachim Nikolin, Dir.-Purchasing

Phone: 49-511-938-01	**Fax:** 49-511-938-81770
Toll-Free:	
Address: Vahrenwalder Strasse 9, Hanover, D-30165 Germany	

GROWTH PLANS/SPECIAL FEATURES:

Continental AG is one of Europe's largest manufacturers of tires and other automotive systems for cars and trucks. With operations in over 35 countries, the company has product offerings in two business groups, with three divisions in each. In the automotive group: Chassis and safety; powertrain; and interior. In the rubber group: passenger and light truck tires; commercial vehicle tires; and ContiTech. The chassis and safety division offers electronic brake systems, hydraulic brake systems, dynamic driving control systems, Advanced Driver Assistance Systems (ADAS), airbag electronics, windshield washer systems, electronic air suspension systems and sensors. The powertrain segment provides products including: engine system components; transmission control units; hybrid and electric vehicle components; sensors and actuators; and fuel systems parts. The company's interior division combines all activities relating to the management and visualization of information in the vehicle, including body and security; connectivity; instrumentation and displays; interior modules; and multimedia. The passenger and light truck tires division designs and manufactures car tires under 11 brand names, including Continental; Semperit; Barum; Viking; and Mabor. The commercial vehicle tires division develops and manufactures truck, bus, off-road and industrial tires. The ContiTech subsidiary manufactures a variety of non-tire rubber products, such as transportation hoses for use in automotive fluid delivery as well as conveyor belts and accessories. ContiTech operates in seven units: air spring systems; Benecke-Kaliko Group; conveyor belt group; Elastomer coatings; fluid technology; power transmission group; and vibration control. In March 2010, ContiTech opened a new production, sales and administrative facility in Jiangsu Province in China. In May 2010, Continental announced the opening of a production facility in Menzel Jemil, Tunisia, which will produce car radios and GPS units for European sale.

FINANCIALS: **Sales and profits are in thousands of dollars—add 000 to get the full amount. 2009 Note: Financial information for 2009 was not available for all companies at press time.**

2009 Sales: $24,816,600	2009 Profits: $-2,036,630	**U.S. Stock Ticker: CON**
2008 Sales: $33,691,800	2008 Profits: $-1,561,700	**Int'l Ticker: CON** Int'l Exchange: Frankfurt-Euronext
2007 Sales: $24,260,000	2007 Profits: $1,490,000	Employees: 139,155
2006 Sales: $19,855,200	2006 Profits: $1,339,870	Fiscal Year Ends: 12/31
2005 Sales: $18,455,089	2005 Profits: $1,269,980	Parent Company:

SALARIES/BENEFITS:

Pension Plan:	ESOP Stock Plan:	Profit Sharing:	Top Exec. Salary: $	Bonus: $
Savings Plan: Y	Stock Purch. Plan:		Second Exec. Salary: $	Bonus: $

OTHER THOUGHTS:

Apparent Women Officers or Directors:
Hot Spot for Advancement for Women/Minorities:

LOCATIONS: ("Y" = Yes)

West:	Southwest:	Midwest:	Southeast:	Northeast:	International:
	Y	Y	Y	Y	Y

CONTINENTAL MOTORS GROUP

www.continentalmotors.com

Industry Group Code: 441110 **Ranks within this company's industry group:** Sales: Profits:

Vehicle Manufacturing:		Dealers:		Parts:		Service:		Finance:		Specialty:	
Cars:		Car Dealer New:	Y	Manufacturers:		General Service:	Y	Leasing:		Information Systems:	
Trucks:		Car Dealer Used:	Y	Retail:	Y	Specialty Service:		Auto Loans:		Online Marketing:	
Motorcycles:		Truck Dealer:		Distributors:		Oil Change:		Insurance:		Other:	
Specialty:		RV Dealer:		Tires:		Paint and Body:				Publishing:	
Buses:		Motorcycle Dealer:		Batteries:						Rental Cars/Trucks:	
RVs:		Specialty Dealer:									

TYPES OF BUSINESS:

Auto Dealers, Retail
New & Used Vehicles
Maintenance Services
Parts Sales

BRANDS/DIVISIONS/AFFILIATES:

Continental Acura
Continental AutoSports
Continental Chrysler Jeep
Continental Honda
Continental Toyota Scion
Continental Audi
Continental Nissan
CarNuts Boutique

CONTACTS:

Note: Officers with more than one job title may be intentionally listed here more than once.

John F. Weinberger, Sr., Pres.
John Stanley, CFO
John F. Weinberger, Sr., Chmn.

Phone: 708-352-8080 **Fax:** 708-352-0678
Toll-Free:
Address: 5800 S. La Grange Rd., Countryside, IL 60525 US

GROWTH PLANS/SPECIAL FEATURES:

Continental Motors Group is one of the largest car dealership groups in the state of Illinois with seven locations. Founded in 1961, the company began as an import repair shop. Continental specializes in the sale of vehicles from diverse automobile brands, including Honda, Acura, Toyota, Nissan, Audi, Scion, Chrysler, Ferrari, Maserati and Jeep. The group's member dealerships include Continental Acura, Continental AutoSports, Continental Chrysler Jeep, Continental Honda, Continental Toyota Scion, Continental Audi and Continental Nissan. The Continental Toyota Scion dealership includes a Collision Center for paintless dent removal, and also offers rental car services. Four of the group's dealerships also maintain detail centers. Continental AutoSports includes the CarNuts Boutique, which offers Maserati and Ferrari apparel as well as models, posters and accessories. Continental Motors also sells parts to its customers through Mopar Performance Parts. The company's web site offers options for both potential buyers and existing owners of vehicles, allowing potential car buyers to compare prices, review vehicle makes and models and determine the value of a trade-in vehicle. Customers are also able to search and view the new and used inventory available for purchase, buy a vehicle, inquire about financing and/or obtain a quick quote online. Existing car owners have the option of scheduling maintenance service, viewing and ordering parts and accessories and obtaining information about extending their warranties through online services.

FINANCIALS:

Sales and profits are in thousands of dollars—add 000 to get the full amount. 2009 Note: Financial information for 2009 was not available for all companies at press time.

2009 Sales: $
2008 Sales: $
2007 Sales: $
2006 Sales: $
2005 Sales: $

2009 Profits: $
2008 Profits: $
2007 Profits: $
2006 Profits: $
2005 Profits: $

U.S. Stock Ticker: Private
Int'l Ticker: Int'l Exchange:
Employees:
Fiscal Year Ends: 12/31
Parent Company:

SALARIES/BENEFITS:

Pension Plan: ESOP Stock Plan: Profit Sharing: Top Exec. Salary: $ Bonus: $
Savings Plan: Stock Purch. Plan: Second Exec. Salary: $ Bonus: $

OTHER THOUGHTS:

Apparent Women Officers or Directors:
Hot Spot for Advancement for Women/Minorities:

LOCATIONS: ("Y" = Yes)

West:	Southwest:	Midwest:	Southeast:	Northeast:	International:
		Y			

COOPER TIRE & RUBBER COMPANY

www.coopertire.com

Industry Group Code: 3262 **Ranks within this company's industry group:** Sales: 8 Profits: 3

Vehicle Manufacturing:		**Dealers:**		**Parts:**		**Service:**		**Finance:**		**Specialty:**	
Cars:		Car Dealer New:		Manufacturers:	Y	General Service:		Leasing:		Information Systems:	
Trucks:		Car Dealer Used:		Retail:		Specialty Service:		Auto Loans:		Online Marketing:	
Motorcycles:		Truck Dealer:		Distributors:		Oil Change:		Insurance:		Other:	
Specialty:		RV Dealer:		Tires:	Y	Paint and Body:				Publishing:	
Buses:		Motorcycle Dealer:		Batteries:						Rental Cars/Trucks:	
RVs:		Specialty Dealer:									

TYPES OF BUSINESS:

Tires
Plastics & Rubber Manufacturing

BRANDS/DIVISIONS/AFFILIATES:

Cooper Chengshan
Cooper Kenda
Cooper Tire & Rubber Company de Mexico

CONTACTS:

Note: Officers with more than one job title may be intentionally listed here more than once.

Roy V. Armes, CEO
Roy V. Armes, Pres.
Bradley E. Hughes, CFO/VP
Brenda S. Harmon, Chief Human Resources Officer
James E. Kline, General Counsel/VP/Corp. Sec.
Roy V. Armes, Chmn.

Phone: 419-423-1321	**Fax:** 419-424-4212
Toll-Free: 800-854-6288	
Address: 701 Lima Ave., Findlay, OH 45840 US	

GROWTH PLANS/SPECIAL FEATURES:

Cooper Tire & Rubber Company is a leading manufacturer of replacement tires, focusing on the manufacture and sale of passenger and light truck replacement tires. In addition, the company manufactures radial medium truck, bias light truck tires, motorcycle tires and racing tires. Cooper owns a purchasing office in Singapore to acquire the principal components of tires, including natural rubber and synthetic rubber. The company operates in two business segments: North American tire operations and international tire operations. Both segments produce replacement tires for passenger cars and light trucks. The North American segment sells its tires indirectly through dealers, distributors and tire chains, and directly through three rental stores owned by the company. The international segment focuses mainly on the U.K., continental Europe, Scandinavia, and China. This segment does not make direct end-user sales, but does make tires for several original equipment manufacturers (OEMs). Cooper has two joint venture manufacturing facilities in China: Cooper Chengshan and Cooper Kenda. The company maintains a 50% hold in Cooper Tire & Rubber Company de Mexico, a joint venture project in charge of selling the Cooper and Pneustone brands.

FINANCIALS:

Sales and profits are in thousands of dollars—add 000 to get the full amount. 2009 Note: Financial information for 2009 was not available for all companies at press time.

2009 Sales: $2,932,575	2009 Profits: $119,570	**U.S. Stock Ticker: CTB**
2008 Sales: $2,881,811	2008 Profits: $-219,380	**Int'l Ticker:** Int'l Exchange:
2007 Sales: $2,932,575	2007 Profits: $119,570	Employees:
2006 Sales: $2,575,218	2006 Profits: $-78,511	Fiscal Year Ends: 12/31
2005 Sales: $2,155,185	2005 Profits: $-9,356	Parent Company:

SALARIES/BENEFITS:

Pension Plan:	ESOP Stock Plan:	Profit Sharing:	Top Exec. Salary: $850,000	Bonus: $1,700,000
Savings Plan: Y	Stock Purch. Plan:		Second Exec. Salary: $408,015	Bonus: $408,015

OTHER THOUGHTS:

Apparent Women Officers or Directors: 2
Hot Spot for Advancement for Women/Minorities:

LOCATIONS: ("Y" = Yes)

West:	Southwest:	Midwest:	Southeast:	Northeast:	International:
Y	Y	Y	Y	Y	Y

COPART INC

www.copart.com

Industry Group Code: 441120 **Ranks within this company's industry group:** Sales: 2 Profits: 1

Vehicle Manufacturing:		Dealers:		Parts:		Service:		Finance:		Specialty:	
Cars:		Car Dealer New:		Manufacturers:		General Service:		Leasing:		Information Systems:	
Trucks:		Car Dealer Used:		Retail:		Specialty Service:		Auto Loans:		Online Marketing:	
Motorcycles:		Truck Dealer:		Distributors:		Oil Change:		Insurance:		Other:	Y
Specialty:		RV Dealer:		Tires:		Paint and Body:				Publishing:	
Buses:		Motorcycle Dealer:		Batteries:						Rental Cars/Trucks:	
RVs:		Specialty Dealer:									

TYPES OF BUSINESS:

Salvage Vehicle Processing
Towing & Storage Services
Online Used Parts Database

BRANDS/DIVISIONS/AFFILIATES:

CoPartfinder
CoPart Dealer Services
CoPartDirect
D. Hales Limited

CONTACTS:

Note: Officers with more than one job title may be intentionally listed here more than once.

A. Jayson Adair, CEO
Russell D. Lowy, COO
Vincent Mitz, Pres.
William E. Franklin, CFO/Sr. VP
Robert Vannuccini, Sr. VP-Mktg.
Thomas E. Wylie, Sr. VP-Human Resources
David L. Bauer, CIO/Sr. VP-IT
Paul A. Styer, General Counsel/Sr. VP/Sec.
Simon E. Rote, VP-Finance
Greg Tucker, Sr. VP-Process Improvement
Willis J. Johnson, Chmn.

Phone: 707-639-5000	**Fax:**
Toll-Free: 888-735-5481	
Address: 4665 Business Center Dr., Fairfield, CA 94534 US	

GROWTH PLANS/SPECIAL FEATURES:

Copart, Inc. provides vehicle sellers, primarily insurance companies, with a full range of remarketing services to process and sell vehicles over the Internet through the company's Virtual Bidding Second Generation Internet auction-style sales technology. The company sells primarily to licensed vehicle dismantlers, rebuilders, repair licensees, used vehicle dealers and exporters. Other customers include banks, charities, car dealerships, fleet operators, vehicle rental companies and private individuals. The firm offers vehicle suppliers a full range of services that expedite each stage of the salvage vehicle sale process and minimize administrative and processing costs. Online tools include online seller access, salvage estimation, end-of-life vehicle processing, Virtual Insured Exchange (VIX) services, transportation services, vehicle inspection, on-demand vehicle reporting and Department of Motor Vehicles (DMV) processing services. The company also maintains a database of registered buyers in the vehicle dismantling, rebuilding, repair, resale and exporting businesses, which allows the firm to notify prospective buyers via e-mail when salvage vehicles matching their vehicle preferences are available. Other services include CoPartfinder, a search engine that helps users locate specific car parts; Copart Dealer Services (CDS), a trade-in sales method for franchise and independent dealerships; and CopartDirect, which allows private individuals to sell their vehicles through the firm's North American facilities. Copart markets its services through an in-house sales force, telemarketing and participation in trade shows and vehicle industry conventions. Copart operates 133 salvage facilities in the U.S., two facilities in Canada and 12 facilities in the U.K. In June 2009, Copart opened a new facility in Warren, Massachusetts. In January 2010, the company announced that it would acquire D. Hales Limited, a vehicle salvage disposal firm with five auction and parts facilities in the U.K.

Copart offers its employees health, dental, vision and life insurance; a flexible spending plan; a 401(k) plan; and an employee stock purchase plan.

FINANCIALS:

Sales and profits are in thousands of dollars—add 000 to get the full amount. 2009 Note: Financial information for 2009 was not available for all companies at press time.

2009 Sales: $743,082	2009 Profits: $141,103	**U.S. Stock Ticker: CPRT**
2008 Sales: $784,848	2008 Profits: $156,932	**Int'l Ticker:** Int'l Exchange:
2007 Sales: $560,680	2007 Profits: $136,338	Employees: 2,713
2006 Sales: $528,571	2006 Profits: $96,947	Fiscal Year Ends: 7/31
2005 Sales: $447,731	2005 Profits: $102,116	Parent Company:

SALARIES/BENEFITS:

Pension Plan:	ESOP Stock Plan:	Profit Sharing:	Top Exec. Salary: $571,155	Bonus: $
Savings Plan: Y	Stock Purch. Plan: Y		Second Exec. Salary: $553,849	Bonus: $

OTHER THOUGHTS:

Apparent Women Officers or Directors:
Hot Spot for Advancement for Women/Minorities:

LOCATIONS: ("Y" = Yes)

West:	Southwest:	Midwest:	Southeast:	Northeast:	International:
Y	Y	Y	Y	Y	Y

CREDIT ACCEPTANCE CORP

www.credaccept.com

Industry Group Code: 522220 **Ranks within this company's industry group:** Sales: 3 Profits: 2

Vehicle Manufacturing:		Dealers:		Parts:		Service:		Finance:		Specialty:	
Cars:		Car Dealer New:		Manufacturers:		General Service:		Leasing:		Information Systems:	
Trucks:		Car Dealer Used:		Retail:		Specialty Service:		Auto Loans:	Y	Online Marketing:	
Motorcycles:		Truck Dealer:		Distributors:		Oil Change:		Insurance:		Other:	
Specialty:		RV Dealer:		Tires:		Paint and Body:				Publishing:	
Buses:		Motorcycle Dealer:		Batteries:						Rental Cars/Trucks:	
RVs:		Specialty Dealer:									

TYPES OF BUSINESS:

Automobile Financing

BRANDS/DIVISIONS/AFFILIATES:

CONTACTS:

Note: Officers with more than one job title may be intentionally listed here more than once.

Brett A. Roberts, CEO
Steven M. Jones, Pres.
Kenneth S. Booth, CFO
Michael P. Miotto, CIO
Charles A. Pearce, Chief Legal Officer
Douglas W. Busk, Treas./Sr. VP
Michael W. Knoblauch, Sr. VP-Loan Servicing
Donald A. Foss, Chmn.

Phone: 248-353-2700	**Fax:** 248-827-8553
Toll-Free: 800-634-1506	
Address: 25505 W. Twelve Mile Rd., Ste. 3000, Southfield, MI 48034-8339 US	

GROWTH PLANS/SPECIAL FEATURES:

Credit Acceptance Corp. provides auto loans to consumers, regardless of their credit history. The company's product is offered through a nationwide network of automobile dealers who benefit from sales of vehicles to consumers who otherwise could not obtain financing; from repeat and referral sales generated by these same customers; and from sales to customers responding to advertisement for the firm's product, but who actually end up qualifying for traditional financing. The firm's target market is a select group of the more than 60,000 independent and franchised automobile dealers in the U.S. Credit Acceptance also services the loans and provides dealers with risk assessment, fraud alert, computerized skip tracing, sales training and other services. Dealers that use Credit Acceptance can offer car buyers disability insurance, vehicle service contracts, collateral protection and credit life. The company's online credit application processing system provides automobile dealerships with the ability to grant credit approval in less than 30 seconds, 24 hours a day and 365 days a year. The company derives revenue from finance charges, which comprise servicing fees, fees earned from the company's third party ancillary product offerings and fees associated with the dealer loan including term extension fees; license fees, which represent monthly fees charged to dealer-partners for access to the firm's Internet-based credit approval processing system; and other income, which primarily consists of remarketing charges, fees charged to dealer-partners for enrolling in the company's program, interest income on secured financing and fees for marketing materials.

Employees are offered medical, dental and life insurance; disability coverage; a 401(k) plan; flexible spending accounts; tuition assistance; and an employee assistance plan.

FINANCIALS:

Sales and profits are in thousands of dollars—add 000 to get the full amount. 2009 Note: Financial information for 2009 was not available for all companies at press time.

2009 Sales: $380,664	2009 Profits: $146,255	**U.S. Stock Ticker: CACC**
2008 Sales: $312,186	2008 Profits: $67,177	**Int'l Ticker:** Int'l Exchange:
2007 Sales: $239,927	2007 Profits: $54,916	Employees:
2006 Sales: $219,332	2006 Profits: $58,640	Fiscal Year Ends: 12/31
2005 Sales: $201,268	2005 Profits: $72,601	Parent Company:

SALARIES/BENEFITS:

Pension Plan:	ESOP Stock Plan:	Profit Sharing:	Top Exec. Salary: $800,000	Bonus: $
Savings Plan: Y	Stock Purch. Plan:		Second Exec. Salary: $525,000	Bonus: $

OTHER THOUGHTS:

Apparent Women Officers or Directors: 1
Hot Spot for Advancement for Women/Minorities:

LOCATIONS: ("Y" = Yes)

West:	Southwest:	Midwest:	Southeast:	Northeast:	International:
Y		Y			

CUMMINS FILTRATION

www.cumminsfiltration.com

Industry Group Code: 3363 **Ranks within this company's industry group:** Sales: Profits:

Vehicle Manufacturing:		Dealers:		Parts:		Service:		Finance:		Specialty:	
Cars:		Car Dealer New:		Manufacturers:	Y	General Service:		Leasing:		Information Systems:	
Trucks:		Car Dealer Used:		Retail:		Specialty Service:		Auto Loans:		Online Marketing:	
Motorcycles:		Truck Dealer:		Distributors:		Oil Change:		Insurance:		Other:	
Specialty:		RV Dealer:		Tires:		Paint and Body:				Publishing:	
Buses:		Motorcycle Dealer:		Batteries:						Rental Cars/Trucks:	
RVs:		Specialty Dealer:									

TYPES OF BUSINESS:

Automobile Part Manufacturing
Filtration Products
Industrial Silencers & Mufflers
Exhaust Systems
Antifreeze & Coolant Additives

BRANDS/DIVISIONS/AFFILIATES:

Cummins Inc
Cummins Filtration
Fleetguard-Valvoline Air Shield DEF
Fleetguard
Fleetschool

CONTACTS: *Note: Officers with more than one job title may be intentionally listed here more than once.*

Jihad Saoud, CEO
Jihad Saoud, Pres.
Kamini Patel, Exec. Dir.-Global Mktg.
Kevin Westerson, Exec. Dir.-Research Tech.
Doug Hudgens, Sr. Advisor-Tech.
Kevin Westerson, Exec. Dir.-Eng.
K.C. Hall, Dir.-Bus. Dev.
Mike Sarris, Dir.-Global Coolants & Chemicals
Pamela Carter, Pres., Cummins Dist. Bus.

Phone: 615-367-0040 **Fax:** 615-399-3650
Toll-Free: 800-777-7064
Address: 2931 Elm Hill Pike, Nashville, TN 37214 US

GROWTH PLANS/SPECIAL FEATURES:

Cummins Filtration, an operating subsidiary of Cummins, Inc., is a manufacturer of filtration and exhaust systems for heavy-duty diesel powered equipment. The firm also supplies products with applications in medium and light duty trucks; industrial equipment for construction, mining, agriculture and marine; power generation; and small engines. The company offers over 14,000 products, which include air intake and filtration systems; exhaust systems and accessories; fluid filtration; centrifugal filtration; coolant and chemical products; closed crankcase ventilation filtration; hydraulic filtration; industrial silencers; service parts; maintenance kits; and fluid analysis and coolant test kits. Its primary brand is Fleetguard. Cummins Filtration's products are produced and sold through more than 23,000 dealer and distribution outlets in global markets throughout North America, South America, Europe, Asia, Africa and the Middle East. The firm operates 23 production plants located in nine countries; 16 distribution centers; and three joint ventures. In August 2009, Cummins Filtration agreed to move its Iowa filter assembly operations to a new facility in Mexico. In January 2010, the company established Fleetschool, an online eLearning program that provides a portfolio of up-to-date market and product training for its dealers, employees and distributors. In February 2010, the firm and Ashland Consumer Markets (Valvoline) agreed to jointly package and market Fleetguard-Valvoline Air Shield DEF, a diesel exhaust fluid.

Cummins Filtration's employees receive access to child care centers; employee assistance; health and wellness programs; housing assistance; and tuition reimbursement. Some employees have the option to telecommute.

FINANCIALS: **Sales and profits are in thousands of dollars—add 000 to get the full amount. 2009 Note: Financial information for 2009 was not available for all companies at press time.**

2009 Sales: $	2009 Profits: $	**U.S. Stock Ticker: Subsidiary**
2008 Sales: $	2008 Profits: $	**Int'l Ticker:** Int'l Exchange:
2007 Sales: $280,300	2007 Profits: $	Employees:
2006 Sales: $	2006 Profits: $	Fiscal Year Ends: 12/31
2005 Sales: $	2005 Profits: $	Parent Company: CUMMINS INC

SALARIES/BENEFITS:

Pension Plan:	ESOP Stock Plan:	Profit Sharing:	Top Exec. Salary: $	Bonus: $
Savings Plan:	Stock Purch. Plan:		Second Exec. Salary: $	Bonus: $

OTHER THOUGHTS:

Apparent Women Officers or Directors: 1
Hot Spot for Advancement for Women/Minorities:

LOCATIONS: ("Y" = Yes)

West:	Southwest:	Midwest:	Southeast:	Northeast:	International:
			Y		Y

CUMMINS INC

www.cummins.com

Industry Group Code: 3363 **Ranks within this company's industry group:** Sales: 11 Profits: 4

Vehicle Manufacturing:		Dealers:		Parts:		Service:		Finance:		Specialty:	
Cars:		Car Dealer New:		Manufacturers:	Y	General Service:		Leasing:		Information Systems:	
Trucks:		Car Dealer Used:		Retail:		Specialty Service:	Y	Auto Loans:		Online Marketing:	
Motorcycles:		Truck Dealer:		Distributors:	Y	Oil Change:		Insurance:		Other:	
Specialty:		RV Dealer:		Tires:		Paint and Body:				Publishing:	
Buses:		Motorcycle Dealer:		Batteries:						Rental Cars/Trucks:	
RVs:		Specialty Dealer:									

TYPES OF BUSINESS:

Automotive Products, Motors & Parts Manufacturing
Engines
Filtration Systems
Power Generation Systems
Alternators
Air Handling Systems
Filtration & Emissions Solutions
Fuel Systems

BRANDS/DIVISIONS/AFFILIATES:

Cummins Power Generation
Onan

CONTACTS:

Note: Officers with more than one job title may be intentionally listed here more than once.

Theodore M. Solso, CEO
Tom Linebarger, COO
Tom Linebarger, Pres.
Patrick J. Ward, CFO/VP
John C. Wall, CTO/VP
Mark Gerstle, Chief Admin. Officer/VP
Marya Rose, General Counsel/VP/Sec.
Marsha Hunt, Controller/VP
Anant Talaulicar, Pres., Components Group
Richard Harris, Chief Investment Officer/VP
Richard Freeland, VP/Pres., Engine Bus.
Livingston Satterthwaite, VP/Pres., Power Generation
Theodore M. Solso, Chmn.
Steven Chapman, VP-China & Russia

Phone: 812-377-5000	**Fax:** 812-377-4937
Toll-Free:	
Address: 500 Jackson St., Columbus, IN 47202 US	

GROWTH PLANS/SPECIAL FEATURES:

Cummins, Inc. designs, manufactures, distributes and services diesel and natural gas engines; electric power generation systems; and engine-related component products, including filtration and emissions solutions, fuel systems, controls and air handling systems. The company's operations are divided into four segments: engine, power generation, components and distribution. The engine segment, which generated 49% of 2009 sales, manufactures and markets diesel and natural gas-powered engines, parts, and services under the Cummins brand name for the heavy- and medium-duty truck, bus, recreational vehicle, light-duty automotive, agricultural, construction, mining, marine, oil and gas, rail and governmental equipment markets. The power generation segment, accounting for 19% of 2009 revenue, designs and manufactures components of power generation systems, including engines, controls, alternators, transfer switches and switchgear. Products are marketed principally under the Cummins Power Generation and Onan brands and include diesel and alternative-fuel electrical generator sets for commercial, institutional and consumer applications, such as office buildings, hospitals, factories, municipalities, utilities, universities, boats and homes. The components segment, which generated 18% of 2009 net sales, produces filters, silencers and intake and exhaust systems and commercial turbochargers. The distribution segment, producing 14% of revenue, consists of 19 company-owned and 18 joint ventures that distribute the company's products and services in over 70 countries and territories. Cummins serves customers through a network of more than 500 company-owned and independent distributor locations and roughly 5,200 dealer locations in more than 190 countries and territories. In October 2009, the company established a new marine center in the Netherlands for the purpose of supporting its marine operations in Europe, Africa and the Middle East.

Employees are offered medical and dental insurance; life insurance; a 401(k) plan; a profit sharing plan; a pension plan; flexible spending accounts; an employee stock purchase plan; and disability coverage.

FINANCIALS:

Sales and profits are in thousands of dollars—add 000 to get the full amount. 2009 Note: Financial information for 2009 was not available for all companies at press time.

2009 Sales: $10,800,000	2009 Profits: $428,000	**U.S. Stock Ticker: CMI**
2008 Sales: $14,342,000	2008 Profits: $755,000	**Int'l Ticker:** Int'l Exchange:
2007 Sales: $13,048,000	2007 Profits: $739,000	Employees: 34,900
2006 Sales: $11,362,000	2006 Profits: $715,000	Fiscal Year Ends: 12/31
2005 Sales: $9,918,000	2005 Profits: $550,000	Parent Company:

SALARIES/BENEFITS:

Pension Plan: Y	ESOP Stock Plan:	Profit Sharing: Y	Top Exec. Salary: $1,139,250	Bonus: $4,452,000
Savings Plan: Y	Stock Purch. Plan: Y		Second Exec. Salary: $678,125	Bonus: $1,236,800

OTHER THOUGHTS:

Apparent Women Officers or Directors: 7
Hot Spot for Advancement for Women/Minorities: Y

LOCATIONS: ("Y" = Yes)

West:	Southwest:	Midwest:	Southeast:	Northeast:	International:
Y	Y	Y	Y	Y	Y

DAIHATSU MOTOR CO LTD

www.daihatsu.com

Industry Group Code: 33611 **Ranks within this company's industry group:** Sales: 17 Profits: 14

Vehicle Manufacturing:		Dealers:		Parts:		Service:		Finance:		Specialty:	
Cars:	Y	Car Dealer New:		Manufacturers:	Y	General Service:		Leasing:		Information Systems:	
Trucks:	Y	Car Dealer Used:		Retail:		Specialty Service:		Auto Loans:		Online Marketing:	
Motorcycles:		Truck Dealer:		Distributors:		Oil Change:		Insurance:		Other:	
Specialty:	Y	RV Dealer:		Tires:		Paint and Body:				Publishing:	
Buses:	Y	Motorcycle Dealer:		Batteries:						Rental Cars/Trucks:	
RVs:		Specialty Dealer:									

TYPES OF BUSINESS:

Automobile Manufacturing
Industrial Engines

BRANDS/DIVISIONS/AFFILIATES:

Toyota Motor Corporation
Cuore
Sirion
Terios
Copen
Materia
Luxio
Boon

CONTACTS:

Note: Officers with more than one job title may be intentionally listed here more than once.

Koichi Ina, Pres.
Katsuyuki Kamio, Exec. VP-Prod. Mktg. & Domestic Sales
Hiroaki Iwabe, Dir.-Global Human Resources
Masanori Mitsui, Exec. VP-R&D Group
Masahiro Takahashi, Dir.-Admin.
Masahiro Takahashi, Dir.-Finance, Acct. & Cost Mgmt. Div.
Katsuhiko Okumura, Vice Chmn.
Takashi Nomoto, Pres., PT Astra Daihatsu Motor
Kenji Baba, Dir.-Sales & Mktg.
Naoto Kitagawa, Dir.-Prod. Mktg. Group & Toyota Mgmt. Dept.
Kousuke Shiramizu, Chmn.
Katsuyuki Kamio, Exec. VP-Overseas Oper.
Masanori Mitsui, Exec. VP-Purchasing

Phone: 81-72-751-8811 **Fax:**
Toll-Free:
Address: 1-1 Daihatsu-cho, Ikeda-city, Osaka, 563-8651 Japan

GROWTH PLANS/SPECIAL FEATURES:

Daihatsu Motor Co., Ltd., headquartered in Osaka, Japan, develops, manufactures and sells small, economy-priced passenger cars. Its models include the MATERIA, TERIOS, Copen, SIRION, Cuore/Charade, Gran Max and DELTA. The firm specializes in compact wagons and SUVs. The company has six factories in Japan and one in both Malaysia and Venezuela. Daihatsu has additional overseas operations in China, Pakistan, Venezuela, Germany and the Netherlands through affiliates, tie-up and consigned companies. The firm sells approximately 635,400 vehicles domestically each year, and exports about 106,600 vehicles. Toyota, Japan's largest automotive company, owns 51.2% of Daihatsu. The company exports its models to over 130 countries. Daihatsu also manufactures industrial engines, and annually sells about 400,000 sets of automotive parts for overseas production. Subsidiaries of Daihatsu include Daihatsu Diesel Mfg. Co.; Daihatsu Motor Kyushu Co.; Aoi Machine Industry Co.; Akashi-kikai Industry Co.; Asano Gear Co.; BOLTZ Co.; Kanbishi Corporation; Metalart Corp.; Daihatsu Car Net; Daihatsu Metal Co.; Daihatsu Techner; and Daihatsu Life Net. In February 2009, the company launched the Luxio, a compact multi-purpose vehicle with rear sliding doors and a low floor, in Indonesia. In August 2009, Daihatsu launched the Mira Cocoa, a mini passenger vehicle, in Japan. In November 2009, the firm and joint venture company Perusahaan Otomobil Kedua Sdn Bhd began sales of the ALZA, a seven-passenger compact car, in Malaysia. In December 2009, the company launched the Tanto Exe and Tanto Exe CUSTOM mini passenger cars in Japan. In January 2010, Daihatsu announced plans to dissolve its interest in FAW Daihatsu (Jilin) Body Parts Co., Ltd., an auto body parts manufacturer in Jilin, China. In February 2010, the firm launched the redesigned Boon, a compact hatchback.

FINANCIALS:

Sales and profits are in thousands of dollars—add 000 to get the full amount. 2009 Note: Financial information for 2009 was not available for all companies at press time.

2009 Sales: $17,867,800	2009 Profits: $241,770	**U.S. Stock Ticker:**
2008 Sales: $16,993,738	2008 Profits: $348,742	**Int'l Ticker: 7262** Int'l Exchange: Tokyo-TSE
2007 Sales: $14,897,800	2007 Profits: $316,000	Employees: 13,198
2006 Sales: $12,266,500	2006 Profits: $305,100	Fiscal Year Ends: 3/31
2005 Sales: $10,703,800	2005 Profits: $235,400	Parent Company:

SALARIES/BENEFITS:

Pension Plan:	ESOP Stock Plan:	Profit Sharing:	Top Exec. Salary: $	Bonus: $
Savings Plan:	Stock Purch. Plan:		Second Exec. Salary: $	Bonus: $

OTHER THOUGHTS:

Apparent Women Officers or Directors:
Hot Spot for Advancement for Women/Minorities:

LOCATIONS: ("Y" = Yes)

West:	Southwest:	Midwest:	Southeast:	Northeast:	International:
					Y

DAIMLER AG

www.daimler.com

Industry Group Code: 33611 **Ranks within this company's industry group:** Sales: 3 Profits: 30

Vehicle Manufacturing:		Dealers:		Parts:		Service:		Finance:		Specialty:	
Cars:	Y	Car Dealer New:		Manufacturers:	Y	General Service:		Leasing:	Y	Information Systems:	
Trucks:	Y	Car Dealer Used:		Retail:		Specialty Service:		Auto Loans:	Y	Online Marketing:	
Motorcycles:		Truck Dealer:		Distributors:		Oil Change:		Insurance:	Y	Other:	Y
Specialty:		RV Dealer:		Tires:		Paint and Body:				Publishing:	
Buses:	Y	Motorcycle Dealer:		Batteries:						Rental Cars/Trucks:	
RVs:		Specialty Dealer:									

TYPES OF BUSINESS:

Automobile Manufacturer
Financial Services & Insurance
Commercial Vehicles, Trucks & Buses
Aerospace & Defense Technology

BRANDS/DIVISIONS/AFFILIATES:

Mercedes-Benz
Mercedes-Benz Canada
Daimler Trucks North America LLC
Automotive Fuel Cell Cooperation
Mitsubishi Fuso Truck of America Inc.
Daimler Financial Services AG
Daimler Financial Services Americas LLC

CONTACTS: *Note: Officers with more than one job title may be intentionally listed here more than once.*

Dieter Zetsche, CEO
Bodo Uebber, Dir.-Finance
Wilfried Porth, Dir.-Human Resources & Labor Rel.
Thomas Weber, Dir.-Group Research
Wolfgang Bernhard, Dir.-Mfg.
Rudiger Grube, Dir.-Corp. Dev.
Michael Muhlbayer, Sr. VP-Investor Rel./Treas.
Bodo Uebber, Dir.-Controlling
Thomas Weber, Dir.-Mercedes-Benz Cars Dev.
Andreas Renschler, Dir.-Trucks
Dieter Zetsche, Head-Mercedes-Benz Cars & Vans
Annette Winkler, Head-smart Product Unit
Dieter Zetsche, Chmn.
Wolfgang Bernhard, Dir.-Procurement

Phone: 49-711-17-0 **Fax:** 49-711-17-22244
Toll-Free:
Address: Mercedesstrasse 137, Stuttgart, 70327 Germany

GROWTH PLANS/SPECIAL FEATURES:

Daimler AG develops, manufactures, distributes and sells a wide range of automotive products, mainly passenger cars, trucks, vans and buses. It also provides financial and other services relating to its automotive businesses. The company reports in five segments: Mercedes-Benz Cars; Daimler Trucks; Daimler Financial Services; Mercedes-Benz Vans; and Daimler Buses. The Mercedes-Benz Cars segment designs, produces and sells Mercedes-Benz passenger cars, Maybach luxury sedans and smart micro compact cars. The Daimler Trucks segment manufactures trucks and specialty vehicles under the Mercedes-Benz, Freightliner, Western Star, Thomas Built Buses, Detroit Diesel and Mitsubishi Fuso brands. Daimler Financial Services primarily provides financing, leasing, insurance and fleet management services. Mercedes-Benz Vans offer privately and commercially used vans, MPVs and camper vans, including the Vito, Viano Sprinter and Vario models; Daimler Buses includes the brands Mercedes-Benz, Setra and Orion. Daimler offers products and services primarily in Western Europe and in the NAFTA region, including the U.S., Canada and Mexico. Approximately 46% of 2009 revenue was derived from sales in Western Europe; 20% from sales in the U.S.; and 15% from sales in Asia. Daimler also owns a 50.1% stake in Automotive Fuel Cell Cooperation. In April 2010, Daimler announced a strategic cooperation with the Renault-Nissan Automotive Alliance which will result in cooperation on the firms' next generation brand line, smart and Twingo, respectively, as well as collaboration in powertrain development. In June 2010, the company announced the production of the Mercedes-Benz Actros truck at the Juiz de Flora facility in Brazil. In July 2010, Daimler announced the establishment of a new Smart product unit within the Mercedes-Benz Cars segment in order to expand the brand and the products under the brand's umbrella.

FINANCIALS: **Sales and profits are in thousands of dollars—add 000 to get the full amount. 2009 Note: Financial information for 2009 was not available for all companies at press time.**

2009 Sales: $107,755,000	2009 Profits: $-3,609,850	**U.S. Stock Ticker: DAI**
2008 Sales: $129,244,000	2008 Profits: $1,906,190	**Int'l Ticker: DAI** Int'l Exchange: Frankfurt-Euronext
2007 Sales: $133,998,000	2007 Profits: $5,372,100	Employees: 256,407
2006 Sales: $198,638,000	2006 Profits: $4,228,560	Fiscal Year Ends: 12/31
2005 Sales: $177,260,000	2005 Profits: $3,368,000	Parent Company:

SALARIES/BENEFITS:

Pension Plan:	ESOP Stock Plan:	Profit Sharing:	Top Exec. Salary: $	Bonus: $
Savings Plan:	Stock Purch. Plan:		Second Exec. Salary: $	Bonus: $

OTHER THOUGHTS:

Apparent Women Officers or Directors: 1
Hot Spot for Advancement for Women/Minorities:

LOCATIONS: ("Y" = Yes)

West:	Southwest:	Midwest:	Southeast:	Northeast:	International:
Y	Y	Y	Y	Y	Y

DAIMLER FINANCIAL SERVICES AG www.daimler-financialservices.com

Industry Group Code: 522220 **Ranks within this company's industry group:** Sales: Profits:

Vehicle Manufacturing:		Dealers:		Parts:		Service:		Finance:		Specialty:	
Cars:		Car Dealer New:		Manufacturers:		General Service:		Leasing:	Y	Information Systems:	Y
Trucks:		Car Dealer Used:		Retail:		Specialty Service:		Auto Loans:	Y	Online Marketing:	
Motorcycles:		Truck Dealer:		Distributors:		Oil Change:		Insurance:	Y	Other:	Y
Specialty:		RV Dealer:		Tires:		Paint and Body:				Publishing:	
Buses:		Motorcycle Dealer:		Batteries:						Rental Cars/Trucks:	
RVs:		Specialty Dealer:									

TYPES OF BUSINESS:

Vehicle Leasing & Financing
Fleet Management Services
Insurance Services
Consulting Services
Toll Collecting Systems
Traffic Routing Systems

BRANDS/DIVISIONS/AFFILIATES:

Daimler AG
Daimler Services Structured Finance GmbH
Daimler Services Fleet Management GmbH
Daimler Services Insurance Solutions, Ltd.
Daimler Services Mobility Management GmbH
Daimler Bank

CONTACTS: *Note: Officers with more than one job title may be intentionally listed here more than once.*

Franz Josef Reiner, Pres.
David H. Olsen, CFO
Dieter Buhl, Dir.-Human Resources
David H. Olsen, Dir.-Financial & Controlling
Alwin Eppe, Dir.-Europe Region
Richard Andrew Howard, Dir. Africa & Asia/Pacific Region
Franz Josef Reiner, Pres./CEO-Daimler Financial Services Americas
Klaus Entemann, Chmn.

Phone: 49-30-2554-1106 **Fax:** 49-30-2554-1113
Toll-Free:
Address: Eichhornstrasse 3, Berlin, 10875 Germany

GROWTH PLANS/SPECIAL FEATURES:

Daimler Financial Services AG, a subsidiary of Daimler AG, is an automotive financial services company with over 100 locations in 40 countries worldwide. Through Daimler Services Structured Finance GmbH, the company provides financial plans customized to suit the requirements of individual customers of all vehicle brands within the Daimler group, including Mercedes-Benz and Maybach. Daimler Services Fleet Management GmbH offers cross-brand fleet management for fleets of 50 or more vehicles, with consulting, leasing and managing/controlling as service components. The company's leasing and financing business covers commercial vehicles, including trucks and vans, as well as personal automobiles. Daimler Services Insurance Solutions, Ltd. has its own business unit that provides dedicated insurance, risk management, employee benefits and consulting services to a range of business sectors in 20 countries. Another subsidiary, Daimler Services Mobility Management GmbH, is divided into two business segments, toll systems and business telematics. This subsidiary supports companies and administrations with tailor-made system solutions in the fields of toll collection and traffic-routing systems. Through the founding of the Daimler Bank, the automobile leasing and financing business will be expanded along with the automotive chain through a variety of attractive investment programs. Daimler Financial Services received approval to provide vehicle financing to the Chinese market. In May 2010, the company, along with Mercedes-Benz Bank, announced the restructuring of its German business operations. As part of the restructuring, Dailmer Financial Services will move its headquarters from Berlin to Stuttgart in the same building as Mercedez-Benz Bank.

FINANCIALS: **Sales and profits are in thousands of dollars—add 000 to get the full amount. 2009 Note: Financial information for 2009 was not available for all companies at press time.**

2009 Sales: $ | 2009 Profits: $
2008 Sales: $ | 2008 Profits: $
2007 Sales: $ | 2007 Profits: $
2006 Sales: $ | 2006 Profits: $
2005 Sales: $ | 2005 Profits: $

U.S. Stock Ticker: Subsidiary
Int'l Ticker: Int'l Exchange:
Employees:
Fiscal Year Ends: 12/31
Parent Company: DAIMLER AG

SALARIES/BENEFITS:

Pension Plan: ESOP Stock Plan: Profit Sharing: Top Exec. Salary: $ Bonus: $
Savings Plan: Stock Purch. Plan: Second Exec. Salary: $ Bonus: $

OTHER THOUGHTS:

Apparent Women Officers or Directors: 1
Hot Spot for Advancement for Women/Minorities:

LOCATIONS: ("Y" = Yes)

West:	Southwest:	Midwest:	Southeast:	Northeast:	International:
					Y

DAIMLER FINANCIAL SERVICES AMERICAS LLC www.daimler-financialservices.com/na

Industry Group Code: 522220 **Ranks within this company's industry group:** Sales: Profits:

Vehicle Manufacturing:		Dealers:		Parts:		Service:		Finance:		Specialty:	
Cars:		Car Dealer New:		Manufacturers:		General Service:		Leasing:	Y	Information Systems:	
Trucks:		Car Dealer Used:		Retail:		Specialty Service:		Auto Loans:	Y	Online Marketing:	
Motorcycles:		Truck Dealer:		Distributors:		Oil Change:		Insurance:	Y	Other:	
Specialty:		RV Dealer:		Tires:		Paint and Body:				Publishing:	
Buses:		Motorcycle Dealer:		Batteries:						Rental Cars/Trucks:	
RVs:		Specialty Dealer:									

TYPES OF BUSINESS:

Vehicle Leasing & Financing
Financing

BRANDS/DIVISIONS/AFFILIATES:

Mercedes-Benz Visa
Mercedes-Benz Financial
Daimler Truck Financial
Daimler Financial Services AG

CONTACTS: *Note: Officers with more than one job title may be intentionally listed here more than once.*

Franz Reiner, CEO
Franz Reiner, Pres.
Brian Stevens, CFO
James Ryan, Dir.-Corp. Mktg.
Jeremy Gump, VP-Human Resources
Udo Neumann, VP-IT Mgmt.
Jeremy Gump, VP-Admin. Svcs.
Matthew Roy, General Counsel/VP/Corp. Sec.
James Ryan, Dir.-Comm.
Brian Stevens, VP-Finance & Controlling
Chris Kaefer, VP-Credit & National Accounts
Richard Howard, VP-Truck Financial U.S.
Janet Marzett, VP-Customer Service, Collections & Remarketing, US
Dietmar Exler, VP-Mercedes-Benz Financial

Phone: 248-991-6700 **Fax:** 248-957-2997
Toll-Free:
Address: 36455 Corporate Dr., Farmington Hills, MI 48331 US

GROWTH PLANS/SPECIAL FEATURES:

Daimler Financial Services Americas LLC (DFSA), a subsidiary of German automobile and truck manufacturer Daimler AG, serves as the financial arm of Daimler in North and South America, providing automobile and truck financing and related services to both dealers and retail customers in the U.S., Canada, Mexico, Brazil and Argentina. DFSA operates in four primary business units: Mercedes-Benz Financial; Daimler Truck Financial; Daimler Financial Services Canada; and Daimler Financial Services Mexico. Mercedes-Benz Financial (MBF) is a full-service automotive financing company that exclusively serves Mercedes-Benz dealers and their customers, including more than 400,000 U.S. Mercedes-Benz owners. MBF offers a number of financing options, including First Class Financing, for customers wishing to finance a vehicle purchase; and First Class Lease, for lease financing. Through its web site, MBF's customers can apply for credit, use an online estimator to compare payment options, check account information and make payments. MBF also offers a Mercedes-Benz Visa card, allowing customers to earn points that can be applied toward vehicle payments or used to purchase Mercedes-Benz merchandise. The Daimler Truck Financial business unit serves as the North American financial services arm of Daimler subsidiary Freightliner LLC, encompassing truck brands such as Freightliner, Western Star and Setra. The unit offers a variety of financing options for truck owner-operators, large and small fleet operations, municipalities and other customers, including RV and pleasure boat financing. Daimler Financial Services Canada and Daimler Financial Services Mexico offer both passenger car and commercial vehicle financing to dealers and customers in Canada and Mexico, respectively. DFSA is affiliated with Daimler Financial Services AG, another Daimler subsidiary, with over 100 offices in approximately 40 countries worldwide.

FINANCIALS: **Sales and profits are in thousands of dollars—add 000 to get the full amount. 2009 Note: Financial information for 2009 was not available for all companies at press time.**

2009 Sales: $ 2009 Profits: $
2008 Sales: $ 2008 Profits: $
2007 Sales: $ 2007 Profits: $
2006 Sales: $ 2006 Profits: $
2005 Sales: $ 2005 Profits: $

U.S. Stock Ticker: Subsidiary
Int'l Ticker: Int'l Exchange:
Employees:
Fiscal Year Ends: 12/31
Parent Company: DAIMLER AG

SALARIES/BENEFITS:

Pension Plan: ESOP Stock Plan: Profit Sharing: Top Exec. Salary: $ Bonus: $
Savings Plan: Stock Purch. Plan: Second Exec. Salary: $ Bonus: $

OTHER THOUGHTS:

Apparent Women Officers or Directors: 1
Hot Spot for Advancement for Women/Minorities:

LOCATIONS: ("Y" = Yes)

West:	Southwest:	Midwest:	Southeast:	Northeast:	International:
	Y	Y			Y

DAIMLER TRUCKS NORTH AMERICA LLC www.daimler-trucksnorthamerica.com

Industry Group Code: 336120 **Ranks within this company's industry group:** Sales: Profits:

Vehicle Manufacturing:		Dealers:		Parts:		Service:		Finance:		Specialty:	
Cars:		Car Dealer New:		Manufacturers:	Y	General Service:		Leasing:		Information Systems:	
Trucks:	Y	Car Dealer Used:		Retail:		Specialty Service:		Auto Loans:		Online Marketing:	
Motorcycles:		Truck Dealer:	Y	Distributors:		Oil Change:		Insurance:		Other:	
Specialty:	Y	RV Dealer:		Tires:		Paint and Body:				Publishing:	
Buses:	Y	Motorcycle Dealer:		Batteries:						Rental Cars/Trucks:	
RVs:		Specialty Dealer:									

TYPES OF BUSINESS:

Truck Manufacturing
Custom-Built Chassis
Van & Bus Manufacturing
Automobile Parts Manufacturing
Specialty Vehicle Manufacturing
Military Vehicle Manufacturing
Used Truck Dealerships
Truck Stops

BRANDS/DIVISIONS/AFFILIATES:

Chrysler LLC
Sterling Trucks
Western Star Trucks
Freightliner Custom Chassis
Thomas Built Buses
SelecTrucks
Detroit Diesel Corporation
TravelCenters of America

CONTACTS: *Note: Officers with more than one job title may be intentionally listed here more than once.*

Martin Daum, CEO
Roger M. Nielsen, COO
Martin Daum, Pres.
Juergen Kritschgau, CFO
Michael Delaney, Sr. VP-Mktg.
Elmar Boeckenhoff, Sr. VP-Tech.
Elmar Boeckenhoff, Sr. VP-Eng.
Juergen Kritschgau, VP-Finance/Controller
Jack Conlan, Sr. VP-Customer Support
Mark Lampert, Sr. VP-Sales

Phone: 503-745-8000 **Fax:** 503-745-8921
Toll-Free:
Address: 4747 N. Channel Ave., Portland, OR 97217 US

GROWTH PLANS/SPECIAL FEATURES:

Daimler Trucks North America LLC (formerly Freightliner LLC), a wholly-owned subsidiary of Daimler AG, is one of the largest manufacturers of medium- and heavy-duty trucks and specialized commercial vehicles in North America. The company sells and services several brands, including Freightliner, its line of medium- and heavy-duty trucks; Sterling, trucks used for vocational applications and local and regional distribution; Western Star, heavy-duty over-the-road and vocational trucks; Freightliner Custom Chassis, for motor homes, school and shuttle buses; and Thomas Built Buses, the company's line of school buses. Daimler Trucks operates a network of over 800 dealers and service centers in North America, including over 40 used truck sales centers (SelecTrucks). The company is also one of the largest exporters of heavy-duty trucks from North America, marketing vehicles in over 35 countries. Daimler Trucks offers a selection of high quality proprietary components, including Mercedes-Benz engines and Alliance parts. The firm is affiliated with Detroit Diesel Corporation, a leading manufacturer of diesel engines for the commercial truck market, and with Axle Alliance Company. The firm is also a partial owner of TravelCenters of America, the largest network of full-service truck stops in the U.S. The company is making efforts to bring diesel hybrid electric engines to market as an alternative for applications such as delivery vans and utility vehicles. Recently, the company began cutting its workforce. Layoffs included 800 from the closure of its Portland, Oregon manufacturing plant; 478 at its Mount Holly, North Carolina truck-making plant; 260 at its Gastonia, North Carolina parts plant; and 1,180 at its Cleveland truck plant in Rowan County, North Carolina. By the time this contraction is complete, the company expects to have cut its workforce by roughly 4,000.

FINANCIALS: **Sales and profits are in thousands of dollars—add 000 to get the full amount. 2009 Note: Financial information for 2009 was not available for all companies at press time.**

2009 Sales: $ | 2009 Profits: $
2008 Sales: $ | 2008 Profits: $
2007 Sales: $ | 2007 Profits: $
2006 Sales: $ | 2006 Profits: $
2005 Sales: $13,000,000 | 2005 Profits: $

U.S. Stock Ticker: Subsidiary
Int'l Ticker: Int'l Exchange:
Employees:
Fiscal Year Ends: 12/31
Parent Company: DAIMLER AG

SALARIES/BENEFITS:

Pension Plan: | ESOP Stock Plan: | Profit Sharing: | Top Exec. Salary: $ | Bonus: $
Savings Plan: Y | Stock Purch. Plan: | Second Exec. Salary: $ | Bonus: $

OTHER THOUGHTS:

Apparent Women Officers or Directors:
Hot Spot for Advancement for Women/Minorities:

LOCATIONS: ("Y" = Yes)

West:	Southwest:	Midwest:	Southeast:	Northeast:	International:
Y		Y	Y	Y	Y

DANA HOLDINGS CORPORATION

www.dana.com

Industry Group Code: 3363 **Ranks within this company's industry group:** Sales: 20 Profits: 55

Vehicle Manufacturing:		Dealers:		Parts:		Service:		Finance:		Specialty:	
Cars:		Car Dealer New:		Manufacturers:		General Service:		Leasing:		Information Systems:	
Trucks:		Car Dealer Used:		Retail:		Specialty Service:		Auto Loans:		Online Marketing:	
Motorcycles:		Truck Dealer:		Distributors:	Y	Oil Change:		Insurance:		Other:	
Specialty:		RV Dealer:		Tires:		Paint and Body:				Publishing:	
Buses:		Motorcycle Dealer:		Batteries:						Rental Cars/Trucks:	
RVs:		Specialty Dealer:									

TYPES OF BUSINESS:

Automotive Products, Motors & Parts Manufacturing
Engine Systems
Fluid Systems
Heavy Vehicle Technologies
Brake Components
Chassis & Drive Train Components
Filtration Products
Financial Services

BRANDS/DIVISIONS/AFFILIATES:

Spicer
Victor Reinz
Parish
Long

CONTACTS: *Note: Officers with more than one job title may be intentionally listed here more than once.*

James E. Sweetnam, CEO
James E. Sweetnam, Pres.
James A. Yost, CFO/Exec. VP
Douglas S. Tracy, CIO/VP
George T. Constand, CTO
Robert H. Marcin, Chief Admin. Officer
Marc S. Levin, General Counsel/Sr. VP/Sec.
Ernesto Gonzalez-Beltran, Sr. VP-Global Oper.
Jacqueline Dedo, Sr. VP-Bus. Dev. & Strategy
Chuck Hartlage, Head-Corp. Media Rel.
Richard Dyer, Chief Acct. Officer/VP
Harro Burmann, Pres., South American Oper.
Mark E. Wallace, Pres., Heavy Vehicle Prod. & Global Oper.
Ken J. Cao, Pres., APAC Oper.
Martin Bryant
Martin Bryant, Pres., Light Vehicle Prod.
John M. Devine, Chmn.
Aziz Aghili, Pres., Europe
Eric Schwarz, Chief Purchasing Officer

Phone: 419-887-3000	**Fax:**
Toll-Free: 800-537-8823	
Address: 3939 Technology Dr., Maumee, OH 43537 US	

GROWTH PLANS/SPECIAL FEATURES:

Dana Holding Corporation supplies axle, driveshaft, structural, sealing and thermal management products for global vehicle manufacturers. With approximately 106 facilities in 23 countries, Dana serves three primary markets: light vehicles, commercial vehicles and off-highway vehicles. Dana's Automotive Systems Group (ASG) business unit sells products mostly into the light vehicle market, while its Heavy Vehicle Technologies and Systems Group (HVTSG) sells products to the commercial vehicle and off-highway markets. The ASG business unit has three operating segments: the light vehicle driveline segment, responsible for front and rear axles, differentials, torque couplings and modular assemblies; the sealing segment, which manufactures gaskets, cover modules, heat shields, and engine sealing systems; and the thermal segment, which offers cooling and heat transfer products. The HVTSG business unit has two operating segments. The commercial vehicle segment is responsible for axles, driveshafts, steering shafts, brakes, suspensions and tire management systems; the off-highway segment produces axles, transaxles, driveshafts, end-fittings, transmissions, torque converters and electronic controls. The company's trademarks include Victor Reinz, Spicer, Parish and Long. In March 2010, Dana Holding Corp. sold structural products operations to light/commercial vehicle structural components manufacturer Metalsa S.A. de C.V.

FINANCIALS: **Sales and profits are in thousands of dollars—add 000 to get the full amount. 2009 Note: Financial information for 2009 was not available for all companies at press time.**

2009 Sales: $5,228,000	2009 Profits: $-436,000	**U.S. Stock Ticker: DAN**
2008 Sales: $8,095,000	2008 Profits: $18,000	**Int'l Ticker:** Int'l Exchange:
2007 Sales: $8,721,000	2007 Profits: $-551,000	Employees:
2006 Sales: $8,504,000	2006 Profits: $-739,000	Fiscal Year Ends: 12/31
2005 Sales: $8,611,000	2005 Profits: $-1,605,000	Parent Company:

SALARIES/BENEFITS:

Pension Plan:	ESOP Stock Plan:	Profit Sharing:	Top Exec. Salary: $1,298,077	Bonus: $500,000
Savings Plan:	Stock Purch. Plan:		Second Exec. Salary: $961,538	Bonus: $250,000

OTHER THOUGHTS:

Apparent Women Officers or Directors: 1
Hot Spot for Advancement for Women/Minorities:

LOCATIONS: ("Y" = Yes)

West:	Southwest:	Midwest:	Southeast:	Northeast:	International:
		Y	Y	Y	Y

DARCARS AUTOMOTIVE GROUP

www.darcars.com

Industry Group Code: 441110 **Ranks within this company's industry group:** Sales: Profits:

Vehicle Manufacturing:		Dealers:		Parts:		Service:		Finance:		Specialty:	
Cars:		Car Dealer New:	Y	Manufacturers:		General Service:	Y	Leasing:		Information Systems:	
Trucks:		Car Dealer Used:	Y	Retail:	Y	Specialty Service:		Auto Loans:		Online Marketing:	Y
Motorcycles:		Truck Dealer:		Distributors:		Oil Change:		Insurance:		Other:	
Specialty:		RV Dealer:		Tires:		Paint and Body:	Y			Publishing:	
Buses:		Motorcycle Dealer:		Batteries:						Rental Cars/Trucks:	Y
RVs:		Specialty Dealer:									

TYPES OF BUSINESS:

Auto Dealers, Retail
Automotive Service & Parts
Car Rental

BRANDS/DIVISIONS/AFFILIATES:

Darcars Rent-A-Car

CONTACTS:

Note: Officers with more than one job title may be intentionally listed here more than once.

Stephanie Eder, Contact-Human Resources
Gary Higgins, Dir.-Fixed Oper.
Tammy Darvish, VP

Phone: 301-622-0300	**Fax:** 301-622-4915
Toll-Free: 800-327-2277	
Address: 12210 Cherry Hill Rd., Silver Spring, MD 20904 US	

GROWTH PLANS/SPECIAL FEATURES:

Darcars Automotive Group, founded in 1977, is a dealership holding company for over 25 car dealerships in Washington, D.C., Maryland and Virginia. Each dealership is dedicated to one primary manufacturer, selling new Ford, Chrysler, Jeep, Scion, Toyota, Kia, Dodge, Volvo, Lincoln, Nissan, Mercury, Chevrolet and Volkswagen. However, the dealerships' used cars may include Mitsubishi, Infiniti, Acura, BMW, Cadillac, GMC, Mercedes-Benz and Saturn models, among other brands. The firm offers a range of additional automotive services through its nine collision centers, including body repair, parts and service departments; as well as car rentals run through its Rockville, Maryland, Toyota and Volvo dealerships. Customers can use the company's web site to locate each individual dealership's web site, which then allows customers to search for used and new cars; research financing options; and order parts online. Darcars is privately-owned and operated by the founding family.

Employees of the firm are offered health; dental; disability and life insurance; company car; paid vacation; and a 401(K) plan.

FINANCIALS:

Sales and profits are in thousands of dollars—add 000 to get the full amount. 2009 Note: Financial information for 2009 was not available for all companies at press time.

2009 Sales: $	2009 Profits: $	**U.S. Stock Ticker: Private**
2008 Sales: $	2008 Profits: $	**Int'l Ticker:** Int'l Exchange:
2007 Sales: $282,200	2007 Profits: $	Employees:
2006 Sales: $	2006 Profits: $	Fiscal Year Ends: 12/31
2005 Sales: $	2005 Profits: $	Parent Company:

SALARIES/BENEFITS:

Pension Plan:	ESOP Stock Plan:	Profit Sharing:	Top Exec. Salary: $	Bonus: $
Savings Plan: Y	Stock Purch. Plan:		Second Exec. Salary: $	Bonus: $

OTHER THOUGHTS:

Apparent Women Officers or Directors: 2
Hot Spot for Advancement for Women/Minorities: Y

LOCATIONS: ("Y" = Yes)

West:	Southwest:	Midwest:	Southeast:	Northeast:	International:
			Y	Y	

DAVID MCDAVID AUTO GROUP

www.mcdavid.com

Industry Group Code: 441110 **Ranks within this company's industry group:** Sales: Profits:

Vehicle Manufacturing:		Dealers:		Parts:		Service:		Finance:		Specialty:	
Cars:		Car Dealer New:	Y	Manufacturers:		General Service:	Y	Leasing:		Information Systems:	
Trucks:		Car Dealer Used:	Y	Retail:	Y	Specialty Service:		Auto Loans:		Online Marketing:	
Motorcycles:		Truck Dealer:		Distributors:		Oil Change:		Insurance:		Other:	
Specialty:		RV Dealer:		Tires:	Y	Paint and Body:				Publishing:	
Buses:		Motorcycle Dealer:		Batteries:						Rental Cars/Trucks:	
RVs:		Specialty Dealer:									

TYPES OF BUSINESS:

Auto Dealers, Retail
Body Parts & Accessories
Wheels & Tires

BRANDS/DIVISIONS/AFFILIATES:

Asbury Automotive Group
McDavid Performance Center
David McDavid Acura
David McDavid Honda
David McDavid Lincoln Mercury
David McDavid Nissan
MCDavid Luxury Motorcars

CONTACTS: *Note: Officers with more than one job title may be intentionally listed here more than once.*

Charles Oglesby, CEO/Pres., Asbury Automotive Group
Craig Monaghan, CFO/Sr. VP-Asbury Automotive Group
Elizabeth B. Chandler, General Counsel/VP-Asbury Automotive Group
Stephan D. McGree, CIO-Asbury Automotive Group

Phone: 972-790-6100	**Fax:** 972-986-5689
Toll-Free:	
Address: 3600 W. Airport Freeway, Irving, TX 75062 US	

GROWTH PLANS/SPECIAL FEATURES:

David McDavid Auto Group, a part of the Asbury Automotive Group, is one of the largest car dealerships in Texas. The company sells new and used Honda, Acura, Pontiac, Buick, GMC, Lincoln, Mercury and Nissan model cars, trucks, SUVs and minivans through its nine domestic and import franchises in four cities throughout Texas. David McDavid has eight dealerships in the Irving, Frisco, Plano, Austin and Houston areas. Dealerships include David McDavid Acura of Austin and Plano; David McDavid Honda of Houston, Frisco and Irving; David McDavid Lincoln Mercury of Plano; and David McDavid Nissan of Houston. In addition, the company sells luxury cars through its MCDavid Luxury Motorcars, based in Houston, Texas. It sells pre-owned BMW, Audi, Nissan, Lexus, Acura, Land Rover, Infiniti, Cadillac, Lincoln and Mercedes-Benz brands. McDavid Performance Center offers body parts and other products such as performance apparel; engine, exhaust, suspension and electrical products; wheels and tires; and interior accessories and graphics. The company's web site also offers customers online financial help through its Second Chance Finance application. The company's founder, David McDavid, started his first car dealership in 1962 at the age of 19. McDavid sold 70% of the company to the Asbury Group in 1998.

.

FINANCIALS: **Sales and profits are in thousands of dollars—add 000 to get the full amount. 2009 Note: Financial information for 2009 was not available for all companies at press time.**

2009 Sales: $	2009 Profits: $	**U.S. Stock Ticker: Private**
2008 Sales: $	2008 Profits: $	**Int'l Ticker:** Int'l Exchange:
2007 Sales: $	2007 Profits: $	Employees:
2006 Sales: $	2006 Profits: $	Fiscal Year Ends: 12/31
2005 Sales: $	2005 Profits: $	Parent Company:

SALARIES/BENEFITS:

Pension Plan:	ESOP Stock Plan:	Profit Sharing:	Top Exec. Salary: $	Bonus: $
Savings Plan:	Stock Purch. Plan:		Second Exec. Salary: $	Bonus: $

OTHER THOUGHTS:

Apparent Women Officers or Directors: 1
Hot Spot for Advancement for Women/Minorities:

LOCATIONS: ("Y" = Yes)

West:	Southwest:	Midwest:	Southeast:	Northeast:	International:
	Y				

DAVID WILSON'S AUTOMOTIVE GROUP www.davidwilsonautogroup.com

Industry Group Code: 441110 **Ranks within this company's industry group:** Sales: Profits:

Vehicle Manufacturing:		Dealers:		Parts:		Service:		Finance:		Specialty:	
Cars:		Car Dealer New:	Y	Manufacturers:		General Service:	Y	Leasing:		Information Systems:	
Trucks:		Car Dealer Used:	Y	Retail:	Y	Specialty Service:		Auto Loans:	Y	Online Marketing:	
Motorcycles:		Truck Dealer:		Distributors:		Oil Change:		Insurance:		Other:	
Specialty:		RV Dealer:		Tires:		Paint and Body:				Publishing:	
Buses:		Motorcycle Dealer:		Batteries:						Rental Cars/Trucks:	
RVs:		Specialty Dealer:									

TYPES OF BUSINESS:

Auto Dealers, Retail
Auto Service
Auto Finance

BRANDS/DIVISIONS/AFFILIATES:

Weir Canyon Honda
Weir Canyon Acura
Tustin Lexus
Desert Lexus
David Wilson's Toyota of Orange
David Wilson's Right Honda
David Wilson's Ford of Orange
David Wilson's South Bay Toyota

CONTACTS:

Note: Officers with more than one job title may be intentionally listed here more than once.

David Wilson, CEO
Ren Rooney, Pres.
Glenn Quintos, CFO

Phone: 714-639-6750	**Fax:** 714-771-0363
Toll-Free:	
Address: 1400 N. Tustin Ave., Orange, CA 92867 US	

GROWTH PLANS/SPECIAL FEATURES:

David Wilson's Automotive Group, founded 1983, is a new and used automobile dealer. It has 13 branches in California, two in Scottsdale, Arizona, and one in Puerto Vallarta, Mexico. California branches include Toyota of Orange; Mazda of Orange; Ford of Orange; Toyota of Riverside; Toyota of Huntington Beach; South Bay Toyota; South Coast Toyota; Freeway Honda; Tustin Lexus; Newport Lexus; Desert Lexus; Weir Canyon Honda; and Weir Canyon Acura. The two branches in Arizona are Right Toyota and Right Honda. The Mexican branch is Toyota Puerto Vallarta. Brands of new vehicles handled by the group include Toyota, Honda, Mazda, Acura, Ford and Lexus. In addition to new and used vehicles sales, the members of David Wilson's Automotive Group also operate parts and services departments. Each branch operates its own web site, with many listing the location's inventory online or offering a search engine to assist customers in finding the vehicle they are looking for. Customers can also apply for financing through the branch web sites, as well as check for dealership specials. Ten of the web sites are offered in both Spanish and English, five are offered only in English and the Toyota Puerto Vallarta site is only in Spanish.

FINANCIALS:

Sales and profits are in thousands of dollars—add 000 to get the full amount. 2009 Note: Financial information for 2009 was not available for all companies at press time.

2009 Sales: $	2009 Profits: $	**U.S. Stock Ticker: Private**
2008 Sales: $	2008 Profits: $	**Int'l Ticker:** Int'l Exchange:
2007 Sales: $1,700,000	2007 Profits: $	Employees:
2006 Sales: $1,700,000	2006 Profits: $	Fiscal Year Ends: 12/31
2005 Sales: $	2005 Profits: $	Parent Company:

SALARIES/BENEFITS:

Pension Plan:	ESOP Stock Plan:	Profit Sharing:	Top Exec. Salary: $	Bonus: $
Savings Plan:	Stock Purch. Plan:		Second Exec. Salary: $	Bonus: $

OTHER THOUGHTS:

Apparent Women Officers or Directors:
Hot Spot for Advancement for Women/Minorities:

LOCATIONS: ("Y" = Yes)

West:	Southwest:	Midwest:	Southeast:	Northeast:	International:
Y	Y				Y

DEERE & CO

www.deere.com

Industry Group Code: 333 **Ranks within this company's industry group:** Sales: 2 Profits: 2

Vehicle Manufacturing:		Dealers:		Parts:		Service:		Finance:		Specialty:	
Cars:		Car Dealer New:		Manufacturers:	Y	General Service:		Leasing:	Y	Information Systems:	Y
Trucks:		Car Dealer Used:		Retail:		Specialty Service:		Auto Loans:	Y	Online Marketing:	
Motorcycles:		Truck Dealer:		Distributors:		Oil Change:		Insurance:		Other:	
Specialty:	Y	RV Dealer:		Tires:		Paint and Body:				Publishing:	
Buses:		Motorcycle Dealer:		Batteries:						Rental Cars/Trucks:	
RVs:		Specialty Dealer:	Y								

TYPES OF BUSINESS:

Construction & Agricultural Equipment
Commercial & Consumer Equipment
Forestry Equipment
Financing

BRANDS/DIVISIONS/AFFILIATES:

John Deere
AutoTrac RowSense Universal
AutoTrac Controller
5105ML Tractor
Load Command
ZTrak PRO 900 Series
Plus-50 II Premium Engine Oil
Ashok Leyland John Deere Construction Eqipment Co

CONTACTS: *Note: Officers with more than one job title may be intentionally listed here more than once.*

Samuel R. Allen, CEO
James M. Field, CFO/Sr. VP
John D. Lagemann, VP-Mktg. & Sales, U.S.
Mary K. W. Jones, VP-Global Human Resources
Barry W. Schaffter, CIO/VP
Klaus G. Hoehn, VP-Advanced Tech.
Klaus G. Hoehn, VP-Eng.
Randal A. Sergesketter, Sr. VP-Mfg. & Eng.
James R. Jenkins, General Counsel/Sr. VP
Ganesh Jayaram, VP-Corp. Bus. Dev.
Frances B. Emerson, VP-Corp. Comm. & Global Brand Mgmt.
Marie Z. Ziegler, VP-Investor Rel.
James A. Davlin, Treas./VP
Kenneth C. Huhn, VP-Labor Rel.
Michael J. Mack, Jr., Pres., Worldwide Construction & Forestry Equipment
James A. Israel, Pres., John Deere Credit Worldwide
Linda E. Newborn, Chief Compliance Officer/VP
Samuel R. Allen, Chmn.
John D. Lagemann, VP-Mktg. & Sales, Canada, Australia & New Zealand
Thomas E. Knoll, VP-Worldwide Supply Mgmt. & Logistics

Phone: 309-765-8000 **Fax:** 309-765-5671
Toll-Free:
Address: 1 John Deere Pl., Moline, IL 61265-8098 US

GROWTH PLANS/SPECIAL FEATURES:

Deere & Co. is known for its John Deere brand name. The firm conducts business in three divisions: agricultural and turf equipment; construction and forestry; and credit. The agricultural and turf segment manufactures and distributes farm, lawn and garden equipment including tractors; combines; harvesters; tillage, seeding and soil preparation machinery; sprayers; hay and forage equipment; material handling equipment; integrated agricultural management systems technology; mowers; golf course equipment; utility tractors; landscape and irrigation equipment; and other outdoor power products. The construction and forestry division offers equipment and service parts used in construction, earthmoving, material handling and timber harvesting, including backhoe loaders; crawler dozers and loaders; four-wheel-drive loaders; excavators; and more. The credit segment provides financing services for products offered by the agricultural and turf and construction/forestry segments. It also offers wholesale financing to dealers of the foregoing equipment, finances retail revolving charge accounts, provides operating loans, invests in wind energy generation and offers certain crop risk mitigation products. Sales are generally conducted through the largely independently-owned 2,565 dealer locations, 1,557 of which sell agricultural equipment. The firm has 19 factories located in 16 countries throughout the world. Its products are sold in over 100 countries. Deere & Co. also offers the John Deere University, an online training resource that provides lessons and courses on basic and advanced technology. In July 2009, the firm's construction and forestry segment and Ashok Leyland Limited agreed to form joint venture Ashok Leyland John Deere Construction Equipment Company Private Limited to manufacture/market backhoes and four-wheel-drive loaders in India. In 2009 and early 2010, Deere & Co. introduced several new products, including the 5105ML Tractor; AutoTrac Controller; AutoTrac RowSense Universal; Load Command; the ZTrak PRO 900 Series; Plus-50 II Premium Engine Oil; and K-Series Wheeled Feller Bunchers. In March 2010, the firm acquired certain assets of Israel-based BHC Manufacturing.

FINANCIALS: Sales and profits are in thousands of dollars—add 000 to get the full amount. 2009 Note: Financial information for 2009 was not available for all companies at press time.

2009 Sales: $23,112,400	2009 Profits: $873,500	**U.S. Stock Ticker: DE**
2008 Sales: $28,438,000	2008 Profits: $2,053,000	**Int'l Ticker:** Int'l Exchange:
2007 Sales: $24,082,200	2007 Profits: $1,821,700	Employees: 51,300
2006 Sales: $22,147,800	2006 Profits: $1,693,800	Fiscal Year Ends: 10/31
2005 Sales: $21,190,800	2005 Profits: $1,446,800	Parent Company:

SALARIES/BENEFITS:

Pension Plan: Y	ESOP Stock Plan:	Profit Sharing:	Top Exec. Salary: $1,512,779	Bonus: $4,864,800
Savings Plan: Y	Stock Purch. Plan: Y		Second Exec. Salary: $795,965	Bonus: $1,606,687

OTHER THOUGHTS:

Apparent Women Officers or Directors: 5
Hot Spot for Advancement for Women/Minorities: Y

LOCATIONS: ("Y" = Yes)

West:	Southwest:	Midwest:	Southeast:	Northeast:	International:
Y	Y	Y	Y	Y	Y

DEI HOLDINGS INC

www.deiholdings.com

Industry Group Code: 334290 **Ranks within this company's industry group:** Sales: Profits:

Vehicle Manufacturing:		**Dealers:**		**Parts:**		**Service:**		**Finance:**		**Specialty:**	
Cars:		Car Dealer New:		Manufacturers:	Y	General Service:		Leasing:		Information Systems:	
Trucks:		Car Dealer Used:		Retail:		Specialty Service:		Auto Loans:		Online Marketing:	
Motorcycles:		Truck Dealer:		Distributors:		Oil Change:		Insurance:		Other:	Y
Specialty:		RV Dealer:		Tires:		Paint and Body:				Publishing:	
Buses:		Motorcycle Dealer:		Batteries:						Rental Cars/Trucks:	
RVs:		Specialty Dealer:									

TYPES OF BUSINESS:

Electronic Equipment-Stolen Vehicle Recovery
Remote Start Systems
Car Audio Equipment
Amplifiers
Speakers
Signal Processors
Mobile Video Systems

BRANDS/DIVISIONS/AFFILIATES:

Directed Electronics Inc
Directed Canada
Definitive Technology
Polk Audio
Astroflex
Clifford
Orion
Viper

CONTACTS:

Note: Officers with more than one job title may be intentionally listed here more than once.

James E. Minarik, CEO
James E. Minarik, Pres.
Kevin Duffy, CFO/Exec. VP
Paul DiComo, Sr. VP-Mktg.
David Peet, Exec. VP-Definitive Tech.
Paul DiComo, Sr. VP-Prod. Dev.
Mike Simmons, Exec. VP
Joe Tristani, COO-Polk Audio
Ben Newhall, VP-Sales, Polk Audio
Jeffrey Nemec, VP-Prod. Dev., Polk Audio
Troy D. Templeton, Chmn.
Julien Joly, Pres., Direct Electronics Canada

Phone: 760-598-6200	**Fax:** 760-598-6400
Toll-Free: 800-876-0800	
Address: 1 Viper Way, Vista, CA 92081 US	

GROWTH PLANS/SPECIAL FEATURES:

DEI Holdings, Inc. (DEI) is a holding company for several consumer electronics firms. Formerly Directed Electronics, Inc., the firm was restructured in recent years to align its corporate structure with its daily operations. DEI Holdings is the now the parent of the following companies: Directed Electronics, Inc., Directed Canada, Polk Audio and Definitive Technology. Directed Electronics and Directed Canada design and market vehicle security and remote start systems; product brand names include XPressKit, Viper, Clifford, Python, Orion, Astroflex and Autostart. Polk Audio and Definitive Technology design and market premium home audio equipment such as floor, bookshelf, in-wall/in-ceiling and surround speakers. In addition, Polk Audio offers car and marine audio equipment; iPod and HD radio systems; and self-powered speaker bars for computer and video games. DEI Holdings operates out of offices in California, Maryland, Europe, Asia and Canada. All of the firm's manufacturing activities are outsourced to third party developers, most of which operate out of locations in Asia. In November 2009, DEI and European insurance telematics provider Octo Telematics S.p.A. agreed to partner to provide telematics services to the vehicle insurance industry in the U.S. and Canada.

FINANCIALS:

Sales and profits are in thousands of dollars—add 000 to get the full amount. 2009 Note: Financial information for 2009 was not available for all companies at press time.

2009 Sales: $	2009 Profits: $	**U.S. Stock Ticker: DEIX**
2008 Sales: $262,917	2008 Profits: $-28,344	**Int'l Ticker:** Int'l Exchange:
2007 Sales: $401,140	2007 Profits: $-139,968	Employees:
2006 Sales: $437,778	2006 Profits: $21,009	Fiscal Year Ends: 12/31
2005 Sales: $304,558	2005 Profits: $-5,137	Parent Company:

SALARIES/BENEFITS:

Pension Plan:	ESOP Stock Plan:	Profit Sharing:	Top Exec. Salary: $	Bonus: $
Savings Plan: Y	Stock Purch. Plan:		Second Exec. Salary: $	Bonus: $

OTHER THOUGHTS:

Apparent Women Officers or Directors:
Hot Spot for Advancement for Women/Minorities:

LOCATIONS: ("Y" = Yes)

West:	Southwest:	Midwest:	Southeast:	Northeast:	International:
Y				Y	Y

DELPHI CORP

www.delphi.com

Industry Group Code: 3363 **Ranks within this company's industry group:** Sales: 8 Profits: 1

Vehicle Manufacturing:		Dealers:		Parts:		Service:		Finance:		Specialty:	
Cars:		Car Dealer New:		Manufacturers:	Y	General Service:		Leasing:		Information Systems:	
Trucks:		Car Dealer Used:		Retail:		Specialty Service:		Auto Loans:		Online Marketing:	
Motorcycles:		Truck Dealer:		Distributors:		Oil Change:		Insurance:		Other:	
Specialty:		RV Dealer:		Tires:		Paint and Body:				Publishing:	
Buses:		Motorcycle Dealer:		Batteries:						Rental Cars/Trucks:	
RVs:		Specialty Dealer:									

TYPES OF BUSINESS:

Automobile Parts Manufacturing
Industrial Components
Dynamics & Propulsion
Safety Systems
Electronics & Mobile Communications
Ride & Handling Systems
Medical Technologies
Fuel Cell & Hybrid Technologies

BRANDS/DIVISIONS/AFFILIATES:

CONTACTS:

Note: Officers with more than one job title may be intentionally listed here more than once.

Rodney O'Neal, CEO
Rodney O'Neal, Pres.
John D. Sheehan, CFO/VP
Karen L. Healy, VP-Mktg.
Kevin M. Butler, VP-Human Resources Mgmt.
Timothy C. McCabe, CIO/VP
David M. Sherbin, General Counsel/Sec./VP
Karen L. Healy, VP-Corp. Affairs
Kevin M. Butler, Exec. VP-Global Bus. Svcs.
Keith D. Stipp, Treas.
David M. Sherbin, Chief Compliance Officer
Jeffrey J. Owens, Pres., Delphi Electronics & Safety
Robert S. Miller, Chmn.
Ronald M. Pirtle, Pres., EMEA
Sidney Johnson, VP-Global Supply Management

Phone: 248-813-2000	**Fax:** 248-813-2673
Toll-Free:	
Address: 5725 Delphi Dr., Troy, MI 48098-2815 US	

GROWTH PLANS/SPECIAL FEATURES:

Delphi Corp. is a supplier of vehicle electronics, transportation components, integrated systems and other electronic technology. Delphi technologies are found in more than 75 million vehicles, as well as communications, computer, energy and medical systems and consumer electronics. The company provides the automotive industry with products such as body electronics; security and vehicle access systems; displays, mechatronics, switches and controls for drive interfaces; electrical architecture and components products; mobile videos; navigation, audio and reception systems; wireless networking; ignition products; heating, venting and cooling products; powertrain cooling; and battery packs for hybrid and electric vehicles. For the medical industry, Delphi offers vital sign monitoring and oxygen concentrators. The firm markets powertrain systems, telematics and connectors (electronic connectors/enclosures, custom interconnects, assemblies and fiber optic connectors) for use in home appliances, cellular phones, TV broadcasting, aerospace and other applications. Wholly-owned subsidiary Delphi Technologies, Inc. is responsible for the creation, management, protection, and leveraging of the company's over 7,000 patents. In October 2009, the company emerged from bankruptcy. It was sold to a group known as Delphi Holdings LLP that includes its lenders and General Motors. Also in October 2009, The Delphi Truck Diagnostic, a diagnostics product for buses, trucks and trailers with brakes; and agreed to sell its global exhaust business to Bienes Turgon for approximately $17 million.

FINANCIALS:

Sales and profits are in thousands of dollars—add 000 to get the full amount. 2009 Note: Financial information for 2009 was not available for all companies at press time.

2009 Sales: $11,755,000	2009 Profits: $9,344,000	**U.S. Stock Ticker: Private**
2008 Sales: $18,060,000	2008 Profits: $3,037,000	**Int'l Ticker:** Int'l Exchange:
2007 Sales: $22,283,000	2007 Profits: $-3,065,000	Employees: 146,600
2006 Sales: $22,737,000	2006 Profits: $-5,464,000	Fiscal Year Ends: 12/31
2005 Sales: $26,947,000	2005 Profits: $-2,357,000	Parent Company: DELPHI HOLDINGS LLP

SALARIES/BENEFITS:

Pension Plan:	ESOP Stock Plan:	Profit Sharing:	Top Exec. Salary: $1,200,000	Bonus: $
Savings Plan:	Stock Purch. Plan:		Second Exec. Salary: $630,000	Bonus: $

OTHER THOUGHTS:

Apparent Women Officers or Directors: 3
Hot Spot for Advancement for Women/Minorities: Y

LOCATIONS: ("Y" = Yes)

West:	Southwest:	Midwest:	Southeast:	Northeast:	International:
Y	Y	Y	Y	Y	Y

DENSO CORPORATION

www.globaldenso.com

Industry Group Code: 3363 **Ranks within this company's industry group:** Sales: 2 Profits: 58

Vehicle Manufacturing:		Dealers:		Parts:		Service:		Finance:		Specialty:	
Cars:		Car Dealer New:		Manufacturers:	Y	General Service:		Leasing:		Information Systems:	
Trucks:		Car Dealer Used:		Retail:		Specialty Service:		Auto Loans:		Online Marketing:	
Motorcycles:		Truck Dealer:		Distributors:		Oil Change:		Insurance:		Other:	
Specialty:		RV Dealer:		Tires:		Paint and Body:				Publishing:	
Buses:		Motorcycle Dealer:		Batteries:						Rental Cars/Trucks:	
RVs:		Specialty Dealer:									

TYPES OF BUSINESS:

Automobile Parts Manufacturer
Engine Components
Automotive Electrical Systems
Automotive Electronic Systems
Thermal Systems
Small Motors
Semiconductors
Industrial Robots

BRANDS/DIVISIONS/AFFILIATES:

Denso Wave, Inc.
DIAS
Denso (China) Investment Co. Ltd.
Denso East Japan Corporation

CONTACTS:

Note: Officers with more than one job title may be intentionally listed here more than once.

Nobuaki Katoh, CEO
Nobuaki Katoh, Pres.
Shigehiro Nishimura, Managing Officer
Hiromi Tokuda, Exec. VP
Shinji Shirasaki, Managing Officer
Shinro Iwatsuki, Exec. VP
Koichi Fukaya, Chmn.
Haruya Maruyama, CEO/Pres., Denso Int'l America, Inc.

Phone: 81-566-25-5850	**Fax:** 81-566-25-4537
Toll-Free:	
Address: 1-1 Showa-cho, Kariya, 448-8661 Japan	

GROWTH PLANS/SPECIAL FEATURES:

Denso Corporation is a global automotive parts manufacturer. The firm operates in 32 countries and regions across North and South America, Europe, Asia and Oceania. Denso's products fall under two categories: its primary automotive components business and a smaller industrial systems division. The automotive division is subdivided into five business groups: Powertrain control systems, which develops and manufactures components and engine management systems for both gasoline and diesel engines; electric systems, which develops and manufactures starters and alternators as well as a line of components for hybrid vehicles; electronic systems, which develops and manufactures electronic control units for automotive control systems; thermal systems, which is responsible for radiators and air conditioners; and information and safety systems, which offers safety systems and body electronics designed to provide driver assistance. Denso's industrial systems output, operated by subsidiary Denso Wave, Inc., consists of automatic identification readers, industrial robots, logic controllers and more. In September 2009, the firm established an aftermarket sales company, Denso Sales RUS LLC, in Russia. In March 2010, Denso announced plans to establish a company in Morocco that will manufacture car air conditioning systems. That same month, the firm announced plans to construct a manufacturing facility in Brazil.

FINANCIALS:

Sales and profits are in thousands of dollars—add 000 to get the full amount. 2009 Note: Financial information for 2009 was not available for all companies at press time.

2009 Sales: $34,011,700	2009 Profits: $-910,020	**U.S. Stock Ticker: DNZOY**
2008 Sales: $40,109,100	2008 Profits: $2,435,570	**Int'l Ticker: 6902** Int'l Exchange: Tokyo-TSE
2007 Sales: $30,590,678	2007 Profits: $1,738,729	Employees: 118,853
2006 Sales: $27,250,684	2006 Profits: $1,449,983	Fiscal Year Ends: 3/31
2005 Sales: $26,033,900	2005 Profits: $1,233,100	Parent Company:

SALARIES/BENEFITS:

Pension Plan:	ESOP Stock Plan:	Profit Sharing:	Top Exec. Salary: $	Bonus: $
Savings Plan:	Stock Purch. Plan:		Second Exec. Salary: $	Bonus: $

OTHER THOUGHTS:

Apparent Women Officers or Directors:
Hot Spot for Advancement for Women/Minorities:

LOCATIONS: ("Y" = Yes)

West:	Southwest:	Midwest:	Southeast:	Northeast:	International:
Y	Y	Y	Y	Y	Y

DEUTZ AG

www.deutz.com

Industry Group Code: 333 **Ranks within this company's industry group:** Sales: 5 Profits: 6

Vehicle Manufacturing:		Dealers:		Parts:		Service:		Finance:		Specialty:	
Cars:		Car Dealer New:		Manufacturers:	Y	General Service:	Y	Leasing:		Information Systems:	
Trucks:		Car Dealer Used:		Retail:		Specialty Service:		Auto Loans:		Online Marketing:	
Motorcycles:		Truck Dealer:		Distributors:		Oil Change:		Insurance:		Other:	
Specialty:		RV Dealer:		Tires:		Paint and Body:				Publishing:	
Buses:		Motorcycle Dealer:		Batteries:						Rental Cars/Trucks:	
RVs:		Specialty Dealer:									

TYPES OF BUSINESS:

Diesel Engines
Maintenance Services

BRANDS/DIVISIONS/AFFILIATES:

DEUTZ Oil Diagnose (DOD) Diagnostic System
DEUTZ Natural Fuel Engines
DEUTZ Agco Motores S.A.
DEUTZ Engine Co., Ltd.
Weifang Weichai-Deutz Diesel Engine Co., Ltd.

CONTACTS: *Note: Officers with more than one job title may be intentionally listed here more than once.*

Helmut Leube, CEO
Margarete Haase, CFO
Margarete Haase, Dir.-Human Resources
Ralf Marquard, Head-R&D
Georg Diderich, Head-Public Rel.
Maria Babilas, Sr. VP-Investor Rel.
Maria Babilas, Sr. VP-Finance
Werner Scherer, Vice Chmn.
Lars-Goran Moberg, Chmn.

Phone: 49-221-822-0	**Fax:** 49-221-822-5850
Toll-Free:	
Address: Ottostrasse 1, Koln-Porz, 51149 Germany	

GROWTH PLANS/SPECIAL FEATURES:

DEUTZ AG manufactures diesel engines for construction, underground mining, compressors, ground support, automotive, agriculture, materials handling, ships, power generation, welding and pumps. The company operates in two business segments: Compact Engines and DEUTZ Customized Solutions. The Compact Engines segment comprises liquid-cooled engines with capacities of less than four liters and engines with capacities of four to eight liters. The division develops, manufactures and sells engines for mobile machinery; automotive and marine applications; and stationary equipment and agricultural machinery. The DEUTZ Customized Solutions segment focuses on air-cooled engines and large liquid-cooled engines with capacities of more than eight liters. The company's field of activity covers development, design, production, sales and services for diesel engines that are cooled by water, oil or air. The company also sells engine oils and cooling system protection and has developed the DEUTZ Oil Diagnose (DOD) diagnostic system to identify and prevent causes of engine damage. DEUTZ has structured most of its compact engines to operate with rape oil methyl ester (RME), a pure vegetable oil, by starting on biofuel, converting to using RME during operation and using biofuel when being shut down. Additionally, DEUTZ Natural Fuel Engines have been approved to run on 100% RME. The firm operates nine distribution companies, nine sales offices and has over 800 sales and service partners in more than 130 countries around the world. It also runs the DEUTZ Agco Motores S.A. joint venture in Argentina and two joint ventures in China: DEUTZ Engine Co., Ltd. and Weifang Weichai-Deutz Diesel Engine Co., Ltd. In July 2010, the firm established a new sales and service subsidiary in Beijing, China.

FINANCIALS: **Sales and profits are in thousands of dollars—add 000 to get the full amount. 2009 Note: Financial information for 2009 was not available for all companies at press time.**

2009 Sales: $1,096,540	2009 Profits: $-157,480	**U.S. Stock Ticker:**
2008 Sales: $2,132,240	2008 Profits: $-11,840	**Int'l Ticker: DEZ** Int'l Exchange: Frankfurt-Euronext
2007 Sales: $2,271,100	2007 Profits: $273,100	Employees:
2006 Sales: $1,763,600	2006 Profits: $91,600	Fiscal Year Ends: 12/31
2005 Sales: $1,694,600	2005 Profits: $91,460	Parent Company:

SALARIES/BENEFITS:

Pension Plan:	ESOP Stock Plan:	Profit Sharing:	Top Exec. Salary: $	Bonus: $
Savings Plan:	Stock Purch. Plan:		Second Exec. Salary: $	Bonus: $

OTHER THOUGHTS:

Apparent Women Officers or Directors: 2
Hot Spot for Advancement for Women/Minorities: Y

LOCATIONS: ("Y" = Yes)

West:	Southwest:	Midwest:	Southeast:	Northeast:	International:
					Y

DISCOUNT TIRE CO

www.discounttire.com

Industry Group Code: 441320 **Ranks within this company's industry group:** Sales: Profits:

Vehicle Manufacturing:		Dealers:		Parts:		Service:		Finance:		Specialty:	
Cars:		Car Dealer New:		Manufacturers:		General Service:		Leasing:		Information Systems:	
Trucks:		Car Dealer Used:		Retail:	Y	Specialty Service:	Y	Auto Loans:		Online Marketing:	Y
Motorcycles:		Truck Dealer:		Distributors:		Oil Change:		Insurance:		Other:	
Specialty:		RV Dealer:		Tires:	Y	Paint and Body:				Publishing:	
Buses:		Motorcycle Dealer:		Batteries:						Rental Cars/Trucks:	
RVs:		Specialty Dealer:									

TYPES OF BUSINESS:

Tire Stores
Mail-Order & Online Tire Sales
Roadside Assistance

BRANDS/DIVISIONS/AFFILIATES:

America's Tire Co.
Discount Tire Direct
DiscountTireDirect.com
CarCareONE

CONTACTS:

Note: Officers with more than one job title may be intentionally listed here more than once.

Tom Englert, CEO
Steve Fournier, COO
Christian Roe, CFO
James Silhasek, General Counsel/Exec. VP
Bruce T. Halle, Chmn.

Phone: 480-606-6000	**Fax:** 480-951-8619
Toll-Free:	
Address: 20225 N. Scottsdale Rd., Scottsdale, AZ 85254 US	

GROWTH PLANS/SPECIAL FEATURES:

Discount Tire Co., based in Arizona, is one of the largest independent tire dealers in the U.S. The firm operates over 750 stores in 22 states across the nation, with concentrations in the Midwest and Southwest. These stores operate under the Discount Tire name, as well as under the America's Tire Co. name in certain areas. Discount Tire carries leading tire brands such as BF Goodrich, Michelin, Goodyear and Bridgestone, as well as private-label tires and wheels. The company also repairs tires, offers tire rotations and balancing to its customers and provides free air pressure checking. Discount Tires provides siping service, a procedure wherein slits, or sipes, are cut at 90-degree angles across tread to provide better tire performance. The firm also sells and delivers tires through its mail-order/online division (Discount Tire Direct) and through its web site. Discount Tire Direct has its own ordering web site, discounttiredirect.com, which provides fast, free shipping to a customer's door. This web site also provides extensive information for its customers on all aspects of wheel and tire care. The firm offers a Discount Tire/America's Tire CarCareONE card, a credit card that also provides emergency roadside assistance. In 2009, 32 store locations were added across the country, including Discount Tire's first in Idaho.

Discount Tires offers its employees benefits including flexible spending accounts; an employee assistance program; medical, vision and dental insurance; a 401(k) plan; and profit sharing plans. Part time employees are eligible for medical insurance and a 401(k).

FINANCIALS:

Sales and profits are in thousands of dollars—add 000 to get the full amount. 2009 Note: Financial information for 2009 was not available for all companies at press time.

2009 Sales: $	2009 Profits: $	**U.S. Stock Ticker: Private**
2008 Sales: $2,410,000	2008 Profits: $	**Int'l Ticker:** Int'l Exchange:
2007 Sales: $2,310,000	2007 Profits: $	Employees: 11,652
2006 Sales: $2,060,000	2006 Profits: $	Fiscal Year Ends: 12/31
2005 Sales: $1,856,000	2005 Profits: $	Parent Company:

SALARIES/BENEFITS:

Pension Plan:	ESOP Stock Plan:	Profit Sharing: Y	Top Exec. Salary: $	Bonus: $
Savings Plan: Y	Stock Purch. Plan:		Second Exec. Salary: $	Bonus: $

OTHER THOUGHTS:

Apparent Women Officers or Directors:
Hot Spot for Advancement for Women/Minorities:

LOCATIONS: ("Y" = Yes)

West:	Southwest:	Midwest:	Southeast:	Northeast:	International:
Y	Y	Y	Y	Y	

DOLLAR THRIFTY AUTOMOTIVE GROUP INC

www.dtag.com

Industry Group Code: 5321 **Ranks within this company's industry group:** Sales: 5 Profits: 1

Vehicle Manufacturing:		Dealers:		Parts:		Service:		Finance:		Specialty:	
Cars:		Car Dealer New:		Manufacturers:		General Service:		Leasing:		Information Systems:	
Trucks:		Car Dealer Used:		Retail:		Specialty Service:		Auto Loans:		Online Marketing:	
Motorcycles:		Truck Dealer:		Distributors:		Oil Change:		Insurance:		Other:	
Specialty:		RV Dealer:		Tires:		Paint and Body:				Publishing:	
Buses:		Motorcycle Dealer:		Batteries:						Rental Cars/Trucks:	Y
RVs:		Specialty Dealer:									

TYPES OF BUSINESS:

Automobile Rental
Used Car Sales
Financial Services

BRANDS/DIVISIONS/AFFILIATES:

Dollar Rent A Car, Inc.
Thrifty, Inc.
Thrifty Car Sales, Inc.
Thrifty Canada, Ltd.
Rental Car Finance Corp.
Dollar Thrifty Funding Corp.
Thrifty Rent-A-Car System, Inc.
DTG Operations, Inc.

CONTACTS:

Note: Officers with more than one job title may be intentionally listed here more than once.

Scott L. Thompson, CEO
Scott L. Thompson, Pres.
H. Clifford Buster, CFO/Exec. VP
Scott Anderson, Sr. Exec. VP-Global Mktg. & Sales
Rick Morris, CIO/Exec. VP
Vicki Vaniman, General Counsel/Sec./Exec. VP
Scott Anderson, Sr. Exec. VP-Corp. & Franchise Oper.
James F. Duffy, Exec. VP-Corp. Oper.
Thomas P. Capo, Chmn.

Phone: 918-660-7700 **Fax:** 918-669-2934
Toll-Free:
Address: 5330 E. 31st St., Tulsa, OK 74135 US

GROWTH PLANS/SPECIAL FEATURES:

Dollar Thrifty Automotive Group, Inc. (DTG) is involved in many aspects of renting and selling vehicles. The firm owns DTG Operations, Inc.; Dollar Rent A Car, Inc. (Dollar); and Thrifty, Inc. (Thrifty). Thrifty owns Thrifty Car Sales, Inc., which operates a franchised retail used car sales network, and Thrifty Rent-A-Car System, Inc., which owns Dollar `Thrifty Automotive Group Canada, Inc. DTG Operations administers company-owned stores under the Dollar and Thrifty brands; provides vehicle leasing to franchisees; and operates reservation centers for both brands. Thrifty Rent-A-Car System, Inc. and Dollar Rent A Car, Inc. conduct franchising, sales and marketing activities for their respective brands. The group has two additional subsidiaries, Rental Car Finance Corp. and Dollar Thrifty Funding Corp., which are special purpose financing companies. Dollar, Thrifty and their respective independent franchisees operate the Dollar and Thrifty vehicle rental systems. The Dollar and Thrifty brands are primarily utilized by leisure customers, including foreign tourists, small businesses, government business and independent business travelers. The Dollar brand's serves the airport and retail market, with most locations either at or near an airport. The brands have 109 in-terminal locations in the U.S., and 613 total locations in the U.S. and Canada. The Thrifty brand serves the airport market, from which 85% of its revenue is derived; and local markets (20%). In 2009, Chrysler vehicles represented approximately 63% of the total U.S. fleet purchases by DTG Operations. In April 2010, the firm signed an agreement to be acquired by Hertz Global Holdings, Inc. for $1.27 billion. In May 2010, Avis Budget Group, Inc. proposed a counterbid to acquire DTG; the offer is under review by the board. During 2010, DTG expanded it operations by opening two new corporate locations and 15 new franchise locations in the U.S.

DTG offers its employees medical, dental and vision coverage; flexible spending accounts; short- and long-term disability; life, AD&D and business travel insurance; and tuition reimbursement.

FINANCIALS:

Sales and profits are in thousands of dollars—add 000 to get the full amount. 2009 Note: Financial information for 2009 was not available for all companies at press time.

2009 Sales: $1,546,249	2009 Profits: $45,022	**U.S. Stock Ticker: DTG**
2008 Sales: $1,697,993	2008 Profits: $-346,718	**Int'l Ticker:** Int'l Exchange:
2007 Sales: $1,760,791	2007 Profits: $1,215	Employees: 6,000
2006 Sales: $1,660,677	2006 Profits: $51,692	Fiscal Year Ends: 12/31
2005 Sales: $1,507,554	2005 Profits: $76,355	Parent Company:

SALARIES/BENEFITS:

Pension Plan:	ESOP Stock Plan:	Profit Sharing: Y	Top Exec. Salary: $550,000	Bonus: $825,000
Savings Plan: Y	Stock Purch. Plan:		Second Exec. Salary: $425,000	Bonus: $478,125

OTHER THOUGHTS:

Apparent Women Officers or Directors: 2
Hot Spot for Advancement for Women/Minorities:

LOCATIONS: ("Y" = Yes)

West:	Southwest:	Midwest:	Southeast:	Northeast:	International:
Y	Y	Y	Y	Y	Y

DONGFENG MOTOR CORPORATION

www.dfmc.com.cn

Industry Group Code: 33611 **Ranks within this company's industry group:** Sales: Profits:

Vehicle Manufacturing:		Dealers:		Parts:		Service:		Finance:		Specialty:	
Cars:	Y	Car Dealer New:		Manufacturers:	Y	General Service:		Leasing:		Information Systems:	
Trucks:	Y	Car Dealer Used:		Retail:		Specialty Service:		Auto Loans:		Online Marketing:	
Motorcycles:		Truck Dealer:		Distributors:		Oil Change:		Insurance:		Other:	
Specialty:	Y	RV Dealer:		Tires:		Paint and Body:				Publishing:	
Buses:	Y	Motorcycle Dealer:		Batteries:						Rental Cars/Trucks:	
RVs:		Specialty Dealer:									

TYPES OF BUSINESS:

Automobile Manufacturing
Truck & Bus Manufacturing
Auto Parts & Components Manufacturing

BRANDS/DIVISIONS/AFFILIATES:

Dongfeng Peugeot Citroen Automobile Co., Limited
Dongfeng-Yueda Kia Automobile Company
Dongfeng Honda Automobile Co., Ltd.
Dongfeng Motor Co., Ltd.
Dongfeng Special-Purpose Vehicle Co., Ltd.
Dongfeng Electric Vehicle Co., Ltd.
Dongfeng Honda Auto Parts Co., Ltd.
Dongfeng Nissan-Diesel Company

CONTACTS: *Note: Officers with more than one job title may be intentionally listed here more than once.*

Xu Ping, Gen. Mgr.
Zhu Fushou, Pres.
Liu Zhangmin, Vice Gen. Mgr.
Li Shaozhu, Vice Gen. Mgr.
Tong Dongcheng, Vice Gen. Mgr.
Liu Weidong, Gen. Mgr.-Dongfeng Peugeot Citroen Automobile Ltd.
Xu Ping, Chmn.

Phone: 86-719-8226-962	**Fax:** 86-719-8226-845
Toll-Free:	
Address: 29 Baiye Rd., Wuhan, 430015 China	

GROWTH PLANS/SPECIAL FEATURES:

Dongfeng Motor Corporation (DFM) is one of China's leading automakers. Established as a state-owned company in 1969, DFM was restructured in the 1990s and has since sought out numerous joint ventures as well as integrating its development with international automotive companies. Subsequently, it has become one of the Chinese automotive companies most heavily vested in foreign partnerships. DFM partnered with PSA Peugeot Citroen to establish Dongfeng Peugeot Citroen Automobile Company Limited, while its other joint-venture partners and affiliates include Nissan Motor Co., Ltd., with which it has created Dongfeng Nissan-Diesel Company; Kia Motors Corporation, with which it formed Dongfeng-Yueda Kia Automobile Company; and Honda Motor Co., Ltd., with which it formed Dongfeng Honda Automobile Co., Ltd. The firm's main subsidiary is Dongfeng Motor Co., Ltd. (Dongfeng Motor). DFM has two primary product lines: commercial vehicles and passenger vehicles. The company's commercial products include semi-trucks, heavy-duty passenger trucks, cement mixers, watering trucks, garbage trucks, dump trucks, freight trucks and buses, mostly manufactured by Dongfeng Motor and other subsidiaries, including Dongfeng Automobile Co., Ltd.; Dongfeng Special-Purpose Vehicle Co., Ltd. ; and Dongfeng Electric Vehicle Co., Ltd. Its passenger vehicles include cars, multi-purpose vehicles (MPVs) and SUVs (Sport Utility Vehicles). The company has passenger vehicle production facilities in Wuhan and Guangzhou; a medium and heavy duty commercial vehicle manufacturing facility in Shiyan; and a light commercial and passenger vehicle production facility in Xiangfan. DFM generally produces over 1 million vehicles annually. In addition to manufacturing vehicles, the firm's subsidiary, Dongfeng Honda Auto Parts Co., Ltd., manufactures auto parts and components.

FINANCIALS: **Sales and profits are in thousands of dollars—add 000 to get the full amount. 2009 Note: Financial information for 2009 was not available for all companies at press time.**

2009 Sales: $	2009 Profits: $	**U.S. Stock Ticker: Government-Owned**
2008 Sales: $	2008 Profits: $	**Int'l Ticker:** Int'l Exchange:
2007 Sales: $	2007 Profits: $	Employees:
2006 Sales: $	2006 Profits: $	Fiscal Year Ends:
2005 Sales: $	2005 Profits: $	Parent Company:

SALARIES/BENEFITS:

Pension Plan:	ESOP Stock Plan:	Profit Sharing:	Top Exec. Salary: $	Bonus: $
Savings Plan:	Stock Purch. Plan:		Second Exec. Salary: $	Bonus: $

OTHER THOUGHTS:

Apparent Women Officers or Directors:
Hot Spot for Advancement for Women/Minorities:

LOCATIONS: ("Y" = Yes)

West:	Southwest:	Midwest:	Southeast:	Northeast:	International:
					Y

DONLEN CORPORATION

www.donlen.com

Industry Group Code: 5321 **Ranks within this company's industry group:** Sales: Profits:

Vehicle Manufacturing:		Dealers:		Parts:		Service:		Finance:		Specialty:	
Cars:		Car Dealer New:		Manufacturers:		General Service:		Leasing:	Y	Information Systems:	
Trucks:		Car Dealer Used:		Retail:		Specialty Service:		Auto Loans:		Online Marketing:	Y
Motorcycles:		Truck Dealer:		Distributors:		Oil Change:		Insurance:		Other:	Y
Specialty:		RV Dealer:		Tires:		Paint and Body:				Publishing:	
Buses:		Motorcycle Dealer:		Batteries:						Rental Cars/Trucks:	
RVs:		Specialty Dealer:									

TYPES OF BUSINESS:

Automobiles-Leasing
Business Vehicles
Fleet Management Services
License & Title Services
Maintenance Services
Asset Management Services

BRANDS/DIVISIONS/AFFILIATES:

FleetWeb
Donlen Driver
Donlen Fleet Leasing, Ltd.
Fleet Management Services
Lifecycle Optimization Tools
Donlen Greenkey.com

CONTACTS: *Note: Officers with more than one job title may be intentionally listed here more than once.*

Gary Rappeport, CEO
Tom Callahan, COO
Tom Callahan, Pres.
Michael Manfred, CFO/Sr. VP
Barry Steel, Sr. VP-Sales
Barry Steel, Sr. VP-Strategy
Dave Lodding, Pres., Fleet Mgmt. Svcs.
Jim Kachidurian, Sr. VP-Client Rel.
Suzanne Deveney, VP-Mktg.

Phone: 847-714-1400	**Fax:** 847-714-1500
Toll-Free:	
Address: 2315 Sanders Rd., Northbrook, IL 60062 US	

GROWTH PLANS/SPECIAL FEATURES:

Donlen Corp., along with subsidiaries Fleet Management Services and Canadian-based Donlen Fleet Leasing, Ltd., provides a range of vehicle leasing, asset management and fleet management services. Donlen currently manages over 135,000 vehicles and its services are accessible in all 50 states in the U.S. The company's asset management team provides leasing, remarketing and ownership programs as well as acquisition, license and title services. Fleet Management Services (FMS) provides clients with flexible management programs in order to reduce operating costs and any administration needed to run an entire fleet. Programs of FMS include preventive maintenance, maintenance consultation, fuel management and accident management, which are all accessed through the company's web-based tracking system, FleetWeb. FleetWeb covers all facets of fleet operations management and supplies a system for order entry and information maintenance. FleetWeb also operates the Donlen Driver web site, where users can compare and order vehicles or submit tax reporting information. In addition, Donlen's corporate web site features an industry news section and the vehicle Lifecycle Calculator, an interactive approach that determines the best value for fleet vehicles. Donlen Greenkey.com an online community for fleet managers, featuring news articles and tips on how to transition to more environmentally friendly fleet programs. Donlen's 'PUSH' (Prevent Unnecessary Spending and Hazards) technology helps to improve preventive maintenance compliance and reduce fleet operating costs. The firm also maintains Lifecycle Optimization Tools, which assists the fleet industry in evaluating asset management decisions, and the National Auction Index (NAI), a large database that publishes vehicle resale transactions. In December 2009, the company launched fleet management apps for the iPhone, which is made available to download for free for Donlen customers.

Employees are offered medical and dental insurance; life insurance; flexible spending accounts; a 401(k) plan; profit sharing; and access to an on-site fitness center.

FINANCIALS: **Sales and profits are in thousands of dollars—add 000 to get the full amount. 2009 Note: Financial information for 2009 was not available for all companies at press time.**

2009 Sales: $	2009 Profits: $	**U.S. Stock Ticker: Private**
2008 Sales: $	2008 Profits: $	**Int'l Ticker:** Int'l Exchange:
2007 Sales: $	2007 Profits: $	Employees:
2006 Sales: $	2006 Profits: $	Fiscal Year Ends: 8/31
2005 Sales: $531,500	2005 Profits: $	Parent Company:

SALARIES/BENEFITS:

Pension Plan:	ESOP Stock Plan:	Profit Sharing: Y	Top Exec. Salary: $	Bonus: $
Savings Plan: Y	Stock Purch. Plan:		Second Exec. Salary: $	Bonus: $

OTHER THOUGHTS:

Apparent Women Officers or Directors:
Hot Spot for Advancement for Women/Minorities:

LOCATIONS: ("Y" = Yes)

West:	Southwest:	Midwest:	Southeast:	Northeast:	International:
Y	Y	Y	Y	Y	Y

DORMAN PRODUCTS INC

www.dormanproducts.com

Industry Group Code: 3363 **Ranks within this company's industry group:** Sales: 55 Profits: 19

Vehicle Manufacturing:		Dealers:		Parts:		Service:		Finance:		Specialty:	
Cars:		Car Dealer New:		Manufacturers:	Y	General Service:		Leasing:		Information Systems:	
Trucks:		Car Dealer Used:		Retail:		Specialty Service:		Auto Loans:		Online Marketing:	
Motorcycles:		Truck Dealer:		Distributors:	Y	Oil Change:		Insurance:		Other:	
Specialty:		RV Dealer:		Tires:		Paint and Body:				Publishing:	
Buses:		Motorcycle Dealer:		Batteries:						Rental Cars/Trucks:	
RVs:		Specialty Dealer:									

TYPES OF BUSINESS:

Automobile Parts Manufacturer
Replacement & Aftermarket Parts

BRANDS/DIVISIONS/AFFILIATES:

Scan-Tech
Dorman Canada
AutoGrade
First Stop
Conduct-Tite
Pik-A-Nut
OE Solutions

CONTACTS:

Note: Officers with more than one job title may be intentionally listed here more than once.

Richard N. Berman, CEO
Steven L. Berman, COO
Steven L. Berman, Pres.
Mathias J. Barton, CFO/Sr. VP
Joseph M. Beretta, Sr. VP-Prod.
Thomas J. Knoblauch, General Counsel/VP
Fred Frigo, Sr. VP-Oper.
Steven L. Berman, Treas./Sec.
Richard N. Berman, Chmn.

Phone: 215-997-1800 **Fax:** 215-997-7968
Toll-Free:
Address: 3400 E. Walnut St., Colmar, PA 18915 US

GROWTH PLANS/SPECIAL FEATURES:

Dorman Products, Inc. is a leading supplier of original equipment automotive replacement parts, fasteners and service line products for the automotive aftermarket. The company designs, packages and markets over 103,000 different automotive replacement parts that are sold primarily in the U.S. to automotive aftermarket retailers such as AutoZone, Advance Auto Parts and O'Reilly; national, regional and local warehouse dealers; specialty markets; and salvage yards. Dorman's automotive replacements parts market is divided into two components: parts for passenger cars and light trucks; and parts for heavy-duty trucks, with most of the firm's parts designed for passenger cars and light trucks. The majority of the company's sales consist of original equipment dealer parts that include intake manifolds, exhaust manifolds, oil cooler lines, window regulators, radiator fan assemblies, power steering pulleys and harmonic balancers. Approximately 90% of the company's products are sold under original brand names, with the remainder sold for resale under customers' private labels or in bulk. Through its Scan-Tech subsidiary and Dorman Canada unit, the company has increased its international distribution of automotive replacement parts through sales in Canada, Europe, the Middle East and Asia. Dorman currently sells its products under a number of proprietary brand names, including OE Solutions, AutoGrade, First Stop, HELP!, Conduct-Tite, Scan-Tech and Pik-A-Nut. In March 2010, the company sold its ignition distributor product line to WAIglobal.

Dorman offers its employees medical, dental and vision coverage; flexible spending accounts; a 401(k) plan; a 529 college savings plan; life and disability insurance; tuition reimbursement; credit union membership; a company-sponsored health club membership; personal protection programs; and auto insurance.

FINANCIALS:

Sales and profits are in thousands of dollars—add 000 to get the full amount. 2009 Note: Financial information for 2009 was not available for all companies at press time.

2009 Sales: $377,378	2009 Profits: $26,495	**U.S. Stock Ticker: DORM**
2008 Sales: $342,325	2008 Profits: $17,813	**Int'l Ticker:** Int'l Exchange:
2007 Sales: $327,725	2007 Profits: $19,193	Employees: 997
2006 Sales: $295,825	2006 Profits: $13,799	Fiscal Year Ends: 12/31
2005 Sales: $278,117	2005 Profits: $17,077	Parent Company:

SALARIES/BENEFITS:

Pension Plan:	ESOP Stock Plan:	Profit Sharing: Y	Top Exec. Salary: $529,973	Bonus: $150,000
Savings Plan: Y	Stock Purch. Plan:		Second Exec. Salary: $529,973	Bonus: $150,000

OTHER THOUGHTS:

Apparent Women Officers or Directors:
Hot Spot for Advancement for Women/Minorities:

LOCATIONS: ("Y" = Yes)

West:	Southwest:	Midwest:	Southeast:	Northeast:	International:
		Y	Y	Y	Y

DRIVETIME AUTOMOTIVE GROUP INC

www.drivetime.com

Industry Group Code: 441110 **Ranks within this company's industry group:** Sales: Profits:

Vehicle Manufacturing:		Dealers:		Parts:		Service:		Finance:		Specialty:	
Cars:		Car Dealer New:		Manufacturers:		General Service:		Leasing:		Information Systems:	
Trucks:		Car Dealer Used:	Y	Retail:		Specialty Service:		Auto Loans:	Y	Online Marketing:	
Motorcycles:		Truck Dealer:		Distributors:		Oil Change:		Insurance:		Other:	
Specialty:		RV Dealer:		Tires:		Paint and Body:				Publishing:	
Buses:		Motorcycle Dealer:		Batteries:						Rental Cars/Trucks:	
RVs:		Specialty Dealer:									

TYPES OF BUSINESS:

Used Auto Dealers
Auto Financing

BRANDS/DIVISIONS/AFFILIATES:

DriveCare Limited Warranty

CONTACTS:

Note: Officers with more than one job title may be intentionally listed here more than once.

Ray Fidel, CEO
Ray Fidel, Pres.
Mark G. Sauder, CFO/Exec. VP
Deborah Powell, Dir.-Human Resources
Jon Ehlinger, General Counsel/Corp. Sec.
Jon Ehlinger, VP-Public Rel.
Al Appelman, VP-Risk & Customer Analytics
Ernest C. Garcia II, Chmn.

Phone: 602-852-6600 **Fax:** 602-852-6686
Toll-Free: 888-418-1212
Address: 4020 E. Indian School Rd., Phoenix, AZ 85018 US

GROWTH PLANS/SPECIAL FEATURES:

DriveTime Automotive Group, Inc. operates a leading chain of buy-here-pay-here used car dealerships. The company targets its products and services to the sub-prime segment of the automobile financing industry. This segment serves customers with limited credit histories, low income or past credit problems who cannot access traditional financing. Advantages of buy-here-pay-here dealerships include the ability to offer customers expanded credit opportunities and flexible payment terms and the ability to make payments at the dealership. The firm finances all of the used cars through retail installment contracts. DriveTime currently operates about 83 dealerships in 25 major metropolitan areas in 13 states: Arizona, California, Colorado, Florida, Georgia, Nevada, New Mexico, North Carolina, Texas and Virginia. The dealerships are located in high-visibility, high-traffic commercial areas and maintain an average inventory of 50-150 used cars, featuring a wide selection of makes and models. The ages of the cars typically range from four to seven years, but all are two years and older. DriveTime acquires its inventory from new or late-model used car dealers, used car wholesalers, used car auctions and customer trade-ins. After purchase, the cars are delivered to one of the company's 13 inspection centers, where they are inspected thoroughly and reconditioned for sale. The firm advertises a 53-point inspection, which is designed to ensure that vehicles are properly inspected before sale, and each vehicle comes with the company's DriveCare limited warranty. The company sells and finances more than 60,000 vehicles per year.

DriveTime offers its employees benefits including medical, dental, vision, disability and life insurance; paid time off; a 401(k); flexible spending accounts; and tuition reimbursement.

FINANCIALS:

Sales and profits are in thousands of dollars—add 000 to get the full amount. 2009 Note: Financial information for 2009 was not available for all companies at press time.

2009 Sales: $
2008 Sales: $
2007 Sales: $
2006 Sales: $
2005 Sales: $

2009 Profits: $
2008 Profits: $
2007 Profits: $
2006 Profits: $
2005 Profits: $

U.S. Stock Ticker: Private
Int'l Ticker: Int'l Exchange:
Employees:
Fiscal Year Ends: 12/31
Parent Company:

SALARIES/BENEFITS:

Pension Plan: ESOP Stock Plan: Profit Sharing: Top Exec. Salary: $ Bonus: $
Savings Plan: Y Stock Purch. Plan: Second Exec. Salary: $ Bonus: $

OTHER THOUGHTS:

Apparent Women Officers or Directors: 1
Hot Spot for Advancement for Women/Minorities:

LOCATIONS: ("Y" = Yes)

West:	Southwest:	Midwest:	Southeast:	Northeast:	International:
Y	Y		Y	Y	

DUCATI MOTOR HOLDING SPA

www.ducati.com

Industry Group Code: 336991 **Ranks within this company's industry group:** Sales: Profits:

Vehicle Manufacturing:		Dealers:		Parts:		Service:		Finance:		Specialty:	
Cars:		Car Dealer New:		Manufacturers:	Y	General Service:		Leasing:		Information Systems:	
Trucks:		Car Dealer Used:		Retail:	Y	Specialty Service:		Auto Loans:		Online Marketing:	Y
Motorcycles:	Y	Truck Dealer:		Distributors:		Oil Change:		Insurance:		Other:	Y
Specialty:		RV Dealer:		Tires:		Paint and Body:				Publishing:	
Buses:		Motorcycle Dealer:	Y	Batteries:						Rental Cars/Trucks:	
RVs:		Specialty Dealer:									

TYPES OF BUSINESS:

Motorcycle Manufacturing & Retail
Apparel & Accessories
Online Retail
Racing Operations

BRANDS/DIVISIONS/AFFILIATES:

Hypermotard
Monster
Multistrada
Sportclassic
Streetfighter
Superbike
Ducati Card Assistance

CONTACTS: *Note: Officers with more than one job title may be intentionally listed here more than once.*

Gabriele Del Torchio, CEO
Enrico D'Onofrio, CFO
Cristiano Silei, VP-Mktg. & Sales
Danilo Bernardini, Mgr.-Human Resources
Daniel Bellini, Dir.-IT
Claudio Domenicali, Dir.-Prod.
Gianfranco Giorgini, Dir.-Oper.
Paolo Poma, Dir.-Planning & Control
Paolo Poma, Dir.-Finance
David Gross, Dir.-Creative
Gabriele Del Torchio, Chmn.

Phone: 39-051-641-3111 **Fax:** 39-051-406-580
Toll-Free:
Address: Via Cavalieri Ducati 3, Bologna, 40132 Italy

GROWTH PLANS/SPECIAL FEATURES:

Ducati Motor Holding S.p.A., founded in Italy in 1926, manufactures six lines of high-performance motorcycles in the sport segment of the road market: Hypermotard; Monster; Multistrada; Sportclassic; Streetfighter; and Superbike. The Hypermotard is capable of speeds exceeding 125 mph and includes such features as fuel injection and 90 Desmo horsepower. The Monster line, with airbrushed fuel tanks, carbon fiber parts and accessories machined from solid aluminum, high performance exhaust systems, was one of the first motorcycles with the absence of fairing, which exposes the engine and reduces body weight. The Multistrada, an all-roads and all-seasons bike, features a 1100 Desmo engine with a quiet wet clutch and comfort-enhancing vibration-isolated handlebars. Its product line includes the Multistrada 1200, Multistrada 1200 S Sport and Multistrada 1200 S Touring. The Sportclassic line is a retro-designed line, and the company offers various accessories including exhaust systems; fiberglass and plastic fibers; electronic components; and chassis and brake systems. The Streetfighter Superbike features 155 horsepower, a clutch dry multiplate with hydraulic control and a variety of accessories. Lastly, the Superbike line offers five twin-cylinder motorcycles: the Superbike 848; the Superbike 1198; the Superbike 1198 S; the Superbike S Corse; and the Superbike 1198 R Corse. The company also sells branded apparel and accessories, including custom exhaust pipes, leather jackets and specially designed Oakley/Ducati sunglasses. Ducati Card Assistance is a maintenance service card offered by Ducati and ACI Global S.p.A., providing such services as emergency roadside assistance, medical consultation and cash advance.

FINANCIALS: **Sales and profits are in thousands of dollars—add 000 to get the full amount. 2009 Note: Financial information for 2009 was not available for all companies at press time.**

2009 Sales: $
2008 Sales: $
2007 Sales: $624,400
2006 Sales: $478,500
2005 Sales: $379,700

2009 Profits: $
2008 Profits: $
2007 Profits: $20,800
2006 Profits: $-13,400
2005 Profits: $-49,100

U.S. Stock Ticker:
Int'l Ticker: DMH Int'l Exchange: Milan-BI
Employees:
Fiscal Year Ends: 12/31
Parent Company:

SALARIES/BENEFITS:

Pension Plan: ESOP Stock Plan: Profit Sharing: Top Exec. Salary: $ Bonus: $
Savings Plan: Stock Purch. Plan: Second Exec. Salary: $ Bonus: $

OTHER THOUGHTS:

Apparent Women Officers or Directors:
Hot Spot for Advancement for Women/Minorities:

LOCATIONS: ("Y" = Yes)

West:	Southwest:	Midwest:	Southeast:	Northeast:	International:
					Y

E I DU PONT DE NEMOURS & CO (DUPONT)

www2.dupont.com

Industry Group Code: 325 **Ranks within this company's industry group:** Sales: 1 Profits: 1

Vehicle Manufacturing:		**Dealers:**		**Parts:**		**Service:**		**Finance:**		**Specialty:**	
Cars:		Car Dealer New:		Manufacturers:	Y	General Service:		Leasing:		Information Systems:	
Trucks:		Car Dealer Used:		Retail:		Specialty Service:		Auto Loans:		Online Marketing:	
Motorcycles:		Truck Dealer:		Distributors:		Oil Change:		Insurance:		Other:	Y
Specialty:		RV Dealer:		Tires:		Paint and Body:				Publishing:	
Buses:		Motorcycle Dealer:		Batteries:						Rental Cars/Trucks:	
RVs:		Specialty Dealer:									

TYPES OF BUSINESS:

Chemicals Manufacturing
Polymers
Performance Coatings
Nutrition & Health Products
Electronics Materials
Agricultural Seeds
Fuel-Cell, Biofuels & Solar Panel Technology
Contract Research & Development

BRANDS/DIVISIONS/AFFILIATES:

Pioneer Hi-Bred International Inc
Teflon
Corian
Kevlar
Tyvek
Solae
DuPont Nomex on Demand
Meyrin Photovoltaic Application Laboratory

CONTACTS:

Note: Officers with more than one job title may be intentionally listed here more than once.

Ellen J. Kullman, CEO
Nicholas C. Farandakis, CFO/Sr. VP
Cynthia C. Green, Chief Mktg. & Sales Officer/VP-Corp. Mktg. & Sales
W. Donald Johnson, Sr. VP-Human Resources
Uma Chowdhry, Chief Science Officer
Phuong Tram, CIO/VP-IT
Uma Chowdhry, CTO/Sr. VP
Thomas M. Connelly, Jr., Chief Innovation Officer/Exec. VP
Jeffrey A. Coe, Sr. VP-Eng.
Thomas L. Sager, General Counsel/Sr. VP-Legal
Jeffrey A. Coe, Sr. VP-Integrated Oper.
David G. Bills, Sr. VP-Corp. Strategy
Karen A. Fletcher, VP-DuPont Investor Rel.
Susan M. Stalnecker, VP-Finance/Treas.
Criag F. Binetti, Sr. VP-DuPont Nutrition & Health
Diane H. Gulyas, Pres., DuPont Performance Polymers
Terry Caloghiris, Pres., DuPont Performance Coatings
Linda J. Fisher, Chief Sustainability Officer
Ellen J. Kullman, Chmn.
Donald D. Wirth, VP-Global Oper.
Keith J. Smith, Chief Procurement Officer/VP-Sourcing & Logistics

Phone: 302-774-1000 **Fax:** 302-773-2631
Toll-Free: 800-441-7515
Address: 1007 Market St., Wilmington, DE 19898 US

GROWTH PLANS/SPECIAL FEATURES:

E. I. du Pont de Nemours & Co. (DuPont), founded in 1802, develops and manufactures products in the biotechnology, electronics, materials science, synthetic fibers and safety and security sectors. DuPont operates in seven segments: Agriculture and Nutrition (A&N); Electronic and Communications (E&C); Performance Coatings, Performance Chemicals; Performance Materials (PM); Safety and Protection (S&P) and Pharmaceuticals. A&N delivers seed products, insecticides, fungicides, herbicides, soy-based food ingredients, food quality diagnostic testing equipment and liquid food packaging systems. Brands include Pioneer seeds and Solae soy proteins. E&C provides a range of advanced materials for the electronics industry, flexographic printing, color communication systems and a range of fluoropolymer and fluorochemical products. The Performance Coatings segment supplies automotive liquid and powder coatings, and general industrial applications such as coatings for heavy equipment, pipes and appliances and electrical insulation. Brands include DuPont, Standox, Spies Hecker and Nason. PM manufactures polymer-based materials, which include engineered polymers, specialized resins and films for use in food packaging, sealants, adhesives, sporting goods and laminated safety glass. The S&P segment provides protective materials and safety consulting services. Significant brands include Teflon fluoropolymers, films, fabric protectors, fibers and dispersions; Corian surfaces; Kevlar high strength material; and Tyvek protective material. The Pharmaceuticals segment involves the worldwide manufacturing and marketing activities of the antihypertensive drugs, Cozaar and Hyzaar. The company has operations in over 70 countries around the world and maintains 75 R&D and customer services labs in 12 countries. In March 2009, the firm launched the DuPont Nomex on Demand smart fiber technology, a material designed for thermal liners in firefighter gear, that expands for thermal insulation in over 250 degree heat. In February 2010, the company opened the Meyrin Photovoltaic Application Laboratory at its European Technical Center in Geneva.

Employees are offered medical, dental and life insurance; disability coverage; dependent care spending accounts; and adoption assistance.

FINANCIALS:

Sales and profits are in thousands of dollars—add 000 to get the full amount. 2009 Note: Financial information for 2009 was not available for all companies at press time.

2009 Sales: $26,109,000	2009 Profits: $1,755,000	**U.S. Stock Ticker: DD**
2008 Sales: $30,529,000	2008 Profits: $2,007,000	**Int'l Ticker:** Int'l Exchange:
2007 Sales: $29,378,000	2007 Profits: $2,988,000	Employees: 58,000
2006 Sales: $27,421,000	2006 Profits: $3,148,000	Fiscal Year Ends: 12/31
2005 Sales: $26,639,000	2005 Profits: $2,053,000	Parent Company:

SALARIES/BENEFITS:

Pension Plan: Y	ESOP Stock Plan:	Profit Sharing:	Top Exec. Salary: $1,369,500	Bonus: $1,932,000
Savings Plan: Y	Stock Purch. Plan:		Second Exec. Salary: $865,992	Bonus: $763,000

OTHER THOUGHTS:

Apparent Women Officers or Directors: 17
Hot Spot for Advancement for Women/Minorities: Y

LOCATIONS: ("Y" = Yes)

West:	Southwest:	Midwest:	Southeast:	Northeast:	International:
Y	Y	Y	Y	Y	Y

EAGLE OTTAWA LEATHER COMPANY LLC www.eagleottawa.com

Industry Group Code: 3363 **Ranks within this company's industry group:** Sales: Profits:

Vehicle Manufacturing:		Dealers:		Parts:		Service:		Finance:		Specialty:	
Cars:		Car Dealer New:		Manufacturers:	Y	General Service:		Leasing:		Information Systems:	
Trucks:		Car Dealer Used:		Retail:		Specialty Service:	Y	Auto Loans:		Online Marketing:	
Motorcycles:		Truck Dealer:		Distributors:		Oil Change:		Insurance:		Other:	
Specialty:		RV Dealer:		Tires:		Paint and Body:				Publishing:	
Buses:		Motorcycle Dealer:		Batteries:						Rental Cars/Trucks:	
RVs:		Specialty Dealer:									

TYPES OF BUSINESS:

Automobile Upholstery Manufacturing
Leather Treatment & Crafting
Engineering & Development Services
Durability Testing Services

BRANDS/DIVISIONS/AFFILIATES:

Everett Smith Group, Ltd.
Maysteel
Dickten & Masch
Trostel, Ltd.

CONTACTS:

Note: Officers with more than one job title may be intentionally listed here more than once.

Jerry L. Sumpter, CEO
Jerry L. Sumpter, Pres.
Bob Carlo, CFO/VP
Tim Brennan, VP-Mktg.
Scott Landis, Dir.-Human Resources
Craig Tonti, Pres., Americas & Europe
Cary Bean, Exec. VP/Pres., Eagle Ottawa China
Pat Catlin, VP-Global Sales & Design
Udo Schnell, Exec. VP/Pres., Eagle Ottawa Europe
Eric Brooks, VP-Global Supply Chain Mgmt.

Phone: 248-364-7400	**Fax:** 248-364-7529
Toll-Free:	
Address: 1885 Pond Run, Auburn Hills, MI 48326 US	

GROWTH PLANS/SPECIAL FEATURES:

Eagle Ottawa Leather Company LLC is a member of the Everett Smith Group of companies. The Everett Smith Group is a privately held company with investments in automotive, leather, sheet metal, rubber, urethanes and thermoplastics. The firm is a world leader in the manufacturing and marketing of upholstery leather for the luxury automotive industry. It operates sales and design centers in Germany, the U.K., the U.S., Italy, South Korea, Japan and China; and manufacturing facilities in Brazil, China, Argentina, Mexico, the U.S., the U.K. and Hungary. The company offers finished hides, cut leather parts, complete seat cover engineering and development services, as well as complete material and seat durability testing services. Its product lines include natural shrunken grain leather, chrome-tanned and non-chrome tanned leather, high-durability leather and automotive-grade semi-aniline leather, varieties that are all used in luxury automotive interiors. Eagle Ottawa procures fresh and cured hides and has the tanning assembly line necessary to produce a colored, embossed and textured finished product for its clients. More than 100 vehicle models produced by 27 automakers worldwide use its leather, with customers including BMW, Audi, Honda, Kia, Nissan, Hummer, Volkswagen, Mercedes-Benz, Lexus, Lincoln, Infiniti, Renault, Land Rover, Mitsubishi, Ford, Chevrolet and Toyota. In January 2010, Eagle Ottawa introduced Ansole, a soil and stain resistant leather finish system.

FINANCIALS:

Sales and profits are in thousands of dollars—add 000 to get the full amount. 2009 Note: Financial information for 2009 was not available for all companies at press time.

2009 Sales: $	2009 Profits: $	**U.S. Stock Ticker: Subsidiary**
2008 Sales: $	2008 Profits: $	**Int'l Ticker:** Int'l Exchange:
2007 Sales: $548,900	2007 Profits: $	Employees:
2006 Sales: $	2006 Profits: $	Fiscal Year Ends: 11/30
2005 Sales: $	2005 Profits: $	Parent Company: EVERETT SMITH GROUP LTD

SALARIES/BENEFITS:

Pension Plan:	ESOP Stock Plan:	Profit Sharing:	Top Exec. Salary: $	Bonus: $
Savings Plan:	Stock Purch. Plan:		Second Exec. Salary: $	Bonus: $

OTHER THOUGHTS:

Apparent Women Officers or Directors:
Hot Spot for Advancement for Women/Minorities:

LOCATIONS: ("Y" = Yes)

West:	Southwest:	Midwest:	Southeast:	Northeast:	International:
Y		Y			Y

EAGLEPICHER CORPORATION

www.epcorp.com

Industry Group Code: 3363 **Ranks within this company's industry group:** Sales: Profits:

Vehicle Manufacturing:		Dealers:		Parts:		Service:		Finance:		Specialty:	
Cars:		Car Dealer New:		Manufacturers:	Y	General Service:		Leasing:		Information Systems:	
Trucks:		Car Dealer Used:		Retail:		Specialty Service:		Auto Loans:		Online Marketing:	
Motorcycles:		Truck Dealer:		Distributors:		Oil Change:		Insurance:		Other:	Y
Specialty:		RV Dealer:		Tires:		Paint and Body:				Publishing:	
Buses:		Motorcycle Dealer:		Batteries:						Rental Cars/Trucks:	
RVs:		Specialty Dealer:									

TYPES OF BUSINESS:

Chemical Manufacturing
Batteries
Specialty Materials
Automotive Parts
Filtration Products & Minerals

BRANDS/DIVISIONS/AFFILIATES:

EP Minerals, LLC
EaglePicher Medical Power
EaglePicher Technologies, LLC
Wolverine Advanced Materials
Carefree
KeeperII

CONTACTS: *Note: Officers with more than one job title may be intentionally listed here more than once.*

David L. Treadwell, CEO
Randy Moore, Pres.
Patrick S. Aubry, CFO
Creed Jones, VP-Human Resources
Greg Miller, VP-Tech.
Greg Miller, VP-Eng.
Rick Estus, VP-Oper.
Michael Retherford, Contractor-Finance
Ronald Nowlin, VP/Gen. Mgr.
Forrest Reed, Dir.-Quality
John Bennett, VP/Gen. Mgr.
Donald L. Ruhnkle, Chmn.

Phone: 313-749-5500	**Fax:** 313-749-5502
Toll-Free:	
Address: 5850 Mercury Dr., Ste. 250, Dearborn, MI 48126 US	

GROWTH PLANS/SPECIAL FEATURES:

EaglePicher Corporation manufactures industrial products for the automotive, defense, space, commercial, power, nuclear, semiconductors, filtration and medical industries through its subsidiaries and manufacturing plants. The company's main subsidiaries include EP Minerals, LLC, which produces diatomaceous earth (DE) products that act as filter aids and fillers for paints, catalyst supports and polyethylene film under the Celatom brand; EaglePicher Medical Power, which supplies implantable medical battery solutions for neuromodulation, neurostimulation, drug pumps, cardiac rhythm management and cardiac monitoring; Wolverine Advanced Materials, which provides vibration damping and sealing materials for the automotive, consumer electronics and industrial markets; EaglePicher Technologies, LLC, which operates through two divisions: commercial power solutions and defense and space; and EaglePicher Technologies Commercial Power Solutions, which offers Carefree and KeeperII batteries and also customizes the packaging of virtually any battery chemistry for its customer's specific needs. The defense and space power sector offers nickel hydrogen cell batteries, lithium-ion cell batteries and electronics.

FINANCIALS: **Sales and profits are in thousands of dollars—add 000 to get the full amount. 2009 Note: Financial information for 2009 was not available for all companies at press time.**

2009 Sales: $	2009 Profits: $	**U.S. Stock Ticker: Private**
2008 Sales: $	2008 Profits: $	**Int'l Ticker:** Int'l Exchange:
2007 Sales: $119,000	2007 Profits: $	Employees:
2006 Sales: $	2006 Profits: $	Fiscal Year Ends: 11/30
2005 Sales: $	2005 Profits: $	Parent Company:

SALARIES/BENEFITS:

Pension Plan:	ESOP Stock Plan:	Profit Sharing:	Top Exec. Salary: $	Bonus: $
Savings Plan:	Stock Purch. Plan:		Second Exec. Salary: $	Bonus: $

OTHER THOUGHTS:

Apparent Women Officers or Directors:
Hot Spot for Advancement for Women/Minorities:

LOCATIONS: ("Y" = Yes)

West:	Southwest:	Midwest:	Southeast:	Northeast:	International:
Y	Y	Y	Y	Y	Y

EARNHARDT'S AUTO CENTERS

www.earnhardt.com

Industry Group Code: 441110 **Ranks within this company's industry group:** Sales: Profits:

Vehicle Manufacturing:		Dealers:		Parts:		Service:		Finance:		Specialty:	
Cars:		Car Dealer New:	Y	Manufacturers:		General Service:	Y	Leasing:		Information Systems:	
Trucks:		Car Dealer Used:	Y	Retail:	Y	Specialty Service:		Auto Loans:	Y	Online Marketing:	
Motorcycles:		Truck Dealer:	Y	Distributors:		Oil Change:		Insurance:	Y	Other:	
Specialty:		RV Dealer:		Tires:		Paint and Body:	Y			Publishing:	
Buses:		Motorcycle Dealer:		Batteries:						Rental Cars/Trucks:	
RVs:		Specialty Dealer:									

TYPES OF BUSINESS:

Auto Dealers, Retail New & Used
Auto Service & Parts
Auto Loans & Insurance
Fleet Sales
RV Sales & Service

BRANDS/DIVISIONS/AFFILIATES:

Earnhardt Auto Body
Earnhardt Honda
Earnhardt Mazda
Earnhardt Chrysler Jeep
Earnhardt Nissan
Earnhardt Scion
Earnhardt Ford
San Tan Hyundai

CONTACTS: *Note: Officers with more than one job title may be intentionally listed here more than once.*

Tex Earnhardt, CEO
Hal J. Earnhardt, III, Pres.
Robbyn McDowell, CFO
Hal J. Earnhardt, Jr., Chmn.

Phone: 480-926-4000 **Fax:** 480-632-7712
Toll-Free: 800-357-6070
Address: 7300 W. Orchid Ln., Chandler, AZ 85226 US

GROWTH PLANS/SPECIAL FEATURES:

Earnhardt's Auto Centers is a new and used automobile dealer with 10 locations in Arizona and one in Texas. The company has locations in six cities: Avondale, Chandler, Gilbert, Mesa and Tempe in Arizona and El Paso, Texas. The dealerships include Earnhardt Honda in Avondale; Earnhardt Mazda and Earnhardt Ford in Chandler; San Tan Hyundai and Earnhardt Dodge in Gilbert; Earnhardt Nissan, Earnhardt Scion and Earnhardt Toyota in Mesa; Earnhardt Ford in Tempe; and Mazda of El Paso and BMW of El Paso. The company currently sells and services nine different automotive brands including: BMW, Dodge, Ford, Honda, Hyundai, Mazda, Nissan, Scion and Toyota. Each of the car dealerships has its own parts and service departments, and the Chandler and Gilbert dealerships also have Earnhardt Auto Body centers adjacent to the local dealerships. Earnhardt Auto Body shops provide full collision repair services and can service all makes and models, not just those sold by Earnhardt's dealerships. The company's web site offers customers an advance look at each dealer's individual inventory and the opportunity to receive a quote on any particular vehicle. The web site also features a build-your-own-vehicle link, which allows the customer to add specific features to a vehicle and receive an instant quote. In addition, commercial customers can use the web site to locate Earnhardt's closest commercial fleet department and receive a quote; and the company provides financing and auto insurance. In June 2010, the firm purchased Pioneer Ford, located in Goodyear, Arizona, from the Penske Automotive Group.

Earnhardt's provides employees with a benefits package that includes a 401(k); medical, dental and life insurance; and a tuition reimbursement program.

FINANCIALS: **Sales and profits are in thousands of dollars—add 000 to get the full amount. 2009 Note: Financial information for 2009 was not available for all companies at press time.**

2009 Sales: $ 2009 Profits: $
2008 Sales: $ 2008 Profits: $
2007 Sales: $ 2007 Profits: $
2006 Sales: $ 2006 Profits: $
2005 Sales: $ 2005 Profits: $

U.S. Stock Ticker: Private
Int'l Ticker: Int'l Exchange:
Employees:
Fiscal Year Ends: 12/31
Parent Company:

SALARIES/BENEFITS:

Pension Plan: ESOP Stock Plan: Profit Sharing: Top Exec. Salary: $ Bonus: $
Savings Plan: Y Stock Purch. Plan: Second Exec. Salary: $ Bonus: $

OTHER THOUGHTS:

Apparent Women Officers or Directors: 1
Hot Spot for Advancement for Women/Minorities:

LOCATIONS: ("Y" = Yes)

West:	Southwest:	Midwest:	Southeast:	Northeast:	International:
	Y				

Note: Financial information, benefits and other data can change quickly and may vary from those stated here.

EAST PENN MANUFACTURING CO INC

www.dekabatteries.com

Industry Group Code: 3363 **Ranks within this company's industry group:** Sales: Profits:

Vehicle Manufacturing:		Dealers:		Parts:		Service:		Finance:		Specialty:	
Cars:		Car Dealer New:		Manufacturers:	Y	General Service:		Leasing:		Information Systems:	
Trucks:		Car Dealer Used:		Retail:		Specialty Service:		Auto Loans:		Online Marketing:	
Motorcycles:		Truck Dealer:		Distributors:		Oil Change:		Insurance:		Other:	Y
Specialty:		RV Dealer:		Tires:		Paint and Body:				Publishing:	
Buses:		Motorcycle Dealer:		Batteries:						Rental Cars/Trucks:	
RVs:		Specialty Dealer:									

TYPES OF BUSINESS:

Battery Manufacturing
Battery Recycling
Fuel Cell Technology
Electric Vehicle Battery Manufacturing

BRANDS/DIVISIONS/AFFILIATES:

Deka

CONTACTS:

Note: Officers with more than one job title may be intentionally listed here more than once.

Robert Flicker, COO/Exec. VP
Daniel R. Langdon, Pres.
DeLight E. Breidegam, Jr., Chmn.

Phone: 610-682-6361	**Fax:** 610-682-4781
Toll-Free:	
Address: Deka Rd., Lyon Station, PA 19536 US	

GROWTH PLANS/SPECIAL FEATURES:

East Penn Manufacturing Co., Inc. manufactures lead-acid batteries, battery accessories, wire and cable products for the industrial, automotive, commercial, marine, and stationary and specialty markets. The Deka line of batteries are available for use in telecommunications, automobiles, boats, RVs (recreational vehicles), farm equipment, motorcycles, ATVs, personal watercraft, snowmobiles, golf carts, military vehicles, construction equipment, railroads and wheelchairs. East Penn also manufactures a line of batteries for the storage of power from alternative energy sources, such as solar and wind power. The company boasts the world's largest battery manufacturing facility, over 2 million square feet on a 490 acre site in Lyon Station, Pennsylvania. The firm also operates a manufacturing, sales and distribution facility in Corydon, Iowa. East Penn safely reuses all parts of used batteries, reclaiming lead, plastic and sulfuric acid and turning sulfur fumes into liquid fertilizer. The company also traps its wastewater and separates it into liquid and solids for separate treatment, resulting in an overall reduction of pollution. In August 2009, East Penn received a $32.5 million grant from the U.S. Department of Energy under the American Recovery and Reinvestment Act to expand its production of advanced lead-acid batteries, to be used in hybrid electric vehicles. The grant has led to an essential restructuring of the company's operations around the production of the electric vehicle batteries under the Deka brand name. This new focus has led to the creation or retention of 89 jobs to operate battery manufacturing equipment.

FINANCIALS:

Sales and profits are in thousands of dollars—add 000 to get the full amount. 2009 Note: Financial information for 2009 was not available for all companies at press time.

2009 Sales: $	2009 Profits: $	**U.S. Stock Ticker: Private**
2008 Sales: $	2008 Profits: $	**Int'l Ticker:** Int'l Exchange:
2007 Sales: $	2007 Profits: $	Employees:
2006 Sales: $	2006 Profits: $	Fiscal Year Ends:
2005 Sales: $	2005 Profits: $	Parent Company:

SALARIES/BENEFITS:

Pension Plan:	ESOP Stock Plan:	Profit Sharing: Y	Top Exec. Salary: $	Bonus: $
Savings Plan: Y	Stock Purch. Plan:		Second Exec. Salary: $	Bonus: $

OTHER THOUGHTS:

Apparent Women Officers or Directors:
Hot Spot for Advancement for Women/Minorities:

LOCATIONS: ("Y" = Yes)

West:	Southwest:	Midwest:	Southeast:	Northeast:	International:
		Y		Y	

EATON CORP

www.eaton.com

Industry Group Code: 3363 **Ranks within this company's industry group:** Sales: 7 Profits: 5

Vehicle Manufacturing:		Dealers:		Parts:		Service:		Finance:		Specialty:	
Cars:		Car Dealer New:		Manufacturers:	Y	General Service:		Leasing:		Information Systems:	
Trucks:		Car Dealer Used:		Retail:		Specialty Service:		Auto Loans:		Online Marketing:	
Motorcycles:		Truck Dealer:		Distributors:		Oil Change:		Insurance:		Other:	Y
Specialty:		RV Dealer:		Tires:		Paint and Body:				Publishing:	
Buses:		Motorcycle Dealer:		Batteries:						Rental Cars/Trucks:	
RVs:		Specialty Dealer:									

TYPES OF BUSINESS:

Hydraulic Products
Electrical Power Distribution & Control Equipment
Truck Transmissions & Axles
Engine Components
Aerospace & Military Components

BRANDS/DIVISIONS/AFFILIATES:

Aeroquip GH810 Ice Champion
Aeroquip MatchMate Global
Pow-R-Flex
UltraShift PLUS
Micro Innovation Holding AG

CONTACTS:

Note: Officers with more than one job title may be intentionally listed here more than once.

Alexander M. Cutler, CEO
Alexander M. Cutler, Pres.
Richard H. Fearon, CFO/Chief Planning Officer
Jeffrey M. Krakowiak, Sr. VP-Mktg. & Sales
James W. McGill, Chief Human Resources Officer/Exec. VP
William W. Blausey, Jr., CIO/Sr. VP
Yannis P. Tsavalas, CTO/Sr. VP
Mark M. McGuire, General Counsel/Exec. VP
Kurt B. McMaken, Sr. VP-Corp. Dev. & Treasury
William B. Doggett, Sr. VP-Comm. & Public Affairs
William C. Hartman, Sr. VP-Investor Rel.
Billie K. Rawot, Controller/Sr. VP
Bradley J. Morton, Pres., Aerospace Group
Joseph P. Palchak, Pres., Vehicle Group
Craig Arnold, COO-Industrial Sector
Thomas S. Gross, COO-Electrical Sector
Alexander M. Cutler, Chmn.
Yannis P. Tsavalas, Pres., EMEA
Craig Reed, Sr. VP-Supply Chain Mgmt.

Phone: 216-523-5000 **Fax:** 216-523-4787
Toll-Free: 800-386-1911
Address: 1111 Superior Ave., Cleveland, OH 44114-2584 US

GROWTH PLANS/SPECIAL FEATURES:

Eaton Corporation is a global designer, manufacturer and marketer of electrical systems and components. The firm operates in two business segments: industrial and electrical. The industrial sector is made up of three divisions: hydraulics, aerospace and vehicle. The hydraulics segment develops and sells fluid power products to industrial, mobile equipment and aerospace customers worldwide. The aerospace business unit serves commercial/military aviation, space, military weapon, marine and off-road applications. The vehicle unit focuses on the powertrain and specialized sensor and actuator areas of passenger cars and light trucks; and the drivetrain systems and components for medium-duty and heavy-duty commercial vehicles. Its primary products include engine air management systems such as superchargers, cylinder head modules, engine valves and lifters; manual and automatic transmissions; clutches; driveshafts; drive and trailer axles; brakes; chassis control systems; and collision warning systems. The electrical segment operates in two geographic divisions: electrical Americas and electrical rest of world. The segment distributes electrical power and control equipment for industrial, commercial and residential markets. The company sells its products to customers in over 150 countries. In 2009, Eaton Corporation introduced several new products, including the CM 120 hydraulic valve; the Aeroquip GH810 Ice Champion wire hose; the Aeroquip MatchMate Global braided and spiral hydraulic hoses; UltraShift PLUS automated transmissions; and the Pow-R-Flex low ampere busway. In July 2009, the company combined its automotive and truck divisions to form the vehicle unit. Also in July 2009, the firm entered a low voltage switchboards and control panel assemblies manufacturing joint venture in United Arab Emirates. In September 2009, Eaton Corporation acquired the remaining 50% interest in the now wholly-owned Micro Innovation Holding AG. In October 2009, the firm opened a new office in Russia.

FINANCIALS:

Sales and profits are in thousands of dollars—add 000 to get the full amount. 2009 Note: Financial information for 2009 was not available for all companies at press time.

2009 Sales: $11,873,000	2009 Profits: $383,000	**U.S. Stock Ticker: ETN**
2008 Sales: $15,376,000	2008 Profits: $1,058,000	**Int'l Ticker:** Int'l Exchange:
2007 Sales: $13,033,000	2007 Profits: $994,000	Employees: 70,000
2006 Sales: $12,232,000	2006 Profits: $950,000	Fiscal Year Ends: 12/31
2005 Sales: $10,874,000	2005 Profits: $805,000	Parent Company:

SALARIES/BENEFITS:

Pension Plan: Y	ESOP Stock Plan:	Profit Sharing:	Top Exec. Salary: $973,248	Bonus: $575,000
Savings Plan: Y	Stock Purch. Plan:		Second Exec. Salary: $574,890	Bonus: $168,906

OTHER THOUGHTS:

Apparent Women Officers or Directors: 2
Hot Spot for Advancement for Women/Minorities: Y

LOCATIONS: ("Y" = Yes)

West:	Southwest:	Midwest:	Southeast:	Northeast:	International:
Y	Y	Y	Y	Y	Y

EDARAN OTOMOBIL NASIONAL BERHAD

www.eon.com.my

Industry Group Code: 441110 **Ranks within this company's industry group:** Sales: Profits:

Vehicle Manufacturing:		Dealers:		Parts:		Service:		Finance:		Specialty:	
Cars:		Car Dealer New:	Y	Manufacturers:		General Service:	Y	Leasing:	Y	Information Systems:	
Trucks:		Car Dealer Used:		Retail:		Specialty Service:	Y	Auto Loans:	Y	Online Marketing:	
Motorcycles:		Truck Dealer:		Distributors:	Y	Oil Change:	Y	Insurance:	Y	Other:	Y
Specialty:		RV Dealer:		Tires:		Paint and Body:	Y			Publishing:	
Buses:		Motorcycle Dealer:		Batteries:						Rental Cars/Trucks:	
RVs:		Specialty Dealer:									

TYPES OF BUSINESS:

Automobile Distribution
Automotive Dealerships
Automotive Service & Modification
Brokerage Services
Life Insurance
Property Development
Banking & Financial Services
General Trading

BRANDS/DIVISIONS/AFFILIATES:

HICOM Holdings Berhad
EON Properties Sdn Bhd
Automotive Conversion Engineering Sdn Bhd
Euromobile Sdn Bhd
Akademi Saga
Sahabat Eon Card
Proton
Mitsubishi Motors Malaysia Sdn Bhd

CONTACTS: *Note: Officers with more than one job title may be intentionally listed here more than once.*

Nik Hamdam bin Nik Hassan, CEO
Encik Badrul Feisal bin Abdul Rahim, COO
Yip Kok Hing, CFO
Chan Choy Lin, Sec.
Encik Abdul Wahab bin Mohd Noor, Head-Proton Oper.
Encik Mohd Asri bin Jusoh, Head-Strategic & Corp. Planning
Stanley Tan Heng Lam, Ceo-Euromobil Sdn Bhd
Encik Ahmad Zaini bin Mohd Ariffin, Mgr.-EON Properties Sdn Bhd
Loh Ling Howe, Head-EON Auto Mart Sdn Bhd
Encik Ahmad Kamal bin Abdul Majid, Head-After Sales Network Support
Marzuki Bin Mohd Noor, Chmn.

Phone: 60-3-7711-2211 **Fax:** 60-3-7806-3882
Toll-Free: 800-88-3003
Address: 2 Persiaran Kerjaya, Taman Perindustrian GS U1, Shah Alam, 40150 Malaysia

GROWTH PLANS/SPECIAL FEATURES:

Edaran Otomobil Nasional Berhad (EON), one of Malaysia's leading automobile distributors, was established in 1984 to distribute the Proton, Malaysia's first national car. The firm is a wholly-owned subsidiary of HICOM Holdings Berhad. While Proton car sales still represent the majority of EON's activity, the firm also markets vehicle brands such as Audi and Mitsubishi; and maintains partnerships with Hyundai, Honda, Inokom, Volkswagen and Suzuki. The company has also expanded its business ventures to include banking and financial services, property development, general trading, stock brokerage and life insurance. EON's wholly-owned subsidiaries include Automotive Conversion Engineering Sdn Bhd, which services and modifies Proton cars; and Euromobil Sdn Bhd, which imports, distributes and services Audi and Volkswagen products in Malaysia. EON offers the Sahabat EON Card that provides free towing services, discounts on products, priority service and various other benefits to its holders. The company's Car Owner Protection Scheme (COPS) is a one-year insurance scheme for purchasers of EON motor vehicles. The firm's non-automotive operations include EON Properties Sdn Bhd., which handles investment in and management of properties; and Akademi Saga, a technical training center. The company also holds partial interests in a number of firms, including a 40% share in SRT-EON Security Services Sdn Bhd; a 40% share in Proton Parts Centre Sdn Bhd; 30% interest in Johnson Controls Automotive Holding (M) Sdn Bhd; 36% interest in HICOM Megah Sdn Bhd; and a 48% interest in Mitsubishi Motors Malaysia Sdn Bhd.

FINANCIALS: **Sales and profits are in thousands of dollars—add 000 to get the full amount. 2009 Note: Financial information for 2009 was not available for all companies at press time.**

2009 Sales: $
2008 Sales: $428,400
2007 Sales: $566,500
2006 Sales: $568,800
2005 Sales: $817,200

2009 Profits: $
2008 Profits: $-12,100
2007 Profits: $18,300
2006 Profits: $1,600
2005 Profits: $20,800

U.S. Stock Ticker: Subsidiary
Int'l Ticker: 5036 Int'l Exchange: Kuala Lumpur-KLSE
Employees:
Fiscal Year Ends: 12/31
Parent Company: HICOM HOLDINGS BERHAD

SALARIES/BENEFITS:

Pension Plan: ESOP Stock Plan: Profit Sharing: Top Exec. Salary: $ Bonus: $
Savings Plan: Stock Purch. Plan: Second Exec. Salary: $ Bonus: $

OTHER THOUGHTS:

Apparent Women Officers or Directors: 3
Hot Spot for Advancement for Women/Minorities: Y

LOCATIONS: ("Y" = Yes)

West:	Southwest:	Midwest:	Southeast:	Northeast:	International:
					Y

EDELBROCK CORPORATION

www.edelbrock.com

Industry Group Code: 3363 **Ranks within this company's industry group:** Sales: Profits:

Vehicle Manufacturing:		Dealers:		Parts:		Service:		Finance:		Specialty:	
Cars:		Car Dealer New:		Manufacturers:	Y	General Service:		Leasing:		Information Systems:	
Trucks:		Car Dealer Used:		Retail:		Specialty Service:		Auto Loans:		Online Marketing:	
Motorcycles:		Truck Dealer:		Distributors:	Y	Oil Change:		Insurance:		Other:	
Specialty:		RV Dealer:		Tires:		Paint and Body:				Publishing:	
Buses:		Motorcycle Dealer:		Batteries:						Rental Cars/Trucks:	
RVs:		Specialty Dealer:									

TYPES OF BUSINESS:

Automobile Parts Manufacturer
Intake Manifolds
Carburetors
Cylinder Heads
Camshafts
Exhaust Systems
Hoses & Fittings
Motorcycle Components

BRANDS/DIVISIONS/AFFILIATES:

RICOR Inertia Active System
Russel Performance
E-Street

CONTACTS: *Note: Officers with more than one job title may be intentionally listed here more than once.*

O. Victor Edelbrock, Jr., CEO
Jeffrey L. Thompson, COO/Exec. VP
O. Victor Edelbrock, Jr., Pres.
Norm Judd, CFO
Jason Snyder, VP-Mktg.
O. Victor Edelbrock, Jr., Chmn.

Phone: 310-781-2222 **Fax:** 310-320-1187
Toll-Free: 800-416-8628
Address: 2700 California St., Torrance, CA 90503 US

GROWTH PLANS/SPECIAL FEATURES:

Edelbrock Corporation, founded in 1938, designs, manufactures, distributes and markets a wide range of performance products designed for cars, light trucks, recreational vehicles, race cars and motorcycles. These products include intake manifolds, carburetors, cylinder heads, camshafts, exhaust systems and other components. The company also manufactures shock absorbers utilizing the patented RICOR Inertia Active System, which offers both a comfortable ride and superior handling. Its subsidiary, Russell Performance, specializes in hoses and fittings for fuel, brake, water and oil systems. In addition, Edelbrock's product line includes motorcycle carburetors, cylinder heads, manifolds and nitrous systems. These products are designed to enhance street, off-road, recreational and competition vehicle performance through increased horsepower, torque and drivability. Edelbrock manufactures carburetors for Harley-Davidson and other motorcycle carburetors and air cleaners for aftermarket activities. It also designs and markets products to enhance engine and vehicle appearance, such as chrome and polished aluminum air cleaners, valve covers and breathers. Edelbrock products are sold in retail automotive chain stores, through mail-order catalog houses, warehouse distributors and performance specialty dealers. The company operates through six locations in California. In early 2009, the firm released E-Street cylinder heads, which are designed for 300-400 horse power street performance engines operating in the idle to 5,500 rpm range.

FINANCIALS: **Sales and profits are in thousands of dollars—add 000 to get the full amount. 2009 Note: Financial information for 2009 was not available for all companies at press time.**

2009 Sales: $ | 2009 Profits: $
2008 Sales: $ | 2008 Profits: $
2007 Sales: $ | 2007 Profits: $
2006 Sales: $ | 2006 Profits: $
2005 Sales: $ | 2005 Profits: $

U.S. Stock Ticker: Private
Int'l Ticker: Int'l Exchange:
Employees:
Fiscal Year Ends: 6/30
Parent Company:

SALARIES/BENEFITS:

Pension Plan: ESOP Stock Plan: Profit Sharing: Top Exec. Salary: $ Bonus: $
Savings Plan: Stock Purch. Plan: Second Exec. Salary: $ Bonus: $

OTHER THOUGHTS:

Apparent Women Officers or Directors:
Hot Spot for Advancement for Women/Minorities:

LOCATIONS: ("Y" = Yes)

West:	Southwest:	Midwest:	Southeast:	Northeast:	International:
Y					

ELDER AUTOMOTIVE GROUP

www.elderautomotivegroup.com

Industry Group Code: 441110 **Ranks within this company's industry group:** Sales: Profits:

Vehicle Manufacturing:		Dealers:		Parts:		Service:		Finance:		Specialty:	
Cars:		Car Dealer New:	Y	Manufacturers:		General Service:	Y	Leasing:		Information Systems:	
Trucks:		Car Dealer Used:	Y	Retail:	Y	Specialty Service:		Auto Loans:	Y	Online Marketing:	
Motorcycles:		Truck Dealer:		Distributors:		Oil Change:		Insurance:		Other:	
Specialty:		RV Dealer:		Tires:		Paint and Body:				Publishing:	
Buses:		Motorcycle Dealer:		Batteries:						Rental Cars/Trucks:	
RVs:		Specialty Dealer:									

TYPES OF BUSINESS:

Auto Dealers, Retail
Parts & Service
Financing

BRANDS/DIVISIONS/AFFILIATES:

Aston Martin of Troy
Jaguar of Tampa
Elder Ford
Land Rover of Lakeside
Saab of Troy
Signature Auto Group
Aston Martin of Tampa
Jaguar of Troy

CONTACTS: *Note: Officers with more than one job title may be intentionally listed here more than once.*

Irma B. Elder, CEO
Tony Elder, Pres.

Phone: 248-585-4000	**Fax:** 248-585-4039
Toll-Free: 888-773-6290	
Address: 777 John R. Rd., Troy, MI 48083 US	

GROWTH PLANS/SPECIAL FEATURES:

Elder Automotive Group (EAG), founded in 1967, is a premier new and pre-owned automobile dealership firm with 11 locations throughout Michigan and Florida. The firm specializes in the Aston Martin, Jaguar, Ford, Jeep, Land Rover, Lincoln, Mercury and Saab brands. Aston Martin of Tampa shares its showroom with Jaguar of Tampa while Aston Martin of Troy shares its showroom with Jaguar of Troy. Jaguar of Lakeside shares its showroom with Land Rover of Lakeside. The Signature Auto Group, which sells Ford, Lincoln, Mercury and Jeep models, has its dealerships in Owosso and Perry. Besides new cars, the dealerships sell parts and pre-owned cars as well as providing maintenance and repair services; and almost all EAG dealerships offers customers financing options. The company is owned by CEO Irma Elder. In early 2009, the company was selected to market and service Fisker Automotive luxury plug-in hybrid vehicles

FINANCIALS: **Sales and profits are in thousands of dollars—add 000 to get the full amount. 2009 Note: Financial information for 2009 was not available for all companies at press time.**

2009 Sales: $	2009 Profits: $	**U.S. Stock Ticker: Private**
2008 Sales: $	2008 Profits: $	**Int'l Ticker:** Int'l Exchange:
2007 Sales: $	2007 Profits: $	Employees:
2006 Sales: $	2006 Profits: $	Fiscal Year Ends:
2005 Sales: $	2005 Profits: $	Parent Company:

SALARIES/BENEFITS:

Pension Plan:	ESOP Stock Plan:	Profit Sharing:	Top Exec. Salary: $	Bonus: $
Savings Plan:	Stock Purch. Plan:		Second Exec. Salary: $	Bonus: $

OTHER THOUGHTS:

Apparent Women Officers or Directors: 1
Hot Spot for Advancement for Women/Minorities:

LOCATIONS: ("Y" = Yes)

West:	Southwest:	Midwest:	Southeast:	Northeast:	International:
		Y	Y		

ENER1 INC

www.ener1.com

Industry Group Code: 33591 **Ranks within this company's industry group:** Sales: 3 Profits: 2

Vehicle Manufacturing:		Dealers:		Parts:		Service:		Finance:		Specialty:	
Cars:		Car Dealer New:		Manufacturers:		General Service:		Leasing:		Information Systems:	
Trucks:		Car Dealer Used:		Retail:		Specialty Service:		Auto Loans:		Online Marketing:	
Motorcycles:		Truck Dealer:		Distributors:		Oil Change:		Insurance:		Other:	
Specialty:		RV Dealer:		Tires:		Paint and Body:				Publishing:	
Buses:		Motorcycle Dealer:		Batteries:	Y					Rental Cars/Trucks:	
RVs:		Specialty Dealer:									

TYPES OF BUSINESS:

Battery Development & Manufacturing

BRANDS/DIVISIONS/AFFILIATES:

EnerDel
EnerFuel
NanoEner
Enertech

CONTACTS:
Note: Officers with more than one job title may be intentionally listed here more than once.

Charles Gassenheimer, CEO
Naoki Ota, COO
Peter Novak, Pres.
Gerard Herlihy, CFO
Peter Novak, CTO
Nicholas Brunero, General Counsel/VP
Jeffrey Seidel, Chief Strategy Officer
Rachel Carroll, VP-Corp. Comm.
Robert Kamischke, CFO/Controller-EnerDel, Inc.
Ulrik Grape, Exec. VP/CEO-EnerDel
Cyrus Ashtiani, CTO-EnerDel
Richard L. Stanley, Pres., EnerDel Inc.
Tae-Hee Yoon, CEO/Chmn.-Enertech International, Inc.
Charles Gassenheimer, Chmn.
Ulrik Grape, Pres., Ener1 Europe

Phone: 212-920-3500	Fax:
Toll-Free:	
Address: 1540 Broadway, Ste. 25C, New York, NY 10036 US	

GROWTH PLANS/SPECIAL FEATURES:

Ener1, Inc. is an alternative energy company focused on designing, developing and manufacturing high-performance, rechargeable lithium-ion batteries and other systems for energy storage. It divides its business into three segments; battery, fuel cell and nanotechnology. The battery segment develops and markets lithium-ion batteries. The fuel cell segment develops fuel cells and fuel cell systems for use in the transportation and stationery power industries. Its nanotechnology business develops nanotechnology related manufacturing processes and materials. The company operates through four subsidiaries: EnerDel, EnerFuel, EnerTech and NanoEner. EnerDel, the company's primary subsidiary, is an end-to-end solutions provider that develops and manufactures products from small cells to complete battery packs. The subsidiary develops lithium-ion batteries for automotive, military and other industrial uses. EnerFuel is developing a hydrogen fuel cell range extender for use in EREVs (extended range electric vehicles) and other electric based automobiles and has successfully created a high temperature fuel cell stack. Other planned products are in early stages of development. EnerTech, based in South Korea, manufactures both large and small format battery cells and packs for use in cell phones, GPS systems and other commercial utilities. NanoEner has built prototype equipment that utilizes a proprietary vapor deposition and solidification process for depositing materials onto battery electrodes as part of the battery cell manufacturing process. NanoEner is developing electrodes produced from this process for testing and is still in research and development phases. In January 2010, the company announced plans to construct a new lithium-ion battery plant in Indiana. In May 2010, the firm began a joint venture with the Chinese auto parts company Wanxiang to produce battery systems for use in passenger and heavy-duty vehicles.

FINANCIALS:
Sales and profits are in thousands of dollars—add 000 to get the full amount. 2009 Note: Financial information for 2009 was not available for all companies at press time.

2009 Sales: $34,800	2009 Profits: $-51,004	**U.S. Stock Ticker: HEV**
2008 Sales: $6,848	2008 Profits: $-52,460	**Int'l Ticker:** Int'l Exchange:
2007 Sales: $ 280	2007 Profits: $-63,938	Employees: 515
2006 Sales: $	2006 Profits: $	Fiscal Year Ends: 12/31
2005 Sales: $	2005 Profits: $	Parent Company:

SALARIES/BENEFITS:

Pension Plan:	ESOP Stock Plan:	Profit Sharing:	Top Exec. Salary: $500,000	Bonus: $250,000
Savings Plan:	Stock Purch. Plan:		Second Exec. Salary: $430,000	Bonus: $

OTHER THOUGHTS:

Apparent Women Officers or Directors: 1
Hot Spot for Advancement for Women/Minorities:

LOCATIONS: ("Y" = Yes)

West:	Southwest:	Midwest:	Southeast:	Northeast:	International:
		Y	Y	Y	Y

ENTERPRISE HOLDINGS

www.enterpriseholdings.com

Industry Group Code: 5321 **Ranks within this company's industry group:** Sales: 1 Profits:

Vehicle Manufacturing:		Dealers:		Parts:		Service:		Finance:		Specialty:	
Cars:		Car Dealer New:		Manufacturers:		General Service:		Leasing:		Information Systems:	
Trucks:		Car Dealer Used:		Retail:		Specialty Service:		Auto Loans:		Online Marketing:	
Motorcycles:		Truck Dealer:		Distributors:		Oil Change:		Insurance:		Other:	Y
Specialty:		RV Dealer:		Tires:		Paint and Body:				Publishing:	
Buses:		Motorcycle Dealer:		Batteries:						Rental Cars/Trucks:	Y
RVs:		Specialty Dealer:									

TYPES OF BUSINESS:

Car & Truck Rental
Vanpool Services

BRANDS/DIVISIONS/AFFILIATES:

Enterprise Rent-a-Car (ERAC)
National Car Rental
Alamo Rent A Car
RideShare
Enterprise Car Sales
WeCar
Enterprise Fleet Management
Enterprise Truck Rental

CONTACTS: *Note: Officers with more than one job title may be intentionally listed here more than once.*

Andrew C. Taylor, CEO
Pamela Nicholson, COO
Pamela Nicholson, Pres.
William W. Snyder, CFO/Exec. VP
Edward Adams, Sr. VP-Human Resources
Craig Kennedy, CIO/Sr. VP
Lee Kaplan, Chief Admin. Officer/Sr. VP
Matthew G. Darrah, Exec. VP-N. American Oper.
Greg Stubblefield, Chief Strategy Officer/Exec. VP
Laura Bryant, Contact-Corp. Comm.
Lisa Martini, Contact-Investor Rel.
Rose Langhorst, Treas./VP
Steve Bloom, Sr. VP-Enterprise Fleet Mgmt. & Car Sales
Andrew C. Taylor, Chmn.

Phone: 314-512-1000	**Fax:** 314-512-4706
Toll-Free:	
Address: 600 Corporate Park Dr., St. Louis, MO 63105 US	

GROWTH PLANS/SPECIAL FEATURES:

Enterprise Holdings, Inc. is the parent company of Alamo Rent A Car, National Car Rental, and Enterprise Rent-A-Car, along with Enterprise Fleet Management, Enterprise Car Sales, Enterprise Commercial Truck Rental, RideShare vanpooling, and WeCar, a car sharing membership program. Enterprise Holdings was formed in 2009 as the final step in the integration of the Alamo and National businesses acquired by Enterprise Rent-A-Car in 2007. The company's combined rental fleet is the largest in the world at 1.1 million vehicles. It serves roughly 7,600 retail and airport locations in the U.S., Canada, Mexico, the Carribean, Latin America, the U.K., Ireland, Germany and Asia. The Enterprise Holdings group of businesses generated $12.1 billion in revenue in 2009. Alamo Rent A Car is a budget rental car company catering to leisure and vacation customers, particularly international travelers visiting North America. Alamo operates 159 self-service kiosks at 65 U.S. locations. National Car Rental is a premium rental brand that serves frequent business travelers and offers the Emerald Club frequent-renter benefits program. Enterprise Rent-A-Car boasts more than 5,000 retail and airport offices in the U.S. Enterprise Car Sales is a used-car reseller that provides non-negotiable pricing and after-market warranties on used cars acquired through trade-in or extracted from the rental fleet. WeCar is a car sharing program that allows customers to rent a car for flexible periods of time through an online membership portal. In March 2010, Tulane University and Loyola University New Orleans launched a car-sharing program in partnership with WeCar for use on their respective campuses.

Enterprise Holdings offers its employees medical, dental, and vision insurance; prescription drug coverage; flexible spending accounts; life insurance; and long-term disability plans.

FINANCIALS: **Sales and profits are in thousands of dollars—add 000 to get the full amount. 2009 Note: Financial information for 2009 was not available for all companies at press time.**

2009 Sales: $13,000,000	2009 Profits: $	**U.S. Stock Ticker: Private**
2008 Sales: $12,100,000	2008 Profits: $	**Int'l Ticker:** Int'l Exchange:
2007 Sales: $	2007 Profits: $	Employees: 75,000
2006 Sales: $	2006 Profits: $	Fiscal Year Ends:
2005 Sales: $	2005 Profits: $	Parent Company:

SALARIES/BENEFITS:

Pension Plan:	ESOP Stock Plan:	Profit Sharing:	Top Exec. Salary: $	Bonus: $
Savings Plan: Y	Stock Purch. Plan:		Second Exec. Salary: $	Bonus: $

OTHER THOUGHTS:

Apparent Women Officers or Directors: 2
Hot Spot for Advancement for Women/Minorities:

LOCATIONS: ("Y" = Yes)

West:	Southwest:	Midwest:	Southeast:	Northeast:	International:
Y	Y	Y	Y	Y	Y

FAULKNER ORGANIZATION (THE)

www.tobesure.com

Industry Group Code: 441110 **Ranks within this company's industry group:** Sales: Profits:

Vehicle Manufacturing:		Dealers:		Parts:		Service:		Finance:		Specialty:	
Cars:		Car Dealer New:	Y	Manufacturers:		General Service:	Y	Leasing:		Information Systems:	
Trucks:		Car Dealer Used:	Y	Retail:	Y	Specialty Service:		Auto Loans:	Y	Online Marketing:	
Motorcycles:		Truck Dealer:		Distributors:		Oil Change:		Insurance:	Y	Other:	
Specialty:		RV Dealer:		Tires:		Paint and Body:	Y			Publishing:	
Buses:		Motorcycle Dealer:		Batteries:						Rental Cars/Trucks:	
RVs:		Specialty Dealer:									

TYPES OF BUSINESS:

Auto Dealers, Retail
Parts & Service
Financing
Fleet Services
Insurance

BRANDS/DIVISIONS/AFFILIATES:

GROWTH PLANS/SPECIAL FEATURES:

Faulkner Organization, founded in 1932 by Henry Faulkner, Sr., is a family-owned and operated car dealer in the Delaware Valley. The company operates a chain of 25 new and used dealerships located throughout Pennsylvania. The firm carries a wide range of domestic and international vehicle brands including Buick, Cadillac, Ford, GMC, Mercury, Pontiac, Saturn, BMW, Toyota, Honda, Mitsubishi and Mazda. The dealerships feature maintenance and service departments, financing, fleet services and insurance. Through the company's web site, customers can search new and used vehicle inventories; obtain quotes; find specials on service and repair work; and apply for pre-qualified auto loans. In addition, Internet specials are announced for auto parts and new and pre-owned vehicles.

CONTACTS: *Note: Officers with more than one job title may be intentionally listed here more than once.*

Gail Faulkner, CEO
Bob Lewis, COO
Bill Sebald, CFO
Bill Sebald, Dir.-Human Resources

Phone: 215-364-3980	**Fax:** 215-364-0706
Toll-Free:	
Address: 4437 Street Rd., Trevose, PA 19053 US	

FINANCIALS: **Sales and profits are in thousands of dollars—add 000 to get the full amount. 2009 Note: Financial information for 2009 was not available for all companies at press time.**

2009 Sales: $	2009 Profits: $	**U.S. Stock Ticker: Private**
2008 Sales: $	2008 Profits: $	**Int'l Ticker:** Int'l Exchange:
2007 Sales: $	2007 Profits: $	Employees:
2006 Sales: $	2006 Profits: $	Fiscal Year Ends: 12/31
2005 Sales: $	2005 Profits: $	Parent Company:

SALARIES/BENEFITS:

Pension Plan:	ESOP Stock Plan:	Profit Sharing:	Top Exec. Salary: $	Bonus: $
Savings Plan:	Stock Purch. Plan:		Second Exec. Salary: $	Bonus: $

OTHER THOUGHTS:

Apparent Women Officers or Directors: 1
Hot Spot for Advancement for Women/Minorities:

LOCATIONS: ("Y" = Yes)

West:	Southwest:	Midwest:	Southeast:	Northeast:	International:
				Y	

FAURECIA SA

www.faurecia.com

Industry Group Code: 3363 **Ranks within this company's industry group:** Sales: 10 Profits: 57

Vehicle Manufacturing:		**Dealers:**		**Parts:**		**Service:**		**Finance:**		**Specialty:**	
Cars:		Car Dealer New:		Manufacturers:	Y	General Service:		Leasing:		Information Systems:	
Trucks:		Car Dealer Used:		Retail:		Specialty Service:		Auto Loans:		Online Marketing:	
Motorcycles:		Truck Dealer:		Distributors:		Oil Change:		Insurance:		Other:	
Specialty:		RV Dealer:		Tires:		Paint and Body:				Publishing:	
Buses:		Motorcycle Dealer:		Batteries:						Rental Cars/Trucks:	
RVs:		Specialty Dealer:									

TYPES OF BUSINESS:

Automobile Part Manufacturing
Vehicle Component Modules
Vehicle Seats
Vehicle Doors
Exhaust Systems
Front End Modules
Acoustic Engineering & Equipment

BRANDS/DIVISIONS/AFFILIATES:

Faurecia University
Plastal Germany
Taco Faurecia Design Center

CONTACTS: *Note: Officers with more than one job title may be intentionally listed here more than once.*

Yann Delabriere, CEO
Frank Imbert, CFO
Jean-Pierre Sounilla, Exec. VP-Group Human Resources
Bruno Montmerle, Exec. VP-Group Strategy
Thierry Lemane, Exec. VP-Group Comm.
Eric-Alain Michelis, VP-Investor Rel.
Jean-Marc Hannequin, Exec. VP-Emission Control
Christophe Schmitt, Exec. VP-Interior Systems
Patrick Koller, Exec. VP-Automotive Seating
Arnaud de David-Beauregard, Exec. VP-Group Dev.
Yann Delabriere, Chmn.
Michael T. Heneka, Pres., Faurecia North America

Phone: 33-1-72-36-70-00 **Fax:** 33-1-72-36-70-07
Toll-Free:
Address: 2 rue Hennape, Nanterre, 92735 France

GROWTH PLANS/SPECIAL FEATURES:

Faurecia S.A., headquartered in France, is a global supplier of vehicle equipment. The firm has approximately 190 production facilities and 28 research and development centers in 29 countries throughout Western Europe, Central Europe, North America, South America and Asia. It divides its design and assembly operations into four major business areas: automotive seating, interior systems, emissions control technologies and automotive exteriors. With regard to seats, the company designs and manufactures foams, frames, adjustment mechanisms and upholstery. Vehicle interior systems manufacturing includes the design and production of instrument panels, central consoles and door panels; in addition, this division provides acoustic engineering and equipment such as floor coverings, carpets and insulators that effectively soundproof a vehicle's interior. The firm engineers and markets a range of complete exhaust systems to control emissions; in addition, it was the originator of the diesel particulate filter, which removes more than 99% of diesel exhaust particulate matter. The company is a lead supplier of exterior modules, which include front-ends such as engine cooling systems; exterior systems such as bumpers; and shock absorb systems. Additionally, the firm is a leader in vehicle architecture, including structure, safety and perceived quality utilizing technologies and processes such as metal-plastic hybrid injection molding. The firm supplies major domestic automotive manufactures such as Peugeot, while Volkswagen, BMW, Ford, Honda and Toyota are among the firm's international clients. In January 2010, Faurecia fully acquired Taco Faurecia Design Center, located in Pune, India. In April 2010, Faurecia completed its acquisition and integration of Plastal Germany, now a part of the firm's Automotive Exteriors, Northern Europe division.

Faurecia offers its employees professional training through its Faurecia University.

FINANCIALS: **Sales and profits are in thousands of dollars—add 000 to get the full amount. 2009 Note: Financial information for 2009 was not available for all companies at press time.**

2009 Sales: $11,391,600	2009 Profits: $-511,580	**U.S. Stock Ticker:**
2008 Sales: $16,001,860	2008 Profits: $-765,810	**Int'l Ticker: EO** Int'l Exchange: Paris-Euronext
2007 Sales: $16,867,850	2007 Profits: $-316,420	Employees: 58,414
2006 Sales: $15,519,560	2006 Profits: $-596,740	Fiscal Year Ends: 12/31
2005 Sales: $14,927,470	2005 Profits: $-248,150	Parent Company:

SALARIES/BENEFITS:

Pension Plan:	ESOP Stock Plan:	Profit Sharing:	Top Exec. Salary: $	Bonus: $
Savings Plan:	Stock Purch. Plan:		Second Exec. Salary: $	Bonus: $

OTHER THOUGHTS:

Apparent Women Officers or Directors:
Hot Spot for Advancement for Women/Minorities:

LOCATIONS: ("Y" = Yes)

West:	Southwest:	Midwest:	Southeast:	Northeast:	International:
		Y		Y	Y

FEDERAL MOGUL CORP

www.federalmogul.com

Industry Group Code: 3363 **Ranks within this company's industry group:** Sales: 19 Profits: 38

Vehicle Manufacturing:		Dealers:		Parts:		Service:		Finance:		Specialty:	
Cars:		Car Dealer New:		Manufacturers:	Y	General Service:		Leasing:		Information Systems:	
Trucks:		Car Dealer Used:		Retail:		Specialty Service:		Auto Loans:		Online Marketing:	
Motorcycles:		Truck Dealer:		Distributors:		Oil Change:		Insurance:		Other:	
Specialty:		RV Dealer:		Tires:		Paint and Body:				Publishing:	
Buses:		Motorcycle Dealer:		Batteries:						Rental Cars/Trucks:	
RVs:		Specialty Dealer:									

TYPES OF BUSINESS:

Aftermarket Products & Services
Powertrain Products
Sealing Systems
Vehicle Safety & Performance Products

BRANDS/DIVISIONS/AFFILIATES:

AE
Glyco
Nüral
Goetze
Fel-Pro
FP Diesel
MicroTorq
IROX

CONTACTS: *Note: Officers with more than one job title may be intentionally listed here more than once.*

Jose Maria Alapont, CEO
Jose Maria Alapont, Pres.
Jeff Kaminski, CFO/Sr. VP
William Bowers, Sr. VP-Sales & Mktg.
Pascal Goachet, Sr. VP-Global Human Resources & Organization
Alston German, CIO/VP
Rene Dalleur, Sr. VP-Global Eng.
Rene Dalleur, Sr. VP-Global Mfg. & Customer Satisfaction
Robert L. Katz, General Counsel/Sr. VP
Jean Brunol, Sr. VP-Bus. & Oper. Strategy
Steven K. Gaut, VP-Corp. Comm. & Gov't Rel.
Alan Haughie, Chief Acct. Officer/VP/Controller
James Burkhart, Sr. VP-Global Aftermarket
Ramzi Hermiz, Sr. VP-Vehicle Safety & Protection
Rainer Jueckstock, Sr. VP-Powertrain Energy
David Bozynksi, Treas./VP
Carl C. Icahn, Chmn.
Markus Wermers, Sr. VP-Global Purchasing

Phone: 248-354-7700	**Fax:** 248-354-8548
Toll-Free:	
Address: 26555 Northwestern Hwy., Southfield, MI 48033 US	

GROWTH PLANS/SPECIAL FEATURES:

Federal-Mogul Corp. is a supplier of vehicle and industrial products for fuel economy, alternative energies, environment and safety systems. The firm sells its products to original equipment manufacturers (OEMs) of automotive, light commercial, heavy-duty, industrial, agricultural, aerospace, marine, rail and off-road vehicles and the worldwide aftermarket. The company operates in five business segments: powertrain energy, accounting for 27% of 2009 sales; powertrain sealings and bearings, accounting for 15%; vehicle safety and protection, 14%; global aftermarket, 44%; and corporate. The powertrain energy segment, offers products that include pistons, piston rings, piston pins, cylinder liners, valve seats and guides and transmission components. Brand names include Federal-Mogul, AE, Champion, Goetze and Nural. The powertrain sealings and bearings segment offers bearings, bushings and thrust washers for engine, transmission and driveline systems. Products are sold under Federal-Mogul, Deva, Fel-Pro, FP Diesel, Glyco, Metafram, Metagliss, National, Payen, Poral and Sintertech brands. The vehicle safety and protection segment offers brake disc pads, brake linings, brake blocks, element resistant systems protection sleeving products and flexible heat shields. Brand names include Abex, Anco, Bentley-Harris, Beral, Champion, Ferodo, Moog, ThermoQuiet and Wagner. The global aftermarket segment sells engine parts, gaskets, seals, chassis, driveline, hub assemblies, disc pads, linings, rotors, spark plugs, wipers, filters and lighting. These products are manufactured within the firm's other segments and are also purchased from outside suppliers. Federal-Mogul has operations in 33 countries and maintains175 manufacturing facilities. In March 2010, the company launched MicroTorq, a crankshaft seal design for vehicles with the ability to reduce friction of up to 70%, and IROX, a polymer coated bearing shell designed to decrease fuel consumption and CO2 emissions.

Employees are offered medical, dental, vision and hearing insurance; flexible spending accounts; life and AD&D insurance; disability coverage; a 401(k) plan; and a pension plan.

FINANCIALS: **Sales and profits are in thousands of dollars—add 000 to get the full amount. 2009 Note: Financial information for 2009 was not available for all companies at press time.**

2009 Sales: $5,330,000	2009 Profits: $-45,000	**U.S. Stock Ticker: FDML**
2008 Sales: $6,865,600	2008 Profits: $-467,900	**Int'l Ticker:** Int'l Exchange:
2007 Sales: $6,913,900	2007 Profits: $1,412,300	Employees: 39,000
2006 Sales: $6,326,400	2006 Profits: $-549,600	Fiscal Year Ends: 12/31
2005 Sales: $6,286,000	2005 Profits: $-334,200	Parent Company:

SALARIES/BENEFITS:

Pension Plan: Y	ESOP Stock Plan:	Profit Sharing:	Top Exec. Salary: $1,500,000	Bonus: $3,075,000
Savings Plan: Y	Stock Purch. Plan:		Second Exec. Salary: $585,650	Bonus: $564,083

OTHER THOUGHTS:

Apparent Women Officers or Directors:
Hot Spot for Advancement for Women/Minorities:

LOCATIONS: ("Y" = Yes)

West:	Southwest:	Midwest:	Southeast:	Northeast:	International:
Y	Y	Y	Y	Y	Y

FEDERAL SIGNAL CORP

www.federalsignal.com

Industry Group Code: 3363 **Ranks within this company's industry group:** Sales: 44 Profits: 20

Vehicle Manufacturing:		Dealers:		Parts:		Service:		Finance:		Specialty:	
Cars:		Car Dealer New:		Manufacturers:	Y	General Service:		Leasing:		Information Systems:	
Trucks:		Car Dealer Used:		Retail:		Specialty Service:		Auto Loans:		Online Marketing:	
Motorcycles:		Truck Dealer:		Distributors:		Oil Change:		Insurance:		Other:	Y
Specialty:	Y	RV Dealer:		Tires:		Paint and Body:				Publishing:	
Buses:		Motorcycle Dealer:		Batteries:						Rental Cars/Trucks:	
RVs:		Specialty Dealer:									

TYPES OF BUSINESS:

Automobile Parts Manufacturing
Customer & Dealer Financing

BRANDS/DIVISIONS/AFFILIATES:

Federal Signal
Bronto Skylift
Jetstream
Guzzler
VAMA
VESystems LLC
Sirit Inc
Diamond Consulting Services Ltd

CONTACTS: *Note: Officers with more than one job title may be intentionally listed here more than once.*

William H. Osborne, CEO
William H. Osborne, Pres.
William G. Barker III, CFO/Sr. VP
John Segvich, Dir.-Mktg. Comm.
Jennifer L. Sherman, Sr. VP-Human Resources
Charles F. Avery, Jr., VP-IT
Jennifer L. Sherman, General Counsel/Corp. Sec.
Fred H. Lietz, VP-Global Oper. Strategy
Leo T. Mahon, VP-Bus. Dev. & Strategy
Daniel J. Hickey, Dir.-Gov't Rel.
Leo T. Mahon, VP-Investor Rel.
Charles F. Avery, Jr., Controller
Esa Peltola, Pres./Managing Dir.-Bronto Skylift
Mark D. Weber, Pres., Environmental Solutions Group
David E. Janek, Pres., Safety & Security Systems Group
Manfred Rietsch, Pres., Federal Signals Tech. Group
James E. Goodwin, Chmn.
Fred H. Lietz, Chief Procurement Officer

Phone: 630-954-2000	**Fax:** 630-954-2030
Toll-Free:	
Address: 1415 W. 22nd St., Ste. 1100, Oak Brook, IL 60523 US	

GROWTH PLANS/SPECIAL FEATURES:

Federal Signal Corp. designs and manufactures products and solutions for municipal, governmental, commercial and industrial customers. The company also provides customer and dealer financing to support the sale of its vehicles. The products manufactured by the firm are divided into three major operating groups. The safety and security systems group designs and manufactures emergency vehicle warning lights and sirens; industrial and outdoor signaling, warning, lighting and communications devices and integrated systems; and parking revenue and access control systems. Products are sold under the Federal Signal, Idris, Target Tech, Federal Signal VAMA, Victor, PIPS and Federal ADP brand names. The fire rescue group manufactures a range of fire rescue apparatus, which are sold under the Bronto Skylift brand. The environmental solutions group manufactures and markets a full range of street cleaning and vacuum loader vehicles and high-performance water blasting equipment; brand names include Vactor, Guzzler, Elgin and Jetstream. Products are also manufactured for the newer markets of hydro-excavation, glycol recovery and surface cleaning. The firm operates 19 manufacturing facilities in seven countries; it serves customers in roughly 100 countries. Roughly 37% of Federal Signal's sales come from U.S. municipal and government customers; 21% from U.S. commercial and industrial customers; and 42% from international clients. In July 2009, the firm sold compact street-sweeper manufacturer Ravo Holding B.V. to Fayat Group. In November 2009, Federal Signal sold subsidiary Pauluhn to Cooper Industries plc for $35 million. In December 2009, the company acquired intelligent transportation systems specialist Diamond Consulting Services, Ltd. for $14.6 million. In March 2010, Federal Signal acquired back-office and customer management systems and services provider VESystems, LLC for $33 million; acquired radio frequency identification technology firm Sirit, Inc.; and agreed to form Federal Signal Technologies Group, a new division comprised of the operations of Diamond Consulting Services, VESystems and Sirit.

FINANCIALS: **Sales and profits are in thousands of dollars—add 000 to get the full amount. 2009 Note: Financial information for 2009 was not available for all companies at press time.**

2009 Sales: $752,500	2009 Profits: $17,700	**U.S. Stock Ticker: FSS**
2008 Sales: $879,000	2008 Profits: $27,200	**Int'l Ticker:** Int'l Exchange:
2007 Sales: $854,800	2007 Profits: $35,100	Employees: 2,614
2006 Sales: $1,211,600	2006 Profits: $42,700	Fiscal Year Ends: 12/31
2005 Sales: $1,119,000	2005 Profits: $-4,600	Parent Company:

SALARIES/BENEFITS:

Pension Plan:	ESOP Stock Plan:	Profit Sharing:	Top Exec. Salary: $617,500	Bonus: $390,137
Savings Plan: Y	Stock Purch. Plan:		Second Exec. Salary: $339,552	Bonus: $

OTHER THOUGHTS:

Apparent Women Officers or Directors: 2
Hot Spot for Advancement for Women/Minorities: Y

LOCATIONS: ("Y" = Yes)

West:	Southwest:	Midwest:	Southeast:	Northeast:	International:
	Y	Y	Y	Y	Y

FERRARI SPA

www.ferrari.com

Industry Group Code: 33611 **Ranks within this company's industry group:** Sales: Profits:

Vehicle Manufacturing:		Dealers:		Parts:		Service:		Finance:		Specialty:	
Cars:	Y	Car Dealer New:		Manufacturers:	Y	General Service:		Leasing:		Information Systems:	
Trucks:		Car Dealer Used:		Retail:		Specialty Service:		Auto Loans:		Online Marketing:	
Motorcycles:		Truck Dealer:		Distributors:		Oil Change:		Insurance:		Other:	Y
Specialty:		RV Dealer:		Tires:		Paint and Body:				Publishing:	Y
Buses:		Motorcycle Dealer:		Batteries:						Rental Cars/Trucks:	
RVs:		Specialty Dealer:	Y								

TYPES OF BUSINESS:

Automobile Manufacturer
Magazine Publication
TV Content Production

BRANDS/DIVISIONS/AFFILIATES:

Fiat S.p.A.
F430
612 Scaglietti
599 GTB Fiorano
Gestione Sportiva
Scaglietti Programe
458 Italia
Ferrari California

CONTACTS:

Note: Officers with more than one job title may be intentionally listed here more than once.

Amedeo Felisa, CEO
Enrico Galliera, Dir.-Brand & Commercial
Mario Mairano, Dir.-Human Resources
Roberto Fedeli, Dir.-Tech.
Italo Valenti, Dir.-Admin.
Mario Mairano, Dir.-Gen. Sec.
Stefano Lai, Dir.-Comm.
Italo Valenti, Dir.-Finance & Control
Piero Ferrari, Vice Chmn.
Mario Almondo, Dir.-Quality
Stefano Domenicali, Dir.-Gestione Sportiva
Sebastiano Rio, Dir.-Industrial
Luca C. di Montezemolo, Chmn.

Phone: 39-0-536-949-111 **Fax:** 39-0-536-949-714
Toll-Free:
Address: Via Abetone Inferiore n. 4, Maranello, I-41053 Italy

GROWTH PLANS/SPECIAL FEATURES:

Ferrari S.p.A., founded in 1928, manufactures high-performance sports cars, selling at prices starting at $140,000. It's 85%-owned by Fiat S.p.A. Other investors include Piero Ferrari, son of Enzo Ferrari, owning 10%, and Mubadala Development Co. of the UAE, with 5%. Current Ferrari vehicles include: the Ferrari California; 599 GTB Fiorano; 458 Italia; and the 612 Scaglietti. Past models have included the F430, F430 Scuderia, and the F430 Spider. The 490-horsepower F430, representing a new generation of Ferrari V-8 berlinettas, was designed by the firm's Gestione Sportiva F1 racing division. It was named after one-tenth its engine displacement, 4308 cubic centimeters (ccs). The 620-horsepower 599 GTB Fiorano is named 599 after one-tenth its engine displacement (5999 ccs), GTB (Gran Turismo Berlinetta) after the most famous Ferrari berlinettas ever made, the classic Gran Turismo luxury cars of the 1960s, and Fiorano after the circuit Ferrari uses to hone its road and track cars. Current prototypes include the FXX, 599 XX, 458 Challenge, F430 GTC and F430 Challenge. In order to maintain high levels of value and exclusivity, Ferrari has self-imposed a limit on its annual production, manufacturing approximately 6,400 cars annually at its single factory near Bologna, Italy. Ferrari offers customers certified pre-owned vehicles through its worldwide dealership network, and its Scaglietti Programe allows customers to have their Ferrari customized for a race or track set-up as long as the car remains street legal. Besides its vehicles, the firm publishes Ferrari magazine, as well as producing Ferrari TV, viewable through the company's web site, which features Ferrari-related content. The firm is currently developing the 599 HY-KERS model, which is a hybrid vehicle. In July 2009, the company launched the Ferrari 458 Italia at the IAA Frankfurt Motor Show. In July 2010, the firm debut the 458 Challenge at the Ferrari's Annual Dealer Meeting.

FINANCIALS:

Sales and profits are in thousands of dollars—add 000 to get the full amount. 2009 Note: Financial information for 2009 was not available for all companies at press time.

2009 Sales: $	2009 Profits: $	**U.S. Stock Ticker: Subsidiary**
2008 Sales: $	2008 Profits: $	**Int'l Ticker:** Int'l Exchange:
2007 Sales: $	2007 Profits: $	Employees:
2006 Sales: $	2006 Profits: $	Fiscal Year Ends: 12/31
2005 Sales: $	2005 Profits: $	Parent Company: FIAT SPA

SALARIES/BENEFITS:

Pension Plan:	ESOP Stock Plan:	Profit Sharing:	Top Exec. Salary: $	Bonus: $
Savings Plan:	Stock Purch. Plan:		Second Exec. Salary: $	Bonus: $

OTHER THOUGHTS:

Apparent Women Officers or Directors:
Hot Spot for Advancement for Women/Minorities:

LOCATIONS: ("Y" = Yes)

West:	Southwest:	Midwest:	Southeast:	Northeast:	International:
Y	Y	Y	Y	Y	Y

FIAT SPA

www.fiatgroup.com

Industry Group Code: 33611 **Ranks within this company's industry group:** Sales: 10 Profits: 27

Vehicle Manufacturing:		Dealers:		Parts:		Service:		Finance:		Specialty:	
Cars:	Y	Car Dealer New:		Manufacturers:	Y	General Service:		Leasing:		Information Systems:	
Trucks:		Car Dealer Used:		Retail:		Specialty Service:		Auto Loans:	Y	Online Marketing:	
Motorcycles:		Truck Dealer:		Distributors:		Oil Change:		Insurance:	Y	Other:	Y
Specialty:	Y	RV Dealer:		Tires:		Paint and Body:				Publishing:	Y
Buses:	Y	Motorcycle Dealer:		Batteries:						Rental Cars/Trucks:	
RVs:		Specialty Dealer:									

TYPES OF BUSINESS:

Automobile Manufacturer
Agricultural & Construction Equipment
Commercial Vehicles
Automotive Retail
Automotive Components
Industrial Automation Systems
Publishing
Business Services

BRANDS/DIVISIONS/AFFILIATES:

Fiat Group Automobiles
Ferrari
Maserati
CNH Global
Iveco
Magneti Marelli
Teksid
Chrysler Group LLC

CONTACTS: *Note: Officers with more than one job title may be intentionally listed here more than once.*

Sergio Marchionne, CEO
Luigi Gubitosi, CFO
Roberto Pucci, Exec. VP-Human Resources
Harold Wester, CTO/Exec. VP
Harold Wester, Head-Eng.
Ferruccio Luppi, Exec. VP-Bus. Dev.
Simone Migliarino, Head-Comm.
Maurizio Francescatti, Head-Treasury
John P. Elkann, Vice Chmn.
Harald Wester, CEO-Alfa Romeo Automobiles
Paolo Rebaudengo, Head-Industrial Rel.
Alfredo Altavilla, CEO-Fiat Powertrain Technologies
Luca C. Di Montezemolo, Chmn.
Giorgio Frasca, Dir.-Int'l Rel.
Gianni Coda, CEO-Purchasing

Phone: 39-011-00-61111	**Fax:** 39-011-00-63798
Toll-Free:	
Address: 250 Via Nizza, Turin, 10126 Italy	

GROWTH PLANS/SPECIAL FEATURES:

Fiat SpA manufactures and sells automobiles, heavy machinery and components. The company is organized in 11 operating sectors: Fiat Group Automobiles; Ferrari; Maserati; agricultural and construction equipment; trucks and commercial vehicles; powertrain technologies; components; metallurgical products; production systems; publishing and communications; and corporate service companies. Fiat Group Automobiles sells Fiat, Lancia and Alfa Romeo cars, as well as light commercial vehicles. Ferrari and Maserati are both majority-owned by Fiat and world-renowned manufacturers of high-end sports cars. The company owns and operates several subsidiaries within the automotive industry. Agricultural and construction equipment is produced by CNH Global, which manufactures the Case IH and New Holland lines. Trucks and commercial vehicles are produced by Iveco, which manufactures light, medium and heavy trucks for on- or off-road uses, as well as buses; special-purpose military vehicles; and diesel, hybrid and hydrogen fuel cell engines. Fiat Powertrain Technologies (FPT) designs and builds engines for passenger and commercial vehicles and for industrial and marine applications. Fiat's components are designed, developed and manufactured by subsidiary Magneti Marelli, and include suspension systems and shock absorbers. Other subsidiaries include Teksid, which manufactures cast metal components and Comau, which designs and produces machine tools and production systems. In addition, Fiat owns Itedi, which publishes the Italian newspaper La Stampa and offers advertising services to more than 100,000 customers. In 2009, the firm plans to introduce two Magneti Marelli-owned joint ventures, one to further its automotive electronic systems operations and one to produce shock absorbers. As a result of Chrysler's 2009 bankruptcy, Chrysler entered into an alliance agreement with Fiat. The alliance gives Fiat an initial 20% stake in Chrysler Group LLC, with the ability to earn further shares, while giving Chrysler access to Fiat small car engineering and technology. If the alliance is successful, Chrysler could quickly be building cars based on Fiat designs for sale in the U.S. and abroad.

FINANCIALS: **Sales and profits are in thousands of dollars—add 000 to get the full amount. 2009 Note: Financial information for 2009 was not available for all companies at press time.**

2009 Sales: $67,624,200	2009 Profits: $-1,131,070	**U.S. Stock Ticker: FIATY**
2008 Sales: $80,147,000	2008 Profits: $2,322,890	**Int'l Ticker: F** Int'l Exchange: Milan-BI
2007 Sales: $78,998,300	2007 Profits: $2,772,350	Employees: 190,014
2006 Sales: $81,376,200	2006 Profits: $1,672,100	Fiscal Year Ends: 12/31
2005 Sales: $73,074,100	2005 Profits: $2,089,700	Parent Company:

SALARIES/BENEFITS:

Pension Plan:	ESOP Stock Plan:	Profit Sharing:	Top Exec. Salary: $	Bonus: $
Savings Plan:	Stock Purch. Plan:		Second Exec. Salary: $	Bonus: $

OTHER THOUGHTS:

Apparent Women Officers or Directors:
Hot Spot for Advancement for Women/Minorities:

LOCATIONS: ("Y" = Yes)

West:	Southwest:	Midwest:	Southeast:	Northeast:	International:
					Y

FINISHMASTER INC

www.finishmaster.com

Industry Group Code: 4246 **Ranks within this company's industry group:** Sales: 1 Profits: 1

Vehicle Manufacturing:		Dealers:		Parts:		Service:		Finance:		Specialty:	
Cars:		Car Dealer New:		Manufacturers:	Y	General Service:		Leasing:		Information Systems:	
Trucks:		Car Dealer Used:		Retail:		Specialty Service:		Auto Loans:		Online Marketing:	
Motorcycles:		Truck Dealer:		Distributors:		Oil Change:		Insurance:		Other:	
Specialty:		RV Dealer:		Tires:		Paint and Body:				Publishing:	
Buses:		Motorcycle Dealer:		Batteries:						Rental Cars/Trucks:	
RVs:		Specialty Dealer:									

TYPES OF BUSINESS:

Automotive Paints & Coatings-Distribution
Industrial & Automotive Paints

BRANDS/DIVISIONS/AFFILIATES:

LDI Ltd., LLC
Tucker Rocky
Automotive Fleet & Industrial Paint Supply, Inc.
SMART
WaterMasters

CONTACTS:

Note: Officers with more than one job title may be intentionally listed here more than once.

John A. Lacy, CEO
John A. Lacy, Pres.
Robert R. Millard, CFO
Daniel A. Courtney, Sr. VP-Oper.
Robert R. Millard, Sr. VP-Finance
David N. Shane, Chmn.

Phone: 317-237-3678	**Fax:** 317-237-2150
Toll-Free: 888-311-3678	
Address: 54 Monument Cir., 8th Fl., Indianapolis, IN 46204 US	

GROWTH PLANS/SPECIAL FEATURES:

FinishMaster, Inc., founded in Indianapolis, Indiana, in 1968, is a leading independent distributor of automotive paints, coatings and related accessories to the automotive collision repair industry. The firm is organized into seven geographic regions: East, Heartland, Midwest, Northwest, South, Southeast and West. Some of the company's products are produced by manufacturers such as BASF, DuPont, PPG and 3M. In addition to FinishMaster's own private brand products, these products are marketed to collision repair shops, automotive dealerships and fleet operators. Products from these manufacturers account for 87% of FinishMaster's sales. The firm also markets its own private label, SMART, for refinishing accessory products, such as body filler and putty, masking and plastic sheeting, undercoat products, detail products, wax and grease remover, glass cleaner, buffing pads, backing plates and adapters, sanders and buffers, paint suits, spray guns and work stands. Through its WaterMasters brand, the company also markets waterborne basecoats for environmentally friendly finisher processes. FinishMaster has 163 sales outlets and three major distribution centers in 28 states. The company is primarily controlled by LDI Ltd, LLC, an investment and operating company that also owns Tucker Rocky, a distributor of motorcycle apparel, parts and accessories. During 2009, FinishMaster acquired the automotive paint operations of Automotive Fleet & Industrial Paint Supply, Inc., which operates one location in Minnesota; and began offering online ordering options through PBEConnection.com

FINANCIALS:

Sales and profits are in thousands of dollars—add 000 to get the full amount. 2009 Note: Financial information for 2009 was not available for all companies at press time.

2009 Sales: $421,391	2009 Profits: $10,946	**U.S. Stock Ticker: FMST**
2008 Sales: $486,013	2008 Profits: $18,060	**Int'l Ticker:** Int'l Exchange:
2007 Sales: $466,626	2007 Profits: $14,934	Employees:
2006 Sales: $450,452	2006 Profits: $22,462	Fiscal Year Ends: 12/31
2005 Sales: $423,803	2005 Profits: $15,647	Parent Company:

SALARIES/BENEFITS:

Pension Plan:	ESOP Stock Plan:	Profit Sharing:	Top Exec. Salary: $	Bonus: $
Savings Plan: Y	Stock Purch. Plan:		Second Exec. Salary: $	Bonus: $

OTHER THOUGHTS:

Apparent Women Officers or Directors:
Hot Spot for Advancement for Women/Minorities:

LOCATIONS: ("Y" = Yes)

West:	Southwest:	Midwest:	Southeast:	Northeast:	International:
Y	Y	Y	Y	Y	

FIRST AUTOMOTIVE GROUP CORPORATION

www.faw.com

Industry Group Code: 33611 **Ranks within this company's industry group:** Sales: Profits:

Vehicle Manufacturing:		Dealers:		Parts:		Service:		Finance:		Specialty:	
Cars:	Y	Car Dealer New:		Manufacturers:	Y	General Service:		Leasing:		Information Systems:	
Trucks:	Y	Car Dealer Used:		Retail:		Specialty Service:		Auto Loans:		Online Marketing:	
Motorcycles:		Truck Dealer:		Distributors:		Oil Change:		Insurance:		Other:	
Specialty:		RV Dealer:		Tires:		Paint and Body:				Publishing:	
Buses:		Motorcycle Dealer:		Batteries:						Rental Cars/Trucks:	
RVs:		Specialty Dealer:									

TYPES OF BUSINESS:

Automobile Manufacturing
Parts Manufacturing
Truck Manufacturing

BRANDS/DIVISIONS/AFFILIATES:

First Automotive Works
Jiefang
Hongqi
Deutz (Dalian) Engine Co. Ltd.
FAW-Volkswagen Automotive Company, Ltd.
ThyssenKrupp Presta Fawer (Changchun) Co. Ltd.
FAW Mazda Motor Sales Co. Ltd.
Valeo Fawer Compressor (Changchun) Co. Ltd.

CONTACTS:

Note: Officers with more than one job title may be intentionally listed here more than once.

Zhu Yanfeng, CEO
Xu Jianyi, Pres.
Teng Tieji, CFO/VP

Phone: 86-431-8590-0715 **Fax:** 86-431-8761-4780
Toll-Free:
Address: No.3025, Dongfeng St., Changchun, 130011 China

GROWTH PLANS/SPECIAL FEATURES:

First Automotive Group Corporation (FAW) is a state-owned Chinese automobile manufacturer. Founded in 1953 as First Automotive Works, it became one of the first vehicle producers in China starting with the 1956 rollout of Jiefang trucks and the 1958 launch of Hongqi cars. Jiefang and Hongqi are still its two major brands. FAW sells about 1.5 million vehicles annually in over 70 countries and has expanded its product line to include six categories: commercial trucks; sport utility vehicles (SUVs) and pickups; mini vehicles; buses and coaches; passenger cars; and components and parts. It has expanded in part through joint ventures, most notably with Volkswagen AG. FAW's partnership with Volkswagen dates to 1991, when FAW-Volkswagen Automotive Company, Ltd. was established by FAW, Volkswagen and Audi. This joint venture produces the Jetta sedan, Bora IV, Caddy MVP, Golf IV, Magotan (European Passat), Sagitar (European Jetta), Audi A4 and Audi A6L. Other joint ventures include the Deutz (Dalian) Engine Co. Ltd. with Deutz AG; ThyssenKrupp Presta Fawer (Changchun) Co. Ltd. with ThyssenKrupp Presta AG; TRW Fawer Automobile Safety Systems Co. Ltd. with TRW Automotive; and Valeo Fawer Compressor (Changchun) Co. Ltd. with France's Valeo. FAW Mazda Motor Sales Co. Ltd., a joint venture between FAW and Mazda Motor Corporation, produces Mazda sports wagons, sports sedans and four door sedans. Lastly, the firm's joint ventures with Toyota produce the Corolla sedan, Vios sedan, Dario Terios Compact SUV, Crown luxury sedan and Reiz (Mark X) performance sedan, as well as engines for Toyota Crown luxury sedans and large automotive stamping dies. Additionally, FAW maintains 28 wholly-owned subsidiaries and has a controlling interest in 18 other subsidiaries. In June 2010, the company, through subsidiary FAW Jilin Automobile Co., Ltd., announced plans to build a new plant at Automobile Industrial Park in Jilin.

FINANCIALS:

Sales and profits are in thousands of dollars—add 000 to get the full amount. 2009 Note: Financial information for 2009 was not available for all companies at press time.

2009 Sales: $	2009 Profits: $	**U.S. Stock Ticker: Government-Owned**
2008 Sales: $	2008 Profits: $	**Int'l Ticker:** Int'l Exchange:
2007 Sales: $	2007 Profits: $	Employees:
2006 Sales: $	2006 Profits: $	Fiscal Year Ends:
2005 Sales: $	2005 Profits: $	Parent Company:

SALARIES/BENEFITS:

Pension Plan:	ESOP Stock Plan:	Profit Sharing:	Top Exec. Salary: $	Bonus: $
Savings Plan:	Stock Purch. Plan:		Second Exec. Salary: $	Bonus: $

OTHER THOUGHTS:

Apparent Women Officers or Directors:
Hot Spot for Advancement for Women/Minorities:

LOCATIONS: ("Y" = Yes)

West:	Southwest:	Midwest:	Southeast:	Northeast:	International:
				Y	Y

FIRST INVESTORS FINANCIAL SERVICES GROUP INC

www.fifsg.com

Industry Group Code: 522220 **Ranks within this company's industry group:** Sales: Profits:

Vehicle Manufacturing:		**Dealers:**		**Parts:**		**Service:**		**Finance:**		**Specialty:**	
Cars:		Car Dealer New:		Manufacturers:		General Service:		Leasing:		Information Systems:	
Trucks:		Car Dealer Used:		Retail:		Specialty Service:		Auto Loans:	Y	Online Marketing:	
Motorcycles:		Truck Dealer:		Distributors:		Oil Change:		Insurance:		Other:	
Specialty:		RV Dealer:		Tires:		Paint and Body:				Publishing:	
Buses:		Motorcycle Dealer:		Batteries:						Rental Cars/Trucks:	
RVs:		Specialty Dealer:									

TYPES OF BUSINESS:

Automobile Financing

BRANDS/DIVISIONS/AFFILIATES:

CONTACTS:

Note: Officers with more than one job title may be intentionally listed here more than once.

Tommy A. Moore, Jr., CEO
Blaise Rodon, COO/Sr. VP
Tommy A. Moore, Jr., Pres.
Bennie H. Duck, CFO/Exec. VP
Bennie H. Duck, Corp. Sec.
Bennie H. Duck, Treas.
Tommy A. Moore, Jr., Chmn.

Phone: 713-977-2600	**Fax:** 800-528-2384
Toll-Free: 800-603-4484	
Address: 675 Bering Dr., Ste. 710, Houston, TX 77057 US	

GROWTH PLANS/SPECIAL FEATURES:

First Investors Financial Services Group, Inc. is a specialized consumer finance company that originates automobile loans. The firm originates its loans through automobile dealers that operate under franchises from major automobile manufacturers, which it refers to as the indirect program. The company also originated loans through utilizing direct marketing, which it referred to as the consumer direct program, but this program was recently suspended. First Investors has active dealership agreements with various dealers, of which approximately 35% are located in Texas, 19% are located in Ohio and 13% are located in Georgia. The company is currently licensed to conduct business in 26 states for direct to consumer loans and indirect loans, and it is actively originating loans in 22 states. It does not generally do business with independent dealers who operate used car lots with no manufacturer affiliation. In addition to originating receivables from its indirect and direct programs, the firm also acquires seasoned receivables in portfolio acquisitions or from other third part originators. The company generally avoids the establishment of branch offices due to various expenses and administrative issues.

First Investors offers its employees medical, dental and vision benefits; healthcare and dependent care flexible spending accounts; short- and long-term disability; basic life and AD&D insurance; a 401(k) plan; service awards; and employee referral rewards.

FINANCIALS:

Sales and profits are in thousands of dollars—add 000 to get the full amount. 2009 Note: Financial information for 2009 was not available for all companies at press time.

2009 Sales: $	2009 Profits: $	**U.S. Stock Ticker: FIFS.PK**
2008 Sales: $	2008 Profits: $	**Int'l Ticker:** Int'l Exchange:
2007 Sales: $62,540	2007 Profits: $3,192	Employees:
2006 Sales: $46,740	2006 Profits: $2,445	Fiscal Year Ends: 4/30
2005 Sales: $36,600	2005 Profits: $ 684	Parent Company:

SALARIES/BENEFITS:

Pension Plan:	ESOP Stock Plan:	Profit Sharing:	Top Exec. Salary: $	Bonus: $
Savings Plan: Y	Stock Purch. Plan:		Second Exec. Salary: $	Bonus: $

OTHER THOUGHTS:

Apparent Women Officers or Directors:
Hot Spot for Advancement for Women/Minorities:

LOCATIONS: ("Y" = Yes)

West:	Southwest:	Midwest:	Southeast:	Northeast:	International:
Y	Y	Y	Y	Y	

FISHER & COMPANY INC

www.fisherco.com

Industry Group Code: 3363 **Ranks within this company's industry group:** Sales: Profits:

Vehicle Manufacturing:		Dealers:		Parts:		Service:		Finance:		Specialty:	
Cars:		Car Dealer New:		Manufacturers:	Y	General Service:		Leasing:		Information Systems:	
Trucks:		Car Dealer Used:		Retail:		Specialty Service:		Auto Loans:		Online Marketing:	
Motorcycles:		Truck Dealer:		Distributors:		Oil Change:		Insurance:		Other:	
Specialty:		RV Dealer:		Tires:		Paint and Body:				Publishing:	
Buses:		Motorcycle Dealer:		Batteries:						Rental Cars/Trucks:	
RVs:		Specialty Dealer:									

TYPES OF BUSINESS:

Auto Parts Manufacturer
Seat Components
Seatbelts

BRANDS/DIVISIONS/AFFILIATES:

Fisher Dynamics
Fisher Dynamics Metal Forming

CONTACTS:

Note: Officers with more than one job title may be intentionally listed here more than once.

Alfred J. (Al) Fisher, III, Pres.
John Whalen, Dir.-Eng.
Alfred J. Fisher, IV, VP
Michael R. Fisher, Pres., Fisher Dynamics
Alfred J. Fisher, Jr., Chmn.

Phone: 586-746-2000 **Fax:** 586-296-1607
Toll-Free:
Address: 33180 Fisher Dr., St. Clair Shores, MI 48082 US

GROWTH PLANS/SPECIAL FEATURES:

Fisher & Company, Inc., through its Fisher Dynamics and Fisher Dynamics Metal Forming subsidiaries, manufactures seating systems and safety-critical precision metal parts for the automotive industry. Fisher Dynamics Metal Forming, founded in 1947 as Fisher Corporation, manufactures a variety of safety-critical precision metal parts, including transmission stampings, engine stampings, vehicle interior stamping components, aerospace stampings, specialized underhood tube formed mounting brackets, seat frame stampings and tight tolerance stampings, for customers in North America, Europe and Asia. The subsidiary has a range of capabilities including mig welding, resistance welding, small-to-medium gauge stampings, fine blanking, tube forming, broaching, reverse extrusion and large stamping. Fisher Dynamics is a leading designer and manufacturer of seat mechanisms for the automotive industry, with manufacturing operations in Michigan, Tennessee, Mexico and China. The subsidiary produces approximately 28 million seat mechanisms annually, including structures, modular seating components, recliners, armrest applications, latches, headrest applications and second and third row mechanisms. Fisher Dynamics additionally maintains sales and engineering facilities in Germany, India and Japan.

FINANCIALS:

Sales and profits are in thousands of dollars—add 000 to get the full amount. 2009 Note: Financial information for 2009 was not available for all companies at press time.

2009 Sales: $	2009 Profits: $	**U.S. Stock Ticker: Private**
2008 Sales: $	2008 Profits: $	**Int'l Ticker:** Int'l Exchange:
2007 Sales: $	2007 Profits: $	Employees:
2006 Sales: $	2006 Profits: $	Fiscal Year Ends:
2005 Sales: $	2005 Profits: $	Parent Company:

SALARIES/BENEFITS:

Pension Plan:	ESOP Stock Plan:	Profit Sharing:	Top Exec. Salary: $	Bonus: $
Savings Plan:	Stock Purch. Plan:		Second Exec. Salary: $	Bonus: $

OTHER THOUGHTS:

Apparent Women Officers or Directors:
Hot Spot for Advancement for Women/Minorities:

LOCATIONS: ("Y" = Yes)

West:	Southwest:	Midwest:	Southeast:	Northeast:	International:
	Y	Y	Y		Y

FISKER AUTOMOTIVE

www.fiskerautomotive.com

Industry Group Code: 33611 **Ranks within this company's industry group:** Sales: Profits:

Vehicle Manufacturing:		Dealers:		Parts:		Service:		Finance:		Specialty:	
Cars:	Y	Car Dealer New:		Manufacturers:		General Service:		Leasing:		Information Systems:	
Trucks:		Car Dealer Used:		Retail:		Specialty Service:		Auto Loans:		Online Marketing:	
Motorcycles:		Truck Dealer:		Distributors:		Oil Change:		Insurance:		Other:	
Specialty:		RV Dealer:		Tires:		Paint and Body:				Publishing:	
Buses:		Motorcycle Dealer:		Batteries:						Rental Cars/Trucks:	
RVs:		Specialty Dealer:									

TYPES OF BUSINESS:

Sports Car Manufacturing

BRANDS/DIVISIONS/AFFILIATES:

Fisker Coachbuild LLC
Quantum Fuel Systems Technologies Worldwide Inc
Karma

CONTACTS:

Note: Officers with more than one job title may be intentionally listed here more than once.

Henrik Fisker, CEO
Bernhard Koehler, COO
Marti Eulberg, VP-Global Mktg. & Sales
Russell Datz, Dir.-Public Rel.

Phone: 714-888-4255	**Fax:** 949-757-4230
Toll-Free:	
Address: 19 Corporate Park, Irvine, CA 92606 US	

GROWTH PLANS/SPECIAL FEATURES:

Fisker Automotive, a joint venture between Fisker Coachbuild LLC and Quantum Fuel Systems Technologies Worldwide, Inc., is a California-based car company that designs, markets and manufactures premium plug-in hybrid automobiles. The company's flagship vehicle, the Karma sedan, is powered by Quantum Technologies' Q-DRIVE technology, which features an electric engine powered by a battery pack, with a gasoline engine supplying backup power. The Karma features two driving modes: Stealth and Sport. The Stealth Drive mode is optimized for efficiency, and the Sport Drive mode delivers the car's full spectrum of power. The car, while achieving an estimated 100 mpg, has the capability of accelerating from 0-60 mph in six seconds and a top speed of 125 mph. The car features a low center of gravity for optimal sport vehicle driving dynamics and regenerative brakes to recapture braking energy. The Karma will be offered in four door sedan and convertible models with pricing to start at $87,900. Initial production is hoped to be 15,000 vehicles annually. Thirty-two retailers have agreed to carry the vehicles. In early 2009, the company received an additional round of venture capital totaling $85 million. The firm's mid-term plan is to introduce a $50,000 automobile by 2014. Fisker outsources all possible manufacturing and design tasks. Manufacturing is contracted out to Valmet Automotive, located in Finland, which is the same plant that assembles Porsche's Boxster and Cayman cars. In September 2009, the company received $528.7 million low-interest loan from the Department of Energy program. The $25 billion program is to fund development of alternative vehicles. The company plans to use $169.3 million to finish the production of its Karma sedan and use majority of the money to develop its next-generation vehicle that would cost $47,400 and would be built in the U.S. In June 2010, the firm bought a former GM factory in Wilmington, Delaware.

FINANCIALS:

Sales and profits are in thousands of dollars—add 000 to get the full amount. 2009 Note: Financial information for 2009 was not available for all companies at press time.

2009 Sales: $	2009 Profits: $	**U.S. Stock Ticker: Joint Venture**
2008 Sales: $	2008 Profits: $	**Int'l Ticker:** Int'l Exchange:
2007 Sales: $	2007 Profits: $	Employees:
2006 Sales: $	2006 Profits: $	Fiscal Year Ends:
2005 Sales: $	2005 Profits: $	Parent Company: QUANTUM FUEL SYSTEMS TECHNOLOGIES WORLDWIDE INC

SALARIES/BENEFITS:

Pension Plan:	ESOP Stock Plan:	Profit Sharing:	Top Exec. Salary: $	Bonus: $
Savings Plan:	Stock Purch. Plan:		Second Exec. Salary: $	Bonus: $

OTHER THOUGHTS:

Apparent Women Officers or Directors:
Hot Spot for Advancement for Women/Minorities:

LOCATIONS: ("Y" = Yes)

West:	Southwest:	Midwest:	Southeast:	Northeast:	International:
Y					

FLETCHER JONES MANAGEMENT GROUP INC www.fletcherjones.com

Industry Group Code: 441110 **Ranks within this company's industry group:** Sales: Profits:

Vehicle Manufacturing:		Dealers:		Parts:		Service:		Finance:		Specialty:	
Cars:		Car Dealer New:	Y	Manufacturers:		General Service:		Leasing:		Information Systems:	
Trucks:		Car Dealer Used:	Y	Retail:		Specialty Service:		Auto Loans:		Online Marketing:	
Motorcycles:		Truck Dealer:		Distributors:		Oil Change:		Insurance:		Other:	
Specialty:		RV Dealer:		Tires:		Paint and Body:				Publishing:	
Buses:		Motorcycle Dealer:		Batteries:						Rental Cars/Trucks:	
RVs:		Specialty Dealer:									

TYPES OF BUSINESS:

Auto Dealers, Retail

BRANDS/DIVISIONS/AFFILIATES:

Mercedez Benz of Chicago
Fletcher Jones of Chicago
Fletcher Jones Imports: Mercedez Benz
Fletcher Jones Toyota
Fletcher Jones Motorcars of Fremont
Porsche of Fremont
Hilo Honda
Landrover of Honolulu

CONTACTS: *Note: Officers with more than one job title may be intentionally listed here more than once.*

Fletcher Jones, Jr., CEO
Tom Downer, COO
Fletcher Jones, Jr., Pres.
Shawn Dettrey, CFO
Garth Blumenthal, Gen. Mgr.

Phone: 702-739-9800	**Fax:** 702-739-0486
Toll-Free:	
Address: 7300 W. Sahara Ave., Las Vegas, NV 89117 US	

GROWTH PLANS/SPECIAL FEATURES:

Fletcher Jones Management Group, Inc. operates 14 automobile dealerships in the west and mid-west U.S. regions. The company has a 225,000-square-foot superstore in Las Vegas, Nevada; an 186,000-square-foot dealership in Newport Beach, California; two in Fremont, California; two dealerships in Chicago; six in Hawaii; and two additional dealerships in Las Vegas, Nevada. Fletcher Jones Management is one of the top Mercedes-Benz dealers in the U.S., with four of its dealerships, including its two largest, specializing in selling Mercedes. Besides Mercedes-Benz, the company sells automobiles from Audi, Ford, Honda, Infiniti, Jaguar, Land Rover, Lexus, Nissan, Porsche, Toyota and Volkswagen.

FINANCIALS: **Sales and profits are in thousands of dollars—add 000 to get the full amount. 2009 Note: Financial information for 2009 was not available for all companies at press time.**

2009 Sales: $	2009 Profits: $	**U.S. Stock Ticker: Private**
2008 Sales: $	2008 Profits: $	**Int'l Ticker:** Int'l Exchange:
2007 Sales: $	2007 Profits: $	Employees:
2006 Sales: $	2006 Profits: $	Fiscal Year Ends:
2005 Sales: $	2005 Profits: $	Parent Company:

SALARIES/BENEFITS:

Pension Plan:	ESOP Stock Plan:	Profit Sharing:	Top Exec. Salary: $	Bonus: $
Savings Plan:	Stock Purch. Plan:		Second Exec. Salary: $	Bonus: $

OTHER THOUGHTS:

Apparent Women Officers or Directors:
Hot Spot for Advancement for Women/Minorities:

LOCATIONS: ("Y" = Yes)

West:	Southwest:	Midwest:	Southeast:	Northeast:	International:
Y		Y			

FORD MOTOR CO

www.ford.com

Industry Group Code: 33611 **Ranks within this company's industry group:** Sales: 4 Profits: 2

Vehicle Manufacturing:		Dealers:		Parts:		Service:		Finance:		Specialty:	
Cars:	Y	Car Dealer New:		Manufacturers:	Y	General Service:		Leasing:	Y	Information Systems:	
Trucks:	Y	Car Dealer Used:		Retail:		Specialty Service:		Auto Loans:	Y	Online Marketing:	
Motorcycles:		Truck Dealer:		Distributors:		Oil Change:		Insurance:	Y	Other:	Y
Specialty:		RV Dealer:		Tires:		Paint and Body:				Publishing:	
Buses:		Motorcycle Dealer:		Batteries:						Rental Cars/Trucks:	
RVs:		Specialty Dealer:									

TYPES OF BUSINESS:

Automobile Manufacturer
Automobile Financing
Fuel-Cell & Hybrid Research

BRANDS/DIVISIONS/AFFILIATES:

Lincoln
Motorcraft
Zhejiang Geely Holding Group
Ford Sync
Ford Mustang
Mazda Motor Corporation
Ford Motor Credit Company (The)

CONTACTS: *Note: Officers with more than one job title may be intentionally listed here more than once.*

Alan Mulally, CEO
Alan Mulally, Pres.
Lewis W. K. Booth, CFO/Exec. VP
James D. Farley, VP-Mktg. & Comm.
Felicia J. Fields, VP-Human Resources & Corp. Svcs.
Gerhard Schmidt, VP-Research
Nicholas J. Smither, CIO/VP
Gerhard Schmidt, CTO
Derrick M. Kuzak, VP-Global Prod. Dev.
Gerhard Schmidt, VP-Advanced Eng.
John Fleming, VP-Global Mfg.
David G. Leitch, General Counsel/Sr. VP
Raymond F. Day, VP-Comm.
Neil M. Schloss, Treas./VP
Michael E. Bannister, Exec. VP/CEO/Chmn.-Ford Motor Credit Co.
Mark Fields, Exec. VP/Pres., Americas
John Fleming, Exec. VP/CEO/Pres., Ford Europe
J C. Mays, VP-Design/Chief Creative Officer
William C. Ford, Jr., Exec. Chmn.
Joseph R. Hinrichs, Exec. VP-APAC & Africa
Thomas K. Brown, Sr. VP-Global Purchasing

Phone: 313-322-3000	**Fax:** 313-845-7512
Toll-Free: 800-392-3673	
Address: 1 American Rd., Dearborn, MI 48126 US	

GROWTH PLANS/SPECIAL FEATURES:

Ford Motor Company is a designer and manufacturer of automobiles and automotive systems. The firm operates in two segments: automotive and financial services. The automotive segment designs, manufactures, sells and services cars and trucks under the brands Ford and Lincoln. The company sells its vehicles to the public via independently owned dealerships, including roughly 11,700 Ford dealerships and 1,370 Lincoln dealerships. In addition to new car sales, these dealerships offer after-sale vehicle services and products such as maintenance and repair; vehicle accessories; and extended-service warranties. Ford markets these products and services under brands including Ford, Ford Extended Service Plan and Motorcraft. Ford has an 11% stake in Mazda Motor Corporation. The firm's financial services segment, run through the Ford Motor Credit Company LLC, offers vehicle-related financing, leasing and insurance. Some of Ford's most popular vehicles include the Ford Mustang sports car, the Ford F150 truck, the compact Ford Focus, the Lincoln Navigator SUV and the Ford Escape Hybrid SUV. Through a partnership with Microsoft, the firm offers Ford Sync, a voice-activated in-car communications and entertainment system for mobile phones and music players. The company hopes to quickly introduce fully electric vehicles to the U.S. market. In 2009, the company introduced hybrid versions of its Ford Fusion. In March 2010, the firm agreed to sell its Volvo Cars unit to Zhejiang Geely Holding Group for $1.8 billion. That same month, Ford launched the Figo compact car, its first vehicle made specifically for the Indian market. In mid 2010, Ford announced that it will close its Mercury division.

The company offers its employees medical, dental and prescription insurance; life and disability insurance; a savings plan; relocation packages; gift matching; dependent scholarships; recreation programs; tuition assistance; and group rates on auto, home, and life insurance.

FINANCIALS: **Sales and profits are in thousands of dollars—add 000 to get the full amount. 2009 Note: Financial information for 2009 was not available for all companies at press time.**

2009 Sales: $105,893,000	2009 Profits: $2,717,000	**U.S. Stock Ticker: F**
2008 Sales: $129,165,000	2008 Profits: $-14,766,000	**Int'l Ticker:** Int'l Exchange:
2007 Sales: $154,379,000	2007 Profits: $-2,795,000	Employees:
2006 Sales: $160,065,000	2006 Profits: $-12,613,000	Fiscal Year Ends: 12/31
2005 Sales: $176,835,000	2005 Profits: $1,440,000	Parent Company:

SALARIES/BENEFITS:

Pension Plan:	ESOP Stock Plan:	Profit Sharing:	Top Exec. Salary: $1,400,003	Bonus: $
Savings Plan: Y	Stock Purch. Plan:		Second Exec. Salary: $1,300,000	Bonus: $

OTHER THOUGHTS:

Apparent Women Officers or Directors: 5
Hot Spot for Advancement for Women/Minorities: Y

LOCATIONS: ("Y" = Yes)

West:	Southwest:	Midwest:	Southeast:	Northeast:	International:
Y	Y	Y	Y	Y	Y

FORD MOTOR COMPANY OF CANADA

www.ford.ca

Industry Group Code: 33611 **Ranks within this company's industry group:** Sales: Profits:

Vehicle Manufacturing:		Dealers:		Parts:		Service:		Finance:		Specialty:	
Cars:	Y	Car Dealer New:	Y	Manufacturers:	Y	General Service:		Leasing:	Y	Information Systems:	
Trucks:	Y	Car Dealer Used:	Y	Retail:		Specialty Service:		Auto Loans:	Y	Online Marketing:	
Motorcycles:		Truck Dealer:		Distributors:	Y	Oil Change:		Insurance:		Other:	
Specialty:		RV Dealer:		Tires:		Paint and Body:				Publishing:	
Buses:		Motorcycle Dealer:		Batteries:						Rental Cars/Trucks:	
RVs:		Specialty Dealer:									

TYPES OF BUSINESS:

Automobiles, Manufacturing
Dealerships
Parts Manufacturing
Auto Financing & Leasing
Hybrid & Electric Vehicles

BRANDS/DIVISIONS/AFFILIATES:

Ford Motor Co
Ford Credit Canada
Ford Parts and Service
Mustang
Explorer
E-Series
Focus
Lincoln

CONTACTS: *Note: Officers with more than one job title may be intentionally listed here more than once.*

David Mondragon, CEO
David Mondragon, Pres.
Jim Farley, VP-Global Mktg., Sales & Svcs.
Stacey Allerton Firth, VP-Human Resources
Dean Stoneley, VP-Mktg.

Phone: 905-845-2511 | **Fax:** 905-844-8085
Toll-Free: 800-565-3673
Address: The Canadian Rd., P.O. Box 2000, Oakville, ON L6J 5E4 Canada

GROWTH PLANS/SPECIAL FEATURES:

Ford Motor Company of Canada Limited (Ford Canada), is a subsidiary of Ford Motor Company, manufactures automobiles. The firm's manufacturing operations are located in Ontario and include vehicle assembly at Oakville and St. Thomas, power train component manufacturing at Windsor. The company's models are available in these segments: cars, trucks, and SUVs and Crossovers. In the car segment, the firm's current models are the Fiesta, Focus, Fusion Hybrid, Fusion, Taurus, Mustang and the Shelby GT500. Current truck models include Ranger, F-150, F-150 Raptor, Explorer Sport Trac, Super Duty and E-Series trucks. In the SUV and Crossover segment, current models include the Escape, Explorer, Expedition and the Edge. Past models include Freestar minivan, the Thunderbird, Five Hundred, Grand Marquis, Escape Hybrid, Freestyle, F-250, F-350, and the Excursion. In addition, Ford also sold Lincoln models, including the Zephyr, LS, Town Car, Mark LT truck Aviator SUV and Navigator SUVs. Ford Canada also operates two parts distribution centers and oversees approximately 540 Ford and Ford-Lincoln dealerships. Ford Parts and Service provide maintenance to its new and used cars at its dealerships. Services provided include oil and filter change; tire rotation and inspection; fill windshield washer fluid; inspection on air conditioning, hoses, belts, battery test, rotors, hydraulic system and steering and suspension components; replacement of front or rear brake pads or shoes. Through Ford Credit Canada, the company provides auto leasing and financing for new and used vehicles.

Employees of the firm are offered health care coverage; tuition refund plan; stock ownership program; vacation and paid holidays. Lastly, employees and their families can purchase Ford and Lincoln vehicles at dealer invoice cost.

FINANCIALS: **Sales and profits are in thousands of dollars—add 000 to get the full amount. 2009 Note: Financial information for 2009 was not available for all companies at press time.**

2009 Sales: $	2009 Profits: $	**U.S. Stock Ticker: Subsidiary**
2008 Sales: $	2008 Profits: $	**Int'l Ticker:** Int'l Exchange:
2007 Sales: $	2007 Profits: $	Employees:
2006 Sales: $	2006 Profits: $	Fiscal Year Ends: 12/31
2005 Sales: $	2005 Profits: $	Parent Company: FORD MOTOR CO

SALARIES/BENEFITS:

Pension Plan:	ESOP Stock Plan: Y	Profit Sharing:	Top Exec. Salary: $	Bonus: $
Savings Plan:	Stock Purch. Plan:		Second Exec. Salary: $	Bonus: $

OTHER THOUGHTS:

Apparent Women Officers or Directors: 1
Hot Spot for Advancement for Women/Minorities:

LOCATIONS: ("Y" = Yes)

West:	Southwest:	Midwest:	Southeast:	Northeast:	International:
					Y

FORD MOTOR CREDIT CO LLC

www.fordcredit.com

Industry Group Code: 522220 **Ranks within this company's industry group:** Sales: 1 Profits: 1

Vehicle Manufacturing:		Dealers:		Parts:		Service:		Finance:		Specialty:	
Cars:		Car Dealer New:		Manufacturers:		General Service:		Leasing:	Y	Information Systems:	
Trucks:		Car Dealer Used:		Retail:		Specialty Service:		Auto Loans:	Y	Online Marketing:	
Motorcycles:		Truck Dealer:		Distributors:		Oil Change:		Insurance:	Y	Other:	
Specialty:		RV Dealer:		Tires:		Paint and Body:				Publishing:	
Buses:		Motorcycle Dealer:		Batteries:						Rental Cars/Trucks:	
RVs:		Specialty Dealer:									

TYPES OF BUSINESS:

Automobile Financing
Insurance
Leasing
Loans & Mortgages
Fleet Financing
Dealer Financing

BRANDS/DIVISIONS/AFFILIATES:

Ford Credit North America
Volvo Car Finance
Mazda American Credit
PRIMUS Financial Services
Ford Motor Co
FCE Bank Plc
TARIC

CONTACTS:

Note: Officers with more than one job title may be intentionally listed here more than once.

Michael E. Bannister, CEO
Kenneth R. Kent, CFO/Vice Chmn.
John T. Noone, Exec. VP/Pres., Global Mktg. & Sales
Terry D. Chenault, Exec. VP/Dir.-Tech. & Risk Mgmt.
Terry D. Chenault, Exec. VP/Dir.-Global Oper.
Kenneth R. Kent, Treas.
Michael E. Bannister, Chmn.

Phone: 313-322-3000	**Fax:** 313-323-2959
Toll-Free: 800-727-7000	
Address: 1 American Rd., Dearborn, MI 48126 US	

GROWTH PLANS/SPECIAL FEATURES:

Ford Motor Credit Co., LLC, formerly Ford Motor Credit Co., an indirect, wholly-owned subsidiary of Ford Motor Company. It is one of the largest companies in the world dedicated to automotive finance, offering financial services to vehicle buyers in 34 countries. The firm offers a wide variety of automotive financing products to and through automotive dealers throughout the world. The company operates through brands such as Ford Credit North America, Ford Financial International, Volvo Car Finance, FCE Bank plc and PRIMUS Financial Services (Ford owns 4% of PRIMUS). Its primary financing products fall into three categories: retail financing, wholesale financing, and other financing. Retail financing includes purchasing retail-installment sale contracts and retail lease contracts from dealers and offering financing to commercial customers, primarily vehicle leasing companies and fleet purchasers, to lease or purchase vehicle fleets. Wholesale financing makes loans to dealers to finance the purchase of vehicle inventory, also known as floor plan financing. Other financing includes making loans to dealers for working capital; such as purchase/finance dealership real estate; and improvements to dealership facilities. The company, also services the finance receivables and leases it originates and purchases; makes loans to Ford affiliates; purchases certain receivables of Ford and its subsidiaries and provides insurance services related to its financing programs. The company earns revenue primarily from: payments made under retail-installment sale contracts and leases that it purchases; interest supplements and other support payments from Ford and affiliated companies; and payments made under wholesale and other dealer loan financing programs. In addition, the firm conducts insurance through TARIC in the U.S., and Canada and through various other insurance subsidiaries worldwide. The insurance covers extended service contracts; physical damage insurance covering vehicles at dealers' locations; in-transit between final assembly plants; and rental vehicles.

FINANCIALS:

Sales and profits are in thousands of dollars—add 000 to get the full amount. 2009 Note: Financial information for 2009 was not available for all companies at press time.

2009 Sales: $12,541,000	2009 Profits: $1,279,000	**U.S. Stock Ticker: FCJ**
2008 Sales: $16,417,000	2008 Profits: $-1,536,000	**Int'l Ticker:** Int'l Exchange:
2007 Sales: $16,716,000	2007 Profits: $775,000	Employees: 8,200
2006 Sales: $17,247,000	2006 Profits: $1,283,000	Fiscal Year Ends: 12/31
2005 Sales: $16,480,000	2005 Profits: $1,904,000	Parent Company: FORD MOTOR CO

SALARIES/BENEFITS:

Pension Plan: Y	ESOP Stock Plan:	Profit Sharing:	Top Exec. Salary: $	Bonus: $
Savings Plan: Y	Stock Purch. Plan: Y		Second Exec. Salary: $	Bonus: $

OTHER THOUGHTS:

Apparent Women Officers or Directors:
Hot Spot for Advancement for Women/Minorities:

LOCATIONS: ("Y" = Yes)

West:	Southwest:	Midwest:	Southeast:	Northeast:	International:
Y	Y	Y	Y	Y	Y

FUEL SYSTEMS SOLUTIONS INC

www.fuelsystemssolutions.com

Industry Group Code: 3363 **Ranks within this company's industry group:** Sales: 51 Profits: 13

Vehicle Manufacturing:		Dealers:		Parts:		Service:		Finance:		Specialty:	
Cars:		Car Dealer New:		Manufacturers:	Y	General Service:		Leasing:		Information Systems:	
Trucks:		Car Dealer Used:		Retail:		Specialty Service:		Auto Loans:		Online Marketing:	
Motorcycles:		Truck Dealer:		Distributors:		Oil Change:		Insurance:		Other:	Y
Specialty:		RV Dealer:		Tires:		Paint and Body:				Publishing:	
Buses:		Motorcycle Dealer:		Batteries:						Rental Cars/Trucks:	
RVs:		Specialty Dealer:									

TYPES OF BUSINESS:

Automobile Parts Manufacturer
Fuel Components & Systems

BRANDS/DIVISIONS/AFFILIATES:

IMPCO Technologies, Inc.
B.R.C. Società a Responsabilità Limitata
IMPCO U.S.
BRC FuelMaker

CONTACTS:

Note: Officers with more than one job title may be intentionally listed here more than once.

Mariano Costamagna, CEO
Robert Olivo, COO
Matthew Beale, Pres.
Matthew Beale, CFO
Matthew Beale, Corp. Sec.
Michael Helfand, Sr. VP-Finance/Chief Acct. Officer
Pier Antonio Costamagna, Managing Dir.-BRC/Dir.-Mechanical Eng., MTM
Richard Nielsen, Gen. Mgr.-IMPCO Technologies
Matthew Beale, Chmn.

Phone: 646-502-7170 **Fax:** 646-502-7171
Toll-Free:
Address: 780 3rd Ave., 25th Fl., New York, NY 10017 US

GROWTH PLANS/SPECIAL FEATURES:

Fuel Systems Solutions, Inc., formerly IMPCO Technologies, Inc., designs, manufactures, installs and supplies alternative fuel components and systems for use in the transportation, industrial and power generation industries. Its components and systems control the pressure and flow of gaseous alternative fuels, such as propane and natural gas used in internal combustion engines, and improve efficiency, enhance power output and reduce emissions by electronically sensing and regulating the proper proportion of fuel and air required by the engine. The company operates in three main segments, organized around its subsidiaries: the industrial segment, including mobile and power generation equipment, consisting of IMPCO Technologies, Inc.; the infrastructure segment, which includes BRC FuelMaker; and the transportation segment, consisting of BRC S.r.L., based in Italy. The company's products include those for fuel delivery, such as pressure regulators, fuel injectors and flow control valves; electronic controls, including solid-state components and proprietary software to monitor and optimize fuel pressure and flow; gaseous fuel internal combustion engines; systems integration; auxiliary power systems; and for natural gas compressors. The company also designs, assembles and markets ancillary components required for complete systems operation on alternative fuels. The firm markets its products through a global network of 360 distributors and dealers in over 70 countries, and more than 100 original equipment manufacturers (OEMs). In August 2009, Fuel Systems Solutions acquired the Power Systems business of Teleflex, Inc.

FINANCIALS:

Sales and profits are in thousands of dollars—add 000 to get the full amount. 2009 Note: Financial information for 2009 was not available for all companies at press time.

2009 Sales: $452,325 — 2009 Profits: $49,841
2008 Sales: $382,697 — 2008 Profits: $23,342
2007 Sales: $265,331 — 2007 Profits: $5,883
2006 Sales: $220,816 — 2006 Profits: $6,912
2005 Sales: $174,539 — 2005 Profits: $-10,354

U.S. Stock Ticker: FSYS
Int'l Ticker: Int'l Exchange:
Employees: 1,767
Fiscal Year Ends: 12/31
Parent Company:

SALARIES/BENEFITS:

Pension Plan: ESOP Stock Plan: Profit Sharing: Top Exec. Salary: $513,241 Bonus: $
Savings Plan: Stock Purch. Plan: Second Exec. Salary: $418,187 Bonus: $58,711

OTHER THOUGHTS:

Apparent Women Officers or Directors:
Hot Spot for Advancement for Women/Minorities:

LOCATIONS: ("Y" = Yes)

West:	Southwest:	Midwest:	Southeast:	Northeast:	International:
Y		Y		Y	Y

FUJI HEAVY INDUSTRIES LTD (SUBARU)

www.fhi.co.jp

Industry Group Code: 33611 **Ranks within this company's industry group:** Sales: 18 Profits: 26

Vehicle Manufacturing:		**Dealers:**		**Parts:**		**Service:**		**Finance:**		**Specialty:**	
Cars:	Y	Car Dealer New:		Manufacturers:	Y	General Service:		Leasing:		Information Systems:	
Trucks:		Car Dealer Used:		Retail:		Specialty Service:		Auto Loans:		Online Marketing:	
Motorcycles:		Truck Dealer:		Distributors:		Oil Change:		Insurance:		Other:	Y
Specialty:	Y	RV Dealer:		Tires:		Paint and Body:				Publishing:	
Buses:	Y	Motorcycle Dealer:		Batteries:						Rental Cars/Trucks:	
RVs:		Specialty Dealer:									

TYPES OF BUSINESS:

Automobile Manufacturing
Buses
Railcars
Aircraft Manufacturing & Components
Heavy-Duty Engines & Equipment
Specialty Vehicles
Sanitation Vehicles
Waste Treatment, Recycling & Alternative Energy Technologies

BRANDS/DIVISIONS/AFFILIATES:

Subaru
Outback
Forester
Impreza
Tribeca
Legacy
Suabru Korea Co., Ltd.

CONTACTS: *Note: Officers with more than one job title may be intentionally listed here more than once.*

Ikuo Mori, CEO
Ikuo Mori, Pres.
Yasuyuki Yoshinage, Exec. VP-Sales & Mktg.
Kazushige Okuhara, Exec. VP-Human Resources
Kazushige Okuhara, Exec. VP-Bus. Process & Info. Mgmt.
Yasuo Kosakai, Exec. VP/Sr. Gen Mgr.-Subaru Mfg.
Kazushige Okuhara, Exec. VP-Gen. Admin.
Kazushige Okuhara, Exec. VP-Legal/Sec.
Jun Kondo, Exec. VP-Strategy Dev. & Subaru Quality Assurance
Kazushige Okuhara, Exec. VP-Corp. Comm.
Kazushige Okuhara, Exec. VP-Finance, Acct. & Internal Audit
Masatsugu Nagato, Exec. VP
Hiroshi Komatsu, Sr. Exec. VP
Jun Kondo, Exec. VP-Industrial Prod., Aerospace & Eco Tech.
Yasuyuki Yoshinaga, VP/Chief Gen. Mgr.-Subaru Japan Sales & Mktg.
Tom Doll, COO/Pres., Subaru of America, Inc.

Phone: 81-3-3347-2111 **Fax:** 81-3-3347-2338
Toll-Free:
Address: Subaru Bldg., 1-7-2 Nishishinjuku, Shinjuku-ku, Tokyo, 160-8316 Japan

GROWTH PLANS/SPECIAL FEATURES:

Fuji Heavy Industries Ltd. (FHI), perhaps best known for its Subaru cars, is a transportation conglomerate that also manufactures buses, railcars, engines, aircraft components and specialty vehicles. It operates four divisions: Subaru Automotive (which generated 91% of 2009 sales), Aerospace (6%), Industrial Products (2%) and Eco Technologies (1%). The Automotive division does business as Subaru, the Japanese name for the Pleiades star-cluster, which also inspired its star-cluster logo. Most of this division's cars are all-wheel-drive vehicles, including the Outback and Forester models, which are unique in that they are built on small-car platforms but have a sport utility vehicle (SUV) look and feel. Other models include Tribeca, Legacy and Impreza. The Subaru engine incorporates an unusual design, called the Horizontally-Opposed Boxer Engine, which the firm claims reduces vibration and is generally more compact than other designs. The Aerospace division includes manufacturing, selling and repairing fixed wing aircraft and parts. In addition to its own branded offerings, including the T-1, T-3 and T-5 defense trainer jets, this division is responsible for the design and building of the center wing section of the Boeing 767 and 777. The Industrial Products division develops, manufactures and sells Robin brand engines and products that utilize these engines, including construction, forestry and agricultural machines and tools. Finally, the Eco Technologies division mainly manufactures, repairs and sells sanitation and recycling vehicles. It also partners with other companies to develop waste treatment, recycling and alternative energy technologies. FHI has over 100 subsidiaries and nine affiliates in Asia, the U.S., Canada and Europe. In January 2010, FHI announced its entry into the South Korean market, through distributor Subaru Korea Co., Ltd. In April 2010, Subaru unveiled its 2011 model of the Impreza WRX STI and WRX.

FINANCIALS: **Sales and profits are in thousands of dollars—add 000 to get the full amount. 2009 Note: Financial information for 2009 was not available for all companies at press time.**

2009 Sales: $15,647,200 | 2009 Profits: $-756,860
2008 Sales: $15,867,800 | 2008 Profits: $186,510
2007 Sales: $14,948,200 | 2007 Profits: $319,000
2006 Sales: $14,763,700 | 2006 Profits: $156,100
2005 Sales: $14,464,900 | 2005 Profits: $182,400

U.S. Stock Ticker:
Int'l Ticker: 7270 Int'l Exchange: Tokyo-TSE
Employees:
Fiscal Year Ends: 3/31
Parent Company:

SALARIES/BENEFITS:

Pension Plan: ESOP Stock Plan: Profit Sharing: Top Exec. Salary: $ Bonus: $
Savings Plan: Stock Purch. Plan: Second Exec. Salary: $ Bonus: $

OTHER THOUGHTS:

Apparent Women Officers or Directors:
Hot Spot for Advancement for Women/Minorities:

LOCATIONS: ("Y" = Yes)

West:	Southwest:	Midwest:	Southeast:	Northeast:	International:
Y		Y		Y	Y

GALPIN MOTORS INC

www.gogalpin.com

Industry Group Code: 441110 **Ranks within this company's industry group:** Sales: Profits:

Vehicle Manufacturing:		Dealers:		Parts:		Service:		Finance:		Specialty:	
Cars:		Car Dealer New:	Y	Manufacturers:		General Service:	Y	Leasing:		Information Systems:	
Trucks:		Car Dealer Used:	Y	Retail:		Specialty Service:	Y	Auto Loans:	Y	Online Marketing:	
Motorcycles:		Truck Dealer:		Distributors:		Oil Change:		Insurance:		Other:	
Specialty:		RV Dealer:		Tires:		Paint and Body:				Publishing:	
Buses:		Motorcycle Dealer:		Batteries:						Rental Cars/Trucks:	Y
RVs:		Specialty Dealer:									

TYPES OF BUSINESS:

Auto Dealers, Retail
Car Rental Services
Vehicle Customization

BRANDS/DIVISIONS/AFFILIATES:

Horseless Carriage Restaurant
Galpinizing
Galpin Auto Sports (G.A.S.)
Pimp My Ride
ShopGalpinAutoSports.com

CONTACTS: *Note: Officers with more than one job title may be intentionally listed here more than once.*

Herbert F. (Bert) Boeckmann II, Pres.
Phil Marshall, CFO/Gen. Bus. Mgr.
Tawny Arnaud, VP-Sales
Beau Boeckmann, Chief-Design/Pres., Galpin Auto Sports
Alan Skobin, General Counsel/VP
Beau Boeckmann, VP-Internet
Karl Boeckmann, VP
Brad Boeckmann, VP
Beau Boeckmann, VP-Promotions, Advertising & Mktg.
Charles McCord, Mgr.-Facilities

Phone: 818-787-3800 **Fax:** 818-778-2210
Toll-Free: 800-256-7137
Address: 15505 Roscoe Blvd., North Hills, CA 91343 US

GROWTH PLANS/SPECIAL FEATURES:

Galpin Motors, Inc. operates nine car dealerships and an integrated series of web sites, selling new and used vehicles in California. Although founded by Frank Galpin in 1946, the company has been owned and operated by the Boeckmann family since the 1960s. The company sells nine main new vehicle makes, Ford, Jaguar, Volvo, Lincoln, Honda, Mazda, Mercury, Saturn and Aston Martin, as well as additional used makes as they are acquired. Customers can also select from a diverse range of high-performance engine options ranging from 500 horse power Ford Racingcrate engines to Roush engines. Galpin's dealerships often have unusual features, such as exhibits, circuses and charity ceremonies. For example, the Galpin Mazda of Santa Clarita location is home to an in-showroom Starbucks Coffee franchise, while its flagship North Hills dealership features an in-house eatery called the Horseless Carriage Restaurant. The Galpin web site offers customers online specials, vehicle inventory search, financing applications, parts ordering and service scheduling. Besides selling cars, Galpin has three vehicle rental facilities, including a Hollywood location with over 1,000 vehicles that it rents to studios for movie production. Additionally, Galpin customizes vehicles in a process it calls Galpinizing, offering distinctive treatments like the Tailgate Party Truck, featuring a built-in barbecue grill, blender, DVD/TV combo and refrigerated beer kegs. Largely in charge of this customization work is Galpin Auto Sports (G.A.S.), the official shop of MTV's Pimp My Ride. The firm also sells rings and G.A.S.-branded merchandise, mainly tee-shirts and hats, through Shopgalpinautosports.com.

Galpin provides its employees benefits including a vehicle purchase plan.

FINANCIALS: **Sales and profits are in thousands of dollars—add 000 to get the full amount. 2009 Note: Financial information for 2009 was not available for all companies at press time.**

2009 Sales: $	2009 Profits: $	**U.S. Stock Ticker: Private**
2008 Sales: $	2008 Profits: $	**Int'l Ticker:** Int'l Exchange:
2007 Sales: $198,900	2007 Profits: $	Employees:
2006 Sales: $	2006 Profits: $	Fiscal Year Ends: 12/31
2005 Sales: $	2005 Profits: $	Parent Company:

SALARIES/BENEFITS:

Pension Plan:	ESOP Stock Plan:	Profit Sharing: Y	Top Exec. Salary: $	Bonus: $
Savings Plan: Y	Stock Purch. Plan:		Second Exec. Salary: $	Bonus: $

OTHER THOUGHTS:

Apparent Women Officers or Directors: 1
Hot Spot for Advancement for Women/Minorities:

LOCATIONS: ("Y" = Yes)

West:	Southwest:	Midwest:	Southeast:	Northeast:	International:
Y					

GAZ GROUP

eng.gazgroup.ru

Industry Group Code: 33611 **Ranks within this company's industry group:** Sales: Profits:

Vehicle Manufacturing:		Dealers:		Parts:		Service:		Finance:		Specialty:	
Cars:	Y	Car Dealer New:		Manufacturers:	Y	General Service:		Leasing:		Information Systems:	
Trucks:	Y	Car Dealer Used:		Retail:		Specialty Service:		Auto Loans:		Online Marketing:	
Motorcycles:		Truck Dealer:		Distributors:		Oil Change:		Insurance:		Other:	
Specialty:	Y	RV Dealer:		Tires:		Paint and Body:				Publishing:	
Buses:	Y	Motorcycle Dealer:		Batteries:						Rental Cars/Trucks:	
RVs:		Specialty Dealer:									

TYPES OF BUSINESS:

Automobile Manufacturing
Auto Parts & Components Manufacturing

BRANDS/DIVISIONS/AFFILIATES:

GAZelle
Sobol
PAZ
Volga Siber
LiAZ
YaMZ
URAL

CONTACTS:

Note: Officers with more than one job title may be intentionally listed here more than once.

Bo Andersson, CEO
Bo Andersson, Pres.
Vyacheslav Shmatov, CFO
Ekaterina Mayorova, Mgr.-Human Resources
Leonid Kuznetsov, Dir.-Strategic Dev.
Leonid Dolgov, Dir.-Passenger Car Div.
Victor Korman, Dir.-Truck & Construction Equipment Div.
Igor Kulgan, Dir.-Powertrain Div.
Andrzej Kasperek, Dir.-Corp. Bus. Dev.
Wolf Siegfried, Chmn.
Yuriy Ushakov, Dir.-Procurement

Phone: 7-831-299-0990	**Fax:**
Toll-Free:	
Address: 88 Lenina Prospect, Nizhny Novgorod, 603950 Russia	

GROWTH PLANS/SPECIAL FEATURES:

Gaz Group is one of Russia's largest automotive manufacturers. The firm manufactures light commercial vehicles (LCVs), buses, passenger cars, road construction machines, industrial trucks and power train components. The company operates 18 automotive manufacturers in 10 regions of Russia. Gaz Group's primary manufacturing locations and plants include the Gorky Automobile Plant, the Pavlovo Bus Plant, the Tver Excavator Plant, the Likino Bus Plant, the Avtodizel Yaroslavl Motor Works and the Ural Automobile Plant. The Gorky Automobile Plant makes GAZelle and Sobol brands of light commercial vehicles, as well as Valdai and Sadko medium duty trucks and Volga Siber passenger cars, built in cooperation with Chrysler. Gaz Group's Pavlovo Bus Plant produces the PAZ brand of buses for urban, suburban and intercity uses. The Tver Excavator Plant manufactures the TvEX brand of crawler excavators and wheel excavators. The firm's Likino Bus Plant manufactures LiAZ brand urban buses. Its Avtodizel Yaroslavl Motor Works produces one of Russia's leading diesel engines and power plants under the YaMZ brand. The Ural Automobile Plant makes URAL brand heavy on- and off-road trucks. The Gaz Group products include the Volga Siber sedan; the minibus models Gazelle and Sobol; the van model GAZelle; the truck models Ural, Valday, Sadko, GAZ Truck and GAZ Dump Truck; the bus models City, Suburban, Coach, School and Special. Construction equipment manufactured by the company includes wheel excavators, crawler excavators, material handlers, forest equipment, motor graders, wheel loaders, asphalt pavers, tracked vehicles, road harrows, trailers and bulldozers. The firm operates a joint-venture with General Motors, called VM Motori S.p.A., established to design and manufacture diesel engines. Gaz Group also manufactures gasoline engines, gearboxes, fuel injection systems, clutches, diesel generators and mobile power units. In April 2010, the company introduced an upgraded GAZelle bus that runs on liquefied petroleum gas.

FINANCIALS:

Sales and profits are in thousands of dollars—add 000 to get the full amount. 2009 Note: Financial information for 2009 was not available for all companies at press time.

2009 Sales: $	2009 Profits: $	**U.S. Stock Ticker: GAZA**
2008 Sales: $4,700,000	2008 Profits: $	**Int'l Ticker:** Int'l Exchange:
2007 Sales: $	2007 Profits: $	Employees:
2006 Sales: $	2006 Profits: $	Fiscal Year Ends:
2005 Sales: $	2005 Profits: $	Parent Company:

SALARIES/BENEFITS:

Pension Plan:	ESOP Stock Plan:	Profit Sharing:	Top Exec. Salary: $	Bonus: $
Savings Plan:	Stock Purch. Plan:		Second Exec. Salary: $	Bonus: $

OTHER THOUGHTS:

Apparent Women Officers or Directors: 1
Hot Spot for Advancement for Women/Minorities:

LOCATIONS: ("Y" = Yes)

West:	Southwest:	Midwest:	Southeast:	Northeast:	International:
					Y

GEICO CORPORATION

www.geico.com

Industry Group Code: 524126 **Ranks within this company's industry group:** Sales: Profits:

Vehicle Manufacturing:		Dealers:		Parts:		Service:		Finance:		Specialty:	
Cars:		Car Dealer New:		Manufacturers:		General Service:		Leasing:		Information Systems:	
Trucks:		Car Dealer Used:		Retail:		Specialty Service:		Auto Loans:		Online Marketing:	
Motorcycles:		Truck Dealer:		Distributors:		Oil Change:		Insurance:	Y	Other:	
Specialty:		RV Dealer:		Tires:		Paint and Body:				Publishing:	
Buses:		Motorcycle Dealer:		Batteries:						Rental Cars/Trucks:	
RVs:		Specialty Dealer:									

TYPES OF BUSINESS:

Insurance-Direct Property & Casualty
Automobile Insurance
Homeowners' Insurance

BRANDS/DIVISIONS/AFFILIATES:

GEICO Casualty
GEICO Direct
GEICO General Insurance
GEICO Indemnity

CONTACTS: *Note: Officers with more than one job title may be intentionally listed here more than once.*

Tony Nicely, CEO
Tony Nicely, Pres.
Mike Campbell, CFO/Sr. VP
Jess Reid, CIO
William C. E. Robinson, Corp. Sec.
Nancy Pierce, VP-Claims Home Office Oper.
Charles G. Schara, Treas.
Lou Simpson, Pres./CEO-Capital Oper.
John Izzo, Regional VP-Mid Atlantic Oper.
Shawn Burklin, Regional VP-Southeast Oper.
John Zinno, Pres., Geico Insurance Agency (GIA)
Tony Nicely, Chmn.

Phone: 301-986-3000	**Fax:** 301-718-5236
Toll-Free:	
Address: 5260 Western Ave., Chevy Chase, MD 20815 US	

GROWTH PLANS/SPECIAL FEATURES:

GEICO Corporation and its affiliates, GEICO General Insurance, GEICO Indemnity and GEICO Casualty, provide automobile, homeowner and other types of insurance under the GEICO and GEICO Direct brand names. The group insures more than 9 million automobile owners representing more than 16 million vehicles. GEICO offers emergency road service and motorcycle insurance. From its 12 regional offices throughout the nation, the company offers 24-hour-a-day service, seven-days-a-week. In addition to auto insurance, the company also provides insurance for boats, all terrain vehicles (ATVs), homes, apartments and mobile homes as well as identity theft protection. The firm utilizes direct marketing, as opposed to insurance agents. Its direct marketing channels include mail, TV, radio and the Internet. GEICO provides e-billing on its web site, offering customers e-mail notification of bills, as well as the ability to view, pay and maintain a billing history online. The company offers discount programs and service options to the U.S. military. GEICO's controlling company, Berkshire Hathaway, Inc., is a global investment and holding conglomerate. Berkshire owns additional insurance industry holdings, including the reinsurance firm General Re and the United States Liability Insurance Group.

The company offers its employees medical and dental coverage; life insurance; disability plans; scholarships programs for associates' children; and paid college tuition for associates.

FINANCIALS: **Sales and profits are in thousands of dollars—add 000 to get the full amount. 2009 Note: Financial information for 2009 was not available for all companies at press time.**

2009 Sales: $
2008 Sales: $12,479,000
2007 Sales: $11,806,000
2006 Sales: $11,055,000
2005 Sales: $10,101,000

2009 Profits: $
2008 Profits: $
2007 Profits: $
2006 Profits: $1,314,000
2005 Profits: $1,221,000

U.S. Stock Ticker: Subsidiary
Int'l Ticker: Int'l Exchange:
Employees:
Fiscal Year Ends: 12/31
Parent Company: BERKSHIRE HATHAWAY INC

SALARIES/BENEFITS:

Pension Plan:	ESOP Stock Plan:	Profit Sharing:	Top Exec. Salary: $	Bonus: $
Savings Plan: Y	Stock Purch. Plan:		Second Exec. Salary: $	Bonus: $

OTHER THOUGHTS:

Apparent Women Officers or Directors:
Hot Spot for Advancement for Women/Minorities:

LOCATIONS: ("Y" = Yes)

West:	Southwest:	Midwest:	Southeast:	Northeast:	International:
Y	Y	Y	Y	Y	

GENERAL MOTORS COMPANY (GM)

www.gm.com

Industry Group Code: 33611 **Ranks within this company's industry group:** Sales: 5 Profits: 1

Vehicle Manufacturing:		Dealers:		Parts:		Service:		Finance:		Specialty:	
Cars:	Y	Car Dealer New:		Manufacturers:	Y	General Service:		Leasing:	Y	Information Systems:	
Trucks:	Y	Car Dealer Used:		Retail:		Specialty Service:		Auto Loans:	Y	Online Marketing:	
Motorcycles:		Truck Dealer:		Distributors:		Oil Change:		Insurance:	Y	Other:	Y
Specialty:	Y	RV Dealer:		Tires:		Paint and Body:				Publishing:	
Buses:		Motorcycle Dealer:		Batteries:						Rental Cars/Trucks:	
RVs:		Specialty Dealer:									

TYPES OF BUSINESS:

Automobile, Truck & Engine Manufacturing
Security & Information Services
Automotive Electronics
Financing & Insurance
Parts & Service
Transmissions
Engines
Locomotives

BRANDS/DIVISIONS/AFFILIATES:

Chevrolet
Buick
Cadillac
GMC
Volt
AmeriCredit Corp.
Opel
Daewoo

CONTACTS:

Note: Officers with more than one job title may be intentionally listed here more than once.

Daniel F. Akerson, CEO
Christopher P. Liddell, CFO/Vice Chmn.
Joel Ewanick, VP-U.S. Mktg.
Mary T. Barra, VP-Global Human Resources
Terry Kline, CIO/VP-IT
Stephen K. Carlisle, VP-Global Prod. Planning
Karl-Friedrich Stracke, VP-Global Vehicle Eng.
John R. Buttermore, VP-Mfg. & Int'l Oper.
Michael P. Millikin, General Counsel/VP
Thomas G. Stephens, Vice Chmn.-Global. Prod. Oper
Stephen J. Girsky, Vice Chmn.-Bus. Dev. & Corp. Strategy
Selim Bingol, VP-Comm.
Daniel Ammann, VP-Finance/Treas.
Jaime Ardila, Pres., GM South America
Mark L. Reuss, Pres., North America
David N. Reilly, Pres., GM Europe
Nicholas S. Cyprus, VP/Controller/Chief Acct. Officer
Edward E. Whitacre, Jr., Chmn.
Timothy E. Lee, Pres., GM Int'l Oper.

Phone: 313- 556-5000	Fax:
Toll-Free:	
Address: 300 Renaissance Ctr., Detroit, MI 48265-3000 US	

GROWTH PLANS/SPECIAL FEATURES:

General Motors Company (GM), formerly General Motors Corp., is engaged in the worldwide development, production and marketing of cars, trucks, automotive systems and locomotives. The firm's major U.S. brands include Chevrolet, Buick, Cadillac and GMC trucks. International brands include Opel, Vauxhall, Daewoo, Isuzu and Holden. GM is organized into three geographically-based segments: General Motors North America (GMNA), which generated 33.2% of 2009 sales; General Motors International Operations (GMIO), which generated 44.5% (more than half of which was sold in China); and General Motors Europe (GME), which generated 22.3%. In April 2009, GM announced plans to phase out the Pontiac brand and plans to launch an electric car concept named Volt. In May 2009, GM announced that it would close about 1,100 dealerships over the near term, and expects to eliminate about 470 further dealerships by selling or closing its Saab and Hummer brands. In June 2009, the firm filed for bankruptcy, and exited a month later under the new name, General Motors Company. GM shed $79 billion in existing debt, while receiving $30 billion in additional government funding. The U.S. government owns about 60% of the reorganized company, and the Canadian government owns about 12.5%, while former bondholders and the UAW union own the balance. In October 2009, GM announced that it would be shutting down its Saturn division, following a failed attempt to sell the company to Penske Automotive Group. In February 2010, the company sold its Saab division to Spyker Cars NV, a Dutch sports car producer. In July 2010, in an effort to return to the auto lending business, the firm agreed to acquire loan provider, AmeriCredit Corp. for $3.5 billion. GM planned an IPO for late 2010 in order to raise as much as $16 billion towards ending government ownership.

FINANCIALS:

Sales and profits are in thousands of dollars—add 000 to get the full amount. 2009 Note: Financial information for 2009 was not available for all companies at press time.

2009 Sales: $104,589,000	2009 Profits: $104,690,000	**U.S. Stock Ticker: Private**
2008 Sales: $148,979,000	2008 Profits: $-30,860,000	**Int'l Ticker:** Int'l Exchange:
2007 Sales: $179,984,000	2007 Profits: $-38,732,000	Employees: 217,000
2006 Sales: $204,467,000	2006 Profits: $-1,978,000	Fiscal Year Ends: 12/31
2005 Sales: $193,050,000	2005 Profits: $-10,417,000	Parent Company:

SALARIES/BENEFITS:

Pension Plan: Y	ESOP Stock Plan:	Profit Sharing:	Top Exec. Salary: $1,379,167	Bonus: $
Savings Plan: Y	Stock Purch. Plan: Y		Second Exec. Salary: $1,208,333	Bonus: $

OTHER THOUGHTS:

Apparent Women Officers or Directors: 9
Hot Spot for Advancement for Women/Minorities: Y

LOCATIONS: ("Y" = Yes)

West:	Southwest:	Midwest:	Southeast:	Northeast:	International:
Y	Y	Y	Y	Y	Y

GENERAL MOTORS OF CANADA LTD

www.gm.ca

Industry Group Code: 33611 **Ranks within this company's industry group:** Sales: Profits:

Vehicle Manufacturing:		Dealers:		Parts:		Service:		Finance:		Specialty:	
Cars:	Y	Car Dealer New:		Manufacturers:	Y	General Service:		Leasing:		Information Systems:	
Trucks:	Y	Car Dealer Used:		Retail:	Y	Specialty Service:		Auto Loans:		Online Marketing:	
Motorcycles:		Truck Dealer:		Distributors:	Y	Oil Change:		Insurance:		Other:	Y
Specialty:	Y	RV Dealer:		Tires:		Paint and Body:				Publishing:	
Buses:		Motorcycle Dealer:		Batteries:						Rental Cars/Trucks:	
RVs:		Specialty Dealer:									

TYPES OF BUSINESS:

Automobiles, Manufacturing
Car & Truck Assembly
Parts Manufacturing & Assembly

BRANDS/DIVISIONS/AFFILIATES:

General Motors Corp (GM)
CAMI Automotive, Inc.
Oshawa Service Parts Operations
Chevrolet Impala
Buick Regal
Chevy Equinox
Cold Weather Development Center
AmeriCredit Corp

CONTACTS: *Note: Officers with more than one job title may be intentionally listed here more than once.*

Kevin W. Williams, Managing Dir.
Kevin W. Williams, Pres.
Shawn Severs, CFO
Marc Comeau, VP-Vehicle Sales, Service & Mktg.
Neil J. Macdonald, General Counsel
Neil J. Macdonald, VP-Corp. Affairs
Shawn Severs, VP-Finance

Phone: **Fax:**
Toll-Free: 800-463-7483
Address: 1908 Colonel Sam Dr., Main Mailing Dept., Oshawa, ON L1H 8P7 Canada

GROWTH PLANS/SPECIAL FEATURES:

General Motors of Canada, Ltd. (GM Canada), a subsidiary of General Motors, is one of Canada's largest assemblers and manufacturers of cars, trucks, engines and components. It operates five factories throughout the country. The firm's car and truck assembly plant, the Oshawa Plant, produces the Chevrolet Impala, the Chevrolet Camaro and Buick Regal cars. The Oshawa metal center produces over 80,000 parts a day for the Oshawa car and truck assembly centers and other GM plants. The St. Catherine's engine plant machines parts and assembles GM's brand of Vortec engines, including the 4.0L, 5.3L and 5.7L V8 GEN III engines and the 3.6L and 2.8L HFV6 engines. This plant also produces specific engine components such as aluminum blocks, cast-iron blocks, cranks, heads, rods and cams. CAMI Automotive, Inc., a joint venture between GM Canada and Suzuki Motor Corp. of Japan, currently produces the Chevy Equinox and GMC Terrain. In addition, the company operates parts distribution centers throughout Canada, as well as Oshawa Service Parts Operations, which provides support for the Canadian parts distribution centers and delivers GM parts and products to dealers and AC Delco distributors. The firm's Canadian Regional Engineering Center uses state-of-the-art technology to design GM's vehicles. Oshawa Service Parts Operations delivers parts to nearly 850 Dealers and AC Delco distributors across Canada. In addition, GM of Canada has a Cold Weather Development Center in Kapuskasing, Ontario, where it tests products for severe weather conditions. Brands of GM include Buick, Cadillac, Chevrolet, GMC, Hummer and Pontiac. In May 2009, GM Canada announced plans to close approximately 42% of its dealerships. In June 2009, GM filed for bankruptcy. In July 2009, GM emerged from bankruptcy. In July 2010, the firm closed its Windsor plant. Also, in July 2010, GM entered into a definitive agreement to acquire AmeriCredit Corp., for approximately $3.5 billion.

FINANCIALS: **Sales and profits are in thousands of dollars—add 000 to get the full amount. 2009 Note: Financial information for 2009 was not available for all companies at press time.**

2009 Sales: $ | 2009 Profits: $
2008 Sales: $ | 2008 Profits: $
2007 Sales: $ | 2007 Profits: $
2006 Sales: $ | 2006 Profits: $
2005 Sales: $ | 2005 Profits: $

U.S. Stock Ticker: Subsidiary
Int'l Ticker: Int'l Exchange:
Employees:
Fiscal Year Ends:
Parent Company: GENERAL MOTORS CORP (GM)

SALARIES/BENEFITS:

Pension Plan: ESOP Stock Plan: Profit Sharing: Top Exec. Salary: $ Bonus: $
Savings Plan: Stock Purch. Plan: Second Exec. Salary: $ Bonus: $

OTHER THOUGHTS:

Apparent Women Officers or Directors:
Hot Spot for Advancement for Women/Minorities:

LOCATIONS: ("Y" = Yes)

West:	Southwest:	Midwest:	Southeast:	Northeast:	International:
					Y

GENTEX CORPORATION

www.gentex.com

Industry Group Code: 3363 **Ranks within this company's industry group:** Sales: 47 Profits: 11

Vehicle Manufacturing:		Dealers:		Parts:		Service:		Finance:		Specialty:	
Cars:		Car Dealer New:		Manufacturers:	Y	General Service:		Leasing:		Information Systems:	
Trucks:		Car Dealer Used:		Retail:		Specialty Service:		Auto Loans:		Online Marketing:	
Motorcycles:		Truck Dealer:		Distributors:		Oil Change:		Insurance:		Other:	Y
Specialty:		RV Dealer:		Tires:		Paint and Body:				Publishing:	
Buses:		Motorcycle Dealer:		Batteries:						Rental Cars/Trucks:	
RVs:		Specialty Dealer:									

TYPES OF BUSINESS:

Specialty Automobile Parts Manufacturer
Electro-Optic Technology
Rearview Mirrors & Mirror Sub-Assemblies
Headlight Systems
Smoke Alarms & Smoke Detectors

BRANDS/DIVISIONS/AFFILIATES:

SmartBeam

CONTACTS: *Note: Officers with more than one job title may be intentionally listed here more than once.*

Fred Bauer, CEO
Steve Dykman, CFO
Mark Newton, VP-North American Sales
Bruce Los, VP-Human Resources
Tom Guarr, VP-Chemical Research
Jeremy Fogg, VP-Mechanical Eng. & Program Mgmt.
Connie Hamblin, Corp. Sec.
John Arnold, VP-Oper.
Robert Vance, VP-Bus. Dev., Japan Automakers
Connie Hamblin, VP-Corp. Comm.
Connie Hamblin, VP-Investor Rel.
Steve Dykman, VP-Finance
Enoch Jen, Sr. VP
Bill Tonar, VP-Advanced Materials & Process Dev.
Scott Edwards, VP-Fire Protection Prod.
John Carter, VP-Quality
Fred Bauer, Chmn.
Jim Hollars, Sr. VP-Int'l
Mark Newton, VP-Purchasing & Electronics

Phone: 616-772-1800	**Fax:** 616-772-7348
Toll-Free:	
Address: 600 N. Centennial St., Zeeland, MI 49464 US	

GROWTH PLANS/SPECIAL FEATURES:

Gentex Corporation designs, develops, manufactures and markets proprietary products. The firm employs electro-optic technology including automatic-dimming rearview mirrors for the automotive industry and fire protection products primarily for the commercial building industry. Its interior auto-dimming mirror uses electrochromic technology and continually varies and automatically darkens to eliminate rearview headlight glare. The company has also introduced an exterior auto-dimming mirror sub-assembly, which works as a complete glare-control system with the interior mirror. Gentex supplies automatic-dimming rearview mirrors for Cadillac, Buick, Chevrolet, Saturn, Ford, Kia, Hummer, BMW, Fiat and other manufacturers. The mirrors are standard or option equipment in over 150 vehicles, including the Ford Expedition, Ford F150, Lincoln Navigator, Lincoln Mark LT, Mazda CX-9 and Toyota Camry. SmartBeam, the company's headlamp control system, automatically turns vehicle high beams on and off according to surrounding traffic conditions. Customers for this product include Opel/Vauxhall, BMW, Toyota, Rolls Royce, Tata/Land Rover and Audi. Gentex is currently making three exterior mirror sub-assembly products: thin glass flat, convex and aspheric. The company also manufactures LED turn signals for side-view mirrors, as well as roughly 60 different models of smoke alarms and smoke detectors, combined with more than 150 different models of signaling appliances. All of its smoke detectors and alarms rely on a photoelectric principle to detect smoke. Gentex also develops dimmable aircraft windows for the passenger compartment of the new Boeing 787 Dreamliner. In May 2009, the company introduced a line of carbon monoxide detectors for its fire safety product catalog.

Gentex offers its employees health, dental, life and disability insurance; a 401(k) plan; tuition reimbursement; quarterly profit sharing; stock options; access to a wellness center; an employee stock purchase plan; and free coffee, tea and soft drinks.

FINANCIALS: **Sales and profits are in thousands of dollars—add 000 to get the full amount. 2009 Note: Financial information for 2009 was not available for all companies at press time.**

2009 Sales: $544,523	2009 Profits: $64,637	**U.S. Stock Ticker: GNTX**
2008 Sales: $623,800	2008 Profits: $62,088	**Int'l Ticker:** Int'l Exchange:
2007 Sales: $653,933	2007 Profits: $122,130	Employees: 2,371
2006 Sales: $572,267	2006 Profits: $108,761	Fiscal Year Ends: 12/31
2005 Sales: $536,483	2005 Profits: $109,527	Parent Company:

SALARIES/BENEFITS:

Pension Plan:	ESOP Stock Plan:	Profit Sharing: Y	Top Exec. Salary: $428,979	Bonus: $39,727
Savings Plan: Y	Stock Purch. Plan: Y		Second Exec. Salary: $242,896	Bonus: $57,389

OTHER THOUGHTS:

Apparent Women Officers or Directors: 1
Hot Spot for Advancement for Women/Minorities:

LOCATIONS: ("Y" = Yes)

West:	Southwest:	Midwest:	Southeast:	Northeast:	International:
		Y			Y

GENUINE PARTS COMPANY

www.genpt.com

Industry Group Code: 441310 **Ranks within this company's industry group:** Sales: 1 Profits: 2

Vehicle Manufacturing:		Dealers:		Parts:		Service:		Finance:		Specialty:	
Cars:		Car Dealer New:		Manufacturers:		General Service:		Leasing:		Information Systems:	
Trucks:		Car Dealer Used:		Retail:	Y	Specialty Service:		Auto Loans:		Online Marketing:	Y
Motorcycles:		Truck Dealer:		Distributors:	Y	Oil Change:		Insurance:		Other:	Y
Specialty:		RV Dealer:		Tires:		Paint and Body:				Publishing:	
Buses:		Motorcycle Dealer:		Batteries:						Rental Cars/Trucks:	
RVs:		Specialty Dealer:									

TYPES OF BUSINESS:

Auto Parts, Retail
Industrial Replacement Parts
Office Products Distribution
Electrical & Electronic Materials

BRANDS/DIVISIONS/AFFILIATES:

NAPA (National Automotive Parts Association)
UAP, Inc.
Motion Industries, Inc.
EIS, Inc.
S.P. Richards Company

CONTACTS: *Note: Officers with more than one job title may be intentionally listed here more than once.*

Thomas C. Gallagher, CEO
Thomas C. Gallagher, Pres.
Jerry W. Nix, CFO
R. Bruce Clayton, Sr. VP-Human Resources
Eric Sundby, VP-IT
Carol B. Yancey, Corp. Sec.
David Haskett, Corp. Controller/Assistant VP
Paul Donahue, Exec. VP/Pres., Automotive Parts Group
Robert J. Susor, Exec. VP
Jerry W. Nix, Vice Chmn.
Carol B. Yancey, Sr. VP-Finance
Thomas C. Gallagher, Chmn.

Phone: 770-953-1700 **Fax:** 770-956-2211
Toll-Free:
Address: 2999 Circle 75 Pkwy., Atlanta, GA 30339 US

GROWTH PLANS/SPECIAL FEATURES:

Genuine Parts Company (GPC) distributes automotive replacement parts, industrial replacement parts, office products and electrical/electronic materials. The Automotive Parts Group distributes automotive replacement parts and accessory items through the National Automotive Parts Association (NAPA), a voluntary trade association for the distribution of automotive parts, of which GPC holds 95% ownership. The Automotive Parts Group includes NAPA stores owned in the U.S. by GPC and stores in Canada operated by UAP, a wholly-owned subsidiary, as well as stores and distribution centers in the U.S., Mexico and Canada owned by majority- and wholly-owned subsidiaries. It provides over 400,000 different parts and operates 58 NAPA automotive parts distribution centers located in 39 states and approximately 1,000 NAPA Auto Parts stores in 43 states. GPC's Industrial Parts Group distributes industrial bearings and power transmission equipment replacement parts, including industrial automation, hydraulic and pneumatic components, industrial supplies and material handling products. Distribution in this sector is done through its wholly-owned subsidiary Motion Industries, Inc. It operates 458 branches, seven distribution centers and 36 service centers in North America, with over 80,000 different items. The Office Products Group, operated through the wholly-owned subsidiary S. P. Richards Company, is engaged in the wholesale distribution of office and other business-related products for the daily operation of businesses, schools, offices and institutions. It distributes more than 50,000 items to nearly 6,000 business product resellers throughout the U.S. and Canada from a network of 43 distribution centers. Lastly, the Electrical/Electronic Materials Group, through EIS, Inc., distributes more than 100,000 items, from insulating and conducive materials to assembly tools and test equipment, to more than 20,000 electrical and electronic manufacturers in North America. EIS also has three manufacturing facilities that provide custom fabricated parts. In March 2010, the company, through Motion Industries, acquired the North American assets of BC Bearing.

FINANCIALS: **Sales and profits are in thousands of dollars—add 000 to get the full amount. 2009 Note: Financial information for 2009 was not available for all companies at press time.**

2009 Sales: $10,057,512	2009 Profits: $399,575	**U.S. Stock Ticker: GPC**
2008 Sales: $11,015,263	2008 Profits: $475,417	**Int'l Ticker:** Int'l Exchange:
2007 Sales: $10,843,195	2007 Profits: $506,339	Employees: 30,300
2006 Sales: $10,457,942	2006 Profits: $475,405	Fiscal Year Ends: 12/31
2005 Sales: $9,783,050	2005 Profits: $437,434	Parent Company:

SALARIES/BENEFITS:

Pension Plan:	ESOP Stock Plan:	Profit Sharing:	Top Exec. Salary: $875,000	Bonus: $812,597
Savings Plan:	Stock Purch. Plan:		Second Exec. Salary: $505,000	Bonus: $330,191

OTHER THOUGHTS:

Apparent Women Officers or Directors: 4
Hot Spot for Advancement for Women/Minorities: Y

LOCATIONS: ("Y" = Yes)

West:	Southwest:	Midwest:	Southeast:	Northeast:	International:
Y	Y	Y	Y	Y	Y

GEORG FISCHER LTD

www.georgfischer.com

Industry Group Code: 3363 **Ranks within this company's industry group:** Sales: 28 Profits: 50

Vehicle Manufacturing:		Dealers:		Parts:		Service:		Finance:		Specialty:	
Cars:		Car Dealer New:		Manufacturers:	Y	General Service:		Leasing:		Information Systems:	
Trucks:		Car Dealer Used:		Retail:		Specialty Service:		Auto Loans:		Online Marketing:	
Motorcycles:		Truck Dealer:		Distributors:		Oil Change:		Insurance:		Other:	
Specialty:		RV Dealer:		Tires:		Paint and Body:				Publishing:	
Buses:		Motorcycle Dealer:		Batteries:						Rental Cars/Trucks:	
RVs:		Specialty Dealer:									

TYPES OF BUSINESS:

Automotive Components
Iron Casting
Manufacturing Technology
Machine Tools
Piping Systems
Design
Control systems

BRANDS/DIVISIONS/AFFILIATES:

Agie Charmilles Group
Actspark
Engemaq
Mikron
Step-Tec
Central Plastics
JRG Gunzenhauser AG

CONTACTS:

Note: Officers with more than one job title may be intentionally listed here more than once.

Yves Serra, CEO
Yves Serra, Pres.
Stephan Wittmann, Dir.-Human Resources
Roland Groebil, Sec.
Yves Serra, Corp. Dev.
Bettina Schmidt, Head-Comm.
Daniel Boesiger, Head-Investor Rel.
Roland Abt, Dir.-Finance & Controlling
Josef Edbauer, Dir.-GF Automotive
Pietro Lori, Dir.-GF Piping Systems
Michael Hauser, Dir.-GF AgieCharmilles
Barbara Senn, Head-Corp. Compliance
Martin Huber, Chmn.

Phone: 41-52-631-1111 **Fax:** 41-52-631-2837
Toll-Free:
Address: Amsler-Laffon-Strasse 9, Schaffhausen, CH-8201 Switzerland

GROWTH PLANS/SPECIAL FEATURES:

Georg Fischer Ltd. is a design and manufacturing firm with 150 subsidiaries operating through three divisions: automotive, piping systems and machine tools. The automotive division designs and manufactures cast components and systems for auto chassis, powertrains and bodies. The firm performs large-scale iron casting, sand and die-casting and pressure die casting of iron and light metals. In addition, the firm sells automotive products such as mounting plates, mounting kits and the TRILEX Wheel System. The piping systems division supplies plastic and metal piping systems for industrial applications, gas and water utilities and construction projects. Products include industrial piping systems; piping system control and regulation products; distribution systems for gas and water; drinking water installation systems; and machines and tools for jointing plastic and metal piping systems. The division has a sales presence in over 100 countries to ensure round-the-clock customer support. The machine tools segment, also known as AgieCharmilles Group, designs and manufactures precision machinery for tool and mold making. The firm's wire-cut and die sinking electric discharge machines (EDM) and high-speed milling (HSM) technologies create forms down to the micro and nano ranges. Molds are produced for the mass production of consumer goods such as phone handsets, as well as for complex, customized precision components. The segment produces products under a number of brand names, including Agie, Charmilles, Actspark, Engemaq, Mikron, Step-Tec, System 3R and Intech EDM. The firm's subsidiaries Central Plastics and JRG Gunzenhauser AG, is a supplier of piping systems to gas and water utilities. In November 2009, Georg Fischer opens a new pipe-manufacturing factory in Ratnagiri, India.

FINANCIALS:

Sales and profits are in thousands of dollars—add 000 to get the full amount. 2009 Note: Financial information for 2009 was not available for all companies at press time.

2009 Sales: $2,735,600	2009 Profits: $-230,860	**U.S. Stock Ticker:**
2008 Sales: $3,949,130	2008 Profits: $61,030	**Int'l Ticker: FI-N** Int'l Exchange: Zurich-SWX
2007 Sales: $3,977,430	2007 Profits: $216,690	Employees: 12,481
2006 Sales: $4,007,500	2006 Profits: $226,700	Fiscal Year Ends: 12/31
2005 Sales: $3,655,100	2005 Profits: $153,500	Parent Company:

SALARIES/BENEFITS:

Pension Plan:	ESOP Stock Plan:	Profit Sharing:	Top Exec. Salary: $	Bonus: $
Savings Plan:	Stock Purch. Plan:		Second Exec. Salary: $	Bonus: $

OTHER THOUGHTS:

Apparent Women Officers or Directors: 3
Hot Spot for Advancement for Women/Minorities: Y

LOCATIONS: ("Y" = Yes)

West:	Southwest:	Midwest:	Southeast:	Northeast:	International:
Y			Y		Y

GKN PLC

www.gknplc.com

Industry Group Code: 3363 **Ranks within this company's industry group:** Sales: 15 Profits: 40

Vehicle Manufacturing:		Dealers:		Parts:		Service:		Finance:		Specialty:	
Cars:		Car Dealer New:		Manufacturers:	Y	General Service:		Leasing:		Information Systems:	
Trucks:		Car Dealer Used:		Retail:		Specialty Service:		Auto Loans:		Online Marketing:	
Motorcycles:		Truck Dealer:		Distributors:		Oil Change:		Insurance:		Other:	Y
Specialty:		RV Dealer:		Tires:		Paint and Body:				Publishing:	
Buses:		Motorcycle Dealer:		Batteries:						Rental Cars/Trucks:	
RVs:		Specialty Dealer:									

TYPES OF BUSINESS:

Automobile Parts-Manufacturing & Engineering
Aerospace Engineering
Driveshaft System Products
Powder Metallurgy
Off Highway Components
Engineering Support Services
Helicopters & Military Vehicles
Propulsion System Components

BRANDS/DIVISIONS/AFFILIATES:

GKN Driveline
GKN Sinter Metals
Hoeganaes
GKN Land Systems
GKN Aerospace

CONTACTS: *Note: Officers with more than one job title may be intentionally listed here more than once.*

Kevin Smith, CEO
Judith Felton, Corp. Sec.
William Seeger, Jr., Dir.-Finance
Nigel Stein, CEO-Automotive
Marcus Bryson, CEO-Aerospace
Andrew Reynolds Smith, CEO-Powder Metallurgy & Industrial Svcs.
Andrew Reynolds Smith, CEO-Land Systems
Roy Brown, Chmn.

Phone: 44-1527-517-715 **Fax:** 44-1527-517-700
Toll-Free:
Address: Ipsley House, Ipsley Church Ln., P.O. Box 55, Redditch, Worcestershire B98 OTL UK

GROWTH PLANS/SPECIAL FEATURES:

GKN PLC is a leading global automotive and aerospace engineering company with operations in over 30 countries. The firm operates in four segments: Automotive, powder metallurgy, land systems and aerospace. In its automotive segment, subsidiary GKN Driveline develops, manufactures and supplies automotive driveline components for light vehicles, including driveshafts, geared components and torque management devices. Additional subsidiaries in the segment are engaged in the manufacture of structural components, engine cylinder liners and substrates for catalytic converters. In the powder metallurgy segment, subsidiary GKN Sinter Metals manufactures precision automotive components for engines, transmissions and steering mechanisms, as well as components for industrial and consumer applications. GKN Sinter Metals operates from 30 global locations, with a majority of its sales generated by automotive customers. Another powder metallurgy subsidiary, Hoeganaes is a leading producer of ferrous metal powder in Europe and North America. GKN Land Systems, formerly the OffHighway division, designs, manufactures and distributes agricultural, construction, mining and industrial machinery components, including torsion axles, wheels, power take-off shafts, gearboxes and tractor attachment systems. The division is currently expanding its reach into the areas of defense, high speed rails and wind power. GKN Aerospace supplies airframe and engine structures, components, assemblies, transparencies and engineering services to aircraft and engine prime contractors. In February 2010, the firm opened a new pre-production facility for the research and development of Environmental Lightweight Fan technology in partnership with Rolls Royce and all-composite fan blades for aircraft engines. In March 2010, GKN Aerospace was selected to assist with composite and metallic work packages for use on F-35 Joint Strike Fighter planes.

FINANCIALS: **Sales and profits are in thousands of dollars—add 000 to get the full amount. 2009 Note: Financial information for 2009 was not available for all companies at press time.**

2009 Sales: $6,491,720	2009 Profits: $-55,340	**U.S. Stock Ticker: GKNLY**
2008 Sales: $6,491,970	2008 Profits: $-158,740	**Int'l Ticker: GKN** Int'l Exchange: London-LSE
2007 Sales: $5,739,820	2007 Profits: $293,740	Employees: 38,147
2006 Sales: $7,147,710	2006 Profits: $357,980	Fiscal Year Ends: 12/31
2005 Sales: $6,366,780	2005 Profits: $102,970	Parent Company:

SALARIES/BENEFITS:

Pension Plan:	ESOP Stock Plan:	Profit Sharing:	Top Exec. Salary: $1,011,199	Bonus: $466,577
Savings Plan:	Stock Purch. Plan:		Second Exec. Salary: $550,841	Bonus: $429,126

OTHER THOUGHTS:

Apparent Women Officers or Directors: 1
Hot Spot for Advancement for Women/Minorities:

LOCATIONS: ("Y" = Yes)

West:	Southwest:	Midwest:	Southeast:	Northeast:	International:
Y	Y	Y	Y	Y	Y

GM DAEWOO AUTO AND TECHNOLOGY CO

www.gmdaewoo.co.kr

Industry Group Code: 33611 **Ranks within this company's industry group:** Sales: Profits:

Vehicle Manufacturing:		Dealers:		Parts:		Service:		Finance:		Specialty:	
Cars:	Y	Car Dealer New:		Manufacturers:	Y	General Service:		Leasing:		Information Systems:	
Trucks:	Y	Car Dealer Used:		Retail:		Specialty Service:		Auto Loans:		Online Marketing:	
Motorcycles:		Truck Dealer:		Distributors:		Oil Change:		Insurance:		Other:	
Specialty:		RV Dealer:		Tires:		Paint and Body:				Publishing:	
Buses:		Motorcycle Dealer:		Batteries:						Rental Cars/Trucks:	
RVs:		Specialty Dealer:									

TYPES OF BUSINESS:

Automobiles, Manufacturing

BRANDS/DIVISIONS/AFFILIATES:

Daewoo Group
Daewoo Motor Co.
General Motors Corp (GM)
Veritas
Lacetti
Winstorm
GM Daewoo Vietnam Auto and Technology

CONTACTS:

Note: Officers with more than one job title may be intentionally listed here more than once.

Mike Arcamone, CEO
Mike Arcamone, Pres.
Mark James, CFO
Rick LaBelle, VP-Mktg. & Sales
Dong-Woo Jang, VP-Personnel Dept.
Steve Clarke, VP-Tech. Center
Tae-Wan Kim, VP-Design Center
Young-Kuk Lee, VP-Mfg. Oper.
Mark James, VP-Admin.
Dwenell Mills, VP-Planning
Jay Cooney, VP-Comm. & Public Policy
Mark James, VP-Finance
James Deluca, VP-Quality
Ronald D. Yuille, VP-Powertrain
Josef Edlinger, VP-Global Purchasing & Supply Chain

Phone: 82-32-520-2114	**Fax:** 82-32-520-4610
Toll-Free:	
Address: 199 Chongchon-dong, Pupyong-ku, Incheon, Korea	

GROWTH PLANS/SPECIAL FEATURES:

GM Daewoo Auto and Technology Company is primarily a manufacturer of vehicles in the Asia-Pacific region. Formerly Daewoo Motor Company and a member of South Korean industrial conglomerate, the Daewoo Group, the firm has been controlled by General Motors since 2002. Currently, GM owns a 70% share of the company. GM Daewoo manufactures 1.5 million vehicles annually through its Bupyung, Gunsan and Changwon manufacturing facilities in Korea; a power train plant for transmission, aluminum head and block production in Boryeong, Korea; and the VIDAMCO assembly plant in Vietnam, operated through subsidiary GM Daewoo Vietnam Auto and Technology. The company also provides brand-specific vehicle kits for assembly at GM facilities in China, Thailand, India, Colombia and Venezuela. Among GM Daewoo's models are the Matiz, Gentra, Lacetti, Tosca and Veritas sedans, as well as the Damas van, Winstorm SUV and Labo medium truck. Approximately 90% of the company's vehicles are exported to over 150 countries under the Chevrolet, Buick and Pontiac names. Aside from manufacturing vehicles, the firm does marketing work to advance GM products in Korea, and is developing hybrid vehicles and hydrogen fuel cells.

FINANCIALS:

Sales and profits are in thousands of dollars—add 000 to get the full amount. 2009 Note: Financial information for 2009 was not available for all companies at press time.

2009 Sales: $	2009 Profits: $	**U.S. Stock Ticker: Subsidiary**
2008 Sales: $	2008 Profits: $	**Int'l Ticker:** Int'l Exchange:
2007 Sales: $	2007 Profits: $	Employees:
2006 Sales: $	2006 Profits: $	Fiscal Year Ends: 12/31
2005 Sales: $	2005 Profits: $	Parent Company: GENERAL MOTORS CORP (GM)

SALARIES/BENEFITS:

Pension Plan:	ESOP Stock Plan:	Profit Sharing:	Top Exec. Salary: $	Bonus: $
Savings Plan:	Stock Purch. Plan:		Second Exec. Salary: $	Bonus: $

OTHER THOUGHTS:

Apparent Women Officers or Directors:
Hot Spot for Advancement for Women/Minorities:

LOCATIONS: ("Y" = Yes)

West:	Southwest:	Midwest:	Southeast:	Northeast:	International:
					Y

GM HOLDEN LTD

www.holden.com.au

Industry Group Code: 33611 **Ranks within this company's industry group:** Sales: Profits:

Vehicle Manufacturing:		Dealers:		Parts:		Service:		Finance:		Specialty:	
Cars:	Y	Car Dealer New:		Manufacturers:	Y	General Service:	Y	Leasing:	Y	Information Systems:	
Trucks:	Y	Car Dealer Used:		Retail:		Specialty Service:		Auto Loans:		Online Marketing:	
Motorcycles:		Truck Dealer:		Distributors:		Oil Change:		Insurance:		Other:	
Specialty:		RV Dealer:		Tires:		Paint and Body:				Publishing:	
Buses:		Motorcycle Dealer:		Batteries:						Rental Cars/Trucks:	
RVs:		Specialty Dealer:									

TYPES OF BUSINESS:

Automobile Manufacturing
Light Commercial Vehicle Manufacturing
Engine and Parts Manufacturing
Retail Dealerships
Fleet Leasing and Management

BRANDS/DIVISIONS/AFFILIATES:

General Motors Corp (GM)
Holden Leasing
Saab Australia
Holden Special Vehicles
Barina
Captiva
Commodore
Ute

CONTACTS: *Note: Officers with more than one job title may be intentionally listed here more than once.*

Mike Devereux, Managing Dir.
Mark Bernhard, CFO
John Elsworth, Exec. Dir.-Sales & Mktg.
Mark Polglaze, Exec. Dir.-Human Resources
Stephen Coletta, CIO
Greg Tyus, Exec. Dir.-Eng.
Martyn Cray, Exec. Dir.-Mfg.
Peter Keley, Exec. Dir.-Planning & Program Mgmt.
Samantha Read, Exec. Dir.-Corp. Affairs
Craig Porritt, Exec. Dir.-Customer Satisfaction & Quality
Mike Devereux, Chmn.
Sean Liang, Exec. Dir.-Global Purchasing & Supply Chain

Phone: 61-3-9647-1111 **Fax:** 61-3-9647-2550
Toll-Free:
Address: 191 Salmon St., Port Melbourne, VIC 3207 Australia

GROWTH PLANS/SPECIAL FEATURES:

GM Holden, Ltd., a subsidiary of General Motors Corp. (GM), is an Australian manufacturer and distributor of vehicles, engines, components and parts, which has produced more than 7 million vehicles since 1948. The company operates through a network of 12 authorized service centers and over 200 dealerships across Australia. The firm's products include a full line of passenger vehicles ranging from economy cars to luxury sedans, such as the Barina, Cruze, Epica, Commodore, Calais, Sportwagon, Statesman, Caprice, Captiva, Ute, Colorado, and the Combo . Sports utility vehicles and light commercial trucks include the Ute, Colorado and Combo models. The firm's largest vehicle export market is the U.S. The Commodore model is exported to markets in the U.S., Canada, Saudi Arabia, Lebanon, the United Arab Emirates, Qatar, Kuwait, Iraq, South Africa, New Zealand, the U.K., Thailand, Malaysia, Singapore, Fiji, Brunei and Brazil. The Statesman and Caprice models are exported to New Zealand, Korea and the Middle East. The Ute model is exported to South Africa and New Zealand. Engine export customers include GM Europe, GM Thailand, GM Daewoo, Shanghai GM and GM South Africa. Associated company Holden Special Vehicles also offers a niche line of premium performance luxury cars. Saab Australia, another associated company, distributes Saab vehicles throughout Australia. Holden Leasing, operated by General Motors Acceptance Corporation (GMAC), offers fleet leasing and management solutions for companies with primarily Holden fleets. In June 2010, figures released by an Australian business agency showed that the Commodore was the best-selling car in the country for 2010.

Holden's employee benefits include continuing education support, on-site medical centers, an employee assistance plan, vehicle purchase and lease plans, subsidized cafeterias and on-site banking.

FINANCIALS: **Sales and profits are in thousands of dollars—add 000 to get the full amount. 2009 Note: Financial information for 2009 was not available for all companies at press time.**

2009 Sales: $	2009 Profits: $	**U.S. Stock Ticker: Subsidiary**
2008 Sales: $	2008 Profits: $	**Int'l Ticker:** Int'l Exchange:
2007 Sales: $4,891,300	2007 Profits: $	Employees:
2006 Sales: $	2006 Profits: $	Fiscal Year Ends: 12/31
2005 Sales: $	2005 Profits: $	Parent Company: GENERAL MOTORS CORP (GM)

SALARIES/BENEFITS:

Pension Plan:	ESOP Stock Plan:	Profit Sharing:	Top Exec. Salary: $	Bonus: $
Savings Plan:	Stock Purch. Plan:		Second Exec. Salary: $	Bonus: $

OTHER THOUGHTS:

Apparent Women Officers or Directors:
Hot Spot for Advancement for Women/Minorities:

LOCATIONS: ("Y" = Yes)

West:	Southwest:	Midwest:	Southeast:	Northeast:	International:
					Y

GMAC INSURANCE HOLDINGS INC

www.gmacinsurance.com

Industry Group Code: 524126 **Ranks within this company's industry group:** Sales: Profits:

Vehicle Manufacturing:		Dealers:		Parts:		Service:		Finance:		Specialty:	
Cars:		Car Dealer New:		Manufacturers:		General Service:		Leasing:		Information Systems:	
Trucks:		Car Dealer Used:		Retail:		Specialty Service:	Y	Auto Loans:		Online Marketing:	
Motorcycles:		Truck Dealer:		Distributors:		Oil Change:		Insurance:	Y	Other:	
Specialty:		RV Dealer:		Tires:		Paint and Body:				Publishing:	
Buses:		Motorcycle Dealer:		Batteries:						Rental Cars/Trucks:	
RVs:		Specialty Dealer:									

TYPES OF BUSINESS:

Insurance, Direct Property & Casualty
Auto Dealership & Auto Insurance
Homeowners Insurance
Roadside Assistance Services
Online Services

BRANDS/DIVISIONS/AFFILIATES:

GM Motor Club
American Capital Acquisition Corporation
AmTrust Financial Services Inc
Maiden Holdings Ltd

CONTACTS: *Note: Officers with more than one job title may be intentionally listed here more than once.*

Larry Pentis, CEO
Wade Bontrager, Sr. VP-Mktg.
Tate Strickland, Contact-Media

Phone: 314-493-8000 **Fax:** 314-493-8114
Toll-Free: 800-325-1190
Address: 500 W. 5th St., Winston-Salem, MO 27152 US

GROWTH PLANS/SPECIAL FEATURES:

GMAC Insurance Holdings, Inc., provides property and casualty insurance and insurance-related products to individuals, automotive dealerships and other businesses. It is a subsidiary of American Capital Acquisition Corporation. The firm primarily provides auto, motorcycle, commercial vehicle and recreational vehicle insurance, but also offers homeowners' insurance, including renters' insurance and condo insurance; insurance for drivers traveling into Mexico; and roadside assistance benefits through the GM Motor Club. The firm divides its products into three segments: consumer products, including physical damage and liability insurance for vehicles and homeowners' insurance; other consumer products, including extended service contracts, mechanical breakdown coverage and maintenance and roadside coverage; and commercial products, including automotive dealer inventory insurance. GMAC Insurance offers inspection, collision repair guarantee, emergency expense allowance, damaged vehicle pick-up, rental car delivery, vehicle replacement, 24-hour claims reporting and additional equipment coverage services. The company offers vehicle and home insurance in the U.S. and internationally through independent agents, affinity groups and the Internet. GMAC Insurance maintains operations in North America, Europe, Latin America and Asia. In October 2009, the company entered into an agreement with American Capital Acquisition Corporation (ACAC). to divest its U.S. property and casualty consumer insurance business. The property and the casualty consumer insurance business include the automobile, commercial vehicle, motorcycle and RV insurance offerings. In March 2010, ACAC acquired the property and the casualty consumer insurance business. The ACAC is a newly formed corporation by the founder of AmTrust Financial Services, Inc. (AFSI) and Maiden Holdings, Ltd. (MHLD).

FINANCIALS: **Sales and profits are in thousands of dollars—add 000 to get the full amount. 2009 Note: Financial information for 2009 was not available for all companies at press time.**

2009 Sales: $ | 2009 Profits: $
2008 Sales: $ | 2008 Profits: $
2007 Sales: $ | 2007 Profits: $
2006 Sales: $5,616,000 | 2006 Profits: $1,127,000
2005 Sales: $4,259,000 | 2005 Profits: $417,000

U.S. Stock Ticker: Subsidiary
Int'l Ticker: Int'l Exchange:
Employees:
Fiscal Year Ends:
Parent Company: AMERICAN CAPITAL ACQUISTION CORPORATION

SALARIES/BENEFITS:

Pension Plan: | ESOP Stock Plan: | Profit Sharing: | Top Exec. Salary: $ | Bonus: $
Savings Plan: | Stock Purch. Plan: | Second Exec. Salary: $ | Bonus: $

OTHER THOUGHTS:

Apparent Women Officers or Directors:
Hot Spot for Advancement for Women/Minorities:

LOCATIONS: ("Y" = Yes)

West:	Southwest:	Midwest:	Southeast:	Northeast:	International:
Y	Y	Y	Y	Y	Y

GOODYEAR TIRE & RUBBER COMPANY (THE) www.goodyear.com

Industry Group Code: 3262 **Ranks within this company's industry group:** Sales: 4 Profits: 8

Vehicle Manufacturing:		Dealers:		Parts:		Service:		Finance:		Specialty:	
Cars:		Car Dealer New:		Manufacturers:	Y	General Service:	Y	Leasing:		Information Systems:	
Trucks:		Car Dealer Used:		Retail:		Specialty Service:		Auto Loans:		Online Marketing:	
Motorcycles:		Truck Dealer:		Distributors:		Oil Change:		Insurance:		Other:	
Specialty:		RV Dealer:		Tires:	Y	Paint and Body:				Publishing:	
Buses:		Motorcycle Dealer:		Batteries:						Rental Cars/Trucks:	
RVs:		Specialty Dealer:									

TYPES OF BUSINESS:

Tire Manufacturing
Automotive Service Shops
Resins & Latex
Synthetic Polymers
Industrial Chemicals
Belts & Hoses
Blimps
Retail Sales

BRANDS/DIVISIONS/AFFILIATES:

Goodyear
Kelly
Lee
Fulda
Sava
Dunlop

CONTACTS: *Note: Officers with more than one job title may be intentionally listed here more than once.*

Richard J. Kramer, CEO
Richard J. Kramer, Pres.
Darren Wells, CFO/Exec. VP
Joseph B. Ruocco, Sr. VP-Human Resources
Jean-Claude Kihn, CTO/Sr. VP
David L. Bialoski, General Counsel/Sr. VP/Sec.
John D. Fish, Sr. VP-Oper.
Laura Thompson, VP-Bus. Dev.
Charles L. Sinclair, Sr. VP-Global Comm.
Scott Honnold, Sr. VP-Finance/Treas.
Isabel H. Jasinowski, VP-Gov't Rel.
Pierre E. Cohade, Pres., Asia Pacific
Eduardo A. Fortunato, Pres., Latin America
Robert J. Keegan, Chmn.
Arthur de Bok, Pres., EMEA
Mark W. Purtilar, Chief Procurement Officer/VP

Phone: 330-796-2121 **Fax:** 330-796-2222
Toll-Free:
Address: 1144 E. Market St., Akron, OH 44316-0001 US

GROWTH PLANS/SPECIAL FEATURES:

The Goodyear Tire & Rubber Company is one of the world's leading manufacturers of tires and rubber-related chemicals for various applications. Goodyear is also one of the world's largest operators of commercial truck service and tire retreading centers. It operates approximately 1,500 tire and auto service center outlets, and manufactures products in 57 manufacturing facilities in 23 countries. Goodyear operates through four business segments: North American Tire, EMEA Tire, Latin American Tire and Asia Pacific Tire. Goodyear manufactures rubber tires for automobiles, trucks, buses, aviation, motorcycles, farm implements, earthmoving equipment, industrial equipment and other applications. The company sells tires under brands including Goodyear, Dunlop, Kelly, Fulda, Debica, Sava, various other Goodyear-owned brands and the private-label brands of certain customers. It also retreads truck, aviation and heavy equipment tires, manufactures and sells tread rubber and other tire retreading materials; provides automotive repair services; and manufactures and sells flaps for truck tires and other types of tires. The company also operates three blimps located in Ohio, California and Florida. Approximately 83% of net sales in 2009 were from the sale of new tires.

Employees are offered medical and welfare benefits, as well as a 401(k) and pension plan.

FINANCIALS: **Sales and profits are in thousands of dollars—add 000 to get the full amount. 2009 Note: Financial information for 2009 was not available for all companies at press time.**

2009 Sales: $16,301,000	2009 Profits: $-375,000	**U.S. Stock Ticker: GT**
2008 Sales: $19,488,000	2008 Profits: $-77,000	**Int'l Ticker:** Int'l Exchange:
2007 Sales: $19,644,000	2007 Profits: $602,000	Employees: 69,000
2006 Sales: $18,751,000	2006 Profits: $-330,000	Fiscal Year Ends: 12/31
2005 Sales: $19,723,000	2005 Profits: $228,000	Parent Company:

SALARIES/BENEFITS:

Pension Plan: Y	ESOP Stock Plan:	Profit Sharing:	Top Exec. Salary: $1,230,000	Bonus: $9,514,895
Savings Plan: Y	Stock Purch. Plan:		Second Exec. Salary: $678,523	Bonus: $3,287,129

OTHER THOUGHTS:

Apparent Women Officers or Directors: 5
Hot Spot for Advancement for Women/Minorities: Y

LOCATIONS: ("Y" = Yes)

West:	Southwest:	Midwest:	Southeast:	Northeast:	International:
Y	Y	Y	Y	Y	Y

GREAT DANE LIMITED PARTNERSHIP

www.greatdanetrailers.com

Industry Group Code: 336214 **Ranks within this company's industry group:** Sales: Profits:

Vehicle Manufacturing:		Dealers:		Parts:		Service:		Finance:		Specialty:	
Cars:		Car Dealer New:		Manufacturers:		General Service:		Leasing:		Information Systems:	
Trucks:	Y	Car Dealer Used:		Retail:		Specialty Service:		Auto Loans:		Online Marketing:	
Motorcycles:		Truck Dealer:	Y	Distributors:	Y	Oil Change:		Insurance:		Other:	
Specialty:		RV Dealer:		Tires:		Paint and Body:				Publishing:	
Buses:		Motorcycle Dealer:		Batteries:						Rental Cars/Trucks:	
RVs:		Specialty Dealer:									

TYPES OF BUSINESS:

Manufacturing-Truck Trailers
Used Trailer Sales
Accessories & Apparel
Replacement Parts

BRANDS/DIVISIONS/AFFILIATES:

CC Industries, Ltd.
Superseal
ThermoGuard
CorroGuard
Composite Van (The)
Freedom
P-Series
i-Van

CONTACTS:

Note: Officers with more than one job title may be intentionally listed here more than once.

William H. Crown, CEO
Phillip Pines, COO/Exec. VP
John J. Sobota, CFO
Brandie Fuller, VP-Mktg.
John J. Sobota, VP-Finance
Phillip Pines, Pres., Pines Trailers Div.
William H. Crown, Chmn.

Phone: 912-644-2100	**Fax:** 912-644-2171
Toll-Free:	
Address: 602 E. Lathrop Ave., Savannah, GA 31402 US	

GROWTH PLANS/SPECIAL FEATURES:

Great Dane Limited Partnership, a unit of the Chicago-based investment group CC Industries, is one of the largest truck trailer manufacturers in North America. The company manufactures refrigerated trailers (reefers); dry freight vans, including drop frame trailers for hauling furniture and electronic equipment; open top trailers for hauling produce; and flatbed or platform trailers for hauling machinery, steel and other oversized or heavy products. The firm's reefer products include the Classic Truckload; the Classic Multi-Temp, which can be divided into three temperature-controlled compartments; and the Super Seal Truckload. Dry freight trailers include the Classic I-Van, which is semi-insulated through the use of reefer press-panel technology; the P-Series; P-101; and SSL trailers. In addition, Great Dane manufactures The Composite Van, a dry freight van featuring a high-strength tubular steel rear frame and reinforced header-to-top-rail connection. The company's platform trailers include the GP and Sentry all-steel trailers and the GPL and Freedom aluminum/steel combination trailers. Great Dane also sells used trailers. The company's web site allows customers to search its used trailer inventory by type, year, length, width and company branch/location. The firm also sells after-market replacement parts through dealers in the U.S., Mexico, Canada and Colombia. The company offers several additional products for its vehicles, including CorroGuard, a spray-in-place thermoplastic coating for superior long-term protection from road abrasion and corrosion; and ThermoGuard, a glass-reinforced, thermoplastic liner for refrigerated trailers. Great Dane has seven manufacturing plants in the U.S., as well as division offices in Savannah, Georgia, and Chicago, Illinois. In February 2010, the firm acquired Johnson Refrigerated Truck Bodies, a manufacturer of refrigerated truck bodies and all-electric refrigeration solutions. In March 2010, the company launched a new, all aluminum platform trailer.

Great Dane offers its employees medical, dental and life insurance; a 401(k) plan; flexible spending accounts; and a profit-sharing plan.

FINANCIALS:

Sales and profits are in thousands of dollars—add 000 to get the full amount. 2009 Note: Financial information for 2009 was not available for all companies at press time.

2009 Sales: $	2009 Profits: $	**U.S. Stock Ticker: Subsidiary**
2008 Sales: $	2008 Profits: $	**Int'l Ticker:** Int'l Exchange:
2007 Sales: $	2007 Profits: $	Employees:
2006 Sales: $	2006 Profits: $	Fiscal Year Ends: 12/31
2005 Sales: $	2005 Profits: $	Parent Company: CC INDUSTRIES LTD

SALARIES/BENEFITS:

Pension Plan:	ESOP Stock Plan:	Profit Sharing: Y	Top Exec. Salary: $	Bonus: $
Savings Plan: Y	Stock Purch. Plan:		Second Exec. Salary: $	Bonus: $

OTHER THOUGHTS:

Apparent Women Officers or Directors: 1
Hot Spot for Advancement for Women/Minorities:

LOCATIONS: ("Y" = Yes)

West:	Southwest:	Midwest:	Southeast:	Northeast:	International:
Y	Y	Y	Y	Y	Y

GROUP 1 AUTOMOTIVE INC

www.group1auto.com

Industry Group Code: 441110 **Ranks within this company's industry group:** Sales: 6 Profits: 5

Vehicle Manufacturing:		Dealers:		Parts:		Service:		Finance:		Specialty:	
Cars:		Car Dealer New:	Y	Manufacturers:		General Service:	Y	Leasing:		Information Systems:	
Trucks:		Car Dealer Used:	Y	Retail:	Y	Specialty Service:		Auto Loans:	Y	Online Marketing:	
Motorcycles:		Truck Dealer:		Distributors:		Oil Change:		Insurance:	Y	Other:	
Specialty:		RV Dealer:		Tires:		Paint and Body:	Y			Publishing:	
Buses:		Motorcycle Dealer:		Batteries:						Rental Cars/Trucks:	
RVs:		Specialty Dealer:									

TYPES OF BUSINESS:

Auto Dealers
Auto Repair Services
Insurance Services
Automotive Replacement Parts
Financing Services
Collision Service Centers

BRANDS/DIVISIONS/AFFILIATES:

Toyota/Scion of Rock Hill

CONTACTS:

Note: Officers with more than one job title may be intentionally listed here more than once.

Earl J. Hesterberg, CEO
Earl J. Hesterberg, Pres.
John C. Rickel, CFO/Sr. VP
J. Brooks O'Hara, VP-Human Resources
James R. Druzbik, VP-Info. Systems
Darryl M. Burman, General Counsel/VP/Corp. Sec.
Wade D. Hubbard, VP-Fixed Oper.
Mark J. Iuppenlatz, VP-Corp. Dev.
Peter C. DeLongchamps, VP-Public Affairs & Manufacturer Rel.
Kim Paper Canning, Mgr.-Investor Rel.
Lance A. Parker, Corp. Controller/VP
Michael D. Welch, Treas.
M. Lee Mitchell, VP-Financial Svcs.
Frank Grese Jr., VP-Central Region
David W. Hult, VP-Eastern Region
John L. Adams, Chmn.
Gigi L. Myung, VP-Purchasing

Phone: 713-647-5700	**Fax:** 713-647-5858
Toll-Free:	
Address: 800 Gessner, Ste. 500, Houston, TX 77024 US	

GROWTH PLANS/SPECIAL FEATURES:

Group 1 Automotive, Inc. is a leading operator in the U.S. and U.K. automotive retailing industry. The company, through its subsidiaries, sells new and used cars and light trucks; provides maintenance and repair services; sells replacement parts; and arranges vehicle financing and insurance through its 101 dealership locations (totaling 136 franchises). The dealerships offer 32 different brands, including Toyota; Honda; Nissan; Ford; BMW; Chevrolet; Dodge; Jeep; and Mercedes-Benz. Import and luxury vehicles account for over 85% of the firm's car sales, while domestic vehicles account for less than15%. Group 1 Automotive dealerships have taken several steps toward building customer confidence in their used vehicle inventory, including participation in manufacturer certification processes. These processes make used vehicles eligible for new vehicle benefits such as new vehicle finance rates and extended manufacturer warranties. In addition to its dealerships, the company owns 25 collision service centers. Group 1 Automotive uses American Auto Exchange's vehicle management software to identify vehicle sales trends, conduct local market analyses and perform current market appraisals. In early 2009, the company sold its World Ford of Kendall dealership in Miami, Florida, and acquired a Hyundai franchise in Houston, Texas. In October 2009, the firm sold two Maxwell Chrysler-Jeep-Dodge dealerships located in Texas. In November 2009, Group 1 Automotive acquired a BMW franchise in Alabama. In March 2010, the company acquired two BMW/Mini dealerships located in the U.K. In April 2010, the firm acquired Harrelson Toyota/Scion (now known as Toyota/Scion of Rock Hill) in South Carolina. In June 2010, Group I Automotive acquired a new Mini franchise in Texas and sold its Pines Ford Lincoln Mercury dealership located in Florida.

FINANCIALS:

Sales and profits are in thousands of dollars—add 000 to get the full amount. 2009 Note: Financial information for 2009 was not available for all companies at press time.

2009 Sales: $4,525,707	2009 Profits: $34,845	**U.S. Stock Ticker: GPI**
2008 Sales: $5,654,087	2008 Profits: $-48,013	**Int'l Ticker:** Int'l Exchange:
2007 Sales: $6,392,997	2007 Profits: $63,415	Employees: 6,990
2006 Sales: $6,083,484	2006 Profits: $88,390	Fiscal Year Ends: 12/31
2005 Sales: $5,969,590	2005 Profits: $54,231	Parent Company:

SALARIES/BENEFITS:

Pension Plan:	ESOP Stock Plan:	Profit Sharing:	Top Exec. Salary: $908,333	Bonus: $1,000,000
Savings Plan:	Stock Purch. Plan: Y		Second Exec. Salary: $408,750	Bonus: $450,000

OTHER THOUGHTS:

Apparent Women Officers or Directors: 4
Hot Spot for Advancement for Women/Minorities: Y

LOCATIONS: ("Y" = Yes)

West:	Southwest:	Midwest:	Southeast:	Northeast:	International:
Y	Y	Y	Y	Y	Y

GROUP LOTUS PLC

www.grouplotus.com

Industry Group Code: 33611 **Ranks within this company's industry group:** Sales: Profits:

Vehicle Manufacturing:		**Dealers:**		**Parts:**		**Service:**		**Finance:**		**Specialty:**	
Cars:	Y	Car Dealer New:	Y	Manufacturers:	Y	General Service:	Y	Leasing:	Y	Information Systems:	
Trucks:		Car Dealer Used:	Y	Retail:	Y	Specialty Service:	Y	Auto Loans:		Online Marketing:	
Motorcycles:		Truck Dealer:		Distributors:		Oil Change:		Insurance:		Other:	Y
Specialty:		RV Dealer:		Tires:		Paint and Body:				Publishing:	
Buses:		Motorcycle Dealer:		Batteries:						Rental Cars/Trucks:	
RVs:		Specialty Dealer:									

TYPES OF BUSINESS:

Automobile Manufacturing
Sports Car Design & Manufacturing
Design & Engineering Services
Consulting Services
Driving Instruction Facilities
New & Pre-owned Sports Car Sales
Automotive Accessories
Lightweight Aluminum Manufacturing

BRANDS/DIVISIONS/AFFILIATES:

Proton Holdings Berhad
Lotus Cars Ltd.
Elise
Europa
Evora
Lotus Lightweight Structures
2-Eleven
Exige

CONTACTS:

Note: Officers with more than one job title may be intentionally listed here more than once.

Dany T. Bahar, CEO
Russell Carr, Head-Lotus Design
Trevor Houghton-Berry, Head-Commercial Oper.
James Stronach, Dir.-Finance
Geraint Castleton-White, Head-Powertrain, Lotus Engineering, Inc.
Paul Newsome, Managing Dir.-Lotus Engineering, Inc.

Phone: 44-1953-608-000 **Fax:** 44-1953-608-300
Toll-Free:
Address: Potash Ln., Norwich, Norfolk NR14 8EZ UK

GROWTH PLANS/SPECIAL FEATURES:

Group Lotus plc, majority owned by Malaysian automobile manufacturer Proton Holdings Berhad, operates a group of automotive divisions. The company's two main lines of business are sports car manufacturing, through Lotus Cars Ltd., and engineering consulting, through Lotus Engineering, Inc. Lotus offers a broad range of sports cars, including the Elise series; the Europa S; the 2-Eleven; the Exige, inspired by racecar design; and the new Evora 2+2 coupe. Lotus Engineering provides consulting services including design, development and testing, as well as manufacturing and sale of finished products, to other carmakers. Lotus Cars USA, Inc. is responsible for sales, distribution and servicing of Lotus cars in North America through its dealer network. In recent years, the company released the Lotus 2-Eleven, a light-weight track car; and the Lotus Exige GT3 concept vehicle, built up to Gran Turismo (GT) racing specs. Lotus Cars retail Lotus automobiles in South Korea through business partner LKO, Ltd. electric vehicles. Group Lotus also operates Lotus Lightweight Structures which manufactures light weight aluminum and composite structures. In April 2010, the firm introduced the 2011 Lotus Elise, available in Lotus Elise R with a 1.8 liter engine, and Lotus Elise SC with a 1.8 liter super charged engine.

FINANCIALS:

Sales and profits are in thousands of dollars—add 000 to get the full amount. 2009 Note: Financial information for 2009 was not available for all companies at press time.

2009 Sales: $	2009 Profits: $	**U.S. Stock Ticker: Subsidiary**
2008 Sales: $	2008 Profits: $	**Int'l Ticker:** Int'l Exchange:
2007 Sales: $	2007 Profits: $	Employees:
2006 Sales: $	2006 Profits: $	Fiscal Year Ends: 3/31
2005 Sales: $303,900	2005 Profits: $-14,000	Parent Company: PROTON HOLDINGS BERHAD

SALARIES/BENEFITS:

Pension Plan: Y	ESOP Stock Plan:	Profit Sharing:	Top Exec. Salary: $	Bonus: $
Savings Plan:	Stock Purch. Plan:		Second Exec. Salary: $	Bonus: $

OTHER THOUGHTS:

Apparent Women Officers or Directors:
Hot Spot for Advancement for Women/Minorities:

LOCATIONS: ("Y" = Yes)

West:	Southwest:	Midwest:	Southeast:	Northeast:	International:
Y	Y	Y	Y	Y	Y

GT TECHNOLOGIES INC

www.gttechnologies.com

Industry Group Code: 3363 **Ranks within this company's industry group:** Sales: Profits:

Vehicle Manufacturing:		Dealers:		Parts:		Service:		Finance:		Specialty:	
Cars:		Car Dealer New:		Manufacturers:	Y	General Service:		Leasing:		Information Systems:	
Trucks:		Car Dealer Used:		Retail:		Specialty Service:		Auto Loans:		Online Marketing:	
Motorcycles:		Truck Dealer:		Distributors:		Oil Change:		Insurance:		Other:	
Specialty:		RV Dealer:		Tires:		Paint and Body:				Publishing:	
Buses:		Motorcycle Dealer:		Batteries:						Rental Cars/Trucks:	
RVs:		Specialty Dealer:									

TYPES OF BUSINESS:

Automotive Systems & Components Manufacturing

BRANDS/DIVISIONS/AFFILIATES:

American Securities
Defiance Precision
Toledo Technologies

CONTACTS:

Note: Officers with more than one job title may be intentionally listed here more than once.

William E. Redmond, Jr., CEO
William E. Redmond, Jr., Pres.
Daniel Brinker, VP-Global Sales
Daniel Brinker, VP-Eng.

Phone: 734-467-8371	**Fax:**
Toll-Free:	
Address: 5859 Executive Dr., Westland, MI 48185-1932 US	

GROWTH PLANS/SPECIAL FEATURES:

GT Technologies, Inc. designs, develops and manufactures performance critical valve actuation components and systems for diesel, gasoline and flex fuel engines. The company, which is owned by private equity firm American Securities, was formed through the merger of Defiance Precision and Toledo Technologies. GT Technologies' primary markets include the power generation, transportation, motorsports and recreational vehicle industries. Its applications range from less than one liter to more than 14 liters in size. The company's products include hydraulic lash adjusting capsules; rocker shaft assemblies; stamped rocker arms and roller finger followers; roller bearings and axles; hydraulic and mechanical roller tappets; and valvetrain actuation assemblies with hydraulic lash compensation. The firm also offers its heavy duty diesel clients with mechanical roller tappets and roller bearings for high pressure fuel injector pumps. GT Technologies' products are all custom-designed to address the specific applications and functional requirements of each client. In addition to its U.S. operations, the company offers its products and services in Europe and Brazil.

FINANCIALS:

Sales and profits are in thousands of dollars—add 000 to get the full amount. 2009 Note: Financial information for 2009 was not available for all companies at press time.

2009 Sales: $	2009 Profits: $	**U.S. Stock Ticker: Private**
2008 Sales: $	2008 Profits: $	**Int'l Ticker:** Int'l Exchange:
2007 Sales: $	2007 Profits: $	Employees:
2006 Sales: $	2006 Profits: $	Fiscal Year Ends:
2005 Sales: $	2005 Profits: $	Parent Company: AMERICAN SECURITIES

SALARIES/BENEFITS:

Pension Plan:	ESOP Stock Plan:	Profit Sharing:	Top Exec. Salary: $	Bonus: $
Savings Plan:	Stock Purch. Plan:		Second Exec. Salary: $	Bonus: $

OTHER THOUGHTS:

Apparent Women Officers or Directors:
Hot Spot for Advancement for Women/Minorities:

LOCATIONS: ("Y" = Yes)

West:	Southwest:	Midwest:	Southeast:	Northeast:	International:
		Y	Y		Y

GUARDIAN INDUSTRIES CORP

www.guardian.com

Industry Group Code: 32712 **Ranks within this company's industry group:** Sales: Profits:

Vehicle Manufacturing:		Dealers:		Parts:		Service:		Finance:		Specialty:	
Cars:		Car Dealer New:		Manufacturers:	Y	General Service:		Leasing:		Information Systems:	
Trucks:		Car Dealer Used:		Retail:		Specialty Service:		Auto Loans:		Online Marketing:	
Motorcycles:		Truck Dealer:		Distributors:		Oil Change:		Insurance:		Other:	
Specialty:		RV Dealer:		Tires:		Paint and Body:				Publishing:	
Buses:		Motorcycle Dealer:		Batteries:						Rental Cars/Trucks:	
RVs:		Specialty Dealer:									

TYPES OF BUSINESS:

Glass Manufacturing
Automotive Products
Building Materials

BRANDS/DIVISIONS/AFFILIATES:

Glass Network
SunGuard Advanced Architectural Glass
DiamondGuard
ClimaGuard Low-E
ClimaGuard SPF
ShowerGuard
Guardian UltraWhite
SRG Global Inc

CONTACTS:

Note: Officers with more than one job title may be intentionally listed here more than once.

Jeffrey A. Knight, CFO
Jeffrey A. Knight, VP-Finance
Russell J. Ebeid, Pres., Glass Group
Russell J. Ebeid, Chmn.

Phone: 248-340-1800	**Fax:** 248-340-9988
Toll-Free:	
Address: 2300 Harmon Rd., Auburn Hills, MI 48326-1714 US	

GROWTH PLANS/SPECIAL FEATURES:

Guardian Industries Corp. is a leading global manufacturer of float glass (a flat, clear glass) and fabricated glass products. The company's product lines include automotive replacement glass, automotive products, building products, glass products and architect resources. Guardian spans the U.S. through its Glass Network, which includes over 4,500 company-owned and independent auto glass centers. The company has 60 plants located throughout five continents, with operations in 21 countries. Products include SunGuard Advanced Architectural Glass; DiamondGuard protective glass coating; ClimaGuard Low-E (low-emissivity) insulating glass; ClimaGuard SPF UV radiation blocking glass; ShowerGuard corrosion and discoloration resistant glass; Guardian UltraWhite low-iron glass with enhanced light-transmitting properties and reduced green tint; Guardian Fiberglass light-density fiberglass; GRIP Tuning automotive aftermarket products; and SatinDeco acid-etched glass. Guardian's automotive products segment specializes in vehicle glass, mouldings, grilles and other exterior trim products. In early 2009, the company announced the creation of SRG Global, Inc., a privately held company that comprises the Guardian Automotive and Siegel-Robert Automotive operations. In October 2009, the firm introduced EcoGuard Mo, a molybdenum-clear glass that optimizes the conductivity of photovoltaic systems. In May 2010, the company opened its second Brazilian float glass manufacturing facility.

The firm offers its employees benefits that include a wellness program.

FINANCIALS:

Sales and profits are in thousands of dollars—add 000 to get the full amount. 2009 Note: Financial information for 2009 was not available for all companies at press time.

2009 Sales: $	2009 Profits: $	**U.S. Stock Ticker: Private**
2008 Sales: $5,600,000	2008 Profits: $	**Int'l Ticker:** Int'l Exchange:
2007 Sales: $	2007 Profits: $	Employees: 19,000
2006 Sales: $5,330,000	2006 Profits: $	Fiscal Year Ends: 12/31
2005 Sales: $5,000,000	2005 Profits: $	Parent Company:

SALARIES/BENEFITS:

Pension Plan:	ESOP Stock Plan:	Profit Sharing:	Top Exec. Salary: $	Bonus: $
Savings Plan:	Stock Purch. Plan:		Second Exec. Salary: $	Bonus: $

OTHER THOUGHTS:

Apparent Women Officers or Directors:
Hot Spot for Advancement for Women/Minorities:

LOCATIONS: ("Y" = Yes)

West:	Southwest:	Midwest:	Southeast:	Northeast:	International:
Y	Y	Y	Y	Y	Y

GULF STATES TOYOTA INC

www.gstcareers.com

Industry Group Code: 42311 **Ranks within this company's industry group:** Sales: Profits:

Vehicle Manufacturing:		Dealers:		Parts:		Service:		Finance:		Specialty:	
Cars:		Car Dealer New:	Y	Manufacturers:		General Service:		Leasing:		Information Systems:	
Trucks:		Car Dealer Used:		Retail:		Specialty Service:		Auto Loans:		Online Marketing:	
Motorcycles:		Truck Dealer:		Distributors:	Y	Oil Change:		Insurance:		Other:	Y
Specialty:		RV Dealer:		Tires:		Paint and Body:				Publishing:	
Buses:		Motorcycle Dealer:		Batteries:						Rental Cars/Trucks:	
RVs:		Specialty Dealer:									

TYPES OF BUSINESS:

Vehicle Distribution-Wholesale
Parts & Accessories Distribution-Wholesale

BRANDS/DIVISIONS/AFFILIATES:

Friedkin Companies
Toyota
Scion
Lexus

CONTACTS:

Note: Officers with more than one job title may be intentionally listed here more than once.

Toby Hynes, Pres./Gen. Mgr.
Frank Gruen, CFO
J.C. Fassino, Sr. VP-Mktg.
Dominic Gallo, VP-Human Resources
Bill Russell, CIO
Thomas Friedkin, Chmn.

Phone: 713-580-3300	**Fax:** 713-580-3332
Toll-Free:	
Address: 7701 Wilshire Place Dr., Houston, TX 77040 US	

GROWTH PLANS/SPECIAL FEATURES:

Gulf States Toyota, Inc. distributes Toyota cars, trucks and SUVs throughout Texas, Arkansas, Louisiana, Oklahoma and Mississippi. It also distributes Lexus luxury automobiles and SUVs and sells parts and accessories to its dealers. The firm is responsible for receiving cars from Toyota, Scion and Lexus when they are shipped to Houston and performing services in preparation for distribution to dealers. Gulf States provides dealership support to approximately 150 dealers in its five-state region. Thomas Friedkin founded Gulf States in 1969, and it is now owned by the Friedkin Companies. It is one of two privately owned companies with exclusive rights to distribute vehicles within the North American Toyota distribution network. The company offers XM Satellite Radio among its dealer-installed options. Gulf States services over 2 million vehicles and generates over $4 billion in sales per year. The firm broke ground on a second vehicle processing center in 2009. The $50 million, 100-acre facility scheduled to open in 2011 will be located in Temple, Texas.

Employees benefits include; medical, dental and prescription plans; life and disability insurance; 401k; employee assistance program; tuition and adoption assistance; discounted pricing on Toyota vehicles and parts; fitness programs and facilities; and discounted pricing on PC hardware, software and wireless devices.

FINANCIALS:

Sales and profits are in thousands of dollars—add 000 to get the full amount. 2009 Note: Financial information for 2009 was not available for all companies at press time.

2009 Sales: $	2009 Profits: $	**U.S. Stock Ticker: Subsidiary**
2008 Sales: $	2008 Profits: $	**Int'l Ticker:** Int'l Exchange:
2007 Sales: $	2007 Profits: $	Employees:
2006 Sales: $	2006 Profits: $	Fiscal Year Ends: 12/31
2005 Sales: $	2005 Profits: $	Parent Company: FRIEDKIN COMPANIES

SALARIES/BENEFITS:

Pension Plan:	ESOP Stock Plan:	Profit Sharing:	Top Exec. Salary: $	Bonus: $
Savings Plan: Y	Stock Purch. Plan:		Second Exec. Salary: $	Bonus: $

OTHER THOUGHTS:

Apparent Women Officers or Directors:
Hot Spot for Advancement for Women/Minorities:

LOCATIONS: ("Y" = Yes)

West:	Southwest:	Midwest:	Southeast:	Northeast:	International:
	Y		Y		

GULF STREAM COACH INC

www.gulfstreamcoach.com

Industry Group Code: 336120 **Ranks within this company's industry group:** Sales: Profits:

Vehicle Manufacturing:		Dealers:		Parts:		Service:		Finance:		Specialty:	
Cars:		Car Dealer New:		Manufacturers:		General Service:		Leasing:		Information Systems:	
Trucks:		Car Dealer Used:		Retail:		Specialty Service:		Auto Loans:		Online Marketing:	
Motorcycles:		Truck Dealer:		Distributors:		Oil Change:		Insurance:		Other:	
Specialty:		RV Dealer:		Tires:		Paint and Body:				Publishing:	Y
Buses:		Motorcycle Dealer:		Batteries:						Rental Cars/Trucks:	
RVs:	Y	Specialty Dealer:									

TYPES OF BUSINESS:

Recreational Vehicle Manufacturing

BRANDS/DIVISIONS/AFFILIATES:

Fairmont Homes Inc
Tourmaster
Main Stream
Gulf Streamers (The)

CONTACTS:

Note: Officers with more than one job title may be intentionally listed here more than once.

Brian J. Shea, Pres.
Chuck Olsen, CFO
Dave Middleton, Mgr.-National Motorized Sales
Dan Miller, Dir.-Info. Systems
Jim Shea, Jr., Chmn.

Phone: 574-773-7761 **Fax:** 574-773-5761
Toll-Free: 800-289-8787
Address: 503 S. Oakland Ave., Nappanee, IN 46550 US

GROWTH PLANS/SPECIAL FEATURES:

Gulf Stream Coach, Inc., a subsidiary of Fairmont Homes, is a leader in the manufacture of a wide variety of recreation vehicles (RVs). The company was founded by the Shea family in rural Indiana, and produced its first model, the Sun Stream, in 1983. Gulf Stream's product offerings are divided between motorized vehicles and travel trailers (fifth wheels), and include 26 brands and more than 100 models. The motorized vehicle line includes Class A, Class C, Toy Movers, Class B Vans and Luxury models. These range from the 42-foot-long Luxury Tourmasters, which look similar to tour buses from the exterior; to the Class B vans, which include a much smaller floor plan but greater maneuverability. Gulf Stream's travel trailers include the categories of Luxury Towables, Towables, Light Weight and Toy Haulers. The firm's RV club, the Gulf Streamers, offers members local chapter activities; a magazine called Main Stream; access to the company's own golf course and recreation complex; and a 100% paid road service. Conquest Motorhomes, the Class C division of Gulf Stream Coach, has an exclusive partnership with International Truck for the production of the chassis in many of its new RVs.

Employees at Gulf Stream are given access to an on-site country club with a swimming pool and golf course. Other employee benefits include health, dental, life and cancer insurance; a prescription card; wellness benefits; and a 401(k) plan.

FINANCIALS:

Sales and profits are in thousands of dollars—add 000 to get the full amount. 2009 Note: Financial information for 2009 was not available for all companies at press time.

2009 Sales: $	2009 Profits: $	**U.S. Stock Ticker: Subsidiary**
2008 Sales: $	2008 Profits: $	**Int'l Ticker:** Int'l Exchange:
2007 Sales: $150,000	2007 Profits: $	Employees:
2006 Sales: $	2006 Profits: $	Fiscal Year Ends: 12/31
2005 Sales: $	2005 Profits: $	Parent Company: FAIRMONT HOMES INC

SALARIES/BENEFITS:

Pension Plan:	ESOP Stock Plan:	Profit Sharing:	Top Exec. Salary: $	Bonus: $
Savings Plan: Y	Stock Purch. Plan:		Second Exec. Salary: $	Bonus: $

OTHER THOUGHTS:

Apparent Women Officers or Directors:
Hot Spot for Advancement for Women/Minorities:

LOCATIONS: ("Y" = Yes)

West:	Southwest:	Midwest:	Southeast:	Northeast:	International:
		Y			

HAHN AUTOMOTIVE WAREHOUSE INC

www.hahnauto.com

Industry Group Code: 423120 **Ranks within this company's industry group:** Sales: Profits:

Vehicle Manufacturing:		Dealers:		Parts:		Service:		Finance:		Specialty:	
Cars:		Car Dealer New:		Manufacturers:		General Service:		Leasing:		Information Systems:	Y
Trucks:		Car Dealer Used:		Retail:	Y	Specialty Service:		Auto Loans:		Online Marketing:	
Motorcycles:		Truck Dealer:		Distributors:	Y	Oil Change:		Insurance:		Other:	Y
Specialty:		RV Dealer:		Tires:		Paint and Body:				Publishing:	Y
Buses:		Motorcycle Dealer:		Batteries:						Rental Cars/Trucks:	
RVs:		Specialty Dealer:									

TYPES OF BUSINESS:

Auto Parts, Retail Stores
Auto Parts, Wholesale Distribution
Auto Repair Instruction & Publication

BRANDS/DIVISIONS/AFFILIATES:

Advantage Auto Stores
Genuine Auto Parts
University of Auto Value Installer Training Guide
Auto Value Service Center Program
Auto Value Group

CONTACTS: *Note: Officers with more than one job title may be intentionally listed here more than once.*

Eli N. Futerman, Co-CEO/Co-Pres.
Daniel J. Chessin, Co-Pres./Co-CEO
Albert J. Van Erp, CFO
Mike Piccolo, VP-Oper.
Albert J. Van Erp, VP-Finance

Phone: 585-235-1595	**Fax:** 585-235-8615
Toll-Free:	
Address: 415 W. Main St., Rochester, NY 14608 US	

GROWTH PLANS/SPECIAL FEATURES:

Hahn Automotive sells automotive aftermarket products to commercial service establishments on a regional basis. Its business is conducted through nine full-service distribution centers and 22 pick-up warehouses to 15 states in the Northeastern and Midwestern U.S. The company also operates an accessory warehouse in New York under the RAAC brand. To complement its distribution centers, Hahn Automotive also operates 80 retail locations under the Advantage Auto Stores and Genuine Auto Parts brands; these locations sell to both professional dealers and do-it-yourself individuals. The company purchases nearly 150,000 automotive aftermarket stock keeping units (SKUs), consisting predominately of nationally branded automotive hard parts, as well as maintenance items, accessories and private-label products, from manufacturers. Hahn Automotive is a member of the Auto Value group, a collection of aftermarket automotive companies, for marketing and support. As a member of the Auto Value group, the stores are affiliated with over 100 distribution centers and more than 1,700 stores throughout North America, including Canada and Mexico. Advantage Auto also supplies its customers with its University of Auto Value Installer Training Guide, which has information on hundreds of publications, clinics, videos and workshops across the country. In addition, the group offers customized marketing assistance, as well as its Auto Value Service Center Program, which provides Auto Value signage, on-hold messaging, installer uniforms, the 1-800 Service Center Locator Service and equipment leasing programs.

FINANCIALS: **Sales and profits are in thousands of dollars—add 000 to get the full amount. 2009 Note: Financial information for 2009 was not available for all companies at press time.**

2009 Sales: $	2009 Profits: $	**U.S. Stock Ticker: Private**
2008 Sales: $	2008 Profits: $	**Int'l Ticker:** Int'l Exchange:
2007 Sales: $140,300	2007 Profits: $	Employees:
2006 Sales: $	2006 Profits: $	Fiscal Year Ends: 9/30
2005 Sales: $	2005 Profits: $	Parent Company:

SALARIES/BENEFITS:

Pension Plan:	ESOP Stock Plan:	Profit Sharing:	Top Exec. Salary: $	Bonus: $
Savings Plan:	Stock Purch. Plan:		Second Exec. Salary: $	Bonus: $

OTHER THOUGHTS:

Apparent Women Officers or Directors:
Hot Spot for Advancement for Women/Minorities:

LOCATIONS: ("Y" = Yes)

West:	Southwest:	Midwest:	Southeast:	Northeast:	International:
		Y		Y	

HANKOOK TIRE CO LTD

global.hankooktire.com

Industry Group Code: 3262 **Ranks within this company's industry group:** Sales: 6 Profits: 1

Vehicle Manufacturing:		Dealers:		Parts:		Service:		Finance:		Specialty:	
Cars:		Car Dealer New:		Manufacturers:	Y	General Service:		Leasing:		Information Systems:	
Trucks:		Car Dealer Used:		Retail:		Specialty Service:		Auto Loans:		Online Marketing:	
Motorcycles:		Truck Dealer:		Distributors:		Oil Change:		Insurance:		Other:	
Specialty:		RV Dealer:		Tires:	Y	Paint and Body:				Publishing:	
Buses:		Motorcycle Dealer:		Batteries:						Rental Cars/Trucks:	
RVs:		Specialty Dealer:									

TYPES OF BUSINESS:

Manufacturing-Tires
Batteries
Alloy Rims & Wheels
Brake Pads & Linings
System Integration Services

BRANDS/DIVISIONS/AFFILIATES:

ATLASBX Co., Ltd.
Daehwa Engineering & Machinery
emFrontier
Frixa
Aurora
Kingstar
Ventus
Enfren

CONTACTS:

Note: Officers with more than one job title may be intentionally listed here more than once.

Seung Hwa Suh, Co-CEO
Ki Yeul Huh, COO
Hwi Joong Kim, Pres./Co-CEO
Hyun Bum Cho, CFO/Exec. VP
Myung Hun An, VP-R&D
Hwi Joong Kim, CTO
Jae Ryong Yoon, Exec. VP-Prod.
Jae Ryong Yoon, Exec. VP-Eng.
Hwi Joong Kim, Chief Prod. Officer
Hyun Shick Cho, Exec. VP/COO-Korea Headquarters
Ho Youl Pae, VP-Market Strategy & Planning
Chang Hwan Kang, Exec. VP-Finance
Ki Yeul Huh, Pres., China Headquarters
Soo Il Lee, VP/COO-America Headquarters
Yang Rai Cho, Chmn.
Jin Wook Choi, Exec. VP/COO-Europe Headquarters

Phone: 82-2-2222-1000 **Fax:** 82-2-2222-1100
Toll-Free:
Address: 647-15 Yeoksam-dong, Gangnam-gu, Seoul, 135-723 Korea

GROWTH PLANS/SPECIAL FEATURES:

Hankook Tire Co., Ltd., based in Korea, is a leading global tire manufacturer. The company manufactures radial tires for passenger cars, SUVs (sport utility vehicles), RVs (recreational vehicles), trucks and buses. The firm's products include automotive batteries through ATLASBX Co., Ltd.; tire manufacturing equipment through Daehwa Engineering & Machinery; system integration services through emFrontier; and brake pads through Frixa. ATLASBX's major products include automotive batteries, taxi batteries, marine batteries, industrial batteries, SUV batteries, absorbent glass mat (AGM) batteries, Micro-HEV batteries, batteries for imported vehicles and batteries for renewable energy storage. Daehwa Engineering & Machinery's product portfolio includes steel belt cutters, bead winders, tire builders, curing presses and uniformity testers. EmFrontier's products include SM/outsourcing services, SI/consulting services and enterprise business application architecture solutions. Lastly, Frixa's portfolio includes brake pads, brake lining, racing brake pads, disc rotors and industrial-use brakes. Hankook is the company's primary brand, which is used internationally, while Aurora is used for its passenger car tires and Kingstar is used for its tires sold outside of Korea. Domestic tire brands include Ventus; Enfren, an environmentally-friendly tire used to curb pollution; Optimo for its premium sedans; Dyna-Pro for its SUVs; and Icebear and Zovac for its winter tires. The firm's global distribution network consists of four regional headquarters in the U.S. and 80 subsidiaries and sales offices. Its products are sold worldwide in about 180 countries, with over 70% of its revenue generated in overseas markets. Sales in Europe generated 30% of 2009 revenues; Americas, 25%; Asia-Pacific, 18%; Korea, 16%; and Middle East and Africa, 11%. In April 2010, the company opened its second Canadian distribution center in Richmond, British Columbia.

FINANCIALS:

Sales and profits are in thousands of dollars—add 000 to get the full amount. 2009 Note: Financial information for 2009 was not available for all companies at press time.

2009 Sales: $4,306,490
2008 Sales: $3,526,140
2007 Sales: $2,834,190
2006 Sales: $
2005 Sales: $3,145,405

2009 Profits: $286,410
2008 Profits: $18,610
2007 Profits: $126,220
2006 Profits: $
2005 Profits: $230,134

U.S. Stock Ticker:
Int'l Ticker: 000240 Int'l Exchange: Seoul-KRX
Employees:
Fiscal Year Ends: 12/31
Parent Company:

SALARIES/BENEFITS:

Pension Plan: ESOP Stock Plan: Profit Sharing: Top Exec. Salary: $ Bonus: $
Savings Plan: Stock Purch. Plan: Second Exec. Salary: $ Bonus: $

OTHER THOUGHTS:

Apparent Women Officers or Directors:
Hot Spot for Advancement for Women/Minorities:

LOCATIONS: ("Y" = Yes)

West:	Southwest:	Midwest:	Southeast:	Northeast:	International:
Y	Y	Y	Y	Y	Y

HARLEY-DAVIDSON INC

www.harley-davidson.com

Industry Group Code: 336991 **Ranks within this company's industry group:** Sales: 2 Profits: 6

Vehicle Manufacturing:		Dealers:		Parts:		Service:		Finance:		Specialty:	
Cars:		Car Dealer New:		Manufacturers:	Y	General Service:		Leasing:		Information Systems:	
Trucks:		Car Dealer Used:		Retail:		Specialty Service:		Auto Loans:	Y	Online Marketing:	
Motorcycles:	Y	Truck Dealer:		Distributors:		Oil Change:		Insurance:	Y	Other:	
Specialty:		RV Dealer:		Tires:		Paint and Body:				Publishing:	
Buses:		Motorcycle Dealer:		Batteries:						Rental Cars/Trucks:	
RVs:		Specialty Dealer:									

TYPES OF BUSINESS:

Motorcycle Manufacturing
Parts & Accessories
Financial Services

BRANDS/DIVISIONS/AFFILIATES:

Harley-Davidson Motor Company
VRSC
Touring
Dyna
Softail
Sportster
Harley-Davidson Financial Services

CONTACTS:

Note: Officers with more than one job title may be intentionally listed here more than once.

Keith E. Wandell, CEO
Keith E. Wandell, Pres.
John A. Olin, CFO/Sr. VP
Mark-Hans Richer, Chief Mktg. Officer/Sr. VP
Tonit Calaway, VP-Human Resources
Paul J. Jones, General Counsel/Sec./VP
James McCaslin, Exec. VP-Corp. Prod. Planning
Joanne Bischmann, VP-Comm.
J. Darrell Thomas, Treas./VP
Lawrence Hund, COO/Pres., Harley-Davidson Financial Svcs.
Matthew Levatich, COO/Pres., Motor Company
Barry K. Allen, Chmn.

Phone: 414-342-4680	**Fax:** 414-343-8230
Toll-Free:	
Address: 3700 W. Juneau Ave., Milwaukee, WI 53208 US	

GROWTH PLANS/SPECIAL FEATURES:

Harley-Davidson, Inc. specializes in the manufacturing and marketing of motorcycles and related products and accessories. The company operates in two segments: motorcycles and related products; and financial services. The motorcycles and related products segment of the firm, which accounts for approximately 75% of total net revenue, designs, manufactures and sells at wholesale primarily heavyweight touring, custom and performance motorcycles, as well as a line of motorcycle parts, accessories, general merchandise and related services. It conducts business on a global basis, with sales in North America, Latin America, Asia/Pacific and Europe/Middle East/Africa. Harley-Davidson currently manufactures five families of motorcycles: VRSC, Touring, Dyna, Softail and Sportster, along with custom model options. This segment also provides a variety of services to its independent dealers, including service and business management training programs; customized dealer software packages; and delivery of its motorcycles. The firm's financial services segment, which does business as Harley-Davidson Financial Services, is engaged in the business of financing and servicing wholesale inventory receivables and retail consumer loans, primarily for the purchase of Harley-Davison motorcycles. It provides property/casualty insurance and also sells extended service contract, gap coverage and debt protection products to motorcycle owners. It conducts business principally in the U.S. and Canada. Harley-Davidson does a significant amount of business abroad, with its international sales accounting for approximately 32% of the net revenue of the motorcycles segment. In October 2009, the company announced its exit from the Buell product line.

Harley-Davidson offers its employees medical, dental and vision insurance; a 401(k) and/or pension plan; life insurance; disability benefits; an employee assistance plan; flexible spending accounts; tuition reimbursement; a stock purchase plan; discounts and financing on company products; and wellness resources.

FINANCIALS:

Sales and profits are in thousands of dollars—add 000 to get the full amount. 2009 Note: Financial information for 2009 was not available for all companies at press time.

2009 Sales: $4,781,909	2009 Profits: $-55,116	**U.S. Stock Ticker: HOG**
2008 Sales: $5,955,384	2008 Profits: $654,718	**Int'l Ticker:** Int'l Exchange:
2007 Sales: $6,143,044	2007 Profits: $933,843	Employees: 7,300
2006 Sales: $5,800,686	2006 Profits: $1,043,153	Fiscal Year Ends: 12/31
2005 Sales: $5,342,214	2005 Profits: $959,604	Parent Company:

SALARIES/BENEFITS:

Pension Plan: Y	ESOP Stock Plan:	Profit Sharing:	Top Exec. Salary: $650,025	Bonus: $780,030
Savings Plan: Y	Stock Purch. Plan: Y		Second Exec. Salary: $508,770	Bonus: $

OTHER THOUGHTS:

Apparent Women Officers or Directors: 3
Hot Spot for Advancement for Women/Minorities: Y

LOCATIONS: ("Y" = Yes)

West:	Southwest:	Midwest:	Southeast:	Northeast:	International:
	Y	Y	Y	Y	Y

HAYES LEMMERZ INTERNATIONAL INC

www.hayes-lemmerz.com

Industry Group Code: 3363 **Ranks within this company's industry group:** Sales: 34 Profits: 54

Vehicle Manufacturing:		Dealers:		Parts:		Service:		Finance:		Specialty:	
Cars:		Car Dealer New:		Manufacturers:	Y	General Service:		Leasing:		Information Systems:	
Trucks:		Car Dealer Used:		Retail:		Specialty Service:		Auto Loans:		Online Marketing:	
Motorcycles:		Truck Dealer:		Distributors:		Oil Change:		Insurance:		Other:	
Specialty:		RV Dealer:		Tires:		Paint and Body:				Publishing:	
Buses:		Motorcycle Dealer:		Batteries:						Rental Cars/Trucks:	
RVs:		Specialty Dealer:									

TYPES OF BUSINESS:

Automobile Part Manufacturing
Automotive & Light Truck Wheels
Commercial Highway Vehicle Wheels

BRANDS/DIVISIONS/AFFILIATES:

CentruStyle
Novachrome

CONTACTS:

Note: Officers with more than one job title may be intentionally listed here more than once.

Curtis J. Clawson, CEO
Fred Bentley, COO
Curtis J. Clawson, Pres.
Mark Brebberman, CFO/VP
Marc Hendrickx, VP-Mktg. & Sales
Tim Welcer, Dir.-Human Resources
Patrick C. Cauley, General Counsel/VP/Sec.
John A. Salvette, VP-Bus. Dev.
Marika Diamond, Dir.-Comm. & Worldwide Public Rel.
David Jorgensen, Corp. Controller
Fred Bentley, Pres., Global Wheel Group
Donald Hampton, VP/Gen. Mgr.-Americas Oper.
David Kasaul, VP-Europe & Africa Oper.
Pieter Klinkers, Pres., Europe, Africa & Asia Pacific
Curtis J. Clawson, Chmn.
Mustafa Zaim, Managing Dir.-Turkish Oper.

Phone: 734-737-5000 **Fax:** 734-737-2198
Toll-Free: 800-521-0515
Address: 15300 Centennial Dr., Northville, MI 48168 US

GROWTH PLANS/SPECIAL FEATURES:

Hayes Lemmerz International, Inc., originally Hayes Wheels, manufactures wheels and wheel-end attachments for major automobile original equipment manufacturers (OEMs). Operating 20 facilities in 12 countries around the world, Hayes Lemmerz supplies major North American, Japanese and European manufacturers of passenger cars and light trucks, as well as commercial highway vehicle customers. The company's main business is designing and manufacturing fabricated steel and cast aluminum wheels for OEMs. Hayes Lemmerz manufactures aluminum wheels with bright finishes such as GemTech machining, Novachrome plating, chrome cladding and premium paints. The firm's aluminum wheels are produced in sizes from 14-24 inches. The steel wheels manufactured by the company include, drop well, bead seat, full face, Versastyle and cladded steel. They range in sizes from 13-20 inches for passenger cars and up to 24.5 inches for commercial vehicles. It offers a variety of tubeless wheels and rims for commercial and military vehicles. Hayes Lemmerz recently expanded its Commercial Highway product line to include the new CentruStyle custom aluminum wheels for tractors and trailers. In March 2009, in response to decreased industry demand, the company, along with some of its U.S. subsidiaries filed petitions under Chapter 11 of the U.S. Bankruptcy code. In December 2009, after completing a restructuring process, the company emerged from Chapter 11.

FINANCIALS:

Sales and profits are in thousands of dollars—add 000 to get the full amount. 2009 Note: Financial information for 2009 was not available for all companies at press time.

2009 Sales: $1,848,400	2009 Profits: $-371,700	**U.S. Stock Ticker: HAYZQ**
2008 Sales: $2,051,900	2008 Profits: $-194,400	**Int'l Ticker:** Int'l Exchange:
2007 Sales: $1,796,800	2007 Profits: $-166,900	Employees: 6,400
2006 Sales: $1,726,200	2006 Profits: $-457,500	Fiscal Year Ends: 1/31
2005 Sales: $1,773,400	2005 Profits: $-62,300	Parent Company:

SALARIES/BENEFITS:

Pension Plan:	ESOP Stock Plan:	Profit Sharing:	Top Exec. Salary: $	Bonus: $
Savings Plan: Y	Stock Purch. Plan:		Second Exec. Salary: $	Bonus: $

OTHER THOUGHTS:

Apparent Women Officers or Directors: 2
Hot Spot for Advancement for Women/Minorities: Y

LOCATIONS: ("Y" = Yes)

West:	Southwest:	Midwest:	Southeast:	Northeast:	International:
		Y			Y

HELLA KGAA HUECK & CO

www.hella.com

Industry Group Code: 3363 **Ranks within this company's industry group:** Sales: Profits:

Vehicle Manufacturing:		Dealers:		Parts:		Service:		Finance:		Specialty:	
Cars:		Car Dealer New:		Manufacturers:	Y	General Service:		Leasing:		Information Systems:	
Trucks:		Car Dealer Used:		Retail:	Y	Specialty Service:		Auto Loans:		Online Marketing:	Y
Motorcycles:		Truck Dealer:		Distributors:		Oil Change:		Insurance:		Other:	
Specialty:		RV Dealer:		Tires:		Paint and Body:				Publishing:	
Buses:		Motorcycle Dealer:		Batteries:						Rental Cars/Trucks:	
RVs:		Specialty Dealer:									

TYPES OF BUSINESS:

Manufacturing, Automotive Parts
Lighting
Electronics
Complete Vehicle Modules
Air Conditioning Systems
Vehicle Wiring Systems
Signal Processing

BRANDS/DIVISIONS/AFFILIATES:

Hella Aftermarket Club
HBPO GmbH
Behr-Hella Thermocontrol GmbH
Intedis
DynaBeam
CELIS
Behr Hella Service
Lane Change Assistant

CONTACTS: *Note: Officers with more than one job title may be intentionally listed here more than once.*

Rolf Breidenbach, CEO
Rolf Breidenbach, Pres.
Hans Sudkamp, CFO
Stefan Osterhage, VP-Human Resources
Tilmann Seubert, VP-Advanced Dev.
Stefan Osterhage, VP-Info. Mgmt. & Logistics
Ulrich Koester, Head-Press & Public Rel.
Wolfgang Ollig, VP-Finance & Controlling
Carsten Albrecht, VP-Aftermarket & Original Equipment Sales
Jurgen Behrend, Chmn.
Carl Brown, Pres., Hella, Inc./Dir.-NAFTA Aftermarket Region

Phone: 49-29-41-38-0	**Fax:** 49-29-41-38-71-33
Toll-Free:	
Address: Rixbecker Str. 75, Lippstadt, 59552 Germany	

GROWTH PLANS/SPECIAL FEATURES:

Hella KGaA Hueck & Co. develops and manufactures lighting and electronics for the automobile industry, with a focus towards products that improve environmental impact and driver safety and comfort. It also produces complete vehicle modules, vehicle electric systems and air conditioning systems through joint venture companies. Hella runs over 70 manufacturing facilities, subsidiaries and joint ventures worldwide. The firm's lighting products division produces VarioX headlamps, Xenon, full-LED headlamps, DynaBeam and the CELIS System. Hella's electronic division produces electronic driver assistance systems, vehicle electric systems and electronic control units. The Lane Change Assistant uses infrared sensor technology and a rear view camera system for the automatic regulation of distance to the next vehicle. The ACC system has sensors which can detect and evaluate the threat of oncoming obstacles, triggering a pre-crash set of activities. The Traffic Sign Detection system informs drivers of changes in speed limit zones. Additionally, Hella has capitalized on the increased demand for fuel efficient technology by developing an intelligent battery sensor and voltage stabilizers that support engine on/off functions. Hella's aftermarket division sells automotive parts and accessories. The firm supplies products through its online catalog, Hella Aftermarket Club, and its business-to-business portal, TecCom. The joint venture, Behr Hella Service, markets vehicle air conditioning and engine cooling parts. Hella develops headlight technology with the Japanese supplier Stanley and Korean supplier SL (formerly Samlip). The firm has a joint venture, HBPO GmbH, with Behr in Germany and Plastic Omnium in France that designs and produces logistics for complete front-end modules. Behr-Hella Thermocontrol GmbH provides system development for vehicle air conditioning and engine cooling. Intedis, a joint venture between Hella and Leoni, produces software-supported design assessment of electronic architectures for all vehicle segments. The firm also develops products outside the automotive industry with LED lighting systems for streets and airports.

FINANCIALS: **Sales and profits are in thousands of dollars—add 000 to get the full amount. 2009 Note: Financial information for 2009 was not available for all companies at press time.**

2009 Sales: $	2009 Profits: $	**U.S. Stock Ticker: Private**
2008 Sales: $	2008 Profits: $	**Int'l Ticker:** Int'l Exchange:
2007 Sales: $	2007 Profits: $	Employees:
2006 Sales: $4,578,870	2006 Profits: $	Fiscal Year Ends: 5/31
2005 Sales: $4,141,890	2005 Profits: $	Parent Company:

SALARIES/BENEFITS:

Pension Plan:	ESOP Stock Plan:	Profit Sharing:	Top Exec. Salary: $	Bonus: $
Savings Plan:	Stock Purch. Plan:		Second Exec. Salary: $	Bonus: $

OTHER THOUGHTS:

Apparent Women Officers or Directors:
Hot Spot for Advancement for Women/Minorities:

LOCATIONS: ("Y" = Yes)

West:	Southwest:	Midwest:	Southeast:	Northeast:	International:
		Y	Y	Y	Y

HENDRICK AUTOMOTIVE GROUP

www.hendrickauto.com

Industry Group Code: 441110 **Ranks within this company's industry group:** Sales: Profits:

Vehicle Manufacturing:		Dealers:		Parts:		Service:		Finance:		Specialty:	
Cars:		Car Dealer New:	Y	Manufacturers:		General Service:	Y	Leasing:		Information Systems:	
Trucks:		Car Dealer Used:	Y	Retail:	Y	Specialty Service:		Auto Loans:	Y	Online Marketing:	
Motorcycles:		Truck Dealer:	Y	Distributors:		Oil Change:		Insurance:		Other:	Y
Specialty:		RV Dealer:		Tires:		Paint and Body:	Y			Publishing:	
Buses:		Motorcycle Dealer:		Batteries:						Rental Cars/Trucks:	
RVs:		Specialty Dealer:									

TYPES OF BUSINESS:

Auto Dealers, Retail
Parts & Service
Accessories
Racing & Motorsports

BRANDS/DIVISIONS/AFFILIATES:

Hendrick Motorsports
Hendrick Marrow Program
Hendrick Autoguard

CONTACTS:

Note: Officers with more than one job title may be intentionally listed here more than once.

James F. Huzl, CEO
James F. Huzl, Pres.
Edward J. Brown, III, CFO
Veronica Zayatz, VP-Acct., Audits & Taxes
J. Richard Hendrick, III, Chmn.

Phone: 704-568-5550	**Fax:** 704-566-3295
Toll-Free:	
Address: 6000 Monroe Rd., Ste. 100, Charlotte, NC 28212 US	

GROWTH PLANS/SPECIAL FEATURES:

Hendrick Automotive Group sells new and used automobiles from more than 20 automakers, including Honda, GMC, Porsche, BMW, Hummer and Volvo. It boasts a network of 59 dealerships in 10 states across the U.S., as well as 87 franchise locations. The firm's automobile offerings include cars as well as light trucks. The company features the Hendrick Advantage, which is comprised of a team-oriented approach to business, an emphasis on customer satisfaction, accountability at all levels and commitment to continuous improvement. Hendrick Automotive offers other services, including financing, maintenance, body repair and parts and accessories. The Automotive Group has 18 collision centers located across the U.S. Customers can access a database of pre-owned and new cars on the company web site. Through the Hendrick Autoguard partner, the company offers warranty and vehicle protection plans for new and used cars and trucks. Hendrick also supports charitable operations including the Hendrick Marrow Program, which recruits potential matching marrow donors, raises funds for tissue typing and offers support for those suffering from leukemia and other blood-related diseases. Hendrick also operates Hendrick Motorsports, which sponsors a number of NASCAR teams. In April 2009, the company acquired Beck Imports, owner of two Mercedes-Benz dealerships.

FINANCIALS:

Sales and profits are in thousands of dollars—add 000 to get the full amount. 2009 Note: Financial information for 2009 was not available for all companies at press time.

2009 Sales: $	2009 Profits: $	**U.S. Stock Ticker: Private**
2008 Sales: $	2008 Profits: $	**Int'l Ticker:** Int'l Exchange:
2007 Sales: $	2007 Profits: $	Employees:
2006 Sales: $	2006 Profits: $	Fiscal Year Ends: 12/31
2005 Sales: $	2005 Profits: $	Parent Company:

SALARIES/BENEFITS:

Pension Plan:	ESOP Stock Plan:	Profit Sharing:	Top Exec. Salary: $	Bonus: $
Savings Plan:	Stock Purch. Plan:		Second Exec. Salary: $	Bonus: $

OTHER THOUGHTS:

Apparent Women Officers or Directors: 1
Hot Spot for Advancement for Women/Minorities:

LOCATIONS: ("Y" = Yes)

West:	Southwest:	Midwest:	Southeast:	Northeast:	International:
Y	Y	Y	Y	Y	

HERB CHAMBERS COMPANIES (THE)

www.herbchambers.com

Industry Group Code: 441110 **Ranks within this company's industry group:** Sales: Profits:

Vehicle Manufacturing:		Dealers:		Parts:		Service:		Finance:		Specialty:	
Cars:		Car Dealer New:	Y	Manufacturers:		General Service:	Y	Leasing:		Information Systems:	
Trucks:		Car Dealer Used:	Y	Retail:	Y	Specialty Service:		Auto Loans:	Y	Online Marketing:	Y
Motorcycles:		Truck Dealer:		Distributors:		Oil Change:		Insurance:		Other:	
Specialty:		RV Dealer:		Tires:		Paint and Body:	Y			Publishing:	
Buses:		Motorcycle Dealer:		Batteries:						Rental Cars/Trucks:	
RVs:		Specialty Dealer:									

TYPES OF BUSINESS:

Auto Dealers, Retail
Online Sales
Parts & Service

BRANDS/DIVISIONS/AFFILIATES:

Herb Chambers Vespa of Boston
Flagship Motorcars
Chambers Motorcars
Herb Chambers Porsche of Boston
Herb Chambers BMW of Boston
Herb Chambers Saab of Braintree
Herb Chambers Toyota of Auburn
Herb Chambers Chrysler Dodge of Millbury

CONTACTS:

Note: Officers with more than one job title may be intentionally listed here more than once.

Herbert G. Chambers, CEO
Herbert G. Chambers, Pres.
Bruce Spatz, CFO

Phone: 617-666-8333	**Fax:** 617-666-8448
Toll-Free:	
Address: 259 McGrath Hwy., Somerville, MA 02145 US	

GROWTH PLANS/SPECIAL FEATURES:

The Herb Chambers Companies operates 46 dealerships throughout New England. It specializes in selling upscale automobiles, including models from Audi, Mercedes-Benz, Maybach, BMW, MINI, Porsche, Infiniti, Lexus, Saab, Cadillac, Jeep, Chrysler, Land Rover, Scion, Toyota, Hummer and Buick; the company also has dealerships offering the Dodge, Ford, Kia, Hyundai and Honda brands, as well as a dealership for Vespas and two for Smart cars. The firm's dealerships also operate parts and service departments. In addition to its dealerships, Herb Chambers maintains four collision centers. The company's web site offers online credit applications, vehicle inventory searching and sales.

FINANCIALS:

Sales and profits are in thousands of dollars—add 000 to get the full amount. 2009 Note: Financial information for 2009 was not available for all companies at press time.

2009 Sales: $	2009 Profits: $	**U.S. Stock Ticker: Private**
2008 Sales: $	2008 Profits: $	**Int'l Ticker:** Int'l Exchange:
2007 Sales: $	2007 Profits: $	Employees:
2006 Sales: $	2006 Profits: $	Fiscal Year Ends: 12/31
2005 Sales: $1,400,000	2005 Profits: $	Parent Company:

SALARIES/BENEFITS:

Pension Plan:	ESOP Stock Plan:	Profit Sharing:	Top Exec. Salary: $	Bonus: $
Savings Plan: Y	Stock Purch. Plan:		Second Exec. Salary: $	Bonus: $

OTHER THOUGHTS:

Apparent Women Officers or Directors:
Hot Spot for Advancement for Women/Minorities:

LOCATIONS: ("Y" = Yes)

West:	Southwest:	Midwest:	Southeast:	Northeast:	International:
				Y	

HERO HONDA MOTORS LTD

www.herohonda.com

Industry Group Code: 336991 **Ranks within this company's industry group:** Sales: 3 Profits: 1

Vehicle Manufacturing:		Dealers:		Parts:		Service:		Finance:		Specialty:	
Cars:		Car Dealer New:		Manufacturers:		General Service:		Leasing:		Information Systems:	
Trucks:		Car Dealer Used:		Retail:		Specialty Service:		Auto Loans:		Online Marketing:	
Motorcycles:	Y	Truck Dealer:		Distributors:		Oil Change:		Insurance:		Other:	
Specialty:		RV Dealer:		Tires:		Paint and Body:				Publishing:	
Buses:		Motorcycle Dealer:	Y	Batteries:						Rental Cars/Trucks:	
RVs:		Specialty Dealer:									

TYPES OF BUSINESS:

Motorcycle Manufacturing & Sales

BRANDS/DIVISIONS/AFFILIATES:

Hero Group
Honda Motor Co Ltd
Daimler AG
Splendor
Glamour
Hunk
Karizma
Daimler Hero Motor Corporation Ltd

CONTACTS: *Note: Officers with more than one job title may be intentionally listed here more than once.*

Pawan Munjal, Managing Dir./CEO
Anil Dua, Sr. VP-Sales, Mktg. & Customer Care
Anadi Pande, VP-Human Resources Mgmt.
Vijay Sethi, VP-Info. Systems
Sumihisa Fukuda, Dir.-Technical
Ilam C. Kamboj, Gen. Mgr.-Legal/Company Sec.
Vikram Kasbekar, Head-Plants Oper.
Anadi Pande, VP-Corp. Planning & Strategy
Toshiaki Nakagawa, Joint Managing Dir.
Brijmohan Lall Munjal, Chmn.
Vikram Kasbekar, Head-Supply Chain

Phone: 91-11-2614-2451 **Fax:** 91-11-2614-3321
Toll-Free:
Address: 34, Community Centre, Basant Lok, Vasant Vihar, New Delhi, 110 057 India

GROWTH PLANS/SPECIAL FEATURES:

Hero Honda Motors Ltd. (HHML), a joint venture between India's Hero Group and Japan-based Honda Motor Company, is a leading manufacturer and marketer of motorcycles in India. Its motorcycles include entry segment, deluxe segment and premium segment models. The company's offerings include its CD-Dawn, CD-Deluxe, Splendor, Splendor+, Splendor NXG, Splendor Super, Glamour, Glamour PGM-FI, Achiever, CBZ X-treme, Hunk and Karizma motorcycle models, as well as the company's Pleasure scooter model. HHML's products are sold and supported through a network of nearly 4,500 dealers, authorized representatives and service centers located in both rural and urban India. The company has three manufacturing plants, in Haridwar, Dharuhera and Gurgaon, with a combined annual capacity of approximately 4.5 million units. The firm also operates zonal offices in New Delhi, Bangalore, Kolkata and Pune, as well as 20 regional offices throughout the country. HHML maintains a joint venture with Daimler AG, Daimler Hero Motor Corporation Ltd., which produces light, medium and heavy-duty commercial vehicles for the Indian market.

FINANCIALS: **Sales and profits are in thousands of dollars—add 000 to get the full amount. 2009 Note: Financial information for 2009 was not available for all companies at press time.**

2009 Sales: $2,627,750 | 2009 Profits: $273,410
2008 Sales: $2,700,000 | 2008 Profits: $257,000
2007 Sales: $2,021,190 | 2007 Profits: $175,150
2006 Sales: $1,779,060 | 2006 Profits: $198,310
2005 Sales: $ | 2005 Profits: $

U.S. Stock Ticker: Joint Venture
Int'l Ticker: Int'l Exchange:
Employees:
Fiscal Year Ends: 3/31
Parent Company:

SALARIES/BENEFITS:

Pension Plan: ESOP Stock Plan: Profit Sharing: Top Exec. Salary: $ Bonus: $
Savings Plan: Stock Purch. Plan: Second Exec. Salary: $ Bonus: $

OTHER THOUGHTS:

Apparent Women Officers or Directors: 1
Hot Spot for Advancement for Women/Minorities:

LOCATIONS: ("Y" = Yes)

West:	Southwest:	Midwest:	Southeast:	Northeast:	International:
					Y

HERTZ GLOBAL HOLDINGS INC

www.hertz.com

Industry Group Code: 5321 **Ranks within this company's industry group:** Sales: 2 Profits: 4

Vehicle Manufacturing:		Dealers:		Parts:		Service:		Finance:		Specialty:	
Cars:		Car Dealer New:		Manufacturers:		General Service:		Leasing:	Y	Information Systems:	
Trucks:		Car Dealer Used:	Y	Retail:		Specialty Service:		Auto Loans:		Online Marketing:	
Motorcycles:		Truck Dealer:		Distributors:		Oil Change:		Insurance:		Other:	Y
Specialty:		RV Dealer:		Tires:		Paint and Body:				Publishing:	
Buses:		Motorcycle Dealer:		Batteries:						Rental Cars/Trucks:	Y
RVs:		Specialty Dealer:									

TYPES OF BUSINESS:

Automobile Rental
Truck Rental
Claims Management
Heavy Equipment Rental
Used Automobile Sales
Leasing
Actuarial Services
Franchising

BRANDS/DIVISIONS/AFFILIATES:

Prestige Collection
Hertz Fun Collection
Green Collection
Hertz Equipment Rental Corporation
1st Call Studio Equipment

CONTACTS:

Note: Officers with more than one job title may be intentionally listed here more than once.

Mark Frissora, CEO
Elyse Douglas, CFO/Exec. VP
Michael P. Senackerib, Chief Mktg. Officer/Sr. VP
LeighAnne Baker, Chief Human Resources Officer/Sr. VP
Joseph F. Eckroth, CIO/Sr. VP
Jeffrey Zimmerman, General Counsel/Sr. VP/Sec.
Jatindar Kapur, Corp. Controller/Sr. VP-Finance
Scott Sider, Exec. VP/Pres., Vehicle Renting & Leasing
Gerald A. Plescia, Exec. VP/Pres., Hertz Equipment Rental Corp.
Lois Boyd, Sr. VP-Process Improvement & Project Mgmt.
Robert J. Stuart, Sr. VP-Global Sales
Mark Frissora, Chmn.
Michael Taride, Exec. VP/Pres., Hertz Int'l
John A. Thomas, Exec. VP-Supply Chain Mgmt.

Phone: 201-307-2000 **Fax:** 201-307-2644
Toll-Free: 800-654-3131
Address: 225 Brae Blvd., Park Ridge, NJ 07656-0713 US

GROWTH PLANS/SPECIAL FEATURES:

Hertz Global Holdings, Inc. owns one of the largest worldwide airport general use car rental brands and one of the largest equipment rental businesses in the U.S. and Canada. The company operates in two segments: car rental and equipment rental. In the car rental business segment, Hertz and its independent licensees accept reservations for car rentals at approximately 8,100 locations in approximately 145 countries. The company generally accepts reservations only for a class of vehicles, but it also accepts reservations for specific makes and models of vehicles in its Prestige Collection national-scale luxury rental program; its Hertz Fun Collection rental program; its Green Collection environmentally friendly rental program; and a limited number of models in high-volume, leisure-oriented destinations. The firm has approximately 2,065 staffed rental locations in the U.S., of which approximately one-fourth are airport locations and three-fourths are off-airport locations. It also rents cars from 1,220 other locations that are not staffed. Hertz has 1,140 staffed rental locations internationally, of which one-fifth are airport locations and four-fifths are off-airport locations, and it rents cars from 120 other locations that are not staffed. The equipment rental business segment, which operates through Hertz Equipment Rental Corporation, rents equipment through 322 branches in the U.S., Canada, France, Spain and China. It offers a broad range of equipment, including earthmoving equipment; material handling equipment; aerial and electrical equipment; air compressors; pumps; generators; small tools; compaction equipment; and construction-related trucks. The car rental segment accounted for 84% of the company's revenue in 2009 and equipment rental, 16%. In April 2010, the firm agreed to acquire competitor Dollar Thrifty Automotive Group, Inc. for $1.27 billion, for the purpose of strengthening its position in the leisure car-rental sector. In July 2010, the company acquired 1st Call Studio Equipment from RoadSafe Holdings.

FINANCIALS:

Sales and profits are in thousands of dollars—add 000 to get the full amount. 2009 Note: Financial information for 2009 was not available for all companies at press time.

2009 Sales: $7,101,500	2009 Profits: $-111,300	**U.S. Stock Ticker: HTZ**
2008 Sales: $8,525,100	2008 Profits: $-1,206,700	**Int'l Ticker:** Int'l Exchange:
2007 Sales: $8,685,600	2007 Profits: $264,500	Employees: 23,050
2006 Sales: $8,058,400	2006 Profits: $115,900	Fiscal Year Ends: 12/31
2005 Sales: $7,314,700	2005 Profits: $371,300	Parent Company:

SALARIES/BENEFITS:

Pension Plan: Y	ESOP Stock Plan:	Profit Sharing:	Top Exec. Salary: $975,769	Bonus: $2,200,000
Savings Plan:	Stock Purch. Plan:		Second Exec. Salary: $571,077	Bonus: $609,840

OTHER THOUGHTS:

Apparent Women Officers or Directors: 3
Hot Spot for Advancement for Women/Minorities: Y

LOCATIONS: ("Y" = Yes)

West:	Southwest:	Midwest:	Southeast:	Northeast:	International:
Y	Y	Y	Y	Y	Y

HILITE INTERNATIONAL INC

www.hilite.com

Industry Group Code: 3363 **Ranks within this company's industry group:** Sales: Profits:

Vehicle Manufacturing:		Dealers:		Parts:		Service:		Finance:		Specialty:	
Cars:		Car Dealer New:		Manufacturers:	Y	General Service:		Leasing:		Information Systems:	
Trucks:		Car Dealer Used:		Retail:		Specialty Service:		Auto Loans:		Online Marketing:	
Motorcycles:		Truck Dealer:		Distributors:		Oil Change:		Insurance:		Other:	
Specialty:		RV Dealer:		Tires:		Paint and Body:				Publishing:	
Buses:		Motorcycle Dealer:		Batteries:						Rental Cars/Trucks:	
RVs:		Specialty Dealer:									

TYPES OF BUSINESS:

Automobile Parts Manufacturer
Transmission Components
Engine Components
Emission Control Systems
Automotive Valves
Clutches
Camphasing Systems

BRANDS/DIVISIONS/AFFILIATES:

Hydraulik-Ring GmbH
Hilite International Marnaz Division

CONTACTS:

Note: Officers with more than one job title may be intentionally listed here more than once.

Joseph W. Carreras, CEO
Michael T. Kestner, CFO
Joseph W. Carreras, Chmn.

Phone: 216-771-6700	**Fax:** 216-574-9956
Toll-Free:	
Address: 127 Public Square, Key Ctr., Cleveland, OH 44114 US	

GROWTH PLANS/SPECIAL FEATURES:

Hilite International, Inc. is a supplier of automotive components, with manufacturing facilities in North America, Europe and Asia. The company's products include engine and transmission system components; Selective Catalytic Reduction (SCR) systems, an emission control technology that reduces fuel consumption, nitrogen oxide (NOx), carbon monoxide and other particulate matter; and valves and other mechanical parts for automotive applications. Hilite's engine products include Camphasing Adjustment Systems, as well as fully variable valvelift systems and hydraulic valves. Transmission products include components for automatic, automated manual, double clutch, continuous and variable transmissions. These components include actuators, valves, integrated solenoids, differential transmissions and electromagnetic clutches for All-Wheel Drive (AWD) systems. Hilite operates in five divisions: Hilite Dallas, based in Carrollton, Texas, which develops and produces hydraulic valves and electromagnetic clutches for AWD systems and climate control applications; the Whitehall division, based in Whitehall, Michigan, responsible for the development and production of hydraulic valves, including pulse wide modulated valves, pressure relief valves and flow control valves, and integrated solenoids and camphasing systems; the Cleveland division, the firm's headquarters and based in Cleveland, Ohio, responsible for the manufacture of engine mounts, heat shields, stamped parts, cross members and transmission mounts; Hilite International Marnaz Division, an international division, which produces machined precision parts and assemblies of mechanical parts; and Hilite International Hydraulik-Ring GmbH, another international section, which produces camphaser systems, pumps, valves, transmission controls and components, dosing units and variable valve controls. The company has three manufacturing facilities in Germany and as well as sales offices in China, South Korea and Japan.

FINANCIALS:

Sales and profits are in thousands of dollars—add 000 to get the full amount. 2009 Note: Financial information for 2009 was not available for all companies at press time.

2009 Sales: $	2009 Profits: $	**U.S. Stock Ticker: Private**
2008 Sales: $	2008 Profits: $	**Int'l Ticker:** Int'l Exchange:
2007 Sales: $145,400	2007 Profits: $	Employees:
2006 Sales: $	2006 Profits: $	Fiscal Year Ends: 6/30
2005 Sales: $	2005 Profits: $	Parent Company:

SALARIES/BENEFITS:

Pension Plan:	ESOP Stock Plan:	Profit Sharing:	Top Exec. Salary: $	Bonus: $
Savings Plan:	Stock Purch. Plan:		Second Exec. Salary: $	Bonus: $

OTHER THOUGHTS:

Apparent Women Officers or Directors:
Hot Spot for Advancement for Women/Minorities:

LOCATIONS: ("Y" = Yes)

West:	Southwest:	Midwest:	Southeast:	Northeast:	International:
	Y	Y			Y

HINO MOTOR SALES (THAILAND) LTD

www.hinothailand.com/en

Industry Group Code: 336120 **Ranks within this company's industry group:** Sales: Profits:

Vehicle Manufacturing:		Dealers:		Parts:		Service:		Finance:		Specialty:	
Cars:		Car Dealer New:		Manufacturers:		General Service:		Leasing:		Information Systems:	
Trucks:		Car Dealer Used:		Retail:		Specialty Service:		Auto Loans:		Online Marketing:	
Motorcycles:		Truck Dealer:	Y	Distributors:	Y	Oil Change:		Insurance:		Other:	
Specialty:		RV Dealer:		Tires:		Paint and Body:				Publishing:	
Buses:		Motorcycle Dealer:		Batteries:						Rental Cars/Trucks:	
RVs:		Specialty Dealer:									

TYPES OF BUSINESS:

Truck & Bus Distribution
Spare Parts Distribution

BRANDS/DIVISIONS/AFFILIATES:

Hino Motors Ltd
Series 3
Series 5
FG1JPKA
FM1JKKA
RM1ESKU
Hino Motors Manufacturing (Thailand) Ltd.

CONTACTS:

Note: Officers with more than one job title may be intentionally listed here more than once.

Takeo Saito, Pres.
Day Yingchol, Gen. Mgr.-Mktg.
Piyasak Sootaranan, Gen. Mgr.-Human Resources & Mgmt.
Sabaithip Osathanugroh, Gen. Mgr.-Admin.
Pholvut Kanchanakittikhun, Gen. Mgr.-Finance
Kimiyoshi Kawano, Exec. VP
Amnuay Pongwicharn, Sr. Managing Dir.
Picharn Angchanpen, VP
Supapong Pemsuwan, Gen. Mgr.-Spare Parts
Narongsak Phiphatsisawat, Gen. Mgr.-Inventory & Logistics

Phone: 66-2900-5000 **Fax:** 66-2900-5288
Toll-Free:
Address: 212 Moo 4 Vibhavadi-Rangsit Rd., Talad Bangkhen, Bangkok, 10210 Thailand

GROWTH PLANS/SPECIAL FEATURES:

Hino Motor Sales (Thailand) Ltd., a 98.3%-owned subsidiary of Japanese firm Hino Motors Ltd., primarily distributes Hino brand trucks in Thailand. It offers 11 different basic truck configurations and two bus models. Its smallest trucks, collectively called Series 3, are comprised of two models of small freight trucks, available in 4- or 6-wheeled configurations. The largest trucks comprise the nine models in the Series 5, and generally consist of 6-, 10- or 12-wheeled freight trucks and semi-truck tractor heads. The Series 5 line also includes the FG1JPKA and FM1JKKA, which are 6- and 10-wheeled natural gas-burning freight trucks, respectively. Its two bus models, the RM1ESKU and the slightly smaller RK8JSLA, seat approximately 44 people. The buses also belong to the Series 5 model vehicles. Many of these vehicles are produced by fellow Hino subsidiary Hino Motors Manufacturing (Thailand) Ltd. Besides new trucks, Hino Motor Sales also offers used Hino vehicles, including 4-, 6- and 10-wheeled cargo trucks, vans and dump trucks. The company's website lists current used vehicle inventory. The firm's vehicles are sold though approximately 73 third-party dealerships in Thailand, divided into six geographic regions: Northern (with 14 dealerships), Northeastern (17), Central (12), Eastern (six), Southern (12) and Bangkok and its vicinity (12). Many of these dealerships also offer auto repair services for Hino trucks, and most retail upwards of 25,000 spare parts for Hino brand vehicles, which are distributed by the company.

FINANCIALS:

Sales and profits are in thousands of dollars—add 000 to get the full amount. 2009 Note: Financial information for 2009 was not available for all companies at press time.

2009 Sales: $	2009 Profits: $	**U.S. Stock Ticker: Subsidiary**
2008 Sales: $	2008 Profits: $	**Int'l Ticker:** Int'l Exchange:
2007 Sales: $	2007 Profits: $	Employees:
2006 Sales: $	2006 Profits: $	Fiscal Year Ends:
2005 Sales: $	2005 Profits: $	Parent Company: HINO MOTORS LTD

SALARIES/BENEFITS:

Pension Plan:	ESOP Stock Plan:	Profit Sharing:	Top Exec. Salary: $	Bonus: $
Savings Plan:	Stock Purch. Plan:		Second Exec. Salary: $	Bonus: $

OTHER THOUGHTS:

Apparent Women Officers or Directors: 3
Hot Spot for Advancement for Women/Minorities: Y

LOCATIONS: ("Y" = Yes)

West:	Southwest:	Midwest:	Southeast:	Northeast:	International:
					Y

HINO MOTORS LTD

www.hino-global.com

Industry Group Code: 336120 **Ranks within this company's industry group:** Sales: 2 Profits: 4

Vehicle Manufacturing:		Dealers:		Parts:		Service:		Finance:		Specialty:	
Cars:	Y	Car Dealer New:		Manufacturers:	Y	General Service:		Leasing:		Information Systems:	
Trucks:	Y	Car Dealer Used:		Retail:		Specialty Service:		Auto Loans:		Online Marketing:	
Motorcycles:		Truck Dealer:	Y	Distributors:		Oil Change:		Insurance:		Other:	
Specialty:	Y	RV Dealer:		Tires:		Paint and Body:				Publishing:	
Buses:	Y	Motorcycle Dealer:		Batteries:						Rental Cars/Trucks:	
RVs:		Specialty Dealer:									

TYPES OF BUSINESS:

Truck & Misc. Automotive Manufacturing
Truck & Bus Sales
Commissioned Auto Manufacturing
Diesel Engine & Parts Manufacturing
Low Emissions Technology

BRANDS/DIVISIONS/AFFILIATES:

Hino Motors Manufacturing (Thailand) Ltd.
Hino 300 Series
Hino 500 Series
Hino 700 Series
Bus Chassis
Land Cruiser Prado
FJ Cruiser
Toyoace

CONTACTS: *Note: Officers with more than one job title may be intentionally listed here more than once.*

Yoshio Shirai, Pres.
Toshiki Inoue, Exec. VP
Masakazu Ichikawa, Exec. VP
Tsunehiko Fujii, Sr. Managing Dir.
Kenji Wagu, Sr. Managing Dir.
Shoji Kondo, Chmn.

Phone: 81-42-586-5111 **Fax:** 81-42-586-5229
Toll-Free:
Address: 3-1-1, Hinodai 3-chome, Hino-shi, Tokyo, 191-8660 Japan

GROWTH PLANS/SPECIAL FEATURES:

Hino Motors, Ltd., founded 1910, manufactures and markets trucks, buses, light commercial vehicles, passenger vehicles and various engines and spare parts. A consolidated subsidiary of Toyota Motor Corporation (which holds a 50% interest), Hino brings together a global network of production and distribution facilities, regional subsidiaries and specialized operations. In Japan, the company produces vehicles and engines at three plants. Its manufacturing operations in other nations include plants for producing trucks, buses and components in Thailand, Vietnam, Indonesia, China, Taiwan, Pakistan and the U.S. Hino's product lines include the Hino 300 Series light-duty trucks; the Hino 500 Series medium-duty trucks; the Hino 700 Series heavy-duty trucks; the Bus Chassis; and both automotive and industrial diesel engines. Between March 2009 and March 2010, the company sold 61,348 trucks and buses overseas, with a combined total of 87,251 domestic and overseas sales of trucks and buses. In addition to trucks and buses, the company is engaged in commissioned manufacture of vehicles and parts for Toyota Motor Corporation, including sport-utility vehicles and passenger cars such as the Land Cruiser Prado, FJ Cruiser, Dyna trucks and Toyoace commercial vehicles. In February 2010, the firm launched the Hino 300 Series Hybrid in Hong Kong. In July 2010, the company, through its wholly-owned subsidiary Hino Motors Manufacturing (Thailand) Ltd., began production of engines for the Hino 500 Series at its Bang Pakong Plant in Chon Buri Province, Thailand.

FINANCIALS: **Sales and profits are in thousands of dollars—add 000 to get the full amount. 2009 Note: Financial information for 2009 was not available for all companies at press time.**

2009 Sales: $11,574,600 | 2009 Profits: $-669,260
2008 Sales: $11,356,500 | 2008 Profits: $-656,650
2007 Sales: $12,454,600 | 2007 Profits: $201,800
2006 Sales: $11,717,800 | 2006 Profits: $182,400
2005 Sales: $10,892,400 | 2005 Profits: $261,200

U.S. Stock Ticker: HINOY
Int'l Ticker: 7205 Int'l Exchange: Tokyo-TSE
Employees: 24,492
Fiscal Year Ends: 3/31
Parent Company: TOYOTA MOTOR CORPORATION

SALARIES/BENEFITS:

Pension Plan: | ESOP Stock Plan: | Profit Sharing: | Top Exec. Salary: $ | Bonus: $
Savings Plan: | Stock Purch. Plan: | | Second Exec. Salary: $ | Bonus: $

OTHER THOUGHTS:

Apparent Women Officers or Directors:
Hot Spot for Advancement for Women/Minorities:

LOCATIONS: ("Y" = Yes)

West:	Southwest:	Midwest:	Southeast:	Northeast:	International:
		Y			Y

HOLMAN ENTERPRISES

www.holmanenterprises.com

Industry Group Code: 441110 **Ranks within this company's industry group:** Sales: Profits:

Vehicle Manufacturing:		Dealers:		Parts:		Service:		Finance:		Specialty:	
Cars:		Car Dealer New:	Y	Manufacturers:		General Service:	Y	Leasing:	Y	Information Systems:	
Trucks:		Car Dealer Used:	Y	Retail:	Y	Specialty Service:	Y	Auto Loans:		Online Marketing:	
Motorcycles:		Truck Dealer:	Y	Distributors:		Oil Change:		Insurance:		Other:	
Specialty:		RV Dealer:		Tires:		Paint and Body:	Y			Publishing:	
Buses:		Motorcycle Dealer:		Batteries:						Rental Cars/Trucks:	
RVs:		Specialty Dealer:									

TYPES OF BUSINESS:

Auto Dealers, Retail
Fleet Management Services

BRANDS/DIVISIONS/AFFILIATES:

Holman Leasing & Rental
Automotive Resources International
Reconditioned Motors & Parts
Fleet Body Equipment
Life Star Rescue, Inc
Steward Financial Services

CONTACTS: *Note: Officers with more than one job title may be intentionally listed here more than once.*

Melinda Holman, CEO
Melinda Holman, Pres.
William Cariss, VP-Dealership Oper.
Robert Campbell, VP-Finance
Melinda Holman, Chmn.

Phone: 856-663-5200	**Fax:** 856-665-3444
Toll-Free:	
Address: 7411 Maple Ave., Pennsauken, NJ 08109 US	

GROWTH PLANS/SPECIAL FEATURES:

Holman Enterprises, a family-owned company, is an automobile dealer. The company owns and operates approximately 10 dealerships in New Jersey and another 12 through its southern operations segment located in Florida. Brands sold include BMW, Cadillac, Ford, Lincoln, Mercury, Honda, Infiniti, MINI, Rolls Royce, Bentley, Saturn, Toyota, Scion, and Volvo. Services include leasing, auctions, pre-owned vehicle location and parts and service. The firm also operates pre-owned vehicle locations, leasing and parts and services centers. Holman Enterprises conducts business through a number of subsidiaries and franchises such as RMP (Reconditioned Motors & Parts); Automotive Resources International, one of the world's largest independent fleet leasing management companies, including over 2,000 fleets consisting of more than 650,000 vehicles; Holman Leasing & Rental, which offers a wide range of leasing options and rental services, with discounts for Holman customers; Life Star Rescue, Inc., which manufactures, reconditions, sells and rents new and used rescue vehicles; and Fleet Body Equipment, a designing and building subsidiary. In December 2009, the RMP franchise acquired Dealers Engine Sales. In 2010, the firm opened a new MINI dealership in Mt. Laurel, NJ, while its southern operations opened its first Audi and Infiniti dealerships. Also in 2010, the company's leasing division began operating under the name Steward Financial Services.

Holman offers its employees medical and dental insurance; a 401(k) plan; long-term disability and life insurance; a pension plan; an employee purchase plan; tuition reimbursement; and an employee assistance plan.

FINANCIALS: **Sales and profits are in thousands of dollars—add 000 to get the full amount. 2009 Note: Financial information for 2009 was not available for all companies at press time.**

2009 Sales: $	2009 Profits: $	**U.S. Stock Ticker: Private**
2008 Sales: $	2008 Profits: $	**Int'l Ticker:** Int'l Exchange:
2007 Sales: $	2007 Profits: $	Employees:
2006 Sales: $	2006 Profits: $	Fiscal Year Ends: 12/31
2005 Sales: $	2005 Profits: $	Parent Company:

SALARIES/BENEFITS:

Pension Plan: Y	ESOP Stock Plan:	Profit Sharing:	Top Exec. Salary: $	Bonus: $
Savings Plan: Y	Stock Purch. Plan: Y		Second Exec. Salary: $	Bonus: $

OTHER THOUGHTS:

Apparent Women Officers or Directors: 1
Hot Spot for Advancement for Women/Minorities:

LOCATIONS: ("Y" = Yes)

West:	Southwest:	Midwest:	Southeast:	Northeast:	International:
			Y	Y	

HOMETOWN AUTO RETAILERS INC

www.hometownautoretailers.com

Industry Group Code: 441110 **Ranks within this company's industry group:** Sales: Profits:

Vehicle Manufacturing:		Dealers:		Parts:		Service:		Finance:		Specialty:	
Cars:		Car Dealer New:	Y	Manufacturers:		General Service:	Y	Leasing:		Information Systems:	
Trucks:		Car Dealer Used:	Y	Retail:	Y	Specialty Service:		Auto Loans:	Y	Online Marketing:	
Motorcycles:		Truck Dealer:		Distributors:		Oil Change:		Insurance:		Other:	
Specialty:		RV Dealer:		Tires:		Paint and Body:	Y			Publishing:	
Buses:		Motorcycle Dealer:		Batteries:						Rental Cars/Trucks:	
RVs:		Specialty Dealer:									

TYPES OF BUSINESS:

Auto Dealers, Retail
Auto Repair
Used Car Sales
Financing Services
Auto Parts

BRANDS/DIVISIONS/AFFILIATES:

Lincoln Mercury Autocare

CONTACTS:

Note: Officers with more than one job title may be intentionally listed here more than once.

Corey E. Shaker, CEO
Corey E. Shaker, Pres.
Charles F. Schwartz, CFO
Charles F. Schwartz, Sec.
Joseph Shaker, VP-Eastern Region
Steven Shaker, VP-Northern Region
William C. Muller, Jr., VP-Southern Region

Phone: 203-756-1300	**Fax:** 203-756-1339
Toll-Free:	
Address: 1309 S. Main St., Waterbury, CT 06706 US	

GROWTH PLANS/SPECIAL FEATURES:

Hometown Auto Retailers, Inc., based in Connecticut, is an individually-owned affiliate dealership of new and used cars and light trucks, serving the U.S. with individual owners and dealerships that place classified ads on the company's web site. These ads then redirect customers to numerous online auction sites, primarily eBay Motors, where bids can be placed for a particular vehicle. The company also provides maintenance and repair services, sells replacements parts for vehicles, and provides related financing, insurance and service contracts through third party and affiliate relationships. Hometown's dealerships market approximately 75 automotive brands including Chevrolet, Chrysler, Dodge, Jeep, Ford, Mazda, Lincoln, Mercury, Nissan and Toyota. Hometown also targets a niche market through the sale of Lincoln town cars and limousines to livery car and livery fleet operators. The company operates a new Ford Motor Company concept service facility branded under the name Lincoln Mercury Autocare. This freestanding neighborhood service center provides off-dealership, fully certified maintenance and light repair of cars and trucks, offering conveniences like extended hours, comfortable customer waiting areas and quick service without prior appointment.

FINANCIALS:

Sales and profits are in thousands of dollars—add 000 to get the full amount. 2009 Note: Financial information for 2009 was not available for all companies at press time.

2009 Sales: $	2009 Profits: $	**U.S. Stock Ticker: Private**
2008 Sales: $	2008 Profits: $	**Int'l Ticker:** Int'l Exchange:
2007 Sales: $	2007 Profits: $	Employees:
2006 Sales: $	2006 Profits: $	Fiscal Year Ends: 12/31
2005 Sales: $233,080	2005 Profits: $1,292	Parent Company:

SALARIES/BENEFITS:

Pension Plan:	ESOP Stock Plan:	Profit Sharing:	Top Exec. Salary: $	Bonus: $
Savings Plan: Y	Stock Purch. Plan:		Second Exec. Salary: $	Bonus: $

OTHER THOUGHTS:

Apparent Women Officers or Directors:
Hot Spot for Advancement for Women/Minorities:

LOCATIONS: ("Y" = Yes)

West:	Southwest:	Midwest:	Southeast:	Northeast:	International:
				Y	

HONDA MOTOR CO LTD

world.honda.com

Industry Group Code: 33611 **Ranks within this company's industry group:** Sales: 6 Profits: 5

Vehicle Manufacturing:		Dealers:		Parts:		Service:		Finance:		Specialty:	
Cars:	Y	Car Dealer New:		Manufacturers:	Y	General Service:		Leasing:		Information Systems:	
Trucks:		Car Dealer Used:		Retail:		Specialty Service:		Auto Loans:		Online Marketing:	
Motorcycles:	Y	Truck Dealer:		Distributors:		Oil Change:		Insurance:		Other:	
Specialty:	Y	RV Dealer:		Tires:		Paint and Body:				Publishing:	
Buses:		Motorcycle Dealer:		Batteries:						Rental Cars/Trucks:	
RVs:		Specialty Dealer:									

TYPES OF BUSINESS:

Automobile Manufacturing
Motorcycles
ATVs & Personal Watercraft
Generators
Marine Engines
Lawn & Garden Equipment
Fuel Cell & Hybrid Vehicles
Airplanes

BRANDS/DIVISIONS/AFFILIATES:

Odyssey
Insight Hybrid
Fit
Honda Life
Acura
CR-V
Honda Motorcycle and Scooter India (Prvt.) Ltd.
Civic

CONTACTS: *Note: Officers with more than one job title may be intentionally listed here more than once.*

Takanobu Ito, CEO
Takanobu Ito, Pres.
Hiroshi Kobayashi, COO-Japanese Sales Oper.
Akio Hamada, Gen. Supervisor-Info. Systems
Akio Hamada, COO-Prod. Oper.
Tsuneo Tanai, COO-Auto Oper.
Hiroshi Soda, COO-Bus. Support Oper.
Hiroshi Soda, Gen. Supervisor-Corp. Comm.
Koichi Kondo, Compliance Officer/Exec. VP
Tetsuo Iwamura, Pres., American Honda Motor Co., Inc.
Hiroyuki Yamada, COO-Customer Service Oper.
Takuji Yamada, COO-Power Prod. Oper.
Satoshi Aoki, Chmn.
Sho Minekawa, COO-Regional Oper., Latin America
Masaya Yamashita, COO-Purchasing Oper.

Phone: 81-3-3423-1111 **Fax:**
Toll-Free:
Address: 1-1, 2-chome, Minami-Aoyama, Minato-ku, Tokyo, 107-8556 Japan

GROWTH PLANS/SPECIAL FEATURES:

Honda Motor Co., Ltd., founded in 1948, develops, produces and manufactures a variety of motor products, ranging from small general-purpose engines and scooters to specialty sports cars. With a network of 22 manufacturing facilities, Honda operates a network of 112 Japanese subsidiaries and 278 overseas subsidiaries. Honda operates through four segments: motorcycles, automobiles, financial services and power products/other. Through its motorcycle unit, Honda produces sport, business and commuter model bikes, which utilize air- or water-cooled gasoline engines with 1-6 cylinders, manufactured by the company. This segment also includes the production of ATVs, personal watercraft and multi utility vehicles (MUVs). Within the automotive segment, the firm manufactures vehicles under the Acura and Honda trademarks. Honda models include the Civic, a sub-compact car; the Accord, an intermediate passenger car; the Fit, a compact passenger car; the Odyssey, a minivan; the Insight Hybrid car; and the CR-V, an SUV. Through the financial services segment, the company offers financial services to its customers and dealers through finance subsidiaries in countries including Japan, the U.S., Canada, the U.K., Germany, Brazil and Thailand. This segment's services include retail lending, leasing to customers and wholesale financing to dealers. Through its power products unit, Honda produces tillers, portable generators, general purpose engines, grass cutters, outboard marine engines, water pumps, snow throwers, power carriers, power sprayers, lawn mowers and lawn tractors. In March 2010, the company, through its wholly-owned subsidiary Honda Motorcycle and Scooter India (Prvt.) Ltd., announced plans to build a second motorcycle production and sales subsidiary in India.

FINANCIALS: **Sales and profits are in thousands of dollars—add 000 to get the full amount. 2009 Note: Financial information for 2009 was not available for all companies at press time.**

2009 Sales: $101,916,000	2009 Profits: $1,395,000	**U.S. Stock Ticker: HMC**
2008 Sales: $119,801,000	2008 Profits: $5,989,000	**Int'l Ticker: 7267** Int'l Exchange: Tokyo-TSE
2007 Sales: $94,240,700	2007 Profits: $5,034,700	Employees: 181,876
2006 Sales: $84,218,000	2006 Profits: $5,074,800	Fiscal Year Ends: 3/31
2005 Sales: $80,705,000	2005 Profits: $4,536,000	Parent Company:

SALARIES/BENEFITS:

Pension Plan: Y	ESOP Stock Plan:	Profit Sharing:	Top Exec. Salary: $	Bonus: $
Savings Plan:	Stock Purch. Plan:		Second Exec. Salary: $	Bonus: $

OTHER THOUGHTS:

Apparent Women Officers or Directors:
Hot Spot for Advancement for Women/Minorities:

LOCATIONS: ("Y" = Yes)

West:	Southwest:	Midwest:	Southeast:	Northeast:	International:
Y	Y	Y	Y	Y	Y

HONDA OF AMERICA MFG INC

www.ohio.honda.com

Industry Group Code: 33611 **Ranks within this company's industry group:** Sales: Profits:

Vehicle Manufacturing:		**Dealers:**		**Parts:**		**Service:**		**Finance:**		**Specialty:**	
Cars:	Y	Car Dealer New:		Manufacturers:	Y	General Service:		Leasing:		Information Systems:	
Trucks:	Y	Car Dealer Used:		Retail:		Specialty Service:		Auto Loans:		Online Marketing:	
Motorcycles:	Y	Truck Dealer:		Distributors:	Y	Oil Change:		Insurance:		Other:	
Specialty:		RV Dealer:		Tires:		Paint and Body:				Publishing:	
Buses:		Motorcycle Dealer:		Batteries:						Rental Cars/Trucks:	
RVs:		Specialty Dealer:									

TYPES OF BUSINESS:

Automobile Manufacturing
Engine & Parts Manufacturing
Motorcycle Manufacturing

BRANDS/DIVISIONS/AFFILIATES:

Honda Motor Co Ltd
Accord
Acura
Civic
CR-V
Accord Crosstour
Honda of Canada Mfg Inc
Midwest Express Inc

CONTACTS:

Note: Officers with more than one job title may be intentionally listed here more than once.

Hidenobu Iwata, CEO
Hidenobu Iwata, Pres.
Makoto Makino, Pres., Honda Eng. North America
Mike Wallace, Mgr.-Honda MRO Purchasing

Phone: 937-642-5000	**Fax:** 937-644-6583
Toll-Free:	
Address: 24000 Honda Pkwy., Marysville, OH 43040-9251 US	

GROWTH PLANS/SPECIAL FEATURES:

Honda of America Manufacturing, Inc. (HAM), a subsidiary of Honda Motor Co., Ltd., manufactures engines, transmissions, motorcycles, cars and light trucks primarily in five Ohio manufacturing plants for the North American market. The firm's main plants are in Marysville, Anna and East Liberty, Ohio. The Marysville auto plant builds approximately 440,000 vehicles per year, including more than 90% of Honda Accord Sedans sold in the U.S. The Anna engine plant produces engine blocks and heads, camshafts, crankshafts, driveshafts, cylinder sleeves and brakes, producing more than 1.1 million V-6 and four-cylinder engines annually. This plant also performs engine testing. The East Liberty auto plant produces Accord Crosstour, Honda Element and CR-V vehicles. The 1.9 million square foot plant produces 240,000 cars and light trucks annually, as well as exporting stamped parts to Honda of Canada Manufacturing, Inc. for the production of its Civic models. The Ohio plants produce the Accord Coupe and Sedan; the Acura TL and RDX; and the CR-V. Honda Motor Co. has other subsidiaries and operations based in Ohio, including research and development and engineering facilities and a transmission manufacturing plant. The company has additional manufacturing operations in Indiana, Alabama, Georgia, North Carolina and South Carolina. The company's Honda plants in Ohio have produced more than 13 million automobiles, 1 million motorcycles, 2 million all-terrain vehicles (ATVs), 17 million engines and nearly 13 million automatic transmissions. In February 2010, the company formed a new material management Center. The goal of the new center is to consolidate parts on-site. Midwest Express, Inc. will handle the operations. This will eliminate the use of shuttle trucks for transport of parts by 130 loads per day.

Employees are offered medical, dental, vision and prescription drug insurance; a post-retirement medical plan; education reimbursement; relocation assistance; credit union membership; and a college savings program.

FINANCIALS:

Sales and profits are in thousands of dollars—add 000 to get the full amount. 2009 Note: Financial information for 2009 was not available for all companies at press time.

2009 Sales: $	2009 Profits: $	**U.S. Stock Ticker: Subsidiary**
2008 Sales: $	2008 Profits: $	**Int'l Ticker:** Int'l Exchange:
2007 Sales: $1,889,200	2007 Profits: $	Employees:
2006 Sales: $	2006 Profits: $	Fiscal Year Ends: 3/31
2005 Sales: $	2005 Profits: $	Parent Company: HONDA MOTOR CO LTD

SALARIES/BENEFITS:

Pension Plan: Y	ESOP Stock Plan:	Profit Sharing:	Top Exec. Salary: $	Bonus: $
Savings Plan: Y	Stock Purch. Plan: Y		Second Exec. Salary: $	Bonus: $

OTHER THOUGHTS:

Apparent Women Officers or Directors:
Hot Spot for Advancement for Women/Minorities:

LOCATIONS: ("Y" = Yes)

West:	Southwest:	Midwest:	Southeast:	Northeast:	International:
		Y	Y	Y	

HYUNDAI MOBIS CO LTD

www.mobis.co.kr

Industry Group Code: 3363 **Ranks within this company's industry group:** Sales: 6 Profits: 2

Vehicle Manufacturing:		**Dealers:**		**Parts:**		**Service:**		**Finance:**		**Specialty:**	
Cars:		Car Dealer New:		Manufacturers:	Y	General Service:		Leasing:		Information Systems:	
Trucks:		Car Dealer Used:		Retail:		Specialty Service:		Auto Loans:		Online Marketing:	
Motorcycles:		Truck Dealer:		Distributors:		Oil Change:		Insurance:		Other:	
Specialty:		RV Dealer:		Tires:		Paint and Body:				Publishing:	
Buses:		Motorcycle Dealer:		Batteries:						Rental Cars/Trucks:	
RVs:		Specialty Dealer:									

TYPES OF BUSINESS:

Automotive Parts Manufacturing
Automotive Parts Development
Automotive Parts Testing

BRANDS/DIVISIONS/AFFILIATES:

Hyundai Motor Company
Kia Motors Corporation
Mobis Technical Research Institute

CONTACTS:

Note: Officers with more than one job title may be intentionally listed here more than once.

Suk-soo Chung, Co-CEO
Seok-Su Jung, Co-Pres./Co-CEO
Dong Hui Hong, VP-Tech. Research
Ui Seon Jung, Co-Pres.
Nam Gi Jung, VP
Chae Yeong Yim, VP
Yeol Heon Hwang, VP
Mong Gu Jung, Chmn./Co-CEO

Phone: 82-2-2018-5114 **Fax:** 82-2-2018-6000
Toll-Free:
Address: Rodamco Tower, 679-4 Yeoksam-dong, Gangnam-gu, Seoul, 135-977 Korea

GROWTH PLANS/SPECIAL FEATURES:

Hyundai Mobis Co., Ltd. (Mobis) is a leading Korean automotive parts manufacturer. The company operates through four divisions: Module; auto parts; quality; and procurement and development. Mobis' module division manufactures chassis, cockpit and front-end modules, with a focus on reducing weight, number of parts and cost, along with convenient assembly and efficient inventory management. In addition to manufacturing basic modules and systems, including CBS (conventional brake system), steering columns, oil pumps, carriers and bumpers, the firm designs and manufactures electronic car control systems including; ESCs (electronic control stability), ABS (antilock brake systems), TCS (traction control systems), advanced airbag systems and MDPS (motor driven power steering). Mobis' auto parts division supplies service parts for all of Hyundai's and Kia's models; totaling 890,000 parts for 143 car models. The firm also supplies LED lamps to BMW. Its quality division provides quality assurance services for all of the company's parts. The firm's procurement and development division develops module parts and supplies parts, production equipment and materials to the module business division. Mobis Technical Research Institute conducts research and development activities in the areas of driver, chassis and front-end module development; safety, brake and air suspension systems development; and development of metal and polymer materials. The Research Institute also works on the casting, forging, sheet stamping, hydro forming and extrusion of lightweight and magnesium parts; and high-tension, high-strength steel parts, including galvanized steel and dual phase ferrite-bainite steel. In November 2009, the firm began a joint venture with LG Chem to develop environmentally-friendly lithium-ion battery packs for use in future Hyundai and Kia hybrid and electric automobiles. The joint venture will operate from Mobis' main hybrid vehicle parts plant. In April 2010, Mobis and KEC Corp. entered a joint development contract for producing power modules in new hybrid cars.

FINANCIALS:

Sales and profits are in thousands of dollars—add 000 to get the full amount. 2009 Note: Financial information for 2009 was not available for all companies at press time.

2009 Sales: $14,421,900	2009 Profits: $1,311,850	**U.S. Stock Ticker:**
2008 Sales: $7,408,730	2008 Profits: $861,530	**Int'l Ticker: 012330** Int'l Exchange: Seoul-KRX
2007 Sales: $6,249,310	2007 Profits: $571,630	Employees:
2006 Sales: $6,011,670	2006 Profits: $505,450	Fiscal Year Ends:
2005 Sales: $	2005 Profits: $	Parent Company:

SALARIES/BENEFITS:

Pension Plan:	ESOP Stock Plan:	Profit Sharing:	Top Exec. Salary: $	Bonus: $
Savings Plan:	Stock Purch. Plan:		Second Exec. Salary: $	Bonus: $

OTHER THOUGHTS:

Apparent Women Officers or Directors:
Hot Spot for Advancement for Women/Minorities:

LOCATIONS: ("Y" = Yes)

West:	Southwest:	Midwest:	Southeast:	Northeast:	International:
			Y	Y	Y

HYUNDAI MOTOR AMERICA

www.hyundaiusa.com

Industry Group Code: 33611 **Ranks within this company's industry group:** Sales: Profits:

Vehicle Manufacturing:		Dealers:		Parts:		Service:		Finance:		Specialty:	
Cars:	Y	Car Dealer New:		Manufacturers:		General Service:		Leasing:		Information Systems:	
Trucks:		Car Dealer Used:		Retail:		Specialty Service:		Auto Loans:		Online Marketing:	
Motorcycles:		Truck Dealer:		Distributors:		Oil Change:		Insurance:		Other:	Y
Specialty:		RV Dealer:		Tires:		Paint and Body:				Publishing:	
Buses:		Motorcycle Dealer:		Batteries:						Rental Cars/Trucks:	
RVs:		Specialty Dealer:									

TYPES OF BUSINESS:

Automobile Distribution

BRANDS/DIVISIONS/AFFILIATES:

Hyundai Motor Company
Elantra
Sonata
Azera
Santa Fe
Tiburon
Accent
Qarmaq

CONTACTS:

Note: Officers with more than one job title may be intentionally listed here more than once.

John Krafcik, CEO
John Krafcik, Pres.
Chris Perry, VP-Mktg.
Kathy Parker, VP-Human Resources & Community Rel.
Michael J. O'Brien, VP-Prod. & Corp. Planning
Erwin Raphael, Dir.-Service Eng. & Prod. Quality
Sam Brnovich, Exec. Dir.-Retail Oper.
Frank Ferrara, Exec. VP-Corp. Planning & Customer Satisfaction
Christopher Hosford, Exec. Dir.-Corp. Comm.
Sukjoon Won, Pres./CEO-Hyundai Capital America
David L. Zuchowski, VP-National Sales
Patricia Romero, Mgr.-National Advertising
Dave Zuchowski, VP-Sales

Phone: 714-965-3000 **Fax:** 801-736-3561
Toll-Free: 800-633-5151
Address: 10550 Talbert Ave., Fountain Valley, CA 92708-6031 US

GROWTH PLANS/SPECIAL FEATURES:

Hyundai Motor America is the U.S. subsidiary of Hyundai Motor Company of Korea. It is responsible for the distribution of Hyundai vehicles nationwide. The company sells Hyundai models such as the Accent, Elantra, Sonata, Azera, Tiburon, Tucson, Santa Fe, Veracruz and Entourage. In addition, the firm has several concept cars in development, including the I-Blue, Nuvis, Qarmaq and Veloster. Hyundai Motor America supports over 800 U.S. Hyundai dealers through its manufacturing facilities in Michigan, Alabama and California. In addition, the parent company has invested millions of dollars in the American market through its manufacturing, engineering and design and research facilities situated nationwide. Hyundai Motor America operates one of the most technologically advanced manufacturing facilities in the world out of Alabama, comprising over 2 million square-feet, with 250 welding robots and the capability to produce approximately 300,000 vehicles annually. Hyundai Motor America's web site possesses shopping tools that allow customer to build their own car, receive quotes, schedule test drives, locate dealers and receive trade-in appraisals. The firm's newest vehicle models include the Elantra Touring, Genesis and Genesis Coupe. In August 2009, Hyundai Motor America announced plans to sell its parent firm's flagship sedan, which is sold under the Equus brand in Korea, in the U.S. starting in late 2010.

Hyundai Motor America offers its employees medical, dental and vision coverage; life, business travel and AD&D insurance; flexible spending accounts; a 401(k); dependent and long-term care programs; an employee assistance program; employee discounts; corporate on-site fitness centers and convenience stores with laundry and tailoring services; education reimbursement; training, mentoring and B.A. and M.B.A. degree programs; and relocation assistance.

FINANCIALS:

Sales and profits are in thousands of dollars—add 000 to get the full amount. 2009 Note: Financial information for 2009 was not available for all companies at press time.

2009 Sales: $	2009 Profits: $	**U.S. Stock Ticker: Subsidiary**
2008 Sales: $	2008 Profits: $	**Int'l Ticker:** Int'l Exchange:
2007 Sales: $	2007 Profits: $	Employees:
2006 Sales: $	2006 Profits: $	Fiscal Year Ends: 12/31
2005 Sales: $	2005 Profits: $	Parent Company: HYUNDAI MOTOR COMPANY

SALARIES/BENEFITS:

Pension Plan:	ESOP Stock Plan:	Profit Sharing:	Top Exec. Salary: $	Bonus: $
Savings Plan: Y	Stock Purch. Plan:		Second Exec. Salary: $	Bonus: $

OTHER THOUGHTS:

Apparent Women Officers or Directors: 2
Hot Spot for Advancement for Women/Minorities:

LOCATIONS: ("Y" = Yes)

West:	Southwest:	Midwest:	Southeast:	Northeast:	International:
Y	Y	Y	Y	Y	

Note: Financial information, benefits and other data can change quickly and may vary from those stated here.

HYUNDAI MOTOR COMPANY

worldwide.hyundai.com

Industry Group Code: 33611 **Ranks within this company's industry group:** Sales: 8 Profits: 3

Vehicle Manufacturing:		Dealers:		Parts:		Service:		Finance:		Specialty:	
Cars:	Y	Car Dealer New:		Manufacturers:	Y	General Service:		Leasing:		Information Systems:	
Trucks:	Y	Car Dealer Used:		Retail:		Specialty Service:		Auto Loans:	Y	Online Marketing:	
Motorcycles:		Truck Dealer:		Distributors:		Oil Change:		Insurance:		Other:	
Specialty:		RV Dealer:		Tires:		Paint and Body:				Publishing:	
Buses:	Y	Motorcycle Dealer:		Batteries:						Rental Cars/Trucks:	
RVs:		Specialty Dealer:									

TYPES OF BUSINESS:

Automobile Manufacturing
Trucks
Buses
Light Commercial Vehicles
Machine Tools
Factory Automation Equipment
Material Handling Equipment
Specialty Vehicle Manufacturing

BRANDS/DIVISIONS/AFFILIATES:

Accent
Sonata
Elantra
Genesis
Hyundai Canada
Kia Motors Corporation
Hyundai Motor America
Hyundai Rotem Company

CONTACTS: *Note: Officers with more than one job title may be intentionally listed here more than once.*

Mong-koo Chung, Co-CEO
Yang Seung Seok, Co-CEO
Yang Seung Seok, Pres., Sales
Ho Don Kang, Co-CEO
Kim Yeong Guk, VP
Yim Heung Su, VP
Baek Hyo Heum, VP
Mong-koo Chung, Chmn.

Phone: 82-2-3464-1114 **Fax:** 82-2-3464-8719
Toll-Free:
Address: 231 Yangjae-dong, Seocho-gu, Seoul, 137-938 Korea

GROWTH PLANS/SPECIAL FEATURES:

Hyundai Motor Company, headquartered in South Korea, is one of the world's leading automobile manufacturers. The firm designs and manufactures passenger cars; recreational vehicles; commercial vehicles, including trucks, buses and tractors; and specialty vehicles, including crane trucks, refrigerated vans and tank trucks for fuel and water transport. Popular export models include the Accent, a sub-compact; the Sonata, a mid-size sedan; the Elantra, a compact sedan; the Santa Fe SUV; and the Genesis, a luxury sedan. Light commercial vehicles include the H-1 cargo van, the H100 Truck and a variety of mini buses. Heavy commercial vehicles include small HD65/72/78 trucks, medium-sized HD120 trucks and busses, as well as cargo, dump, mixer and tractor trucks. Hyundai also makes machine tools for factory automation and material handling and owns approximately 39% of Kia Motors Corporation. Subsidiary Hyundai Motor America oversees U.S. operations, including primary facilities in Alabama, Michigan and California. The subsidiary also distributes Hyundai vehicles in the U.S., which are sold and serviced by more than 600 dealerships. In addition to its U.S. operations, the firm has other overseas plants in Europe, India and China, as well as research and development centers in North America, Japan and Europe. In November 2009, the firm announced plans to invest an initial $173 million towards the development of a small passenger car for the Indian market. In December 2009, Hyundai announced a new joint venture in China, with Baotou Bei Ben Heavy-Duty Truck Co., Ltd., to focus on the sale of commercial vehicles. In March 2010, the company announced that, in cooperation with Spain-based Santander Consumer Finance, it was establishing a new firm, Hyundai Capital Germany GmbH, to offer automotive financing services to customers in Europe.

Hyundai offers employee benefits including medical, dental and vision coverage; life and disability insurance; a 401(k) plan; and an employee assistance program.

FINANCIALS: **Sales and profits are in thousands of dollars—add 000 to get the full amount. 2009 Note: Financial information for 2009 was not available for all companies at press time.**

2009 Sales: $81,951,000	2009 Profits: $2,664,240	**U.S. Stock Ticker: HYMTF.PK**
2008 Sales: $60,240,800	2008 Profits: $648,030	**Int'l Ticker: 005380** Int'l Exchange: Seoul-KRX
2007 Sales: $68,740,000	2007 Profits: $1,360,000	Employees:
2006 Sales: $68,468,000	2006 Profits: $1,355,000	Fiscal Year Ends: 12/31
2005 Sales: $46,358,200	2005 Profits: $1,472,600	Parent Company:

SALARIES/BENEFITS:

Pension Plan:	ESOP Stock Plan:	Profit Sharing:	Top Exec. Salary: $	Bonus: $
Savings Plan: Y	Stock Purch. Plan:		Second Exec. Salary: $	Bonus: $

OTHER THOUGHTS:

Apparent Women Officers or Directors:
Hot Spot for Advancement for Women/Minorities:

LOCATIONS: ("Y" = Yes)

West:	Southwest:	Midwest:	Southeast:	Northeast:	International:
Y		Y	Y	Y	Y

INCHCAPE PLC

www.inchcape.com

Industry Group Code: 441110 **Ranks within this company's industry group:** Sales: 3 Profits: 2

Vehicle Manufacturing:		Dealers:		Parts:		Service:		Finance:		Specialty:	
Cars:		Car Dealer New:	Y	Manufacturers:		General Service:		Leasing:	Y	Information Systems:	
Trucks:		Car Dealer Used:	Y	Retail:		Specialty Service:		Auto Loans:	Y	Online Marketing:	Y
Motorcycles:		Truck Dealer:		Distributors:	Y	Oil Change:		Insurance:	Y	Other:	Y
Specialty:		RV Dealer:		Tires:		Paint and Body:				Publishing:	
Buses:		Motorcycle Dealer:		Batteries:						Rental Cars/Trucks:	
RVs:		Specialty Dealer:									

TYPES OF BUSINESS:

Auto Dealers, Retail
Import & Distribution Services
Financial Services
Logistics
Refurbishment
e-Commerce

BRANDS/DIVISIONS/AFFILIATES:

Inchcape Retail
Inchcape Fleet Solutions
Inchcape Automotive Retail
Subaru Australia/New Zealand

CONTACTS:

Note: Officers with more than one job title may be intentionally listed here more than once.

Andre Lacroix, CEO
Tony George, Group Dir.-Human Resources
Claire Chapman, General Counsel/Group Company Sec.
Dale Butcher, Group Dir.-Bus. Dev.
Ken Lee, Group Dir.-Comm.
John McConnell, Group Dir.-Finance
Connor McCormack, CEO-Inchcape, U.K.
Koh Ching Hong, Managing Dir.-Inchcape, South Asia
Spencer Lock, CEO-Inchcape, Australaisa
George Ashford, CEO-Toyota Belgium
Ken Hanna, Chmn.
Patrick S. Lee, Managing Dir.-Inchcape, North Asia
Martin Taylor, CEO-Europe Dist., Africa & South America

Phone: 44-20-7546-0022 **Fax:** 44-20-7546-0010
Toll-Free:
Address: 22A St. James's Sq., London, SW1Y 5LP UK

GROWTH PLANS/SPECIAL FEATURES:

Inchcape plc is an international automotive services company. Its operations include distribution and auto dealerships. The firm's primary markets are Australia, Europe, Hong Kong, Singapore, the U.K. and Russia. The company has additional operations in China, Poland, Brunei, Chile, Ethiopia, Guam, New Zealand, Peru and Saipan. Inchcape operates two businesses in the U.K., Inchcape Retail and Inchcape Fleet Solutions. Inchcape Retail is a leading U.K. dealer, with 128 franchised retail centers, focusing its operations on premium brands, including Audi, BMW/MINI, Honda, Mercedes-Benz, Porsche, Toyota/Lexus and Volkswagen. Inchcape Fleet Solutions provides management and leasing services. Sales to the U.K. represented approximately 37% of the group's total in 2009. In Australia, the company operates three businesses: Inchcape Automotive Retail, with over 20 retail centers; Subaru Australia/New Zealand, retailing roughly 7,000 new and used vehicles annually; and AutoNexus, a parts and vehicle logistics business. Sales from this region were 14% of the total. The European region's sales, composed of markets in Belgium, Luxembourg, Greece and Finland, represented 18% of the group's total. In Europe, the firm sells and distributes through its 21 owned retail centers Toyota and Lexus in Belgium and Greece; Jaguar, Toyota and Lexus in Luxembourg; and in Finland Jaguar, Land Rover and Mazda. The company's business in South Asia, where it has 10 franchise locations and distributes Toyota, Lexus, HinoTrucks and Suzuki, comprised 10% of its total sales. In North Asia, Inchcape has 21 franchised retail centers, selling Toyota, Lexus, HinoTrucks, Daihatsu, Jaguar, Chevrolet, Scion and Mazda. This region generated roughly 6% of the firm's 2009 total sales.

FINANCIALS:

Sales and profits are in thousands of dollars—add 000 to get the full amount. 2009 Note: Financial information for 2009 was not available for all companies at press time.

2009 Sales: $8,660,540	2009 Profits: $147,350	**U.S. Stock Ticker:**
2008 Sales: $10,331,680	2008 Profits: $84,830	**Int'l Ticker: INCH** Int'l Exchange: London-LSE
2007 Sales: $9,996,630	2007 Profits: $291,150	Employees: 13,677
2006 Sales: $9,481,800	2006 Profits: $346,200	Fiscal Year Ends: 12/31
2005 Sales: $7,881,110	2005 Profits: $228,982	Parent Company:

SALARIES/BENEFITS:

Pension Plan:	ESOP Stock Plan:	Profit Sharing:	Top Exec. Salary: $1,154,706	Bonus: $1,385,653
Savings Plan:	Stock Purch. Plan:		Second Exec. Salary: $343,664	Bonus: $343,664

OTHER THOUGHTS:

Apparent Women Officers or Directors: 2
Hot Spot for Advancement for Women/Minorities: Y

LOCATIONS: ("Y" = Yes)

West:	Southwest:	Midwest:	Southeast:	Northeast:	International:
					Y

INERGY AUTOMOTIVE

www.inergyautomotive.com

Industry Group Code: 3363 **Ranks within this company's industry group:** Sales: Profits:

Vehicle Manufacturing:		**Dealers:**		**Parts:**		**Service:**		**Finance:**		**Specialty:**	
Cars:		Car Dealer New:		Manufacturers:	Y	General Service:		Leasing:		Information Systems:	
Trucks:		Car Dealer Used:		Retail:		Specialty Service:		Auto Loans:		Online Marketing:	
Motorcycles:		Truck Dealer:		Distributors:		Oil Change:		Insurance:		Other:	
Specialty:		RV Dealer:		Tires:		Paint and Body:				Publishing:	
Buses:		Motorcycle Dealer:		Batteries:						Rental Cars/Trucks:	
RVs:		Specialty Dealer:									

TYPES OF BUSINESS:

Automotive Fuel Systems
Diesel Particulate Filters
Selective Catalytic Reduction Systems

BRANDS/DIVISIONS/AFFILIATES:

Plastic Omnium
Solvay
CAPLESS

CONTACTS: *Note: Officers with more than one job title may be intentionally listed here more than once.*

Pierre Lecocq, CEO
Jean-Francois Berard, VP-Mktg.
Eric Constant, VP-Human Resources & Internal Comm.
Jean-Francois Berard, VP-R&D
Jean-Francois Berard, VP-Strategy
Eric Constant, VP-Corp. Affairs
Laure Hauseux, VP-Finance
Gerd Behnstedt, VP-Sales
Jorge Santos, VP-Quality
Mark Sullivan, VP-North America
Jan Van Den Oetelaar, VP-Europe
Claude Clement, VP-Asia
Hans Georg Malner, VP-Purchasing

Phone: 331-5602-2121 **Fax:** 331-4526-1151
Toll-Free:
Address: 15-25 Blvd. de l'Amiral Bruix, Paris, 75016 France

GROWTH PLANS/SPECIAL FEATURES:

Inergy Automotive Systems is a joint venture between Plastic Omnium and Solvay SA that designs and manufactures automotive fuel systems. The company develops innovative systems that store, handle, deliver and regulate energy in automotive vehicles. It accomplishes this through its expertise in polymer technology, industrial processes and systems architecture. The Inergy system includes a fuel tank, fuel-filler neck, on-board refueling vapor recovery system, fuel pump, fuel delivery module, vapor canister, on-board diagnostic sensor, fuel-level sensor, fuel lines, wiring harness and roll-over valves. The company has also developed CAPLESS, a refueling system that involves no fuel tank cap. The fuel-delivery systems are designed for OEMs (original equipment manufacturers) such as Toyota, General Motors, Nissan, BMW, Volkswagen, DaimlerChrysler and Peugeot. The company designs components, systems and processes for customers who need to comply with technical and environmental demands such as partial zero emissions vehicle (PZEV), reduced carbon dioxide emissions, low emissions vehicle (LEV) II and zero emissions vehicles (ZEV). Systems are designed for recycling and adapted to process alternative fuels. The company has 22 facilities in 17 countries. Headquartered in Paris, Inergy has four plant locations in France, two in Spain, two in the U.S. and other locations in Mexico, Canada, Africa, Asia, Europe and South America. Europe and South Africa account for approximately 56% of Inergy Automotive's sales; North America, 24%; Asia, 15%; and South America, 5%.

FINANCIALS: **Sales and profits are in thousands of dollars—add 000 to get the full amount. 2009 Note: Financial information for 2009 was not available for all companies at press time.**

2009 Sales: $	2009 Profits: $	**U.S. Stock Ticker: Joint Venture**
2008 Sales: $	2008 Profits: $	**Int'l Ticker:** Int'l Exchange:
2007 Sales: $	2007 Profits: $	Employees:
2006 Sales: $	2006 Profits: $	Fiscal Year Ends: 12/31
2005 Sales: $	2005 Profits: $	Parent Company:

SALARIES/BENEFITS:

Pension Plan:	ESOP Stock Plan:	Profit Sharing:	Top Exec. Salary: $	Bonus: $
Savings Plan:	Stock Purch. Plan:		Second Exec. Salary: $	Bonus: $

OTHER THOUGHTS:

Apparent Women Officers or Directors: 1
Hot Spot for Advancement for Women/Minorities:

LOCATIONS: ("Y" = Yes)

West:	Southwest:	Midwest:	Southeast:	Northeast:	International:
				Y	Y

INGERSOLL-RAND PLC

company.ingersollrand.com

Industry Group Code: 3334 **Ranks within this company's industry group:** Sales: 1 Profits: 1

Vehicle Manufacturing:		**Dealers:**		**Parts:**		**Service:**		**Finance:**		**Specialty:**	
Cars:		Car Dealer New:		Manufacturers:	Y	General Service:		Leasing:		Information Systems:	
Trucks:		Car Dealer Used:		Retail:		Specialty Service:		Auto Loans:		Online Marketing:	
Motorcycles:		Truck Dealer:		Distributors:		Oil Change:		Insurance:		Other:	Y
Specialty:	Y	RV Dealer:		Tires:		Paint and Body:				Publishing:	
Buses:		Motorcycle Dealer:		Batteries:						Rental Cars/Trucks:	
RVs:		Specialty Dealer:									

TYPES OF BUSINESS:

Refrigeration Systems & Controls
Heating, Ventilation & Air Conditioning (HVAC) Systems
Stationary & Mobile Food Refrigeration Systems
Industrial Products-Compressed Air Systems
Golf Carts & Utility Vehicles
Security Products-Doors & Locks
Electronic & Biometric Access Control Systems & Software
Time, Attendance & Personnel Scheduling Systems

BRANDS/DIVISIONS/AFFILIATES:

Hussman
Thermo King
Trane
American Standard
Schlage
Club Car
CISA
Von Duprin

CONTACTS: *Note: Officers with more than one job title may be intentionally listed here more than once.*

Michael W. Lamach, CEO
Michael W. Lamach, Pres.
Steven R. Shawley, CFO/Sr. VP
Marcia J. Avedon, Sr. VP-Human Resources
Patricia Nachtigal, General Counsel/Sr. VP
Todd Wyman, Sr. VP-Global Oper.
Marcia J. Avedon, Sr. VP-Comm.
Richard W. Randall, VP-Finance
Didier Teirlinck, Sr. VP/Pres., Climate Solutions Sector
Robert G. Zafari, Pres., Industrial Tech. Sector
John W. Conover IV, Sr. VP/Pres., Security Tech. Sector
Steven B. Hochhauser, Sr. VP/Pres., Residential Solutions
Michael W. Lamach, Chmn.
Jeff Song, Pres., Ingersoll Rand China
Todd Wyman, Sr. VP-Integrated Supply Chain

Phone: 353-01-8707400	**Fax:**
Toll-Free:	
Address: 170/175 Lakeview Dr., Airside Business Park, Swords, UK	

GROWTH PLANS/SPECIAL FEATURES:

Ingersoll-Rand plc primarily manufactures heating and cooling systems and industrial products. It operates in four segments: climate solutions; residential solutions; industrial technologies; and security technologies. The climate solutions segment delivers energy-efficient refrigeration and Heating, Ventilation and Air Conditioning (HVAC) solutions. It offers customers a broad range of products, services and solutions to manage controlled temperature environments. It includes the Hussman, Thermo King and Trane brands. The residential solutions segment offers customers products, services and solutions including mechanical and electronic locks, energy-efficient HVAC systems, indoor air quality solutions, advanced controls, portable security systems and remote home management. Its brands include American Standard, Schlage and Trane. The industrial technologies segment's products include compressed air systems, tools, pumps, fluid handling systems, environmentally friendly micro turbines and golf and utility vehicles. Its primary brands are Ingersoll-Rand and Club Car. Lastly, the security technologies segment includes electronic and biometric access control systems and software; locks and locksets; door closers, exit devices, steel doors and frames; and portable security devices. It also offers time, attendance and personnel scheduling systems. Its primary brands are CISA, LCN, Schlage and Von Duprin. The climate solutions segment accounted for 55% of 2009 revenues; residential solutions, 15%; industrial technologies, 17%; and security technologies, 13%.

Employees are offered developmental programs; savings and retirement programs; life and accident insurance; short- and long-term disability coverage; wellness programs; medical coverage; and employee assistance programs.

FINANCIALS: **Sales and profits are in thousands of dollars—add 000 to get the full amount. 2009 Note: Financial information for 2009 was not available for all companies at press time.**

2009 Sales: $13,195,300	2009 Profits: $462,900	**U.S. Stock Ticker: IR**
2008 Sales: $13,227,400	2008 Profits: $-2,567,400	**Int'l Ticker:** Int'l Exchange:
2007 Sales: $8,763,100	2007 Profits: $733,100	Employees: 57,000
2006 Sales: $8,033,700	2006 Profits: $765,000	Fiscal Year Ends: 12/31
2005 Sales: $7,263,700	2005 Profits: $1,054,200	Parent Company:

SALARIES/BENEFITS:

Pension Plan: Y	ESOP Stock Plan:	Profit Sharing:	Top Exec. Salary: $1,275,000	Bonus: $2,446,000
Savings Plan:	Stock Purch. Plan:		Second Exec. Salary: $688,542	Bonus: $850,927

OTHER THOUGHTS:

Apparent Women Officers or Directors: 5
Hot Spot for Advancement for Women/Minorities: Y

LOCATIONS: ("Y" = Yes)

West:	Southwest:	Midwest:	Southeast:	Northeast:	International:
Y	Y	Y	Y	Y	Y

INOUE RUBBER (THAILAND) PCL

www.ircthailand.com

Industry Group Code: 3262 **Ranks within this company's industry group:** Sales: 10 Profits: 6

Vehicle Manufacturing:		Dealers:		Parts:		Service:		Finance:		Specialty:	
Cars:		Car Dealer New:		Manufacturers:	Y	General Service:		Leasing:		Information Systems:	
Trucks:		Car Dealer Used:		Retail:		Specialty Service:		Auto Loans:		Online Marketing:	
Motorcycles:		Truck Dealer:		Distributors:		Oil Change:		Insurance:		Other:	
Specialty:		RV Dealer:		Tires:	Y	Paint and Body:				Publishing:	
Buses:		Motorcycle Dealer:		Batteries:						Rental Cars/Trucks:	
RVs:		Specialty Dealer:									

TYPES OF BUSINESS:

Industrial Rubber Parts Manufacturing
Motorcycle Tire & Tube Manufacturing
Motorcycle Wheel Set Assembly

BRANDS/DIVISIONS/AFFILIATES:

Inoue Rubber Co., Ltd.
IRC
IRC (Asia) Research Co., Ltd.
Kinno Hoshi Engineering Co., Ltd.
Inoue Rubber Vietnam Co., Ltd.

CONTACTS: *Note: Officers with more than one job title may be intentionally listed here more than once.*

Takeshi Arakawa, Managing Dir.
Pimjai Laochinda, Pres.
Yuchawan Paoin, Sec.
Soichi Inoue, Vice Chmn.-IRC/Pres., Inoue Rubber Co., Ltd.
Koji Yamauchi, Exec. Dir.
Nareothai Boothong, Exec. Dir.
Surlyan Chalprome, Exec. Dir.

Phone: 662-996-0890	**Fax:** 662-996-1439
Toll-Free:	
Address: 258 Soi Rangsit-Nakornnayok 49, Prachatipat, 12130 Thailand	

GROWTH PLANS/SPECIAL FEATURES:

Inoue Rubber (Thailand) PCL (IRC) manufactures industrial elastomer parts, as well as motorcycle tires and tubes. The company started in 1969 as collaboration between Japanese firm Inoue Rubber Co., Ltd. (Inoue Japan) and shareholders from the Leeissaranukul family, who have a long history in Thailand's automotive industry. Today, Inoue Japan owns 34.3% of the firm. IRC's industrial elastomer parts mainly comprise rubber components for automobiles and motorcycles, including gaskets, bumpers, weather stripping, door sponges and engine mountings. It also supplies rubber parts used in other industries (including agriculture), such as insulators, gaskets and hoses. Its main customers include Ford, Toyota, Suzuki, Honda, Isuzu, Kawasaki and Mitsubishi. The firm's motorcycle tires, comprising off-road tires, on-road tires, heavy tires and scooter tires, as well as its motorcycle tubes, are supplied to both domestic and overseas motorcycle manufacturers. As a value added service, the company also assembles its tires and tubes into complete wheels. IRC has two primary facilities, both located in Thailand, which manufacture products under the IRC brand name. At its headquarters in Prachathipat, in the Thanyaburi district of Pathumthanee province, it manufactures motorcycle tires and tubes and assembles wheel sets, while it manufactures its industrial rubber parts at a plant in Lam Sai, in the Wang Noi district of Ayutthaya province. By product category, industrial elastomer parts generated the largest share (42%) of 2009 sales, followed by motorcycle tires (39.1%), motorcycle tubes (13.1%) and wheel set assembly (5.5%). By region, domestic sales generated 76.1% of 2009 sales, with exports generating the remaining 23.9%. The company has two 99.99%-owned subsidiaries: IRC (Asia) Research Co., Ltd. and Kinno Hoshi Engineering Co., Ltd., as well as 10%-owned Inoue Rubber Vietnam Co., Ltd. IRC (Asia) conducts research and development in IRC's product areas, along with Inoue Japan. Kinno manufactures metal molds that IRC uses to manufacture rubber auto parts.

FINANCIALS: **Sales and profits are in thousands of dollars—add 000 to get the full amount. 2009 Note: Financial information for 2009 was not available for all companies at press time.**

2009 Sales: $144,220	2009 Profits: $8,280	**U.S. Stock Ticker:**
2008 Sales: $164,890	2008 Profits: $8,030	**Int'l Ticker: IRC** Int'l Exchange: Bangkok-BAK
2007 Sales: $142,920	2007 Profits: $84,080	Employees: 1,666
2006 Sales: $	2006 Profits: $	Fiscal Year Ends: 12/31
2005 Sales: $	2005 Profits: $	Parent Company: INOUE RUBBER CO LTD

SALARIES/BENEFITS:

Pension Plan:	ESOP Stock Plan:	Profit Sharing:	Top Exec. Salary: $	Bonus: $
Savings Plan:	Stock Purch. Plan:		Second Exec. Salary: $	Bonus: $

OTHER THOUGHTS:

Apparent Women Officers or Directors: 4
Hot Spot for Advancement for Women/Minorities: Y

LOCATIONS: ("Y" = Yes)

West:	Southwest:	Midwest:	Southeast:	Northeast:	International:
					Y

INTERNET BRANDS INC

www.internetbrands.com

Industry Group Code: 519130 **Ranks within this company's industry group:** Sales: 1 Profits: 1

Vehicle Manufacturing:		Dealers:		Parts:		Service:		Finance:		Specialty:	
Cars:		Car Dealer New:		Manufacturers:		General Service:		Leasing:		Information Systems:	
Trucks:		Car Dealer Used:		Retail:		Specialty Service:		Auto Loans:		Online Marketing:	Y
Motorcycles:		Truck Dealer:		Distributors:		Oil Change:		Insurance:		Other:	Y
Specialty:		RV Dealer:		Tires:		Paint and Body:				Publishing:	
Buses:		Motorcycle Dealer:		Batteries:						Rental Cars/Trucks:	
RVs:		Specialty Dealer:									

TYPES OF BUSINESS:

Auto Sales-Online
Home & Home Improvement Web Sites
Online Travel Directories
Career Web Sites
Financial Research Web Sites
Health Web Sites

BRANDS/DIVISIONS/AFFILIATES:

Autodata Solutions, Inc.
Autodata Solutions Company
vBulletin Solutions Inc.
CarsDirect.com
CVTips.com
HealthNews.org
BusinessMart.com
TrekEarth.com

CONTACTS: *Note: Officers with more than one job title may be intentionally listed here more than once.*

Robert N. Brisco, CEO
Lisa Morita, COO
Robert N. Brisco, Pres.
Scott A. Friedman, CFO
Chuck Hoover, Chief Mktg. Officer
Joe Rosenblum, CTO
B. Lynn Walsh, General Counsel
B. Lynn Walsh, Exec. VP-Corp. Dev.
Gregory T. Perrier, CEO/Pres., Autodata Solutions Co.
Howard Morgan, Chmn.

Phone: 310-280-4000 **Fax:**
Toll-Free: 800-692-2200
Address: 909 N. Sepulveda Blvd., 11th Fl., El Segundo, CA 90245 US

GROWTH PLANS/SPECIAL FEATURES:

Internet Brands, Inc. owns and operates e-commerce and community sites. The firm operates more than 230 web sites grouped into seven categories: automotive; careers; health; home-related; money and business; shopping; and travel and leisure. The automotive segment operates e-commerce automotive web sites that enable consumers to research and buy new and used cars, including Autos.com, CarsDirect.com and NewCarTestDrive.com. The careers segment operates job listings sites, portfolio sites and community sites, including CVTips.com, GrooveJob.com, ModelMayhem.com and WAHM.com. The health segment includes websites focusing on three categories: medical procedures, health-related support communities and fitness and nutrition. Its web sites include HealthNews.org, DermaNetwork.org, InfertilitySpecialist.com and FitDay.com. The home-related segment includes web sites involving housing selection and home improvement. Home web sites include ApartmentRatings.com, Craftster.org and DoItYourself.com. Web sites in the money and business segment provide visitors with forums and resources to manage their finances and run their business, including Mortgage101.com, BusinessMart.com and FinWeb.com. The shopping segment offers sites with a focus on online discounts and certain high value categories, such as consumer electronics. Sites include UltimateCoupons.com, HighDefDigest.com and Bargainist.com. Lastly, the travel and leisure web sites include accommodation and community sites, such as BikeForums.net, TrekEarth.com and BBOnline.com. The company licenses certain Internet technology products and services through its Autodata Solutions division, which is comprised of Autodata Solutions, Inc. and Autodata Solutions Company. It also owns and operates vBulletin software through its subsidiary, vBulletin Solutions Inc. In February 2010, the company expanded its health and home categories by acquiring seven websites, including DentalFind.com and Gardens.com. In March 2010, the firm acquired Tjoos.com, an online coupon website. In April 2010, the company acquired ExpertHub, a network of websites that connects consumers with attorneys and other professionals.

Employees are offered medical, dental, vision and life insurance; short- and long-term disability; flexible spending accounts; an employee assistance program; and casual dress.

FINANCIALS: **Sales and profits are in thousands of dollars—add 000 to get the full amount. 2009 Note: Financial information for 2009 was not available for all companies at press time.**

2009 Sales: $99,756	2009 Profits: $12,388	**U.S. Stock Ticker: INET**
2008 Sales: $104,036	2008 Profits: $11,559	**Int'l Ticker:** Int'l Exchange:
2007 Sales: $89,889	2007 Profits: $ 311	Employees: 649
2006 Sales: $84,804	2006 Profits: $93,067	Fiscal Year Ends: 12/31
2005 Sales: $78,100	2005 Profits: $13,400	Parent Company:

SALARIES/BENEFITS:

Pension Plan:	ESOP Stock Plan:	Profit Sharing:	Top Exec. Salary: $360,000	Bonus: $385,000
Savings Plan: Y	Stock Purch. Plan:		Second Exec. Salary: $280,000	Bonus: $102,000

OTHER THOUGHTS:

Apparent Women Officers or Directors: 3
Hot Spot for Advancement for Women/Minorities: Y

LOCATIONS: ("Y" = Yes)

West:	Southwest:	Midwest:	Southeast:	Northeast:	International:
Y					

INTERSTATE BATTERY SYSTEM OF AMERICA

www.interstatebatteries.com

Industry Group Code: 33591 **Ranks within this company's industry group:** Sales: Profits:

Vehicle Manufacturing:		Dealers:		Parts:		Service:		Finance:		Specialty:	
Cars:		Car Dealer New:		Manufacturers:	Y	General Service:		Leasing:		Information Systems:	
Trucks:		Car Dealer Used:		Retail:	Y	Specialty Service:		Auto Loans:		Online Marketing:	Y
Motorcycles:		Truck Dealer:		Distributors:	Y	Oil Change:		Insurance:		Other:	
Specialty:		RV Dealer:		Tires:		Paint and Body:				Publishing:	
Buses:		Motorcycle Dealer:		Batteries:	Y					Rental Cars/Trucks:	
RVs:		Specialty Dealer:									

TYPES OF BUSINESS:

Battery Manufacturing
Retail Battery Sales
Battery Distribution

BRANDS/DIVISIONS/AFFILIATES:

All Battery Centers
PowerCare
Mega-Tron
Workaholic
Aerotron
PowerVolt
Pinnacle

CONTACTS:

Note: Officers with more than one job title may be intentionally listed here more than once.

Carlos Sepulveda, CEO
Carlos Sepulveda, Pres.
Lisa Huntsberry, CFO/VP
Dennis Brown, Chief Mktg. Officer/Sr. VP
Chris Willis, VP-Human Resources
Merv Tarde, CIO/VP-IT
Chris Willis, General Counsel
Jane Koenecke, VP-Creative Comm. & Events
Mickey Elam, Sr. VP-Independent Dist. Group
Scott Miller, VP-All Battery Group
Walt Holmes, Chief Legal Officer/Sr. VP
Billy Norris, VP-National Accounts
Norm Miller, Chmn.
Chris Antoniou, VP-Supply Chain Mgmt.

Phone: 972-991-1444	**Fax:** 972-458-8288
Toll-Free: 866-842-5368	
Address: 12770 Merit Dr., Ste. 400, Dallas, TX 75251 US	

GROWTH PLANS/SPECIAL FEATURES:

Interstate Battery System of America, Inc. (IBSA) produces and distributes batteries through its distributors, dealers, All Battery Centers stores and the Internet. The company's batteries are used in the automotive and marine industries; motorcycles; snowmobiles; 4-wheelers; watercrafts; recreational vehicles; lawn mowers; watches; households; laptops; hearing-aids; wheelchairs/mobility scooters; forklifts; cordless/cellular phones; and backup power supplies for the industrial and telecommunications industries. More than 200,000 retail dealers sell Interstate batteries throughout the U.S. and Canada. IBSA also has roughly 340 wholesale distributors. At its retailer locations, an Interstate regional manager comes at regular intervals to rotate stock and pick up old batteries for recycling in order to keep the stock fresh. The firm's PowerCare division provides batteries and battery services to the power industry. The company's All Battery Centers network provides over 16,000 different types of household and business batteries. These batteries utilize NiCad, NiMH, SLA, Lithium, Alkaline, Zinc Air and Silver Oxide cell technology. Household batteries are used for products such as flashlights and camcorders, and business batteries are used for products such as pagers and computer backup power. Consumers are also able to purchase many of the company's batteries online. The company does business with automotive manufacturers such as Toyota, Lexus, Volvo and Subaru. Brand names include Aerotron, Workaholic, Mega-Tron, Pinnacle and PowerVolt. In May 2010, IBSA signed three new All Battery Centers franchisees located in Florida, Connecticut and Louisiana. In July 2010, the firm signed a new franchisee in Texas.

The company offers its employees health and life insurance; paid holidays; tuition reimbursement; and wellness programs.

FINANCIALS:

Sales and profits are in thousands of dollars—add 000 to get the full amount. 2009 Note: Financial information for 2009 was not available for all companies at press time.

2009 Sales: $	2009 Profits: $	**U.S. Stock Ticker: Private**
2008 Sales: $	2008 Profits: $	**Int'l Ticker:** Int'l Exchange:
2007 Sales: $1,500,000	2007 Profits: $	Employees: 1,415
2006 Sales: $1,000,000	2006 Profits: $	Fiscal Year Ends:
2005 Sales: $754,900	2005 Profits: $	Parent Company:

SALARIES/BENEFITS:

Pension Plan:	ESOP Stock Plan:	Profit Sharing: Y	Top Exec. Salary: $	Bonus: $
Savings Plan: Y	Stock Purch. Plan:		Second Exec. Salary: $	Bonus: $

OTHER THOUGHTS:

Apparent Women Officers or Directors: 2
Hot Spot for Advancement for Women/Minorities:

LOCATIONS: ("Y" = Yes)

West:	Southwest:	Midwest:	Southeast:	Northeast:	International:
Y	Y	Y	Y	Y	Y

ISUZU MOTORS AMERICA INC

www.isuzu.com

Industry Group Code: 33611 **Ranks within this company's industry group:** Sales: Profits:

Vehicle Manufacturing:		Dealers:		Parts:		Service:		Finance:		Specialty:	
Cars:		Car Dealer New:		Manufacturers:		General Service:		Leasing:		Information Systems:	
Trucks:		Car Dealer Used:		Retail:		Specialty Service:		Auto Loans:		Online Marketing:	
Motorcycles:		Truck Dealer:		Distributors:	Y	Oil Change:		Insurance:		Other:	
Specialty:		RV Dealer:		Tires:		Paint and Body:				Publishing:	
Buses:		Motorcycle Dealer:		Batteries:						Rental Cars/Trucks:	
RVs:		Specialty Dealer:									

TYPES OF BUSINESS:

Distribution-SUVs
Commercial Vehicles & Diesel Engines

BRANDS/DIVISIONS/AFFILIATES:

Isuzu Motors Ltd
Isuzu Manufacturing Services of America

CONTACTS:

Note: Officers with more than one job title may be intentionally listed here more than once.

J. Terry Maloney, COO
J. Terry Maloney, Pres.
Robert B. Trawick, VP-Dealer Network Dev. & Bus. Mgmt.
Yoshitomo Utaka, Chmn.

Phone: 714-935-9300 **Fax:** 714-935-5200
Toll-Free: 800-255-6727
Address: 1400 S. Douglass Rd., Ste. 100, Anaheim, CA 92806 US

GROWTH PLANS/SPECIAL FEATURES:

Isuzu Motors America, Inc. (IMA), a subsidiary of Isuzu Motors, Ltd., provides parts and service operations for Isuzu vehicles, sports utility vehicles and industrial diesel engines throughout the U.S. The firm's parent company, Isuzu Motors, is one of the world's largest manufactures of medium- and heavy-duty trucks. Isuzu Motors America focuses mainly on SUV offerings, which include the 5-passenger Ascender SUV and the i290 and i370 pickups. The company's subsidiary, Isuzu Manufacturing Services of America (IMSA), provides research and development, engineering and production support functions for Isuzu's commercial vehicle, sports utility vehicle and powertrain operations. The company's powertrain division distributes approximately 30 models of industrial diesel engines that offer up to 300 horsepower. Isuzu's trucks division has a partnership with General Motors that provides diesel engines to Chevy and GMC's heavy-duty pickups; this partnership continued after General Motor's divesture of Isuzu shares. In January 2009, Isuzu Motors America ceased distribution of new Isuzu passenger vehicles in North America. This move is the result of diminished sales and GM's decision to discontinue the Ascender, i-290 and i-370, which it manufactured for Isuzu. The firm's parts and service operations will continue for both vehicle owners and dealers, including parts warranties, roadside assistance, and the customer call-center. Isuzu will also continue to sell commercial trucks in the North American market through its subsidiary, Isuzu Commercial Truck of America, Inc.

FINANCIALS:

Sales and profits are in thousands of dollars—add 000 to get the full amount. 2009 Note: Financial information for 2009 was not available for all companies at press time.

2009 Sales: $	2009 Profits: $	**U.S. Stock Ticker: Subsidiary**
2008 Sales: $	2008 Profits: $	**Int'l Ticker:** Int'l Exchange:
2007 Sales: $	2007 Profits: $	Employees:
2006 Sales: $	2006 Profits: $	Fiscal Year Ends: 3/31
2005 Sales: $	2005 Profits: $	Parent Company: ISUZU MOTORS LTD

SALARIES/BENEFITS:

Pension Plan:	ESOP Stock Plan:	Profit Sharing:	Top Exec. Salary: $	Bonus: $
Savings Plan:	Stock Purch. Plan:		Second Exec. Salary: $	Bonus: $

OTHER THOUGHTS:

Apparent Women Officers or Directors:
Hot Spot for Advancement for Women/Minorities:

LOCATIONS: ("Y" = Yes)

West:	Southwest:	Midwest:	Southeast:	Northeast:	International:
Y	Y	Y	Y	Y	

ISUZU MOTORS LTD

www.isuzu.co.jp

Industry Group Code: 33611 **Ranks within this company's industry group:** Sales: 19 Profits: 22

Vehicle Manufacturing:		Dealers:		Parts:		Service:		Finance:		Specialty:	
Cars:	Y	Car Dealer New:		Manufacturers:	Y	General Service:		Leasing:		Information Systems:	
Trucks:	Y	Car Dealer Used:		Retail:		Specialty Service:		Auto Loans:		Online Marketing:	
Motorcycles:		Truck Dealer:		Distributors:		Oil Change:		Insurance:		Other:	
Specialty:		RV Dealer:		Tires:		Paint and Body:				Publishing:	
Buses:	Y	Motorcycle Dealer:		Batteries:						Rental Cars/Trucks:	
RVs:		Specialty Dealer:									

TYPES OF BUSINESS:

Automobile Manufacturing
Trucks & Buses
Diesel Engines
Logistics Services

BRANDS/DIVISIONS/AFFILIATES:

Tri Petch Isuzu Sales Co Ltd
Isuzu Motors America Inc
Isuzu Automotive Europe
Isuzu Truck South Africa (Pty) Limited
Isuzu-OAO Severstal-Auto
Isuzu Commercial Truck of America, Inc.
DMAX, Ltd.
Isuzu North America Corporation

CONTACTS: *Note: Officers with more than one job title may be intentionally listed here more than once.*

Susumu Hosoi, Pres.
Yoshihiro Tadaki, Exec. VP-Sales & Quality Assurance
Ryozo Tsukioka, Managing Exec. Officer-Eng. Div.
Masanori Katayama, Sr. Exec. Officer-Mfg. Div.
Makoto Kawahara, Exec. Officer-Corp. Planning
Makoto Kawahara, Exec. Officer-Finance
Eizou Kawasaki, Managing Exec. Officer-Powertrain Bus. Div.
Chikao Mitsuzaki, Sr. Exec. Officer-Japan Sales Div.
Shunichi Tokunaga, Sr. Exec. Officer-China Oper.
Katsumasa Nagai, Sr. Exec. Officer-Prod. Planning & Integration
Yoshinori Ida, Chmn.
Yoshifumi Komura, Exec. Officer-North American Oper.
Yasuaki Shimizu, Managing Exec. Officer-Purchasing

Phone: 81-3-5471-1141 **Fax:** 81-3-5471-1043
Toll-Free:
Address: 6-26-1 Minami-oi, Shinagawa-ku, Tokyo, 140-8722 Japan

GROWTH PLANS/SPECIAL FEATURES:

Isuzu Motors, Ltd., headquartered in Tokyo, Japan, manufactures and sells automobiles, sport-utility vehicles (SUVs), pickups, freight trucks, buses, automobile parts and diesel engines. Its SUV line includes the Ascender, the MU-7 in Thailand and the Panther in Indonesia, while its pick-up trucks include the D-MAX. Truck models come in heavy, medium and light-duty varieties, with models that include tractor-trailers, dump trucks and concrete trucks. Isuzu sells its buses under the Erga brand name, offering a standard-size version and a smaller version known as the Erga Mio, both of which offer natural gas and diesel-run options. The company has focused on the development of fuel-efficient and low-emissions diesel engines for years, and currently produces a wide variety of diesel engine models sold to the automotive, industrial and maritime markets. The firm has more than 50 subsidiaries around the world, and its products are currently sold in more than 100 countries. Isuzu has a number of partnerships, including Isuzu Automotive Europe, a joint venture with Mitsubishi Corp. to expand sales in Europe; Isuzu Truck South Africa (Pty) Limited, a joint venture with GM South Africa; and Isuzu-OAO Severstal-Auto, which implements local production and sales of light-duty commercial trucks in Russia. Subsidiaries of the firm based in the U.S. include Isuzu Motors America, LLC, focused on industrial engine sales and service; Isuzu Commercial Truck of America, Inc., which manages Isuzu's North American commercial vehicle business, including importing and distribution; DMAX, Ltd., a manufacturer and seller of diesel engines; and Isuzu North America Corporation, which oversees North American subsidiaries and provides administrative support to local operations. In February 2009, the company announced plans to build a plant near Mexico City, Isuzu's first in Latin America, where it will manufacture midsize 4-ton trucks.

FINANCIALS: **Sales and profits are in thousands of dollars—add 000 to get the full amount. 2009 Note: Financial information for 2009 was not available for all companies at press time.**

2009 Sales: $15,419,000	2009 Profits: $-290,670	**U.S. Stock Ticker:**
2008 Sales: $19,180,300	2008 Profits: $757,330	**Int'l Ticker: 7202** Int'l Exchange: Tokyo-TSE
2007 Sales: $16,570,500	2007 Profits: $920,750	Employees:
2006 Sales: $13,452,100	2006 Profits: $	Fiscal Year Ends: 3/31
2005 Sales: $13,425,818	2005 Profits: $539,250	Parent Company:

SALARIES/BENEFITS:

Pension Plan:	ESOP Stock Plan:	Profit Sharing:	Top Exec. Salary: $	Bonus: $
Savings Plan:	Stock Purch. Plan:		Second Exec. Salary: $	Bonus: $

OTHER THOUGHTS:

Apparent Women Officers or Directors:
Hot Spot for Advancement for Women/Minorities:

LOCATIONS: ("Y" = Yes)

West:	Southwest:	Midwest:	Southeast:	Northeast:	International:
Y		Y			Y

JAGUAR CARS LTD

www.jaguar.com

Industry Group Code: 33611 **Ranks within this company's industry group:** Sales: Profits:

Vehicle Manufacturing:		Dealers:		Parts:		Service:		Finance:		Specialty:	
Cars:	Y	Car Dealer New:		Manufacturers:		General Service:		Leasing:	Y	Information Systems:	
Trucks:		Car Dealer Used:		Retail:		Specialty Service:		Auto Loans:	Y	Online Marketing:	
Motorcycles:		Truck Dealer:		Distributors:		Oil Change:		Insurance:	Y	Other:	
Specialty:		RV Dealer:		Tires:		Paint and Body:				Publishing:	
Buses:		Motorcycle Dealer:		Batteries:						Rental Cars/Trucks:	
RVs:		Specialty Dealer:									

TYPES OF BUSINESS:

Automobiles, Manufacturing
Racing

BRANDS/DIVISIONS/AFFILIATES:

Tata Motors Limited
Tata Group
R-Type
XF
XJ
XK
Land Rover
Ford Motor Co.

CONTACTS: *Note: Officers with more than one job title may be intentionally listed here more than once.*

David M. Smith, CEO
Mike O'Driscoll, Managing Dir.
Ian Callum, Dir.-Design
Gary Temple, Pres., Jaguar Land Rover North America, LLC

Phone: 44-24-7640-2121	**Fax:**
Toll-Free:	
Address: Abbey Rd., Whitley, Coventry, CV3 4LF UK	

GROWTH PLANS/SPECIAL FEATURES:

Jaguar Cars, Ltd., based in the U.K. and founded in 1922, manufactures a distinctive line of luxury sedans and sports cars. The company is a subsidiary of Tata Motors Limited. Tata Motors, based in India, is part of the Tata Group conglomerate, which includes businesses ranging from steel production and retailing to compact car manufacturing. Jaguar's current line includes four models: the XF, XJ, XK and the R-Type. The Jaguar XF, available in different four models is a sports sedan with a 5.0-liter V8 Supercharged engine, as well as features such as Bluetooth phone connectivity, a portable audio interface and voice-controlled navigation options. The company's flagship model, the XJ sedan features a monocoque alloy bodyshell, a 470 hp supercharged engine and 510 hp engine, Bluetooth wireless technology and automatic climate control. Jaguar's XK series includes XK and XKR coupes and convertibles. The R-Type premium model is available in the XF and XK models, features A-J V8 Gen-3 direct injection engine; touch screen navigational system; and 19-inch Tamana alloy wheels. Jaguar Cars Finance offers finance and payment packages for leasing or purchasing new and used Jaguars, in addition to car insurance. The firm has a collaboration with Lotus Engineering and Queen's University Belfast to develop an engine that maximizes fuel efficiency when running on renewable fuels. In April 2009, the XKR and the XFR were introduced to the market. In June 2009, Jaguar and Land Rover brands entered the Indian market. In July 2009, the Jaguar Heritage Museum in Coventry, U.K. was re-launched.

FINANCIALS: **Sales and profits are in thousands of dollars—add 000 to get the full amount. 2009 Note: Financial information for 2009 was not available for all companies at press time.**

2009 Sales: $	2009 Profits: $	**U.S. Stock Ticker: Subsidiary**
2008 Sales: $	2008 Profits: $	**Int'l Ticker:** Int'l Exchange:
2007 Sales: $	2007 Profits: $	Employees:
2006 Sales: $	2006 Profits: $	Fiscal Year Ends: 12/31
2005 Sales: $	2005 Profits: $	Parent Company: TATA MOTORS LIMITED

SALARIES/BENEFITS:

Pension Plan:	ESOP Stock Plan:	Profit Sharing:	Top Exec. Salary: $	Bonus: $
Savings Plan:	Stock Purch. Plan:		Second Exec. Salary: $	Bonus: $

OTHER THOUGHTS:

Apparent Women Officers or Directors:
Hot Spot for Advancement for Women/Minorities:

LOCATIONS: ("Y" = Yes)

West:	Southwest:	Midwest:	Southeast:	Northeast:	International:
Y	Y	Y	Y	Y	Y

JARDINE CYCLE AND CARRIAGE

www.jcclgroup.com

Industry Group Code: 33611 **Ranks within this company's industry group:** Sales: 21 Profits: 9

Vehicle Manufacturing:		Dealers:		Parts:		Service:		Finance:		Specialty:	
Cars:		Car Dealer New:	Y	Manufacturers:		General Service:	Y	Leasing:		Information Systems:	
Trucks:		Car Dealer Used:		Retail:		Specialty Service:		Auto Loans:	Y	Online Marketing:	
Motorcycles:		Truck Dealer:	Y	Distributors:	Y	Oil Change:		Insurance:	Y	Other:	Y
Specialty:		RV Dealer:		Tires:		Paint and Body:				Publishing:	
Buses:		Motorcycle Dealer:	Y	Batteries:						Rental Cars/Trucks:	
RVs:		Specialty Dealer:									

TYPES OF BUSINESS:

Automobiles, Retailing
Auto Distribution
Auto Dealers
Auto Service
Auto Insurance

BRANDS/DIVISIONS/AFFILIATES:

Cycle & Carriage Ltd.
Cycle & Carriage Bintang
Jardine Matheson Group
PT Astra International Tbk
Tunas Ridean
Truong Hai Auto Corporation

CONTACTS: *Note: Officers with more than one job title may be intentionally listed here more than once.*

Benjamin Keswick, Group Managing Dir.
Chiew Sin Cheok, Dir.-Group Finance
Jason Wen, Dir.-Human Resources, Group Motor Oper.
Ho Yeng Tat, Corp. Sec.
Cheah Kim Teck, CEO-Group Motor Oper.
Ho Yeng Tat, Dir.-Corp. Affairs
Wong Kin Foo, COO-Cycle & Carriage Bintang Berhad
Anton Setiawan, Pres./Dir.-PT Tunas Ridean Tbk
Tron Ba Duong, Chmn./Gen. Dir.-Truong Hai Auto Corp.
Anthony Nightingale, Chmn.
Prijono Sugiarto, Pres./Dir.-PT Astra Int'l Tbk

Phone: 65-6473-3122 **Fax:** 65-6475-7088
Toll-Free:
Address: 239 Alexandra Rd., Singapore, 159930 Singapore

GROWTH PLANS/SPECIAL FEATURES:

Jardine Cycle & Carriage (JC&C) manages a variety of Singapore and Southeast Asian business interests in motor vehicle distribution and retailing. The company operates its motor vehicle distribution, sales and after-sales businesses under its well-established brand name, Cycle & Carriage. It is a member of a conglomerate, the Jardine Matheson Group, which operates in the fields of engineering, insurance broking, property investment, retailing, hotels, motor vehicles, financial services, mining and agribusiness. A leader in Singapore's auto market, Cycle & Carriage is the country's major dealer of Mercedes-Benz, Kia, Mitsubishi, and Citroen. Cycle & Carriage also offers related financing and comprehensive insurance brokerage. In Malaysia, the company's motor vehicle operations are run under the name Cycle & Carriage Bintang, 59.1% controlled by JC&C, specializing in the distribution of Mercedes-Benz vehicles. The firm also owns a 43.8% interest in Tunas Ridean, an independent automotive dealer in Indonesia representing Toyota, Daihatsu, BMW and Peugeot motor vehicles and Honda motorcycles; and a 29.1% interest in Truong Hai Auto Corporation (THACO), an automotive manufacture, assembly, distribution, retail, repair and maintenance company based in Vietnam, representing Kia, Foton, King Long and Hyundai. The company additionally holds a 50.1% interest in PT Astra International Tbk, an Indonesian conglomerate engaged in auto distribution, financial services, agribusiness, heavy equipment and mining, information technology and infrastructure. The company's interest in PT Astra International greatly extends its regional reach, with Astra representing one of the largest independent automotive groups in Southeast Asia. Astra's motor vehicle brands include Honda motorcycles and Toyota, Daihatsu, Isuzu, Peugeot, Nissan Diesel and BMW cars and trucks. In June 2009, the company announced the liquidation of Cycle & Carriage (Mauritius) Ltd., a dormant subsidiary. In December 2009, JC&C acquired an additional 5.8% interest in THACO.

FINANCIALS: **Sales and profits are in thousands of dollars—add 000 to get the full amount. 2009 Note: Financial information for 2009 was not available for all companies at press time.**

2009 Sales: $10,640,400	2009 Profits: $502,800	**U.S. Stock Ticker:**
2008 Sales: $11,192,000	2008 Profits: $448,000	**Int'l Ticker: C07** Int'l Exchange: Singapore-SIN
2007 Sales: $8,921,000	2007 Profits: $340,100	Employees: 137,000
2006 Sales: $7,186,000	2006 Profits: $223,800	Fiscal Year Ends: 12/31
2005 Sales: $3,798,000	2005 Profits: $426,000	Parent Company:

SALARIES/BENEFITS:

Pension Plan:	ESOP Stock Plan:	Profit Sharing:	Top Exec. Salary: $	Bonus: $
Savings Plan:	Stock Purch. Plan:		Second Exec. Salary: $	Bonus: $

OTHER THOUGHTS:

Apparent Women Officers or Directors:
Hot Spot for Advancement for Women/Minorities:

LOCATIONS: ("Y" = Yes)

West:	Southwest:	Midwest:	Southeast:	Northeast:	International:
					Y

JASON INC

www.jasoninc.com

Industry Group Code: 3363 **Ranks within this company's industry group:** Sales: Profits:

Vehicle Manufacturing:		Dealers:		Parts:		Service:		Finance:		Specialty:	
Cars:		Car Dealer New:		Manufacturers:	Y	General Service:		Leasing:		Information Systems:	
Trucks:		Car Dealer Used:		Retail:		Specialty Service:		Auto Loans:		Online Marketing:	
Motorcycles:		Truck Dealer:		Distributors:		Oil Change:		Insurance:		Other:	Y
Specialty:		RV Dealer:		Tires:		Paint and Body:				Publishing:	
Buses:		Motorcycle Dealer:		Batteries:						Rental Cars/Trucks:	
RVs:		Specialty Dealer:									

TYPES OF BUSINESS:

Automobile Parts Manufacturing
Seats
Non-Woven Acoustical Fiber Insulation
Finishing Products
Precision Components

BRANDS/DIVISIONS/AFFILIATES:

Atlanta Brush
Janesville Acoustics
Milsco Manufacturing Company
Assembled Products
JacksonLea
Metalex
Osborn International
Sealeze

CONTACTS:

Note: Officers with more than one job title may be intentionally listed here more than once.

David Westgate, CEO
David Westgate, Pres.
David Westgate, Chmn.

Phone: 414-277-9300	**Fax:** 414-277-9445
Toll-Free:	
Address: 411 E. Wisconsin Ave., Ste. 2120, Milwaukee, WI 53202 US	

GROWTH PLANS/SPECIAL FEATURES:

Jason Incorporated is a diversified manufacturing corporation operating in two segments: Motor Vehicle and Industrial. Established in 1985 and headquartered in Milwaukee, Wisconsin, Jason Incorporated was taken private through a management-led buyout in 2000. The firm's Motor Vehicle Group has businesses that include large manufacturers of non-woven acoustical fiber insulation for the automotive industry. It also includes seating products made for motorcycles, boats and a range of off-road mobile equipment. The segment includes the companies Milsco Manufacturing Company and Janesville Acoustics. These subsidiaries are second-tier suppliers to many of the world's major auto manufacturers. Additionally, Jason Incorporated's subsidiary Milsco Manufacturing has been the sole supplier of motorcycle seats to Harley-Davidson for almost 70 years. Jason's industrial businesses are among the largest U.S. manufacturers of finishing products, such as industrial brushes and buffing products, for industrial applications and precision components for original equipment manufacturers worldwide. This segment includes Jason Precision Components, located in Shanghai, China; JacksonLea; Assembled Products; Advance Wire Products; Metalex; Osborn International; Sealeze; and Atlanta Brush. The industrial segment has operations in the U.S., Mexico, Canada, China, Brazil, Germany, Romania, Sweden, Denmark, Spain and the U.K.

FINANCIALS:

Sales and profits are in thousands of dollars—add 000 to get the full amount. 2009 Note: Financial information for 2009 was not available for all companies at press time.

2009 Sales: $	2009 Profits: $	**U.S. Stock Ticker: Private**
2008 Sales: $	2008 Profits: $	**Int'l Ticker:** Int'l Exchange:
2007 Sales: $385,900	2007 Profits: $	Employees:
2006 Sales: $	2006 Profits: $	Fiscal Year Ends: 12/31
2005 Sales: $	2005 Profits: $	Parent Company:

SALARIES/BENEFITS:

Pension Plan:	ESOP Stock Plan:	Profit Sharing:	Top Exec. Salary: $	Bonus: $
Savings Plan:	Stock Purch. Plan:		Second Exec. Salary: $	Bonus: $

OTHER THOUGHTS:

Apparent Women Officers or Directors:
Hot Spot for Advancement for Women/Minorities:

LOCATIONS: ("Y" = Yes)

West:	Southwest:	Midwest:	Southeast:	Northeast:	International:
Y		Y	Y	Y	Y

JAYCO INC

www.jayco.com

Industry Group Code: 336120 **Ranks within this company's industry group:** Sales: Profits:

Vehicle Manufacturing:		Dealers:		Parts:		Service:		Finance:		Specialty:	
Cars:		Car Dealer New:		Manufacturers:		General Service:		Leasing:		Information Systems:	
Trucks:		Car Dealer Used:		Retail:		Specialty Service:		Auto Loans:		Online Marketing:	
Motorcycles:		Truck Dealer:		Distributors:		Oil Change:		Insurance:		Other:	
Specialty:		RV Dealer:		Tires:		Paint and Body:				Publishing:	
Buses:		Motorcycle Dealer:		Batteries:						Rental Cars/Trucks:	
RVs:	Y	Specialty Dealer:									

TYPES OF BUSINESS:

Recreational Vehicle Manufacturing
Motor Homes
Camping Trailers

BRANDS/DIVISIONS/AFFILIATES:

Jay Series
Baja
Select
Jay Feather
Jay Flight
Eagle
Designer
Jayco Travel Club

CONTACTS: *Note: Officers with more than one job title may be intentionally listed here more than once.*

Wilbur Bontrager, CEO
Derald L. Bontrager, COO
Derald L. Bontrager, Pres.
Wilbur Bontrager, Chmn.

Phone: 574-825-5861	**Fax:** 574-825-7354
Toll-Free:	
Address: 903 S. Main St., Middlebury, IN 46540 US	

GROWTH PLANS/SPECIAL FEATURES:

Jayco, Inc. is a leading manufacturer of recreation vehicles (RVs). A family-owned business, the company began in a farmhouse in 1968, and now consists of a large-scale production operation with a dealership network of 300 locations. The company's recreation vehicles include camping trailers, lightweight trailers, park and travel trailers, fifth wheels, motor homes and toy haulers. Jayco's camping trailers include the Jay Series, which sleeps up to eight people and comes equipped with such standard amenities as a carryout stove, a sofa and a dinette area; the Baja, which combines the features of a trailer and toy hauler and comes equipped with a Bike Port deck, capable of holding up to 1,500 pounds; and the Select camping trailer, which sleeps six to eight and includes added storage features. Jayco's lightweight trailers are sold under the Jay Feather and Skylark brand; its park and travel trailers are sold under the Jay Flight and Eagle brands; its fifth wheels are sold under the Eagle and Designer brands; and its toy haulers are sold under the Octane and Recon brands. Its motor homes, sold under the Greyhawk, Melbourne, Seneca, Precept, Embark and Insignia brands, include amenities such as solid wood cabinets, patio awnings and increased storage capacity and sleep between five and seven people. Owners of Jayco trailers can be part of the Jayco Travel Club, an organization that plans activities and trips each year with over 50 chapters across the U.S. and Canada. Models range in price from about $8,000 to $225,000. Jayco products are marketed in the U.S., Canada, Chile, China, Germany, Japan, Jordan, Korea, Kuwait, Mexico, Puerto Rico, Slovakia, Switzerland, the United Arab Emirates and the U.K.

FINANCIALS: **Sales and profits are in thousands of dollars—add 000 to get the full amount. 2009 Note: Financial information for 2009 was not available for all companies at press time.**

2009 Sales: $	2009 Profits: $	**U.S. Stock Ticker: Private**
2008 Sales: $	2008 Profits: $	**Int'l Ticker:** Int'l Exchange:
2007 Sales: $585,000	2007 Profits: $	Employees:
2006 Sales: $	2006 Profits: $	Fiscal Year Ends: 8/31
2005 Sales: $	2005 Profits: $	Parent Company:

SALARIES/BENEFITS:

Pension Plan:	ESOP Stock Plan:	Profit Sharing:	Top Exec. Salary: $	Bonus: $
Savings Plan:	Stock Purch. Plan:		Second Exec. Salary: $	Bonus: $

OTHER THOUGHTS:

Apparent Women Officers or Directors:
Hot Spot for Advancement for Women/Minorities:

LOCATIONS: ("Y" = Yes)

West:	Southwest:	Midwest:	Southeast:	Northeast:	International:
		Y			

JB POINDEXTER & CO INC

www.jbpoindexter.com

Industry Group Code: 336211 **Ranks within this company's industry group:** Sales: Profits:

Vehicle Manufacturing:		Dealers:		Parts:		Service:		Finance:		Specialty:	
Cars:		Car Dealer New:		Manufacturers:	Y	General Service:		Leasing:		Information Systems:	
Trucks:	Y	Car Dealer Used:		Retail:		Specialty Service:		Auto Loans:		Online Marketing:	
Motorcycles:		Truck Dealer:		Distributors:	Y	Oil Change:		Insurance:		Other:	Y
Specialty:	Y	RV Dealer:		Tires:		Paint and Body:				Publishing:	
Buses:		Motorcycle Dealer:		Batteries:						Rental Cars/Trucks:	
RVs:		Specialty Dealer:									

TYPES OF BUSINESS:

Truck Body Manufacturing
Step Van Manufacturing
Truck Accessories
Specialty Industrial Products
Contract Machining
Expandable Foam Products
Cargo Handling Equipment
Specialty Vehicles

BRANDS/DIVISIONS/AFFILIATES:

Morgan Corporation
Commercial Babcock
Morgan Olson
Truck Accessories Group
Specialty Manufacturing Group
MIC Group
EFP Corporation
Federal Coach

CONTACTS: *Note: Officers with more than one job title may be intentionally listed here more than once.*

John B. Poindexter, CEO
Robert Preston, COO
Jay Krishnamurthy, VP-IT
Larry Wolfe, VP-Admin.
Larry Wolfe, Sec.
Phil Schull, VP-Risk Mgmt.
John B. Poindexter, Chmn.
Andy Lu, VP-Int'l Dev.
Michael Picone, VP-Procurement

Phone: 713-655-9800 **Fax:** 713-951-9038
Toll-Free:
Address: 600 Travis St., Ste. 200, Houston, TX 77002 US

GROWTH PLANS/SPECIAL FEATURES:

J.B. Poindexter & Co., Inc is a diversified manufacturing company serving the transportation industry and the industrial products markets. The company brings together an extended network of subsidiaries operating independently in a decentralized structure. The primary businesses are focused in five groups: truck bodies, step vans, truck accessories, specialty manufacturing and specialty vehicles. The truck bodies businesses include Morgan Corporation, which is one of largest manufacturers in the U.S. of Class 3-7 refrigerated and dry truck bodies, designed for Ryder, Penske and FedEx. The group also includes Commercial Babcock, a Canadian company which manufactures and markets medium duty truck bodies. The step vans group is comprised of local delivery trucks for foodservice, vending, uniform and linen companies, and are manufactured and distributed by Morgan Olson through its 381,000 square foot facility in Sturgis, Michigan. J.B. Poindexter's Truck Accessories Group manufactures pickup truck caps, covers, lids and campers marketed under brand names Leer, Century, Raider, LoRider, Pace Edwards, State Wide Aluminum and BOXTOP. The group has manufacturing facilities in Pennsylvania, Indiana, Washington and California, and distributes its products through independent dealers to individuals, small businesses and fleets. The company's Specialty Manufacturing Group offers manufacturing capabilities including precision machining, fabrication and expandable foam product manufacturing. The group operates through two main subsidiaries: MIC Group, a contract machining company with services including electron beam welding, precision machining and gun-drilling; and EFP Corporation, an industrial manufacturer of expandable foam packaging products. The specialty vehicles group is operated by subsidiaries Federal Coach in Arkansas, which produces a line of Cadillac and Lincoln funeral coaches, limousines and mid-sized buses for individuals, local governments and fleet services; and Eagle Coach in Ohio, a manufacturer and marketer of funeral coaches and other funeral specialty vehicles.

FINANCIALS: **Sales and profits are in thousands of dollars—add 000 to get the full amount. 2009 Note: Financial information for 2009 was not available for all companies at press time.**

2009 Sales: $	2009 Profits: $	**U.S. Stock Ticker: Private**
2008 Sales: $706,400	2008 Profits: $6,800	**Int'l Ticker:** Int'l Exchange:
2007 Sales: $792,200	2007 Profits: $- 800	Employees: 3,462
2006 Sales: $795,400	2006 Profits: $8,200	Fiscal Year Ends: 12/31
2005 Sales: $	2005 Profits: $	Parent Company:

SALARIES/BENEFITS:

Pension Plan:	ESOP Stock Plan:	Profit Sharing:	Top Exec. Salary: $	Bonus: $
Savings Plan:	Stock Purch. Plan:		Second Exec. Salary: $	Bonus: $

OTHER THOUGHTS:

Apparent Women Officers or Directors:
Hot Spot for Advancement for Women/Minorities:

LOCATIONS: ("Y" = Yes)

West:	Southwest:	Midwest:	Southeast:	Northeast:	International:
Y	Y	Y	Y	Y	Y

JD POWER & ASSOCIATES

www.jdpower.com

Industry Group Code: 541910 **Ranks within this company's industry group:** Sales: Profits:

Vehicle Manufacturing:		Dealers:		Parts:		Service:		Finance:		Specialty:	
Cars:		Car Dealer New:		Manufacturers:		General Service:		Leasing:		Information Systems:	Y
Trucks:		Car Dealer Used:		Retail:		Specialty Service:		Auto Loans:		Online Marketing:	
Motorcycles:		Truck Dealer:		Distributors:		Oil Change:		Insurance:		Other:	Y
Specialty:		RV Dealer:		Tires:		Paint and Body:				Publishing:	Y
Buses:		Motorcycle Dealer:		Batteries:						Rental Cars/Trucks:	
RVs:		Specialty Dealer:									

TYPES OF BUSINESS:

Global Marketing Information Services
Automotive Industry Research
Consumer Satisfaction Surveys

BRANDS/DIVISIONS/AFFILIATES:

McGraw Hill Cos Inc

CONTACTS:

Note: Officers with more than one job title may be intentionally listed here more than once.

Finbarr O'Neill, Pres.
Peter Marlow, VP/Gen. Mgr.-Mktg.
Alexander Arrieta, Sr. Dir.-Human Resources
Kevin Keegan, VP/Gen. Mgr.-Global Research Oper.
Richard Belanger, VP/Gen. Mgr.-IT
John Humphrey, Sr. VP-Global Automotive Oper.
Peter Marlow, VP/Gen. Mgr.-Corp. Comm.
Nilo Ramos, VP-Corp. Finance
Geoffrey D. Broderick, VP/Gen. Mgr.-Automotive Revenue Mgmt. Group
Stuart Greif, VP/Gen. Mgr.-Global Travel & Hospitality
John Tews, Dir.-Media Rel.
Aimee Canlas, Mgr.-Media Rel.
Gary B. Tucker, Sr. VP-Global Svcs. & Emerging Markets

Phone: 805-418-8000 **Fax:** 805-418-8900
Toll-Free: 888-537-6937
Address: 2625 Townsgate Rd., Ste. 100, Westlake Village, CA 91361 US

GROWTH PLANS/SPECIAL FEATURES:

J.D. Power & Associates is a market researching company specializing in consumer satisfaction. Although it covers a wide variety of industries, the company is best known for its research work in the automotive industry. Since its founding in 1968 by James D. Power, III, the company has specialized in analyzing market information such as product quality and buyer behavior. In addition, the company conducts private tracking studies, media studies, forecasting and training services, often using independent, unbiased surveys to cull information. The firm surveys recent new car buyers each year in order to create its well-known automobile quality ratings. With this consumer data, the company can establish the qualifications of customer satisfaction, identify the strengths and weaknesses of individual companies and provide recommendations on how companies can improve themselves. The company has an intelligence network that links forecasting experts in the Americas, Europe and Asia Pacific regions. Automotive forecasting services include production and sales forecasting; global product advance; and engine and transmission reports. Other industries served by J.D. Power include telecommunications, travel, real estate, finance, marine, healthcare, utilities, commercial vehicles, sports/entertainment, retail, electronics and professional services. In addition to its market research business, the company also provides consultation services in the areas of design, manufacturing and development; and the sales and marketing process of a product. Moreover, the firm offers market consultant training services. J.D. Power is a business unit of publishing company McGraw-Hill.

J.D. Power offers its employees a complete benefits package including prescription drug coverage; medical, dental , disability, AD&D and vision insurance; flexible spending accounts; a 401(k); and automobile and homeowner's coverage.

FINANCIALS:

Sales and profits are in thousands of dollars—add 000 to get the full amount. 2009 Note: Financial information for 2009 was not available for all companies at press time.

2009 Sales: $	2009 Profits: $	**U.S. Stock Ticker: Subsidiary**
2008 Sales: $	2008 Profits: $	**Int'l Ticker:** Int'l Exchange:
2007 Sales: $	2007 Profits: $	Employees:
2006 Sales: $	2006 Profits: $	Fiscal Year Ends: 12/31
2005 Sales: $	2005 Profits: $	Parent Company: MCGRAW HILL COS INC

SALARIES/BENEFITS:

Pension Plan: Y	ESOP Stock Plan:	Profit Sharing: Y	Top Exec. Salary: $	Bonus: $
Savings Plan: Y	Stock Purch. Plan:		Second Exec. Salary: $	Bonus: $

OTHER THOUGHTS:

Apparent Women Officers or Directors: 1
Hot Spot for Advancement for Women/Minorities:

LOCATIONS: ("Y" = Yes)

West:	Southwest:	Midwest:	Southeast:	Northeast:	International:
Y		Y		Y	Y

JIM KOONS AUTOMOTIVE COMPANIES INC

www.koons.com

Industry Group Code: 441110 **Ranks within this company's industry group:** Sales: Profits:

Vehicle Manufacturing:		Dealers:		Parts:		Service:		Finance:		Specialty:	
Cars:		Car Dealer New:	Y	Manufacturers:		General Service:	Y	Leasing:		Information Systems:	
Trucks:		Car Dealer Used:	Y	Retail:	Y	Specialty Service:		Auto Loans:		Online Marketing:	Y
Motorcycles:		Truck Dealer:		Distributors:		Oil Change:		Insurance:		Other:	
Specialty:		RV Dealer:		Tires:		Paint and Body:	Y			Publishing:	
Buses:		Motorcycle Dealer:		Batteries:						Rental Cars/Trucks:	
RVs:		Specialty Dealer:									

TYPES OF BUSINESS:

Auto Dealers, Retail
Collision Repair Centers
Commercial Sales
Online Sales
Parts

BRANDS/DIVISIONS/AFFILIATES:

Sterling Ford
Lexus of Wilmington
Tysons Chevrolet-Chrysler
Koons Lincoln-Mercury/Volvo
Falls Church Ford-Dodge

CONTACTS:

Note: Officers with more than one job title may be intentionally listed here more than once.

James E. Koons, CEO
Ed Waugh, Controller

Phone: 703-356-0400	**Fax:** 703-442-5765
Toll-Free: 800-782-0191	
Address: 2000 Chain Bridge Rd., 112, VA 22182 US	

GROWTH PLANS/SPECIAL FEATURES:

Jim Koons Automotive Companies, Inc. sells new and used vehicles. Founded in 1964 by John Koons Sr., the first auto dealer to enter the Automotive Hall of Fame, the firm is now run by his son Jim Koons. Brands including Chevrolet, Chrysler, Dodge, Ford, Lexus, Lincoln, Mercury, Scion, Toyota and Volvo are sold through the company's 20 plus locations in Maryland and Virginia. Koons' commercial sales department offers manufactured and customized vehicles to meet the needs of any business. The company also operates several collision repair centers. Koon's web site features a virtual showroom of its new and used vehicles with information regarding special purchase deals, rebates and repair service specials. Customers are also able to value a trade-in vehicle, schedule a maintenance appointment, order customized vehicles, purchase accessories and parts and apply for credit online. The company's locations include Koons Tyson's Toyota/Scion, which provides an expansive location for car tune-ups, as well as new car sales; Lexus of Wilmington; Sterling Ford; Tysons Chevrolet-Chrysler; Koons Lincoln-Mercury/Volvo; and Falls Church Ford-Dodge.

Jim Koons Automotive Companies, Inc. offers its employees a benefits package including health, dental, life, and disability insurance and a 401(k) plan.

FINANCIALS:

Sales and profits are in thousands of dollars—add 000 to get the full amount. 2009 Note: Financial information for 2009 was not available for all companies at press time.

2009 Sales: $	2009 Profits: $	**U.S. Stock Ticker: Private**
2008 Sales: $	2008 Profits: $	**Int'l Ticker:** Int'l Exchange:
2007 Sales: $	2007 Profits: $	Employees:
2006 Sales: $	2006 Profits: $	Fiscal Year Ends: 12/31
2005 Sales: $	2005 Profits: $	Parent Company:

SALARIES/BENEFITS:

Pension Plan:	ESOP Stock Plan:	Profit Sharing:	Top Exec. Salary: $	Bonus: $
Savings Plan: Y	Stock Purch. Plan:		Second Exec. Salary: $	Bonus: $

OTHER THOUGHTS:

Apparent Women Officers or Directors:
Hot Spot for Advancement for Women/Minorities:

LOCATIONS: ("Y" = Yes)

West:	Southwest:	Midwest:	Southeast:	Northeast:	International:
				Y	

JL FRENCH AUTOMOTIVE CASTINGS

www.jlfrench.com

Industry Group Code: 336350 **Ranks within this company's industry group:** Sales: Profits:

Vehicle Manufacturing:		Dealers:		Parts:		Service:		Finance:		Specialty:	
Cars:		Car Dealer New:		Manufacturers:	Y	General Service:		Leasing:		Information Systems:	
Trucks:		Car Dealer Used:		Retail:		Specialty Service:		Auto Loans:		Online Marketing:	
Motorcycles:		Truck Dealer:		Distributors:		Oil Change:		Insurance:		Other:	Y
Specialty:		RV Dealer:		Tires:		Paint and Body:				Publishing:	
Buses:		Motorcycle Dealer:		Batteries:						Rental Cars/Trucks:	
RVs:		Specialty Dealer:									

TYPES OF BUSINESS:

Automobile Parts Manufacturing
Aluminum Die Casting
Power Train Components
Aluminum Smelting

BRANDS/DIVISIONS/AFFILIATES:

Allotech International
Windward Capital Partners LP

CONTACTS:

Note: Officers with more than one job title may be intentionally listed here more than once.

Thomas Musgrave, CEO
Thomas Musgrave, Pres.
Cathy Voskuil, Contact-Media
Mark Dlugopolski, Contact-Media
Thomas Musgrave, Chmn.
Thomas Bischoff, Contact-European Sales Office

Phone: 920-458-7724 **Fax:** 920-458-0140
Toll-Free:
Address: 3101 S. Taylor Dr., Sheboygan, WI 53082-1024 US

GROWTH PLANS/SPECIAL FEATURES:

J. L. French Automotive Castings, Inc. (French), based in Wisconsin, is a leading global supplier of die cast aluminum components to the automotive industry, specializing in power train components. Windward Capital Partners LP owns the company. The firm's products, which include cam covers, transmission cases, engine front covers, bedplates, engine blocks, brackets, and oil pans, are utilized in most high-volume automotive platforms. French's capabilities include design, modeling, prototyping, cast production, machining and assembly. It offers die cast machines from 300 tons to 3,500 tons. The company has 34 semi-automated assembly lines. The company operates five manufacturing facilities on the three Continents and five sales/customer support offices around the world. The company's North American headquarters are in Sheboygan, Wisconsin, and the headquarters for its European operations are in Ansola, Spain. Through its Allotech International subsidiary, French is also a leading aluminum secondary smelter in North America. The firm produces castings for many OEMs and Tier 1 suppliers, including GM, Ford, DaimlerChrysler, Audi and Nissan-Renault. French provides components for over 20 Ford models, including the Explorer, Taurus and F-Series pickup trucks. In July 2009, the firm filed for bankruptcy.

J.L. French Automotive Castings, Inc. offers its employees educational assistance, flexible spending accounts, medical benefits and life insurance.

FINANCIALS:

Sales and profits are in thousands of dollars—add 000 to get the full amount. 2009 Note: Financial information for 2009 was not available for all companies at press time.

2009 Sales: $	2009 Profits: $	**U.S. Stock Ticker: Private**
2008 Sales: $	2008 Profits: $	**Int'l Ticker:** Int'l Exchange:
2007 Sales: $293,000	2007 Profits: $	Employees:
2006 Sales: $	2006 Profits: $	Fiscal Year Ends: 12/31
2005 Sales: $	2005 Profits: $	Parent Company: WINDWARD CAPITAL PARTNERS LP

SALARIES/BENEFITS:

Pension Plan: Y	ESOP Stock Plan:	Profit Sharing:	Top Exec. Salary: $	Bonus: $
Savings Plan:	Stock Purch. Plan:		Second Exec. Salary: $	Bonus: $

OTHER THOUGHTS:

Apparent Women Officers or Directors: 1
Hot Spot for Advancement for Women/Minorities:

LOCATIONS: ("Y" = Yes)

West:	Southwest:	Midwest:	Southeast:	Northeast:	International:
		Y			Y

JM FAMILY ENTERPRISES

www.jmfamily.com

Industry Group Code: 42311 **Ranks within this company's industry group:** Sales: Profits:

Vehicle Manufacturing:		**Dealers:**		**Parts:**		**Service:**		**Finance:**		**Specialty:**	
Cars:		Car Dealer New:	Y	Manufacturers:		General Service:		Leasing:	Y	Information Systems:	
Trucks:		Car Dealer Used:	Y	Retail:		Specialty Service:		Auto Loans:	Y	Online Marketing:	
Motorcycles:		Truck Dealer:		Distributors:	Y	Oil Change:		Insurance:	Y	Other:	Y
Specialty:		RV Dealer:		Tires:		Paint and Body:				Publishing:	
Buses:		Motorcycle Dealer:		Batteries:						Rental Cars/Trucks:	
RVs:		Specialty Dealer:									

TYPES OF BUSINESS:

Automobile Distribution-Wholesale
Automobile Dealer
Parts Distribution
Financing & Insurance
Dealership Financing
Consulting Services

BRANDS/DIVISIONS/AFFILIATES:

JM Lexus
JM&A Group
JM Service Center (JMSC)
Southeast Toyota Distributors, LLC
World Omni Financial Corp. (WOFC)

CONTACTS:

Note: Officers with more than one job title may be intentionally listed here more than once.

Colin Brown, CEO
Colin Brown, Pres.
Brent Burns, CFO/Exec. VP
Ken Yerves, CIO/Exec. VP
Ken Yerves, Chief Admin. Officer
Carmen Johnson, General Counsel/Sr. VP
Eric Gebhard, Treas.
Frank Armstrong, Exec. VP/Pres., World Omni Financial Corp.
Ron Coombs, Sr. VP/COO-JM&A Group
Forrest Heathcott, Exec. VP/Pres., JM&A Group
Ed Sheehy, Exec. VP/Pres., Southeast Toyota Distributors, LLC

Phone: 954-429-2000	**Fax:** 954-429-2300
Toll-Free:	
Address: 100 Jim Moran Blvd., Deerfield Beach, FL 33442 US	

GROWTH PLANS/SPECIAL FEATURES:

JM Family Enterprises, Inc. is a leading family-owned diversified automotive company. Through its subsidiaries, JM is a leading global distributor of Toyotas and Scions; a diversified financial services company; a leading provider of finance and insurance products; a leading provider of integrated software systems for automotive dealers; and a leading global Lexus dealership. Subsidiary JM Lexus is one of the highest volume Lexus dealerships in the world, selling roughly 7,700 new and 2,000 pre-owned vehicles annually. The firm's JM&A Group subsidiary is a leading independent provider of finance and insurance products in the automotive industry, currently servicing over 2,800 dealer customers nationwide. JM Service Center (JMSC) is JM's internal shared services center. Its Southeast Toyota Distributors, LLC subsidiary is a leading independent global distributor of Toyotas and Scions, distributing cars, trucks, vans, parts and accessories to over 173 independent Toyota dealers. Southeast Toyota accounts for approximately 20% of U.S. Toyota sales. Subsidiary World Omni Financial Corp. (WOFC) is a diversified financial services company and a leading provider in the areas of indirect consumer retail and lease financing; commercial dealership financing; third-party portfolio management and servicing; remarketing services; wholesale floorplan accounting and risk management systems; and field services such as floorplan audit services and vehicle inspection services.

JM offers its employees educational assistance and development programs; flextime; adoption assistance; an onsite fitness center, cafeteria and credit union; massage therapy; health and dependent care spending accounts; and medical, dental, vision, prescription, life and disability insurance.

FINANCIALS:

Sales and profits are in thousands of dollars—add 000 to get the full amount. 2009 Note: Financial information for 2009 was not available for all companies at press time.

2009 Sales: $	2009 Profits: $	**U.S. Stock Ticker: Private**
2008 Sales: $10,100,000	2008 Profits: $	**Int'l Ticker:** Int'l Exchange:
2007 Sales: $12,200,000	2007 Profits: $	Employees: 4,000
2006 Sales: $10,500,000	2006 Profits: $	Fiscal Year Ends: 12/31
2005 Sales: $9,400,000	2005 Profits: $	Parent Company:

SALARIES/BENEFITS:

Pension Plan: Y	ESOP Stock Plan:	Profit Sharing: Y	Top Exec. Salary: $	Bonus: $
Savings Plan: Y	Stock Purch. Plan:		Second Exec. Salary: $	Bonus: $

OTHER THOUGHTS:

Apparent Women Officers or Directors: 1
Hot Spot for Advancement for Women/Minorities:

LOCATIONS: ("Y" = Yes)

West:	Southwest:	Midwest:	Southeast:	Northeast:	International:
		Y	Y	Y	Y

JOHNSON CONTROLS INC

www.johnsoncontrols.com

Industry Group Code: 3363 **Ranks within this company's industry group:** Sales: 3 Profits: 53

Vehicle Manufacturing:		Dealers:		Parts:		Service:		Finance:		Specialty:	
Cars:		Car Dealer New:		Manufacturers:	Y	General Service:		Leasing:		Information Systems:	
Trucks:		Car Dealer Used:		Retail:		Specialty Service:		Auto Loans:		Online Marketing:	
Motorcycles:		Truck Dealer:		Distributors:		Oil Change:		Insurance:		Other:	Y
Specialty:		RV Dealer:		Tires:		Paint and Body:				Publishing:	
Buses:		Motorcycle Dealer:		Batteries:						Rental Cars/Trucks:	
RVs:		Specialty Dealer:									

TYPES OF BUSINESS:

Automobile Parts & Controls
Automotive Batteries
Facilities Management
Automotive Interior Components
Energy Management Services
Building Security, Lighting & HVAC Systems

BRANDS/DIVISIONS/AFFILIATES:

National Energy Services
Johnson Controls-Saft Advanced Power Solutions
Automotive Experience
Optima
Varta
Metasys Sustainability Manager
Heliar
LTH

CONTACTS: *Note: Officers with more than one job title may be intentionally listed here more than once.*

Stephen A. Roell, CEO
Keith Wandell, COO
Stephen A. Roell, Pres.
R. Bruce McDonald, CFO/Exec. VP
Susan F. Davis, Exec. VP-Human Resources
Colin Boyd, CIO/VP-IT
Jerome D. Okarma, General Counsel/VP/Sec.
Jacqueline F. Strayer, VP-Corp. Comm.
Glen Ponczak, Exec. Dir.-Investor Rel.
Frank A. Voltolina, Corp. Treas./VP
C. David Meyers, VP/Pres., Building Efficiency
Jeffrey G. Augustin, VP-Finance, Building Efficiency
Alex A. Molinaroli, VP/Pres., Power Solutions
Charles A. Harvey, VP-Public Affairs & Diversity
Stephen A. Roell, Chmn.
Jeffrey S. Edwards, VP-Automotive Experience, Japan & APAC

Phone: 414-524-1200	**Fax:** 414-524-2070
Toll-Free: 800-524-6220	
Address: 5757 N. Green Bay Ave., Milwaukee, WI 53209 US	

GROWTH PLANS/SPECIAL FEATURES:

Johnson Controls, Inc. is a leader in automotive interiors/batteries, building efficiency and facility management. The firm's Automotive Experience segment, which accounts for roughly 42% of the company's sales, designs and manufactures concept cars; complete seat systems; seating components; electronics; instrument panels; overhead, door and cargo management systems; cockpits; and interior trim for manufacturers of cars and light trucks. The division operates approximately 175 wholly- and majority-owned manufacturing/assembly plants in 32 countries. Johnson Control's Power Solutions division (14% of sales) manufactures and replaces automotive batteries, focusing on innovations for hybrid electric vehicles. Its battery brands include Optima, Varta, Heliar (in South America), and LTH (in Mexico). The segment produces roughly 110 million lead-acid batteries annually in approximately 55 wholly- and majority-owned manufacturing/assembly facilities in 21 countries. The Building Efficiency division (44% of sales) operates in 59 countries, supplying systems designed for heating; ventilation; air conditioning; lighting; security; and fire management. The U.S. Department of Defense utilizes Johnson Controls for the Pentagon's energy management and environmental control systems. Global WorkPlace Solutions, part of Building Efficiency, provides companies with a real-estate based approach to shareholder value. The Building Efficiency division also does facility management, using its patented Metasys Building Management System. It handles school districts, hospitals, factories, airports and government facilities. Johnson Controls has a joint venture with Saft SA, a battery company, called Johnson Controls-Saft Advanced Power Solutions. In January 2010, the firm opened two new laboratories in Pennsylvania for the testing of commercial air-conditioning equipment. In February 2010, the company and IBM agreed to jointly develop a program to reduce energy and water consumption in buildings. In March 2010, Johnson Controls acquired lighting services firm National Energy Services.

The firm offers employees benefits including health care coverage, tuition reimbursement and a 401(k) plan.

FINANCIALS: **Sales and profits are in thousands of dollars—add 000 to get the full amount. 2009 Note: Financial information for 2009 was not available for all companies at press time.**

2009 Sales: $28,497,000	2009 Profits: $-338,000	**U.S. Stock Ticker: JCI**
2008 Sales: $38,062,000	2008 Profits: $979,000	**Int'l Ticker:** Int'l Exchange:
2007 Sales: $34,624,000	2007 Profits: $1,252,000	Employees: 130,000
2006 Sales: $32,235,000	2006 Profits: $1,028,000	Fiscal Year Ends: 9/30
2005 Sales: $27,479,400	2005 Profits: $909,400	Parent Company:

SALARIES/BENEFITS:

Pension Plan:	ESOP Stock Plan:	Profit Sharing:	Top Exec. Salary: $1,371,500	Bonus: $1,097,000
Savings Plan: Y	Stock Purch. Plan:		Second Exec. Salary: $817,000	Bonus: $470,000

OTHER THOUGHTS:

Apparent Women Officers or Directors: 4
Hot Spot for Advancement for Women/Minorities: Y

LOCATIONS: ("Y" = Yes)

West:	Southwest:	Midwest:	Southeast:	Northeast:	International:
Y	Y	Y	Y	Y	Y

JORDAN AUTOMOTIVE GROUP

www.jordanauto.com

Industry Group Code: 441110 **Ranks within this company's industry group:** Sales: Profits:

Vehicle Manufacturing:		Dealers:		Parts:		Service:		Finance:		Specialty:	
Cars:		Car Dealer New:	Y	Manufacturers:		General Service:	Y	Leasing:		Information Systems:	
Trucks:		Car Dealer Used:	Y	Retail:		Specialty Service:		Auto Loans:		Online Marketing:	
Motorcycles:		Truck Dealer:	Y	Distributors:		Oil Change:		Insurance:		Other:	
Specialty:		RV Dealer:		Tires:		Paint and Body:	Y			Publishing:	
Buses:		Motorcycle Dealer:		Batteries:						Rental Cars/Trucks:	
RVs:		Specialty Dealer:	Y								

TYPES OF BUSINESS:

Auto Dealers, Retail
Fleet Sales
Repair Services
Agricultural & Industrial Vehicles

BRANDS/DIVISIONS/AFFILIATES:

Jordan Fleet Sales
WayCool Rewards Club

CONTACTS:

Note: Officers with more than one job title may be intentionally listed here more than once.

Craig Kapson, Pres.
Melissa Stone, Mgr.-Mktg.
Robert Hayden, VP-Oper.
Melissa Stone, Mgr.-eCommerce

Phone: 574-259-1981	**Fax:** 574-254-7552
Toll-Free: 800-837-1981	
Address: 609 E. Jefferson Blvd., Mishawaka, IN 46545 US	

GROWTH PLANS/SPECIAL FEATURES:

Jordan Automotive Group sells new and used vehicles through its five Indiana franchises. The group sells Ford, Toyota, Volvo, and Scion vehicles. The company also provides repair services for these brands and operates a body shop. Jordan has a national and commercial fleet sales division, Jordan Fleet Sales, and offers commercial and fleet services. This division sells heavy-duty trucks used for agricultural, construction, ambulance and rental needs. Potential customers and pre-existing owners can obtain a quick quote, schedule a maintenance appointment and view images and information on new and used vehicles through the company's web site. Also online, customers can apply for financing through the firm's finance department. It also has a pre-owned superstore that comes equipped with a search feature for customers to browse cars, trucks and vans of differing makes and models. Jordan offers a WayCool rewards club for customers, who get their vehicles serviced at Jordan dealerships, or at their collision centers. The rewards club can be used for discounts and to earn points at select other merchants. Customers who buy from the group also receive benefits such as free car washes for life and free first year of scheduled maintenance on certified pre-owned vehicles.

FINANCIALS:

Sales and profits are in thousands of dollars—add 000 to get the full amount. 2009 Note: Financial information for 2009 was not available for all companies at press time.

2009 Sales: $	2009 Profits: $	**U.S. Stock Ticker: Private**
2008 Sales: $	2008 Profits: $	**Int'l Ticker:** Int'l Exchange:
2007 Sales: $	2007 Profits: $	Employees:
2006 Sales: $	2006 Profits: $	Fiscal Year Ends: 12/31
2005 Sales: $	2005 Profits: $	Parent Company:

SALARIES/BENEFITS:

Pension Plan:	ESOP Stock Plan:	Profit Sharing:	Top Exec. Salary: $	Bonus: $
Savings Plan:	Stock Purch. Plan:		Second Exec. Salary: $	Bonus: $

OTHER THOUGHTS:

Apparent Women Officers or Directors: 1
Hot Spot for Advancement for Women/Minorities:

LOCATIONS: ("Y" = Yes)

West:	Southwest:	Midwest:	Southeast:	Northeast:	International:
		Y			

KANTO AUTO WORKS LTD

www.kanto-aw.co.jp/en/

Industry Group Code: 336211 **Ranks within this company's industry group:** Sales: 2 Profits: 2

Vehicle Manufacturing:		Dealers:		Parts:		Service:		Finance:		Specialty:	
Cars:		Car Dealer New:		Manufacturers:	Y	General Service:		Leasing:		Information Systems:	
Trucks:		Car Dealer Used:		Retail:		Specialty Service:		Auto Loans:		Online Marketing:	
Motorcycles:		Truck Dealer:		Distributors:		Oil Change:		Insurance:		Other:	Y
Specialty:		RV Dealer:		Tires:		Paint and Body:				Publishing:	
Buses:		Motorcycle Dealer:		Batteries:						Rental Cars/Trucks:	
RVs:		Specialty Dealer:									

TYPES OF BUSINESS:

Motor Vehicle Body Manufacturing
Automobile Assembly
Housing Manufacturing
Engineering Services
Food Services

BRANDS/DIVISIONS/AFFILIATES:

Toyota Group
Toyota Motor Corporation
Kanto Shoji Co., Ltd.
Kanto Kosan Co., Ltd.
K.E. Protec Co., Ltd.
K.F. Service Co., Ltd.
Patrafour
TETRAS

CONTACTS: *Note: Officers with more than one job title may be intentionally listed here more than once.*

Tetsuo Hattori, Pres.
Tokuo Fukuichi, Sr. Dir.-Tech.
Toshikazu Sano, Dir.-Planning
Naoto Tanoue, Mgr.-Iwate Plant
Yasuhiko Ichihashi, VP
Yoshiaki Ishii, Sr. Managing Dir.
Masahito Kanai, Sr. Managing Dir.
Makoto Suzuki, Dir.-Overseas Bus. Planning

Phone: 81-46-861-5111 **Fax:**
Toll-Free:
Address: Tauraminato-cho, Yokosuka, Kanegawa, 237-8585 Japan

GROWTH PLANS/SPECIAL FEATURES:

Kanto Auto Works, Ltd., a Toyota Group company, manufactures automotive car bodies for Toyota Motor Corporation. Kanto's corporate partnership with Toyota began in 1948, when it signed a contract to assemble bodies for the chassis of Toyota's Toyopet passenger car. The firm currently manufactures compact cars and luxury vehicles from its Higashi Fuji plant in Shizuoka and its Iwate plant in Iwate. At its Higashi Fuji plant, Kanto manufactures Toyota models including the Century, Crown Sedan, Crown Comfort, Comfort, Isis, Corolla Fielder, Lexus SC430 and Corolla (exclusively for export). At its Iwate plant, the company manufactures Toyota models including the Belta, Auris, Blade, Corolla Rumion and Ractis, as well as the ist, a subcompact car. The firm also operates several additional facilities, including the Higashi Fuji Machinery Engineering plant, the Yamanashi Housing works facility and the Higashi Fuji Integration Center. In addition to cars, the company offers the Patrafour electric wheelchair and the TETRAS automatic vehicle maintenance lift. The Patrafour features an all-wheel drive system and is sold in Japan by Nissin Medical Industries Co., Ltd. The TETRAS maintenance lift is sold at Anzen Motor Car outlets in Japan. The company manufactures approximately 314,100 vehicles per year. Kanto's subsidiaries include Kanto Shoji Co., Ltd., for business commerce; Kanto Kosan Co., Ltd., for facilities construction; K.E. Protec Co., Ltd., for automotive plant engineering services; and K.F. Service Co., Ltd., for food services. The company has two overseas plants: Kanjiko Do Brasil Industria Automotiva Ltda., in Sao Paulo, Brazil, which manufactures press components for cars; and Auto CS Engineering Co., Ltd., in Thailand, which manufactures and sells press and resin molds primarily for cars.

FINANCIALS: **Sales and profits are in thousands of dollars—add 000 to get the full amount. 2009 Note: Financial information for 2009 was not available for all companies at press time.**

2009 Sales: $6,615,180	2009 Profits: $3,810	**U.S. Stock Ticker:**
2008 Sales: $8,491,810	2008 Profits: $105,440	**Int'l Ticker: 7223** Int'l Exchange: Tokyo-TSE
2007 Sales: $7,617,520	2007 Profits: $83,360	Employees:
2006 Sales: $6,786,800	2006 Profits: $73,600	Fiscal Year Ends: 3/31
2005 Sales: $5,679,460	2005 Profits: $64,260	Parent Company:

SALARIES/BENEFITS:

Pension Plan:	ESOP Stock Plan:	Profit Sharing:	Top Exec. Salary: $	Bonus: $
Savings Plan:	Stock Purch. Plan:		Second Exec. Salary: $	Bonus: $

OTHER THOUGHTS:

Apparent Women Officers or Directors:
Hot Spot for Advancement for Women/Minorities:

LOCATIONS: ("Y" = Yes)

West:	Southwest:	Midwest:	Southeast:	Northeast:	International:
					Y

KAR AUCTION SERVICES INC

www.karholdings.com

Industry Group Code: 453998 **Ranks within this company's industry group:** Sales: 1 Profits: 1

Vehicle Manufacturing:		Dealers:		Parts:		Service:		Finance:		Specialty:	
Cars:		Car Dealer New:		Manufacturers:		General Service:		Leasing:		Information Systems:	
Trucks:		Car Dealer Used:		Retail:		Specialty Service:		Auto Loans:		Online Marketing:	
Motorcycles:		Truck Dealer:		Distributors:		Oil Change:		Insurance:		Other:	Y
Specialty:		RV Dealer:		Tires:		Paint and Body:				Publishing:	
Buses:		Motorcycle Dealer:		Batteries:						Rental Cars/Trucks:	
RVs:		Specialty Dealer:	Y								

TYPES OF BUSINESS:

Vehicle Auctions
Financial Services

BRANDS/DIVISIONS/AFFILIATES:

ADESA
Insurance Auto Auctions Inc
Automotive Finance Corporation
AutoVIN
Automotive Finance Consumer Division
PAR North America
I-bid LIVE
KAR Holdings Inc

CONTACTS:

Note: Officers with more than one job title may be intentionally listed here more than once.

James P. Hallett, CEO
Eric M. Loughmiller, CFO/Exec. VP
John R. Nordin, CIO/Exec. VP
Rebecca C. Polak, General Counsel/Exec. VP/Sec.
Benjamin Skuy, Exec. VP-Strategic Initiatives
Thomas Caruso, CEO/Pres., ADESA
Donald S. Gottwald, CEO/Pres., Automotive Finance Corp.
Thomas C. O'Brien, CEO/Pres., Insurance Auto Auctions, Inc.
David Vignes, Exec. VP-Enterprise Optimization
Brian T. Clingen, Chmn.
Benjamin Skuy, Exec. VP-Int'l Markets

Phone:	Fax:
Toll-Free: 800-923-3725	
Address: 13085 Hamilton Crossing Blvd., Carmel, IN 46032 US	

GROWTH PLANS/SPECIAL FEATURES:

KAR Auction Services, Inc., formerly KAR Holdings, Inc., provides auction services for both whole car and salvage auctions. The firm operates through the following subsidiaries: ADESA Auctions; Insurance Auto Auctions, Inc. (IAAI); Automotive Finance Corporation (AFC); AutoVIN the Automated Vehicle Information Network; PAR North America (PAR); and Automotive Finance Consumer Division (AFCD). ADESA Auctions has 62 used vehicle sites providing wholesale used vehicle auctions. This division also provides inbound and outbound logistics; reconditioning; vehicle inspection and certification; titling; and administrative services. IAAI offers salvage vehicle auctions and services, with 153 sites. The auctions sell damaged vehicles designated as total losses by insurance companies; recovered stolen vehicles for which an insurance settlement has been made; and older model vehicles donated to charity or sold by dealers. Services provided by this segment also include inbound and outbound logistics; inspections; evaluations; titling; and settlement administrative services. I-bid LIVE, IAAI's Internet solution, connects to live auctions allowing buyers to bid along with those physically present. AFC provides short-term inventory-secured financing and/or floorplan financing to independent used vehicle dealers from 88 loan production offices in the U.S. and Canada. AutoVIN provides field information services including vehicle condition reporting, inventory verification, program compliance auditing and facility inspections. PAR works with over 100 auctions nationwide and in Canada to provide centralized repossessions, vehicle titling, remarketing services, lease end-of-term, online tools, and vehicle transition services. AFCD provides financial products and services to automotive dealerships, including AFCD Dealer Desktop, powered by Nowcom; virtual financial and insurance services; vehicle service contracts; and GAP insurance coverage. In 2009 and 2010, IAAI opened several new locations in Pennsylvania and Mississippi, Louisiana and Alaska. In September 2009, ADESA opened a new location in Guadalajara, Mexico. In November 2009, KAR Holdings changed its name to KAR Auction Services and became publicly traded.

FINANCIALS:

Sales and profits are in thousands of dollars—add 000 to get the full amount. 2009 Note: Financial information for 2009 was not available for all companies at press time.

2009 Sales: $1,729,600	2009 Profits: $23,200	**U.S. Stock Ticker: Private**
2008 Sales: $1,771,400	2008 Profits: $-216,200	**Int'l Ticker:** Int'l Exchange:
2007 Sales: $1,102,800	2007 Profits: $-38,300	Employees: 12,648
2006 Sales: $	2006 Profits: $	Fiscal Year Ends: 12/31
2005 Sales: $	2005 Profits: $	Parent Company:

SALARIES/BENEFITS:

Pension Plan:	ESOP Stock Plan:	Profit Sharing:	Top Exec. Salary: $592,250	Bonus: $784,456
Savings Plan: Y	Stock Purch. Plan:		Second Exec. Salary: $482,281	Bonus: $505,610

OTHER THOUGHTS:

Apparent Women Officers or Directors: 1
Hot Spot for Advancement for Women/Minorities:

LOCATIONS: ("Y" = Yes)

West:	Southwest:	Midwest:	Southeast:	Northeast:	International:
		Y	Y		Y

KAWASAKI HEAVY INDUSTRIES LTD

www.khi.co.jp

Industry Group Code: 333 **Ranks within this company's industry group:** Sales: 3 Profits: 3

Vehicle Manufacturing:		**Dealers:**		**Parts:**		**Service:**		**Finance:**		**Specialty:**	
Cars:		Car Dealer New:		Manufacturers:	Y	General Service:		Leasing:		Information Systems:	
Trucks:		Car Dealer Used:		Retail:		Specialty Service:		Auto Loans:		Online Marketing:	
Motorcycles:	Y	Truck Dealer:		Distributors:		Oil Change:		Insurance:		Other:	Y
Specialty:	Y	RV Dealer:		Tires:		Paint and Body:				Publishing:	
Buses:		Motorcycle Dealer:		Batteries:						Rental Cars/Trucks:	
RVs:		Specialty Dealer:									

TYPES OF BUSINESS:

Recreational Vehicle & Machinery Manufacturing
Motorcycles, ATVs & Personal Watercraft
Helicopter & Aerospace Manufacturing
Industrial Machinery
Gas Turbines, Engines & Generators
Locomotives, Ships & Submarines
Plant & Infrastructure Manufacturing
Power Plant Construction

BRANDS/DIVISIONS/AFFILIATES:

India Kawasaki Motors Pvt. Ltd.
Kawasaki Precision Machinery Trading Co., Ltd.

CONTACTS:

Note: Officers with more than one job title may be intentionally listed here more than once.

Satoshi Hasegawa, Pres.
Mitsutoshi Takao, Sr. VP-Corp. Planning
Hiroshi Takata, Sr. VP/Pres., Motorcycle & Engine Company
Yuichi Asano, Sr. VP/Pres., Gas Turbine & Machinery Company
Shigeru Murayama, Sr. VP/Pres., Aerospace Company
Kyohei Matsuoka, Sr. VP/Pres., Rolling Stock Company
Tadaharu Ohashi, Chmn.

Phone: 81-78-371-9530 **Fax:** 81-78-371-9568
Toll-Free:
Address: Kobe Crystal Tower,1-3 Higashikawasaki-cho 1-chome, Hyogo, 650-8680 Japan

GROWTH PLANS/SPECIAL FEATURES:

Kawasaki Heavy Industries, Ltd. (KHI) manufactures a range of transportation equipment and industrial goods. KHI operates through seven business segments: shipbuilding, which accounted for 12.9% of 2009 revenue; rolling stock, 14.2%; aerospace, 16.1%; gas turbines and machinery, 16.3%; plant and infrastructure engineering, 7.7%; motorcycle and engine, 18.4%; and precision machinery, 5.8%. The shipbuilding segment manufactures liquefied natural gas (LNG) and liquefied petroleum gas (LPG) carriers; container ships; VLCCs (Very Large Crude Carriers); submarines; and maritime application equipment. The rolling stock business segment manufactures Shinkansen bullet electric train cars; electric and diesel locomotives; passenger coaches; integrated transit systems; monorail cars; and platform screen doors. The aerospace business segment manufactures CH-47, OH-1 and BK117 helicopters; component parts for the Boeing 777, 787 and 767 passenger airplanes; component parts for the Embraer 170 and 190 jet aircraft; missiles; electronic equipment; and space equipment. The gas turbines and machinery segment manufactures jet engines; small and medium-sized gas turbine generators; gas turbine cogeneration systems; gas turbines for naval vessels; gas engines; gas compression modules; diesel engines; and marine propulsion systems. The plant and infrastructure engineering segment manufactures cement, chemical, power and municipal refuse incineration plants; crushing machines; shield machines; LNG and LPG tanks; and tunnel-boring machines. The motorcycle and engine segment manufactures motorcycles, ATVs, utility vehicles, personal watercraft and general-purpose gasoline engines. Lastly, the precision machinery segment manufactures industrial hydraulic products and industrial robots. In April 2010, KHI launched India Kawasaki Motors Pvt. Ltd., a wholly-owned subsidiary specializing in motorcycle imports and sales. In June 2010, the company established Shanghai-based Kawasaki Precision Machinery Trading (Shanghai) Co., Ltd., a wholly-owned subsidiary specializing in sales of hydraulic components and equipment for construction machinery and ships.

FINANCIALS:

Sales and profits are in thousands of dollars—add 000 to get the full amount. 2009 Note: Financial information for 2009 was not available for all companies at press time.

2009 Sales: $14,380,400	2009 Profits: $125,980	**U.S. Stock Ticker: KWHIY**
2008 Sales: $14,981,008	2008 Profits: $350,709	**Int'l Ticker: 7012** Int'l Exchange: Tokyo-TSE
2007 Sales: $12,182,395	2007 Profits: $252,113	Employees: 30,563
2006 Sales: $11,258,083	2006 Profits: $140,180	Fiscal Year Ends: 3/31
2005 Sales: $11,149,457	2005 Profits: $103,080	Parent Company:

SALARIES/BENEFITS:

Pension Plan:	ESOP Stock Plan:	Profit Sharing:	Top Exec. Salary: $	Bonus: $
Savings Plan:	Stock Purch. Plan:		Second Exec. Salary: $	Bonus: $

OTHER THOUGHTS:

Apparent Women Officers or Directors:
Hot Spot for Advancement for Women/Minorities:

LOCATIONS: ("Y" = Yes)

West:	Southwest:	Midwest:	Southeast:	Northeast:	International:
	Y	Y	Y	Y	Y

KELLEY AUTOMOTIVE GROUP

www.drivekelley.com

Industry Group Code: 441110 **Ranks within this company's industry group:** Sales: Profits:

Vehicle Manufacturing:		Dealers:		Parts:		Service:		Finance:		Specialty:	
Cars:		Car Dealer New:	Y	Manufacturers:		General Service:	Y	Leasing:		Information Systems:	
Trucks:		Car Dealer Used:	Y	Retail:	Y	Specialty Service:		Auto Loans:		Online Marketing:	Y
Motorcycles:		Truck Dealer:		Distributors:		Oil Change:		Insurance:		Other:	Y
Specialty:		RV Dealer:		Tires:		Paint and Body:	Y			Publishing:	
Buses:		Motorcycle Dealer:		Batteries:						Rental Cars/Trucks:	
RVs:		Specialty Dealer:									

TYPES OF BUSINESS:

Auto Dealers, Retail
New & Used Cars
Automotive Parts & Service

BRANDS/DIVISIONS/AFFILIATES:

Courtesy Motors
Kelley Chevrolet
Saturn of Fort Wayne
Tom Kelley Buik Pontiac GMC
Tom Kelley Cadillac
Tom Kelley Hummer
Tom Kelley Saab
Courtesy Ford

CONTACTS: *Note: Officers with more than one job title may be intentionally listed here more than once.*

Thomas W. Kelley, CEO
Thomas W. Kelley, Pres.
Gary Thelen, CFO
Jim Kelley, VP-Oper., Tom Kelley Cadillac Saab Hummer
Trent Waybright, Gen. Mgr.-Saturn of Fort Wayne
Chuck Kelley, Gen. Mgr.-Kelley Chevrolet
Thomas W. Kelley, Chmn.

Phone: 260-434-4750	**Fax:** 260-434-4707
Toll-Free: 877-853-5539	
Address: 633 Ave. of Autos, Fort Wayne, IN 46804 US	

GROWTH PLANS/SPECIAL FEATURES:

Kelley Automotive Group is a family owned group of new and pre-owned vehicle dealers. In addition to vehicle sales, the company also handles parts, services and body work. The group has 12 dealership locations that span from Fort Wayne, Indiana to Atlanta, Georgia, including Courtesy Ford; Tom Kelley Hummer; Saturn of Fort Wayne; Tom Kelley Saab; Courtesy Motors; and Tom Kelley Volvo. Brands handled by the dealerships include Volvo, Hummer, Ford, Chevrolet, Buick, Cadillac, Saab, GMC, Pontiac and Saturn. Kelley's inventory can be viewed online, where customers can search new or used inventory, or by year, make, model, vehicle type, MSRP or location. In addition, customers can compare up to five vehicles at once. The company's web site also allows customers to apply for financing, schedule service appointments, view print ads online, request a part online and locate affiliated body shops. In April 2010, Dealership Holdings, LLC, a new company partially owned by the Kelley family, acquired substantially all the assets of Kelley Automotive Group, which has ceased operations.

FINANCIALS: **Sales and profits are in thousands of dollars—add 000 to get the full amount. 2009 Note: Financial information for 2009 was not available for all companies at press time.**

2009 Sales: $	2009 Profits: $	**U.S. Stock Ticker: Private**
2008 Sales: $	2008 Profits: $	**Int'l Ticker:** Int'l Exchange:
2007 Sales: $	2007 Profits: $	Employees:
2006 Sales: $	2006 Profits: $	Fiscal Year Ends:
2005 Sales: $	2005 Profits: $	Parent Company:

SALARIES/BENEFITS:

Pension Plan:	ESOP Stock Plan:	Profit Sharing:	Top Exec. Salary: $	Bonus: $
Savings Plan:	Stock Purch. Plan:		Second Exec. Salary: $	Bonus: $

OTHER THOUGHTS:

Apparent Women Officers or Directors:
Hot Spot for Advancement for Women/Minorities:

LOCATIONS: ("Y" = Yes)

West:	Southwest:	Midwest:	Southeast:	Northeast:	International:
		Y	Y		

KEY PLASTICS LLC

www.keyplastics.com

Industry Group Code: 3363 **Ranks within this company's industry group:** Sales: Profits:

Vehicle Manufacturing:		Dealers:		Parts:		Service:		Finance:		Specialty:	
Cars:		Car Dealer New:		Manufacturers:	Y	General Service:		Leasing:		Information Systems:	
Trucks:		Car Dealer Used:		Retail:		Specialty Service:		Auto Loans:		Online Marketing:	
Motorcycles:		Truck Dealer:		Distributors:		Oil Change:		Insurance:		Other:	
Specialty:		RV Dealer:		Tires:		Paint and Body:				Publishing:	
Buses:		Motorcycle Dealer:		Batteries:						Rental Cars/Trucks:	
RVs:		Specialty Dealer:									

TYPES OF BUSINESS:

Automotive Part Manufacturing
Injection Molding

BRANDS/DIVISIONS/AFFILIATES:

Wayzata Investment Partners LLC
OLHO GmbH

CONTACTS:

Note: Officers with more than one job title may be intentionally listed here more than once.

Terrence G. Gohl, CEO
Ralph Ralston, COO
Ralph Ralston, Pres.
Nuno Romero, Corp. Contact-Europe
Gene Davis, Chmn.
Miguel Ferraz, Gen. Mgr.-Shanghai Key Automotive Plastic

Phone: 248-449-6100 **Fax:** 248-449-4105
Toll-Free:
Address: 21700 Haggerty Rd., Ste. 100N, Northville, MI 48167 US

GROWTH PLANS/SPECIAL FEATURES:

Key Plastics LLC offers a full range of engineering, program management and production services to the automotive industry. The company operates through 23 facilities, nine of which are located in North America, 12 in Europe and two in Asia. In addition, the company has four technical centers. Key Plastics provides exterior, interior, trim and under hood products. Exterior products include wheel covers, molding and license plate buckets. The company's interior products include air vents and ducts; bezels and fascias for radios, climate, navigation and steering wheel controls; cup holders; ashtrays; glove boxes; control panel covers; instrument clusters; speaker grilles; decorative trims; assist handles; floor console assemblies; seat belt adjusters; and head rest assemblies. Trim products include radio bezel assemblies; HVAC bezel assemblies; ignition bobbins and spools; ignition case assemblies; seat trim products; air louvers; air bag covers; and speaker grilles. Key Plastics' under hood products include battery trays; electric and electronic component supports; cable channels; and fan and shrouds. Additionally, the firm offers program management and technical services, which include in-house rapid prototyping, painting, thermoforming, in-house performance testing and layouts and local program management for all services. Customers include most domestic and transplant original equipment manufacturers (OEMs) and Tier One suppliers in the industry. In February 2009, the firm completed a restructuring. This reorganization resulted in Wayzata Investment Partners LLC becoming the controlling shareholder of Key Plastics from The Ewing Management Group. In April 2010, the firm acquired OLHO GmbH business in Janovice, Czech Republic and the equipment and inventory of the OLHO facility in Lohne, Germany. The company plans to strength its portfolio by supplying air vents and interior mechanisms to its automotive customers.

FINANCIALS:

Sales and profits are in thousands of dollars—add 000 to get the full amount. 2009 Note: Financial information for 2009 was not available for all companies at press time.

2009 Sales: $
2008 Sales: $
2007 Sales: $673,000
2006 Sales: $
2005 Sales: $

2009 Profits: $
2008 Profits: $
2007 Profits: $
2006 Profits: $
2005 Profits: $

U.S. Stock Ticker: Private
Int'l Ticker: Int'l Exchange:
Employees:
Fiscal Year Ends: 12/31
Parent Company: WAYZATA INVESTMENT PARTNERS LLC

SALARIES/BENEFITS:

Pension Plan: ESOP Stock Plan: Profit Sharing: Top Exec. Salary: $ Bonus: $
Savings Plan: Stock Purch. Plan: Second Exec. Salary: $ Bonus: $

OTHER THOUGHTS:

Apparent Women Officers or Directors:
Hot Spot for Advancement for Women/Minorities:

LOCATIONS: ("Y" = Yes)

West:	Southwest:	Midwest:	Southeast:	Northeast:	International:
		Y		Y	Y

KEY SAFETY SYSTEMS INC

www.keysafetyinc.com

Industry Group Code: 3363 **Ranks within this company's industry group:** Sales: Profits:

Vehicle Manufacturing:		**Dealers:**		**Parts:**		**Service:**		**Finance:**		**Specialty:**	
Cars:		Car Dealer New:		Manufacturers:	Y	General Service:		Leasing:		Information Systems:	
Trucks:		Car Dealer Used:		Retail:		Specialty Service:		Auto Loans:		Online Marketing:	
Motorcycles:		Truck Dealer:		Distributors:		Oil Change:		Insurance:		Other:	
Specialty:		RV Dealer:		Tires:		Paint and Body:				Publishing:	
Buses:		Motorcycle Dealer:		Batteries:						Rental Cars/Trucks:	
RVs:		Specialty Dealer:									

TYPES OF BUSINESS:

Automotive Safety Components Manufacturing
Seat Belts
Steering Wheels
Airbags
Electronic Sensors
Testing & Engineering Services

BRANDS/DIVISIONS/AFFILIATES:

KSS-Abhishek Safety Systems Pvt., Ltd.
Yanfeng Key
Hamlin Electronics
Crestview Partners, L.P.

CONTACTS:

Note: Officers with more than one job title may be intentionally listed here more than once.

Jason Luo, CEO
Jason Luo, Pres.
Dave Smith, CFO
Ron Feldeisen, Sr. VP-Global Sales & Mktg.
Larry Casey, Sr. VP-Global Human Resources
Jim Scarpa, Sr. VP-Mfg. & Quality
Tom Dono, General Counsel/Sr. VP-Legal Affairs
Greg Heald, Sr. VP-Bus. Dev.
Mark Wehner, Pres., Safety Prod. Bus. Unit
Dave Smith, Sr. VP-Specialty Bus. Unit
Greg Heald, Sr. VP-Procurement

Phone: 586-726-3800	**Fax:**
Toll-Free:	
Address: 7000 Nineteen Mile Rd., Sterling Heights, MI 48314 US	

GROWTH PLANS/SPECIAL FEATURES:

Key Safety Systems, Inc. (KSS) is a leading designer, developer and manufacturer of automotive safety components and systems including airbags, standard and inflatable seat belts, inflators and airbag-equipped steering wheels. Company founder Allen Breed is credited with inventing the automotive airbag. KSS's airbag components and assemblies include sensors, inflators, steering-wheel airbag combinations and driver-side and side-impact supplemental restraint systems. The firm's products are used by carmakers around the world in more than 300 models produced by about 60 manufacturers globally. KSS also makes specialty vehicle safety products for over OEM (original equipment manufacturer) customers in the heavy truck and bus, agriculture, construction, exotic automobile, military vehicle, recreation and utility vehicle and automotive aftermarket segments. The firm also develops and manufactures sensor technology through Hamlin Electronics. Additionally, KSS provides testing and engineering services to customers in various industries. Solutions include product design and consulting services, such as failure analysis, compliance testing, laboratory design, injury and crash data analysis and biomechanical studies; testing services, including physical and environmental, mechanical, durability, electrical and static deployment testing; and prototyping services, including metal forming, fixture creation, plastic injection molding and dimensional inspection solutions. The company supports this client base from 35 manufacturing, technical and sales facilities in a dozen countries, including four primary technical centers in the U.S., Germany, China and Japan. The firm also maintains several joint ventures, including Yanfeng Key, which provides engineering services; and KSS-Abhishek Safety Systems Pvt., Ltd., which manufactures advanced safety products. KSS is owned by private equity firm Crestview Partners, LP. In November 2009, the company introduced the first automotive inflatable seatbelt. In April 2010, the company established a new manufacturing facility in Romania; and announced plans to expand airbag inflator production at its wholly-owned plant in Huzhou, China.

FINANCIALS:

Sales and profits are in thousands of dollars—add 000 to get the full amount. 2009 Note: Financial information for 2009 was not available for all companies at press time.

2009 Sales: $	2009 Profits: $	**U.S. Stock Ticker: Private**
2008 Sales: $	2008 Profits: $	**Int'l Ticker:** Int'l Exchange:
2007 Sales: $	2007 Profits: $	Employees:
2006 Sales: $	2006 Profits: $	Fiscal Year Ends:
2005 Sales: $	2005 Profits: $	Parent Company: CRESTVIEW PARTNERS LP

SALARIES/BENEFITS:

Pension Plan:	ESOP Stock Plan:	Profit Sharing:	Top Exec. Salary: $	Bonus: $
Savings Plan:	Stock Purch. Plan:		Second Exec. Salary: $	Bonus: $

OTHER THOUGHTS:

Apparent Women Officers or Directors:
Hot Spot for Advancement for Women/Minorities:

LOCATIONS: ("Y" = Yes)

West:	Southwest:	Midwest:	Southeast:	Northeast:	International:
	Y	Y	Y		Y

Note: Financial information, benefits and other data can change quickly and may vary from those stated here.

KEYSTONE AUTOMOTIVE INDUSTRIES INC www.keystone-auto.com

Industry Group Code: 423120 **Ranks within this company's industry group:** Sales: Profits:

Vehicle Manufacturing:		Dealers:		Parts:		Service:		Finance:		Specialty:	
Cars:		Car Dealer New:		Manufacturers:	Y	General Service:		Leasing:		Information Systems:	
Trucks:		Car Dealer Used:		Retail:		Specialty Service:		Auto Loans:		Online Marketing:	
Motorcycles:		Truck Dealer:		Distributors:	Y	Oil Change:		Insurance:		Other:	
Specialty:		RV Dealer:		Tires:		Paint and Body:				Publishing:	
Buses:		Motorcycle Dealer:		Batteries:						Rental Cars/Trucks:	
RVs:		Specialty Dealer:									

TYPES OF BUSINESS:

Auto Parts-Distribution
Collision Replacement Parts
Wheels & Rims

BRANDS/DIVISIONS/AFFILIATES:

KLQ Corporation
Auto Panels Plus

CONTACTS: *Note: Officers with more than one job title may be intentionally listed here more than once.*

Richard L. Keister, CEO
Richard L. Keister, Pres.
Jeffrey T. Gray, CFO/VP
Christopher Northup, VP-Mktg. & Oper.
Robert E. Hedrick, Chief People Officer/VP
Jesus Arriaga, CIO/VP
John G. Arena, General Counsel/VP/Corp. Sec.
D. Currey Hall, VP-Oper.
James T. Tuttle, VP-Finance
Carl F. Hartman, VP-Oper.
Arnold B. Kohorst, VP-Oper.
Daniel G. Morrissey, VP-Oper.
James M. Pundt, VP-Oper.
Ronald G. Foster, Chmn.
Charles Fischer, VP-Supply Chain Mgmt.

Phone: 909-624-8041 **Fax:** 909-624-9136
Toll-Free: 800-772-5557
Address: 700 E. Bonita Ave., Pomona, CA 91767 US

GROWTH PLANS/SPECIAL FEATURES:

Keystone Automotive Industries, Inc., wholly-owned by LKQ Corp., distributes aftermarket collision replacement parts produced by independent manufacturers for automobiles and light trucks. Through its 300 distribution centers and 13 depots throughout the U.S. and Canada, the company distributes nearly 100,000 products to over 25,000 collision repair shops. In addition, the company recycles and produces chrome-plated and plastic bumpers and remanufactures alloy and steel wheels. Keystone operates 56 plastic and steel bumper recycling facilities and 13 wheel remanufacturing facilities. The firm's principal product lines consist of automotive body parts, bumpers, lights, cooling products, paint, remanufactured alloy wheels and light truck accessories. Automotive body parts include fenders, hoods, radiators, condensers and head and tail light assemblies, and make up the majority of the company's net sales. The firm also electroplates approximately 250,000 steel plated bumpers for automobiles and light trucks every year and sells paint and related materials, such as sandpaper, abrasives, masking products and plastic filler. In addition to selling steel wheels, caps and covers, the company operates 13 facilities that remanufacture collision-damaged alloy wheels and one plant that remanufactures steel wheels.

FINANCIALS: **Sales and profits are in thousands of dollars—add 000 to get the full amount. 2009 Note: Financial information for 2009 was not available for all companies at press time.**

2009 Sales: $
2008 Sales: $
2007 Sales: $713,955
2006 Sales: $628,328
2005 Sales: $557,705

2009 Profits: $
2008 Profits: $
2007 Profits: $30,324
2006 Profits: $22,258
2005 Profits: $14,260

U.S. Stock Ticker: Subsidiary
Int'l Ticker: Int'l Exchange:
Employees:
Fiscal Year Ends: 3/31
Parent Company: LKQ CORP

SALARIES/BENEFITS:

Pension Plan: | ESOP Stock Plan: | Profit Sharing: | Top Exec. Salary: $ | Bonus: $
Savings Plan: Y | Stock Purch. Plan: | Second Exec. Salary: $ | Bonus: $

OTHER THOUGHTS:

Apparent Women Officers or Directors:
Hot Spot for Advancement for Women/Minorities:

LOCATIONS: ("Y" = Yes)

West:	Southwest:	Midwest:	Southeast:	Northeast:	International:
Y	Y	Y	Y	Y	Y

KIA MOTORS CORPORATION

www.kiamotors.com

Industry Group Code: 33611 **Ranks within this company's industry group:** Sales: 15 Profits: 6

Vehicle Manufacturing:		**Dealers:**		**Parts:**		**Service:**		**Finance:**		**Specialty:**	
Cars:	Y	Car Dealer New:		Manufacturers:		General Service:		Leasing:		Information Systems:	
Trucks:	Y	Car Dealer Used:		Retail:		Specialty Service:		Auto Loans:		Online Marketing:	
Motorcycles:		Truck Dealer:		Distributors:		Oil Change:		Insurance:		Other:	
Specialty:	Y	RV Dealer:		Tires:		Paint and Body:				Publishing:	
Buses:	Y	Motorcycle Dealer:		Batteries:						Rental Cars/Trucks:	
RVs:		Specialty Dealer:									

TYPES OF BUSINESS:

Automobiles, Manufacturing
Buses
Military Vehicles
Passenger Vehicles

BRANDS/DIVISIONS/AFFILIATES:

Hyundai Motor Company
Optima
Spectra
Mohave
Rio
Sorento
Picanto
Cadenza

CONTACTS: *Note: Officers with more than one job title may be intentionally listed here more than once.*

Sung-Eun Chung, Co-CEO
Young-Jong Seo, Pres./Co-CEO
Jae-Rok Lee, Head-Finance
Mong-Koo Chung, Chmn.

Phone: 82-2-3464-1114	**Fax:** 82-2-3464-6820
Toll-Free:	
Address: 231 Yangjae-dong, Seocho-gu, Seoul, 137-938 Korea	

GROWTH PLANS/SPECIAL FEATURES:

Kia Motors Corporation, one of the largest automobile manufacturers in Korea, is an affiliate of Hyundai Motor Company. Hyundai won approval to increase its ownership to a 51% controlling interest after Kia went bankrupt in 1997, though Hyundai now controls 38.67%. Kia has the capacity to produce 1.5 million vehicles a year in 13 manufacturing facilities in eight countries. Kia offers different models of cars which include: passenger cars including the Soul, Cerato/Forte, Picanto, Rio, cee'd, Optima/Magentis, Cadenza and Opirus; SUV and MPV's, including the Venga, Rondo/Carens, Carnival, Mohave, Sportage and Sorento; commercial vehicles, including trucks and passenger buses; and concept cars, including the Kia Ray, a plug-in hybrid. The company also produces buses and military vehicles. Kia has additional facilities located around the world, with its high-capacity plants in Korea, China and Slovakia. It also maintains research and design facilities in Korea, Germany, the U.S. and Japan. Additionally, Kia is actively involved in sports marketing, acting as a major sponsor of the Australian Open and the FIFA World Cup. The firm has a number of subsidiaries including Kia Motors America, Inc. which provides a complete line of vehicles through 640 dealers across the U.S. and Kia Motors Europe, the European sales arm based in Frankfurt. In November 2009, Kia began production at its first manufacturing plant in the U.S. Located in Georgia, the plant is capable of producing 300,000 cars annually. Also in November, the firm launched its new Cadenza sedan in Korea under the name K7, with global sales to begin in 2010.

FINANCIALS: **Sales and profits are in thousands of dollars—add 000 to get the full amount. 2009 Note: Financial information for 2009 was not available for all companies at press time.**

2009 Sales: $26,430,100	2009 Profits: $879,130	**U.S. Stock Ticker:**
2008 Sales: $12,501,100	2008 Profits: $86,990	**Int'l Ticker: 000270** Int'l Exchange: Seoul-KRX
2007 Sales: $12,170,680	2007 Profits: $10,680	Employees:
2006 Sales: $17,134,700	2006 Profits: $38,650	Fiscal Year Ends: 12/31
2005 Sales: $16,351,300	2005 Profits: $695,880	Parent Company:

SALARIES/BENEFITS:

Pension Plan:	ESOP Stock Plan:	Profit Sharing:	Top Exec. Salary: $	Bonus: $
Savings Plan:	Stock Purch. Plan:		Second Exec. Salary: $	Bonus: $

OTHER THOUGHTS:

Apparent Women Officers or Directors:
Hot Spot for Advancement for Women/Minorities:

LOCATIONS: ("Y" = Yes)

West:	Southwest:	Midwest:	Southeast:	Northeast:	International:
Y		Y	Y		Y

KOENIGSEGG AUTOMOTIVE AB

www.koenigsegg.com

Industry Group Code: 33611 **Ranks within this company's industry group:** Sales: Profits:

Vehicle Manufacturing:		Dealers:		Parts:		Service:		Finance:		Specialty:	
Cars:	Y	Car Dealer New:		Manufacturers:		General Service:		Leasing:		Information Systems:	
Trucks:		Car Dealer Used:		Retail:		Specialty Service:		Auto Loans:		Online Marketing:	
Motorcycles:		Truck Dealer:		Distributors:		Oil Change:		Insurance:		Other:	
Specialty:	Y	RV Dealer:		Tires:		Paint and Body:				Publishing:	
Buses:		Motorcycle Dealer:		Batteries:						Rental Cars/Trucks:	
RVs:		Specialty Dealer:									

TYPES OF BUSINESS:

Automotive Manufacturing

BRANDS/DIVISIONS/AFFILIATES:

Agera
Trevita
CCX
CCXR
Ghost Light

CONTACTS:

Note: Officers with more than one job title may be intentionally listed here more than once.

Christian V. Koenigsegg, CEO
Patrik Nilsson, Mgr.-Sales
Jon Gunner, Dir.-Tech
Halldora Von Koenigsegg, Exec. Mgr.
Magnus Arntell, Mgr.-Purchasing

Phone: 46-421-45-44-60	**Fax:** 46-431-45-44-61
Toll-Free:	
Address: Barkakravagen 70, Angelholm, 262 74 Sweden	

GROWTH PLANS/SPECIAL FEATURES:

Koenigsegg Automotive AB is a Swedish sportscar manufacturer that focuses on individually crafted automobiles designed for speed and handling. The company produces its cars at the former site of a Swedish Air Force squadron. Every car Koenigsegg makes is crafted at its Angelholm facility by a 45-person staff comprised of seven engineers, four research and design staff, four composite technicians, five pre-assembly staff, three engine assembly technicians, 14 final assembly staff, three storage staff and five public relations, sales, administration and leadership staff. Koenigsegg has a production capacity of seven cars simultaneously. The company's full line of cars includes the Trevita, which featured a limited production of only three units, has a top speed of 250 miles per hour and an acceleration time from zero to 62 miles per hour of 2.9 seconds; the Special Edition, which featured a limited production of only two units, has a top speed of 250 miles per hour and an acceleration time from zero to 62 miles per hour of 2.9 seconds; the CCX, which boasts 806 horsepower and a top speed of 245 miles per hour; the CCXR, which can run on ethanol-based E85 or E100 biofuel as well as gasoline, and features a top speed of 250 miles per hour and horsepower of 1018 when run on biofuel; and the CCX and CCXR Edition models, which are offered in limited production runs and are specifically designed for track performance. In 2005, the company's legacy CCR model beat the Guinness Top Speed by a Production Model Vehicle record formerly held by the McClaren F1. In March 2010, the company unveiled the Agera at the Geneva Motor Show, a car capable of 910 horsepower and outfitted with a proprietary form of interior illumination known as Ghost Light, which utilizes invisible nanotubes.

FINANCIALS:

Sales and profits are in thousands of dollars—add 000 to get the full amount. 2009 Note: Financial information for 2009 was not available for all companies at press time.

2009 Sales: $	2009 Profits: $	**U.S. Stock Ticker: Private**
2008 Sales: $	2008 Profits: $	**Int'l Ticker:** Int'l Exchange:
2007 Sales: $	2007 Profits: $	Employees:
2006 Sales: $	2006 Profits: $	Fiscal Year Ends:
2005 Sales: $	2005 Profits: $	Parent Company:

SALARIES/BENEFITS:

Pension Plan:	ESOP Stock Plan:	Profit Sharing:	Top Exec. Salary: $	Bonus: $
Savings Plan:	Stock Purch. Plan:		Second Exec. Salary: $	Bonus: $

OTHER THOUGHTS:

Apparent Women Officers or Directors: 1
Hot Spot for Advancement for Women/Minorities:

LOCATIONS: ("Y" = Yes)

West:	Southwest:	Midwest:	Southeast:	Northeast:	International:
					Y

KOITO MANUFACTURING CO LTD

www.koito.co.jp/english

Industry Group Code: 3363 **Ranks within this company's industry group:** Sales: 24 Profits: 14

Vehicle Manufacturing:		Dealers:		Parts:		Service:		Finance:		Specialty:	
Cars:		Car Dealer New:		Manufacturers:	Y	General Service:		Leasing:		Information Systems:	
Trucks:		Car Dealer Used:		Retail:		Specialty Service:		Auto Loans:		Online Marketing:	
Motorcycles:		Truck Dealer:		Distributors:		Oil Change:		Insurance:		Other:	Y
Specialty:		RV Dealer:		Tires:		Paint and Body:				Publishing:	
Buses:		Motorcycle Dealer:		Batteries:						Rental Cars/Trucks:	
RVs:		Specialty Dealer:									

TYPES OF BUSINESS:

Automotive Lighting Systems
LED Products
Airplane, Train & Railway Components
Electrical Devices
Measuring Equipment
Adaptive Front Lighting Systems
Near Infrared Lamps

BRANDS/DIVISIONS/AFFILIATES:

North American Lighting, Inc.
Koito Europe NV
Koito Europe Limited
Koito Czech s.r.o.
Koito Kyushu Limited
Koito Transport Co., Ltd.
Shizuokadenso Co., Ltd.
Haibara Machine & Tools Co., Ltd.

CONTACTS: *Note: Officers with more than one job title may be intentionally listed here more than once.*

Masahiro Ohtake, Pres.
Shuichi Goto, Exec. VP
Mitsuo Kikuchi, Exec. VP
Hiroshi Koishihara, Exec. Sr. Managing Dir.
Toshiharu Suzuki, Exec. Sr. Managing Dir.
Takashi Ohtake, Chmn.

Phone: 81-3-3443-7111 **Fax:** 81-3-3447-1520
Toll-Free:
Address: 4-8-3, Takanawa, Minato-ku, Tokyo, 108-8711 Japan

GROWTH PLANS/SPECIAL FEATURES:

Koito Manufacturing Co., Ltd., established in 1915, is a global manufacturer of automotive lighting equipment; components for airplanes, trains and railways; electrical devices; and measuring equipment. It is also involved in related financial and distribution operations. Koito's research and development activities include developing adaptive front lighting systems (AFS), which are capable of automatically controlling headlights to respond to changing road conditions such as turns, weather conditions, road types and other driving factors. Koito was the first company to receive approval from the Japanese Ministry of Land, Infrastructure and Transport (MLIT) for testing its Intelligent AFS prototype on public roads. The company is also researching a near infrared lamp to assist with night driving by helping drivers detect pedestrians and other obstacles outside the reach of headlamp illumination. The company operates an overseas network of 13 subsidiaries located in the U.S., Belgium, U.K., Czech Republic, China, Thailand, Taiwan, Indonesia and India. It also operates 15 domestic subsidiaries and operates four plants in the Shizuoka prefecture in Japan. Koito's primary U.S. subsidiary, North American Lighting, Inc., is a leading independent auto lamp manufacturer in North America, serving both U.S. and Japanese transplant automakers. Koito Europe NV, the firm's primary European subsidiary, oversees its European operations, which are developed by two manufacturing bases: Koito Europe Limited in England and Koito Czech s.r.o. in Zatec, Czech Republic. Some of its other subsidiaries include Koito Kyushu Limited; Koito Transport Co., Ltd.; Shizuokadenso Co., Ltd.; Haibara Machine and Tools Co., Ltd.; Minatsu, Ltd.; and KPS N.A., Inc. In May 2010, the company announced plans to establish Pt. Indonesia Koito, a new automotive lighting equipment subsidiary in Indonesia.

FINANCIALS: **Sales and profits are in thousands of dollars—add 000 to get the full amount. 2009 Note: Financial information for 2009 was not available for all companies at press time.**

2009 Sales: $4,438,340	2009 Profits: $44,820	**U.S. Stock Ticker: KOTMF**
2008 Sales: $4,970,480	2008 Profits: $164,550	**Int'l Ticker: 7276** Int'l Exchange: Tokyo-TSE
2007 Sales: $4,282,900	2007 Profits: $141,800	Employees:
2006 Sales: $4,117,900	2006 Profits: $121,700	Fiscal Year Ends: 3/31
2005 Sales: $3,366,021	2005 Profits: $84,673	Parent Company:

SALARIES/BENEFITS:

Pension Plan:	ESOP Stock Plan:	Profit Sharing:	Top Exec. Salary: $	Bonus: $
Savings Plan:	Stock Purch. Plan:		Second Exec. Salary: $	Bonus: $

OTHER THOUGHTS:

Apparent Women Officers or Directors:
Hot Spot for Advancement for Women/Minorities:

LOCATIONS: ("Y" = Yes)

West:	Southwest:	Midwest:	Southeast:	Northeast:	International:
Y		Y		Y	Y

KOLBENSCHMIDT PIERBURG AG

www.kspg-ag.de

Industry Group Code: 3363 **Ranks within this company's industry group:** Sales: Profits:

Vehicle Manufacturing:		Dealers:		Parts:		Service:		Finance:		Specialty:	
Cars:		Car Dealer New:		Manufacturers:	Y	General Service:		Leasing:		Information Systems:	
Trucks:		Car Dealer Used:		Retail:	Y	Specialty Service:		Auto Loans:		Online Marketing:	
Motorcycles:		Truck Dealer:		Distributors:		Oil Change:		Insurance:		Other:	
Specialty:		RV Dealer:		Tires:		Paint and Body:				Publishing:	
Buses:		Motorcycle Dealer:		Batteries:						Rental Cars/Trucks:	
RVs:		Specialty Dealer:									

TYPES OF BUSINESS:

Automobile Parts Manufacturing
Pistons & Piston Compressors
Air Supply Products & Pumps
Emission Control Products
Bearings
Aluminum Engine Blocks
Hybrid & Fuel Cell Technologies

BRANDS/DIVISIONS/AFFILIATES:

Pierburg GmbH
Pierburg Pump Technology GmbH
KS Kolbenschmidt GmbH
KS Gleitlager GmbH
KS Aluminium-Technologie AG
MSI Motor Service International GmbH
ALUSIL
Permaglide

CONTACTS: *Note: Officers with more than one job title may be intentionally listed here more than once.*

Gerd Kleinert, CEO
Gerd Kleinert, Dir.-Mktg.
Peter-Sebastian Krause, Dir.-Human Resources
Peter P. Merten, Dir.-IT
Peter-Sebastian Krause, Dir.-Legal Affairs
Gerd Kleinert, Dir.-Oper.
Gerd Kleinert, Dir.-Strategy
Peter P. Merten, Dir.-Finance/Controlling
Klaus Eberhardt, Chmn.

Phone: 49-7132-33-0 **Fax:** 49-7132-33-27-96
Toll-Free:
Address: Karl-Schmidt-Strasse, Neckarsulm, 74172 Germany

GROWTH PLANS/SPECIAL FEATURES:

Kolbenschmidt Pierburg AG (KP AG) is a Germany-based holding company that, through its subsidiaries, provides products for the automotive industry. The company specializes in products for air supply, emission control and pumps, as well as in the development, manufacture and aftermarket supply of pistons, engine blocks and plain bearings. The company has six autonomous divisions: Pierburg GmbH; Pierburg Pump Technology GmbH; KS Kolbenschmidt GmbH; KS Gleitlager GmbH; KS Aluminium-Technologie GmbH; and MSI Motor Service International GmbH. Pierburg, the air management division, manufactures individual systems and components for air supply and emission control through six locations worldwide. Pierburg Pump Technology's product portfolio includes oil pumps, vacuum pumps, coolant pumps and recirculating water pumps. The division has a presence in five locations worldwide. KS Kolbenschmidt develops, produces and sells gasoline and diesel engine pistons for cars and commercial vehicles; pistons for two-cycle and compressor engines; and large pistons for stationary, marine and locomotive engines. It has a presence in nine locations worldwide. KS Gleitlager, the group's plain bearings division, manufactures engine bearings and dry bearings, the latter under the brand name of Permaglide. The division has five locations worldwide and its product line include more than 3,000 items. KS Aluminium-Technologie produces hypereutectic aluminum-silicon alloy engine blocks under the ALUSIL brand and develops casting techniques for ALUSIL engine blocks. The division has locations in Germany and China. Lastly, MSI Motor Service is the sales organization for KP AG's worldwide aftermarket activities. Through its network, the division sells company products to wholesalers, engine repairers and independent workshops in 130 countries.

FINANCIALS: **Sales and profits are in thousands of dollars—add 000 to get the full amount. 2009 Note: Financial information for 2009 was not available for all companies at press time.**

2009 Sales: $	2009 Profits: $
2008 Sales: $5,540,680	2008 Profits: $193,330
2007 Sales: $5,876,380	2007 Profits: $220,090
2006 Sales: $5,320,280	2006 Profits: $180,470
2005 Sales: $2,626,190	2005 Profits: $110,170

U.S. Stock Ticker:
Int'l Ticker: KPG Int'l Exchange: Frankfurt-Euronext
Employees: 21,020
Fiscal Year Ends: 12/31
Parent Company:

SALARIES/BENEFITS:

Pension Plan: ESOP Stock Plan: Profit Sharing: Top Exec. Salary: $ Bonus: $
Savings Plan: Stock Purch. Plan: Second Exec. Salary: $ Bonus: $

OTHER THOUGHTS:

Apparent Women Officers or Directors:
Hot Spot for Advancement for Women/Minorities:

LOCATIONS: ("Y" = Yes)

West:	Southwest:	Midwest:	Southeast:	Northeast:	International:
		Y		Y	Y

KUMHO TIRE CO LTD

www.kumhotire.com

Industry Group Code: 3262 **Ranks within this company's industry group:** Sales: 9 Profits: 9

Vehicle Manufacturing:		**Dealers:**		**Parts:**		**Service:**		**Finance:**		**Specialty:**	
Cars:		Car Dealer New:		Manufacturers:		General Service:		Leasing:		Information Systems:	
Trucks:		Car Dealer Used:		Retail:		Specialty Service:		Auto Loans:		Online Marketing:	
Motorcycles:		Truck Dealer:		Distributors:		Oil Change:		Insurance:		Other:	
Specialty:		RV Dealer:		Tires:	Y	Paint and Body:				Publishing:	
Buses:		Motorcycle Dealer:		Batteries:						Rental Cars/Trucks:	
RVs:		Specialty Dealer:									

TYPES OF BUSINESS:

Tire Manufacturing
Ultra-High-Performance Tires

BRANDS/DIVISIONS/AFFILIATES:

Kumho Asiana Group
Kumho USA, Inc.

CONTACTS:

Note: Officers with more than one job title may be intentionally listed here more than once.

Park Sam Gu, Co-CEO
Kim Jong Ho, Pres./Co-CEO
Dong Jin Hwang, VP
Han Seop Lee, Managing Dir.
Chun Taek Cho, Managing Dir.
Du Hyeong Son, Assistant Managing Dir.
Park Sam Gu, Chmn.
J.B. Kim, Pres., Kumho Tire USA, Inc.

Phone: 82-62-940-2114	**Fax:**
Toll-Free:	
Address: 555, Sochon-dong, Gwangsan-gu, Gwangju, 506-040 Korea	

GROWTH PLANS/SPECIAL FEATURES:

Kumho Tire Co., Ltd., headquartered in Seoul, South Korea, is a leading global manufacturer of tires and part of the Kumho Asiana Group. With nine manufacturing plants in Asia and one in development in the U.S., the company has an annual manufacturing capacity of approximately 75 million tires. The firm's overseas sales office network includes locations in the U.S., Canada, Germany, France, Austria, the U.K., Spain, Italy, Russia, Australia, Japan, Thailand, China, Vietnam, Singapore, Turkey, Saudi Arabia, Egypt, the United Arab Emirates, South Africa, Panama, Chile, Brazil and Mexico. Additionally, Kumho maintains three primary research and development centers, located in the U.S., the U.K. and China. Kumho sells its tires, which include passenger car, SUV, light truck, commercial truck, competition and specialty tires, in roughly 180 countries worldwide. Some of the company's specialty tires include aviation tires, racing tires, ultra-high-performance (UHP) tires, run-flat tires, aroma tires and colored-smoke tires. Kumho was among the first Korean companies to develop military aviation tires and is one of the only Korean companies to produce aviation tires. Kumho's run-flat tires can be safely driven at speeds of up to 50 miles an hour, even after sustaining significant puncture damage. Aroma tires contain scented oils that release slowly over the tire's lifespan. Colored-smoke tires use a dye mixture built into the tread of the tire to produce a colored smoke effect for racing applications. The company's supplies original equipment (OE) tires to a number of international automobile manufacturers, including Mercedes-Benz and Ford Motor Co. In early 2009, the company opened a new 150,000-square-foot warehouse facility in South Brunswick, New Jersey to serve customer in the northeastern U.S. In March 2010, subsidiary Kumho USA, Inc. announced the introduction of several new tires that offer a balance between high traction, vehicle performance and reduced environmental impact.

FINANCIALS:

Sales and profits are in thousands of dollars—add 000 to get the full amount. 2009 Note: Financial information for 2009 was not available for all companies at press time.

2009 Sales: $1,547,590	2009 Profits: $-633,970	**U.S. Stock Ticker:**
2008 Sales: $1,891,260	2008 Profits: $-157,980	**Int'l Ticker: 073240** Int'l Exchange: Seoul-KRX
2007 Sales: $1,861,890	2007 Profits: $-22,230	Employees:
2006 Sales: $1,929,900	2006 Profits: $1,000	Fiscal Year Ends: 12/31
2005 Sales: $1,736,500	2005 Profits: $96,200	Parent Company:

SALARIES/BENEFITS:

Pension Plan:	ESOP Stock Plan:	Profit Sharing:	Top Exec. Salary: $	Bonus: $
Savings Plan:	Stock Purch. Plan:		Second Exec. Salary: $	Bonus: $

OTHER THOUGHTS:

Apparent Women Officers or Directors:
Hot Spot for Advancement for Women/Minorities:

LOCATIONS: ("Y" = Yes)

West:	Southwest:	Midwest:	Southeast:	Northeast:	International:
Y		Y	Y	Y	Y

LACKS ENTERPRISES INC

www.lacksenterprises.com

Industry Group Code: 3363 **Ranks within this company's industry group:** Sales: Profits:

Vehicle Manufacturing:		Dealers:		Parts:		Service:		Finance:		Specialty:	
Cars:		Car Dealer New:		Manufacturers:	Y	General Service:		Leasing:		Information Systems:	
Trucks:		Car Dealer Used:		Retail:		Specialty Service:		Auto Loans:		Online Marketing:	
Motorcycles:		Truck Dealer:		Distributors:		Oil Change:		Insurance:		Other:	
Specialty:		RV Dealer:		Tires:		Paint and Body:				Publishing:	
Buses:		Motorcycle Dealer:		Batteries:						Rental Cars/Trucks:	
RVs:		Specialty Dealer:									

TYPES OF BUSINESS:

Plastic Parts & Accessories
Injection Molding
Wheel Components & Systems
Automotive Trim
Turn-Key Solutions
Logistics & Supply Chain Management

BRANDS/DIVISIONS/AFFILIATES:

Lacks Wheel Trim Systems, Inc.
Lacks Trim Systems, Inc.
Plastic Plate, Inc.
High Impact Plated Plastic (HIPP-140)
Chromtec
Platinum Chrome
Spinelle Metal Finish
Flexlamp

CONTACTS: *Note: Officers with more than one job title may be intentionally listed here more than once.*

Richard Lacks, Jr., CEO
Richard Lacks, Jr., Pres.
Jenn Groendyke, VP-Public Rel. & Comm.
Kurt P. Lacks, Chmn./Exec. VP

Phone: 616-949-6570	**Fax:**
Toll-Free:	
Address: 5460 Cascade Rd. SE, Grand Rapids, MI 49546 US	

GROWTH PLANS/SPECIAL FEATURES:

Lacks Enterprises, Inc. is a manufacturer and supplier of plastic parts and accessories for the automotive and consumer electronics industries. The company comprises three business operations: Lacks Wheel Trim Systems, Inc., a supplier of automotive wheel components and systems; Lacks Trim Systems, a global provider of complex components and systems for the exterior and interior automotive trim market; and Plastic-Plate, Inc., a provider of plastic molding and plating services. The company introduced High Impact Plated Plastic (HIPP-140), a chrome-plated plastic alternative to expensive metal trim for grilles and bumper molding, with enhanced impact, fatigue and temperature performance. Lacks' patented Chromtec technology was developed as an alternative to chrome-plated steel and aluminum wheels, providing resistance to rusting, peeling, dents and abrasions. Platinum Chrome is the company's electroplating process, providing a smooth matte finish. Lack's Spinelle Metal Finish is a multi-coat system providing metal finishes. The company's patented Flexlamp uses advanced composite polymers to create external automotive lighting that can be located in the vehicle's impact zone. Plastic-Plate Inc., a division of the firm, is currently developing conductive painting techniques, electroless shielding technologies and selective double-sided plating processes. It manufactures molding and finishing and works with OEM (Original Equipment Manufacturer) partners to produce a product. In addition to its 17 facilities located in Michigan (including the firm's research and development facility), the company operates facilities in Sweden and Germany.

Employees of the firm are offered training and development opportunities; insurance plans; profit sharing; a 401(k) plan; and tuition reimbursement.

FINANCIALS: **Sales and profits are in thousands of dollars—add 000 to get the full amount. 2009 Note: Financial information for 2009 was not available for all companies at press time.**

2009 Sales: $	2009 Profits: $	**U.S. Stock Ticker: Private**
2008 Sales: $	2008 Profits: $	**Int'l Ticker:** Int'l Exchange:
2007 Sales: $172,400	2007 Profits: $	Employees:
2006 Sales: $	2006 Profits: $	Fiscal Year Ends:
2005 Sales: $	2005 Profits: $	Parent Company:

SALARIES/BENEFITS:

Pension Plan:	ESOP Stock Plan:	Profit Sharing: Y	Top Exec. Salary: $	Bonus: $
Savings Plan: Y	Stock Purch. Plan:		Second Exec. Salary: $	Bonus: $

OTHER THOUGHTS:

Apparent Women Officers or Directors: 1
Hot Spot for Advancement for Women/Minorities:

LOCATIONS: ("Y" = Yes)

West:	Southwest:	Midwest:	Southeast:	Northeast:	International:
		Y			Y

LAND ROVER

www.landrover.com

Industry Group Code: 33611 **Ranks within this company's industry group:** Sales: Profits:

Vehicle Manufacturing:		Dealers:		Parts:		Service:		Finance:		Specialty:	
Cars:	Y	Car Dealer New:		Manufacturers:		General Service:		Leasing:		Information Systems:	
Trucks:		Car Dealer Used:		Retail:		Specialty Service:		Auto Loans:		Online Marketing:	
Motorcycles:		Truck Dealer:		Distributors:		Oil Change:		Insurance:		Other:	
Specialty:		RV Dealer:		Tires:		Paint and Body:				Publishing:	
Buses:		Motorcycle Dealer:		Batteries:						Rental Cars/Trucks:	
RVs:		Specialty Dealer:									

TYPES OF BUSINESS:

Auto Manufacturing
Luxury Vehicles
Off-Road Vehicles

BRANDS/DIVISIONS/AFFILIATES:

Tata Motors Limited
Jaguar Land Rover
Range Rover Sport
Freelander
Discovery
Range Rover
Defender
LR3

CONTACTS: *Note: Officers with more than one job title may be intentionally listed here more than once.*

Carl-Peter Forster, CEO-Jaguar Land Rover
Kenneth Gregor, CFO-Jaguar Land Rover
Des Thurlby, Dir.-Human Resources, Jaguar Land Rover
Michael Ali, Dir.-IT, Jaguar Land Rover
Phil Hodgkinson, Dir.-Prod. Dev., Jaguar Land Rover
Bob Joyce, Group Dir.-Eng., Jaguar Land Rover
Paul Cope, Dir.-Mfg., Jaguar Land Rover
Simon Warr, Dir.-Corp. Comm. & Pub. Affairs, Jaguar Land Rover
Phil Popham, Managing Dir.
Gerry McGovern, Dir.-Design
Tim Davis, Dir.-Quality, Jaguar Land Rover
Ermal M. Faulkner, Dir.-Purchasing, Jaguar Land Rover

Phone: 44-1926-649-111	**Fax:** 44-1926-641-597
Toll-Free:	
Address: B523 Banbury Rd., Gaydon, Warwick, CV35 0RR UK	

GROWTH PLANS/SPECIAL FEATURES:

Land Rover is a world leader in the design and production of 4x4 vehicles. The company is part of the Jaguar Land Rover division of Japan-based Tata Motors Company. Currently, Land Rover markets four models in the U.S.: Range Rover, Range Rover Sport, LR3 and LR2. The U.S. is Land Rover's largest export market. The firm also markets Discovery, Freelander and Defender in other areas of the world. The firm's newest Range Rover starts at about $79,275, and comes with a V8 engine, a six-speed automatic transmission, GPS navigation technology, a rear view camera and a DVD player. If customers choose to design their own vehicle, they can do so through the company's web site. Land Rover models are designed for durability and off-road capability, and the company duly hosts a number of expeditions for adventurers and environmental researchers around the globe. The firm has dealerships available in nearly every state in the U.S. and most areas of U.K. Land Rover includes information on its web site offering a range of technical information, special tools, diagnostic equipment and training materials. Land Rover introduced the LRX concept car, which is smaller than other Land Rovers, lighter in weight and relatively low to the ground. In May 2009, the firm agreed to begin importing vehicles to India. In June 2009, Jaguar Land Rover opened a new parts distribution center in China. In September 2009, Jaguar Land Rover agreed to close one of its U.K.-based manufacturing plants.

FINANCIALS: **Sales and profits are in thousands of dollars—add 000 to get the full amount. 2009 Note: Financial information for 2009 was not available for all companies at press time.**

2009 Sales: $	2009 Profits: $	**U.S. Stock Ticker: Subsidiary**
2008 Sales: $	2008 Profits: $	**Int'l Ticker:** Int'l Exchange:
2007 Sales: $	2007 Profits: $	Employees:
2006 Sales: $	2006 Profits: $	Fiscal Year Ends: 12/31
2005 Sales: $	2005 Profits: $	Parent Company: TATA MOTORS LIMITED

SALARIES/BENEFITS:

Pension Plan: Y	ESOP Stock Plan:	Profit Sharing:	Top Exec. Salary: $	Bonus: $
Savings Plan:	Stock Purch. Plan:		Second Exec. Salary: $	Bonus: $

OTHER THOUGHTS:

Apparent Women Officers or Directors:
Hot Spot for Advancement for Women/Minorities:

LOCATIONS: ("Y" = Yes)

West:	Southwest:	Midwest:	Southeast:	Northeast:	International:
Y	Y	Y	Y	Y	Y

LARRY H MILLER GROUP

www.lhm.com

Industry Group Code: 441110 **Ranks within this company's industry group:** Sales: Profits:

Vehicle Manufacturing:		Dealers:		Parts:		Service:		Finance:		Specialty:	
Cars:		Car Dealer New:	Y	Manufacturers:		General Service:	Y	Leasing:		Information Systems:	
Trucks:		Car Dealer Used:	Y	Retail:	Y	Specialty Service:		Auto Loans:	Y	Online Marketing:	
Motorcycles:		Truck Dealer:		Distributors:		Oil Change:		Insurance:		Other:	Y
Specialty:		RV Dealer:		Tires:		Paint and Body:	Y			Publishing:	
Buses:		Motorcycle Dealer:		Batteries:						Rental Cars/Trucks:	
RVs:		Specialty Dealer:									

TYPES OF BUSINESS:

Auto Dealers, Retail
Auto Financing & Service
Sports Arenas
Movie Theaters
Professional Sports Teams
TV Station
Sports Apparel Stores

BRANDS/DIVISIONS/AFFILIATES:

Utah Jazz
Megaplex Theaters
Delta Center
KJZZ
Fanzz
Jordan Commons
Prestige Financial Services
Miller Motorsports Park

CONTACTS: *Note: Officers with more than one job title may be intentionally listed here more than once.*

Greg Miller, CEO
Robert Tingey, General Counsel
Jay Francis, Exec. VP-Oper.
Clark Whitworth, CFO-Automotive
Robert Hyde, CFO-Sports & Entertainment
Steve Starks, Exec. VP-Oper.

Phone: 801-563-4100	**Fax:** 801-563-4198
Toll-Free:	
Address: 9350 S.150 E., Ste. 1000, Sandy, UT 84070 US	

GROWTH PLANS/SPECIAL FEATURES:

Larry H. Miller Group (LMG) is a holding company that operates a large range of subsidiary companies in several business segments: retail stores, sports franchises, financial services, entertainment venues, movie theaters, media outlets and most prominently, car dealerships. LMG owns approximately 45 new and used automobile dealerships in Arizona, Colorado, Idaho, New Mexico, Oregon and Utah. The firm sells a wide variety of automotive brands including Ford, Cadillac, Lexus, Toyota, Honda, Chevrolet and Jeep. LMG offers credit through Prestige Financial Services and through Landcar Agency, two subsidiary companies dedicated to providing financing and bankruptcy loans to customers. The company also owns and manages several Megaplex theaters all over Utah, numbering over 60 screens. These standard multi-screen movie theaters are located around Salt Lake City, Lehi, South Jordan and Ogden, Utah. LMG also operates major stadiums and arenas, including the Miller Motorsports Park, which sponsors a range of events and races including the National Basketball Association (NBA) team the Utah Jazz and its home arena, the Delta Center; the Salt Lake Bees baseball club and its home, the Franklin Covey Field; and the Energy Solutions Arena, which hosts concerts, ice shows and circuses. Other assets include Salt Lake-based television station KJZZ; Fanzz, a sports apparel store with approximately 50 locations in California, Colorado, Idaho, New Mexico, Nevada, Kansas, Texas and Utah; and Sandy, Utah-based Jordan Commons, an entertainment center with a theater, restaurants and a 10-story office tower.

FINANCIALS: **Sales and profits are in thousands of dollars—add 000 to get the full amount. 2009 Note: Financial information for 2009 was not available for all companies at press time.**

2009 Sales: $	2009 Profits: $	**U.S. Stock Ticker: Private**
2008 Sales: $	2008 Profits: $	**Int'l Ticker:** Int'l Exchange:
2007 Sales: $	2007 Profits: $	Employees:
2006 Sales: $	2006 Profits: $	Fiscal Year Ends: 12/31
2005 Sales: $	2005 Profits: $	Parent Company:

SALARIES/BENEFITS:

Pension Plan:	ESOP Stock Plan:	Profit Sharing:	Top Exec. Salary: $	Bonus: $
Savings Plan:	Stock Purch. Plan:		Second Exec. Salary: $	Bonus: $

OTHER THOUGHTS:

Apparent Women Officers or Directors:
Hot Spot for Advancement for Women/Minorities:

LOCATIONS: ("Y" = Yes)

West:	Southwest:	Midwest:	Southeast:	Northeast:	International:
Y	Y				

LDI LTD

www.ldiltd.com

Industry Group Code: 336991 **Ranks within this company's industry group:** Sales: Profits:

Vehicle Manufacturing:		Dealers:		Parts:		Service:		Finance:		Specialty:	
Cars:		Car Dealer New:		Manufacturers:		General Service:		Leasing:		Information Systems:	
Trucks:		Car Dealer Used:		Retail:		Specialty Service:		Auto Loans:		Online Marketing:	
Motorcycles:		Truck Dealer:		Distributors:	Y	Oil Change:		Insurance:		Other:	Y
Specialty:		RV Dealer:		Tires:		Paint and Body:				Publishing:	
Buses:		Motorcycle Dealer:		Batteries:						Rental Cars/Trucks:	
RVs:		Specialty Dealer:									

TYPES OF BUSINESS:

Auto Parts Distribution
Aftermarket Parts & Accessories-Motorcycles & Specialty
Automotive Paints & Coatings Distribution
Harley-Davidson Accessories
Specialty Services

BRANDS/DIVISIONS/AFFILIATES:

Tucker Rocky Distributing
FinishMaster, Inc.
Lacy Diversified Industries
Biker's Choice
Malcolm Smith Racing
QuadBoss
Firstgear

CONTACTS: *Note: Officers with more than one job title may be intentionally listed here more than once.*

David Shane, CEO
David Shane, Pres.
Michael P. Hutson, CFO/Sr. VP-Finance
Paula K. Bachert, VP-Strategic Planning & Dev.
Margot L. Eccles, VP-Community Rel.
Margot L. Eccles, VP-Shareholder Rel.
Gary M. Bilsland, Treas.
Marc D. Johnson, VP-Investments & Corp. Dev.
Andre B. Lacy, Chmn.

Phone: 317-237-5400	**Fax:** 317-237-3444
Toll-Free:	
Address: 54 Monument Cir., Ste. 800, Indianapolis, IN 46204 US	

GROWTH PLANS/SPECIAL FEATURES:

LDI, Ltd., formerly known as Lacy Diversified Industries, is the holding company for one wholly-owned subsidiary and one majority-owned company. The company's two business units are Tucker Rocky and FinishMaster. Subsidiary Tucker Rocky is a leading wholesale distributor of aftermarket parts and accessories for enthusiasts of motorcycles, personal watercraft, all-terrain vehicles and snowmobiles. Tucker Rocky also operates Biker's Choice, which distributes and markets brand name bike accessories aftermarket retailers. Some of the other subsidiaries of Tucker Rocky include Malcolm Smith Racing (MSR), an off-road motorcycle apparel company; Firstgear, a line of technical apparel for street bike riders; Answer Racing, a motocross apparel and parts company. In addition, Tucker Rocky has also developed its own QuadBoss brand of ATV accessories and parts. Through TRDealer.com, dealers can search for products, check stock, check backorders, place orders, see pricing, view invoices and credit memos. While the firm does not sell items directly to the public, it does offer a sponsored web site which consumers can search products and their suggested retail prices, then print a wish list to take to a dealer where they can actually purchase the items. Tucker Rocky stocks over 100,000 products at distribution centers in Texas, California, Oregon, Colorado, Illinois, Florida and Pennsylvania, each of which provides next-day delivery to power sports dealers across the U.S. and exports products to foreign markets. Tucker has seven distribution centers. FinishMaster, Inc., majority-owned by LDI, is a leading distributor of automotive paints, coatings and related products to the collision repair industry. The company has over 180 sales branches and three distribution centers in 28 states, with headquarters located in Indianapolis, Indiana. FinishMaster provides finishing products in addition to value-added services, including computerized color matching and profitability consulting. The firm distributes paints from BASF, DuPont, PPG and 3M.

FINANCIALS: **Sales and profits are in thousands of dollars—add 000 to get the full amount. 2009 Note: Financial information for 2009 was not available for all companies at press time.**

2009 Sales: $	2009 Profits: $	**U.S. Stock Ticker: Private**
2008 Sales: $	2008 Profits: $	**Int'l Ticker:** Int'l Exchange:
2007 Sales: $427,100	2007 Profits: $	Employees:
2006 Sales: $	2006 Profits: $	Fiscal Year Ends: 12/31
2005 Sales: $	2005 Profits: $	Parent Company:

SALARIES/BENEFITS:

Pension Plan:	ESOP Stock Plan:	Profit Sharing:	Top Exec. Salary: $	Bonus: $
Savings Plan:	Stock Purch. Plan:		Second Exec. Salary: $	Bonus: $

OTHER THOUGHTS:

Apparent Women Officers or Directors: 2
Hot Spot for Advancement for Women/Minorities:

LOCATIONS: ("Y" = Yes)

West:	Southwest:	Midwest:	Southeast:	Northeast:	International:
Y	Y	Y	Y	Y	

LEAR CORP

www.lear.com

Industry Group Code: 3363 **Ranks within this company's industry group:** Sales: 13 Profits: 3

Vehicle Manufacturing:		Dealers:		Parts:		Service:		Finance:		Specialty:	
Cars:		Car Dealer New:		Manufacturers:	Y	General Service:		Leasing:		Information Systems:	
Trucks:		Car Dealer Used:		Retail:		Specialty Service:		Auto Loans:		Online Marketing:	
Motorcycles:		Truck Dealer:		Distributors:		Oil Change:		Insurance:		Other:	
Specialty:		RV Dealer:		Tires:		Paint and Body:				Publishing:	
Buses:		Motorcycle Dealer:		Batteries:						Rental Cars/Trucks:	
RVs:		Specialty Dealer:									

TYPES OF BUSINESS:

Automobile Components
Automotive Interiors
Electrical Systems
Instrument Panels
Seat Systems
Flooring Systems
Entertainment & Wireless Systems
Keyless Entry Systems

BRANDS/DIVISIONS/AFFILIATES:

ProTec Plus Self-Aligning Head Restraint
SoyFoam

CONTACTS:

Note: Officers with more than one job title may be intentionally listed here more than once.

Robert E. Rossiter, CEO
Robert E. Rossiter, Pres.
Matthew J. Simoncini, CFO/Sr. VP
Melvin Stephens, Sr. VP-Human Resources
Terrence B. Larkin, General Counsel/Sr. VP/Corp. Sec.
Melvin Stephens, Sr. VP-Corp. Rel. & Comm.
Wendy L. Foss, Controller/VP
Shari Burgess, VP/Treas.
Louis R. Salvatore, Sr. VP/Pres., Global Seating Systems
Ray E Scott, Sr. VP/Pres., Global Electrical Power Systems
Robert E. Rossiter, Chmn.

Phone: 248-447-1500	**Fax:** 248-447-1722
Toll-Free: 800-413-5327	
Address: 21557 Telegraph Rd., Southfield, MI 48033 US	

GROWTH PLANS/SPECIAL FEATURES:

Lear Corp. is one of the world's largest automotive interior systems suppliers, serving every major automotive manufacturer, including General Motors, Ford, Daimler, BMW, Fiat, Volkswagen, Renault-Nissan, Hyundai and PSA Peugeot Citroen. The firm currently operates 197 facilities in 36 countries. Its business is conducted through two segments: seating and electrical power management systems. The seating segment, accounting for 80% of the firm's revenues, consists of the manufacture, assembly and supply of vehicle seating requirements. Products include the ProTec Plus Self-Aligning Head Restraint, which provides longer and earlier support for an occupant's head in a rear-impact collision; and SoyFoam seating made from recyclable materials and designs. The electronic power management segment, accounting for 20% of revenue comprises four categories: electrical distribution systems; smart junction boxes and body control modules; wireless systems; and specialty electronics. New electronic technology allows the integration of wiring and electronic products within the overall electrical architecture of the vehicle. Lear has the ability to integrate engineering, research, design, development and validation testing of all automotive interior systems with its research and development studio, its six advanced technology centers and its product engineering centers worldwide. In November 2009, the emerged from Chapter 11 bankruptcy protection, after filing in July 2009.

Employees are offered medical, dental and vision insurance; flexible spending accounts; an employee assistance program; life insurance; disability coverage; a 401(k) plan; a pension plan; a financial planning program and tuition reimbursement.

FINANCIALS:

Sales and profits are in thousands of dollars—add 000 to get the full amount. 2009 Note: Financial information for 2009 was not available for all companies at press time.

2009 Sales: $9,739,600	2009 Profits: $826,700	**U.S. Stock Ticker: LEA**
2008 Sales: $13,570,500	2008 Profits: $-689,900	**Int'l Ticker:** Int'l Exchange:
2007 Sales: $15,995,000	2007 Profits: $241,500	Employees: 52,000
2006 Sales: $17,838,900	2006 Profits: $-707,500	Fiscal Year Ends: 12/31
2005 Sales: $17,089,200	2005 Profits: $-1,381,500	Parent Company:

SALARIES/BENEFITS:

Pension Plan: Y	ESOP Stock Plan:	Profit Sharing:	Top Exec. Salary: $1,240,530	Bonus: $5,404,375
Savings Plan: Y	Stock Purch. Plan:		Second Exec. Salary: $635,152	Bonus: $1,494,202

OTHER THOUGHTS:

Apparent Women Officers or Directors: 2
Hot Spot for Advancement for Women/Minorities:

LOCATIONS: ("Y" = Yes)

West:	Southwest:	Midwest:	Southeast:	Northeast:	International:
Y	Y	Y	Y	Y	Y

LES SCHWAB TIRE CENTERS

www.lesschwab.com

Industry Group Code: 441320 **Ranks within this company's industry group:** Sales: Profits:

Vehicle Manufacturing:		Dealers:		Parts:		Service:		Finance:		Specialty:	
Cars:		Car Dealer New:		Manufacturers:		General Service:		Leasing:		Information Systems:	
Trucks:		Car Dealer Used:		Retail:	Y	Specialty Service:	Y	Auto Loans:		Online Marketing:	
Motorcycles:		Truck Dealer:		Distributors:		Oil Change:		Insurance:		Other:	
Specialty:		RV Dealer:		Tires:	Y	Paint and Body:				Publishing:	
Buses:		Motorcycle Dealer:		Batteries:	Y					Rental Cars/Trucks:	
RVs:		Specialty Dealer:									

TYPES OF BUSINESS:

Tires, Retail
Alignments, Shock & Brake Service
Battery & Shock Retail

BRANDS/DIVISIONS/AFFILIATES:

CONTACTS:
Note: Officers with more than one job title may be intentionally listed here more than once.

Dick Borgman, CEO
John Cuniff, CFO
Dale Thompson, Chief Mktg. Officer
Jodie Hueske, VP-Human Resources
Philip Wick, Chmn.
Ken Edwards, VP-Supply Chain Mgmt.

Phone: 541-447-4136 **Fax:** 541-416-5488
Toll-Free:
Address: 20900 Cooley Rd., Bend, OR 97701 US

GROWTH PLANS/SPECIAL FEATURES:

Les Schwab Tire Centers independently operates a chain of stores that sell tires, wheels and batteries, in addition to performing alignments, shock and brake services. The company's founder Les Schwab started the company in 1952 with the purchase of one tire store, and has expanded the group since to include over 400 company-owned stores and member dealer locations in the western U.S. Stores are located throughout California, Idaho, Montana, Nevada, Oregon, Utah, Alaska and Washington. The company's corporate operations are in central Oregon, where it runs one of the largest retreading facilities in the country and maintains a distribution center that is more than 2 million square feet. The company provides tires for passenger cars, light trucks, SUVs, farm vehicles as well as specialty tires, such as ATV, motor home, boat and trailer, golf cart and lawn and garden tires. The firm's Fleet Tire System offers services to its commercial accounts. Additionally, the firm markets custom wheels and snow wheels. Les Schwab Tire Centers also retails a variety of batteries for cars; buses; farm equipment; lawn and garden; aircraft and military; light trucks; motor homes; industrial equipment; RVs and boat trailers; golf carts; heavy trucks and equipment; motorcycles; ATVs and floor sweepers. In addition, the firm retails a variety of shocks for light trucks, SUVs, lifted light trucks and passenger cars. The company's services include complete front-disc brake service, complete rear-drum brake services, performance suspension lifting and lowering solutions, as well as standard, thrust and four-wheel alignment services.

Les Schwab Tire Centers offer its employees a benefits package that includes a retiree health plan, profit sharing, an employee bonus program, an employee purchase plan, an employee assistance program and adoption assistance.

FINANCIALS:
Sales and profits are in thousands of dollars—add 000 to get the full amount. 2009 Note: Financial information for 2009 was not available for all companies at press time.

2009 Sales: $	2009 Profits: $	**U.S. Stock Ticker: Private**
2008 Sales: $	2008 Profits: $	**Int'l Ticker:** Int'l Exchange:
2007 Sales: $1,480,000	2007 Profits: $	Employees:
2006 Sales: $1,360,000	2006 Profits: $	Fiscal Year Ends: 12/31
2005 Sales: $1,200,000	2005 Profits: $	Parent Company:

SALARIES/BENEFITS:

Pension Plan:	ESOP Stock Plan:	Profit Sharing: Y	Top Exec. Salary: $	Bonus: $
Savings Plan:	Stock Purch. Plan: Y		Second Exec. Salary: $	Bonus: $

OTHER THOUGHTS:

Apparent Women Officers or Directors: 1
Hot Spot for Advancement for Women/Minorities:

LOCATIONS: ("Y" = Yes)

West:	Southwest:	Midwest:	Southeast:	Northeast:	International:
Y					

LINAMAR CORP

www.linamar.com

Industry Group Code: 3363 **Ranks within this company's industry group:** Sales: 36 Profits: 39

Vehicle Manufacturing:		Dealers:		Parts:		Service:		Finance:		Specialty:	
Cars:		Car Dealer New:		Manufacturers:	Y	General Service:		Leasing:		Information Systems:	
Trucks:		Car Dealer Used:		Retail:		Specialty Service:		Auto Loans:		Online Marketing:	
Motorcycles:		Truck Dealer:		Distributors:	Y	Oil Change:		Insurance:		Other:	Y
Specialty:		RV Dealer:		Tires:		Paint and Body:				Publishing:	
Buses:		Motorcycle Dealer:		Batteries:						Rental Cars/Trucks:	
RVs:		Specialty Dealer:									

TYPES OF BUSINESS:

Automobile Parts Manufacturing
Machined Components, Assemblies & Castings
Industrial Products

BRANDS/DIVISIONS/AFFILIATES:

Skyjack, Inc.
Powertrain Asia Group

CONTACTS: *Note: Officers with more than one job title may be intentionally listed here more than once.*

Linda S. Hasenfratz, CEO
Jim Jarrell, COO
Jim Jarrell, Pres.
Edward A. Mahood, CFO
Mark Stoddart, Exec. VP-Mktg.
Roger Fulton, Exec. VP-Human Resources
Edward A. Mahood, Exec. VP-IT
Mark Stoddart, CTO
Brian Wade, VP-Mfg.& Quality
Roger Fulton, General Counsel/Corp. Sec.
Edward A. Mahood, Treas.
Ken McDougall, Pres., Powertrain Mexico
Phil McCulloch, Pres., Energy & Heavy Machining
Ken Myers, Pres., Powertrain Canada & U.S.
Nick Adams, VP-Powertrain Sales
Frank J. Hasenfratz, Chmn.
Csaba Havasi, Group Pres., Hungary/VP-Oper., Europe

Phone: 519-836-7550	**Fax:** 519-824-8479
Toll-Free:	
Address: 287 Speedvale Ave. W., Guelph, ON N1H 1C5 Canada	

GROWTH PLANS/SPECIAL FEATURES:

Linamar Corp. designs, develops and manufactures precision machined components and other engineered products, the bulk of which are sold to OEM and Tier 1 customers in the automotive industry. The company also sells products with industrial and agricultural applications. The firm operates five product development centers, 37 manufacturing locations and 11 sales offices in Canada, the U.S., Mexico, Germany, Hungary, the U.K., China, Korea and Japan. The firm operates through two reportable segments: powertrain/driveline and industrial. The power/driveline segment consists of the transmission and engine groups. Together these groups manufacture and assemble all of the precision-machined components and assemblies used in high quality transmission systems, as well as every key mechanical component of a modern engine. The groups focus on core components such as power transfer units, transmission cases, pumps, steering knuckles, gears, joints, power steering pumps, cylinder blocks, camshaft assemblies, crankshaft assemblies and connecting rods. The industrial group, represented by wholly-owned subsidiary Skyjack, Inc., handles non-automotive products, such as aerial work platforms. This division focuses on reliable scissor lifts, telescopic boom lifts and telehandlers. Linamar's European operations are focused on machines components and assemblies that are used in engine and transmission/driveline systems. All of the company's products and services are also offered in Asia through the company's Powertrain Asia Group. In December 2009, the company announced the closure of Ontario-based Invar Manufacturing Corporation, one of its wholly-owned subsidiaries.

FINANCIALS: **Sales and profits are in thousands of dollars—add 000 to get the full amount. 2009 Note: Financial information for 2009 was not available for all companies at press time.**

2009 Sales: $1,607,870	2009 Profits: $-45,000	**U.S. Stock Ticker: LNR**
2008 Sales: $2,092,720	2008 Profits: $65,230	**Int'l Ticker: LNR** Int'l Exchange: Toronto-TSX
2007 Sales: $2,197,900	2007 Profits: $103,900	Employees:
2006 Sales: $2,149,000	2006 Profits: $94,600	Fiscal Year Ends: 12/31
2005 Sales: $2,041,729	2005 Profits: $945,001	Parent Company:

SALARIES/BENEFITS:

Pension Plan: Y	ESOP Stock Plan:	Profit Sharing:	Top Exec. Salary: $472,432	Bonus: $1,359,456
Savings Plan:	Stock Purch. Plan:		Second Exec. Salary: $324,923	Bonus: $1,087,034

OTHER THOUGHTS:

Apparent Women Officers or Directors: 1
Hot Spot for Advancement for Women/Minorities:

LOCATIONS: ("Y" = Yes)

West:	Southwest:	Midwest:	Southeast:	Northeast:	International:
		Y			Y

LITHIA MOTORS INC

www.lithia.com

Industry Group Code: 441110 **Ranks within this company's industry group:** Sales: 8 Profits: 9

Vehicle Manufacturing:		Dealers:		Parts:		Service:		Finance:		Specialty:	
Cars:		Car Dealer New:	Y	Manufacturers:		General Service:	Y	Leasing:		Information Systems:	
Trucks:		Car Dealer Used:	Y	Retail:	Y	Specialty Service:		Auto Loans:	Y	Online Marketing:	
Motorcycles:		Truck Dealer:		Distributors:		Oil Change:	Y	Insurance:	Y	Other:	
Specialty:		RV Dealer:		Tires:		Paint and Body:	Y			Publishing:	
Buses:		Motorcycle Dealer:		Batteries:						Rental Cars/Trucks:	
RVs:		Specialty Dealer:									

TYPES OF BUSINESS:

Auto Dealers, Retail
Automotive Repair & Maintenance
Insurance & Financing

BRANDS/DIVISIONS/AFFILIATES:

CONTACTS:

Note: Officers with more than one job title may be intentionally listed here more than once.

Sidney B. DeBoer, CEO
Bryan B. DeBoer, COO
Bryan B. DeBoer, Pres.
Jeffrey B. DeBoer, CFO/Sr. VP
Tom Dobry, VP-Mktg.
Kyra Drennan, VP-Info. Systems
Sidney B. DeBoer, Corp. Sec.
Scott Hiller, Sr. VP-Oper.
Chris Holzshu, VP-Financial Planning & Analysis
R. Bradford Gray, Exec. VP
Mark D. DeBoer, VP-Real Estate
Brian Evans, VP-Mergers & Acquisitions
Fred Stoner, VP-Fixed Oper.
Sidney B. DeBoer, Chmn.

Phone: 541-776-6868 **Fax:** 541-774-7617
Toll-Free: 877-331-3084
Address: 360 E. Jackson St., Medford, OR 97501 US

GROWTH PLANS/SPECIAL FEATURES:

Lithia Motors, Inc. is a leading operator of automotive dealerships, retailing both new and used vehicles through 84 stores in the U.S. and over the Internet. The company operates stores in Oregon, California, Texas, Washington, Iowa, Idaho, Colorado, Alaska, Montana, Nevada, Nebraska and New Mexico. Lithia also operates 13 collision repair centers. The firm sells new and used cars and light trucks; sells replacement parts; provides vehicle maintenance, warranty, paint and repair services; and arranges related financing, service contracts, protection products and credit insurance for its automotive customers. Lithia's dealerships offer customers vehicles under 26 domestic and imported brands, including Ford, Toyota, BMW, Suzuki, Hyundai and General Motors. Chrysler, which includes Chrysler, Dodge and Jeep, accounts for the largest single revenue share of the company, approximately 15%. The company markets its parts and service products by notifying the owners of vehicles purchased at its franchises when their vehicles are due for periodic service. The firm's other marketing efforts include periodic direct-mail ads to previous customers, as well as newspaper, television and radio ads. The Lithia web site offers users several services, such as viewing new and used vehicle inventories and scheduling service appointments. The company also offers financing and insurance to customers that purchase new or used vehicles. In July 2010, the company opened a franchise in Bend, Oregon while closing one in Fresno, California.

Employees are offered medical, dental and vision insurance; short- and long-term disability coverage; life insurance; an employee stock purchase plan; a 401(k) plan; and employee discounts.

FINANCIALS:

Sales and profits are in thousands of dollars—add 000 to get the full amount. 2009 Note: Financial information for 2009 was not available for all companies at press time.

2009 Sales: $1,749,315	2009 Profits: $9,151	**U.S. Stock Ticker: LAD**
2008 Sales: $2,063,000	2008 Profits: $-252,586	**Int'l Ticker:** Int'l Exchange:
2007 Sales: $2,585,100	2007 Profits: $21,549	Employees: 3,930
2006 Sales: $3,050,537	2006 Profits: $37,304	Fiscal Year Ends: 12/31
2005 Sales: $2,851,698	2005 Profits: $53,627	Parent Company:

SALARIES/BENEFITS:

Pension Plan:	ESOP Stock Plan:	Profit Sharing:	Top Exec. Salary: $840,000	Bonus: $679,200
Savings Plan: Y	Stock Purch. Plan: Y		Second Exec. Salary: $624,000	Bonus: $493,120

OTHER THOUGHTS:

Apparent Women Officers or Directors: 1
Hot Spot for Advancement for Women/Minorities:

LOCATIONS: ("Y" = Yes)

West:	Southwest:	Midwest:	Southeast:	Northeast:	International:
Y	Y	Y			

LKQ CORP

www.lkqcorp.com

Industry Group Code: 3363 **Ranks within this company's industry group:** Sales: 30 Profits: 9

Vehicle Manufacturing:		Dealers:		Parts:		Service:		Finance:		Specialty:	
Cars:	Y	Car Dealer New:		Manufacturers:		General Service:		Leasing:		Information Systems:	
Trucks:		Car Dealer Used:		Retail:	Y	Specialty Service:		Auto Loans:		Online Marketing:	
Motorcycles:		Truck Dealer:		Distributors:	Y	Oil Change:		Insurance:		Other:	
Specialty:		RV Dealer:		Tires:		Paint and Body:				Publishing:	
Buses:		Motorcycle Dealer:		Batteries:						Rental Cars/Trucks:	
RVs:		Specialty Dealer:									

TYPES OF BUSINESS:

Remanufactured OEM Parts
Aftermarket Replacement Parts
Vehicle Salvage
Scrap/Bulk Automotive Parts
Refurbished Aluminum Wheels

BRANDS/DIVISIONS/AFFILIATES:

Greenleaf Auto Recyclers, LLC

CONTACTS: *Note: Officers with more than one job title may be intentionally listed here more than once.*

Joseph M. Holsten, CEO
Joseph M. Holsten, Pres.
John S. Quinn, CFO/Exec. VP
Victor M. Casini, General Counsel/VP/Corp. Sec.
Robert L. Wagman, VP-Oper., Wholesale Parts Div.
Walter P. Hanley, Sr. VP-Dev.
Frank P. Erlain, VP-Finance/Controller
Leonard A. Damron, Sr. VP-Southeast Region
H. Bradley Willen, VP-Midwest Region
Steven H. Jones, VP-Central Region & Core Oper.
Donald F. Flynn, Chmn.

Phone: 312-621-1950 **Fax:** 312-621-1969
Toll-Free:
Address: 120 N. LaSalle St., Ste. 3300, Chicago, IL 60602 US

GROWTH PLANS/SPECIAL FEATURES:

LKQ Corporation is one of the largest providers of recycled OEM (original equipment manufacturer) automotive parts and related services in the U.S. LKQ operates approximately 295 facilities around the world. In the U.S. and Canada, the company has a network of 92 locations that supply wholesale recycled OEM parts, 74 of which include a combination of processing, sales and redistribution operations, and 18 of which are primarily redistribution facilities. The firm's aftermarket parts business operates from facilities that serve as sales, warehousing or distribution centers, with a total of 145 facilities in the U.S. and Canada. LKQ also has locations providing self-service retail recycled vehicle products. The company refurbishes bumpers and wheels at 51 locations in the U.S. and Canada and one location in northeast Mexico. It also refurbishes head lamps and tail lamps at a facility in Michigan. The firm procures salvage vehicles, primarily at auctions, using its local professionals and centralized purchasing systems, and directly from insurance companies, automobile manufacturers and other suppliers. Once LKQ has received the proper title, assuring that the vehicles have not been stolen, it dismantles it for recycled parts. The firm's customers include collision and mechanical repair shops and, indirectly, insurance companies, including extended-warranty companies. LKQ's most popular products include engines, vehicle front-end assemblies, doors, transmissions, trunk lids, bumper assemblies, wheels, head and tail lamp assemblies and mirrors. In October 2009, the company acquired Greenleaf Auto Recyclers, LLC, a wholesale auto parts recycling business, from Schnitzer Steel Industries, Inc. Concurrent with the acquisition, the firm sold four self service facilities and certain assets associated with three other self service locations to Schnitzer. In January 2010, LKQ sold Schnitzer two additional self service recycling facilities.

FINANCIALS: **Sales and profits are in thousands of dollars—add 000 to get the full amount. 2009 Note: Financial information for 2009 was not available for all companies at press time.**

2009 Sales: $2,047,942	2009 Profits: $127,521	**U.S. Stock Ticker: LKQX**
2008 Sales: $1,908,532	2008 Profits: $99,899	**Int'l Ticker:** Int'l Exchange:
2007 Sales: $1,112,351	2007 Profits: $65,901	Employees: 10,000
2006 Sales: $789,381	2006 Profits: $44,395	Fiscal Year Ends: 12/31
2005 Sales: $547,392	2005 Profits: $30,887	Parent Company:

SALARIES/BENEFITS:

Pension Plan:	ESOP Stock Plan:	Profit Sharing:	Top Exec. Salary: $675,000	Bonus: $1,614,412
Savings Plan: Y	Stock Purch. Plan:		Second Exec. Salary: $414,404	Bonus: $483,417

OTHER THOUGHTS:

Apparent Women Officers or Directors:
Hot Spot for Advancement for Women/Minorities:

LOCATIONS: ("Y" = Yes)

West:	Southwest:	Midwest:	Southeast:	Northeast:	International:
Y	Y	Y	Y	Y	

LOJACK CORPORATION

www.lojack.com

Industry Group Code: 334290 **Ranks within this company's industry group:** Sales: 1 Profits: 1

Vehicle Manufacturing:		Dealers:		Parts:		Service:		Finance:		Specialty:	
Cars:		Car Dealer New:		Manufacturers:		General Service:		Leasing:		Information Systems:	
Trucks:		Car Dealer Used:		Retail:		Specialty Service:		Auto Loans:		Online Marketing:	
Motorcycles:		Truck Dealer:		Distributors:		Oil Change:		Insurance:		Other:	Y
Specialty:		RV Dealer:		Tires:		Paint and Body:				Publishing:	
Buses:		Motorcycle Dealer:		Batteries:						Rental Cars/Trucks:	
RVs:		Specialty Dealer:									

TYPES OF BUSINESS:

Electronic Equipment-Stolen Vehicle Recovery
Asset Monitoring & Recovery

BRANDS/DIVISIONS/AFFILIATES:

LoJack Stolen Vehicle Recovery System
LoJack Early Warning Recovery System
Boomerang Tracking
LoJack for Laptops
LoJack SafetyNet
SC-Integrity

CONTACTS: *Note: Officers with more than one job title may be intentionally listed here more than once.*

Richard T. Riley, CEO
Richard T. Riley, Pres.
Timothy P. O'Connor, CFO/Exec. VP
Kevin M. Mullins, Sr. VP/Gen. Mgr.-Sales
Mark Bornemann, VP-Human Resources
Kathleen Lundy, General Counsel/Exec. VP
Scott Tripp, VP-Oper. N. America
Thomas A. Wooters, VP-Regulatory Strategy
Paul McMahon, VP-Corp. & Mktg. Comm.
Paul Weichselbaum, Exec. VP-Business Management
Paul Marosy, Gen. Mgr.-Lojack SafetyNet
Chris Knorr, VP-National Accounts
Richard T. Riley, Chmn.
Thomas M. Camp, Sr. VP/Gen. Mgr.-Int'l
Robert Furtado, Pres./CEO-Lojack Supply Chain Integrity

Phone: 781-251-4130 **Fax:**
Toll-Free:
Address: 200 Lowder Brook Dr., Ste. 1000, Westwood, MA 02090 US

GROWTH PLANS/SPECIAL FEATURES:

LoJack Corporation creates and markets technology products and services for the tracking and recovery of valuable mobile assets. The company operates in three segments: The North America segment, 71% of revenues in 2009, involves U.S. domestic operations and Boomerang in Canada; the International segment, 27% of revenue, involves the sale of licenses and branded products; and the All Other segment, 2%, involves LoJack SafetyNet and SC-Integrity. The LoJack System, based on radio frequency (RF) technology, is comprised of a Registration System, maintained and operated by LoJack; a Sector Activation System and Vehicle Tracking Units, both operated by law enforcement officials; and a LoJack Unit, a VHF transponder. If a car equipped with a LoJack unit is stolen, its owner reports the theft and a radio signal is transmitted automatically to the unit in the stolen vehicle, activating its tracking signal. The Boomerang System is based on RF and cellular technology and uses internally developed tracking devices and a wireless telecommunications network for locating and tracking stolen assets. The coverage area for Boomerang's tracking includes most of North America; however, it primarily operates in Canada. LoJack SafetyNet is designed to monitor the location and aid in the discovery and rescue of people who could potentially wander off, such as individuals with Alzheimer's and Down syndrome. LoJack Supply Chain Integrity (SCI), through its InTransit system, covertly monitors shipped cargo and aid in recovery if it is stolen. LoJack operates in 28 U.S. states and Washington, D.C. and in over 30 countries internationally. LoJack licenses its name to Absolute Software, which markets LoJack for Laptops, a computer theft recovery product. In April 2010, the company expanded its operations into Utah.

LoJack offers employees medical and dental coverage; flexible spending accounts; a college funding plan; and adoption assistance.

FINANCIALS: **Sales and profits are in thousands of dollars—add 000 to get the full amount. 2009 Note: Financial information for 2009 was not available for all companies at press time.**

2009 Sales: $135,013	2009 Profits: $-35,282	**U.S. Stock Ticker: LOJN**
2008 Sales: $198,679	2008 Profits: $-32,530	**Int'l Ticker:** Int'l Exchange:
2007 Sales: $222,749	2007 Profits: $21,405	Employees: 700
2006 Sales: $213,288	2006 Profits: $16,507	Fiscal Year Ends: 12/31
2005 Sales: $190,726	2005 Profits: $18,439	Parent Company:

SALARIES/BENEFITS:

Pension Plan:	ESOP Stock Plan:	Profit Sharing: Y	Top Exec. Salary: $525,192	Bonus: $
Savings Plan: Y	Stock Purch. Plan: Y		Second Exec. Salary: $490,034	Bonus: $

OTHER THOUGHTS:

Apparent Women Officers or Directors: 2
Hot Spot for Advancement for Women/Minorities: Y

LOCATIONS: ("Y" = Yes)

West:	Southwest:	Midwest:	Southeast:	Northeast:	International:
Y	Y	Y	Y	Y	Y

LUCOR INC

www.jiffylube.com

Industry Group Code: 811191 **Ranks within this company's industry group:** Sales: Profits:

Vehicle Manufacturing:		Dealers:		Parts:		Service:		Finance:		Specialty:	
Cars:		Car Dealer New:		Manufacturers:		General Service:	Y	Leasing:		Information Systems:	
Trucks:		Car Dealer Used:		Retail:		Specialty Service:		Auto Loans:		Online Marketing:	
Motorcycles:		Truck Dealer:		Distributors:		Oil Change:	Y	Insurance:		Other:	
Specialty:		RV Dealer:		Tires:		Paint and Body:				Publishing:	
Buses:		Motorcycle Dealer:		Batteries:						Rental Cars/Trucks:	
RVs:		Specialty Dealer:									

TYPES OF BUSINESS:

Automotive Oil Change & Lubrication Shops

BRANDS/DIVISIONS/AFFILIATES:

Jiffy Lube International

CONTACTS:

Note: Officers with more than one job title may be intentionally listed here more than once.

Stephen P. Conway, CEO
Jerry B. Conway, COO
Jerry B. Conway, Pres.
Stephen P. Conway, Chmn.

Phone: 919-828-9511	**Fax:** 919-828-4847
Toll-Free:	
Address: 790 Pershing Rd., Raleigh, NC 27608 US	

GROWTH PLANS/SPECIAL FEATURES:

Lucor, Inc. is one of largest franchisers of Jiffy Lube International in the U.S. Jiffy Lube is known for its fast oil changes, which it provides across North America with more than 2,000 locations. Jiffy Lube is one of the largest systems of franchised service centers in the fast lube industry. Lucor operates a chain of about 175 of these automotive service shops, with locations in North Carolina, Tennessee, Virginia, Pennsylvania, Kentucky, Ohio, Michigan and Georgia. Lucor's service centers offer basic maintenance services including oil and oil filter changes, chassis lubrication, battery checks, air filter replacement, tire inflation, vacuuming and window washing, as well as preventative maintenance services such as emissions inspections. The shops also check lights and wiper blades and replenish fluids, among other services. The private company is partially owned by Stephen and Jerry Conway, brothers who co-founded the company in 1986.

FINANCIALS:

Sales and profits are in thousands of dollars—add 000 to get the full amount. 2009 Note: Financial information for 2009 was not available for all companies at press time.

2009 Sales: $	2009 Profits: $	**U.S. Stock Ticker: Private**
2008 Sales: $	2008 Profits: $	**Int'l Ticker:** Int'l Exchange:
2007 Sales: $100,500	2007 Profits: $	Employees:
2006 Sales: $	2006 Profits: $	Fiscal Year Ends: 12/31
2005 Sales: $	2005 Profits: $	Parent Company:

SALARIES/BENEFITS:

Pension Plan:	ESOP Stock Plan:	Profit Sharing:	Top Exec. Salary: $	Bonus: $
Savings Plan:	Stock Purch. Plan:		Second Exec. Salary: $	Bonus: $

OTHER THOUGHTS:

Apparent Women Officers or Directors:
Hot Spot for Advancement for Women/Minorities:

LOCATIONS: ("Y" = Yes)

West:	Southwest:	Midwest:	Southeast:	Northeast:	International:
				Y	

LUND INTERNATIONAL INC

www.lundinternational.com

Industry Group Code: 3363 **Ranks within this company's industry group:** Sales: Profits:

Vehicle Manufacturing:		**Dealers:**		**Parts:**		**Service:**		**Finance:**		**Specialty:**	
Cars:		Car Dealer New:		Manufacturers:	Y	General Service:		Leasing:		Information Systems:	
Trucks:		Car Dealer Used:		Retail:	Y	Specialty Service:		Auto Loans:		Online Marketing:	
Motorcycles:		Truck Dealer:		Distributors:		Oil Change:		Insurance:		Other:	
Specialty:		RV Dealer:		Tires:		Paint and Body:				Publishing:	
Buses:		Motorcycle Dealer:		Batteries:						Rental Cars/Trucks:	
RVs:		Specialty Dealer:									

TYPES OF BUSINESS:

Automobile Parts Manufacturer
Appearance Products, Automotive
Exterior Visors
Running Boards
Hood Shields
Bumpers
Truck Liners
Spoilers

BRANDS/DIVISIONS/AFFILIATES:

Nifty Products, Inc.
Belmor
Deflecta-Shield Corp.
Auto Ventshade
Lund Truck Accessories
Resilience Capital Partners
Trenz
Linsalata Capital Partners

CONTACTS:

Note: Officers with more than one job title may be intentionally listed here more than once.

George Scherff, CEO
Reginald Fields, Chief Acct. Officer/VP-Finance

Phone: 678-804-3767	**Fax:**
Toll-Free: 888-588-6049	
Address: 4325 Hamilton Mill Road, Ste. 400, Buford, GA 30518 US	

GROWTH PLANS/SPECIAL FEATURES:

Lund International, Inc., wholly-owned by Linsalata Capital Partners and Resilience Capital Partners, is a group of specialty companies that design, manufacture and market accessories for the automotive market. Its brands include Auto Ventshade, Deflecta-Shield, Trenz, Nifty, Belmor and Lund. The firm sells over 150 product lines, which include exterior visors, hood shields, running boards, air deflectors, bed covers and protection, bumpers, toolboxes, cab bars and other styling accessories. Subsidiary Auto Ventshade's products include floor mats, reflectors and headlight covers. Deflecta-Shield also produces a line of accessories for light trucks, SUVs and vans, such as toolboxes, bed protection products and mud flaps. Trenz makes exterior and interior accessories, including custom grills for aftermarket warehouses and catalogs. Nifty Products provides custom-molded floor mats, carpet mats, rear cargo bay trays and truck liners for cars and trucks. Belmor designs and manufactures accessories for heavy trucks, such as bug deflectors, bug screens, rock guards and winter fronts. Lund produces car accessories such as light covers, grille inserts, hood shields, spoilers and vents; along with truck accessories such as cargo covers, window accessories and running boards. The company sells its products through a network of dealers, warehouse distributors, specialty chain stores and catalog companies. Lund's products are produced with thermoforming, plastic injection molding, cut-and-sew, metal forming, fiberglass molding, dye cutting and top coating.

FINANCIALS:

Sales and profits are in thousands of dollars—add 000 to get the full amount. 2009 Note: Financial information for 2009 was not available for all companies at press time.

2009 Sales: $	2009 Profits: $	**U.S. Stock Ticker: Private**
2008 Sales: $	2008 Profits: $	**Int'l Ticker:** Int'l Exchange:
2007 Sales: $116,100	2007 Profits: $	Employees:
2006 Sales: $	2006 Profits: $	Fiscal Year Ends: 12/31
2005 Sales: $	2005 Profits: $	Parent Company: LINSALATA CAPITAL PARTNERS

SALARIES/BENEFITS:

Pension Plan:	ESOP Stock Plan:	Profit Sharing:	Top Exec. Salary: $	Bonus: $
Savings Plan:	Stock Purch. Plan:		Second Exec. Salary: $	Bonus: $

OTHER THOUGHTS:

Apparent Women Officers or Directors:
Hot Spot for Advancement for Women/Minorities:

LOCATIONS: ("Y" = Yes)

West:	Southwest:	Midwest:	Southeast:	Northeast:	International:
Y		Y	Y		

LUPIENT AUTOMOTIVE GROUP

www.lupient.com

Industry Group Code: 441110 **Ranks within this company's industry group:** Sales: Profits:

Vehicle Manufacturing:		Dealers:		Parts:		Service:		Finance:		Specialty:	
Cars:		Car Dealer New:	Y	Manufacturers:		General Service:	Y	Leasing:		Information Systems:	
Trucks:		Car Dealer Used:	Y	Retail:	Y	Specialty Service:		Auto Loans:	Y	Online Marketing:	
Motorcycles:		Truck Dealer:		Distributors:		Oil Change:		Insurance:		Other:	Y
Specialty:		RV Dealer:		Tires:		Paint and Body:	Y			Publishing:	
Buses:		Motorcycle Dealer:		Batteries:						Rental Cars/Trucks:	
RVs:		Specialty Dealer:									

TYPES OF BUSINESS:

Auto Dealers, Retail
Auto Finance
Auto Service
Fleet Sales
Water Park

BRANDS/DIVISIONS/AFFILIATES:

Jim Lupient Infiniti of Golden Valley
Lupient Brooklyn Park Imports
Lupient Chevrolet of Bloomington
Lupient Viking Buick Pontiac GMC Nissan
Lupient Bothun Chrysler of Eau Claire

CONTACTS:

Note: Officers with more than one job title may be intentionally listed here more than once.

James W. Lupient, CEO
James W. Lupient, Chmn.

Phone: 763-544-6666	**Fax:** 763-513-5517
Toll-Free:	
Address: 7100 Wayzata Blvd., Golden Valley, MN 55426 US	

GROWTH PLANS/SPECIAL FEATURES:

Lupient Auto Group is the largest Minnesota-based new and pre-owned automotive dealer. It features 15 locations in the Great Lakes area. The dealer's locations include the Jim Lupient Infiniti of Golden Valley; Lupient Chevrolet of Bloomington; Lupient Viking Buick Pontiac GMC Nissan; Lupient Brooklyn Park Imports; and Lupient Bothun Chrysler of Eau Claire. Lupient sells and services a wide variety of automobiles including Saturn, Kia, Nissan, Chevrolet, Infiniti, Pontiac, Buick, GMC and Dodge. In addition to individual automobiles, the firm generates revenues from large fleet sale operations. It also offers title and license administration and nationwide delivery, as well as providing warranty, maintenance and service work. Through the company's web site, customers can link to each of the dealerships and view inventory, get an instant quote on any vehicle or schedule service appointments. Lupient operates four body shops including one in Wisconsin. Lupient also operates a water park featuring three large water slides, various water-park-related activities and covered shelters that are available for reservation.

FINANCIALS:

Sales and profits are in thousands of dollars—add 000 to get the full amount. 2009 Note: Financial information for 2009 was not available for all companies at press time.

2009 Sales: $	2009 Profits: $	**U.S. Stock Ticker: Private**
2008 Sales: $	2008 Profits: $	**Int'l Ticker:** Int'l Exchange:
2007 Sales: $	2007 Profits: $	Employees:
2006 Sales: $	2006 Profits: $	Fiscal Year Ends:
2005 Sales: $	2005 Profits: $	Parent Company:

SALARIES/BENEFITS:

Pension Plan:	ESOP Stock Plan:	Profit Sharing:	Top Exec. Salary: $	Bonus: $
Savings Plan:	Stock Purch. Plan:		Second Exec. Salary: $	Bonus: $

OTHER THOUGHTS:

Apparent Women Officers or Directors:
Hot Spot for Advancement for Women/Minorities:

LOCATIONS: ("Y" = Yes)

West:	Southwest:	Midwest:	Southeast:	Northeast:	International:
		Y			

MAACO ENTERPRISES INC

www.maaco.com

Industry Group Code: 8111 **Ranks within this company's industry group:** Sales: Profits:

Vehicle Manufacturing:		Dealers:		Parts:		Service:		Finance:		Specialty:	
Cars:		Car Dealer New:		Manufacturers:		General Service:		Leasing:		Information Systems:	
Trucks:		Car Dealer Used:		Retail:		Specialty Service:		Auto Loans:		Online Marketing:	
Motorcycles:		Truck Dealer:		Distributors:		Oil Change:		Insurance:		Other:	
Specialty:		RV Dealer:		Tires:		Paint and Body:	Y			Publishing:	
Buses:		Motorcycle Dealer:		Batteries:						Rental Cars/Trucks:	
RVs:		Specialty Dealer:									

TYPES OF BUSINESS:

Automotive Repair & Maintenance
Auto Painting
Collision Repair

BRANDS/DIVISIONS/AFFILIATES:

MAACO Collision Repair & Auto Painting Centers
Ambassador
Presidential
Supreme
Signature
MAACO Franchising, Inc.
Driven Brands, Inc.

CONTACTS: *Note: Officers with more than one job title may be intentionally listed here more than once.*

David M. Lapps, Pres.
Patrick Donohue, VP
Mark A. Martino, Chmn.

Phone: 610-265-6606 **Fax:** 610-337-6113
Toll-Free:
Address: 381 Brooks Rd., King of Prussia, PA 19406 US

GROWTH PLANS/SPECIAL FEATURES:

MAACO Enterprises, Inc. provides auto body repair and painting through its franchise network of nearly 500 MAACO Collision Repair and Auto Painting Centers. Since 1972, these franchised centers across the U.S., Canada and Puerto Rico have repaired more than 16.5 million cars. MAACO offers individualized services and options to take care of dents, chips, dings, rust and other minor accident damage. Ranging in cost from a couple hundred dollars to over a thousand dollars, MAACO offers the Ambassador, the Presidential, the Supreme and the Signature service packages. The Ambassador package includes an exterior coat of high grade automotive enamel. The Presidential package includes an exterior coat of a catalyzed enamel material that is more resistant to environmental chemicals, weather extremes and tough road conditions than ordinary enamel. The Supreme package includes an exterior coat of a highly durable, easy to care for, UV-ray resistant, single-stage polyurethane paint with a sealer. Finally, the Signature package includes a two-step application of base coat and clear coat, which duplicates the color and gloss of a factory paint job, and is durable and easy to care for. These services come with coast-to-coast warranty, quality assurance, central billing, original factory color matching and quality name-brand paints and parts. The firm has color match systems in its auto body shops designed to match paint using Sherwin-Williams and DuPont paint systems. In addition to personal vehicle repair, the company offers fleet maintenance services. These services include accident management, remarketing and re-identification. MAACO's fleet clients include Aramark, DHL, Enterprise and USPS. MAACO's franchising division, MAACO Franchising, Inc., is owned by Driven Brands, Inc.

FINANCIALS: **Sales and profits are in thousands of dollars—add 000 to get the full amount. 2009 Note: Financial information for 2009 was not available for all companies at press time.**

2009 Sales: $	2009 Profits: $	**U.S. Stock Ticker: Private**
2008 Sales: $	2008 Profits: $	**Int'l Ticker:** Int'l Exchange:
2007 Sales: $	2007 Profits: $	Employees:
2006 Sales: $	2006 Profits: $	Fiscal Year Ends: 10/31
2005 Sales: $	2005 Profits: $	Parent Company:

SALARIES/BENEFITS:

Pension Plan:	ESOP Stock Plan:	Profit Sharing:	Top Exec. Salary: $	Bonus: $
Savings Plan:	Stock Purch. Plan:		Second Exec. Salary: $	Bonus: $

OTHER THOUGHTS:

Apparent Women Officers or Directors:
Hot Spot for Advancement for Women/Minorities:

LOCATIONS: ("Y" = Yes)

West:	Southwest:	Midwest:	Southeast:	Northeast:	International:
Y	Y	Y	Y	Y	Y

MACK TRUCKS INC

www.macktrucks.com

Industry Group Code: 336120 **Ranks within this company's industry group:** Sales: Profits:

Vehicle Manufacturing:		Dealers:		Parts:		Service:		Finance:		Specialty:	
Cars:		Car Dealer New:		Manufacturers:	Y	General Service:		Leasing:	Y	Information Systems:	Y
Trucks:	Y	Car Dealer Used:		Retail:	Y	Specialty Service:	Y	Auto Loans:		Online Marketing:	
Motorcycles:		Truck Dealer:	Y	Distributors:		Oil Change:		Insurance:		Other:	Y
Specialty:		RV Dealer:		Tires:		Paint and Body:				Publishing:	
Buses:		Motorcycle Dealer:		Batteries:						Rental Cars/Trucks:	
RVs:		Specialty Dealer:									

TYPES OF BUSINESS:

Truck Manufacturer
Heavy-Duty Trucks
Replacement Parts
Customer Support Services
Construction Services

BRANDS/DIVISIONS/AFFILIATES:

AB Volvo
Mack Canada Inc
Mack Trucks Australia
Vision Sleepers
Titan
OneCall Complete Care
Granite
InfoMax Wireless

CONTACTS: *Note: Officers with more than one job title may be intentionally listed here more than once.*

Dennis R. Slagle, CEO
Dennis R. Slagle, Pres.
Kevin Flaherty, Sr. VP-Mktg. & Sales
David McKenna, Dir.-Powertrain Mktg. & Sales
John Thomas, VP-Western Region
David Barletta, VP-Central Region
Patrick Meehan, VP-Northeast Region
Carl Heikel, Sr. VP-Int'l Oper.

Phone: 336-291-9001	**Fax:** 336-291-9202
Toll-Free: 800-866-1177	
Address: 7825 National Service Rd., Greensboro, NC 27409 US	

GROWTH PLANS/SPECIAL FEATURES:

Mack Trucks, Inc., a subsidiary of Volvo Group, produces heavy-duty and medium-duty trucks and product components in the U.S. These components are sold in over 45 countries through over 670 sales, parts and service centers. Its international subsidiaries include Mack Canada, Inc.; Mack Trucks Australia Pty. Ltd.; and Mack de Venezuela C.A. Mack's trucks are grouped into five core product lines: the highway series, heavy haul series, powertrain series, construction series and refuse series. The highway series include the Pinnacle SmartWay, Pinnacle Sleepers and Pinnacle DayCabs for long hauls and steep grades. Mack's most powerful model, the Titan, makes up the heavy haul series. Powertrain products include electronics, front/rear axles and transmissions. The construction series includes the Granite, Granite Axle Back and Granite Axle Forward models used for construction and logging. The Mack Refuse line-up includes the TerraPro and Granite series as its durable models for garbage collection and refuse haulage. Mack's OneCall Complete Care program offers roadside assistance, protection plans, a leasing program, warranty and Mack-certified technicians. The company also provides fleet managers with InfoMax Wireless, which accesses and monitors onboard data logs on a seamless, automated basis. In 2010, Mack Trucks introduced MVASIST, a web-based service for truck fleet managers; Mack C150/151 rear axle carriers; Bendix Extended Service brakes; the Mack mDRIVE automated manual transmission; and the Mack ClearTech selective catalytic reduction system.

FINANCIALS: **Sales and profits are in thousands of dollars—add 000 to get the full amount. 2009 Note: Financial information for 2009 was not available for all companies at press time.**

2009 Sales: $	2009 Profits: $	**U.S. Stock Ticker: Subsidiary**
2008 Sales: $	2008 Profits: $	**Int'l Ticker:** Int'l Exchange:
2007 Sales: $	2007 Profits: $	Employees:
2006 Sales: $	2006 Profits: $	Fiscal Year Ends: 12/31
2005 Sales: $	2005 Profits: $	Parent Company: AB VOLVO

SALARIES/BENEFITS:

Pension Plan:	ESOP Stock Plan:	Profit Sharing:	Top Exec. Salary: $	Bonus: $
Savings Plan:	Stock Purch. Plan:		Second Exec. Salary: $	Bonus: $

OTHER THOUGHTS:

Apparent Women Officers or Directors:
Hot Spot for Advancement for Women/Minorities:

LOCATIONS: ("Y" = Yes)

West:	Southwest:	Midwest:	Southeast:	Northeast:	International:
Y	Y	Y	Y	Y	Y

MAGNA INTERNATIONAL INC

www.magna.com

Industry Group Code: 3363 **Ranks within this company's industry group:** Sales: 5 Profits: 56

Vehicle Manufacturing:		Dealers:		Parts:		Service:		Finance:		Specialty:	
Cars:		Car Dealer New:		Manufacturers:	Y	General Service:		Leasing:		Information Systems:	
Trucks:		Car Dealer Used:		Retail:		Specialty Service:		Auto Loans:		Online Marketing:	
Motorcycles:		Truck Dealer:		Distributors:		Oil Change:		Insurance:		Other:	Y
Specialty:		RV Dealer:		Tires:		Paint and Body:				Publishing:	
Buses:		Motorcycle Dealer:		Batteries:						Rental Cars/Trucks:	
RVs:		Specialty Dealer:									

TYPES OF BUSINESS:

Automobile Parts Manufacturer
Vehicle Assembly Services
Seating & Interior Products
Closure Systems
Body & Chassis Systems
Mirror, Lighting & Glass Systems
Exterior Decorative Systems
Drivetrain Components

BRANDS/DIVISIONS/AFFILIATES:

Intier Automotive Inc
Magna Donnelly
Decoma International Inc
Cosma International
Magna Powertrain
Magna Seating
Magna Car Top Systems

CONTACTS: *Note: Officers with more than one job title may be intentionally listed here more than once.*

Donald Walker, Co-CEO
Vincent J. Galifi, CFO/Exec. VP
Gerd R. Brusius, Exec. VP-Corp. Sales & Mktg
Marc Neeb, Exec. VP-Global Human Resources
Jeffrey O. Palmer, Chief Legal Officer/Exec. VP
Peter Koob, Exec. VP-Corp. Dev.
Louis Tonelli, VP-Investor Rel.
Patrick W. D. McCann, VP-Finance
Herbert Demel, COO-Vehicles & Powertrain
Tom Skudutis, COO-Exteriors & Interiors
Joachim Volker Hirsch, VP-Special Projects
Siegfried Wolf, Co-CEO
Frank Stronach, Chmn.
Manfred Eibeck, Exec. VP-Magna Europe

Phone: 905-726-2462 **Fax:** 905-726-7164
Toll-Free:
Address: 337 Magna Dr., Aurora, ON L4G 7K1 Canada

GROWTH PLANS/SPECIAL FEATURES:

Magna International, Inc. is a global supplier of high-tech automotive components, systems and complete modules. The firm designs, engineers and manufactures a full range of interior and exterior systems, in addition to providing complete vehicle assembly services to major automotive manufacturers. The company operates in three geographic segments North America, Europe and rest of the world that include 238 manufacturing operations, 79 product development, engineering and sales centers that are located in over 25 countries. Through its divisions and subsidiaries, the company provides metallic body and chassis systems, hydro-formed components and assemblies, seating and interior systems, power train products, closure systems, mirror systems, roof systems, electronic systems and exterior body products, as well as engine, transmission and fueling systems and components. Magna's primary operating subsidiaries include Cosma International; Magna Powertrain; Decoma International; Magna Seating; Magna Mirrors; Magna Electronics; Magna Steyr; Magna Donnelly; and Intier Automotive, Inc. Some of the company's notable customers are Chrysler Group; Daimler AG; Porsche; Toyota; General Motors; BMW; Volkswagen; Nissan; Lexus; Mitsubishi; Tata Automotive; and Ford Motor Company. In February 2010, the company's subsidiary, Magna Steyr, acquired Karmann Japan, Co. Ltd., a convertible systems supplier. In April 2010, the company announced a joint venture with Hollingsworth Logistics, Chattanooga Seating Systems, which will supply complete seating systems for Volkswagen Group of America.

The company provides its employees with a whole range of benefits including profit sharing; an employee assistance program; competitive wages and benefits; job counseling and training; and an employee disaster relief fund.

FINANCIALS: **Sales and profits are in thousands of dollars—add 000 to get the full amount. 2009 Note: Financial information for 2009 was not available for all companies at press time.**

2009 Sales: $17,367,000	2009 Profits: $-493,000	**U.S. Stock Ticker: MGA**
2008 Sales: $23,704,000	2008 Profits: $71,000	**Int'l Ticker: MG.A** Int'l Exchange: Toronto-TSX
2007 Sales: $26,067,000	2007 Profits: $663,000	Employees: 74,350
2006 Sales: $24,180,000	2006 Profits: $528,000	Fiscal Year Ends: 12/31
2005 Sales: $22,811,000	2005 Profits: $639,000	Parent Company:

SALARIES/BENEFITS:

Pension Plan:	ESOP Stock Plan:	Profit Sharing:	Top Exec. Salary: $	Bonus: $
Savings Plan:	Stock Purch. Plan:		Second Exec. Salary: $	Bonus: $

OTHER THOUGHTS:

Apparent Women Officers or Directors: 2
Hot Spot for Advancement for Women/Minorities:

LOCATIONS: ("Y" = Yes)

West:	Southwest:	Midwest:	Southeast:	Northeast:	International:
		Y	Y	Y	Y

MAGNA MIRRORS

www.magnamirrors.com

Industry Group Code: 3363 **Ranks within this company's industry group:** Sales: Profits:

Vehicle Manufacturing:		Dealers:		Parts:		Service:		Finance:		Specialty:	
Cars:		Car Dealer New:		Manufacturers:	Y	General Service:		Leasing:		Information Systems:	
Trucks:		Car Dealer Used:		Retail:		Specialty Service:		Auto Loans:		Online Marketing:	
Motorcycles:		Truck Dealer:		Distributors:		Oil Change:		Insurance:		Other:	
Specialty:		RV Dealer:		Tires:		Paint and Body:				Publishing:	
Buses:		Motorcycle Dealer:		Batteries:						Rental Cars/Trucks:	
RVs:		Specialty Dealer:									

TYPES OF BUSINESS:

Automobile Parts Manufacturer
Window & Door Systems
Vision Systems
Glass & Coating Products
Automotive Mirrors

BRANDS/DIVISIONS/AFFILIATES:

Magna International, Inc.
Magna Donnelly
Total BlindZoneManagement
VideoMirror
Frameless
CornerVue360
NaviMirror
ReversAid

CONTACTS:

Note: Officers with more than one job title may be intentionally listed here more than once.

Jim Brodie, VP/Gen. Mgr.
Donald J. Walker, Co-CEO-Magna International
Siegfried Wolf, Co-CEO-Magna International

Phone: 616-786-7000	**Fax:**
Toll-Free:	
Address: 49 W. 3rd St., Holland, MI 49423 US	

GROWTH PLANS/SPECIAL FEATURES:

Magna Mirrors, formerly Magna Donnelly, is a subsidiary of Magna International, Inc., a Canadian auto parts firm, that supplies automotive customers around the world with automotive mirror and vision systems. The firm focuses on developing features and technologies around its core products, including exterior and interior mirror systems; actuators; electrochromic (EC) glass; and door handle systems. The company divides its products into five segments: interior mirrors, both prismatic and EC; exterior mirrors, including auto-dimming glass; actuators; electronic vision systems, including lane change and blind zone assistance systems; and door handle and overhead console technologies. Products include the VideoMirror rearview mirror, which contains an LCD screen that allows video zooming features, navigation and multiple camera inputs; Frameless exterior EC mirrors, which utilize a reflective frame around exterior mirrors to maximize visibility; and the Total BlindZoneManagement (TBZM) system, which combines camera systems, mirrors and lighting to eliminate blind spots around a vehicle. Features of the TBZM system include predictive front lighting, which lights curves during nighttime driving; CornerVue360, for corner visibility; NaviMirror and MirrorPilot are a navigation and telematics system; CabinVue, an interior cabin display; ReversAid, a display system for reverse driving; and the BlindZoneMirror, which uses a small mirror integrated into a vehicle's side mirrors to increase visibility of side blind zones. The firm operates manufacturing divisions and engineering facilities in the U.S., Mexico, Austria, Germany, France, Spain, Sweden, Slovakia, China, Japan, India and South Africa. Magna Mirrors produces over 26 million interior mirrors and 28 million exterior mirrors annually. Customers include Daimler, Chrysler, Ford, General Motors, Honda, Mazda, Ferrari, Suzuki, Hyundai, BMW, Volkswagen and Volvo.

FINANCIALS:

Sales and profits are in thousands of dollars—add 000 to get the full amount. 2009 Note: Financial information for 2009 was not available for all companies at press time.

2009 Sales: $	2009 Profits: $	**U.S. Stock Ticker: Subsidiary**
2008 Sales: $	2008 Profits: $	**Int'l Ticker:** Int'l Exchange:
2007 Sales: $	2007 Profits: $	Employees:
2006 Sales: $	2006 Profits: $	Fiscal Year Ends:
2005 Sales: $	2005 Profits: $	Parent Company: MAGNA INTERNATIONAL INC

SALARIES/BENEFITS:

Pension Plan:	ESOP Stock Plan:	Profit Sharing:	Top Exec. Salary: $	Bonus: $
Savings Plan:	Stock Purch. Plan:		Second Exec. Salary: $	Bonus: $

OTHER THOUGHTS:

Apparent Women Officers or Directors:
Hot Spot for Advancement for Women/Minorities:

LOCATIONS: ("Y" = Yes)

West:	Southwest:	Midwest:	Southeast:	Northeast:	International:
		Y		Y	Y

MAGNETI MARELLI HOLDING SPA

www.magnetimarelli.com

Industry Group Code: 3363 **Ranks within this company's industry group:** Sales: 18 Profits: 18

Vehicle Manufacturing:		Dealers:		Parts:		Service:		Finance:		Specialty:	
Cars:		Car Dealer New:		Manufacturers:	Y	General Service:		Leasing:		Information Systems:	
Trucks:		Car Dealer Used:		Retail:		Specialty Service:		Auto Loans:		Online Marketing:	
Motorcycles:		Truck Dealer:		Distributors:		Oil Change:		Insurance:		Other:	Y
Specialty:		RV Dealer:		Tires:		Paint and Body:				Publishing:	
Buses:		Motorcycle Dealer:		Batteries:						Rental Cars/Trucks:	
RVs:		Specialty Dealer:									

TYPES OF BUSINESS:

Automotive Components
Power Train Systems
Motor Sport Components
Lighting
Automotive Performance Research Equipment

BRANDS/DIVISIONS/AFFILIATES:

Fiat SpA
Cofa
Step9

CONTACTS:
Note: Officers with more than one job title may be intentionally listed here more than once.

Eugenio Razelli, CEO
Eugenio Razelli, Pres.
Donatella Penati, CFO
Gianpaolo Accossato, General Counsel
Sergio Garue, Sr. VP-Purchasing

Phone: 39-02-9722-7454 **Fax:** 39-02-9722-7510
Toll-Free:
Address: Viale Aldo Borletti 61/63, Milano, 20011 Italy

GROWTH PLANS/SPECIAL FEATURES:

Magneti Marelli Holding S.p.A, a subsidiary of Fiat, designs and manufactures components and systems for lighting, suspension, exhaust and powertrain applications. Magneti Marelli has supplied major car manufacturers such as Renault, Citroen, Peugeot, the Fiat Group, Ford, Volkswagen, Audi, Seat, BMW, DaimlerChrysler, GM-Opel, Volvo, Saab, Nissan, Toyota and Daewoo. Magneti Marelli also maintains a motor sport division that offers a line of performance-enhancing products, including the Step9 engine and chassis control unit, capable of driving an engine at speeds of up to 20,000 rpm. The unit also has product lines in alternators, motors and voltage regulators; fuel systems and ignition; sensors; electronic control systems; data acquisition, display and lap trigger; and software. Magneti Marelli has industrial and research facilities in Italy, France, Spain, Great Britain, Germany, Poland, Czech Republic, Russia, Turkey, the U.S., Mexico, Brazil, Argentina, China, Malaysia and South Africa. Magneti Marelli maintains several joint ventures with companies including: Endurance Technologies to manufacture shock absorbers for motor vehicles in India and Thailand; Suzuki Motor Corporation and Maruti Suzuki India Limited for the production of electronic control units for diesel engine; Sumi Motherson Group for engine control components; and Telecom Italia to create onboard infomobility services. In April 2009, the company opened a new plant in China. In August 2009, the firm partnered with FAAM, a producer of starter batteries and industrial traction batteries, to develop and market lithium traction batteries and related control management systems. In November 2009, the company entered a partnership with Samsung Mobile Display to develop display-based products for instrument clusters, infotainment and car navigation.

FINANCIALS:
Sales and profits are in thousands of dollars—add 000 to get the full amount. 2009 Note: Financial information for 2009 was not available for all companies at press time.

2009 Sales: $5,706,220	2009 Profits: $31,700	**U.S. Stock Ticker: Subsidiary**
2008 Sales: $	2008 Profits: $	**Int'l Ticker:** Int'l Exchange:
2007 Sales: $	2007 Profits: $	Employees: 32,000
2006 Sales: $6,069,200	2006 Profits: $	Fiscal Year Ends: 12/31
2005 Sales: $5,183,660	2005 Profits: $	Parent Company: FIAT SPA

SALARIES/BENEFITS:

Pension Plan:	ESOP Stock Plan:	Profit Sharing:	Top Exec. Salary: $	Bonus: $
Savings Plan:	Stock Purch. Plan:		Second Exec. Salary: $	Bonus: $

OTHER THOUGHTS:

Apparent Women Officers or Directors: 1
Hot Spot for Advancement for Women/Minorities:

LOCATIONS: ("Y" = Yes)

West:	Southwest:	Midwest:	Southeast:	Northeast:	International:
		Y			Y

MAHINDRA & MAHINDRA LIMITED

www.mahindra.com

Industry Group Code: 33611 **Ranks within this company's industry group:** Sales: 24 Profits: 10

Vehicle Manufacturing:		Dealers:		Parts:		Service:		Finance:		Specialty:	
Cars:	Y	Car Dealer New:		Manufacturers:		General Service:		Leasing:		Information Systems:	
Trucks:	Y	Car Dealer Used:		Retail:		Specialty Service:		Auto Loans:		Online Marketing:	
Motorcycles:	Y	Truck Dealer:		Distributors:		Oil Change:		Insurance:		Other:	
Specialty:	Y	RV Dealer:		Tires:		Paint and Body:				Publishing:	
Buses:		Motorcycle Dealer:		Batteries:						Rental Cars/Trucks:	
RVs:		Specialty Dealer:									

TYPES OF BUSINESS:

Automotive & Farm Equipment Manufacturing & Distribution
Software Engineering
Real Estate Development
Hotels
Financial Services
Automobile Finance
Housing Finance
Information Technology

BRANDS/DIVISIONS/AFFILIATES:

Mahindra & Mahindra Financial Services Ltd
Mahindra Rural Housing Finance Ltd
Mahindra Intertrade Limited
Mahindra Lifescapes

CONTACTS:

Note: Officers with more than one job title may be intentionally listed here more than once.

Anand G. Mahindra, Managing Dir./Vice Chmn.
Bharat N. Doshi, CFO
Rajeev Dubey, Pres., Human Resources
Ulhas n. Yargop, Pres., IT Sector
Sandhya G. Sharma, Sr. Gen. Mgr.-Investor Rel.
Uday Phadke, Pres., Finance
Hemant Luthra, Pres., Systech Sector
Anjanikumar Choudhari, Pres., Farm Equipment Sector
Pawan Goenka, Pres., Automotive Sector
Keshub Mahindra, Chmn.

Phone: 91-22-5652-6000 **Fax:** 91-22-2496-1649
Toll-Free:
Address: Mahindra Towers, G.M. Bhosale Marg, Mumbai, 400 018 India

GROWTH PLANS/SPECIAL FEATURES:

Mahindra & Mahindra Limited is one of the largest industrial companies in India and a leading producer of multi-utility vehicles. The company operates in six sectors: automotive; farm equipment; financial services; trade, retail and logistics; infrastructure development; and information technology. The automotive sector is in the business of manufacturing and marketing utility vehicles and light commercial vehicles, including three-wheelers. In addition to Indian sales, the group exports its vehicles to several countries in Europe, Africa, South Asia and the Middle East. The farm equipment sector is a leading producer of tractors, with plants in India, the U.S., China and Australia. The financial services sector operates through subsidiaries such as Mahindra & Mahindra Financial Services Ltd., providing financing for utility vehicles, tractors and cars in rural and semi-urban areas; and Mahindra Rural Housing Finance Ltd., serving the housing finance needs of rural and semi-urban customers throughout India. The trade, retail and logistics sector, through subsidiaries such as Mahindra Intertrade Limited, is involved in the trading of various commodities, with a particular emphasis on steel and steel-related services. The infrastructure development sector is involved in real estate, the hospitality industry, project engineering and design services. Subsidiary Mahindra Lifescapes is a corporate property developer in India. The information technology sector, through subsidiaries such as Tech Mahindra Limited, provides software engineering and related services for telecom service providers, equipment manufacturers, software vendors and systems integrators.

FINANCIALS:

Sales and profits are in thousands of dollars—add 000 to get the full amount. 2009 Note: Financial information for 2009 was not available for all companies at press time.

2009 Sales: $5,787,960 | 2009 Profits: $302,170
2008 Sales: $5,495,500 | 2008 Profits: $286,900
2007 Sales: $3,491,850 | 2007 Profits: $303,810
2006 Sales: $2,407,660 | 2006 Profits: $257,650
2005 Sales: $ | 2005 Profits: $

U.S. Stock Ticker:
Int'l Ticker: 500520 Int'l Exchange: Bombay-BSE
Employees: 16,094
Fiscal Year Ends: 3/31
Parent Company:

SALARIES/BENEFITS:

Pension Plan: ESOP Stock Plan: Profit Sharing: Top Exec. Salary: $ Bonus: $
Savings Plan: Stock Purch. Plan: Second Exec. Salary: $ Bonus: $

OTHER THOUGHTS:

Apparent Women Officers or Directors:
Hot Spot for Advancement for Women/Minorities:

LOCATIONS: ("Y" = Yes)

West:	Southwest:	Midwest:	Southeast:	Northeast:	International:
					Y

MAJOR AUTOMOTIVE COMPANIES INC

www.majorworld.com

Industry Group Code: 441110 **Ranks within this company's industry group:** Sales: Profits:

Vehicle Manufacturing:		Dealers:		Parts:		Service:		Finance:		Specialty:	
Cars:		Car Dealer New:	Y	Manufacturers:		General Service:	Y	Leasing:		Information Systems:	
Trucks:		Car Dealer Used:	Y	Retail:	Y	Specialty Service:		Auto Loans:	Y	Online Marketing:	
Motorcycles:		Truck Dealer:		Distributors:		Oil Change:		Insurance:		Other:	
Specialty:		RV Dealer:		Tires:		Paint and Body:				Publishing:	
Buses:		Motorcycle Dealer:		Batteries:						Rental Cars/Trucks:	
RVs:		Specialty Dealer:									

TYPES OF BUSINESS:

Auto Dealers-Retail
Auto Financing
Parts & Repair Service
Used Car Sales

BRANDS/DIVISIONS/AFFILIATES:

Major World
MajorWorld.com
Major Dealer Group

CONTACTS:

Note: Officers with more than one job title may be intentionally listed here more than once.

Bruce Bendell, CEO
Bruce Bendell, COO
Bruce Bendell, Pres.
Bruce Bendell, Chmn.

Phone: 866-614-2884	**Fax:**
Toll-Free: 888-326-2567	
Address: 43-40 Northern Blvd., Long Island City, NY 11101 US	

GROWTH PLANS/SPECIAL FEATURES:

Major Automotive Companies, Inc., is a holding company for Major Dealer Group, one of the largest-volume automobile retailers in the New York metropolitan area. From its dealership in Long Island City, New York, Major Dealer Group sells new cars including such makes as Acura, BMW, Toyota, Kia, Ford, Volkswagen, Hyundai, Porsche, Cadillac, Chevrolet, Chrysler, Dodge and Jeep. In addition to its new cars, the company also sells used vehicles of virtually all makes. Major Automotive focuses on the sale of used vehicles, which affords it the opportunity to generate additional customer traffic from a wide variety of prospective buyers, increase new and used vehicle sales by aggressively pursuing customer trade-ins and generate incremental revenues from customers financially unable or indisposed to purchase a new vehicle. Major has established the Major World brand and MajorWorld.com Internet brand for its current used car operations and those of the Major Dealer Group's participating regional dealerships. Customers can search for available used and new cars, obtain a valuation of a used vehicle trade-in and apply for financing through the company's web site. In order to market to diverse populations, the company employs a multilingual sales force. Additionally, its customized telephone interactive voice response provides price quotes, places orders, answers frequently asked questions and approves credit in multiple languages. The firm also offers related financing, replacement parts and vehicle repair services through its dealerships.

FINANCIALS:

Sales and profits are in thousands of dollars—add 000 to get the full amount. 2009 Note: Financial information for 2009 was not available for all companies at press time.

2009 Sales: $	2009 Profits: $	**U.S. Stock Ticker: MJRC.PK**
2008 Sales: $	2008 Profits: $	**Int'l Ticker:** Int'l Exchange:
2007 Sales: $	2007 Profits: $	Employees:
2006 Sales: $	2006 Profits: $	Fiscal Year Ends: 12/31
2005 Sales: $	2005 Profits: $	Parent Company:

SALARIES/BENEFITS:

Pension Plan:	ESOP Stock Plan:	Profit Sharing:	Top Exec. Salary: $	Bonus: $
Savings Plan:	Stock Purch. Plan:		Second Exec. Salary: $	Bonus: $

OTHER THOUGHTS:

Apparent Women Officers or Directors:
Hot Spot for Advancement for Women/Minorities:

LOCATIONS: ("Y" = Yes)

West:	Southwest:	Midwest:	Southeast:	Northeast:	International:
				Y	

MARANGONI SPA

www.marangoni.com

Industry Group Code: 3262 **Ranks within this company's industry group:** Sales: Profits:

Vehicle Manufacturing:		Dealers:		Parts:		Service:		Finance:		Specialty:	
Cars:		Car Dealer New:		Manufacturers:	Y	General Service:		Leasing:		Information Systems:	
Trucks:		Car Dealer Used:		Retail:	Y	Specialty Service:		Auto Loans:		Online Marketing:	
Motorcycles:		Truck Dealer:		Distributors:	Y	Oil Change:		Insurance:		Other:	
Specialty:		RV Dealer:		Tires:	Y	Paint and Body:				Publishing:	
Buses:		Motorcycle Dealer:		Batteries:						Rental Cars/Trucks:	
RVs:		Specialty Dealer:									

TYPES OF BUSINESS:

Plastics & Rubber, Manufacturing
Tire Sales & Distribution
Retreading Systems
Tire Technology & Equipment
Car Accessories

BRANDS/DIVISIONS/AFFILIATES:

Marangoni Tread
Ellerbrock GmbH
Eurorubber S.p.a.
RINGTREAD
Marangoni Pneumatici
Marangoni Meccanica
Pneusmarket S.p.a.
Marangoni do Brasil Ltda.

CONTACTS:

Note: Officers with more than one job title may be intentionally listed here more than once.

Mario Marangoni, Managing Dir.
Massimo De Alessandri, Managing Dir.
Mario Marangoni, Chmn.

Phone: 39-045-921-5100 **Fax:** 39-045-823-2830
Toll-Free:
Address: Via E. Fermi 11/b, Verona, 37135 Italy

GROWTH PLANS/SPECIAL FEATURES:

Marangoni SpA operates integrated businesses that design, develop, manufacture, retread and distribute tires. It engages in every aspect of tire production and retreading from the processing of raw materials, through development, manufacture, sales and distribution to scrap tire disposal. The retreading systems division provides products and services including hot and cold retreading materials, machinery and accessories for retreading and assistance and marketing support. Its retreading subsidiaries operate throughout the world and include Marangoni Tread; Ellerbrock GmbH; Eurorubber Spa; Marangoni do Brasil Ltda; and Marangoni Tread North America Inc. The company's specialty lies in cold retreading, for which it makes use of its proprietary RINGTREAD system, involving procured rings as opposed to the more traditional strip method. Marangoni, as Marangoni Pneumatici, also produces tires for cars, light-duty transportation and industrial vehicles. Through Marangoni Meccanica, the company designs and manufactures tire production and retreading equipment, plants and technologies. Marangoni's distribution division, Pneusmarket S.p.a., manages a wholesale distribution network of more than 40 sales outlets, offering various car services and accessories in addition to tires. The company places a lifetime warranty on all of its tires.

FINANCIALS:

Sales and profits are in thousands of dollars—add 000 to get the full amount. 2009 Note: Financial information for 2009 was not available for all companies at press time.

2009 Sales: $	2009 Profits: $	**U.S. Stock Ticker: Private**
2008 Sales: $	2008 Profits: $	**Int'l Ticker:** Int'l Exchange:
2007 Sales: $	2007 Profits: $	Employees:
2006 Sales: $	2006 Profits: $	Fiscal Year Ends: 12/31
2005 Sales: $	2005 Profits: $	Parent Company:

SALARIES/BENEFITS:

Pension Plan:	ESOP Stock Plan:	Profit Sharing:	Top Exec. Salary: $	Bonus: $
Savings Plan:	Stock Purch. Plan:		Second Exec. Salary: $	Bonus: $

OTHER THOUGHTS:

Apparent Women Officers or Directors:
Hot Spot for Advancement for Women/Minorities:

LOCATIONS: ("Y" = Yes)

West:	Southwest:	Midwest:	Southeast:	Northeast:	International:
			Y		Y

MARUTI SUZUKI INDIA LIMITED

www.marutisuzuki.com

Industry Group Code: 33611 **Ranks within this company's industry group:** Sales: 26 Profits: 13

Vehicle Manufacturing:		Dealers:		Parts:		Service:		Finance:		Specialty:	
Cars:	Y	Car Dealer New:		Manufacturers:	Y	General Service:	Y	Leasing:		Information Systems:	
Trucks:		Car Dealer Used:		Retail:	Y	Specialty Service:		Auto Loans:	Y	Online Marketing:	
Motorcycles:		Truck Dealer:		Distributors:		Oil Change:		Insurance:	Y	Other:	Y
Specialty:		RV Dealer:		Tires:		Paint and Body:				Publishing:	
Buses:		Motorcycle Dealer:		Batteries:						Rental Cars/Trucks:	
RVs:		Specialty Dealer:									

TYPES OF BUSINESS:

Automobile Manufacturer
Financial Services
Auto Accessories
Driving Training School

BRANDS/DIVISIONS/AFFILIATES:

Suzuki Motor Corporation
SX4
A-Star
Ritz
Grand Vitara
WagonR
Dzire
Maruti Driving School

CONTACTS:

Note: Officers with more than one job title may be intentionally listed here more than once.

Shinzo Nakanishi, CEO/Managing Dir.
Tsuneo. Ohashi, Dir./Managing Exec. Officer-Prod.
S. Ravi Aiyar, Chief Legal Officer/Sec.
R. C. Bhargava, Chmn.

Phone: 91-11-4678-1124 **Fax:** 91-11-4615-0525
Toll-Free:
Address: Plot Number 1, Nelson Mandela Rd., Vasant Kunj, New Delhi, 110 070 India

GROWTH PLANS/SPECIAL FEATURES:

Maruti Suzuki India Limited (MSIL), formerly Maruti Udyog Limited, is a 54%-owned subsidiary of Suzuki Motor Corporation and one of India's foremost automobile manufacturing companies, accounting for more than 55% of the domestic car market. The company began in 1982 as a joint venture between the government of India and Suzuki. The firm operates in five segments: marketing and sales; research and development; manufacturing; administration; and supply chain. MSIL has two integrated production facilities in India, which together have an annual production capacity of approximately one million vehicles. Vehicles include 13 models and more than 150 variants on those models, such as the sedans SX4, Alto and DZire; the sports utility vehicles Grand Vitara and WagonR; the compact Maruti 800, Swift, A-Star, Ritz and Zen Estilo; the Eeco and Omni vans; and the Maruti Gypsy King jeep. MSIL sells its vehicles through a network of 802 sales outlets in 555 cities in India, and provides maintenance and support to customers through 2,740 workshops in 1,335 cities. The company also exports its vehicles to over 100 countries, primarily in Africa, Latin America and Southeast Asia. The firm also offers automobile accessories, such as wheel and body covers, graphics kits, seat and steering wheel covers, mud flaps, door visors, sun visors, fog lamps, floor mats, media systems, car frames, security systems and car care products. The Maruti Driving School (MDS) offers on-the-road, classroom and MDS simulator training. In January 2010, the company announced the Eeco, a large five-door can designed specifically for the Indian market.

FINANCIALS:

Sales and profits are in thousands of dollars—add 000 to get the full amount. 2009 Note: Financial information for 2009 was not available for all companies at press time.

2009 Sales: $4,392,010	2009 Profits: $260,900	**U.S. Stock Ticker: Subsidiary**
2008 Sales: $3,848,250	2008 Profits: $380,470	**Int'l Ticker: 532500** Int'l Exchange: Bombay-BSE
2007 Sales: $3,143,460	2007 Profits: $337,610	Employees:
2006 Sales: $	2006 Profits: $	Fiscal Year Ends: 3/31
2005 Sales: $	2005 Profits: $	Parent Company: SUZUKI MOTOR CORPORATION

SALARIES/BENEFITS:

Pension Plan:	ESOP Stock Plan:	Profit Sharing:	Top Exec. Salary: $	Bonus: $
Savings Plan:	Stock Purch. Plan:		Second Exec. Salary: $	Bonus: $

OTHER THOUGHTS:

Apparent Women Officers or Directors: 1
Hot Spot for Advancement for Women/Minorities:

LOCATIONS: ("Y" = Yes)

West:	Southwest:	Midwest:	Southeast:	Northeast:	International:
					Y

MAYBACH

www.maybach-manufaktur.com

Industry Group Code: 33611 **Ranks within this company's industry group:** Sales: Profits:

Vehicle Manufacturing:		Dealers:		Parts:		Service:		Finance:		Specialty:	
Cars:	Y	Car Dealer New:	Y	Manufacturers:	Y	General Service:		Leasing:		Information Systems:	
Trucks:		Car Dealer Used:		Retail:		Specialty Service:		Auto Loans:		Online Marketing:	
Motorcycles:		Truck Dealer:		Distributors:		Oil Change:		Insurance:		Other:	Y
Specialty:		RV Dealer:		Tires:		Paint and Body:				Publishing:	
Buses:		Motorcycle Dealer:		Batteries:						Rental Cars/Trucks:	
RVs:		Specialty Dealer:									

TYPES OF BUSINESS:

Automobile Manufacturing
Luxury Automobiles
Automobile Customization

BRANDS/DIVISIONS/AFFILIATES:

Daimler AG
Mercedes-Benz Group
Maybach-Manufaktur
Maybach Car Demonstrator
Landaulet
Maybach Zeppelin

CONTACTS: *Note: Officers with more than one job title may be intentionally listed here more than once.*

Dieter Zetsche, CEO-Daimler AG

Phone: 49-0711-17-0	**Fax:**
Toll-Free:	
Address: Epplestrabe 225, Stuttgart, 70567 Germany	

GROWTH PLANS/SPECIAL FEATURES:

Maybach, a subsidiary of Daimler AG and a sister brand to Mercedes-Benz, produces expensive luxury automobiles intended to cater the world's elite. The company operates as part of the Mercedes Benz Group, and distributes vehicles in the U.S., Europe and Asia. Its automobiles are based on the opulent cars built by Wilhelm Maybach and his son, Karl, between 1921 and 1941. Today, Maybach vehicles are in league with the automobiles produced by Rolls-Royce and Bentley. The company's Maybach-Manufaktur facility in Sindelfingen, Germany is capable of producing 1,000 special-order vehicles per year. The Center of Excellence is a studio from which prospective customers order vehicles built to exact specifications, which include everything from technical components to wood, leather and paint selections. The results are displayed on the Maybach Car Demonstrator, a video program that depicts each step of the model configuration. The current Maybach models are the Maybach 57 and the longer Maybach 62. Both are available in an 'S' model: the upgrade includes a more powerful engine, as well as minor aesthetic changes. Some of the features of the car include, 19-inch television screen located on the back of the passenger seat; reclining rear seat; and high-speed WLAN (Wireless Local Area Network) router. The company offers knowledgeable sales representatives, many associated with Mercedes-Benz, who are available in any of the national Maybach Centers located in the U.S., Italy, France, Hong Kong Japan, Jordan, Kuwait and other countries around the world. The firm's fifth model called the Landaulet, which features an extra-large folding roof over the rear-seat area and a renovated chauffeur's quarters. In 2009, the company introduced the new Maybach Zeppelin luxury sedan.

FINANCIALS: **Sales and profits are in thousands of dollars—add 000 to get the full amount. 2009 Note: Financial information for 2009 was not available for all companies at press time.**

2009 Sales: $	2009 Profits: $	**U.S. Stock Ticker: Subsidiary**
2008 Sales: $	2008 Profits: $	**Int'l Ticker:** Int'l Exchange:
2007 Sales: $	2007 Profits: $	Employees:
2006 Sales: $	2006 Profits: $	Fiscal Year Ends: 12/31
2005 Sales: $	2005 Profits: $	Parent Company: DAIMLER AG

SALARIES/BENEFITS:

Pension Plan:	ESOP Stock Plan:	Profit Sharing:	Top Exec. Salary: $	Bonus: $
Savings Plan:	Stock Purch. Plan:		Second Exec. Salary: $	Bonus: $

OTHER THOUGHTS:

Apparent Women Officers or Directors:
Hot Spot for Advancement for Women/Minorities:

LOCATIONS: ("Y" = Yes)

West:	Southwest:	Midwest:	Southeast:	Northeast:	International:
				Y	Y

MAZDA MOTOR CORPORATION

www.mazda.com

Industry Group Code: 33611 **Ranks within this company's industry group:** Sales: 14 Profits: 24

Vehicle Manufacturing:		Dealers:		Parts:		Service:		Finance:		Specialty:	
Cars:	Y	Car Dealer New:		Manufacturers:		General Service:		Leasing:		Information Systems:	
Trucks:	Y	Car Dealer Used:		Retail:		Specialty Service:		Auto Loans:		Online Marketing:	
Motorcycles:		Truck Dealer:		Distributors:		Oil Change:		Insurance:		Other:	
Specialty:		RV Dealer:		Tires:		Paint and Body:				Publishing:	
Buses:		Motorcycle Dealer:		Batteries:						Rental Cars/Trucks:	
RVs:		Specialty Dealer:									

TYPES OF BUSINESS:

Automobiles, Manufacturing
Commercial Vans & Trucks
Hydrogen Engine Technology

BRANDS/DIVISIONS/AFFILIATES:

Mazda5
Mazda Canada
Ford Motor Company
MCM Energy Service Company
Miata
Bongo
Titan
Mazda Carol

CONTACTS: *Note: Officers with more than one job title may be intentionally listed here more than once.*

Takashi Yamanouchi, CEO
Takashi Yamanouchi, Pres.
Kiyoshi Ozaki, CFO/Sr. Managing Exec. Officer
Masahiro Moro, Exec. Officer-Global Mktg.
Koji Kurosawa, Managing Exec. Officer-Human Resources
Masaharu Yamaki, Exec. VP-R&D
Philip G. Spender, Exec. VP-IT
Masaharu Yamaki, Exec. VP-Prod. & Quality
Masamichi Kogai, Managing Exec. Officer-Prod. Eng. Div.
Takashi Yamanouchi, Exec. VP-Admin.
Koji Kurosawa, Sec.
Akira Marumoto, Managing Exec. Officer-Corp. Planning
Yuji Harada, Managing Exec. Officer-Corp. Comm.
Yuji Nakamine, Managing Exec. Officer-Overseas Sales
Seita Kanai, Pres., Mazda Engineering & Technology Co., Ltd.
James J. O'Sullivan, Pres./CEO-Mazda Motor of America, Inc.
Keishi Egawa, Exec. VP/COO-Mazda Motor of America, Inc.
Hisakazu Imaki, Chmn.
Jeffrey H. Guyton, Pres./CEO-Mazda Motor Europe GmbH
Masaharu Yamaki, Exec. VP-Purchasing

Phone: 81-82-282-1111 **Fax:** 81-82-287-5190
Toll-Free:
Address: 3-1 Shinchi, Fuchu-cho, Aki-gun, Hiroshima, 730-8670 Japan

GROWTH PLANS/SPECIAL FEATURES:

Mazda Motor Corporation, established in 1920, is one of Japan's largest automakers. Mazda operates four production facilities in Japan and 13 overseas facilities, including joint ventures in the U.S. (Missouri), China, Taiwan, Thailand, the Philippines and South Africa with Ford Motor Company, which holds a 13.8% share in the firm. The company has been exporting cars to the U.S. and Europe for almost 40 years, and with Mazda cars and trucks now being sold in nearly 130 countries, overseas sales account for over two-thirds of annual revenues. Working closely with Ford, the company has recently revamped much of its passenger car, truck, minivan and utility vehicle product line, rolling out new models including the Mazda 6, Mazda 3, Mazda 8 and the RX-8, a high-performance sports car. Other popular models include the Miata sports-convertible, the Tribute sport utility vehicle and the BT-50 pick-up. The company's line of commercial vehicles targets the light industrial sector with high-efficiency diesel vans and trucks. Marketed under brand names including Bongo, Titan, Mazda E-Series and Mazda T-Series, these vehicles are available in various configurations of cargo bed and cabin size. Many of these vehicles are produced on an outsourced basis, with Bongo vans and trucks being built by Nissan and Mitsubishi. Mazda markets passenger micro-mini vans and trucks under the model name Scrum, with vehicles being manufactured on a third-party OEM basis by Suzuki Motor Corporation. The firm operates a joint venture with Mitsubishi named MCM Energy Service Company, which provides electricity and steam to two of Mazda's Japanese production facilities. In December 2009, Mazda released the 20CS Smart Edition Premacy (known as the Mazda5 internationally) and the Mazda Carol micro-mini in Japan.

FINANCIALS: **Sales and profits are in thousands of dollars—add 000 to get the full amount. 2009 Note: Financial information for 2009 was not available for all companies at press time.**

2009 Sales: $27,445,000 — 2009 Profits: $-513,950
2008 Sales: $37,617,000 — 2008 Profits: $993,890
2007 Sales: $27,640,000 — 2007 Profits: $630,000
2006 Sales: $24,830,200 — 2006 Profits: $
2005 Sales: $24,212,280 — 2005 Profits: $413,118

U.S. Stock Ticker: MZDAF.PK
Int'l Ticker: 7261 Int'l Exchange: Tokyo-TSE
Employees:
Fiscal Year Ends: 3/31
Parent Company:

SALARIES/BENEFITS:

Pension Plan: ESOP Stock Plan: Profit Sharing: Top Exec. Salary: $ Bonus: $
Savings Plan: Stock Purch. Plan: Second Exec. Salary: $ Bonus: $

OTHER THOUGHTS:

Apparent Women Officers or Directors:
Hot Spot for Advancement for Women/Minorities:

LOCATIONS: ("Y" = Yes)

West:	Southwest:	Midwest:	Southeast:	Northeast:	International:
Y	Y	Y	Y	Y	Y

MAZDA NORTH AMERICAN OPERATIONS

www.mazdausa.com

Industry Group Code: 33611 **Ranks within this company's industry group:** Sales: Profits:

Vehicle Manufacturing:		Dealers:		Parts:		Service:		Finance:		Specialty:	
Cars:		Car Dealer New:	Y	Manufacturers:		General Service:	Y	Leasing:	Y	Information Systems:	
Trucks:		Car Dealer Used:	Y	Retail:		Specialty Service:		Auto Loans:		Online Marketing:	
Motorcycles:		Truck Dealer:		Distributors:	Y	Oil Change:		Insurance:		Other:	Y
Specialty:		RV Dealer:		Tires:		Paint and Body:				Publishing:	
Buses:		Motorcycle Dealer:		Batteries:						Rental Cars/Trucks:	
RVs:		Specialty Dealer:									

TYPES OF BUSINESS:

Car & Truck Dealerships
Customer Parts & Services Operations
Vehicle Research & Development

BRANDS/DIVISIONS/AFFILIATES:

Mazda Motor Corporation
MNAO
Mazda Motor of America Inc
Mazda Canada Inc
Mazda Motor de Mexico S de RL de SV
Tribute
Mazda5
Mazda6

CONTACTS:

Note: Officers with more than one job title may be intentionally listed here more than once.

James J. O'Sullivan, CEO
Keishi Egawa, COO/VP
James J. O'Sullivan, Pres.
Donald Romano, Chief Mktg. Officer
Renee Lewis, VP-Human Resources
James DiMarzio, CIO
Robert T. Davis, Sr. VP-Prod. Dev. & Quality
Shawn Murphy, General Counsel/Corp. Sec./VP
Eric Johnston, VP-Strategic Planning & Market Integration
Jay Amestoy, VP-Public & Gov't Affairs
Ron Stettner, VP-Sales
Takashi Yamanouchi, Pres./CEO-Mazda Motor Corporation
Nobuyuki Sato, VP-Mazda Canada
Leopoldo Orellana, Managing Dir.-Mazda Motor de Mexico
Donald Romano, Pres., Mazda Canada

Phone: 949-727-6220 **Fax:** 949-727-6813
Toll-Free: 800-222-5500
Address: 7755 Irvine Center Dr., Irvine, CA 92623 US

GROWTH PLANS/SPECIAL FEATURES:

Mazda North American Operations (MNAO), a subsidiary of Mazda Motor Corporation (Mazda), provides sales, marketing, parts and customer service support operations for Mazda vehicles in the U.S., Canada and Mexico. The company comprises Mazda Motor of America, Inc., which handles the firm's U.S. sales and distribution operations, as well as providing product planning, product development, research, evaluation testing and vehicle certification services; Mazda Canada, Inc., based in Ontario, which manages the company's operations in Canada; and Mazda Motor de Mexico S. de R.L. de S.V., based in Mexico City, which controls operations in Mexico. MNAO sells and leases its line of new and used cars, trucks, minivans and SUVs through roughly 859 dealerships across North America, roughly 700 of which are located in the U.S. The firm's models include the Mazda3 5-Door; Mazda3 4-Door; MazdaSpeed3; Mazda5; Mazda6; MX-5 Miata roadster; RX-8 sports car; CX7 SUV; CX9 SUV; and the Tribute Hybrid SUV. Approximately 60% of Mazda vehicles sold in North America are sold through dealerships that exclusively offer the Mazda brand. All recent model Mazda cars are equipped with Bluetooth hands-free voice-command or steering mounted controls for making and receiving phone calls. MNAO's online shopping tools allow customers to build their own vehicles, search existing inventory, appraise trade-ins, request a quote, estimate payments, compare vehicles, locate a dealer and apply for credit.

Mazda offers its employees life, AD&D, disability, medical, dental and vision insurance; healthcare and childcare flexible spending accounts; mental health and substance abuse programs; an employee assistance program; paid holidays; a new and used vehicle purchase program; lease and temporary rental vehicle programs; flex time scheduling; and an incentive plan.

FINANCIALS:

Sales and profits are in thousands of dollars—add 000 to get the full amount. 2009 Note: Financial information for 2009 was not available for all companies at press time.

2009 Sales: $ | 2009 Profits: $
2008 Sales: $ | 2008 Profits: $
2007 Sales: $ | 2007 Profits: $
2006 Sales: $ | 2006 Profits: $
2005 Sales: $ | 2005 Profits: $

U.S. Stock Ticker: Subsidiary
Int'l Ticker: Int'l Exchange:
Employees:
Fiscal Year Ends: 3/31
Parent Company: MAZDA MOTOR CORPORATION

SALARIES/BENEFITS:

Pension Plan: | ESOP Stock Plan: | Profit Sharing: | Top Exec. Salary: $ | Bonus: $
Savings Plan: Y | Stock Purch. Plan: | | Second Exec. Salary: $ | Bonus: $

OTHER THOUGHTS:

Apparent Women Officers or Directors: 1
Hot Spot for Advancement for Women/Minorities:

LOCATIONS: ("Y" = Yes)

West:	Southwest:	Midwest:	Southeast:	Northeast:	International:
Y	Y	Y	Y	Y	

MCLAREN PERFORMANCE TECHNOLOGIES

www.mclarenperformance.com

Industry Group Code: 3363 **Ranks within this company's industry group:** Sales: Profits:

Vehicle Manufacturing:		**Dealers:**		**Parts:**		**Service:**		**Finance:**		**Specialty:**	
Cars:		Car Dealer New:		Manufacturers:	Y	General Service:		Leasing:		Information Systems:	
Trucks:		Car Dealer Used:		Retail:		Specialty Service:		Auto Loans:		Online Marketing:	
Motorcycles:		Truck Dealer:		Distributors:		Oil Change:		Insurance:		Other:	Y
Specialty:	Y	RV Dealer:		Tires:		Paint and Body:				Publishing:	
Buses:		Motorcycle Dealer:		Batteries:						Rental Cars/Trucks:	
RVs:		Specialty Dealer:									

TYPES OF BUSINESS:

Automotive Products, Motors & Parts Manufacturing
Power Train Products
Testing & Development Services
Vehicle Development & Fabrication
Engineering Services
Performance Products
Engine Testing

BRANDS/DIVISIONS/AFFILIATES:

Linamar Corp

CONTACTS:

Note: Officers with more than one job title may be intentionally listed here more than once.

Linda S. Hasenfratz, CEO
Jim Jarrell, COO
Jim Jarrell, Pres.
Phil Guys, VP-Eng.

Phone: 248-477-6240	**Fax:** 248-477-3349
Toll-Free:	
Address: 32233 W. Eight Mile Rd., Livonia, MI 48152 US	

GROWTH PLANS/SPECIAL FEATURES:

McLaren Performance Technologies, Inc., a subsidiary of Linamar Corp., specializes in powertrain products. The parent company, Linamar, is a world leader in the design and integration of precision-machined components and other modules and systems for the automobile industry. McLaren is divided into four segments: engine testing; engineering services; performance products; and vehicle development and fabrication. The engine testing division houses a 24-hour facility that contains 16 standardized dynamometer test cells, with the capability of computerized simulation and analysis. McLaren's engineering services division offers development, manufacturing and assembling of powertrain systems. The division also provides its clients with engine quality audit and validation through processing warranty returns and performing inspections and audits of in-use products. The company's performance products sector produces high performance custom parts and complete engine assemblies for racing professionals and others in the automobile industry. The vehicle development and fabrication division offers custom services, such as the designing, fabricating, assembling, painting and testing of concept; prototype; and performance vehicles. The vehicles can be customized to highlight powertrains or other parts. The company has prototyping and fabrication facilities with 14 hoist-equipped bays. McLaren Performance Technologies has provided its services to Ford, BMW and General Motors. In August 2009, the firm expanded its corporate headquarters by roughly 10,000 square feet.

FINANCIALS:

Sales and profits are in thousands of dollars—add 000 to get the full amount. 2009 Note: Financial information for 2009 was not available for all companies at press time.

2009 Sales: $	2009 Profits: $	**U.S. Stock Ticker: Subsidiary**
2008 Sales: $	2008 Profits: $	**Int'l Ticker:** Int'l Exchange:
2007 Sales: $	2007 Profits: $	Employees:
2006 Sales: $	2006 Profits: $	Fiscal Year Ends: 12/31
2005 Sales: $	2005 Profits: $	Parent Company: LINAMAR CORP

SALARIES/BENEFITS:

Pension Plan:	ESOP Stock Plan:	Profit Sharing:	Top Exec. Salary: $	Bonus: $
Savings Plan:	Stock Purch. Plan:		Second Exec. Salary: $	Bonus: $

OTHER THOUGHTS:

Apparent Women Officers or Directors: 1
Hot Spot for Advancement for Women/Minorities:

LOCATIONS: ("Y" = Yes)

West:	Southwest:	Midwest:	Southeast:	Northeast:	International:
		Y			

MERCEDES-BENZ USA LLC

www.mbusa.com

Industry Group Code: 33611 **Ranks within this company's industry group:** Sales: Profits:

Vehicle Manufacturing:		Dealers:		Parts:		Service:		Finance:		Specialty:	
Cars:		Car Dealer New:	Y	Manufacturers:		General Service:		Leasing:		Information Systems:	
Trucks:		Car Dealer Used:	Y	Retail:		Specialty Service:		Auto Loans:		Online Marketing:	
Motorcycles:		Truck Dealer:		Distributors:	Y	Oil Change:		Insurance:		Other:	Y
Specialty:		RV Dealer:		Tires:		Paint and Body:				Publishing:	
Buses:		Motorcycle Dealer:		Batteries:						Rental Cars/Trucks:	
RVs:		Specialty Dealer:									

TYPES OF BUSINESS:

Automobiles-Import & Distribution
Marketing & Sales Services
Dealership

BRANDS/DIVISIONS/AFFILIATES:

Daimler AG
Maybach
Mercedes-Benz Manhattan, Inc.
S-Class
M-Class
GL-Class
mbrace
ML450 HYBRID 4MATIC

CONTACTS:

Note: Officers with more than one job title may be intentionally listed here more than once.

Ernst Lieb, CEO
Ernst Lieb, Pres.
Norbert H. Litzkow, CFO
Lisa Rosenfeld, Gen. Mgr.-Human Resources
Peter Patrone, Gen. Mgr.-IT
Tracey L. Matura, General Counsel/Sec.
Geoff Day, Dir.-Corp. Comm.
Herbert Werner, VP-Finance

Phone: 201-573-0600 **Fax:** 201-573-0117
Toll-Free: 800-367-6372
Address: 3 Mercedes Dr., Montvale, NJ 07645 US

GROWTH PLANS/SPECIAL FEATURES:

Mercedes-Benz USA LLC (MBUSA), a wholly-owned subsidiary of Daimler AG, sells, services, distributes and markets Mercedes-Benz cars and light trucks and Maybach super-luxury sedans throughout the U.S. MBUSA's vehicles include the C-, E- and S-Class sedans; E-, CLS- and CL-Class coupes; SLK-, SL- and SLS-Class roadsters; the GLK-, M-, GL- and G-Class light trucks and SUVs; the CLK-Class convertible; and the R-Class crossover. The firm sells these vehicles through a network of 348 independently owned dealerships in the U.S. MBUSA also provides sales, marketing and other services to Mercedes-Benz dealerships. The company serves the dealerships through regional offices in Parsippany, New Jersey; Rosemont, Illinois; Jacksonville, Florida; and Costa Mesa, California. MBUSA also has vehicle preparation centers in Brunswick, Georgia; Jacksonville, Florida; Carson, California; and Belcamp and Baltimore, Maryland. It has parts distribution centers in Forth Worth, Texas; Carol Stream, Illinois; and Robinsville, New Jersey. It also has a marshalling yard in Tuscaloosa, Alabama. In addition, the firm owns and operates one dealership in the U.S., Mercedes-Benz Manhattan, Inc., located in New York City. In November 2009, the company introduced the ML450 HYBRID 4MATIC, one of the first European full hybrids in the U.S. Also in November 2009, the company introduced mbrace, a telematics product that allows customers to perform applications such as locking or locating their vehicle through their smartphones. In May 2010, the firm opened a new vehicle preparation in Brunswick, Georgia.

FINANCIALS:

Sales and profits are in thousands of dollars—add 000 to get the full amount. 2009 Note: Financial information for 2009 was not available for all companies at press time.

2009 Sales: $	2009 Profits: $	**U.S. Stock Ticker: Subsidiary**
2008 Sales: $	2008 Profits: $	**Int'l Ticker:** Int'l Exchange:
2007 Sales: $	2007 Profits: $	Employees:
2006 Sales: $	2006 Profits: $	Fiscal Year Ends: 12/31
2005 Sales: $	2005 Profits: $	Parent Company: DAIMLER AG

SALARIES/BENEFITS:

Pension Plan:	ESOP Stock Plan:	Profit Sharing:	Top Exec. Salary: $	Bonus: $
Savings Plan:	Stock Purch. Plan:		Second Exec. Salary: $	Bonus: $

OTHER THOUGHTS:

Apparent Women Officers or Directors: 1
Hot Spot for Advancement for Women/Minorities:

LOCATIONS: ("Y" = Yes)

West:	Southwest:	Midwest:	Southeast:	Northeast:	International:
Y	Y	Y	Y	Y	

METALDYNE LLC

www.metaldyne.com

Industry Group Code: 3363 **Ranks within this company's industry group:** Sales: Profits:

Vehicle Manufacturing:		**Dealers:**		**Parts:**		**Service:**		**Finance:**		**Specialty:**	
Cars:		Car Dealer New:		Manufacturers:	Y	General Service:		Leasing:		Information Systems:	
Trucks:		Car Dealer Used:		Retail:		Specialty Service:		Auto Loans:		Online Marketing:	
Motorcycles:		Truck Dealer:		Distributors:		Oil Change:		Insurance:		Other:	
Specialty:		RV Dealer:		Tires:		Paint and Body:				Publishing:	
Buses:		Motorcycle Dealer:		Batteries:						Rental Cars/Trucks:	
RVs:		Specialty Dealer:									

TYPES OF BUSINESS:

Automobile Parts Manufacturer
Chassis Components
Engine Components
Driveline Components

BRANDS/DIVISIONS/AFFILIATES:

MD Investors Corp
Dynaturn
Carlyle Group (The)

CONTACTS:

Note: Officers with more than one job title may be intentionally listed here more than once.

Thomas A. Amato, CEO
Tom Chambers, COO
Tom A. Amato, Pres.
Terry Iwasaki, CFO/VP
Kimberly A. Kovac, VP-Human Resources
Jim Hudak, VP-Eng.
Terry Iwasaki, Treas.
Linda Theisen, VP-Commercial & Quality
Ben Schmidt, VP/Gen. Mgr.-Mataldyne Americas
Thomas Amato, Chmn.
Denis Bardou, VP/Gen. Mgr.-Metaldyne Europe

Phone: 734-207-6200	**Fax:** 734-207-6500
Toll-Free:	
Address: 47659 Halyard Dr., Plymouth, MI 48170 US	

GROWTH PLANS/SPECIAL FEATURES:

Metaldyne, LLC, formerly Metaldyne Corp., designs and produces engine, driveline and chassis products for automakers and Tier 1 suppliers worldwide. The company combines one of the largest independent machining and assembly capabilities and the manufacturing of thin-wall precision die castings for automotive applications. Products are divided into five groups: sintered products, forging products, vibration control products, powertrain products and chassis products. Sintered products include powder metal conducting rods, powder metal main bearing caps, powder metals carriers and fracture-split camshaft caps. The forging products segment encompasses bevel gears, complex parts, housings, sliding sleeves, splined sleeves, transmission shafts and aluminum and copper products. Vibration control products include dampers, isolation pulleys and viscous dampers. The powertrain group includes products such as balance shaft modules, clutch modules, front engine module assemblies and net-shape side and pinion gears. Metaldyne's chassis group has commercialized its patented process Dynaturn for the assembly of a wheel-end, mini-corner module that improves reliability and reduces brake warranty repairs. Products in this group include ball joints, corner modules, control arms, knuckles and independent rear suspension. Additionally, the company is the world's largest supplier of aluminum valve bodies. The firm owns 23 facilities in 12 countries, including South Korea, China and the Czech Republic. In early 2009, the firm filed for Chapter 11 bankruptcy protection. In June 2009, the company announced it had agreed to sell its European and some North American assets of sintered, vibration control and powertrain segments to RHJ International for $100 million. In October 2009, former parent firm Asahi Tec sold substantially all of the assets of Metaldyne to MD Investors Corporation, a group lead by private equity firm The Carlyle Group. In April 2010, the firm sold its Hamburg, Michigan-based Tubular Products plant to Hyspan Precision Products of Chula Vista, California.

FINANCIALS:

Sales and profits are in thousands of dollars—add 000 to get the full amount. 2009 Note: Financial information for 2009 was not available for all companies at press time.

2009 Sales: $	2009 Profits: $	**U.S. Stock Ticker: Private**
2008 Sales: $	2008 Profits: $	**Int'l Ticker:** Int'l Exchange:
2007 Sales: $1,817,369	2007 Profits: $-45,806	Employees:
2006 Sales: $1,849,000	2006 Profits: $-181,300	Fiscal Year Ends: 3/31
2005 Sales: $1,886,939	2005 Profits: $-261,907	Parent Company: MD INVESTORS CORP

SALARIES/BENEFITS:

Pension Plan:	ESOP Stock Plan:	Profit Sharing:	Top Exec. Salary: $	Bonus: $
Savings Plan:	Stock Purch. Plan:		Second Exec. Salary: $	Bonus: $

OTHER THOUGHTS:

Apparent Women Officers or Directors: 3
Hot Spot for Advancement for Women/Minorities: Y

LOCATIONS: ("Y" = Yes)

West:	Southwest:	Midwest:	Southeast:	Northeast:	International:
		Y		Y	Y

MIDAS INC

www.midasinc.com

Industry Group Code: 8111 **Ranks within this company's industry group:** Sales: 2 Profits: 2

Vehicle Manufacturing:		Dealers:		Parts:		Service:		Finance:		Specialty:	
Cars:		Car Dealer New:		Manufacturers:		General Service:	Y	Leasing:		Information Systems:	
Trucks:		Car Dealer Used:		Retail:		Specialty Service:	Y	Auto Loans:		Online Marketing:	
Motorcycles:		Truck Dealer:		Distributors:		Oil Change:	Y	Insurance:		Other:	
Specialty:		RV Dealer:		Tires:	Y	Paint and Body:				Publishing:	
Buses:		Motorcycle Dealer:		Batteries:						Rental Cars/Trucks:	
RVs:		Specialty Dealer:									

TYPES OF BUSINESS:

Automotive Repair & Maintenance
Real Estate Operations

BRANDS/DIVISIONS/AFFILIATES:

Midas International Corporation
Midas
SpeeDee

CONTACTS:

Note: Officers with more than one job title may be intentionally listed here more than once.

Alan D. Feldman, CEO
Alan D. Feldman, Pres.
William M. Guzik, CFO/Exec. VP
Rick Dow, Chief Mktg. Officer/Sr. VP
Ben Parma, VP-Human Resources
Alvin K. Marr, General Counsel/Sr. VP/Corp. Sec.
Mike Gould, Sr. VP-Retail Oper.
John A. Warzecha, Sr. VP-Franchise Bus. Dev.
James M. Haeger, Controller/VP
Alan D. Feldman, Chmn.

Phone: 630-438-3000 **Fax:** 630-438-3880
Toll-Free: 800-621-8545
Address: 1300 Arlington Heights Rd., Itasca, IL 60143 US

GROWTH PLANS/SPECIAL FEATURES:

Midas, Inc. provides auto repair and maintenance services in the U.S., Canada, Europe, Australia, the Middle East, Latin America and the Caribbean through company-operated and franchised shops. The firm operates under numerous subsidiaries including Midas International Corporation. Under the Midas brand, the company offers exhaust, brake, suspension, air conditioning and maintenance services. Midas farms out its wholesale parts distribution and quick-delivery operations through companies such as Uni-Select, Inc.; National Automotive Parts Association; and CarQuest Corporation. Subsidiary Midas Realty Corporation selects, leases and acquires sites and constructs facilities for company-operated and franchised shops throughout North America. It also enters into contingent operating lease agreements in order to ensure control of the real estate used by Midas shops. There are roughly 2,435 Midas shops in 14 countries around the world. North American operations account for approximately 1,602 of these shops, with company-owned shops accounting for nearly 98 locations and franchises for approximately 1,576 locations. The firm also operates the SpeeDee brand of oil change and tune-up shops; there are roughly 112 SpeeDee locations in 12 states and 57 in Mexico. Approximately 11% of Midas' retail business is generated by exhaust; 34% by brakes; 10% by suspension, shocks and struts; and 45% from new Midas categories, which include tires and related services, fleet maintenance services and general maintenance. In August 2009, the firm added SpeeDee services to 11 existing Midas shops in Northern California. In January 2010, Midas acquired 22 franchised Midas locations (also in Northern California) from Maurice I. Glad for roughly $5.8 million.

FINANCIALS:

Sales and profits are in thousands of dollars—add 000 to get the full amount. 2009 Note: Financial information for 2009 was not available for all companies at press time.

2009 Sales: $182,800	2009 Profits: $2,600	**U.S. Stock Ticker: MDS**
2008 Sales: $187,400	2008 Profits: $7,800	**Int'l Ticker:** Int'l Exchange:
2007 Sales: $178,200	2007 Profits: $13,000	Employees: 890
2006 Sales: $174,900	2006 Profits: $10,300	Fiscal Year Ends: 12/31
2005 Sales: $192,500	2005 Profits: $2,200	Parent Company:

SALARIES/BENEFITS:

Pension Plan:	ESOP Stock Plan:	Profit Sharing:	Top Exec. Salary: $725,000	Bonus: $157,637
Savings Plan:	Stock Purch. Plan:		Second Exec. Salary: $295,000	Bonus: $45,135

OTHER THOUGHTS:

Apparent Women Officers or Directors: 1
Hot Spot for Advancement for Women/Minorities:

LOCATIONS: ("Y" = Yes)

West:	Southwest:	Midwest:	Southeast:	Northeast:	International:
Y	Y	Y	Y	Y	Y

MILLER INDUSTRIES INC

www.millerind.com

Industry Group Code: 3363 **Ranks within this company's industry group:** Sales: 57 Profits: 26

Vehicle Manufacturing:		Dealers:		Parts:		Service:		Finance:		Specialty:	
Cars:		Car Dealer New:		Manufacturers:	Y	General Service:		Leasing:	Y	Information Systems:	
Trucks:		Car Dealer Used:		Retail:		Specialty Service:	Y	Auto Loans:		Online Marketing:	
Motorcycles:		Truck Dealer:		Distributors:		Oil Change:		Insurance:		Other:	Y
Specialty:		RV Dealer:		Tires:		Paint and Body:				Publishing:	
Buses:		Motorcycle Dealer:		Batteries:						Rental Cars/Trucks:	
RVs:		Specialty Dealer:									

TYPES OF BUSINESS:

Wrecker Equipment
Trailer Body & Car Carrier Manufacturing

BRANDS/DIVISIONS/AFFILIATES:

Century
Challenger
Eagle
Vulcan
Chevron
Holmes
Titan
Boniface

CONTACTS: *Note: Officers with more than one job title may be intentionally listed here more than once.*

William G. Miller, Co-CEO
Jeffrey I. Badgley, Pres.
J. Vincent Mish, CFO/Exec. VP
Frank Madonia, General Counsel/Sec./Exec. VP
J. Vincent Mish, Treas.
Jeffrey I. Badgley, Co-CEO
William G. Miller, Chmn.

Phone: 423-238-4171 **Fax:** 423-238-5371
Toll-Free: 800-292-0330
Address: 8503 Hilltop Dr., Ooltewah, TN 37363 US

GROWTH PLANS/SPECIAL FEATURES:

Miller Industries, Inc. is one of the world's leading integrated providers of vehicle towing and recovery equipment and services. It offers a broad range of towing and recovery equipment products that meet most customer design, capacity and cost requirements. Miller manufactures the bodies of wreckers, trailer bodies and car carriers for installation on truck chassis manufactured by third parties. The wreckers range in capacity from 8-75 tons, and are used to remove abandoned, illegally parked or disabled vehicles, as well as for commercial towing. Other uses of wreckers include removing vehicles from accident scenes or to recover overturned tractor trailers, busses, motor homes and other large vehicles. The firm's trailer bodies are used primarily by auto dealers, leasing companies and similar businesses and can generally haul 6-8 vehicles. The firm's specialized trailers are designed, engineered and manufactured for military applications. The car carriers are primarily used for long-distance hauling of autos and industrial equipment. Miller markets towing and recovery equipment under several brand names: Century, Challenger, Eagle, Champion, Vulcan, Chevron, Holmes, Titan, Boniface and Jige. The company's products are sold primarily through independent distributors that serve all 50 U.S. states, Canada and Mexico, as well as other foreign markets in Europe, the Pacific Rim, South America, Africa and the Middle East. The firm's four domestic manufacturing operations are located in Tennessee and Pennsylvania, while its two foreign manufacturing operations are located in France and the U.K. The company has approximately 120 independent distributors network that serve all 50 states and approximately 50 distributors that serve foreign markets. Recently, Miller launched many new products in 2009, both vehicles and accessories, including the Holmes 220 Snatcher rack, a towing attachment that can be installed in a standard three-quarter ton pickup to add 3,500 pounds of towing capacity.

FINANCIALS: **Sales and profits are in thousands of dollars—add 000 to get the full amount. 2009 Note: Financial information for 2009 was not available for all companies at press time.**

2009 Sales: $237,567 | 2009 Profits: $6,016
2008 Sales: $270,989 | 2008 Profits: $3,586
2007 Sales: $400,032 | 2007 Profits: $16,331
2006 Sales: $409,421 | 2006 Profits: $45,343
2005 Sales: $351,884 | 2005 Profits: $18,586

U.S. Stock Ticker: MLR
Int'l Ticker: Int'l Exchange:
Employees: 680
Fiscal Year Ends: 12/31
Parent Company:

SALARIES/BENEFITS:

Pension Plan: ESOP Stock Plan: Profit Sharing: Top Exec. Salary: $294,286 Bonus: $
Savings Plan: Y Stock Purch. Plan: Second Exec. Salary: $293,086 Bonus: $

OTHER THOUGHTS:

Apparent Women Officers or Directors:
Hot Spot for Advancement for Women/Minorities:

LOCATIONS: ("Y" = Yes)

West:	Southwest:	Midwest:	Southeast:	Northeast:	International:
			Y	Y	Y

MITSUBISHI FUSO TRUCK OF AMERICA INC

www.mitfuso.com

Industry Group Code: 336120 **Ranks within this company's industry group:** Sales: Profits:

Vehicle Manufacturing:		**Dealers:**		**Parts:**		**Service:**		**Finance:**		**Specialty:**	
Cars:		Car Dealer New:		Manufacturers:		General Service:		Leasing:		Information Systems:	
Trucks:	Y	Car Dealer Used:		Retail:		Specialty Service:		Auto Loans:		Online Marketing:	
Motorcycles:		Truck Dealer:		Distributors:		Oil Change:		Insurance:		Other:	
Specialty:		RV Dealer:		Tires:		Paint and Body:				Publishing:	
Buses:		Motorcycle Dealer:		Batteries:						Rental Cars/Trucks:	
RVs:		Specialty Dealer:									

TYPES OF BUSINESS:

Commercial Truck Manufacturing

BRANDS/DIVISIONS/AFFILIATES:

Daimler AG
Mitsubishi Fuso Truck and Bus Corporation

CONTACTS:

Note: Officers with more than one job title may be intentionally listed here more than once.

Todd Bloom, CEO
Matthew Stevenson, COO
Todd Bloom, Pres.
Takeo Ishimaru, CFO
Michael Rumsey, VP-Sales Oper.
Leighton Good, Mgr.-Prod. & Applications
Len Doherty, Dir.-Parts Oper.
Joshua Treager, Mgr.-Corp. Comm.
Albert Kirchmann, Pres./CEO-Mitsubishi Fuso Truck & Bus Corp.
Dominick Genes, Mgr.-Prod. Support
Jim Metz, Mgr.-National Service

Phone: 856-467-4500	**Fax:** 856-467-2781
Toll-Free:	
Address: 2015 Center Square Rd., Logan Township, NJ 08085 US	

GROWTH PLANS/SPECIAL FEATURES:

Mitsubishi Fuso Truck of America, Inc. (MFTA) is the U.S. operating arm of Mitsubishi Fuso Truck and Bus Corporation (MFTBC), a part of Daimler AG's Trucks Division. The company manufactures and markets a line of Class 3 through Class 7 diesel-powered, medium-duty cabover trucks through more than 200 dealers across the U.S., Puerto Rico and Canada. The firm's trucks are used for dry freight, landscaping, refrigerated delivery, vehicle recovery, public works and beverage vending applications, and are also used as contractor vehicles for carpenters, plumbers, electricians and energy, utility and telecommunications companies. Mitsubishi Fuso has sold more than 100,000 standard, four-wheel-drive and crew cab trucks vehicles in the U.S. and Canada since its inception in 1985. The company's truck models include the FE, which is available in three gross vehicle weigh ratings that include FE-125 (12,500 pounds), FE-145 (14,500 pounds) and FE-180 (17,995 pounds); the FE Crew Cab, which has a crew cab that can hold up to seven people; the FG 4X4, designed with all-terrain tires, heavy duty axles, shocks and springs for off-road landscaping and utility uses (14,050 pounds); the FK200 (19,850 pounds); the FK260 (25,995 pounds); and the FM330 (32,900 pounds). The FK and FM series trucks utilize a Fuso 6M60 7.5L (460 cubic inches) in-line SOHC six-cylinder turbocharged diesel engine.

FINANCIALS:

Sales and profits are in thousands of dollars—add 000 to get the full amount. 2009 Note: Financial information for 2009 was not available for all companies at press time.

2009 Sales: $	2009 Profits: $	**U.S. Stock Ticker: Subsidiary**
2008 Sales: $	2008 Profits: $	**Int'l Ticker:** Int'l Exchange:
2007 Sales: $250,000	2007 Profits: $	Employees:
2006 Sales: $	2006 Profits: $	Fiscal Year Ends: 12/31
2005 Sales: $	2005 Profits: $	Parent Company: DAIMLER AG

SALARIES/BENEFITS:

Pension Plan:	ESOP Stock Plan:	Profit Sharing:	Top Exec. Salary: $	Bonus: $
Savings Plan:	Stock Purch. Plan:		Second Exec. Salary: $	Bonus: $

OTHER THOUGHTS:

Apparent Women Officers or Directors:
Hot Spot for Advancement for Women/Minorities:

LOCATIONS: ("Y" = Yes)

West:	Southwest:	Midwest:	Southeast:	Northeast:	International:
Y	Y	Y	Y	Y	Y

MITSUBISHI MOTORS (THAILAND) CO LTD www.mitsubishi-motors.co.th

Industry Group Code: 33611 **Ranks within this company's industry group:** Sales: Profits:

Vehicle Manufacturing:		Dealers:		Parts:		Service:		Finance:		Specialty:	
Cars:	Y	Car Dealer New:		Manufacturers:	Y	General Service:		Leasing:		Information Systems:	
Trucks:	Y	Car Dealer Used:		Retail:		Specialty Service:		Auto Loans:		Online Marketing:	
Motorcycles:		Truck Dealer:		Distributors:		Oil Change:		Insurance:		Other:	
Specialty:		RV Dealer:		Tires:		Paint and Body:				Publishing:	
Buses:		Motorcycle Dealer:		Batteries:						Rental Cars/Trucks:	
RVs:		Specialty Dealer:									

TYPES OF BUSINESS:

Passenger Automobile & Truck Manufacturing

BRANDS/DIVISIONS/AFFILIATES:

Pajero
Pajero Sport
Lancer 1.6 GLX
Triton
Triton Plus
Mitsubishi Motors Corporation
MMTh Engine Co., Ltd

GROWTH PLANS/SPECIAL FEATURES:

Mitsubishi Motors (Thailand) Co. Ltd. (MMTh) is the Thai subsidiary of international car manufacturer Mitsubishi Motors Corporation. The firm manufactures and distributes Mitsubishi pickup trucks and passenger cars. While the vast majority of manufactured vehicles are exported worldwide, approximately 10% of them are produced specifically for Thailand's domestic market. The company's manufacturing facility, located in Chonburi, has an annual production capacity of 200,000 units. The company's vehicles include an SUV called the Pajero; the Pajero Sport line of two and four wheel drive SUVs; the Lancer 1.6 GLX car series; the Space Wagon mini van; and the Triton and Triton Plus truck series. MMTh also runs a subsidiary that manufactures engines, MMTh Engine Co., Ltd. Parent company Mitsubishi Motors Corporation, based in Japan, has 14 manufacturing facilities, five research facilities and approximately 50 subsidiaries; the firm offers its products in over 160 countries.

CONTACTS: *Note: Officers with more than one job title may be intentionally listed here more than once.*

Nobuyuki Takahashi, Pres.
Terut Butloetcharoen, Head-Corp. Comm.
Koji Nakahara, Exec. VP

Phone: 0-2529-9000	**Fax:** 0-2529-9090
Toll-Free:	
Address: 688 Phaholyothin Rd., Klongluang, 12120 Thailand	

FINANCIALS: **Sales and profits are in thousands of dollars—add 000 to get the full amount. 2009 Note: Financial information for 2009 was not available for all companies at press time.**

2009 Sales: $	2009 Profits: $	**U.S. Stock Ticker: Subsidiary**
2008 Sales: $	2008 Profits: $	**Int'l Ticker:** Int'l Exchange:
2007 Sales: $	2007 Profits: $	Employees:
2006 Sales: $	2006 Profits: $	Fiscal Year Ends: 3/31
2005 Sales: $	2005 Profits: $	Parent Company: MITSUBISHI MOTORS CORP

SALARIES/BENEFITS:

Pension Plan:	ESOP Stock Plan:	Profit Sharing:	Top Exec. Salary: $	Bonus: $
Savings Plan:	Stock Purch. Plan:		Second Exec. Salary: $	Bonus: $

OTHER THOUGHTS:

Apparent Women Officers or Directors:
Hot Spot for Advancement for Women/Minorities:

LOCATIONS: ("Y" = Yes)

West:	Southwest:	Midwest:	Southeast:	Northeast:	International:
					Y

MITSUBISHI MOTORS CORP

www.mitsubishi-motors.com

Industry Group Code: 33611 **Ranks within this company's industry group:** Sales: 16 Profits: 25

Vehicle Manufacturing:		Dealers:		Parts:		Service:		Finance:		Specialty:	
Cars:	Y	Car Dealer New:		Manufacturers:	Y	General Service:		Leasing:	Y	Information Systems:	
Trucks:	Y	Car Dealer Used:		Retail:		Specialty Service:		Auto Loans:	Y	Online Marketing:	
Motorcycles:		Truck Dealer:		Distributors:	Y	Oil Change:		Insurance:		Other:	
Specialty:		RV Dealer:		Tires:		Paint and Body:				Publishing:	
Buses:	Y	Motorcycle Dealer:		Batteries:						Rental Cars/Trucks:	
RVs:		Specialty Dealer:									

TYPES OF BUSINESS:

Automobiles, Manufacturing
Automobile Parts
Agricultural Machinery & Industrial Engines

BRANDS/DIVISIONS/AFFILIATES:

Mitsubishi Group
Colt
Galant Fortis
Outlander
Triton
Town Box
i-MiEV
Mitsubishi Motors North America, Inc. (MMNA)

CONTACTS:

Note: Officers with more than one job title may be intentionally listed here more than once.

Osamu Masuko, Pres.
Hiizu Ichikawa, Managing Dir.-Finance
Tetsuro Aikawa, Managing Dir.-Domestic Sales
Gayu Uesugi, Dir.-Prod. Strategy & Dev.
Hiroshi Harunari, Managing Dir.-Overseas Oper.
Hiizu Ichikawa, Managing Dir.-Corp. Affairs
Shuichi Aoto, Dir.-Acct. & Controlling Group
Makoto Maeda, Exec. VP/Head-Russian Bus. Dev. & MiEV Bus. Mgmt.
Seiichi Ohta, Head-Quality Affairs Group
Osamu Matsumoto, Head-Prod. Group
Shinichi Kurihara, CEO/Pres., Mitsubishi Motors North America, Inc.
Takashi Nishioka, Chmn.
Hiroshi Harunari, Corp. Gen. Mgr.-EMEA
Hiroshi Kuroda, Head-Procurement Group

Phone: 81-3-3456-1111	**Fax:**
Toll-Free:	
Address: 33-8, Shiba 5-chome, Minato-ku, Tokyo, 108-8410 Japan	

GROWTH PLANS/SPECIAL FEATURES:

Mitsubishi Motors Corp. (MMC), part of Mitsubishi Group, designs, manufactures, sells and distributes automobiles, trucks, buses and parts. It also designs, manufactures, sells and imports agricultural machinery and industrial engines. MMC has 72 subsidiaries and affiliates and sold almost 1 million vehicles between March 2009 and March 2010 in 160 countries, with sales outside Japan generating 80% of total automobile sales. The Mitsubishi brand includes the Colt coupe, Galant Fortis sedan, Outlander SUV, Triton pickup, Town Box minivan and all-electric i-MiEV. The firm has seven car manufacturing facilities in five countries; seven engine, transmission and parts manufacturing facilities in four countries; and five research and development centers in four countries. Mitsubishi Motors North America, Inc. (MMNA) oversees all of the company's North American operations, including sales, manufacturing, finance and research and development. It manufactures and markets coupes, convertibles, sedans and sport utility vehicles through a network of almost 700 dealers in the U.S., Canada, Mexico and the Caribbean. Mitsubishi Motors Credit of America, Inc. provides Mitsubishi retailers with a variety of wholesale financing and retail options to assist clients in purchasing or leasing Mitsubishi brand vehicles. Some of the firm's other subsidiaries include Hokkaido Mitsubishi Motors Sales Co., Ltd.; Mitsubishi Motors R&D of America, Inc. (MRDA); Mitsubishi Motors Deutschland GmbH; Mitsubishi Motors France S.A.S; Mitsubishi Motors Belgium nv; Mitsubishi Motors Australia, Ltd. (MMAL); Mitsubishi Motors (Thailand) Co., Ltd. (MMTH); Asian Transmission Corp. (ATC); and Mitsubishi Motor Parts Sales of Gulf FZE. In April 2010, the company and PSA Peugeot Citroen began vehicle production at PCMA Rus, the firms' joint plant in Russia, of which MMC owns 30%.

FINANCIALS:

Sales and profits are in thousands of dollars—add 000 to get the full amount. 2009 Note: Financial information for 2009 was not available for all companies at press time.

2009 Sales: $21,359,100	2009 Profits: $-593,980	**U.S. Stock Ticker:**
2008 Sales: $26,726,600	2008 Profits: $345,880	**Int'l Ticker: 7211** Int'l Exchange: Tokyo-TSE
2007 Sales: $21,951,200	2007 Profits: $87,140	Employees:
2006 Sales: $21,200,700	2006 Profits: $-921,700	Fiscal Year Ends: 3/31
2005 Sales: $21,226,300	2005 Profits: $-4,747,800	Parent Company:

SALARIES/BENEFITS:

Pension Plan:	ESOP Stock Plan:	Profit Sharing:	Top Exec. Salary: $	Bonus: $
Savings Plan:	Stock Purch. Plan:		Second Exec. Salary: $	Bonus: $

OTHER THOUGHTS:

Apparent Women Officers or Directors:
Hot Spot for Advancement for Women/Minorities:

LOCATIONS: ("Y" = Yes)

West:	Southwest:	Midwest:	Southeast:	Northeast:	International:
Y		Y			Y

MODINE MANUFACTURING COMPANY

www3.modine.com

Industry Group Code: 3363 **Ranks within this company's industry group:** Sales: 38 Profits: 47

Vehicle Manufacturing:		**Dealers:**		**Parts:**		**Service:**		**Finance:**		**Specialty:**	
Cars:		Car Dealer New:		Manufacturers:	Y	General Service:		Leasing:		Information Systems:	
Trucks:		Car Dealer Used:		Retail:		Specialty Service:		Auto Loans:		Online Marketing:	
Motorcycles:		Truck Dealer:		Distributors:	Y	Oil Change:		Insurance:		Other:	
Specialty:		RV Dealer:		Tires:		Paint and Body:				Publishing:	
Buses:		Motorcycle Dealer:		Batteries:						Rental Cars/Trucks:	
RVs:		Specialty Dealer:									

TYPES OF BUSINESS:

Automobile Parts Manufacturer
Heat Exchangers & Systems
Oil Cores
Electronics Cooling
Heating & Air Conditioning Products
Radiator Cores
Fuel Cells

BRANDS/DIVISIONS/AFFILIATES:

CONTACTS:

Note: Officers with more than one job title may be intentionally listed here more than once.

Thomas A. Burke, CEO
Thomas A. Burke, Pres.
Michael B. Lucareli, CFO/VP-Finance/Corp. Treas.
Gregory T. Troy, Chief Human Resources Officer/VP
Thomas A. Burke, CTO
Scott D. Wollenberg, VP-Global Eng.
Margaret C. Kelsey, General Counsel/Corp. Sec.
Margaret C. Kelsey, VP-Corp. Dev.
Susan Fisher, Dir.-Corp. Comm.
Susan Fisher, Dir.-Investor Rel.
Robert R. Kampstra, Corp. Controller/Chief Acct. Officer/VP
Thomas F. Marry, VP-Asia & Commercial Prod. Group
Matthew J. McBurney, Dir.-Commercial Prod., North America
Scott L. Browser, Regional VP-Americas
Gary L. Neale, Chmn.
Klaus A. Feldmann, Regional VP-Europe

Phone: 262-636-1200 **Fax:** 262-636-1424
Toll-Free:
Address: 1500 DeKoven Ave., Racine, WI 53403-2552 US

GROWTH PLANS/SPECIAL FEATURES:

Modine Manufacturing Company is a worldwide leader in thermal management technology. The firm serves the vehicular; industrial; commercial; fuel cell; and building heating, ventilating, air conditioning and refrigeration (HVAC&R) markets. Modine develops, produces and markets thermal management products, components and systems such as radiators, charge air coolers, exhaust gas recirculation (EGR) coolers and oil coolers. Its primary customers are original equipment manufacturers (OEMs) in various industries, including the commercial truck, bus and specialty vehicle markets; the firm also caters to construction contractors and wholesalers of plumbing and heating equipment. The company is organized into five segments: original equipment-North America, original equipment-Asia, original equipment-Europe, South America and commercial products. The three original equipment units sell radiators, charge-air-coolers, EGR coolers, fan shrouds, engine oil coolers, fuel coolers, intake air coolers and HVAC system modules such as condensers, evaporators and heater cores. The original equipment-North America segment also maintains the fuel cell business segment. The South America segment sells products for construction and agricultural applications; automotive OEM and industrial applications; aftermarket radiators, charge-air-coolers, oil coolers, auxiliary coolers and engine cooling modules; and HVAC system modules. The company's commercial segment offers products such as unit heaters; duct furnaces; infrared units; hydronic products; roof mounted fired makeup air units; unit ventilators; close control units for precise temperature and humidity control applications; chiller units; ceiling cassettes; condensing units; and coils for heating, refrigeration, air conditioning and vehicular applications. In December 2009, the firm sold subsidiary Modine Korea LLC, its vehicular HVAC business, to KB Synthetics as part of a refocusing strategy. In line with this strategy, the firm has closed several of its facilities in the U.S. and Europe, including, most recently, its Harrodsburg, Kentucky facility.

Modine offers employees medical benefits, educational assistance, retirement plans, life insurance and flexible spending accounts.

FINANCIALS:

Sales and profits are in thousands of dollars—add 000 to get the full amount. 2009 Note: Financial information for 2009 was not available for all companies at press time.

2009 Sales: $1,408,714	2009 Profits: $-108,612	**U.S. Stock Ticker: MOD**
2008 Sales: $1,601,672	2008 Profits: $-68,633	**Int'l Ticker:** Int'l Exchange:
2007 Sales: $1,525,492	2007 Profits: $42,691	Employees: 6,953
2006 Sales: $1,595,622	2006 Profits: $7,641	Fiscal Year Ends: 3/31
2005 Sales: $1,342,416	2005 Profits: $61,662	Parent Company:

SALARIES/BENEFITS:

Pension Plan: Y	ESOP Stock Plan:	Profit Sharing:	Top Exec. Salary: $627,750	Bonus: $
Savings Plan: Y	Stock Purch. Plan:		Second Exec. Salary: $454,530	Bonus: $

OTHER THOUGHTS:

Apparent Women Officers or Directors: 3
Hot Spot for Advancement for Women/Minorities: Y

LOCATIONS: ("Y" = Yes)

West:	Southwest:	Midwest:	Southeast:	Northeast:	International:
	Y	Y	Y	Y	Y

MONRO MUFFLER BRAKE INC

www.monro.com

Industry Group Code: 8111 **Ranks within this company's industry group:** Sales: 1 Profits: 1

Vehicle Manufacturing:		Dealers:		Parts:		Service:		Finance:		Specialty:	
Cars:		Car Dealer New:		Manufacturers:		General Service:	Y	Leasing:		Information Systems:	
Trucks:		Car Dealer Used:		Retail:		Specialty Service:		Auto Loans:		Online Marketing:	
Motorcycles:		Truck Dealer:		Distributors:		Oil Change:	Y	Insurance:		Other:	Y
Specialty:		RV Dealer:		Tires:	Y	Paint and Body:				Publishing:	
Buses:		Motorcycle Dealer:		Batteries:						Rental Cars/Trucks:	
RVs:		Specialty Dealer:									

TYPES OF BUSINESS:

Automotive Repair & Maintenance
Under-Car Repair Services
Inspection Services
Tires

BRANDS/DIVISIONS/AFFILIATES:

Monro Muffler Brake & Service
Mr. Tire
Tread Quarters Discount Tire
Monro Muffler Brake & Service
Monro Service Corporation

CONTACTS: *Note: Officers with more than one job title may be intentionally listed here more than once.*

Robert G. Gross, CEO
John W. Van Heel, Pres.
Catherine D'Amico, CFO
John W. Van Heel, Sec.
Joseph Tomarchio, Jr., Exec. VP-Store Oper.
Catherine D'Amico, Exec. VP-Finance/Treas.
Craig L. Hoyle, Div. VP-Southern Oper.
Christopher R. Hoornbeck, Div. VP-Western Oper.
Robert G. Gross, Chmn.

Phone: 585-647-6400	**Fax:** 585-647-0945
Toll-Free:	
Address: 200 Holleder Pkwy., Rochester, NY 14615 US	

GROWTH PLANS/SPECIAL FEATURES:

Monro Muffler Brake, Inc., based in Rochester, New York, operates through a chain of 777 company-operated stores and 14 dealer-operated stores providing automotive under-car repair and tire services in the U.S. These stores are typically located in high-visibility locations in suburban and small towns in New York, Pennsylvania, Ohio, Connecticut, Massachusetts, West Virginia, Virginia, Maryland, Vermont, New Hampshire, New Jersey, North Carolina, South Carolina, Indiana, Rhode Island, Delaware and Maine. The stores operate under the names Monro Muffler Brake & Service, Tread Quarters Discount Tire and Mr. Tire. In 2009, the firm's stores serviced approximately 3.9 million vehicles. Monro provides a range of services on passenger cars, light trucks and vans for brakes; mufflers and exhaust systems; and steering, drive train, suspension and wheel alignment. Other products and services offered by the company include tires and routine maintenance services, such as state inspections. The company specializes in the repair and replacement of parts that must be periodically replaced due to normal wear and tear. Typically, the firm does not perform under-the-hood repair, except for oil change services, heating and cooling system flush and fill services and some minor tune-ups. Monro operates one subsidiary, Monro Service Corporation, which provides purchasing, distribution, merchandising, advertising, accounting and other store support functions. In June 2009, Monro acquired Autotire Car Care Center, comprising 26 locations in Missouri, for approximately $10 million. In September 2009, the firm acquired Tire Warehouse Central for approximately $34 million and Midwest Tire & Auto Repair for approximately $2 million. In January 2010, Mr. Tire Auto Service Center opened a new location in Carnegie, Pennsylvania. In March 2010, the company agreed to acquire Import Export Tire, Co., a Pittsburgh, Pennsylvania based tire chain.

Monro offers its employees ASE certification reimbursement, recreational discounts, an employee assistance program, tool insurance and medical, dental, life and disability insurance.

FINANCIALS: **Sales and profits are in thousands of dollars—add 000 to get the full amount. 2009 Note: Financial information for 2009 was not available for all companies at press time.**

2009 Sales: $476,106	2009 Profits: $24,088	**U.S. Stock Ticker: MNRO**
2008 Sales: $439,389	2008 Profits: $21,921	**Int'l Ticker:** Int'l Exchange:
2007 Sales: $417,226	2007 Profits: $22,271	Employees: 4,277
2006 Sales: $368,727	2006 Profits: $22,666	Fiscal Year Ends: 3/31
2005 Sales: $337,409	2005 Profits: $19,669	Parent Company:

SALARIES/BENEFITS:

Pension Plan:	ESOP Stock Plan: Y	Profit Sharing:	Top Exec. Salary: $769,125	Bonus: $150,000
Savings Plan: Y	Stock Purch. Plan:		Second Exec. Salary: $360,000	Bonus: $

OTHER THOUGHTS:

Apparent Women Officers or Directors: 1
Hot Spot for Advancement for Women/Minorities:

LOCATIONS: ("Y" = Yes)

West:	Southwest:	Midwest:	Southeast:	Northeast:	International:
		Y		Y	

MONTUPET SA

www.montupet.fr

Industry Group Code: 3363 **Ranks within this company's industry group:** Sales: 56 Profits: 33

Vehicle Manufacturing:		Dealers:		Parts:		Service:		Finance:		Specialty:	
Cars:		Car Dealer New:		Manufacturers:	Y	General Service:		Leasing:		Information Systems:	
Trucks:		Car Dealer Used:		Retail:	Y	Specialty Service:		Auto Loans:		Online Marketing:	
Motorcycles:		Truck Dealer:		Distributors:	Y	Oil Change:		Insurance:		Other:	
Specialty:		RV Dealer:		Tires:		Paint and Body:				Publishing:	
Buses:		Motorcycle Dealer:		Batteries:						Rental Cars/Trucks:	
RVs:		Specialty Dealer:									

TYPES OF BUSINESS:

Automobile Parts Manufacturing
Cast Aluminum Parts

BRANDS/DIVISIONS/AFFILIATES:

Montupet Limitee
Montupet UK Ltd.
Calcast Ltd.
Torreon
Chateauroux
Nogent/Laigneville
Alumalsa

CONTACTS:
Note: Officers with more than one job title may be intentionally listed here more than once.

Stephane Magnan, Managing Dir.
Didier Crozet, Managing Dir.
Marc Majus, Managing Dir.
Stephane Magnan, Chmn.

Phone: 33-1-47-56-47-56 **Fax:** 33-1-47-39-77-93
Toll-Free:
Address: 202 Quai de Clichy, Clichy, BP77-92112 France

GROWTH PLANS/SPECIAL FEATURES:

Montupet SA, established in 1894, is a major manufacturer of molded car parts in aluminum alloys. The company makes three product ranges in cast aluminum: finished motor parts, including cylinder heads, cylinder blocks and intake manifolds; machined and painted wheels and rims; and finished structure parts, suspension and braking parts. The firm also manufactures part of the tooling necessary to its production. Montupet's products are made either through gravity casting, which relies on the weight of the liquid metal to fill a die; or through low pressure casting, which forces liquid metal into a die via a tube to more accurately control how the die fills. Montupet designs and manufactures parts mainly for Renault, Ford-Volvo, GM-Saab and PSA. It also manufactures parts for Audi-VW, Bosch, Autres, Iveco, Lucas, Delphi and John Deere. The firm has several subsidiaries for commercial representation, manufacturing and distribution in multiple countries in Europe and North America, including production plants such as Montupet Limitee in Canada, which mainly manufactures cylinder heads; Montupet UK Ltd. and Calcast Ltd. in North Ireland, which mainly manufacture aluminum wheels and cylinder heads; Torreon in Mexico, which manufactures cylinder heads; Chateauroux and Nogent/Laigneville in France, which mainly manufacture cylinder heads and structural components; and Alumalsa in Spain, which mainly manufactures manifolds; as well as sales offices in the U.S., U.K., Sweden, Germany, Italy, Spain and France. In March 2010, the company acquired three aluminum smelting works facilities.

FINANCIALS:
Sales and profits are in thousands of dollars—add 000 to get the full amount. 2009 Note: Financial information for 2009 was not available for all companies at press time.

2009 Sales: $260,330	2009 Profits: $-20,540	**U.S. Stock Ticker:**
2008 Sales: $566,220	2008 Profits: $-1,140	**Int'l Ticker: MON** Int'l Exchange: Paris-Euronext
2007 Sales: $701,000	2007 Profits: $-11,420	Employees:
2006 Sales: $672,900	2006 Profits: $2,900	Fiscal Year Ends: 12/31
2005 Sales: $605,300	2005 Profits: $11,500	Parent Company:

SALARIES/BENEFITS:

Pension Plan:	ESOP Stock Plan:	Profit Sharing:	Top Exec. Salary: $	Bonus: $
Savings Plan:	Stock Purch. Plan:		Second Exec. Salary: $	Bonus: $

OTHER THOUGHTS:

Apparent Women Officers or Directors:
Hot Spot for Advancement for Women/Minorities:

LOCATIONS: ("Y" = Yes)

West:	Southwest:	Midwest:	Southeast:	Northeast:	International:
		Y			Y

MORGAN MOTOR COMPANY (THE)

www.morgan-motor.co.uk

Industry Group Code: 33611 **Ranks within this company's industry group:** Sales: Profits:

Vehicle Manufacturing:		Dealers:		Parts:		Service:		Finance:		Specialty:	
Cars:	Y	Car Dealer New:		Manufacturers:		General Service:		Leasing:		Information Systems:	
Trucks:		Car Dealer Used:		Retail:		Specialty Service:		Auto Loans:		Online Marketing:	
Motorcycles:		Truck Dealer:		Distributors:		Oil Change:		Insurance:	Y	Other:	
Specialty:	Y	RV Dealer:		Tires:		Paint and Body:				Publishing:	
Buses:		Motorcycle Dealer:		Batteries:						Rental Cars/Trucks:	
RVs:		Specialty Dealer:									

TYPES OF BUSINESS:

Automobile Design & Manufacture
Insurance

BRANDS/DIVISIONS/AFFILIATES:

Roadster
Aero 8
AeroMax
LIFECar
LIFECar2

CONTACTS:

Note: Officers with more than one job title may be intentionally listed here more than once.

Charles Peter Henry Morgan, Managing Dir.
Steve Morris, Dir.-Prod.
Tim Whitworth, Dir.-Finance

Phone: 44-1684-573104 **Fax:** 44-1684-892295
Toll-Free:
Address: Pickerleigh Rd., Malvern Link, Worcestershire WR14 2LL UK

GROWTH PLANS/SPECIAL FEATURES:

Morgan Motor Company, a family-owned company since its inception in 1909, specializes in designing and building high-quality retro-stylized vehicles. The Morgan factory in Malvern, England builds approximately 500 sports cars per year, at a rate of around 23 days per car. Morgan's standard models include the +4 two-seater, which starts at approximately \$51,000; the 4/4, at around \$45,000; the Roadster, at \$63,000; and the four-seat Roadster, at \$68,000. The Aero 8 race car models start at approximately \$114,000. Morgan has also developed limited edition and concept cars including; AeroMax, which was limited to 100 models and the LIFECar concept vehicle, which features a fuel cell hybrid power train. The company has created an insurance policy exclusively designed by Morgan for Morgan drivers, while Morgan car clubs have proliferated around the world for those interested in maintaining and upgrading their cars. The company's Internet site offers a wide range of Morgan merchandise such as clothing, books and videos, posters, gifts and racing event bookings. Morgan cars can also be rented from the factory for special events for approximately \$263 a day for the Roadster (\$197 for the Sport), \$443 for overnight (\$312), \$986 for a weekend (\$690) and \$1,972 for seven days (\$1232). Cars are sold in the U.S., U.K., Australia, New Zealand, South Africa, Austria, Belgium, Denmark, France, Germany, Italy, Japan and many other countries. It is currently collaborating with three U.K. universities to develop LIFECar2.

FINANCIALS:

Sales and profits are in thousands of dollars—add 000 to get the full amount. 2009 Note: Financial information for 2009 was not available for all companies at press time.

2009 Sales: \$	2009 Profits: \$	**U.S. Stock Ticker: Private**
2008 Sales: \$	2008 Profits: \$	**Int'l Ticker:** Int'l Exchange:
2007 Sales: \$	2007 Profits: \$	Employees:
2006 Sales: \$	2006 Profits: \$	Fiscal Year Ends: 12/31
2005 Sales: \$	2005 Profits: \$	Parent Company:

SALARIES/BENEFITS:

Pension Plan:	ESOP Stock Plan:	Profit Sharing:	Top Exec. Salary: \$	Bonus: \$
Savings Plan:	Stock Purch. Plan:		Second Exec. Salary: \$	Bonus: \$

OTHER THOUGHTS:

Apparent Women Officers or Directors:
Hot Spot for Advancement for Women/Minorities:

LOCATIONS: ("Y" = Yes)

West:	Southwest:	Midwest:	Southeast:	Northeast:	International:
					Y

MORSE OPERATIONS INC

www.edmorse.com

Industry Group Code: 441110 **Ranks within this company's industry group:** Sales: Profits:

Vehicle Manufacturing:		Dealers:		Parts:		Service:		Finance:		Specialty:	
Cars:		Car Dealer New:	Y	Manufacturers:		General Service:	Y	Leasing:		Information Systems:	
Trucks:		Car Dealer Used:	Y	Retail:	Y	Specialty Service:		Auto Loans:	Y	Online Marketing:	
Motorcycles:		Truck Dealer:	Y	Distributors:		Oil Change:		Insurance:		Other:	
Specialty:		RV Dealer:		Tires:		Paint and Body:	Y			Publishing:	
Buses:		Motorcycle Dealer:		Batteries:						Rental Cars/Trucks:	
RVs:		Specialty Dealer:									

TYPES OF BUSINESS:

Auto Dealers, Retail
Fleet Sales
Maintenance Services

BRANDS/DIVISIONS/AFFILIATES:

Saturn of Brandon
Saturn of Lakeland
Saturn of Tampa
Ed Morse Fleet Sales

CONTACTS: *Note: Officers with more than one job title may be intentionally listed here more than once.*

Ted Morse, CEO
Carmine Colella, COO/Exec. VP
Ted Morse, Pres.
Betty Anne Beaver, VP-Risk Mgmt.
Ed Morse, Chmn.

Phone: 954-351-0055	**Fax:** 954-771-7214
Toll-Free:	
Address: 6363 NW 6th Way, Ste. 400, Fort Lauderdale, FL 33309 US	

GROWTH PLANS/SPECIAL FEATURES:

Morse Operations, Inc., headquartered in Fort Lauderdale, Florida, sells vehicles through its 12 in-state dealerships and one dealership in Mobile, Alabama. The company has a total of 16 separate franchises, each of which offers 10 brands of cars; including Buick, Cadillac, Chevrolet, Ford, Honda, Saturn and Toyota. Its three Saturn locations (which are the only dealerships that do not bear the Morse name) are called Saturn of Brandon, Saturn of Lakeland and Saturn of Tampa. Morse Operations also offers buses; commercial sales vans and trucks; and pre-owned vehicles. Ed Morse Fleet Sales caters to businesses interested in renting vehicles for a variety of purposes. The fleet division offers brands such as Jeep, Chevrolet, Buick, Honda, Cadillac, Mazda and Toyota; the division delivers anywhere in the U.S. Morse Operations offers financing for its vehicles as well as service and parts, which are available at all dealerships. In addition, all of the company's body shops are equipped to serve automotive paint and body needs. The firm's web site allows customers to search new inventory, research new and used vehicles, schedule service maintenance and order parts.

Morse Operations offers employees benefits which include health, dental, vision, paid vacation, 401(k) savings plans.

FINANCIALS: Sales and profits are in thousands of dollars—add 000 to get the full amount. 2009 Note: Financial information for 2009 was not available for all companies at press time.

2009 Sales: $	2009 Profits: $	**U.S. Stock Ticker: Private**
2008 Sales: $	2008 Profits: $	**Int'l Ticker:** Int'l Exchange:
2007 Sales: $	2007 Profits: $	Employees:
2006 Sales: $	2006 Profits: $	Fiscal Year Ends: 12/31
2005 Sales: $	2005 Profits: $	Parent Company:

SALARIES/BENEFITS:

Pension Plan:	ESOP Stock Plan:	Profit Sharing:	Top Exec. Salary: $	Bonus: $
Savings Plan: Y	Stock Purch. Plan:		Second Exec. Salary: $	Bonus: $

OTHER THOUGHTS:

Apparent Women Officers or Directors: 1
Hot Spot for Advancement for Women/Minorities:

LOCATIONS: ("Y" = Yes)

West:	Southwest:	Midwest:	Southeast:	Northeast:	International:
			Y		

MOTOR COACH INDUSTRIES INTERNATIONAL www.mcicoach.com

Industry Group Code: 336120 **Ranks within this company's industry group:** Sales: Profits:

Vehicle Manufacturing:		Dealers:		Parts:		Service:		Finance:		Specialty:	
Cars:		Car Dealer New:		Manufacturers:	Y	General Service:	Y	Leasing:		Information Systems:	
Trucks:		Car Dealer Used:		Retail:		Specialty Service:		Auto Loans:		Online Marketing:	
Motorcycles:		Truck Dealer:		Distributors:		Oil Change:		Insurance:		Other:	Y
Specialty:		RV Dealer:		Tires:		Paint and Body:				Publishing:	
Buses:	Y	Motorcycle Dealer:		Batteries:						Rental Cars/Trucks:	
RVs:		Specialty Dealer:	Y								

TYPES OF BUSINESS:

Motor Coach Manufacturing
Luxury Buses
Customization
Parts & Service
Refurbishing
Apparel & Accessories
Financing

BRANDS/DIVISIONS/AFFILIATES:

JLL Partners
Prevost
Van Hool
MCI J4500
MCI E4500
MCI D4505
MCI D4005

CONTACTS: *Note: Officers with more than one job title may be intentionally listed here more than once.*

Tom Sorrells, II, CEO
Tom Sorrells, III, COO
Tom Sorrells, III, Pres.
Christopher Motogawa,
Ana Budisin, VP-Sales Oper.
Pete Tully, Sr. VP-Human Resources
Timothy Nalepka, General Counsel/Sec./Sr. VP
Tom Wagner, Dir.-Bus. Dev, Public Sector
Patricia Plodzeen, Public Rel.
Patricia Ziska, VP/Chief Customer Officer
Bob Graf, Mgr.-Customer Solutions
Michael Melaniphy, VP-Public Sector
Peter Cotter, Sr. VP/Gen. Mgr.
Todd Pankey, VP-Supply Chain

Phone: 847-285-2000	**Fax:** 847-285-2013
Toll-Free: 866-624-2622	
Address: 1700 E. Golf Rd., Ste. 300, Schaumburg, IL 60173 US	

GROWTH PLANS/SPECIAL FEATURES:

Motor Coach Industries (MCI) designs, builds, sells, services and finances motor coaches up to 45 feet in length. The firm is headquartered in Schaumburg, Illinois, with sales and service centers located across the U.S. as well as in Canada and Mexico. The company operates seven sales centers and nine MCI fleet Support service centers. MCI creates vehicles as intercity coaches and for long-distance travel, offers motor coach conversion, coach-related parts and services for the North American market. Customers include local transit authorities, prison authorities and other organizations. The firm has opened a certified pre-owned program, assuring customers of better access to select late-model MCI coaches. The firm also assists in the customization of vehicles, such as that of NFL broadcaster John Madden's fully equipped luxury coach. The company constructs luxury buses under the following model names: MCI E4500, J4500, D4505 and D4005. Pre-owned buses are sold under the MCI, Prevost and Van Hool brands. MCI Luxury buses can feature hot showers, and commuter coaches often feature vacuum flush toilets and six-monitor video systems. The MCI unit also manufactures coaches for public transit, government agencies, universities and correctional facilities. It also offers motor coach service, financing and refurbishing. JLL Partners, an investment firm, owns a controlling share of the firm. MCI offers Diesel Particulate Filters, which reduce muffler components and helps to reduce particulate matter or black smoke, by up to 90%. This is in response to the new EPA clean diesel standards. MCI also offers diesel-hybrid models, as part of its effort to supply eco-conscious customers.

MCI employee benefits include medical, dental, vision insurances; educational reimbursement; paid vacation/holidays; and employee recognition programs.

FINANCIALS: **Sales and profits are in thousands of dollars—add 000 to get the full amount. 2009 Note: Financial information for 2009 was not available for all companies at press time.**

2009 Sales: $	2009 Profits: $	**U.S. Stock Ticker: Private**
2008 Sales: $	2008 Profits: $	**Int'l Ticker:** Int'l Exchange:
2007 Sales: $692,400	2007 Profits: $	Employees:
2006 Sales: $	2006 Profits: $	Fiscal Year Ends: 12/31
2005 Sales: $	2005 Profits: $	Parent Company:

SALARIES/BENEFITS:

Pension Plan:	ESOP Stock Plan:	Profit Sharing:	Top Exec. Salary: $	Bonus: $
Savings Plan: Y	Stock Purch. Plan:		Second Exec. Salary: $	Bonus: $

OTHER THOUGHTS:

Apparent Women Officers or Directors: 2
Hot Spot for Advancement for Women/Minorities: Y

LOCATIONS: ("Y" = Yes)

West:	Southwest:	Midwest:	Southeast:	Northeast:	International:
Y	Y	Y	Y	Y	Y

MOTORCAR PARTS OF AMERICA INC

www.motorcarparts.com

Industry Group Code: 3363 **Ranks within this company's industry group:** Sales: 58 Profits: 27

Vehicle Manufacturing:		**Dealers:**		**Parts:**		**Service:**		**Finance:**		**Specialty:**	
Cars:		Car Dealer New:		Manufacturers:	Y	General Service:		Leasing:		Information Systems:	
Trucks:		Car Dealer Used:		Retail:		Specialty Service:		Auto Loans:		Online Marketing:	
Motorcycles:		Truck Dealer:		Distributors:		Oil Change:		Insurance:		Other:	
Specialty:		RV Dealer:		Tires:		Paint and Body:				Publishing:	
Buses:		Motorcycle Dealer:		Batteries:						Rental Cars/Trucks:	
RVs:		Specialty Dealer:									

TYPES OF BUSINESS:

Replacement Alternators & Starters

BRANDS/DIVISIONS/AFFILIATES:

Quality-Built
Talon
Xtreme
Reliance

CONTACTS:

Note: Officers with more than one job title may be intentionally listed here more than once.

Selwyn Joffe, CEO
Steve Kratz, COO
Selwyn Joffe, Pres.
David Lee, CFO
Tom Stricker, Exec. VP-Sales
Doug Schooner, VP-Mfg.
Michael Umansky, General Counsel/VP/Corp. Sec.
Kevin Daly, Chief Acct. Officer
Rick Mochulsky, VP-Traditional Sales
Selwyn Joffe, Chmn.
Meryvn McCulloch, VP-Acquisitions

Phone: 310-212-7910	**Fax:** 310-212-6315
Toll-Free: 800-890-9988	
Address: 2929 California St., Torrance, CA 90503 US	

GROWTH PLANS/SPECIAL FEATURES:

Motorcar Parts of America, Inc. (MPA) remanufactures and distributes replacement alternators and starters for import and domestic cars and light trucks. MPA's product line features over 1,600 alternator models and more than 900 starter models; the company also manufactures starter ignition wire sets. The firm's products are sold throughout the U.S. to more than 7,700 automotive parts stores, including some of the largest chains of retail automotive stores such as AutoZone, Pep Boys, CSK Automotive and O'Reilly Automotive. MPA also gears its marketing and sales efforts toward traditional warehouse distributors and supplies remanufactured alternators and starters to General Motors. Approximately 91% of the firm's products are sold for resale under customer private labels, with the remaining 5% sold under brand names such as Quality-Built, Reliance, Talon, and Xtreme. The company has remanufacturing, warehousing and shipping operations in California, Oregon, Tennessee, North Carolina and New Jersey; a logistics facility in Singapore; an alternator manufacturing facility in Malaysia; and a manufacturing facility in Mexico. In August 2009, the firm acquired certain assets of alternators and starters manufacturer Reliance Automotive, Inc.

FINANCIALS:

Sales and profits are in thousands of dollars—add 000 to get the full amount. 2009 Note: Financial information for 2009 was not available for all companies at press time.

2009 Sales: $134,866	2009 Profits: $3,857	**U.S. Stock Ticker: MPAA**
2008 Sales: $133,337	2008 Profits: $4,607	**Int'l Ticker:** Int'l Exchange:
2007 Sales: $136,323	2007 Profits: $-2,475	Employees: 256
2006 Sales: $108,397	2006 Profits: $6,298	Fiscal Year Ends: 3/31
2005 Sales: $95,785	2005 Profits: $6,288	Parent Company:

SALARIES/BENEFITS:

Pension Plan:	ESOP Stock Plan:	Profit Sharing:	Top Exec. Salary: $500,000	Bonus: $500,100
Savings Plan:	Stock Purch. Plan:		Second Exec. Salary: $406,000	Bonus: $40,100

OTHER THOUGHTS:

Apparent Women Officers or Directors:
Hot Spot for Advancement for Women/Minorities:

LOCATIONS: ("Y" = Yes)

West:	Southwest:	Midwest:	Southeast:	Northeast:	International:
Y				Y	Y

NAVISTAR INC

www.navistar.com

Industry Group Code: 336120 **Ranks within this company's industry group:** Sales: Profits:

Vehicle Manufacturing:		Dealers:		Parts:		Service:		Finance:		Specialty:	
Cars:		Car Dealer New:		Manufacturers:	Y	General Service:		Leasing:	Y	Information Systems:	
Trucks:	Y	Car Dealer Used:		Retail:		Specialty Service:		Auto Loans:		Online Marketing:	
Motorcycles:		Truck Dealer:		Distributors:	Y	Oil Change:		Insurance:		Other:	
Specialty:		RV Dealer:		Tires:		Paint and Body:				Publishing:	
Buses:	Y	Motorcycle Dealer:		Batteries:						Rental Cars/Trucks:	
RVs:		Specialty Dealer:									

TYPES OF BUSINESS:

Commercial Truck Manufacturing
Diesel Engines
Bus Manufacturing
Financial Services
Parts

BRANDS/DIVISIONS/AFFILIATES:

Navistar International Corporation
MaxxForce
Ford Motor Co
DuraStar Hybrid
Monaco RV
Monaco Coach Corp.

CONTACTS:

Note: Officers with more than one job title may be intentionally listed here more than once.

Daniel C. Ustian, CEO
Daniel C. Ustian, Pres.
Andrew J. Cederoth, CFO/Exec. VP
Heather Kos, Contact-Investor Rel.
Daniel C. Ustian, Chmn.

Phone: 630-753-5000 **Fax:** 630-753-3982
Toll-Free: 800-448-7825
Address: 4201 Winfield Rd., Warrenville, IL 60555 US

GROWTH PLANS/SPECIAL FEATURES:

Navistar, Inc., formerly International Truck and Engine Corporation (ITEC), is a wholly-owned subsidiary of Navistar International. The company manufactures heavy-duty trucks that bear the International brand name. These vehicles include city tractor, liquid and bulk dry, long-haul and regional-haul trucks. Navistar also manufactures medium-duty trucks and service trucks for applications including construction and waste collection. In addition, the firm is one of the industry's largest school bus manufacturers. Formed in 1902, it made the world's first factory-built school bus in 1907, and today more students ride International-brand buses than all other brands combined. The company also manufactures commercial buses. Additionally, the firm provides parts through nearly 1,000 dealer locations in the U.S., Brazil, Canada, and Mexico; manufactures diesel engines, including the V-8 engines for Ford's Power Stroke pickup; and offers financial services, including debt financing and leasing, through International Finance Group. Navistar also offers its products in 90 countries worldwide through 60 different dealers. In recent years, the company became the first to begin hybrid commercial truck production with its DuraStar Hybrid, a diesel hybrid electric medium-duty truck. In May 2010, Navistar introduced its first all-electric commercial truck, the EStar, and announced that FedEx will receive its first production unit.

Navistar, Inc. offers its employees medical, dental and vision insurance; short- and long-term disability insurance; tuition reimbursement; and flexible spending accounts.

FINANCIALS:

Sales and profits are in thousands of dollars—add 000 to get the full amount. 2009 Note: Financial information for 2009 was not available for all companies at press time.

2009 Sales: $	2009 Profits: $	**U.S. Stock Ticker: Subsidiary**
2008 Sales: $	2008 Profits: $	**Int'l Ticker:** Int'l Exchange:
2007 Sales: $236,100	2007 Profits: $	Employees:
2006 Sales: $	2006 Profits: $	Fiscal Year Ends: 10/31
2005 Sales: $	2005 Profits: $	Parent Company: NAVISTAR INTERNATIONAL CORP

SALARIES/BENEFITS:

Pension Plan:	ESOP Stock Plan:	Profit Sharing:	Top Exec. Salary: $	Bonus: $
Savings Plan: Y	Stock Purch. Plan:		Second Exec. Salary: $	Bonus: $

OTHER THOUGHTS:

Apparent Women Officers or Directors:
Hot Spot for Advancement for Women/Minorities:

LOCATIONS: ("Y" = Yes)

West:	Southwest:	Midwest:	Southeast:	Northeast:	International:
Y	Y	Y	Y	Y	Y

NAVISTAR INTERNATIONAL CORP

www.navistar.com

Industry Group Code: 336120 **Ranks within this company's industry group:** Sales: 3 Profits: 1

Vehicle Manufacturing:		Dealers:		Parts:		Service:		Finance:		Specialty:	
Cars:		Car Dealer New:		Manufacturers:	Y	General Service:	Y	Leasing:	Y	Information Systems:	
Trucks:	Y	Car Dealer Used:		Retail:		Specialty Service:		Auto Loans:		Online Marketing:	
Motorcycles:		Truck Dealer:		Distributors:	Y	Oil Change:		Insurance:		Other:	
Specialty:	Y	RV Dealer:		Tires:		Paint and Body:				Publishing:	
Buses:	Y	Motorcycle Dealer:		Batteries:						Rental Cars/Trucks:	
RVs:	Y	Specialty Dealer:									

TYPES OF BUSINESS:

Truck Manufacturing
Diesel Engines
Financial Services
Bus Manufacturing
Low-Emission Vehicles
Diesel-Electric Hybrid Vehicles

BRANDS/DIVISIONS/AFFILIATES:

International
Navistar Defense
IC
WCC
Monaco
Navistar Financial Corp.
Continental Mfg. Company

CONTACTS: *Note: Officers with more than one job title may be intentionally listed here more than once.*

Daniel C. Ustian, CEO
Daniel C. Ustian, Pres.
Andrew J. (A. J.) Cederoth, CFO/Sr. VP
Greg Elliott, Sr. VP-Human Resources
Dave Allendorph, Chief Designer
Greg Elliott, Sr. VP-Admin.
Steven Covey, General Counsel/Sr. VP/Chief Ethics Officer
Jack Allen, Pres., North American Truck Group
Phyllis Cochran, Sr. VP/Gen. Mgr.-Navistar Parts
David Johanneson, CEO/Pres., Navistar Financial Corp.
Archie Massicotte, Pres., Navistar Defense, LLC
Daniel C. Ustian, Chmn.

Phone: 630-753-5000 | **Fax:** 630-753-2303
Toll-Free: 800-448-7825
Address: 4201 Winfield Rd., P.O. Box 1488, Warrenville, IL 60555 US

GROWTH PLANS/SPECIAL FEATURES:

Navistar International Corporation is a manufacturer of commercial trucks, buses, diesel engines, chassis, recreational vehicles and military vehicles. Additionally, the firm provides service parts for trucks and trailers and is a private-label designer and manufacturer of diesel engines for the pickup truck, van and sport utility vehicle (SUV) markets. The company operates in four segments: Truck, Engine, Parts and Financial Services. In its Truck segment, Navistar manufactures and distributes class four through eight trucks and buses in the common carrier, private carrier, government, leasing, construction, energy, military, student and commercial transportation markets under the International, Navistar Defense and IC brands. The segment also produces chassis for motor homes and commercial step-van vehicles under the WCC brand and recreational vehicles under the Monaco family of brands. The Engine segment designs and manufactures diesel engines across the 50 through 475 horsepower range for use primarily in its class six and seven medium trucks, military vehicles and buses; for use in certain class eight heavy truck models; and for sale to original equipment manufacturers (OEMs) of SUVs and pick-ups. The firm's Parts segment provides proprietary products and standard truck, trailer and engine service parts. Navistar's financial services segment provides retail, wholesale and lease financing of products sold by its Truck and Parts segments and its dealers within the U.S. and Mexico. The segment provided wholesale financing for 96% of the company's new truck inventory sold in the U.S. during 2009. In December 2009, the company acquired Continental Mfg. Company, one of the largest privately-held mixer manufacturers in North America.

Navistar, Inc. offers its employees medical, dental and vision insurance; short- and long-term disability insurance; tuition reimbursement; and flexible spending accounts.

FINANCIALS: **Sales and profits are in thousands of dollars—add 000 to get the full amount. 2009 Note: Financial information for 2009 was not available for all companies at press time.**

2009 Sales: $11,569,000	2009 Profits: $320,000	**U.S. Stock Ticker: NAV**
2008 Sales: $14,724,000	2008 Profits: $134,000	**Int'l Ticker:** Int'l Exchange:
2007 Sales: $12,295,000	2007 Profits: $-120,000	Employees: 17,900
2006 Sales: $14,200,000	2006 Profits: $301,000	Fiscal Year Ends: 10/31
2005 Sales: $12,124,000	2005 Profits: $139,000	Parent Company:

SALARIES/BENEFITS:

Pension Plan:	ESOP Stock Plan:	Profit Sharing:	Top Exec. Salary: $1,180,000	Bonus: $1,946,000
Savings Plan: Y	Stock Purch. Plan:		Second Exec. Salary: $655,000	Bonus: $

OTHER THOUGHTS:

Apparent Women Officers or Directors: 2
Hot Spot for Advancement for Women/Minorities:

LOCATIONS: ("Y" = Yes)

West:	Southwest:	Midwest:	Southeast:	Northeast:	International:
Y	Y	Y	Y	Y	Y

NAVTEQ CORPORATION

www.navteq.com

Industry Group Code: 511210N **Ranks within this company's industry group:** Sales: Profits:

Vehicle Manufacturing:		Dealers:		Parts:		Service:		Finance:		Specialty:	
Cars:		Car Dealer New:		Manufacturers:		General Service:		Leasing:		Information Systems:	Y
Trucks:		Car Dealer Used:		Retail:		Specialty Service:		Auto Loans:		Online Marketing:	
Motorcycles:		Truck Dealer:		Distributors:		Oil Change:		Insurance:		Other:	Y
Specialty:		RV Dealer:		Tires:		Paint and Body:				Publishing:	
Buses:		Motorcycle Dealer:		Batteries:						Rental Cars/Trucks:	
RVs:		Specialty Dealer:									

TYPES OF BUSINESS:

Digital Map Information
Route Planning Technology
Vehicle Navigation
Internet-Based Mapping
Location-Based Services
Geographic Information Systems

BRANDS/DIVISIONS/AFFILIATES:

Nokia Corporation
T-Systems Traffic GmbH
Motorway Junction Objects
Navteq LocationPoint

CONTACTS:

Note: Officers with more than one job title may be intentionally listed here more than once.

Judson Green, CEO
Judson Green, Pres.
Jeff Mize, Exec. VP-Sales
Tiffany Treacy, VP-Global Prod. Mgmt.
Kirk Mitchell, Dir.-Bus. Dev.
Bob Richter, Public Rel.
Marc Naddell, VP-Partner & Dev. Programs
Roy Kolstad, VP/Gen. Mgr.-Enterprise North America
Christopher Rothey, VP-Market Dev. & Advertising
Cindy Paulauskas, VP-Map & Content Prod., Americas
Helder Azevedo, Gen. Dir.-Latin America

Phone: 312-894-7000 **Fax:** 312-894-7050
Toll-Free: 866-462-8837
Address: 425 W. Randolph St., Chicago, IL 60606 US

GROWTH PLANS/SPECIAL FEATURES:

Navteq Corporation, a subsidiary of Nokia Corp., is a provider of digital map, traffic and location data for automotive navigation systems, mobile navigation devices and Internet mapping applications. The firm maintains and continuously upgrading its geographical database, through 192 offices in 43 countries. The database covers millions of points of interest in 78 countries on six continents. Products are offered to both businesses and individuals and consist of a broad range of navigation tools, including databases of urban and rural transportation grids that are often incorporated into GPS products by systems manufacturers and mobile navigation device manufacturers. The firm also offers a route-planning tool that allows for driving directions and route optimization via the Internet and is used by web sites such as MapQuest, Microsoft/MSN, Autodesk, Toshiba and Yahoo!. In addition, location-based services provide geographic information about specific locations tailored to the proximity of a specific user, primarily utilized by mobile directory assistance services and emergency response systems. Geographic information systems (GIS) render geographic representations of information for use in infrastructure cataloging and tracking by government agencies and utility companies, as well as asset tracking and fleet management for commercial logistics companies. Navteq generally sells its products to mobile device and handset manufacturers, automobile manufacturers and dealers, navigation systems manufacturers, software developers, Internet portals, parcel and overnight delivery services companies and government entities. In January 2009, the firm completed its acquisition of T-Systems Traffic GmbH, a provider of traffic services in Germany. In May 2009, the company launched Navteq LocationPoint, a location-based advertising service, in Europe. In June 2009, Navteq released Motorway Junction Objects, an in-vehicle, three-dimensional display to assist drivers in navigating complex junctions and motorway rings, in Australia. In January 2010, the company was selected by United States Postal Service (USPS) to provide map data for eFMS (Electronic Facilities Management System).

FINANCIALS:

Sales and profits are in thousands of dollars—add 000 to get the full amount. 2009 Note: Financial information for 2009 was not available for all companies at press time.

2009 Sales: $	2009 Profits: $	**U.S. Stock Ticker: Subsidiary**
2008 Sales: $	2008 Profits: $	**Int'l Ticker:** Int'l Exchange:
2007 Sales: $853,387	2007 Profits: $172,950	Employees:
2006 Sales: $581,619	2006 Profits: $109,970	Fiscal Year Ends: 12/31
2005 Sales: $496,512	2005 Profits: $170,830	Parent Company: NOKIA CORPORATION

SALARIES/BENEFITS:

Pension Plan:	ESOP Stock Plan:	Profit Sharing:	Top Exec. Salary: $	Bonus: $
Savings Plan:	Stock Purch. Plan:		Second Exec. Salary: $	Bonus: $

OTHER THOUGHTS:

Apparent Women Officers or Directors: 2
Hot Spot for Advancement for Women/Minorities:

LOCATIONS: ("Y" = Yes)

West:	Southwest:	Midwest:	Southeast:	Northeast:	International:
		Y			Y

NEWCOR INC

www.newcor.com

Industry Group Code: 3363 **Ranks within this company's industry group:** Sales: Profits:

Vehicle Manufacturing:		Dealers:		Parts:		Service:		Finance:		Specialty:	
Cars:		Car Dealer New:		Manufacturers:	Y	General Service:		Leasing:		Information Systems:	
Trucks:		Car Dealer Used:		Retail:		Specialty Service:		Auto Loans:		Online Marketing:	
Motorcycles:		Truck Dealer:		Distributors:	Y	Oil Change:		Insurance:		Other:	
Specialty:		RV Dealer:		Tires:		Paint and Body:				Publishing:	
Buses:		Motorcycle Dealer:		Batteries:						Rental Cars/Trucks:	
RVs:		Specialty Dealer:									

TYPES OF BUSINESS:

Automobile Parts Manufacturer
Power Train Components
Agricultural Products
Foundry Castings
Machined Components
Rubber & Plastic Products
Custom Machines & Systems

BRANDS/DIVISIONS/AFFILIATES:

EXX Inc
Deco Engineering Inc
Machine Tool & Gear Inc
Rochester Gear Inc

GROWTH PLANS/SPECIAL FEATURES:

Newcor, Inc., a subsidiary of holding company EXX, Inc., produces products for the automotive, industrial and heavy-duty truck markets. The firm operates in one segment: precision-machined products. This segment consists of three subsidiaries: Deco Engineering, Inc.; Rochester Gear, Inc.; and Machine Tool & Gear, Inc. Deco Engineering produces high-volume precision machined engine and power train components and assemblies, such as rocker arms and power steering pumps, primarily for the heavy-duty truck market. Rochester Gear and Machine Tool & Gear produce high-quality shafts, axles, transmission parts, differential pins and gears, rear axle shafts and other machined components. Newcor and these subsidiaries have four locations in Michigan: one dedicated to sales (operated directly by Newcor) and three that are used for manufacturing (one operated by each subsidiary). The firm's customers include Chrysler LLC and Deere and Company. In February 2010, Newcor sold its Wisconsin-based injection molding subsidiary, Plastronics Plus, Inc., to EPC-Missouri, Inc., a division of Engineered Plastic Components, Inc.

CONTACTS:

Note: Officers with more than one job title may be intentionally listed here more than once.

David A. Segal, CEO
David A. Segal, Chmn.

Phone: 248-409-1070 **Fax:** 248-409-1076
Toll-Free:
Address: 1771 Harmon Rd., Ste. 200, Auburn Hills, MI 48326 US

FINANCIALS:

Sales and profits are in thousands of dollars—add 000 to get the full amount. 2009 Note: Financial information for 2009 was not available for all companies at press time.

2009 Sales: $	2009 Profits: $	**U.S. Stock Ticker: Subsidiary**
2008 Sales: $	2008 Profits: $	**Int'l Ticker:** Int'l Exchange:
2007 Sales: $	2007 Profits: $	Employees:
2006 Sales: $	2006 Profits: $	Fiscal Year Ends: 12/31
2005 Sales: $	2005 Profits: $	Parent Company: EXX INC

SALARIES/BENEFITS:

Pension Plan:	ESOP Stock Plan:	Profit Sharing:	Top Exec. Salary: $	Bonus: $
Savings Plan:	Stock Purch. Plan:		Second Exec. Salary: $	Bonus: $

OTHER THOUGHTS:

Apparent Women Officers or Directors:
Hot Spot for Advancement for Women/Minorities:

LOCATIONS: ("Y" = Yes)

West:	Southwest:	Midwest:	Southeast:	Northeast:	International:
		Y			

NEWMAR CORP

www.newmarcorp.com

Industry Group Code: 336120 **Ranks within this company's industry group:** Sales: Profits:

Vehicle Manufacturing:		Dealers:		Parts:		Service:		Finance:		Specialty:	
Cars:		Car Dealer New:		Manufacturers:		General Service:		Leasing:		Information Systems:	
Trucks:		Car Dealer Used:		Retail:		Specialty Service:		Auto Loans:		Online Marketing:	
Motorcycles:		Truck Dealer:		Distributors:		Oil Change:		Insurance:		Other:	
Specialty:		RV Dealer:		Tires:		Paint and Body:				Publishing:	
Buses:		Motorcycle Dealer:		Batteries:						Rental Cars/Trucks:	
RVs:	Y	Specialty Dealer:									

TYPES OF BUSINESS:

Recreational Vehicle Manufacturing

BRANDS/DIVISIONS/AFFILIATES:

Cypress
Torrey Pine
Kountry Aire
X-Aire
Bay Star
Canyon Star
Dutch Star
Mountain Aire

GROWTH PLANS/SPECIAL FEATURES:

Newmar Corp. is a recreation vehicle manufacturer specializing in motorhomes and fifth wheels (also known as trailers). The firm's fifth wheel lineup includes the Cypress Fifth Wheel, the Torrey Pine Fifth Wheel, the X-Aire Fifth Wheel and the Cypress Fifth Wheel. The company's motorhomes include the Bay Star, the Canyon Star, the Dutch Star and the Ventana while the luxury motorhomes include the Mountain Aire, the King Aire and the Essex. Both motorhomes and trailers come equipped with wood cabinetry, furniture, a television, an oven, a bathroom with plumbing, a sound system, air conditioning and many other features. Newmar also offers full-paint exterior graphics on its vehicles. These graphics are applied in its 18,900-square-foot paint facility. The firm owns a company country club that goes by the name Kountry Klub for RV owners. All purchases come with a Newmar Express Limited Warranty, which insures the vehicle for the first year after purchase. The company's Newmar Canyon Star, released in July 2010, features a rear garage that can store most sizes of off-road vehicles.

CONTACTS: *Note: Officers with more than one job title may be intentionally listed here more than once.*

Richard Parks, CEO
John Sammut, VP-Mktg. & Sales
Keith Weirich, Dir.-Human Resources
Wayne Quigley, Dir.-IT
Kevin Bogan, VP-Mfg.
Richard Parks, Chmn.

Phone: 574-773-7791	**Fax:** 574-773-2895
Toll-Free:	
Address: 355 N. Delaware St., Nappanee, IN 46550-0030 US	

FINANCIALS: **Sales and profits are in thousands of dollars—add 000 to get the full amount. 2009 Note: Financial information for 2009 was not available for all companies at press time.**

2009 Sales: $	2009 Profits: $	**U.S. Stock Ticker: Private**
2008 Sales: $	2008 Profits: $	**Int'l Ticker:** Int'l Exchange:
2007 Sales: $400,000	2007 Profits: $	Employees:
2006 Sales: $	2006 Profits: $	Fiscal Year Ends:
2005 Sales: $	2005 Profits: $	Parent Company:

SALARIES/BENEFITS:

Pension Plan:	ESOP Stock Plan:	Profit Sharing:	Top Exec. Salary: $	Bonus: $
Savings Plan:	Stock Purch. Plan:		Second Exec. Salary: $	Bonus: $

OTHER THOUGHTS:

Apparent Women Officers or Directors:
Hot Spot for Advancement for Women/Minorities:

LOCATIONS: ("Y" = Yes)

West:	Southwest:	Midwest:	Southeast:	Northeast:	International:
		Y			

NIHON PLAST CO LTD

www.n-plast.co.jp

Industry Group Code: 3363 **Ranks within this company's industry group:** Sales: 41 Profits: 37

Vehicle Manufacturing:		Dealers:		Parts:		Service:		Finance:		Specialty:	
Cars:		Car Dealer New:		Manufacturers:	Y	General Service:		Leasing:		Information Systems:	
Trucks:		Car Dealer Used:		Retail:		Specialty Service:		Auto Loans:		Online Marketing:	
Motorcycles:		Truck Dealer:		Distributors:		Oil Change:		Insurance:		Other:	
Specialty:		RV Dealer:		Tires:		Paint and Body:				Publishing:	
Buses:		Motorcycle Dealer:		Batteries:						Rental Cars/Trucks:	
RVs:		Specialty Dealer:									

TYPES OF BUSINESS:

Manufacturing-Automobile Components
Airbags
Steering Wheels
Instrument Panel Parts
Interior & Exterior Trim Parts
Air Spoilers

BRANDS/DIVISIONS/AFFILIATES:

Nihon Kaken Co., Ltd.
NP Service Co., Ltd.
Neaton Auto Products MFG, Inc.
Neaton Rome Inc.
P.T. Nihon Plast Indonesia P.T.
Nihon Plast Mexicana S.A de C.V.
Nihon Magnesio S.A de C.V.
Nihon Plast (Zhongshan) Co., Ltd.

CONTACTS: *Note: Officers with more than one job title may be intentionally listed here more than once.*

Makato Hirose, Pres.
Nobuhiro Abe, Sr. Managing Dir.
Kazutoshi Sugimoto, Managing Dir.
Masayuki Furugoori, Managing Dir.
Haruo Furugoori, Managing Dir.

Phone: 81-545-52-0481	**Fax:** 81-545-53-5687
Toll-Free:	
Address: 218 Aoshima Cho, Fuji, 417-0047 Japan	

GROWTH PLANS/SPECIAL FEATURES:

Nihon Plast Co., Ltd. makes airbag, plastic molding and occupant protection components primarily for passenger cars. The company primarily manufactures, processes and sells synthetic resins, die cast metal mold, automotive parts and electrical components. Nihon Plast's 10 subsidiaries are Nihon Kaken Co., Ltd.; NP Service Co., Ltd.; Neaton Auto Products MFG, Inc.; Neaton Rome Inc.; P.T. Nihon Plast Indonesia P.T.; Nihon Plast Mexicana S.A de C.V; Nihon Magnesio S.A de C.V; Nihon Plast (Zhongshan) Co., Ltd.; Nihon Plast (Wuhan) Co., Ltd; and Nihon Plast Thailand Co., Ltd. Nihon Plast's products are divided into five categories: safety parts; instrument panel parts; interior trim parts; exterior trim parts; and air spoilers. The safety parts division includes steering wheels and SRS airbag modules. Instrumental panel parts consist of glove boxes, ventilators, air conditioning ducts, console boxes, cup holders, column covers and shift knobs. Its interior trim parts include interior components with decorative covering. Its exterior trim parts include cover cowl tops and fender protectors. Lastly, it manufactures air spoilers in a variety of colors and sizes. The firm has manufacturing facilities in Fuji, Isesaki and Kyushu, which utilize various molding and manufacturing techniques, including injection molding, blow molding, decorative processing, RIM molding, combination molding, high reflective coating applicators and vibration welding. Nihon Plast's Technical Center has facilities to test equipment, such as crash simulation, airbag deployment and burst and durability tests. The facility also has vibration test equipment to simulated high-speed driving and rough road testing conditions. The company is affiliated with NP Kasei Co., Ltd.; Tousen Plant Co., Ltd.; and Nihon Plast Distribution Co., Ltd. Primary clients include Nissan Motor Co. Ltd.; Honda Motor Co. Ltd.; Calsonic Kansei Corp.; Suzuki Motor Corp.; and Honda Access Corp.

FINANCIALS: **Sales and profits are in thousands of dollars—add 000 to get the full amount. 2009 Note: Financial information for 2009 was not available for all companies at press time.**

2009 Sales: $984,940	2009 Profits: $-37,550	**U.S. Stock Ticker:**
2008 Sales: $1,116,490	2008 Profits: $21,050	**Int'l Ticker: 7291** Int'l Exchange: Tokyo-TSE
2007 Sales: $923,800	2007 Profits: $20,400	Employees:
2006 Sales: $880,200	2006 Profits: $26,100	Fiscal Year Ends: 3/31
2005 Sales: $772,600	2005 Profits: $-8,700	Parent Company:

SALARIES/BENEFITS:

Pension Plan:	ESOP Stock Plan:	Profit Sharing:	Top Exec. Salary: $	Bonus: $
Savings Plan:	Stock Purch. Plan:		Second Exec. Salary: $	Bonus: $

OTHER THOUGHTS:

Apparent Women Officers or Directors:
Hot Spot for Advancement for Women/Minorities:

LOCATIONS: ("Y" = Yes)

West:	Southwest:	Midwest:	Southeast:	Northeast:	International:
					Y

NIPPON PISTON RING CO LTD

www.npr.co.jp

Industry Group Code: 3363 **Ranks within this company's industry group:** Sales: 48 Profits: 42

Vehicle Manufacturing:		Dealers:		Parts:		Service:		Finance:		Specialty:	
Cars:		Car Dealer New:		Manufacturers:	Y	General Service:		Leasing:		Information Systems:	
Trucks:		Car Dealer Used:		Retail:		Specialty Service:		Auto Loans:		Online Marketing:	
Motorcycles:		Truck Dealer:		Distributors:	Y	Oil Change:		Insurance:		Other:	
Specialty:		RV Dealer:		Tires:		Paint and Body:				Publishing:	
Buses:		Motorcycle Dealer:		Batteries:						Rental Cars/Trucks:	
RVs:		Specialty Dealer:									

TYPES OF BUSINESS:

Automobile Parts Manufacturing
Internal Combustion Engine Components
Piston Rings, Cylinder Liners & Valve Train Parts
Appliance Components
Industrial Machinery Components

BRANDS/DIVISIONS/AFFILIATES:

Metal Injection Molding (MIM)
NPR of America, Inc.
NPR Manufacturing Kentucky, LLC
NPR Manufacturing Michigan, LLC
NPR of Europe GmbH
Seojin Cam Co., Ltd.
NPR Auto Parts Manufacturing Co., Ltd.
IP Rings, Ltd.

CONTACTS: *Note: Officers with more than one job title may be intentionally listed here more than once.*

Shigeo Takahashi, Pres.
Yuji Sakamoto, Dir.-Sales
Hidebumi Mori, Exec. VP-Info. Systems Dept.
Teruo Takahashi, Dir.-Tech. Eng. Dept.
Masaaki Otani, Dir.-Prod. Div.
Masaaki Otani, Dir.-Prod. Eng. Div.
Akira Yamamoto, Dir.-Overseas Oper. Div.
Akira Yamamoto, Dir.-Corp. Planning Dept.
Hidebumi Mori, Exec. VP-Gen. Affairs Dept.
Tatsuya Tsuji, Dir.-Acct. & Finance Dept.
Koji Takeuchi, Dir.-Quality Assurance Dept.
Hidebumi Mori, Exec. VP-Corp. Mgmt.
Yuji Sakamoto, Dir.-Bus. Planning Dept.
Hidebumi Mori, Exec. VP-Int'l Bus.

Phone: 81-48-856-5022 **Fax:** 81-48-856-5038
Toll-Free:
Address: 12-10, 5-Chome, Honmachi-Higashi, Chuo-ku, Saitama City, 338-8503 Japan

GROWTH PLANS/SPECIAL FEATURES:

Nippon Piston Rings (NPR) is a leading Japanese manufacturer and marketer of production and replacement parts for domestic and overseas automobile, marine and land engines. These components include piston rings, cylinder liners and seal rings; valve train parts for internal combustion engines, such as valve seat inserts, cast iron and composite camshafts, valve rocker arms, valve guides and rocker bridges; engine parts; synchronizer rings; compressor parts for household electronic appliances; components for industrial machinery; and casting, sintering and plastic working parts. Most of the company's business relates to domestic operations, supplying both original equipment components to Japanese auto makers and aftermarket parts to distributors, with overseas operations serving markets in the U.S., Germany, India, China and other parts of Southeast Asia. Almost half of the company's total sales (approximately 40.9%) relate to piston rings, with valve train parts making up another 32.1%, cylinder liners accounting for 17.2% and other products constituting the remaining 9.8% of sales. NPR utilizes a technique called metal injection molding (MIM). MIM products are manufactured using a multi-stage compacting press technique and are used as functional parts for various engines and automobiles. Some of the firm's major clients include Toyota Motor Corporation; Nissan Motor Co., Ltd.; Mitsubishi Motors Corporation; Mazda Motor Corporation; Isuzu Motors, Ltd.; and Honda Motor Co., Ltd. NPR's U.S. distribution and sales are managed by NPR of America LLC, which has offices in California and Michigan. NPR Manufacturing also has facilities in Michigan and Kentucky. The company's subsidiaries include Seojin Cam Co., Ltd., in Korea; NPR Auto Parts Manufacturing Co., Ltd., in China; NPR of Europe GmbH in Germany; IP Rings, Ltd., in India; and Siam NPR Co., Ltd., in Thailand. In 2009, the firm voluntarily dissolved Chinese subsidiary NPR Trading (Shanghai) Co., Ltd.

FINANCIALS: **Sales and profits are in thousands of dollars—add 000 to get the full amount. 2009 Note: Financial information for 2009 was not available for all companies at press time.**

2009 Sales: $531,610	2009 Profits: $-58,340	**U.S. Stock Ticker:**
2008 Sales: $473,010	2008 Profits: $-51,910	**Int'l Ticker: 6461** Int'l Exchange: Tokyo-TSE
2007 Sales: $482,900	2007 Profits: $4,900	Employees:
2006 Sales: $447,800	2006 Profits: $6,900	Fiscal Year Ends: 3/31
2005 Sales: $420,000	2005 Profits: $	Parent Company:

SALARIES/BENEFITS:

Pension Plan:	ESOP Stock Plan:	Profit Sharing:	Top Exec. Salary: $	Bonus: $
Savings Plan:	Stock Purch. Plan:		Second Exec. Salary: $	Bonus: $

OTHER THOUGHTS:

Apparent Women Officers or Directors:
Hot Spot for Advancement for Women/Minorities:

LOCATIONS: ("Y" = Yes)

West:	Southwest:	Midwest:	Southeast:	Northeast:	International:
Y		Y			Y

NISSAN DIESEL (THAILAND) CO LTD

www.nissandiesel.co.th

Industry Group Code: 336120 **Ranks within this company's industry group:** Sales: Profits:

Vehicle Manufacturing:		Dealers:		Parts:		Service:		Finance:		Specialty:	
Cars:		Car Dealer New:		Manufacturers:	Y	General Service:		Leasing:		Information Systems:	
Trucks:	Y	Car Dealer Used:		Retail:		Specialty Service:		Auto Loans:		Online Marketing:	
Motorcycles:		Truck Dealer:		Distributors:		Oil Change:		Insurance:		Other:	
Specialty:		RV Dealer:		Tires:		Paint and Body:				Publishing:	
Buses:	Y	Motorcycle Dealer:		Batteries:						Rental Cars/Trucks:	
RVs:		Specialty Dealer:									

TYPES OF BUSINESS:

Commercial Truck Manufacturing
Automotive Parts Manufacturing

BRANDS/DIVISIONS/AFFILIATES:

TC Machinery Co Ltd
PKB214
CDA214
CWA214
CWM454M
CWM454HM
JP252
CWM454HT

CONTACTS:

Note: Officers with more than one job title may be intentionally listed here more than once.

Yeong Yue Sun, Managing Dir.
Yeong Yue Sun, Pres.
Chua Tong Guan, Dir.-Finance & Acct.
Pichit Rachawong, Exec. VP
Kiyoshi Chigira, VP
Chow Sheng Choy, Managing Dir.
Yeong Yue Sun, Chmn.

Phone: 66-2567-2882	**Fax:** 66-2567-2883
Toll-Free:	
Address: 59 Moo 1, Rangsit-Pathumthani Rd., Ban Klang, 12000 Thailand	

GROWTH PLANS/SPECIAL FEATURES:

Nissan Diesel (Thailand) Co., Ltd. (NDT) primarily manufactures heavy-duty trucks for the Thai market. It was established in1987 as a joint venture between two Thai firms (Siam Motor Co., Ltd. and Marubeni Thailand Co., Ltd.) and two Japanese firms (Marubeni Corporation and Nissan Diesel Motor Co., Ltd.). Subsequently, the firm became a wholly-owned subsidiary of TC Machinery Co., Ltd. in 2002. NDT's vehicles comprise the PKB214 6-wheeled freight truck; three models of 10-wheeled trucks, consisting of the CDA214 and CWA214 freight trucks and the CWM454M dump truck; and four other models, comprising the CWM454HM cement mixer, the JP252 bus chassis and two models of the CWM454HT full air brake semi-truck tractor. These vehicles, as well as the firm's replacement parts, are sold under the UD brand name. The UD brand was introduced to Thailand in 1955 by Siam Motors, and became part of the firm's portfolio when the joint venture was formed in1987. The company also sells other automotive materials, such as engine coolant, under other brands, including NDT. The firm's products are distributed by 64 dealers all across Thailand, divided into six areas: Central Thailand (with 14 dealers), Northern Thailand (10), Eastern Thailand (six), Northeastern Thailand (11), Southern Thailand (12) and the Bangkok area (11). Of these dealers, all sell parts, 15 also offer repair services and only 12 sell vehicles, generally in addition to offering parts, services or both. Besides its domestic sales network, NDT exports its vehicles to 65 countries worldwide. The company maintains one factory, located in Bang Sao Thong, in Thailand's Samut Prakarn province.

FINANCIALS:

Sales and profits are in thousands of dollars—add 000 to get the full amount. 2009 Note: Financial information for 2009 was not available for all companies at press time.

2009 Sales: $	2009 Profits: $	**U.S. Stock Ticker: Subsidiary**
2008 Sales: $	2008 Profits: $	**Int'l Ticker:** Int'l Exchange:
2007 Sales: $	2007 Profits: $	Employees:
2006 Sales: $	2006 Profits: $	Fiscal Year Ends:
2005 Sales: $	2005 Profits: $	Parent Company: TC MACHINERY CO LTD

SALARIES/BENEFITS:

Pension Plan:	ESOP Stock Plan:	Profit Sharing:	Top Exec. Salary: $	Bonus: $
Savings Plan:	Stock Purch. Plan:		Second Exec. Salary: $	Bonus: $

OTHER THOUGHTS:

Apparent Women Officers or Directors:
Hot Spot for Advancement for Women/Minorities:

LOCATIONS: ("Y" = Yes)

West:	Southwest:	Midwest:	Southeast:	Northeast:	International:
					Y

NISSAN MOTOR CO LTD

www.nissan-global.com

Industry Group Code: 33611 **Ranks within this company's industry group:** Sales: 7 Profits: 29

Vehicle Manufacturing:		Dealers:		Parts:		Service:		Finance:		Specialty:	
Cars:	Y	Car Dealer New:		Manufacturers:		General Service:		Leasing:	Y	Information Systems:	
Trucks:	Y	Car Dealer Used:		Retail:		Specialty Service:		Auto Loans:	Y	Online Marketing:	
Motorcycles:		Truck Dealer:		Distributors:		Oil Change:		Insurance:		Other:	Y
Specialty:		RV Dealer:		Tires:		Paint and Body:				Publishing:	
Buses:		Motorcycle Dealer:		Batteries:						Rental Cars/Trucks:	
RVs:		Specialty Dealer:									

TYPES OF BUSINESS:

Automobiles, Manufacturing
Research & Development
Industrial Machinery
Marine Equipment
Logistics Services
Alternative Fuels Research

BRANDS/DIVISIONS/AFFILIATES:

Rogue
Nissan (China) Investment Co Ltd
Fairlady Z Roadster
Renault-Nissan
Altima
Infinity
LEAF
Pathfinder

CONTACTS:

Note: Officers with more than one job title may be intentionally listed here more than once.

Carlos Ghosn, CEO
Toshiyuki Shiga, COO
Carlos Ghosn, Pres.
Joseph G. Peter, CFO
Junichi Endo, Sr. VP-Global Mktg. & Sales
Greg Kelly, Sr. VP-Human Resources
Mitsuhiko Yamashita, Exec. VP-R&D
Minoru Shinohara, Sr. VP-Tech. Dev. Div.
Atsushi Shizuta, Sr. VP-Prod. Dev. Div.
Toshiharu Sakai, Sr. VP-Industrial Eng. Div.
Hidetoshi Imazu, Exec. VP-Mfg.
Greg Kelly, Sr. VP-Legal/Sec.
Carlos Tavares, Exec. VP-American Oper.
Andy Palmer, Sr. VP-Corp. Planning
Hitoshi Kawaguchi, Sr. VP-External & Gov't Affairs
Joseph G. Peter, Sr. VP-Investor Rel.
Joseph G. Peter, Sr. VP-Finance, Acct. & Control
Shiro Nakamura, Sr. VP-Design & Brand Mgmt.
Takao Katagiri, Sr. VP-Japan Mktg. & Sales
Kazumasa Katoh, Sr. VP-Total Customer Satisfaction Function
Carlos Ghosn, Chmn.

Phone: 81-3-3543-5523 **Fax:** 81-3-5565-2228
Toll-Free:
Address: 1-1, Takashima 1-chome, Nishi-ku, Yokohama-shi, 220-8686 Japan

GROWTH PLANS/SPECIAL FEATURES:

Nissan Motor Co., Ltd. develops, manufactures, sells and services automotive products in over 160 countries. The company's products, which are sold both in Japan and overseas (principally in North America and Europe), include passenger cars, busses and trucks, along with related components. Brands include Nissan, Infiniti and Forklift, with model offerings such as Nissan Sentra, Nissan Versa, Nissan Altima, Nissan Rogue and Nissan Pathfinder. The Forklift brand offers material handling equipment, including pallet trucks, tow tractors and lifts. Through Nissan Marine, the firm also produces/sells pleasure boats, operates a marina business and exports outboard engines. The company operates offices and production plants in Japan, Africa, North America, Australia, Europe, Asia and the Middle East. Abroad, Nissan and Renault, a French company, manage an alliance that allows each company to maintain its distinct corporate culture and brand identity, while enduring the challenges of market globalization and the accelerating change of technology. Renault-Nissan ranks as one of the world's leading automotive groups, and the two companies operate a joint venture factory in the eastern Indian city of Chennai. The allied firm promotes intensive research and development in alternative fuel technologies. Nissan has been increasing investments in its research and development operations, and plans to produce additional gasoline-electric vehicles as well as subcompact electric cars powered by firm-developed lithium-ion batteries. In June 2009, Nissan Motor opened a production plant in Russia. In 2009, the firm introduced Nissan LEAF, a medium-sized, zero-emission hatchback; and the Fairlady Z Roadster two-seat convertible. In October 2009, the company and Sumitomo Corporation agreed to establish a joint venture to recycle and reuse lithium ion batteries for electric cars. In March 2010, subsidiary Nissan (China) Investment Co., Ltd. opened a new design studio in China.

FINANCIALS:

Sales and profits are in thousands of dollars—add 000 to get the full amount. 2009 Note: Financial information for 2009 was not available for all companies at press time.

2009 Sales: $89,102,300	2009 Profits: $-2,469,180	**U.S. Stock Ticker: NSANY**
2008 Sales: $108,242,000	2008 Profits: $4,823,000	**Int'l Ticker: 7201** Int'l Exchange: Tokyo-TSE
2007 Sales: $88,717,000	2007 Profits: $3,905,000	Employees: 155,659
2006 Sales: $80,583,700	2006 Profits: $4,427,800	Fiscal Year Ends: 3/31
2005 Sales: $79,700,000	2005 Profits: $4,760,000	Parent Company:

SALARIES/BENEFITS:

Pension Plan:	ESOP Stock Plan:	Profit Sharing:	Top Exec. Salary: $	Bonus: $
Savings Plan: Y	Stock Purch. Plan:		Second Exec. Salary: $	Bonus: $

OTHER THOUGHTS:

Apparent Women Officers or Directors:
Hot Spot for Advancement for Women/Minorities:

LOCATIONS: ("Y" = Yes)

West:	Southwest:	Midwest:	Southeast:	Northeast:	International:
Y	Y	Y	Y	Y	Y

NISSAN NORTH AMERICA INC

www.nissanusa.com

Industry Group Code: 33611 **Ranks within this company's industry group:** Sales: Profits:

Vehicle Manufacturing:		Dealers:		Parts:		Service:		Finance:		Specialty:	
Cars:	Y	Car Dealer New:		Manufacturers:	Y	General Service:		Leasing:	Y	Information Systems:	
Trucks:	Y	Car Dealer Used:		Retail:		Specialty Service:		Auto Loans:	Y	Online Marketing:	
Motorcycles:		Truck Dealer:		Distributors:	Y	Oil Change:		Insurance:		Other:	Y
Specialty:	Y	RV Dealer:		Tires:		Paint and Body:				Publishing:	
Buses:		Motorcycle Dealer:		Batteries:						Rental Cars/Trucks:	
RVs:		Specialty Dealer:									

TYPES OF BUSINESS:

Automobiles, Manufacturing
Car & Truck Manufacturing
Engine & Part Manufacturing
Car & Parts Distribution
Car Design & Engineering
Financing & Leasing

BRANDS/DIVISIONS/AFFILIATES:

Nissan Motor Co., Ltd.
Nissan Technical Center North America
Nissan Diesel Motor Co., Ltd.
Nissan Canada, Inc.
Nissan Canada Finance
Nissan Motor Acceptance Corp.
Nissan Mexicana, S.A. de C.V.

CONTACTS: *Note: Officers with more than one job title may be intentionally listed here more than once.*

Brian Carolin, Sr. VP-Sales & Mktg.
Bill Krueger, Sr. VP-Mfg.
Scott Becker, VP-Legal & Gov't Affairs
Alan J. Buddendeck, VP-Corp. Comm.
Catherine Perez, VP-Purchasing
Victor Nacif, VP-Design Bus. Aspects Nissan Design America
Bill Krueger, Sr. VP-Supply Chain & Purchasing

Phone: 615-725-1000 **Fax:** 615-725-3343
Toll-Free:
Address: 1 Nissan Way, Franklin, TN 37067 US

GROWTH PLANS/SPECIAL FEATURES:

Nissan North America, Inc. (NNA), a subsidiary of Nissan Motor Co., Ltd., coordinates Nissan's operations in the U.S., Canada and Mexico, including automotive styling, consumer and corporate financing and engineering. Vehicle lines marketed by the firm include the Rogue, Murano, Titan, Maxima, Xterra, Pathfinder, Frontier, Quest and Altima, as well as Nissan's luxury Infiniti vehicles, through 1,100 dealers in the continental U.S. NNA has several manufacturing plants in the U.S. and Mexico. Its Smyrna, Tennessee plant manufactures the Frontier, Maxima, Pathfinder, Xterra and Altima models, with an annual production capacity of 550,000 vehicles. The firm's Decherd, Tennessee facility produces all engines, crankshafts and cylinder block casting for all Nissan and Infiniti vehicles. Nissan Mexicana, S.A. de C.V., manufactures Nissan vehicles for North America and has an annual production capacity of more than 300,000. It also produces engines and other parts for global distribution. Nissan Technical Center North America designs, develops and tests new Nissan vehicles, while Nissan Design America has created or influenced the design of many of Nissan's vehicles. Nissan Canada, Inc. markets and distributes Nissan and Infiniti vehicles to Canadian dealerships, while Nissan Canada Finance provides financial and training services to Canada's Infiniti and Nissan dealers. Nissan Motor Acceptance Corp. is the financial arm of NNA and offers financing for Nissan and Infiniti vehicles sold in the U.S. Nissan Diesel of America, the American distributor of trucks by Nissan Diesel Motor Co., Ltd., distributes commercial diesel trucks under the UD TRUCKS brand name through 95 dealerships in the U.S. In August 2009, Nissan announced that it will offer a new, all-electric car called the Leaf by late 2012. In conjunction with this announcement, the firm released plans to construct a battery manufacturing facility adjacent to its current facility in Smyrna, Tennessee, which it expects to be operational by 2012.

FINANCIALS: **Sales and profits are in thousands of dollars—add 000 to get the full amount. 2009 Note: Financial information for 2009 was not available for all companies at press time.**

2009 Sales: $ | 2009 Profits: $
2008 Sales: $ | 2008 Profits: $
2007 Sales: $ | 2007 Profits: $
2006 Sales: $ | 2006 Profits: $
2005 Sales: $ | 2005 Profits: $

U.S. Stock Ticker: Subsidiary
Int'l Ticker: Int'l Exchange:
Employees:
Fiscal Year Ends: 3/31
Parent Company: NISSAN MOTOR CO LTD

SALARIES/BENEFITS:

Pension Plan: ESOP Stock Plan: Profit Sharing: Top Exec. Salary: $ Bonus: $
Savings Plan: Stock Purch. Plan: Second Exec. Salary: $ Bonus: $

OTHER THOUGHTS:

Apparent Women Officers or Directors: 1
Hot Spot for Advancement for Women/Minorities:

LOCATIONS: ("Y" = Yes)

West:	Southwest:	Midwest:	Southeast:	Northeast:	International:
Y			Y		Y

NISSAN SHATAI CO LTD

www.nissan-shatai.co.jp

Industry Group Code: 336211 **Ranks within this company's industry group:** Sales: 3 Profits: 1

Vehicle Manufacturing:		Dealers:		Parts:		Service:		Finance:		Specialty:	
Cars:		Car Dealer New:		Manufacturers:	Y	General Service:		Leasing:		Information Systems:	
Trucks:		Car Dealer Used:		Retail:		Specialty Service:		Auto Loans:		Online Marketing:	
Motorcycles:		Truck Dealer:		Distributors:		Oil Change:		Insurance:		Other:	
Specialty:		RV Dealer:		Tires:		Paint and Body:				Publishing:	
Buses:		Motorcycle Dealer:		Batteries:						Rental Cars/Trucks:	
RVs:		Specialty Dealer:									

TYPES OF BUSINESS:

Automobile Manufacturer
Vehicle Bodies

BRANDS/DIVISIONS/AFFILIATES:

Nissan Motor Co., Ltd.
NV200
AD
AD Expert
Urvan
Cedric
Civilian
Caravan Coach

CONTACTS:

Note: Officers with more than one job title may be intentionally listed here more than once.

Yoshiaki Watanabe, Pres.
Yoshimitsu Mitake, Managing Exec. Officer
Makoto Monda, Managing Exec. Officer
Shuichi Ohtani, Managing Exec. Officer
Itaru Koeda, Chmn.

Phone: 81-463-21-8012	**Fax:** 81-463-8155
Toll-Free:	
Address: 10-1 Amanuma, Hiratsuka, Kanagawa, 254-8610 Japan	

GROWTH PLANS/SPECIAL FEATURES:

Nissan Shatai Co., Ltd., based in Japan, is a major parts and vehicle manufacturer for Nissan Motor Co., Ltd. The firm makes and assembles car bodies and parts exclusively for Nissan. Nissan Shatai has manufacturing divisions in passenger car bodies, commercial vehicle bodies, automobile parts and small bus bodies. The company manufactures three product categories: light commercial vehicles (LCVs), multipurpose vehicles (MPVs) and special equipment vehicles (SEVs). The LCV segment includes vans and trucks, such as the NV200, AD, AD Expert and Urvan; business sedans, including the Cedric; pickup trucks; and microbuses, such as the Civilian and the Caravan Coach. The MPV product line manufactures minivans, such as the ElGrand, the Serena and the Caravan Silkroad; station wagons, including the Wingroad; and sport utility vehicles (SUVs), including the Patrol Safari. The SEV product line includes ambulances based on the ElGrand frame; lifter vans based on the Caravan frame; and commercial trucks. The firm uses 3D-CAD and Intelligent Body Assembly System (IBS) technologies to design and assemble vehicle bodies.

FINANCIALS:

Sales and profits are in thousands of dollars—add 000 to get the full amount. 2009 Note: Financial information for 2009 was not available for all companies at press time.

2009 Sales: $4,915,900	2009 Profits: $108,510	**U.S. Stock Ticker:**
2008 Sales: $6,471,290	2008 Profits: $193,020	**Int'l Ticker: 7222** Int'l Exchange: Tokyo-TSE
2007 Sales: $5,576,100	2007 Profits: $166,300	Employees:
2006 Sales: $5,166,900	2006 Profits: $110,800	Fiscal Year Ends: 12/31
2005 Sales: $5,826,000	2005 Profits: $151,200	Parent Company:

SALARIES/BENEFITS:

Pension Plan:	ESOP Stock Plan:	Profit Sharing:	Top Exec. Salary: $	Bonus: $
Savings Plan:	Stock Purch. Plan:		Second Exec. Salary: $	Bonus: $

OTHER THOUGHTS:

Apparent Women Officers or Directors:
Hot Spot for Advancement for Women/Minorities:

LOCATIONS: ("Y" = Yes)

West:	Southwest:	Midwest:	Southeast:	Northeast:	International:
					Y

NYX INC

www.nyxinc.com

Industry Group Code: 3363 **Ranks within this company's industry group:** Sales: Profits:

Vehicle Manufacturing:		Dealers:		Parts:		Service:		Finance:		Specialty:	
Cars:		Car Dealer New:		Manufacturers:	Y	General Service:		Leasing:		Information Systems:	
Trucks:		Car Dealer Used:		Retail:		Specialty Service:		Auto Loans:		Online Marketing:	
Motorcycles:		Truck Dealer:		Distributors:		Oil Change:		Insurance:		Other:	Y
Specialty:		RV Dealer:		Tires:		Paint and Body:				Publishing:	
Buses:		Motorcycle Dealer:		Batteries:						Rental Cars/Trucks:	
RVs:		Specialty Dealer:									

TYPES OF BUSINESS:

Automobile Parts Manufacturer
Interior & Exterior Components
Under-Hood Assemblies
Plastics Processing
Steel Stamping
Design Services

BRANDS/DIVISIONS/AFFILIATES:

CONTACTS:

Note: Officers with more than one job title may be intentionally listed here more than once.

Chain S. Sandhu, CEO
Jatinder-bir Sandhu, Pres.
Daniel E. Laible, Dir.-Human Resources
Mark R. Greer, Dir.-Finance

Phone: 734-462-2385	**Fax:** 734-464-4830
Toll-Free:	
Address: 36800 Plymouth Rd., Livonia, MI 48150-1055 US	

GROWTH PLANS/SPECIAL FEATURES:

NYX, Inc. provides custom-engineered interior, under-hood and technology systems and parts to the automotive industry. It specializes in plastics processing, engineered plastics and rubber extrusion, steel stamping and assembly. NYX divides its products into two main categories: interior subsystem solutions and under-hood solutions. Interior subsystems products include center and overhead consoles; instrument panel sub-assemblies; trim, step pads and sill plates; seating components; door panels; door and glove box latches and handles; and electrical carriers. Under-hood products comprise fluid and air handling systems, including speed control subsystems; cowl vent grills; sun drain tubes; wash fluid handling tubes; under-hood hoses; powertrain emissions, ventilation and fluid management systems; and air and vacuum management systems. The company has production facilities located throughout the Metro Detroit area, with additional facilities in Lobelville, Tennessee; and Windsor, Ontario. Additionally, the firm maintains a design center in Chandigarh, India, that offers around-the-clock engineering and design services and support to improve customer time-to-market. The company's engineering technologies include computer-aided design (CAD), computer-aided manufacturing (CAM) and computer-aided engineering (CAE) capabilities. The firm supplies original equipment manufacturers, including General Motors, Chrysler, Ford, Nissan, Honda, Lear, Collins & Aikman, Intier Automotive, Visteon, Delphi and Siemens. NYX has been owned by its current CEO, Chain S. Sandhu, since 1989.

FINANCIALS:

Sales and profits are in thousands of dollars—add 000 to get the full amount. 2009 Note: Financial information for 2009 was not available for all companies at press time.

2009 Sales: $	2009 Profits: $	**U.S. Stock Ticker: Private**
2008 Sales: $	2008 Profits: $	**Int'l Ticker:** Int'l Exchange:
2007 Sales: $	2007 Profits: $	Employees:
2006 Sales: $	2006 Profits: $	Fiscal Year Ends: 12/31
2005 Sales: $	2005 Profits: $	Parent Company:

SALARIES/BENEFITS:

Pension Plan:	ESOP Stock Plan:	Profit Sharing:	Top Exec. Salary: $	Bonus: $
Savings Plan:	Stock Purch. Plan:		Second Exec. Salary: $	Bonus: $

OTHER THOUGHTS:

Apparent Women Officers or Directors:
Hot Spot for Advancement for Women/Minorities:

LOCATIONS: ("Y" = Yes)

West:	Southwest:	Midwest:	Southeast:	Northeast:	International:
		Y	Y		Y

ONSTAR CORPORATION

www.onstar.com

Industry Group Code: 334220 **Ranks within this company's industry group:** Sales: Profits:

Vehicle Manufacturing:		Dealers:		Parts:		Service:		Finance:		Specialty:	
Cars:		Car Dealer New:		Manufacturers:		General Service:		Leasing:		Information Systems:	
Trucks:		Car Dealer Used:		Retail:		Specialty Service:	Y	Auto Loans:		Online Marketing:	
Motorcycles:		Truck Dealer:		Distributors:		Oil Change:		Insurance:		Other:	Y
Specialty:		RV Dealer:		Tires:		Paint and Body:				Publishing:	
Buses:		Motorcycle Dealer:		Batteries:						Rental Cars/Trucks:	
RVs:		Specialty Dealer:									

TYPES OF BUSINESS:

Vehicle Telematics
Safety Services
Roadside Assistance
Accident Assistance
Communications Services
Stolen Vehicle Recovery
GPS Systems

BRANDS/DIVISIONS/AFFILIATES:

General Motors Corp (GM)
Directions & Connections Plan
Safe & Sound Plan
OnStar Hands-Free Calling

CONTACTS: *Note: Officers with more than one job title may be intentionally listed here more than once.*

Chris Preuss, Pres.
Anthony DiSalle, VP-Sales, Service & Mktg.
Nick Pudar, VP-Planning & Bus. Dev.
Jocelyn Allen, VP-Corp. Comm.
Jim Kobus, Mgr.-Internal Comm.

Phone: 248-588-6050	**Fax:** 313-667-0822
Toll-Free: 888-466-7827	
Address: 400 Renaissance Ctr., Detroit, MI 48265 US	

GROWTH PLANS/SPECIAL FEATURES:

OnStar Corporation, a subsidiary of General Motors Corp., provides in-vehicle safety and security services by means of its three-button system. These services include 24-hour-a-day access to trained service advisors, a connection to emergency assistance and access to OnStar Hands-Free Calling. The company's technological field is telematics, which is the transmission of data communications betweens systems and devices. OnStar's in-vehicle safety, security and information services use global positioning system (GPS) satellite and cellular technology to link the vehicle and driver to the OnStar Center. If an airbag deploys, or if service is requested, a message is sent to the OnStar Center through a cellular antenna installed on the vehicle. The company's subscriber base numbers over 2 million. Because OnStar uses a stronger cell antenna than portable cell phones, calls can be made from more remote locations. Vehicles that are equipped with an OnStar package include certain models of Chevrolet, Pontiac, Buick, Cadillac, GMC, Saturn, Hummer and SAAB.

FINANCIALS: **Sales and profits are in thousands of dollars—add 000 to get the full amount. 2009 Note: Financial information for 2009 was not available for all companies at press time.**

2009 Sales: $	2009 Profits: $	**U.S. Stock Ticker: Subsidiary**
2008 Sales: $	2008 Profits: $	**Int'l Ticker:** Int'l Exchange:
2007 Sales: $	2007 Profits: $	Employees:
2006 Sales: $	2006 Profits: $	Fiscal Year Ends:
2005 Sales: $	2005 Profits: $	Parent Company: GENERAL MOTORS CORP (GM)

SALARIES/BENEFITS:

Pension Plan:	ESOP Stock Plan:	Profit Sharing:	Top Exec. Salary: $	Bonus: $
Savings Plan: Y	Stock Purch. Plan:		Second Exec. Salary: $	Bonus: $

OTHER THOUGHTS:

Apparent Women Officers or Directors: 1
Hot Spot for Advancement for Women/Minorities:

LOCATIONS: ("Y" = Yes)

West:	Southwest:	Midwest:	Southeast:	Northeast:	International:
		Y			Y

ORBITAL CORPORATION LTD

www.orbeng.com.au

Industry Group Code: 3363 **Ranks within this company's industry group:** Sales: 61 Profits: 30

Vehicle Manufacturing:		Dealers:		Parts:		Service:		Finance:		Specialty:	
Cars:		Car Dealer New:		Manufacturers:	Y	General Service:		Leasing:		Information Systems:	
Trucks:		Car Dealer Used:		Retail:		Specialty Service:		Auto Loans:		Online Marketing:	
Motorcycles:		Truck Dealer:		Distributors:		Oil Change:		Insurance:		Other:	Y
Specialty:		RV Dealer:		Tires:		Paint and Body:				Publishing:	
Buses:		Motorcycle Dealer:		Batteries:						Rental Cars/Trucks:	
RVs:		Specialty Dealer:									

TYPES OF BUSINESS:

Automobile Parts Manufacturer
Fuel Injection Engines
Combustion Engines
Control System Technologies
Engineering Services

BRANDS/DIVISIONS/AFFILIATES:

FlexDI
Orbital Consulting
Synerject LLC
Continental AG
M3 Electronic Control Unit
Orbital Autogas Systems

CONTACTS: *Note: Officers with more than one job title may be intentionally listed here more than once.*

Terry Dewayne Stinson, CEO/Managing Dir.
Keith Anthony Halliwell, CFO
David Worth, Dir.-Sales & Mktg.
Geoff Paul Cathcart, Dir.-Eng.
Ian Veitch, Sec.
Geoff Paul Cathcart, Dir.-Oper.
Steven Ahern, Dir.-Intellectual Property Mgmt. & Planning
Brian Anthony (Tony) Fitzgerald, Managing Dir.-Orbital Autogas Systems
Phil Westlake, Mgr.-Bus. Dev., Orbital Autogas Systems
William Peter Day, Chmn.

Phone: 61-8-9441-2311 **Fax:** 61-8-9441-2133
Toll-Free:
Address: 4 Whipple St., Balcatta, Western Australia 6021 Australia

GROWTH PLANS/SPECIAL FEATURES:

Orbital Corporation, Ltd. is an international developer of engine technologies. It provides design, production development and operational improvement services to engine and engine management system producers, regulators and end users. Orbital's products are utilized in motorcycles, boats, recreational vehicles and automobiles. Orbital's main technology, FlexDI, is a combustion system that allows a vehicle to use almost any type of common fuel (including gasoline, ethanol, compressed natural gas and hydrogen, or mixtures of these) without redesigning the base engine. The company also provides contract- or consultancy-based engineering and testing services through Orbital Consulting. Through its recently formed division, Orbital Autogas Systems (OAGS), the company is developing Liquid, an aftermarket LPG (liquid propane gas) injection kit for car and light commercial vehicle applications. It also supplies this technology to Ford Australia for use in its E-Gas vehicles. In addition, it is working on other alternative fuel technologies utilizing compressed natural gas and liquid natural gas. Orbital has subsidiaries in Australia, the U.S. and the U.K., and it maintains strategic alliances and joint ventures with Continental AG (which acquired Siemens-VDO) and others. One of its main joint ventures, Synerject LLC, with Continental, offers fuel injection systems for the marine, lawn and garden, motorcycle and recreation industries, covering both two- and four-stroke engines. Synerject has recently begun a new phase of growth in Asian markets. For example, its M3 Electronic Control Unit (ECU) module, designed for the single-cylinder motorcycle and scooter market, is manufactured at a facility in Changchun, China. Synerject has offices in the U.S. and France.

FINANCIALS: **Sales and profits are in thousands of dollars—add 000 to get the full amount. 2009 Note: Financial information for 2009 was not available for all companies at press time.**

2009 Sales: $18,871	2009 Profits: $-2,250	**U.S. Stock Ticker: OBTLY**
2008 Sales: $12,640	2008 Profits: $ 390	**Int'l Ticker: OEC** Int'l Exchange: Sydney-ASX
2007 Sales: $12,800	2007 Profits: $1,120	Employees: 93
2006 Sales: $8,700	2006 Profits: $- 700	Fiscal Year Ends: 6/30
2005 Sales: $8,834	2005 Profits: $-1,688	Parent Company:

SALARIES/BENEFITS:

Pension Plan:	ESOP Stock Plan:	Profit Sharing:	Top Exec. Salary: $220,902	Bonus: $
Savings Plan: Y	Stock Purch. Plan:		Second Exec. Salary: $203,621	Bonus: $

OTHER THOUGHTS:

Apparent Women Officers or Directors: 1
Hot Spot for Advancement for Women/Minorities:

LOCATIONS: ("Y" = Yes)

West:	Southwest:	Midwest:	Southeast:	Northeast:	International:
		Y		Y	Y

O'REILLY AUTOMOTIVE INC

www.oreillyauto.com

Industry Group Code: 441310 **Ranks within this company's industry group:** Sales: 4 Profits: 3

Vehicle Manufacturing:		**Dealers:**		**Parts:**		**Service:**		**Finance:**		**Specialty:**	
Cars:		Car Dealer New:		Manufacturers:		General Service:		Leasing:		Information Systems:	
Trucks:		Car Dealer Used:		Retail:	Y	Specialty Service:		Auto Loans:		Online Marketing:	
Motorcycles:		Truck Dealer:		Distributors:	Y	Oil Change:		Insurance:		Other:	
Specialty:		RV Dealer:		Tires:		Paint and Body:				Publishing:	
Buses:		Motorcycle Dealer:		Batteries:						Rental Cars/Trucks:	
RVs:		Specialty Dealer:									

TYPES OF BUSINESS:

Auto Parts, Retail
Tools
Auto Accessories

BRANDS/DIVISIONS/AFFILIATES:

O'Reilly Auto Parts
Power Torque
BrakeBest
Checker Auto Parts
Master-Pro
Omnispark
Super Start
Ultima

CONTACTS: *Note: Officers with more than one job title may be intentionally listed here more than once.*

Greg L. Henslee, CEO/Co-Pres.
Ted F. Wise, COO
Ted F. Wise, Co-Pres.
Tom McFall, CFO
Doug Ruble, VP-Advertising & Mktg.
Phillip Thompson, VP-Human Resources
Steve Jasinski, VP-Info. Systems
Mike Williams, VP-Advanced Tech.
Mike Swearengin, Sr. VP-Merch.
Phyllis Evans, VP-Store Admin.
Tricia Headley, Corp. Sec./VP
Jeff Shaw, Sr. VP-Store Sales & Oper.
Jeremy Fletcher, Exec. VP-Finance/Controller
Doug Ruble, VP-Advertising & Mktg.
Alan Fears, VP-Store Acquisitions & Expansion
Greg Johnson, Sr. VP-Dist. Oper.
Barry Sabor, VP-Loss Prevention
David E. O'Reilly, Chmn.
Greg Beck, VP-Purchasing

Phone: 417-829-5727	**Fax:**
Toll-Free: 800-755-6759	
Address: 233 S. Patterson Ave., Springfield, MO 65802 US	

GROWTH PLANS/SPECIAL FEATURES:

O'Reilly Automotive, Inc., founded in 1957, is one of the largest specialty retailers of automotive aftermarket parts, tools, supplies, equipment and accessories in the U.S., selling products to both do-it-yourself (DIY) customers and professional installers. The company operates 3,421 stores in 38 states across the U.S. Stores carry an extensive product line consisting of new and remanufactured automotive hard parts, such as alternators, starters, brake system components, batteries, chassis parts and engine parts; maintenance items, such as oil, antifreeze, fluids, wiper blades, lighting, engine additives and appearance products; accessories, such as floor mats, truck accessories seat covers; and a complete line of auto body paint and related materials, automotive tools and professional service equipment. Store merchandise generally consists of nationally recognized, well-advertised, name-brand products such as AC Delco, Moog, Wagner, Gates Rubber, Federal Mogul, Monroe, Prestone, Quaker State, Pennzoil, Castrol, Valvoline, STP, BWD, Cardone, Wix, Armor All and Turtle Wax. In addition to name-brand products, stores carry a wide variety of high-quality private-label products under the BestTest, BrakeBest, Master Pro, MicroGard, Murray, Power Torque, Super Start, Ultima and Omnispark name brands. O'Reilly operates 21 distribution centers, each equipped with highly automated material handling equipment that expedites the movement of products to loading areas for shipment to individual stores on a nightly basis.

O'Reilly offers its employees a benefits package that includes medical, dental, vision, pharmacy and life insurance; a credit union membership; and an employee assistance program.

FINANCIALS: **Sales and profits are in thousands of dollars—add 000 to get the full amount. 2009 Note: Financial information for 2009 was not available for all companies at press time.**

2009 Sales: $4,847,062	2009 Profits: $307,498	**U.S. Stock Ticker: ORLY**
2008 Sales: $3,576,553	2008 Profits: $186,232	**Int'l Ticker:** Int'l Exchange:
2007 Sales: $2,522,319	2007 Profits: $193,988	Employees: 44,822
2006 Sales: $2,283,222	2006 Profits: $178,085	Fiscal Year Ends: 12/31
2005 Sales: $2,045,318	2005 Profits: $164,266	Parent Company:

SALARIES/BENEFITS:

Pension Plan:	ESOP Stock Plan:	Profit Sharing: Y	Top Exec. Salary: $784,615	Bonus: $2,303,251
Savings Plan: Y	Stock Purch. Plan: Y		Second Exec. Salary: $576,154	Bonus: $1,335,886

OTHER THOUGHTS:

Apparent Women Officers or Directors: 3
Hot Spot for Advancement for Women/Minorities: Y

LOCATIONS: ("Y" = Yes)

West:	Southwest:	Midwest:	Southeast:	Northeast:	International:
Y	Y	Y	Y	Y	

ORION BUS INDUSTRIES

www.orionbus.com

Industry Group Code: 33611 **Ranks within this company's industry group:** Sales: Profits:

Vehicle Manufacturing:		Dealers:		Parts:		Service:		Finance:		Specialty:	
Cars:		Car Dealer New:		Manufacturers:	Y	General Service:		Leasing:		Information Systems:	
Trucks:		Car Dealer Used:		Retail:		Specialty Service:		Auto Loans:		Online Marketing:	
Motorcycles:		Truck Dealer:		Distributors:		Oil Change:		Insurance:		Other:	
Specialty:		RV Dealer:		Tires:		Paint and Body:				Publishing:	
Buses:	Y	Motorcycle Dealer:		Batteries:						Rental Cars/Trucks:	
RVs:		Specialty Dealer:									

TYPES OF BUSINESS:

Bus Manufacturing
Hybrid Electric Buses

BRANDS/DIVISIONS/AFFILIATES:

Daimler Commercial Buses of North America
HybriDrive
Daimler AG

CONTACTS: *Note: Officers with more than one job title may be intentionally listed here more than once.*

Andreas Strecker, CEO
Martin Walz, COO
Andreas Strecker, Pres.
Harry Rendel, CFO
Tom Utrup, Regional Mgr.-Sales, Western Buses
Ludwig Mueller, Exec. VP-Eng.
Patrick Scully, Chief Commercial Officer

Phone: 315-223-5100 **Fax:** 315-768-6520
Toll-Free:
Address: 165 Base Rd., Oriskany, NY 13424-0748 US

GROWTH PLANS/SPECIAL FEATURES:

Orion Bus Industries, a division of Daimler Buses North America, manufactures commuter buses for cities in the U.S. and Canada. Orion begins the production of each of its buses in its Ontario factory, where the integrated chassis and body structure of each bus is assembled. That structure then is shipped to a plant in Oriskany, New York, where the seating, axles, electrical, engines, transmissions, heating and air conditioning systems are installed. The New York factory also completes all final finishing and testing of the firm's buses. The company produces the Orion VII Next Generation, Orion's new hybrid transit bus, powered by the HybriDrive propulsion system with up to 35% improved fuel economy, significantly reduced emissions. It is one of the first hybrid buses available with lithium-ion battery technology. The Orion VII Next Generation comes in three lengths- 30, 35, and 40 foot- and is capable of seating up to 44 passengers. Orion also offers aftermarket parts and services for all of the vehicles it sells, as well as for most other transit buses on the market. Special features of Orion's parts system include its Most Requested Items, an inventory of approximately 600 parts replenished weekly; Monthly Specials, a monthly flyer featuring sale prices or new products; customized spares lists, which Orion can tailor to a specific fleet's needs; Detroit Diesel Parts Distribution Center, which ships nearly a million items per year; and original equipment standards on part sourcing. In May 2010, Orion introduced its updated Orion VII transit bus, which utilizes selective catalytic reduction (SCR) technology to maximize fuel efficiency and reduce emissions.

FINANCIALS: **Sales and profits are in thousands of dollars—add 000 to get the full amount. 2009 Note: Financial information for 2009 was not available for all companies at press time.**

2009 Sales: $ 2009 Profits: $
2008 Sales: $ 2008 Profits: $
2007 Sales: $110,600 2007 Profits: $
2006 Sales: $ 2006 Profits: $
2005 Sales: $ 2005 Profits: $

U.S. Stock Ticker: Subsidiary
Int'l Ticker: Int'l Exchange:
Employees:
Fiscal Year Ends: 12/31
Parent Company: DAIMLER AG

SALARIES/BENEFITS:

Pension Plan: ESOP Stock Plan: Profit Sharing: Top Exec. Salary: $ Bonus: $
Savings Plan: Stock Purch. Plan: Second Exec. Salary: $ Bonus: $

OTHER THOUGHTS:

Apparent Women Officers or Directors:
Hot Spot for Advancement for Women/Minorities:

LOCATIONS: ("Y" = Yes)

West:	Southwest:	Midwest:	Southeast:	Northeast:	International:
				Y	Y

OSHKOSH CORPORATION

www.oshkoshcorporation.com

Industry Group Code: 336120 **Ranks within this company's industry group:** Sales: 4 Profits: 5

Vehicle Manufacturing:		Dealers:		Parts:		Service:		Finance:		Specialty:	
Cars:		Car Dealer New:		Manufacturers:		General Service:		Leasing:		Information Systems:	
Trucks:	Y	Car Dealer Used:		Retail:		Specialty Service:		Auto Loans:		Online Marketing:	
Motorcycles:		Truck Dealer:		Distributors:		Oil Change:		Insurance:		Other:	
Specialty:	Y	RV Dealer:		Tires:		Paint and Body:				Publishing:	
Buses:		Motorcycle Dealer:		Batteries:						Rental Cars/Trucks:	
RVs:		Specialty Dealer:									

TYPES OF BUSINESS:

Fire & Emergency Vehicles
Military Trucks
Truck Bodies
Specialty Trucks
Cement Mixers
Refuse Trucks

BRANDS/DIVISIONS/AFFILIATES:

Oshkosh
JLG
Pierce
JerrDan

CONTACTS:
Note: Officers with more than one job title may be intentionally listed here more than once.

Robert G. Bohn, CEO
Charles L. Szews, COO
Charles L. Szews, Pres.
David M. Sagehorn, CFO/Exec. VP
Ann T. Stawski, VP-Mktg. Comm.
Stephen M. Subasic, VP-Human Resources
Michael S. Guzowski, VP-IT
Donald H. Verhoff, Exec. VP-Tech.
Josef Matosevic, Exec. VP-Global Mfg. Oper.
Michael K. Rohrkaste, Chief Admin. Officer/Exec. VP
Bryan J. Blankfield, General Counsel/Sec./Exec. VP
Mark M. Radue, VP-Bus. Dev.
Joseph H. (Jay) Kimmitt, Exec. VP-Industry Rel. & Gov't Oper.
Patrick N. Davidson, VP-Investor Rel.
Thomas J. Polnaszek, Sr. VP-Finance/Controller
R. Andrew (Andy) Hove, Exec. VP/Pres., Defense
Wilson R. Jones, Exec. VP/Pres., Access Equipment
James W. Johnson, Exec. VP/Pres., Fire & Emergency
Michael J. Wuest, Exec. VP/Pres., Commercial
Robert G. Bohn, Chmn.
Gregory L. Fredericksen, Chief Procurement Officer/Exec. VP

Phone: 920-235-9151	**Fax:** 920-233-9251
Toll-Free:	
Address: 2307 Oregon St., Oshkosh, WI 54902 US	

GROWTH PLANS/SPECIAL FEATURES:

Oshkosh Corporation is a leading designer, manufacturer and marketer of specialty vehicles and vehicle bodies. The company operates in four segments: Defense; access equipment; fire and emergency; and commercial. The defense segment, accounting for 49% of the company's 2009 sales, supplies severe-duty, heavy-payload tactical trucks to the U.S. Department of Defense (DoD). The access equipment segment, through subsidiary JLG, manufactures aerial work platforms, telehandlers, scissor lifts and vertical masts used in construction, agricultural, industrial, institutional and general maintenance applications. JLG markets its products in over 3,500 locations worldwide. This segment accounted for 20% of 2009 sales. The fire and emergency segment, through subsidiary Pierce, is a leading domestic manufacturer of fire apparatus assembled on custom chassis. It also manufactures fire apparatus assembled on commercially-available chassis, snow removal vehicles and emergency vehicles, including pumpers; aerial and ladder trucks; tankers; light-, medium- and heavy-duty rescue vehicles; rough terrain response vehicles; mobile command and control centers; bomb squad vehicles; and hazardous materials control vehicles. The segment sells aircraft rescue and fire fighting (ARFF) vehicles to domestic and international airports. Through its JerrDan subsidiary, the segment also manufactures towing and recovery equipment in the U.S. The fire and emergency segment accounted for 21% of sales. The commercial segment, representing 10% of sales, manufactures rear- and front-discharge concrete mixers; refuse collection vehicles; mobile and stationary compactors and waste transfer units; portable and stationary concrete batch plants; and vehicle components. In October 2009, the company sold its 75% interest in its European fire apparatus business, Bai.

Employees are offered medical, dental and life insurance; disability coverage; and a pension plan.

FINANCIALS:
Sales and profits are in thousands of dollars—add 000 to get the full amount. 2009 Note: Financial information for 2009 was not available for all companies at press time.

2009 Sales: $5,295,200	2009 Profits: $-1,098,800	**U.S. Stock Ticker: OSK**
2008 Sales: $6,936,400	2008 Profits: $79,300	**Int'l Ticker:** Int'l Exchange:
2007 Sales: $6,139,300	2007 Profits: $268,100	Employees: 12,300
2006 Sales: $3,427,388	2006 Profits: $205,529	Fiscal Year Ends: 9/30
2005 Sales: $2,959,900	2005 Profits: $160,205	Parent Company:

SALARIES/BENEFITS:

Pension Plan: Y	ESOP Stock Plan:	Profit Sharing:	Top Exec. Salary: $1,015,807	Bonus: $527,813
Savings Plan:	Stock Purch. Plan: Y		Second Exec. Salary: $583,377	Bonus: $244,116

OTHER THOUGHTS:

Apparent Women Officers or Directors: 2
Hot Spot for Advancement for Women/Minorities: Y

LOCATIONS: ("Y" = Yes)

West:	Southwest:	Midwest:	Southeast:	Northeast:	International:
Y	Y	Y	Y	Y	Y

OURISMAN AUTOMOTIVE ENTERPRISES

www.ourisman.com

Industry Group Code: 441110 **Ranks within this company's industry group:** Sales: Profits:

Vehicle Manufacturing:		Dealers:		Parts:		Service:		Finance:		Specialty:	
Cars:		Car Dealer New:	Y	Manufacturers:		General Service:	Y	Leasing:		Information Systems:	
Trucks:		Car Dealer Used:	Y	Retail:	Y	Specialty Service:		Auto Loans:	Y	Online Marketing:	
Motorcycles:		Truck Dealer:	Y	Distributors:		Oil Change:		Insurance:		Other:	
Specialty:		RV Dealer:		Tires:		Paint and Body:	Y			Publishing:	
Buses:		Motorcycle Dealer:		Batteries:						Rental Cars/Trucks:	
RVs:		Specialty Dealer:									

TYPES OF BUSINESS:

Auto Dealers, Retail
Auto Service
Auto Financing
Fleet Sales

BRANDS/DIVISIONS/AFFILIATES:

Ourisman Honda
Ourisman Dodge
Ourisman Chevrolet
Ourisman Toyota
Orusiman Lincoln Mercury Ford
Ourisman Jeep
Ourisman Volkswagen
Ourisman Chantilly Scion

CONTACTS: *Note: Officers with more than one job title may be intentionally listed here more than once.*

John Ourisman, Pres.
Mohamed Reshed, CFO
Mandell J. Ourisman, Chmn.

Phone: 301-423-4028	**Fax:** 301-423-5725
Toll-Free:	
Address: 4400 Branch Ave., Marlow Heights, MD 20748 US	

GROWTH PLANS/SPECIAL FEATURES:

Ourisman Automotive Enterprises is a family-owned automobile dealership company in the Washington, D.C. area. The company operates 26 new and pre-owned automobile franchise dealerships, at 17 locations, throughout Maryland and Virginia. Ourisman sells vehicles from such automakers as Hyundai, Dodge, Honda, Ford, Chevrolet, Mazda, Volkswagen, Toyota, Mitsubishi, Suzuki, Scion, Chrysler, Lincoln, Mercury and Jeep. In addition, Ourisman's Ford dealerships sell and service a full line of commercial trucks. Via the company's web site, customers can link to individual dealerships' sites where they can search new and pre-owned inventory, schedule service appointments and apply for financing. Additionally, the web site features Ourisman's Used Car Center, a searchable database of all 1,500 used cars across the company's entire dealership. The site also provides credit checks, payment calculations and detailed information regarding each used vehicle. Each individual dealer's web site also features a lemon check, which allows a customer to receive a free CARFAX vehicle history report.

FINANCIALS: **Sales and profits are in thousands of dollars—add 000 to get the full amount. 2009 Note: Financial information for 2009 was not available for all companies at press time.**

2009 Sales: $	2009 Profits: $	**U.S. Stock Ticker: Private**
2008 Sales: $	2008 Profits: $	**Int'l Ticker:** Int'l Exchange:
2007 Sales: $	2007 Profits: $	Employees:
2006 Sales: $	2006 Profits: $	Fiscal Year Ends: 12/31
2005 Sales: $	2005 Profits: $	Parent Company:

SALARIES/BENEFITS:

Pension Plan:	ESOP Stock Plan:	Profit Sharing:	Top Exec. Salary: $	Bonus: $
Savings Plan:	Stock Purch. Plan:		Second Exec. Salary: $	Bonus: $

OTHER THOUGHTS:

Apparent Women Officers or Directors:
Hot Spot for Advancement for Women/Minorities:

LOCATIONS: ("Y" = Yes)

West:	Southwest:	Midwest:	Southeast:	Northeast:	International:
				Y	

PACCAR INC

www.paccar.com

Industry Group Code: 33611 **Ranks within this company's industry group:** Sales: 22 Profits: 16

Vehicle Manufacturing:		Dealers:		Parts:		Service:		Finance:		Specialty:	
Cars:		Car Dealer New:		Manufacturers:	Y	General Service:		Leasing:	Y	Information Systems:	
Trucks:	Y	Car Dealer Used:		Retail:		Specialty Service:		Auto Loans:		Online Marketing:	
Motorcycles:		Truck Dealer:		Distributors:	Y	Oil Change:		Insurance:	Y	Other:	Y
Specialty:		RV Dealer:		Tires:		Paint and Body:				Publishing:	
Buses:		Motorcycle Dealer:		Batteries:						Rental Cars/Trucks:	
RVs:		Specialty Dealer:									

TYPES OF BUSINESS:

Truck Manufacturer
Premium Truck Manufacturer
Parts Distribution
Finance, Lease and Insurance Services

BRANDS/DIVISIONS/AFFILIATES:

PACCAR International
DAF Trucks
Peterbilt Motors
Kenworth Truck Company
PacLease
PACCAR Financial Services

CONTACTS: *Note: Officers with more than one job title may be intentionally listed here more than once.*

Mark C. Pigott, CEO
James. G. Cardillo, Pres.
T. Kyle Quinn, CIO/VP
David C. Anderson, General Counsel/VP
Michael T. Barkley, Controller/VP
Thomas E. Plimpton, Vice Chmn.
Robert J. Christensen, Sr. VP
Ronald E. Armstrong, Sr. VP
Daniel D.Sobic, Exec. VP
Mark C. Pigott, Chmn.

Phone: 425-468-7400	**Fax:** 425-468-8216
Toll-Free:	
Address: 777 106th Ave. NE, Bellevue, WA 98004 US	

GROWTH PLANS/SPECIAL FEATURES:

PACCAR, Inc. is a leading manufacturer of premium light-, medium- and heavy-duty trucks. The firm operates in two major divisions: trucks and financing/leasing. The truck subsidiaries include Kenworth Truck Company, Peterbilt Motors and DAF Trucks. The vehicles are used worldwide for over-the-road and off-highway hauling of freight, petroleum, wood products, construction and other materials. The Kenworth and Peterbilt nameplates are manufactured and distributed by separate divisions in the U.S. and foreign plants in Canada, Mexico and Australia. Headquartered in the Netherlands, DAF Trucks comprises the European component of PACCAR, with distribution throughout Europe, Asia and Africa. Another group, PACCAR International, is based in the U.S. and offers the Kenworth, Peterbilt and DAF brands outside of their primary markets. Products and services are available worldwide through a network of approximately 1,800 locations in more than 100 countries, with customer call centers operating continuously. Substantially all trucks and related parts are sold to independent dealers. The company's financing/leasing segment, which operates through wholly-owned subsidiaries PACCAR Financial and PacLease, maintains a presence in over 18 countries and owns a fleet of more than 150,000 vehicles. This division provides financing and leasing arrangements, mainly for its manufactured trucks. The company's share of the U.S. and Canadian Class 8 truck market was 25.1% in 2009. Commercial trucks and related replacement parts comprise the largest segment of the company's business, accounting for approximately 86.5% of net sales. In January 2010, the firm launched the new PACCAR MX diesel engine for its Kenworth and Peterbilt models in order to meet more stringent emissions requirements.

PACCAR offers its employees medical, dental and vision coverage; life and AD&D insurance; short- and long-term disability; a 401(k) plan; a pension plan; flexible spending accounts; an employee assistance program; tuition reimbursement; charitable gift matching; college scholarship; an employee stock purchase plan; and an employee computer purchase plan.

FINANCIALS: **Sales and profits are in thousands of dollars—add 000 to get the full amount. 2009 Note: Financial information for 2009 was not available for all companies at press time.**

2009 Sales: $8,086,500	2009 Profits: $111,900	**U.S. Stock Ticker: PCAR**
2008 Sales: $14,972,500	2008 Profits: $1,017,900	**Int'l Ticker:** Int'l Exchange:
2007 Sales: $15,221,700	2007 Profits: $1,227,300	Employees: 18,700
2006 Sales: $16,454,100	2006 Profits: $1,496,000	Fiscal Year Ends: 12/31
2005 Sales: $13,298,400	2005 Profits: $1,133,200	Parent Company:

SALARIES/BENEFITS:

Pension Plan: Y	ESOP Stock Plan:	Profit Sharing:	Top Exec. Salary: $1,350,000	Bonus: $
Savings Plan: Y	Stock Purch. Plan: Y		Second Exec. Salary: $800,000	Bonus: $

OTHER THOUGHTS:

Apparent Women Officers or Directors: 3
Hot Spot for Advancement for Women/Minorities: Y

LOCATIONS: ("Y" = Yes)

West:	Southwest:	Midwest:	Southeast:	Northeast:	International:
Y	Y	Y	Y	Y	Y

PARK-OHIO HOLDINGS CORP

www.pkoh.com

Industry Group Code: 333 **Ranks within this company's industry group:** Sales: 7 Profits: 5

Vehicle Manufacturing:		Dealers:		Parts:		Service:		Finance:		Specialty:	
Cars:		Car Dealer New:		Manufacturers:	Y	General Service:		Leasing:		Information Systems:	
Trucks:		Car Dealer Used:		Retail:		Specialty Service:		Auto Loans:		Online Marketing:	
Motorcycles:		Truck Dealer:		Distributors:	Y	Oil Change:		Insurance:		Other:	Y
Specialty:		RV Dealer:		Tires:		Paint and Body:				Publishing:	
Buses:		Motorcycle Dealer:		Batteries:						Rental Cars/Trucks:	
RVs:		Specialty Dealer:									

TYPES OF BUSINESS:

Logistics & Supply Chain Services
Automobile Parts Manufacturing
Aluminum Components
Industrial Equipment Manufacturing

BRANDS/DIVISIONS/AFFILIATES:

Park-Ohio Industries, Inc.

CONTACTS:

Note: Officers with more than one job title may be intentionally listed here more than once.

Edward F. Crawford, CEO
Matthew V. Crawford, COO
Matthew V. Crawford, Pres.
Jeffrey L. Rutherford, CFO/VP
Robert D. Vilsack, General Counsel/Corp. Sec.
Patrick W. Fogarty, Dir.-Corp. Dev.
Edward F. Crawford, Chmn.

Phone: 440-947-2000	**Fax:** 440-947-2099
Toll-Free:	
Address: 6065 Parkland Blvd., Cleveland, OH 44124 US	

GROWTH PLANS/SPECIAL FEATURES:

Park-Ohio Holdings Corp., through its subsidiary Park-Ohio Industries, Inc., is an industrial supply chain logistics and diversified manufacturing business. The firm operates through three segments: the Supply Technologies segment, the Aluminum Products segment and the Manufactured Products segment. The Supply Technologies segment, which accounted for approximately 47% of 2009 sales, provides integrated supply chain and logistics services for a broad range of high-volume, specialty production components. Supply Technologies provides various value-added services, such as engineering and design; part usage; cost analysis; supplier selection; quality assurance; bar coding; product packaging and tracking; just-in-time and point-of-use delivery; electronic billing services; and ongoing technical support. This segment operates 40 logistics service centers in the U.S., Mexico, Canada, Puerto Rico, Scotland, Ireland, Hungary, China, Taiwan, Singapore and India; it also maintains production sourcing and support centers in Asia. The segment's primary customers are in the heavy-duty truck; automotive and vehicle parts; electrical distribution and controls; power sports/fitness equipment; heating, ventilation and air conditioning; aerospace and defense; electrical components; appliance; and semiconductor industries. Park-Ohio's Aluminum Products segment, which accounted for 16%, casts and machines aluminum engine, transmission, brake, suspension and other components for automotive, agricultural equipment, construction equipment, heavy-duty truck and marine equipment used by original equipment manufacturers, primarily on a sole-source basis. The Manufactured Products segment, comprising 37%, operates a diverse group of niche manufacturing businesses that design and manufacture a range of highly engineered products, including induction heating and melting systems, pipe threading systems, rubber products and forged and machined products. This segment operates 21 facilities in the U.S., Canada, Mexico, the U.K., Belgium, Germany, China and Japan. This segment's principal customers are original equipment manufacturers and end-users in the aerospace, automotive, steel, forging, railroad, truck, oil, food processing and consumer appliance industries.

FINANCIALS:

Sales and profits are in thousands of dollars—add 000 to get the full amount. 2009 Note: Financial information for 2009 was not available for all companies at press time.

2009 Sales: $701,047	2009 Profits: $-5,209	**U.S. Stock Ticker: PKOH**
2008 Sales: $1,068,757	2008 Profits: $-119,803	**Int'l Ticker:** Int'l Exchange:
2007 Sales: $1,071,441	2007 Profits: $21,197	Employees: 350
2006 Sales: $1,056,246	2006 Profits: $24,179	Fiscal Year Ends: 12/31
2005 Sales: $932,900	2005 Profits: $30,808	Parent Company:

SALARIES/BENEFITS:

Pension Plan: Y	ESOP Stock Plan:	Profit Sharing:	Top Exec. Salary: $687,500	Bonus: $
Savings Plan:	Stock Purch. Plan: Y		Second Exec. Salary: $366,666	Bonus: $

OTHER THOUGHTS:

Apparent Women Officers or Directors: 1
Hot Spot for Advancement for Women/Minorities:

LOCATIONS: ("Y" = Yes)

West:	Southwest:	Midwest:	Southeast:	Northeast:	International:
	Y	Y	Y	Y	Y

PENSKE AUTOMOTIVE GROUP INC

www.penskeautomotive.com

Industry Group Code: 441110 **Ranks within this company's industry group:** Sales: 2 Profits: 3

Vehicle Manufacturing:		Dealers:		Parts:		Service:		Finance:		Specialty:	
Cars:		Car Dealer New:	Y	Manufacturers:		General Service:	Y	Leasing:		Information Systems:	
Trucks:		Car Dealer Used:	Y	Retail:		Specialty Service:		Auto Loans:		Online Marketing:	
Motorcycles:		Truck Dealer:		Distributors:	Y	Oil Change:		Insurance:		Other:	
Specialty:		RV Dealer:		Tires:		Paint and Body:	Y			Publishing:	
Buses:		Motorcycle Dealer:		Batteries:						Rental Cars/Trucks:	
RVs:		Specialty Dealer:									

TYPES OF BUSINESS:

Auto Dealers, Retail
Automotive Leasing
Online Car Retail

BRANDS/DIVISIONS/AFFILIATES:

Penske Corporation
smart USA Distributor LLC
Penske Truck Leasing Co.

CONTACTS: *Note: Officers with more than one job title may be intentionally listed here more than once.*

Roger S. Penske, CEO
Robert H. Kurnick, Jr., Pres.
Robert O'Shaughnessy, CFO
Calvin C. Sharp, Exec. VP-Human Resources
Shane M. Spradlin, General Counsel/Exec. VP/Corp. Sec.
R. Whitfield Ramonat, Exec. VP-Central Oper. & Financial Svcs.
Anthony R. Pordon, Sr. VP-Corp. Comm.
Anthony R. Pordon, Sr. VP-Investor Rel.
Robert O'Shaughnessy, Exec. VP-Finance
Bernie Wolfe, Exec. VP-East Oper.
George Brochick, Exec. VP-West Oper.
Roger S. Penske, Chmn.

Phone: 248-648-2500 **Fax:** 248-648-2525
Toll-Free:
Address: 2555 Telegraph Rd., Bloomfield Hills, MI 48302-0954 US

GROWTH PLANS/SPECIAL FEATURES:

Penske Automotive Group, Inc. (PAG), formerly called United Auto Group, is a leading automotive retailer, owning and operating 158 franchises in the U.S. and 148 franchises outside of the U.S., primarily in the U.K. The firm offers a full range of vehicle brands, with 95% of its total revenue in 2009 generated from brands of non-U.S. based manufacturers and 65% generated from premium brands, including Audi, BMW, Cadillac and Porsche. Typically, customers can choose from an inventory of over 1,250 new and used vehicles and have access to approximately 253 service bays with the capacity to service approximately 1,000 vehicles per day. Every PAG dealership maintains a web site where customers can review vehicle inventories and obtain photos, prices, promotions, specifications, reviews, financial information and tools to schedule service appointments. PAG has also partnered with CarsDirect.com, a leading online car buying service that provides consumers with a full menu of research features. The firm also offers distribution services through wholly-owned subsidiary smart USA Distributor, LLC, which is the exclusive distributor of the smart fortwo vehicle in the U.S. and Puerto Rico via a network of over 75 smart dealerships. Penske Corporation and its affiliates own approximately 51% of the stock of Penske Automotive Group. The firm recently acquired a 9% limited partnership interest in Penske Truck Leasing Co. In January 2010, the company acquired two Audi and Volkswagen dealerships in Santa Ana, California.

FINANCIALS: **Sales and profits are in thousands of dollars—add 000 to get the full amount. 2009 Note: Financial information for 2009 was not available for all companies at press time.**

2009 Sales: $9,523,105	2009 Profits: $76,920	**U.S. Stock Ticker: PAG**
2008 Sales: $11,637,136	2008 Profits: $-418,903	**Int'l Ticker:** Int'l Exchange:
2007 Sales: $12,781,717	2007 Profits: $122,233	Employees: 13,950
2006 Sales: $11,126,719	2006 Profits: $124,701	Fiscal Year Ends: 12/31
2005 Sales: $9,661,393	2005 Profits: $118,973	Parent Company:

SALARIES/BENEFITS:

Pension Plan:	ESOP Stock Plan:	Profit Sharing:	Top Exec. Salary: $1,000,000	Bonus: $
Savings Plan: Y	Stock Purch. Plan:		Second Exec. Salary: $600,000	Bonus: $

OTHER THOUGHTS:

Apparent Women Officers or Directors: 1
Hot Spot for Advancement for Women/Minorities:

LOCATIONS: ("Y" = Yes)

West:	Southwest:	Midwest:	Southeast:	Northeast:	International:
Y	Y	Y	Y	Y	Y

PENSKE CORPORATION

www.penske.com

Industry Group Code: 532120 **Ranks within this company's industry group:** Sales: Profits:

Vehicle Manufacturing:		Dealers:		Parts:		Service:		Finance:		Specialty:	
Cars:		Car Dealer New:	Y	Manufacturers:	Y	General Service:	Y	Leasing:	Y	Information Systems:	
Trucks:		Car Dealer Used:		Retail:	Y	Specialty Service:		Auto Loans:		Online Marketing:	
Motorcycles:		Truck Dealer:		Distributors:		Oil Change:		Insurance:		Other:	Y
Specialty:		RV Dealer:		Tires:		Paint and Body:				Publishing:	
Buses:		Motorcycle Dealer:		Batteries:						Rental Cars/Trucks:	Y
RVs:		Specialty Dealer:									

TYPES OF BUSINESS:

Truck Rental
Auto Racing
Auto Sales & Service
Supply Chain Solutions
Auto Accessories Manufacturing & Retail
Fuel Management Systems
Fleet Management Services
Vehicle Components & Systems

BRANDS/DIVISIONS/AFFILIATES:

Penske Automotive Group
Penske Truck Leasing
DAVCO Technology, LLC
VM Motori S.p.A.
QEK Global Solutions
Penske Logistics
Bright Truck Leasing
Bright Distribution

CONTACTS: *Note: Officers with more than one job title may be intentionally listed here more than once.*

Roger S. Penske, CEO
Robert H. Kurnick, Jr., Pres.
J. Patrick Conroy, CFO/Exec. VP
Randy Ryerson, Dir.-Corp. Comm.
Robert H. Kurnick, Jr., Pres., Penske Automotive Group
Calvin C. Sharp, Exec. VP-Human Resources, Penske Automotive Group
Anthony R. Pordon, Sr. VP-Penske Automotive Group
Vince Hartnett Jr,, Pres., Penske Logistics
Roger S. Penske, Chmn.

Phone: 248-648-2000	**Fax:** 248-648-2005
Toll-Free:	
Address: 2550 Telegraph Rd., Bloomfield Hills, MI 48302 US	

GROWTH PLANS/SPECIAL FEATURES:

Penske Corporation is a diversified transportation company that participates in a variety of automotive markets through its network of subsidiaries. Its markets include auto sales and service, truck rental, supply chain solutions, vehicle headlight design and development, vehicle lighting and harness safety systems, fluid management and automobile racing. Penske Automotive Group (PAG) runs over 300 franchised dealerships, primarily in 19 U.S. states, Puerto Rico, Germany and the U.K. PAG focuses on the sale of high-end automobile brands such as Toyota, Lexus, Mercedes-Benz, Jaguar and Honda. Penske Motor Group owns and operates automobile dealerships in California. Penske Truck Leasing offers fleet management services including service leasing, truck rentals, logistics, used trucks for sale and felt services for utility and transit companies with municipalities. Italian subsidiary VM Motori S.p.A. specializes in the design and production of diesel engines. QEK Global Solutions provides integrated support services to manufacturers and their primary suppliers. Penske Logistics focuses on supply chain solutions, providing solutions designed to cut costs, reduce cycle time, improve service and integrate technology into the operations of its customers. Truck-Lite Co., Inc. is responsible for creating vehicle lighting and harness safety systems for fleet vehicles. DAVCO Technology, LLC provides diesel fuel management with its line of filters, fuel/water separators and fuel warmers. DAVCO products include the Sea Pro for marine applications; Diesel Pro for medium trucks; and the REN line of industrial automatic oil replenishment systems with fluid level switches and slow flow meters. Penske Racing's operations include teams competing in NASCAR Sprint Cup Series, IndyCar Series, NASCAR Nationwide Series and American Le Mans Series. The firm partnered with Ford Motor Company to provide logistics services at Ford's Southampton, U.K. facility. In March 2010, the firm's subsidiary Penske Truck Leasing Co., L.P acquired Texas based Bright Truck Leasing and Bright Distribution.

FINANCIALS: **Sales and profits are in thousands of dollars—add 000 to get the full amount. 2009 Note: Financial information for 2009 was not available for all companies at press time.**

2009 Sales: $	2009 Profits: $	**U.S. Stock Ticker: Private**
2008 Sales: $	2008 Profits: $	**Int'l Ticker:** Int'l Exchange:
2007 Sales: $	2007 Profits: $	Employees:
2006 Sales: $	2006 Profits: $	Fiscal Year Ends: 12/31
2005 Sales: $	2005 Profits: $	Parent Company:

SALARIES/BENEFITS:

Pension Plan:	ESOP Stock Plan:	Profit Sharing:	Top Exec. Salary: $	Bonus: $
Savings Plan:	Stock Purch. Plan:		Second Exec. Salary: $	Bonus: $

OTHER THOUGHTS:

Apparent Women Officers or Directors:
Hot Spot for Advancement for Women/Minorities:

LOCATIONS: ("Y" = Yes)

West:	Southwest:	Midwest:	Southeast:	Northeast:	International:
Y	Y	Y	Y	Y	Y

PEP BOYS-MANNY MOE & JACK (THE)

www.pepboys.com

Industry Group Code: 441310 **Ranks within this company's industry group:** Sales: 5 Profits: 5

Vehicle Manufacturing:		Dealers:		Parts:		Service:		Finance:		Specialty:	
Cars:		Car Dealer New:		Manufacturers:		General Service:	Y	Leasing:		Information Systems:	
Trucks:		Car Dealer Used:		Retail:	Y	Specialty Service:		Auto Loans:		Online Marketing:	
Motorcycles:		Truck Dealer:		Distributors:		Oil Change:	Y	Insurance:		Other:	
Specialty:		RV Dealer:		Tires:	Y	Paint and Body:				Publishing:	
Buses:		Motorcycle Dealer:		Batteries:	Y					Rental Cars/Trucks:	
RVs:		Specialty Dealer:									

TYPES OF BUSINESS:

Auto Parts, Retail
Automotive Services
Installation Services
Used Vehicle Inspections

BRANDS/DIVISIONS/AFFILIATES:

Pep Express
Pep Boys Supercenter
Pep Boys Service and Tire Center
Florida Tire, Inc.

CONTACTS:

Note: Officers with more than one job title may be intentionally listed here more than once.

Michael R. Odell, CEO
Raymond L. Arthur, CFO/Exec. VP
Scott A. Webb, Exec. VP-Mktg.
Troy E. Fee, Sr. VP-Human Resources
Scott A. Webb, Exec. VP-Merch.
Brian David Zuckerman, General Counsel/Sec./Sr. VP
Joseph A. Cirelli, Sr. VP-Corp. Dev.
Alexandra Spooner, Mgr.-Comm.
William E. Shull, III, Exec. VP-Stores
Max Lukens, Chmn.

Phone: 215-430-9000	Fax: 215-226-2323
Toll-Free: 800-737-2697	
Address: 3111 W. Allegheny Ave., Philadelphia, PA 19132 US	

GROWTH PLANS/SPECIAL FEATURES:

The Pep Boys-Manny, Moe & Jack operates a leading automotive retail and service chain specializing in the sale, installation and servicing of automotive parts, tires and accessories. Pep Boys has 590 locations in 35 states and Puerto Rico, comprising 554 Supercenters, nine Pep Express stores and 27 Service & Tire center. These locations total over 11.7 million square feet of retail space, including the company's 6,027 service bays. Supercenters average approximately 20,700 square feet; Pep Express stores, 9,500 square feet; and Service & Tire Centers, 6,800 square feet. Supercenters carry approximately 25,000 items and Service & Tire Centers, 4,000 items. These items include tires, batteries and new and remanufactured car parts; chemicals and maintenance items; fashion, electronic and performance accessories; personal transportation merchandise; and garage and repair shop products. The company sells products under national brand names and private labels including Cornell, Futura, Definity, Procool, Proline, Prostart, Prosteer, Prostop and ValueGrade. Professional automotive services are available at Supercenters or the Service & Tire location, with the average Supercenter housing 11 service bays. Services cover oil changes; transmission and engine flushes; brake services; tire alignments; suspension work; tune-ups and diagnostics; state inspections and emissions testing; and air conditioning services. Parts and accessories sales account for 63.9% of Pep Boys' total revenue, service labor charges accounted for 19.7% and tire sales, 16.4%. In October 2009, the company acquired Florida Tire, Inc., consisting of 10 service locations.

Employees are offered medical, dental and vision insurance; flexible spending accounts; a 401(k) savings plan; disability coverage; tuition reimbursement; and merchandise discounts.

FINANCIALS:

Sales and profits are in thousands of dollars—add 000 to get the full amount. 2009 Note: Financial information for 2009 was not available for all companies at press time.

2009 Sales: $1,927,788	2009 Profits: $-30,429	**U.S. Stock Ticker: PBY**
2008 Sales: $2,138,075	2008 Profits: $-41,039	**Int'l Ticker:** Int'l Exchange:
2007 Sales: $2,243,855	2007 Profits: $-2,549	Employees: 18,458
2006 Sales: $2,208,974	2006 Profits: $-37,528	Fiscal Year Ends: 1/31
2005 Sales: $2,269,974	2005 Profits: $23,579	Parent Company:

SALARIES/BENEFITS:

Pension Plan:	ESOP Stock Plan:	Profit Sharing:	Top Exec. Salary: $800,000	Bonus: $1,145,600
Savings Plan: Y	Stock Purch. Plan:		Second Exec. Salary: $500,000	Bonus: $607,313

OTHER THOUGHTS:

Apparent Women Officers or Directors: 1
Hot Spot for Advancement for Women/Minorities:

LOCATIONS: ("Y" = Yes)

West:	Southwest:	Midwest:	Southeast:	Northeast:	International:
Y	Y	Y	Y	Y	Y

PETERSON MANUFACTURING CO

www.pmlights.com

Industry Group Code: 3363 **Ranks within this company's industry group:** Sales: Profits:

Vehicle Manufacturing:		**Dealers:**		**Parts:**		**Service:**		**Finance:**		**Specialty:**	
Cars:		Car Dealer New:		Manufacturers:	Y	General Service:		Leasing:		Information Systems:	
Trucks:		Car Dealer Used:		Retail:		Specialty Service:		Auto Loans:		Online Marketing:	
Motorcycles:		Truck Dealer:		Distributors:		Oil Change:		Insurance:		Other:	
Specialty:		RV Dealer:		Tires:		Paint and Body:				Publishing:	
Buses:		Motorcycle Dealer:		Batteries:						Rental Cars/Trucks:	
RVs:		Specialty Dealer:									

TYPES OF BUSINESS:

Automotive Lighting Products
Mirrors & Reflectors
Antennas

BRANDS/DIVISIONS/AFFILIATES:

Piranha
PM
Auto Select
Nightwatcher
Great White
BladeLights
Maxi-Seal

CONTACTS:

Note: Officers with more than one job title may be intentionally listed here more than once.

Don R. Armacost, Jr., CEO
Don R. Armacost, Jr., Pres.
Mark Assenmacher, Dir.-Mktg.
Brian McMahon, VP-Human Resources
Jim Rowden, VP-Eng.
Steve Hickerson, VP-Finance
Allyn Leake, Mgr.-Heavy Duty Sales
Ryan Eichhorn, Mgr.-OEM Sales

Phone: 816-765-2000	**Fax:** 816-761-6693
Toll-Free:	
Address: 4200 E. 135th St., Grandview, MO 64030 US	

GROWTH PLANS/SPECIAL FEATURES:

Peterson Manufacturing Co. develops and manufactures a complete line of vehicle safety lights, mirrors, reflectors, antennas and other related products. The company sells products both to automotive manufacturers and to major retailers. Some of its major customers include Harley-Davidson, John Deere, Caterpillar, Wal-Mart, Fleetwood and EZ Loader. The company offers a line of over 2,200 products, which include LED lights, incandescent lights, specialty lights (such as dome and interior lights, as well as tow and snow plow lights), halogen lights, mounting and electrical accessories. The firm also offers a line of reflectors, emergency lights, mirrors and antennas. Peterson's Piranha LED light brand lights up faster than ordinary lights and has six times the life expectancy. The company's standard lighting products are sold under the PM brand. The Auto Select brand covers its imported automotive products. Nightwatcher is Peterson's trademark for fog driving and off-road lights. Other brands include BladeLights, for snowplow and emergency lights; Maxi-Seal, for custom wire harness systems for the heavy-duty trucking industry and for its aftermarket electrical accessory program; and Great White, for back-up and utility lights. Peterson Manufacturing oversees 11 business units in different industries, including the maritime, aviation, rail and motor racing industries, although the group is primarily focused on automotive lighting products. These companies include Anderson Marine; Maxi-Seal Harness Systems, Inc.; Mission Plastics Arkansas and Mission Plastics North; D&D Aviation, Inc.; Kansas City Aviation Center; Midwest Aviation Center; Renzenberger Inc., Transportation Services; Transworld Products, Inc.; Motorsport Marketing; and Vector Tools & Engineering.

FINANCIALS:

Sales and profits are in thousands of dollars—add 000 to get the full amount. 2009 Note: Financial information for 2009 was not available for all companies at press time.

2009 Sales: $	2009 Profits: $	**U.S. Stock Ticker: Private**
2008 Sales: $	2008 Profits: $	**Int'l Ticker:** Int'l Exchange:
2007 Sales: $	2007 Profits: $	Employees:
2006 Sales: $	2006 Profits: $	Fiscal Year Ends:
2005 Sales: $	2005 Profits: $	Parent Company:

SALARIES/BENEFITS:

Pension Plan:	ESOP Stock Plan:	Profit Sharing:	Top Exec. Salary: $	Bonus: $
Savings Plan:	Stock Purch. Plan:		Second Exec. Salary: $	Bonus: $

OTHER THOUGHTS:

Apparent Women Officers or Directors:
Hot Spot for Advancement for Women/Minorities:

LOCATIONS: ("Y" = Yes)

West:	Southwest:	Midwest:	Southeast:	Northeast:	International:
		Y			

PHIL LONG DEALERSHIPS INC

www.phillong.com

Industry Group Code: 441110 **Ranks within this company's industry group:** Sales: Profits:

Vehicle Manufacturing:		Dealers:		Parts:		Service:		Finance:		Specialty:	
Cars:		Car Dealer New:	Y	Manufacturers:		General Service:	Y	Leasing:		Information Systems:	
Trucks:		Car Dealer Used:	Y	Retail:		Specialty Service:		Auto Loans:	Y	Online Marketing:	
Motorcycles:		Truck Dealer:	Y	Distributors:		Oil Change:	Y	Insurance:		Other:	
Specialty:		RV Dealer:		Tires:		Paint and Body:	Y			Publishing:	
Buses:		Motorcycle Dealer:		Batteries:						Rental Cars/Trucks:	
RVs:		Specialty Dealer:	Y								

TYPES OF BUSINESS:

Auto Dealers
Auto Service
Auto Finance
Collision Repair

BRANDS/DIVISIONS/AFFILIATES:

Phil Long Collision Repair Center

GROWTH PLANS/SPECIAL FEATURES:

Phil Long Automobile Dealerships is a new and used automobile dealer that operates 14 dealerships in Colorado. The dealer showrooms offer new and used cars, trucks, vans and SUVs. The dealerships sell and service 10 different makes, including Ford, Saturn, Hyundai, Jeep, Chrysler, Mercedes-Benz, Audi, Suzuki and Kia. Phil Long's web site offers a link to each individual dealership's web site, where customers can apply for credit; search both new and pre-owned inventory; and make appointments with the service or collision departments. Each Phil Long dealership has its own parts and service department as well as a signature Phil Long Collision Repair Center. The Phil Long Collision Repair Center is exclusive to the company's dealerships and stocks parts with equivalent fit and finish of the original equipment manufacturer. The company also operates the Phil Long Expo Center, an indoor, multi-purpose event venue.

CONTACTS: *Note: Officers with more than one job title may be intentionally listed here more than once.*

Jay Cimino, CEO
Jay Cimino, Pres.
Raymond Turner, CFO
Michelle Narron, Mgr.-Corp. Comm.
Jay Cimino, Chmn.

Phone: 719-575-7000	**Fax:** 719-575-7837
Toll-Free:	
Address: 1212 Motor City Dr., Colorado Springs, CO 80906 US	

FINANCIALS: **Sales and profits are in thousands of dollars—add 000 to get the full amount. 2009 Note: Financial information for 2009 was not available for all companies at press time.**

2009 Sales: $	2009 Profits: $	**U.S. Stock Ticker: Private**
2008 Sales: $	2008 Profits: $	**Int'l Ticker:** Int'l Exchange:
2007 Sales: $	2007 Profits: $	Employees:
2006 Sales: $	2006 Profits: $	Fiscal Year Ends:
2005 Sales: $	2005 Profits: $	Parent Company:

SALARIES/BENEFITS:

Pension Plan:	ESOP Stock Plan:	Profit Sharing:	Top Exec. Salary: $	Bonus: $
Savings Plan:	Stock Purch. Plan:		Second Exec. Salary: $	Bonus: $

OTHER THOUGHTS:

Apparent Women Officers or Directors: 1
Hot Spot for Advancement for Women/Minorities:

LOCATIONS: ("Y" = Yes)

West:	Southwest:	Midwest:	Southeast:	Northeast:	International:
Y					

PIAGGIO & C SPA

www.piaggio.com

Industry Group Code: 336991 **Ranks within this company's industry group:** Sales: 5 Profits: 3

Vehicle Manufacturing:		Dealers:		Parts:		Service:		Finance:		Specialty:	
Cars:		Car Dealer New:		Manufacturers:	Y	General Service:		Leasing:		Information Systems:	
Trucks:		Car Dealer Used:		Retail:		Specialty Service:		Auto Loans:		Online Marketing:	Y
Motorcycles:	Y	Truck Dealer:		Distributors:		Oil Change:		Insurance:		Other:	
Specialty:	Y	RV Dealer:		Tires:		Paint and Body:				Publishing:	
Buses:		Motorcycle Dealer:		Batteries:						Rental Cars/Trucks:	
RVs:		Specialty Dealer:									

TYPES OF BUSINESS:

Motorcycle Manufacturing
Scooters
Mopeds
Accessories
Engines
Two-Wheel Recreational Vehicles

BRANDS/DIVISIONS/AFFILIATES:

Piaggio
Vespa
Gilera
Aprilia
Moto Guzzi
Scarabeo
Derbi
Liberty

CONTACTS:

Note: Officers with more than one job title may be intentionally listed here more than once.

Roberto Colaninno, CEO
Maurizio Roman, Gen. Mgr.-Prod. Strategies
Alessandra Simonotto, Dir.-Admin.
Maurizio Roman, Gen. Mgr.-Dev.
Francesco Delzio, Mgr.-Public Rel. & Institutional Affairs
Michele Pallottini, Gen. Mgr.-Finance & Svcs.
Alessandra Simonotto, Dir.-Credit Management
Matteo Colaninno, Deputy Chmn.
Roberto Colaninno, Chmn.

Phone: 39-587-27-21-11 **Fax:** 39-587-27-23-44
Toll-Free:
Address: 25 Viale Rinaldo Piaggio, Pontedera, Pisa, 56025 Italy

GROWTH PLANS/SPECIAL FEATURES:

Piaggio & C. S.p.A. is a leading manufacturer of motorized two-wheel vehicles, including racing scooters, mopeds, motorcycles and personal two-wheel recreational vehicles. The company has a commercial presence in over 50 countries in Europe, India, Asia and America. It operates seven production facilities located in Italy, Spain, India and Vietnam. The company's products are sold under brands including Piaggio, Vespa, Gilera, Aprilia, Moto Guzzi, Scarabeo and Derbi. The firm's scooter range includes 50cc's, such as the Liberty, the NRG, the Fly and the Zip, as well as 500cc's. Scooters over 50cc's include the larger Fly and Zip models; the three-wheeled MP3, which is also available in the hybrid version; and the high wheelers Beverly, Carnaby and Liberty. Its motorbikes, which are marketed under the Gilera and Derbi brands, include the Runner, Nexus, Fuoco 500, GP 800, Senda, Atlantis, Boulevard and GPR product lines. In addition, Piaggio produces three- and four-wheeled light transport vehicles under the Piaggio, Ape, Quargo and Porter brands, as well as related accessories. Through its engine division, the company also manufactures a variety of engines, which cover the range of company vehicles: mopeds, scooters, motorcycles and work vehicles. Through VespaVintage.com, customers can purchase an exclusive line of replacement parts for classic Vespas. Piaggio is 55% owned by IMMSI S.p.A. In June 2010, the company launched the Piaggio Mp3 scooter on the Chinese market. In that same month, it announced plans to construct a new production facility in India and launch the Vespa LX 123 model on the Indian market.

FINANCIALS:

Sales and profits are in thousands of dollars—add 000 to get the full amount. 2009 Note: Financial information for 2009 was not available for all companies at press time.

2009 Sales: $1,885,460	2009 Profits: $58,330
2008 Sales: $1,990,970	2008 Profits: $54,530
2007 Sales: $2,145,670	2007 Profits: $75,580
2006 Sales: $2,120,700	2006 Profits: $92,800
2005 Sales: $1,719,300	2005 Profits: $

U.S. Stock Ticker:
Int'l Ticker: PIA Int'l Exchange: Milan-BI
Employees:
Fiscal Year Ends: 12/31
Parent Company:

SALARIES/BENEFITS:

Pension Plan:	ESOP Stock Plan:	Profit Sharing:	Top Exec. Salary: $	Bonus: $
Savings Plan:	Stock Purch. Plan:		Second Exec. Salary: $	Bonus: $

OTHER THOUGHTS:

Apparent Women Officers or Directors: 2
Hot Spot for Advancement for Women/Minorities:

LOCATIONS: ("Y" = Yes)

West:	Southwest:	Midwest:	Southeast:	Northeast:	International:
					Y

PILKINGTON PLC

www.pilkington.com

Industry Group Code: 3272 **Ranks within this company's industry group:** Sales: Profits:

Vehicle Manufacturing:		Dealers:		Parts:		Service:		Finance:		Specialty:	
Cars:		Car Dealer New:		Manufacturers:	Y	General Service:		Leasing:		Information Systems:	
Trucks:		Car Dealer Used:		Retail:		Specialty Service:		Auto Loans:		Online Marketing:	
Motorcycles:		Truck Dealer:		Distributors:		Oil Change:		Insurance:		Other:	
Specialty:		RV Dealer:		Tires:		Paint and Body:				Publishing:	
Buses:		Motorcycle Dealer:		Batteries:						Rental Cars/Trucks:	
RVs:		Specialty Dealer:									

TYPES OF BUSINESS:

Glass Production
Auto Glass
Building Glass
Glass Fiber

BRANDS/DIVISIONS/AFFILIATES:

Pilkington Automotive
Nippon Sheet Glass
Pilkington Solar (Taicang), Limited
Activ

CONTACTS:

Note: Officers with more than one job title may be intentionally listed here more than once.

Mike Powell, Dir.-Finance
Stephen Pownall, VP-Worldwide Info. Systems
David Roycroft, Head-Corp. Affairs
Mark Lyons, Pres., Building Prod. Worldwide
Craig Naylor, CEO-NSG Group
Mike Fallon, Pres., Automotive Prod. Worldwide
Keiji Yoshikawa, Pres., Specialty Glass Worldwide
Katsuji Fujimoto, Chmn., NSG Group

Phone: 44-1744-288-82 **Fax:** 44-1744-692-660
Toll-Free:
Address: Alexandra Business Park Prescot Rd., St. Helens, Merseyside WA10 3TT UK

GROWTH PLANS/SPECIAL FEATURES:

Pilkington plc, a subsidiary of Nippon Sheet Glass Company, is a glass manufacturer for the architecture and automotive industries. The company maintains manufacturing operations in 29 countries and sales teams in over 130 countries. Worldwide operations are divided into two business lines: building products, which supplies original equipment and refurbished glass to the domestic and commercial construction industry; automotive products, which provides glass products and glazing systems to automotive original equipment and aftermarket clients; and specialty glass, which provides glass fiber and IT glass products. Pilkington offers building use glass products such as the self-cleaning glass Activ, which uses natural UV radiation to activate processes to break down dirt in conjunction with a water sheeting finish that allows rain to wash the glass clean; Eclipse Advantage and Suncool, which are coated with a pyrolytic substance to block heat; K Glass, Opitherm, Spacia, energiKare and Optiwhite, which provide thermal insulation; Pyroshield, Pyroclear, Pyrodur and Pyrostop, which provide protection from fires; Optiphon, which controls noise; Optifloat T and Optilam, which are toughened to provide security; as well as other models that provide decoration, architectural flexibility, solar energy and other special applications. Pilkington Automotive, the company's auto glass operations and related business subsidiary, supplies major auto manufacturers on an original equipment basis. These products incorporate glazing designed to reduce the effects of solar heat build-up, allow rainwater to clear easily and provide a noise barrier. In addition, the company manufactures auto glass with antennae incorporated into the glaze. Pilkington's automotive operations comprise some 44 locations in 20 countries around the world. In May 2010, NSG acquired the remaining 50% stake in Taicang Pilkington China Glass Special Glass from China Glass Holdings and will rename the now wholly-owned subsidiary, Pilkington Solar (Taicang), Limited.

FINANCIALS:

Sales and profits are in thousands of dollars—add 000 to get the full amount. 2009 Note: Financial information for 2009 was not available for all companies at press time.

2009 Sales: $	2009 Profits: $
2008 Sales: $	2008 Profits: $
2007 Sales: $	2007 Profits: $
2006 Sales: $	2006 Profits: $
2005 Sales: $5,061,200	2005 Profits: $187,900

U.S. Stock Ticker: Subsidiary
Int'l Ticker: Int'l Exchange:
Employees:
Fiscal Year Ends:
Parent Company: NIPPON SHEET GLASS COMPANY LIMITED

SALARIES/BENEFITS:

Pension Plan:	ESOP Stock Plan:	Profit Sharing:	Top Exec. Salary: $	Bonus: $
Savings Plan:	Stock Purch. Plan:		Second Exec. Salary: $	Bonus: $

OTHER THOUGHTS:

Apparent Women Officers or Directors:
Hot Spot for Advancement for Women/Minorities:

LOCATIONS: ("Y" = Yes)

West:	Southwest:	Midwest:	Southeast:	Northeast:	International:
Y	Y	Y	Y	Y	Y

PININFARINA SPA

www.pininfarina.it

Industry Group Code: 33611 **Ranks within this company's industry group:** Sales: 33 Profits: 18

Vehicle Manufacturing:		Dealers:		Parts:		Service:		Finance:		Specialty:	
Cars:	Y	Car Dealer New:		Manufacturers:	Y	General Service:		Leasing:		Information Systems:	
Trucks:		Car Dealer Used:		Retail:		Specialty Service:	Y	Auto Loans:		Online Marketing:	
Motorcycles:		Truck Dealer:		Distributors:		Oil Change:		Insurance:		Other:	Y
Specialty:		RV Dealer:		Tires:		Paint and Body:				Publishing:	
Buses:		Motorcycle Dealer:		Batteries:						Rental Cars/Trucks:	
RVs:		Specialty Dealer:									

TYPES OF BUSINESS:

Automotive Design & Engineering Services
Aeronautics Design
Mass Transit Design
Consumer Products Design
Retractable Roof Systems
Engineering Services
Prototype Testing
Automobile Design

BRANDS/DIVISIONS/AFFILIATES:

Pininfarina Extra S.r.l.
Pininfarina Sverige AB
RHTU Sverige AB
Pininfarina Deutschland GmbH
Pininfarina Extra USA Corp.
mpx Entwicklung GmbH
Matra Automobile Engineering Maroc S.A.S.

CONTACTS: *Note: Officers with more than one job title may be intentionally listed here more than once.*

Silvio Angori, CEO
Silvio Angori, COO
Gianfranco Albertini, CFO
Giorgio Astesano, Dir.-Sales & Prod.
Roberto Mattio, Dir.-Human Resources
Gino Mazzucco, Dir.-Prod. Dev.
Gabriella Isoardi, Dir.-Legal
Leonardo Salazzari, Dir.-Oper.
Giorgio Astesano, Dir.-Bus. Dev.
Silvio Pietro Angori, Dir.-Comm. & Image
Gianfranco Albertini, Gen. Mgr.-Investor Rel.
Lowie Vermeersch, Dir.-Design
Paolo Pininfarina, Chmn.
Leonardo Salazzari, Interim Dir.-Purchasing

Phone: 39-011-547260 **Fax:** 39-011-7091721
Toll-Free:
Address: 6 Via Bruno Buozzi, Turin, 10121 Italy

GROWTH PLANS/SPECIAL FEATURES:

Pininfarina SpA specializes in providing automotive and general manufacturers with services through all stages of product development, from planning, designing and development to engineering, manufacturing and end product consultation. The firm's subsidiaries include Pininfarina Extra S.r.l.; Pininfarina Sverige AB; RHTU Sverige AB; Pininfarina Deutschland GmbH; Pininfarina Extra USA Corp.; mpx Entwicklung GmbH; and Matra Automobile Engineering Maroc S.A.S. In the aeronautics and aeroacoustics industry, the company designs the interior and exterior forms of its vehicles using its own automotive wind tunnels. It does design work for trains, planes and boats, as well as non-transportation products such as shoes, cellular phones, coffee machines, ski boots and watches. The firm's current production includes the Alfa Romeo Brera, Volvo C70, Alfa Romeo Spider, Mitsubishi Colt CZC and Ford Focus CC. The company's customers include car makers such as Ferrari, General Motors, Lancia, Maserati, Fiat, Alfa Romeo, Hyundai, Peugeot, Citroen, Jaguar, Daewoo, Honda, Brilliance, AviChina – Hafei, Chery, JAC, Ford, Volvo, Mitsubishi and Rolls-Royce; industrial vehicle makers including BMC; bus and truck makers including BredaMenarinibus, IVECO and Hispano; railway makers including AnsaldoBreda, Bombardier and Eurostar; nautical and aeronautical clients including Beneteau, Derecktor Shipyards, Ferretti Yachts and BAE Systems; and other clients, including Leitner Ropeways, Poma and Solex. In December 2009, the company signed the final contract for the sale of certain business operations to De Tomaso Automobili S.p.A. for $2.6 million. In that same month, it also signed a final agreement for the sale of its Grugliasco industrial facility to Sviluppo Investimenti Territorio S.r.l.

FINANCIALS: **Sales and profits are in thousands of dollars—add 000 to get the full amount. 2009 Note: Financial information for 2009 was not available for all companies at press time.**

2009 Sales: $237,130 — 2009 Profits: $-38,930
2008 Sales: $711,720 — 2008 Profits: $-275,520
2007 Sales: $962,300 — 2007 Profits: $-154,580
2006 Sales: $713,570 — 2006 Profits: $-29,670
2005 Sales: $629,085 — 2005 Profits: $-11,047

U.S. Stock Ticker:
Int'l Ticker: PINF Int'l Exchange: Milan-BI
Employees:
Fiscal Year Ends: 12/31
Parent Company:

SALARIES/BENEFITS:

Pension Plan: ESOP Stock Plan: Profit Sharing: Top Exec. Salary: $ Bonus: $
Savings Plan: Stock Purch. Plan: Second Exec. Salary: $ Bonus: $

OTHER THOUGHTS:

Apparent Women Officers or Directors: 1
Hot Spot for Advancement for Women/Minorities:

LOCATIONS: ("Y" = Yes)

West:	Southwest:	Midwest:	Southeast:	Northeast:	International:
					Y

PIRELLI & C SPA

www.pirelli.com

Industry Group Code: 3262 **Ranks within this company's industry group:** Sales: 5 Profits: 4

Vehicle Manufacturing:		Dealers:		Parts:		Service:		Finance:		Specialty:	
Cars:		Car Dealer New:		Manufacturers:		General Service:		Leasing:		Information Systems:	
Trucks:		Car Dealer Used:		Retail:		Specialty Service:		Auto Loans:		Online Marketing:	
Motorcycles:		Truck Dealer:		Distributors:		Oil Change:		Insurance:		Other:	
Specialty:		RV Dealer:		Tires:	Y	Paint and Body:				Publishing:	
Buses:		Motorcycle Dealer:		Batteries:						Rental Cars/Trucks:	
RVs:		Specialty Dealer:									

TYPES OF BUSINESS:

Tire Manufacturing
Real Estate
Broadband Technology

BRANDS/DIVISIONS/AFFILIATES:

Pirelli Tyre
Pirelli Ambiente
Pirelli Eco technologies
Pirelli RE
PZero Moda S.r.l.
Pirelli Labs
Pirelli Broadband Solutions

CONTACTS: *Note: Officers with more than one job title may be intentionally listed here more than once.*

Marco T. Provera, CEO
Luciano Gobbi, CFO
Gustavo Bracco, Dir.-Human Resources
Francesco Chiappetta, General Counsel
Luciano Gobbi, Chief Strategic Planning Officer
Maurizio Abet, Dir.-Media Comm.
Valeria Leone, Investor Rel. Officer
Francesco Tanzi, Dir.-Finance
Franceso Gori, Managing Dir.-Pirelli Tyre
Franceso Gori, CEO-Pirelli Tyre
Antonio Calabro, Dir.-Institutional & Cultural Affairs
Marco T. Provera, Chmn.

Phone: 39-02-64421 **Fax:** 39-02-6442-2670
Toll-Free:
Address: 25 Viale Piero e Alberto Pirelli N., Milan, 20126 Italy

GROWTH PLANS/SPECIAL FEATURES:

Pirelli & C. S.p.A. is an Italian company best known for its sale of tires, although it is also active in the real estate, broadband, renewable energies, and environmental technologies sectors. Pirelli manufactures tires for cars, industrial/commercial vehicles, motorcycles and farm equipment. It is a multinational corporation that operates in more than 169 countries and has 24 factories on four continents. Pirelli real estate segment invests in real estate companies and provides financing services. Pirelli Broadband Solutions is active in the technological fields of broadband access and second-generation photonics based on nanotechnology. Through Pirelli Labs, the firm develops innovations in the field of photonics, nanotechnologies and broadband access systems, both wired and wireless. Pirelli Ambiente, the company's renewable energy segment, is involved in three main businesses: the creation of quality fuel from waste matter, photovoltaic energy, and environmental cleanup. Pirelli's Eco Technology business produces low environmental impact fuel as well as anti-particulate filters, which can be retrofitted onto older diesel vehicles to reduce emissions. The firm operates the Vizzola test track, a 915,000-square-foot facility with an 82-foot tower; it is home to many of the company's prototype designs. In September 2009, Pirelli announced an agreement with Chinese partner Hixih Group to build a particulate filter factory in Yanzhou, China. In that same month, the company announced the restructuring of its business to focus on the core business of tires. All operations involved with the production, sale or design of that core business will be regrouped under the new Tyre and Parts Department. In May 2010, Pirelli announced plans for the separation of its real estate business, Pirelli RE.

FINANCIALS: **Sales and profits are in thousands of dollars—add 000 to get the full amount. 2009 Note: Financial information for 2009 was not available for all companies at press time.**

2009 Sales: $5,622,600	2009 Profits: $28,480	**U.S. Stock Ticker:**
2008 Sales: $6,545,720	2008 Profits: $-580,130	**Int'l Ticker: PC** Int'l Exchange: Milan-BI
2007 Sales: $6,390,000	2007 Profits: $455,110	Employees: 29,570
2006 Sales: $6,552,860	2006 Profits: $-1,473,490	Fiscal Year Ends: 12/31
2005 Sales: $5,716,690	2005 Profits: $501,750	Parent Company:

SALARIES/BENEFITS:

Pension Plan:	ESOP Stock Plan:	Profit Sharing:	Top Exec. Salary: $3,093,731	Bonus: $
Savings Plan: Y	Stock Purch. Plan:		Second Exec. Salary: $727,607	Bonus: $

OTHER THOUGHTS:

Apparent Women Officers or Directors: 3
Hot Spot for Advancement for Women/Minorities: Y

LOCATIONS: ("Y" = Yes)

West:	Southwest:	Midwest:	Southeast:	Northeast:	International:
					Y

POLARIS INDUSTRIES INC

www.polarisindustries.com

Industry Group Code: 336999 **Ranks within this company's industry group:** Sales: 1 Profits: 1

Vehicle Manufacturing:		Dealers:		Parts:		Service:		Finance:		Specialty:	
Cars:		Car Dealer New:		Manufacturers:	Y	General Service:		Leasing:		Information Systems:	
Trucks:		Car Dealer Used:		Retail:		Specialty Service:		Auto Loans:		Online Marketing:	
Motorcycles:	Y	Truck Dealer:		Distributors:	Y	Oil Change:		Insurance:		Other:	Y
Specialty:	Y	RV Dealer:		Tires:		Paint and Body:				Publishing:	
Buses:		Motorcycle Dealer:		Batteries:						Rental Cars/Trucks:	
RVs:		Specialty Dealer:									

TYPES OF BUSINESS:

All-Terrain Vehicle Manufacturing
Snowmobile Manufacturing
Parts & Accessories
Motorcycles
Clothing
Low-Emission Vehicles (LEV)

BRANDS/DIVISIONS/AFFILIATES:

RANGER
Victory Vegas
Kingpin
Vegas Jackpot
Eight Ball
Victory Vision
Polaris Breeze

CONTACTS: *Note: Officers with more than one job title may be intentionally listed here more than once.*

Scott W. Wine, CEO
Bennett J. Morgan, COO
Bennett J. Morgan, Pres.
Michael W. Malone, CFO
Michael Jonikas, VP-Mktg. & Sales
John B. Corness, VP-Human Resources
William Fisher, CIO/VP
David C Longren, CTO/VP
Stacy L. Bogart, General Counsel/Corp. Sec/VP
Wesley W. Barker, VP-Oper.
Todd M. Balan, VP-Corp. Dev.
Michael W. Malone, VP-Finance
Mark E. Blackwell, VP-Victory Motorcycles
Scott Swenson, VP/Gen. Mgr.-Snowmobile & PG&A
Michael Dougherty, VP-Global New Market Dev.
Matthew J. Homan, VP-Off-Road Vehicles
Gregory R. Palen, Chmn.
Mark E. Blackwell, VP-Int'l
Suresh Krishna, VP-Supply Chain & Integration

Phone: 763-542-0500	**Fax:** 763-542-0599
Toll-Free: 800-765-2747	
Address: 2100 Hwy. 55, Medina, MN 55340 US	

GROWTH PLANS/SPECIAL FEATURES:

Polaris Industries, Inc. designs, engineers and manufactures off-road vehicles, including side-by-side and all-terrain recreational and utility vehicles (ATVs), as well as snowmobiles and motorcycles. The firm markets these together with related accessories, clothing and replacement parts through 1,500 independent dealers in North America and nine subsidiaries and 43 distributors in approximately 130 countries around the world. The firm's line of ATVs consists of 33 models, including general purpose, sport, side-by-side, four-wheel-drive and the RANGER line of utility ATVs. The company's RANGER 6x6 is one of the only six-wheel-drive vehicles in production. The company also offers the Ranger EV, an all-electric side-by-side vehicle. ATV accessories include winches, bumpers, brush guards, plows, racks, mowers, tires, pull-behinds, cabs, cargo box accessories, tracks and oil. Polaris' line of snowmobiles contains 27models, including youth, utility, economy, performance and competition models. Snowmobile accessories include covers, traction products, reverse kits, electric starters, tracks, bags, windshields, oil and lubricants. Polaris' Victory line of V-twin cruiser motorcycles includes the Victory Vision line of luxury touring models, as well as the Vegas Low, Kingpin, Eight-Ball, Kingpin Tour, Vegas and Vegas Jackpot and some limited edition models. Motorcycle accessories include saddle bags, handlebars, backrests, exhaust, windshields, seats, oil and various chrome accessories. Polaris also markets the Polaris Breeze, an electric-powered low emission vehicle (LEV) used for suburban communities and golf courses. In addition to the variety of replacement parts and accessories for its vehicles, Polaris markets a full line of recreational clothing, which includes helmets, jackets, bibs and pants, leathers and hats for each of its product lines. The company also has a strategic alliance with Bobcat Company, a work vehicle company, for the technology collaboration, co-development and supply of work vehicles. In May 2010, Polaris introduced two new Breeze LEV products, the Breeze 2 Passenger and the Breeze SL.

Polaris offers its employees tuition and health club reimbursement, a flexible spending plan and an employee assistance program.

FINANCIALS: **Sales and profits are in thousands of dollars—add 000 to get the full amount. 2009 Note: Financial information for 2009 was not available for all companies at press time.**

2009 Sales: $1,565,887	2009 Profits: $101,017	**U.S. Stock Ticker: PII**
2008 Sales: $1,948,254	2008 Profits: $117,395	**Int'l Ticker:** Int'l Exchange:
2007 Sales: $1,780,009	2007 Profits: $111,650	Employees: 3,000
2006 Sales: $1,656,518	2006 Profits: $106,985	Fiscal Year Ends: 12/31
2005 Sales: $1,869,819	2005 Profits: $136,714	Parent Company:

SALARIES/BENEFITS:

Pension Plan:	ESOP Stock Plan: Y	Profit Sharing: Y	Top Exec. Salary: $586,058	Bonus: $445,404
Savings Plan: Y	Stock Purch. Plan: Y		Second Exec. Salary: $407,692	Bonus: $309,846

OTHER THOUGHTS:

Apparent Women Officers or Directors: 1
Hot Spot for Advancement for Women/Minorities:

LOCATIONS: ("Y" = Yes)

West:	Southwest:	Midwest:	Southeast:	Northeast:	International:
		Y			Y

PORSCHE AUTOMOBIL HOLDING SE

www.porsche-se.com

Industry Group Code: 33611 **Ranks within this company's industry group:** Sales: 23 Profits: 33

Vehicle Manufacturing:		Dealers:		Parts:		Service:		Finance:		Specialty:	
Cars:	Y	Car Dealer New:		Manufacturers:	Y	General Service:		Leasing:	Y	Information Systems:	
Trucks:		Car Dealer Used:		Retail:		Specialty Service:	Y	Auto Loans:	Y	Online Marketing:	
Motorcycles:		Truck Dealer:		Distributors:		Oil Change:		Insurance:	Y	Other:	
Specialty:		RV Dealer:		Tires:		Paint and Body:				Publishing:	
Buses:		Motorcycle Dealer:		Batteries:						Rental Cars/Trucks:	
RVs:		Specialty Dealer:									

TYPES OF BUSINESS:

Automobile Manufacturing
Sports Cars
Engineering Services
Financial Services
Consulting Services
Driving School
Racing
Apparel & Accessories

BRANDS/DIVISIONS/AFFILIATES:

Volkswagen AG
Dr. Ing. h.c. F. Porsche AG
Porsche Cars North America
Cayenne
911 Turbo
911 Carerra
Cayman S
Panamera

CONTACTS: *Note: Officers with more than one job title may be intentionally listed here more than once.*

Martin Winterkorn, CEO
Hans Dieter Potsch, CFO
Thomas Edig, Dir.-Human Resources & Labor Rel.
Wolfgang Durheimer, Dir.-R&D
Wolfgang Glabus, Dir.-Comm.
Michael Macht, Chmn.

Phone: 49-711-911-0	**Fax:** 49-711-911-25777
Toll-Free:	
Address: Porscheplatz 1, Stuttgart, 70435 Germany	

GROWTH PLANS/SPECIAL FEATURES:

Porsche Automobil Holding SE is a holding company that controls 100% of Dr. Ing. h.c. F. Porsche AG (Porsche). The company, through its Porsche subsidiary, is a leading global manufacturer of sports cars. The company's production has been streamlined to five model lines: the 911, the newly introduced Panamera, the Cayman, the Boxster and the Cayenne SUV. The 911 is available in many model iterations, including Carrera, Carrera 4, Carrera S, Carrera Cabriolet, Carrera S Cabriolet, Carrera 4 Cabriolet, Carrera 4S, Carrera 4S Cabriolet and Turbo. Most are priced between roughly $76,000 and $195,000. The Boxster ranges in price up to $56,700. Its models include the Boxster and Boxster S. The Cayman line offers the Cayman and Cayman S priced up to $60,200. Cayenne SUVs include the Cayenne, Cayenne S, Cayenne S Transsyberia, Cayenne GTS, Cayenne Turbo and Cayenne Turbo S, which range in price from $45,000 to $124,800. Panamera models include Panamera S, Panamera 4S and Panamera Turbo, ranging in price from $89,800 to $132,600. Porsche AG is controlled by descendants of its founding family. In May 2009, Volkswagen and Porsche announced that they were in talks to merge the operations of the two companies, and in August 2009 they announced an agreement that would have VW purchase an approximate 42% stake in Porsche's sports car business by the end of 2009, with the remainder of Porsche being merged into VW's operations by 2011. Later in August 2009, Qatar Holding LLC, a commercial arm of the Emirate of Qatar, signed a purchase agreement for Qatar to acquire 10% of the shares of Porsche SE.

FINANCIALS: **Sales and profits are in thousands of dollars—add 000 to get the full amount. 2009 Note: Financial information for 2009 was not available for all companies at press time.**

2009 Sales: $7,765,930	2009 Profits: $-5,594,549	**U.S. Stock Ticker: POAHF.PK**
2008 Sales: $9,935,620	2008 Profits: $8,371,000	**Int'l Ticker: PSHG** Int'l Exchange: Frankfurt-Euronext
2007 Sales: $9,804,510	2007 Profits: $5,644,870	Employees: 375,959
2006 Sales: $9,655,630	2006 Profits: $1,888,380	Fiscal Year Ends: 12/31
2005 Sales: $7,971,600	2005 Profits: $948,900	Parent Company:

SALARIES/BENEFITS:

Pension Plan:	ESOP Stock Plan:	Profit Sharing:	Top Exec. Salary: $	Bonus: $
Savings Plan:	Stock Purch. Plan:		Second Exec. Salary: $	Bonus: $

OTHER THOUGHTS:

Apparent Women Officers or Directors:
Hot Spot for Advancement for Women/Minorities:

LOCATIONS: ("Y" = Yes)

West:	Southwest:	Midwest:	Southeast:	Northeast:	International:
					Y

POTAMKIN AUTOMOTIVE GROUP

www.planetautomotive.com

Industry Group Code: 441110 **Ranks within this company's industry group:** Sales: Profits:

Vehicle Manufacturing:		Dealers:		Parts:		Service:		Finance:		Specialty:	
Cars:		Car Dealer New:	Y	Manufacturers:		General Service:	Y	Leasing:		Information Systems:	
Trucks:		Car Dealer Used:	Y	Retail:		Specialty Service:		Auto Loans:		Online Marketing:	
Motorcycles:		Truck Dealer:		Distributors:		Oil Change:		Insurance:		Other:	
Specialty:		RV Dealer:		Tires:		Paint and Body:				Publishing:	
Buses:		Motorcycle Dealer:		Batteries:						Rental Cars/Trucks:	
RVs:		Specialty Dealer:									

TYPES OF BUSINESS:

Auto Dealers, Retail

BRANDS/DIVISIONS/AFFILIATES:

Potamkin Automotive Group

CONTACTS:

Note: Officers with more than one job title may be intentionally listed here more than once.

Barry Frieder, COO
Barry Frieder, Pres.
David Yusko, CFO
Ralph Perkins, VP-Mktg.
Joel Verity, Dir.-IT
John Hickey, Exec. Legal Council
Andrew Pfeifer, Sr. VP-Corp. Oper.
Ralph Perkins, VP-Bus. Dev.
Ralph Perkins, VP-e-commerce
David Winton, Treas./Exec. VP
Robert Potamkin, Co-Chmn.
Bill Mercado, VP-Fixed Oper.
Alan Potamkin, Co-Chmn.
David Frieder, VP-Purchasing & Vendor Rel.

Phone: 305-774-7690 **Fax:** 305-774-7696
Toll-Free:
Address: 6600 Cowpen Rd., Miami Lakes, FL 33014 US

GROWTH PLANS/SPECIAL FEATURES:

Potamkin Automotive Group is a privately owned car dealership network based out of Florida, and one of the largest automotive dealer groups in the U.S. The firm operates by partnering with some of the best dealerships in the country and providing them with financial backing, financial contracts, appealing advertising rates on a local and regional basis, manufacturer relationships and discounts from suppliers and vendors. After having given its dealer partners the tools needed to succeed, Potamkin allows them to remain individually operated and managed in order to allow them to best serve their local markets. This style of partnership is labeled as corporate decentralizing. The firm currently has 28 dealerships and roughly 48 franchises in California, Texas, Florida, New York, Pennsylvania and Massachusetts. All Potamkin dealerships offer their clients several exclusive deals: a no-haggle, no-hassle pricing program; a 3-Day/100-Mile money back guarantee; a 10% discount on service, parts and accessories; free car washes for the life of the vehicle ownership; and numerous financing plans. Models sold by Potamkin dealerships include Audi, Buick, Honda, GMC, Mazda, Chevrolet, Jeep, Kia, Toyota and Volkswagon.

Potamkin Automotive provides its employees with a 401(k) plan; flexible spending accounts; disability, basic life, dependant life and accident insurance; business travel insurance; and a medical, dental and vision plan.

FINANCIALS:

Sales and profits are in thousands of dollars—add 000 to get the full amount. 2009 Note: Financial information for 2009 was not available for all companies at press time.

2009 Sales: $	2009 Profits: $
2008 Sales: $1,500,000	2008 Profits: $
2007 Sales: $	2007 Profits: $
2006 Sales: $	2006 Profits: $
2005 Sales: $	2005 Profits: $

U.S. Stock Ticker: Private
Int'l Ticker: Int'l Exchange:
Employees: 1,500
Fiscal Year Ends: 12/31
Parent Company:

SALARIES/BENEFITS:

Pension Plan:	ESOP Stock Plan:	Profit Sharing:	Top Exec. Salary: $	Bonus: $
Savings Plan: Y	Stock Purch. Plan:		Second Exec. Salary: $	Bonus: $

OTHER THOUGHTS:

Apparent Women Officers or Directors:
Hot Spot for Advancement for Women/Minorities:

LOCATIONS: ("Y" = Yes)

West:	Southwest:	Midwest:	Southeast:	Northeast:	International:
Y	Y		Y	Y	

PPG INDUSTRIES INC

www.ppg.com

Industry Group Code: 325510 **Ranks within this company's industry group:** Sales: 1 Profits: 1

Vehicle Manufacturing:		Dealers:		Parts:		Service:		Finance:		Specialty:	
Cars:		Car Dealer New:		Manufacturers:	Y	General Service:		Leasing:		Information Systems:	
Trucks:		Car Dealer Used:		Retail:		Specialty Service:		Auto Loans:		Online Marketing:	
Motorcycles:		Truck Dealer:		Distributors:		Oil Change:		Insurance:		Other:	
Specialty:		RV Dealer:		Tires:		Paint and Body:				Publishing:	
Buses:		Motorcycle Dealer:		Batteries:						Rental Cars/Trucks:	
RVs:		Specialty Dealer:									

TYPES OF BUSINESS:

Automotive Paints
Coatings
Glass
Chemicals
Fiberglass
Industrial Products

BRANDS/DIVISIONS/AFFILIATES:

Aquacron
Clarvista
Transitions
Teslin

CONTACTS:
Note: Officers with more than one job title may be intentionally listed here more than once.

Charles E. Bunch, CEO
Robert J. Dellinger, CFO
Patrick J. Kenny, VP-Corp. Mktg.
Charles W. Wise, VP-Human Resources
Charles F. Kahle II, VP-Coatings R&D
Werner Baer, VP-IT
Charles F. Kahle II, CTO
James C. Diggs, General Counsel/Sr. VP
Aziz S. Giga, VP-Strategic Planning/Treas.
Lynne D. Schmidt, VP-Gov't & Community Affairs
Vince Morales, VP-Investor Rel.
Robert J. Dellinger, Sr. VP-Finance
J. Rich Alexander, Sr. VP-Performance Coatings
Douglas S. Pegg, VP-Packaging Coatings
Thomas S. Mauck, VP-Protective & Marine Coatings
Richard A. Beuke, VP-Silicas
Charles E. Bunch, Chmn.
Viktor Sekmakas, Pres., PPG Asia/Pacific/VP-Industrial Coatings
Stephen T. Lampe, VP-Purchasing & Dist.

Phone: 412-434-3131	**Fax:** 412-434-2125
Toll-Free:	
Address: 1 PPG Pl., Pittsburgh, PA 15272 US	

GROWTH PLANS/SPECIAL FEATURES:

PPG Industries, Inc. is a manufacturing company that operates in six business segments: performance coatings; industrial coatings; architectural coatings-EMEA; optical and specialty materials; commodity chemicals; and glass. The performance coatings, industrial coatings and architectural coatings-EMEA segments each supply protective and decorative finishes for customers in various markets such as industrial equipment; automotive and marine. The optical and specialty materials segment comprises the optical products and silicas businesses. Its primary products are Transitions lenses, sunlenses, optical materials and polarized film; amorphous precipitated silicas for tire, battery separator and other end-use markets; and Teslin synthetic printing sheet used in waterproof labels, e-passports and identification cards. The commodity chemicals segment produces chlor-alkali and derivative products including chlorine, caustic soda, vinyl chloride monomer, chlorinated solvents, calcium hypochlorite, ethylene dichloride and phosgene derivatives. Most of these products are sold directly to manufacturing companies in the chemical processing, rubber and plastics, paper, minerals, metals and water treatment industries. The glass segment comprises the performance glazings and fiber glass businesses. PPG's major markets within this segment are commercial and residential construction, as well as wind energy, energy infrastructure, transportation and electronics. The company operates in over 60 countries worldwide. In November 2009, PPG launched a new water-based coating called Aquacron, to be used for light industrial applications. In May 2010, the firm introduced Clarvista shower glass, for shower doors and bath enclosures. The new product features a coating designed to shield against surface scratches and other signs of wear and tear.

Employees are offered medical, dental and life insurance, as well as disability coverage.

FINANCIALS:
Sales and profits are in thousands of dollars—add 000 to get the full amount. 2009 Note: Financial information for 2009 was not available for all companies at press time.

2009 Sales: $12,239,000	2009 Profits: $336,000	**U.S. Stock Ticker: PPG**
2008 Sales: $15,849,000	2008 Profits: $538,000	**Int'l Ticker:** Int'l Exchange:
2007 Sales: $12,220,000	2007 Profits: $834,000	Employees: 39,900
2006 Sales: $10,938,000	2006 Profits: $711,000	Fiscal Year Ends: 12/31
2005 Sales: $10,201,000	2005 Profits: $596,000	Parent Company:

SALARIES/BENEFITS:

Pension Plan:	ESOP Stock Plan:	Profit Sharing:	Top Exec. Salary: $1,050,000	Bonus: $1,500,000
Savings Plan:	Stock Purch. Plan:		Second Exec. Salary: $577,466	Bonus: $587,674

OTHER THOUGHTS:

Apparent Women Officers or Directors: 8
Hot Spot for Advancement for Women/Minorities: Y

LOCATIONS: ("Y" = Yes)

West:	Southwest:	Midwest:	Southeast:	Northeast:	International:
Y	Y	Y	Y	Y	Y

PRIMEARTH EV ENERGY CO LTD

www.peve.jp

Industry Group Code: 33591 **Ranks within this company's industry group:** Sales: Profits:

Vehicle Manufacturing:		Dealers:		Parts:		Service:		Finance:		Specialty:	
Cars:		Car Dealer New:		Manufacturers:	Y	General Service:		Leasing:		Information Systems:	
Trucks:		Car Dealer Used:		Retail:		Specialty Service:		Auto Loans:		Online Marketing:	
Motorcycles:		Truck Dealer:		Distributors:		Oil Change:		Insurance:		Other:	
Specialty:		RV Dealer:		Tires:		Paint and Body:				Publishing:	
Buses:		Motorcycle Dealer:		Batteries:						Rental Cars/Trucks:	
RVs:		Specialty Dealer:									

TYPES OF BUSINESS:

Battery Manufacturing-Hybrid Cars
Battery Management Systems

BRANDS/DIVISIONS/AFFILIATES:

Panasonic Corporation
Toyota Motor Corporation
Battery ECU
Panasonic Automotive Systems of America
Panasonic Corporation of North America

CONTACTS: *Note: Officers with more than one job title may be intentionally listed here more than once.*

Yoshiro Hayashi, Pres.

Phone:	**Fax:**
Toll-Free: 800-211-7262	
Address: 20 Okasaki, Kosai, Shizuoka, 431-0422 Japan	

GROWTH PLANS/SPECIAL FEATURES:

Primearth EV Energy Co., Ltd., formerly Panasonic EV Energy Co., Ltd., develops, manufactures and sells nickel metal-hydride batteries, primarily for hybrid electric vehicles (HEVs). Founded in 1996, it is a joint venture between Panasonic Corporation and Toyota Motor Corporation, with Toyota holding a majority stake of 80.5%. Primearth manufactures two HEV rechargeable batteries, the metal case prismatic and the plastic case prismatic modules, which both take up 14% less volume than conventional HEV batteries. Additionally, the metal case battery has a 40% higher cooling performance, and the plastic case battery is approximately 25% lighter than conventional HEV battery modules. Besides batteries, Primearth offers a battery management system known as Battery ECU, which monitors and controls the battery's functions, such as temperature and voltage. The firm's products are used in several current production model vehicles, including the Lexus LS600h, LS600hL, RX450h and GS450h; Toyota Prius, Crown Hybrid, Kluger Hybrid, Camry Hybrid and Estima Hybrid; Daihatsu Hijet Cargo Hybrid; and the Hino Dutro Hybrid. Although not its primary line of business, the company has historically supplied batteries for pure electric vehicles (PEVs). The firm's U.S. sales group consists of Panasonic Automotive Systems of America, a division of Panasonic Corporation of North America, while its Japanese sales group comprises the Automotive Systems Company of Panasonic Corporation. Primearth's main battery production facility is located in Kosai, Japan. The firm has recently opened two new plants; the Sakaijuku plant, also in Kosai and the Miyagi plant, located in Taiwa, Japan. In November 2009, the firm began producing a limited amount of lithium-ion batteries to be tested in Toyota's Prius PHV (plug-in hybrid). In June 2010, the company changed its name to Primearth EV Energy Co., Ltd. and reached an accumulated battery pack production of 3 million pieces.

FINANCIALS: **Sales and profits are in thousands of dollars—add 000 to get the full amount. 2009 Note: Financial information for 2009 was not available for all companies at press time.**

2009 Sales: $	2009 Profits: $	**U.S. Stock Ticker: Joint Venture**
2008 Sales: $	2008 Profits: $	**Int'l Ticker:** Int'l Exchange:
2007 Sales: $539,300	2007 Profits: $	Employees: 1,800
2006 Sales: $	2006 Profits: $	Fiscal Year Ends: 3/31
2005 Sales: $	2005 Profits: $	Parent Company: TOYOTA MOTOR CORPORATION

SALARIES/BENEFITS:

Pension Plan:	ESOP Stock Plan:	Profit Sharing:	Top Exec. Salary: $	Bonus: $
Savings Plan:	Stock Purch. Plan:		Second Exec. Salary: $	Bonus: $

OTHER THOUGHTS:

Apparent Women Officers or Directors:
Hot Spot for Advancement for Women/Minorities:

LOCATIONS: ("Y" = Yes)

West:	Southwest:	Midwest:	Southeast:	Northeast:	International:
					Y

PROGRESSIVE CORPORATION (THE)

www.progressive.com

Industry Group Code: 524126 **Ranks within this company's industry group:** Sales: 3 Profits: 1

Vehicle Manufacturing:		Dealers:		Parts:		Service:		Finance:		Specialty:	
Cars:		Car Dealer New:		Manufacturers:		General Service:		Leasing:		Information Systems:	
Trucks:		Car Dealer Used:		Retail:		Specialty Service:		Auto Loans:		Online Marketing:	
Motorcycles:		Truck Dealer:		Distributors:		Oil Change:		Insurance:	Y	Other:	
Specialty:		RV Dealer:		Tires:		Paint and Body:				Publishing:	
Buses:		Motorcycle Dealer:		Batteries:						Rental Cars/Trucks:	
RVs:		Specialty Dealer:									

TYPES OF BUSINESS:

Insurance, Direct Property & Casualty
Automobile Insurance

BRANDS/DIVISIONS/AFFILIATES:

ProgressiveResponds.com
Progressive Direct

CONTACTS:

Note: Officers with more than one job title may be intentionally listed here more than once.

Glenn M. Renwick, CEO
Glenn M. Renwick, Pres.
Brian Domeck, CFO
Valerie Krasowski, Chief Human Resources Officer
Ray Voelker, CIO
Chuck Jarrett, Chief Legal Officer/Sec./VP
Jeffrey W. Basch, Chief Acct. Officer/VP
John P. Sauerland, Pres., Personal Lines Group
John Barbagallo, Pres., Commercial Lines Group
Bill Cody, Chief Investment Officer
Tricia Griffith, Chief Claims Officer
Peter B. Lewis, Chmn.

Phone: 440-461-5000 **Fax:** 440-446-7436
Toll-Free: 800-776-4737
Address: 6300 Wilson Mills Rd., Mayfield Village, OH 44143 US

GROWTH PLANS/SPECIAL FEATURES:

The Progressive Corporation, together with its 53 subsidiaries and one affiliated mutual insurance company, is one of the largest auto insurers in the U.S., with more than 10 million policies in force. Progressive is divided into three business areas: personal lines, commercial auto and claims. The firm's personal lines segment writes insurance for private passenger automobiles and recreational and other vehicles, motorcycles, ATVs, RVs, mobile homes, watercraft and snowmobiles. The personal lines business accounts for 89% of total net premiums. The commercial auto business writes primary liability and physical damage insurance for automobiles and trucks owned by small businesses and represents 11% of Progressive's total net premiums. The firm manages its claims business on a companywide basis through approximately 370 claims offices located throughout the U.S. The company has 54 centers in 41 metropolitan areas across the country that provide end-to-end resolution for auto physical damage losses. Customers can choose to bring their vehicles to one of these sites, where they can pick up a rental vehicle. Progressive's representatives will then write the estimate, select a qualified repair shop, arrange the vehicle's repair, pick-up and delivery and inspect the vehicle once the repairs are complete. Progressive maintains a catastrophe web site, ProgressiveResponds.com, to provide consumers with information about how to stay safe and protect their vehicles and boats during a catastrophic event. The company also has provides policy issuance and claims adjusting services for the Commercial Auto Insurance Procedures/Plans (CAIP), state-supervised plans active in 43 states. In 2009, the firm expanded its coverage to coal haulers and began offering car insurance in Australia through a new business, Progressive Direct.

Progressive offers its employees health, dental, vision and life insurance; tuition assistance; flexible spending accounts; an employee assistance program; on-site fitness and health centers; adoption assistance; and a 401(k) plan.

FINANCIALS:

Sales and profits are in thousands of dollars—add 000 to get the full amount. 2009 Note: Financial information for 2009 was not available for all companies at press time.

2009 Sales: $14,563,600	2009 Profits: $1,057,500	**U.S. Stock Ticker: PGR**
2008 Sales: $12,840,100	2008 Profits: $-70,000	**Int'l Ticker:** Int'l Exchange:
2007 Sales: $14,686,800	2007 Profits: $1,182,500	Employees: 24,661
2006 Sales: $14,786,400	2006 Profits: $1,647,500	Fiscal Year Ends: 12/31
2005 Sales: $14,303,400	2005 Profits: $1,393,900	Parent Company:

SALARIES/BENEFITS:

Pension Plan:	ESOP Stock Plan:	Profit Sharing:	Top Exec. Salary: $750,000	Bonus: $798,750
Savings Plan: Y	Stock Purch. Plan:		Second Exec. Salary: $380,000	Bonus: $269,800

OTHER THOUGHTS:

Apparent Women Officers or Directors: 6
Hot Spot for Advancement for Women/Minorities: Y

LOCATIONS: ("Y" = Yes)

West:	Southwest:	Midwest:	Southeast:	Northeast:	International:
Y	Y	Y	Y	Y	Y

PROTON HOLDINGS BERHAD

www.proton.com

Industry Group Code: 33611 **Ranks within this company's industry group:** Sales: 28 Profits: 19

Vehicle Manufacturing:		Dealers:		Parts:		Service:		Finance:		Specialty:	
Cars:	Y	Car Dealer New:		Manufacturers:	Y	General Service:		Leasing:		Information Systems:	
Trucks:		Car Dealer Used:		Retail:		Specialty Service:		Auto Loans:		Online Marketing:	
Motorcycles:		Truck Dealer:		Distributors:	Y	Oil Change:		Insurance:		Other:	
Specialty:	Y	RV Dealer:		Tires:		Paint and Body:				Publishing:	
Buses:		Motorcycle Dealer:		Batteries:						Rental Cars/Trucks:	
RVs:		Specialty Dealer:									

TYPES OF BUSINESS:

Automobile Manufacturing
Motorcycles
Bicycles
Distribution
Manufacturing Consulting
Financial Services
Property Investments

BRANDS/DIVISIONS/AFFILIATES:

Waja
Gen.2
Persona
Saga
Wira
Savvy
Satria
Elise

CONTACTS: *Note: Officers with more than one job title may be intentionally listed here more than once.*

Syed Zainal Abidin B Syed Mohamed Tahir, Managing Dir.
Hamdan Bin Mohd Nor, Gen. Mgr.-Int'l Sales & Svcs.
Hasnah Binti Ismail, Dir.-Human Resources Div.
Zamariah Binti Ismail, Gen. Mgr.-Info. & Comm. Tech.
Tajul Zahari Bin Abu Bakar, Dir.-Eng.
Muhammad Aris Bin Anuar, Gen. Mgr.-Mfg., Shah Alam
Michelle Kythe Lim Beng Sze, Gen. Mgr.-Legal Div.
Badrulhisham Bin Mohd Ghazali, Gen. Mgr.-Corp. Planning
Faridahanom Binti Idris, Sr. Mgr.-Corp. Comm. & Events
Kelvin Low, Contact-Investor Rel.
Vimala Menon, Dir.-Finance & Corp. Affairs Div.
Mohamed Shukor Bin Ibrahim, CEO-Proton Edar Sdn Bhd
Mohd Nizamuddin Bin Mokhtar, Gen. Mgr.-Secretarial & Compliance Div.
Claudius Meynert, Dir.-Export Markets Div.
Michael J. Kimberley, CEO-Group Lotus Plc.
Mohd Nadzmi Bin Mohd Salleh, Chmn.
Brian Collier, Managing Dir.-Proton Cars U.K. Ltd.
Razif Bin Ahmad, Dir.-Procurement Div.

Phone: 603-5191-1055	**Fax:** 603-5191-1255
Toll-Free:	
Address: HICOM Industrial Estate, Batu Tiga, Selangor, Shah Alam, 40000 Malaysia	

GROWTH PLANS/SPECIAL FEATURES:

Proton Holdings Berhad designs and produces a diverse line of consumer cars. The company is one of only four automakers in Malaysia. Proton currently exports its vehicles to 15 overseas markets, including the U.K., the Middle East, Southeast Asia and Australia, while exploring export potential in countries like Iran, Syria, China and Indonesia. Its portfolio includes the Waja family sedan, Gen.2, Arena, Saga, Wira, Savvy, Satria, Chancellor and Persona. It also manufactures the sports cars Elise and Exige through its Lotus division. Proton also produces and distributes passenger cars and motorcycles through its Proton Edar subsidiary, as well as mountain and road bicycles through its T-Bikes unit. Proton manufactures its cars in Malaysia and the U.K. The company also has manufacturing joint ventures in Vietnam and Indonesia. Proton conducts research for new technologies in facilities in the U.S. and Malaysia. Subsidiary Group Lotus manufactures cars, operates as an engineering consultant and provides automotive sales and servicing in the U.S. and the U.K. In Tanjun Malim, Malaysia, Proton boasts a 1,280-acre site featuring Proton City, a plant five times larger than any other Proton manufacturing plant and capable of manufacturing approximately 1 million cars a year. The company's next largest plant is in Shah Alam, Malaysia, with 250 acres and capable of producing approximately 230,000 cars a year. The business of the company has been enlarged and expanded to include engineering consultancy, manufacturing, distribution, financial services and property investments.

FINANCIALS: **Sales and profits are in thousands of dollars—add 000 to get the full amount. 2009 Note: Financial information for 2009 was not available for all companies at press time.**

2009 Sales: $1,836,660	2009 Profits: $-85,450	**U.S. Stock Ticker:**
2008 Sales: $1,591,740	2008 Profits: $52,270	**Int'l Ticker: 5304** Int'l Exchange: Kuala Lumpur-KLSE
2007 Sales: $1,327,190	2007 Profits: $-166,920	Employees: 11,500
2006 Sales: $1,406,200	2006 Profits: $-176,900	Fiscal Year Ends: 3/31
2005 Sales: $2,303,700	2005 Profits: $219,900	Parent Company:

SALARIES/BENEFITS:

Pension Plan:	ESOP Stock Plan:	Profit Sharing:	Top Exec. Salary: $	Bonus: $
Savings Plan:	Stock Purch. Plan:		Second Exec. Salary: $	Bonus: $

OTHER THOUGHTS:

Apparent Women Officers or Directors: 3
Hot Spot for Advancement for Women/Minorities: Y

LOCATIONS: ("Y" = Yes)

West:	Southwest:	Midwest:	Southeast:	Northeast:	International:
				Y	Y

PSA PEUGEOT CITROEN SA

www.psa-peugeot-citroen.com

Industry Group Code: 33611 **Ranks within this company's industry group:** Sales: 11 Profits: 28

Vehicle Manufacturing:		**Dealers:**		**Parts:**		**Service:**		**Finance:**		**Specialty:**	
Cars:	Y	Car Dealer New:		Manufacturers:	Y	General Service:		Leasing:		Information Systems:	
Trucks:		Car Dealer Used:		Retail:		Specialty Service:		Auto Loans:	Y	Online Marketing:	
Motorcycles:	Y	Truck Dealer:		Distributors:		Oil Change:		Insurance:		Other:	Y
Specialty:	Y	RV Dealer:		Tires:		Paint and Body:				Publishing:	
Buses:		Motorcycle Dealer:		Batteries:						Rental Cars/Trucks:	
RVs:		Specialty Dealer:									

TYPES OF BUSINESS:

Automobiles, Manufacturing
Automotive Equipment & Components
Transportation & Logistics Services
Motorcycles
Financial Services
Industrial Equipment
Engines
Clean Diesel & Hybrid Engine Technology

BRANDS/DIVISIONS/AFFILIATES:

Peugeot
Citroen
Faurecia
Gefco
Banque PSA Finance
Peugeot Motorcycles
Dongfeng Peugeot Citroen Automobile

CONTACTS: *Note: Officers with more than one job title may be intentionally listed here more than once.*

Philippe Varin, CEO
Denis Martin, VP-Human Resources
Pascal Henault, VP-Research & Automotive Innovation
Alain Sartoris, VP-IT & Exec. Dev.
Roland Vardanega, Managing Dir.-Mfg.
Jean-Claude Hanus, VP-Legal Affairs/Institutional Rel./Internal Audit
Liliane Lacourt, VP-Corp. Comm.
Isabel Marey-Semper, VP-Finance
Jean-Philippe Collin, Managing Dir.-Automobiles Peugeot
Gregoire Olivier, Exec. VP/Managing Dir.-Programs
Daniel Marteau, Dir.-Replacement Parts
Roland Vardanega, Interim Chmn.
Claude Vajsman, Dir.-China
Jean-Christophe Quemard, Dir.-Purchasing

Phone: 01-40-66-55-11	**Fax:**
Toll-Free:	
Address: 75 Ave. de la Grande-Armee, Paris, 75116 France	

GROWTH PLANS/SPECIAL FEATURES:

PSA Peugeot Citroen S.A. (PSAPC) is a leading automobile manufacturer in Europe, producing cars and light commercial vehicles under the Peugeot and Citroen brand names. The firm operates in approximately 150 countries and is focused on producing more environmentally friendly vehicles. The firms vehicles feature HDi (High-pressure Direct Injection) diesel engine technology, which helps the diesel burn more effectively, which greatly reduces solid particles in emissions. The firm also developed the Diesel Particulate Filter System (DPFS), which eliminates virtually all fine particle diesel emissions by burning them while still in the cylinder, and trapping any resulting soot in the exhaust system. Besides creating cleaner diesel engines, the company developed a hybrid Citroen engine equipped with its Stop & Start system, which turns the engine off when the vehicle reaches a full stop and starts the engine again when the accelerator is pressed. In addition to car manufacturing, PSAPC also operates the following four subsidiaries: Faurecia, a European leader in manufacturing automotive equipment and components, such as seats and exhaust systems; Gefco, a France-based provider of transportation and logistics services; Banque PSA Finance, a federation of the group's finance companies; Peugeot Motocycles, a manufacturer of 50cc-125cc scooters and motorcycles in Europe. Additionally, the firm has a joint venture with Chinese automaker Dongfeng Motor, called Dongfeng Peugeot Citroen Automobile (DPCA). This joint venture operates two manufacturing facilities in Hubei. In recent years, the company formed a joint venture with Mitsubishi Motors Corporation to produce Peugeot, Citroen and Mitsubishi vehicles in Russia. In 2009, the firm introduced several new vehicles, including The Peugeot 3008 a concept car fusion between an SUV, hatchback and multi-purpose vehicle; the Citroen C3 compact car; and the RCZ 308 coupe.

FINANCIALS: **Sales and profits are in thousands of dollars—add 000 to get the full amount. 2009 Note: Financial information for 2009 was not available for all companies at press time.**

2009 Sales: $64,595,500	2009 Profits: $-1,889,160	**U.S. Stock Ticker:**
2008 Sales: $73,365,900	2008 Profits: $-462,960	**Int'l Ticker: UG** Int'l Exchange: Paris-Euronext
2007 Sales: $79,196,800	2007 Profits: $1,194,510	Employees: 186,000
2006 Sales: $75,428,100	2006 Profits: $234,960	Fiscal Year Ends: 12/31
2005 Sales: $72,260,021	2005 Profits: $1,321,479	Parent Company:

SALARIES/BENEFITS:

Pension Plan:	ESOP Stock Plan:	Profit Sharing: Y	Top Exec. Salary: $	Bonus: $
Savings Plan:	Stock Purch. Plan:		Second Exec. Salary: $	Bonus: $

OTHER THOUGHTS:

Apparent Women Officers or Directors: 2
Hot Spot for Advancement for Women/Minorities: Y

LOCATIONS: ("Y" = Yes)

West:	Southwest:	Midwest:	Southeast:	Northeast:	International:
				Y	Y

PT ASTRA INTERNATIONAL TBK

www.astra.co.id

Industry Group Code: 33611 **Ranks within this company's industry group:** Sales: Profits:

Vehicle Manufacturing:		Dealers:		Parts:		Service:		Finance:		Specialty:	
Cars:	Y	Car Dealer New:		Manufacturers:	Y	General Service:		Leasing:		Information Systems:	
Trucks:		Car Dealer Used:		Retail:	Y	Specialty Service:		Auto Loans:	Y	Online Marketing:	
Motorcycles:	Y	Truck Dealer:		Distributors:	Y	Oil Change:		Insurance:	Y	Other:	Y
Specialty:	Y	RV Dealer:		Tires:		Paint and Body:				Publishing:	
Buses:		Motorcycle Dealer:		Batteries:						Rental Cars/Trucks:	
RVs:		Specialty Dealer:									

TYPES OF BUSINESS:

Automobiles, Manufacturing
Heavy Equipment
Financial Services
Agribusiness
Information Technology
Infrastructure
Motorcycles & Four-Wheelers
Customer Relationship Management

BRANDS/DIVISIONS/AFFILIATES:

AstraWorld
PT Astra Agro Lestari Tbk
Jardine Cycle and Carriage
PT General Electric Services

CONTACTS: *Note: Officers with more than one job title may be intentionally listed here more than once.*

Prijono Sugiarto, Pres.
Simon Collier Dixon, Dir.-IT
Arief Istanto, Chief Corp. Comm.
Simon Collier Dixon, Dir.-Corp. Finance
Gunawan Geniusahardja

Gunawan Geniusahardja, Dir.-Financial Svcs. Group
Budi Setiadharma, Pres., Board of Commissioners

Phone: 62-21-652-2555 **Fax:** 62-21-651-2058
Toll-Free:
Address: 8 Jalan Gaya Motor Raya, Sunter II, Jakarta Utara, 14330 Indonesia

GROWTH PLANS/SPECIAL FEATURES:

PT Astra International, based in Indonesia, is an automotive manufacturer. In addition to its automotive business, the firm operates in an additional five business sectors: heavy equipment, financial services, agribusiness, information technology and the general infrastructure and logistic value chain. The company's automotive segment manufactures, distributes and sells various automobile brands, including Toyota, Daihatsu, Isuzu, Nissan Diesel Trucks, Lexus, Peugeot and BMW. The segment also manufactures and distributes Honda motorcycles through a joint-venture with Honda; manufactures and distributes automobile and motorcycle parts; and provides customer relationship management services through its AstraWorld subsidiary. Astra's financing segment provides automotive financing, motorcycle financing, banking services, general insurance and heavy equipment financing. The firm's heavy equipment segment manufactures construction machinery, provides mining contracting and operates two coal mines in Kalimantan, Indonesia. The company's agribusiness segment, through subsidiary PT Astra Agro Lestari Tbk (AAL) is involved in the total cultivation, harvesting and processing of palm oil, with 20 operating mills and a total plantation area of 264 thousand hectares. Astra's information technology segment, through several subsidiaries, is a provider of document solutions and IT services in Indonesia. The segment operates through 21 branch offices throughout Indonesia. The firm's infrastructure division provides general infrastructure and transportation services, such as rental car and taxi services. Jardine Cycle and Carriage owns approximately 50.1% of the company. In June 2010, the company purchased 47% of the shares of PT General Electric Services (GES), increasing its shares in GES to 100%.

FINANCIALS: **Sales and profits are in thousands of dollars—add 000 to get the full amount. 2009 Note: Financial information for 2009 was not available for all companies at press time.**

2009 Sales: $ | 2009 Profits: $
2008 Sales: $9,686,990 | 2008 Profits: $917,260
2007 Sales: $7,621,190 | 2007 Profits: $707,960
2006 Sales: $6,050,000 | 2006 Profits: $403,120
2005 Sales: $6,215,100 | 2005 Profits: $554,500

U.S. Stock Ticker:
Int'l Ticker: ASII Int'l Exchange: Jakarta-JSX
Employees: 73,000
Fiscal Year Ends: 12/31
Parent Company:

SALARIES/BENEFITS:

Pension Plan: ESOP Stock Plan: Profit Sharing: Top Exec. Salary: $ Bonus: $
Savings Plan: Stock Purch. Plan: Second Exec. Salary: $ Bonus: $

OTHER THOUGHTS:

Apparent Women Officers or Directors:
Hot Spot for Advancement for Women/Minorities:

LOCATIONS: ("Y" = Yes)

West:	Southwest:	Midwest:	Southeast:	Northeast:	International:
					Y

REMY INTERNATIONAL INC

www.remyinc.com

Industry Group Code: 3363 **Ranks within this company's industry group:** Sales: 42 Profits: 21

Vehicle Manufacturing:		Dealers:		Parts:		Service:		Finance:		Specialty:	
Cars:		Car Dealer New:		Manufacturers:	Y	General Service:		Leasing:		Information Systems:	
Trucks:		Car Dealer Used:		Retail:		Specialty Service:		Auto Loans:		Online Marketing:	
Motorcycles:		Truck Dealer:		Distributors:	Y	Oil Change:		Insurance:		Other:	
Specialty:		RV Dealer:		Tires:		Paint and Body:				Publishing:	
Buses:		Motorcycle Dealer:		Batteries:						Rental Cars/Trucks:	
RVs:		Specialty Dealer:									

TYPES OF BUSINESS:

Electrical Components
Aftermarket Remanufacturing
Original Equipment Manufacturing
Hybrid and Electric Motors

BRANDS/DIVISIONS/AFFILIATES:

Delco Remy
World Wide Automotive
Remy Electric Motor Technologies
HVH250
Western Reman Industrial
Remy Power Products

CONTACTS:

Note: Officers with more than one job title may be intentionally listed here more than once.

John H. Weber, CEO
John H. Weber, Pres.
Fred Knechtel, CFO/Sr. VP
Jerry Mills, Sr. VP/Chief Human Resources Officer
Quinn Williams, General Counsel
James Steel, Corp. Treas./VP
Kevin Quinn, Gen. Mgr.-Remy Electric Motor Technologies
Jay Pittas, Sr. VP/Pres., Remy Inc
Jay Sanchez, Sr. VP/Pres., Remy Power Products
Harold K. Sperlich, Chmn.
Phillipe James, Pres./Managing Dir.-Europe

Phone: 765-778-6499 **Fax:** 765-778-6404
Toll-Free: 800-372-3555
Address: 600 Corporation Dr., Pendleton, IN 46064 US

GROWTH PLANS/SPECIAL FEATURES:

Remy International, Inc. is a manufacturer of electrical components for automobiles, light trucks and heavy-duty vehicles, with additional operations focusing on the aftermarket remanufacture of electrical, powertrain and drivetrain components. Under the brand names Delco Remy and World Wide Automotive, Remy markets a full line of starter motors, alternators, engines, torque converters and fuel systems. The company also provides private-label and original equipment manufacturer (OEM) contract products directly to manufacturers. In addition to automotive products, Remy manufactures a line of engine components for trains, marine, and industrial vehicles through its Western Reman Industrial business unit. The company's Remy Power Products unit is North America's largest re-manufacturer of starters and alternators, disassembling cores into their sub-components, which are then cleaned, inspected, combined with new parts and reassembled into finished products. Its European operations consist of a manufacturing plant in Hungary and another in Tunisia and distribution centers in the U.K. and Belgium. The firm has over 3,500 customers principally in North America, Europe, Latin America and Asia, which include General Motors, DaimlerChrysler, Toyota, Honda and Hyundai/Kia. Remy additionally supplies consumer outlets like Advance Auto Parts and AutoZone. In February 2010, the company formed a new business segment, Remy Electric Motor Technologies, in order to focus on the EV and HEV (electric and hybrid-electric vehicle) markets. This new segment will provide high-output electric drive motors, including its HVH250 motor it debuted in 2009, to the automotive, truck, bus and heavy equipment markets.

FINANCIALS:

Sales and profits are in thousands of dollars—add 000 to get the full amount. 2009 Note: Financial information for 2009 was not available for all companies at press time.

2009 Sales: $910,745
2008 Sales: $1,100,805
2007 Sales: $1,129,000
2006 Sales: $1,255,546
2005 Sales: $1,115,305

2009 Profits: $14,060
2008 Profits: $-5,776
2007 Profits: $
2006 Profits: $-122,517
2005 Profits: $-96,984

U.S. Stock Ticker: Private
Int'l Ticker: Int'l Exchange:
Employees:
Fiscal Year Ends: 12/31
Parent Company:

SALARIES/BENEFITS:

Pension Plan: Y ESOP Stock Plan: Profit Sharing: Top Exec. Salary: $ Bonus: $
Savings Plan: Y Stock Purch. Plan: Second Exec. Salary: $ Bonus: $

OTHER THOUGHTS:

Apparent Women Officers or Directors:
Hot Spot for Advancement for Women/Minorities:

LOCATIONS: ("Y" = Yes)

West:	Southwest:	Midwest:	Southeast:	Northeast:	International:
	Y	Y	Y	Y	Y

RENAULT SA

www.renault.com

Industry Group Code: 33611 **Ranks within this company's industry group:** Sales: 12 Profits: 31

Vehicle Manufacturing:		Dealers:		Parts:		Service:		Finance:		Specialty:	
Cars:	Y	Car Dealer New:		Manufacturers:		General Service:	Y	Leasing:	Y	Information Systems:	
Trucks:		Car Dealer Used:		Retail:		Specialty Service:		Auto Loans:	Y	Online Marketing:	
Motorcycles:		Truck Dealer:		Distributors:		Oil Change:		Insurance:		Other:	
Specialty:	Y	RV Dealer:		Tires:		Paint and Body:				Publishing:	
Buses:		Motorcycle Dealer:		Batteries:						Rental Cars/Trucks:	
RVs:		Specialty Dealer:									

TYPES OF BUSINESS:

Automobiles, Manufacturing
Financial Services
Commercial Vehicles
Two-Wheelers
Farm Machinery
Automotive Maintenance Service

BRANDS/DIVISIONS/AFFILIATES:

Renault Samsung Motors
Dacia
RCI Banque
Renault-Nissan BV
Renault Agriculture
Renault Minute
Nissan Motor Co Ltd
AvtoVAZ OAO

CONTACTS: *Note: Officers with more than one job title may be intentionally listed here more than once.*

Carlos Ghosn, CEO
Patrick Pelata, COO
Dominique Thormann, CFO/Exec. VP
Jerome Stoll, Exec. VP-Sales & Mktg./Leader-Europe Mgmt.
Gerard Leclercq, Sr. VP-Human Resources
Philippe Klein, Exec. VP-Prod. Planning, Plan & Programs
Odile Desforges, Exec. VP-Eng. & Quality
Michel Gornet, Exec. VP-Mfg. & Logistics
Christian Husson, Sr. VP-Legal Dept. & Public Affairs
Marie-Francoise Damesin, Sr. VP-Comm.
Michel Balthazard, Sr. VP-Pre-Eng., Projects & Requirements
Bernard Cambier, Sr. VP-Market Area France
Christian Mardrus, Sr. VP/Dir.-Global Logistics
Nadine Leclair, Sr. VP-Vehicle Eng.
Carlos Ghosn, Chmn.
Katsumi Nakamura, Exec. VP/Leader-Asia Africa Mgmt. Committee
Michel Faivre-Duboz, Sr. VP-Global Supply Chain

Phone: 33-1-76-84-04-04 **Fax:** 33-1-76-84-50-33
Toll-Free:
Address: 13-15 Quai le Gallo, Boulogne Billancourt, 92513 France

GROWTH PLANS/SPECIAL FEATURES:

Renault S.A. is a leading automobile manufacturer in France. The company's automobile division consists of the Renault, Renault Samsung Motors (RSM) and Dacia brands based in South Korea and Romania, respectively. It designs, develops and markets a line of small to mid-size cars, including hatchbacks and minivans, as well as light commercial vehicles and two-wheelers, such as scooters. Some of Renault's brands include the Twingo, Clio, Megane, Scenic, Modus, Laguna and Kangoo. The Kangoo Express, Trafic and Master are all light commercial vehicles. Dacia's models include the Duster, a SUV; Logan, available in a 4-door sedan and Sandero, a 4-door hatchback. RSM brands include the QM5, SM3, SM5 and SM7, all 4-door sedans. Renault's sales and finance division is comprised of RCI Banque and its subsidiaries, a total of approximately 45 companies, which provide sales, services and cash management for the group. In addition, the firm operates Renault Agriculture, a subsidiary that manufactures and markets farm machinery. The firm also has an agreement with Claas, a leader in harvesting and haymaking machinery, making Claas the majority shareholder in Renault Agriculture. Renault operates a host of automotive maintenance locations under the name Renault Minute and Motrio. There are 1,200 Renault Minute centers in 22 countries and 1,100 Motrio centers in five countries. Through its joint venture Renault-Nissan B.V., Renault owns approximately 44% of Japan-based Nissan Motor Co. Ltd. Nissan, in turn, owns approximately 15% of Renault. The French government has a 16% stake in Renault. The firm has a partnership and stake in Russian automaker AvtoVAZ OAO. In June 2009, Renault announced plans to begin manufacturing cars in Chennai, India by 2011. In April 2010, Renault-Nissan Alliance announced a partnership with Daimler AG. The Renault-Nissan Alliance will have a 3.1% stake in Daimler and Daimler a 3.1% in Renault and a 3.1% stake in Nissan.

FINANCIALS: **Sales and profits are in thousands of dollars—add 000 to get the full amount. 2009 Note: Financial information for 2009 was not available for all companies at press time.**

2009 Sales: $45,865,500 | 2009 Profits: $-4,251,590
2008 Sales: $47,578,900 | 2008 Profits: $754,140
2007 Sales: $64,891,000 | 2007 Profits: $4,360,950
2006 Sales: $54,787,900 | 2006 Profits: $3,882,700
2005 Sales: $52,749,800 | 2005 Profits: $4,406,240

U.S. Stock Ticker: RNO
Int'l Ticker: RNO Int'l Exchange: Paris-Euronext
Employees:
Fiscal Year Ends: 12/31
Parent Company:

SALARIES/BENEFITS:

Pension Plan: | ESOP Stock Plan: | Profit Sharing: | Top Exec. Salary: $ | Bonus: $
Savings Plan: | Stock Purch. Plan: | Second Exec. Salary: $ | Bonus: $

OTHER THOUGHTS:

Apparent Women Officers or Directors: 5
Hot Spot for Advancement for Women/Minorities: Y

LOCATIONS: ("Y" = Yes)

West:	Southwest:	Midwest:	Southeast:	Northeast:	International:
					Y

RENT-A-WRECK OF AMERICA INC

www.rentawreck.com

Industry Group Code: 5321 **Ranks within this company's industry group:** Sales: Profits:

Vehicle Manufacturing:		Dealers:		Parts:		Service:		Finance:		Specialty:	
Cars:		Car Dealer New:		Manufacturers:		General Service:		Leasing:		Information Systems:	
Trucks:		Car Dealer Used:		Retail:		Specialty Service:		Auto Loans:		Online Marketing:	
Motorcycles:		Truck Dealer:		Distributors:		Oil Change:		Insurance:	Y	Other:	
Specialty:		RV Dealer:		Tires:		Paint and Body:				Publishing:	
Buses:		Motorcycle Dealer:		Batteries:						Rental Cars/Trucks:	Y
RVs:		Specialty Dealer:									

TYPES OF BUSINESS:

Automobile Rental
Franchising

BRANDS/DIVISIONS/AFFILIATES:

LeasePlan USA
JJF Management Services, Inc.

CONTACTS:

Note: Officers with more than one job title may be intentionally listed here more than once.

Bill Cash, Pres.
Jason Manelli, Dir.-Mktg.
Jason Manelli, Dir.-Comm.
Mike DeLorenzo, VP
Dale Tripp, Dir.-Franchise Sales

Phone: 240-581-1350	**Fax:**
Toll-Free:	
Address: 105 Main St., Laurel, MD 20707 US	

GROWTH PLANS/SPECIAL FEATURES:

Rent-A-Wreck of America (RAWA) is a leading provider of vehicle rental services, with operations in approximately 400 locations in the U.S. and internationally in Scandinavia and Iceland. Through its Rent-A-Wreck and Priceless Rent-A-Car brands, the company rents used-vehicles. RAWA offers its Rent-A-Wreck franchises to qualified franchisees, who may either rent or lease vehicles. All of the company's franchisees offer various vehicles to their customers depending on local demand, which provides them with the flexibility to offer an appropriate range of vehicles for their areas. These vehicles can range anywhere from budgets cars to pickup trucks, vans, station wagons or luxury cars. The firm's marketing strategies have relied heavily on the use of its strange name, but the firm has also involved a few slogans, such as Don't Let the Name Fool You! and The Smart Alternative. The company also offers the option of adding a franchise service to existing businesses. Recently, RAWA completed a merger with MBFG, Inc., a subsidiary of J.J.F. Management Services, Inc. J.J.F., headquartered in Maryland, operates 24 automobile and truck rental and dealership franchises across the country, totaling about 2,500 vehicles. The company recently partnered with LeasePlan USA for emergency roadside service for its rental vehicles. Recently, the company opened new branches in Fontana, California and Baton Rouge, Louisiana.

FINANCIALS:

Sales and profits are in thousands of dollars—add 000 to get the full amount. 2009 Note: Financial information for 2009 was not available for all companies at press time.

2009 Sales: $	2009 Profits: $	**U.S. Stock Ticker: Private**
2008 Sales: $	2008 Profits: $	**Int'l Ticker:** Int'l Exchange:
2007 Sales: $	2007 Profits: $	Employees:
2006 Sales: $	2006 Profits: $	Fiscal Year Ends: 3/31
2005 Sales: $	2005 Profits: $	Parent Company:

SALARIES/BENEFITS:

Pension Plan:	ESOP Stock Plan:	Profit Sharing:	Top Exec. Salary: $	Bonus: $
Savings Plan:	Stock Purch. Plan:		Second Exec. Salary: $	Bonus: $

OTHER THOUGHTS:

Apparent Women Officers or Directors:
Hot Spot for Advancement for Women/Minorities:

LOCATIONS: ("Y" = Yes)

West:	Southwest:	Midwest:	Southeast:	Northeast:	International:
Y	Y	Y	Y	Y	Y

REXHALL INDUSTRIES INC

www.rexhall.com

Industry Group Code: 336120 **Ranks within this company's industry group:** Sales: Profits:

Vehicle Manufacturing:		Dealers:		Parts:		Service:		Finance:		Specialty:	
Cars:		Car Dealer New:		Manufacturers:		General Service:		Leasing:		Information Systems:	
Trucks:		Car Dealer Used:		Retail:		Specialty Service:		Auto Loans:		Online Marketing:	
Motorcycles:		Truck Dealer:		Distributors:		Oil Change:		Insurance:		Other:	
Specialty:		RV Dealer:		Tires:		Paint and Body:				Publishing:	
Buses:		Motorcycle Dealer:		Batteries:						Rental Cars/Trucks:	
RVs:	Y	Specialty Dealer:									

TYPES OF BUSINESS:

RV Manufacturing

BRANDS/DIVISIONS/AFFILIATES:

Aerbus
Rexair
Vision
BaseCamp
Sanscape
TREX
RoseAir

CONTACTS: *Note: Officers with more than one job title may be intentionally listed here more than once.*

William J. Rex, CEO
William J. Rex, Pres.
Michael R. Pieper, CFO
Michael R. Pieper, VP-Admin.
James C. Rex, VP/Gen. Mgr.-Consumer Affairs
William J. Rex, Chmn.

Phone: 661-726-0565 **Fax:** 661-726-5813
Toll-Free: 800-765-7500
Address: 46147 7th St. W., Lancaster, CA 93534 US

GROWTH PLANS/SPECIAL FEATURES:

Rexhall Industries, Inc. designs, manufactures and sells Class A recreational vehicles (RVs). The firm's 2010 brands are RexAir, RoseAir and Aerbus, three deluxe motorhomes with a variety of available features. Rexhall has also manufactured the Vision, BaseCamp and the Sanscape, which are now referred to as the company's standard brands. The models range in size from 27-40 feet long. All of the company's models have optional patented TREX slide rooms, which allow the width of the vehicle, in certain rooms, to be increased when parked. The company's vehicles feature a steel frame that is 100% welded, instead of the traditional fastened method of constructing an RV frame. The benefit of this method is that it provides more strength and stability, as well as a quieter ride, than the traditional methods. Rexhall manufactures its own molded fiberglass components, upholstered items, cabinetry, counter tops, driver doors, front entry doors and exterior storage compartment doors from its manufacturing facilities in Lancaster, California.

FINANCIALS: **Sales and profits are in thousands of dollars—add 000 to get the full amount. 2009 Note: Financial information for 2009 was not available for all companies at press time.**

2009 Sales: $	2009 Profits: $	**U.S. Stock Ticker: REXLQ**
2008 Sales: $	2008 Profits: $	**Int'l Ticker:** Int'l Exchange:
2007 Sales: $	2007 Profits: $	Employees:
2006 Sales: $	2006 Profits: $	Fiscal Year Ends: 12/31
2005 Sales: $	2005 Profits: $	Parent Company:

SALARIES/BENEFITS:

Pension Plan:	ESOP Stock Plan:	Profit Sharing:	Top Exec. Salary: $	Bonus: $
Savings Plan:	Stock Purch. Plan:		Second Exec. Salary: $	Bonus: $

OTHER THOUGHTS:

Apparent Women Officers or Directors:
Hot Spot for Advancement for Women/Minorities:

LOCATIONS: ("Y" = Yes)

West:	Southwest:	Midwest:	Southeast:	Northeast:	International:
Y					

RHEINMETALL AG

www.rheinmetall.com

Industry Group Code: 3363 **Ranks within this company's industry group:** Sales: 22 Profits: 44

Vehicle Manufacturing:		Dealers:		Parts:		Service:		Finance:		Specialty:	
Cars:		Car Dealer New:		Manufacturers:	Y	General Service:		Leasing:		Information Systems:	
Trucks:		Car Dealer Used:		Retail:		Specialty Service:		Auto Loans:		Online Marketing:	
Motorcycles:		Truck Dealer:		Distributors:		Oil Change:		Insurance:		Other:	Y
Specialty:	Y	RV Dealer:		Tires:		Paint and Body:				Publishing:	
Buses:		Motorcycle Dealer:		Batteries:						Rental Cars/Trucks:	
RVs:		Specialty Dealer:									

TYPES OF BUSINESS:

Automotive Components Manufacturing
Military Vehicles
Weapons & Ammunition
Defense Electronics
Air Defense Systems
Command & Control Systems
Reconnaissance Systems
Training & Simulator Operations

BRANDS/DIVISIONS/AFFILIATES:

Kolbenschmidt Pierburg AG
KS Kolbenschmidt
Pierburg GmbH
Pierburg Pump Technology
KS Aluminum-Technologie AG
KS Gleitlager GmbH
Permaglide
MS Motor Systems International GmbH

CONTACTS: *Note: Officers with more than one job title may be intentionally listed here more than once.*

Klaus Eberhardt, CEO/Chmn.-Defense Sector
Herbert Muller, CFO
Gerd Kleinert, Head-Mktg., Automotive Sector
Ingo Hecke, Head-Human Resources
Ludwig Dammer, Head-Prototypes Svcs., Pierburg GmbH
Ludwig Dammer, Head-Tech.
Andreas Beyer, Head-Law/Internal Auditing/Mergers & Acquisitions
Gerd Kleinert, Head-Oper., Automotive Sector
Gerd Kleinert, Head-Strategy, Automotive Sector
Peter Rucker, Head-Corp. Comm.
Franz-Bernd Reich, Head-Investor Rel.
Peter P. Merten, Head-Finance/Controlling/IT, Automotive Sector
Helmut P. Merch, Head-IT/Finance/Controlling, Defense Sector
Gerd Kleinert, Chmn.-Automotive/CEO-Kolbenschmidt Pierburg AG
Detlef Moog, Head-Land Systems/Weapons/Munitions/Propellants
Gero Voss, CEO-Rheinmetall Denel Munition (Pty) Ltd.
Klaus Greinert, Chmn.
Shaun Liebenberg, Head-Int'l Bus. Dev., Defense Sector

Phone: 49-211-473-01	Fax: 49-211-473-4746
Toll-Free:	
Address: Rheinmetall Platz 1, Dusseldorf, 40476 Germany	

GROWTH PLANS/SPECIAL FEATURES:

Rheinmetall AG, established in 1889, makes automotive components and military defense equipment. The automotive sector, run by Kolbenschmidt Pierburg AG, specializes in module and systems production. This sector exclusively supplies the new Audi A6 gasoline engine block. Kolbenschmidt operates the following divisions. KS Kolbenschmidt manufactures various pistons. Pierburg GmbH manufactures air management, actuator, emission control systems and solenoid valves. Pierburg Pump Technology offers oil, vacuum and water pumps. KS Aluminum-Technologie AG manufactures aluminum engine blocks and cylinder heads. KS Gleitlager GmbH manufactures various bearings, including continuous casting products and its Permaglide brand dry bearings. Lastly, MS Motor Service International GmbH mainly sells parts for the aftermarket sector. Rheinmetall's defense sector business, one of Europe's top land forces equipment suppliers, supplying many European military bases, operates the following six divisions. The land systems division mainly manufactures combat vehicles including bridge-laying tanks, mine-clearing systems and armored recovery vehicles, as well as offering turrets and weapons stations. The weapons and munitions division manufactures lethal ammunition, such as the 120 millimeter shells for the Leopard 2 tank, and non-lethal weapons such as medium-energy lasers. The propellants division mainly manufactures artillery charges, but also develops automotive, aviation, medical and fastening applications for its products. The air defense division primarily manufactures short-range antiaircraft systems. The C4ISTAR division manufactures technology packages that assist reconnaissance systems, command and control systems, fire control units, ground surveillance sensors and thermal-imaging systems. Lastly, the defense sector also operates a simulation and training division, which manufactures air, land and sea training simulators.

FINANCIALS: **Sales and profits are in thousands of dollars—add 000 to get the full amount. 2009 Note: Financial information for 2009 was not available for all companies at press time.**

2009 Sales: $4,661,110	2009 Profits: $-78,910	**U.S. Stock Ticker:**
2008 Sales: $5,154,670	2008 Profits: $179,860	**Int'l Ticker: RHM** Int'l Exchange: Frankfurt-Euronext
2007 Sales: $5,335,860	2007 Profits: $199,850	Employees: 21,020
2006 Sales: $4,830,920	2006 Profits: $163,870	Fiscal Year Ends: 12/31
2005 Sales: $4,413,870	2005 Profits: $150,790	Parent Company:

SALARIES/BENEFITS:

Pension Plan:	ESOP Stock Plan:	Profit Sharing:	Top Exec. Salary: $	Bonus: $
Savings Plan:	Stock Purch. Plan:		Second Exec. Salary: $	Bonus: $

OTHER THOUGHTS:

Apparent Women Officers or Directors:
Hot Spot for Advancement for Women/Minorities:

LOCATIONS: ("Y" = Yes)

West:	Southwest:	Midwest:	Southeast:	Northeast:	International:
		Y		Y	Y

RICART AUTOMOTIVE INC

www.ricart.com

Industry Group Code: 441110 **Ranks within this company's industry group:** Sales: Profits:

Vehicle Manufacturing:		Dealers:		Parts:		Service:		Finance:		Specialty:	
Cars:		Car Dealer New:	Y	Manufacturers:		General Service:	Y	Leasing:		Information Systems:	
Trucks:		Car Dealer Used:	Y	Retail:	Y	Specialty Service:		Auto Loans:	Y	Online Marketing:	
Motorcycles:		Truck Dealer:		Distributors:		Oil Change:		Insurance:		Other:	Y
Specialty:		RV Dealer:	Y	Tires:		Paint and Body:				Publishing:	
Buses:		Motorcycle Dealer:		Batteries:						Rental Cars/Trucks:	
RVs:		Specialty Dealer:	Y								

TYPES OF BUSINESS:

Auto Dealers, Retail
Reconditioned Airplane Sales
Mortgage Services
Van & RV Sales

BRANDS/DIVISIONS/AFFILIATES:

Ricart Ford
Ricart RV Land
Central Ohio Credit Corp.
Ricart Aviation Sales
Ricart Credit Solutions
Ricart Cares
Ricart Chevrolet
Ricart Imports

CONTACTS:

Note: Officers with more than one job title may be intentionally listed here more than once.

Paul Fred Ricart, Jr., Co-CEO
Rhett C. Ricart, Pres./Co-CEO

Phone: 614-836-6265	**Fax:** 614-836-6563
Toll-Free:	
Address: 4255 S. Hamilton Rd., Columbus, OH 43125 US	

GROWTH PLANS/SPECIAL FEATURES:

Ricart Automotive, Inc. is one of the world's largest new and used car dealership. The company offers several vehicle brands, including Ford, Nissan, Hyundai, Kia, Chevrolet, Mazda and Mitsubishi at most of its dealerships, including its 66-acre Ricart Mega Mall. Ricart provides service, parts and financing. From the company web site, customers can search inventory by make, model, year and price; apply for financing; get a quote; or check the Ask Patty web site, which gives automotive advice to women. The firm also operates Ricart RV Land which offers recreational vehicles, and features brands such as Forest River Rockwood, Forest River Roo and Four Winds Dutchman. The company is also a supplier of RV parts and accessories. In addition, Ricart operates non-automotive businesses through Central Ohio Credit Corp., Ricart Credit Solutions and Ricart Aviation Sales, which purchases and sells reconditioned airplanes. The company is owned by the Ricart family, which has owned the firm since its inception in 1953. Brothers Fred and Rhett Ricart acquired the firm in 1982 from their father, and have since added nine dealerships in the Columbus, Ohio region.

FINANCIALS:

Sales and profits are in thousands of dollars—add 000 to get the full amount. 2009 Note: Financial information for 2009 was not available for all companies at press time.

2009 Sales: $	2009 Profits: $	**U.S. Stock Ticker: Private**
2008 Sales: $	2008 Profits: $	**Int'l Ticker:** Int'l Exchange:
2007 Sales: $152,300	2007 Profits: $	Employees:
2006 Sales: $	2006 Profits: $	Fiscal Year Ends: 12/31
2005 Sales: $	2005 Profits: $	Parent Company:

SALARIES/BENEFITS:

Pension Plan:	ESOP Stock Plan:	Profit Sharing:	Top Exec. Salary: $	Bonus: $
Savings Plan:	Stock Purch. Plan:		Second Exec. Salary: $	Bonus: $

OTHER THOUGHTS:

Apparent Women Officers or Directors:
Hot Spot for Advancement for Women/Minorities:

LOCATIONS: ("Y" = Yes)

West:	Southwest:	Midwest:	Southeast:	Northeast:	International:
		Y			

RIETER HOLDING LTD

www.rieter.com

Industry Group Code: 3363 **Ranks within this company's industry group:** Sales: 33 Profits: 49

Vehicle Manufacturing:		Dealers:		Parts:		Service:		Finance:		Specialty:	
Cars:		Car Dealer New:		Manufacturers:	Y	General Service:		Leasing:		Information Systems:	
Trucks:		Car Dealer Used:		Retail:		Specialty Service:		Auto Loans:		Online Marketing:	
Motorcycles:		Truck Dealer:		Distributors:		Oil Change:		Insurance:		Other:	Y
Specialty:		RV Dealer:		Tires:		Paint and Body:				Publishing:	
Buses:		Motorcycle Dealer:		Batteries:						Rental Cars/Trucks:	
RVs:		Specialty Dealer:									

TYPES OF BUSINESS:

Auto Parts Manufacturing
Interior Trim
Noise Control Systems
Thermal Insulation Products
Dash Assemblies
Plastic Extrusion Systems
Textile Spinning Systems
Automotive Carpets

BRANDS/DIVISIONS/AFFILIATES:

Rieter Textile Systems
Rieter Automotive Systems

CONTACTS:

Note: Officers with more than one job title may be intentionally listed here more than once.

Hartmut Reuter, CEO
Urs Leinhauser, CFO
Thomas Anwander, Corp. Sec.
Peter Gradel, Head-Corp. Comm.
Peter Gnagi, CEO-Textile Systems
Wolfgang Drees, CEO-Automotive Systems
Erwin Stoller, Chmn.

Phone: 41-52-208-79-55	**Fax:** 41-52-208-70-60
Toll-Free:	
Address: Schlosstalstrasse 43, Winterthur, CH-8406 Switzerland	

GROWTH PLANS/SPECIAL FEATURES:

Rieter Holding, Ltd. is a Swiss-based industrial group that provides systems and services for the automotive, textile and plastics industries. The group is composed of two divisions: Rieter Textile Systems (representing 27% of the firm's total sales), which develops and produces machinery and integrated systems for converting fibers and plastics into yarns, nonwovens and pellets, and whose products include spinning systems, extrusion systems, pelletizing and plastic machinery and parts; and Rieter Automotive Systems (73% of total sales), which develops and produces components, modules and integrated systems from fibers, plastics and metals, to provide acoustic comfort and thermal insulation in motor vehicles. Reiter Automotive's products include noise control, thermal insulation and trim products, such as absorbers and dampers, headliners, heat shields, flooring mats and systems, engine compartments and encapsulations, door panel inserts, dash assemblies and insulators, molded carpets and trim parts, package trays, trunk trim, under-floor systems and wheelhouse treatments. Rieter's customer base includes Audi, BMW, Daimler, Chrysler, GM and Toyota. Rieter operates about 70 facilities, with subsidiaries and associated companies in 21 countries around the world, including Argentina, Belgium, Brazil, China, Germany, France, Great Britain, India, Italy, Canada, The Netherlands, Poland, Portugal, Spain, Turkey, Czech Republic and the U.S. In April 2009, the company sold its Rieter Real Estate Ltd. subsidy as part of a plan to restructure the firm's activities down to its core components. In 2010, the firm continued its restructuring plan by selling subsidiaries Rieter Perfojet, part of its textile systems division, and Idea Institute, an Italian design and engineering firm that was part of its automotive division.

FINANCIALS:

Sales and profits are in thousands of dollars—add 000 to get the full amount. 2009 Note: Financial information for 2009 was not available for all companies at press time.

2009 Sales: $1,860,310	2009 Profits: $-220,660	**U.S. Stock Ticker:**
2008 Sales: $2,961,940	2008 Profits: $-373,910	**Int'l Ticker: RIEN** Int'l Exchange: Zurich-SWX
2007 Sales: $3,484,200	2007 Profits: $181,400	Employees: 12,761
2006 Sales: $3,164,100	2006 Profits: $135,600	Fiscal Year Ends: 12/31
2005 Sales: $2,598,810	2005 Profits: $114,960	Parent Company:

SALARIES/BENEFITS:

Pension Plan:	ESOP Stock Plan:	Profit Sharing:	Top Exec. Salary: $	Bonus: $
Savings Plan:	Stock Purch. Plan: Y		Second Exec. Salary: $	Bonus: $

OTHER THOUGHTS:

Apparent Women Officers or Directors:
Hot Spot for Advancement for Women/Minorities:

LOCATIONS: ("Y" = Yes)

West:	Southwest:	Midwest:	Southeast:	Northeast:	International:
		Y	Y		Y

RIZZA AUTOMOTIVE GROUP

www.rizzacars.com

Industry Group Code: 441110 **Ranks within this company's industry group:** Sales: Profits:

Vehicle Manufacturing:		Dealers:		Parts:		Service:		Finance:		Specialty:	
Cars:		Car Dealer New:	Y	Manufacturers:		General Service:	Y	Leasing:		Information Systems:	
Trucks:		Car Dealer Used:	Y	Retail:	Y	Specialty Service:		Auto Loans:	Y	Online Marketing:	
Motorcycles:		Truck Dealer:		Distributors:		Oil Change:		Insurance:		Other:	
Specialty:		RV Dealer:		Tires:		Paint and Body:				Publishing:	
Buses:		Motorcycle Dealer:		Batteries:						Rental Cars/Trucks:	
RVs:		Specialty Dealer:									

TYPES OF BUSINESS:

Auto Dealers, Retail
Parts & Service
Financing

BRANDS/DIVISIONS/AFFILIATES:

Rizza Rewards
Rizza Cash
Joe Rizza Porsche
Joe Rizza Ford
Rizza Chevrolet

CONTACTS: *Note: Officers with more than one job title may be intentionally listed here more than once.*

Joseph R. Rizza, CEO
Dan McMillan, CFO
Jim Mac, Gen. Sales Mgr.-Joe Rizza Acura

Phone: 708-364-2200 **Fax:** 708-364-2428
Toll-Free:
Address: 8150 W. 159th St., Orland Park, IL 60462 US

GROWTH PLANS/SPECIAL FEATURES:

Rizza Automotive Group operates a chain of new and used car dealerships in the Chicago area. The group has eight locations in Naperville, Tinley Park, Orland Park, North Riverside and Bridgeview. Rizza carries makes including Ford, Chevrolet, Lincoln, Mercury, Cadillac, Buick, Saab, Kia, Suzuki, Subaru and Acura, as well as high-end brands such as Porsche and Hummer. The company also sells pre-owned vehicles, Ford fleets sales and each dealership has a parts and services department. When a customer purchases a vehicle from a Rizza dealership, they receive a Rizza Rewards card that allows the customer to earn Rizza Cash when they bring the vehicle back for servicing. Rizza Cash is good towards the purchase of a new vehicle or further parts and services visits. At the Rizza web site, customers can search the new and used inventory, schedule a test drive and access the company's finance department. In addition, the company provides separate web sites to search the firm's inventory of vehicles, the combined inventory of used cars or the bargain lot, which contains all of the company's bargain priced vehicles. Rizza dealerships include Joe Rizza Porsche, Joe Rizza Ford and Rizza Chevrolet.

FINANCIALS: **Sales and profits are in thousands of dollars—add 000 to get the full amount. 2009 Note: Financial information for 2009 was not available for all companies at press time.**

2009 Sales: $ 2009 Profits: $
2008 Sales: $ 2008 Profits: $
2007 Sales: $ 2007 Profits: $
2006 Sales: $ 2006 Profits: $
2005 Sales: $ 2005 Profits: $

U.S. Stock Ticker: Private
Int'l Ticker: Int'l Exchange:
Employees:
Fiscal Year Ends: 12/31
Parent Company:

SALARIES/BENEFITS:

Pension Plan: ESOP Stock Plan: Profit Sharing: Top Exec. Salary: $ Bonus: $
Savings Plan: Stock Purch. Plan: Second Exec. Salary: $ Bonus: $

OTHER THOUGHTS:

Apparent Women Officers or Directors:
Hot Spot for Advancement for Women/Minorities:

LOCATIONS: ("Y" = Yes)

West:	Southwest:	Midwest:	Southeast:	Northeast:	International:
		Y			

ROBERT BOSCH GMBH

www.bosch.com

Industry Group Code: 3363 **Ranks within this company's industry group:** Sales: 1 Profits: 60

Vehicle Manufacturing:		Dealers:		Parts:		Service:		Finance:		Specialty:	
Cars:		Car Dealer New:		Manufacturers:	Y	General Service:		Leasing:		Information Systems:	
Trucks:		Car Dealer Used:		Retail:		Specialty Service:		Auto Loans:		Online Marketing:	
Motorcycles:		Truck Dealer:		Distributors:		Oil Change:		Insurance:		Other:	
Specialty:		RV Dealer:		Tires:		Paint and Body:				Publishing:	
Buses:		Motorcycle Dealer:		Batteries:						Rental Cars/Trucks:	
RVs:		Specialty Dealer:									

TYPES OF BUSINESS:

Auto Parts Manufacturing
Gasoline Systems
Motor, Control & Motion Products
Chassis Systems
Electronics & Multimedia
Energy & Body Systems
Security Systems
Power Tools

BRANDS/DIVISIONS/AFFILIATES:

Bosch Security Systems
Aethon Inc
ZF Steering Systems GmbH
Bosch Rexroth
Blaupunkt
Bosch-Siemens Hausgerate
Accu Industries Inc
Shenzhen Wei Ning Da Industrial Co Ltd

CONTACTS:

Note: Officers with more than one job title may be intentionally listed here more than once.

Franz Fehrenbach, Managing Dir.
Gerhard Kummel, Dir.-Finance & Financial Statements
Peter Tyroller, Dir.-Sales & Mktg.
Wolfgang Malchow, Dir.-Human Resources & Social Svcs.
Siegfried Dais, Dir.-Research
Siegfried Dais, Dir.-IT
Siegfried Dais, Dir.-Advance Eng
Peter J. Marks, Dir.-Mfg. Coordination
Gerhard Kummel, Dir.-Bus. Admin.
Wolfgang Malchow, Dir.-Legal Svcs., Taxes & Internal Auditing
Franz Fehrenbach, Dir.-Corp. Planning, Real Estate & Facilities
Franz Fehrenbach, Dir.-Corp. Comm.
Gerhard Kummel, Dir.-Planning & Controlling
Peter Tyroller, Dir.-Original Equipment Sales
Bernd Bohr, Chmn.-Automotive Group & Systems Integration
Peter J. Marks, CEO/Chmn./Pres., North & South America
Volkmar Denner, Dir.-Electrical Drives & Automotive Electronics
Franz Fehrenbach, Chmn.
Uwe Raschke, Dir.-Asia Pacific
Rudolf Colm, Dir.-Purchasing, Logistics & Insurance

Phone: 49-711-811-0	**Fax:** 49-711-811-6630
Toll-Free:	
Address: Postfach 106050, Stuttgart, 70049 Germany	

GROWTH PLANS/SPECIAL FEATURES:

Robert Bosch GmbH is one of the world's leading manufacturers of automotive components. It has operations in more than 50 countries. The company operates in four business sectors: automotive technology; industrial technology; and consumer goods and building technology. Its automotive divisions deal in gasoline systems; diesel systems; chassis systems; energy and body systems; car multimedia; automotive electronics; and automotive aftermarket products. Bosch's products include braking and fuel injection systems, starters and alternators. The segment is also involved in a joint venture with ZH Friedrichshafen AG called ZF Steering Systems GmbH, which develops, produces and sells steering technology for passenger and commercial vehicles. The industrial technology unit includes Bosch Rexroth, which supplies a range of motor, control and motion products, and the packaging technology division. The consumer goods and building technology group deals in power tools, thermotechnology, household appliances, security systems, communications and broadband networks. The Blaupunkt unit is a major name in car audio equipment. The firm also owns 50% of European appliance maker Bosch-Siemens Hausgerate. Bosch is a leader in antilock brake technology, clean diesel technology and factory automation. Some of the subsidiaries of Bosch include Accu Industries Inc., a vehicle equipment manufacturer, and Shenzhen Wei Ning Da Industrial Co Ltd (Weicon), a Shenzhen, China-based diagnostics equipment specialist. In December 2009, the firm formed a joint venture called Bosch Emission Systems GmbH & Co. KG with Eberspacher GmbH & Co. KG, to provide diesel exhaust after treatment to the automobile industry. In April 2010, the company announced a $5 million partnership with Aethon, Inc., to collaborate on future engineering products.

Employees of Bosch USA are offered benefits, including medical, dental and vision coverage; long-term care insurance; life and accidental death and dismemberment insurance; travel accident insurance; paid vacations; short and long-term disability coverage; and an educational assistance program.

FINANCIALS:

Sales and profits are in thousands of dollars—add 000 to get the full amount. 2009 Note: Financial information for 2009 was not available for all companies at press time.

2009 Sales: $50,929,800	2009 Profits: $-1,596,980	**U.S. Stock Ticker: Private**
2008 Sales: $60,222,300	2008 Profits: $496,440	**Int'l Ticker:** Int'l Exchange:
2007 Sales: $61,814,400	2007 Profits: $3,803,350	Employees:
2006 Sales: $68,104,700	2006 Profits: $3,383,100	Fiscal Year Ends: 12/31
2005 Sales: $64,638,900	2005 Profits: $3,819,620	Parent Company:

SALARIES/BENEFITS:

Pension Plan: Y	ESOP Stock Plan:	Profit Sharing:	Top Exec. Salary: $	Bonus: $
Savings Plan: Y	Stock Purch. Plan:		Second Exec. Salary: $	Bonus: $

OTHER THOUGHTS:

Apparent Women Officers or Directors:
Hot Spot for Advancement for Women/Minorities:

LOCATIONS: ("Y" = Yes)

West:	Southwest:	Midwest:	Southeast:	Northeast:	International:
Y	Y	Y	Y	Y	Y

ROLLS ROYCE MOTOR CAR LIMITED

www.rolls-roycemotorcars.com

Industry Group Code: 33611 **Ranks within this company's industry group:** Sales: Profits:

Vehicle Manufacturing:		Dealers:		Parts:		Service:		Finance:		Specialty:	
Cars:	Y	Car Dealer New:	Y	Manufacturers:	Y	General Service:		Leasing:		Information Systems:	
Trucks:		Car Dealer Used:	Y	Retail:		Specialty Service:		Auto Loans:		Online Marketing:	
Motorcycles:		Truck Dealer:		Distributors:		Oil Change:		Insurance:		Other:	
Specialty:		RV Dealer:		Tires:		Paint and Body:				Publishing:	
Buses:		Motorcycle Dealer:		Batteries:						Rental Cars/Trucks:	
RVs:		Specialty Dealer:									

TYPES OF BUSINESS:

Automobile Design & Manufacture
Luxury Automobile Sales
Automobile Customizing
Pre-owned Luxury Automobile Sales

BRANDS/DIVISIONS/AFFILIATES:

BMW (Bayerische Motoren Weke AG)
Bentley Motors
Phantom
RR4
Drophead Coupe
Bespoke
Ghost

CONTACTS:

Note: Officers with more than one job title may be intentionally listed here more than once.

Torsten Muller-Otvos, CEO
Jolyon Nash, Dir.-Mktg. & Sales
Nigel Wonnacott, Mgr.-Prod. Comm.
Helmut Riedl, Dir.-Eng.
Xaver Franz, Dir.-Mfg.
Richard Carter, Dir.-Global Comm.
Andrew B. Shilston, Dir.-Finance
Paul Harris, Dir.-APAC
Brenda Pek, Gen. Mgr.-South & East APAC
James Crichton, Dir.-Middle East
Ian Robertson, Chmn.
David Archibald, Dir.-Europe & South Africa

Phone: 44-1234-384000	**Fax:** 44-1234-384100
Toll-Free:	
Address: The Drive, Westhampnett, Chichester, West Sussex PO18 0SH UK	

GROWTH PLANS/SPECIAL FEATURES:

Rolls-Royce Motor Car Ltd., a subsidiary of BMW, is a predominant designer and manufacturer of fully customizable luxury automobiles. Bespoke, the company's automobile modification program, allows customers to intricately customize any aspect of the automobile. The company's dealer network, closely allied with that of Bentley Motors, Inc., spans the globe with locations in 31 countries. The firm currently offers four primary vehicle models: the Phantom, Phantom Coupe, Phantom Drophead Coupe and the Phantom Extended Wheelbase. The company also has experimental models such as the 100EX and 101EX. Rolls-Royce maintains a pre-owned service through its dealership network. Through the years, the company's models have included the Phantom V and VI, from 1959 to 1991; the Silver Shadow I and II, from 1965 to 1981; the Corniche I-IV, from 1971 to 1996; the Camargue 1975 to 1986; the Silver Spirit lines, from 1980 to 1989; the Corniche, from 2000 to 2002; and the Phantom, from 2003 to present. The Phantom remains the flagship automobile for Rolls-Royce. In early 2009, Roll-Royce officially named the RR4 the Rolls-Royce Ghost.

FINANCIALS:

Sales and profits are in thousands of dollars—add 000 to get the full amount. 2009 Note: Financial information for 2009 was not available for all companies at press time.

2009 Sales: $	2009 Profits: $	**U.S. Stock Ticker: Subsidiary**
2008 Sales: $	2008 Profits: $	**Int'l Ticker:** Int'l Exchange:
2007 Sales: $	2007 Profits: $	Employees:
2006 Sales: $	2006 Profits: $	Fiscal Year Ends: 12/31
2005 Sales: $	2005 Profits: $	Parent Company: BMW (BAYERISCHE MOTOREN WERKE AG)

SALARIES/BENEFITS:

Pension Plan:	ESOP Stock Plan:	Profit Sharing:	Top Exec. Salary: $	Bonus: $
Savings Plan:	Stock Purch. Plan:		Second Exec. Salary: $	Bonus: $

OTHER THOUGHTS:

Apparent Women Officers or Directors: 1
Hot Spot for Advancement for Women/Minorities:

LOCATIONS: ("Y" = Yes)

West:	Southwest:	Midwest:	Southeast:	Northeast:	International:
					Y

ROSENTHAL AUTOMOTIVE ORGANIZATION www.rosenthalauto.com

Industry Group Code: 441110 **Ranks within this company's industry group:** Sales: Profits:

Vehicle Manufacturing:		Dealers:		Parts:		Service:		Finance:		Specialty:	
Cars:		Car Dealer New:	Y	Manufacturers:		General Service:	Y	Leasing:		Information Systems:	
Trucks:		Car Dealer Used:	Y	Retail:	Y	Specialty Service:		Auto Loans:		Online Marketing:	Y
Motorcycles:		Truck Dealer:		Distributors:		Oil Change:		Insurance:		Other:	
Specialty:		RV Dealer:		Tires:		Paint and Body:				Publishing:	
Buses:		Motorcycle Dealer:		Batteries:						Rental Cars/Trucks:	
RVs:		Specialty Dealer:									

TYPES OF BUSINESS:

Auto Dealer
Fleet Sales
Repair Service
Online Service Appointment Scheduling

BRANDS/DIVISIONS/AFFILIATES:

Rosenthal Chevrolet
Rosenthal Chrysler
Rosenthal Fairfax Honda
Rosenthal Landmark Honda
Rosenthal Jaguar Tysons
Rosenthal Jaguar Chantilly
Rosenthal Jeep
Rosenthal Land Rover Tysons

CONTACTS: *Note: Officers with more than one job title may be intentionally listed here more than once.*

Phone:	**Fax:**
Toll-Free: 877-300-6394	
Address: 3100 Jefferson Davis Highway, Arlington, VA 22202 US	

GROWTH PLANS/SPECIAL FEATURES:

Rosenthal Automotive Organization is an automotive dealership operating through approximately seven locations in the Washington, D.C. Metro area, Maryland and Virginia. The firm sells cars, trucks and SUVs (sport utility vehicles). Brands sold include BMW, Audi, Chevrolet, Jeep, Chrysler, Honda, Mazda, Porsche, Volvo, Acura, Jaguar, Land Rover and Volkswagen. Rosenthal Automotive additionally sells used cars and offers online service appointment scheduling and an online parts order form. The company's dealerships in Virginia include Rosenthal Chevrolet, Rosenthal Chrysler, Rosenthal Fairfax Honda, BMW of Arlington, Rosenthal Landmark Honda, Rosenthal Jaguar Tysons, Rosenthal Jaguar Chantilly, Rosenthal Jeep, Rosenthal Land Rover Tysons, Rosenthal Land Rover Chantilly, Rosenthal Arlington Mazda, Rosenthal Fairfax Volvo, Porsche of Arlington and Rosenthal Fairfax Volkswagen. Rosenthal Automotive's Maryland dealerships include Rosenthal Gaithersburg Acura and Rosenthal Gaithersburg Mazda.

FINANCIALS: **Sales and profits are in thousands of dollars—add 000 to get the full amount. 2009 Note: Financial information for 2009 was not available for all companies at press time.**

2009 Sales: $	2009 Profits: $	**U.S. Stock Ticker: Private**
2008 Sales: $	2008 Profits: $	**Int'l Ticker:** Int'l Exchange:
2007 Sales: $	2007 Profits: $	Employees:
2006 Sales: $	2006 Profits: $	Fiscal Year Ends:
2005 Sales: $	2005 Profits: $	Parent Company:

SALARIES/BENEFITS:

Pension Plan:	ESOP Stock Plan:	Profit Sharing:	Top Exec. Salary: $	Bonus: $
Savings Plan:	Stock Purch. Plan:		Second Exec. Salary: $	Bonus: $

OTHER THOUGHTS:

Apparent Women Officers or Directors:
Hot Spot for Advancement for Women/Minorities:

LOCATIONS: ("Y" = Yes)

West:	Southwest:	Midwest:	Southeast:	Northeast:	International:
				Y	

RUSH ENTERPRISES INC

www.rushenterprises.com

Industry Group Code: 441110 **Ranks within this company's industry group:** Sales: 9 Profits: 10

Vehicle Manufacturing:		Dealers:		Parts:		Service:		Finance:		Specialty:	
Cars:		Car Dealer New:		Manufacturers:		General Service:	Y	Leasing:	Y	Information Systems:	
Trucks:	Y	Car Dealer Used:		Retail:	Y	Specialty Service:	Y	Auto Loans:		Online Marketing:	
Motorcycles:		Truck Dealer:	Y	Distributors:	Y	Oil Change:		Insurance:	Y	Other:	Y
Specialty:		RV Dealer:		Tires:	Y	Paint and Body:	Y			Publishing:	
Buses:		Motorcycle Dealer:		Batteries:						Rental Cars/Trucks:	Y
RVs:		Specialty Dealer:	Y								

TYPES OF BUSINESS:

Truck Dealerships
New & Used Construction Equipment
Truck Parts
Repair Services
Financing & Insurance
Leasing
Construction Equipment Rental

BRANDS/DIVISIONS/AFFILIATES:

Rush Truck Centers
Perfection Equipment
Rush Truck Leasing
World Wide Tires
John Deere
Rush Equipment Centers

CONTACTS:

Note: Officers with more than one job title may be intentionally listed here more than once.

W. M. Rush, CEO
W. M. Rush, Pres.
Steven L. Keller, CFO/VP
David C. Orf, Sr. VP-Mktg., Fleets & Specialized Equipment
Derrek Weaver, General Counsel/VP
Daryl J. Gorup, Sr. VP-Dealership Oper.
Scott Anderson, Sr. VP-Finance & Insurance
James E. Thor, Sr. VP-Retail Sales
Richard Hall, VP-Insurance
Martin A. Naegelin Jr., Exec. VP
Richard J. Ryan, Sr. VP-Navistar Dealerships
W. Marvin Rush, Chmn.

Phone: 830-626-5200	**Fax:**
Toll-Free: 800-973-7874	
Address: 555 IH-35 S., Ste. 500, New Braunfels, TX 78130 US	

GROWTH PLANS/SPECIAL FEATURES:

Rush Enterprises, Inc. is a full-service, integrated retailer and servicer of premium transportation and construction equipment and related services. The company currently has two business segments: the truck segment and the construction equipment segment. The truck segment operates a network of Rush Truck Centers that provide retail sales of new and used medium-duty and heavy-duty trucks; aftermarket parts, service and body shop facilities; and financial services, including the financing of new and used truck purchases, insurance products and truck leasing and rentals. Perfection Equipment, a Rush Enterprises subsidiary, offers installation of equipment, equipment repair, parts installation, and paint and body repair. Rush Truck Leasing offers leasing and rental opportunities for Class 6, Class 7 and Class 8 trucks, heavy-duty cranes and refuse haulers. The company also sells a complete line of property and casualty insurance through its truck centers. Additionally, the company operates three World Wide Tires stores, which sell tires for use on Class 8 trucks. The construction equipment segment's operations include the sale of new and used construction equipment; aftermarket parts and service facilities; and the financing of new and used construction equipment. It operates two full-service John Deere construction equipment dealerships in Southeastern Texas. Its Rush Equipment Centers provide a full line of John Deere construction equipment, including backhoe loaders, crawler-dozers, hydraulic excavators and four-wheel drive loaders. In May 2010, the firm acquired certain assets of Lake City International for $38.7 million. It also plans to purchase real estate owned by one of Lake City International's affiliates for $34.5 million. In the same month, it created a new Navistar division within the company. In June 2010, the company signed an agreement to sell its John Deere construction equipment business, including its Rush Equipment Centers in Houston and Beaumont, to Doggett Heavy Machinery Services, LLC for $37 million.

FINANCIALS:

Sales and profits are in thousands of dollars—add 000 to get the full amount. 2009 Note: Financial information for 2009 was not available for all companies at press time.

2009 Sales: $1,239,289	2009 Profits: $5,884	**U.S. Stock Ticker: RUSHA**
2008 Sales: $1,654,956	2008 Profits: $28,865	**Int'l Ticker:** Int'l Exchange:
2007 Sales: $2,030,779	2007 Profits: $51,492	Employees: 2,706
2006 Sales: $2,350,523	2006 Profits: $58,786	Fiscal Year Ends: 12/31
2005 Sales: $1,864,770	2005 Profits: $44,625	Parent Company:

SALARIES/BENEFITS:

Pension Plan:	ESOP Stock Plan:	Profit Sharing:	Top Exec. Salary: $900,000	Bonus: $307,000
Savings Plan: Y	Stock Purch. Plan: Y		Second Exec. Salary: $584,040	Bonus: $409,000

OTHER THOUGHTS:

Apparent Women Officers or Directors:
Hot Spot for Advancement for Women/Minorities:

LOCATIONS: ("Y" = Yes)

West:	Southwest:	Midwest:	Southeast:	Northeast:	International:
Y	Y	Y	Y		

RUSS DARROW GROUP INC

www.russdarrow.com

Industry Group Code: 441110 **Ranks within this company's industry group:** Sales: Profits:

Vehicle Manufacturing:		Dealers:		Parts:		Service:		Finance:		Specialty:	
Cars:		Car Dealer New:	Y	Manufacturers:		General Service:	Y	Leasing:	Y	Information Systems:	
Trucks:		Car Dealer Used:	Y	Retail:		Specialty Service:		Auto Loans:	Y	Online Marketing:	
Motorcycles:		Truck Dealer:		Distributors:		Oil Change:		Insurance:		Other:	
Specialty:		RV Dealer:		Tires:		Paint and Body:	Y			Publishing:	
Buses:		Motorcycle Dealer:		Batteries:						Rental Cars/Trucks:	
RVs:		Specialty Dealer:									

TYPES OF BUSINESS:

Auto Dealers, Retail
Fleet Sales
Leasing
Repair Services
Financing

BRANDS/DIVISIONS/AFFILIATES:

Russ Darrow Leasing

CONTACTS:

Note: Officers with more than one job title may be intentionally listed here more than once.

Russell Darrow, Jr., CEO
Phil Harrington, CFO
Russell Darrow, Jr., Chmn.

Phone: 262-250-9600	**Fax:** 262-253-7530
Toll-Free:	
Address: W133 N8569 Executive Pkwy., Menomonee Falls, WI 53051 US	

GROWTH PLANS/SPECIAL FEATURES:

Russ Darrow Group is a leading automobile dealer in Wisconsin, with approximately 20 locations throughout the state. The group sells both new and used vehicles, with a focus on the brands Honda, Toyota, Nissan, Jeep, Dodge, Kia, Mitsubishi, Mazda, Cadillac and GMC. The firm also has 16 parts, service and collision centers that are located within its dealerships. Russ Darrow Group's web site features a search engine for new and pre-owned vehicles, as well as for vehicles that are priced under $10,000. Customers can also check Internet specials; contact and make appointments with the service, parts and collision departments; and fill out a finance application. In addition to selling new and used vehicles, the company also has Russ Darrow Leasing, which leases and finances trucks and commercial fleets. Russ Darrow Leasing offers a fleet maintenance management program and a fleet fuel card program in conjunction with its commercial fleet services offering.

Russ Darrow offers its employees technician apprenticeship training, an employee assistance program, vehicle purchase discounts, a bi-annual family zoo party, tenure benefits, flexible spending accounts and medical, dental, disability and life insurance.

FINANCIALS:

Sales and profits are in thousands of dollars—add 000 to get the full amount. 2009 Note: Financial information for 2009 was not available for all companies at press time.

2009 Sales: $	2009 Profits: $	**U.S. Stock Ticker: Private**
2008 Sales: $	2008 Profits: $	**Int'l Ticker:** Int'l Exchange:
2007 Sales: $147,300	2007 Profits: $	Employees:
2006 Sales: $	2006 Profits: $	Fiscal Year Ends: 12/31
2005 Sales: $	2005 Profits: $	Parent Company:

SALARIES/BENEFITS:

Pension Plan:	ESOP Stock Plan:	Profit Sharing:	Top Exec. Salary: $	Bonus: $
Savings Plan:	Stock Purch. Plan:		Second Exec. Salary: $	Bonus: $

OTHER THOUGHTS:

Apparent Women Officers or Directors:
Hot Spot for Advancement for Women/Minorities:

LOCATIONS: ("Y" = Yes)

West:	Southwest:	Midwest:	Southeast:	Northeast:	International:
		Y			

RYBROOK HOLDINGS LIMITED

www.rybrookcars.co.uk

Industry Group Code: 441110 **Ranks within this company's industry group:** Sales: Profits:

Vehicle Manufacturing:		Dealers:		Parts:		Service:		Finance:		Specialty:	
Cars:		Car Dealer New:	Y	Manufacturers:		General Service:		Leasing:	Y	Information Systems:	
Trucks:		Car Dealer Used:	Y	Retail:		Specialty Service:		Auto Loans:		Online Marketing:	
Motorcycles:		Truck Dealer:	Y	Distributors:		Oil Change:		Insurance:		Other:	
Specialty:		RV Dealer:		Tires:		Paint and Body:				Publishing:	
Buses:		Motorcycle Dealer:	Y	Batteries:						Rental Cars/Trucks:	
RVs:		Specialty Dealer:									

TYPES OF BUSINESS:

Auto Dealers, Retail
Auto Leasing

BRANDS/DIVISIONS/AFFILIATES:

Ryland Group
Rybrook

GROWTH PLANS/SPECIAL FEATURES:

Rybrook Holdings, formerly Ryland Group, is a leading private car dealership in the U.K., with roughly 18 dealerships operating under the Ryland and Rybrook names. The firm carries 10 different makes of vehicles, including Bentley, BMW, Honda, Jaguar, Land Rover, Mercedes-Benz, MINI, Rolls-Royce, Smart and Volvo. The group also sells used cars. Ryland's web site assists customers in valuing their current automobiles and in selecting new models. For corporate customers, the firm offers car and fuel benefit calculators and a sales group committed to company fleet sales. In addition, Ryland's dealerships feature parts and service departments and personal financing. For businesses, the firm offers fleet services for up to 250 vehicles in most of the models of its new cars. In July 2010, Rybrook was chosen by McLaren Automotive as a partner for its dealership in Birmingham, England.

CONTACTS: *Note: Officers with more than one job title may be intentionally listed here more than once.*

Peter W. Whale, CEO
Keith Hampson, Dir.-Finance
Nigel Thomas, Dir.-Fleet Dev.
Peter W. Whale, Chmn.

Phone: 44-1675-466-566	**Fax:** 44-1675-466-567
Toll-Free:	
Address: 6 Athena Court, Athena Dr., Tachbrook Park, Warwick, Birmingham CV34-6RT UK	

FINANCIALS: **Sales and profits are in thousands of dollars—add 000 to get the full amount. 2009 Note: Financial information for 2009 was not available for all companies at press time.**

2009 Sales: $	2009 Profits: $	**U.S. Stock Ticker: Private**
2008 Sales: $	2008 Profits: $	**Int'l Ticker:** Int'l Exchange:
2007 Sales: $3,032,000	2007 Profits: $-334,000	Employees:
2006 Sales: $4,757,216	2006 Profits: $359,942	Fiscal Year Ends:
2005 Sales: $4,817,566	2005 Profits: $447,052	Parent Company:

SALARIES/BENEFITS:

Pension Plan:	ESOP Stock Plan:	Profit Sharing:	Top Exec. Salary: $	Bonus: $
Savings Plan:	Stock Purch. Plan:		Second Exec. Salary: $	Bonus: $

OTHER THOUGHTS:

Apparent Women Officers or Directors:
Hot Spot for Advancement for Women/Minorities:

LOCATIONS: ("Y" = Yes)

West:	Southwest:	Midwest:	Southeast:	Northeast:	International:
					Y

RYGOR GROUP LTD

www.rygor.co.uk

Industry Group Code: 441110 **Ranks within this company's industry group:** Sales: Profits:

Vehicle Manufacturing:		Dealers:		Parts:		Service:		Finance:		Specialty:	
Cars:		Car Dealer New:		Manufacturers:		General Service:	Y	Leasing:		Information Systems:	
Trucks:		Car Dealer Used:		Retail:	Y	Specialty Service:	Y	Auto Loans:		Online Marketing:	
Motorcycles:		Truck Dealer:	Y	Distributors:		Oil Change:		Insurance:		Other:	Y
Specialty:		RV Dealer:		Tires:		Paint and Body:				Publishing:	
Buses:		Motorcycle Dealer:		Batteries:						Rental Cars/Trucks:	Y
RVs:		Specialty Dealer:	Y								

TYPES OF BUSINESS:

Auto Dealers, Retail
Commercial Sales
Parts & Service
Distribution Services
Rental Services
Warehousing Services

BRANDS/DIVISIONS/AFFILIATES:

Rygor Commercials, Ltd.
Rygor Group Services

CONTACTS:

Note: Officers with more than one job title may be intentionally listed here more than once.

Khanh Dinh, Mgr.-Mktg.
Jim Pascoe, Mgr.-Group Oper.
Graham Drake, Dir.-Finance
Tim Stacey, Dealer Principal
Paul Reed, Dir.-After Sales
Bill Kingsmill, Mgr.-Truck Sales
Tim Page, Mgr.-Van Sales

Phone: 44-1373-855-555 **Fax:** 44-1373-855-525
Toll-Free:
Address: The Broadway, W. Wilts Trading Estate, Westbury, BA13 4JX UK

GROWTH PLANS/SPECIAL FEATURES:

Rygor Group, Ltd., based in southern England, provides vehicle sales and services through two divisions: Rygor Commercials, Ltd. and Rygor Group Services. Subsidiary Rygor Commercials sells both new and used vans, minibuses and heavy-duty and light trucks under the Mercedes-Benz brand name to commercial and corporate customers in the U.K. It also offers optional parts and service contracts and warrantees, as an official Mercedes-Benz dealer. The subsidiary has six locations, with four of those offering sales of new and used vehicles and all offering services. The commercial truck Benz models include the Atego, the Axor, the Actros and the Econic. The company also offers the Mistubishi Fuso Canter, a truck that ranges in weight from 3.5 to 7.5 tons. Other industrial vehicles offered include the Vito, which comes as a panel van, a traveliner, a dualiner and as a refrigerator vehicle; the Sprinter, which is a panel van, a traveliner, a chassis cab and a dropside; and the Vario, which is offered as a panel van and a chassis cab. The firm offers finance, insurance and leasing contracts on its web site, through Mercedes-Benz CharterWay, the commercial vehicle financial services, contract hire and fleet management division of Daimler AG. Rygor Group Services provides distribution services, trailer rental, contract hire and warehousing services to commercial customers. In March 2010, the firm introduced the Mercedes Vito Lavida, a custom built motor home available in the standard option or can be tailored to fit a consumer's needs.

FINANCIALS:

Sales and profits are in thousands of dollars—add 000 to get the full amount. 2009 Note: Financial information for 2009 was not available for all companies at press time.

2009 Sales: $	2009 Profits: $	**U.S. Stock Ticker: Private**
2008 Sales: $	2008 Profits: $	**Int'l Ticker:** Int'l Exchange:
2007 Sales: $	2007 Profits: $	Employees:
2006 Sales: $	2006 Profits: $	Fiscal Year Ends:
2005 Sales: $	2005 Profits: $	Parent Company:

SALARIES/BENEFITS:

Pension Plan:	ESOP Stock Plan:	Profit Sharing:	Top Exec. Salary: $	Bonus: $
Savings Plan:	Stock Purch. Plan:		Second Exec. Salary: $	Bonus: $

OTHER THOUGHTS:

Apparent Women Officers or Directors:
Hot Spot for Advancement for Women/Minorities:

LOCATIONS: ("Y" = Yes)

West:	Southwest:	Midwest:	Southeast:	Northeast:	International:
					Y

S&T MOTORS CO LTD

www.hisntmotors.com/abroad

Industry Group Code: 336991 **Ranks within this company's industry group:** Sales: Profits:

Vehicle Manufacturing:		Dealers:		Parts:		Service:		Finance:		Specialty:	
Cars:		Car Dealer New:		Manufacturers:		General Service:		Leasing:		Information Systems:	
Trucks:		Car Dealer Used:		Retail:		Specialty Service:		Auto Loans:		Online Marketing:	
Motorcycles:	Y	Truck Dealer:		Distributors:		Oil Change:		Insurance:		Other:	
Specialty:	Y	RV Dealer:		Tires:		Paint and Body:				Publishing:	
Buses:		Motorcycle Dealer:		Batteries:						Rental Cars/Trucks:	
RVs:		Specialty Dealer:									

TYPES OF BUSINESS:

Manufacturing-Motorcycles
Manufacturing-Scooters
Manufacturing-ATVs

BRANDS/DIVISIONS/AFFILIATES:

S&T Group
Hyosung Motors America, Inc.
Hyosung Motors Australia Pty. Ltd.
Chongqing Yinxiang Motorcycle (Group) Co.
ATK Motor Company, Inc.

CONTACTS:

Note: Officers with more than one job title may be intentionally listed here more than once.

Taekwon Kim, CEO
Taekwon Kim, Pres.

Phone: 82-55-282-7011 **Fax:** 82-55-282-2664
Toll-Free:
Address: 77, Sungsan-dong, Changwon, Kyungsangnamdo, 641-314 Korea

GROWTH PLANS/SPECIAL FEATURES:

S&T Motors Co., Ltd., an S&T Group company, is a manufacturer of motorcycles, scooters and ATVs. The firm has two subsidiaries that manufacture and sell its products: Hyosung Motors America, Inc., headquartered in Norcross, Georgia; and Hyosung Motors Australia Pty. Ltd., based in Australia. It has also established an automotive parts manufacturing joint venture in China with Chongqing Yinxiang Motorcycle (Group) Co. S&T Motors manufactures six vehicle categories: Road sports, street bikes, cruisers, scooters, off-roads and ATVs. Its road sports category offers the GT650R and the GT250R motorcycles, intended for speed and high-performance. The firm's street bike category is similar to its road sports category, but includes motorcycles designed more for luxury than for speed. The cruiser category includes larger motorcycles designed for long distance travel. The company's scooters include models for everyday use and for commuting. The off-road category of motorcycles is designed to handle mud, rugged mountain terrain and jumps. The ATV category includes three models of four-wheeled ATVs including the Wow50, a smaller version designed for younger riders. Including its two subsidiaries, S&T Motors has 42 firms distributing its products in as many countries. In November 2009, the company announced a partnership with American motorcycle manufacturer ATK Motor Company, Inc. Through the partnership S&T will send products to be assembled by ATK in the U.S., which will then be sold through select Harley-Davidson dealerships.

FINANCIALS:

Sales and profits are in thousands of dollars—add 000 to get the full amount. 2009 Note: Financial information for 2009 was not available for all companies at press time.

2009 Sales: $	2009 Profits: $	**U.S. Stock Ticker: Subsidiary**
2008 Sales: $100,550	2008 Profits: $-7,710	**Int'l Ticker: 000040** Int'l Exchange: Seoul-KRX
2007 Sales: $111,010	2007 Profits: $10,410	Employees:
2006 Sales: $	2006 Profits: $	Fiscal Year Ends:
2005 Sales: $	2005 Profits: $	Parent Company: S&T HOLDINGS CO LTD

SALARIES/BENEFITS:

Pension Plan:	ESOP Stock Plan:	Profit Sharing:	Top Exec. Salary: $	Bonus: $
Savings Plan:	Stock Purch. Plan:		Second Exec. Salary: $	Bonus: $

OTHER THOUGHTS:

Apparent Women Officers or Directors:
Hot Spot for Advancement for Women/Minorities:

LOCATIONS: ("Y" = Yes)

West:	Southwest:	Midwest:	Southeast:	Northeast:	International:
			Y		Y

SAAB AUTOMOBILE AB

www.saab.com

Industry Group Code: 33611 **Ranks within this company's industry group:** Sales: Profits:

Vehicle Manufacturing:		Dealers:		Parts:		Service:		Finance:		Specialty:	
Cars:	Y	Car Dealer New:		Manufacturers:		General Service:		Leasing:		Information Systems:	
Trucks:		Car Dealer Used:		Retail:		Specialty Service:		Auto Loans:		Online Marketing:	
Motorcycles:		Truck Dealer:		Distributors:		Oil Change:		Insurance:		Other:	Y
Specialty:		RV Dealer:		Tires:		Paint and Body:				Publishing:	
Buses:		Motorcycle Dealer:		Batteries:						Rental Cars/Trucks:	
RVs:		Specialty Dealer:									

TYPES OF BUSINESS:

Automobiles, Manufacturing
Automobile Distribution
Merchandise & Accessories Retail

BRANDS/DIVISIONS/AFFILIATES:

Spyker Cars NV
9-3 SportCombi
9-3 Sport Sedan
9-5 Sedan
9-3 Convertible
9-3X
Saab-i Digital Newsletter

CONTACTS:

Note: Officers with more than one job title may be intentionally listed here more than once.

Jan-Ake Jonsson, Managing Dir.
Victor Muller, Chmn.

Phone: 46-520-85000	**Fax:** 46-520-35016
Toll-Free:	
Address: 461 80, Trollhattan, Sweden	

GROWTH PLANS/SPECIAL FEATURES:

Saab Automobile AB, based in Sweden, designs and manufactures automobiles. Saab has operations in more than 60 countries around the globe, with a particular emphasis on the U.S., Switzerland, U.K., Sweden, Italy, The Netherlands, Norway, Germany, Australia and France. The company's U.S. subsidiary is headquartered in Detroit, Michigan. The firm's five car models are the 9-3 Sport Sedan, 9-3 SportCombi, 9-3 Convertible, the luxury 9-5 Sedan and the 9-3X, which is able to run on bioethanol. International and Diplomat sales account for a large portion of Saab's sales. The company offers Saab customers the Saab-i Digital Newsletter, which is published seven or eight times per year and relates to the characteristics of Saab cars and the driving experience in general. Saab enthusiasts may purchase merchandise through the Saab Expressions line, such as pen and pencil sets, toys, watches and martini glasses. The firm's web site offers online shopping tools that allow customers to request a quote, receive competitive comparisons, estimate payments, receive trade-in appraisals, locate dealers, build their own and request a test drive. In early 2009, the company filed for bankruptcy protection. In February 2010, former parent company General Motors sold Saab to Dutch sports car producer Spyker Cars N.V.

FINANCIALS:

Sales and profits are in thousands of dollars—add 000 to get the full amount. 2009 Note: Financial information for 2009 was not available for all companies at press time.

2009 Sales: $	2009 Profits: $	**U.S. Stock Ticker: Subsidiary**
2008 Sales: $	2008 Profits: $	**Int'l Ticker:** Int'l Exchange:
2007 Sales: $	2007 Profits: $	Employees:
2006 Sales: $3,073,100	2006 Profits: $	Fiscal Year Ends: 12/31
2005 Sales: $	2005 Profits: $	Parent Company: SPYKER CARS NV

SALARIES/BENEFITS:

Pension Plan:	ESOP Stock Plan:	Profit Sharing:	Top Exec. Salary: $	Bonus: $
Savings Plan:	Stock Purch. Plan:		Second Exec. Salary: $	Bonus: $

OTHER THOUGHTS:

Apparent Women Officers or Directors:
Hot Spot for Advancement for Women/Minorities:

LOCATIONS: ("Y" = Yes)

West:	Southwest:	Midwest:	Southeast:	Northeast:	International:
		Y			Y

SAAB CARS NORTH AMERICA INC

www.saabusa.com

Industry Group Code: 33611 **Ranks within this company's industry group:** Sales: Profits:

Vehicle Manufacturing:		Dealers:		Parts:		Service:		Finance:		Specialty:	
Cars:		Car Dealer New:	Y	Manufacturers:		General Service:		Leasing:	Y	Information Systems:	
Trucks:		Car Dealer Used:		Retail:		Specialty Service:		Auto Loans:	Y	Online Marketing:	
Motorcycles:		Truck Dealer:		Distributors:		Oil Change:		Insurance:		Other:	Y
Specialty:		RV Dealer:		Tires:		Paint and Body:				Publishing:	
Buses:		Motorcycle Dealer:		Batteries:						Rental Cars/Trucks:	
RVs:		Specialty Dealer:									

TYPES OF BUSINESS:

Automobiles-Import & Distribution

BRANDS/DIVISIONS/AFFILIATES:

Saab Aero X
Saab Automobile AB
Spyker Cars NV
GMAC Financial Services
Saab 9-5
Saab 9-7X
Saab 9-3

CONTACTS: *Note: Officers with more than one job title may be intentionally listed here more than once.*

Mike Colleran, COO
Mike Colleran, Pres.
Michele Tinson, Dir.-Comm.
Victor R. Muller, CEO-Spyker Cars N.V.
Jan Ake Jonsson, CEO-Saab Automobile AB

Phone: **Fax:**
Toll-Free: 800-722-2872
Address: 4327 Delemere Ct., Royal Oak, MI 48073 US

GROWTH PLANS/SPECIAL FEATURES:

Saab Cars North America (SCNA), formerly Saab Cars USA, Inc., is the importing and distributing subsidiary of Saab Automobile AB. Saab Automobile AB is a wholly-owned subsidiary of Spyker Cars N.V. The company distributes Saab cars across the U.S. through a network of dealerships. The firm offers all Saab models, including the 9-3, available in a sport sedan and a convertible; 93X, a sports sedan and the luxury 9-5, available as both a sedan and a wagon. Saab's most recent offerings include its first SUV, the Saab 9-7X. The firm has four concept vehicles. The Saab 9-X, features a new style of a convertible, with a driver-focused cockpit design. The 9-X BioHybrid, uses biothanol fuel. The company's 9-X BioPower, has 300 hp (horsepower) and runs on E85 ethanol. Lastly, the Saab Aero-X, a two-seat sports coupe with a glass cockpit, which lifts to allow entrance, inspired by the firm's aircraft heritage, sports a 400 hp ethanol-fueled engine. The company features a build your own Saab, which allows customers to customize their vehicles. In February 2009, Saab Automobile AB filed for bankruptcy in Sweden. In February 2010, former parent company General Motors sold Saab to Dutch sports car producer Spyker Cars N.V. In March 2010, the company moved its headquarters to Royal Oak, Michigan. SCNA plans to invest $2.4 million to enhance North American Sales and Marketing Operations. In addition, more than 2,000 jobs are planned to be created over the next few years. Also, in March 2010, the firm selected GMAC Financial Services as the provider of wholesale and retail financial services for customers and qualified Saab dealers worldwide.

FINANCIALS: **Sales and profits are in thousands of dollars—add 000 to get the full amount. 2009 Note: Financial information for 2009 was not available for all companies at press time.**

2009 Sales: $
2008 Sales: $
2007 Sales: $
2006 Sales: $
2005 Sales: $

2009 Profits: $
2008 Profits: $
2007 Profits: $
2006 Profits: $
2005 Profits: $

U.S. Stock Ticker: Subsidiary
Int'l Ticker: Int'l Exchange:
Employees:
Fiscal Year Ends: 12/31
Parent Company: SPYKER CARS NV

SALARIES/BENEFITS:

Pension Plan: ESOP Stock Plan: Profit Sharing: Top Exec. Salary: $ Bonus: $
Savings Plan: Stock Purch. Plan: Second Exec. Salary: $ Bonus: $

OTHER THOUGHTS:

Apparent Women Officers or Directors:
Hot Spot for Advancement for Women/Minorities:

LOCATIONS: ("Y" = Yes)

West:	Southwest:	Midwest:	Southeast:	Northeast:	International:
Y	Y	Y	Y	Y	Y

SAIC-GM-WULING AUTOMOBILE COMPANY

www.sgmw.com.cn

Industry Group Code: 33611 **Ranks within this company's industry group:** Sales: Profits:

Vehicle Manufacturing:		Dealers:		Parts:		Service:		Finance:		Specialty:	
Cars:	Y	Car Dealer New:		Manufacturers:	Y	General Service:		Leasing:		Information Systems:	
Trucks:	Y	Car Dealer Used:		Retail:		Specialty Service:		Auto Loans:		Online Marketing:	
Motorcycles:		Truck Dealer:		Distributors:		Oil Change:		Insurance:		Other:	
Specialty:		RV Dealer:		Tires:		Paint and Body:				Publishing:	
Buses:		Motorcycle Dealer:		Batteries:						Rental Cars/Trucks:	
RVs:		Specialty Dealer:									

TYPES OF BUSINESS:

Automobile Manufacturing
Gasoline Engine Manufacturing

BRANDS/DIVISIONS/AFFILIATES:

Shanghai Automotive Industry Corp (SAIC)
General Motors Corp (GM)
Liuzhou Wuling Motors Co. Ltd.
Hongtu
Xingwang
Rongguang
Sunshine
Chevrolet Spark

CONTACTS:

Note: Officers with more than one job title may be intentionally listed here more than once.

Shen Yang, Gen. Mgr.
Jason Ding, Sales Contact-Asia & Europe
Hong Chen, Chmn.
Dylan Wu, Sales Contact-Africa

Phone: 86-772-3751331	**Fax:** 86-772-3751340
Toll-Free:	
Address: No. 18 Hexi Rd., Liuzhou, 545007 China	

GROWTH PLANS/SPECIAL FEATURES:

SAIC-GM-Wuling Automobile Company (SGMW) is a Chinese automaker that specializes in mini-vans and light trucks. It is a three way joint venture between Shanghai Automobile Industry Corp. (SAIC), with a 50.1% stake, General Motors China (34%) and Liuzhou Wuling Motors Co. Ltd. (15.9%). The firm primarily manufactures six models, all sold under the Wuling moniker: the Hongtu, Rongguang, Sunshine and Xingwang minivans, as well as the 1025 and PN series pickups. The Hongtu and Rongguang minivans seat four and have additional folding seats. The Sunshine, a rear box minivan, has higher gas mileage but considerably less horsepower than the firm's other minivans, and seats 7-8 passengers. The Xingwang is the company's economy-priced minivan. Lastly, the 1025 and PN series pickups come in either a single- or double-cab configurations, which seat two and four people, respectively. These vehicles resemble a minivan with the back end replaced with a truck bed. Although all these vehicles carry the Wuling name, some are actually rebranded versions of other cars, including the Chevrolet N200, which was rebranded the Wuling Hongtu. Additionally, besides its Wuling vehicles, the firm produces the Chevrolet Spark mini-car. The company also produces the Wuling B10, B11 and B12 gas engines. SGMW has two vehicle manufacturing facilities, in Liuzhou and Qingdao, China, as well as an engine factory. These plants benefit from the General Motors (GM) Global Manufacturing System. SGMW, which is highly focused on exporting its products, currently sells its vehicles in 40 countries in the Middle East, Africa, Southeast Asia and South America.

FINANCIALS:

Sales and profits are in thousands of dollars—add 000 to get the full amount. 2009 Note: Financial information for 2009 was not available for all companies at press time.

2009 Sales: $	2009 Profits: $	**U.S. Stock Ticker: Joint Venture**
2008 Sales: $	2008 Profits: $	**Int'l Ticker:** Int'l Exchange:
2007 Sales: $1,685,100	2007 Profits: $	Employees:
2006 Sales: $	2006 Profits: $	Fiscal Year Ends:
2005 Sales: $	2005 Profits: $	Parent Company: SHANGHAI AUTOMOTIVE INDUSTRY CORP (SAIC)

SALARIES/BENEFITS:

Pension Plan:	ESOP Stock Plan:	Profit Sharing:	Top Exec. Salary: $	Bonus: $
Savings Plan:	Stock Purch. Plan:		Second Exec. Salary: $	Bonus: $

OTHER THOUGHTS:

Apparent Women Officers or Directors:
Hot Spot for Advancement for Women/Minorities:

LOCATIONS: ("Y" = Yes)

West:	Southwest:	Midwest:	Southeast:	Northeast:	International:
					Y

SALEEN PERFORMANCE VEHICLES

www.saleen.com

Industry Group Code: 33611 **Ranks within this company's industry group:** Sales: Profits:

Vehicle Manufacturing:		Dealers:		Parts:		Service:		Finance:		Specialty:	
Cars:	Y	Car Dealer New:		Manufacturers:	Y	General Service:		Leasing:		Information Systems:	
Trucks:		Car Dealer Used:		Retail:		Specialty Service:	Y	Auto Loans:		Online Marketing:	Y
Motorcycles:		Truck Dealer:		Distributors:		Oil Change:		Insurance:		Other:	Y
Specialty:	Y	RV Dealer:		Tires:		Paint and Body:				Publishing:	
Buses:		Motorcycle Dealer:		Batteries:						Rental Cars/Trucks:	
RVs:		Specialty Dealer:									

TYPES OF BUSINESS:

Specialty Automobiles
Performance Parts
Clothing & Collectible Merchandise

BRANDS/DIVISIONS/AFFILIATES:

MJ Acquisitions
Saleen, Inc.
Saleen Speedlab
Saleen Club of America
Control-Tec LLC
Power-Tec Engineering LLC
Arrow Racing Engines
S302

CONTACTS: *Note: Officers with more than one job title may be intentionally listed here more than once.*

Michael F. Shields, CEO
Michael Timarac, Dir.-Sales
Jesse Albright, Mgr.-Oper.
Michael Timarac, Mgr.-Brand
David Byron, Dir.-Design

Phone:	**Fax:** 248-499-5333
Toll-Free: 800-888-8945	
Address: 33603 Dequindre Rd., Troy, MI 48083 US	

GROWTH PLANS/SPECIAL FEATURES:

Saleen Performance Vehicles, formerly Saleen, Inc. is a manufacturer of specialty high-performance street and racing cars. Saleen vehicles emphasize speed, such as the S302, launched in June 2010, which features a 425 horsepower (hp) V8 engine, six-speed manual transmission, Saleen Racecraft suspension and is capable of speeds up to 200 miles per hour (mph). Other Saleen vehicles include the 435S, which offers 435 hp and a five-speed manual transmission; and the S281, featuring a 475-hp V8 engine, sport-tuned coil springs and nitrogen-pressurized shocks. Through Saleen Speedlab, the company also sells aftermarket car parts for high performance markets. Parts range from suspension assemblies, wheels and tires, engine upgrade components and driveline systems to aesthetic components, such as pedal sets, trim, vents and grilles, body panels and decals, as well as Saleen accessories and apparel. The firm also runs a fan club called the Saleen Club of America. Saleen is owned by MJ Acquisitions, a group with interests in the full service engineering, design, manufacturing, assembly and control system segments of the automotive industry. Other MJ Acquisitions group companies include Control-Tec LLC, a provider of design, calibration, validation and certification services for powertrain control systems; Power-Tec Engineering LLC, a provider of engineering design, R&D, testing, calibrations, validation and prototype manufacturing services to the automotive market; Arrow Racing Engines, with operations in engine design, building, testing and research and development. In February 2009, MJ Acquisitions acquired the assets of Saleen, Inc., after which it was renamed Saleen Performance Vehicles.

FINANCIALS: **Sales and profits are in thousands of dollars—add 000 to get the full amount. 2009 Note: Financial information for 2009 was not available for all companies at press time.**

2009 Sales: $	2009 Profits: $	**U.S. Stock Ticker: Private**
2008 Sales: $	2008 Profits: $	**Int'l Ticker:** Int'l Exchange:
2007 Sales: $	2007 Profits: $	Employees:
2006 Sales: $	2006 Profits: $	Fiscal Year Ends: 12/31
2005 Sales: $	2005 Profits: $	Parent Company: MJ ACQUISITIONS

SALARIES/BENEFITS:

Pension Plan:	ESOP Stock Plan:	Profit Sharing:	Top Exec. Salary: $	Bonus: $
Savings Plan:	Stock Purch. Plan:		Second Exec. Salary: $	Bonus: $

OTHER THOUGHTS:

Apparent Women Officers or Directors:
Hot Spot for Advancement for Women/Minorities:

LOCATIONS: ("Y" = Yes)

West:	Southwest:	Midwest:	Southeast:	Northeast:	International:
		Y			

SAM SWOPE AUTO GROUP INC

www.samswope.com

Industry Group Code: 441110 **Ranks within this company's industry group:** Sales: Profits:

Vehicle Manufacturing:		Dealers:		Parts:		Service:		Finance:		Specialty:	
Cars:		Car Dealer New:	Y	Manufacturers:		General Service:	Y	Leasing:		Information Systems:	
Trucks:		Car Dealer Used:	Y	Retail:	Y	Specialty Service:		Auto Loans:	Y	Online Marketing:	
Motorcycles:		Truck Dealer:	Y	Distributors:		Oil Change:		Insurance:		Other:	
Specialty:		RV Dealer:		Tires:		Paint and Body:	Y			Publishing:	
Buses:		Motorcycle Dealer:		Batteries:						Rental Cars/Trucks:	
RVs:		Specialty Dealer:	Y								

TYPES OF BUSINESS:

Auto Dealers, Retail
Parts
Service
Trailers, Retail

BRANDS/DIVISIONS/AFFILIATES:

Swope Advantage

CONTACTS:

Note: Officers with more than one job title may be intentionally listed here more than once.

Richard S. Swope, CEO
Richard S. Swope, Pres.
Michael Sanderson, CFO/Exec. VP
Patti Swope, Exec. VP-Bus. Dev.
Patti Swope, Spokesperson
Willie N. Mitchell, Mgr.-Commercial Sales
Samuel G. Swope, Chmn.

Phone: 502-499-5000	**Fax:** 502-499-5009
Toll-Free:	
Address: 10 Swope Autocenter Dr., Louisville, KY 40299 US	

GROWTH PLANS/SPECIAL FEATURES:

Sam Swope Auto Group is comprised of 15 wholly-owned automobile dealerships in Louisville, Kentucky and eight affiliated dealerships in Lexington, Radcliff and Elizabethtown, Kentucky. The firm's dealerships sell makes including Pontiac, Buick, GMC, Cadillac, Saturn, Suzuki, Honda, Toyota, Scion, smart car, Infiniti, Mitsubishi, Volvo, BMW and Lexus. The company's web site provides customers with information regarding financing under the Swope Advantage plan, including quick quotes, specials and credit applications. The Swope Advantage plan turns the Swope group of dealerships into buy-here/pay-here facilities, offering customers in-house loans for their vehicle purchase. The plan also offers a referral program, where customers can earn $100 for every person they refer who purchases a vehicle through the Swope Advantage plan. In addition, customers are able to schedule repair and maintenance service appointments, order parts and view a virtual showroom of available new and used cars online. Sam Swope Auto offers a body shop, parts and service.

FINANCIALS:

Sales and profits are in thousands of dollars—add 000 to get the full amount. 2009 Note: Financial information for 2009 was not available for all companies at press time.

2009 Sales: $	2009 Profits: $	**U.S. Stock Ticker: Private**
2008 Sales: $	2008 Profits: $	**Int'l Ticker:** Int'l Exchange:
2007 Sales: $434,300	2007 Profits: $	Employees:
2006 Sales: $	2006 Profits: $	Fiscal Year Ends: 12/31
2005 Sales: $	2005 Profits: $	Parent Company:

SALARIES/BENEFITS:

Pension Plan:	ESOP Stock Plan:	Profit Sharing:	Top Exec. Salary: $	Bonus: $
Savings Plan:	Stock Purch. Plan:		Second Exec. Salary: $	Bonus: $

OTHER THOUGHTS:

Apparent Women Officers or Directors: 1
Hot Spot for Advancement for Women/Minorities:

LOCATIONS: ("Y" = Yes)

West:	Southwest:	Midwest:	Southeast:	Northeast:	International:
		Y			

SANLUIS CORPORACION SAB DE CV

www.sanluisrassini.com

Industry Group Code: 3363 **Ranks within this company's industry group:** Sales: 54 Profits: 35

Vehicle Manufacturing:		Dealers:		Parts:		Service:		Finance:		Specialty:	
Cars:		Car Dealer New:		Manufacturers:	Y	General Service:		Leasing:		Information Systems:	
Trucks:		Car Dealer Used:		Retail:	Y	Specialty Service:		Auto Loans:		Online Marketing:	
Motorcycles:		Truck Dealer:		Distributors:		Oil Change:		Insurance:		Other:	
Specialty:		RV Dealer:		Tires:		Paint and Body:				Publishing:	
Buses:		Motorcycle Dealer:		Batteries:						Rental Cars/Trucks:	
RVs:		Specialty Dealer:									

TYPES OF BUSINESS:

Parts-Suspension System Components
Parts-Brake Components
Parts-Elastomer Manufacturing

BRANDS/DIVISIONS/AFFILIATES:

SANLUIS Rassini
SANLUIS Rassini Suspensions
Rassini, S.A. de C.V.
Rassini NHK Autopecas, S.A.
Rassini Torsion Bars, S.A. de C.V.
Rassini Chassis Systems, LLC
SANLUIS Rassini Brakes
SANLUIS Investments, LLC

CONTACTS: *Note: Officers with more than one job title may be intentionally listed here more than once.*

Antonio Madero, CEO
Enrique Villasenor, Pres.
Sergio Visintini, CFO
Robert Anderson, Pres., Tech. Center
Enrique Villasenor, Pres., Suspension Group
Hector Galvan, Pres., Brakes Group
Eugenio Madero, VP-Suspension Group
Sergio Mendlowicz, Dir.-Rassini NHK Autopecas
Antonio Madero, Chmn.

Phone: 52-55-5229-5800	**Fax:** 52-55-5202-6604
Toll-Free:	
Address: 220 Monte Pelvoux, 8th Fl., Lomas de Chapultepec, 11000 Mexico	

GROWTH PLANS/SPECIAL FEATURES:

SANLUIS Corporacion S.A.B. de C.V. designs and produces auto parts for suspension and break systems through its SANLUIS Rassini brand. It manufactures leaf springs, coil springs, bushings, rotors and drums for original equipment manufacturers (OEMs). It primarily operates in the North America and Brazil markets and has seven production facilities and three commercial offices in the Americas, Europe and Asia. The company is divided into two operating groups: suspensions, which generated 89% of the company's 2009 revenue; and brakes, 11%. The suspension segment, which operates as SANLUIS Rassini Suspensions, includes sales of multi-leaf springs and parabolic leaf springs, coil springs, torsion bars and stabilizing bars. Suspension group subsidiaries include Rassini, S.A. de C.V., manufacturing leaf and coil springs; Rassini NHK Autopecas, S.A., manufacturing leaf and coil springs; Rassini Torsion Bars, S.A. de C.V., manufacturing torsion bars; and Rassini Chassis Systems, LLC, manufacturing coil springs. The company's brakes group, which operates as SANLUIS Rassini Brakes, sells rotors, disks, drums and hubs for brake systems. Brake group subsidiaries include SANLUIS Investments, LLC; SANLUIS Developments, LLC; Fundimak, S.A. de C.V.; SR Holding, S.A. de C.V.; Rassini Frenos, S.A. de C.V.; and Brembo Rassini, S.A. de C.V. SANLUIS Rassini also produces high-density rubbers through subsidiary SANLUIS Rassini-BYPASA. The firm has a research and development center in Plymouth, Michigan which uses RASCAL, a type of software developed in-house specifically for coil spring design, as well as CAD (Computer Aided Design) software such as UNIGRAPHICS and other off-the-shelf software. The company's customers include Ford, General Motors, Chrysler, BMW, Honda, Mitsubishi, Nissan, Toyota, Volkswagen and American Axle, among others.

FINANCIALS: **Sales and profits are in thousands of dollars—add 000 to get the full amount. 2009 Note: Financial information for 2009 was not available for all companies at press time.**

2009 Sales: $415,900	2009 Profits: $-28,790	**U.S. Stock Ticker:**
2008 Sales: $511,090	2008 Profits: $-36,090	**Int'l Ticker: SANLUISA** Int'l Exchange: Mexico City-BMV
2007 Sales: $587,620	2007 Profits: $-79,830	Employees:
2006 Sales: $699,560	2006 Profits: $	Fiscal Year Ends: 12/31
2005 Sales: $	2005 Profits: $	Parent Company:

SALARIES/BENEFITS:

Pension Plan:	ESOP Stock Plan:	Profit Sharing:	Top Exec. Salary: $	Bonus: $
Savings Plan:	Stock Purch. Plan:		Second Exec. Salary: $	Bonus: $

OTHER THOUGHTS:

Apparent Women Officers or Directors:
Hot Spot for Advancement for Women/Minorities:

LOCATIONS: ("Y" = Yes)

West:	Southwest:	Midwest:	Southeast:	Northeast:	International:
		Y			Y

SANSONE AUTO NETWORK

www.sansoneauto.com

Industry Group Code: 441110 **Ranks within this company's industry group:** Sales: Profits:

Vehicle Manufacturing:		Dealers:		Parts:		Service:		Finance:		Specialty:	
Cars:		Car Dealer New:	Y	Manufacturers:		General Service:	Y	Leasing:		Information Systems:	
Trucks:		Car Dealer Used:	Y	Retail:		Specialty Service:		Auto Loans:	Y	Online Marketing:	
Motorcycles:		Truck Dealer:		Distributors:		Oil Change:		Insurance:		Other:	
Specialty:		RV Dealer:		Tires:		Paint and Body:				Publishing:	
Buses:		Motorcycle Dealer:		Batteries:						Rental Cars/Trucks:	
RVs:		Specialty Dealer:									

TYPES OF BUSINESS:

Auto Dealers, Retail
Parts
Service
Financing

BRANDS/DIVISIONS/AFFILIATES:

Route 1 Automall
Route 35 Automall

GROWTH PLANS/SPECIAL FEATURES:

Sansone Auto Network, comprising 17 franchises at three automall locations in New Jersey, sells new and used vehicles. The automall offers vehicle brands including Dodge, Nissan, Ford, Toyota, Chrysler, Mazda, Scion and Kia. Sansone's automobile services include auto repair and financing. Customers can schedule service appointments and apply for financing online, as well as search for vehicles and obtain Internet specials on new and used vehicles. The online finance department has the ability to pre-qualify loan applicants. Sansone is a certified dealer of Saleen/SVT, an enhancer of Ford Mustang products. In 2009, Paul Sansone, Jr. took over the automall on route 66, renaming it Sansone Jr's 66 Automall.

CONTACTS: *Note: Officers with more than one job title may be intentionally listed here more than once.*

Paul Sansone, CEO
Joseph Massaro, CFO
Debbie Yaniga, Dir.-Human Resources

Phone: 732-815-0500	**Fax:** 732-815-2395
Toll-Free:	
Address: 3401 Route 66 N., Neptune, NJ 07753 US	

FINANCIALS: **Sales and profits are in thousands of dollars—add 000 to get the full amount. 2009 Note: Financial information for 2009 was not available for all companies at press time.**

2009 Sales: $	2009 Profits: $	**U.S. Stock Ticker: Private**
2008 Sales: $	2008 Profits: $	**Int'l Ticker:** Int'l Exchange:
2007 Sales: $	2007 Profits: $	Employees:
2006 Sales: $	2006 Profits: $	Fiscal Year Ends:
2005 Sales: $	2005 Profits: $	Parent Company:

SALARIES/BENEFITS:

Pension Plan:	ESOP Stock Plan:	Profit Sharing:	Top Exec. Salary: $	Bonus: $
Savings Plan:	Stock Purch. Plan:		Second Exec. Salary: $	Bonus: $

OTHER THOUGHTS:

Apparent Women Officers or Directors: 1
Hot Spot for Advancement for Women/Minorities:

LOCATIONS: ("Y" = Yes)

West:	Southwest:	Midwest:	Southeast:	Northeast:	International:
				Y	

SANTA MONICA FORD LINCOLN MERCURY

www.smford.com

Industry Group Code: 441110 **Ranks within this company's industry group:** Sales: Profits:

Vehicle Manufacturing:		Dealers:		Parts:		Service:		Finance:		Specialty:	
Cars:		Car Dealer New:	Y	Manufacturers:		General Service:	Y	Leasing:		Information Systems:	
Trucks:		Car Dealer Used:	Y	Retail:	Y	Specialty Service:		Auto Loans:	Y	Online Marketing:	
Motorcycles:		Truck Dealer:	Y	Distributors:		Oil Change:		Insurance:		Other:	
Specialty:		RV Dealer:		Tires:		Paint and Body:	Y			Publishing:	
Buses:		Motorcycle Dealer:		Batteries:						Rental Cars/Trucks:	
RVs:		Specialty Dealer:									

TYPES OF BUSINESS:

Auto Dealers, Retail
Fleet Sales
Parts & Service

BRANDS/DIVISIONS/AFFILIATES:

I-CAR

GROWTH PLANS/SPECIAL FEATURES:

Santa Monica Ford Lincoln Mercury is a major dealership that services the greater Los Angeles area, selling over 40,000 vehicles a year. The company's high sales volume comes largely from fleet sales to corporate customers. Santa Monica Ford offers both new and pre-owned Ford, Lincoln and Mercury vehicles at its dealership and to customers throughout the country through its online showrooms. Models sold by the firm include Ford Expedition, Ford Mustang, Lincoln Navigator, Ford Edge, Ford Escape Hybrid, Mercury Mariner, Mercury Milan and Lincoln Town Car. Santa Monica Ford's web site also provides detailed statistics and pictures for all of the vehicles in its inventory, in addition to possessing online quotes and finance applications forms. The firm also operates an I-CAR certified collision center that offers free estimates and lifetime warranties and that can perform painting, refinishing and frame alignment and measuring. Santa Monica Ford's other operational divisions include its auto financing and leasing services, a parts department and a service department.

CONTACTS: *Note: Officers with more than one job title may be intentionally listed here more than once.*

Ronald Davis, Pres.
Billy Lourie, Bus. Dev.
Larry Rosen, Controller

Phone: 310-451-1588 **Fax:** 310-394-0643
Toll-Free: 888-875-3867
Address: 1230 Santa Monica Blvd., Santa Monica, CA 90404 US

FINANCIALS: **Sales and profits are in thousands of dollars—add 000 to get the full amount. 2009 Note: Financial information for 2009 was not available for all companies at press time.**

2009 Sales: $	2009 Profits: $	**U.S. Stock Ticker: Private**
2008 Sales: $	2008 Profits: $	**Int'l Ticker:** Int'l Exchange:
2007 Sales: $	2007 Profits: $	Employees:
2006 Sales: $	2006 Profits: $	Fiscal Year Ends:
2005 Sales: $	2005 Profits: $	Parent Company:

SALARIES/BENEFITS:

Pension Plan:	ESOP Stock Plan:	Profit Sharing:	Top Exec. Salary: $	Bonus: $
Savings Plan:	Stock Purch. Plan:		Second Exec. Salary: $	Bonus: $

OTHER THOUGHTS:

Apparent Women Officers or Directors:
Hot Spot for Advancement for Women/Minorities:

LOCATIONS: ("Y" = Yes)

West:	Southwest:	Midwest:	Southeast:	Northeast:	International:
Y					

SCANIA AB

www.scania.com

Industry Group Code: 336120 **Ranks within this company's industry group:** Sales: Profits:

Vehicle Manufacturing:		**Dealers:**		**Parts:**		**Service:**		**Finance:**		**Specialty:**	
Cars:		Car Dealer New:	Y	Manufacturers:	Y	General Service:		Leasing:		Information Systems:	
Trucks:	Y	Car Dealer Used:		Retail:		Specialty Service:		Auto Loans:		Online Marketing:	
Motorcycles:		Truck Dealer:	Y	Distributors:	Y	Oil Change:		Insurance:		Other:	
Specialty:	Y	RV Dealer:		Tires:		Paint and Body:				Publishing:	Y
Buses:	Y	Motorcycle Dealer:		Batteries:						Rental Cars/Trucks:	
RVs:		Specialty Dealer:	Y								

TYPES OF BUSINESS:

Trucks & Buses, Manufacturing
Buses & Coaches
Industrial & Marine Engines
Auto Sales
Parts & Accessories
Construction & Specialty Vehicles
Fire & Rescue Vehicles
Repair & Assistance

BRANDS/DIVISIONS/AFFILIATES:

Scania USA, Inc.
Scania Irizar PB
Scania World Magazine
Scania Power Magazine
Scania Fleet Management
Scania Assistance
Volkswagen AB

CONTACTS: *Note: Officers with more than one job title may be intentionally listed here more than once.*

Leif Ostling, CEO
Leif Ostling, Pres.
Jan Ytterberg, CFO/Exec. VP
Urban Erdtman, Exec. VP-Sales & Svcs. Mgmt.
Magnus Hahn, Sr. VP-Human Resources Support
Per Hallberg, Exec. VP-R&D
Carl Riben, General Counsel/Sr. VP
Erik Ljungberg, Sr. VP-Corp. Rel.
Per Hillstrom, Head-Investor Rel.
Martin Lundstedt, Exec. VP-Franchise & Factory Sales
John Hofstedt, Sr. VP-Powertrain Dev.
Henrik Henrikson, Sr. VP-Franchise & Factory Sales, Trucks
Martin Winterkorn, Chmn.
Anders Nielsen, Exec. VP-Production & Logistics

Phone: 46-8-55-38-10-00	**Fax:** 46-8-55-38-10-37
Toll-Free:	
Address: Scania AB, Sodertalje, SE-151 87 Sweden	

GROWTH PLANS/SPECIAL FEATURES:

Scania AB, a member of the Volkswagen group, manufactures heavy trucks and buses and sells them in over 100 countries around the globe. It manufactures a range of vehicles for construction and specialty purposes including tractors, trailers, concrete mixers, garbage trucks and fire and rescue vehicles. In addition, the firm manufactures industrial and marine engines for applications in boats, generators and other machinery. Scania offers its customers financial services, roadside assistance, computer-based fleet management rentals, parts, and workshop services. Supplementary to selling its own branded buses, Scania sells vehicles manufactured by companies including Volvo, Mercedes and Renault. Scania's ethanol-run bus and coach range includes the Scania Irizar PB tourist coach, featuring a 470 hp engine. One of the only bus manufacturers in the BioEthanol for Sustainable Transport (BEST) project, Scania began large-scale development of ethanol-powered vehicles in collaboration with Storstockholms Lokaltrafik (SL), the Swedish capital's regional transport company. Scania has been using ethanol engines for more than 15 years and delivers its ethanol buses into worldwide markets. The company also offers vehicles that run on Rapeseed Methyl Ester (RME), ethanol, biogas or natural gas. The Scania World Magazine and Scania Power Magazine offer information about Scania's products and services and news in the trucking industry, available in five languages. The firm also maintains services such as Scania Assistance, which consists of professionals who send out service vehicles and arrange for replacement vehicles, as well as running credit checks and providing workshop estimates; and Scania Fleet Management, a program in which customers can monitor their fleet from an office computer. In January 2010, the company signed an agreement with Terex Corporation to supply engines for the vehicles and heavy equipment Terex manufactures and sells.

FINANCIALS: **Sales and profits are in thousands of dollars—add 000 to get the full amount. 2009 Note: Financial information for 2009 was not available for all companies at press time.**

2009 Sales: $
2008 Sales: $12,532,500
2007 Sales: $11,899,900
2006 Sales: $11,251,700
2005 Sales: $8,762,878

2009 Profits: $
2008 Profits: $1,252,170
2007 Profits: $1,320,000
2006 Profits: $944,663
2005 Profits: $645,480

U.S. Stock Ticker:
Int'l Ticker: SCVB Int'l Exchange: Stockholm-SSE
Employees:
Fiscal Year Ends: 12/31
Parent Company: VOLKSWAGEN AG

SALARIES/BENEFITS:

Pension Plan:	ESOP Stock Plan:	Profit Sharing:	Top Exec. Salary: $	Bonus: $
Savings Plan:	Stock Purch. Plan:		Second Exec. Salary: $	Bonus: $

OTHER THOUGHTS:

Apparent Women Officers or Directors: 1
Hot Spot for Advancement for Women/Minorities:

LOCATIONS: ("Y" = Yes)

West:	Southwest:	Midwest:	Southeast:	Northeast:	International:
	Y				Y

SEAT SA

www.seat.com

Industry Group Code: 33611 **Ranks within this company's industry group:** Sales: Profits:

Vehicle Manufacturing:		Dealers:		Parts:		Service:		Finance:		Specialty:	
Cars:	Y	Car Dealer New:		Manufacturers:		General Service:		Leasing:		Information Systems:	
Trucks:		Car Dealer Used:		Retail:		Specialty Service:		Auto Loans:		Online Marketing:	
Motorcycles:		Truck Dealer:		Distributors:		Oil Change:		Insurance:		Other:	
Specialty:		RV Dealer:		Tires:		Paint and Body:				Publishing:	
Buses:		Motorcycle Dealer:		Batteries:						Rental Cars/Trucks:	
RVs:		Specialty Dealer:									

TYPES OF BUSINESS:

Automobile Manufacturing

BRANDS/DIVISIONS/AFFILIATES:

Volkswagon AG
Altea
Exeo
Alhambra
Ibiza
Leon
ECOMOTIVE
Audi Q3

CONTACTS:

Note: Officers with more than one job title may be intentionally listed here more than once.

James Muir, Pres.
Jan-Henrik Lafrentz, Exec. VP-Sales & Mktg.
Ramon Paredes, Exec. VP-Human Resources
Frank Bekemeier, Exec. VP-R&D
Wolfram Thomas, Exec. VP-Prod.
Serafi del Arco Majon, Head-Corp. Comm.
Holger Kintscher, Exec. VP-Finance
Luc Donckerwolke, Head-Design
Artur Martins, Head-Mktg., Spain
Francisco Javier Garcia Sanz, Chmn.
Deiter Seemann, Exec. VP-Purchases

Phone: 34-93-708-5000	**Fax:** 34-93-708-5502
Toll-Free:	
Address: Autovia A2, Km. 585, Martorell, 08760 Spain	

GROWTH PLANS/SPECIAL FEATURES:

SEAT SA, a subsidiary of Volkswagen AG and a member of the Audi brand group, is a Spanish designer and manufacturer of automobiles with operations in more than 70 countries worldwide. SEAT produces nine models: the Ibiza, Ibiza SC, Ibiza ST the Altea, the Altea XL, Altea Freetrack, the Leon, the Alhambra, the Exeo and the Exeo ST. The Ibiza models are compact hatchbacks available with either three or five doors. The Altea is a five-door MPV (multi-purpose vehicle), the Altea XL is a larger version of the Altea and the Altea Freetrack is a four-wheel drive version of the Altea. The Leon is a five-door compact car. The Alhambra is a five-door minivan. Finally, the Exeo, introduced in 2009, is a four-door saloon-style sedan, also available in a five-door station wagon version, the Exeo ST. The Alhambra, manufactured in Palmela, Portugal, is the only model not manufactured at the company's Martorell factory. The company has an annual vehicle production capacity of about 400,000 vehicles, and its Martorell factory has a daily output of about 2,000 units. The Martorell factory's total 2009 production was 301, 287 vehicles. The company's top-selling models were the Leon and the Ibiza. The company also manufactures the Audi Q3 at its Martorell factory. In July 2010, the company introduced its new line of engines, including a new TDI diesel engine for the Ibiza as well as the ECOMOTIVE engine which features significantly reduced emissions.

FINANCIALS:

Sales and profits are in thousands of dollars—add 000 to get the full amount. 2009 Note: Financial information for 2009 was not available for all companies at press time.

2009 Sales: $	2009 Profits: $	**U.S. Stock Ticker: Subsidiary**
2008 Sales: $	2008 Profits: $	**Int'l Ticker:** Int'l Exchange:
2007 Sales: $9,154,000	2007 Profits: $	Employees:
2006 Sales: $7,580,190	2006 Profits: $-67,110	Fiscal Year Ends: 12/31
2005 Sales: $7,204,910	2005 Profits: $-85,460	Parent Company: VOLKSWAGEN AG

SALARIES/BENEFITS:

Pension Plan:	ESOP Stock Plan:	Profit Sharing:	Top Exec. Salary: $	Bonus: $
Savings Plan:	Stock Purch. Plan:		Second Exec. Salary: $	Bonus: $

OTHER THOUGHTS:

Apparent Women Officers or Directors:
Hot Spot for Advancement for Women/Minorities:

LOCATIONS: ("Y" = Yes)

West:	Southwest:	Midwest:	Southeast:	Northeast:	International:
					Y

SEGWAY LLC

www.segway.com

Industry Group Code: 336991 **Ranks within this company's industry group:** Sales: Profits:

Vehicle Manufacturing:		Dealers:		Parts:		Service:		Finance:		Specialty:	
Cars:		Car Dealer New:		Manufacturers:		General Service:		Leasing:		Information Systems:	
Trucks:		Car Dealer Used:		Retail:		Specialty Service:		Auto Loans:		Online Marketing:	
Motorcycles:		Truck Dealer:		Distributors:		Oil Change:		Insurance:		Other:	
Specialty:	Y	RV Dealer:		Tires:		Paint and Body:				Publishing:	
Buses:		Motorcycle Dealer:		Batteries:						Rental Cars/Trucks:	
RVs:		Specialty Dealer:									

TYPES OF BUSINESS:

Personal Transportation Devices
Robotic Cargo Transportation Devices

BRANDS/DIVISIONS/AFFILIATES:

Segway Personal Transporter
Segway Robotic Mobility Platform
Project P.U.M.A.
i2 Cargo
x2
x2 Golf
i2
Segway Robotic Mobility Platform (RMP)

CONTACTS: *Note: Officers with more than one job title may be intentionally listed here more than once.*

James Norrod, CEO
James Norrod, Pres.
Monique Apter, VP-Sales
Carol Valianti, VP-Global Comm.
Eric Fleming, Dir.-Creative Svcs.
Claude Le Blond, VP-Int'l Bus.

Phone: 603-222-6000	**Fax:** 603-222-6001
Toll-Free: 866-473-4929	
Address: 14 Technology Dr., Bedford, NH 03110 US	

GROWTH PLANS/SPECIAL FEATURES:

Segway, LLC manufactures and distributes a unique battery-powered personal transportation device, featuring two parallel wheels, called the Segway Personal Transporter (PT). The PT, with a range of 24 miles per charge and a top speed of 12 miles per hour, uses computer processors to mimic human equilibrium, moving forward, backward or turning in response to the rider's body movements. The device was designed for use in congested urban areas, as well as for various commercial uses. Available in a variety of customized models, the PT works both indoors and outdoors, in a range of climates and terrain conditions. The U.S. Postal Service has tested it for use by its mail carriers, and the Segway Patrol models were devised to suit police, military and security agencies. It features extra reflective markings, expanded cargo options, an integrated lighting system and an optional accessory bar. Other models include the i2, a general commuter model; the i2 Cargo, which can haul up to 15 pounds of payload in its two saddle-bag like storage bins; the x2, featuring low pressure tires to handle more difficult terrain; and the x2 Golf, designed to accommodate a golf club bag. Third-party dealers distribute the PT in 43 U.S. states, as well as in Canada, Latin America, Europe, Asia, the Middle East and Australia. Other product offerings include the Segway Robotic Mobility Platform (RMP), a family of four battery powered devices, controlled by either a USB or CAN serial bus interface, that are used to move heavy payloads in tight spaces over a variety of rough terrain. The RMP devices, mainly designed for business customers, range from $7,500 to $32,000. In April 2009, Segway introduced Project P.U.M.A. (Personal Urban Mobility & Accessibility), a prototype two-passenger, enclosed version of the PT, with a top speed of 35 mph and range of 35 miles.

FINANCIALS: **Sales and profits are in thousands of dollars—add 000 to get the full amount. 2009 Note: Financial information for 2009 was not available for all companies at press time.**

2009 Sales: $	2009 Profits: $	**U.S. Stock Ticker: Private**
2008 Sales: $	2008 Profits: $	**Int'l Ticker:** Int'l Exchange:
2007 Sales: $	2007 Profits: $	Employees:
2006 Sales: $	2006 Profits: $	Fiscal Year Ends:
2005 Sales: $	2005 Profits: $	Parent Company:

SALARIES/BENEFITS:

Pension Plan:	ESOP Stock Plan:	Profit Sharing:	Top Exec. Salary: $	Bonus: $
Savings Plan:	Stock Purch. Plan:		Second Exec. Salary: $	Bonus: $

OTHER THOUGHTS:

Apparent Women Officers or Directors: 2
Hot Spot for Advancement for Women/Minorities:

LOCATIONS: ("Y" = Yes)

West:	Southwest:	Midwest:	Southeast:	Northeast:	International:
				Y	

SEQUA CORP

www.sequa.com

Industry Group Code: 33641 **Ranks within this company's industry group:** Sales: Profits:

Vehicle Manufacturing:		Dealers:		Parts:		Service:		Finance:		Specialty:	
Cars:		Car Dealer New:		Manufacturers:	Y	General Service:		Leasing:		Information Systems:	
Trucks:		Car Dealer Used:		Retail:		Specialty Service:		Auto Loans:		Online Marketing:	
Motorcycles:		Truck Dealer:		Distributors:		Oil Change:		Insurance:		Other:	
Specialty:		RV Dealer:		Tires:		Paint and Body:				Publishing:	
Buses:		Motorcycle Dealer:		Batteries:						Rental Cars/Trucks:	
RVs:		Specialty Dealer:									

TYPES OF BUSINESS:

Aerospace
Automotive Accessories
Metal Coatings
Specialty Chemicals
Industrial Machinery

BRANDS/DIVISIONS/AFFILIATES:

Carlyle Group (The)
Precoat Metals
ARC Automotive, Inc.
Casco Products Corporation
Chromalloy Gas Turbine Corporation

GROWTH PLANS/SPECIAL FEATURES:

Sequa Corp. is a highly diversified company with interests in the aerospace, automotive, metal coating, specialty chemicals, industrial machinery and men's formalwear industries. The aerospace segment consists of Chromalloy Gas Turbine Corporation, Sequa's largest operating unit. Chromalloy repairs and manufactures components for commercial and US military jet aircraft engines, as well as marine and land-based aero engines. The automotive segment is composed of two businesses: ARC Automotive, Inc. and Casco Products Corporation. ARC Automotive produces inflators for driver, passenger-side impact and curtain airbag modules. Casco Products is a leading supplier of automotive cigarette lighters, power outlets and automotive accessories. The metal coating segment operates solely through Precoat Metals, which applies protective and decorative coatings to continuous steel and aluminum coil.

CONTACTS: *Note: Officers with more than one job title may be intentionally listed here more than once.*

Armand F. Lauzon, Jr., CEO
Donna Costello, CFO
Andrew Farrant, VP-Mktg.
John Bollman, VP-Human Resources
Steven R. Lowson, General Counsel/Corp. Sec.
Andrew Farrant, VP-Corp. Comm.
David G. Albert, VP-External Affairs
Peter J. Clare, Chmn.

Phone: 813-434-4522 **Fax:**
Toll-Free:
Address: 3000 Bayport Dr., Ste. 880, Tampa, FL 33607 US

FINANCIALS: **Sales and profits are in thousands of dollars—add 000 to get the full amount. 2009 Note: Financial information for 2009 was not available for all companies at press time.**

2009 Sales: $	2009 Profits: $	**U.S. Stock Ticker: Private**
2008 Sales: $	2008 Profits: $	**Int'l Ticker:** Int'l Exchange:
2007 Sales: $	2007 Profits: $	Employees:
2006 Sales: $2,183,816	2006 Profits: $65,606	Fiscal Year Ends: 12/31
2005 Sales: $1,997,558	2005 Profits: $27,323	Parent Company: CARLYLE GROUP (THE)

SALARIES/BENEFITS:

Pension Plan:	ESOP Stock Plan:	Profit Sharing:	Top Exec. Salary: $	Bonus: $
Savings Plan:	Stock Purch. Plan:		Second Exec. Salary: $	Bonus: $

OTHER THOUGHTS:

Apparent Women Officers or Directors: 1
Hot Spot for Advancement for Women/Minorities:

LOCATIONS: ("Y" = Yes)

West:	Southwest:	Midwest:	Southeast:	Northeast:	International:
Y	Y	Y	Y	Y	Y

SHANGHAI AUTOMOTIVE INDUSTRY CORP (SAIC)

www.saicgroup.com

Industry Group Code: 33611 **Ranks within this company's industry group:** Sales: Profits:

Vehicle Manufacturing:		Dealers:		Parts:		Service:		Finance:		Specialty:	
Cars:	Y	Car Dealer New:	Y	Manufacturers:	Y	General Service:	Y	Leasing:	Y	Information Systems:	
Trucks:	Y	Car Dealer Used:	Y	Retail:	Y	Specialty Service:		Auto Loans:	Y	Online Marketing:	
Motorcycles:	Y	Truck Dealer:		Distributors:	Y	Oil Change:		Insurance:	Y	Other:	
Specialty:	Y	RV Dealer:		Tires:		Paint and Body:				Publishing:	
Buses:	Y	Motorcycle Dealer:		Batteries:						Rental Cars/Trucks:	Y
RVs:		Specialty Dealer:									

TYPES OF BUSINESS:

Automobile Manufacturing
Motorcycle Manufacturing
Bus Manufacturing
Car Rental Services
Tractor & Heavy Equipment Manufacturing
Parts Manufacturing, Distribution & Retailing
Consumer Finance & Leasing
Insurance

BRANDS/DIVISIONS/AFFILIATES:

SAIC Motor Corporation, Ltd. (SAIC Motor)
Shanghai Motor Manufacturing Co., Ltd.
Shanghai Automobile Import and Export Corp.
Shanghai General Motors
Shanghai Volkswagen Automotive Co., Ltd.
SAIC GM Wuling Automobile Co.
Roewe
Istana

CONTACTS: *Note: Officers with more than one job title may be intentionally listed here more than once.*

Shen Jianhua, Pres.
Zhe Genlin, VP-Finance
Zhang Guangsheng, Co-Vice Chmn.
Chen Hong, Co-Vice Chmn.-SAIC Group/Pres., SAIC Motor
Chen Zhixin, Exec. VP-SAIC Motor
Ye Yongming, VP
Hu Maoyuan, Chmn.

Phone: 86-21-2201-1688 **Fax:** 86-21-2201-1188
Toll-Free:
Address: 489 WeiHai Rd., Shanghai, 200041 China

GROWTH PLANS/SPECIAL FEATURES:

Shanghai Automotive Industry Corp. (SAIC), a state-owned entity, is one of China's largest automotive companies. The group operates roughly 50 manufacturing facilities, mainly near Shanghai, that make passenger cars, tractors, motorcycles, trucks, buses and automotive parts. SAIC has branches in Korea, Japan, Hong Kong, the U.S., the U.K. and Europe. Annually, the firm sells nearly 1.8 million vehicles, comprising over 1 million passenger cars and 708,000 commercial vehicles. Additional group operations include automotive service, insurance, parts distribution and retail, consumer automotive financing and car rental services. SAIC's primary operating subsidiary is 83.83%-owned SAIC Motor Corporation, Ltd. (SAIC Motor). Subsidiaries under SAIC Motor include Shanghai Motor Manufacturing Co., Ltd.; 51.33%-owned Ssangyong Motor of South Korea; and Sunwin Motor Group. SAIC Motor's main joint ventures are a 50-50 joint venture with General Motors Corp. (GM) called Shanghai General Motors (SGM); and a 50-50 joint venture with Volkswagen AG called Shanghai Volkswagen Automotive Co., Ltd. (SVW). SAIC GM Wuling Automobile Co., a three-way joint venture between SAIC Group, GM and Liuzhou Wuling Motors Co., has the capability to manufacture more than 340,000 vehicles annually. Finished vehicles are branded under the Wuling name for sale domestically and under export to more than 19 countries in Southeast Asia, the Middle East, South America and Western Europe. Service and trade subsidiaries include Shanghai Automobile Import and Export Corp. (SACO), which exports vehicles and parts and oversees importation of high-precision machines, testing and inspection devices and other related items to support SAIC's manufacturing technologies. The company's passenger vehicles are sold under brands including Roewe, MG, Volkswagen, Skoda, Buick, Cadillac and Ssangyong, while its commercial vehicle brands include Wulin, Huizhong, Hongyan, Sunwin, Istana and Yuejin.

FINANCIALS: **Sales and profits are in thousands of dollars—add 000 to get the full amount. 2009 Note: Financial information for 2009 was not available for all companies at press time.**

2009 Sales: $	2009 Profits: $	**U.S. Stock Ticker:**
2008 Sales: $24,882,200	2008 Profits: $52,900	**Int'l Ticker: SAIC** Int'l Exchange: Shanghai-SHE
2007 Sales: $	2007 Profits: $	Employees:
2006 Sales: $	2006 Profits: $	Fiscal Year Ends: 12/31
2005 Sales: $	2005 Profits: $	Parent Company:

SALARIES/BENEFITS:

Pension Plan:	ESOP Stock Plan:	Profit Sharing:	Top Exec. Salary: $	Bonus: $
Savings Plan:	Stock Purch. Plan:		Second Exec. Salary: $	Bonus: $

OTHER THOUGHTS:

Apparent Women Officers or Directors:
Hot Spot for Advancement for Women/Minorities:

LOCATIONS: ("Y" = Yes)

West:	Southwest:	Midwest:	Southeast:	Northeast:	International:
		Y			Y

SHEEHY AUTO STORES

www.sheehy.com

Industry Group Code: 441110 **Ranks within this company's industry group:** Sales: Profits:

Vehicle Manufacturing:		Dealers:		Parts:		Service:		Finance:		Specialty:	
Cars:		Car Dealer New:	Y	Manufacturers:		General Service:	Y	Leasing:	Y	Information Systems:	
Trucks:		Car Dealer Used:	Y	Retail:	Y	Specialty Service:		Auto Loans:	Y	Online Marketing:	
Motorcycles:		Truck Dealer:		Distributors:		Oil Change:		Insurance:		Other:	
Specialty:		RV Dealer:		Tires:		Paint and Body:	Y			Publishing:	
Buses:		Motorcycle Dealer:		Batteries:						Rental Cars/Trucks:	
RVs:		Specialty Dealer:									

TYPES OF BUSINESS:

Auto Dealers, Retail
Auto Service
Auto Finance
Collision Repair

BRANDS/DIVISIONS/AFFILIATES:

Sheehy Markdown

CONTACTS:

Note: Officers with more than one job title may be intentionally listed here more than once.

Vincent A. Sheehy, IV, Pres.
Michael Larkin, CFO
Vincent Sheehy III, Chmn.

Phone: 703-802-3480 **Fax:** 703-802-3481
Toll-Free:
Address: 12701 Fair Lakes Cir., Ste. 250, Fairfax, VA 22033 US

GROWTH PLANS/SPECIAL FEATURES:

Sheehy Auto Stores is a new and pre-owned automobile dealer with 20 stores and 17 locations throughout Virginia and Maryland, including Springfield, Richmond, Powhatan, Ashland, Manassas, Annapolis, Glen Burnie, Mechanicsville and Alexandria. The company was founded in 1965 as Sheehy Ford, a small, family-owned car dealership just off the Washington, D.C. beltway. Today, the company sells automobiles from a wide variety of manufacturers: Ford, Nissan, Infiniti, Chevrolet, Honda, Mazda, Hyundai, Lexus, Mitsubishi and Subaru. Sheehy is one of the largest retailers of Fords in the mid-Atlantic region, selling approximately 30,000 vehicles annually. All cars sold by Sheehy carry a three-day money back guarantee and the Sheehy Markdown, which ensures that all new vehicles are priced below list price and all used vehicles are priced below blue book; it even features a bargain lot, on which customers can find automobiles for less than $9,995. The company has an in-house collision center as well. Sheehy's web site provides links to each of the dealerships, where customers can browse inventory, schedule service appointments or apply for financing.

Sheehy offers its employees medical and dental insurance; flexible spending accounts; a 401(k); paid vacation; short/long term disability insurance; and life insurance.

FINANCIALS:

Sales and profits are in thousands of dollars—add 000 to get the full amount. 2009 Note: Financial information for 2009 was not available for all companies at press time.

2009 Sales: $	2009 Profits: $	**U.S. Stock Ticker: Private**
2008 Sales: $	2008 Profits: $	**Int'l Ticker:** Int'l Exchange:
2007 Sales: $	2007 Profits: $	Employees:
2006 Sales: $	2006 Profits: $	Fiscal Year Ends: 12/31
2005 Sales: $	2005 Profits: $	Parent Company:

SALARIES/BENEFITS:

Pension Plan:	ESOP Stock Plan:	Profit Sharing:	Top Exec. Salary: $	Bonus: $
Savings Plan: Y	Stock Purch. Plan:		Second Exec. Salary: $	Bonus: $

OTHER THOUGHTS:

Apparent Women Officers or Directors:
Hot Spot for Advancement for Women/Minorities:

LOCATIONS: ("Y" = Yes)

West:	Southwest:	Midwest:	Southeast:	Northeast:	International:
				Y	

SIEMENS AG

www.siemens.com

Industry Group Code: 335 **Ranks within this company's industry group:** Sales: 1 Profits: 1

Vehicle Manufacturing:		Dealers:		Parts:		Service:		Finance:		Specialty:	
Cars:		Car Dealer New:		Manufacturers:		General Service:		Leasing:		Information Systems:	Y
Trucks:		Car Dealer Used:		Retail:		Specialty Service:		Auto Loans:		Online Marketing:	
Motorcycles:		Truck Dealer:		Distributors:		Oil Change:		Insurance:		Other:	Y
Specialty:		RV Dealer:		Tires:		Paint and Body:				Publishing:	
Buses:		Motorcycle Dealer:		Batteries:						Rental Cars/Trucks:	
RVs:		Specialty Dealer:									

TYPES OF BUSINESS:

Electrical Equipment Manufacturing
Energy & Power Plant Systems & Consulting
IT Systems & Consulting
Lighting & Optical Systems
Automation Systems
Transportation & Logistics Systems
Photovoltaic Equipment
Medical and Health Care Services and Equipment

BRANDS/DIVISIONS/AFFILIATES:

CTI Molecular Imaging
Siemens Building Technologies
Siemens Canada
Siemens Corporate Technology
Siemens Energy & Automation Inc
Siemens Energy Services
Siemens Healthcare
Solel Solar Systems

CONTACTS: *Note: Officers with more than one job title may be intentionally listed here more than once.*

Peter H. Loscher, CEO
Peter H. Loscher, Pres.
Joe Kaeser, Head-Finance
Siegfried Russwurm, Head-Human Resources/Dir.-Labor
Heinrich Hiesinger, CIO
Hermann Requardt, Head-Corp. Tech.
Peter Y. Solmssen, Head-Legal & Compliance
Joe Kaeser, Controller
Hermann Requardt, Sector CEO-Healthcare
Heinrich Hiesinger, Sector CEO-Industry
Wolfgang Dehen, Sector CEO-Energy/Dir.-Asia & Australia
Eric Spiegel, CEO/Pres., Siemens Corp.
Gerhard Cromme, Chmn.
Peter Y. Solmssen, Dir.-The Americas
Barbara Kux, Head-Supply Chain Mgmt. & Sustainability

Phone: 49-69-797-6660	**Fax:**
Toll-Free:	
Address: Wittelsbacherplatz 2, Munich, 80333 Germany	

GROWTH PLANS/SPECIAL FEATURES:

Siemens AG is one of the largest electrical engineering and manufacturing companies in the world. Based in Germany, the firm sells products and services to approximately 190 countries around the globe, including all 50 states in the U.S. The company is organized in three primary sectors: industry, energy and healthcare. The industry sector's offerings range from industry automation products and services to building, lighting and mobility systems and services, as well as system integration for plant businesses. Additionally, this sector provides networking technology for transportation systems, including airport logistics, postal automation and railway electrification. The energy sector offers a broad range of products and services related to the generation, transmission and distribution of power, as well as for the extraction, conversion and transportation of oil and gas. The healthcare sector develops, manufactures and markets diagnostic and therapeutic systems, devices and consumables, as well as information technology systems for clinical and healthcare administration settings. Besides these activities, subsidiaries Siemens IT Solutions & Services as well as Siemens Financial Services support sector activities as business partners, meanwhile continuing to build up their own business with external customers. Recently, the company announced layoffs of approximately 4.2% of its workforce, totaling nearly 16,750 jobs. The firm has also begun to consolidate its more than 1,800 separate businesses to fewer than 1,000, realigning its operations regionally as cost-saving measures. The company has also sold a number of its telecommunications businesses in order to focus on the core sectors of health care, energy and industrial equipment. In July 2009, the firm sold its 50% stake in Fujitsu Siemens Computers, an IT infrastructure provider, to Fujitsu Limited for roughly $670 million. In October 2009, Siemens announced that it would acquire Israel-based Solel Solar Systems Limited for $418 million.

FINANCIALS: **Sales and profits are in thousands of dollars—add 000 to get the full amount. 2009 Note: Financial information for 2009 was not available for all companies at press time.**

2009 Sales: $113,842,000	2009 Profits: $3,404,080	**U.S. Stock Ticker: SI**
2008 Sales: $107,580,000	2008 Profits: $8,189,070	**Int'l Ticker: SIE** Int'l Exchange: Frankfurt-Euronext
2007 Sales: $115,406,000	2007 Profits: $3,535,760	Employees: 427,000
2006 Sales: $113,740,000	2006 Profits: $3,950,360	Fiscal Year Ends: 9/30
2005 Sales: $90,670,000	2005 Profits: $2,702,000	Parent Company:

SALARIES/BENEFITS:

Pension Plan:	ESOP Stock Plan:	Profit Sharing:	Top Exec. Salary: $	Bonus: $
Savings Plan:	Stock Purch. Plan:		Second Exec. Salary: $	Bonus: $

OTHER THOUGHTS:

Apparent Women Officers or Directors: 5
Hot Spot for Advancement for Women/Minorities: Y

LOCATIONS: ("Y" = Yes)

West:	Southwest:	Midwest:	Southeast:	Northeast:	International:
Y	Y	Y	Y	Y	Y

SIRIUS XM RADIO INC

www.sirius.com

Industry Group Code: 515210A **Ranks within this company's industry group:** Sales: 1 Profits: 1

Vehicle Manufacturing:		Dealers:		Parts:		Service:		Finance:		Specialty:	
Cars:		Car Dealer New:		Manufacturers:		General Service:		Leasing:		Information Systems:	
Trucks:		Car Dealer Used:		Retail:		Specialty Service:		Auto Loans:		Online Marketing:	
Motorcycles:		Truck Dealer:		Distributors:		Oil Change:		Insurance:		Other:	Y
Specialty:		RV Dealer:		Tires:		Paint and Body:				Publishing:	
Buses:		Motorcycle Dealer:		Batteries:						Rental Cars/Trucks:	
RVs:		Specialty Dealer:									

TYPES OF BUSINESS:

Satellite Radio Broadcasting
Mobile Television Content

BRANDS/DIVISIONS/AFFILIATES:

Sirius
Liberty Media Corp.
XM Radio
XM SkyDock

CONTACTS: *Note: Officers with more than one job title may be intentionally listed here more than once.*

Mel Karmazin, CEO
Scott Greenstein, Pres.
David J. Frear, CFO/Exec. VP
James Meyer, Pres., Sales
Dara Altman, Chief Admin. Officer/Exec. VP
Patrick L. Donnelly, General Counsel/Exec. VP/Sec.
James Meyer, Pres., Oper.
Sal Resendez, Contact-Media Rel.
Scott Greenstein, Chief Content Officer
Hillary Schupf, Contact-Media, Talk & Entertainment Content
Andrew Fitzpatrick, Contact-Media, Sports Content
Samantha Bowman, Contact-Media, Music & Entertainment Content
Eddy W. Hartenstein, Chmn.

Phone: 212-584-5100 **Fax:** 212-584-5353
Toll-Free:
Address: 1221 Ave. of the Americas, Fl. 36, New York, NY 10020 US

GROWTH PLANS/SPECIAL FEATURES:

Sirius XM Radio, Inc. is a satellite radio provider in the U.S. It offers 135 channels to its subscribers, 69 channels of 100% commercial-free music and 66 channels of sports, news, talk, entertainment, traffic and weather. The company's primary source of revenue is subscription fees, with most of its customers subscribing to Sirius on an annual, semi-annual, quarterly or monthly basis. The firm has nearly 19 million subscribers. Most subscribers receive service through Sirius radios, which are sold through its web site and by automakers and national and regional retailers. Sirius radios for the car, truck, home, RV, boat, office and store are available in more than 20,000 retail locations, including Best Buy, Crutchfield, Costco, Target, Wal-Mart, Sam's Club and RadioShack. Sirius has agreements with every major automaker to offer its radios as factory or dealer-installed options in their vehicles. Sirius Internet Radio is an Internet-only version of the firm's service, which delivers a simulcast of select music and non-music channels. The company also offers Backseat TV, a television content service designed primarily for children in the backseat of a vehicle. Sirius' music channels are also available through an application for the Apple iPod and iPod touch. The company also offers service in Canada. In early 2009, Sirius XM after years of massive losses, agreed to a new alliance with Liberty Media, which also owns a major stake in satellite TV firm DirecTV. In total, Liberty will provide loans totaling $530 million in exchange for a 40% stake in the company. In November 2009, the company launched the XM SkyDock, a satellite radio controlled by an Apple iPod.

The company offers its employees medical, dental and vision insurance; domestic partner benefits; an employee assistance program; life and AD&D insurance; healthcare spending accounts; transportation and parking reimbursement programs; short- and long-term disability insurance; a 401(k) plan; and a profit sharing plan.

FINANCIALS: **Sales and profits are in thousands of dollars—add 000 to get the full amount. 2009 Note: Financial information for 2009 was not available for all companies at press time.**

2009 Sales: $2,472,638	2009 Profits: $-342,790	**U.S. Stock Ticker: SIRI**
2008 Sales: $1,663,992	2008 Profits: $-5,313,288	**Int'l Ticker:** Int'l Exchange:
2007 Sales: $922,066	2007 Profits: $-565,252	Employees: 1,514
2006 Sales: $637,235	2006 Profits: $-1,104,867	Fiscal Year Ends: 12/31
2005 Sales: $242,245	2005 Profits: $-862,997	Parent Company:

SALARIES/BENEFITS:

Pension Plan:	ESOP Stock Plan:	Profit Sharing: Y	Top Exec. Salary: $1,250,000	Bonus: $7,000,000
Savings Plan: Y	Stock Purch. Plan:		Second Exec. Salary: $950,000	Bonus: $1,250,000

OTHER THOUGHTS:

Apparent Women Officers or Directors: 4
Hot Spot for Advancement for Women/Minorities: Y

LOCATIONS: ("Y" = Yes)

West:	Southwest:	Midwest:	Southeast:	Northeast:	International:
				Y	

SIXT AKTIENGESELLSCHAFT

ag.sixt.com

Industry Group Code: 5321 **Ranks within this company's industry group:** Sales: 3 Profits: 2

Vehicle Manufacturing:		Dealers:		Parts:		Service:		Finance:		Specialty:	
Cars:		Car Dealer New:		Manufacturers:		General Service:		Leasing:	Y	Information Systems:	
Trucks:		Car Dealer Used:	Y	Retail:		Specialty Service:		Auto Loans:		Online Marketing:	
Motorcycles:		Truck Dealer:		Distributors:		Oil Change:		Insurance:		Other:	Y
Specialty:		RV Dealer:		Tires:		Paint and Body:				Publishing:	
Buses:		Motorcycle Dealer:		Batteries:						Rental Cars/Trucks:	Y
RVs:		Specialty Dealer:									

TYPES OF BUSINESS:

Automobile Rental
e-Commerce
Automobile Leasing
Used Car Sales
Fleet Management
Insurance Services

BRANDS/DIVISIONS/AFFILIATES:

SIXTI GmbH
Sixt Leasing AG
Sixt VIP Services GMBH
Sixt SAS
United Rental Group, Ltd.
Europa Service Car, Ltd.

CONTACTS: *Note: Officers with more than one job title may be intentionally listed here more than once.*

Detlev Patsch, COO
Julian zu Pulitz, CFO
Frank Feist, Dir.-Sales
Julian zu Pulitz, Controller
Thierry Antinori, Deputy Chmn.-Supervisory Board
Gunter Thielen, Chmn.-Supervisory Board
Erich Sixt, Chmn.
Detlef Krehahn, VP-Int'l Franchise

Phone: 49-89-744444-260	**Fax:** 49-89-744448-4260
Toll-Free:	
Address: Zugspitzstrasse 1, Pullach im Isartal, 82049 Germany	

GROWTH PLANS/SPECIAL FEATURES:

Sixt Aktiengesellschaft, along with its subsidiaries, provides automobile rentals, full-service leasing, used car sales and e-commerce solutions in over 85 countries throughout the world. Together with its licensees and partners, the company has a worldwide presence of 3,500 service points, with 1,923 rental locations worldwide, including 530 in Germany. The company operates through two business units. The vehicle rental unit rents automobiles, including cars, trucks and holiday cars to corporate and private customers; it also offers a limousine service and used car sales. It possesses one of the largest fleets of BMW and Mercedes Benz vehicles in the world. SIXTI GmbH, a subsidiary of Sixt, offers no-frills car rental with rates as low as about $14 per day. SIXTI provides customers with Smart Car and Ford Fiesta for its MicroDrive service, and Ford Focus and Peugeot 307 models for its slightly more expensive Mididrive service. The other business unit is the leasing unit, which provides a broad range of leasing services, including pure-play finance leasing, full-service leasing, fleet management, fleet consulting, billing and reporting. Sixt's online platform offers access to its vehicle rental and leasing offers, the sale of new and used vehicles, travel management and insurance services. The company has partnership collaborations with various airlines and hotel groups worldwide. In November 2009, the company partnered with Traveldoo to provide its service and its entire car rental fleet for direct online access and purchase. In March 2010, the company expanded its North African operations into Libya with services in Tripoli. In July 2010, Sixt added the high-performance Germany luxury brand Porsche to its roster of rental cars.

Sixt offers all its employees a company car. The firm prefers internal promotion to external recruitment and offers continuous training and development programs for its workers.

FINANCIALS: **Sales and profits are in thousands of dollars—add 000 to get the full amount. 2009 Note: Financial information for 2009 was not available for all companies at press time.**

2009 Sales: $2,032,500	2009 Profits: $13,200	**U.S. Stock Ticker:**
2008 Sales: $2,518,570	2008 Profits: $123,090	**Int'l Ticker: SIX2** Int'l Exchange: Frankfurt-Euronext
2007 Sales: $2,306,200	2007 Profits: $137,500	Employees: 2,981
2006 Sales: $2,121,400	2006 Profits: $108,400	Fiscal Year Ends: 12/31
2005 Sales: $1,963,500	2005 Profits: $82,100	Parent Company:

SALARIES/BENEFITS:

Pension Plan:	ESOP Stock Plan:	Profit Sharing:	Top Exec. Salary: $	Bonus: $
Savings Plan: Y	Stock Purch. Plan: Y		Second Exec. Salary: $	Bonus: $

OTHER THOUGHTS:

Apparent Women Officers or Directors: 1
Hot Spot for Advancement for Women/Minorities:

LOCATIONS: ("Y" = Yes)

West:	Southwest:	Midwest:	Southeast:	Northeast:	International:
					Y

SKODA AUTO AS

www.skoda-auto.com

Industry Group Code: 33611 **Ranks within this company's industry group:** Sales: Profits:

Vehicle Manufacturing:		**Dealers:**		**Parts:**		**Service:**		**Finance:**		**Specialty:**	
Cars:	Y	Car Dealer New:		Manufacturers:	Y	General Service:		Leasing:		Information Systems:	
Trucks:		Car Dealer Used:		Retail:		Specialty Service:		Auto Loans:		Online Marketing:	
Motorcycles:		Truck Dealer:		Distributors:	Y	Oil Change:		Insurance:		Other:	
Specialty:	Y	RV Dealer:		Tires:		Paint and Body:				Publishing:	
Buses:		Motorcycle Dealer:		Batteries:						Rental Cars/Trucks:	
RVs:		Specialty Dealer:									

TYPES OF BUSINESS:

Automobile Manufacturer
Automobile Parts Manufacturer

BRANDS/DIVISIONS/AFFILIATES:

SkodaAuto Deutschland GmbH
SKODA AUTO Slovensko, s.r.o.
Skoda Auto Polska S.A.
Skoda Auto India Private Ltd.
Volkswagen AG

CONTACTS:

Note: Officers with more than one job title may be intentionally listed here more than once.

Libor Myska, Head-Sales Control
Miroslava Nigrinova, Head-Human Resources Care
Andreas Hafemann, Head-Info. Systems & Organization
Markus Steiner, Head-Brand Prod. Planning
David Kavan, Head-Legal Dept.
Martin Lauer, Head-Corp. Comm.
Jana Sramova, Head-Acct.
Arne Gruber, Head-Prod. & Logistics Controlling
Lukas Folc, Head-Sales, Subsidiaries & Divisions Controlling
Manfred Bort, Head-Quality Mgmt..
Jozef Kaban, Head-Design
Winfried Vahland, Chmn.
Christian Wiegal, Head-Int'l Sales
Walther Schlogl, Head-Purchasing

Phone: 42-326-811-111 **Fax:** 42-326-721-328
Toll-Free:
Address: Vaclava Klementa 869, Mlada Boleslav, 293 60 Czech Republic

GROWTH PLANS/SPECIAL FEATURES:

Skoda Auto AS, a subsidiary of Volkswagen AG, is a major designer and manufacturer of automobiles in the Czech Republic. The company is engaged in the development, production and sale of passenger and utility cars, engines, components, original parts and car accessories, as well as providing related repair and maintenance services. Skoda offers four different models: the Fabia, the Octavia, the Roomster/Praktik, the Yeti and the Superb. The Fabia is a small hatchback based on the Volkswagen Polo platform. The Octavia is based on the Volkswagen Jetta platform. The Roomster is a small 5-door multi-purpose vehicle. The model also comes in a panel van version called the Praktik. The Yeti is the first compact SUV Skoda has offered. The Superb is a four-door sedan based on a Volkswagen Passat platform. The Superb is available in three different trims, the Comfort, the Ambition and the Elegance, as well as additional 4x4 and GreenLine variants. Each of Skoda's models comes with the option of gasoline or diesel engines and many feature a Combi variant model, which extends the car's interior space and capacity. The firm also offers vehicle fleet sales. In addition to complete vehicles, the firm manufactures vehicle components for itself and other Volkswagen group companies. These components include engines, gear boxes and steel and cast-iron semi-finished parts. Skoda operates in over 100 markets, with subsidiaries in the Czech Republic, Russia, Slovakia, Germany, Poland and India. These subsidiaries include Skoda Auto Deutschland GmbH; SKODA AUTO Slovensko, s.r.o.; Skoda Auto Polska S.A.; and Skoda Auto India Private Ltd. In June 2010, the company began production of the Fabia RS, a sports model variation of the hatchback, and the Fabia Combi GreenLine, which offers a high-pressure direct injection engine for improved fuel economy and reduced CO2 emissions.

FINANCIALS:

Sales and profits are in thousands of dollars—add 000 to get the full amount. 2009 Note: Financial information for 2009 was not available for all companies at press time.

2009 Sales: $	2009 Profits: $	**U.S. Stock Ticker: Subsidiary**
2008 Sales: $	2008 Profits: $	**Int'l Ticker:** Int'l Exchange:
2007 Sales: $	2007 Profits: $	Employees:
2006 Sales: $	2006 Profits: $	Fiscal Year Ends: 12/31
2005 Sales: $	2005 Profits: $	Parent Company: VOLKSWAGEN AG

SALARIES/BENEFITS:

Pension Plan:	ESOP Stock Plan:	Profit Sharing:	Top Exec. Salary: $	Bonus: $
Savings Plan:	Stock Purch. Plan:		Second Exec. Salary: $	Bonus: $

OTHER THOUGHTS:

Apparent Women Officers or Directors: 2
Hot Spot for Advancement for Women/Minorities:

LOCATIONS: ("Y" = Yes)

West:	Southwest:	Midwest:	Southeast:	Northeast:	International:
					Y

SKYLINE CORPORATION

www.skylinecorp.com

Industry Group Code: 332311 **Ranks within this company's industry group:** Sales: 1 Profits: 1

Vehicle Manufacturing:		Dealers:		Parts:		Service:		Finance:		Specialty:	
Cars:		Car Dealer New:		Manufacturers:		General Service:		Leasing:		Information Systems:	
Trucks:		Car Dealer Used:		Retail:		Specialty Service:		Auto Loans:		Online Marketing:	
Motorcycles:		Truck Dealer:		Distributors:		Oil Change:		Insurance:		Other:	Y
Specialty:		RV Dealer:		Tires:		Paint and Body:				Publishing:	
Buses:		Motorcycle Dealer:		Batteries:						Rental Cars/Trucks:	
RVs:	Y	Specialty Dealer:									

TYPES OF BUSINESS:

Manufactured Housing
Recreational Vehicles
Prefabricated Metal Buildings & Components

BRANDS/DIVISIONS/AFFILIATES:

Nomad
Shyline Homes
Aljo
Weekender
Hillcrest Homes
Rampage
Trailrider
Wagoneer

CONTACTS:

Note: Officers with more than one job title may be intentionally listed here more than once.

Thomas G. Deranek, CEO
Jon S. Pilarski, CFO
Terrence M. Decio, VP-Mktg. & Sales
Charles W. Chambliss, VP-Prod. Dev.
Charles W. Chambliss, VP-Eng.
Martin R. Fransted, Sec.
Christopher R. Leader, VP-Oper.
Jon S. Pilarski, VP-Finance/Treas.
Bruce G. Page, VP-Oper.
Martin R. Fransted, Corp. Controller
Thomas G. Deranek, Chmn.

Phone: 574-294-6521 **Fax:** 574-293-7574
Toll-Free: 800-348-7469
Address: 2520 By-Pass Rd., P.O. Box 743, Elkhart, IN 46515 US

GROWTH PLANS/SPECIAL FEATURES:

Skyline Corporation, along with its consolidated subsidiaries, designs, produces and distributes manufactured housing, including single-section, multi-section and modular homes and towable RVs, including travel trailers, fifth wheels and park models. The firm sold 2,712 manufactured homes in 2009. The company also sold 2,832 recreational vehicles in 2009, which are sold under a number of trademarks for travel trailers, fifth wheels and park models. Skyline has 14 manufacturing facilities in 10 states; of which 11 produce housing and 3 produce RVs. The firm's manufactured homes are distributed by approximately 240 independent dealers at 400 locations throughout the U.S., and its RVs are distributed by approximately 130 independent dealers at 150 locations throughout the U.S. The company sells a variety of RVs: Aljo; Aljo Ultra-Lite; Layton; Layton Ultra-Lite; Mountain View; Nomad; Nomad Ultra-Lite; Texan; Wagoneer; Weekender; Freestyle; Trail Rider; and Rampage. The RV market is made up primarily of vacationing middle-income families, retired couples traveling around the country and sports enthusiasts pursuing four-season hobbies. Housing options include Skyline Homes, Hillcrest Homes and Skyline Park Models. Skyline Homes and Hillcrest Homes by Skyline can range from a one bedroom, 400 square foot home to a 5 bedroom, 2,700 square foot multi-sectional modular home, nearly indistinguishable from conventionally built homes, which can be assembled on commercial lots. The Skyline Park Models are meant for temporary use and are commonly used in resort or vacation locations.

FINANCIALS:

Sales and profits are in thousands of dollars—add 000 to get the full amount. 2009 Note: Financial information for 2009 was not available for all companies at press time.

2009 Sales: $166,676	2009 Profits: $-15,434	**U.S. Stock Ticker: SKY**
2008 Sales: $301,765	2008 Profits: $-5,556	**Int'l Ticker:** Int'l Exchange:
2007 Sales: $365,473	2007 Profits: $2,593	Employees: 1,300
2006 Sales: $508,543	2006 Profits: $14,292	Fiscal Year Ends: 5/31
2005 Sales: $454,324	2005 Profits: $5,452	Parent Company:

SALARIES/BENEFITS:

Pension Plan:	ESOP Stock Plan:	Profit Sharing:	Top Exec. Salary: $300,000	Bonus: $
Savings Plan:	Stock Purch. Plan:		Second Exec. Salary: $290,000	Bonus: $

OTHER THOUGHTS:

Apparent Women Officers or Directors:
Hot Spot for Advancement for Women/Minorities:

LOCATIONS: ("Y" = Yes)

West:	Southwest:	Midwest:	Southeast:	Northeast:	International:
Y	Y	Y	Y	Y	

SMART GMBH

www.smart.com

Industry Group Code: 33611 **Ranks within this company's industry group:** Sales: Profits:

Vehicle Manufacturing:		Dealers:		Parts:		Service:		Finance:		Specialty:	
Cars:	Y	Car Dealer New:		Manufacturers:		General Service:		Leasing:		Information Systems:	
Trucks:		Car Dealer Used:		Retail:		Specialty Service:		Auto Loans:		Online Marketing:	
Motorcycles:		Truck Dealer:		Distributors:		Oil Change:		Insurance:		Other:	
Specialty:		RV Dealer:		Tires:		Paint and Body:				Publishing:	
Buses:		Motorcycle Dealer:		Batteries:						Rental Cars/Trucks:	
RVs:		Specialty Dealer:									

TYPES OF BUSINESS:

Automobile Manufacturer
Ultra-Compact Cars

BRANDS/DIVISIONS/AFFILIATES:

Daimler AG
Mercedes-Benz Cars
smart fortwo
smart fortwo coupe
smart fortwo cabrio
Carbiolet
smart USA Distributor LLC
smart-BARBUS GmbH

CONTACTS: *Note: Officers with more than one job title may be intentionally listed here more than once.*

Dieter Zetsche, Chmn.-Daimler AG/Head-Mercedes Benz
Anders Sundt Jensen, Head-Brand Mgmt., Daimler AG Mercedes-Benz Unit
Wolfgang Bernhard, VP-Prod. & Procurement, Daimler AG
Wilried Porth, VP-Human Resources, Daimler AG

Phone: 49-7031-9071-163 **Fax:** 49-7031-9071-241
Toll-Free:
Address: 2 Leibnizstrasse, Boeblingen, D-71032 Germany

GROWTH PLANS/SPECIAL FEATURES:

Smart GmbH (smart), part of Daimler AG's Mercedes-Benz Cars group, manufactures ultra-compact cars primarily sold in the European market. Its sole model, the two-seat fortwo, is just eight feet long, with 7.8 cubic feet of trunk space and 12 cubic feet total storage space, including the roof. The gasoline model, with a top speed of 90 MPH (miles per hour), is rated at 48 MPG (miles per gallon) and the diesel model at 50 MPG, under standard driving conditions. The fortwo comes in two basic models: the coupe and the cabrio (or cabriolet in the U.S.). The coupe features a three-cylinder engine and plastic exterior body panels that can be exchanged and recycled. The cabriolet, in almost all other respects similar to the coupe, offers a convertible top. Additionally, smart offers the edition limited three, featuring what smart calls a micro hybrid drive, which turns the car off when breaking, reducing fuel consumption by up to 20%. The 2009 smart fortwo is available in three trim levels: an entry-level pure for under $12,000, a well-equipped passion coupe, starting at under $14,000, and a convertible, the passion cabriolet, starting at under $17,000. The fortwo is one of six cars displayed in New York's Museum of Modern Art, and is the only car in the display currently in production. smart has sold over 1 million cars in 37 countries since producing its first car in 1998. Headquartered in Bloomfield Hills, Michigan, smart USA Distributor LLC, a wholly-owned subsidiary of Penske Automotive Group, Inc., is the exclusive distributor of the smart fortwo in the U.S. and Puerto Rico. smart USA has 74 dealerships in 31 U.S. states. In March 2009, joint venture smart-BARBUS GmbH unveiled the smart fortwo BARBUS electric-drive concept car.

FINANCIALS: **Sales and profits are in thousands of dollars—add 000 to get the full amount. 2009 Note: Financial information for 2009 was not available for all companies at press time.**

2009 Sales: $	2009 Profits: $	**U.S. Stock Ticker: Subsidiary**
2008 Sales: $	2008 Profits: $	**Int'l Ticker:** Int'l Exchange:
2007 Sales: $	2007 Profits: $	Employees:
2006 Sales: $	2006 Profits: $	Fiscal Year Ends: 12/31
2005 Sales: $	2005 Profits: $	Parent Company: DAIMLER AG

SALARIES/BENEFITS:

Pension Plan:	ESOP Stock Plan:	Profit Sharing:	Top Exec. Salary: $	Bonus: $
Savings Plan:	Stock Purch. Plan:		Second Exec. Salary: $	Bonus: $

OTHER THOUGHTS:

Apparent Women Officers or Directors:
Hot Spot for Advancement for Women/Minorities:

LOCATIONS: ("Y" = Yes)

West:	Southwest:	Midwest:	Southeast:	Northeast:	International:
Y	Y	Y	Y	Y	Y

SOGEFI SPA

www.sogefi.it

Industry Group Code: 3363 **Ranks within this company's industry group:** Sales: 40 Profits: 32

Vehicle Manufacturing:		Dealers:		Parts:		Service:		Finance:		Specialty:	
Cars:		Car Dealer New:		Manufacturers:	Y	General Service:		Leasing:		Information Systems:	
Trucks:		Car Dealer Used:		Retail:	Y	Specialty Service:		Auto Loans:		Online Marketing:	
Motorcycles:		Truck Dealer:		Distributors:		Oil Change:		Insurance:		Other:	
Specialty:		RV Dealer:		Tires:		Paint and Body:				Publishing:	
Buses:		Motorcycle Dealer:		Batteries:						Rental Cars/Trucks:	
RVs:		Specialty Dealer:									

TYPES OF BUSINESS:

Automotive Parts Manufacturing
Fluid Filters
Suspension Parts

BRANDS/DIVISIONS/AFFILIATES:

Cir S.p.A
Purflux
Crosland
Tecnocar
Coopers
FIAAM
Fram
Allevard Rejena

CONTACTS:

Note: Officers with more than one job title may be intentionally listed here more than once.

Emanuele Bosio, Managing Dir.
Giancarlo Coppa, CFO
Pierre L'Alloret, Gen. Mgr.-Sales & Dev., Filters Div. OEM & OES
Alberto Obert, Mgr.-Human Resources
Giancarlo Coppa, Mgr.-Investor Rel.
Corrado Passera, Oper. Gen. Mgr.-Suspension Compnents
Giampietro Dell'Orto, Mgr.-Kaizen Project
Keith Drew, Oper. Gen. Mgr.-Filters Div.
Giorgio F. Imposimato, Mgr.-Internal Audit & Risk
Rodolfo De Benedetti, Chmn.
Roberto Fabris, Mgr.-Purchasing

Phone: 39-02-467501	Fax: 39-02-43511348
Toll-Free:	
Address: Via Flavio Gioia, 8, Milano, 20149 Italy	

GROWTH PLANS/SPECIAL FEATURES:

SOGEFI S.p.A., managed and supervised by Cir S.p.A, is an Italian company that manufactures automotive components, specializing in filters and suspension parts. Filters generated roughly 53.1% of its 2009 sales and suspension components generated 46.9%. Approximately 61.6% of its products are sold in the original equipment manufacturing (OEM) market; 224.7% are sold in the independent aftermarket (IAM); and 13.7% are sold as original equipment spares (OES). The firm's filtration products include engine and cabin air filters; oil filters; and fuel filters for both diesel and petrol engines. These filters are sold under the brand names Purflux, Crosland, Tecnocar, Coopers, FIAAM and Fram. Its suspension and precision products include track adjusters; stabilizer and torsion bars; leaf and precision springs; coil springs for shock absorbers; and stabilinks. These products are sold under the commercial brand names Rejna, Allevard Rejena and United Springs. SOGEFI maintains 505 offices and 39 plants in 13 countries across three continents. It has a presence in Argentina, Brazil, the U.S., China, India, Italy, France, the U.K., the Netherlands, Germany, Sweden, Spain and Slovenia. Its largest market is France, which generated 24.3% of sales in 2009. Its other large markets include Mercosur (in English, the Southern Common Market, a regional trade agreement between Argentina, Brazil, Uruguay and Paraguay), which generated 19.6%; and Germany, 13.3%. The firm's corporate customers include car makers such as Peugeot-Citroen, Renault, Ford, Fiat, Volkswagen, BMW, Daimler, Chrysler, General Motors, Toyota, Honda and Nissan; truck makers such as Iveco, Mercedes-Benz, DAF, CNH, Caterpillar, Man, SCANIA and John Deere; railway vehicle manufacturers Bombardier and Alstom; and others, including Berco and Valeo.

FINANCIALS:

Sales and profits are in thousands of dollars—add 000 to get the full amount. 2009 Note: Financial information for 2009 was not available for all companies at press time.

2009 Sales: $997,990	2009 Profits: $-9,710	**U.S. Stock Ticker:**
2008 Sales: $1,455,380	2008 Profits: $40,770	**Int'l Ticker: SGFI** Int'l Exchange: Milan-BI
2007 Sales: $1,533,050	2007 Profits: $74,660	Employees: 5,770
2006 Sales: $1,578,800	2006 Profits: $78,700	Fiscal Year Ends: 12/31
2005 Sales: $1,399,030	2005 Profits: $61,100	Parent Company:

SALARIES/BENEFITS:

Pension Plan:	ESOP Stock Plan:	Profit Sharing:	Top Exec. Salary: $	Bonus: $
Savings Plan:	Stock Purch. Plan:		Second Exec. Salary: $	Bonus: $

OTHER THOUGHTS:

Apparent Women Officers or Directors: 1
Hot Spot for Advancement for Women/Minorities:

LOCATIONS: ("Y" = Yes)

West:	Southwest:	Midwest:	Southeast:	Northeast:	International:
		Y		Y	Y

SONIC AUTOMOTIVE INC

www.sonicautomotive.com

Industry Group Code: 441110 **Ranks within this company's industry group:** Sales: 5 Profits: 6

Vehicle Manufacturing:		Dealers:		Parts:		Service:		Finance:		Specialty:	
Cars:		Car Dealer New:	Y	Manufacturers:		General Service:	Y	Leasing:		Information Systems:	
Trucks:		Car Dealer Used:	Y	Retail:	Y	Specialty Service:		Auto Loans:	Y	Online Marketing:	
Motorcycles:		Truck Dealer:		Distributors:		Oil Change:		Insurance:	Y	Other:	
Specialty:		RV Dealer:		Tires:		Paint and Body:	Y			Publishing:	
Buses:		Motorcycle Dealer:		Batteries:						Rental Cars/Trucks:	
RVs:		Specialty Dealer:									

TYPES OF BUSINESS:

Auto Dealers, Retail
Collision Repair Centers
Auto Parts
Insurance
Financing

BRANDS/DIVISIONS/AFFILIATES:

CONTACTS:

Note: Officers with more than one job title may be intentionally listed here more than once.

O. Bruton Smith, CEO
B. Scott Smith, Pres.
David P. Cosper, CFO
Stephen K. Coss, General Counsel/Sr. VP/Sec.
Jeff Dyke, Exec. VP-Oper.
B. Scott Smith, Chief Strategic Officer
J. Todd Atenhan, Contact-Investor Rel.
Greg Young, VP-Finance
David B. Smith, Exec. VP
O. Bruton Smith, Chmn.

Phone: 704-566-2400	**Fax:** 704-536-5116
Toll-Free:	
Address: 6415 Idlewild Blvd., Ste. 109, Charlotte, NC 28212 US	

GROWTH PLANS/SPECIAL FEATURES:

Sonic Automotive, Inc. is one of the leading U.S. automotive retailers, operating 145 dealership franchises nationwide. The firm's dealerships offer new and used cars and trucks; replacement parts; and services such as repair, finance and insurance. These dealerships feature a total of 29 brands of cars and light trucks, including Honda, Ford, BMW, General Motors, Toyota, Chrysler, Nissan, Volkswagen, Hyundai, Porsche, Volvo, and Mercedes. The firm derives 53% of its revenue from the sale of new vehicles; 27% from the sale of used vehicles; 18% from vehicle maintenance, warranty, paint and repair services; and 2% from financing, insurance and other items. Most of the company's dealerships sell either luxury or mid-line import brands, but Sonic is also involved in the sale of certified pre-owned and value used vehicles, which are vehicles that originate as trade-ins and would normally be wholesaled, but are instead sold for $10,000 or less. In addition to its dealerships, Sonic operates 26 collision repair centers in 15 states. Sonic has an aggressive expansion strategy focused primarily on metropolitan markets in the Southeast, Southwest, Midwest and California, which are experiencing rapid population growth. This strategy involves acquiring dealerships currently performing at or below the industry average but which have attractive product lines or key locations. It also involves increasing sales of products and services such as finance, insurance, parts and service and repair, because these products and services have higher profit margins than automobiles. During 2009, Sonic disposed of 18 franchises.

FINANCIALS:

Sales and profits are in thousands of dollars—add 000 to get the full amount. 2009 Note: Financial information for 2009 was not available for all companies at press time.

2009 Sales: $6,131,709	2009 Profits: $31,548	**U.S. Stock Ticker: SAH**
2008 Sales: $7,008,108	2008 Profits: $-692,349	**Int'l Ticker:** Int'l Exchange:
2007 Sales: $7,907,112	2007 Profits: $89,563	Employees: 9,200
2006 Sales: $7,985,079	2006 Profits: $81,117	Fiscal Year Ends: 12/31
2005 Sales: $7,278,720	2005 Profits: $91,861	Parent Company:

SALARIES/BENEFITS:

Pension Plan:	ESOP Stock Plan:	Profit Sharing:	Top Exec. Salary: $1,100,000	Bonus: $1,760,000
Savings Plan: Y	Stock Purch. Plan:		Second Exec. Salary: $950,000	Bonus: $1,520,000

OTHER THOUGHTS:

Apparent Women Officers or Directors:
Hot Spot for Advancement for Women/Minorities:

LOCATIONS: ("Y" = Yes)

West:	Southwest:	Midwest:	Southeast:	Northeast:	International:
Y	Y	Y	Y	Y	

SPARTAN MOTORS INC

www.spartanmotors.com

Industry Group Code: 3363 **Ranks within this company's industry group:** Sales: 52 Profits: 24

Vehicle Manufacturing:		Dealers:		Parts:		Service:		Finance:		Specialty:	
Cars:		Car Dealer New:		Manufacturers:	Y	General Service:		Leasing:		Information Systems:	
Trucks:		Car Dealer Used:		Retail:		Specialty Service:		Auto Loans:		Online Marketing:	
Motorcycles:		Truck Dealer:		Distributors:	Y	Oil Change:		Insurance:		Other:	
Specialty:	Y	RV Dealer:		Tires:		Paint and Body:				Publishing:	
Buses:		Motorcycle Dealer:		Batteries:						Rental Cars/Trucks:	
RVs:	Y	Specialty Dealer:									

TYPES OF BUSINESS:

Heavy-Duty Chassis Manufacturing
Custom Chassis
Aerial Ladder Components

BRANDS/DIVISIONS/AFFILIATES:

Spartan Motors Chassis, Inc.
Road Rescue, Inc.
Crimson Fire
Crimson Fire Aerials, Inc.
EVTeam
Spartan Motors Chassis, Inc.

CONTACTS: *Note: Officers with more than one job title may be intentionally listed here more than once.*

John E. Sztykiel, CEO
Thomas W. Gorman, COO
John E. Sztykiel, Pres.
Joseph M. Nowicki, CFO
Thomas T. Kivell, General Counsel/VP/Corp. Sec.
William F. Foster, VP
Hugh Sloan, Chmn.

Phone: 517-543-6400	**Fax:** 517-543-9269
Toll-Free:	
Address: 1000 Reynolds Rd., Charlotte, MI 48813 US	

GROWTH PLANS/SPECIAL FEATURES:

Spartan Motors, Inc. is a world leader in the engineering, design and manufacturing of heavy-duty custom platforms and emergency vehicles. The company has five wholly-owned subsidiaries: Spartan Motors Chassis, Inc., located at the corporate headquarters in Charlotte, Michigan (Spartan Chassis); Crimson Fire, Inc. located in Brandon, South Dakota (Crimson); Crimson Fire Aerials, Inc., located in Lancaster, Pennsylvania (Crimson Aerials); Road Rescue, Inc., located in Marion, South Carolina (Road Rescue); and Utilimaster. The firm has three operating segments: Spartan Chassis, emergency vehicle team (EVTeam) and Utilimaster. Spartan Chassis engineers, manufactures and markets chassis for fire trucks, motor homes and specialty applications such as military vehicles, trolleys, utility trucks and crash-rescue vehicles. The chassis consist of a frame assembly, engine, transmission, electrical system, running gear and some specialty chassis applications. Spartan Chassis manufactures chassis only upon receipt of confirmed purchase orders; thus, it does not have significant amounts of completed product inventory. Spartan Chassis generated roughly 81% of consolidated sales in 2009. Spartan Chassis markets its custom manufactured chassis throughout the U.S. and Canada, primarily through the direct contact of its sales department with original equipment manufacturers (OEMs), dealers and end users. The company's EVTeam consists of its three wholly-owned subsidiaries: Crimson; Crimson Aerials, Inc.; and Road Rescue, Inc. Crimson and Road Rescue engineer and manufacture emergency vehicles built on chassis platforms purchased from either Spartan chassis or outside sources. Crimson Aerials engineers and manufactures aerial ladder components for fire trucks. Utilimaster, which the firm acquired in 2009, manufactures customer specific specialty vehicles in the delivery and service market, including walk-in and hi-cube vans. In June 2010, Spartan announced plans to cease operations of its Road Rescue ambulance business.

FINANCIALS: **Sales and profits are in thousands of dollars—add 000 to get the full amount. 2009 Note: Financial information for 2009 was not available for all companies at press time.**

2009 Sales: $429,926	2009 Profits: $11,772	**U.S. Stock Ticker: SPAR**
2008 Sales: $844,390	2008 Profits: $42,714	**Int'l Ticker:** Int'l Exchange:
2007 Sales: $681,922	2007 Profits: $24,504	Employees: 720
2006 Sales: $445,378	2006 Profits: $16,828	Fiscal Year Ends: 12/31
2005 Sales: $343,007	2005 Profits: $8,292	Parent Company:

SALARIES/BENEFITS:

Pension Plan:	ESOP Stock Plan:	Profit Sharing:	Top Exec. Salary: $338,058	Bonus: $88,799
Savings Plan:	Stock Purch. Plan:		Second Exec. Salary: $158,530	Bonus: $10,437

OTHER THOUGHTS:

Apparent Women Officers or Directors:
Hot Spot for Advancement for Women/Minorities:

LOCATIONS: ("Y" = Yes)

West:	Southwest:	Midwest:	Southeast:	Northeast:	International:
		Y		Y	

SPECIAL DEVICES INCORPORATED

www.specialdevices.com

Industry Group Code: 3363 **Ranks within this company's industry group:** Sales: Profits:

Vehicle Manufacturing:		Dealers:		Parts:		Service:		Finance:		Specialty:	
Cars:		Car Dealer New:		Manufacturers:	Y	General Service:		Leasing:		Information Systems:	
Trucks:		Car Dealer Used:		Retail:		Specialty Service:		Auto Loans:		Online Marketing:	
Motorcycles:		Truck Dealer:		Distributors:		Oil Change:		Insurance:		Other:	Y
Specialty:		RV Dealer:		Tires:		Paint and Body:				Publishing:	
Buses:		Motorcycle Dealer:		Batteries:						Rental Cars/Trucks:	
RVs:		Specialty Dealer:									

TYPES OF BUSINESS:

Airbags Initiator Systems
Propellants
Electronic Detonator Products
Micro Gas Generators
Composite Molded Assemblies

BRANDS/DIVISIONS/AFFILIATES:

Wayzata Investment Partners
Ensign-Bickford Aerospace & Defense Company

CONTACTS: *Note: Officers with more than one job title may be intentionally listed here more than once.*

Christopher Hunter, CEO
Christopher Hunter, Pres.

Phone: 805-553-1200	**Fax:** 805-553-1201
Toll-Free:	
Address: 14370 White Sage Rd., Moorpark, CA 93021 US	

GROWTH PLANS/SPECIAL FEATURES:

Special Devices, Inc. (SDI), owned by Wayzata Investment Partners, provides engineered energetic devices for the automotive; industrial and mining; and blasting industries. SDI was founded in the 1950s as a special effects company. The company operates from domestic facilities in California and Arizona, as well as international facilities in Thailand, Japan and Germany. SDI's automotive products include initiators, which are pyrotechnic devices used primarily in automotive airbag systems. The initiator activates the inflator of an airbag, which then causes the deployment of the actual bag. In addition to initiators, the company also makes micro gas generators that remove seatbelt slack in the event of a collision, as well as composite molded assemblies, that reduce total product cost by molding certain design features into the initiator assembly, and by replacing expensive machined components. SDI's technology has the potential to reduce cost by eliminating components in certain applications of the design process. In the industrial segment, the firm makes explosive bolts and nuts, that release and separate bolted connections on command; gas generators, that inflation of many types of products or devices; pyrotechnic electrical disconnects, that terminate electrical circuits at a high speed; cable cutters, for severing electrical cables, structural cables, tubing and cords; fire suppression systems, the disperse liquid, solid and gaseous suppressants; pin pullers and pin pushers, that provide rapid movement of latch/ locking mechanisms; and propelling cartridges, that eject or launch projectiles using pyrotechnic energy. The company makes electronic detonator products for the mining and blasting industries. In March 2009, the firm laid off 117 workers at its Moorpark location, slashing the company's local work force by about a third. In March 2010, SDI sold its defense and aerospace division to Ensign-Bickford Aerospace & Defense Company (EBA&D) for an undisclosed amount.

FINANCIALS: **Sales and profits are in thousands of dollars—add 000 to get the full amount. 2009 Note: Financial information for 2009 was not available for all companies at press time.**

2009 Sales: $	2009 Profits: $	**U.S. Stock Ticker: Private**
2008 Sales: $	2008 Profits: $	**Int'l Ticker:** Int'l Exchange:
2007 Sales: $	2007 Profits: $	Employees:
2006 Sales: $	2006 Profits: $	Fiscal Year Ends:
2005 Sales: $	2005 Profits: $	Parent Company: WAYZATA INVESTMENT PARTNERS

SALARIES/BENEFITS:

Pension Plan:	ESOP Stock Plan:	Profit Sharing:	Top Exec. Salary: $	Bonus: $
Savings Plan:	Stock Purch. Plan:		Second Exec. Salary: $	Bonus: $

OTHER THOUGHTS:

Apparent Women Officers or Directors:
Hot Spot for Advancement for Women/Minorities:

LOCATIONS: ("Y" = Yes)

West:	Southwest:	Midwest:	Southeast:	Northeast:	International:
Y	Y				Y

Note: Financial information, benefits and other data can change quickly and may vary from those stated here.

SPECTRA PREMIUM INDUSTRIES INC

www.spectrapremium.com

Industry Group Code: 3363 **Ranks within this company's industry group:** Sales: Profits:

Vehicle Manufacturing:		Dealers:		Parts:		Service:		Finance:		Specialty:	
Cars:		Car Dealer New:		Manufacturers:	Y	General Service:		Leasing:		Information Systems:	
Trucks:		Car Dealer Used:		Retail:		Specialty Service:		Auto Loans:		Online Marketing:	
Motorcycles:		Truck Dealer:		Distributors:	Y	Oil Change:		Insurance:		Other:	
Specialty:		RV Dealer:		Tires:		Paint and Body:				Publishing:	
Buses:		Motorcycle Dealer:		Batteries:						Rental Cars/Trucks:	
RVs:		Specialty Dealer:									

TYPES OF BUSINESS:

Aftermarket Remanufactured Parts
Heat-Transfer Products
Underbody Components

BRANDS/DIVISIONS/AFFILIATES:

American Designers

CONTACTS:

Note: Officers with more than one job title may be intentionally listed here more than once.

Jacques Mombleau, CEO
Jacques Mombleau, Pres.
Denis Poirier, CFO/Exec. VP
Jason Best, VP-Sales & Mktg., Aftermarket
Richard J. Grenier, VP-Human Resources
Bernard Blouin, VP-Eng.
Kerry Best, VP-Mfg.
Louis Juneau, VP-Legal Affairs/Corp. Sec.
Cathi Owen, VP-Oper., Heat Transfer Prod.
Daniel Mais, VP/Corp. Controller
Denis Charest, Chmn.
Peter Butler, Pres., Spectra Premium Europe
Rick Calagoure, VP-Int'l Sourcing & Aftermarket Dev.

Phone: 450-641-3090 **Fax:** 450-641-3866
Toll-Free: 888-910-8888
Address: 1421 Ampere St., Boucherville, QC J4B 5Z5 Canada

GROWTH PLANS/SPECIAL FEATURES:

Spectra Premium Industries, Inc. manufactures passenger automobile and heavy-duty industrial truck parts for original equipment manufacturers (OEMs) and the aftermarket sector. It primarily supplies heat-transfer and underbody components, such as radiators and fuel tanks, with additional operations focused on other cooling system elements (such as condensers and compressors), heater cores, oil sending units, fuel pumps and replacement body panels (sold under the brand name American Designers) for classic cars. The firm's fuel tanks are compatible with more than 500 models of foreign, domestic and classic cars. Spectra Premium's OEM contracts include supplying steel fuel tanks and aluminum radiators for companies such as Daimler AG and Bombardier Recreational Products. Spectra Premium North America operates the company's five manufacturing plants, all of which are located in Canada. The three Quebec plants manufacture fuel tanks, oil pans, industrial cores and full radiators and radiator components, while the Nova Scotia and Alberta plants manufacture radiator components and industrial cores, respectively. Its distribution network consists of a global network of 17 company-operated distribution centers in Canada and the U.S., with third-party retailers operating an additional 200 warehouses and 10,000 points of sale. The firm is privately-owned following its merger with 6551399 Canada, Inc., a company controlled by Spectra Premium's senior management. In April 2009, following the loss of its main customer (General Motors Corp.) subsidiary Trimag S.E.C. filed for bankruptcy protection and ceased all operations in June 2009. Trimag had operated two of Spectra Premium's manufacturing facilities.

FINANCIALS:

Sales and profits are in thousands of dollars—add 000 to get the full amount. 2009 Note: Financial information for 2009 was not available for all companies at press time.

2009 Sales: $	2009 Profits: $	**U.S. Stock Ticker:**
2008 Sales: $	2008 Profits: $	**Int'l Ticker: SPD** Int'l Exchange: Toronto-TSX
2007 Sales: $	2007 Profits: $	Employees:
2006 Sales: $231,800	2006 Profits: $	Fiscal Year Ends: 1/31
2005 Sales: $216,972	2005 Profits: $-1,169	Parent Company:

SALARIES/BENEFITS:

Pension Plan:	ESOP Stock Plan:	Profit Sharing:	Top Exec. Salary: $	Bonus: $
Savings Plan:	Stock Purch. Plan:		Second Exec. Salary: $	Bonus: $

OTHER THOUGHTS:

Apparent Women Officers or Directors: 1
Hot Spot for Advancement for Women/Minorities:

LOCATIONS: ("Y" = Yes)

West:	Southwest:	Midwest:	Southeast:	Northeast:	International:
	Y	Y			Y

SPITZER MANAGEMENT INC

www.spitzer.com

Industry Group Code: 441110 **Ranks within this company's industry group:** Sales: Profits:

Vehicle Manufacturing:		Dealers:		Parts:		Service:		Finance:		Specialty:	
Cars:		Car Dealer New:	Y	Manufacturers:		General Service:	Y	Leasing:		Information Systems:	
Trucks:		Car Dealer Used:	Y	Retail:	Y	Specialty Service:		Auto Loans:	Y	Online Marketing:	
Motorcycles:		Truck Dealer:		Distributors:		Oil Change:		Insurance:		Other:	Y
Specialty:		RV Dealer:		Tires:		Paint and Body:	Y			Publishing:	
Buses:		Motorcycle Dealer:		Batteries:						Rental Cars/Trucks:	
RVs:		Specialty Dealer:									

TYPES OF BUSINESS:

Auto Dealers, Retail
Property Management
Parts & Service
Marina Management
Golf Course Management
Financing

BRANDS/DIVISIONS/AFFILIATES:

Spitzer Collision Center
Spitzer Marinas
Pheasant Run Golf Course

GROWTH PLANS/SPECIAL FEATURES:

Spitzer Management, Inc. is a new and pre-owned automobile dealer with approximately 20 automobile dealerships in Ohio, Pennsylvania and Florida. Spitzer offers car financing and sells both new and used vehicles from such model brands as Acura, Chevrolet, Dodge, Ford, Kia, Mitsubishi, Scion, Toyota and Volkswagen. Through the company's web site, customers are able to search the inventory, build a vehicle, compare vehicles, apply for credit and obtain product information. Spitzer Collision Center, one of the company's other operating divisions, offers complete auto body repair with frame and unibody repair, state-of-the-art color matching, lifetime guarantees, replacement car rentals and 24-hour-a-day towing. Vehicle owners can schedule service and maintenance, request parts and set up an appointment with the collision center via the company's web site. Spitzer also owns Spitzer Marinas, which operates two marinas in Lorain, Ohio and Pheasant Run Golf Course, a public 18-hole golf course located in La Grange, Ohio.

CONTACTS:

Note: Officers with more than one job title may be intentionally listed here more than once.

Alan Spitzer, CEO
Alan Spitzer, Pres.
Tom Bury, CFO
Ed Grasso, Dir.-Tech.
Alan Spitzer, Chmn.

Phone: 440-323-4671	**Fax:** 440-323-3623
Toll-Free:	
Address: 150 E. Bridge St., Elyria, OH 44035 US	

FINANCIALS:

Sales and profits are in thousands of dollars—add 000 to get the full amount. 2009 Note: Financial information for 2009 was not available for all companies at press time.

2009 Sales: $	2009 Profits: $	**U.S. Stock Ticker: Private**
2008 Sales: $	2008 Profits: $	**Int'l Ticker:** Int'l Exchange:
2007 Sales: $	2007 Profits: $	Employees:
2006 Sales: $	2006 Profits: $	Fiscal Year Ends: 12/31
2005 Sales: $	2005 Profits: $	Parent Company:

SALARIES/BENEFITS:

Pension Plan:	ESOP Stock Plan:	Profit Sharing:	Top Exec. Salary: $	Bonus: $
Savings Plan:	Stock Purch. Plan:		Second Exec. Salary: $	Bonus: $

OTHER THOUGHTS:

Apparent Women Officers or Directors:
Hot Spot for Advancement for Women/Minorities:

LOCATIONS: ("Y" = Yes)

West:	Southwest:	Midwest:	Southeast:	Northeast:	International:
		Y	Y	Y	

SRG GLOBAL INC

www.srob.com

Industry Group Code: 3261 **Ranks within this company's industry group:** Sales: Profits:

Vehicle Manufacturing:		Dealers:		Parts:		Service:		Finance:		Specialty:	
Cars:		Car Dealer New:		Manufacturers:	Y	General Service:		Leasing:		Information Systems:	
Trucks:		Car Dealer Used:		Retail:		Specialty Service:		Auto Loans:		Online Marketing:	
Motorcycles:		Truck Dealer:		Distributors:		Oil Change:		Insurance:		Other:	Y
Specialty:		RV Dealer:		Tires:		Paint and Body:				Publishing:	
Buses:		Motorcycle Dealer:		Batteries:						Rental Cars/Trucks:	
RVs:		Specialty Dealer:									

TYPES OF BUSINESS:

Automotive Components
Trim Products & Systems
Front End Systems
Bodyside Systems
Rear End Systems
Greenhouse Systems
Interior systems
Non-Automotive Products

BRANDS/DIVISIONS/AFFILIATES:

Siegel-Robert Automotive
Guardian Automotive
Guardian Industries Corp
Lab Radio
G-Coat

CONTACTS:

Note: Officers with more than one job title may be intentionally listed here more than once.

Kevin Baird, Pres.
Dave Prater, VP-Prod. Dev.
Dave Prater, VP-Prod. Eng.
Amy Hennes, Contact-Media Rel.
Russell J. Ebeid, Chmn.-Guardian Industries Corp.

Phone: 586-757-7800 **Fax:** 586-757-8329
Toll-Free:
Address: 23751 Amber Ave., Warren, MI 48089 US

GROWTH PLANS/SPECIAL FEATURES:

SRG Global, Inc., a wholly-owned subsidiary of Guardian Industries Corp., is an industrial manufacturer of metal and plastic components for the worldwide automotive industry. The company was formed in March 2009 from the combination of Guardian Automotive, Siegel-Robert Automotive and Lab. Radio (Guardian Automotive's European trim operations). The firm specializes in the production of automotive trim products, including grilles, bodyside moldings and nameplates. SRG Global operates 11 facilities in North America, Asia and Europe. The firm utilizes G-Coat, a patented formula used to improve paint adhesion to chrome. The company's products fall into six categories: front-end systems; bodyside systems; rear end systems; greenhouse systems; interior systems; and non-automotive. Front-end systems include grilles, emblems and hood moldings. SRG Global bodyside products include rockside moldings, rocker panels, wheel covers and step pads. The rear end products offered are license plate garnishes, tailgate finishers, spoilers and nameplates. Greenhouse systems include window surround and door belt moldings, as well as Cowl/Leaf Screens. The firm offers instrument bezels and door trim interior systems products. SRG Global offers non-automotive products for commercial trucks, motorcycles and appliances. In May 2010, the company opened a new chrome-plated plastics manufacturing facility in Taylor, Michigan.

FINANCIALS:

Sales and profits are in thousands of dollars—add 000 to get the full amount. 2009 Note: Financial information for 2009 was not available for all companies at press time.

2009 Sales: $ | 2009 Profits: $
2008 Sales: $ | 2008 Profits: $
2007 Sales: $523,000 | 2007 Profits: $
2006 Sales: $ | 2006 Profits: $
2005 Sales: $ | 2005 Profits: $

U.S. Stock Ticker: Subsidiary
Int'l Ticker: Int'l Exchange:
Employees:
Fiscal Year Ends: 12/31
Parent Company: GUARDIAN INDUSTRIES CORP

SALARIES/BENEFITS:

Pension Plan: ESOP Stock Plan: Profit Sharing: Top Exec. Salary: $ Bonus: $
Savings Plan: Stock Purch. Plan: Second Exec. Salary: $ Bonus: $

OTHER THOUGHTS:

Apparent Women Officers or Directors: 1
Hot Spot for Advancement for Women/Minorities:

LOCATIONS: ("Y" = Yes)

West:	Southwest:	Midwest:	Southeast:	Northeast:	International:
		Y			Y

SSANGYONG MOTOR CO

www.smotor.com

Industry Group Code: 33611 **Ranks within this company's industry group:** Sales: 30 Profits: 23

Vehicle Manufacturing:		Dealers:		Parts:		Service:		Finance:		Specialty:	
Cars:	Y	Car Dealer New:		Manufacturers:	Y	General Service:		Leasing:		Information Systems:	
Trucks:	Y	Car Dealer Used:		Retail:		Specialty Service:		Auto Loans:		Online Marketing:	
Motorcycles:		Truck Dealer:		Distributors:		Oil Change:		Insurance:		Other:	
Specialty:		RV Dealer:		Tires:		Paint and Body:				Publishing:	
Buses:		Motorcycle Dealer:		Batteries:						Rental Cars/Trucks:	
RVs:		Specialty Dealer:									

TYPES OF BUSINESS:

Auto Manufacturer
SUVs
Passenger Cars
Multi-Purpose Vehicles

BRANDS/DIVISIONS/AFFILIATES:

Shanghai Automotive Industry Corp (SAIC)
Musso Sports
Rexton
New Kyron
Actyon
Actyon Sports
Chairman
Rodius/Stavic

CONTACTS: *Note: Officers with more than one job title may be intentionally listed here more than once.*

Yeong Tae Park, Co-CEO
Yu Yil Lee, Co-CEO
Gwan Bong Ha, VP
Jong Sik Choi, VP
Jae Wan Lee, VP

Phone: 82-31-610-1114 **Fax:** 82-31-610-3700
Toll-Free:
Address: 150-3 Chilgoi-dong, Pyungtaek-si, Gyeonggi-do, 459-711 Korea

GROWTH PLANS/SPECIAL FEATURES:

SsangYong Motor Co., controlled 51 % by Shanghai Automotive Industry Corp (SAIC), is a leading Korean automobile manufacturer specializing in luxury SUVs, passenger cars, sports utility trucks and multi-purpose vehicles (MPVs). The company has historically manufactured commercial trucks, jeeps, special purpose vehicles and construction equipment, but now focuses mainly on light commercial vehicles. SsangYong was the first company to introduce a sports utility truck, the Musso Sports, to the Korean market. Currently, the company produces four SUVs, including the Rexton, New Kyron, Actyon and Actyon Sports. The firm's luxury passenger car, the Chairman, has a Mercedes-Benz 6-cylinder engine and has options for an electronic leg supporter, a variable air purification system and power massagers in the seats. The Rodius/Stavic is SsangYong's MPV, which features seating variation for between nine and 11 passengers, as well swing doors similar to passenger car doors, a rear obstacle warning system and an immobilizer for panic alarm, vehicle-finding and automatic door lock functions. The company's global network spans Europe, including the Commonwealth of Independent States; the Middle East; Asia, with particular focus on China; the Pacific region and Oceania, including Australia; Central and South America; and Africa. SsangYong's primary manufacturing plant is located just south of Seoul in Pyungtaek, South Korea and has an annual manufacturing capacity of 210,000 vehicles. This facility also contains the company's head office and research and development center. A second plant in Changwon, South Korea manufactures gasoline and diesel engines, transmissions, transaxles and rear ends for SsangYong's SUVs and passenger cars. In June 2010, the company signed an agreement with Sollers, its Russian partner, to export about 160,000 vehicles to Russia until 2017.

FINANCIALS: **Sales and profits are in thousands of dollars—add 000 to get the full amount. 2009 Note: Financial information for 2009 was not available for all companies at press time.**

2009 Sales: $906,540	2009 Profits: $-292,730	**U.S. Stock Ticker:**
2008 Sales: $2,106,970	2008 Profits: $-598,920	**Int'l Ticker: 003620** Int'l Exchange: Seoul-KRX
2007 Sales: $2,652,550	2007 Profits: $9,740	Employees: 7,100
2006 Sales: $3,175,384	2006 Profits: $-210,802	Fiscal Year Ends: 12/31
2005 Sales: $3,661,464	2005 Profits: $-111,188	Parent Company:

SALARIES/BENEFITS:

Pension Plan:	ESOP Stock Plan:	Profit Sharing:	Top Exec. Salary: $	Bonus: $
Savings Plan:	Stock Purch. Plan:		Second Exec. Salary: $	Bonus: $

OTHER THOUGHTS:

Apparent Women Officers or Directors:
Hot Spot for Advancement for Women/Minorities:

LOCATIONS: ("Y" = Yes)

West:	Southwest:	Midwest:	Southeast:	Northeast:	International:
					Y

STACKPOLE LIMITED COMPANY

www.stackpole.on.ca

Industry Group Code: 336350 **Ranks within this company's industry group:** Sales: Profits:

Vehicle Manufacturing:		Dealers:		Parts:		Service:		Finance:		Specialty:	
Cars:		Car Dealer New:		Manufacturers:	Y	General Service:		Leasing:		Information Systems:	
Trucks:		Car Dealer Used:		Retail:		Specialty Service:		Auto Loans:		Online Marketing:	
Motorcycles:		Truck Dealer:		Distributors:		Oil Change:		Insurance:		Other:	
Specialty:		RV Dealer:		Tires:		Paint and Body:				Publishing:	
Buses:		Motorcycle Dealer:		Batteries:						Rental Cars/Trucks:	
RVs:		Specialty Dealer:									

TYPES OF BUSINESS:

Automobile Parts Manufacturing
Engine & Transmission Components
Gears

BRANDS/DIVISIONS/AFFILIATES:

Tomkins plc
Formflo Limited

CONTACTS:

Note: Officers with more than one job title may be intentionally listed here more than once.

Eric R. Cozens, Pres.
Andrew Linley, CFO
Ronald J. Duke, VP-New Bus. Dev.

Phone: 905-822-6015 **Fax:** 905-855-7363
Toll-Free:
Address: 2430 Royal Windsor Dr., Mississauga, ON L5J 1K7 Canada

GROWTH PLANS/SPECIAL FEATURES:

Stackpole Limited, a business division of the Gates Corporation (subsidiary of Tomkins plc), is a manufacturer and assembler of highly engineered, technologically differentiated automotive powertrain systems and components. The firm focuses on products with applications in transfer cases, automatic transmissions, manual transmissions and engines. These products include gears and sprockets; clutch components; synchronizer assemblies; automotive pumps; planetary carriers; and engine components. Stackpole has seven business divisions: the automotive gear division and the engineered products division, located in Mississagua, Ontario; the carrier systems division, located in Stratford, Ontario; a second engineered products division and the precision metal components division in Ancaster, Ontario; the FormFlo Limited division in the U.K.; and the Stackpole sales office division in Michigan. Much of Stackpole Limited's research and development efforts are dedicated to powder metal technology, which form many of its auto components, as well as many of the technologies of other Tomkins companies. Automotive customers for the company include General Motors Corporation; BorgWarner, Inc.; DaimlerChrysler; Ford Motor Company; Getrag GmbH; and ZF Industries, Inc. Non-automotive customers include Blount International, Inc.; General Kinetics Incorporated; Whirlpool Corporation; and Mid-South Manufacturing, Inc.

FINANCIALS:

Sales and profits are in thousands of dollars—add 000 to get the full amount. 2009 Note: Financial information for 2009 was not available for all companies at press time.

2009 Sales: $	2009 Profits: $	**U.S. Stock Ticker: Subsidiary**
2008 Sales: $	2008 Profits: $	**Int'l Ticker:** Int'l Exchange:
2007 Sales: $192,100	2007 Profits: $	Employees:
2006 Sales: $	2006 Profits: $	Fiscal Year Ends: 12/31
2005 Sales: $	2005 Profits: $	Parent Company: TOMKINS PLC

SALARIES/BENEFITS:

Pension Plan:	ESOP Stock Plan:	Profit Sharing:	Top Exec. Salary: $	Bonus: $
Savings Plan:	Stock Purch. Plan:		Second Exec. Salary: $	Bonus: $

OTHER THOUGHTS:

Apparent Women Officers or Directors:
Hot Spot for Advancement for Women/Minorities:

LOCATIONS: ("Y" = Yes)

West:	Southwest:	Midwest:	Southeast:	Northeast:	International:
		Y			Y

STANADYNE CORPORATION

www.stanadyne.com

Industry Group Code: 3363 **Ranks within this company's industry group:** Sales: Profits:

Vehicle Manufacturing:		**Dealers:**		**Parts:**		**Service:**		**Finance:**		**Specialty:**	
Cars:		Car Dealer New:		Manufacturers:	Y	General Service:		Leasing:		Information Systems:	
Trucks:		Car Dealer Used:		Retail:	Y	Specialty Service:		Auto Loans:		Online Marketing:	
Motorcycles:		Truck Dealer:		Distributors:	Y	Oil Change:		Insurance:		Other:	
Specialty:		RV Dealer:		Tires:		Paint and Body:				Publishing:	
Buses:		Motorcycle Dealer:		Batteries:						Rental Cars/Trucks:	
RVs:		Specialty Dealer:									

TYPES OF BUSINESS:

Engine Components Manufacturing
Parts Distribution & Sale

BRANDS/DIVISIONS/AFFILIATES:

KKR & Co LP (Kohlberg Kravis Roberts & Co)
Precision Products
Stanadyne S.p.A.
Amalgamations Private Limited
Stanadyne Amalgamations Private Limited

CONTACTS:

Note: Officers with more than one job title may be intentionally listed here more than once.

M. David Jones, CEO
M. David Jones, Pres.
Stephen S. Langin, CFO/VP
Leonello Forte, Dir.-Sales & Mktg., Europe
Jean S. McCarthy, VP-Human Resources
John Pinson, CTO/VP
Stephen S. Langin, Corp. Sec.
Paul W. Hegwood, VP-Oper.
James D. Wiggins, Chmn.
Joseph M. Vorih, VP-Int'l

Phone: 860-525-0821	**Fax:** 860-683-4500
Toll-Free:	
Address: 92 Deerfield Rd., Windsor, CT 06095 US	

GROWTH PLANS/SPECIAL FEATURES:

Stanadyne Corporation, established as Hartford Machine Screw Company and currently wholly-owned by KKR & Co., designs and manufactures engine components, including fuel injection equipment for diesel engines and hydraulic valve lifters primarily for gasoline engines. The company's products find use in a variety of applications, including agricultural and construction vehicles and equipment, industrial products, automobiles, light-duty trucks and marine equipment. It also sells replacement parts through service organizations and its own network of dealers and distributors. Stanadyne possesses a broad range of manufacturing technology and is capable of high-volume production runs, machining high-quality components within tolerances of smaller than one micron. Stanadyne operates through its Precision Products and Technologies segment, which manufactures proprietary products, including pumps for gasoline and diesel engines and injectors and filtration systems for diesels. The primary focus is the agricultural and industrial off-highway segments of the market. The segment's largest customers include Deere & Company, Daimler AG, General Engine Products, Inc. and Cummins, Inc. Stanadyne and Deere have a supply agreement through 2011. The firm has international locations in Italy (Stanadyne S.p.A.), China and India. In India, it has a joint venture with Amalgamations Private Limited, called Stanadyne Amalgamations Private Limited, a diesel fuel injection equipment manufacturer. In April 2009, the company decided to cease operations at its Connecticut manufacturing plant.

FINANCIALS:

Sales and profits are in thousands of dollars—add 000 to get the full amount. 2009 Note: Financial information for 2009 was not available for all companies at press time.

2009 Sales: $	2009 Profits: $	**U.S. Stock Ticker: Private**
2008 Sales: $	2008 Profits: $	**Int'l Ticker:** Int'l Exchange:
2007 Sales: $	2007 Profits: $	Employees:
2006 Sales: $	2006 Profits: $	Fiscal Year Ends: 12/31
2005 Sales: $	2005 Profits: $	Parent Company: KKR & CO LP (KOHLBERG KRAVIS ROBERTS & CO)

SALARIES/BENEFITS:

Pension Plan:	ESOP Stock Plan:	Profit Sharing:	Top Exec. Salary: $468,125	Bonus: $
Savings Plan:	Stock Purch. Plan:		Second Exec. Salary: $261,250	Bonus: $

OTHER THOUGHTS:

Apparent Women Officers or Directors: 1
Hot Spot for Advancement for Women/Minorities:

LOCATIONS: ("Y" = Yes)

West:	Southwest:	Midwest:	Southeast:	Northeast:	International:
				Y	Y

STANDARD MOTOR PRODUCTS INC

www.smpcorp.com

Industry Group Code: 3363 **Ranks within this company's industry group:** Sales: 45 Profits: 28

Vehicle Manufacturing:		**Dealers:**		**Parts:**		**Service:**		**Finance:**		**Specialty:**	
Cars:		Car Dealer New:		Manufacturers:	Y	General Service:		Leasing:		Information Systems:	
Trucks:		Car Dealer Used:		Retail:		Specialty Service:		Auto Loans:		Online Marketing:	
Motorcycles:		Truck Dealer:		Distributors:	Y	Oil Change:		Insurance:		Other:	
Specialty:		RV Dealer:		Tires:		Paint and Body:				Publishing:	
Buses:		Motorcycle Dealer:		Batteries:						Rental Cars/Trucks:	
RVs:		Specialty Dealer:									

TYPES OF BUSINESS:

Automobile Parts Manufacturer
Engine Management Products
Ignition Parts
Emission Control Parts
Fuel System Parts
Battery Cables

BRANDS/DIVISIONS/AFFILIATES:

Standard
Intermotor
BWD
Imperial
Hayden
Four Seasons
Factory Air

CONTACTS:

Note: Officers with more than one job title may be intentionally listed here more than once.

Lawrence I. Sills, CEO
John P. Gethin, COO
John P. Gethin, Pres.
James J. Burke, CFO/VP-Finance
Michael J. Fitzgerald, VP-Mktg.
Thomas S. Tesoro, VP-Human Resources
Ray Nicholas, VP-IT
Carmine J. Broccole, General Counsel/Sec./VP
William J. Fazio, Chief Acct. Officer
Dale Burks, VP-Temperature Control Div.
Robert H. Martin, Treas.
Eric Sills, VP-Engine Mgmt. Div.
Lawrence I. Sills, Chmn.
Robert Kimbro, VP-Dist. Sales

Phone: 718-392-0200	**Fax:** 718-472-0122
Toll-Free:	
Address: 37-18 Northern Blvd., Long Island City, NY 11101 US	

GROWTH PLANS/SPECIAL FEATURES:

Standard Motor Products, Inc. (SMP) is a leading independent manufacturer and distributor of replacement parts for motor vehicles, primarily in the automotive aftermarket industry. It is organized into two major operating segments, each of which focuses on a specific line of replacement parts. The company's engine management segment manufactures ignition and emission parts, ignition wires, battery cables and fuel system parts. Its temperature control segment manufactures and remanufactures air conditioning compressors, clutch assemblies, small motors, fan clutches, filter dryers, evaporators, transmission coolers, accumulators and hoses, heater cores and valves, engine cooling system parts, power window accessories, windshield washer system parts and other air conditioning and heating parts. SMP sells its products primarily to warehouse distributors and large auto parts retail chains, original equipment manufacturers and original equipment service part operations in the U.S., Canada and Latin America. The company does business in Europe through its wholly-owned European subsidiary, SMP Holdings Limited. SMP's customers consist of many top warehouse distributors and auto parts retail chains, including Pep Boys, Advance Auto Parts, O'Reilly Automotive, AutoZone, CARQUEST and NAPA Auto Parts. The company distributes parts under its own brand names, such as Standard, Intermotor, BWD, Four Seasons, Hayden and Imperial, as well as under private labels for key customers. The firm generated 68.2% of sales from engine products and 26.8% from temperature control products in 2009. In November 2009, the company sold its subsidiary Standard Motor Products Holdings, Ltd., which had served as its European distribution arm, for $3 million to the managers of the business. The company maintains a manufacturing operation in Poland.

SMP offers its employee medical, dental, life and disability insurance; flexible spending accounts; tuition assistance; and optional additional insurance.

FINANCIALS:

Sales and profits are in thousands of dollars—add 000 to get the full amount. 2009 Note: Financial information for 2009 was not available for all companies at press time.

2009 Sales: $735,424	2009 Profits: $3,483	**U.S. Stock Ticker: SMP**
2008 Sales: $775,241	2008 Profits: $-22,894	**Int'l Ticker:** Int'l Exchange:
2007 Sales: $790,185	2007 Profits: $2,275	Employees: 2,000
2006 Sales: $812,024	2006 Profits: $9,411	Fiscal Year Ends: 12/31
2005 Sales: $830,413	2005 Profits: $-3,545	Parent Company:

SALARIES/BENEFITS:

Pension Plan:	ESOP Stock Plan: Y	Profit Sharing:	Top Exec. Salary: $538,000	Bonus: $544,292
Savings Plan: Y	Stock Purch. Plan:		Second Exec. Salary: $460,000	Bonus: $676,954

OTHER THOUGHTS:

Apparent Women Officers or Directors: 1
Hot Spot for Advancement for Women/Minorities:

LOCATIONS: ("Y" = Yes)

West:	Southwest:	Midwest:	Southeast:	Northeast:	International:
Y	Y	Y	Y	Y	Y

STATE FARM INSURANCE COMPANIES

www.statefarm.com

Industry Group Code: 524126 **Ranks within this company's industry group:** Sales: 1 Profits: 3

Vehicle Manufacturing:		Dealers:		Parts:		Service:		Finance:		Specialty:	
Cars:		Car Dealer New:		Manufacturers:		General Service:		Leasing:		Information Systems:	
Trucks:		Car Dealer Used:		Retail:		Specialty Service:		Auto Loans:		Online Marketing:	
Motorcycles:		Truck Dealer:		Distributors:		Oil Change:		Insurance:	Y	Other:	Y
Specialty:		RV Dealer:		Tires:		Paint and Body:				Publishing:	
Buses:		Motorcycle Dealer:		Batteries:						Rental Cars/Trucks:	
RVs:		Specialty Dealer:									

TYPES OF BUSINESS:

Insurance, Direct Property & Casualty
Accident Insurance
Health Insurance
Life Insurance
Annuities
Automobile Insurance
Banking/Savings Association
Mutual Funds

BRANDS/DIVISIONS/AFFILIATES:

State Farm Bank, F.S.B.
State Farm Life & Accident Assurance Co.
State Farm Fire & Casualty Co.
State Farm Automobile Insurance Company
State Farm General Insurance Company
State Farm Guaranty Insurance Company
State Farm Associate and Retail Mutual Funds
Canadian Zone of State Farm Insurance (The)

CONTACTS:

Note: Officers with more than one job title may be intentionally listed here more than once.

Edward B. Rust, Jr., CEO
Edward B. Rust, Jr., Pres.
Michael L. Tipsord, CFO/Sr. VP
Michael C. Davidson, Chief Agency & Mktg. Officer
Laura Haas, Asst. VP-Human Resources & Diversity
Susan D. Waring, Chief Admin. Officer/Exec. VP
Kim Brunner, Chief Legal Officer/Sec./Exec. VP
Dan Kinney, VP-Oper.
Mike Fernandez, VP-Public Affairs
Paul J. Smith, Treas.
Jim Broach, Dir.-Admin. Svcs.
Mark Gibson, Assistant VP-Advertising
Laurette Stiles, VP-Strategic Resources
Karl Brondell, Asst. VP-Claims
Edward B. Rust, Jr., Chmn.

Phone: 309-766-2311 **Fax:**
Toll-Free: 877-734-2265
Address: 1 State Farm Plaza, Bloomington, IL 61710-0001 US

GROWTH PLANS/SPECIAL FEATURES:

State Farm Insurance Companies is a mutual company providing personal property and casualty insurance through 30 operation centers and 343 claim offices across the U.S. and Canada. The company provides auto, homeowners, renter's, life and annuities, health, disability, long-term care, business, boat, farm and ranch, flood, motorcycle, personal and volcano damage insurance. Over half of its 78.8 million policies are auto policies. The group's major insurance companies include State Farm Automobile Insurance Company; State Farm Life and Accident Assurance Company; State Farm Fire and Casualty Company; State Farm General Insurance Company; State Farm Lloyds; and State Farm Guaranty Insurance Company. Through State Farm Bank, F.S.B., the company provides bank account, credit card and loan services, including individual retirement accounts (IRA), money market, checking, savings and health savings accounts; and home mortgage and home equity, vehicle and business loans. The firm also manages over 424,000 mutual fund accounts through State Farm Associate and Retail Mutual Funds and State Farm Investment Management Corp. State Farm is also a leading insurer in Canada through The Canadian Zone of State Farm Insurance, serving over 1.2 million households in Alberta, New Brunswick and Ontario.

State Farm offers its employees medical, dental and vision plans; flexible spending accounts; long-term care and disability insurance; tuition reimbursement; credit union membership; mutual funds; adoption leave; an employee assistance program; a tobacco cessation program; and relocation assistance.

FINANCIALS:

Sales and profits are in thousands of dollars—add 000 to get the full amount. 2009 Note: Financial information for 2009 was not available for all companies at press time.

2009 Sales: $32,064,000	2009 Profits: $570,000
2008 Sales: $31,584,000	2008 Profits: $1,036,000
2007 Sales: $61,611,600	2007 Profits: $5,463,700
2006 Sales: $60,528,000	2006 Profits: $5,315,500
2005 Sales: $59,223,900	2005 Profits: $3,241,800

U.S. Stock Ticker: Mutual Company
Int'l Ticker: Int'l Exchange:
Employees: 68,517
Fiscal Year Ends: 12/31
Parent Company:

SALARIES/BENEFITS:

Pension Plan: Y	ESOP Stock Plan:	Profit Sharing:	Top Exec. Salary: $	Bonus: $
Savings Plan: Y	Stock Purch. Plan:		Second Exec. Salary: $	Bonus: $

OTHER THOUGHTS:

Apparent Women Officers or Directors: 5
Hot Spot for Advancement for Women/Minorities: Y

LOCATIONS: ("Y" = Yes)

West:	Southwest:	Midwest:	Southeast:	Northeast:	International:
Y	Y	Y	Y	Y	Y

STELLICAN LTD

www.stellican.com

Industry Group Code: 336991 **Ranks within this company's industry group:** Sales: Profits:

Vehicle Manufacturing:		Dealers:		Parts:		Service:		Finance:		Specialty:	
Cars:		Car Dealer New:		Manufacturers:		General Service:		Leasing:		Information Systems:	
Trucks:		Car Dealer Used:		Retail:		Specialty Service:		Auto Loans:		Online Marketing:	
Motorcycles:	Y	Truck Dealer:		Distributors:		Oil Change:		Insurance:		Other:	Y
Specialty:	Y	RV Dealer:		Tires:		Paint and Body:				Publishing:	
Buses:		Motorcycle Dealer:		Batteries:						Rental Cars/Trucks:	
RVs:		Specialty Dealer:									

TYPES OF BUSINESS:

Capital Investment
Motorcycle Manufacturing
Boat Manufacturing
Cash Registers, Soft Drinks & Sports Teams

BRANDS/DIVISIONS/AFFILIATES:

Indian Motorcycle Co
Chris-Craft Corp.
Cantieri Riva s.p.a.
Sweda Group
Sarema S.p.A.
Vicenza Calcio S.p.A.
La Casera
Indian Chief

CONTACTS: *Note: Officers with more than one job title may be intentionally listed here more than once.*

Stephen M. Julius, Managing Dir.
Nick Glaja, VP-Eng.
Bob Greenberg, VP-Oper., Chris-Craft Corp.
Stephen M. Julius, Chmn.-Chris-Craft Corp. & Indian Motorcycle Co.
Stephen F. Heese, CEO/Pres., Chris-Craft Corp.
Stephen F. Heese, Pres., Indian Motorcycle Co.
Chris Bernauer, Gen. Mgr.-Indian Motorcycle Co.

Phone: 44-20-72448159 **Fax:** 44-20-73707206
Toll-Free:
Address: 4 Collingham Gardens, London, SW5 0HW UK

GROWTH PLANS/SPECIAL FEATURES:

Stellican Ltd. is a private equity, corporate finance and principal investment firm that specializes in the acquisition and turnaround of distressed businesses. Most of the firm's investments are in recreational products and heritage brands. Acquisitions have included luxury motorboat manufacturer Chris-Craft Corp.; Italian yacht maker Cantieri Riva S.p.A.; American motorcycle manufacturer Indian Motorcycle Co.; Italian soccer team Vicenza Calcio S.p.A.; Italian cash register makers Sweda Group and Sarema S.p.A.; and Spanish soft drink maker La Casera. Stellican has acquired the trademarks and intellectual property of Indian Motorcycle Co., including trademark model divisions Chief, Spirit and Scout, as well as design items including signature Indian-head fender lights and logo treatments. Indian Motorcycle, founded in 1901, manufactures all of its models in-house using classic designs and modern technological updates to the engine and other internal components. Chris-Craft Corp., founded in 1874, manufactures luxury motorboats featuring deep-v hulls, reverse transoms, flared bows, large cabin house windows, perforated plate dashboards, bow sit pits and premium exterior and interior hardwoods. Chris-Craft's boat models include the Silver Bullet, Lancer, Catalina, Launch, Corsair and Roamer.

FINANCIALS: **Sales and profits are in thousands of dollars—add 000 to get the full amount. 2009 Note: Financial information for 2009 was not available for all companies at press time.**

2009 Sales: $	2009 Profits: $	**U.S. Stock Ticker: Private**
2008 Sales: $	2008 Profits: $	**Int'l Ticker:** Int'l Exchange:
2007 Sales: $	2007 Profits: $	Employees:
2006 Sales: $	2006 Profits: $	Fiscal Year Ends: 12/31
2005 Sales: $	2005 Profits: $	Parent Company:

SALARIES/BENEFITS:

Pension Plan:	ESOP Stock Plan:	Profit Sharing:	Top Exec. Salary: $	Bonus: $
Savings Plan:	Stock Purch. Plan:		Second Exec. Salary: $	Bonus: $

OTHER THOUGHTS:

Apparent Women Officers or Directors:
Hot Spot for Advancement for Women/Minorities:

LOCATIONS: ("Y" = Yes)

West:	Southwest:	Midwest:	Southeast:	Northeast:	International:
	Y	Y	Y	Y	Y

STERLING AUTOBODY CENTERS

www.sterlingautobody.com

Industry Group Code: 8111 **Ranks within this company's industry group:** Sales: Profits:

Vehicle Manufacturing:		Dealers:		Parts:		Service:		Finance:		Specialty:	
Cars:		Car Dealer New:		Manufacturers:		General Service:		Leasing:		Information Systems:	
Trucks:		Car Dealer Used:		Retail:		Specialty Service:		Auto Loans:		Online Marketing:	
Motorcycles:		Truck Dealer:		Distributors:		Oil Change:		Insurance:		Other:	Y
Specialty:		RV Dealer:		Tires:		Paint and Body:	Y			Publishing:	
Buses:		Motorcycle Dealer:		Batteries:						Rental Cars/Trucks:	
RVs:		Specialty Dealer:									

TYPES OF BUSINESS:

Automotive Repair & Maintenance
Collision Repair

BRANDS/DIVISIONS/AFFILIATES:

Allstate Insurance Corporation (The)
Enterprise Rent-A-Car

CONTACTS:

Note: Officers with more than one job title may be intentionally listed here more than once.

Nick Notte, Pres.
Sharon Mazanec, VP-Mktg. & Sales
Mike Nuxoll, VP-Human Resources & Training
John Donohue, VP-IT
Tony Giannola, VP-Admin.
Bob Benjamin, VP-Oper.
Tony Giannola, VP-Finance
Roger Wright, VP-Strategic Design & Process Implementation
Sharon Mazanec, VP-Real Estate
Tony Giannola, VP-Procurement

Phone:	**Fax:** 508-653-9538
Toll-Free: 800-653-5310	
Address: 9 Tech Cir., Natick, MA 01760 US	

GROWTH PLANS/SPECIAL FEATURES:

Sterling Autobody Centers, a subsidiary of Allstate Corporation, operates a line of automobile collision repair centers. It operates over 60 centers across 16 U.S. states: California, Nevada, Arizona, Utah, Colorado, Texas, Illinois, Michigan, Ohio, Pennsylvania, New York, Maryland, Virginia, North Carolina, Georgia and Florida. Known for its customer service, the company picks up the damaged car, delivers the repaired car, has all cars professionally cleaned and offers a limited lifetime warranty on all work performed. Through a partnership with Enterprise Rent-a-Car, the firm will also deliver and return a rental car for its customers. Sterling works exclusively with Enterprise Rent-A-Car for replacement cars during repair. In February 2010, Sterling opened a new 12,000 square-foot repair facility in Oakland, California. In April 2010, the company opened a new 16,000 square-foot facility in Ontario and a 24,000 square-foot facility in Chicago.

Sterling offers its employees medical, dental, and vision care; short and long-term disability; life insurance; and Sterling University, a company-wide program that teaches a variety of technical and managerial skills, to train and advance its employees.

FINANCIALS:

Sales and profits are in thousands of dollars—add 000 to get the full amount. 2009 Note: Financial information for 2009 was not available for all companies at press time.

2009 Sales: $	2009 Profits: $	**U.S. Stock Ticker: Subsidiary**
2008 Sales: $	2008 Profits: $	**Int'l Ticker:** Int'l Exchange:
2007 Sales: $	2007 Profits: $	Employees:
2006 Sales: $	2006 Profits: $	Fiscal Year Ends:
2005 Sales: $	2005 Profits: $	Parent Company: ALLSTATE CORPORATION (THE)

SALARIES/BENEFITS:

Pension Plan:	ESOP Stock Plan:	Profit Sharing:	Top Exec. Salary: $	Bonus: $
Savings Plan: Y	Stock Purch. Plan:		Second Exec. Salary: $	Bonus: $

OTHER THOUGHTS:

Apparent Women Officers or Directors: 1
Hot Spot for Advancement for Women/Minorities:

LOCATIONS: ("Y" = Yes)

West:	Southwest:	Midwest:	Southeast:	Northeast:	International:
Y	Y	Y	Y	Y	

STONERIDGE INC

www.stoneridge.com

Industry Group Code: 3363 **Ranks within this company's industry group:** Sales: 49 Profits: 36

Vehicle Manufacturing:		**Dealers:**		**Parts:**		**Service:**		**Finance:**		**Specialty:**	
Cars:		Car Dealer New:		Manufacturers:	Y	General Service:		Leasing:		Information Systems:	
Trucks:		Car Dealer Used:		Retail:		Specialty Service:		Auto Loans:		Online Marketing:	
Motorcycles:		Truck Dealer:		Distributors:		Oil Change:		Insurance:		Other:	
Specialty:		RV Dealer:		Tires:		Paint and Body:				Publishing:	
Buses:		Motorcycle Dealer:		Batteries:						Rental Cars/Trucks:	
RVs:		Specialty Dealer:									

TYPES OF BUSINESS:

Automotive Electronic Components
Vehicle Power Distribution Systems
Actuator & Sensor Products
Instrumentation & Display Products
Wiring Systems
Switch Products

BRANDS/DIVISIONS/AFFILIATES:

Stoneridge Hi-Stat Manufacturing
Stoneridge Pollak
Stoneridge Electronics North America
Stoneridge Electronics Europe
PST Eletronica
Minda Stoneridge Instruments Ltd.
Bolton Conductive Systems, LLC

CONTACTS: *Note: Officers with more than one job title may be intentionally listed here more than once.*

John C. Corey, CEO
John C. Corey, Pres.
George E. Strickler, CFO
Thomas A. Beaver, VP-Global Sales
Thomas A. Beaver, VP-Systems Eng.
Avery S. Cohen, Sec.
George E. Strickler, Treas./Exec. VP
Mark J. Tervalon, VP/Pres., Stoneridge Electronics Div.
Steven J. Syzdek, VP/Gen. Mgr.-Stoneridge Asia Pacific
Mike Carnahan, VP/Gen. Mgr.-Electronics, North America
Michael D. Sloan, VP/Pres., Control Devices Div.
William M. Lasky, Chmn.
Peter Kruk, Managing Dir.-Stoneridge Electronics, Europe

Phone: 330-856-2443 **Fax:** 330-856-3618
Toll-Free:
Address: 9400 E. Market St., Warren, OH 44484 US

GROWTH PLANS/SPECIAL FEATURES:

Stoneridge, Inc. is a leading independent designer and manufacturer of highly engineered electrical and electronic components, modules and systems focused principally on the automotive, medium- and heavy-duty truck, agricultural and off-road vehicle markets. Stoneridge has 17 manufacturing and design centers and 14 sales and engineering support offices at various locations around the world. The company operates in two segments: electronics and control devices. Core electronics products include vehicle electrical power and distribution systems; electronic instrumentation; and information display products. These products collect, store and display vehicle information such as speed, pressure, maintenance data, operator performance, temperature and distance traveled. The power distribution systems regulate, coordinate and direct the operation of the entire electrical system within a vehicle compartment. The firm's control devices segment manufactures products that monitor, measure or activate a specific function within a vehicle. These products include electronic switches and sensors that control emissions, braking, steering and suspension systems. Stoneridge operates five divisions under its two reportable segments. The electronics division includes Stoneridge Electronics North America-Wiring, Stoneridge Electronics North America-Transportation and Stoneridge Electronics Europe. The control devices division includes Stoneridge Pollak and Stoneridge Hi-Stat Manufacturing. In 2009, the electronics segment generated 63% of sales, while control devices generated 37%. The company also operates through joint ventures, including PST Eletronica of Brazil, in which it holds a 50% interest; and Minda Stoneridge Instruments Ltd. of India, in which it holds a 49% stake. In October 2009, the firm acquired a controlling stake in Bolton Conductive Systems, LLC, a military and specialty vehicle wiring and electronics supplier. In March 2010, Stoneridge opened a technical center and sales office in Shanghai as part of its expansion into the Asian market.

Stoneridge offers its employees health and life insurance; a 401(k); savings plans; flexible spending accounts; and long term disability coverage.

FINANCIALS: **Sales and profits are in thousands of dollars—add 000 to get the full amount. 2009 Note: Financial information for 2009 was not available for all companies at press time.**

2009 Sales: $475,152	2009 Profits: $-32,326	**U.S. Stock Ticker: SRI**
2008 Sales: $752,698	2008 Profits: $-97,527	**Int'l Ticker:** Int'l Exchange:
2007 Sales: $727,120	2007 Profits: $16,671	Employees: 5,200
2006 Sales: $708,699	2006 Profits: $14,513	Fiscal Year Ends: 12/31
2005 Sales: $671,584	2005 Profits: $ 933	Parent Company:

SALARIES/BENEFITS:

Pension Plan:	ESOP Stock Plan:	Profit Sharing:	Top Exec. Salary: $615,439	Bonus: $204,800
Savings Plan: Y	Stock Purch. Plan:		Second Exec. Salary: $324,430	Bonus: $72,765

OTHER THOUGHTS:

Apparent Women Officers or Directors: 1
Hot Spot for Advancement for Women/Minorities:

LOCATIONS: ("Y" = Yes)

West:	Southwest:	Midwest:	Southeast:	Northeast:	International:
Y	Y	Y	Y	Y	Y

STRATTEC SECURITY CORP

www.strattec.com

Industry Group Code: 3363 **Ranks within this company's industry group:** Sales: 59 Profits: 31

Vehicle Manufacturing:		Dealers:		Parts:		Service:		Finance:		Specialty:	
Cars:		Car Dealer New:		Manufacturers:	Y	General Service:		Leasing:		Information Systems:	
Trucks:		Car Dealer Used:		Retail:		Specialty Service:		Auto Loans:		Online Marketing:	
Motorcycles:		Truck Dealer:		Distributors:		Oil Change:		Insurance:		Other:	
Specialty:		RV Dealer:		Tires:		Paint and Body:				Publishing:	
Buses:		Motorcycle Dealer:		Batteries:						Rental Cars/Trucks:	
RVs:		Specialty Dealer:									

TYPES OF BUSINESS:

Vehicle Security Systems
Automotive Locks & Keys
Electronic Security Systems
Ancillary Automotive Power Systems

BRANDS/DIVISIONS/AFFILIATES:

Vehicle Access Systems Technology (VAST) Alliance
Strattec Power Access, LLC
STRATTEC Power Access de Mexico
Vehicle Access Systems Technology LLC

CONTACTS: *Note: Officers with more than one job title may be intentionally listed here more than once.*

Harold M. Stratton, II, CEO
Frank J. Krejci, COO
Frank J. Krejci, Pres.
Patrick J. Hansen, CFO/Sr. VP
Dennis A. Kazmierski, VP-Mktg. & Sales
Patrick J. Hansen, Sec.
Kathryn E. Scherbarth, VP-Milwaukee Oper.
Patrick J. Hansen, Treas.
Brian J. Reetz, VP-Security Products
Richard P. Messina, VP-Strattec Power Access LLC
Harold M. Stratton, II, Chmn.
Rolondo J. Guillot, VP-Mexican Oper.

Phone: 414-247-3333 **Fax:** 414-247-3329
Toll-Free:
Address: 3333 W. Good Hope Rd., Milwaukee, WI 53209 US

GROWTH PLANS/SPECIAL FEATURES:

Strattec Security Corp. is one of the world's largest producers of automotive locks and keys. It designs, manufactures and markets automotive security products, including mechanical and electronically-enhanced locks and keys, steering column and instrument panel ignition lock housings, as well as access control products including latches, power sliding door systems, power lift gate systems, power deck lid systems, door handles and related access control products. It maintains one manufacturing facility at its headquarters in Wisconsin and two manufacturing facilities in Juarez, Mexico, as well as a warehouse in El Paso, Texas and a sales and engineering office in Troy, Michigan. The firm's four principle customers, which together accounted for roughly 71% of 2009 sales, are General Motors Corp. (GM); Delphi Corp.; Ford Motor Company; and Chrysler Group LLC. Strattec is involved in the Vehicle Access Systems Technology (VAST) Alliance, with WITTE Automotive, a German lock maker, and Michigan-based ADAC Automotive, Inc. The VAST Alliance provides a cross-licensing agreement, allowing the three companies to manufacture and sell each other's products: WITTE manufactures and sells Strattec and ADAC products in Europe and Strattec and ADAC manufacture and sell WITTE products in North America. The three companies also maintain a joint venture, Vehicle Access Systems Technology LLC (VAST LLC) which was set up to take advantage of market opportunities outside Europe and North America. Currently, the joint venture maintains three manufacturing facilities in China and one in Brazil as well as supporting sales throughout Asia and Latin America. In 2009, Strattec and Witte formed a subsidiary called STRATTEC Power Access, LLC, which designs, manufactures and sells ancillary automotive power systems, including for power sliding side doors, and also operates its own subsidiary in Mexico called STRATTEC Power Access de Mexico, which operates out of the manufacturing facilities in Juarez.

Employees of Strattec receive medical, dental, vision, life insurance and disability plans.

FINANCIALS: **Sales and profits are in thousands of dollars—add 000 to get the full amount. 2009 Note: Financial information for 2009 was not available for all companies at press time.**

2009 Sales: $126,097	2009 Profits: $-6,122	**U.S. Stock Ticker: STRT**
2008 Sales: $159,642	2008 Profits: $3,267	**Int'l Ticker:** Int'l Exchange:
2007 Sales: $167,707	2007 Profits: $8,183	Employees: 1,655
2006 Sales: $181,197	2006 Profits: $12,477	Fiscal Year Ends: 6/30
2005 Sales: $190,314	2005 Profits: $15,038	Parent Company:

SALARIES/BENEFITS:

Pension Plan:	ESOP Stock Plan: Y	Profit Sharing:	Top Exec. Salary: $373,814	Bonus: $
Savings Plan: Y	Stock Purch. Plan: Y		Second Exec. Salary: $217,134	Bonus: $

OTHER THOUGHTS:

Apparent Women Officers or Directors: 1
Hot Spot for Advancement for Women/Minorities:

LOCATIONS: ("Y" = Yes)

West:	Southwest:	Midwest:	Southeast:	Northeast:	International:
	Y	Y			Y

SUPERIOR INDUSTRIES INTERNATIONAL INC

www.supind.com

Industry Group Code: 3363 **Ranks within this company's industry group:** Sales: 53 Profits: 46

Vehicle Manufacturing:		**Dealers:**		**Parts:**		**Service:**		**Finance:**		**Specialty:**	
Cars:		Car Dealer New:		Manufacturers:	Y	General Service:		Leasing:		Information Systems:	
Trucks:		Car Dealer Used:		Retail:		Specialty Service:		Auto Loans:		Online Marketing:	
Motorcycles:		Truck Dealer:		Distributors:	Y	Oil Change:		Insurance:		Other:	Y
Specialty:		RV Dealer:		Tires:		Paint and Body:				Publishing:	
Buses:		Motorcycle Dealer:		Batteries:						Rental Cars/Trucks:	
RVs:		Specialty Dealer:									

TYPES OF BUSINESS:

Automobile Parts Manufacturer
Aluminum Road Wheels

BRANDS/DIVISIONS/AFFILIATES:

GROWTH PLANS/SPECIAL FEATURES:

Superior Industries International is a designer, manufacturer and supplier of aluminum road wheels to original equipment manufacturers (OEMs) in the automotive industry. The firm operates five manufacturing plants in the U.S. and Mexico. Superior's primary product is an aluminum road wheel, used in production of passenger cars and light trucks by domestic and international OEMs. Superior maintains clients all over the world, with the biggest (GM, Ford Motor Company and Chrysler) accounting for 81% of net sales in 2009. Other customers include BMW, Fiat, Jaguar, Land Rover, Mazda, Mercedes Benz, Mitsubishi and Nissan, among others. The firm manufactures 69% of its wheels in Mexico and the remaining 31% in the U.S. Customers in North America represent the biggest market for the company, with 80% of products sold domestically and 20% internationally. In January 2009, the firm closed its southern California manufacturing plant and eliminated 290 jobs. In June 2010, the firm acquired an equity interest in aluminum wheel manufacturer Synergies Castings Limited, an India-based company. Superior also announced in June that it would divest its 50% stake in Suoftec Light Metal Products Production & Distribution, Ltd., its Hungarian joint venture with OTTO FUCHS KG.

CONTACTS:

Note: Officers with more than one job title may be intentionally listed here more than once.

Steven J. Borick, CEO
Steven J. Borick, Pres.
Emil J. Fanelli, Acting CFO
Michael J. O'Rourke, Exec. VP-Sales & Mktg.
Eddie Rodriguez, VP-Human Resources
Ross Perian, CIO
Parveen Kakar, Sr. VP-Prod. Dev.
Parveen Kakar, Sr. VP-Corp. Eng.
Kenneth A. Stakas, Sr. VP-Mfg.
Robert A. Earnest, General Counsel/VP/Corp. Sec.
Michael J. O'Rourke, Exec. VP-Oper.
Steven A. Gamble, VP/Treas.
Robert Bracy, Sr. VP-Project Mgmt.
Steven J. Borick, Chmn.
Gabriel Soto, VP-Mexico Oper.
Cameron Toyne, VP-Supply Chain Mgmt.

Phone: 818-781-4973 **Fax:** 818-780-3500
Toll-Free:
Address: 7800 Woodley Ave., Van Nuys, CA 91406-1788 US

FINANCIALS:

Sales and profits are in thousands of dollars—add 000 to get the full amount. 2009 Note: Financial information for 2009 was not available for all companies at press time.

2009 Sales: $418,846	2009 Profits: $-94,142	**U.S. Stock Ticker: SUP**
2008 Sales: $754,894	2008 Profits: $-26,053	**Int'l Ticker:** Int'l Exchange:
2007 Sales: $956,892	2007 Profits: $9,292	Employees: 3,500
2006 Sales: $789,862	2006 Profits: $-10,799	Fiscal Year Ends: 12/31
2005 Sales: $804,161	2005 Profits: $20,219	Parent Company:

SALARIES/BENEFITS:

Pension Plan:	ESOP Stock Plan:	Profit Sharing:	Top Exec. Salary: $850,000	Bonus: $
Savings Plan:	Stock Purch. Plan:		Second Exec. Salary: $291,250	Bonus: $10,000

OTHER THOUGHTS:

Apparent Women Officers or Directors: 1
Hot Spot for Advancement for Women/Minorities:

LOCATIONS: ("Y" = Yes)

West:	Southwest:	Midwest:	Southeast:	Northeast:	International:
Y			Y		Y

SUPREME INDUSTRIES INC

www.supremeind.com

Industry Group Code: 336211 **Ranks within this company's industry group:** Sales: 5 Profits: 3

Vehicle Manufacturing:		Dealers:		Parts:		Service:		Finance:		Specialty:	
Cars:		Car Dealer New:		Manufacturers:	Y	General Service:		Leasing:		Information Systems:	
Trucks:		Car Dealer Used:		Retail:		Specialty Service:		Auto Loans:		Online Marketing:	
Motorcycles:		Truck Dealer:		Distributors:		Oil Change:		Insurance:		Other:	
Specialty:		RV Dealer:		Tires:		Paint and Body:				Publishing:	
Buses:		Motorcycle Dealer:		Batteries:						Rental Cars/Trucks:	
RVs:		Specialty Dealer:									

TYPES OF BUSINESS:

Specialized Vehicles
Specialized Truck Bodies & Shuttle Buses
Vertically Integrated Fiberglass Products
Fiberglass Wind Deflectors

BRANDS/DIVISIONS/AFFILIATES:

Supreme Corp.
Signature Van
Iner-City
Spartan
Spartan MX
Astro Body
Kold King
Surpreme Specialty Vehicles

CONTACTS:

Note: Officers with more than one job title may be intentionally listed here more than once.

Herbert M. Gardner, CEO
Robert W. Wilson, COO
Robert W. Wilson, Pres.
Jeffery D. Mowery, CFO
Bob Besse, VP-Mktg. & Sales
William J. Barrett, Corp. Sec.
William J. Barrett, Exec. VP-Long Range & Strategic Planning
Jeffery D. Mowery, Treas.
Mark Beer, Dir.-Strategic Accounts
Herbert M. Gardner, Chmn.

Phone: 574-642-3070 **Fax:** 574-642-3208
Toll-Free: 800-642-4889
Address: 2581 E. Kercher Rd., P.O. Box 237, Goshen, IN 46528 US

GROWTH PLANS/SPECIAL FEATURES:

Supreme Industries, Inc., through its wholly-owned subsidiary Supreme Corp., manufactures specialized vehicles, including trucks, buses and armored vehicles. Supreme has manufacturing, distribution and service facilities in nine states across the continental U.S. The company has two operating segments: specialized vehicles and vertically integrated fiberglass products. The specialized vehicle industry consists of companies that manufacture and distribute specialized truck bodies and shuttle buses. Depending on the product, it is either built directly on a truck chassis or built separately and installed at a later date. The firm makes its own fiberglass wind deflectors under the Fuel Shark brand. Supreme's products include Signature Van bodies, which range from 10-28 feet in length; Iner-City cutaway van bodies, which are manufactured on cutaway chassis allowing access from the cab to the cargo area; Spartan cargo vans, which are available in lengths of 10-14 feet; Spartan MX insulated bodies, which are designed for companies making frequent hand-loaded refrigerated deliveries; the Astro Body, a molded fiberglass van that mounts to a pickup chassis; Kold King insulated van bodies for temperature controlled applications; Stake bodies, which are flatbeds with various configurations of removable sides; Suburbans with armored protection against hostile fire; armored trucks, which are available in aluminum, galvaneal or stainless steel; and Surpreme Specialty Vehicles (SSV), which are designed for emergency response and homeland security personnel. Additional products include StarTrans shuttle buses under the Senator and Candidate brands, which have seating capacities for 12-29 people; StarTrans mid-size buses under the President and Ambassador brands, which have seating capacities of up to 25 passengers; StarTrans trolleys, which are marketed to resort areas and theme parks; the StarTrans Tourliner, which provides transportation for up to 39 passengers; and the StarTrans Activity Bus, which is marketed to churches, schools and day care centers.

FINANCIALS:

Sales and profits are in thousands of dollars—add 000 to get the full amount. 2009 Note: Financial information for 2009 was not available for all companies at press time.

2009 Sales: $192,036 | 2009 Profits: $-8,743
2008 Sales: $257,903 | 2008 Profits: $-3,061
2007 Sales: $301,655 | 2007 Profits: $4,164
2006 Sales: $340,747 | 2006 Profits: $4,595
2005 Sales: $341,253 | 2005 Profits: $8,341

U.S. Stock Ticker: STS
Int'l Ticker: Int'l Exchange:
Employees: 1,400
Fiscal Year Ends: 12/31
Parent Company:

SALARIES/BENEFITS:

Pension Plan: | ESOP Stock Plan: | Profit Sharing: | Top Exec. Salary: $150,000 | Bonus: $
Savings Plan: Y | Stock Purch. Plan: | | Second Exec. Salary: $91,800 | Bonus: $

OTHER THOUGHTS:

Apparent Women Officers or Directors:
Hot Spot for Advancement for Women/Minorities:

LOCATIONS: ("Y" = Yes)

West:	Southwest:	Midwest:	Southeast:	Northeast:	International:
Y	Y	Y	Y	Y	

SUZUKI AUTOMOBILE (THAILAND) CO LTD

www.suzuki.co.th

Industry Group Code: 42311 **Ranks within this company's industry group:** Sales: Profits:

Vehicle Manufacturing:		Dealers:		Parts:		Service:		Finance:		Specialty:	
Cars:		Car Dealer New:	Y	Manufacturers:		General Service:		Leasing:		Information Systems:	
Trucks:		Car Dealer Used:		Retail:		Specialty Service:		Auto Loans:		Online Marketing:	
Motorcycles:		Truck Dealer:		Distributors:	Y	Oil Change:		Insurance:		Other:	
Specialty:		RV Dealer:		Tires:		Paint and Body:				Publishing:	
Buses:		Motorcycle Dealer:		Batteries:						Rental Cars/Trucks:	
RVs:		Specialty Dealer:									

TYPES OF BUSINESS:

Automobile Imports & Exports

BRANDS/DIVISIONS/AFFILIATES:

Suzuki Motor Corporation
Siam International Corp. Ltd.
Carry
APV
Grand Vitara
Swift
Thai Suzuki Motor Co., Ltd.

GROWTH PLANS/SPECIAL FEATURES:

Suzuki Automobile (Thailand) Co., Ltd., established in 2003, imports and distributes Suzuki brand cars and parts in Thailand. It is a joint venture that is 60%-owned by Suzuki Motor Corporation, 20%-owned by Siam International Corp. Ltd. and 20%-owned by Phornpong Phornprapha, who is the President of Siam International and chairman of the company. The firm's product line-up includes the Suzuki Carry commercial vehicle, as well as passenger vehicles such as the compact Suzuki Swift, the Suzuki APV (All Purpose Vehicle) and the Suzuki Grand Vitara compact SUV. In total, Suzuki Automobile (Thailand) has a network of 41 dealerships spread throughout Thailand. Its affiliates include auto manufacturer Thai Suzuki Motor Co., Ltd., a fellow Suzuki subsidiary that produces and markets Suzuki motorcycles.

CONTACTS: *Note: Officers with more than one job title may be intentionally listed here more than once.*

Phornpong Phornprapha, Chmn.

Phone: 66-2245-5734	**Fax:** 66-2247-9396
Toll-Free:	
Address: Siam International Bldg., Fl 2, 5/15 Phayathai Rd., Bangkok, 10400 Thailand	

FINANCIALS: **Sales and profits are in thousands of dollars—add 000 to get the full amount. 2009 Note: Financial information for 2009 was not available for all companies at press time.**

2009 Sales: $	2009 Profits: $	**U.S. Stock Ticker: Joint Venture**
2008 Sales: $	2008 Profits: $	**Int'l Ticker:** Int'l Exchange:
2007 Sales: $	2007 Profits: $	Employees:
2006 Sales: $	2006 Profits: $	Fiscal Year Ends:
2005 Sales: $	2005 Profits: $	Parent Company: SUZUKI MOTOR CORPORATION

SALARIES/BENEFITS:

Pension Plan:	ESOP Stock Plan:	Profit Sharing:	Top Exec. Salary: $	Bonus: $
Savings Plan:	Stock Purch. Plan:		Second Exec. Salary: $	Bonus: $

OTHER THOUGHTS:

Apparent Women Officers or Directors:
Hot Spot for Advancement for Women/Minorities:

LOCATIONS: ("Y" = Yes)

West:	Southwest:	Midwest:	Southeast:	Northeast:	International:
					Y

SUZUKI MOTOR CORPORATION

www.globalsuzuki.com

Industry Group Code: 33611 **Ranks within this company's industry group:** Sales: 13 Profits: 11

Vehicle Manufacturing:		Dealers:		Parts:		Service:		Finance:		Specialty:	
Cars:	Y	Car Dealer New:		Manufacturers:	Y	General Service:		Leasing:		Information Systems:	
Trucks:		Car Dealer Used:		Retail:		Specialty Service:		Auto Loans:		Online Marketing:	
Motorcycles:	Y	Truck Dealer:		Distributors:		Oil Change:		Insurance:		Other:	
Specialty:	Y	RV Dealer:		Tires:		Paint and Body:				Publishing:	
Buses:		Motorcycle Dealer:		Batteries:						Rental Cars/Trucks:	
RVs:		Specialty Dealer:									

TYPES OF BUSINESS:

Automobiles, Manufacturing
Motorcycles
ATVs
Marine Products
Wheelchairs
Industrial Equipment

BRANDS/DIVISIONS/AFFILIATES:

Suzuki Automobile (Thailand) Co Ltd
Maruti Suzuki India, Ltd.
Suzuki New Zealand, Ltd.
Suzuki International Europe GmbH
Suzuki Italia S.p.A.
Suzuki Motor Poland SP.Z.O.O.
American Suzuki Motor Corp.
Vitara

CONTACTS: *Note: Officers with more than one job title may be intentionally listed here more than once.*

Osamu Suzuki, CEO
Osamu Suzuki, COO
Minoru Tamura, Sr. Managing Exec. Officer-Domestic Mktg.
Hiroyasu Uchida, Gen. Mgr.-Human Resources
Takashi Nakayama, Gen. Mgr.-Automobile Eng.
Naoki Aizawa, Sr. Managing Officer-Mfg.
Toyokazu Sugimoto, Sr. Managing Officer-Admin.
Toyokazu Sugimoto, Gen. Mgr.-Corp. Planning
Takashi Nakayama, Sr. Managing Exec. Officer
Minoru Tamura, Pres., Suzuki Finance, Inc.
Takao Hirosawa, Sr. Managing Exec. Officer/Mgr.-Tokyo Branch
Masanori Atsumi, Sr. Managing Officer-Motorcycle Eng.
Osamu Suzuki, Chmn.
Shinzo Nakanishi, Dir.-Global Mktg./CEO-Maruti Suzuki India Ltd.
Eiji Mochizuki, Sr. Managing Officer-Purchasing

Phone: 81-53-440-2904 **Fax:**
Toll-Free:
Address: 300 Takatsuka-cho, Minami-ku, Hamamatsu, 432-8611 Japan

GROWTH PLANS/SPECIAL FEATURES:

Suzuki Motor Corporation designs and manufactures all terrain vehicles (ATVs), motorcycles, outboard motors, passenger cars, compact and subcompact cars, commercial vehicles and other products. The firm also manufactures boats, electric scooters, motorized wheelchairs and industrial equipment. The company is one of the largest manufacturers of minicars and motorcycles in Japan, producing about 2,500 automobiles and 3,300 motorcycles annually. Suzuki's main production facilities are spread throughout 20 countries. The company's network serves 187 countries and areas. The firm's products include the Vitara and Grand Vitara, SX4, Splash, Jimny, Swift and Alto automobiles; and the Bandit, Gladius and Suzuki Boulevard motorcycles. Automobiles account for about 81.7% of the company's sales, with motorcycles comprising 15.1% and its other products accounting for the remaining 3.2%. Suzuki has developed an ultra-low-emission, direct-injection turbo engine for the minicar category in Japan, as well as a line of motorcycles incorporating an electronically controlled, continuously variable transmission. Major overseas subsidiaries include Suzuki International Europe GmbH in Germany; Suzuki Italia S.p.A. in Italy; Suzuki Motor Poland SP.Z.O.O. in Poland; American Suzuki Motor Corp. in the U.S.; Maruti Suzuki India, Ltd., in India; and Suzuki New Zealand, Ltd., in New Zealand. Suzuki's recent products include the Ritz compact car, launched in India in 2009; the Kizashi four-wheel-drive sedan; the Alto minivehicle, available in Japan; and the Wagon R compact car, launched in India in 2009. In November 2009, the company announced plans for a new automobile plant with pressing, welding, painting, assembly and engine production capabilities in Thailand. In December 2009, Suzuki agreed to sell its 50% stake in joint venture CAMI Automotive Inc. to General Motors (GM), its ownership partner; and entered a product, distribution and manufacturing partnership with Volkswagen AG.

FINANCIALS: **Sales and profits are in thousands of dollars—add 000 to get the full amount. 2009 Note: Financial information for 2009 was not available for all companies at press time.**

2009 Sales: $32,281,200 | 2009 Profits: $294,670
2008 Sales: $29,911,000 | 2008 Profits: $273,000
2007 Sales: $26,799,405 | 2007 Profits: $635,394
2006 Sales: $23,380,045 | 2006 Profits: $561,379
2005 Sales: $20,806,000 | 2005 Profits: $415,000

U.S. Stock Ticker: SZKMY
Int'l Ticker: 7269 Int'l Exchange: Tokyo-TSE
Employees:
Fiscal Year Ends: 3/31
Parent Company:

SALARIES/BENEFITS:

Pension Plan: ESOP Stock Plan: Profit Sharing: Top Exec. Salary: $ Bonus: $
Savings Plan: Stock Purch. Plan: Second Exec. Salary: $ Bonus: $

OTHER THOUGHTS:

Apparent Women Officers or Directors:
Hot Spot for Advancement for Women/Minorities:

LOCATIONS: ("Y" = Yes)

West:	Southwest:	Midwest:	Southeast:	Northeast:	International:
Y					Y

SYTNER GROUP PLC

www.sytner.co.uk

Industry Group Code: 441110 **Ranks within this company's industry group:** Sales: Profits:

Vehicle Manufacturing:		Dealers:		Parts:		Service:		Finance:		Specialty:	
Cars:		Car Dealer New:	Y	Manufacturers:		General Service:	Y	Leasing:		Information Systems:	
Trucks:		Car Dealer Used:	Y	Retail:	Y	Specialty Service:		Auto Loans:	Y	Online Marketing:	
Motorcycles:		Truck Dealer:		Distributors:		Oil Change:		Insurance:		Other:	Y
Specialty:		RV Dealer:		Tires:		Paint and Body:	Y			Publishing:	
Buses:		Motorcycle Dealer:		Batteries:						Rental Cars/Trucks:	Y
RVs:		Specialty Dealer:									

TYPES OF BUSINESS:

Auto Dealers, Retail
Auto Parts & Service

BRANDS/DIVISIONS/AFFILIATES:

Penske Automotive Group Inc
ALPINA
Nick Whale Ferrari & Maserati Dealership
Graypaul Birmingham

CONTACTS:

Note: Officers with more than one job title may be intentionally listed here more than once.

Gerard Nieuwenhuys, Managing Dir.
Melvin Rogers, Head-Human Resources

Phone: 44-845-481-0148	**Fax:** 44-116-282-1010
Toll-Free:	
Address: 2 Penman Way, Grove Park, Leicester, LE19 1ST UK	

GROWTH PLANS/SPECIAL FEATURES:

Sytner Group plc is a retailer of new and pre-owned vehicles, specializing in high-end, luxury vehicles in the U.K., operating over 137 dealerships. It is a wholly-owned subsidiary of the Penske Automotive Group, Inc. (formerly United Auto Group), a Detroit-based automotive company that owns and operates 310 franchises across the U.S., Mexico, Germany, Puerto Rico and, through Sytner, the U.K. Sytner sells a total of 24 premier brands of new cars, including Ferrari, Lamborghini, Porsche, Jaguar, Maserati, Bentley, Audi, BMW, Mercedes-Benz, Honda, SEAT, Rolls-Royce, smart, MINI, Lexus, Chrysler, Saab, Toyota and Volvo. The firm also offers used cars for many of the same brands. Sytner allows customers to order customized new cars that meet their specifications, and works with specialist builder ALPINA to offer individually tailored BMW's. The company also offers after-sale body shop, parts and repair services; including tailored solutions for most of its brands and its Sytner Drive vehicle replacement plan, which provides customers with a replacement vehicle of the same standard as their own vehicle, if it is damaged in an accident. Sytner's web site provides links to each individual dealership where customers can browse new and used inventory. In February 2009, Sytner acquired the Nick Whale Ferrari and Maserati Dealership in Birmingham, U.K. The business will now operate under the name Graypaul Birmingham. In June 2010, the firm was chosen by sports car manufacturer McLaren Automotive to be its retailer in the north and northwest regions of England and Scotland.

FINANCIALS:

Sales and profits are in thousands of dollars—add 000 to get the full amount. 2009 Note: Financial information for 2009 was not available for all companies at press time.

2009 Sales: $	2009 Profits: $	**U.S. Stock Ticker: Subsidiary**
2008 Sales: $	2008 Profits: $	**Int'l Ticker:** Int'l Exchange:
2007 Sales: $	2007 Profits: $	Employees:
2006 Sales: $	2006 Profits: $	Fiscal Year Ends: 12/31
2005 Sales: $	2005 Profits: $	Parent Company: PENSKE AUTOMOTIVE GROUP INC

SALARIES/BENEFITS:

Pension Plan:	ESOP Stock Plan:	Profit Sharing:	Top Exec. Salary: $	Bonus: $
Savings Plan:	Stock Purch. Plan:		Second Exec. Salary: $	Bonus: $

OTHER THOUGHTS:

Apparent Women Officers or Directors:
Hot Spot for Advancement for Women/Minorities:

LOCATIONS: ("Y" = Yes)

West:	Southwest:	Midwest:	Southeast:	Northeast:	International:
					Y

TATA GROUP

www.tata.com

Industry Group Code: 55111 **Ranks within this company's industry group:** Sales: 1 Profits:

Vehicle Manufacturing:		**Dealers:**		**Parts:**		**Service:**		**Finance:**		**Specialty:**	
Cars:	Y	Car Dealer New:		Manufacturers:	Y	General Service:		Leasing:		Information Systems:	
Trucks:	Y	Car Dealer Used:		Retail:		Specialty Service:		Auto Loans:		Online Marketing:	
Motorcycles:		Truck Dealer:		Distributors:		Oil Change:		Insurance:		Other:	
Specialty:	Y	RV Dealer:		Tires:		Paint and Body:				Publishing:	
Buses:		Motorcycle Dealer:		Batteries:						Rental Cars/Trucks:	
RVs:		Specialty Dealer:									

TYPES OF BUSINESS:

Engineering Products
Communication & Information Systems
Steel
Energy Utilities
Solar Power
Automobiles
Hotels & Resorts
Pharmaceuticals & Chemicals

BRANDS/DIVISIONS/AFFILIATES:

Infiniti Retail
Tata Global Beverages
Tata AIG General Insurance
Tata Realty and Infrastructure
Tata Motors Limited
Tata Sons
Advinus Therapeutics
TRF

CONTACTS: *Note: Officers with more than one job title may be intentionally listed here more than once.*

Ishaat Hussain, Dir.-Finance
R. Gopalakrishnan, Member-Group Exec. Office & Group Corp. Center
Srinath Narasimhan, CEO-Tata Communications
Kishor A. Chaukar, Managing Dir.-Tata Industries
Patrick McGoldrick, CEO-Tata Technologies
Ratan N. Tata, Chmn.

Phone: 91 22-6665-7183	**Fax:** 91-22-5665-7974
Toll-Free:	
Address: 24 Homi Mody Street, Mumbai, VA 400 001 India	

GROWTH PLANS/SPECIAL FEATURES:

Tata Group comprises approximately 116 companies operating worldwide across seven business sectors: information technology and communications; engineering; materials; services; energy; consumer products; and chemicals. One of India's largest business conglomerates, Tata Group has operations in over 80 countries spanning six continents. The group's 28 publicly listed companies include Tata Steel, Tata Consultancy Services, Tata Motors and Tata Tea. Tata's engineering sector includes automotive company Tata AutoComp Systems and engineering products company TAL Manufacturing Solutions. The group's materials sector includes Tata Advanced Materials, a manufacturer of armor products, telecommunication products and composite panels for cargo containers. Tata's energy sector includes power companies North Delhi Power and Tata BP Solar Tata's chemicals companies include Rallis India, Tata Chemicals and pharmaceutical company Advinus Therapeutics. The group's services sector includes Indian Hotels Company Limited (IHCL), Tata Realty and Infrastructure and financial services companies such as Tata AIG General Insurance and Tata Financial Services. Tata consumer products companies include Infiniti Retail, Tata Ceramics and Alliance Coffee. Tata's information systems and communications sector includes information systems companies Nelito Systems and Tata Technologies; and Nelco, a manufacturer of consumer electronic products. Tata Sons promotes and holds majority shares in Tata Group's key companies. Tata Industries is a promoter company of Tata Group which focuses in particular on high-tech business areas. In May 2010, Tata Tea announced that all the beverage companies under its umbrella, including Tata Tea, Tetley, and Eight O'clock Coffee will now be known collectively as Tata Global Beverages. In April 2010, TRF, a company in TATA's engineering segment, acquired Hewitt Robins International, a producer of bulk material handling vibratory equipment, for approximately $4.8 million. Also in April 2010, Tata Realty and Infrastructure announced a joint-venture with Actis, a private equity investor, to invest $200 million for road and highway projects in India.

FINANCIALS: **Sales and profits are in thousands of dollars—add 000 to get the full amount. 2009 Note: Financial information for 2009 was not available for all companies at press time.**

2009 Sales: $70,900,000	2009 Profits: $	**U.S. Stock Ticker: Private**
2008 Sales: $62,500,000	2008 Profits: $	**Int'l Ticker:** Int'l Exchange:
2007 Sales: $28,500,000	2007 Profits: $	Employees: 363,039
2006 Sales: $21,675,600	2006 Profits: $	Fiscal Year Ends: 3/31
2005 Sales: $17,878,000	2005 Profits: $	Parent Company:

SALARIES/BENEFITS:

Pension Plan:	ESOP Stock Plan:	Profit Sharing:	Top Exec. Salary: $	Bonus: $
Savings Plan:	Stock Purch. Plan:		Second Exec. Salary: $	Bonus: $

OTHER THOUGHTS:

Apparent Women Officers or Directors:
Hot Spot for Advancement for Women/Minorities:

LOCATIONS: ("Y" = Yes)

West:	Southwest:	Midwest:	Southeast:	Northeast:	International:
				Y	Y

TATA MOTORS LIMITED

www.tatamotors.com

Industry Group Code: 33611 **Ranks within this company's industry group:** Sales: 20 Profits: 8

Vehicle Manufacturing:		Dealers:		Parts:		Service:		Finance:		Specialty:	
Cars:	Y	Car Dealer New:		Manufacturers:		General Service:		Leasing:		Information Systems:	
Trucks:	Y	Car Dealer Used:		Retail:		Specialty Service:		Auto Loans:		Online Marketing:	
Motorcycles:		Truck Dealer:		Distributors:		Oil Change:		Insurance:		Other:	
Specialty:		RV Dealer:		Tires:		Paint and Body:				Publishing:	
Buses:	Y	Motorcycle Dealer:		Batteries:						Rental Cars/Trucks:	
RVs:		Specialty Dealer:									

TYPES OF BUSINESS:

Automobile Manufacturing
Light & Medium Commercial Vehicles Manufacturing
Heavy Commercial Vehicles Manufacturing
Passenger Vehicles Manufacturing

BRANDS/DIVISIONS/AFFILIATES:

Jaguar Cars Ltd
Land Rover
Tata Nano

CONTACTS: *Note: Officers with more than one job title may be intentionally listed here more than once.*

Carl Peter Forster, Managing Dir.
C. Ramakrishnan, CFO/Exec. Dir.
S.N. Ambardekar, Head-Mfg. Oper.
R. Bagga, VP-Legal
A. Gajendragadkar, VP-Bus. Planning
Debasis Ray, Head-Corp. Comm.
H.K. Sethna, Head-Investor Rel./Company Sec.
P.Y. Gurav, VP-Corp. Finance
Ravi Pisharody, Pres., Commercial Vehicles Bus. Unit
S.B. Borwankar, Head-Jamshedpur Plant
Akshaykumar Mankad, Head-Car Plant
Rajiv Dube, Pres., Passenger Cars
Ratan N. Tata, Chmn.
B.B. Parekh, Chief-Strategic Sourcing

Phone: 91-22-6665-8282 **Fax:** 91-22-6665-7260
Toll-Free:
Address: Bombay House, 24, Homi Mody St., Mumbai, 400 001 India

GROWTH PLANS/SPECIAL FEATURES:

Tata Motors Limited is one of India's largest automobile manufacturers. The company manufactures commercial and passenger vehicles, and also provides automobile financing services. Tata's products include passenger vehicles, representing 31.8% of 2009 revenues; utility vehicles, 23.7%; light commercial vehicles, including pick-up trucks, at 23.9%; and medium and heavy commercial vehicles, 20.6%. Measuring by number of units sold, passenger cars represented 33% of 2009 sales; utility vehicles, 7.7%; light commercial vehicles, 31.9%; and medium and heavy commercial vehicles, 27.4%. Through its subsidiaries, the firm is also engaged in areas such as engineering; construction equipment manufacturing; vehicle components manufacturing; supply chain management; factory automation; and automotive retailing and servicing. The company employs a significant number of engineers and scientists and maintains R&D centers in India, South Korea, Spain and the U.K. Tata is among the world's leading bus manufacturers, and the company has expanded these activities through strategic partnerships with Hispano Carrocera, a Spanish bus and coach manufacturer, as well as Marcopolo, a Brazil-based company engaged in the manufacture of bodies for buses and coaches. The firm has also expanded its international presence through such activities as the manufacture and marketing of pick-up trucks in Thailand and the marketing of Fiat-branded cars in India, as well as through vehicle sales in several countries in Europe, Africa, the Middle East, Australia and Asia. Tata Motors also owns the Jaguar and Land Rover brands previously held by Ford Motor Co., an operation encompassing roughly 26 vehicle sales subsidiaries worldwide. In July 2009, Tata Motors began distributing its inexpensive Tata Nano; the Nano, a small four-seat vehicle, cost just over 100,000 Rupees (approximately $2,200) at its launch, a price that is expected to fundamentally affect the availability of passenger cars in India.

FINANCIALS: **Sales and profits are in thousands of dollars—add 000 to get the full amount. 2009 Note: Financial information for 2009 was not available for all companies at press time.**

2009 Sales: $14,455,320 — 2009 Profits: $510,500
2008 Sales: $9,998,600 — 2008 Profits: $355,100
2007 Sales: $7,270,000 — 2007 Profits: $500,000
2006 Sales: $5,409,500 — 2006 Profits: $337,400
2005 Sales: $4,548,100 — 2005 Profits: $304,000

U.S. Stock Ticker: TTM
Int'l Ticker: 500570 Int'l Exchange: Bombay-BSE
Employees: 36,364
Fiscal Year Ends: 3/31
Parent Company: TATA GROUP

SALARIES/BENEFITS:

Pension Plan:	ESOP Stock Plan:	Profit Sharing:	Top Exec. Salary: $971,045	Bonus: $
Savings Plan:	Stock Purch. Plan:		Second Exec. Salary: $643,733	Bonus: $

OTHER THOUGHTS:

Apparent Women Officers or Directors:
Hot Spot for Advancement for Women/Minorities:

LOCATIONS: ("Y" = Yes)

West:	Southwest:	Midwest:	Southeast:	Northeast:	International:
					Y

TBC CORPORATION

www.tbccorp.com

Industry Group Code: 441320 **Ranks within this company's industry group:** Sales: Profits:

Vehicle Manufacturing:		Dealers:		Parts:		Service:		Finance:		Specialty:	
Cars:		Car Dealer New:		Manufacturers:		General Service:	Y	Leasing:		Information Systems:	
Trucks:		Car Dealer Used:		Retail:		Specialty Service:		Auto Loans:		Online Marketing:	
Motorcycles:		Truck Dealer:		Distributors:	Y	Oil Change:	Y	Insurance:		Other:	
Specialty:		RV Dealer:		Tires:	Y	Paint and Body:				Publishing:	
Buses:		Motorcycle Dealer:		Batteries:	Y					Rental Cars/Trucks:	
RVs:		Specialty Dealer:									

TYPES OF BUSINESS:

Tire Stores
Wholesale Tire Distribution

BRANDS/DIVISIONS/AFFILIATES:

Sumitomo Corporation
Tire Kingdom Inc
Cordovan
Big O Tires Inc
Sigma
National Tire & Battery
Carroll Tire Company
Treadways

CONTACTS: *Note: Officers with more than one job title may be intentionally listed here more than once.*

Lawrence C. Day, CEO
Lawrence C. Day, Pres.
Timothy J. Miller, CFO
Erik R. Olsen, Chief Mktg. Officer/Exec. VP
Peter Wellman, CIO/Sr. VP
Terry L. Trantina, General Counsel/Sr. VP/Sec.
Timothy J. Miller, Treas./Exec. VP
Martin S. Krcelic, Sr. VP-TBC Brands
Orland M. Wolford, Pres./CEO-TBC Retail Group
N. Willian Inhken, Exec. VP/COO-Tire Kingdom Group
Kevin A. Kormondy, Exec. VP/COO-Big O Tires
Lawrence C. Day, Chmn.
J. Glen Gravatt, Pres., Purchasing & Dist. Div.

Phone: 561-383-3100	**Fax:** 531-383-3149
Toll-Free:	
Address: 4300 TBC Way, Palm Beach Gardens, FL 33410 US	

GROWTH PLANS/SPECIAL FEATURES:

TBC Corporation markets and distributes replacement automobile tires through wholesale and retail operations. TBC's wholesale business markets and distributes its proprietary brands of tires, as well as other tires and related products, to regional tire chains and distributors serving independent tire dealers covering the U.S., Canada and Mexico. The company also markets directly to independent tire dealers in the U.S. through its 36 Carroll Tire wholesale distribution centers. Tires marketed under the company's proprietary brands Multi-Mile, Cordovan, Sigma and Vanderbilt are manufactured and marketed through subsidiary TBC Private Brands. TBC Private Brands specializes in passenger, commercial, farm and specialty tires. The Treadways subsidiary provides high performance, passenger, light and medium truck, farm and industrial tires under the Sumitomo, Eldorado, Telstar and Jetzon brands. The company's retail segment operates over 1,200 franchised and company-owned tire centers. These consist of both the franchised retail tire business, Big O Tires, Inc., and the company-owned stores operated through TBC Retail Group under the brands Tire Kingdom; National Tire and Battery; and Merchant's Tire and Auto Centers. Tire Kingdom International sells wholesale tires in domestic and international markets, including Sonar and Cyclone in the U.S.; Dominator Tires in Central and South America and the Middle East; and Sigma tires in all markets excluding the United States. TBC is owned by the Sumitomo Corporation, one of Japan's largest integrated trading and investment business organizations. In October 2009, the firm announced plans to expand its wholesale distribution center into a 1.1 million square foot facility in Charleston, South Carolina.

FINANCIALS: **Sales and profits are in thousands of dollars—add 000 to get the full amount. 2009 Note: Financial information for 2009 was not available for all companies at press time.**

2009 Sales: $	2009 Profits: $	**U.S. Stock Ticker: Subsidiary**
2008 Sales: $	2008 Profits: $	**Int'l Ticker:** Int'l Exchange:
2007 Sales: $1,779,400	2007 Profits: $	Employees: 9,500
2006 Sales: $	2006 Profits: $	Fiscal Year Ends: 12/31
2005 Sales: $	2005 Profits: $	Parent Company: SUMITOMO CORPORATION

SALARIES/BENEFITS:

Pension Plan:	ESOP Stock Plan:	Profit Sharing:	Top Exec. Salary: $	Bonus: $
Savings Plan:	Stock Purch. Plan:		Second Exec. Salary: $	Bonus: $

OTHER THOUGHTS:

Apparent Women Officers or Directors:
Hot Spot for Advancement for Women/Minorities:

LOCATIONS: ("Y" = Yes)

West:	Southwest:	Midwest:	Southeast:	Northeast:	International:
Y	Y	Y	Y	Y	

TELEFLEX INC

www.teleflex.com

Industry Group Code: 3363 **Ranks within this company's industry group:** Sales: 32 Profits: 6

Vehicle Manufacturing:		Dealers:		Parts:		Service:		Finance:		Specialty:	
Cars:		Car Dealer New:		Manufacturers:	Y	General Service:		Leasing:		Information Systems:	
Trucks:		Car Dealer Used:		Retail:		Specialty Service:		Auto Loans:		Online Marketing:	
Motorcycles:		Truck Dealer:		Distributors:		Oil Change:		Insurance:		Other:	Y
Specialty:		RV Dealer:		Tires:		Paint and Body:				Publishing:	
Buses:		Motorcycle Dealer:		Batteries:						Rental Cars/Trucks:	
RVs:		Specialty Dealer:									

TYPES OF BUSINESS:

Diversified Manufacturing
General & Specialized Surgical Products
Automotive Products & Controls
Marine Products & Controls
Industrial Products & Services
Hospital Products & Equipment

BRANDS/DIVISIONS/AFFILIATES:

Nordisk Aviation Products
Arrow International, Inc.
Telair International, Inc.
Nordisk Aviation Products

CONTACTS: *Note: Officers with more than one job title may be intentionally listed here more than once.*

Jeffrey P. Black, CEO
Richard A. Meier, CFO/Exec. VP
Randall P. Gaboriault, CIO/Sr. VP
Laurence G. Miller, General Counsel/Exec. VP/Corp. Sec.
John Sickler, Jr,, VP-Corp. Dev.
Jake Elguicze, VP-Investor Rel.
C. Jeffrey Jacobs, Treas.
Gregg Winter, VP-Taxes
Charles E. Williams, Corp. Controller/Chief Acct. Officer
John B. Suddarth, Pres., Aerospace & Commercial
R. Ernest Waaser, Pres., Medical
Jeffrey P. Black, Chmn.
Vince Northfield, VP-Global Oper., Medical

Phone: 610-948-5100 **Fax:** 610-948-5101
Toll-Free:
Address: 155 S. Limerick Rd., Limerick, PA 19468-1699 US

GROWTH PLANS/SPECIAL FEATURES:

Teleflex, Inc. manufactures specialty engineered products for the commercial marine, medical and aerospace industries. The company sells its products to customers in over 140 countries through its own operations and through local direct sales and distribution networks. The firm operates in three segments: medical (77% of revenue in 2009), commercial (13%), and aerospace (10%). The medical sector designs, develops, manufactures and supplies medical devices for critical care and surgical applications. Medical products are categorized into four product groups: Critical Care, Surgical, Cardiac Care, and OEM and Development Services. The critical care product category is largest product category in the segment, representing 65% of 2009 medical revenues, and consists of single-use products utilized for vascular access, respiratory care, anesthesia and airway management, treatment of urologic conditions and other specialty procedures. The commercial sector designs and manufactures steering and throttle controls and engine drive assemblies primarily for the recreational marine market. Key products include shift and throttle cables; mechanical, hydraulic and electronic steering systems and throttle controls; engine drive parts; associated parts and products; and outdoor power components. The aerospace segment provides cargo handling systems and equipment for wide body and narrow body aircraft; cargo containment devices fir air cargo and passenger baggage; and actuators for applications in commercial and military aircraft. Leading brand names include Telair International and Nordisk Aviation Products. Sales to customers in commercial aviation markets represent more than 95% of revenues in this segment. In August 2009, Teleflex sold its Power Systems business to Fuel Systems Solutions, Inc. In March 2010, the company completed the sale of its SSI Surgical Services Inc. subsidiary to a private multi-service line healthcare company. In June 2010, Teleflex sold its Rigging Services business to Houston Wire & Cable Company.

Teleflex offers its employees medical, prescription, dental and vision coverage; flexible spending accounts; life insurance; short- and long-term disability; an employee assistance program; and tuition assistance.

FINANCIALS: **Sales and profits are in thousands of dollars—add 000 to get the full amount. 2009 Note: Financial information for 2009 was not available for all companies at press time.**

2009 Sales: $1,890,062	2009 Profits: $302,994	**U.S. Stock Ticker: TFX**
2008 Sales: $2,066,731	2008 Profits: $119,774	**Int'l Ticker:** Int'l Exchange:
2007 Sales: $1,575,082	2007 Profits: $146,484	Employees: 12,700
2006 Sales: $1,690,809	2006 Profits: $139,430	Fiscal Year Ends: 12/31
2005 Sales: $2,514,552	2005 Profits: $138,817	Parent Company:

SALARIES/BENEFITS:

Pension Plan:	ESOP Stock Plan:	Profit Sharing:	Top Exec. Salary: $900,000	Bonus: $1,458,000
Savings Plan: Y	Stock Purch. Plan:		Second Exec. Salary: $427,500	Bonus: $532,238

OTHER THOUGHTS:

Apparent Women Officers or Directors: 1
Hot Spot for Advancement for Women/Minorities:

LOCATIONS: ("Y" = Yes)

West:	Southwest:	Midwest:	Southeast:	Northeast:	International:
Y	Y	Y	Y	Y	Y

TENNECO INC

www.tenneco.com

Industry Group Code: 3363 **Ranks within this company's industry group:** Sales: 23 Profits: 43

Vehicle Manufacturing:		**Dealers:**		**Parts:**		**Service:**		**Finance:**		**Specialty:**	
Cars:		Car Dealer New:		Manufacturers:	Y	General Service:		Leasing:		Information Systems:	
Trucks:		Car Dealer Used:		Retail:		Specialty Service:		Auto Loans:		Online Marketing:	
Motorcycles:		Truck Dealer:		Distributors:		Oil Change:		Insurance:		Other:	
Specialty:		RV Dealer:		Tires:		Paint and Body:				Publishing:	
Buses:		Motorcycle Dealer:		Batteries:						Rental Cars/Trucks:	
RVs:		Specialty Dealer:									

TYPES OF BUSINESS:

Automotive Parts Manufacturer
Advanced Suspension Technologies
Ride Control Products
Emissions Systems
Performance Mufflers
Noise Control Systems

BRANDS/DIVISIONS/AFFILIATES:

Beijing Hainachuan Automotive Parts Company
Marzocchi
Quiet-Flow
Monroe
Walker
DynoMax
Rancho
Changchun FAW Sihuan Group Ltd.

CONTACTS:

Note: Officers with more than one job title may be intentionally listed here more than once.

Gregg Sherrill, CEO
Kenneth R. Trammell, CFO/Exec. VP
Barbara A. Kluth, VP-Human Resources
H. William Haser, CIO/VP
Timothy E. Jackson, CTO/Sr. VP
Michael Charlton, VP-Mfg.
James Harrington, General Counsel/Sr. VP/Corp. Sec.
Maritza Gibbons, VP-Bus. Dev. & Strategic Planning
James K. Spangler, VP-Global Comm.
John Kunz, Treas./VP-Tax
Guillermo Minuzzi, Managing Dir.-South America
Neal Yanos, Exec. VP-North America
Jeff Jarrell, VP-Japan & Korea Global OEM Bus.
Paul D. Novas, VP/Controller
Gregg Sherrill, Chmn.
Hari N. Nair, Pres., Int'l/Exec. VP
Michael Charlton, VP-Global Supply Chain Mgmt.

Phone: 847-482-5000 **Fax:** 847-482-5940
Toll-Free:
Address: 500 N. Field Dr., Lake Forest, IL 60045 US

GROWTH PLANS/SPECIAL FEATURES:

Tenneco, Inc. is a leading manufacturer of automotive emission control and ride control products and systems for both original equipment manufacturers (OEMs) and aftermarket retailers. The firm designs, manufactures and sells individual components for vehicles, as well as groups of components that are combined as modules or systems within vehicles. The firm maintains 54 emission control manufacturing facilities across six continents. Tenneco's primary brands are Monroe ride control products and Walker exhaust products. Other brands include Rancho shock absorbers; Quiet-Flow mufflers; Clevite Elastomers, elastomeric vibration control components; Monroe Sensa-Trac and Reflex shocks and struts; Lukey performance exhaust and filters; DynoMax performance mufflers; and Marzocchi forks and suspensions. Tenneco sells to over 65 OEMs worldwide, mainly to General Motors, which accounts for 16% of net sales, and Ford, 14%. In the aftermarket, Tenneco's customers include full-line and specialty warehouse distributors, retailers, jobbers, installer chains and car dealers, such as National Auto Parts Association (NAPA), Advance Auto Parts, Pep Boys and O'Reilly Automotive. The firm's products are sold primarily in North America (45% of sales) and Europe, South America and India (48%). The remaining revenue comes from the Asian Pacific market and intergroup sales. In February 2009, the company and GE Transportation signed a joint agreement to develop Hydrocarbon-Selective Catalytic Reduction (SCR), an aftermarket treatment for diesel engines aimed at reducing harmful emissions. In June 2009, the firm created a joint venture with Beijing Hainachuan Automotive Parts Company to manufacture emission control parts for the Chinese OEM market. In September 2009, Tenneco announced plans to close its Cozad, Nebraska, original equipment (OE) ride control plant. In March 2010, the company formed a joint venture in China with Changchun FAW Sihuan Group Ltd. to supply emission control components and systems for cars, trucks and commercial vehicles.

FINANCIALS:

Sales and profits are in thousands of dollars—add 000 to get the full amount. 2009 Note: Financial information for 2009 was not available for all companies at press time.

2009 Sales: $4,649,000	2009 Profits: $-73,000	**U.S. Stock Ticker: TEN**
2008 Sales: $5,916,000	2008 Profits: $-415,000	**Int'l Ticker:** Int'l Exchange:
2007 Sales: $6,184,000	2007 Profits: $-5,000	Employees: 21,000
2006 Sales: $4,682,000	2006 Profits: $49,000	Fiscal Year Ends: 12/31
2005 Sales: $4,441,000	2005 Profits: $58,000	Parent Company:

SALARIES/BENEFITS:

Pension Plan:	ESOP Stock Plan: Y	Profit Sharing:	Top Exec. Salary: $885,000	Bonus: $475,000
Savings Plan:	Stock Purch. Plan:		Second Exec. Salary: $578,125	Bonus: $234,375

OTHER THOUGHTS:

Apparent Women Officers or Directors: 2
Hot Spot for Advancement for Women/Minorities:

LOCATIONS: ("Y" = Yes)

West:	Southwest:	Midwest:	Southeast:	Northeast:	International:
Y	Y	Y	Y	Y	Y

TEREX CORPORATION

www.terex.com

Industry Group Code: 333 **Ranks within this company's industry group:** Sales: 4 Profits: 7

Vehicle Manufacturing:		Dealers:		Parts:		Service:		Finance:		Specialty:	
Cars:		Car Dealer New:		Manufacturers:		General Service:		Leasing:		Information Systems:	
Trucks:	Y	Car Dealer Used:		Retail:		Specialty Service:		Auto Loans:		Online Marketing:	
Motorcycles:		Truck Dealer:		Distributors:		Oil Change:		Insurance:		Other:	
Specialty:	Y	RV Dealer:		Tires:		Paint and Body:				Publishing:	
Buses:		Motorcycle Dealer:		Batteries:						Rental Cars/Trucks:	
RVs:		Specialty Dealer:									

TYPES OF BUSINESS:

Heavy Equipment
Cranes
Mining Equipment
Aerial Work Platforms
Road Building Equipment
Utility Products
Construction Equipment
Materials Handling Equipment

BRANDS/DIVISIONS/AFFILIATES:

Terex
Noell Crane
Fantuzzi Industries Sarl
Terex Aerial Work Platforms
Terex Construction
Terex Materials Processing
Terex Cranes

CONTACTS:

Note: Officers with more than one job title may be intentionally listed here more than once.

Ronald M. DeFeo, CEO
Tom Riordan, COO
Tom Riordan, Pres.
Phillip C. Widman, CFO/Sr. VP
Kevin A. Barr, Sr. VP-Human Resources
Eric I. Cohen, General Counsel/Sr. VP/Corp. Sec.
Brian J. Henry, Sr. VP-Bus. Dev.
Tom Gelston, VP-Investor Rel.
Brian J. Henry, Sr. VP-Finance
Tim Ford, Pres., Terex Aerial Work Platforms
Mark Clair, VP/Controller/Chief Acct. Officer
Eric Nielsen, Pres., Terex Materials Processing & Mining
Richard Nichols, Pres., Terex Cranes
Ronald M. DeFeo, Chmn.

Phone: 203-222-7170	**Fax:** 203-222-7976
Toll-Free:	
Address: 200 Nyala Farm Rd., Westport, CT 06880 US	

GROWTH PLANS/SPECIAL FEATURES:

Terex Corporation is a diversified global manufacturer of capital equipment. The company specializes in providing solutions for the construction, infrastructure, quarrying, shipping, transportation and utility industries. The company operates in four business segments: Terex Aerial Work Platforms; Terex Construction; Terex Cranes; and Terex Materials Processing. The Terex Aerial Work Platforms segment designs, manufactures and markets products such as material lifts, portable aerial work platforms, trailer-mounted articulating booms, self-propelled articulating and telescopic booms, scissor lifts, construction trailers and related components and parts. The Terex Construction segment designs, manufactures and markets roadbuilding, heavy and compact construction equipment. Roadbuilding equipment includes asphalt and concrete pavers, transfer devices, reclaimers/stabilizers, plants, mixers, placers and cold planers; landfill compactors; and bridge inspection equipment. Heavy equipment includes hydraulic excavators, off-highway trucks, large wheel loaders and material handlers. Compact equipment includes excavators, site dumpers, loader backhoes, compaction equipment and skid steer loaders. The Terex Cranes segment produces mobile telescopic cranes, tower cranes, lattice boom crawler cranes and truck-mounted cranes, as well as their related replacement parts and components. It also offers specialized port and rail equipment such as straddle carriers; gantry cranes; mobile harbor cranes; ship-to-shore cranes; telescopic container stackers; lift trucks; and forklifts, as well as related replacement parts and components. The Terex Materials Processing segment produces crushers, apron feeders, washing systems, screens and related components and replacement parts. Terex sells its products worldwide and operates manufacturing facilities in North America, South America, Europe, Australia and Asia. In July 2009, the firm acquired the port equipment operations of Noell Crane and Fantuzzi Industries S.a.r.l. In August 2009, Terex agreed to shut down its manufacturing plant in Cedar Rapids, Iowa. In December 2009, the firm divested its power buggy product line. In February 2010, the company sold its mining division to Bucyrus International, Inc. for $1.3 billion.

FINANCIALS:

Sales and profits are in thousands of dollars—add 000 to get the full amount. 2009 Note: Financial information for 2009 was not available for all companies at press time.

2009 Sales: $4,043,100	2009 Profits: $-398,400	**U.S. Stock Ticker: TEX**
2008 Sales: $8,387,000	2008 Profits: $71,900	**Int'l Ticker:** Int'l Exchange:
2007 Sales: $7,976,100	2007 Profits: $613,900	Employees: 15,900
2006 Sales: $	2006 Profits: $	Fiscal Year Ends: 12/31
2005 Sales: $	2005 Profits: $	Parent Company:

SALARIES/BENEFITS:

Pension Plan:	ESOP Stock Plan:	Profit Sharing:	Top Exec. Salary: $1,150,000	Bonus: $
Savings Plan:	Stock Purch. Plan:		Second Exec. Salary: $780,000	Bonus: $

OTHER THOUGHTS:

Apparent Women Officers or Directors: 1
Hot Spot for Advancement for Women/Minorities:

LOCATIONS: ("Y" = Yes)

West:	Southwest:	Midwest:	Southeast:	Northeast:	International:
Y	Y	Y	Y	Y	Y

TESLA MOTORS INC

www.teslamotors.com

Industry Group Code: 33611 **Ranks within this company's industry group:** Sales: Profits:

Vehicle Manufacturing:		Dealers:		Parts:		Service:		Finance:		Specialty:	
Cars:	Y	Car Dealer New:		Manufacturers:	Y	General Service:		Leasing:		Information Systems:	
Trucks:		Car Dealer Used:		Retail:		Specialty Service:		Auto Loans:		Online Marketing:	
Motorcycles:		Truck Dealer:		Distributors:		Oil Change:		Insurance:		Other:	
Specialty:	Y	RV Dealer:		Tires:		Paint and Body:				Publishing:	
Buses:		Motorcycle Dealer:		Batteries:						Rental Cars/Trucks:	
RVs:		Specialty Dealer:									

TYPES OF BUSINESS:

Automobile Manufacturing, All-Electric
Battery Manufacturing
Lithium Ion Battery Storage Technologies

BRANDS/DIVISIONS/AFFILIATES:

Tesla Roadster
Model S
Tesla Energy Group
VantagePoint Venture Partners
Draper Fisher Jervetson
Compass Venture Partners
Technology Partners
Toyota Motor Corporation

CONTACTS: *Note: Officers with more than one job title may be intentionally listed here more than once.*

Elon Musk, CEO/Prod. Architect
Deepak Ahuja, CFO
John Walker, VP-Sales, North America
Arnnon Geshuri, VP-Human Resources
Evelyn Chiang, VP-IT
J. B. Straubel, CTO
Peter Rawlinson, Chief Engineer/VP-Vehicle Eng.
Gilbert Passin, VP-Mfg.
Craig Harding, General Counsel/Sec.
Diarmuid O'Connell, VP-Bus. Dev.
Ricardo Reyes, VP-Comm.
Mike Taylor, VP-Finance
Franz von Holzhausen, Chief Designer
Jim Dunlay, VP-Powertrain Hardware Eng.
Elon Musk, Chmn.
Cristiano Carlutti, VP-European Sales & Oper.
Evelyn Chiang, VP-Supply Chain

Phone: 650-681-5000 **Fax:**
Toll-Free:
Address: 3500 Deer Creek, Palo Alto, CA 94304 US

GROWTH PLANS/SPECIAL FEATURES:

Tesla Motors, Inc. manufactures high-performance electric automobiles. Its first model, the two-seat Tesla Roadster, accelerates from 0-60 miles per hour (mph) in 3.9 seconds, has a top speed of 125 mph, runs for approximately 170-244 miles per charge and has a base price of $109,000. The vehicle's power supply consists of 6,831 lithium-ion battery cells linked together in the trunk. It offers regenerative braking, meaning it uses braking friction to charge the battery, and also carries an on-board charging unit that can pull power from standard wall outlets or from optional mobile charge kits. A full charge can take as little as 4 hours. The company's second model, the four-door, seven-passenger sports sedan named Model S will be available in 2012 and sell for around $57,000. The Model S seats seven, has a 160-300 mile range, will go from 0-60 mph in 5.6 seconds, and feature a top speed of 120 mph. Tesla is backed by a number of investors including VantagePoint Venture Partners, Draper Fisher Jervetson, Compass Venture Partners and Technology Partners. In May 2010, the Toyota Motor Corporation purchased a $50 million stake in the firm. As part of the deal, Tesla will take over a large car manufacturing plant in Freemont, California that was formerly operated as a joint venture of Toyota and GM. The new funds and manufacturing facility will give Tesla significant expansion capability. In June 2010, Tesla Motors went public. In July 2010, Tesla and Toyota announced an agreement to begin developing an electric version of the Toyota sport utility vehicle, the RAV4.

FINANCIALS: **Sales and profits are in thousands of dollars—add 000 to get the full amount. 2009 Note: Financial information for 2009 was not available for all companies at press time.**

2009 Sales: $	2009 Profits: $	**U.S. Stock Ticker: TSLA**
2008 Sales: $	2008 Profits: $	**Int'l Ticker:** Int'l Exchange:
2007 Sales: $	2007 Profits: $	Employees:
2006 Sales: $	2006 Profits: $	Fiscal Year Ends: 12/31
2005 Sales: $	2005 Profits: $	Parent Company:

SALARIES/BENEFITS:

Pension Plan:	ESOP Stock Plan:	Profit Sharing:	Top Exec. Salary: $	Bonus: $
Savings Plan:	Stock Purch. Plan:		Second Exec. Salary: $	Bonus: $

OTHER THOUGHTS:

Apparent Women Officers or Directors: 1
Hot Spot for Advancement for Women/Minorities:

LOCATIONS: ("Y" = Yes)

West:	Southwest:	Midwest:	Southeast:	Northeast:	International:
Y	Y				Y

THOR INDUSTRIES INC

www.thorindustries.com

Industry Group Code: 336214 **Ranks within this company's industry group:** Sales: 1 Profits: 1

Vehicle Manufacturing:		Dealers:		Parts:		Service:		Finance:		Specialty:	
Cars:		Car Dealer New:		Manufacturers:	Y	General Service:		Leasing:		Information Systems:	
Trucks:		Car Dealer Used:		Retail:		Specialty Service:		Auto Loans:		Online Marketing:	
Motorcycles:		Truck Dealer:		Distributors:		Oil Change:		Insurance:		Other:	
Specialty:		RV Dealer:	Y	Tires:		Paint and Body:				Publishing:	
Buses:	Y	Motorcycle Dealer:		Batteries:						Rental Cars/Trucks:	
RVs:	Y	Specialty Dealer:									

TYPES OF BUSINESS:

Recreational Vehicle Manufacturing
Motor Homes
Automotive Parts & Accessories
Buses

BRANDS/DIVISIONS/AFFILIATES:

Airstream, Inc.
Dutchmen Manufacturing, Inc.
Four Winds International, Inc.
Keystone RV Company
SJC Industries
Champion Bus, Inc.
ElDorado National, Inc.
Goshen Coach, Inc.

CONTACTS: *Note: Officers with more than one job title may be intentionally listed here more than once.*

Peter B. Orthwein, CEO
Peter B. Orthwein, Pres.
Christian G. Farman, CFO/Sr. VP
Walter L. Bennett, Chief Admin. Officer
Walter L. Bennett, Corp. Sec./Exec. VP
Richard E. Riegel III, Dir.-Bus. Dev.
Richard E. Riegel III, Contact-Corp. Comm.
Richard E. Riegel II, Sr. Group Pres., Bus Group
Ron Fenech, Sr. Group Pres., RV Group
Andrew Imanse, Group Pres., Comm. Bus Division
Bob Martin, Pres., Keystone RV
Peter B. Orthwein, Chmn.

Phone: 937-596-6849	**Fax:** 937-596-6539
Toll-Free:	
Address: 419 W. Pike St., Jackson Center, OH 45334 US	

GROWTH PLANS/SPECIAL FEATURES:

Thor Industries, Inc. is a leading manufacturer of a wide range of recreation vehicles (RVs) and small and midsize commercial buses. In addition, the firm provides related parts, services and accessories for all vehicles they manufacture. The company's primary RV subsidiaries are Airstream, Inc.; Dutchmen Manufacturing, Inc.; Crossroads RV; Four Winds International, Inc.; Keystone RV Company; Komfort Corp.; Damon Corporation; Citair, Inc.; and Damon Corporation, Inc. Together they produce conventional travel trailers, fifth wheels, park models, which aremobile homes designed for recreational living, and Class A, B and C motor homes. In 2009, towable RVs generated 63% of the firm's sales and motorized RVs accounted for 10%. The firm markets its recreational vehicles through approximately 1,418 dealers throughout the U.S. and Canada. Thor's small and midsize bus operating subsidiaries are Champion Bus, Inc.; El Dorado National California, Inc.; El Dorado National Kansas, Inc; General Coach, Inc.; and Goshen Coach, Inc. Product applications include transit buses, airport car rental and hotel shuttles, paramedical transit for hospitals and nursing homes and tour and charter buses. Bus sales generated 27% of the firm's 2009 sales. Thor also has a joint venture with Cruise America, Inc. called CAT Joint Venture LLC, which makes short-term rentals of motorized recreation vehicles to the public. In March 2010, Thor announced the acquisition of SJC Industries, an Indiana-based manufacturer of ambulances, for roughly $20 million.

FINANCIALS: **Sales and profits are in thousands of dollars—add 000 to get the full amount. 2009 Note: Financial information for 2009 was not available for all companies at press time.**

2009 Sales: $1,521,896	2009 Profits: $17,143	**U.S. Stock Ticker: THO**
2008 Sales: $2,640,680	2008 Profits: $92,706	**Int'l Ticker:** Int'l Exchange:
2007 Sales: $2,856,308	2007 Profits: $134,731	Employees: 5,378
2006 Sales: $3,066,276	2006 Profits: $163,405	Fiscal Year Ends: 7/31
2005 Sales: $2,558,141	2005 Profits: $119,143	Parent Company:

SALARIES/BENEFITS:

Pension Plan:	ESOP Stock Plan:	Profit Sharing:	Top Exec. Salary: $500,000	Bonus: $172,375
Savings Plan: Y	Stock Purch. Plan:		Second Exec. Salary: $419,231	Bonus: $50,000

OTHER THOUGHTS:

Apparent Women Officers or Directors:
Hot Spot for Advancement for Women/Minorities:

LOCATIONS: ("Y" = Yes)

West:	Southwest:	Midwest:	Southeast:	Northeast:	International:
Y		Y			Y

TI AUTOMOTIVE

www.tiautomotive.com

Industry Group Code: 336350 **Ranks within this company's industry group:** Sales: Profits:

Vehicle Manufacturing:		Dealers:		Parts:		Service:		Finance:		Specialty:	
Cars:		Car Dealer New:		Manufacturers:	Y	General Service:		Leasing:		Information Systems:	
Trucks:		Car Dealer Used:		Retail:		Specialty Service:		Auto Loans:		Online Marketing:	
Motorcycles:		Truck Dealer:		Distributors:		Oil Change:		Insurance:		Other:	
Specialty:		RV Dealer:		Tires:		Paint and Body:				Publishing:	
Buses:		Motorcycle Dealer:		Batteries:						Rental Cars/Trucks:	
RVs:		Specialty Dealer:									

TYPES OF BUSINESS:

Automobile Parts Manufacturing
Fuel Storage & Fluid Transfer Systems
Fluid Systems Analysis

BRANDS/DIVISIONS/AFFILIATES:

Fluid Carrying Systems
Fluid Delivery Systems
Fluid Storage Systems
Fluid Systems Analysis
Walbro
Marwal Systems
TU Pierburg
Oak Tree Capital Management

CONTACTS: *Note: Officers with more than one job title may be intentionally listed here more than once.*

William L. Kozyra, CEO
William L. Kozyra, Pres.
Tim Knutson, CFO
Jim Kroop, Chief Sales Officer
Domenic Milicia, Chief Human Resources Officer
Al Deane, CTO
Tim Guerriero, General Counsel/Sec.
Domenic Milicia, Chief Comm. Officer
Phil Stephenson, Exec. VP-Global Fluid Carrying Systems
Thomas Buchholz, VP-Global Powertrain Components
Hans Dieltjens, Exec. VP-Global Tank Systems
Jan Svec, VP-Global HVAC Fluid Systems
William L. Kozyra, Chmn.
Jay Phillion, Chief Purchasing & Quality Officer

Phone: 44-1865-871-820	**Fax:** 44-1865-871-866
Toll-Free:	
Address: 4650 Kingsgate, Oxford Business Park S., Oxford, OX4 2SU UK	

GROWTH PLANS/SPECIAL FEATURES:

TI Automotive is a global supplier of integrated fuel storage and delivery systems and fluid carrying systems for braking and power train applications for cars and trucks. The company is owned by a consortium of funds managed by Oaktree Capital Management LP and Duquesne Capital Management LLC. TI operates 126 facilities in 27 countries. It maintains relationships with every major automobile maker in the world, and its components are used in roughly half of the cars built worldwide. TI operates through four technology groups: The Fluid Carrying Systems, Fluid Delivery Systems, Fluid Storage Systems, and Fluid Systems Analysis. The company offers original-equipment and aftermarket products, including replacement fuel pumps and modules that are designed to fit in popular vehicle models. The firm sells its products under five division lines: Fluid Carrying Systems, Powertrain Components, Tank Systems, HVAC Fluid Systems and Pump and Module Systems. These products are marketed globally under the brand names Walbro, Marwal Systems and TU Pierburg. The company has recently begun shifting its operations into high growth markets by opening manufacturing plants in Poland, Turkey, China, Korea, Thailand, Indonesia and India. In February 2009, TI opened a new plant in Russia.

FINANCIALS: **Sales and profits are in thousands of dollars—add 000 to get the full amount. 2009 Note: Financial information for 2009 was not available for all companies at press time.**

2009 Sales: $	2009 Profits: $	**U.S. Stock Ticker: Private**
2008 Sales: $2,900,000	2008 Profits: $	**Int'l Ticker:** Int'l Exchange:
2007 Sales: $1,500,000	2007 Profits: $	Employees:
2006 Sales: $	2006 Profits: $	Fiscal Year Ends: 12/31
2005 Sales: $	2005 Profits: $	Parent Company: OAKTREE CAPITAL MANAGEMENT

SALARIES/BENEFITS:

Pension Plan:	ESOP Stock Plan:	Profit Sharing:	Top Exec. Salary: $	Bonus: $
Savings Plan:	Stock Purch. Plan:		Second Exec. Salary: $	Bonus: $

OTHER THOUGHTS:

Apparent Women Officers or Directors:
Hot Spot for Advancement for Women/Minorities:

LOCATIONS: ("Y" = Yes)

West:	Southwest:	Midwest:	Southeast:	Northeast:	International:
	Y	Y	Y		Y

TITAN INTERNATIONAL INC

www.titan-intl.com

Industry Group Code: 3363 **Ranks within this company's industry group:** Sales: 46 Profits: 34

Vehicle Manufacturing:		Dealers:		Parts:		Service:		Finance:		Specialty:	
Cars:		Car Dealer New:		Manufacturers:	Y	General Service:		Leasing:		Information Systems:	
Trucks:		Car Dealer Used:		Retail:		Specialty Service:		Auto Loans:		Online Marketing:	
Motorcycles:		Truck Dealer:		Distributors:		Oil Change:		Insurance:		Other:	
Specialty:		RV Dealer:		Tires:	Y	Paint and Body:				Publishing:	
Buses:		Motorcycle Dealer:		Batteries:						Rental Cars/Trucks:	
RVs:		Specialty Dealer:									

TYPES OF BUSINESS:

Tire Manufacturing
Specialty Tires & Wheels

BRANDS/DIVISIONS/AFFILIATES:

Titan Tire Corporations
Titan Wheel

CONTACTS:

Note: Officers with more than one job title may be intentionally listed here more than once.

Maurice M. Taylor, Jr., CEO
Cheri T. Holley, General Counsel/VP/Corp. Sec.
Kent W. Hackamack, VP-Finance/Treas.
Maurice M. Taylor, Jr., Chmn.

Phone: 217-228-6011	**Fax:** 217-228-3166
Toll-Free:	
Address: 2701 Spruce St., Quincy, IL 62301 US	

GROWTH PLANS/SPECIAL FEATURES:

Titan International, Inc. manufactures wheels, tires and assemblies for off-highway vehicles used in the agricultural, earthmoving, construction and consumer markets. The company primarily operates through two wholly-owned subsidiaries: Titan Tire Corp., one of North America's largest manufacturers of off-highway tires; and Titan Wheel, one of the world's largest makers of off-highway wheels. The company's agricultural rims, wheels and tires are manufactured for use on tractors, combines, skidders, plows, planters and irrigation equipment. Its earthmoving and construction rims and wheels are used on skid steers, aerial lifts, cranes, graders and levelers, scrapers, self-propelled shovel loaders, load transporters, haul trucks and backhoe loaders. In the consumer market, Titan builds a wheels and tires for all-terrain vehicles (ATV), turf, golf and trailer applications. It also provides brakes, actuators and components for consumer applications. Agricultural sales account for roughly 77% of the company's sales. Earthmoving/construction segment accounts for 20% of Titan's sales, while the consumer market contributed the remaining 3%. Titan also produces various wheels, tires and components for the U.S. government, primarily for military vehicles such as trucks, trailers, tanks and personnel carriers. Its various wheels and rims range in diameter from 5-63 inches and its construction wheels can weigh up to 7,000 pounds. Titan sells its products directly to original equipment manufacturers, independent distributors and equipment dealers, as well as through its own distribution centers. In April 2010, Titan Tire launched the Ultimate series of deeply threaded tires. In June 2010, Titan Tire acquired all of the assets (with the exception of the machinery, land and buildings) of bankrupt Denman Tire for roughly $4.4 million.

FINANCIALS:

Sales and profits are in thousands of dollars—add 000 to get the full amount. 2009 Note: Financial information for 2009 was not available for all companies at press time.

2009 Sales: $727,599	2009 Profits: $-24,645	**U.S. Stock Ticker: TWI**
2008 Sales: $1,036,700	2008 Profits: $13,337	**Int'l Ticker:** Int'l Exchange:
2007 Sales: $837,021	2007 Profits: $-7,247	Employees: 2,400
2006 Sales: $679,454	2006 Profits: $5,144	Fiscal Year Ends: 12/31
2005 Sales: $470,133	2005 Profits: $11,042	Parent Company:

SALARIES/BENEFITS:

Pension Plan:	ESOP Stock Plan:	Profit Sharing:	Top Exec. Salary: $693,750	Bonus: $1,125,000
Savings Plan: Y	Stock Purch. Plan:		Second Exec. Salary: $268,125	Bonus: $100,000

OTHER THOUGHTS:

Apparent Women Officers or Directors: 1
Hot Spot for Advancement for Women/Minorities:

LOCATIONS: ("Y" = Yes)

West:	Southwest:	Midwest:	Southeast:	Northeast:	International:
Y	Y	Y	Y	Y	Y

TOKAI RIKA CO LTD

www.tokai-rika.co.jp

Industry Group Code: 3363 **Ranks within this company's industry group:** Sales: 26 Profits: 23

Vehicle Manufacturing:		**Dealers:**		**Parts:**		**Service:**		**Finance:**		**Specialty:**	
Cars:		Car Dealer New:		Manufacturers:	Y	General Service:		Leasing:		Information Systems:	
Trucks:		Car Dealer Used:		Retail:	Y	Specialty Service:		Auto Loans:		Online Marketing:	
Motorcycles:		Truck Dealer:		Distributors:	Y	Oil Change:		Insurance:		Other:	
Specialty:		RV Dealer:		Tires:		Paint and Body:				Publishing:	
Buses:		Motorcycle Dealer:		Batteries:						Rental Cars/Trucks:	
RVs:		Specialty Dealer:									

TYPES OF BUSINESS:

Automobile Parts Manufacturing
Human Interface Systems
Security Systems
Seat Belts
Controls
Aftermarket Parts
Housing Facilities & Equipment

BRANDS/DIVISIONS/AFFILIATES:

TRAM, Inc.
TAC Manufacturing, Inc.
TRMI, Inc.
Quality Safety Systems Company
Wuxi Risho Technology Co., Ltd.
TRP, Inc.
Thai Seat Belt Co., Ltd.
TRB Limited

CONTACTS: *Note: Officers with more than one job title may be intentionally listed here more than once.*

Yuzo Ushiyama, Pres.
Takaoki Tsuchiya, Exec. VP
Shigeru Kato, Exec. VP
Yoshiteru Sasaki, Senior Managing Dir.
Takafumi Mizuno, Senior Managing Dir.
Kiyoshi Kinoshita, Chmn.

Phone: 81-587-95-5211 **Fax:** 81-587-95-1917
Toll-Free:
Address: 3-260 Toyota, Oguchi-Cho, Niwa-Gun, Aichi, 480-0195 Japan

GROWTH PLANS/SPECIAL FEATURES:

Tokai Rika Co. Ltd. is a manufacturer of automobile parts and components. It divides its vehicle products into four categories: switches/human machine interface systems; security systems; safety systems; and electronics and others. The switches/human machine interface systems category includes devices that facilitate communication between drivers and automobiles, creating car systems that imitate the extension of human sensations and impulses. Its products include the Electro Shiftmatic, the Multi-function Switch and the Push Start Switch. The security systems category includes both mechanical and electronic anti-theft functions. Its products include the Immobilizer; the Smart Key Portable Device and Emergency Key; and the Remote Key and Receiver. The company's safety systems devices include seatbelts, wood steering wheels and car mirrors. Lastly, the company electronics and others category includes housing facilities and equipment, including La Lock, the Hallway Immobilizer Key System and the Window Lock Monitoring System; automotive electronics products, including the Power Supply ECU; automotive accessories; and switches, sensors and electronic control circuits for combines and tractors. Toyota Motor is one of the company's major customers. The company has five domestic plants and 28 subsidiaries: eight in Japan; six in North America; 10 in Asia; and four in Europe and elsewhere. Its subsidiaries include TRAM, Inc.; TAC Manufacturing, Inc.; TRMI, Inc.; Quality Safety Systems Company; Wuxi Risho Technology Co., Ltd.; TRP, Inc.; Thai Seat Belt Co., Ltd.; TRB Limited; and Tokai Rika Belgium N.V.

FINANCIALS: **Sales and profits are in thousands of dollars—add 000 to get the full amount. 2009 Note: Financial information for 2009 was not available for all companies at press time.**

2009 Sales: $3,741,760 — 2009 Profits: $11,790
2008 Sales: $4,669,730 — 2008 Profits: $225,870
2007 Sales: $3,674,680 — 2007 Profits: $162,790
2006 Sales: $3,296,310 — 2006 Profits: $134,660
2005 Sales: $2,802,280 — 2005 Profits: $97,530

U.S. Stock Ticker:
Int'l Ticker: 6995 Int'l Exchange: Tokyo-TSE
Employees: 14,776
Fiscal Year Ends: 3/31
Parent Company:

SALARIES/BENEFITS:

Pension Plan: ESOP Stock Plan: Profit Sharing: Top Exec. Salary: $ Bonus: $
Savings Plan: Stock Purch. Plan: Second Exec. Salary: $ Bonus: $

OTHER THOUGHTS:

Apparent Women Officers or Directors:
Hot Spot for Advancement for Women/Minorities:

LOCATIONS: ("Y" = Yes)

West:	Southwest:	Midwest:	Southeast:	Northeast:	International:
		Y			Y

TORESCO ENTERPRISES INC

www.1800autoland.com

Industry Group Code: 441110 **Ranks within this company's industry group:** Sales: Profits:

Vehicle Manufacturing:		Dealers:		Parts:		Service:		Finance:		Specialty:	
Cars:		Car Dealer New:	Y	Manufacturers:		General Service:	Y	Leasing:		Information Systems:	
Trucks:		Car Dealer Used:	Y	Retail:		Specialty Service:		Auto Loans:	Y	Online Marketing:	
Motorcycles:		Truck Dealer:	Y	Distributors:		Oil Change:		Insurance:		Other:	
Specialty:		RV Dealer:		Tires:		Paint and Body:				Publishing:	
Buses:		Motorcycle Dealer:		Batteries:						Rental Cars/Trucks:	
RVs:		Specialty Dealer:									

TYPES OF BUSINESS:

Auto Dealers, Retail
Fleet Sales
Repair Services
Financing

BRANDS/DIVISIONS/AFFILIATES:

Autoland
Dodgeland

CONTACTS:

Note: Officers with more than one job title may be intentionally listed here more than once.

Steven Iauruzio, Gen. Mgr.-Sales
Kashif Qureshi, Dir.-Finance
Mark Montenero, VP/Gen. Mgr.
Nelson Castanheira, Mgr.-Parts
Joe Scibilia, Dir.-Service & Parts
Donald Toresco, Chmn.

Phone: 973-467-2900	**Fax:** 973-467-1824
Toll-Free:	
Address: 170 Rte. 22 E., Springfield, NJ 07081 US	

GROWTH PLANS/SPECIAL FEATURES:

Toresco Enterprises, Inc., established in the mid 1940s by the Toresco family, operates Autoland, an automobile mall in New Jersey. Autoland sells both used and pre-owned automobiles and offers financing, maintenance services and parts. Toresco has two Autoland locations: Autoland Chrysler Jeep Dodge and Autoland Toyota Scion, both located in Springfield, New Jersey. Through the firm's web site, customers can search new and used inventories; schedule a test drive; schedule a service appointment; place an order for parts; and fill out a finance application. Its web site also provides a financing payment calculator and coupons for its cars, services and parts. New automobiles sold by Autoland include Toyota, Scion, Chrysler, Jeep and Dodge cars, trucks and SUVs. Dodgeland, one of Toresco's earliest dealerships, was one of the first in the Northeast to use computers to store and print bank contracts and other paperwork. The company's current owner, Donald Toresco, opened the first Autoland location in 1985.

FINANCIALS:

Sales and profits are in thousands of dollars—add 000 to get the full amount. 2009 Note: Financial information for 2009 was not available for all companies at press time.

2009 Sales: $	2009 Profits: $	**U.S. Stock Ticker: Private**
2008 Sales: $	2008 Profits: $	**Int'l Ticker:** Int'l Exchange:
2007 Sales: $	2007 Profits: $	Employees:
2006 Sales: $	2006 Profits: $	Fiscal Year Ends: 12/31
2005 Sales: $	2005 Profits: $	Parent Company:

SALARIES/BENEFITS:

Pension Plan:	ESOP Stock Plan:	Profit Sharing:	Top Exec. Salary: $	Bonus: $
Savings Plan:	Stock Purch. Plan:		Second Exec. Salary: $	Bonus: $

OTHER THOUGHTS:

Apparent Women Officers or Directors:
Hot Spot for Advancement for Women/Minorities:

LOCATIONS: ("Y" = Yes)

West:	Southwest:	Midwest:	Southeast:	Northeast:	International:
				Y	

TOWER AUTOMOTIVE LLC

www.towerautomotive.com

Industry Group Code: 3363 **Ranks within this company's industry group:** Sales: Profits:

Vehicle Manufacturing:		Dealers:		Parts:		Service:		Finance:		Specialty:	
Cars:		Car Dealer New:		Manufacturers:	Y	General Service:		Leasing:		Information Systems:	
Trucks:		Car Dealer Used:		Retail:		Specialty Service:		Auto Loans:		Online Marketing:	
Motorcycles:		Truck Dealer:		Distributors:		Oil Change:		Insurance:		Other:	
Specialty:		RV Dealer:		Tires:		Paint and Body:				Publishing:	
Buses:		Motorcycle Dealer:		Batteries:						Rental Cars/Trucks:	
RVs:		Specialty Dealer:									

TYPES OF BUSINESS:

Automobile Parts Manufacturer
Body Components & Assemblies

BRANDS/DIVISIONS/AFFILIATES:

Cerberus Capital Management LP

CONTACTS:

Note: Officers with more than one job title may be intentionally listed here more than once.

Mark Malcolm, CEO
Mark Malcolm, Pres.
Gyula Meleghy, Pres., Tower Automotive Int'l Oper.

Phone: 248-675-6000	**Fax:** 248-675-6800
Toll-Free:	
Address: 17672 N. Laurel Park Dr., Ste. 400 E., Livonia, MI 48152 US	

GROWTH PLANS/SPECIAL FEATURES:

Tower Automotive LLC, owned by Cerberus Capital Management L.P., is a leading designer and producer of body structure metal components and assemblies. The firm's products are used by such global automotive manufacturers as Ford Motor Company, Hyundai, Kia, Renault, Volkswagen, Chrysler, Fiat Auto, BMW, Daimler, Honda and Toyota. Operating through 43 facilities in 10 countries throughout the Americas, Europe and Asia, Tower manufactures body structural stampings and assemblies; chassis structural stampings and assemblies, including full frames and cradles; suspension components, modules and systems; and exposed sheet metal surfaces. The firm's technological capabilities include CAE (computer-aided engineering), CAD (computer-aided design) and CAM (computer-aided manufacturing); physical testing; and prototyping. Its physical testing capabilities include single and multi-channel durability testing; mechanical and chemical materials testing; static stiffness, yield and ultimate strength testing; and vibration testing. Tower's process technologies include tool and die design; body-in-white assembly; stamping, hydroforming and roll-forming; and lightweight and high-strength materials experience.

FINANCIALS:

Sales and profits are in thousands of dollars—add 000 to get the full amount. 2009 Note: Financial information for 2009 was not available for all companies at press time.

2009 Sales: $
2008 Sales: $
2007 Sales: $3,000,000
2006 Sales: $2,884,400
2005 Sales: $2,932,209

2009 Profits: $
2008 Profits: $
2007 Profits: $
2006 Profits: $-202,066
2005 Profits: $-373,372

U.S. Stock Ticker: Private
Int'l Ticker: Int'l Exchange:
Employees:
Fiscal Year Ends: 12/31
Parent Company: CERBERUS CAPITAL MANAGEMENT LP

SALARIES/BENEFITS:

Pension Plan:	ESOP Stock Plan:	Profit Sharing:	Top Exec. Salary: $	Bonus: $
Savings Plan:	Stock Purch. Plan:		Second Exec. Salary: $	Bonus: $

OTHER THOUGHTS:

Apparent Women Officers or Directors:
Hot Spot for Advancement for Women/Minorities:

LOCATIONS: ("Y" = Yes)

West:	Southwest:	Midwest:	Southeast:	Northeast:	International:
		Y	Y		Y

TOYO TIRE & RUBBER CO LTD

www.toyojapan.com

Industry Group Code: 3262 **Ranks within this company's industry group:** Sales: 7 Profits: 7

Vehicle Manufacturing:		Dealers:		Parts:		Service:		Finance:		Specialty:	
Cars:		Car Dealer New:		Manufacturers:	Y	General Service:		Leasing:		Information Systems:	
Trucks:		Car Dealer Used:		Retail:		Specialty Service:		Auto Loans:		Online Marketing:	
Motorcycles:		Truck Dealer:		Distributors:		Oil Change:		Insurance:		Other:	Y
Specialty:		RV Dealer:		Tires:	Y	Paint and Body:				Publishing:	
Buses:		Motorcycle Dealer:		Batteries:						Rental Cars/Trucks:	
RVs:		Specialty Dealer:									

TYPES OF BUSINESS:

Plastics & Rubber Manufacturing
Tire Production
Automotive Parts Manufacturing
Auto Racing
Thermal Insulation
Chemical & Industrial Products

BRANDS/DIVISIONS/AFFILIATES:

Divertech Company

CONTACTS:

Note: Officers with more than one job title may be intentionally listed here more than once.

Kenji Nakakura, CEO
Kenji Nakakura, Pres.
Yasuo Onodera, CFO
Kenji Takada, Dir.-Tire Mfg.

Phone: 81-6-6441-8801 **Fax:**
Toll-Free:
Address: 1-17-18 Edobori, Nishi-ku, Osaka, 550-8661 Japan

GROWTH PLANS/SPECIAL FEATURES:

Toyo Tire & Rubber Co., Ltd. is a worldwide corporation specializing in the production of rubber and polyurethane products. The company operates in three divisions: Tires, chemicals and industrial products, and automotive parts. Toyo's primary business unit is its tire division, which is focused on the manufacturing of tires for cars, trucks, buses and commercial and off-road vehicles, as well as tires for heavy construction machinery and studless snow tires. Its tire business is divided into three departments: original equipment sales, replacement tires and overseas tire operations. Team Toyo, the company's racing division, outfits numerous racing circuits and markets a range of branded apparel. Toyo's chemical and industrial products division creates a wide range of industrial rubber and polyurethane products, such as seismic-isolation rubber bearings for bridges, flexible polyurethane foam, waterproof and sealing sheets. It also creates thermal insulation products, as well as components for information technology equipment. Toyo's automotive parts division is primarily concerned with developing anti-vibration products, such as engine mounts and seat cushions, specifically for automobiles. Toyo also controls Divertech Company, which was created with the goal of improving product power, production technologies, manufacturing methods and facilities for Toyo's non-tire businesses. Collectively, Toyo and its 37 consolidated subsidiaries operate in 11 countries and distribute products in over 100 countries. In January 2010, the firm announced plans to establish a wholly-owned subsidiary in Zhangjiangang City, Jiangsu Province, China. The new subsidiary will manufacture passenger and light truck tires.

FINANCIALS:

Sales and profits are in thousands of dollars—add 000 to get the full amount. 2009 Note: Financial information for 2009 was not available for all companies at press time.

2009 Sales: $3,485,000
2008 Sales: $3,565,565
2007 Sales: $2,980,000
2006 Sales: $2,792,300
2005 Sales: $2,510,800

2009 Profits: $-113,790
2008 Profits: $61,264
2007 Profits: $55,900
2006 Profits: $50,000
2005 Profits: $69,600

U.S. Stock Ticker:
Int'l Ticker: 5105 Int'l Exchange: Tokyo-TSE
Employees: 7,248
Fiscal Year Ends: 3/31
Parent Company:

SALARIES/BENEFITS:

Pension Plan: ESOP Stock Plan: Profit Sharing: Top Exec. Salary: $ Bonus: $
Savings Plan: Stock Purch. Plan: Second Exec. Salary: $ Bonus: $

OTHER THOUGHTS:

Apparent Women Officers or Directors:
Hot Spot for Advancement for Women/Minorities:

LOCATIONS: ("Y" = Yes)

West:	Southwest:	Midwest:	Southeast:	Northeast:	International:
Y		Y	Y		Y

TOYODA GOSEI CO LTD

www.toyoda-gosei.com

Industry Group Code: 3363 **Ranks within this company's industry group:** Sales: 17 Profits: 16

Vehicle Manufacturing:		Dealers:		Parts:		Service:		Finance:		Specialty:	
Cars:		Car Dealer New:		Manufacturers:	Y	General Service:		Leasing:		Information Systems:	
Trucks:		Car Dealer Used:		Retail:		Specialty Service:		Auto Loans:		Online Marketing:	
Motorcycles:		Truck Dealer:		Distributors:		Oil Change:		Insurance:		Other:	Y
Specialty:		RV Dealer:		Tires:		Paint and Body:				Publishing:	
Buses:		Motorcycle Dealer:		Batteries:						Rental Cars/Trucks:	
RVs:		Specialty Dealer:									

TYPES OF BUSINESS:

Automotive Components
LEDs & Optoelectronics
Consumer Products
Airbags
Cell Phone Cases
Wheelchair Cushions

BRANDS/DIVISIONS/AFFILIATES:

Toyota Group

CONTACTS:

Note: Officers with more than one job title may be intentionally listed here more than once.

Hajime Wakayama, Pres.
Takayasu Hiramatsu, Vice Chmn.
Tsuneji Obara, Exec. VP
Muneo Furutani, Exec. VP
Kuniaki Osaka, Sr. Managing Dir.
Akio Matsubara, Chmn.

Phone: 81-52-400-1055	**Fax:** 81-52-409-7491
Toll-Free:	
Address: 1 Haruhinagahata Kiyosu, Aichi, 452-8564 Japan	

GROWTH PLANS/SPECIAL FEATURES:

Toyoda Gosei Co., Ltd., a member of the Toyota Group, produces and distributes automotive components. The company has 45 consolidated subsidiaries operating in 16 nations and regions around the world. The firm's automotive business operates in four segments: interior and exterior parts, which accounted for 29% of sales in 2009; body sealing products, 16.2%; functional parts, 19.1%; and safety system products, 30.5%. The interior and exterior parts division produces instrument panel modules and components, such as integrated center clusters, registers, cup holders, audio covers and glove compartments; interior parts, such as assist grips, front pillar garnishes and lighting illumination scuff plates; exterior parts, such as radiator grilles, side protection molding, roof spoilers, hybrid wheels, mud guards and wheel caps; applied LED products; and automobile accessories, such as console boxes, blue light grilles and front bumper spoilers. The body sealing products division primarily makes weather stripping. The functional parts division develops fuel tanks and components; power train parts, such as water and air hoses, cylinder head covers and insulation plates for hybrid cars; and chassis and drive-train parts, including brake hoses, piston cups, pinion boots and dust covers. The safety system products division makes steering wheels and airbags. The company also produces optoelectronic products and general industry products. In the optoelectronic products division, which accounted for 3.7% of 2009 sales, Toyoda offers LED lighting and LED lamps/chips. The company also produces a variety of other consumer products, which accounted for 1.5% of 2009 sales and include communications equipment components, air-conditioning products, home-related components and construction and production machinery components. The company has LED patent agreements with Sharp Corporation and Showa Denko K. K.

FINANCIALS:

Sales and profits are in thousands of dollars—add 000 to get the full amount. 2009 Note: Financial information for 2009 was not available for all companies at press time.

2009 Sales: $5,798,730	2009 Profits: $41,930	**U.S. Stock Ticker:**
2008 Sales: $6,612,408	2008 Profits: $307,443	**Int'l Ticker: 7282** Int'l Exchange: Tokyo-TSE
2007 Sales: $5,027,145	2007 Profits: $135,059	Employees:
2006 Sales: $4,243,021	2006 Profits: $91,833	Fiscal Year Ends: 3/31
2005 Sales: $4,055,673	2005 Profits: $98,567	Parent Company:

SALARIES/BENEFITS:

Pension Plan:	ESOP Stock Plan:	Profit Sharing:	Top Exec. Salary: $	Bonus: $
Savings Plan:	Stock Purch. Plan:		Second Exec. Salary: $	Bonus: $

OTHER THOUGHTS:

Apparent Women Officers or Directors:
Hot Spot for Advancement for Women/Minorities:

LOCATIONS: ("Y" = Yes)

West:	Southwest:	Midwest:	Southeast:	Northeast:	International:
	Y	Y			Y

TOYOTA AUTO BODY CO LTD

www.toyota-body.co.jp

Industry Group Code: 336211 **Ranks within this company's industry group:** Sales: 1 Profits: 4

Vehicle Manufacturing:		Dealers:		Parts:		Service:		Finance:		Specialty:	
Cars:	Y	Car Dealer New:		Manufacturers:	Y	General Service:		Leasing:		Information Systems:	
Trucks:	Y	Car Dealer Used:		Retail:		Specialty Service:		Auto Loans:		Online Marketing:	
Motorcycles:		Truck Dealer:		Distributors:		Oil Change:		Insurance:		Other:	
Specialty:	Y	RV Dealer:		Tires:		Paint and Body:				Publishing:	
Buses:		Motorcycle Dealer:		Batteries:						Rental Cars/Trucks:	
RVs:		Specialty Dealer:									

TYPES OF BUSINESS:

Motor Vehicle Body Manufacturing
Commercial Vans & Trucks
Auto Parts Manufacturing

BRANDS/DIVISIONS/AFFILIATES:

Toyota Motor Corporation
P.T. Sugity Creatives Co., Ltd.
Chun Shyang Shin Yeh Industry Co., Ltd.
Toyota Auto Body Malaysia Sdn. Bhd.
Thai Auto Conversion Co., Ltd.
Auto Parts Manufacturing Mississippi, Inc.

CONTACTS:

Note: Officers with more than one job title may be intentionally listed here more than once.

Takuji Amioka, Pres.
Toshio Mizushima, Chmn.

Phone: 81-566-36-2121	**Fax:**
Toll-Free:	
Address: 100 Kanayama, Ichiriyama-cho Kariya, Aichi, 448-8666 Japan	

GROWTH PLANS/SPECIAL FEATURES:

Toyota Auto Body Co., Ltd., founded in 1945 in Japan, operates as a subsidiary of Toyota Motor Corporation. Its main business is composed of body assembly for passenger cars, minivans, SUVs and commercial vans and trucks and, through a series of subsidiaries, parts manufacturing. The firm also assembles specialty equipped vehicles, including vehicles with refrigeration and freezer capabilities, container vans, vans with power lifters and welfare service vehicles and machinery, such as detachable seat and ramp-type wheelchair-customized vehicles. It produces the hybrid electric Prius sedans; and was instrumental in the production of Japan's first all-steel, large-sized truck. It also produces the mini vans Alphard, Vellfire, Estima, Estima Hybrid, Voxy and Noah. SUVs assembled include the Toyota Land Cruiser 200 and the Lexus LX570. The firm's domestic plants include Kariya, Inabe, Yoshiwara and Fujimatsu, along with the Kotobuki New Development Center; and internationally, the company operates subsidiaries in Indonesia, Thailand, Taiwan and Malaysia. Overseas subsidiaries include P.T. Sugity Creatives Co., Ltd.; Chun Shyang Shin Yeh Industry Co., Ltd.; Toyota Auto Body Malaysia Sdn. Bhd.; and Thai Auto Conversion Co., Ltd. Toyota Motor Corporation owns approximately 50% of the company. In conjunction with Toyota's new plant in Mississippi, Toyota Auto Body plans to open a plant in Mississippi to supply stamped body parts, body weld parts and plastic parts for the Toyota plant. The subsidiary, named Auto Parts Manufacturing Mississippi, Inc., is scheduled to begin operation in late 2010.

FINANCIALS:

Sales and profits are in thousands of dollars—add 000 to get the full amount. 2009 Note: Financial information for 2009 was not available for all companies at press time.

2009 Sales: $19,586,700	2009 Profits: $-12,950
2008 Sales: $18,640,900	2008 Profits: $134,100
2007 Sales: $13,181,800	2007 Profits: $122,300
2006 Sales: $11,876,400	2006 Profits: $130,500
2005 Sales: $9,132,300	2005 Profits: $102,600

U.S. Stock Ticker: Subsidiary
Int'l Ticker: 7221 Int'l Exchange: Tokyo-TSE
Employees: 16,447
Fiscal Year Ends: 3/31
Parent Company: TOYOTA MOTOR CORPORATION

SALARIES/BENEFITS:

Pension Plan:	ESOP Stock Plan:	Profit Sharing:	Top Exec. Salary: $	Bonus: $
Savings Plan:	Stock Purch. Plan:		Second Exec. Salary: $	Bonus: $

OTHER THOUGHTS:

Apparent Women Officers or Directors:
Hot Spot for Advancement for Women/Minorities:

LOCATIONS: ("Y" = Yes)

West:	Southwest:	Midwest:	Southeast:	Northeast:	International:
			Y		Y

TOYOTA MOTOR CORPORATION

www.toyota.co.jp

Industry Group Code: 33611 **Ranks within this company's industry group:** Sales: 1 Profits: 32

Vehicle Manufacturing:		**Dealers:**		**Parts:**		**Service:**		**Finance:**		**Specialty:**	
Cars:	Y	Car Dealer New:		Manufacturers:	Y	General Service:		Leasing:	Y	Information Systems:	
Trucks:	Y	Car Dealer Used:		Retail:		Specialty Service:		Auto Loans:	Y	Online Marketing:	
Motorcycles:		Truck Dealer:		Distributors:		Oil Change:		Insurance:		Other:	Y
Specialty:	Y	RV Dealer:		Tires:		Paint and Body:				Publishing:	
Buses:		Motorcycle Dealer:		Batteries:						Rental Cars/Trucks:	
RVs:		Specialty Dealer:									

TYPES OF BUSINESS:

Automobiles, Manufacturing
Manufactured Housing
Advertising & e-Commerce Services
Financial Services
Telecommunications Services
Information Technology
Nanotechnology Research

BRANDS/DIVISIONS/AFFILIATES:

Lexus
Daihatsu Motor Co.
Hino Motors
Toyota Financial Services Corporation
Toyota Motor Credit Corporation
Toyota South Africa (Pty) Ltd.
BSI-TOYOTA Collaboration Center
Tesla Motors Inc

CONTACTS: *Note: Officers with more than one job title may be intentionally listed here more than once.*

Akio Toyoda, Pres.
Takahiko Ijichi, CEO-Human Resources
Takeshi Uchiyamada, Exec. VP-R&D & Prod. Mgmt./CEO-Design Group
Nobuyori Kodaira, CEO-IT
Tadashi Yamashina, CEO-Tech. Admin. Group
Atsushi Niimi, Exec. VP-Strategic Prod. Planning
Atsushi Niimi, Exec. VP-Prod. Eng. & Planning
Atsushi Niimi, Exec. VP-Mfg.
Takahiko Ijichi, CEO-Gen. Admin.
Mamuro Furuhashi, Sr. Managing Dir- Tokyo Secretarial Div.
Yukitoshi Funo, Exec. VP-Oper. Planning & Support
Nobuyori Kodaira, CEO-Bus. Dev., Corp. Planning
Mamuro Furuhashi, CEO-Gov't & Public Affairs
Takahiko Ijichi, CEO-Acct.
Atsushi Niimi, Exec. VP-North America, China
Nobuyori Kodaira, CEO-Environment Affairs Div./CEO-eToyota Div.
Akira Okabe, CEO-Asia & Oceania Oper.
Teiji Tachibana, CEO-Housing/Sr. Managing Dir.-Housing Planning
Fujio Cho, Chmn.
Yukitoshi Funo, Exec VP-Middle East, Africa & Latin America Oper.
Shinichi Sasaki, Exec. VP-Purchasing, Quality & Customer Service

Phone: 81-0565-28-2121	**Fax:** 81-0565-23-5800
Toll-Free:	
Address: 1 Toyota-Cho, Toyota City, Aichi, 471-8571 Japan	

GROWTH PLANS/SPECIAL FEATURES:

Toyota Motor Corporation (TMC) designs, manufactures, assembles and sells passenger cars, minivans, commercial vehicles and related parts and accessories in 170 countries under the Toyota, Lexus, Daihatsu and Hino brands. The firm operates in three segments: automotive, financial and other. Its primary automotive markets are Japan, which generated 29.9% of its 2010 sales; North America, which generated 29%; Europe, which generated 11.9%; and Asia, which generated 13.5%. Other markets generated 15.7% of its 2010 automotive sales. Toyota produces both conventional engine vehicles and hybrid vehicles, with automobile types including subcompact and compact cars; mini-vehicles; mid-size, luxury, sports and specialty cars; recreational and sport-utility vehicles; pickup trucks; minivans; and buses. Subsidiary Daihatsu Motor Co. produces and sells mini-vehicles and compact cars. Another subsidiary, Hino Motors, produces and sells commercial vehicles such as trucks and buses. Toyota produces automobiles and related components through over 50 manufacturing companies in 26 countries. During 2009, 60% of the firm's vehicles sold in North America were produced in North America, and 57% of its vehicles sold in Europe were produced in Europe. The company offers financial services in 33 countries through subsidiary Toyota Financial Services Corporation; in the U.S. through subsidiary Toyota Motor Credit Corporation; and in 32 additional countries through various subsidiaries. Approximately 47% of Toyota's 2010 unit sales in the U.S. included a financing or lease arrangement with Toyota. In March 2010, following months of recalls on various models for serious safety issues, Toyota announced a restructuring of its operations, establishing the TMC Special Committee for Global Quality, that will aim to prevent future lapses in overall product quality. In May 2010, the firm acquired a stake in Tesla Motors for $50 million and in July 2010, the two companies reached an agreement to develop an electric version of Toyota's RAV4 sport utility vehicle.

FINANCIALS:

Sales and profits are in thousands of dollars—add 000 to get the full amount. 2009 Note: Financial information for 2009 was not available for all companies at press time.

2009 Sales: $220,547,000	2009 Profits: $-4,693,960	**U.S. Stock Ticker: TM**
2008 Sales: $262,394,000	2008 Profits: $17,146,000	**Int'l Ticker: 7203** Int'l Exchange: Tokyo-TSE
2007 Sales: $185,752,000	2007 Profits: $13,927,000	Employees: 320,808
2006 Sales: $179,083,000	2006 Profits: $11,681,000	Fiscal Year Ends: 3/31
2005 Sales: $159,046,000	2005 Profits: $10,037,000	Parent Company:

SALARIES/BENEFITS:

Pension Plan:	ESOP Stock Plan:	Profit Sharing:	Top Exec. Salary: $	Bonus: $
Savings Plan:	Stock Purch. Plan:		Second Exec. Salary: $	Bonus: $

OTHER THOUGHTS:

Apparent Women Officers or Directors:
Hot Spot for Advancement for Women/Minorities:

LOCATIONS: ("Y" = Yes)

West:	Southwest:	Midwest:	Southeast:	Northeast:	International:
Y	Y	Y	Y	Y	Y

TOYOTA MOTOR CREDIT CORP

www.toyotafinancial.com

Industry Group Code: 522220 **Ranks within this company's industry group:** Sales: 2 Profits: 4

Vehicle Manufacturing:		Dealers:		Parts:		Service:		Finance:		Specialty:	
Cars:		Car Dealer New:		Manufacturers:		General Service:		Leasing:	Y	Information Systems:	
Trucks:		Car Dealer Used:		Retail:		Specialty Service:		Auto Loans:	Y	Online Marketing:	
Motorcycles:		Truck Dealer:		Distributors:		Oil Change:		Insurance:	Y	Other:	
Specialty:		RV Dealer:		Tires:		Paint and Body:				Publishing:	
Buses:		Motorcycle Dealer:		Batteries:						Rental Cars/Trucks:	
RVs:		Specialty Dealer:									

TYPES OF BUSINESS:

Automobile Financing
Leasing
Insurance

BRANDS/DIVISIONS/AFFILIATES:

Toyota Motor Corporation
Toyota Financial Services
Lexus Financial Services
Toyota Financial Services Americas Corporation
Toyota Financial Services Corporation

CONTACTS: *Note: Officers with more than one job title may be intentionally listed here more than once.*

George E. Borst, CEO
George E. Borst, Pres.
Chris Ballinger, CFO/VP
David Pelliccioni, Chief Admin. Officer
David Pellicioni, Corp. Sec./Sr. VP
Ichiro Yajima, Treas./Exec. VP

Phone: 310-468-1310 **Fax:** 310-468-7800
Toll-Free:
Address: 19001 S. Western Ave., Torrance, CA 90509 US

GROWTH PLANS/SPECIAL FEATURES:

Toyota Motor Credit Corporation (TMCC) is a financial and insurance firm. The company provides retail and wholesale financing, retail leasing and certain other financial products and services to authorized Toyota, Lexus and Scion vehicle dealers and to other domestic and import franchised dealers and their customers in the U.S. and Puerto Rico. The firm is a wholly-owned subsidiary of Toyota Financial Services Americas Corporation, which is a subsidiary of Toyota Financial Services Corporation, which in turn is a subsidiary of Toyota Motor Corporation. TMCC has approximately 30 company branches and three customer service centers across the U.S. The company's services are marketed under the Toyota Financial Services and Lexus Financial Services brands. TMCC also offers financing for various industrial and commercial products such as forklifts, light and medium-duty trucks and electric vehicles. Subsidiaries of TMCC sell insurance, acquire and securitize lease and financing receivables from other lenders and provide retail and wholesale lease financing.

The firm offers its employees a benefits package that includes life, disability, medical, dental and vision insurance; a health care flexible spending account; a 401(k) plan; a dependent care reimbursement account; a pension plan; an associate support and assistance plan; LifeCare resources; adoption assistance; flextime; a fitness center discount; tuition aid; discounted vehicles; and an associate vehicle lease.

FINANCIALS: **Sales and profits are in thousands of dollars—add 000 to get the full amount. 2009 Note: Financial information for 2009 was not available for all companies at press time.**

2009 Sales: $8,800,000	2009 Profits: $-623,000	**U.S. Stock Ticker: Subsidiary**
2008 Sales: $8,192,000	2008 Profits: $-223,000	**Int'l Ticker:** Int'l Exchange:
2007 Sales: $7,296,000	2007 Profits: $432,000	Employees: 3,300
2006 Sales: $5,585,000	2006 Profits: $580,000	Fiscal Year Ends: 3/31
2005 Sales: $4,086,000	2005 Profits: $762,000	Parent Company: TOYOTA MOTOR CORPORATION

SALARIES/BENEFITS:

Pension Plan: Y	ESOP Stock Plan:	Profit Sharing:	Top Exec. Salary: $	Bonus: $
Savings Plan: Y	Stock Purch. Plan:		Second Exec. Salary: $	Bonus: $

OTHER THOUGHTS:

Apparent Women Officers or Directors:
Hot Spot for Advancement for Women/Minorities:

LOCATIONS: ("Y" = Yes)

West:	Southwest:	Midwest:	Southeast:	Northeast:	International:
Y	Y	Y	Y	Y	Y

TOYOTA MOTOR THAILAND CO LTD

www.toyota.co.th

Industry Group Code: 33611 **Ranks within this company's industry group:** Sales: Profits:

Vehicle Manufacturing:		Dealers:		Parts:		Service:		Finance:		Specialty:	
Cars:	Y	Car Dealer New:		Manufacturers:		General Service:		Leasing:		Information Systems:	
Trucks:	Y	Car Dealer Used:		Retail:		Specialty Service:	Y	Auto Loans:		Online Marketing:	
Motorcycles:		Truck Dealer:		Distributors:		Oil Change:		Insurance:		Other:	Y
Specialty:		RV Dealer:		Tires:		Paint and Body:				Publishing:	
Buses:		Motorcycle Dealer:		Batteries:						Rental Cars/Trucks:	
RVs:		Specialty Dealer:									

TYPES OF BUSINESS:

Automobile Manufacturing
Automotive Repair Services
Rice Production
Ethanol-based Fuel Production

BRANDS/DIVISIONS/AFFILIATES:

Toyota Motor Corporation
Vios
Camry Hybrid
Vigo
Alphard
Avanza
Fortuner
Rachamongkol Rice Co., Ltd.

CONTACTS:

Note: Officers with more than one job title may be intentionally listed here more than once.

Kyoichi Tanada, Pres.
Wichien Emprasertsuk, Sr. VP-Mktg.
Ekachai Ratanachaiwong, Sr. VP-Tech., Mfg.
Apinont Suchewaboripont, Sr. VP-Mfg.
Vudhigorn Suriyachantananont, Sr. VP-Admin.
Kohei Nakao, Treas.
Ninnart Chaithirapinyo, Vice Chmn.
Nigorn Prasertsom, VP-Mktg.
Apichai Sidrattakul, VP-Mfg.
Charnchai Suppayakom, VP-Mfg.
Pramon Sutivong, Chmn.

Phone: 66-2-386-1000 **Fax:**

Toll-Free:

Address: 186/1 Moo Old Railway Rd., Samrong Tai, 10130 Thailand

GROWTH PLANS/SPECIAL FEATURES:

Toyota Motor Thailand Co., Ltd. (TMT), a subsidiary of Toyota Motor Corporation, is a Thai manufacturer of Toyota brand automobiles. It currently produces 15 models, comprising four passenger vehicles, eight commercial vehicles and three multipurpose vehicles. The passenger vehicles, mostly sedans, range from the low-priced Vios, to the mid-range Camry and Camry Hybrid. Other passenger models include the Yaris and Altis. Commercial vehicle models range from the Vigo truck, available with either a standard or extra cab configuration, to the Alphard van. The firm also produces two other Vigo models, the Vigo Double Cab and Vigo Smart Cab, as well as the Hiace, Commuter, Ventury and Majesty vans. Lastly, TMT's multi-purpose vehicles comprise the Avanza, the Innova and the Fortuner. The firm has three manufacturing facilities: the Samrong Plant, with a production capacity of 250,000 units per year; the Gateway Plant, 200,000 units per year; and the Ban Pho Plant, 100,000 units per year. TMT's vehicles are sold though 119 Toyota dealerships and are on display at 319 showrooms. Many of these dealerships also offer repair services. To facilitate repairs covered under warranty, the firm offers the Warranty Plus Card, which stores all the most pertinent information about the customer's car, including model, vehicle identification number (VIN), maintenance history and claim record. Permanent information, such as the model and VIN, is printed on the card, while changeable information, such as repair history, is stored in a memory chip implanted in the card. Other companies in Toyota's Thailand Group, which serve as affiliates of TMT, include Toyota Automotive Technical School and Rachamongkol Rice Co., Ltd., which operates a rice mill that TMT uses to produce Gasohol E-10, a 10%-ethanol fuel.

FINANCIALS:

Sales and profits are in thousands of dollars—add 000 to get the full amount. 2009 Note: Financial information for 2009 was not available for all companies at press time.

2009 Sales: $ | 2009 Profits: $
2008 Sales: $ | 2008 Profits: $
2007 Sales: $ | 2007 Profits: $
2006 Sales: $ | 2006 Profits: $
2005 Sales: $ | 2005 Profits: $

U.S. Stock Ticker: Subsidiary
Int'l Ticker: Int'l Exchange:
Employees:
Fiscal Year Ends:
Parent Company: TOYOTA MOTOR CORPORATION

SALARIES/BENEFITS:

Pension Plan:	ESOP Stock Plan:	Profit Sharing:	Top Exec. Salary: $	Bonus: $
Savings Plan:	Stock Purch. Plan:		Second Exec. Salary: $	Bonus: $

OTHER THOUGHTS:

Apparent Women Officers or Directors:
Hot Spot for Advancement for Women/Minorities:

LOCATIONS: ("Y" = Yes)

West:	Southwest:	Midwest:	Southeast:	Northeast:	International:
					Y

TREADWAYS CORP

www.treadwayscorp.com

Industry Group Code: 441320 **Ranks within this company's industry group:** Sales: Profits:

Vehicle Manufacturing:		Dealers:		Parts:		Service:		Finance:		Specialty:	
Cars:		Car Dealer New:		Manufacturers:		General Service:		Leasing:		Information Systems:	
Trucks:		Car Dealer Used:		Retail:		Specialty Service:		Auto Loans:		Online Marketing:	
Motorcycles:		Truck Dealer:		Distributors:	Y	Oil Change:		Insurance:		Other:	
Specialty:		RV Dealer:		Tires:	Y	Paint and Body:				Publishing:	
Buses:		Motorcycle Dealer:		Batteries:						Rental Cars/Trucks:	
RVs:		Specialty Dealer:									

TYPES OF BUSINESS:

Private-Label Tire Distribution

BRANDS/DIVISIONS/AFFILIATES:

Sumitomo Corporation
Sumitomo Tire
Eldorado Tire
TreadNet
Jetzon Tire
Telstar Tire
TBC Corporation

CONTACTS:

Note: Officers with more than one job title may be intentionally listed here more than once.

John Rigney, CFO
William F. Hirst, Exec. VP-Sales & Customer Service
Kyle Iwasawa, Exec. VP-Oper.

Phone: 610-615-8000	**Fax:** 610-615-8001
Toll-Free: 800-895-1449	
Address: 2000 Campus Ln., East Norriton, PA 19403 US	

GROWTH PLANS/SPECIAL FEATURES:

Treadways Corp. is a private-brand supplier of automobile and truck tires with distribution centers around the U.S. The firm is a wholly-owned subsidiary of TBC Corporation, which in turn is a wholly-owned subsidiary of Japanese holding company Sumitomo Corporation. Its commercial brands are sourced from manufacturers including Sumitomo Tire, Cooper Tire and Rubber, B.F. Goodrich and Goodyear. The company distributes these products to tire retail and automotive service centers through its four branded divisions: Sumitomo Tire, Eldorado Tire, Telstar Tire and Jetzon Tire. The company's current brands are based on assets obtained through a series of acquisitions made throughout the 1990s. Treadways maintains an integrated TreadNet online ordering and distribution service, with access across the catalogs of all four divisions. The company's tires are sold to over 4,000 customers, including dealers and distributors; these products include a variety of high performance, passenger, farm tire and industrial tire product lines.

FINANCIALS:

Sales and profits are in thousands of dollars—add 000 to get the full amount. 2009 Note: Financial information for 2009 was not available for all companies at press time.

2009 Sales: $	2009 Profits: $	**U.S. Stock Ticker: Subsidiary**
2008 Sales: $	2008 Profits: $	**Int'l Ticker:** Int'l Exchange:
2007 Sales: $	2007 Profits: $	Employees:
2006 Sales: $	2006 Profits: $	Fiscal Year Ends: 3/31
2005 Sales: $	2005 Profits: $	Parent Company: SUMITOMO CORPORATION

SALARIES/BENEFITS:

Pension Plan:	ESOP Stock Plan:	Profit Sharing:	Top Exec. Salary: $	Bonus: $
Savings Plan: Y	Stock Purch. Plan:		Second Exec. Salary: $	Bonus: $

OTHER THOUGHTS:

Apparent Women Officers or Directors:
Hot Spot for Advancement for Women/Minorities:

LOCATIONS: ("Y" = Yes)

West:	Southwest:	Midwest:	Southeast:	Northeast:	International:
Y	Y	Y	Y	Y	

TRELLEBORG AB

www.trelleborg.com

Industry Group Code: 3261 **Ranks within this company's industry group:** Sales: 1 Profits: 1

Vehicle Manufacturing:		Dealers:		Parts:		Service:		Finance:		Specialty:	
Cars:		Car Dealer New:		Manufacturers:	Y	General Service:		Leasing:		Information Systems:	
Trucks:		Car Dealer Used:		Retail:		Specialty Service:		Auto Loans:		Online Marketing:	
Motorcycles:		Truck Dealer:		Distributors:		Oil Change:		Insurance:		Other:	Y
Specialty:		RV Dealer:		Tires:	Y	Paint and Body:				Publishing:	
Buses:		Motorcycle Dealer:		Batteries:						Rental Cars/Trucks:	
RVs:		Specialty Dealer:									

TYPES OF BUSINESS:

Polymer Technology-Based Customized Solutions
Polymer-Based Automotive Components
Industrial Fluid Systems
Building Materials

BRANDS/DIVISIONS/AFFILIATES:

Trelleborg Engineered Systems
Trelleborg Automotive
Trelleborg Sealing Solutions
Trelleborg Wheel Systems
Elastopipe
Trelline
Vulcan
Mataki

CONTACTS: *Note: Officers with more than one job title may be intentionally listed here more than once.*

Peter Nilsson, CEO
Peter Nilsson, Pres.
Bo Jacobsson, CFO/Exec. VP
Soren Andersson, Sr. VP-Human Resources
Peter Svenburg, Sr. VP-IT
Ulf Graden, General Counsel/Sr. VP/Sec.
Viktoria Bergman, Sr. VP-Corp. Comm.
Conny Torstensson, VP-Investor Rel.
Claes Jorwall, Sr. VP-Taxes
Lennart Johansson, Pres., Trelleborg Engineered Systems
Maurizio Vischi, Pres., Trelleborg Wheel Systems
Roger Johansson, Pres., Trelleborg Automotive
Claus Barsoe, Pres., Trelleborg Sealing Solutions
Anders Narvinger, Chmn.

Phone: 46-410-670-00	**Fax:** 46-410-427-63
Toll-Free:	
Address: P.O. Box 153, Trelleborg, 231 22 Sweden	

GROWTH PLANS/SPECIAL FEATURES:

Trelleborg AB provides customized solutions based on polymer technology and application. The firm operates four business units: Trelleborg Engineered Systems, which accounted for 41% of sales in 2009; Trelleborg Automotive, 30.8%; Trelleborg Sealing Solutions, 17.2%; and Trelleborg Wheel Systems, 11%. Trelleborg Engineered Solutions produces hoses, elastomer laminates and polymer-coated fabrics; dredging systems and pipe seals; protective and diving suits; marine fender systems; support bearings expansion joints for bridges; and tunnel seals and niche products for the offshore oil/gas extraction sector. Some of its brands include Elastopipe, Trelline, Vulcan, Dipro, ETM, Mataki and Uraduct. Trelleborg Automotive develops and manufactures polymer-based components and systems for noise and vibration damping in light and industrial vehicles, as well as rail, marine and off-road vehicles. Products include thermoplastic boots, brake shims and damping materials. Trelleborg Sealing Solutions supplies advanced sealing solutions in specialty materials designed for a range of industrial applications. The largest product groups are O-rings, rotary seals and hydraulic seals. It also produces safety-critical aircraft seals for engines, flight control actuators, airframes and landing gear; vehicle seals for fuel systems, steering, climate control and exhaust systems; and seals for trains, construction and agricultural machinery. Lastly, Trelleborg Wheel Systems produces tires and complete wheel systems for farm and forest machines; lift trucks; and other materials-handling vehicles. The firm has production units in Europe, Asia, the Middle East, North America and Australia. In April 2010, Trelleborg Automotive launched a fully-owned production facility in Nizhny Novgorod, Russia. In that same month, Trelleborg Sealing Solutions launched a production center in Bangalore, India. In May 2010, Trelleborg Automotive announced plans to divest its Fluid Solutions operation to German-based Bavaria Industriekapital AG.

Trelleborg offers internships and summer work opportunities as well as offering employees training and management programs.

FINANCIALS: **Sales and profits are in thousands of dollars—add 000 to get the full amount. 2009 Note: Financial information for 2009 was not available for all companies at press time.**

2009 Sales: $3,585,020	2009 Profits: $54,190	**U.S. Stock Ticker:**
2008 Sales: $4,062,850	2008 Profits: $-33,530	**Int'l Ticker: TRELB** Int'l Exchange: Stockholm-SSE
2007 Sales: $4,024,900	2007 Profits: $108,900	Employees: 21,119
2006 Sales: $4,568,800	2006 Profits: $108,900	Fiscal Year Ends: 12/31
2005 Sales: $3,996,500	2005 Profits: $197,400	Parent Company:

SALARIES/BENEFITS:

Pension Plan:	ESOP Stock Plan:	Profit Sharing:	Top Exec. Salary: $	Bonus: $
Savings Plan:	Stock Purch. Plan:		Second Exec. Salary: $	Bonus: $

OTHER THOUGHTS:

Apparent Women Officers or Directors: 5
Hot Spot for Advancement for Women/Minorities: Y

LOCATIONS: ("Y" = Yes)

West:	Southwest:	Midwest:	Southeast:	Northeast:	International:
Y	Y	Y	Y	Y	Y

TRI PETCH ISUZU SALES CO LTD

www.isuzu-tis.com

Industry Group Code: 336120 **Ranks within this company's industry group:** Sales: Profits:

Vehicle Manufacturing:		Dealers:		Parts:		Service:		Finance:		Specialty:	
Cars:		Car Dealer New:		Manufacturers:	Y	General Service:	Y	Leasing:		Information Systems:	
Trucks:	Y	Car Dealer Used:		Retail:		Specialty Service:		Auto Loans:		Online Marketing:	
Motorcycles:		Truck Dealer:		Distributors:		Oil Change:		Insurance:		Other:	
Specialty:	Y	RV Dealer:		Tires:		Paint and Body:				Publishing:	
Buses:		Motorcycle Dealer:		Batteries:						Rental Cars/Trucks:	
RVs:		Specialty Dealer:									

TYPES OF BUSINESS:

Passenger Truck Manufacturing
Diesel Engine Manufacturing

BRANDS/DIVISIONS/AFFILIATES:

Isuzu Motors Ltd
Mitsubishi Corp
Spark
Hi-Lander
Cab 4
Forward
MU-7
i-TEQ

GROWTH PLANS/SPECIAL FEATURES:

Tri Petch Isuzu Sales Co., Ltd. (TIS), established in 1974, mainly produces, distributes and services Isuzu pickups and medium-duty trucks in Thailand. All of its products are sold under the Isuzu banner. Specific brands include the Spark, Hi-Lander, Cab 4, Spacecab and Rodeo light trucks. The firm recently began offering an enhanced line of its trucks under the D-Max Super Platinum edition tag. This line of its trucks focuses on providing a more stylized truck body and advanced entertainment packages. The company also produces the Isuzu Forward line of commercial trucks and the Isuzu MU-7, which is a SUV-type car based on the Isuzu D-Max light truck. The firm's distribution and service centers network includes almost 300 locations throughout Thailand. Besides vehicles, TIS also produces Isuzu i-TEQ diesel engines. The company is a joint venture between Japanese firms Isuzu Motors Ltd. and Mitsubishi Corp.

CONTACTS: *Note: Officers with more than one job title may be intentionally listed here more than once.*

Hiroshi Nakagawa, Pres.
Panatda Chennavasin, VP-Corp. Strategies
Panatda Chennavasin, VP-Corp. Rel.

Phone: 66-2966-2111	**Fax:** 66-2966-1291
Toll-Free:	
Address: 1088 Vibhavadi Rangsit Rd., Ladyao, Chatuchak, Bangkok, 10900 Thailand	

FINANCIALS: **Sales and profits are in thousands of dollars—add 000 to get the full amount. 2009 Note: Financial information for 2009 was not available for all companies at press time.**

2009 Sales: $	2009 Profits: $	**U.S. Stock Ticker: Joint Venture**
2008 Sales: $	2008 Profits: $	**Int'l Ticker:** Int'l Exchange:
2007 Sales: $	2007 Profits: $	Employees:
2006 Sales: $	2006 Profits: $	Fiscal Year Ends:
2005 Sales: $	2005 Profits: $	Parent Company: ISUZU MOTORS LTD

SALARIES/BENEFITS:

Pension Plan:	ESOP Stock Plan:	Profit Sharing:	Top Exec. Salary: $	Bonus: $
Savings Plan:	Stock Purch. Plan:		Second Exec. Salary: $	Bonus: $

OTHER THOUGHTS:

Apparent Women Officers or Directors: 1
Hot Spot for Advancement for Women/Minorities:

LOCATIONS: ("Y" = Yes)

West:	Southwest:	Midwest:	Southeast:	Northeast:	International:
					Y

TRW AUTOMOTIVE HOLDINGS CORP

www.trw.com

Industry Group Code: 3363 **Ranks within this company's industry group:** Sales: 9 Profits: 12

Vehicle Manufacturing:		Dealers:		Parts:		Service:		Finance:		Specialty:	
Cars:		Car Dealer New:		Manufacturers:	Y	General Service:		Leasing:		Information Systems:	
Trucks:		Car Dealer Used:		Retail:		Specialty Service:		Auto Loans:		Online Marketing:	
Motorcycles:		Truck Dealer:		Distributors:		Oil Change:		Insurance:		Other:	
Specialty:		RV Dealer:		Tires:		Paint and Body:				Publishing:	
Buses:		Motorcycle Dealer:		Batteries:						Rental Cars/Trucks:	
RVs:		Specialty Dealer:									

TYPES OF BUSINESS:

Automotive Systems & Components
Safety Systems

BRANDS/DIVISIONS/AFFILIATES:

TRW Asia Pacific Co Ltd

CONTACTS:

Note: Officers with more than one job title may be intentionally listed here more than once.

John C. Plant, CEO
Steven Lunn, COO/Exec. VP
John C. Plant, Pres.
Joseph S. Cantie, CFO/Exec. VP
Peter J. Lake, Exec. VP-Sales
Neil E. Marchuk, Exec. VP-Human Resources
Alexander Heilig, Dir.-Global Eng.
Robin Walker-Lee, General Counsel/Exec. VP/Sec.
Peter J. Lake, Exec. VP-Bus. Dev.
Neil P. Simpkins, Chmn.

Phone: 734-855-2600	**Fax:** 734-855-2999
Toll-Free:	
Address: 12001 Tech Ctr. Dr., Livonia, MI 48150 US	

GROWTH PLANS/SPECIAL FEATURES:

TRW Automotive Holdings Corp. is one of the world's largest suppliers of automotive systems, modules and components to global automotive original equipment manufacturers (OEMs) and related aftermarkets. Through an extensive network of subsidiaries, TRW supplies products and services to over 40 major vehicle manufacturers. Through approximately 184 facilities around the world, the company produces braking, steering, suspension, cruise control, commercial steering, airbag, seat belt and heating/air conditioning systems. The firm also develops a line of safety products for the automobile industry that includes active safety systems, such as tire pressure monitoring systems and vehicle rollover sensors; and passive safety systems, such as airbag sensors. TRW uses tire pressure monitoring systems that can tell drivers which tires are under-inflated, by how much and how fast they are losing pressure. The company also uses advanced technology in its occupant weight sensing system. The system uses strain gauges at each corner of the front passenger seat frame to directly measure the occupant's seating weight and classify them to determine the appropriate air bag deployment strength. TRW also offers automotive service, parts, technical support and diagnostic support through its aftermarket business unit. The company's three largest customers are Volkswagen (19.1% of sales), Ford (15.6%) and General Motors (11.1%). Roughly 85% of the firm's sales are to original equipment manufacturers. In November 2009, the firm opened a new North American Driver Assist Systems Engineering Center at its Michigan headquarters. In December 2009, the company introduced an airbag module that is less than 50% the size of standard driver airbag modules; it also launched the ACR2 Basic seatbelt retractor. In March 2010, subsidiary TRW Asia Pacific Co., Ltd. agreed to form a joint venture with Xi'an Dong Fang Group Co., Ltd. to establish an airbag inflator and seat belt pretensioner manufacturing plant in China.

FINANCIALS:

Sales and profits are in thousands of dollars—add 000 to get the full amount. 2009 Note: Financial information for 2009 was not available for all companies at press time.

2009 Sales: $11,614,000	2009 Profits: $55,000	**U.S. Stock Ticker: TRW**
2008 Sales: $14,995,000	2008 Profits: $-779,000	**Int'l Ticker:** Int'l Exchange:
2007 Sales: $14,702,000	2007 Profits: $90,000	Employees: 63,600
2006 Sales: $13,144,000	2006 Profits: $176,000	Fiscal Year Ends: 12/31
2005 Sales: $12,643,000	2005 Profits: $204,000	Parent Company:

SALARIES/BENEFITS:

Pension Plan: Y	ESOP Stock Plan:	Profit Sharing:	Top Exec. Salary: $1,680,000	Bonus: $4,200,000
Savings Plan: Y	Stock Purch. Plan:		Second Exec. Salary: $798,650	Bonus: $1,269,044

OTHER THOUGHTS:

Apparent Women Officers or Directors: 2
Hot Spot for Advancement for Women/Minorities:

LOCATIONS: ("Y" = Yes)

West:	Southwest:	Midwest:	Southeast:	Northeast:	International:
	Y	Y	Y	Y	Y

TUTTLE-CLICK AUTOMOTIVE GROUP

www.tuttleclick.com

Industry Group Code: 441110 **Ranks within this company's industry group:** Sales: Profits:

Vehicle Manufacturing:		Dealers:		Parts:		Service:		Finance:		Specialty:	
Cars:		Car Dealer New:	Y	Manufacturers:		General Service:	Y	Leasing:		Information Systems:	
Trucks:		Car Dealer Used:	Y	Retail:	Y	Specialty Service:		Auto Loans:		Online Marketing:	
Motorcycles:		Truck Dealer:		Distributors:		Oil Change:		Insurance:		Other:	
Specialty:		RV Dealer:		Tires:		Paint and Body:				Publishing:	
Buses:		Motorcycle Dealer:		Batteries:						Rental Cars/Trucks:	
RVs:		Specialty Dealer:									

TYPES OF BUSINESS:

Auto Dealers, Retail
Maintenance & Repair

BRANDS/DIVISIONS/AFFILIATES:

Irvine Auto Mall
Tustin Auto Mall

CONTACTS:

Note: Officers with more than one job title may be intentionally listed here more than once.

Chris Cotter, Pres.
James H. Click, Chmn.

Phone: 949-598-4800	**Fax:** 949-830-0980
Toll-Free:	
Address: 41 Auto Center Dr., Irvine, CA 92618 US	

GROWTH PLANS/SPECIAL FEATURES:

Tuttle-Click Automotive Group sells new and used cars at dealerships in Irvine, Tustin and Orange County California. The company's dealership network represents seven franchises, which sell Chrysler, Dodge, Ford, Lincoln Mercury, Mitsubishi and Jeep vehicles. Its service centers deal primarily with repair and maintenance of Ford and Chrysler models. The groups operations include the Tustin Auto Mall, which is a dealership and service center that specializes in the Chrysler, Jeep and Dodge model cars; the Irvine Auto Center, which is a primarily a Lincoln Mercury dealership and service center, but also works with Ford and Mitsubishi; and its Commercial Truck Centers, which offers sales and maintenance of Ford and Dodge model trucks in the Orange County area. The company also operates an online dealership that assists visitors in choosing, purchasing and financing any of its new or used vehicles. The web site displays detailed information for each car in its inventory, including specifications, prices, mileage and pictures. Customers who buy new cars and trucks are also able to customize the vehicle online to satisfy their personal preferences. Founded by Holmes Tuttle and James Click, the company has been in business for over 60 years.

FINANCIALS:

Sales and profits are in thousands of dollars—add 000 to get the full amount. 2009 Note: Financial information for 2009 was not available for all companies at press time.

2009 Sales: $	2009 Profits: $	**U.S. Stock Ticker: Private**
2008 Sales: $	2008 Profits: $	**Int'l Ticker:** Int'l Exchange:
2007 Sales: $677,500	2007 Profits: $	Employees:
2006 Sales: $	2006 Profits: $	Fiscal Year Ends: 12/31
2005 Sales: $	2005 Profits: $	Parent Company:

SALARIES/BENEFITS:

Pension Plan:	ESOP Stock Plan:	Profit Sharing:	Top Exec. Salary: $	Bonus: $
Savings Plan:	Stock Purch. Plan:		Second Exec. Salary: $	Bonus: $

OTHER THOUGHTS:

Apparent Women Officers or Directors:
Hot Spot for Advancement for Women/Minorities:

LOCATIONS: ("Y" = Yes)

West:	Southwest:	Midwest:	Southeast:	Northeast:	International:
Y					

UD TRUCKS CORP

www.udtrucks.com

Industry Group Code: 336120 **Ranks within this company's industry group:** Sales: Profits:

Vehicle Manufacturing:		Dealers:		Parts:		Service:		Finance:		Specialty:	
Cars:		Car Dealer New:		Manufacturers:	Y	General Service:		Leasing:		Information Systems:	
Trucks:	Y	Car Dealer Used:		Retail:		Specialty Service:		Auto Loans:		Online Marketing:	
Motorcycles:		Truck Dealer:		Distributors:	Y	Oil Change:		Insurance:		Other:	Y
Specialty:	Y	RV Dealer:		Tires:		Paint and Body:				Publishing:	
Buses:	Y	Motorcycle Dealer:		Batteries:						Rental Cars/Trucks:	
RVs:		Specialty Dealer:									

TYPES OF BUSINESS:

Truck & Bus Manufacturing
Engines & Transmissions
Vehicle & Parts Distribution

BRANDS/DIVISIONS/AFFILIATES:

AB Volvo
Quon
Condor
Spacewing
Spacearrow
Columbian Motor Corp.
PT Astra Nissan Diesel Indonesia
UD Trucks North America

CONTACTS:

Note: Officers with more than one job title may be intentionally listed here more than once.

Satoru Takeuchi, Pres.
Yusuke Sakaue, Exec. VP-Info. Systems
Toshimitsu Kurihara, Sr. VP-Eng.
Toshimitsu Kurihara, Sr. VP-Prod. Control
Keishi Abe, Sr. VP-Domestic Strategy Planning
Yusuke Sakaue, Exec. VP-Acct. & Finance Dept.
Mikio Miyamura, Sr. VP
Tadamichi Harada, Sr. VP-Volvo PT Japan
Par Ostberg, Chmn.
Claes Svedberg, Sr. VP-Overseas Sales

Phone: 81-48-726-7601 **Fax:** 81-48-781-6349
Toll-Free:
Address: 1-1 Ageo-shi, Saitama, 362-8523 Japan

GROWTH PLANS/SPECIAL FEATURES:

UD Trucks Corporation, formerly Nissan Diesel Motor Co., Ltd., a wholly-owned subsidiary of AB Volvo, manufactures light-, medium- and heavy-duty diesel trucks and buses, as well as bus chassis and special-purpose vehicles. The firm's products include diesel engines (the GEI 3 series and the MD92TB), compressed natural gas engines (the FU6 and PU6), gas engines (the PA6 and RA10) and transmissions (the ESCOT and MRT23). Other major products include the Quon, Condor and Capacitor Hybrid trucks. In addition, the company manufactures buses for the Asian transportation market. Models offered include, Spacewing, Spacearrow and Spacerunner. The company has several facilities in Japan and a number of international subsidiaries. The Ageo Complex produces heavy- and light-duty trucks, tractors, buses and other vehicles, as well as housing the firm's research and development division. The Kounsou Plant manufactures cast components for diesel engines, transmissions, brakes and other vehicle parts. The Hanyu Plant manufactures 5-12 speed transmissions for heavy- and medium-duty trucks, including the ESCOT automatic transmission. The Motegi Proving Ground provides a comprehensive proving course, as well as inspection facilities that support the ongoing development of products and new technologies in such areas as safety, durability, economy and pollution control. UD's international subsidiaries include; Columbian Motor Corp., located in Manila; PT Astra Nissan Diesel Indonesia; Ghandhara Nissan, Ltd., located in Pakistan; UD Finance Netherlands, B.V.; and UD Trucks North America, Inc., located in Irving, Texas. The company exports its vehicles and parts worldwide, including the UD line of commercial truck, which is distributed in the U.S. by UD Trucks North America, Inc. In February 2010, the firm began selling Volvo trucks in Japanese markets. In the same month, the firm changed its name to UD Trucks Corporation.

FINANCIALS:

Sales and profits are in thousands of dollars—add 000 to get the full amount. 2009 Note: Financial information for 2009 was not available for all companies at press time.

2009 Sales: $	2009 Profits: $	**U.S. Stock Ticker: Subsidiary**
2008 Sales: $	2008 Profits: $	**Int'l Ticker: 7210** Int'l Exchange: Tokyo-TSE
2007 Sales: $4,243,200	2007 Profits: $182,800	Employees:
2006 Sales: $4,393,700	2006 Profits: $264,700	Fiscal Year Ends: 3/31
2005 Sales: $4,287,900	2005 Profits: $279,100	Parent Company: AB VOLVO

SALARIES/BENEFITS:

Pension Plan:	ESOP Stock Plan:	Profit Sharing:	Top Exec. Salary: $	Bonus: $
Savings Plan:	Stock Purch. Plan:		Second Exec. Salary: $	Bonus: $

OTHER THOUGHTS:

Apparent Women Officers or Directors:
Hot Spot for Advancement for Women/Minorities:

LOCATIONS: ("Y" = Yes)

West:	Southwest:	Midwest:	Southeast:	Northeast:	International:
	Y				Y

UNIPART GROUP OF COMPANIES

www.unipart.co.uk

Industry Group Code: 3363 **Ranks within this company's industry group:** Sales: Profits:

Vehicle Manufacturing:		Dealers:		Parts:		Service:		Finance:		Specialty:	
Cars:		Car Dealer New:		Manufacturers:	Y	General Service:	Y	Leasing:		Information Systems:	
Trucks:		Car Dealer Used:		Retail:		Specialty Service:		Auto Loans:		Online Marketing:	
Motorcycles:		Truck Dealer:		Distributors:	Y	Oil Change:		Insurance:		Other:	Y
Specialty:		RV Dealer:		Tires:		Paint and Body:				Publishing:	
Buses:		Motorcycle Dealer:		Batteries:						Rental Cars/Trucks:	
RVs:		Specialty Dealer:									

TYPES OF BUSINESS:

Automobile Parts Manufacturer
Supply Chain Management
Consulting Services
Railroad Supplies
Automobile Parts Warehousing & Distribution
Marine Parts & Accessories
Recreational Vehicle & Camping Accessories

BRANDS/DIVISIONS/AFFILIATES:

Unipart Logistics
Unipart Automotive
Unipart Manufacturing Group
Unipart Rail
Unipart Expert Practices
Unipart Leisure and Marine
Unipart Conference Center
Intertruck

CONTACTS: *Note: Officers with more than one job title may be intentionally listed here more than once.*

John M. Neill, CEO
John-Paul Warner, Group Mgr.-Comm.
Tony Morgue, Dir.-Finance
Frank Nigriello, Dir.-Corp. Affairs

Phone: 44-1865-778-966 **Fax:** 44-1865-383-763
Toll-Free:
Address: Unipart House, Garsington Rd., Cowley, Oxford, OX4 2PG UK

GROWTH PLANS/SPECIAL FEATURES:

The Unipart Group of Companies (UGC) is a logistics and automotive parts and accessories company in Europe. UGC operates in 11 business sectors: logistics, consulting, automotive, rail, security, commercial vehicles, manufacturing, leisure & marine, car care centers, conferences and Unipart international. Unipart Logistics aids companies in identifying the most cost efficient and effective methods of managing various areas of business, such as inventory management and supplier development. The consultancy sector, operating as Unipart Expert Practices, partners with clients to reduce costs and aid productivity and quality. Unipart Automotive is one of the largest suppliers of aftermarket components in the U.K. It carries components for cars, light vans and commercial vehicles, as well as garage equipment, workshop and bodyshop planning and design, and bodyshop consumables. Unipart Rail supplies materials for infrastructure, traction and rolling stock; assists with manufacture, service and repair; LED signaling and handles logistics and supply chain management. Unipart Security Solutions offers manned guarding, control room services and security consultancy. Unipart commercial vehicle, comprised of Truck & Trailer Components and Intertruck, provides aftermarket parts and services for its customers. Unipart Manufacturing Group makes vehicle equipment for the automotive industry. Its joint ventures include Unipart Eberspacher Exhaust Systems, which manufactures exhaust systems, catalytic converters, fabricated manifolds and steel fuel tanks, and Kautex Unipart Ltd, which manufactures plastic fuel tanks and fuel systems. Unipart Leisure and Unipart Marine are wholesale suppliers of caravans, motor homes, camping and marine accessories and parts. Unipart Car Care Centers is a network of over 1,300 independent repair garages. The Unipart Conference Center is a nine room facility that provides conference space, leisure suites and catering. Unipart International provides services and products to the truck and bus aftermarket and the collision parts industry through a mixture of distribution, service and manufacturing companies.

FINANCIALS: **Sales and profits are in thousands of dollars—add 000 to get the full amount. 2009 Note: Financial information for 2009 was not available for all companies at press time.**

2009 Sales: $	2009 Profits: $	**U.S. Stock Ticker: Private**
2008 Sales: $	2008 Profits: $	**Int'l Ticker:** Int'l Exchange:
2007 Sales: $2,281,800	2007 Profits: $	Employees:
2006 Sales: $2,291,730	2006 Profits: $29,270	Fiscal Year Ends: 12/31
2005 Sales: $2,329,990	2005 Profits: $101,090	Parent Company:

SALARIES/BENEFITS:

Pension Plan:	ESOP Stock Plan:	Profit Sharing:	Top Exec. Salary: $	Bonus: $
Savings Plan:	Stock Purch. Plan:		Second Exec. Salary: $	Bonus: $

OTHER THOUGHTS:

Apparent Women Officers or Directors:
Hot Spot for Advancement for Women/Minorities:

LOCATIONS: ("Y" = Yes)

West:	Southwest:	Midwest:	Southeast:	Northeast:	International:
					Y

UNI-SELECT INC

www.uni-select.com

Industry Group Code: 423120 Ranks within this company's industry group: Sales: 1 Profits: 1

Vehicle Manufacturing:		Dealers:		Parts:		Service:		Finance:		Specialty:	
Cars:		Car Dealer New:		Manufacturers:		General Service:		Leasing:		Information Systems:	
Trucks:		Car Dealer Used:		Retail:	Y	Specialty Service:		Auto Loans:		Online Marketing:	
Motorcycles:		Truck Dealer:		Distributors:	Y	Oil Change:		Insurance:		Other:	Y
Specialty:		RV Dealer:		Tires:		Paint and Body:				Publishing:	
Buses:		Motorcycle Dealer:		Batteries:						Rental Cars/Trucks:	
RVs:		Specialty Dealer:									

TYPES OF BUSINESS:

Automobile Parts Manufacturer
Auto Parts Dealer
Auto Parts Distribution
Product & Market Development Services
Marketing & Support Services

BRANDS/DIVISIONS/AFFILIATES:

Auto Parts Plus
Auto Plus
Bumper to Bumper
Parts Plus
Parts Holding, LLC
Consumer Auto Parts, Inc.
Replacement Parts Depot Limited
Uni-Select USA, Inc.

CONTACTS: *Note: Officers with more than one job title may be intentionally listed here more than once.*

Richard G. Roy, CEO
Richard G. Roy, Pres.
Denis Mathieu, CFO/VP
Brent Windom, VP-Mktg.
Luc L'Esperance, VP-Human Resources
Jean-Pierre Beaulieu, CIO/VP
Brent Windom, VP-Prod. Dev.
Robert Buzzard, VP-Admin.
Pierre Chesnay, VP-Legal Affairs/Sec.
Guy M. Archambault, VP-Corp. Dev.
Martin Labrecque, VP-Finance & Control
Gary O'Connor, Exec. VP-Automotive Group Canada
Jean Rivard, Exec. VP-Heavy Duty Group
Jean Rivard, VP-Special Projects
Jean-Louis Dulac, Chmn.
James Buzzard, Sr. VP-Corp. Dev., USA
Michel Laverdure, VP-Corp. Purchasing

Phone: 450-641-2440	**Fax:** 450-449-4908
Toll-Free:	
Address: 170 Industrial Blvd., Boucherville, QC J4B 2X3 Canada	

GROWTH PLANS/SPECIAL FEATURES:

Uni-Select, Inc. is a wholesale distributor and marketer of automotive and heavy-duty replacement parts and accessories. The firm is linked with a network of auto parts dealers in North America, with 56 distribution centers in the U.S. and 14 in Canada that supply access to roughly 350,000 different types of auto parts. The company splits its business into two segments: Canadian Automotive Group and USA Automotive Group. The Canadian Automotive Group specializes in distributing replacement parts for light cars under the Auto Parts Plus, Auto Plus and Bumper to Bumper brands. The group distributes parts through 12 distribution centers to over 700 independent stores and 2,000 repair shops. It also supplies its merchant customers with services that support their operations such as differentiating marketing programs, training activities, IT management tools and financing. The USA Automotive Group distributes parts for light cars under the Parts Plus and Auto Plus brands. This group, operated by the firm's subsidiary Uni-Select USA, Inc., supplies coverage for approximately 70% of registered vehicles in the U.S. as well as offering supplementary services to merchant customers. The company recently acquired Parts Depot, Inc., a Mid-Atlantic parts distributor with 67 stores in the Eastern and Southeastern U.S. In August 2009, the firm completed the sale of its heavy duty parts distribution segment to UAP, Inc. and Enterprise Robert Thibert, Inc. In February 2010, Uni-Select acquired the U.S. based Automotive Information Management, Inc., a program distribution group that provides access to better purchase terms offered by manufacturers for its members.

FINANCIALS: **Sales and profits are in thousands of dollars—add 000 to get the full amount. 2009 Note: Financial information for 2009 was not available for all companies at press time.**

2009 Sales: $1,339,730	2009 Profits: $36,680	**U.S. Stock Ticker:**
2008 Sales: $1,193,700	2008 Profits: $41,610	**Int'l Ticker: UNS** Int'l Exchange: Toronto-TSX
2007 Sales: $1,144,900	2007 Profits: $40,000	Employees:
2006 Sales: $1,101,400	2006 Profits: $41,400	Fiscal Year Ends: 12/31
2005 Sales: $1,083,997	2005 Profits: $37,144	Parent Company:

SALARIES/BENEFITS:

Pension Plan:	ESOP Stock Plan:	Profit Sharing:	Top Exec. Salary: $434,782	Bonus: $132,514
Savings Plan:	Stock Purch. Plan:		Second Exec. Salary: $284,519	Bonus: $

OTHER THOUGHTS:

Apparent Women Officers or Directors:
Hot Spot for Advancement for Women/Minorities:

LOCATIONS: ("Y" = Yes)

West:	Southwest:	Midwest:	Southeast:	Northeast:	International:
Y	Y	Y	Y	Y	Y

UTILIMASTER CORP

www.utilimaster.com

Industry Group Code: 336120 **Ranks within this company's industry group:** Sales: Profits:

Vehicle Manufacturing:		Dealers:		Parts:		Service:		Finance:		Specialty:	
Cars:		Car Dealer New:		Manufacturers:		General Service:		Leasing:		Information Systems:	
Trucks:	Y	Car Dealer Used:		Retail:	Y	Specialty Service:		Auto Loans:		Online Marketing:	
Motorcycles:		Truck Dealer:		Distributors:		Oil Change:		Insurance:		Other:	
Specialty:	Y	RV Dealer:		Tires:		Paint and Body:				Publishing:	
Buses:		Motorcycle Dealer:		Batteries:						Rental Cars/Trucks:	
RVs:		Specialty Dealer:									

TYPES OF BUSINESS:

Truck Manufacturer
Custom Vehicles

BRANDS/DIVISIONS/AFFILIATES:

Spartan Motors, Inc.
Metromaster
Utilivan
Trademaster
Vehicle Control Access System (VCAS)
Aeromaster
Energywise Utilivan

CONTACTS:

Note: Officers with more than one job title may be intentionally listed here more than once.

Larry Doyle, CEO
Larry Doyle, Pres.
Scott Sargent, VP-Sales & Mktg.
Steve Campbell, Dir.-Parts Sales
DeRay Steffenson, Dir.-Customer Service

Phone: 574-862-4561 **Fax:** 574-862-4517
Toll-Free: 800-582-3454 x 3000
Address: 65906 State Rd. 19, Wakarusa, IN 46573-0585 US

GROWTH PLANS/SPECIAL FEATURES:

Utilimaster Corp., acquired by Spartan Motors, Inc. in 2009, designs and builds custom commercial vehicles. Utilimaster works extensively with and offers specialized solutions to four major industries: Parcel, baking & snack, textile and utility. Its products include Aeromaster walk-in vans (also called step-vans), parcel delivery vans (PDVs) and truck bodies for corporations. Walk-in vans, which feature direct access from cab to cargo area, are primarily used to haul cargo, such as bakery goods or textiles, as well as parcel delivery. PDVs, such as the Metromaster, Utilivan and Trademaster, are used in many other industries besides parcel delivery, such as construction and utility service. They have optional walk-in access and over-cab storage space. The company's large cargo capacity, fully-enclosed truck bodies are mounted on a chassis with the original cab. Some other vehicle options for the company's models include cargo load bars, grab handles, luxury seats, radios and lift gates. Common customization projects include installing flood lights, ventilation systems, adjustable shelves, side roll-up doors, loading ramps, diesel generators and workbenches. In addition, the company offers servicing for its vehicles, and its customers can purchase parts online. Customers for the company include FedEx (Federal Express Corporation), USPS (United States Postal Service), Canada Post, UPS, Budget, Penske, Ryder TRS, Aramark, Frito-Lay, Purolator Parcel Delivery, The Salvation Army, Utz Snack Foods and Wabash Canada. In partnership with STRATTEC and FedEx, the company developed the Vehicle Control Access System (VCAS), a keyless vehicle that utilizes an electronic bracelet to unlock and start the vehicle. In March 2010, the company launched a new, fuel efficient van, the Energywise Utilivan.

Employees of Utilmaster receive medical, dental and vision insurance; paid time off; an employee assistance program; and discounts on GM and Ford products.

FINANCIALS:

Sales and profits are in thousands of dollars—add 000 to get the full amount. 2009 Note: Financial information for 2009 was not available for all companies at press time.

2009 Sales: $	2009 Profits: $	**U.S. Stock Ticker: Subsidiary**
2008 Sales: $	2008 Profits: $	**Int'l Ticker:** Int'l Exchange:
2007 Sales: $138,600	2007 Profits: $	Employees:
2006 Sales: $	2006 Profits: $	Fiscal Year Ends: 12/31
2005 Sales: $96,600	2005 Profits: $	Parent Company: SPARTAN MOTORS INC

SALARIES/BENEFITS:

Pension Plan:	ESOP Stock Plan:	Profit Sharing:	Top Exec. Salary: $	Bonus: $
Savings Plan: Y	Stock Purch. Plan:		Second Exec. Salary: $	Bonus: $

OTHER THOUGHTS:

Apparent Women Officers or Directors:
Hot Spot for Advancement for Women/Minorities:

LOCATIONS: ("Y" = Yes)

West:	Southwest:	Midwest:	Southeast:	Northeast:	International:
		Y			

UTILITY TRAILER MANUFACTURING CO

www.utilitytrailer.com

Industry Group Code: 336120 **Ranks within this company's industry group:** Sales: Profits:

Vehicle Manufacturing:		Dealers:		Parts:		Service:		Finance:		Specialty:	
Cars:		Car Dealer New:		Manufacturers:		General Service:		Leasing:		Information Systems:	
Trucks:		Car Dealer Used:		Retail:		Specialty Service:		Auto Loans:		Online Marketing:	
Motorcycles:		Truck Dealer:		Distributors:		Oil Change:		Insurance:		Other:	
Specialty:	Y	RV Dealer:		Tires:		Paint and Body:				Publishing:	
Buses:		Motorcycle Dealer:		Batteries:						Rental Cars/Trucks:	
RVs:		Specialty Dealer:									

TYPES OF BUSINESS:

Trailer Manufacturing
Parts & Service

BRANDS/DIVISIONS/AFFILIATES:

Barrier Door
Tautliner
Grocery 2000R
Distributor 2000R
Centerseal 2000R
Utilitopics

CONTACTS:

Note: Officers with more than one job title may be intentionally listed here more than once.

Paul Bennett, CEO
Craig Bennett, Sr. VP-Mktg. & Sales
Todd Bennett, Dir.-Finance
Stephen F. Bennett, VP-Purchasing

Phone: 626-965-1541	**Fax:** 626-965-2790
Toll-Free:	
Address: 17295 E. Railroad St., City of Industry, CA 91748 US	

GROWTH PLANS/SPECIAL FEATURES:

Utility Trailer Manufacturing Co. designs, engineers, builds and services a complete line of trailers, including flatbeds, refrigerated trailers (reefers), dry-freight vans and curtain-sided trailers. It has developed numerous technologies, including the cold flow floor design, its patented Barrier Door, the use of polyurethane foam in refrigerated trailers, the shockless pintle hook and a completely waterproof electrical system. The firm was one of the first companies in the U.S. to introduce and manufacture curtain-sided trailers. Sold under the brand Tautliner, these trailers feature load-bearing curtains that slide back for immediate access to the load. The Tautliner is one of the company's most popular brands. The firm's 3000R reefer, one of the top selling reefers in the world, is used on five continents and is available in three different size models: Grocery, Distributor and Centerseal. The company operates five trailer manufacturing plants throughout the U.S., and its products are sold by 100 dealers in the U.S., Canada, Mexico and Chile. Its North American facilities also offer parts and servicing for all of the company's trailers. The firm also publishes Utilitopics, a newsletter sent to company employees, customers and dealers, covering market conditions and other topics. Utility Trailer has been owned and operated by the Bennett family since brothers H. C. and E. W. Bennett founded the company in 1914. In February 2010, Utility introduced two new side skirt designs, the USS-120 and USS-160, created with UV protected one-piece fiberglass reinforced plastic, which offer 4% and 5% gains in fuel efficiency, respectively.

FINANCIALS:

Sales and profits are in thousands of dollars—add 000 to get the full amount. 2009 Note: Financial information for 2009 was not available for all companies at press time.

2009 Sales: $	2009 Profits: $	**U.S. Stock Ticker: Private**
2008 Sales: $	2008 Profits: $	**Int'l Ticker:** Int'l Exchange:
2007 Sales: $	2007 Profits: $	Employees:
2006 Sales: $	2006 Profits: $	Fiscal Year Ends:
2005 Sales: $	2005 Profits: $	Parent Company:

SALARIES/BENEFITS:

Pension Plan:	ESOP Stock Plan:	Profit Sharing:	Top Exec. Salary: $	Bonus: $
Savings Plan:	Stock Purch. Plan:		Second Exec. Salary: $	Bonus: $

OTHER THOUGHTS:

Apparent Women Officers or Directors:
Hot Spot for Advancement for Women/Minorities:

LOCATIONS: ("Y" = Yes)

West:	Southwest:	Midwest:	Southeast:	Northeast:	International:
Y	Y	Y	Y	Y	Y

VALEO

www.valeo.com

Industry Group Code: 3363 **Ranks within this company's industry group:** Sales: 12 Profits: 48

Vehicle Manufacturing:		Dealers:		Parts:		Service:		Finance:		Specialty:	
Cars:		Car Dealer New:		Manufacturers:	Y	General Service:		Leasing:		Information Systems:	
Trucks:		Car Dealer Used:		Retail:		Specialty Service:		Auto Loans:		Online Marketing:	
Motorcycles:		Truck Dealer:		Distributors:		Oil Change:		Insurance:		Other:	
Specialty:		RV Dealer:		Tires:		Paint and Body:				Publishing:	
Buses:		Motorcycle Dealer:		Batteries:						Rental Cars/Trucks:	
RVs:		Specialty Dealer:									

TYPES OF BUSINESS:

Automobile Parts Manufacturing
Security Systems
Electrical & Electronic Systems
Lighting Systems
Thermal Systems
Aftermarket Products
Transmission Components

BRANDS/DIVISIONS/AFFILIATES:

Foshan Valeo Ichikoh Auto Lighting Systems Co
Michelin Group

CONTACTS:

Note: Officers with more than one job title may be intentionally listed here more than once.

Jacques Aschenbroich, CEO
Luc Bleriot, COO
Robert Charvier, CFO
Hans-Peter Kunze, Sr. VP-Sales & Bus. Dev.
Michel Boulain, VP-Human Resources
Martin Haub, VP-R&D
Andre Gold, Sr. VP-Tech.
Geric Lebedoff, General Counsel
Edouard de Pirey, VP-Corp. Strategy & Planning
Kate Philipps, Dir.-Comm.
Robert de la Serve, Sr. VP-Valeo Service Activity
France Curis, Dir.-Taxation
Quintin Testa, Dir.-Quality
Pascal Colombani, Chmn.

Phone: 33-1-40-55-20-20	**Fax:** 33-1-40-55-21-71
Toll-Free:	
Address: 43 rue Bayen Cedex 17, Paris, 75848 France	

GROWTH PLANS/SPECIAL FEATURES:

Valeo SA is an independent industrial group focused on the design, production and sale of components, systems and modules for cars and trucks, both in the original equipment market and the aftermarket. Valeo is a supplier to major global automakers including Ford Motor Company, General Motors, Porsche, Toyota, Volkswagen Group and many others. The firm is organized into four divisions that group together 10 product family branches and one branch dedicated to aftermarket products. While marketing and logistics activities are shared to improve efficiency, each branch maintains its own customer interface to provide the best solutions for specific customer requirements. The electrical systems division represents approximately half of Valeo's sales and covers the lighting, wipers, switches and detection, electronics and connective systems, security and engine management branches. The thermal systems division represents approximately a quarter of the firm's sales and covers climate control and engine cooling branches. The transmissions division produces products such as friction materials and clutch systems. Valeo's aftermarket business operates two industrial branches: OES for the sale of original equipment spare parts to automakers and IAM for sales to the independent aftermarket. Additionally, the company operates a joint venture, Foshan Valeo Ichikoh Auto Lighting Systems Co., Ltd., with Ichikoh, a Japanese manufacturer of lighting systems. The firm has a presence in 28 countries and operates approximately 125 production sites, 62 research and development centers and nine distribution centers. Approximately two-thirds of Valeo's revenues are generated within Europe, with other major markets in North America, Asia and, to a lesser extent, South America. In February 2009, the company announced a partnership with Michelin Group to coordinate the development of electric and rechargeable hybrid vehicle systems. In May 2009, the firm restructured its office infrastructure with a new collaborative working platform based on Google Apps Premier Edition.

FINANCIALS:

Sales and profits are in thousands of dollars—add 000 to get the full amount. 2009 Note: Financial information for 2009 was not available for all companies at press time.

2009 Sales: $10,188,400	2009 Profits: $-207,870	**U.S. Stock Ticker: VLEEY**
2008 Sales: $11,365,800	2008 Profits: $-273,200	**Int'l Ticker: FR** Int'l Exchange: Paris-Euronext
2007 Sales: $13,150,000	2007 Profits: $210,000	Employees: 52,110
2006 Sales: $13,556,200	2006 Profits: $225,710	Fiscal Year Ends: 12/31
2005 Sales: $13,238,000	2005 Profits: $201,240	Parent Company:

SALARIES/BENEFITS:

Pension Plan:	ESOP Stock Plan:	Profit Sharing:	Top Exec. Salary: $	Bonus: $
Savings Plan:	Stock Purch. Plan:		Second Exec. Salary: $	Bonus: $

OTHER THOUGHTS:

Apparent Women Officers or Directors: 2
Hot Spot for Advancement for Women/Minorities:

LOCATIONS: ("Y" = Yes)

West:	Southwest:	Midwest:	Southeast:	Northeast:	International:
		Y	Y	Y	Y

VAUXHALL MOTORS LTD

www.vauxhall.co.uk

Industry Group Code: 33611 **Ranks within this company's industry group:** Sales: Profits:

Vehicle Manufacturing:		Dealers:		Parts:		Service:		Finance:		Specialty:	
Cars:	Y	Car Dealer New:		Manufacturers:	Y	General Service:	Y	Leasing:		Information Systems:	
Trucks:		Car Dealer Used:	Y	Retail:		Specialty Service:		Auto Loans:		Online Marketing:	
Motorcycles:		Truck Dealer:		Distributors:		Oil Change:		Insurance:		Other:	Y
Specialty:		RV Dealer:		Tires:		Paint and Body:				Publishing:	
Buses:		Motorcycle Dealer:		Batteries:						Rental Cars/Trucks:	Y
RVs:		Specialty Dealer:									

TYPES OF BUSINESS:

Automobiles, Manufacturing
Used Vehicle Sales
Car & Van Rental
Light Commercial Vehicles

BRANDS/DIVISIONS/AFFILIATES:

General Motors Corp. (GM)
GM Europe
Insignia
Corsa
Vauxhall Rental
Antara
Vivaro
Insignia ecoFLEX

CONTACTS:

Note: Officers with more than one job title may be intentionally listed here more than once.

Duncan Aldred, Managing Dir.
Rory Harvey, Dir.-Retail Sales
Andy Gilson, Dir.-Corp. Strategy
Richard G. Molyneux, Dir.-Finance
Peter Hope, Dir.-Mktg.
Jonathan Browning, Chmn.

Phone: 44-1582-721-122 **Fax:** 44-1582-427-400
Toll-Free:
Address: Griffin House, Osborne Rd., Luton, Bedfordshire LU1 3YT UK

GROWTH PLANS/SPECIAL FEATURES:

Vauxhall Motors, Ltd., a subsidiary of General Motors Corporation (GM), is a U.K.-based manufacturer of passenger cars and light commercial vehicles. The firm collaborates many of its operations with GM Europe. The firm's car models include Agila, Antara, Astra and Astra TwinTop, Corsa, Insignia, Meriva, Tigra, VXR8 and Zafira, as well as the Astravan, Combo, Corsavan, Movano and Vivaro van models. The company is also associated with GM's manufacturing plants at Ellesmere Port, Cheshire, and Luton, Bedfordshire, and maintains an after-sales warehouse in Chalton, Bedfordshire. The Vauxhall Heritage Centre houses a variety of classic Vauxhall models, as well as the PA Cresta, Viva and multiple generations of the Cavalier model. Vauxhall Heritage Services offers owners or prospective owners of classic Vauxhall vehicles part and technical support services, as well as information on related clubs and events. Vauxhall Network Q provides performance certification and warranty services for used Vauxhall vehicles. In March 2009, the company launched the Insignia ecoFLEX range, equipped with a common-rail turbo diesel engine for improved carbon dioxide emissions. As GM's finances began to show improvement in late 2009 the company decided against previous plans to sell Vauxhall, and in February 2010, GM committed a significant amount of money to ensure Vauxhall's continued viability. Also In February 2010, Vauxhall unveiled its prototype Ampera, an electric operated automobile with a range of 40 miles on its lithium-ion battery and a backup gas system for extended mobility of up to 300 miles. The Ampera is expected to become commercially available in the U.K. in 2012.

FINANCIALS:

Sales and profits are in thousands of dollars—add 000 to get the full amount. 2009 Note: Financial information for 2009 was not available for all companies at press time.

2009 Sales: $	2009 Profits: $	**U.S. Stock Ticker: Subsidiary**
2008 Sales: $	2008 Profits: $	**Int'l Ticker:** Int'l Exchange:
2007 Sales: $	2007 Profits: $	Employees:
2006 Sales: $	2006 Profits: $	Fiscal Year Ends: 12/31
2005 Sales: $	2005 Profits: $	Parent Company: GENERAL MOTORS CORP (GM)

SALARIES/BENEFITS:

Pension Plan:	ESOP Stock Plan:	Profit Sharing:	Top Exec. Salary: $	Bonus: $
Savings Plan:	Stock Purch. Plan:		Second Exec. Salary: $	Bonus: $

OTHER THOUGHTS:

Apparent Women Officers or Directors:
Hot Spot for Advancement for Women/Minorities:

LOCATIONS: ("Y" = Yes)

West:	Southwest:	Midwest:	Southeast:	Northeast:	International:
					Y

VISTA PRO AUTOMOTIVE LLC

www.vistaproauto.com

Industry Group Code: 3363 **Ranks within this company's industry group:** Sales: Profits:

Vehicle Manufacturing:		Dealers:		Parts:		Service:		Finance:		Specialty:	
Cars:		Car Dealer New:		Manufacturers:	Y	General Service:		Leasing:		Information Systems:	
Trucks:		Car Dealer Used:		Retail:		Specialty Service:		Auto Loans:		Online Marketing:	
Motorcycles:		Truck Dealer:		Distributors:		Oil Change:		Insurance:		Other:	
Specialty:		RV Dealer:		Tires:		Paint and Body:				Publishing:	
Buses:		Motorcycle Dealer:		Batteries:						Rental Cars/Trucks:	
RVs:		Specialty Dealer:									

TYPES OF BUSINESS:

Automotive Aftermarket Parts
Climate Control Products
Heat Transfer Products
Starters
Alternators
Heavy Duty Truck & Tractor Parts
Industrial Radiators

BRANDS/DIVISIONS/AFFILIATES:

Vista-Pro
Grilledensers
Tractor Tough
Truck Tough
Ultra-Seal
Ready-Aire
CTR (Complete Truck Radiator)
CIR (Complete Industrial Radiator)

CONTACTS: *Note: Officers with more than one job title may be intentionally listed here more than once.*

Steve Scharnhorst, CEO
Steve Scharnhorst, Pres.
Jeffrey Degen, VP-Mktg.
Jeffrey Degen, VP-Strategic Planning
Jeffrey Degen, Contact-Comm.

Phone:	**Fax:** 615-622-2302
Toll-Free: 888-250-2676	
Address: 15 Century Blvd., Ste. 600, Nashville, TN 37214 US	

GROWTH PLANS/SPECIAL FEATURES:

Vista-Pro Automotive, LCC, designs, manufactures and distributes aftermarket climate control, heat transfer, and starter and alternator products for the automotive and heavy-duty markets. Vista-Pro is the result of the merger of Visteon Remanufacturing, Inc. and Proliance International Distributors, in 2010. The company has locations in 15 states, including California, Colorado, Georgia, Montana, Illinois, Ohio, Utah, Connecticut, Missouri, Oklahoma, Washington, Florida, Mississippi, and Tennessee, where its headquarters are located. Vista-Pro also has production plants in Mexico in the cities of Nuevo Laredo and Mexico City. Its products fall into three categories: engine cooling, which includes radiators, charge air coolers and intercoolers; temperature control, which includes compressors, heaters, condensers, evaporators, accumulators, filters, driers, and hose assemblies; and heavy duty, which includes truck radiators, tractor radiators, charge air coolers, industrial radiators, AC condensers and radiator replacement cores. In June 2010, Vista-Pro introduced nine new radiators, six new condensers and one new heater core to its product line.

FINANCIALS: **Sales and profits are in thousands of dollars—add 000 to get the full amount. 2009 Note: Financial information for 2009 was not available for all companies at press time.**

2009 Sales: $	2009 Profits: $	**U.S. Stock Ticker: Private**
2008 Sales: $	2008 Profits: $	**Int'l Ticker:** Int'l Exchange:
2007 Sales: $	2007 Profits: $	Employees:
2006 Sales: $	2006 Profits: $	Fiscal Year Ends:
2005 Sales: $	2005 Profits: $	Parent Company:

SALARIES/BENEFITS:

Pension Plan:	ESOP Stock Plan:	Profit Sharing:	Top Exec. Salary: $	Bonus: $
Savings Plan:	Stock Purch. Plan:		Second Exec. Salary: $	Bonus: $

OTHER THOUGHTS:

Apparent Women Officers or Directors:
Hot Spot for Advancement for Women/Minorities:

LOCATIONS: ("Y" = Yes)

West:	Southwest:	Midwest:	Southeast:	Northeast:	International:
Y	Y	Y	Y	Y	Y

VISTEON CORPORATION

www.visteon.com

Industry Group Code: 3363 **Ranks within this company's industry group:** Sales: 14 Profits: 8

Vehicle Manufacturing:		**Dealers:**		**Parts:**		**Service:**		**Finance:**		**Specialty:**	
Cars:		Car Dealer New:		Manufacturers:	Y	General Service:		Leasing:		Information Systems:	
Trucks:		Car Dealer Used:		Retail:		Specialty Service:		Auto Loans:		Online Marketing:	
Motorcycles:		Truck Dealer:		Distributors:		Oil Change:		Insurance:		Other:	
Specialty:		RV Dealer:		Tires:		Paint and Body:				Publishing:	
Buses:		Motorcycle Dealer:		Batteries:						Rental Cars/Trucks:	
RVs:		Specialty Dealer:									

TYPES OF BUSINESS:

Automobile Parts
Climate Control Products
Interior & Exterior Components
Chassis & Power Train Components
Multimedia Systems
Fuel Storage & Delivery Products

BRANDS/DIVISIONS/AFFILIATES:

3M

CONTACTS:

Note: Officers with more than one job title may be intentionally listed here more than once.

Donald J. Stebbins, CEO
Donald J. Stebbins, Pres.
William G. Quigley III, CFO/Exec. VP
Dorothy L. Stephenson, Sr. VP-Human Resources
James F. Sistek, CIO/VP
Michael K. Sharnas, General Counsel/VP
Julie A. Fream, VP-Strategy & Global Comm.
Jim Fisher, Corp. Comm.
Michael J. Widgren, Chief Acct. Officer/VP/Controller
Steve Meszaros, VP-Electronics Prod. Group
Joy M. Greenway, VP/Pres., Climate Prod. Group
Robert Pallash, Sr. VP/Pres., Global Customer Group
Donald J. Stebbins, Chmn.
Jonathan K. Maples, VP-Global Purchasing

Phone: **Fax:** 734-736-5560
Toll-Free: 800-847-8366
Address: 1 Village Center Dr., Van Buren Township, MI 48111 US

GROWTH PLANS/SPECIAL FEATURES:

Visteon Corp. supplies automotive systems, modules and components to global vehicle manufacturers and the aftermarket for replacement and appearance enhancement parts. The company is in the process of restructuring, and as a result, operations have split into five segments: Climate, Electronics, Interiors, Services and Other. Climate operations produce products such as climate air handling modules; engine induction systems; powertrain cooling modules; heat exchangers; compressors; fluid transport; and climate controls. The Electronics sector primarily manufactures infotainment, driver information and audio systems; powertrain, feature and electronic control modules; and lighting. The Interiors division mainly produces door trim, instrument panels, floor consoles and cockpit modules. The Services sector offers transition services for divestiture transactions, primarily those involving ACH Transactions and Chassis Divestiture. The Other division is primarily involved in the production of parts sold and distributed to the automotive aftermarket, as well as fuel and powertrain products. The firm has a partnership with 3M to develop new technology for the automobile industry. The company operates through regional headquarters in the U.S., and it maintains manufacturing sites, sales offices and joint ventures in North and South America, Africa, Europe and the Asia-Pacific region. Ford makes up 39% of the firm's sales. In May 2009, the firm filed for bankruptcy protection, which does not include its overseas units. Visteon is the largest supplier to Ford, which agreed to supply some financing for ongoing operations during Visteon's bankruptcy. In March 2010, the company filed an amended plan of reorganization and disclosure statement with the U.S. Bankruptcy Court. Under the amended plan would provide recoveries to bondholders, unsecured creditors and trade creditors.

FINANCIALS:

Sales and profits are in thousands of dollars—add 000 to get the full amount. 2009 Note: Financial information for 2009 was not available for all companies at press time.

2009 Sales: $6,685,000	2009 Profits: $128,000	**U.S. Stock Ticker: VSTNQ**
2008 Sales: $9,544,000	2008 Profits: $-681,000	**Int'l Ticker:** Int'l Exchange:
2007 Sales: $11,275,000	2007 Profits: $-372,000	Employees: 29,500
2006 Sales: $11,256,000	2006 Profits: $-163,000	Fiscal Year Ends: 12/31
2005 Sales: $16,976,000	2005 Profits: $-270,000	Parent Company:

SALARIES/BENEFITS:

Pension Plan: Y	ESOP Stock Plan:	Profit Sharing:	Top Exec. Salary: $1,283,333	Bonus: $2,579,197
Savings Plan:	Stock Purch. Plan:		Second Exec. Salary: $1,076,186	Bonus: $1,650,750

OTHER THOUGHTS:

Apparent Women Officers or Directors: 4
Hot Spot for Advancement for Women/Minorities: Y

LOCATIONS: ("Y" = Yes)

West:	Southwest:	Midwest:	Southeast:	Northeast:	International:
	Y	Y	Y		Y

VOLKSWAGEN AG

www.volkswagenag.com

Industry Group Code: 33611 **Ranks within this company's industry group:** Sales: 2 Profits: 4

Vehicle Manufacturing:		Dealers:		Parts:		Service:		Finance:		Specialty:	
Cars:	Y	Car Dealer New:		Manufacturers:	Y	General Service:		Leasing:	Y	Information Systems:	
Trucks:	Y	Car Dealer Used:		Retail:		Specialty Service:		Auto Loans:	Y	Online Marketing:	
Motorcycles:		Truck Dealer:		Distributors:		Oil Change:		Insurance:		Other:	
Specialty:		RV Dealer:		Tires:		Paint and Body:				Publishing:	
Buses:		Motorcycle Dealer:		Batteries:						Rental Cars/Trucks:	Y
RVs:		Specialty Dealer:									

TYPES OF BUSINESS:

Automobiles, Manufacturing
Truck Manufacturing
Car Rental Services
Consumer Financing

BRANDS/DIVISIONS/AFFILIATES:

SEAT SA
Porsche Automobile Holding SE
Bentley Motors
Skoda Auto AS
Volkswagen Financial Services AG
Volkswagen Bank GmbH
Volkswagen Leasing GmbH
LeasePlan Corporation NV

CONTACTS: *Note: Officers with more than one job title may be intentionally listed here more than once.*

Martin Winterkorn, CEO
Hans Dieter Potsch, CFO
Horst Neumann, Dir.-Human Resources & Labor
Jochem Heizmann, Dir.-Prod.
Christine Ritz, Group Head-Investor Rel.
Hans D. Potsch, Controller
Oliver Larkin, Sr. VP-Investor Rel., London Office
Alexander Hunger, Sr. VP-Investor Rel., Wolfsburg Office
Hans Dieter Pötsch, CFO-Porsche Automobil Holding SE
Martin Winterkorn, Chmn.
Francisco Javier Garcia Sanz, Dir.-Procurement

Phone: 49-53-61-90 **Fax:** 49-53-619-30411
Toll-Free: 800-822-8987
Address: VHH 11. Fl., P.O. Box 1849, Wolfsburg, D-38436 Germany

GROWTH PLANS/SPECIAL FEATURES:

Volkswagen AG (VW) is one of the world's leading automobile manufacturers and the number-one automobile manufacturer in Europe, with yearly production of more than 6 million cars, trucks and vans. The company's two primary divisions are Automotive and Financial Services. The automotive group is made up of nine brands from six European countries: Volkswagen, Audi, Bentley, Bugatti, Lamborghini, SEAT, Skoda, Scania and Volkswagen Commercial Vehicles. Each brand operates as an independent entity on the market, with products ranging from low-consumption small cars to luxury class vehicles. Models offered under the Volkswagen brand include the New Beetle, Jetta, Passat, Golf, Fox and Polo. In the commercial vehicle segment, products include pick-ups, busses and heavy trucks. The financial services division, operated through wholly-owned subsidiary Volkswagen Financial Services AG, is responsible for coordinating the worldwide financial services of the company, with offerings including vehicle financing; direct bank business, offered through Volkswagen Bank GmbH; and fleet management, including the activities of subsidiaries Volkswagen Leasing GmbH and LeasePlan Corporation N.V. In January 2009, the company established a vehicle finance arm to serve the Indian market. The company has been utilizing planned short-term stoppages at its manufacturing facilities to contend with slowing international demand in late 2008 and early 2009. In addition, as of January 2009, Porsche Automobil Holding SE had raised its stake in Volkswagen to roughly 50% and had been attempting a takeover before credit problems and falling global auto sales forced a change in its plans. In May 2009, Volkswagen and Porsche announced that they were in talks to merge the operations of the two companies, and in August 2009, they announced an agreement that would have VW purchase an approximate 42% stake in Porsche's sports car business by the end of 2009, with the remainder of Porsche being merged into VW's operations by 2011.

FINANCIALS: **Sales and profits are in thousands of dollars—add 000 to get the full amount. 2009 Note: Financial information for 2009 was not available for all companies at press time.**

2009 Sales: $143,666,000 | 2009 Profits: $2,533,280
2008 Sales: $150,559,000 | 2008 Profits: $6,201,850
2007 Sales: $144,062,000 | 2007 Profits: $5,453,080
2006 Sales: $137,750,000 | 2006 Profits: $3,610,000
2005 Sales: $112,825,900 | 2005 Profits: $1,326,400

U.S. Stock Ticker: VLKAY
Int'l Ticker: VOW Int'l Exchange: Frankfurt-Euronext
Employees: 369,928
Fiscal Year Ends: 12/31
Parent Company:

SALARIES/BENEFITS:

Pension Plan: Y | ESOP Stock Plan: | Profit Sharing: | Top Exec. Salary: $9,093,830 | Bonus: $
Savings Plan: | Stock Purch. Plan: | | Second Exec. Salary: $4,753,757 | Bonus: $

OTHER THOUGHTS:

Apparent Women Officers or Directors: 2
Hot Spot for Advancement for Women/Minorities:

LOCATIONS: ("Y" = Yes)

West:	Southwest:	Midwest:	Southeast:	Northeast:	International:
				Y	Y

VOLKSWAGEN GROUP OF AMERICA INC

www.volkswagengroupamerica.com

Industry Group Code: 33611 **Ranks within this company's industry group:** Sales: Profits:

Vehicle Manufacturing:		Dealers:		Parts:		Service:		Finance:		Specialty:	
Cars:		Car Dealer New:	Y	Manufacturers:		General Service:		Leasing:	Y	Information Systems:	
Trucks:		Car Dealer Used:	Y	Retail:	Y	Specialty Service:		Auto Loans:	Y	Online Marketing:	Y
Motorcycles:		Truck Dealer:		Distributors:		Oil Change:		Insurance:		Other:	
Specialty:		RV Dealer:		Tires:		Paint and Body:				Publishing:	
Buses:		Motorcycle Dealer:		Batteries:						Rental Cars/Trucks:	
RVs:		Specialty Dealer:									

TYPES OF BUSINESS:

Automobile Distribution
Vehicle Importing
Vehicle Financing & Leasing

BRANDS/DIVISIONS/AFFILIATES:

Volkswagen AG
VW Credit Inc
Audi
Bentley
Bugatti
Lamborghini
Jetta
Beetle

CONTACTS:

Note: Officers with more than one job title may be intentionally listed here more than once.

Jonathan Browning, CEO
Mark Barnes, Interim Pres.
Kerry Christopher, Mgr.-Prod. Comm.
David Geanacopoulos, General Counsel
Jill Bratina, VP-Corp. Comm.
Johan de Nysschen, Exec. VP-Audi of America, Inc.
Christophe Georges, COO-Bentley Motors, Inc.
Kevin V. Kelly, Pres., Volkswagen Credit, Inc.
David Geanacopoulos, Exec. VP-Public Affairs

Phone: 703-364-7000 **Fax:**
Toll-Free:
Address: 2200 Ferdinand Porsche Dr., Herndon, VA 20171 US

GROWTH PLANS/SPECIAL FEATURES:

Volkswagen Group of America (VGA) is the U.S. importing and distribution branch of Volkswagen AG. The firm handles all of Volkswagen's brands, including Volkswagen, Audi, Bentley, Bugatti and Lamborghini. Wholly-owned subsidiary VW Credit, Inc. offers leasing and financial services through brands Volkswagen Credit, Audi Financial Services and Bentley Financial Services. It also manages and markets co-branded financial services through third-party providers. VGA operates parts distribution centers in California, Florida, New Jersey, Texas and Wisconsin; ports and post production facilities in California, Georgia, Rhode Island and Texas; corporate research, development and technical facilities in California, Arizona and New Jersey; and financial service centers in Illinois and Oregon. The company operates approximately 600 Volkswagen and 270 Audi dealerships in the U.S. Volkswagen's models include Rabbit, Jetta, Jetta SportWagen, GTI, Passat, Passat Wagon, Beetle, Touareg and Eos. Audi models include the TT Coupe, A3-A6, A8, Q7 and the R8 supersportscar. VGA retails car accessories, apparel and other logo merchandise through its e-commerce web site. All of the firm's 2010 model year vehicles come standard equipped with Electronic Stabilization Program (ESP), which works in conjunction with anti-lock brakes and helps reduce loss of control, rollovers and other types of crashes. In June 2010, VGA opened a new training center at its plant in Chattanooga, Tennessee.

FINANCIALS:

Sales and profits are in thousands of dollars—add 000 to get the full amount. 2009 Note: Financial information for 2009 was not available for all companies at press time.

2009 Sales: $	2009 Profits: $	**U.S. Stock Ticker: Subsidiary**
2008 Sales: $	2008 Profits: $	**Int'l Ticker:** Int'l Exchange:
2007 Sales: $	2007 Profits: $	Employees:
2006 Sales: $	2006 Profits: $	Fiscal Year Ends: 12/31
2005 Sales: $	2005 Profits: $	Parent Company: VOLKSWAGEN AG

SALARIES/BENEFITS:

Pension Plan:	ESOP Stock Plan:	Profit Sharing:	Top Exec. Salary: $	Bonus: $
Savings Plan:	Stock Purch. Plan:		Second Exec. Salary: $	Bonus: $

OTHER THOUGHTS:

Apparent Women Officers or Directors: 1
Hot Spot for Advancement for Women/Minorities:

LOCATIONS: ("Y" = Yes)

West:	Southwest:	Midwest:	Southeast:	Northeast:	International:
Y	Y	Y	Y	Y	Y

VOLVO CAR CORPORATION

www.volvocars.com

Industry Group Code: 33611 **Ranks within this company's industry group:** Sales: Profits:

Vehicle Manufacturing:		Dealers:		Parts:		Service:		Finance:		Specialty:	
Cars:	Y	Car Dealer New:		Manufacturers:		General Service:		Leasing:		Information Systems:	
Trucks:		Car Dealer Used:		Retail:		Specialty Service:		Auto Loans:		Online Marketing:	
Motorcycles:		Truck Dealer:		Distributors:		Oil Change:		Insurance:		Other:	
Specialty:		RV Dealer:		Tires:		Paint and Body:				Publishing:	
Buses:		Motorcycle Dealer:		Batteries:						Rental Cars/Trucks:	
RVs:		Specialty Dealer:									

TYPES OF BUSINESS:

Car Manufacturer

BRANDS/DIVISIONS/AFFILIATES:

Vattenfall AB
S60
C70
XC60
City Safety
FlexiFuel
Partial Zero Emission Vehicle (PZEV)

CONTACTS:

Note: Officers with more than one job title may be intentionally listed here more than once.

Stephen Odell, CEO
Steven Armstrong, COO
Stephen Odell, Pres.
Gerry Keaney, Sr. VP-Mktg. Sales & Customer Service
Bjorn Sallstrom, Sr. VP-Human Resources
Magnus Jonsson, Sr. VP-Prod. Dev.
Magnus Hellsten, Sr. VP-Mfg.
Elisabet Wenzlaff, General Counsel/Sr. VP
Olle Axelson, Sr. VP-Public Affairs
Stuart Rowley, Sr. VP-Finance
Bengt Banck, Sr. VP-Quality & Customer Satisfaction
John Fleming, Chmn.
Bernt Ejbyfeldt, Sr. VP-Purchasing

Phone: 46-31-59-00-00 **Fax:**
Toll-Free:
Address: VAK Bldg., Assar Gabrielssons vag Goteborg, Goteborg, Sweden

GROWTH PLANS/SPECIAL FEATURES:

Volvo Car Corporation, founded in 1927, is a Swedish designer, developer and manufacturer of cars known for safety and reliability. Volvo's largest markets are the U.K., the U.S., Germany and Sweden, with additional sales centers in Europe and Japan. The firm sold over 374,000 vehicles in 2008 through approximately 2,340 independent dealerships. Volvo cars are manufactured at six facilities, with the largest in Sweden and Belgium and smaller plants in China and Southeast Asia. Its current models include the S40, S60 and S80 sedans; the V50 and V70 versatility models; the XC70 and XC90 SUVs; and the C70 convertible. It recently launched the XC60 crossover, featuring the City Safety automatic low-speed breaking function, and plans to unveil low-emission versions of seven models during 2009. Volvo's convertibles are manufactured by 40%-owned joint venture Pininfarina Sverige AB, with Pininfarina S.p.A., at the Uddevalla, Sweden factory. The firm's cars have won numerous awards for safety, design, environmental issues and overall value. It offers environmentally savvy FlexiFuel cars (so named because they can run on either ethanol or gasoline), and hopes to expand its production of those models. PremAir is the company's smog-reducing technology, developed in collaboration with the Engelhard Corporation, which converts ground-level ozone passing through the radiator into oxygen. Available in California and certain Northeastern states in the U.S., Volvo's PZEV (Partial Zero Emission Vehicle) engines produce exhaust which, in heavy city traffic, may be cleaner than the ambient air. In March 2010, Volvo's owner, Ford Motor Co., agreed to sell Volvo to Zhejiang Geely Holding Group, based in Hangzhou, China. The buyer intends to maintain production in Sweden and will likely build an additional plant in China.

FINANCIALS:

Sales and profits are in thousands of dollars—add 000 to get the full amount. 2009 Note: Financial information for 2009 was not available for all companies at press time.

2009 Sales: $	2009 Profits: $	**U.S. Stock Ticker: Subsidiary**
2008 Sales: $	2008 Profits: $	**Int'l Ticker:** Int'l Exchange:
2007 Sales: $	2007 Profits: $	Employees:
2006 Sales: $	2006 Profits: $	Fiscal Year Ends: 12/31
2005 Sales: $	2005 Profits: $	Parent Company: ZHEJIANG GEELY HOLDING GROUP

SALARIES/BENEFITS:

Pension Plan:	ESOP Stock Plan:	Profit Sharing:	Top Exec. Salary: $	Bonus: $
Savings Plan:	Stock Purch. Plan:		Second Exec. Salary: $	Bonus: $

OTHER THOUGHTS:

Apparent Women Officers or Directors: 2
Hot Spot for Advancement for Women/Minorities:

LOCATIONS: ("Y" = Yes)

West:	Southwest:	Midwest:	Southeast:	Northeast:	International:
Y	Y	Y	Y	Y	Y

VOLVO CARS OF NORTH AMERICA INC

www.volvocars.com/us

Industry Group Code: 441110 **Ranks within this company's industry group:** Sales: Profits:

Vehicle Manufacturing:		Dealers:		Parts:		Service:		Finance:		Specialty:	
Cars:	Y	Car Dealer New:	Y	Manufacturers:	Y	General Service:		Leasing:	Y	Information Systems:	
Trucks:		Car Dealer Used:	Y	Retail:		Specialty Service:		Auto Loans:	Y	Online Marketing:	
Motorcycles:		Truck Dealer:		Distributors:		Oil Change:		Insurance:		Other:	Y
Specialty:		RV Dealer:		Tires:		Paint and Body:				Publishing:	
Buses:		Motorcycle Dealer:		Batteries:						Rental Cars/Trucks:	
RVs:		Specialty Dealer:									

TYPES OF BUSINESS:

Automobiles-Distribution & Marketing
Fleet Sales
Auto Financing
Roadside Assistance
Replacement Parts

BRANDS/DIVISIONS/AFFILIATES:

Volvo Car Corporation
Ford Motor Co.
Volvo Finance
Zhejiang Geely Holding Group
S80
S40
C30
XC90

CONTACTS:

Note: Officers with more than one job title may be intentionally listed here more than once.

Doug Speck, CEO
Doug Speck, Pres.
Juanita Ragland Doby, VP-Human Resources
Wendi McAden, VP-Corp. Comm.

Phone:	**Fax:**
Toll-Free: 800-458-1552	
Address: 1 Volvo Drive, Rockleigh, NJ 07647 US	

GROWTH PLANS/SPECIAL FEATURES:

Volvo Cars of North America, Inc., a subsidiary of Sweden-based Volvo Car Corporation, itself a subsidiary of Ford Motor Company, distributes, sells and markets Volvo-brand coupes, sedans, station wagons, sports utility vehicles (SUVs) and convertibles in the U.S. and Canada. The company is connected to Volvo Finance, which provides leasing and financing for new vehicles, including variable and customized payment plans, and advance payment programs. The company's web site includes a customization tool through which a purchaser can create and order a personalized vehicle. Volvo's vehicle models include the S40, starting at $26,200; S60, starting at $37,700; S80, starting at $39,200; V50, starting at $28,700; V70, starting at $33,550; C30, starting at $24,600; C70, starting at $39,950; XC70, starting at $37,950; XC60, starting at $32,395; and XC90 starting at $37,700. Vehicle accessories include backseat entertainment systems, portable navigation systems, booster cushions, Sirius Satellite Radio with six-month introductory subscription, parking assist software, reversible luggage compartment mat, electric cooler, protective bumper cover, bicycle carrier, specialized trim, gearshift knobs, steering wheels and other merchandise. The company also provides overseas delivery; pre-owned vehicles; special Internet offers; fleet sales for corporations; care and maintenance services through Volvo Service Centers across North America; spare and replacement parts; roadside assistance; and high-definition and satellite radio services for its vehicles. In March 2010, Volvo agreed to be acquired by the Zhejiang Geely Holding Group, based in Hangzhou, China. The buyer will maintain production in Sweden and will likely build an additional plant in China.

FINANCIALS:

Sales and profits are in thousands of dollars—add 000 to get the full amount. 2009 Note: Financial information for 2009 was not available for all companies at press time.

2009 Sales: $	2009 Profits: $	**U.S. Stock Ticker: Subsidiary**
2008 Sales: $	2008 Profits: $	**Int'l Ticker:** Int'l Exchange:
2007 Sales: $	2007 Profits: $	Employees:
2006 Sales: $	2006 Profits: $	Fiscal Year Ends: 12/31
2005 Sales: $	2005 Profits: $	Parent Company: FORD MOTOR COMPANY

SALARIES/BENEFITS:

Pension Plan:	ESOP Stock Plan:	Profit Sharing:	Top Exec. Salary: $	Bonus: $
Savings Plan:	Stock Purch. Plan:		Second Exec. Salary: $	Bonus: $

OTHER THOUGHTS:

Apparent Women Officers or Directors: 2
Hot Spot for Advancement for Women/Minorities:

LOCATIONS: ("Y" = Yes)

West:	Southwest:	Midwest:	Southeast:	Northeast:	International:
Y	Y	Y	Y	Y	Y

WABASH NATIONAL CORP

www.wabashnational.com

Industry Group Code: 33611 **Ranks within this company's industry group:** Sales: 32 Profits: 20

Vehicle Manufacturing:		Dealers:		Parts:		Service:		Finance:		Specialty:	
Cars:		Car Dealer New:		Manufacturers:	Y	General Service:		Leasing:	Y	Information Systems:	
Trucks:		Car Dealer Used:		Retail:		Specialty Service:		Auto Loans:		Online Marketing:	
Motorcycles:		Truck Dealer:		Distributors:		Oil Change:		Insurance:		Other:	
Specialty:	Y	RV Dealer:		Tires:		Paint and Body:				Publishing:	
Buses:		Motorcycle Dealer:		Batteries:						Rental Cars/Trucks:	
RVs:		Specialty Dealer:	Y								

TYPES OF BUSINESS:

Trailer Manufacturer
Trailer Dealerships
Repair Parts
Leasing & Financing
Trailer Rental

BRANDS/DIVISIONS/AFFILIATES:

Wabash National Trailer Center
DuraPlate
Benson
RoadRailer
FreightPro
SolarGuard
Eagle
Transcraft Corporation

CONTACTS:
Note: Officers with more than one job title may be intentionally listed here more than once.

Richard J. Giromini, CEO
Richard J. Giromini, Pres.
Mark J. Weber, CFO/Sr. VP
Bruce Ewald, Sr. VP-Mktg. & Sales
Timothy J. Monahan, Sr. VP-Human Resources
Rodney P. Ehrich, CTO/Sr. VP
Joe Zachman, Sr. VP-Mfg.
Erin J. Roth, General Counsel/VP/Corp. Sec.
Martin C. Jischke, Chmn.

Phone: 765-771-5300	**Fax:** 765-771-5474
Toll-Free: 800-937-4784	
Address: 1000 Sagamore Pkwy. S., Lafayette, IN 47905 US	

GROWTH PLANS/SPECIAL FEATURES:

Wabash National Corp., headquartered in Lafayette, Indiana, designs, manufactures and markets standard and customized truck trailers and related transportation equipment, including dry vans, refrigerated vans, flat trailers, dump trailers, tank trailers and container chassis under the Wabash trademark. Company operations are conducted through two wholly-owned subsidiaries: Transcraft Corporation, which develops and manufactures flatbed and drop deck trailers; and Wabash National Trailer Centers, which markets and sells new and used trailers as well as parts for the industry. The products are distributed through a company-owned national network of dealerships, as well as a network of 119 independent dealers with 210 locations. The firm also sells used trailers from other manufacturers. Wabash supplies trailers to Schneider National, Werner Enterprises, Heartland Express, Swift Transportation, GE Trailer Fleet Services, Crete Carrier Corporation, Safeway, U.S. Xpress Enterprises, Knight Transportation and others. The company markets freight trailer brands from Wabash include the DuraPlate dry van trailer to the RoadRailer bi-modal system, which is able to travel on highways and railways. The firm also offers FreightPro smooth aluminum trailers; Transcraft, Eagle and Benson platform trailers; dump equipment; and SolarGuard refrigerated trailers, which enables customers to achieve lower costs through reduced fuel consumption and reduced operating hours. The company operates two subsidiaries, Transcraft Corporation, a manufacturer of flatbed and drop deck trailers; and Wabash National Trailer Centers, a retail distributor of new and used trailers and aftermarket parts throughout the U.S. and Canada. The firm also has an agreement with PODS Enterprises to use the Wabash DuraPlate segment to produce and service PODS mobile storage containers. In June 2010, the company announced the initiation of production of 350 new ArcticLite refrigerated van trailers for Frozen Food Express Industries, Inc.

FINANCIALS:
Sales and profits are in thousands of dollars—add 000 to get the full amount. 2009 Note: Financial information for 2009 was not available for all companies at press time.

2009 Sales: $337,840	2009 Profits: $-101,765	**U.S. Stock Ticker: WNC**
2008 Sales: $836,213	2008 Profits: $-125,826	**Int'l Ticker:** Int'l Exchange:
2007 Sales: $1,102,544	2007 Profits: $16,285	Employees: 1,600
2006 Sales: $1,312,180	2006 Profits: $9,420	Fiscal Year Ends: 12/31
2005 Sales: $1,213,711	2005 Profits: $111,087	Parent Company:

SALARIES/BENEFITS:

Pension Plan:	ESOP Stock Plan:	Profit Sharing:	Top Exec. Salary: $533,796	Bonus: $
Savings Plan:	Stock Purch. Plan:		Second Exec. Salary: $253,984	Bonus: $

OTHER THOUGHTS:

Apparent Women Officers or Directors:
Hot Spot for Advancement for Women/Minorities:

LOCATIONS: ("Y" = Yes)

West:	Southwest:	Midwest:	Southeast:	Northeast:	International:
Y	Y	Y	Y	Y	Y

WANXIANG AMERICA CORPORATION

www.wanxiang.com

Industry Group Code: 3363 **Ranks within this company's industry group:** Sales: Profits:

Vehicle Manufacturing:		Dealers:		Parts:		Service:		Finance:		Specialty:	
Cars:		Car Dealer New:		Manufacturers:	Y	General Service:		Leasing:		Information Systems:	
Trucks:		Car Dealer Used:		Retail:		Specialty Service:		Auto Loans:		Online Marketing:	
Motorcycles:		Truck Dealer:		Distributors:		Oil Change:		Insurance:		Other:	
Specialty:		RV Dealer:		Tires:		Paint and Body:				Publishing:	
Buses:		Motorcycle Dealer:		Batteries:						Rental Cars/Trucks:	
RVs:		Specialty Dealer:									

TYPES OF BUSINESS:

Automobile Parts Manufacturer
Agricultural Engineering
Aquaculture
Real Estate Development
Restaurant & Hotel Management
Power Plant Construction
Leasing & Financial Services
Infrastructure Development & Construction

BRANDS/DIVISIONS/AFFILIATES:

QC Bearing Company
QC Driveline Company
Wanxiang Group Corporation
Universal Automotive Industries
Rockford Powertrain
Universal LED
Universal Solar

CONTACTS: *Note: Officers with more than one job title may be intentionally listed here more than once.*

Gary E. Wetzel, COO
Pin Ni, Pres.
Gary E. Wetzel, CFO
Michael J. Schaal, Gen. Mgr.

Phone: 847-622-8838	**Fax:** 847-931-4838
Toll-Free:	
Address: 88 Airport Rd., Elgin, IL 60123 US	

GROWTH PLANS/SPECIAL FEATURES:

Wanxiang America Corporation, a subsidiary of Wanxiang Group Corporation, is a supplier of universal joints, bearings, CV joints, drive shafts and other drivetrain parts to customers in over 40 countries around the world. It specializes in casting, forging, stamping, heat treatment, machining and grinding industrial processes. The firm's subsidiary, The QC Bearing Company, operates in southern China, producing a line of bearings and components, alongside sister company QC Driveline, which produces CV joints, auto batteries, shock absorbers, leaf springs, brake discs and tools. Additionally the company operates a renewable energy subsidiary Wanxiang Energy. This division is subdivided into Universal LED, which provides LED lighting solutions for a variety of household and municipal applications, and Universal Solar, a supplier of solar panels. Wanxiang owns significant stakes in six companies in the U.S., including Universal Automotive Industries and Rockford Powertrain. The Wanxiang America division also operates in Canada; Central and South America; and Europe. The firm's parent, Wanxiang Group Corporation, serves domestic and international clients such as Volkswagen AG; PAS Peugot Citroen S.A.; Toyota Motor Corporation; Iveco SpA; and Isuzu Motors Limited. It also supplies parts to General Motors, Ford Motor Co.; Daimler AG; Caterpillar, Inc.; and Deere & Company. In addition to auto parts, the Wanxiang Group is involved in agricultural engineering; aquaculture, raising eels and snakes; real estate development; restaurant and hotel management; power plant construction; leasing and financial services; and infrastructure development and construction. In February 2010, Wanxiang America finished construction on a new solar panel manufacturing facility in Rockford, Illinois.

FINANCIALS: **Sales and profits are in thousands of dollars—add 000 to get the full amount. 2009 Note: Financial information for 2009 was not available for all companies at press time.**

2009 Sales: $	2009 Profits: $	**U.S. Stock Ticker: Subsidiary**
2008 Sales: $	2008 Profits: $	**Int'l Ticker:** Int'l Exchange:
2007 Sales: $160,000	2007 Profits: $	Employees:
2006 Sales: $	2006 Profits: $	Fiscal Year Ends:
2005 Sales: $	2005 Profits: $	Parent Company: WANXIANG GROUP CORPORATION

SALARIES/BENEFITS:

Pension Plan:	ESOP Stock Plan:	Profit Sharing:	Top Exec. Salary: $	Bonus: $
Savings Plan:	Stock Purch. Plan:		Second Exec. Salary: $	Bonus: $

OTHER THOUGHTS:

Apparent Women Officers or Directors:
Hot Spot for Advancement for Women/Minorities:

LOCATIONS: ("Y" = Yes)

West:	Southwest:	Midwest:	Southeast:	Northeast:	International:
		Y			Y

WANXIANG GROUP CORPORATION

www.wanxiang.com.cn

Industry Group Code: 3363 **Ranks within this company's industry group:** Sales: Profits:

Vehicle Manufacturing:		Dealers:		Parts:		Service:		Finance:		Specialty:	
Cars:		Car Dealer New:		Manufacturers:	Y	General Service:		Leasing:	Y	Information Systems:	
Trucks:		Car Dealer Used:		Retail:		Specialty Service:		Auto Loans:		Online Marketing:	
Motorcycles:		Truck Dealer:		Distributors:		Oil Change:		Insurance:		Other:	Y
Specialty:		RV Dealer:		Tires:		Paint and Body:				Publishing:	
Buses:		Motorcycle Dealer:		Batteries:						Rental Cars/Trucks:	
RVs:		Specialty Dealer:									

TYPES OF BUSINESS:

Automotive Parts Manufacturer
Agricultural Engineering
Aquaculture
Restaurant & Hotel Management
Road & Bridge Construction
Power Plant Construction
Leasing & Financial Services
Trade Consulting

BRANDS/DIVISIONS/AFFILIATES:

Wanxiang America Corporation
QC Bearing Company (The)
QC Driveline
Wanxiang Technical Center

CONTACTS: *Note: Officers with more than one job title may be intentionally listed here more than once.*

Weiding Lu, CEO
Gary E. Wetzel, COO/CFO-Wanxiang America Corp.
Guanqui Lu, Chmn.
Pin Ni, Pres., Wanxiang America Corp.

Phone: 86-571-8283-2999	**Fax:** 86-571-8283-3999
Toll-Free:	
Address: Wang Xiang Rd., Xiao Shan District, Hangzhou, 311215 China	

GROWTH PLANS/SPECIAL FEATURES:

Wanxiang Group Corporation is one of China's largest auto parts manufacturers, supplying universal joints, bearings and CV joints to customers in over 40 countries. The company serves domestic and international clients such as Volkswagen AG; PAS Peugot Citroen S.A.; Toyota Motor Corporation; Iveco SpA; and Isuzu Motors Limited. In addition to auto parts, the Wanxiang Group is involved in agricultural engineering; aquaculture, raising eels and snakes; restaurant and hotel management; bridge and road development; international trading; power plant construction; leasing and financial services; and China trade consulting. The company operates through several subsidiaries, including Wanxiang America Corporation (WAC), which is based in Illinois and supplies support services to customers in the U.S., Canada, Central and South America and Europe. Another division of WAC, the QC Bearing Company, operates in southern China, producing a line of bearings and components for the original equipment manufacturer (OEM) and aftermarket segments, alongside sister company QC Driveline, which produces universal joints, CV joints, drive shafts, batteries, shock absorbers, leaf springs, coil springs, brake discs and tools. The Wanxiang Technical Center, based in Zhejiang, China, is the research and development division of the Wanxiang group. In April 2009, Wanxiang announced plans to begin producing lithium batteries and electric vehicles from its new plant in Hangzhou, China. The facility is expected to have an annual production capacity of 1,000 electric vehicles and 1 billion watts of lithium battery by 2010. In May 2010, Wanxiang and Ener1, Inc., based in the U.S., agreed to form a joint venture to produce battery systems for the passenger and heavy-duty markets.

FINANCIALS: **Sales and profits are in thousands of dollars—add 000 to get the full amount. 2009 Note: Financial information for 2009 was not available for all companies at press time.**

2009 Sales: $	2009 Profits: $	**U.S. Stock Ticker: Private**
2008 Sales: $	2008 Profits: $	**Int'l Ticker:** Int'l Exchange:
2007 Sales: $	2007 Profits: $	Employees:
2006 Sales: $	2006 Profits: $	Fiscal Year Ends:
2005 Sales: $	2005 Profits: $	Parent Company:

SALARIES/BENEFITS:

Pension Plan:	ESOP Stock Plan:	Profit Sharing:	Top Exec. Salary: $	Bonus: $
Savings Plan:	Stock Purch. Plan:		Second Exec. Salary: $	Bonus: $

OTHER THOUGHTS:

Apparent Women Officers or Directors:
Hot Spot for Advancement for Women/Minorities:

LOCATIONS: ("Y" = Yes)

West:	Southwest:	Midwest:	Southeast:	Northeast:	International:
		Y			Y

WESCAST INDUSTRIES INC

www.wescast.com

Industry Group Code: 3363 **Ranks within this company's industry group:** Sales: Profits:

Vehicle Manufacturing:		Dealers:		Parts:		Service:		Finance:		Specialty:	
Cars:		Car Dealer New:		Manufacturers:	Y	General Service:		Leasing:		Information Systems:	
Trucks:		Car Dealer Used:		Retail:		Specialty Service:		Auto Loans:		Online Marketing:	
Motorcycles:		Truck Dealer:		Distributors:		Oil Change:		Insurance:		Other:	
Specialty:		RV Dealer:		Tires:		Paint and Body:				Publishing:	
Buses:		Motorcycle Dealer:		Batteries:						Rental Cars/Trucks:	
RVs:		Specialty Dealer:									

TYPES OF BUSINESS:

Engine Components
Powertrain Components
Exhaust Manifolds
Turbine Housing

BRANDS/DIVISIONS/AFFILIATES:

Wescast Hungary Zrt.
United Machining, Inc.

CONTACTS:

Note: Officers with more than one job title may be intentionally listed here more than once.

Edward G. Frackowiak, CEO
Rick Legate, COO
Teresa Fortney, CFO
Jay McNaughton, VP-Sales & Innovation
Alan Blignaut, VP-Human Resources
Andrea K. Kelman, Corp. Sec.
Thomas K. Shea, Dir.-Corp. Finance
Edward G. Frackowiak, Chmn.

Phone: 519-750-0000 **Fax:** 519-720-1629
Toll-Free:
Address: 150 Savannah Oaks Dr., Brantford, ON N3T 5L8 Canada

GROWTH PLANS/SPECIAL FEATURES:

Wescast Industries, Inc., based in Ontario, Canada, is one of the world's largest suppliers of exhaust manifolds for passenger cars and light trucks. The firm designs, casts, machines and assembles exhaust system components for automotive original equipment manufacturers (OEMs) in North America, Europe and Asia. The production of cast iron exhaust manifolds consists of first casting, which is the pouring of molten iron into sand moulds, and then machining, which is the finishing of the raw exhaust manifold by milling, drilling, tapping, assembling and testing by highly-automated machines. In this way, the company prepares the exhaust manifold for final assembly on the engine. In addition to exhaust manifolds, the firm produces integrated turbo manifolds, turbine housings, catalytic converter containers, differential cases and wheel hubs. Wescast conducts business primarily with General Motors, Ford Motor Company and Chrysler; these three clients accounted for approximately 64% of the firm's 2009 consolidated sales. The company operates eight production facilities and five sales and design centers in North America, Europe and Asia. Wescast also maintains several subsidiaries, including wholly-owned subsidiary United Machining, Inc., which operates a flexible machining facility in Michigan. The firm's European power-train operations, which accounts for approximately 36% of sales, are managed by the subsidiary Wescast Hungary Zrt. European clients include Renault; Honeywell TT; BorgWarner TS; Volkswagen; Sata (Fiat); JCB; BMW; Mitsubishi Heavy; Audi; Ford of Europe; PSA; and GM Isuzu. The company also has a foundry and machining operation located in Wuhan, China.

FINANCIALS:

Sales and profits are in thousands of dollars—add 000 to get the full amount. 2009 Note: Financial information for 2009 was not available for all companies at press time.

2009 Sales: $	2009 Profits: $	**U.S. Stock Ticker: WCSTF**
2008 Sales: $273,740	2008 Profits: $101,380	**Int'l Ticker: WCS.A** Int'l Exchange: Toronto-TSX
2007 Sales: $382,700	2007 Profits: $-11,400	Employees:
2006 Sales: $367,300	2006 Profits: $4,000	Fiscal Year Ends: 12/31
2005 Sales: $364,097	2005 Profits: $-24,561	Parent Company:

SALARIES/BENEFITS:

Pension Plan:	ESOP Stock Plan:	Profit Sharing:	Top Exec. Salary: $364,366	Bonus: $ 217
Savings Plan:	Stock Purch. Plan: Y		Second Exec. Salary: $244,571	Bonus: $108,327

OTHER THOUGHTS:

Apparent Women Officers or Directors: 2
Hot Spot for Advancement for Women/Minorities: Y

LOCATIONS: ("Y" = Yes)

West:	Southwest:	Midwest:	Southeast:	Northeast:	International:
		Y			Y

WINNEBAGO INDUSTRIES INC

www.winnebagoind.com

Industry Group Code: 336120 **Ranks within this company's industry group:** Sales: 5 Profits: 3

Vehicle Manufacturing:		Dealers:		Parts:		Service:		Finance:		Specialty:	
Cars:		Car Dealer New:		Manufacturers:	Y	General Service:		Leasing:		Information Systems:	
Trucks:		Car Dealer Used:		Retail:		Specialty Service:		Auto Loans:		Online Marketing:	
Motorcycles:		Truck Dealer:		Distributors:		Oil Change:		Insurance:		Other:	Y
Specialty:		RV Dealer:	Y	Tires:		Paint and Body:				Publishing:	
Buses:		Motorcycle Dealer:		Batteries:						Rental Cars/Trucks:	
RVs:	Y	Specialty Dealer:									

TYPES OF BUSINESS:

Motor Home Manufacturing
Commercial Vehicles
Component Products
Extruded Aluminum

BRANDS/DIVISIONS/AFFILIATES:

Itasca
Winnebago
Spirit
Meridian
Aspect
Outlook
Cambria
Ellipse

CONTACTS: *Note: Officers with more than one job title may be intentionally listed here more than once.*

Robert J. Olson, CEO
Robert J. Olson, Pres.
Sarah N. Nielsen, CFO/VP
Roger W. Martin, VP-Mktg. & Sales
William J. O'Leary, VP-Prod. Dev.
Daryl Krieger, VP-Mfg.
Robert Gossett, VP-Admin.
Raymond M. Beebe, General Counsel/VP/Sec.
Randy J. Potts, Sr. VP-Strategic Planning
Donald L. Heidemann, Treas.
Brian J. Hrubes, Controller
Robert J. Olson, Chmn.

Phone: 641-585-3535	**Fax:** 641-585-6966
Toll-Free:	
Address: 605 W. Crystal Lake Rd., Forest City, IA 50436 US	

GROWTH PLANS/SPECIAL FEATURES:

Winnebago Industries, Inc. is a leading U.S. manufacturer of motor homes and related products and services. The company sells its motor homes through 245 dealers in the U.S. and Canada under the Winnebago, Itasca and ERA brand names. Although motor home sales represent approximately 92% of annual revenue, the company offers other products consisting principally of extruded aluminum and a variety of parts and components for other manufacturers. The company's line of motor homes includes the Winnebago View, Aspect, Access, Sightseer and Adventurer, Tour, and Journey, among several others, as well as the Itasca Navion, Cambria, Impulse, Suncruiser, Meridian and Ellipse, among others. Winnebago Sells Class A and Class C motor homes, making up about 47% and 50% of sales respectively, which both usually include living accommodations for up to seven people; kitchen, dining, sleeping and bath areas; and in some models, a lounge. These vehicles are sold with the option of gas or diesel engines. The Class B models, which account for the remaining sales, are sold under the Era brand name and come exclusively with diesel engines. These motor homes include luxury amenity choices for customers, such as home theater systems, generators, king-sized beds, leather upholstery and a choice of several different decors. In addition, the company offers customers choices of floor plans, cabinet finishes and other design elements in many of its models.

Winnebago offers its employees health and dental insurance, as well as education reimbursement.

FINANCIALS: **Sales and profits are in thousands of dollars—add 000 to get the full amount. 2009 Note: Financial information for 2009 was not available for all companies at press time.**

2009 Sales: $211,519	2009 Profits: $-78,766	**U.S. Stock Ticker: WGO**
2008 Sales: $604,352	2008 Profits: $2,784	**Int'l Ticker:** Int'l Exchange:
2007 Sales: $870,152	2007 Profits: $41,564	Employees: 1,630
2006 Sales: $864,403	2006 Profits: $44,744	Fiscal Year Ends: 8/31
2005 Sales: $991,975	2005 Profits: $65,073	Parent Company:

SALARIES/BENEFITS:

Pension Plan:	ESOP Stock Plan:	Profit Sharing:	Top Exec. Salary: $401,539	Bonus: $
Savings Plan: Y	Stock Purch. Plan:		Second Exec. Salary: $236,408	Bonus: $

OTHER THOUGHTS:

Apparent Women Officers or Directors: 1
Hot Spot for Advancement for Women/Minorities:

LOCATIONS: ("Y" = Yes)

West:	Southwest:	Midwest:	Southeast:	Northeast:	International:
		Y			

YAMAHA MOTOR CO LTD

www.yamaha-motor.co.jp

Industry Group Code: 336991 **Ranks within this company's industry group:** Sales: 1 Profits: 4

Vehicle Manufacturing:		Dealers:		Parts:		Service:		Finance:		Specialty:	
Cars:		Car Dealer New:		Manufacturers:	Y	General Service:		Leasing:		Information Systems:	
Trucks:		Car Dealer Used:		Retail:		Specialty Service:		Auto Loans:		Online Marketing:	
Motorcycles:	Y	Truck Dealer:		Distributors:		Oil Change:		Insurance:		Other:	Y
Specialty:	Y	RV Dealer:		Tires:		Paint and Body:				Publishing:	
Buses:		Motorcycle Dealer:		Batteries:						Rental Cars/Trucks:	
RVs:		Specialty Dealer:									

TYPES OF BUSINESS:

Motorcycle Manufacturing
Personal Water Vehicles
Snowmobiles
Boats
Golf Carts
Motors
Generators
All-Terrain Vehicles

BRANDS/DIVISIONS/AFFILIATES:

India Yamaha Motor Private Limited
Mitsui & Co. Ltd.

CONTACTS: *Note: Officers with more than one job title may be intentionally listed here more than once.*

Hiroyuki Yanagi, Pres.
Toshizumi Kato, Sr. Gen. Mgr.-Sales Section
Yoshiaki Hashimoto, Sr. Gen. Mgr.-Human Resources Dev.
Toyoo Ohtsubo, Exec. Gen. Mgr.-Tech.
Toshizumi Kato, Sr. Gen. Mgr.-Motorcycle Bus. Oper.
Takaaki Kimura, Sr. Exec. Officer/Gen. Mgr.-Marine Bus. Oper.
Masanori Sugita, Gen. Mgr.-Procurement Quality Control Div.
Shigeo Hayakawa, Pres., Yamaha Motor do Brasil Ltda.
Yoshihiko Takahashi, Pres., Yamaha Motor de Mexico S.A. de C.V.
Tsuneji Togami, Chmn.
Hajime Yamaji, Pres., Yamaha Motor Europe N.V.

Phone: 81-5-3832-1103 **Fax:** 81-5-3837-4252
Toll-Free:
Address: 2500 Shingai, Iwata-shi, Shizuoka, 438-8501 Japan

GROWTH PLANS/SPECIAL FEATURES:

Yamaha Motor Co., Ltd., which consists of Yamaha Motor Co., Ltd. and its 141 associated companies (108 subsidiaries and 26 affiliates), is a Japanese manufacturer and seller of motorcycles, boats, outboard motors, personal watercraft, snowmobiles, all-terrain vehicles (ATVs), golf carts, water pumps, automotive engines, intelligent machinery, industrial-use unmanned helicopters and electrical power units for wheelchairs. The company operates in four segments: motorcycles, marine products, power products and other products. The motorcycles segment manufactures and sells motorcycles and parts for overseas production. The marine products segment manufactures and sells outboard motors, personal watercraft, recreational-use boats, fiberglass-reinforced plastic pools, fishing boats, utility boats and diesel engines, as well as related products. The power products segment offers ATVs, side-by-side vehicles, snowmobiles, generators, golf carts, multipurpose engines and snow throwers. The other products segment provides automobile engines, surface mounters, industrial robots, electro-hybrid bicycles, industrial-use unmanned helicopters, electrically powered wheelchairs and intermediate parts for all business segments. Additionally, the company imports and sells various types of products used in the development of tourist businesses and the management of leisure and recreational facilities. The company maintains an Indian joint venture, India Yamaha Motor Private Limited, with Mitsui & Co., Ltd. (Mitsui). Yamaha and its subsidiaries, affiliated companies and joint ventures operate in approximately 35 countries worldwide. In September 2009, the company launched the 2010 YZ250F, a 4-stroke, single-cylinder 250cc engine motocrosser. In July 2010, the firm introduced the EC-03, a zero-emissions electric scooter.

FINANCIALS: **Sales and profits are in thousands of dollars—add 000 to get the full amount. 2009 Note: Financial information for 2009 was not available for all companies at press time.**

2009 Sales: $17,841,400 | 2009 Profits: $20,590
2008 Sales: $17,031,100 | 2008 Profits: $19,660
2007 Sales: $15,700,000 | 2007 Profits: $640,000
2006 Sales: $13,282,900 | 2006 Profits: $648,400
2005 Sales: $11,818,220 | 2005 Profits: $

U.S. Stock Ticker:
Int'l Ticker: 7272 Int'l Exchange: Tokyo-TSE
Employees: 49,761
Fiscal Year Ends: 3/31
Parent Company:

SALARIES/BENEFITS:

Pension Plan: | ESOP Stock Plan: | Profit Sharing: | Top Exec. Salary: $ | Bonus: $
Savings Plan: | Stock Purch. Plan: | | Second Exec. Salary: $ | Bonus: $

OTHER THOUGHTS:

Apparent Women Officers or Directors:
Hot Spot for Advancement for Women/Minorities:

LOCATIONS: ("Y" = Yes)

West:	Southwest:	Midwest:	Southeast:	Northeast:	International:
Y	Y	Y	Y	Y	Y

YAZAKI NORTH AMERICA INC

www.yazaki-na.com

Industry Group Code: 3363 **Ranks within this company's industry group:** Sales: Profits:

Vehicle Manufacturing:		Dealers:		Parts:		Service:		Finance:		Specialty:	
Cars:		Car Dealer New:		Manufacturers:	Y	General Service:		Leasing:		Information Systems:	
Trucks:		Car Dealer Used:		Retail:		Specialty Service:		Auto Loans:		Online Marketing:	
Motorcycles:		Truck Dealer:		Distributors:		Oil Change:		Insurance:		Other:	
Specialty:		RV Dealer:		Tires:		Paint and Body:				Publishing:	
Buses:		Motorcycle Dealer:		Batteries:						Rental Cars/Trucks:	
RVs:		Specialty Dealer:									

TYPES OF BUSINESS:

Vehicle Power & Data Networks
Wire Products
Electric Motor Products

BRANDS/DIVISIONS/AFFILIATES:

YTC America Inc
Yazaki Energy Systems Inc
Y-Connect Operations
Yazaki Europe
TATA Yazaki Autocomp LTD
Yazaki Do Brazil LTDA
Australian Arrow PTY LTD
IntelliTow

CONTACTS: *Note: Officers with more than one job title may be intentionally listed here more than once.*

Dieter Ehrmanntraut, CEO
Dieter Ehrmanntraut, Pres.
Lynn Weaver, VP-Human Resources
Jim Romine, Exec. VP-Eng.
Marcia Goffney, General Counsel/VP/Sec.
Nigel Thompson, Exec. VP-Bus. Planning
Shefali Cromer, Contact-Media
Nigel Thompson, Exec. VP-Finance
Don Winn, VP-Finance
Tom Blankinship, VP-EDS Eng.
Rich Tajer, VP-Component Bus. Unit
Sheryl Leanza, Mgr.-Customs
Max Yamashita, Chmn.
Olga Alavanou, VP-Purchasing & Logistics

Phone: 734-983-1000	**Fax:** 734-983-1105
Toll-Free:	
Address: 6801 Haggerty Rd., Canton, MI 48187 US	

GROWTH PLANS/SPECIAL FEATURES:

Yazaki North America, Inc. is a manufacturer of vehicle power, data networks and electronic technologies to the automotive industry. The firm produces solid-state power centers, instrumentation, electronics, electrical distribution systems, fiber optics and connection systems. It is one of the world's largest privately owned auto suppliers, with facilities in more than 39 countries including 87 manufacturing operations. The firm's product lines are IntelliTow, connectors, electrical distribution systems, electronics, high voltage components and systems, power and data network and vehicle information products. These products and services include wire manufacturing, wire harnesses, power distribution components, injection molding, circuit-board production, electronics assembly, plastic extrusion, small-parts stamping, connectors and instrumentation. The company is also a leading supplier of vehicle power and data solutions to the automotive industry. Yazaki offers automotive high-voltage products for gasoline-electric hybrids and other vehicles employing electric drive technology. Its components include connection systems for motors, inverters, battery packs, battery bus bar modules, high-voltage cables, and high-voltage junction blocks. Yazaki supplies hybrid vehicles including Ford's Escape and Mercury's Mariner. The firm's subsidiaries include YTC America, Inc., Yazaki Energy Systems, Inc. and Y-Connect Operations in the U.S; Yazaki Europe; TATA Yazaki Autocomp LTD. in India; Yazaki Do Brazil LTDA; and Australian Arrow PTY. LTD.

Employees are offered life, medical and dental insurance; flexible spending accounts; an employee assistance program; a 401(k) savings and retirement plan; and disability coverage.

FINANCIALS: **Sales and profits are in thousands of dollars—add 000 to get the full amount. 2009 Note: Financial information for 2009 was not available for all companies at press time.**

2009 Sales: $	2009 Profits: $	**U.S. Stock Ticker: Private**
2008 Sales: $	2008 Profits: $	**Int'l Ticker:** Int'l Exchange:
2007 Sales: $191,500	2007 Profits: $	Employees:
2006 Sales: $	2006 Profits: $	Fiscal Year Ends: 12/31
2005 Sales: $	2005 Profits: $	Parent Company:

SALARIES/BENEFITS:

Pension Plan: Y	ESOP Stock Plan:	Profit Sharing:	Top Exec. Salary: $	Bonus: $
Savings Plan: Y	Stock Purch. Plan:		Second Exec. Salary: $	Bonus: $

OTHER THOUGHTS:

Apparent Women Officers or Directors: 6
Hot Spot for Advancement for Women/Minorities: Y

LOCATIONS: ("Y" = Yes)

West:	Southwest:	Midwest:	Southeast:	Northeast:	International:
Y	Y	Y	Y	Y	Y

YUASA BATTERY (THAILAND) PCL

www.yuasathai.com

Industry Group Code: 33591 **Ranks within this company's industry group:** Sales: 2 Profits: 1

Vehicle Manufacturing:		Dealers:		Parts:		Service:		Finance:		Specialty:	
Cars:		Car Dealer New:		Manufacturers:		General Service:		Leasing:		Information Systems:	
Trucks:		Car Dealer Used:		Retail:		Specialty Service:		Auto Loans:		Online Marketing:	
Motorcycles:		Truck Dealer:		Distributors:		Oil Change:		Insurance:		Other:	
Specialty:		RV Dealer:		Tires:		Paint and Body:				Publishing:	
Buses:		Motorcycle Dealer:		Batteries:	Y					Rental Cars/Trucks:	
RVs:		Specialty Dealer:									

TYPES OF BUSINESS:

Automotive Battery Manufacturing
Industrial Battery Manufacturing
Battery Sales & Distribution

BRANDS/DIVISIONS/AFFILIATES:

GS Yuasa International Ltd.
Yuasa
Yucon
Thunderlite
Yuasa Sales & Distribution Co., Ltd.

CONTACTS: *Note: Officers with more than one job title may be intentionally listed here more than once.*

Katsumi Nakato, CEO
Subhavas Bandhuvadh, COO/Sr. Exec. VP
Katsumi Nakato, Acting CFO
Ichiro Murata, Chief Exec. Engineer
Sukthae Ruengwattanachot, Sec.
Sukthae Ruengwattanachot, Gen. Mgr.-Oper.
Pataraporn Tasanasewee, Mgr.-Finance & Acct.
Komson Arunpan, Gen. Mgr.-Samut Prakam Plant
Akihiko Tsubota, Gen. Mgr.-Cha Cheang Sao Plant
Chan Manutham, Chmn.
Chan Manutham, Chmn.-Yuasa Sales & Distribution Co., Ltd.

Phone: 66-2258-0545 **Fax:** 66-2259-0201
Toll-Free:
Address: Manutham Mansion, 33 Soi 51, Sukhumvit Rd., Bangkok, 10110 Thailand

GROWTH PLANS/SPECIAL FEATURES:

Yuasa Battery Thailand PCL manufactures and imports batteries, primarily for automobiles and industrial applications. It was started as a joint venture with Japanese firm Yuasa Corporation, which subsequently merged with Japan Storage Battery Co., Ltd. to form GS Yuasa International Ltd. (GYIN). GYIN is currently the largest shareholder of the firm, owning a 40.69% interest. Yuasa's batteries are sold under the Yuasa (used with permission from GYIN), Yucon and Thunderlite brand names. The company pays GYIN a royalty fee for all its batteries, regardless of the brand, based on either number of batteries sold or number manufactured, depending on the type of battery. In general, Yuasa produces car batteries, motorcycle batteries and industrial power supply batteries. Although all of its automobile batteries utilize a lead-acid design, it does offer a range of nickel-cadmium industrial batteries, often used in marine or rail vehicles or for emergency power supplies, as well as some solar powered industrial batteries. The firm has two factories, located in the Samut Prakan and Cha Cheang Sao provinces. Its primary subsidiary is Yuasa Sales & Distribution Co., Ltd., which markets Yuasa's batteries.

FINANCIALS: **Sales and profits are in thousands of dollars—add 000 to get the full amount. 2009 Note: Financial information for 2009 was not available for all companies at press time.**

2009 Sales: $45,930 — 2009 Profits: $1,410
2008 Sales: $52,940 — 2008 Profits: $-1,000
2007 Sales: $58,320 — 2007 Profits: $-5,260
2006 Sales: $ — 2006 Profits: $
2005 Sales: $ — 2005 Profits: $

U.S. Stock Ticker: Subsidiary
Int'l Ticker: YUASA Int'l Exchange: Bangkok-BAK
Employees:
Fiscal Year Ends: 12/31
Parent Company: GS YUASA INTERNATIONAL LTD

SALARIES/BENEFITS:

Pension Plan: ESOP Stock Plan: Profit Sharing: Top Exec. Salary: $ Bonus: $
Savings Plan: Stock Purch. Plan: Second Exec. Salary: $ Bonus: $

OTHER THOUGHTS:

Apparent Women Officers or Directors: 3
Hot Spot for Advancement for Women/Minorities: Y

LOCATIONS: ("Y" = Yes)

West:	Southwest:	Midwest:	Southeast:	Northeast:	International:
					Y

YULON MOTOR CO LTD

www.yulon-motor.com.tw

Industry Group Code: 33611 **Ranks within this company's industry group:** Sales: 29 Profits: 17

Vehicle Manufacturing:		Dealers:		Parts:		Service:		Finance:		Specialty:	
Cars:	Y	Car Dealer New:	Y	Manufacturers:	Y	General Service:		Leasing:		Information Systems:	
Trucks:		Car Dealer Used:		Retail:		Specialty Service:		Auto Loans:		Online Marketing:	
Motorcycles:		Truck Dealer:		Distributors:	Y	Oil Change:		Insurance:		Other:	
Specialty:		RV Dealer:		Tires:		Paint and Body:				Publishing:	
Buses:		Motorcycle Dealer:		Batteries:						Rental Cars/Trucks:	
RVs:		Specialty Dealer:									

TYPES OF BUSINESS:

Automobiles, Manufacturing
Automotive Components & Accessories

BRANDS/DIVISIONS/AFFILIATES:

Yulon-Nissan Motor Co. Ltd.
Yulon General Motors
Luxgen
Luxgen Motor (Zhejiang)

CONTACTS: *Note: Officers with more than one job title may be intentionally listed here more than once.*

Guorong Chen, Gen. Mgr.
F. J. Pan, CEO-Yulon General Motors
Lilian Chen, Managing Dir.
Kenneth Yen, CEO-Yulon Group
Kaitai Yan, Chmn.

Phone: 886-37-871801	**Fax:** 886-37-874790
Toll-Free:	
Address: 39-1 Pau-Kon Keun, Xihu, Sanyi, Miao li Hsien, Taiwan	

GROWTH PLANS/SPECIAL FEATURES:

Yulon Motor Co., Ltd., established in 1953 and operated by Yulon Group, is one of Taiwan's largest automobile manufacturers, with an annual production capacity of 150,000 units. The company makes vehicles, automotive components, automobile accessories and peripherals exclusively for Nissan vehicles sold in Taiwan and mainland China. In addition to manufacturing, Yulon sells vehicles through subsidiary companies. Yulon General Motors, a wholly-owned subsidiary of Yulon, sells Buick, Cadillac and Opel vehicles in Taiwan. The company also sells other select brands of vehicles in Taiwan, including Luxgen (a self-designed brand), Infiniti, Nissan, Renault and Nissan Diesel. Yulon Motor has a joint venture with Nissan Motor Co., Japan, called Yulon-Nissan Motor Co., Ltd. The joint venture was formed by dividing Yulon Motor into two parts, with 60% of the new company owned by Yulon Motor, and the remaining 40% by a consolidated subsidiary of Nissan Motor Company. The joint venture focuses on the development of the Nissan brand in Taiwan and other Asian markets and sells models including the New Bluebird, Livina, Serena, Murano, Rogue and X-Trail. In July 2010, Yulon announced plans to manufacture and sell its Luxgen MPV car (a seven seat, luxury multi-purpose vehicle) in mainland China. The operations will be undertaken through a joint venture, Luxgen Motor (Zhejiang), with Zhejiang Zhongyu Holding Group. An annual capacity of 240,000 units is expected when the company begins production in 2011.

FINANCIALS: **Sales and profits are in thousands of dollars—add 000 to get the full amount. 2009 Note: Financial information for 2009 was not available for all companies at press time.**

2009 Sales: $1,525,110	2009 Profits: $35,220	**U.S. Stock Ticker: Subsidiary**
2008 Sales: $1,120,390	2008 Profits: $12,520	**Int'l Ticker: 2201** Int'l Exchange: Taipei-TPE
2007 Sales: $1,287,610	2007 Profits: $96,940	Employees:
2006 Sales: $	2006 Profits: $	Fiscal Year Ends: 12/31
2005 Sales: $	2005 Profits: $	Parent Company: YULON GROUP

SALARIES/BENEFITS:

Pension Plan:	ESOP Stock Plan:	Profit Sharing:	Top Exec. Salary: $	Bonus: $
Savings Plan:	Stock Purch. Plan:		Second Exec. Salary: $	Bonus: $

OTHER THOUGHTS:

Apparent Women Officers or Directors: 1
Hot Spot for Advancement for Women/Minorities:

LOCATIONS: ("Y" = Yes)

West:	Southwest:	Midwest:	Southeast:	Northeast:	International:
					Y

ZAP

www.zapworld.com

Industry Group Code: 336991 **Ranks within this company's industry group:** Sales: 6 Profits: 5

Vehicle Manufacturing:		Dealers:		Parts:		Service:		Finance:		Specialty:	
Cars:	Y	Car Dealer New:	Y	Manufacturers:	Y	General Service:		Leasing:		Information Systems:	
Trucks:	Y	Car Dealer Used:		Retail:		Specialty Service:		Auto Loans:		Online Marketing:	
Motorcycles:	Y	Truck Dealer:	Y	Distributors:	Y	Oil Change:		Insurance:		Other:	Y
Specialty:	Y	RV Dealer:		Tires:		Paint and Body:				Publishing:	
Buses:		Motorcycle Dealer:		Batteries:						Rental Cars/Trucks:	
RVs:		Specialty Dealer:									

TYPES OF BUSINESS:

Light Electric Vehicles
Electric Bicycles & Scooters
Electric ATVs
Lithium Batteries
Electric Fleet Vehicle Manufacturing

BRANDS/DIVISIONS/AFFILIATES:

Xebra
ZAPPY
Zapino
Recharge-It-All
iZAP
Voltage Vehicles
ZAPWorld Stores, Inc.
ZAP Manufacturing, Inc.

CONTACTS: *Note: Officers with more than one job title may be intentionally listed here more than once.*

Steven Schneider, CEO
H. David Jones, COO
Gary Dodd, Pres.
William Hartman, CFO
William Hartman, Sec.
Gary Dodd, Pres., Global Oper.
Amos Kazzaz, Pres., Voltage Vehicles
Eqbal Al Yousuf, Chmn.

Phone: 707-525-8658	**Fax:**
Toll-Free: 800-251-4555	
Address: 501 Fourth St., Santa Rosa, CA 95401 US	

GROWTH PLANS/SPECIAL FEATURES:

ZAP is a provider of electric and other advanced technology vehicles. The firm markets many forms of advanced transportation vehicles, including electric automobiles, scooters, and all terrain vehicles. The company's products are focused on two primary businesses: ZAP Electric Vehicles and ZAP Recharge-It-All. The company's vehicles include the zero-emission ZAPPY and Zapino electric scooters; ZAP Dude electric ATVs; the XEBRA 100% electric sedan and utility pick-up truck; the XEBRA Xero Solar Panel, which slowly recharges the vehicle's battery; the ZAPTRUCK XL utility truck; and the ZAPVAN SHUTTLE. The firm is currently taking reservations for its upcoming Alias vehicle. The firm's Recharge-It-All rechargeable lithium battery pack technology is designed to work with cell phones, digital cameras, laptops, hand-held computers and more. The iZAP charger, a derivative of Recharge-It-All, is designed for use with Apple Computer's iPods. The company's Portable Energy line includes USB and car charger products for the Apple iPhone and iPod, Blackberries, PSP, BlueTooth items, digital cameras and more. ZAP has a number of wholly-owned subsidiaries, such as Voltage Vehicles, engaged primarily in the distribution and sale of advanced technology and conventional automobiles; ZAPWorld Stores, Inc., engaged primarily in consumer sales of ZAP products; ZAP Manufacturing, Inc., primarily involved in the distribution of ZAP products; and ZAP Retail Outlet. ZAP owns 16 U.S. patents. The company has begun refocusing its operations on servicing the growing appetite for electric vehicles in the fleet and taxi markets. ZAP has worked on projects for the Taxi fleet market in China; qualified as a supplier for the U.S. General Service Administration; and designed electric vehicles for a proposal for the conversion to an all-electric USPS fleet.

FINANCIALS: **Sales and profits are in thousands of dollars—add 000 to get the full amount. 2009 Note: Financial information for 2009 was not available for all companies at press time.**

2009 Sales: $4,068	2009 Profits: $-10,687	**U.S. Stock Ticker: ZAAP.OB**
2008 Sales: $7,588	2008 Profits: $9,807	**Int'l Ticker:** Int'l Exchange:
2007 Sales: $5,712	2007 Profits: $-28,006	Employees: 35
2006 Sales: $10,830	2006 Profits: $-11,915	Fiscal Year Ends: 12/31
2005 Sales: $3,602	2005 Profits: $-23,501	Parent Company:

SALARIES/BENEFITS:

Pension Plan:	ESOP Stock Plan:	Profit Sharing:	Top Exec. Salary: $179,000	Bonus: $
Savings Plan:	Stock Purch. Plan:		Second Exec. Salary: $125,000	Bonus: $

OTHER THOUGHTS:

Apparent Women Officers or Directors: 1
Hot Spot for Advancement for Women/Minorities:

LOCATIONS: ("Y" = Yes)

West:	Southwest:	Midwest:	Southeast:	Northeast:	International:
Y	Y	Y	Y	Y	

ZF FRIEDRICHSHAFEN AG

www.zf.com

Industry Group Code: 336350 **Ranks within this company's industry group:** Sales: 1 Profits: 3

Vehicle Manufacturing:		Dealers:		Parts:		Service:		Finance:		Specialty:	
Cars:		Car Dealer New:		Manufacturers:	Y	General Service:	Y	Leasing:		Information Systems:	
Trucks:		Car Dealer Used:		Retail:		Specialty Service:	Y	Auto Loans:		Online Marketing:	
Motorcycles:		Truck Dealer:		Distributors:	Y	Oil Change:		Insurance:		Other:	
Specialty:		RV Dealer:		Tires:		Paint and Body:				Publishing:	
Buses:		Motorcycle Dealer:		Batteries:						Rental Cars/Trucks:	
RVs:		Specialty Dealer:									

TYPES OF BUSINESS:

Automotive Components
Transmissions & Power Trains
Axles
Steering Systems
Chassis Components
Repair Services
Agricultural & Construction Machinery
Boat & Helicopter Transmissions

BRANDS/DIVISIONS/AFFILIATES:

ZF Lenksysteme
ZF Sachs AG
ZF Boge Elastmetall
ZF Services
ZF-AS Tronic Mid
ZF-AS Tronic Lite
ZF Lemforder
ZF Electronics GmbH

CONTACTS:

Note: Officers with more than one job title may be intentionally listed here more than once.

Hans-Georg Härter, CEO
Konstantin Sauer, CFO
Thomas Sigi, Exec. VP-Human Resources & Service Companies
Michael Paul, Exec. VP-R&D
Willi Berchtold, Exec. VP-IT
Andreas Hartman, VP-Corp. Strategy
Willi Berchtold, Exec. VP-Finance & Controlling
Michael Paul, Exec. VP-Tech. Div.
Wolfgang Vogel, Exec. VP-Aviation Tech. & Marine Propulsion
Reinhard Buhl, Group Exec.-ZF Lemforder GmbH
Andreas Hartmann, Chief Compliance Officer
Rainer Thieme, Chmn.
Manfred Schwab, Exec. VP-Asia Pacific

Phone: 49-7541-77-0 **Fax:** 49-7541-77-90-80-00
Toll-Free:
Address: Graf-von-Soden-Platz 1, Friedrichshafen, 88046 Germany

GROWTH PLANS/SPECIAL FEATURES:

ZF Friedrichshafen AG designs and manufactures automatic and manual transmissions for commercial vehicles, cars, aircraft, and marine vessels. It operates approximately 125 production plants in 26, with six primary development locations. The company also makes industrial drives such as servo gearboxes, as well as rail transmissions. Its off-road division makes transmissions for construction equipment and farm machinery. ZF's chassis unit makes automotive rear-axle systems and suspension modules. Through subsidiary ZF Lenksysteme (a joint venture with Robert Bosch GmbH), the company makes steering systems. Subsidiary ZF Sachs AG produces vibration dampers and other components for chassis regulation. ZF Boge Elastmetall, the rubber-metal technology business unit, develops and produces components and modules for vibration damping. The marine propulsion systems division produces transmissions for all types of pleasure boats and commercial marine craft. The aviation technology division develops, produces and maintains helicopter transmissions. ZF Electronics GmbH produces switching systems, sensor technologies and controls for the automobile industry. ZF Services is responsible for the worldwide aftermarket business for Sachs, Boge and Lemforder products; the company has approximately 40 such aftermarket trading businesses. In addition, the firm has 600 service partners located around the world. Prominent customers of the company include: AB Volvo; BMW Group; Chrysler LLC; Fiat S.p.A.; Ford Motor Company Inc.; General Motors Corporation; Honda Motor Co. Ltd; Renault-Nissan BV; Tata Group; Toyota Motor Corporation; and Volkswagen AG. In March 2010, the company partnered with Intel Corp. to create a telematics system that will include a hardware and software platform called Openmatics; this platform will be initially utilized by metro buses. In April 2010, the company announced the release of its 2010 Sachs heavy-duty clutch product line for class 8 trucks.

FINANCIALS:

Sales and profits are in thousands of dollars—add 000 to get the full amount. 2009 Note: Financial information for 2009 was not available for all companies at press time.

2009 Sales: $12,006,700	2009 Profits: $-539,410	**U.S. Stock Ticker: Private**
2008 Sales: $17,849,800	2008 Profits: $619,700	**Int'l Ticker:** Int'l Exchange:
2007 Sales: $18,061,100	2007 Profits: $739,640	Employees: 61,156
2006 Sales: $18,308,740	2006 Profits: $	Fiscal Year Ends: 12/31
2005 Sales: $13,843,500	2005 Profits: $304,650	Parent Company:

SALARIES/BENEFITS:

Pension Plan:	ESOP Stock Plan:	Profit Sharing:	Top Exec. Salary: $	Bonus: $
Savings Plan:	Stock Purch. Plan:		Second Exec. Salary: $	Bonus: $

OTHER THOUGHTS:

Apparent Women Officers or Directors:
Hot Spot for Advancement for Women/Minorities:

LOCATIONS: ("Y" = Yes)

West:	Southwest:	Midwest:	Southeast:	Northeast:	International:
Y	Y	Y	Y	Y	Y

ZHEJIANG GEELY HOLDING GROUP

www.geely.com

Industry Group Code: 33611 **Ranks within this company's industry group:** Sales: Profits:

Vehicle Manufacturing:		**Dealers:**		**Parts:**		**Service:**		**Finance:**		**Specialty:**	
Cars:	Y	Car Dealer New:		Manufacturers:	Y	General Service:		Leasing:		Information Systems:	
Trucks:		Car Dealer Used:		Retail:		Specialty Service:		Auto Loans:		Online Marketing:	
Motorcycles:		Truck Dealer:		Distributors:		Oil Change:		Insurance:		Other:	
Specialty:	Y	RV Dealer:		Tires:		Paint and Body:				Publishing:	
Buses:		Motorcycle Dealer:		Batteries:						Rental Cars/Trucks:	
RVs:		Specialty Dealer:									

TYPES OF BUSINESS:

Automobile Manufacturer

BRANDS/DIVISIONS/AFFILIATES:

Ford Motor Co
Volvo
Geely Automobile Holdings
Drivetrain Systems International Pty Ltd
Shanghai LTI Automobile Components Co Ltd
Manganese Bronze Holdings
Geely
Shanghai Geely International Corporation

CONTACTS:

Note: Officers with more than one job title may be intentionally listed here more than once.

Yang Jian, Pres.
Yin Daqing, CFO/VP
Zhao Fuquan, CTO/VP
Yang Xueliang, Dir.-Public Rel.
Wen-Ming Chen, VP
An Cong Hui, VP
Liu Jinliang, VP
Li Shufu, Chmn.

Phone: 400-88-69-888 **Fax:**
Toll-Free:
Address: 1760 Province Jiangling Rd., Binjiang District, Hangzhou, Zhejiang Province 310051 China

GROWTH PLANS/SPECIAL FEATURES:

Zhejiang Geely Holding Group Co., Ltd., founded in 1986, is an auto manufacturer based in China. The company's wholly-owned subsidiary, Geely Automobile Holdings operates the automotive business and is a fully integrated car manufacturer. It has independent research and design capabilities for vehicles, engines, transmissions and hybrid technologies. The firm operates in three divisions: research and development; manufacturing; and marketing and services. In the research and development segment, the company has more than 1,200 patents, 30 of which were granted internationally as of September 2009. The company has two prototypes that use methyl as an alternative fuel. In addition, the firm plans to develop five hybrid models over the coming years incorporating plug-in, stop-run, hybrid systems and electric only systems. Geely cars are manufactured in six assembly and power-train manufacturing plants in China. Manufacturing plants are located in Lanzhou (Gansu province), Linhai (Zhejiang province), Luqiao (Zhejiang province), Ningbo (Zhejiang province), Shanghai and Xiangtan (Hunan province). In the marketing and service segment, the company has a distribution network that extends to 45 countries across five continents with 500 retail distributors and by nearly 300 dealers. In addition, Geely has nearly 600 service stations. The firm has five key brand groups: Geely, Maple, Gleagle, Emgrand and Englon. Shanghai Geely International Corporation is the company's import and export subsidiary. Shanghai LTI Automobile Components Co., Ltd. is a joint venture with Manganese Bronze Holdings, to produce the iconic London Taxi. In March 2009, the company acquired Drivetrain Systems International Pty Ltd, transmission developer headquartered in Australia. In March 2010, the firm agreed to purchase Ford Motor Company's Volvo Cars unit for $1.8 billion. In July 2010, the company announced plans to plans to construct a local research and development facility and build a new factory with an annual production capacity of 300,000 vehicles for Volvo.

FINANCIALS:

Sales and profits are in thousands of dollars—add 000 to get the full amount. 2009 Note: Financial information for 2009 was not available for all companies at press time.

2009 Sales: $ | 2009 Profits: $
2008 Sales: $ | 2008 Profits: $
2007 Sales: $ | 2007 Profits: $
2006 Sales: $ | 2006 Profits: $
2005 Sales: $ | 2005 Profits: $

U.S. Stock Ticker: Private
Int'l Ticker: Int'l Exchange:
Employees:
Fiscal Year Ends: 12/31
Parent Company:

SALARIES/BENEFITS:

Pension Plan: ESOP Stock Plan: Profit Sharing: Top Exec. Salary: $ Bonus: $
Savings Plan: Stock Purch. Plan: Second Exec. Salary: $ Bonus: $

OTHER THOUGHTS:

Apparent Women Officers or Directors:
Hot Spot for Advancement for Women/Minorities:

LOCATIONS: ("Y" = Yes)

West:	Southwest:	Midwest:	Southeast:	Northeast:	International:
		Y		Y	Y

ZIEBART INTERNATIONAL CORP

www.ziebart.com

Industry Group Code: 8111 **Ranks within this company's industry group:** Sales: Profits:

Vehicle Manufacturing:		Dealers:		Parts:		Service:		Finance:		Specialty:	
Cars:		Car Dealer New:		Manufacturers:		General Service:		Leasing:		Information Systems:	
Trucks:		Car Dealer Used:		Retail:	Y	Specialty Service:	Y	Auto Loans:		Online Marketing:	
Motorcycles:		Truck Dealer:		Distributors:		Oil Change:		Insurance:		Other:	
Specialty:		RV Dealer:		Tires:		Paint and Body:	Y			Publishing:	
Buses:		Motorcycle Dealer:		Batteries:						Rental Cars/Trucks:	
RVs:		Specialty Dealer:									

TYPES OF BUSINESS:

Automotive Repair & Maintenance
Aftermarket Accessories Installation
Detailing
Paint & Fabric Protection
Window Tinting
Rust Protection

BRANDS/DIVISIONS/AFFILIATES:

Renu-A-Shine
Inner-Clean
Protect-A-Shine
Diamond Gloss
Inner Guard
ZeeGuard
Gold Shield
Formula Z

CONTACTS: *Note: Officers with more than one job title may be intentionally listed here more than once.*

Thomas E. Wolfe, CEO
Thomas E. Wolfe, Pres.
James L. Levagood, VP-IT
Sue Spriet, Dir.-Admin.
William R. Patterson, Treas./VP
Michael W. Riley, Sr. VP
Michael A. Pino, Sr. VP
Daniel C. Baker, Sr. VP
Thomas E. Wolfe, Chmn.
Bruce Weir, VP-Int'l Oper.

Phone: 248-588-4100	**Fax:** 248-588-1444
Toll-Free: 800-877-1312	
Address: 1290 E. Maple Rd., Troy, MI 48083 US	

GROWTH PLANS/SPECIAL FEATURES:

Ziebart International Corp. is a leading global provider of automotive appearance and protection services, with a network of 400 locations in 29 countries. The company's services include detailing; paint and fabric protection; window tinting; rust protection; and installation of electronic systems, sunroofs and alarm systems. The company specializes in truck accessories, such as bed liners, trailer hitches, toolboxes, bedrails, as well as scratch, and scuff paint repair for bed liners. Ziebart's detailing products include Aquapel, Renu-A-Shine and Inner-Clean. Its other brand names include Protect-A-Shine, Diamond Gloss, Z-Liner, Ziebart TidyCar, Ziebart Shield, ZeeGaurd, Formula Z, Express Shine, Preserv-A-Shine, Shatter Bloc, Artech, Gold Shield, Ziebart Anti-Bacterial Process and Inner Guard. The company also provides spray-on truck bed liners; glass repair and replacement; and remote starter installation. The firm maintains strategic business partnerships with groups including Speedy Auto Glass and Rhino Linings. Ziebart also offers management; marketing; construction design, location scouting, and layout of a new store; business development; grand opening support; monthly publications, ongoing support for franchise owners; marketing meetings and technical, sales and marketing training for its franchisees. The company has been named to Entrepreneur's list of the Top 500 Franchisers for 15 consecutive years; Success magazine's Franchise Gold 100 for four consecutive years; Income Opportunities' Platinum 200 list; and as one of Franchise Times magazine's Top 200.

FINANCIALS: **Sales and profits are in thousands of dollars—add 000 to get the full amount. 2009 Note: Financial information for 2009 was not available for all companies at press time.**

2009 Sales: $	2009 Profits: $	**U.S. Stock Ticker: Private**
2008 Sales: $	2008 Profits: $	**Int'l Ticker:** Int'l Exchange:
2007 Sales: $114,000	2007 Profits: $	Employees:
2006 Sales: $	2006 Profits: $	Fiscal Year Ends:
2005 Sales: $	2005 Profits: $	Parent Company:

SALARIES/BENEFITS:

Pension Plan:	ESOP Stock Plan: Y	Profit Sharing:	Top Exec. Salary: $	Bonus: $
Savings Plan:	Stock Purch. Plan:		Second Exec. Salary: $	Bonus: $

OTHER THOUGHTS:

Apparent Women Officers or Directors: 1
Hot Spot for Advancement for Women/Minorities:

LOCATIONS: ("Y" = Yes)

West:	Southwest:	Midwest:	Southeast:	Northeast:	International:
Y	Y	Y	Y	Y	Y

ZIPCAR INC

www.zipcar.com

Industry Group Code: 5321 **Ranks within this company's industry group:** Sales: Profits:

Vehicle Manufacturing:		Dealers:		Parts:		Service:		Finance:		Specialty:	
Cars:		Car Dealer New:		Manufacturers:		General Service:		Leasing:		Information Systems:	
Trucks:		Car Dealer Used:		Retail:		Specialty Service:		Auto Loans:		Online Marketing:	
Motorcycles:		Truck Dealer:		Distributors:		Oil Change:		Insurance:		Other:	
Specialty:		RV Dealer:		Tires:		Paint and Body:				Publishing:	
Buses:		Motorcycle Dealer:		Batteries:						Rental Cars/Trucks:	Y
RVs:		Specialty Dealer:									

TYPES OF BUSINESS:

Car Sharing Service
Car Rental
Fleet Management Software

BRANDS/DIVISIONS/AFFILIATES:

CONTACTS:

Note: Officers with more than one job title may be intentionally listed here more than once.

Scott Griffith, CEO
Mark Norman, COO
Mark Norman, Pres.
Ed Goldfinger, CFO
Vicki Godfrey, Chief Mktg. Officer
Sean Quimby, VP-Human Resources
Luke Schneider, CTO
Doug Williams, VP-Eng.
Jon Zeitler, Exec. VP-Corp. Dev.
Scott Griffith, Chmn.

Phone: 617-995-4231	**Fax:** 617-995-4300
Toll-Free: 866-494-7227	
Address: 25 First St., 4th Fl., Cambridge, MA 02141 US	

GROWTH PLANS/SPECIAL FEATURES:

Zipcar, Inc. is a membership-based car sharing company that offers shared access to automobiles and trucks for users in a growing number of urban areas across the U.S., Canada and the U.K. Originating in Boston, Massachusetts in 1999, Zipcar has since established a presence in urban areas such as New York, Philadelphia, San Francisco, Washington D.C., Atlanta, Chicago, Portland and Seattle. In all, Zipcar has vehicles in more than 55 cities in 25 U.S. states. Internationally, the company has set up Canadian operations in Toronto and Vancouver, as well as U.K. operations in London. Members reserve vehicles ahead of time (either online or by phone), then pay an hourly or daily fee for the use of the vehicle; the rental price includes all gas and insurance costs, as well as 180 free miles. Members can reserve cars for an hour at a time, or for longer periods of up to four days. The program is marketed to a range of customers, from those who normally use public transportation but occasionally want access to a car, to those who need a car as a primary mode of transportation but wish to avoid the costs and logistics involved in ownership. Zipcar offers a number of plans that reward members who use the service more often with reduced hourly and daily rates. Zipcar has also established partnerships with a number of business and university clients, and the university program has grown to include cars on over 60 U.S. campuses, including Yale, Stanford, Arizona State, Johns Hopkins, Wellesley College, the University of Michigan and Dartmouth. Members use Zipcards, which make use of radio frequency identification (RFID) technology, to unlock cars, while global positioning system (GPS) technology combined with new smart phone software allows members to locate cars nearby and make reservations on-the-go from their mobile phones. In mid-2009, the firm had a membership of about 325,000. In June 2010, the company filed to go public.

FINANCIALS:

Sales and profits are in thousands of dollars—add 000 to get the full amount. 2009 Note: Financial information for 2009 was not available for all companies at press time.

2009 Sales: $	2009 Profits: $	**U.S. Stock Ticker: Private**
2008 Sales: $130,000	2008 Profits: $	**Int'l Ticker:** Int'l Exchange:
2007 Sales: $	2007 Profits: $	Employees:
2006 Sales: $	2006 Profits: $	Fiscal Year Ends: 12/31
2005 Sales: $	2005 Profits: $	Parent Company:

SALARIES/BENEFITS:

Pension Plan:	ESOP Stock Plan:	Profit Sharing:	Top Exec. Salary: $	Bonus: $
Savings Plan:	Stock Purch. Plan:		Second Exec. Salary: $	Bonus: $

OTHER THOUGHTS:

Apparent Women Officers or Directors: 1
Hot Spot for Advancement for Women/Minorities:

LOCATIONS: ("Y" = Yes)

West:	Southwest:	Midwest:	Southeast:	Northeast:	International:
Y	Y	Y	Y	Y	Y

ADDITIONAL INDEXES

Contents:

INDEX OF FIRMS NOTED AS HOT SPOTS FOR ADVANCEMENT FOR WOMEN & MINORITIES

INDEX OF SUBSIDIARIES, BRAND NAMES AND AFFILIATIONS

Brand or subsidiary, followed by the name of the related corporation

INDEX OF SUBSIDIARIES, BRAND NAMES AND AFFILIATIONS, CONT.

INDEX OF SUBSIDIARIES, BRAND NAMES AND AFFILIATIONS, CONT.

INDEX OF SUBSIDIARIES, BRAND NAMES AND AFFILIATIONS, CONT.

INDEX OF SUBSIDIARIES, BRAND NAMES AND AFFILIATIONS, CONT.

INDEX OF SUBSIDIARIES, BRAND NAMES AND AFFILIATIONS, CONT.

INDEX OF SUBSIDIARIES, BRAND NAMES AND AFFILIATIONS, CONT.

INDEX OF SUBSIDIARIES, BRAND NAMES AND AFFILIATIONS, CONT.

INDEX OF SUBSIDIARIES, BRAND NAMES AND AFFILIATIONS, CONT.

INDEX OF SUBSIDIARIES, BRAND NAMES AND AFFILIATIONS, CONT.

INDEX OF SUBSIDIARIES, BRAND NAMES AND AFFILIATIONS, CONT.

INDEX OF SUBSIDIARIES, BRAND NAMES AND AFFILIATIONS, CONT.

INDEX OF SUBSIDIARIES, BRAND NAMES AND AFFILIATIONS, CONT.

INDEX OF SUBSIDIARIES, BRAND NAMES AND AFFILIATIONS, CONT.

INDEX OF SUBSIDIARIES, BRAND NAMES AND AFFILIATIONS, CONT.

INDEX OF SUBSIDIARIES, BRAND NAMES AND AFFILIATIONS, CONT.

INDEX OF SUBSIDIARIES, BRAND NAMES AND AFFILIATIONS, CONT.

INDEX OF SUBSIDIARIES, BRAND NAMES AND AFFILIATIONS, CONT.

INDEX OF SUBSIDIARIES, BRAND NAMES AND AFFILIATIONS, CONT.

INDEX OF SUBSIDIARIES, BRAND NAMES AND AFFILIATIONS, CONT.

INDEX OF SUBSIDIARIES, BRAND NAMES AND AFFILIATIONS, CONT.

INDEX OF SUBSIDIARIES, BRAND NAMES AND AFFILIATIONS, CONT.

INDEX OF SUBSIDIARIES, BRAND NAMES AND AFFILIATIONS, CONT.

INDEX OF SUBSIDIARIES, BRAND NAMES AND AFFILIATIONS, CONT.

INDEX OF SUBSIDIARIES, BRAND NAMES AND AFFILIATIONS, CONT.

INDEX OF SUBSIDIARIES, BRAND NAMES AND AFFILIATIONS, CONT.

INDEX OF SUBSIDIARIES, BRAND NAMES AND AFFILIATIONS, CONT.

INDEX OF SUBSIDIARIES, BRAND NAMES AND AFFILIATIONS, CONT.

LaVergne, TN USA
27 March 2011
221725LV00001B/2/P

9 781593 921811